FOREWORD

This dictionary has been designed to provide detailed coverage of the central areas of modern English and German. The user will see that, instead of merely giving *lists* of various possible but different translations, entries are divided up to give more precise information. For example, where a headword has several different meanings the relevant translations for each meaning are marked off by explanatory words in italics. Thus: **disagree** *vi* nicht übereinstimmen; *(quarrel)* (sich) streiten; *(food)* nicht bekommen *(with dat)*. Of these explanatory words some act as definitions – *(quarrel)* – and some are typical subjects – *(food)*. So if the user wants to know the translation for 'disagree' in the sense of 'quarrel' the dictionary tells him the correct German expression; if it is something that somebody has eaten that 'disagrees' with him then the dictionary gives the proper German equivalent. Again where a headword can be used together with other words in various ways these possibilities are indicated. For example: **abhören** *vt Vokabeln* test; *Telefongespräch* tap; *Tonband etc* listen to. The translations here are related each to a particular context, and by this means confusion and error are avoided. The user will also see that in many cases where a one-word translation is not possible whole phrases have been included, making the dictionary even more useful.

The editors are confident that with its precise analytical treatment and up-to-date wordlist this dictionary will serve the user as a most informative and reliable guide.

VORWORT

Dieses Wörterbuch hat sich eine detaillierte Behandlung der wichtigsten Bereiche der modernen englischen und deutschen Sprache zum Ziel gesetzt. Anstatt mehrere mögliche, aber in der Bedeutung verschiedene Übersetzungen nur einfach aneinanderzureihen, werden dem Benutzer anhand einer Aufgliederung des Eintrags genauere Auskünfte über Sinn und Gebrauch des Wortes gegeben. Wenn zum Beispiel ein Stichwort unterschiedliche Bedeutungen hat, werden die entsprechenden Übersetzungen mit kursiv gedruckten, erklärenden Bezeichnungen voneinander abgegrenzt. So zum Beispiel: **aufsteigen** *vi irreg (auf etw)* get onto; *(hochsteigen)* climb; *(Rauch)* rise. Von diesen erklärenden Bezeichnungen sind manche Definitionen oder Quasisynonyme – *(hochsteigen)* – und manche typische Subjekte – *(Rauch)*. Wenn also der Benutzer die Entsprechung für ‚aufsteigen' in der Bedeutung von ‚hochsteigen' sucht, zum Beispiel im Zusammenhang mit Bergsteigern, findet er hier auf Anhieb die korrekte Übersetzung; handelt es sich um Rauch, weiß er, daß ‚rise' das richtige englische Wort dafür ist. Auch wo ein Stichwort je nach Satzzusammenhang unterschiedlich angewendet und übersetzt wird, werden diese Möglichkeiten aufgezeigt. Zum Beispiel: *abhören* vt *Vokabeln* test; *Telefongespräch* tap; *Tonband etc* listen to. Die Übersetzungen beziehen sich auf den genannten Zusammenhang, und dadurch werden Verwirrung und Fehler vermieden. Außerdem werden in Fällen, in denen eine Übersetzung durch ein einziges entsprechendes Wort nicht möglich ist, ganze Satzkonstruktionen aufgeführt, was den praktischen Wert des Wörterbuchs noch um ein weiteres erhöht.

Die Herausgeber sind der Überzeugung, daß sich dem Benutzer auf Grund dieser detaillierten Aufgliederung der Einträge und der zeitgemäßen Auswahl der Stichwörter ein aufschlußreiches und zuverlässiges Wörterbuch bietet.

editors
Veronika Calderwood-Schnorr
Ute Nicol
Peter Terrell

assistant editor
Anne Dickinson

Regular German noun endings
Regelmäßige Endungen

nom		gen	pl	nom		gen	pl
-ant	m	-anten	-anten	-ion	f	-ion	-ionen
-anz	f	-anz	-anzen	-ist	m	-isten	-isten
-ar	m	-ar(e)s	-are	-ium	nt	-iums	-ien
-chen	nt	-chens	-chen	-ius	m	-ius	-iusse
-ei	f	-ei	-eien	-ive	f	-ive	-iven
-elle	f	-elle	-ellen	-keit	f	-keit	-keiten
-ent	m	-enten	-enten	-lein	nt	-lein	-lein
-enz	f	-enz	-enzen	-ling	m	-lings	-linge
-ette	f	-ette	-etten	-ment	nt	-ments	-mente
-eur	m	-eurs	-eure	-mus	m	-mus	-men
-euse	f	-euse	-eusen	-schaft	f	-schaft	-schaften
-heit	f	-heit	-heiten	-tät	f	-tät	-täten
-ie	f	-ie	-ien	-tor	m	-tors	-toren
-ik	f	-ik	-iken	-ung	f	-ung	-ungen
-in	f	-in	-innen	-ur	f	-ur	-uren
-ine	f	-ine	-inen				

v

Phonetic symbols
Lautschrift

[ː] *length mark* Längezeichen   ['] *stress mark* Betonung
[ˈ] *glottal stop* Knacklaut

all vowel sounds are approximate only
alle Vokallaute sind nur ungefähre Entsprechungen

lie	[aɪ]	weit	day	[eɪ]	
now	[aʊ]	Haut	girl	[ɜː]	
above	[ə]	bitte	board	[ɔː]	
green	[iː]	viel	root	[uː]	Hut
pity	[i]	Bischof	come	[ʌ]	Butler
rot	[ɒ,ɔ]	Post	salon	[ɔ̃]	Champignon
full	[ʊ]	Pult	avant (garde)	[ɑ̃]	Ensemble
			fair	[ɛə]	mehr
bet	[b]	Ball	beer	[ɪə]	Bier
dim	[d]	dann	toy	[ɔɪ]	Heu
face	[f]	Faß	pure	[ʊə]	
go	[g]	Gast	wine	[w]	
hit	[h]	Herr	thin	[θ]	
you	[j]	ja	this	[ð]	
eat	[k]	kalt			
lick	[l]	Last	Hast	[a]	mash
must	[m]	Mast	Ensemble	[ã]	avant (garde)
nut	[n]	Nuß	Metall	[e]	meths
bang	[ŋ]	lang	häßlich	[ɛ]	
pepper	[p]	Pakt	Cousin	[ɛ̃]	
sit	[s]	Rasse	vital	[i]	
shame	[ʃ]	Schal	Moral	[o]	
tell	[t]	Tal	Champignon	[õ]	salon
vine	[v]	was	ökonomisch	[ø]	
loch	[x]	Bach	gönnen	[œ]	
zero	[z]	Hase	Heu	[ɔy]	toy
leisure	[ʒ]	Genie	kulant	[u]	
			physisch	[y]	
bat	[æ]	Bahn	Müll	[ʏ]	
farm	[ɑː]	Bahn	ich	[ç]	
set	[e]	Kette			

[ʳ]   r *can be pronounced before a vowel;* Bindungs-R

Abbreviations used in text
Im Text verwendete Abkürzungen

a	adjective	Adjektiv	*Astrol*	astrology	Astrologie
abbr	abbreviation	Abkürzung	*Astron*	astronomy	Astronomie
acc	accusative	Akkusativ	*attr*	attributive	attributiv
ad	adverb	Adverb	*Aut*	automobiles	Kraftfahr-
Agr	agriculture	Landwirt-			zeuge
		schaft	*aux*	auxiliary	Hilfsverb
Anat	anatomy	Anatomie	*Aviat*	aviation	Luftfahrt
Archit	architecture	Architektur	*Biol*	biology	Biologie
art	article	Artikel	*Bot*	botany	Botanik
Art	art	Kunst	*Brit*	British	britisch

Cards		Kartenspiel	old		veraltet
Chem	chemistry	Chemie	o.s.	oneself	sich
Cine	cinema	Film	Parl	parliament	Parlament
cj	conjunction	Konjunktion	pej	pejorative	abschätzig
col	colloquial	umgangssprachlich	Phot	photography	Photographie
			Phys	physics	Physik
Comm	commerce	Handel	pl	plural	Plural
comp	comparative	Komparativ	Pol	politics	Politik
Cook	cooking	Kochen und Backen	poss	possessive	besitzanzeigend
cpd	compound	zusammengesetztes Wort	pref	prefix	Präfix, Vorsilbe
dat	dative	Dativ	prep	preposition	Präposition
Eccl	ecclesiastical	kirchlich	Press		Presse
Elec	electricity	Elektrizität	Print	printing	Typographie
esp	especially	besonders	pron	pronoun	Pronomen, Fürwort
etc	et cetera	und so weiter			
etw	something	etwas	Psych	psychology	Psychologie
euph	euphemism	Euphemismus, Hüllwort	pt	past	1. Vergangenheit, Imperfekt
f	feminine	Femininum	ptp	past participle	Partizip Perfekt
fig	figurative	übertragen			
Fin	finance	Finanzwesen	Rad	radio	Radio
gen	genitive	Genitiv	Rail	railways	Eisenbahn
Geog	geography	Geographie	rel	relative	Relativ-
Gram	grammar	Grammatik	Rel	religion	Religion
Hist	history	Geschichte	sb	someone, somebody	jemand (—en, —em)
impers	impersonal	unpersönlich			
indef	indefinite	unbestimmt	Sch	school	Schulwesen
insep	inseparable	nicht getrennt gebraucht	Sci	science	Naturwissenschaft
interj	interjection	Interjektion, Ausruf	Scot	Scottish	schottisch
interrog	interrogative	interrogativ, Frage(wort)	sing	singular	Singular, Einzahl
			Ski	skiing	Skisport
inv	invariable	unveränderlich	sth	something	etwas
irreg	irregular	unregelmäßig	suff	suffix	Suffix, Nachsilbe
jd	somebody	jemand	superl	superlative	Superlativ
jdm	(to) somebody	jemandem	Tech	technology	Technik
			Tel	telecommunications	Nachrichtentechnik
jdn	somebody	jemanden			
jds	somebody's	jemandes	Theat	theatre	Theater
Jur	law	Rechtswesen	TV	television	Fernsehen
Ling	linguistics	Sprachwissenschaft	Univ	university	Hochschulwesen
lit	literal	wörtlich	US	(North) America	(nord-)amerikanisch
liter	literary	literarisch			
Liter	literature	Literatur	usu	usually	gewöhnlich
m	masculine	Maskulinum	v	verb	Verb
Math	mathematics	Mathematik	vi	intransitive verb	intransitives Verb
Med	medicine	Medizin			
Met	meteorology	Meteorologie	vr	reflexive verb	reflexives Verb
Mil	military	militärisch			
Min	mining	Bergbau	vt	transitive verb	transitives Verb
Mus	music	Musik			
n	noun	Substantiv, Hauptwort	Zool	zoology	Zoologie
			~	change of speaker	zwischen zwei Sprechern
Naut	nautical, naval	nautisch, Seefahrt	≈	cultural equivalent	ungefähre Entsprechung
nom	nominative	Nominativ			
nt	neuter	Neutrum	®	registered trademark	eingetragenes Warenzeichen
num	numeral	Zahlwort			
obj	object	Objekt			

A

A, a [a:] *nt* A, a.
Aal [a:l] *m* -(e)s, -e eel.
Aas [a:s] *nt* -es, -e *or* **Äser** carrion; **—geier** *m* vulture.
ab [ap] *prep* +*dat* from; *ad* off; **links —** to the left; **— und zu** *or* an now and then *or* again; **von da — from** then on; **der Knopf ist —** the button has come off.
Abänderung ['ap'ɛndərʊŋ] *f* alteration.
abarbeiten ['ap'arbaɪtən] *vr* wear o.s. out, slave away.
Abart ['ap'a:rt] *f* (*Biol*) variety; **a—ig** *a* abnormal.
Abbau ['apbaʊ]- *m* -(e)s dismantling; (*Verminderung*) reduction (*gen* in); (*Verfall*) decline (*gen* in); (*Min*) mining; quarrying; (*Chem*) decomposition; **a—en** *vt* dismantle; (*Min*) mine; quarry; (*verringern*) reduce; (*Chem*) break down.
abbeißen ['apbaɪsən] *vt irreg* bite off.
abberufen ['apbərʊ:fən] *vt irreg* recall.
Abberufung *f* recall.
abbestellen ['apbəʃtɛlən] *vt* cancel.
abbezahlen ['apbətsa:lən] *vt* pay off.
abbiegen ['apbi:gən] *irreg vi* turn off; (*Straße*) bend; *vt* bend; (*verhindern*) ward off.
Abbild ['apbɪlt] *nt* portrayal; (*einer Person*) image, likeness; **a—en** ['apbɪldən] *vt* portray; **—ung** *f* illustration.
Abbitte ['apbɪtə] *f*: **— leisten** *or* **tun** make one's apologies (*bei* to).
abblasen ['apbla:zən] *vt irreg* blow off; (*fig*) call off.
abblenden ['apblɛndən] *vti* (*Aut*) dip, dim (*US*).
Abblendlicht *nt* dipped *or* dimmed (*US*) headlights *pl.*
abbrechen ['apbrɛçən] *vti irreg* break off; (*Gebäude*) pull down; *Zelt* take down; (*aufhören*) stop.
abbrennen ['apbrɛnən] *irreg vt* burn off; *Feuerwerk* let off; *vi* (*aux sein*) burn down; **abgebrannt sein** (*col*) be broke.
abbringen ['apbrɪŋən] *vt irreg*: **jdn von etw —** dissuade sb from sth; **jdn vom Weg —** divert sb; **ich bringe den Verschluß nicht ab** (*col*) I can't get the top off.
abbröckeln ['apbrœkəln] *vti* crumble off *or* away.
Abbruch ['apbrʊx] *m* (*von Verhandlungen etc*) breaking off; (*von Haus*) demolition; **jdm/etw — tun** harm sb/sth; **a—reif** *a* only fit for demolition.
abbrühen ['apbry:ən] *vt* scald; **abgebrüht** (*col*) hard-boiled.
abbuchen ['apbu:xən] *vt* debit.
abbürsten ['apbyrstən] *vt* brush off.
abdanken ['apdaŋkən] *vi* resign; (*König*) abdicate.
Abdankung *f* resignation; abdication.

abdecken ['apdɛkən] vt uncover; Tisch clear; Loch cover.

abdichten ['apdiçtən] vt seal; (Naut) caulk.

abdrängen ['apdrɛŋən] vt push off.

abdrehen ['apdre:ən] vt Gas turn off; Licht switch off; Film shoot; jdm den Hals — wring sb's neck; vi (Schiff) change course.

abdrosseln ['apdrosəln] vt throttle; (Aut) stall; Produktion cut back.

Abdruck ['apdrʊk] m (Nachdrucken) reprinting; (Gedrucktes) reprint; (Gips—, Wachs—) impression; (Finger—) print; a—en vt print, publish.

abdrücken ['apdrʏkən] vt make an impression of; Waffe fire; Person hug, squeeze; jdm die Luft — squeeze all the breath out of sb; vr leave imprints; (abstoßen) push o.s. away.

abebben ['ap'ɛbən] vi ebb away.

Abend ['a:bənt] m -s, -e evening; zu — essen have dinner or supper; a— ad evening; (am —) essen 'nt supper; a—füllend taking up the whole evening; —kurs m evening classes pl; —land nt West; a—lich a evening; —mahl nt Holy Communion; —rot nt sunset; a—s ad in the evening.

Abenteuer ['a:bəntɔʏər] nt -s, - adventure; a—lich a adventurous.

Abenteurer m -s, - adventurer; —in f adventuress.

aber ['a:bər] cj but; (jedoch) however; das ist — schön that's really nice; nun ist — Schluß! now that's enough!; ad tausend und — tausend thousands upon thousands; A— nt but; A—glaube m superstition; —gläubisch a superstitious.

aberkennen ['ap'ɛrkɛnən] vt irreg: jdm etw — deprive sb of sth, take sth (away) from sb.

Aberkennung f taking away.

aber- cpd: —malig a repeated; —mals ad once again.

abfahren ['apfa:rən] irreg vi leave, depart; vt take or cart away; Strecke drive; Reifen wear; Fahrkarte use.

Abfahrt ['ap-fa:rt] f departure; (Ski) descent; (Piste) run; —slauf m (Ski) descent, run down; —s-tag m day of departure; —szeit f departure time.

Abfall ['ap-fal] m waste; (von Speisen etc) rubbish, garbage (US); (Neigung) slope; (Verschlechterung) decline; —eimer m rubbish bin, garbage can (US); a—en vi irreg (lit, fig) fall or drop off; (Pol, vom Glauben) break away; (sich neigen) fall or drop away.

abfällig ['ap-fɛlɪç] a disparaging, deprecatory.

abfangen ['ap-faŋən] vt irreg intercept; Person catch; (unter Kontrolle bringen) check.

abfärben ['ap-fɛrbən] vi (lit) lose its colour; (Wäsche) run; (fig) rub off.

abfassen ['ap-fasən] vt write, draft.

abfertigen ['ap-fɛrtɪgən] vt prepare for dispatch, process; (an der Grenze) clear; Kundschaft attend to; jdn kurz — give sb short shrift.

Abfertigung f preparing for dispatch, processing; clearance.

abfeuern ['ap-fɔʏərn] vt fire.

abfinden ['ap-fɪndən] irreg vt pay off; vr come to terms; sich mit jdm —/nicht — put up with/not get on with sb.

Abfindung f (von Gläubigern) payment ; (Geld) sum in settlement.

abflauen ['ap-flauən] vi (Wind, Erregung) die away, subside ; (Nachfrage, Geschäft) fall or drop off.

abfliegen ['ap-fli:gən] irreg vi (Flugzeug) take off ; (Passagier auch) fly ; vt Gebiet fly over.

abfließen ['ap-fli:sən] vi irreg drain away.

Abflug ['ap-flu:k] m departure ; (Start) take-off ; —zeit f departure time.

Abfluß ['ap-flus] m draining away ; (Öffnung) outlet.

abfragen ['ap-fra:gən] vt test ; jdn or jdm etw — question sb on sth.

Abfuhr ['ap-fu:r] f -, -en removal ; (fig) snub, rebuff.

Abführ- ['ap-fy:r] cpd: a—en vt lead away ; Gelder, Steuern pay ; vi (Med) have a laxative effect ; —mittel nt laxative, purgative.

abfüllen ['ap-fylən] vt draw off ; (in Flaschen) bottle.

Abgabe ['apga:bə] f handing in ; (von Ball) pass ; (Steuer) tax ; (eines Amtes) giving up ; (einer Erklärung) giving ; a—nfrei a tax-free ; a—npflichtig a liable to tax.

Abgang ['apgaŋ] m (von Schule) leaving ; (Theat) exit ; (Med: Ausscheiden) passing ; (Fehlgeburt) miscarriage ; (Abfahrt) departure ; (der Post, von Waren) dispatch.

Abgas ['apga:s] nt waste gas ; (Aut) exhaust.

abgeben ['apge:bən] irreg vt Gegenstand hand or give in ; Ball pass ; Wärme give off ; Amt hand over ; Schuß fire ; Erklärung, Urteil give ; (darstellen, sein) make ; jdm etw — (überlassen) let sb have sth ; vr:

sich mit jdm/etw — associate with sb/bother with sth.

abgedroschen ['apgədrɔʃən] a hackneyed ; Witz corny.

abgefeimt ['apgəfaimt] a cunning.

abgegriffen ['apgəgrifən] a Buch well-thumbed ; Redensart hackneyed.

abgehen ['apge:ən] irreg vi go away, leave ; (Theat) exit ; (Post) go ; (Med) be passed ; (Baby) die ; (Knopf etc) come off ; (abgezogen werden) be taken off ; (Straße) branch off ; etw geht jdm ab (fehlt) sb lacks sth ; vt Strecke go or walk along.

abgelegen ['apgəle:gən] a remote.

abgemacht ['apgəmaxt] a fixed ; —! done.

abgeneigt ['apgənaikt] a averse to, disinclined.

Abgeordnete(r) ['apgə'ɔrdnətə(r)] mf member of parliament ; elected representative.

Abgesandte(r) ['apgəzantə(r)] mf delegate ; (Pol) envoy.

abgeschmackt ['apgəʃmakt] a tasteless ; A—heit f lack of taste ; (Bemerkung) tasteless remark.

abgesehen ['apgəze:ən] a: es auf jdn/etw —haben be after sb/sth ; — von... apart from...

abgespannt ['apgəʃpant] a tired out.

abgestanden ['apgəʃtandən] a stale ; Bier auch flat.

abgestorben ['apgəʃtɔrbən] a numb ; (Biol, Med) dead.

abgetakelt ['apgəta:kəlt] a (col) decrepit, past it.

abgetragen ['apgətra:gən] a shabby, worn out.

abgewinnen ['apgəvinən] vt irreg: jdm Geld — win money from sb ;

einer Sache etw/Geschmack — get sth/pleasure from sth.

abgewöhnen ['apgəvø:nən] *vt:* jdm/sich etw — cure sb of sth/give sth up.

abgleiten ['apglaɪtən] *vi irreg.* slip, slide.

Abgott ['apgɔt] *m* idol.

abgöttisch ['apgœtɪʃ] *a:* — lieben idolize.

abgrenzen ['apgrɛntsən] *vt* (*lit, fig*) mark off; fence off.

Abgrund ['apgrʊnt] *m* (*lit, fig*) abyss.

abgründig ['apgrʏndɪç] *a* unfathomable; *Lächeln* cryptic.

abhacken ['aphakən] *vt* chop off.

abhaken ['apha:kən] *vt* tick off.

abhalten ['aphaltən] *vt irreg Versammlung* hold; jdn von etw — (*fernhalten*) keep sb away from sth; (*hindern*) keep sb from sth.

abhandeln ['aphandəln] *vt Thema* deal with; jdm die Waren/8 Mark — do a deal with sb for the goods/beat sb down 8 marks.

abhanden [ap'handən] *a:* — kommen get lost.

Abhandlung ['aphandlʊŋ] *f* treatise, discourse.

Abhang ['aphaŋ] *m* slope.

abhängen ['aphɛŋən] *irreg vt Bild* take down; *Anhänger* uncouple; *Verfolger* shake off; *vi* (*Fleisch*) hang; von jdm/etw — depend on sb/sth.

abhängig ['aphɛŋɪç] *a* dependent (*von* on); A—keit *f* dependence (*von* on).

abhärten ['aphɛrtən] *vtr* toughen (o.s.) up; sich gegen etw — inure o.s. to sth.

abhauen ['aphauən] *irreg vt* cut

off; *Baum* cut down; *vi* (*col*) clear off *or* out.

abheben ['aphe:bən] *irreg vt* lift (up); *Karten* cut; *Masche* slip; *Geld* withdraw, take out; *vi* (*Flugzeug*) take off; (*Rakete*) lift off; (*Cards*) cut; *vr* stand out (*von* from), contrast (*von* with).

abhelfen ['aphɛlfən] *vi irreg* (+ *dat*) remedy.

abhetzen ['aphɛtsən] *vr* wear *or* tire o.s. out.

Abhilfe ['aphɪlfə] *f* remedy; — schaffen put things right.

abholen ['apho:lən] *vt Gegenstand* fetch, collect; *Person* call for; (*am Bahnhof etc*) pick up, meet.

abhorchen ['aphɔrçən] *vt* (*Med*) auscultate, sound.

abhören ['aphø:rən] *vt Vokabeln* test; *Telefongespräch* tap; *Tonband etc* listen to.

Abhörgerät *nt* bug.

Abitur [abi'tu:r] *nt* -s, -e German school leaving examination; —i'ent(in *f*) *m* candidate for school leaving certificate.

abkämmen ['apkɛmən] *vt Gegend* comb, scour.

abkanzeln ['apkantsəln] *vt* (*col*) bawl out.

abkapseln ['apkapsəln] *vr* shut *or* cut o.s. off.

abkaufen ['apkaufən] *vt:* jdm etw — buy sth from sb.

abkehren ['apke:rən] *vt Blick* avert, turn away; *vr* turn away.

Abklatsch ['apklatʃ] *m* -es, -e (*fig*) (poor) copy.

abklingen ['apklɪŋən] *vi irreg* die away; (*Radio*) fade out.

abknöpfen ['apknœpfən] *vt* unbutton; jdm etw — (*col*) get sth off sb.

abkochen ['apkɔxən] *vt* boil.

abkommen ['apkɔmən] *vi irreg* get away; **von der Straße/von einem Plan** — leave the road/give up a plan; **A— *nt* -s, -** agreement.

abkömmlich ['apkœmliç] *a.* available, free.

abkratzen ['apkratsən] *vt* scrape off; *vi (col)* kick the bucket.

abkühlen ['apky:lən] *vt* cool down; *vr (Mensch)* cool down *or* off; *(Wetter)* get cool; *(Zuneigung)* cool.

Abkunft ['apkʊnft] *f -* origin, birth.

abkürzen ['apkʏrtsən] *vt* shorten; *Wort auch* abbreviate; **den Weg —** take a short cut.

Abkürzung *f (Wort)* abbreviation; *(Weg)* short cut.

abladen ['apla:dən] *vt irreg* unload.

Ablage ['apla:gə] *f -, -n (für Akten)* tray; *(für Kleider)* cloakroom; **a—rn** *vt* deposit; *vr* be deposited; *vi* mature.

ablassen ['aplasən] *irreg vt Wasser, Dampf* let off; *(vom Preis)* knock off; *vi:* **von etw —** give sth up, abandon sth.

Ablauf ['aplaʊf] *m (Abfluß)* drain; *(von Ereignissen)* course; *(einer Frist, Zeit)* expiry; **a—en** *irreg vi (abfließen)* drain away; *(Ereignisse)* happen; *(Frist, Zeit, Paß)* expire; *vt Sohlen* wear (down *or* out); **jdm den Rang a—en** steal a march on sb.

ablegen ['aple:gən] *vt* put *or* lay down; *Kleider* take off; *Gewohnheit* get rid of; *Prüfung* take, sit; *Zeugnis* give.

Ableger *m -s, -* layer; *(fig)* branch, offshoot.

ablehnen ['aple:nən] *vt* reject; *Einladung* decline, refuse; *vi* decline, refuse.

Ablehnung *f* rejection; refusal.

ableiten ['aplaɪtən] *vt Wasser* divert; *(deduzieren)* deduce; *Wort* derive.

Ableitung *f* diversion; deduction; derivation; *(Wort)* derivative.

ablenken ['aplɛŋkən] *vt* turn away, deflect; *(zerstreuen)* distract; *vi* change the subject.

Ablenkung *f* distraction.

ablesen ['aple:zən] *vt irreg* read out; *Meßgeräte* read.

ableugnen ['aplɔʏgnən] *vt* deny.

ablichten ['aplɪçtən] *vt* photocopy; photograph.

abliefern ['apli:fərn] *vt* deliver; **etw bei jdm/einer Dienststelle —** hand sth over to sb/in at an office.

Ablieferung *f* delivery; **—sschein** *m* delivery note.

abliegen ['apli:gən] *vi irreg* be some distance away; *(fig)* be far removed.

ablisten ['aplɪstən] *vt:* **jdm etw —** trick *or* con sb out of sth.

ablösen ['aplø:zən] *vt (abtrennen)* take off, remove; *(in Amt)* take over from; *Wache* relieve.

Ablösung *f* removal; relieving.

abmachen ['apmaxən] *vt* take off; *(vereinbaren)* agree.

Abmachung *f* agreement.

abmagern ['apma:gərn] *vi* get thinner.

Abmagerungskur *f* diet; **eine — machen** go on a diet.

Abmarsch ['apmarʃ] *m* departure; **a—bereit** *a* ready to start; **a—ieren** *vi* march off.

abmelden ['apmɛldən] *vt Zeitungen* cancel; *Auto* take off the road; **jdn bei der Polizei —** register sb's departure with the police; *vr* give notice of one's departure; (im Hotel) check out.

abmessen ['apmɛsən] vt irreg measure.

Abmessung f measurement.

abmontieren ['apmɔnti:rən] vt take off.

abmühen ['apmy:ən] vr wear o.s. out.

Abnäher ['apnɛ:ər] m -s, - dart.

Abnahme ['apna:mə] f -, -n removal; (Comm) buying; (Verringerung) decrease (gen in).

abnehmen ['apne:mən] irreg vt take off, remove; Führerschein take away; Geld get (jdm out of sb); (kaufen, col: glauben) buy (jdm from sb); Prüfung hold; Maschen decrease; jdm Arbeit — take work off sb's shoulders; vi decrease; (schlanker werden) lose weight.

Abnehmer m -s, - purchaser, customer.

Abneigung ['apnaigʊŋ] f aversion, dislike.

abnorm [ap'nɔrm] a abnormal.

abnötigen ['apnø:tɪgən] vt: jdm etw/Respekt — force sth from sb/gain sb's respect.

abnutzen ['apnʊtsən] vt wear out.

Abnutzung f wear (and tear).

Abonnement [abɔn(e)'mã:] nt -s, -s subscription.

Abonnent(in f) [abɔ'nɛnt(ɪn)] m subscriber.

abonnieren [abɔ'ni:rən] vt subscribe to.

abordnen ['ap'ɔrdnən] vt delegate.

Abordnung f delegation.

Abort [a'bɔrt] m -(e)s, -e lavatory.

abpacken ['apakən] vt pack.

abpassen ['apasən] vt Person,

Gelegenheit wait for; (in Größe) Stoff etc adjust.

abpfeifen . ['appfaifən] vti irreg (Sport) (das Spiel) — blow the whistle (for the end of game).

Abpfiff ['appfɪf] m final whistle.

abplagen ['appla:gən] vr wear o.s. out.

Abprall ['appral] m rebound; (von Kugel) ricochet; a—en vi bounce off; ricochet.

abputzen ['apputsən] vt clean.

abquälen ['ap-kvɛ:lən] vr drive o.s. frantic; sich mit etw — struggle with sth.

abraten [ap'ra:tən] vi irreg advise, warn (jdm von etw sb against sth).

abräumen ['aprɔymən] vt clear up or away.

abreagieren [apreagi:rən] vt Zorn work off (an + dat on); vr calm down.

abrechnen ['aprɛçnən] vt deduct, take off; vi (lit) settle up; (fig) get even.

Abrechnung f settlement; (Rechnung) bill.

Abrede ['apre:də] f: etw in — stellen deny or dispute sth.

abregen ['apre:gən] vr (col) calm or cool down.

abreiben ['apraibən] vtr irreg rub off; (säubern) wipe; jdn mit einem Handtuch — towel sb down.

Abreise ['apraizə] f departure; a—n vi leave, set off.

abreißen ['apraisən] vt irreg Haus tear down; Blatt tear off.

abrichten ['apriçtən] vt train.

abriegeln ['apri:gəln] vt Tür bolt; Straße, Gebiet seal off.

Abriß ['apris] m -sses, -sse (Übersicht) outline.

Abruf [ˈapruːf] *m*: auf — on call; a—en *vt irreg* Mensch call away; (*Comm*) Ware request delivery of.

abrunden [ˈaprʊndən] *vt* round off.

abrüsten [ˈaprʏstən] *vi* disarm.

Abrüstung *f* disarmament.

abrutschen [ˈaprʊtʃən] *vi* slip; (*Aviat*) sideslip.

Absage [ˈapzaːgə] *f* -, -n refusal; a—n *vt* cancel, call off; Einladung turn down; *vi* cry off; (*ablehnen*) decline.

absägen [ˈapzɛːgən] *vt* saw off.

absahnen [ˈapzaːnən] *vt* (*lit*) skim; das beste für sich — take the cream.

Absatz [ˈapzats] *m* (*Comm*) sales *pl*; (*Bodensatz*) deposit; (*neuer Abschnitt*) paragraph; (*Treppen—*) landing; (*Schuh—*) heel; —flaute *f* slump in the market; —gebiet *nt* (*Comm*) market.

abschaben [ˈapʃaːbən] *vt* scrape off; Möhren scrape.

abschaffen [ˈapʃafən] *vt* abolish, do away with.

Abschaffung *f* abolition.

abschalten [ˈapʃaltən] *vti* (*lit, col*) switch off.

abschattieren [ˈapʃatiːrən] *vt* shade.

abschätzen [ˈapʃɛtsən] *vt* estimate; Lage assess; Person size up.

abschätzig [ˈapʃɛtsɪç] a disparaging, derogatory.

Abschaum [ˈapʃaʊm] *m* -(e)s scum.

Abscheu [ˈapʃɔy] *m* -(e)s loathing, repugnance; a—erregend a repulsive, loathsome; a—lich [apˈʃɔylɪç] a abominable.

abschicken [ˈapʃɪkən] *vt* send off.

abschieben [ˈapʃiːbən] *vt irreg* push away; Person pack off.

Abschied [ˈapʃiːt] *m* -(e)s, -e parting; (*von Armee*) discharge; — nehmen say good-bye (*von jdm* to sb), take one's leave (*von jdm* of sb); seinen — nehmen (*Mil*) apply for discharge; zum — on parting; —sbrief *m* farewell letter; —sfeier *f* farewell party.

abschießen [ˈapʃiːsən] *vt irreg* Flugzeug shoot down; Geschoß fire; (*col*) Minister get rid of.

abschirmen [ˈapʃɪrmən] *vt* screen.

abschlagen [ˈapʃlaːgən] *vt irreg* (*abhacken*, Comm) knock off; (*ablehnen*) refuse; (*Mil*) repel.

abschlägig [ˈapʃlɛːgɪç] a negative. **Abschlagszahlung** *f* interim payment.

abschleifen [ˈapʃlaifən] *irreg vt* grind down; Rost polish off; *vr* wear off.

Abschlepp- [ˈapʃlɛp] *cpd*: —dienst *m* (*Aut*) breakdown service; a—en *vt* take in tow; —seil *nt* towrope.

abschließen [ˈapʃliːsən] *irreg vt* Tür lock; (*beenden*) conclude, finish; Vertrag, Handel conclude; *vr* (*sich isolieren*) cut o.s. off.

Abschluß [ˈapʃlʊs] *m* (*Beendigung*) close, conclusion; (*Comm: Bilanz*) balancing; (*von Vertrag, Handel*) conclusion; zum — in conclusion; —feier *f* end-of-term party; —rechnung *f* final account.

abschmieren [ˈapʃmiːrən] *vt* (*Aut*) grease, lubricate.

abschneiden [ˈapʃnaidən] *irreg vt* cut off; *vi* do, come off.

Abschnitt [ˈapʃnɪt] *m* section; (*Mil*) sector; (*Kontroll—*) counterfoil; (*Math*) segment; (*Zeit—*) period.

abschnüren [ˈapʃnyːrən] *vt* constrict.

abschöpfen ['ap-ʃœpfən] vt skim off.

abschrauben ['ap-ʃraubən] vt unscrew.

abschrecken ['ap-ʃrɛkən] vt deter, put off; (mit kaltem Wasser) plunge in cold water; **–d** a deterrent; **–des Beispiel** warning.

abschreiben ['ap-ʃraibən] vt irreg copy; (verlorengeben) write off; (Comm) deduct.

Abschreibung f (Comm) deduction; (Wertverminderung) depreciation.

Abschrift ['ap-ʃrift] f copy.

abschürfen ['ap-ʃyrfən] vt graze.

Abschuß ['ap-ʃus] m (eines Geschützes) firing; (Herunterschießen) shooting down; (Tötung) shooting.

abschüssig ['ap-ʃʏsɪç] a steep.

abschütteln ['ap-ʃʏtəln] vt shake off.

abschwächen ['ap-ʃvɛçən] vt lessen; Behauptung, Kritik tone down; vr lessen.

abschweifen ['ap-ʃvaifən] vi wander.

Abschweifung f digression.

abschwellen ['ap-ʃvɛlən] vi irreg (Geschwulst) go down; (Lärm) die down.

abschwenken ['ap-ʃvɛŋkən] vi turn away.

abschwören ['ap-ʃvøːrən] vi irreg (+ dat) renounce.

abseh- ['apze:] cpd: **–bar** a foreseeable; **in –barer Zeit** in the foreseeable future; **das Ende ist –bar** the end is in sight; **–en** irreg vt Ende, Folgen foresee; **jdm etw –en** (erlernen) copy sth from sb; vi: **von etw –en** refrain from sth;

(nicht berücksichtigen) leave sth out of consideration.

abseits ['apzaits] ad out of the way; prep + gen away from; **A–nt** (Sport) offside; **im A–** stehen be offside.

Absend- ['apzɛnd] cpd: **a–en** vt irreg send off, dispatch; **–er** m **-s, - sender**; **–ung** f dispatch.

absetz- ['apzɛts] cpd: **–bar a** Beamter dismissible; Waren saleable; (von Steuer) deductible; **–en** vt (niederstellen, aussteigen lassen) put down; (abnehmen) take off; (Comm: verkaufen) sell; (Fin: abziehen) deduct; (entlassen) dismiss; König depose; (streichen) drop; (hervorheben) pick out; vr (sich entfernen) clear off; (sich ablagern) be deposited; **A–ung** f (Fin: Abzug) deduction; (Entlassung) dismissal; (von König) deposing; (Streichung) dropping.

absichern ['apzɪçərn] vtr make safe; (schützen) safeguard.

Absicht ['apzɪçt] f intention; **mit –** on purpose; **a–lich** a intentional, deliberate; **a–slos** a unintentional.

absinken ['apzɪŋkən] vi irreg sink; (Temperatur, Geschwindigkeit) decrease.

absitzen ['apzɪtsən] irreg vi dismount; vt Strafe serve.

absolut [apzo'lu:t] a absolute; **A–ismus** [-'tɪsmus] m absolutism.

absolvieren [apzɔl'vi:rən] vt (Sch) complete.

absonder- ['apzɔndər] cpd: **–lich** [ap'zɔndərlɪç] a odd, strange; **–n** vt separate; (ausscheiden) give off, secrete; vr cut o.s. off; **A–ung** f separation; (Med) secretion.

abspalten ['ap-ʃpaltən] vt split off.

Abspannung ['ap-ʃpanuŋ] f (Ermüdung) exhaustion.

absparen ['ap-ʃpaːrən] *vt*: sich (dat) etw — scrimp and save for sth.

abspeisen ['ap-ʃpaɪzən] *vt* (*fig*) fob off.

abspenstig ['ap-ʃpɛnstɪç]: — machen lure away (*jdm* from sb).

absperren ['ap-ʃpɛrən] *vt* block or close off; Tür lock.

Absperrung *f* (Vorgang) blocking or closing off; (Sperre) barricade.

abspielen ['ap-ʃpiːlən] *vt* Platte, Tonband play; (Sport) Ball pass; vom Blatt — (Mus) sight-read; *vr* happen.

absplittern ['ap-ʃplɪtərn] *vt* chip off.

Absprache ['ap-ʃpraːxə] *f* arrangement.

absprechen ['ap-ʃprɛçən] *vt irreg* (vereinbaren) arrange; jdm etw — deny sb sth.

abspringen ['ap-ʃprɪŋən] *vi irreg* jump down/off; (Farbe, Lack) flake off; (Aviat) bale out; (sich distanzieren) back out.

Absprung ['ap-ʃprʊŋ] *m* jump.

abspülen ['ap-ʃpyːlən] *vt* rinse; Geschirr wash up.

abstammen ['ap-ʃtamən] *vi* be descended; (Wort) be derived.

Abstammung *f* descent; derivation.

Abstand ['ap-ʃtant] *m* distance; (zeitlich) interval; davon — nehmen, etw zu tun refrain from doing sth; — halten (Aut) keep one's distance; mit — der beste by far the best; —ssumme *f* compensation.

abstatten ['ap-ʃtatən] *vt* Dank give; Besuch pay.

abstauben ['ap-ʃtaʊbən] *vti* dust;

(col: stehlen) pinch; (den Ball) — (Sport) tuck the ball away.

abstechen ['ap-ʃtɛçən] *irreg vt* cut; Tier cut the throat of; *vi* contrast (gegen, von with).

Abstecher *m* -s, - detour.

abstecken ['ap-ʃtɛkən] *vt* (losmachen) unpin; Fläche mark out.

abstehen ['ap-ʃteːən] *vi irreg* (Ohren, Haare) stick out; (entfernt sein) stand away.

absteigen ['ap-ʃtaɪgən] *vi irreg* (vom Rad etc) get off, dismount; (in Gasthof) put up (in + dat at); (Sport) be relegated (in + acc to).

abstellen ['ap-ʃtɛlən] *vt* (niederstellen) put down; (entfernt stellen) pull out; (hinstellen) Auto park; (ausschalten) turn or switch off; Mißstand, Unsitte stop; (ausrichten) gear (auf + acc to).

Abstellgleis *nt* siding.

abstempeln ['ap-ʃtɛmpəln] *vt* stamp.

absterben ['ap-ʃtɛrbən] *vi irreg* die; (Körperteil) go numb.

Abstieg ['ap-ʃtiːk] *m* -(e)s, -e descent; (Sport) relegation; (fig) decline.

abstimmen ['ap-ʃtɪmən] *vi* vote; *vt* Instrument tune (auf + acc to); Interessen match (auf + acc with); Termine, Ziele fit in (auf + acc with); *vr* agree.

Abstimmung *f* vote.

abstinent [apstiˈnɛnt] *a* abstemious; (von Alkohol) teetotal.

Abstinenz [apstiˈnɛnts] *f* abstinence; teetotalism; —ler *m* -s, - teetotaller.

abstoßen ['ap-ʃtoːsən] *vt irreg* push off or away; (verkaufen) unload; (anekeln) repel, repulse; —d a repulsive.

abstrahieren [apstraˈhiːrən] *vti* abstract.

abstrakt [apˈstrakt] *a* abstract; *ad* abstractly, in the abstract; **A—ion** [apstraktsiˈoːn] *f* abstraction; **A—um** *nt* **-s, -kta** abstract concept/noun.

abstreiten [ˈap-ʃtraitən] *vt irreg* deny.

Abstrich [ˈap-ʃtriç] *m* (*Abzug*) cut; (*Med*) smear; **—e machen** lower one's sights.

abstufen [ˈap-ʃtuːfən] *vt* Hang terrace; *Farben* shade; *Gehälter* grade.

abstumpfen [ˈap-ʃtumpfən] *vt* (*lit, fig*) dull, blunt; *vi* (*lit, fig*) become dulled.

Absturz [ˈap-ʃturts] *m* fall; (*Aviat*) crash.

abstürzen [ˈap-ʃtYrtsən] *vi* fall; (*Aviat*) crash.

absuchen [ˈapzuːxən] *vt* scour, search.

absurd [apˈzurt] *a* absurd.

Abszeß [apsˈtsɛs] *m* **-sses, -sse** abscess.

Abt [apt] *m* **-(e)s, ̈e** abbot.

abtasten [ˈaptastən] *vt* feel, probe.

abtauen [ˈaptauən] *vti* thaw.

Abtei [apˈtai] *f* **-, -en** abbey.

Abteil [apˈtail] *nt* **-(e)s, -e** compartment; **'a—en** *vt* divide up; (*abtrennen*) divide off; **—ung** *f* (*in Firma, Kaufhaus*) department; (*Mil*) unit; **—ungsleiter** *m* head of department.

abtönen [ˈaptøːnən] *vt* (*Phot*) tone down.

abtragen [ˈaptraːgən] *vt irreg* Hügel, Erde level down; *Essen* clear away; *Kleider* wear out; *Schulden* pay off.

abträglich [ˈaptrɛːkliç] *a* harmful (*dat* to).

abtransportieren [ˈaptransportiːrən] *vt* take away, remove.

abtreiben [ˈaptraibən] *irreg vt* Boot, Flugzeug drive off course; *Kind* abort; *vi* be driven off course; abort.

Abtreibung *f* abortion; **—sversuch** *m* attempted abortion.

abtrennen [ˈaptrɛnən] *vt* (*lostrennen*) detach; (*entfernen*) take off; (*abteilen*) separate off.

abtreten [ˈaptreːtən] *irreg vt* wear out; (*überlassen*) hand over, cede (*jdm to sb*); *vi* go off; (*zurücktreten*) step down.

Abtritt [ˈaptrɪt] *m* resignation.

abtrocknen [ˈaptrɔknən] *vti* dry.

abtrünnig [ˈaptrYnɪç] *a* renegade.

abtun [ˈaptuːn] *vt irreg* take off; (*fig*) dismiss.

aburteilen [ˈapʔurtailən] *vt* condemn.

abverlangen [ˈap-fɛrlaŋən] *vt*: jdm etw — demand sth from sb.

abwägen [ˈapvɛːgən] *vt irreg* weigh up.

abwählen [ˈapvɛːlən] *vt* vote out (of office).

abwandeln [ˈapvandəln] *vt* adapt.

abwandern [ˈapvandərn] *vi* move away.

abwarten [ˈapvartən] *vt* wait for; *vi* wait.

abwärts [ˈapvɛrts] *ad* down.

Abwasch [ˈapvaʃ] *m* **-(e)s** washing-up; **a—en** *vt irreg* Schmutz wash off; *Geschirr* wash (up).

Abwasser [ˈapvasər] *nt* **-s, -wässer** sewage.

abwechseln [ˈapvɛksəln] *vir* alternate; (*Personen*) take turns; **—d** *a* alternate.

Abweg ['apve:k] *m*: auf —e geraten/führen go/lead astray; a—ig ['apve:giç] a wrong.

Abwehr ['apve:r] *f* – defence; (*Schutz*) .protection; (—dienst) counter-intelligence (service); a—en *vt* ward off; *Ball* stop; a—ende Geste dismissive gesture.

abweichen ['apvaiçən] *vi irreg* deviate; (*Meinung*) differ; —d a deviant; differing.

abweisen ['apvaizən] *vt irreg* turn away; *Antrag* turn down; —d a Haltung cold.

abwenden ['apvɛndən] *irreg vt* avert; *vr* turn away.

abwerben ['apvɛrbən] *vt irreg* woo away (*jdm* from sb).

abwerfen ['apvɛrfən] *vt irreg* throw off; *Profit* yield; (*aus Flugzeug*) drop; *Spielkarte* discard.

abwerten ['apvɛrtən] *vt* (*Fin*) devalue.

abwesend ['apve:zənt] a absent.

Abwesenheit ['apve:zənhait] *f* absence.

abwickeln ['apvikəln] *vt* unwind; *Geschäft* wind up.

abwiegen ['apvi:gən] *vt irreg* weigh out.

abwimmeln ['apviməln] *vt* (*col*) *Person* get rid of; *Auftrag* get out of.

abwinken ['apviŋkən] *vi* wave it/him *etc* aside.

abwirtschaften ['apvirt-ʃaftən] *vi* go downhill.

abwischen ['apviʃən] *vt* wipe off or away; (*putzen*) wipe.

abwracken ['apvrakən] *vt Schiff* break (up); abgewrackter Mensch wreck of a person.

Abwurf ['apvurf] *m* throwing off;

(*von Bomben etc*) dropping; (*von Reiter, Sport*) throw.

abwürgen ['apvYrgən] *vt* (*col*) scotch; *Motor* stall.

abzahlen ['aptsa:lən] *vt* pay off.

abzählen ['aptsɛ:lən] *vti* count (up).

Abzahlung *f* repayment; auf — kaufen buy on hire purchase.

abzapfen ['aptsapfən] *vt* draw off; jdm Blut/Geld — take blood from sb/bleed sb.

abzäunen ['aptsɔYnən] *vt* fence off.

Abzeichen ['aptsaiçən] *nt* badge; (*Orden*) decoration.

abzeichnen ['aptsaiçnən] *vt* draw, copy; *Dokument* initial; *vr* stand out; (*fig: bevorstehen*) loom.

Abziehbild *nt* transfer.

abziehen ['aptsi:ən] *irreg vt* take off; *Tier* skin; *Bett* strip; *Truppen* withdraw; (*subtrahieren*) take away, subtract; (*kopieren*) run off; *vi* go away; (*Truppen*) withdraw.

abzielen ['aptsi:lən] *vi* be aimed (auf +*acc* at).

Abzug ['aptsu:k] *m* departure; (*von Truppen*) withdrawal; (*Kopie*) copy; (*Subtraktion*) subtraction; (*Betrag*) deduction; (*Rauch*—) flue; (*von Waffen*) trigger.

abzüglich ['aptsY:kliç] *prep* +*gen* less.

abzweigen ['aptsvaigən] *vi* branch off; *vt* take aside.

Abzweigung *f* junction.

Accessoires [akseso'a:rs] *pl* accessories *pl*.

ach [ax] *interj* oh; mit A— und Krach by the skin of one's teeth.

Achse ['aksə] *f* -, -n axis; (*Aut*) axle; auf — sein be on the move.

Achsel ['aksəl] *f* -, -n shoulder;

—höhle f armpit; —zucken nt shrug (of one's shoulders).

Achsenbruch m (Aut) broken axle.

Acht [axt] f - attention; (Hist) proscription; sich in — nehmen be careful (vor +dat of), watch out (vor +dat for); etw außer a— lassen disregard sth; — f -, -en, a— num eight; a— Tage a week; a—bar a worthy; a—e(r,s) a eighth; —el num eighth; a—en vt respect; vi pay attention (auf +acc to); darauf a—en, daß ... be careful that ...

ächten ['ɛçtən] vt outlaw, ban.

Achter- cpd: —bahn f big dipper, roller coaster; —deck nt (Naut) afterdeck.

acht- cpd: —fach a eightfold; —geben vi irreg take care (auf +acc of); —los a careless; —mal ad eight times; —sam a attentive.

Achtung ['axtʊŋ] f attention; (Ehrfurcht) respect; interj look out!; (Mil) attention!; —, Lebensgefahr/Stufe! danger/mind the step!

acht- cpd: —zehn num eighteen; —zig num eighty; A—ziger(in f) m -s, - octogenarian; A—zigerjahre pl eighties pl.

ächzen ['ɛçtsən] vi groan (vor +dat with).

Acker ['akər] m -s, ¨ field; —bau m agriculture; a—n vti plough; (col) slog away.

addieren [a'di:rən] vt add (up).

Addition [aditsi'o:n] f addition.

Ade [a'de:] nt -s, -s, a— interj farewell, adieu.

Adel ['a:dəl] m -s nobility; a—ig, adlig a noble.

Ader ['a:dər] f -, -n vein.

Adjektiv ['atjɛktiːf] nt -s, -e adjective.

Adler ['a:dlər] m -s, - eagle.

Admiral [atmi'ra:l] m -s, -e admiral; —ität f admiralty.

adopt- cpd: —ieren [adɔp'ti:rən] vt adopt; A—ion [adɔptsi'o:n] f adoption; A—iveltern [adɔp'ti:f-] pl adoptive parents pl; A—ivkind nt adopted child.

Adress- cpd: —ant [adrɛ'sant] m sender; —at [adrɛ'sa:t] m -en, -en addressee; —e [a'drɛsə] f -, -n address; a—ieren [adrɛ'si:rən] vt address (an +acc to).

Advent [at'vɛnt] m -s, -e Advent; —skranz m Advent wreath.

Adverb [at'vɛrp] nt adverb; a—ial [atvɛrbi'a:l] a adverbial.

aero- [aero] pref aero-.

Affäre [a'fɛ:rə] f -, -n affair.

Affe ['afə] m -en, -en monkey.

affektiert [afɛk'ti:rt] a affected.

Affen- cpd: a—artig a like a monkey; mit a—artiger Geschwindigkeit like a flash; —hitze f (col) incredible heat; —schande f (col) crying shame.

affig ['afɪç] a affected.

After ['aftər] m -s, - anus.

Agent [a'gɛnt] m agent; —ur [-'tu:r] f agency.

Aggregat [agre'ga:t] nt -(e)s, -e aggregate; (Tech) unit; —zustand m (Phys) state.

Aggress- cpd: —ion [agrɛsi'o:n] f aggression; a—iv [agrɛ'si:f] a aggressive; —ivität [agrɛsivi'tɛ:t] f aggressiveness.

Agitation [agitatsi'o:n] f agitation.

Agrar- cpd: —politik f agricultural policy; —staat m agrarian state.

aha [a'ha] interj aha.

Ahn [a:n] m -en, -en forebear.

ähneln ['ɛːnəln] vi (+dat) be like, resemble; vr be alike or similar.

ahnen ['aːnən] vt suspect; Tod, Gefahr have a presentiment of; du ahnst es nicht you have no idea.

ähnlich ['ɛːnlɪç] a similar (dat to); Ä—keit f similarity.

Ahnung ['aːnʊŋ] f idea, suspicion; presentiment; a—slos a unsuspecting.

Ahorn ['aːhɔrn] m -s, -e maple.

Ähre ['ɛːrə] f -, -n ear.

Akademie [akade'miː] f academy.

Akademiker(in f) [aka'deːmikər(ɪn)] m -s, - university graduate.

akademisch a academic.

akklimatisieren [aklimati'ziːrən] vr become acclimatized.

Akkord [a'kɔrt] m -(e)s, -e (Mus) chord; im - arbeiten do piecework; —arbeit f piecework; —eon [a'kɔrdeɔn] nt -s, -s accordion.

Akkusativ [akuzatiːf] m -s, -e accusative (case).

Akrobat(in f) [akro'baːt(ɪn)] m -en, -en acrobat.

Akt [akt] m -(e)s, -e act; (Art) nude.

Akte ['aktə] f -, -n file; etw zu den —n legen (lit, fig) file sth away; a—nkundig a on the files; —nschrank m filing cabinet; —ntasche f briefcase.

Aktie ['aktsiə] f -, -n share; —ngesellschaft f joint-stock company; —nkurs m share price.

Aktion [aktsi'oːn] f campaign; (Polizei-, Such-) action; —är [ˈɛ:r] m -s, -e shareholder.

aktiv [ak'tiːf] a active; (Mil) regular; A— nt -s (Gram) active (voice); A—a [ak'tiːva] pl assets pl; —ieren [-'viːrən] vt activate;

A—i'tät f activity; A—saldo m (Comm) credit balance.

Aktualität [aktualiˈtɛːt] f topicality; (einer Mode) up-to-dateness.

aktuell [aktu'el] a topical; up-to-date.

Akustik [a'kʊstɪk] f acoustics pl.

akut [a'kuːt] a acute.

Akzent [ak'tsɛnt] m accent; (Betonung) stress.

akzeptieren [aktsep'tiːrən] vt accept.

Alarm [a'larm] m -(e)s, -e alarm; a—bereit a standing by; —bereitschaft f stand-by; a—ieren ['-'miːrən] vt alarm.

albern ['albərn] a silly.

Album ['album] nt -s, **Alben** album.

Algebra ['algebra] f - algebra.

alias ['aːlias] ad alias.

Alibi ['aːlibi] nt -s, -s alibi.

Alimente [ali'mɛntə] pl alimony.

Alkohol ['alkohol] m -s, -e alcohol a—frei a non-alcoholic; —iker(in f) [alko'hoːlikər(ɪn)] m -s, -, alcoholic; a—isch a alcoholic; —verbot nt ban on alcohol.

All [al] nt -s universe; a—'abendlich a every evening; a—bekannt a universally known; a—e(r,s) a all; wir —e all of us; —e beide both of us/you etc; —e vier Jahre every four years; ad (col: zu Ende) finished; etw —e machen finish sth up.

Allee [a'leː] f -, -n avenue.

allein [a'laɪn] a/ad alone; (ohne Hilfe) on one's own, by oneself; nicht — (nicht nur) not only; cj but, only; A—gang m: im A—gang on one's own; A—herrscher m autocrat; A—hersteller m sole manufacturer; —stehend a single.

alle- *cpd*: **—mal** *ad* (*jedesmal*) always; (*ohne weiteres*) with no bother; **ein für —mal** once and for all; **—nfalls** *ad* at all events; (*höchstens*) at most; **—rbeste(r,s)** *a* very best; **—rdings** *ad* (*zwar*) admittedly; (*gewiß*) certainly.

allerg- *cpd*: **—isch** [a'lɛrgɪʃ] *a* allergic; **A—ie** [-'gi:] *f* allergy.

aller- ['alar] *cpd*: **—hand** *a inv* (*col*) all sorts of; **das ist doch —hand!** that's a bit thick; **—hand!** (*lobend*) good show!; **A—'heiligen** *nt* All Saints' Day; **—höchste(r,s)** *a* very highest; **—höchstens** *ad* at the very most; **—lei** *a inv* all sorts of; **—letzte(r,s)** *a* very last; **—seits** *ad* on all sides; **prost —seits!** cheers everyone!; **—wenigste(r,s)** *a* very least.

alles *pron* everything; **— in allem** all in all.

allgemein ['algə'maɪn] *a* general; **—gültig** *a* generally accepted; **A—heit** *f* (*Menschen*) general public; (*pl: Redensarten*) general remarks *pl*.

Alliierte(r) [ali'i:rtə(r)] *m* ally.

all- *cpd*: **—jährlich** *a* annual; **—mählich** *a* gradual; **A—tag** *m* everyday life; **—täglich** *a,ad* daily; (*gewöhnlich*) commonplace; **—tags** *ad* on weekdays; **—'wissend** *a* omniscient; **—zu** *ad* all too; **—zuoft** *ad* all too often; **—zuviel** *ad* too much.

Almosen ['almo:zən] *nt* -s, - alms *pl*.

Alpen ['alpən] *pl* Alps *pl*; **—blume** *f* alpine flower.

Alphabet [alfa'be:t] *nt* -(e)s, -e alphabet; **a—isch** *a* alphabetical.

Alptraum ['alptraum] *m* nightmare.

als [als] *cj* (*zeitlich*) when; (*comp*) than; (*Gleichheit*) as; **nichts —** nothing but; **— ob** as if.

also ['alzo] *cj* so; (*folglich*) therefore; **ich komme — morgen** so I'll come tomorrow; **— gut** *or* **schön!** okay then; **—, so was!** well really!; **na —!** there you are then!

alt [alt] *a* old; **ich bin nicht mehr der —e** I am not the man I was; **alles beim —en lassen** leave everything as it was; **A— m** -s, **-e** (*Mus*) alto; **A—ar** [al'ta:r] *m* -(e)s, -äre altar; **—bekannt** *a* long-known; **A—'eisen** *nt* scrap iron.

Alter ['altər] *nt* -s, - age; (*hohes*) old age; **im — von** at the age of; **a—n** *vi* grow old, age; **—na'tive** *f* alternative; **—sgrenze** *f* age limit; **—sheim** *nt* old people's home; **—sversorgung** *f* old age pension; **—tum** *nt* antiquity.

alt- *cpd*: **—'hergebracht** *a* traditional; **—klug** *a* precocious; **—modisch** *a* old-fashioned; **A—papier** *nt* waste paper; **A—stadt** *f* old town; **A—stimme** *f* alto; **A—'weibersommer** *m* Indian summer.

Aluminium [alu'mi:niʊm] *nt* -s aluminium, aluminum (*US*); **—folie** *f* tinfoil.

am [am] = **an dem**; **— Sterben** on the point of dying; **— 15. März** on March 15th; **— besten/schönsten** best/most beautiful.

Amalgam [amal'ga:m] *nt* -s, -e amalgam.

Amateur [ama'tø:r] *m* amateur.

Amboß ['ambɔs] *m* -sses, -sse anvil.

ambulant [ambu'lant] *a* outpatient.

Ameise ['a:maɪzə] *f* -, -n ant.

Ampel ['ampəl] *f* -, -n traffic lights *pl*.

amphibisch [amˈfiːbɪʃ] *a* amphibious.

amputieren [ampuˈtiːrən] *vt* amputate.

Amsel [ˈamzəl] *f* -, -n blackbird.

Amt [amt] *nt* -(e)s, ¨er office; (*Pflicht*) duty; (*Tel*) exchange; **a—ieren** [amˈtiːrən] *vi* hold office; **a—lich** *a* official; **—sperson** *f* official; **—srichter** *m* district judge; **—sstunden** *pl* office hours *pl*; **—szeit** *f* period of office.

amüsant [amyˈzant] *a* amusing.

Amüsement [amyzəˈmãː] *nt* amusement.

amüsieren [amyˈziːrən] *vt* amuse; *vr* enjoy o.s.

an [an] *prep* +*dat* (*räumlich*) at; (*auf, bei*) on; (*nahe bei*) near; (*zeitlich*) on; +*acc* (*räumlich*) (on)to; — Ostern at Easter; — diesem Ort/Tag at this place/on this day; am Anfang at the beginning; — und für sich actually; *ad*: von ... — from ... on; — die 5 DM around 5 marks; das Licht ist — the light is on.

analog [anaˈloːk] *a* analogous; **A—ie** [-ˈgiː] *f* analogy.

Analyse [anaˈlyːzə] *f* -, -n analysis.

analysieren [analyˈziːrən] *vt* analyse.

Ananas [ˈananas] *f* -, - *or* -se pineapple.

Anarchie [anarˈçiː] *f* anarchy.

Anatomie [anatoˈmiː] *f* anatomy.

anbahnen [ˈanbaːnən] *vtr* open up.

anbändeln [ˈanbɛndəln] *vi* (*col*) flirt.

Anbau [ˈanbau] *m* (*Agr*) cultivation; (*Gebäude*) extension; **a—en** *vt* (*Agr*) cultivate; *Gebäudeteil* build on.

anbehalten [ˈanbəhaltən] *vt irreg* keep on.

anbei [anˈbai] *ad* enclosed.

anbeißen [ˈanbaisən] *irreg vt* bite into; *vi* (*lit*) bite; (*fig*) swallow the bait; **zum A—** (*col*) good enough to eat.

anbelangen [ˈanbəlaŋən] *vt* concern; was mich anbelangt as far as I am concerned.

anberaumen [ˈanbəraumən] *vt* fix.

anbeten [ˈanbeːtən] *vt* worship.

Anbetracht [ˈanbətraxt] *m*: in — (+*gen*) in view of.

Anbetung *f* worship.

anbiedern [ˈanbiːdərn] *vr* make up (*bei* to).

anbieten [ˈanbiːtən] *irreg vt* offer; *vr* volunteer.

anbinden [ˈanbɪndən] *irreg vt* tie up; *vi* mit jdm — start something with sb; kurz angebunden (*fig*) curt.

Anblick [ˈanblɪk] *m* sight; a—en *vt* look at.

anbrechen [ˈanbrɛçən] *irreg vt* start; *Vorräte* break into; *vi* start; (*Tag*) break; (*Nacht*) fall.

anbrennen [ˈanbrɛnən] *vi irreg* catch fire; (*Cook*) burn.

anbringen [ˈanbrɪŋən] *vt irreg* bring; *Ware* sell; (*festmachen*) fasten.

Anbruch [ˈanbrux] *m* beginning; — des Tages/der Nacht dawn/nightfall.

anbrüllen [ˈanbrylən] *vt* roar at.

Andacht [ˈandaxt] *f* -, -en devotion; (*Gottesdienst*) prayers *pl*.

andächtig [ˈandɛçtɪç] *a* devout.

andauern [ˈandauərn] *vi* last, go on; **—d** *a* continual.

Andenken [ˈandɛŋkən] *nt* -s, - memory; souvenir.

andere(r,s) ['andərə(r,z)] a other; (verschieden) different; am —n Tage the next day; ein —s Mal another time; kein —r nobody else; von etw —m sprechen talk about sth else ;'—nteils, —rseits ad on the other hand.

ändern ['ɛndərn] vt alter, change; vr change.

ander- cpd: —nfalls ad otherwise; —s ad differently (als from); wer —s? who else?; jd/irgendwo —s sb/somewhere else; —s aussehen/klingen look/sound different; —sartig a different; —seits ad on the other hand; —sfarbig a of a different colour; —sgläubig a of a different faith; —sherum ad the other way round; —swo ad elsewhere; —swoher ad from elsewhere; —swohin ad elsewhere.

anderthalb ['andərt'halp] a one and a half.

Änderung ['ɛndəruŋ] f alteration, change.

anderweitig ['andər'vartıç] a other; ad otherwise; (anderswo) elsewhere.

andeuten ['andɔytən] vt indicate; (Wink geben) hint at.

Andeutung f indication; hint.

Andrang ['andraŋ] m crush.

andrehen ['andre:ən] vt turn or switch on; (col) jdm etw — unload sth onto sb.

androhen ['andro:ən] vt: jdm etw — threaten sb with sth.

aneignen ['an'aıgnən] vt: sich (dat) etw — acquire sth; (widerrechtlich) appropriate sth.

aneinander ['an'ar'nandər] ad at/on/to etc one another or each other; —fügen vt put together; —geraten vi irreg clash; —legen vt put together.

anekeln ['an'e:kəln] vt disgust.

Anemone [ane'mo:nə] f -, -n anemone.

anerkannt ['an'ɛrkant] a recognized, acknowledged.

anerkennen ['an'ɛrkɛnən] vt irreg recognize, acknowledge; (würdigen) appreciate; —d a appreciative; —swert a praiseworthy.

Anerkennung f recognition, acknowledgement; appreciation.

anfachen ['anfaxən] vt (lit) fan into flame; (fig) kindle.

anfahren ['anfa:rən] irreg vt deliver; (fahren gegen) hit; Hafen put into; (fig) bawl out; vi drive up; (losfahren) drive off.

Anfall ['anfal] m (Med) attack; a—en irreg vt attack; (fig) overcome; vi (Arbeit) come up; (Produkt) be obtained.

anfällig ['anfɛlıç] a delicate; — für etw prone to sth.

Anfang ['anfaŋ] m -(e)s, -fänge beginning, start; von — an right from the beginning; zu — at the beginning; — Mai at the beginning of May; a—en irreg begin, start; (machen) do.

Anfänger(in f) ['anfɛŋər(ın)] m -s, - beginner.

anfänglich ['anfɛŋlıç] a initial.

anfangs ad at first; A—buchstabe m initial or first letter; A—stadium nt initial stages pl.

anfassen ['anfasən] vt handle; (berühren) touch; vi lend a hand; vr feel.

anfechten ['anfɛçtən] vt irreg dispute; (beunruhigen) trouble.

anfertigen ['anfɛrtıgən] vt make.

anfeuern ['anfɔyərn] vt (fig) spur on.

anflehen ['anfle:ən] vt implore.

anfliegen ['anfli:gən] irreg vt fly to; vi fly up.

Anflug ['anflu:k] m (Aviat) approach; (Spur) trace.

anfordern ['anfordərn] vt demand.

Anforderung f demand (gen for).

Anfrage ['anfra:gə] f inquiry; **a—n** vi inquire.

anfreunden ['anfrɔyndən] vr make friends.

anfügen ['anfy:gən] vt add; (beifügen) enclose.

anfühlen ['anfy:lən] vtr feel.

anführen ['anfy:rən] vt lead; (zitieren) quote; (col: betrügen) lead up the garden path.

Anführer m leader.

Anführung f leadership; (Zitat) quotation; **—sstriche, —szeichen** pl quotation marks pl, inverted commas pl.

Angabe ['anga:bə] f statement; (Tech) specification; (col: Prahlerei) boasting; (Sport) service; **—n** pl (Auskunft) particulars pl.

angeben ['ange:bən] irreg vt give; (anzeigen) inform on; (bestimmen) set; vi (col) boast; (Sport) serve.

Angeber m -s, - (col) show-off; **—ei** ['-'rai] f (col) showing off.

angeblich ['ange:pliç] a alleged.

angeboren ['angəbo:rən] a inborn, innate (jdm in sb).

Angebot ['angəbo:t] nt offer; (Comm) supply (an + dat of).

angebracht ['angəbraxt] a appropriate, in order.

angegriffen ['angəgrifən] a exhausted.

angeheitert ['angəhaitərt] a tipsy.

angehen ['ange:ən] irreg vt concern; (angreifen) attack; (bitten) approach (um for); vi (Feuer) light; (col: beginnen) begin; **—d** a prospective; er ist ein —der Vierziger he is approaching forty.

angehören ['angəhø:rən] vi belong (dat to).

Angehörige(r) mf relative.

Angeklagte(r) ['angəkla:ktə(r)] mf accused.

Angel ['aŋəl] f -, -n fishing rod; (Tür—) hinge.

Angelegenheit ['angəle:gənhait] f affair, matter.

Angel- cpd: **—haken** m fish hook; **a—n** vt catch; vi fish; **—n** nt -s angling, fishing; **—rute** f fishing rod.

angemessen ['angəmɛsən] a appropriate, suitable.

angenehm ['angəne:m] a pleasant; **—!** (bei Vorstellung) pleased to meet you; jdm — sein be welcome.

angenommen ['angənɔmən] a assumed; **—, wir ...** assuming we....

angesehen ['angəze:ən] a respected.

angesichts ['angəziçts] prep +gen in view of, considering.

angespannt ['angəʃpant] a Aufmerksamkeit close; Arbeit hard.

Angestellte(r) ['angəʃtɛltə(r)] mf employee.

angetan ['angəta:n] a: von jdm/etw — sein be impressed by sb/sth; es jdm — haben appeal to sb.

angewiesen ['angəvi:zən] a: auf jdn/etw — sein be dependent on sb/sth.

angewöhnen ['angəvø:nən] vt: jdm/sich etw — get sb/become accustomed to sth.

Angewohnheit ['angəvo:nhait] f habit.

angleichen ['anglaiçən] vtr irreg adjust (dat to).

Angler ['aŋlər] m -s, - angler.

angreifen ['angraɪfən] vt irreg attack; (anfassen) touch; Arbeit tackle; (beschädigen) damage.

Angreifer m -s, - attacker.

Angriff ['angrɪf] m attack; etw in — nehmen make a start on sth.

Angst [aŋst] f -, ⁼e fear; — haben be afraid or scared (vor + dat of); — haben um jdn/etw be worried about sb/sth; nur keine —! don't be scared; a— a: jdm. ist a— sb is afraid or scared; jdm a— machen scare sb; —hase m (col) chicken, scaredy-cat.

ängst- [εŋst] cpd: —igen vt frighten; vr worry (o.s.) (vor + dat, um about); —lich a nervous; (besorgt) worried; Ä—lichkeit f nervousness.

anhaben ['anha:bən] vt irreg have on; er kann mir nichts — he can't hurt me.

anhalt- ['anhalt] cpd: —en irreg vt stop; (gegen etw halten) hold up (jdm against sb); jdn zur Arbeit/Höflichkeit — make sb work/be polite; vi stop; (andauern) persist; —end a persistent; A—er m -s, - hitch-hiker; per A—er fahren hitch-hike; A—spunkt m clue.

anhand [an'hant] prep + gen with.

Anhang ['anhaŋ] m appendix; (Leute) family; supporters pl.

anhäng- ['anhɛŋ] cpd: —en vt irreg hang up; Wagen couple up; Zusatz add (on); sich an jdn —en attach o.s. to sb; A—er m -s, - supporter; (Aut) trailer; (am Koffer) tag; (Schmuck) pendant; A—erschaft f supporters pl; A—sel nt appendage; a—lich a attached; A—lichkeit f devotion; A—sel nt -s, - appendage.

Anhäufung ['anhɔʏfʊŋ] f accumulation.

anheben ['anhe:bən] vt irreg lift up; Preise raise.

anheimelnd ['anhaɪməlnt] a comfortable, cosy.

anheimstellen [an'haɪmʃtεlən] vt: jdm etw — leave sth up to sb.

Anhieb ['anhi:b] m: auf — at the very first go; (kurz entschlossen) on the spur of the moment.

Anhöhe ['anhø:ə] f hill.

anhören ['anhø:rən] vt listen to; (anmerken) hear; vr sound.

animieren [ani'mi:rən] vt encourage, urge on.

Anis [a'ni:s] m -es, -e aniseed.

ankaufen ['ankaʊfən] vt purchase, buy.

Anker ['aŋkər] m -s, - anchor; vor — gehen drop anchor; a—n vti anchor; —platz m anchorage.

Anklage ['ankla:gə] f accusation; (Jur) charge; —bank f dock; a—n vt accuse; (Jur) charge (gen with).

Ankläger ['anklε:gər] m accuser.

Anklang ['anklaŋ] m: bei jdm — finden meet with sb's approval.

Ankleide- ['anklaɪdə] cpd: —kabine f changing cubicle; a—n vtr dress.

anklopfen ['anklɔpfən] vi knock.

anknüpfen ['anknʏpfən] vt fasten or tie on; (fig) start; vi (anschließen) refer (an + acc to).

ankommen ['ankɔmən] vi irreg arrive; (näherkommen) approach; (Anklang finden) go down (bei with); es kommt darauf an it depends; (wichtig sein) it depends; (wichtig sein) that (is what) matters; es kommt auf ihn an it depends on him; es darauf — lassen let things take their course; gegen jdn/etw — cope with sb/sth.

ankündigen ['ankʏndɪgən] vt announce.

Ankündigung f announcement.

Ankunft ['ankʊnft] f -, -künfte arrival; —szeit f time of arrival.

ankurbeln ['ankʊrbəln] vt (Aut) crank; (fig) boost.

Anlage' ['anlaːgə] f disposition; (Begabung) talent; (Park) gardens pl; (Beilage) enclosure; (Tech) plant; (Fin) investment; (Entwurf) layout.

anlangen ['anlaŋən] vi arrive.

Anlaß ['anlas] m -sses, -lässe cause (zu for); (Ereignis) occasion; aus — (+gen) on the occasion of; — zu etw geben give rise to sth; etw zum — nehmen take the opportunity of sth.

anlassen irreg vt leave on; Motor start; vr (col) start off.

Anlasser m -s, - (Aut) starter.

anläßlich ['anlɛslɪç] prep +gen on the occasion of.

Anlauf ['anlaʊf] m run-up; a—en irreg vi begin; (Film) show; (Sport) run up; (Fenster) mist up; (Metall) tarnish; rot a—en colour; gegen etw a—en run into or up against sth; angelaufen kommen come running up; vt call at.

anläuten ['anlɔʏtən] vi ring.

anlegen ['anleːgən] vt put (an +acc against/on); (anziehen) put on; (gestalten) lay out; Geld invest; Gewehr aim (auf +acc at); es auf etw (acc) — be out for sth/to do sth; sich mit jdm — (col) quarrel with sb; vi dock.

Anlegestelle f, **Anlegeplatz** m landing place.

anlehnen ['anleːnən] vt lean (an

+acc against); Tür leave ajar; vr lean (an +acc on).

anleiten ['anlaɪtən] vt instruct.

Anleitung f instructions pl.

anlernen ['anlɛrnən] vt teach, instruct.

anliegen ['anliːgən] vi irreg (Kleidung) cling; A— nt -s, - matter; (Wunsch) wish; —d a adjacent; (beigefügt) enclosed.

Anlieger m -s, - resident.

anliegen ['anlyːgən] vt irreg lie to.

anmachen ['anmaxən] vt attach; Elektrisches put on; Salat dress.

anmaßen ['anmaːsən] vt: sich (dat) etw — lay claim to sth; —d a arrogant.

Anmaßung f presumption.

Anmeld- ['anmɛld] cpd: —eformular nt registration form; a—en vt announce; vr (sich ankündigen) make an appointment; (polizeilich, für Kurs etc) register; —ung f announcement; appointment; registration.

anmerken ['anmɛrkən] vt observe; (anstreichen) mark; jdm etw — notice sb's sth; sich (dat) nichts — lassen not give anything away.

Anmerkung f note.

Anmut ['anmuːt] f - grace; a—en vt give a feeling; a—ig a charming.

annähen ['annɛːən] vt sew on.

annähern ['annɛːərn] vr get closer; —d a approximate.

Annäherung f approach; —sversuch m advances pl.

Annahme ['annaːmə] f -, -n acceptance; (Vermutung) assumption.

annehm- ['anneːm] cpd: —bar a acceptable; —en irreg vt accept; Namen take; Kind adopt; (vermuten) suppose, assume; angenommen, das ist so assuming that is so; *vr* take care (*gen* of); A—lichkeit *f* comfort.

annektieren [anɛk'tiːrən] *vt* annex.

Annonce [a'nõːsə] *f* -, -n advertisement.

annoncieren [anõ'siːrən] *vti* advertise.

annullieren [anʊ'liːrən] *vt* annul.

Anode [a'noːdə] *f* -, -n anode.

anöden ['an'øːdən] *vt* (col) bore stiff.

anonym [ano'nyːm] *a* anonymous.

Anorak ['anorak] *m* -s, -s anorak.

anordnen ['an'ɔrdnən] *vt* arrange; (befehlen) order.

Anordnung *f* arrangement; order.

anorganisch ['an'ɔrgaːnɪʃ] *a* inorganic.

anpacken ['anpakən] *vt* grasp; (fig) tackle; mit — lend a hand.

anpassen ['anpasən] *vt* fit (jdm sb); (fig) adapt (dat to); *vr* adapt.

Anpassung *f* fitting; adaptation; a—sfähig *a* adaptable.

Anpfiff ['anpfɪf] *m* (Sport) (starting) whistle; kick-off; (col) rocket.

anpöbeln ['anpøːbəln] *vt* abuse.

Anprall ['anpral] *m* collision (gegen, an +acc with).

anprangern ['anpraŋərn] *vt* denounce.

anpreisen ['anpraɪzən] *vt irreg* extol.

Anprobe ['anproːbə] *f* trying on.

anprobieren ['anprobiːrən] *vt* try on.

anrechnen ['anrɛçnən] *vt* charge; (fig) count; jdm etw hoch — value sb's sth greatly.

Anrecht ['anrɛçt] *nt* right (auf +acc to).

Anrede ['anreːdə] *f* form of address; a—n *vt* address; (belästigen) accost.

anregen ['anreːgən] *vt* stimulate; angeregte Unterhaltung lively discussion; —d *a* stimulating.

Anregung *f* stimulation; (Vorschlag) suggestion.

anreichern ['anraɪçərn] *vt* enrich.

Anreise ['anraɪzə] *f* journey; a—n *vi* arrive.

Anreiz ['anraɪts] *m* incentive.

Anrichte ['anrɪçtə] *f* -, -n sideboard; a—n *vt* serve up; Unheil a—n make mischief.

anrüchig ['anryçɪç] *a* dubious.

anrücken ['anrʏkən] *vi* approach; (Mil) advance.

Anruf ['anruːf] *m* call; a—en *vt irreg* call out to; (bitten) call on; (Tel) ring up, phone, call.

anrühren ['anryːrən] *vt* touch; (mischen) mix.

ans [ans] = an das.

Ansage ['anzaːgə] *f* -, -n announcement; a—n *vt* announce; er say one will come; —r(in *f*) *m* -s, - announcer.

ansammeln ['anzaməln] *vtr* collect.

Ansammlung *f* collection; (Leute) crowd.

ansässig ['anzɛsɪç] *a* resident.

Ansatz ['anzats] *m* start; (Haar—) hairline; (Hals—) base; (Verlängerungsstück) extension; (Veranschlagung) estimate; die ersten Ansätze zu etw the beginnings of sth; —punkt *m* starting point.

anschaffen ['anʃafən] *vt* buy, purchase.

Anschaffung *f* purchase.

anschalten ['anʃaltən] *vt* switch on.

anschau- ['anʃau] *cpd*: —en *vt* look at; —lich *a* illustrative; A—ung *f* (Meinung) view; aus eigener A—ung from one's own experience; A—ungsmaterial *nt* illustrative material.

Anschein ['anʃaɪn] *m* appearance; allem — nach to all appearances; den — haben seem, appear; a—end a apparent.

Anschlag ['anʃlaːk] *m* notice; (*Attentat*) attack; (*Comm*) estimate; (*auf Klavier*) touch; (*Schreibmaschine*) character; a—en ['anʃlaːgən] *irreg vt* put up; (*beschädigen*) chip; (*Akkord*) strike; *Kosten* estimate; *vi* hit (*an +acc* against); (*wirken*) have an effect; (*Glocke*) ring; (*Hund*) bark; —zettel *m* notice.

anschließen ['anʃliːsən] *irreg vt* connect up; *Sender* link up; *vr:* (*sich*) an etw (*acc*) — adjoin sth; (*zeitlich*) follow sth; *vr* join (*jdm/etw* sb/sth); (*beipflichten*) agree (*jdm/etw* with sb/sth); —d a adjacent; (*zeitlich*) subsequent; *ad* afterwards; —d an (+*acc*) following.

Anschluß ['anʃlʊs] *m* (*Elec, Rail*) connection; (*von Wasser etc*) supply; im — an (+*acc*) following; — finden make friends.

anschmiegsam ['anʃmiːkzaːm] *a* affectionate.

anschmieren ['anʃmiːrən] *vt* smear; (*col*) take in.

anschnallen ['anʃnalən] *vt* buckle on; *vr* fasten one's seat belt.

anschneiden ['anʃnaɪdən] *vt irreg* cut into; *Thema* broach.

Anschnitt ['anʃnɪt] *m* first slice.

anschreiben ['anʃraɪbən] *vt irreg* write (up); (*Comm*) charge up; (*benachrichtigen*) write to; bei jdm gut/schlecht angeschrieben sein be well/badly thought of by sb, be in sb's good/bad books.

anschreien ['anʃraɪən] *vt irreg* shout at.

Anschrift ['anʃrɪft] *f* address.

Anschuldigung ['anʃʊldɪgʊŋ] *f* accusation.

anschwellen ['anʃvɛlən] *vi irreg* swell (up).

anschwemmen ['anʃvɛmən] *vt* wash ashore.

anschwindeln ['anʃvɪndəln] *vt* lie to.

ansehen ['anzeːən] *vt irreg* look at; jdm etw — see sth (from sb's face); jdn/etw als etw — look on sb/sth as sth; — für consider; A— *nt* -s respect; (*Ruf*) reputation.

ansehnlich ['anzeːnlɪç] *a* fine-looking; (*beträchtlich*) considerable.

ansein ['anzaɪn] *vi irreg* (*col*) be on.

ansetzen ['anzɛtsən] *vt* (*anfügen*) fix on (*an +acc* to); (*anlegen, an Mund etc*) put (*an +acc* to); (*festlegen*) fix; (*entwickeln*) develop; *Fett* put on; *Blätter* grow; (*zubereiten*) prepare; jdn/etw auf jdn/etw — set sb/sth on sb/sth; *vi* (*anfangen*) start, begin; (*Entwicklung*) set in; (*dick werden*) put on weight; zu etw — prepare to do sth; *vr* (*Rost etc*) start to develop.

Ansicht ['anzɪçt] *f* (*Anblick*) sight; (*Meinung*) view, opinion; zur — on approval; meiner — nach in my opinion; —skarte *f* picture postcard; —ssache *f* matter of opinion.

anspannen ['anʃpanən] *vt* harness; *Muskel* strain.

Anspannung *f* strain.

Anspiel ['anʃpiːl] *nt* (*Sport*) start; a—en *vi* (*Sport*) start play; auf etw (*acc*) a—en refer *or* allude to sth; —ung *f* reference, allusion (*auf +acc* to).

Ansporn ['anʃpɔrn] *m* -(e)s incentive.

Ansprache ['anʃprɑːxə] *f* address.

ansprechen ['anʃprɛçən] *irreg vt* speak to; (*bitten, gefallen*) appeal to; jdn auf etw (*acc*) (hin) — ask sb about sth; etw als etw — regard sth as sth; *vi* react (*auf + acc* to); —d a attractive.

anspringen ['anʃprɪŋən] *vi irreg* (*Aut*) start.

Anspruch ['anʃprʊx] *m* (*Recht*) claim (*auf + acc* to); hohe Ansprüche stellen/haben demand/expect a lot; jdn/etw in — nehmen occupy sb/take up sth; a—slos a undemanding; a—svoll a demanding.

anspucken ['anʃpʊkən] *vt* spit at.

anstacheln ['anʃtaxəln] *vt* spur on.

Anstalt ['anʃtalt] *f* -, -en institution; —en machen, etw zu tun prepare to do sth.

Anstand ['anʃtant] *m* decency.

anständig ['anʃtɛndɪç] a decent; (*col*) proper; (*groß*) considerable; A—keit *f* propriety, decency.

anstandslos ad without any ado.

anstarren ['anʃtarən] *vt* stare at.

anstatt [an'ʃtat] *prep + gen* instead of; *cj*: — etw zu tun instead of doing sth.

anstechen ['anʃtɛçən] *vt irreg* prick; Faß tap.

Ansteck- ['anʃtɛk] *cpd*: a—en *vt* pin on; (*Med*) infect; Pfeife light; Haus set fire to; *vr*: ich habe mich bei ihm angesteckt I caught it from him; *vi* (*fig*) be infectious; a—end a infectious; —ung *f* infection.

anstehen ['anʃteːən] *vi irreg* queue (up), line up (*US*).

anstelle [an'ʃtɛlə] *prep + gen* in place of; —n ['an-] *vt* (*einschalten*)

turn on; (*Arbeit geben*) employ; (*machen*) do; *vr* queue (up), line up (*US*); (*col*) act.

Anstellung *f* employment; (*Posten*) post, position.

Anstieg ['anʃtiːk] *m* -(e)s, -e climb; (*fig: von Preisen etc*) increase (*gen* in).

anstift- ['anʃtɪft] *cpd*: —en *vt* Unglück cause; jdn zu etw —en put sb up to sth; A—er *m* -s, - instigator.

anstimmen ['anʃtɪmən] *vt* Lied strike up with; Geschrei set up; *vi* strike up.

Anstoß ['anʃtoːs] *m* impetus; (*Ärgernis*) offence; (*Sport*) kick-off; der erste — the initiative; — nehmen an (+ *dat*) take offence at; a—en *irreg vt* push; (*mit Fuß*) kick; *vi* knock, bump; (*mit der Zunge*) lisp; (*mit Gläsern*) drink (a toast) (*auf + acc* to); an etw (*acc*) a—en (*angrenzen*) adjoin sth.

anstößig ['anʃtøːsɪç] a offensive, indecent; A—keit *f* indecency, offensiveness.

anstreben ['anʃtreːbən] *vt* strive for.

anstreichen ['anʃtraɪçən] *vt irreg* paint.

Anstreicher *m* -s, - painter.

anstrengen ['anʃtrɛŋən] *vt* strain; (*Jur*) bring; *vr* make an effort; angestrengt ad as hard as one can; —d a tiring.

Anstrengung *f* effort.

Anstrich ['anʃtrɪç] *m* coat of paint.

Ansturm ['anʃtʊrm] *m* rush; (*Mil*) attack.

ansuchen ['anzuːxən] *vi*: um etw — apply for sth; A—nt -s,- request.

Antagonismus [antago'nɪsmʊs] *m* antagonism.

antasten 23 Anzahl

antasten ['antastən] vt touch; *Recht* infringe upon; *Ehre* question.

Anteil ['antaɪl] m -s, -e share (*an* + *dat* in); (*Mitgefühl*) sympathy; — **nehmen an** (+ *dat*) share in; (*sich interessieren*) take an interest in; —**nahme** f - sympathy.

Antenne [an'tɛnə] f -, -n aerial; (*Zool*) antenna.

Anthrazit [antra'tsiːt] m -s, -e anthracite.

Anti- ['anti] *in cpds* anti; —**alkoholiker** m teetotaller; **a—autoritär** a anti-authoritarian; —**biotikum** [antibi'oːtikum] nt -s, -**ka** antibiotic.

antik [an'tiːk] a antique; A—e f -, -**n** (*Zeitalter*) ancient world; (*Kunstgegenstand*) antique.

Antikörper m antibody.

Antilope [anti'loːpə] f -, -**n** antelope.

Antipathie [antipa'tiː] f antipathy.

Antiquariat [antikvari'aːt] nt -(e)s, -e secondhand bookshop.

Antiquitäten [antikviˈtɛːtən] pl antiques pl; —**handel** m antique business; —**händler** m antique dealer.

Antrag ['antraːk] m -(e)s, -**träge** proposal; (*Parl*) motion; (*Gesuch*) application.

antreffen ['antrɛfən] vt irreg meet.

antreiben ['antraɪbən] irreg vt drive on; *Motor* drive; (*anschwemmen*) wash up; vi be washed up.

antreten ['antreːtən] irreg vt *Amt* take up; *Erbschaft* come into; *Beweis* offer; *Reise* start, begin; (*Mil*) fall in; (*Sport*) line up; **gegen jdn** — play/fight against sb.

Antrieb ['antriːp] m (*lit,fig*) drive; **aus eigenem** — one's own accord.

antrinken ['antriŋkən] vt irreg *Flasche, Glas* start... to drink from; **sich** (*dat*) **Mut/einen Rausch** — give oneself Dutch courage/get drunk; **angetrunken sein** be tipsy.

Antritt ['antrit] m beginning, commencement; (*eines Amts*) taking up.

antun ['antuːn] vt irreg: **jdm etw** — do sth to sb; **sich** (*dat*) **Zwang** — force o.s.

Antwort ['antvɔrt] f-, -**en** answer, reply; um — **wird gebeten** RSVP; **a—en** vi answer, reply.

anvertrauen ['anfɛrtrauən] vt: **jdm etw** — entrust sb with sth; **sich jdm** — confide in sb.

anwachsen ['anvaksən] vi irreg grow; (*Pflanze*) take root.

Anwalt ['anvalt] m -(e)s, -**wälte**, **Anwältin** ['anvɛltɪn] f solicitor; lawyer; (*fig*) champion.

Anwandlung ['anvandluŋ] f caprice; **eine** — **von etw** a fit of sth.

Anwärter ['anvɛrtər] m candidate.

anweisen ['anvaɪzən] vt irreg instruct; (*zuteilen*) assign (*jdm etw* sth to sb).

Anweisung f instruction; (*Comm*) remittance; (*Post—, Zahlungs—*) money order.

anwend- ['anvɛnd] cpd: —**bar** ['anvɛnt-] a practicable, applicable; —**en** vt irreg use, employ; *Gesetz, Regel* apply; A—**ung** f use; application.

Anwesen- ['anveːzən] cpd: **a—d** a present; **die** —**den** those present; —**heit** f presence; —**heitsliste** f attendance register.

anwidern ['anviːdərn] vt disgust.

Anwuchs ['anvuːks] m growth.

Anzahl ['antsaːl] f number (*an* + *dat* of); **a—en** vt pay on account; —ung f deposit, payment on account.

anzapfen ['antsapfən] vt tap; Person (um Geld) touch.

Anzeichen ['antsaiçən] nt sign, indication.

Anzeige ['antsaigə] f -, -n (Zeitungs—) announcement; (Werbung) advertisement; (bei Polizei) report; — erstatten gegen jdn report sb (to the police); a—n vt (zu erkennen geben) show; (bekanntgeben) announce; (bei Polizei) report; —nteil m advertisements pl; —r m indicator.

anzetteln ['antsetəln] vt (col) instigate.

anziehen ['antsi:ən] irreg vt attract; Kleidung put on; Mensch dress; Schraube, Seil pull tight; Knie draw up; Feuchtigkeit absorb; vr get dressed; —d a attractive.

Anziehung f (Reiz) attraction; —skraft f power of attraction; (Phys) force of gravitation.

Anzug ['antsu:k] m suit; im — sein be approaching.

anzüglich ['antsy:kliç] a personal; (anstößig) offensive; A—keit f offensiveness; (Bemerkung) personal remark.

anzünden ['antsyndən] vt light.

Anzünder m lighter.

anzweifeln ['antsvaifəln] vt doubt.

apart [a'part] a distinctive.

Apathie [apa'ti:] f apathy.

apathisch [a'pa:tiʃ] a apathetic.

Apfel ['apfəl] m -s, = apple; —saft m apple juice; —sine [apfəl'zi:nə] f -, -n orange; —wein m cider.

Apostel [a'pɔstəl] m -s, - apostle.

Apostroph [apo'stro:f] m -s, -e apostrophe.

Apotheke [apo'te:kə] f -, -n chemist's (shop), drugstore (US); —r(in f) m -s,- chemist, druggist (US).

Apparat [apa'ra:t] m -(e)s, -e piece of apparatus; camera; telephone; (Rad, TV) set; am — bleiben hold the line; —ur [-'tu:r] f apparatus.

Appartement [apart(ə)'mã:] nt -s, -s flat.

Appell [a'pɛl] m -s, -e (Mil) muster, parade; (fig) appeal; a—ieren [ape'li:rən] vi appeal (an + acc to).

Appetit [ape'ti:t] m -(e)s, -e appetite; guten — enjoy your meal; a—lich a appetizing; —losigkeit f lack of appetite.

Applaus [a'plaus] m -es, -e applause.

Appretur [apre'tu:r] f finish.

Aprikose [apri'ko:zə] f -, -n apricot.

April [a'prɪl] m -(s), -e April; —wetter nt April showers pl.

Aquaplaning [akva'pla:nɪŋ] nt (-s) aquaplaning.

Aquarell [akva'rɛl] nt -s, -e watercolour.

Aquarium [a'kva:rium] nt aquarium.

Äquator [ɛ'kva:tor] m -s equator.

Arbeit ['arbait] f -, -en work (no art); (Stelle) job; (Erzeugnis) piece of work; (wissenschaftliche) dissertation; (Klassen—) test; das war eine — that was a hard job; a—en vi work; vt work, make; —er(in f) m -s, - worker; (ungelernt) labourer; —erschaft f workers pl, labour force; —geber m -s, - employer; —nehmer m -s, - employee; a—sam a industrious.

Arbeits- in cpds labour; **—amt** nt employment exchange; **a—fähig** a fit for work, able-bodied; **—gang** m operation; **—gemeinschaft** f study group; **—kräfte** pl workers pl, labour; **a—los** a unemployed, out-of-work; **—losigkeit** f unemployment; **—platz** m job; place of work; **a—scheu** a work-shy; **—tag** m work(ing) day; **—teilung** f division of labour; **a—unfähig** a unfit for work; **—zeit** f working hours pl.

Archäologe [arçeɔ'loːɡə] m -n, -n archaeologist.

Architekt(in f) [arçi'tekt(m)] m -en, -en architect; **—ur** [-'tuːr] f architecture.

Archiv [ar'çiːf] nt -s, -e archive.

arg [ark] a bad, awful; ad awfully, very.

Ärger ['ɛrɡər] m -s (Wut) anger; (Unannehmlichkeit) trouble; **ä—lich** a (zornig) angry; (lästig) annoying, aggravating; **ä—n** vt annoy; vr get annoyed; **—nis** nt -ses, -se annoyance; öffentliches **—nis erregen** be a public nuisance.

arg- cpd: **—listig** a cunning, insidious; **—los** a guileless, innocent; **A—losigkeit** f guilelessness, innocence; **A—ument** [arɡu'ment] nt argument; **A—wohn** m suspicion; **—wöhnisch** a suspicious.

Arie ['aːrjə] f -, -n aria.

Aristokrat [aristo'kraːt] m -en,-en aristocrat **—ie** [-'tiː] f aristocracy; **a—isch** a aristocratic.

arithmetisch [arit'meːtiʃ] a arithmetical.

arm [arm] a poor; **A—** m -(e)s, -e arm; (Fluß-) branch; **A—a'tur** f (Elec) armature; **A—a'turenbrett** nt instrument panel; (Aut) dashboard; **A—band** nt bracelet;

A—banduhr f (wrist) watch; **A—e(r)** mf poor man/woman; **die A—en** the poor; **A—ee** [ar'meː] f -, -n army; **A—eekorps** nt army corps.

Ärmel ['ɛrməl] m -s, - sleeve; etw aus dem **—** schütteln (fig) produce sth just like that.

ärmlich ['ɛrmlɪç] a poor.

armselig a wretched, miserable.

Armut ['armuːt] f - poverty.

Aroma [a'roːma] nt -s, Aromen aroma; **a—tisch** [aro'maːtɪʃ] a aromatic.

arrangieren [arã'ʒiːrən] vt arrange; vr come to an arrangement.

Arrest [a'rest] m -(e)s, -e detention.

arrogant [aro'ɡant] a arrogant.

Arroganz f arrogance.

Arsch [arʃ] m -es, ⁓e (col) arse, bum.

Art [aːrt] f -, -en (Weise) way; (Sorte) kind, sort; (Biol) species; **eine — (von) Frucht** a kind of fruit; **Häuser aller —** houses of all kinds; **es ist nicht seine —, das zu tun** it's not like him to do that; **ich mache das auf meine —** I do that my (own) way; **nach — des Hauses** à la maison; **a—en** vi: nach jdm **a—en** take after sb; **der Mensch ist so geartet, daß ... human nature** is such that ...

Arterie [ar'teːrjə] f artery; **—nver-kalkung** f arteriosclerosis.

artig ['aːrtɪç] a good, well-behaved.

Artikel [ar'tiːkəl] m -s, - article.

Artillerie [artilə'riː] f artillery.

Arznei [aːrts'naɪ] f medicine; **—mittel** nt medicine, medicament.

Arzt [aːrtst] m -es, ⁓e, **Ärztin** ['ɛːrtstɪn] f doctor.

ärztlich ['ɛːrtstlıç] a medical.

As [as] nt -ses, -se ace.

Asbest [as'bɛst] m -(e)s, -e asbestos.

Asche ['aʃə] f -, -n ash, cinder; —nbahn f cinder track; —nbecher m ashtray; —nbrödel nt Cinderella; —rmittwoch m Ash Wednesday.

asozial ['azotsiaːl] a antisocial; Familien asocial.

Aspekt [as'pɛkt] m -(e)s, -e aspect.

Asphalt [as'falt] m -(e)s, -e asphalt; a—ieren [-'tiːrən] vt asphalt; —straße f asphalt road.

Assistent(in f) [asıs'tɛnt(ın)] m assistant.

Assoziation [asotsiatsi'oːn] f association.

Ast [ast] m -(e)s, ≈e bough, branch; —er f -, -n aster.

ästhetisch [ɛs'teːtıʃ] a aesthetic.

Asthma ['astma] nt -s asthma; —tiker(in f) [ast'maːtikər(ın)] m -s, - asthmatic.

Astro- [astro] cpd: —'loge m -n, -n astrologer; —lo'gie f astrology; —'naut m -en, -en astronaut; —'nautik f astronautics; —'nom m -en, -en astronomer; —no'mie f astronomy.

Asyl [a'zyːl] nt -s, -e asylum; (Heim) home; (Obdachlosen—) shelter.

Atelier [atəli'eː] nt -s, -s studio.

Atem ['aːtəm] m -s breath; den —anhalten hold one's breath; außer — out of breath; a—beraubend a breath-taking; a—los a breathless; —pause f breather; —zug m breath.

Atheismus [ate'ısmʊs] m atheism.

Atheist m atheist; a—isch a atheistic.

Äther ['ɛːtər] m -s, - ether.

Athlet [at'leːt] m -en, -en athlete; —ik f athletics.

Atlas ['atlas] m - or -ses, -se or At'lanten atlas.

atmen ['aːtmən] vti breathe.

Atmosphäre [atmo'sfɛːrə] f -, -n atmosphere.

atmosphärisch a atmospheric.

Atmung [a'tmʊŋ] f respiration.

Atom [a'toːm] nt -s, -e atom; a—ar [ato'maːr] a atomic; —bombe f atom bomb; —energie f atomic or nuclear energy; —kern m atomic nucleus; —kernforschung f nuclear research; —kraftwerk nt nuclear power station; —krieg m nuclear or atomic war; —macht f nuclear or atomic power; —müll m atomic waste; —sperrvertrag m (Pol) nuclear non-proliferation treaty; —versuch m atomic .test; —waffen pl. atomic weapons pl; —zeitalter nt atomic age.

Attentat [atɛn'taːt] nt -(e)s, -e (attempted) assassination· (auf + acc of).

Attentäter [atɛn'tɛːtər] m (would-be) assassin.

Attest [a'tɛst] nt -(e)s, -e certificate.

attraktiv [atrak'tiːf] a attractive.

Attrappe [a'trapə] f -, -n dummy.

Attribut [atri'buːt] nt -(e)s, -e (Gram) attribute.

ätzen ['ɛtsən] vi be caustic.

auch [aux] cf also, too, as well; (selbst, sogar) even; (wirklich) really; oder — or; — das ist schön that's nice too or as well; das habe ich — nicht gemacht I didn't do it either; ich — nicht nor I, me neither; — wenn das Wetter schlecht ist even if the weather is bad; wer/was — whoever/whatever; so sieht es — aus it looks like it too; — das noch! not that as well!

auf [aʊf] *prep* +acc or dat (räumlich) on; (hinauf: +acc) up; (in Richtung: +acc) to; (nach) after; — der Reise on the way; — der Post/dem Fest at the post office/party; — das Land into the country; — der Straße on the road; — dem Land/der ganzen Welt in the country/the whole world; — deutsch in German; — Lebenszeit for sb's lifetime; bis — ihn except for him; — einmal at once; ad: — und ab up and down; — und davon up and away; —! (los) come on!; — sein (col) (Person) be up; (Tür) be open; von Kindheit — from childhood onwards; — daß so that.

aufatmen ['aʊfʔaːtmən] *vi* heave a sigh of relief.

aufbahren ['aʊfbaːrən] *vt* lay out.

Aufbau ['aʊfbaʊ] *m* (Bauen) building, construction; (Struktur) structure; (aufgebautes Teil) superstructure; a—en *vt* erect, build (up); Existenz make; (gestalten) construct; (gründen) found, base (auf + dat on).

aufbäumen ['aʊfbɔymən] *vr* rear; (fig) revolt, rebel.

aufbauschen ['aʊfbaʊʃən] *vt* puff out; (fig) exaggerate.

aufbehalten ['aʊfbəhaltən] *vt irreg* keep on.

aufbekommen ['aʊfbəkɔmən] *vt irreg* (öffnen) get open; Hausaufgaben be given.

aufbessern ['aʊfbɛsərn] *vt* Gehalt increase.

aufbewahren ['aʊfbəvaːrən] *vt* keep; Gepäck put in the left-luggage office.

Aufbewahrung *f* (safe)keeping; (Gepäck—) left-luggage office; jdm etw zur — geben give sb sth for safekeeping; —sort *m* storage place.

aufbieten ['aʊfbiːtən] *vt irreg* Kraft summon (up), exert; Armee, Polizei mobilize; Brautpaar publish the banns of.

aufblasen ['aʊfblaːzən] *irreg vt* blow up, inflate; *vr* (col) become big-headed.

aufbleiben ['aʊfblaɪbən] *vi irreg* (Laden) remain open; (Person) stay up.

aufblenden ['aʊfblɛndən] *vt* Scheinwerfer turn on full beam.

aufblicken ['aʊfblɪkən] *vi* (lit, fig) look up (zu (lit) at, (fig) to).

aufblühen ['aʊfblyːən] *vi* blossom, flourish.

aufbrauchen ['aʊfbraʊxən] *vt* use up.

aufbrausen ['aʊfbraʊzən] *vi* (fig) flare up; —d a hot-tempered.

aufbrechen ['aʊfbrɛçən] *irreg vt* break or prize open; *vi* burst open; (gehen) start, set off.

aufbringen ['aʊfbrɪŋən] *vt irreg* (öffnen) open; (in Mode) bring into fashion; (beschaffen) procure; (Fin) raise; (ärgern) irritate; Verständnis für etw — be able to understand sth.

Aufbruch ['aʊfbrʊx] *m* departure.

aufbrühen ['aʊfbryːən] *vt* Tee make.

aufbürden ['aʊfbyrdən] *vt* burden (jdm etw sb with sth).

aufdecken ['aʊfdɛkən] *vt* uncover.

aufdrängen ['aʊfdrɛŋən] *vt* force (jdm on sb); *vr* intrude (jdm on sb).

aufdringlich ['aufdrɪŋlɪç] *a* pushy.
aufeinander [auf'ar'nandər] *ad* achten after each other; schießen at each other; vertrauen each other; **A—folge** *f* succession, series; **—folgen** *vi* follow one another; **—folgend** *a* consecutive; **—legen** *vt* lay on top of one another; **—prallen** *vi* hit one another.
Aufenthalt ['auf'ɛnthalt] *m* stay; (Verzögerung) delay; (Rail: Halten) stop; (Ort) haunt; **—sgenehmigung** *f* residence permit.
auferlegen ['auf'ɛrle:gən] *vt* impose (jdm etw sth upon sb).
Auferstehung · ['auf'ɛrʃte:uŋ] *f* resurrection.
aufessen ['auf'ɛsən] *vt irreg* eat up.
auffahr- ['auffa:r] *cpd:* **—en** *irreg vi* (Auto) run, crash (auf +acc into); (herankommen) draw up; (hochfahren) jump up; (wütend werden) flare up; (in den Himmel) ascend; *vt* Kanonen, Geschütz bring up; **—end** *a* hot-tempered; **A—t** *f* (Haus—) drive; (Autobahn—) slip road; **A—unfall** *m* pile-up.
auffallen ['auffalən] *vi irreg* be noticeable; jdm — strike sb; **—d** *a* striking.
auffällig ['auffɛlɪç] *a* conspicuous, striking.
auffang- ['auffaŋ] *cpd:* **—en** *vt irreg* catch; Funkspruch intercept; Preise peg; **A—lager** *nt* refugee camp.
auffassen ['auffasən] *vt* understand, comprehend; (auslegen) see, view.
Auffassung *f* (Meinung) opinion; (Auslegung) view, concept; (also **—sgabe**) grasp.

auffindbar ['auffɪntba:r] *a* to be found.
auffordern ['auffɔrdərn] *vt* (befehlen) call upon, order; (bitten) ask.
Aufforderung *f* (Befehl) order; (Einladung) invitation.
auffrischen ['auffrɪʃən] *vt* freshen up; Kenntnisse brush up; Erinnerungen reawaken; *vi* (Wind) freshen.
aufführen ['auffy:rən] *vt* (Theat) perform; (in einem Verzeichnis) list, specify; *vr* (sich benehmen) behave.
Aufführung *f* (Theat) performance; (Liste) specification.
Aufgabe ['aufga:bə] *f* **-, -n** task; (Sch) exercise; (Haus—) homework; (Verzicht) giving up; (von Gepäck) registration; (von Post) posting; (von Inserat) insertion.
Aufgang ['aufgaŋ] *m* ascent; (Sonnen—) rise; (Treppe) staircase.
aufgeben ['aufge:bən] *irreg vt* (verzichten) give up; Paket send, post; Gepäck register; Bestellung give; Inserat insert; Rätsel, Problem set; *vi* give up.
Aufgebot ['aufgəbo:t] *nt* supply; (von Kräften) utilization; (Ehe—) banns *pl.*
aufgedreht ['aufgədre:t] *a* (col) excited.
aufgedunsen ['aufgədunzən] *a* swollen, puffed up.
aufgehen ['aufge:ən] *vi irreg* (Sonne, Teig) rise; (sich öffnen) open; (klarwerden) become clear (jdm to sb); (Math) come out exactly; (sich widmen) be absorbed (in +dat in); in Rauch/Flammen — go up in smoke/flames.
aufgeklärt ['aufgəklɛ:rt] *a* en-

lightened; (sexuell) knowing the facts of life.

aufgelegt ['aufgəle:kt] a: gut/schlecht — sein be in a good/bad mood; zu etw — sein be in the mood for sth.

aufgeregt ['aufgəre:kt] a excited.

aufgeschlossen ['aufgəʃlɔsən] a open, open-minded.

aufgeweckt ['aufgəvɛkt] a bright, intelligent.

aufgießen ['aufgi:sən] vt irreg Wasser pour over; Tee infuse.

aufgreifen ['aufgraifən] vt irreg Thema take up; Verdächtige pick up, seize.

aufgrund [auf'grunt] prep +gen on the basis of; (wegen) because of.

aufhaben ['aufha:bən] vt irreg have on; Arbeit have to do.

aufhalsen ['aufhalzən] vt (col) jdm etw — saddle or lumber sb with sth.

aufhalten ['aufhaltən] irreg vt Person detain; Entwicklung check; Tür, Hand hold open; Augen keep open; vr (wohnen) live; (bleiben) stay; sich über etw/jdn — go on about sth/sb; sich mit etw — waste time over.

aufhängen ['aufhɛŋən] irreg vt Wäsche hang up; Menschen hang; vr hang o.s.

Aufhänger m -s, - (am Mantel) hook; (fig) peg.

aufheben ['aufhe:bən] irreg vt (hochheben) raise, lift; Sitzung wind up; Urteil annul; Gesetz repeal, abolish; (aufbewahren) keep; bei jdm gut aufgehoben sein be well looked after at sb's; vr cancel o.s. out; viel A—(s) machen make a fuss (von about).

aufheitern ['aufhaitərn] vtr (Him-

mel, Miene) brighten; Mensch cheer up.

aufhellen ['aufhɛlən] vtr clear up; Farbe, Haare lighten.

aufhetzen ['aufhɛtsən] vt stir up (gegen against).

aufholen ['aufho:lən] vt make up; vi catch up.

aufhorchen ['aufhɔrçən] vi prick up one's ears.

aufhören ['aufhø:rən] vi stop; etw zu tun stop doing sth.

aufklappen ['aufklapən] vt open.

aufklären ['aufklɛ:rən] vt Geheimnis etc clear up; Person enlighten; (sexuell) tell the facts of life to; (Mil) reconnoitre; vr clear up.

Aufklärung f (von Geheimnis) clearing up; (Unterrichtung, Zeitalter) enlightenment; (sexuell) sex education; (Mil, Aviat) reconnaissance.

aufkleben ['aufkle:bən] vt stick on.

Aufkleber m -s, - sticker.

aufknöpfen ['aufknœpfən] vt unbutton.

aufkommen ['aufkɔmən] vi irreg (Wind) come up; (Zweifel, Gefühl) arise; (Mode) start; für jdn/etw — be liable or responsible for sth/sb.

aufladen ['aufla:dən] vt irreg load.

Auflage ['aufla:gə] f edition; (Zeitung) circulation; (Bedingung) condition; jdm etw zur — machen make sth a condition for sb.

auflassen ['auflasən] vt (offen) leave open; (aufgesetzt) leave on.

auflauern ['auflauərn] vi: jdm — lie in wait for sb.

Auflauf ['auflauf] m (Cook) pudding; (Menschen—) crowd.

aufleben ['aufle:bən] vi revive.

auflegen ['aʊfleːgən] vt put on; Telefon hang up; (Print) print.
auflehnen ['aʊfleːnən] vt lean on; vr rebel (gegen against).
Auflehnung f rebellion.
auflesen ['aʊfleːzən] vt irreg pick up.
aufleuchten ['aʊflɔʏçtən] vi light up.
aufliegen ['aʊfliːgən] vi irreg lie on; (Comm) be available.
auflockern ['aʊflɔkərn] vt loosen; (fig) Eintönigkeit etc liven up.
auflösen ['aʊfløːzən] vtr dissolve; Haare etc loosen; Mißverständnis sort out; (in Tränen) aufgelöst sein be in tears.
Auflösung f dissolving; (fig) solution.
aufmachen ['aʊfmaxən] vt open; Kleidung undo; (zurechtmachen) do up; vr set out.
Aufmachung f (Kleidung) outfit, get-up; (Gestaltung) format.
aufmerksam ['aʊfmɛrkzaːm] a attentive; jdn auf etw (acc) — machen point sth out to sb; A—keit f attention, attentiveness.
aufmuntern ['aʊfmʊntərn] vt (ermutigen) encourage; (erheitern) cheer up.
Aufnahme ['aʊfnaːmə] f -, -n reception; (Beginn) beginning; (in Verein etc) admission; (in Liste etc) inclusion; (Notieren) taking down; (Phot) shot; (auf Tonband etc) recording; a—fähig a receptive; —prüfung f entrance test.
aufnehmen ['aʊfneːmən] vt irreg receive; (hochheben) pick up; (beginnen) take up; (in Verein etc) admit; (in Liste etc) include; (fassen) hold; (notieren) take down; (photographieren) photo-

graph; (auf Tonband, Platte) record; (Fin: leihen) take out; es mit jdm — können be able to compete with sb.
aufopfern ['aʊfʔɔpfərn] vtr sacrifice; —d a selfless.
aufpassen ['aʊfpasən] vi (aufmerksam sein) pay attention; auf jdn/etw — look after or watch sb/sth; aufgepaßt look out!
Aufprall ['aʊfpral] m -s, -e impact; a—en vi hit, strike.
Aufpreis ['aʊfpraɪs] m extra charge.
aufpumpen ['aʊfpʊmpən] vt pump up.
aufputschen ['aʊfpʊtʃən] vt (aufhetzen) inflame; (erregen) stimulate.
aufraffen ['aʊfrafən] vr rouse o.s.
aufräumen ['aʊfrɔʏmən] vti Dinge clear away; Zimmer tidy up.
aufrecht ['aʊfrɛçt] a (lit, fig) upright; —erhalten vt irreg maintain.
aufreg- ['aʊfreːg] cpd: —en vt excite; vr get excited; —end a exciting; A—ung f excitement.
aufreiben ['aʊfraɪbən] vt irreg Haut rub open; (erschöpfen) exhaust; —d a strenuous.
aufreißen ['aʊfraɪsən] vt irreg Umschlag tear open; Augen open wide; Tür throw open; Straße take up.
aufreizen ['aʊfraɪtsən] vt incite, stir up; —d a exciting, stimulating.
aufrichten ['aʊfrɪçtən] vt put up, erect; (moralisch) console; vr rise (moralisch) take heart (an + dat from).
aufrichtig ['aʊfrɪçtɪç] a sincere, honest; A—keit f sincerity.
aufrücken ['aʊfrʏkən] vi move up; (beruflich) be promoted.

Aufruf ['aʊfruːf] m summons; (zur Hilfe) call; (des Namens) calling out; a—en vt irreg (auffordern) call upon (zu for); Namen call out.

Aufruhr ['aʊfruːr] m -(e)s, -e uprising, revolt; in — sein be in uproar.

aufrührerisch ['aʊfryːrərɪʃ] a rebellious.

aufrunden ['aʊfrʊndən] vt Summe round up.

Aufrüstung ['aʊfrʏstʊŋ] f rearmament.

aufrütteln ['aʊfrʏtəln] vt (lit, fig) shake up.

aufs [aʊfs] = auf das.

aufsagen ['aʊfzaːgən] vt Gedicht recite; Freundschaft put an end to.

aufsammeln ['aʊfzaməln] vt gather up.

aufsässig ['aʊfzɛsɪç] a rebellious.

Aufsatz ['aʊfzats] m (Geschriebenes) essay; (auf Schrank etc) top.

aufsaugen ['aʊfzaʊgən] vt irreg soak up.

aufschauen ['aʊfʃaʊən] vi look up.

aufscheuchen ['aʊfʃɔʏçən] vt scare or frighten away.

aufschieben ['aʊfʃiːbən] vt irreg push open; (verzögern) put off, postpone.

Aufschlag ['aʊfʃlaːk] m (Ärmel—) cuff; (Jacken—) lapel; (Hosen—) turn-up; (Aufprall) impact; (Preis—) surcharge; (Tennis) service; a—en irreg vt (öffnen) open; (verwunden) cut; (hochschlagen) turn up; (aufbauen) Zelt, Lager pitch, erect; Wohnsitz take up; vi (aufprallen) hit; (teurer werden) go up; (Tennis) serve.

aufschließen ['aʊfʃliːsən] irreg vt open up, unlock; vi (aufrücken) close up.

Aufschluß ['aʊfʃlʊs] m information; a—reich a informative, illuminating.

aufschnappen ['aʊfʃnapən] vt (col) pick up; vi fly open.

aufschneiden ['aʊfʃnaɪdən] irreg vt Geschwür cut open; Brot cut up; (Med) lance; vi brag.

Aufschneider m -s, - boaster, braggart.

Aufschnitt ['aʊfʃnɪt] m (slices of) cold meat.

aufschnüren ['aʊfʃnyːrən] vt unlace; Paket untie.

aufschrauben ['aʊfʃraʊbən] vt (fest—) screw on; (lösen) unscrew.

aufschrecken ['aʊfʃrɛkən] vt startle; vi irreg start up.

Aufschrei ['aʊfʃraɪ] m cry; a—en vi irreg cry out.

aufschreiben ['aʊfʃraɪbən] vt irreg write down.

Aufschrift ['aʊfʃrɪft] f (Inschrift) inscription; (auf Etikett) label.

Aufschub ['aʊfʃuːp] m -(e)s, -schübe delay, postponement.

aufschwatzen ['aʊfʃvatsən] vt: jdm etw — talk sb into (getting/having etc) sth.

Aufschwung ['aʊfʃvʊŋ] m (Elan) boost; (wirtschaftlich) upturn, boom; (Sport) circle.

aufsehen ['aʊfzeːən] vi irreg (lit, fig) look up (zu lit at, (fig) to); A— nt -s sensation, stir; —erregend a sensational.

Aufseher(in f) m -s, - guard; (im Betrieb) supervisor; (Museums—) attendant; (Park—) keeper.

aufsein ['aʊfzaɪn] vi irreg (col) be open; (Person) be up.

aufsetzen ['aʊfzɛtsən] vt put on; Flugzeug put down; Dokument draw up; *vr* sit upright; *vi* (*Flugzeug*) touch down.

Aufsicht ['aufzɪçt] *f* supervision; die — haben be in charge.

aufsitzen ['aufzɪtsən] *vi irreg* (*aufrecht hinsitzen*) sit up; (*aufs Pferd, Motorrad*) mount, get on; (*Schiff*) run aground; jdm — lassen (*col*) stand sb up; jdm — (*col*) be taken in by sb.

aufspalten ['aufʃpaltən] *vt* split.

aufsparen ['aufʃpaːrən] *vt* save (up).

aufsperren ['aufʃpɛrən] *vt* unlock; *Mund* open wide.

aufspielen ['aufʃpiːlən] *vr* show off; **sich als etw** — try to come on as sth.

aufspießen ['aufʃpiːsən] *vt* spear.

aufspringen ['aufʃprɪŋən] *vi irreg* jump (*auf* +*acc* onto); (*hochspringen*) jump up; (*sich öffnen*) spring open; (*Hände, Lippen*) become chapped.

aufspüren ['aufʃpyːrən] *vt* track down; trace.

aufstacheln ['aufʃtaxəln] *vt* incite.

Aufstand ['aufʃtant] *m* insurrection, rebellion.

aufständisch ['aufʃtɛndɪʃ] *a* rebellious, mutinous.

aufstechen ['aufʃteçən] *vt irreg* prick open, puncture.

aufstecken ['aufʃtɛkən] *vt* stick on, pin up; (*col*) give up.

aufstehen ['aufʃteːən] *vi irreg* get up; (*Tür*) be open.

aufsteigen ['aufʃtaɪgən] *vi irreg* (*auf etw*) get onto; (*hochsteigen*) climb; (*Rauch*) rise.

aufstellen ['aufʃtɛlən] *vt* (*aufrecht stellen*) put up; (*aufreihen*) line up; (*nominieren*) put up; (*formu-*

lieren) *Programm etc* draw up; (*leisten*) *Rekord* set up.

Aufstieg ['aufʃtiːk] *m* -(e)s, -e (*auf Berg*) ascent; (*Fortschritt*) rise; (*beruflich, Sport*) promotion.

aufstoßen ['aufʃtoːsən] *irreg vt* push open; *vi* belch.

aufstrebend ['aufʃtreːbənd] *a* ambitious; *Land* up-and-coming.

Aufstrich ['aufʃtrɪç] *m* spread.

aufstülpen ['aufʃtʏlpən] *vt Ärmel* turn up; *Hut* put on.

aufstützen ['aufʃtʏtsən] *vr* lean (*auf* +*acc* on); *vt Körperteil* prop, lean; *Person* prop up.

aufsuchen ['aufzuːxən] *vt* (*besuchen*) visit; (*konsultieren*) consult.

auftakeln ['auftaːkəln] *vt* (*Naut*) rig (out); *vr* (*col*) deck o.s. out.

Auftakt ['auftakt] *m* (*Mus*) upbeat; (*fig*) prelude.

auftanken ['auftaŋkən] *vi* get petrol; *vt* refuel.

auftauchen ['auftauxən] *vi* appear; (*aus Wasser etc*) emerge; (*U-Boot*) surface; (*Zweifel*) arise.

auftauen ['auftauən] *vti* thaw; (*fig*) relax.

aufteilen ['auftaɪlən] *vt* divide up; *Raum* partition.

Aufteilung *f* division; partition.

auftischen ['auftɪʃən] *vt* serve (up); (*fig*) tell.

Auftrag ['auftraːk] *m* -(e)s, -träge order; (*Anweisung*) commission; (*Aufgabe*) mission; im — von on behalf of; a—en [-gən] *irreg vt* Essen serve; *Farbe* put on; *Kleidung* wear out; jdm etw a—en tell sb sth; *vi* (*dick machen*) make you/me *etc* look fat; dick a—en (*fig*) exaggerate; **-geber** *m* -s, -

(Comm) purchaser, customer.

auftreiben ['aʊftraɪbən] vt irreg (col: beschaffen) raise.

auftreten ['aʊftreːtən] irreg vt kick open; vi appear; (mit Füßen) tread; (sich verhalten) behave; A— nt -s (Vorkommen) appearance; (Benehmen) behaviour.

Auftrieb ['aʊftriːp] m (Phys) buoyancy, lift; (fig) impetus.

Auftritt ['aʊftrɪt] m (des Schauspielers) entrance; (lit, fig: Szene) scene.

auftun ['aʊftuːn] irreg vt open; vr open up. .

aufwachen ['aʊfvaxən] vi wake up.

aufwachsen ['aʊfvaksən] vi irreg grow up.

Aufwand ['aʊfvant] m -(e)s expenditure; (Kosten auch) expense; (Luxus) show; bitte, keinen —! please don't go out of your way.

aufwärmen ['aʊfvɛrmən] vt warm up; alte Geschichten rake up.

aufwärts ['aʊfvɛrts] ad upwards; A—entwicklung f upward trend; —gehen vi irreg look up.

aufwecken ['aʊfvɛkən] vt wake(n) up.

aufweichen ['aʊfvaɪçən] vt soften, soak.

aufweisen ['aʊfvaɪzən] vt irreg show.

aufwenden ['aʊfvɛndən] vt irreg expend; Geld spend; Sorgfalt devote.

aufwendig a costly.

aufwerfen ['aʊfvɛrfən] irreg vt Fenster etc throw open; Probleme throw up, raise; vr: sich zu etw — make o.s. out to be sth.

aufwerten ['aʊfvɛrtən] vt (Fin) revalue; (fig) raise in value.

aufwiegeln ['aʊfviːgəln] vt stir up, incite.

aufwiegen ['aʊfviːgən] vt irreg make up for.

Aufwind ['aʊfvɪnt] m up-current.

aufwirbeln ['aʊfvɪrbəln] vt whirl up; Staub — (fig) create a stir.

aufwischen ['aʊfvɪʃən] vt wipe up.

aufzählen ['aʊftsɛːlən] vt count out.

aufzeichnen ['aʊftsaɪçnən] vt sketch; (schriftlich) jot down; (auf Band) record.

Aufzeichnung f (schriftlich) note; (Tonband—) recording; (Film—) record.

aufzeigen ['aʊftsaɪgən] vt show, demonstrate.

aufziehen ['aʊftsiːən] vt irreg (hochziehen) raise, draw up; (öffnen) pull open; Uhr wind; (col: necken) tease; (großziehen) Kinder raise, bring up; Tiere rear.

Aufzug ['aʊftsuːk] m (Fahrstuhl) lift, elevator; (Aufmarsch) procession, parade; (Kleidung) getup; (Theat) act.

aufzwingen ['aʊftsvɪŋən] vt irreg: jdm etw — force sth upon sb.

Aug- ['aʊg] cpd: —apfel m eyeball; (fig) apple of one's eye; —e nt -s, -n eye; (Fett—) globule of fat; unter vier —en in private; —enblick m moment; im —enblick at the moment; a—enblicklich a (sofort) instantaneous; (gegenwärtig) present; —enbraue f eyebrow; a—enscheinlich a obvious; —enweide f sight for sore eyes; —enzeuge m eye witness.

August [aʊ'gʊst] m -(e)s or -, -e August.

Auktion [aʊktsi'oːn] f auction; —ator [-'naːtɔr] m auctioneer.

Aula ['aʊla] f -, Aulen or -s assembly hall.

aus [aus] *prep* +*dat* out of; (*von ... her*) from; (*Material*) made of; — ihr wird nie etwas she'll never get anywhere; *ad* out; (*beendet*) finished, over; (*ausgezogen*) off; — und ein gehen come and go; (*bei jdm*)·visit frequently; weder — noch ein wissen be at sixes and sevens; auf etw (*acc*) — sein be after sth; vom Fenster — out of the window; von Rom — from Rome; von sich — of one's own accord; A— *nt* - outfield; ins A— gehen go out.

ausarbeiten ['aus'arbaitən] *vt* work out.

ausarten ['aus'artən] *vi* degenerate; (*Kind*) become overexcited.

ausatmen ['aus'a:tmən] *vi* breathe out.

ausbaden ['ausba:dən] *vt*: etw — müssen (*col*) carry the can for sth.

Ausbau ['ausbau] *m* extension, expansion; removal; a—en *vt* extend, expand; (*herausnehmen*) take out, remove; a—fähig *a* (*fig*) worth ·developing.

ausbedingen ['ausbədɪŋən] *vt irreg*: sich (*dat*) etw — insist on sth.

ausbessern ['ausbɛsərn] *vt* mend, repair.

ausbeulen ['ausbɔylən] *vt* beat out.

Ausbeute ['ausbɔytə] *f* yield; (*Fische*) catch; a—n *vt* exploit; (*Min*) work.

ausbild- ['ausbɪld] *cpd*: —en *vt* educate; *Lehrling, Soldat* instruct, train; *Fähigkeiten* develop; *Geschmack* cultivate; - A—er *m* -s, - instructor; A—ung *f* education; training, instruction; development, cultivation.

ausbitten ['ausbɪtən] *vt irreg*: sich

(*dat*) etw — (*erbitten*) ask for sth (*verlangen*) insist on sth.

ausbleiben ['ausblaibən] *vi irreg* (*Personen*) stay away, not come (*Ereignisse*) fail to happen, no happen.

Ausblick ['ausblɪk] *m* (*lit, fig*) prospect, outlook, view.

ausbomben ['ausbombən] *vt* bomb out.

ausbrechen ['ausbrɛçən] *irreg vi* break out; in Tränen/Gelächter — burst into tears/out laughing; v break off.

ausbreiten ['ausbraitən] *vt* spread (out); *Arme* stretch out; v spread; (*über Thema*) expand, en large (*über* +*acc* on).

ausbrennen ['ausbrɛnən] *irreg vt* scorch; *Wunde* cauterize; *vi* burr out.

ausbringen ['ausbrɪŋən] *vt irreg* ein Hoch propose.

Ausbruch ['ausbrux] *m* outbreak (*von Vulkan*) eruption; (*Gefühls*—outburst; (*von Gefangenen*) escape.

ausbrüten ['ausbry:tən] *vt* (*lit, fig*) hatch.

Ausbuchtung ['ausbuxtuŋ] *f* bulge; (*Küste*) projection, pro tuberance.

ausbuhen ['ausbu:ən] *vt* boo.

ausbürsten ['ausbyrstən] *vt* brush out.

Ausdauer ['ausdauər] *f* persever ance, stamina; a—nd *a* persevering

ausdehnen ['ausde:nən] *vtr* (*räum lich*) expand; *Gummi* stretch (*Nebel*) extend; (*zeitlich*) stretch (*fig*) *Macht* extend.

ausdenken ['ausdɛŋkən] *vt irreg* (*zu Ende denken*) think through; sich (*dat*) etw — think sth up.

ausdiskutieren ['ausdɪskuti:rən] vt talk out.

ausdrehen ['ausdre:ən] vt turn or switch off; Licht auch turn out.

Ausdruck ['ausdrʊk] m expression, phrase; (Kundgabe, Gesichts—) expression.

ausdrücken ['ausdrʏkən] vt (also vr: formulieren, zeigen) express; Zigarette put out; Zitrone squeeze.

ausdrücklich a express, explicit.

ausdrucks- cpd: **—los** a expressionless, blank; **—voll** a expressive; **A—weise** f mode of expression.

auseinander [aus'aɪ'nandər] ad (getrennt) apart; **—** schreiben write as separate words; **—bringen** vt irreg separate; **—fallen** vi irreg fall apart; **—gehen** vi irreg (Menschen) separate; (Meinungen) differ; (Gegenstand) fall apart; (col: dick werden) put on weight; **—halten** vt irreg tell apart; **—nehmen** vt irreg take to pieces, dismantle; **—setzen** vt (erklären) set forth, explain; vr (sich verständigen) come to terms, settle; (sich befassen) concern o.s.; **A—setzung** f argument.

auserlesen [aus'erle:zən] a select, choice.

ausfahren ['ausfa:rən] irreg vi drive out; (Naut) put out (to sea); vt take out; (Tech) Fahrwerk drive out; ausgefahrene Wege rutted roads.

Ausfahrt f (des Zuges etc) leaving, departure; (Autobahn—, Garagen—) exit, way out; (Spazierfahrt) drive, excursion.

Ausfall ['ausfal] m loss; (Nichtstattfinden) cancellation; (Mil) sortie; (Fechten) lunge; (radioaktiv) fall-out; **a—en** vi irreg (Zähne, Haare) fall or come out;

(nicht stattfinden) be cancelled; (wegbleiben) be omitted; (Person) drop out; (Lohn) be stopped; (nicht funktionieren) break down; (Resultat haben) turn out; wie ist das Spiel ausgefallen? what was the result of the game?; **a—end** a impertinent; **—straße** f arterial road.

ausfegen ['ausfe:gən] vt sweep out.

ausfeilen ['ausfailən] vt file out; Stil polish up.

ausfertigen ['ausfertɪgən] vt draw up; Rechnung make out; doppelt **—** duplicate.

Ausfertigung f drawing up; making out; (Exemplar) copy.

ausfindig machen ['ausfɪndɪç maxən] vt discover.

ausfliegen ['ausfli:gən] vti irreg fly away; sie sind ausgeflogen (col) they're out.

ausflippen ['ausflɪpən] vi (col) freak out.

Ausflucht ['ausflʊxt] f **-, -flüchte** excuse.

Ausflug ['ausflu:k] m excursion, outing.

Ausflügler ['ausfly:klər] m **-s, -** tripper.

Ausfluß ['ausflʊs] m outlet; (Med) discharge.

ausfragen ['ausfra:gən] vt interrogate, question.

ausfransen ['ausfranzən] vi fray.

ausfressen ['ausfresən] vt irreg eat up; (aushöhlen) corrode; (col: anstellen) be up to.

Ausfuhr ['ausfu:r] f **-, -en** export, exportation; in cpds export.

ausführ- ['ausfy:r] cpd: **—bar** a feasible; (Comm) exportable; **—en** vt (verwirklichen) carry out; Person take out; Hund take for a walk; (Comm) export; (erklären) give details of; **—lich** a detailed; **ad** in detail; **A—lichkeit** f detail; **A—ung** f execution, performance; (*Durchführung*) completion; (*Herstellungsart*) version; (*Erklärung*) explanation.

ausfüllen ['ausfylən] vt fill up; *Fragebogen etc* fill in; (*Beruf*) be fulfilling for.

Ausgabe ['ausga:bə] f (*Geld*) expenditure, outlay; (*Aushändigung*) giving out; (*Gepäck—*) left-luggage office; (*Buch*) edition; (*Nummer*) issue.

Ausgang ['ausgaŋ] m way out, exit; (*Ende*) end; (*Ausgangspunkt*) starting point; (*Ergebnis*) result; (*Ausgehtag*) free time, time off; **kein —** no exit; **—sbasis** f, **—spunkt** m starting point; **—ssperre** f curfew.

ausgeben ['ausge:bən] *irreg* vt *Geld* spend; (*austeilen*) issue, distribute; vr: **sich für etw/jdn —** pass o.s. off as sth/sb.

ausgebucht ['ausgəbu:xt] a fully booked.

ausgedient ['ausgədi:nt] a *Soldat* discharged; (*verbraucht*) no longer in use; **— haben** have done good service.

ausgefallen ['ausgəfalən] a (*ungewöhnlich*) exceptional.

ausgeglichen ['ausgəgliçən] a (well-balanced), **A—heit** f balance; (*von Mensch*) even-temperedness.

Ausgeh- ['ausge:] cpd: **—anzug** m good suit; **a—en** vi *irreg* go out; (*zu Ende gehen*) come to an end; (*Benzin*) run out; (*Haare, Zähne*) fall or come out; (*Feuer, Ofen, Licht*) go out; (*Strom*) go off; (*Resultat haben*) turn out; **mir ging das Benzin aus** I ran out of petrol; **von etw** (*acc*) **a—en** aim at sth; **von**

etw **a—en** (*wegführen*) lead away from sth; (*herrühren*) come from sth; (*zugrunde legen*) proceed from sth; **wir können davon a—en, daß ...** we can proceed from the assumption that ..., we can take as our starting point that ...; **leer a—en** get nothing; **schlecht a—en** turn out badly; **—verbot** nt curfew.

ausgelassen ['ausgəlasən] a boisterous, high-spirited; **A—heit** f boisterousness, high spirits pl, exuberance.

ausgelastet ['ausgəlastət] a fully occupied.

ausgelernt ['ausgəlɛrnt] a trained, qualified.

ausgemacht ['ausgəmaxt] a (*col*) settled; *Dummkopf etc* out-and-out, downright; **es gilt als —, daß ...** it is settled that ...; **es war eine —e Sache, daß ...** it was a foregone conclusion that ...

ausgenommen ['ausgənomən] *prep* +*gen* or *dat*, *cj* except; **Anwesende sind —** present company excepted.

ausgeprägt ['ausgəprɛ:kt] a prominent.

ausgerechnet ['ausgərɛçnət] ad just, precisely; **— du/heute** you of all people/today of all days.

ausgeschlossen ['ausgəʃlosən] a (*unmöglich*) impossible, out of the question; **es ist nicht —, daß ...** it cannot be ruled out that ...

ausgeschnitten ['ausgəʃnitən] a *Kleid* low-necked.

ausgesprochen ['ausgəʃproxən] a *Faulheit, Lüge etc* out-and-out; (*unverkennbar*) marked; ad decidedly.

ausgezeichnet ['ausgətsaiçnət] a excellent.

usgiebig ['ausgi:biç] a Gebrauch thorough, good; Essen generous, avish; — schlafen have. a good sleep.

Ausgleich ['ausglaiç] m -(e)s, -e balance; (Vermittlung) reconciliation; (Sport) equalization; zum— — (+ gen) in order to offset; das ist ein guter — that's very relaxing; a—en irreg vt balance (out); reconcile; Höhe even up; vi (Sport) equalize; —stor nt equalizer.

usgraben ['ausgra:bən] vt irreg dig up; Leichen exhume; (fig) unearth.

Ausgrabung f excavation; (Ausgraben auch) digging up.

Ausguß ['ausgus] m (Spüle) sink; (Abfluß) outlet; (Tülle) spout.

ushaben ['ausha:bən] vt irreg (col) Kleidung have taken off; Buch have finished.

ushalten ['ausha:ltən] irreg vt bear, stand; Geliebte keep; vi hold out; das ist nicht zum A— that is unbearable.

ushandeln ['aushandəln] vt negotiate.

ushändigen ['aushɛndɪgən] vt: jdm etw — hand sth over to sb.

Aushang ['aushaŋ] m notice.

ushängen ['aushɛŋən] irreg vt Meldung put up; Fenster take off its hinges; vi be displayed; vr hang out.

Aushängeschild nt (shop) sign.

usharren ['aushaɾən] vi hold out.

usheben ['aushe:bən] vt irreg Erde lift out; Grube hollow out; Tür take off its hinges; Diebesnest clear out; (Mil) enlist.

ushecken ['aushɛkən] vt (col) concoct, think up.

aushelfen ['aushɛlfən] vi irreg: jdm — help sb out.

Aushilfe ['aushɪlfə] f help, assistance; (Person) (temporary) worker.

Aushilfs- cpd: —kraft f temporary worker; a—weise ad temporarily, as a stopgap.

ausholen ['ausho:lən] vi swing one's arm back; (zur Ohrfeige) raise one's arm to; (beim Gehen) take long strides; weit — (fig) be expansive.

aushorchen ['aushoɾçən] vt sound out, pump.

aushungern ['aushuŋərn] vt starve out.

auskennen ['auskɛnən] vr irreg know thoroughly; (an einem Ort) know one's way about; (in Fragen etc) be knowledgeable.

auskippen ['auskɪpən] vt empty.

ausklammern ['ausklamərn] vt Thema exclude, leave out.

Ausklang ['ausklaŋ] m end.

auskleiden ['ausklaidən] vr undress; vt Wand line.

ausklingen ['ausklɪŋən] vi irreg (Ton, Lied) die away; (Fest) peter out.

ausklopfen ['ausklopfən] vt Teppich beat; Pfeife knock out.

auskochen ['auskoxən] vt boil; (Med) sterilize; ausgekocht (fig) out-and-out.

auskommen ['auskɔmən] vi irreg: mit jdm — get on with sb; mit etw — get by with sth; A— nt -s: sein A— haben get by.

auskosten ['auskɔstən] vt enjoy to the full.

auskugeln ['ausku:gəln] vt (col) Arm dislocate.

auskundschaften ['aus-kunt-ʃaftən] vt spy out; *Gebiet* reconnoitre.

Auskunft ['auskunft] f -, **-künfte** information; (*nähere*) details pl, particulars pl; (*Stelle*) information office; (*Tel*) inquiries'; jdm — **erteilen** give sb information.

auskuppeln ['auskupəln] vi disengage the clutch.

auslachen ['auslaxən] vt laugh at, mock.

ausladen ['ausla:dən] irreg vt unload; (*col*) *Gäste* cancel an invitation to; vi stick out.

Auslage ['ausla:gə] f shop window (display); **—n** pl outlay, expenditure.

Ausland ['auslant] nt foreign countries pl; im/ins — abroad.

Ausländer(in f) ['auslɛndər(ɪn)] m -s, - foreigner.

ausländisch a foreign.

Auslands- cpd: **—gespräch** nt international call; **—korrespondent(in** f) m foreign correspondent; **—reise** f trip abroad.

auslassen ['auslasən] irreg vt leave out; *Wort etc auch* omit; *Fett* melt; *Kleidungsstück* let out; *Wut, Ärger* vent (an +dat on); vr: sich über etw (acc) — speak one's mind about sth.

Auslassung f omission; **—szeichen** nt apostrophe.

Auslauf ['auslauf] m (*für Tiere*) run; (*Ausfluß*) outflow, outlet; **a—en** vi irreg run out; (*Behälter*) leak; (*Naut*) put out (to sea); (*langsam aufhören*) run down.

Ausläufer ['auslɔyfər] m (*von Gebirge*) spur; (*Pflanze*) runner; (*Met*) (*von Hoch*) ridge; (*von Tief*) trough.

ausleeren ['ausle:rən] vt empty.

auslegen ['ausle:gən] vt *Waren* lay out; *Köder* put down; *Geld* lend; (*bedecken*) cover; *Text etc* interpret.

Auslegung- f interpretation.

Ausleihe ['auslaɪə] f -, -n issuing; (*Stelle*) issue desk; **a—n** vt irreg (*verleihen*) lend; sich (*dat*) etw **a—en** borrow sth.

Auslese ['ausle:zə] f -, -n selection; (*Elite*) elite; (*Wein*) choice wine; **a—n** vt irreg select; (*col: zu Ende lesen*) finish.

ausliefern ['auslɪ:fərn] vt deliver (up), hand over; (*Comm*) deliver; jdm/etw ausgeliefert sein be at the mercy of sb/sth; vr: sich jdm — give o.s. up to sb.

auslöschen ['auslœʃən] vt extinguish; (*fig*) wipe out, obliterate.

auslosen ['auslo:zən] vt draw lots for.

auslösen ['auslø:zən] vt *Explosion, Schuß* set off; (*hervorrufen*) cause, produce; *Gefangene* ransom; *Pfand* redeem.

Auslöser m -s, - (*Phot*) release.

ausmachen ['ausmaxən] vt *Licht, Radio* turn off; *Feuer* put out; (*entdecken*) make out; (*vereinbaren*) agree; (*beilegen*) settle; (*Anteil darstellen, betragen*) represent; (*bedeuten*) matter; das macht ihm nichts aus it doesn't matter to him; macht es Ihnen etwas aus, wenn ...? would you mind if ...?

ausmalen ['ausma:lən] vt paint; (*fig*) describe; sich (*dat*) etw — imagine sth.

Ausmaß ['ausma:s] nt dimension; (*fig auch*) scale.

ausmerzen ['ausmɛrtsən] vt eliminate.

usmessen ['ausmɛsən] vt irreg
measure.

Ausnahme ['ausna:mə] f -, -n
exception; **eine — machen** make an
exception; **—fall** m exceptional
case; **—zustand** m state of
emergency.

ausnahms- cpd: —los ad without
exception; **—weise** ad by way of
exception, for once.

ausnehmen ['ausne:mən] irreg vt
take out, remove; Tier gut; Nest
rob; (col: Geld abnehmen) clean
out; (ausschließen) make an
exception of; vr look, appear; **—d**
a exceptional.

ausnützen ['ausnytsən] vt Zeit,
Gelegenheit ' use, turn to good
account; Einfluß use; Mensch,
Gutmütigkeit exploit.

auspacken ['auspakən] vt unpack.

auspfeifen ['auspfaifən] vt irreg
hiss/boo at.

ausplaudern ['ausplaudərn] vt
Geheimnis blab.

ausprobieren ['ausprobi:rən] vt
try (out).

Auspuff ['auspuf] m -(e)s, -e
(Tech) exhaust; **—rohr** nt exhaust
(pipe); **—topf** m (Aut) silencer.

ausradieren ['ausradi:rən] vt
erase, rub out.

ausrangieren ['ausrãʒi:rən] vt
(col) chuck out.

ausrauben ['ausraubən] vt rob.

ausräumen ['ausrɔymən] vt Dinge
clear away; Schrank, Zimmer
empty; Bedenken put aside.

ausrechnen ['ausrɛçnən] vt calculate, reckon.

Ausrechnung f calculation, reckoning.

Ausrede ['ausre:də] f excuse; **a—n**

vi have one's say; vt: **jdm etw a—n**
talk sb out of sth.

ausreichen ['ausraiçən] vi suffice,
be enough; **—d** a sufficient,
adequate; (Sch) adequate.

Ausreise ['ausraizə] f departure;
bei der — when leaving the country; **—erlaubnis** f exit visa; **a—n**
vi leave the country.

ausreißen ['ausraisən] irreg vt tear
or pull out; vi (Riß bekommen)
tear; (col) make off, scram.

ausrenken ['ausrɛŋkən] vt
dislocate.

ausrichten ['ausriçtən] vt Botschaft deliver; Gruß pass on; Hochzeit etc arrange; (erreichen) get
anywhere (bei with); (in gerade
Linie bringen) get in a straight line;
(angleichen) bring into line; **jdm
etw —** take a message for sb; **ich
werde es ihm —** I'll tell him.

ausrotten ['ausrɔtən] vt stamp out,
exterminate.

ausrücken ['ausrykən] vi (Mil)
move off; (Feuerwehr, Polizei) be
called out; (col: weglaufen) run
away.

Ausruf ['ausru:f] m (Schrei) cry,
exclamation; (Verkünden) proclamation; **a—en** vt irreg cry out,
exclaim; call out; **—ezeichen** nt
exclamation mark.

ausruhen ['ausru:ən] vtr rest.

ausrüsten ['ausrystən] vt equip, fit
out.

Ausrüstung f equipment.

ausrutschen ['ausrutʃən] vi slip.

Aussage ['ausza:gə] f -, -n (Jur)
statement; **a—n** vt say, state; vi
(Jur) give evidence.

ausschalten ['ausʃaltən] vt switch
off; (fig) eliminate.

Ausschank ['ausʃaŋk] m -(e)s,

-schänke dispensing, giving out; (Comm) selling; (Theke) bar.

Ausschau ['ausʃau] f: — **halten** look out, watch (nach for); a—en vi look out (nach for), be on the look-out.

ausscheiden ['ausʃaidən] irreg vt separate; (Med) give off, secrete; vi leave (aus etw sth); (Sport) be eliminated or knocked out; er scheidet für den Posten aus he can't be considered for the job.

Ausscheidung f separation; retiral; elimination.

ausschenken ['ausʃɛŋkən] vt pour out; (Comm) sell.

ausschimpfen ['ausʃɪmpfən] vt scold, tell off.

ausschlachten ['ausʃlaxtən] vt Auto cannibalize; (fig) make a meal of.

ausschlafen ['ausʃlaːfən] irreg vir have a long lie (in); vt sleep off; ich bin nicht ausgeschlafen I didn't have or get enough sleep.

Ausschlag ['ausʃlaːk] m (Med) rash; (Pendel—) swing; (Nadel) deflection; den — geben (fig) tip the balance; a—en [-gən] irreg vt knock out; (auskleiden) deck out; (verweigern) decline; vi (Pferd) kick out; (Bot) sprout; (Zeiger) be deflected; a—gebend a decisive.

ausschließen ['ausʃliːsən] vt irreg shut or lock out; (fig) exclude; ich will mich nicht — myself not excepted.

ausschließlich a, ad exclusive(ly); prep + gen excluding, exclusive of.

Ausschluß ['ausʃlus] m exclusion.

ausschmücken ['ausʃmykən] vt decorate; (fig) embellish.

ausschneiden ['ausʃnaidən] vt irreg cut out; Büsche trim.

Ausschnitt ['ausʃnɪt] m (Teil) section; (von Kleid) neckline; (Zeitungs—) cutting; (aus Film etc) excerpt.

ausschreiben ['ausʃraibən] v irreg (ganz schreiben) write out (in full); (ausstellen) write (out); Stelle, Wettbewerb etc announce, advertise.

Ausschreitung ['ausʃraituŋ] f excess.

Ausschuß ['ausʃus] m committee, board; (Abfall) waste, scraps pl (Comm: also —ware f) reject.

ausschütten ['ausʃytən] vt pour out; Eimer empty; Geld pay; vr shake (with laughter).

ausschweifend ['ausʃvaifənt] a Leben dissipated, debauched; Phantasie extravagant.

Ausschweifung f excess.

ausschweigen ['ausʃvaigən] vr irreg keep silent.

ausschwitzen ['ausʃvitsən] vt exude; (Mensch) sweat out.

aussehen ['auszeːən] vi irreg look; das sieht nach nichts aus that doesn't look anything special; es sieht nach Regen aus it looks like rain; es sieht schlecht aus things look bad; A— nt -s appearance.

aussein ['auszain] vi irreg (col) be out; (zu Ende) be over.

außen ['ausən] ad outside; (nach —) outwards; — ist es rot it's red (on the) outside; A—antenne f outside aerial; A—bordmotor m outboard motor.

aussenden ['auszɛndən] vt irreg send out, emit.

Außen- cpd: —dienst m outside or field service; (von . Diplomat) foreign service; —handel m foreign trade; —minister m foreign minister; —ministerium nt foreign office; —politik f foreign policy; —seite f outside; —seiter m -s, -, —stehende(r) mf outsider; —welt f outside world.

außer ['ausər] prep +dat (räumlich) out of; (abgesehen von) except; — Gefahr sein be out of danger; — Zweifel beyond any doubt; — Betrieb out of order; — sich (dat) sein/geraten be beside o.s.; — Dienst retired; — Landes abroad; cj (ausgenommen) except; — wenn unless; — daß except; —amtlich a unofficial, private; —dem cj besides, in addition; —dienstlich a unofficial.

äußere(r,s) ['oysərə(r,z)] a outer, external.

außer- cpd: —ehelich a extramarital; —gewöhnlich a unusual; —halb prep +gen, ad outside; A—kraftsetzung f putting out of action.

äußer- cpd: —lich a, ad external; —n vt utter, express; (zeigen) show; vr give one's opinion; (sich zeigen) show itself.

außer- cpd: —ordentlich a extraordinary; —planmäßig a unscheduled; —'stande ad not in a position, unable.

äußerst ['oysərst] ad extremely, most; —e(r,s) a utmost; (räumlich) farthest; Termin last possible; Preis highest; —enfalls ad if the worst comes to the worst.

aussetzen ['auszetsən] vt Kind, Tier abandon; Boote lower; Belohnung offer; Urteil, Verfahren postpone; jdn/sich etw (dat) — lay sb/o.s. open to sth; jdm/etw ausgesetzt sein be exposed to sb/sth; an jdm/etw etwas — find fault with sb/sth; vi (aufhören) stop; (Pause machen) drop out.

Aussicht ['auszıçt] f view; (in Zukunft) prospect; in — sein be in view; etw in — haben have sth in view; a—slos a hopeless; —spunkt m viewpoint; a—sreich a promising; —sturm m observation tower.

aussöhnen ['auszø:nən] vt reconcile; vr reconcile o.s., become reconciled.

Aussöhnung f reconciliation.

aussondern ['auszɔndərn] vt separate, select.

aussortieren ['auszɔrti:rən] vt sort out.

ausspannen ['ausʃpanən] vt spread or stretch out; Pferd unharness; (col) Mädchen. steal (jdm from sb); vi relax.

aussparen ['ausʃpa:rən] vt leave open.

aussperren ['ausʃpɛrən] vt lock out.

ausspielen ['ausʃpi:lən] vt Karte lead; Geldprämie offer as a prize; jdn gegen jdn — play sb off against sb; vi (Cards) lead; ausgespielt haben be finished.

Aussprache ['ausʃpra:xə] f pronunciation; (Unterredung) (frank) discussion.

aussprechen ['ausʃprɛçən] irreg vt pronounce; (zu Ende sprechen) speak; (äußern) say, express; vr (sich äußern) speak (über +acc about); (sich anvertrauen) unburden o.s.; (diskutieren) discuss; vi (zu Ende sprechen) finish speaking.

Ausspruch ['ausʃprux] m saying, remark.

ausspülen ['ausʃpy:lən] vt wash out; Mund rinse.

ausstaffieren ['ausʃtafi:rən] vt equip, kit out; Zimmer furnish.

Ausstand ['ausʃtant] m strike; **in den —** treten go on strike.

ausstatten ['ausʃtatən] vt Zimmer etc furnish; **jdn mit etw —** equip sb or kit sb out with sth.

Ausstattung f (Ausstatten) provision; (Kleidung) outfit; (Aussteuer) dowry; (Aufmachung) make-up; (Einrichtung) furnishing.

ausstechen ['ausʃtɛçən] vt irreg Augen, Rasen, Graben dig out; Kekse cut out; (übertreffen) outshine.

ausstehen ['ausʃte:ən] irreg vt stand, endure; vi (noch nicht da-sein) be outstanding.

aussteigen ['ausʃtaigən] vi irreg get out, alight.

ausstellen ['ausʃtɛlən] vt exhibit, display; (col: ausschalten) switch off; Rechnung etc make out; Paß, Zeugnis issue.

Ausstellung f exhibition; (Fin) drawing up; (einer Rechnung) making out; (eines Passes etc) issuing.

aussterben ['ausʃtɛrbən] vi irreg die out.

Aussteuer ['ausʃtɔyər] f dowry.

ausstopfen ['ausʃtɔpfən] vt stuff.

ausstoßen ['ausʃtoːsən] vt irreg Luft, Rauch give off, emit; (aus Verein etc) expel, exclude; Auge poke out.

ausstrahlen ['ausʃtraːlən] vti radiate; (Rad) broadcast.

Ausstrahlung f radiation; (fig) charisma.

ausstrecken ['ausʃtrɛkən] vtr stretch out.

ausstreichen ['ausʃtraiçən] vt irreg cross out; (glätten) smooth out.

ausströmen ['ausʃtrøːmən] vi (Gas) pour out, escape; vt give off; (fig) radiate.

aussuchen ['auszuːxən] vt select, pick out.

Austausch ['austauʃ] m exchange; **a—bar** a exchangeable; **a—en** vt exchange, swop; **—motor** m reconditioned engine.

austeilen ['austailən] vt distribute, give out.

Auster ['austər] f -, -n oyster.

austoben ['austoːbən] vr (Kind) run wild; (Erwachsene) sow one's wild oats.

austragen ['austraːgən] vt irreg Post deliver; Streit etc decide; Wettkämpfe hold.

Austräger ['austrɛːgər] m delivery boy; (Zeitungs—) newspaper boy.

austreiben ['austraibən] vt irreg drive out, expel; Geister exorcize.

austreten ['austreːtən] irreg vi (zur Toilette) be excused; **aus etw —** leave sth; vt Feuer tread out, trample; Schuhe wear out; Treppe wear down.

austrinken ['austrɪŋkən] irreg vt Glas drain; Getränk drink up; vi finish one's drink, drink up.

Austritt ['austrɪt] m emission; (aus Verein, Partei etc) retirement, withdrawal.

austrocknen ['austrɔknən] vti dry up.

ausüben ['aus'yːbən] vt Beruf practise, carry out; Funktion perform; Einfluß exert; Reiz, Wirkung exercise, have (auf jdn on sb).

Ausübung f practice, exercise.

Ausverkauf ['ausfɛrkauf] m sale; **a—en** vt sell out; Geschäft sell up; **a—t** a Karten, Artikel sold out; (Theat) Haus full.

Auswahl ['ausva:l] f selection, choice (an + dat of).

auswählen ['ausvɛ:lən] vt select, choose.

Auswander- ['ausvandər] cpd: —er m emigrant; a—n vi emigrate; —ung f emigration.

auswärtig ['ausvɛrtɪç] a (nicht am/vom Ort) out-of-town; (ausländisch) foreign; A—e(s) Amt nt Foreign Office, State Department (US).

auswärts ['ausvɛrts] ad outside; (nach · außen) outwards; — essen eat out; A—spiel nt away game.

auswechseln ['ausvɛksəln] vt change, substitute.

Ausweg ['ausve:k] m way out; a—los a hopeless.

ausweichen ['ausvaiçən] vi irreg: jdm/etw — (lit) move aside or make way for sb/sth; (fig) side-step sb/sth; —d a evasive.

ausweinen ['ausvaimən] vr have a (good) cry.

Ausweis ['ausvais] m -es, -e identity card, passport; (Mitglieds—, Bibliotheks— etc) card; a—en [-zən] irreg vt expel, banish; vr prove one's identity; —karte f; —papiere pl identity papers pl; —ung f expulsion.

ausweiten ['ausvaitən] vt stretch.

auswendig ['ausvɛndɪç] ad by heart; — lernen vt learn by heart.

auswert- ['ausvɛrt] cpd: —en vt evaluate; A—ung f evaluation, analysis; (Nutzung) utilization.

auswirk- ['ausvɪrk] cpd: —en vr have an effect; A—ung f effect.

auswischen ['ausvɪʃən] vt wipe out; jdm eins — (col) put one over on sb.

Auswuchs ['ausvu:ks] m (out)-growth; · (fig) product.

auswuchten ['ausvʊxtən] vt (Aut) balance.

auszacken ['austsakən] vt Stoff etc pink.

auszahlen ['austsa:lən] vt Lohn, Summe pay out; Arbeiter pay off; Miterbe buy out; vr (sich lohnen) pay.

auszählen ['austsɛ:lən] vt Stimmen count; (Boxen) count out.

auszeichnen ['austsaiçnən] vt honour; (Mil) decorate; (Comm) price; vr distinguish o.s.

Auszeichnung f distinction; (Comm) pricing; (Ehrung) award-ing of decoration; (Ehre) honour; (Orden) decoration; mit — with distinction.

ausziehen ['austsi:ən] irreg vt Kleidung take off; Haare, Zähne, Tisch etc pull out; (nachmalen) trace; vr undress; vi (aufbrechen) leave; (aus · Wohnung) move out.

Auszug ['austsu:k] m (aus Wohnung) removal; (aus Buch etc) extract; (Konto—) statement; (Ausmarsch) departure.

Auto ['auto] nt -s, -s (motor-)car; — fahren drive; —bahn f motor-way; —fahrer(in f) m motorist, driver; —fahrt f drive; a—gen [-'ge:n] a autogenous; —'gramm nt autograph; —'mat m -en, -en machine; a—'matisch a automatic; a—'nom [-'no:m] a autonomous.

Autopsie [auto'psi:] f post-mortem, autopsy.

Autor ['autor] m -s, -en, **Autorin** [au'to:rɪn] f author.

Auto- cpd: —radio nt car radio; —reifen m car tyre; —rennen nt motor racing.

autoritär [autori'tɛ:r] a authori-tarian.

Autorität f authority.
Auto- cpd: —unfall m car or motor

accident; —verleih m car hire.
Axt [akst] f -, ‡e axe.

B

B, b [be:] nt B, b.
Baby ['be:bi] nt -s, -s baby;
—ausstattung f layette; —sitter ['be:bizitər] m -s, - baby-sitter.
Bach [bax] m -(e)s, ‡e stream, brook.
Back- [bak] cpd: —blech nt baking tray; —bord m -(e)s, -e (Naut) port; —e f -, -n cheek; **b—en** vti irreg bake; —enbart m sideboards pl; —enzahn m molar.
Bäcker ['bɛkər] m -s, - baker; —ei [-'rai] f bakery; (—laden) baker's (shop).
Back- cpd: —form f baking tin; —hähnchen nt roast chicken; —obst nt dried fruit; —ofen m oven; —pflaume f prune; —pulver nt baking powder; —stein m brick.
Bad [ba:t] nt -(e)s, ‡er bath; (Schwimmen) bathe; (Ort) spa.
Bade- ['ba:də] cpd: —anstalt f (swimming) baths pl; —anzug m bathing suit; —hose f bathing or swimming trunks pl; —kappe f bathing cap; —mantel m bath(ing) robe; —meister m baths attendant; **b—n** vi bathe, have a bath; vt bath; —ort m spa; —tuch nt bath towel; —wanne f bath (tub); —zimmer nt bathroom.
baff [baf] a: — sein (col) be flabbergasted.
Bagatelle [baga'tɛlə] f -, -n trifle.
Bagger ['bagər] m -s, - excavator; (Naut) dredger; **b—n** vti excavate,

(Naut) dredge.
Bahn [ba:n] f -, -en railway, railroad (US); (Weg) road, way; (Spur) lane; (Renn—) track; (Astron) orbit; (Stoff—) length; **b—brechend** a pioneering; **b—en** vt: sich/jdm einen Weg **b—en** clear a way/a way for sb; —fahrt f railway journey; —hof m station; auf dem —hof at the station; —hofshalle f station concourse; —hofsvorsteher m stationmaster; —hofswirtschaft f station restaurant; —linie f (railway) line; —steig m platform; —steigkarte f platform ticket; —strecke f (railway) line; —übergang m level crossing, grade crossing (US); —wärter m signalman.
Bahre ['ba:rə] f -, -n stretcher.
Bajonett [bajo'nɛt] nt -(e)s, -e bayonett.
Bakelit® [bake'li:t] nt -s Bakelite®.
Bakterien [bak'te:riən] pl bacteria pl.
Balance [ba'lãːsə] f -, -n balance, equilibrium.
balan'cieren vti balance.
bald [balt] ad (zeitlich) soon; (beinahe) almost; —..., —... now..., now...; —ig ['baldıç] a early, speedy; —möglichst ad as soon as possible.
Baldrian ['baldria:n] m -s, -e valerian.
Balken ['balkən] m -s, - beam; (Trag—) girder; (Stütz—) prop.

Balkon [bal'kõ:] m -s, -s or -e balcony ; (*Theat*) (dress) circle.

Ball [bal] m -(e)s, ⁼s ball ; (*Tanz*) dance, ball.

Ballade [ba'la:də] f -, -n ballad.

Ballast [ba'last] m -(e)s, -e ballast ; (*fig*) weight, burden.

Ballen ['balən] m -s, - bale ; (*Anat*) ball ; b— vt (*formen*) make into a ball ; *Faust* clench ; vr build up ; (*Menschen*) gather.

Ballett [ba'let] nt -(e)s, -e ballet ; —(t)änzer(in f) m ballet dancer.

Ball- cpd: —junge 'm ball boy ; —kleid nt evening dress.

Ballon [ba'lõ:] m -s, -s or -e balloon.

Ballspiel nt ball game.

Ballung ['balʊŋ] f concentration ; (*von Energie*) build-up ; —sgebiet nt conurbation.

Bambus ['bambʊs] m -ses, -se bamboo ; —rohr nt bamboo cane.

Bammel ['baməl] m -s (col) (einen)⁂ — haben vor jdm/etw be scared of sb/sth.

banal [ba'na:l] a banal ; B—ität [banali'tɛ:t] f banality.

Banane [ba'na:nə] f -, -n banana.

Banause [ba'naʊzə] m -n, -n philistine.

Band [bant] m -(e)s, ⁼e (*Buch*) volume ; nt -(e)s, ⁼er (*Stoff*—) ribbon, tape ; (*Fließ*—) production line ; (*Faß*—) hoop ; (*Ton*—) tape ; (*Anat*) ligament ; etw auf — aufnehmen tape sth ; am laufenden — (col) non-stop ; nt -(e)s, -e (*Freundschafts*— etc) bond ; [bɛnt] f -, -s band, group.

Bandage [ban'da:ʒə] f -, -n bandage.

banda'gieren vt bandage.

Bande ['bandə] f -, -n band ; (*Straßen*—) gang.

bändigen ['bɛndɪgən] vt *Tier* tame ; *Trieb, Leidenschaft* control, restrain.

Bandit [ban'di:t] m -en, -en bandit.

Band- cpd: —maß nt tape measure ; —säge f band saw ; —scheibe f (*Anat*) disc ; —wurm m tapeworm.

bange ['baŋə] a scared ; (*besorgt*) anxious ; jdm wird es — sb is becoming scared ; jdm — machen scare sb ; B—macher m -s, - scaremonger ; —n vi: um jdn/etw —n be anxious or worried about sb/sth.

Banjo ['banjo, 'bɛndʒo] nt -s, -s banjo.

Bank[1] [baŋk] f -, ⁼e (*Sitz*—) bench ; (*Sand*— etc) (sand)bank or -bar.

Bank[2] [baŋk] f -, -en (*Geld*—) bank ; —anweisung f banker's order ; —beamte(r) m bank clerk.

Bankett [baŋ'kɛt] nt -(e)s, -e (*Essen*) banquet ; (*Straßenrand*) verge.

Bankier [baŋki'e:] m -s, -s banker.

Bank- cpd: —konto m bank account ; —note f banknote ; —raub m bank robbery.

Bankrott [baŋ'krɔt] m -(e)s, -e bankruptcy ; —machen go bankrupt ; b— a bankrupt.

Bann [ban] m -(e)s, -e (*Hist*) ban ; (*Kirchen*—) excommunication ; (*fig: Zauber*) spell ; b—en vt *Geister* exorcise ; *Gefahr* avert ; (*bezaubern*) enchant ; (*Hist*) banish ; —er nt -s, - banner, flag.

bar [ba:r] a (*unbedeckt*) bare ; (*frei von*) lacking (*gen* in) ; (*offenkundig*) utter, sheer ; —(e)s Geld cash ; etw (in) — bezahlen pay sth (in) cash ; etw für —e Münze nehmen (*fig*) take sth at its face value; **B—** *f* **-, -s** bar.

Bär [bɛːr] *m* **-en, -en** bear.

Baracke [ba'rakə] *f* **-, -n** hut, barrack.

barbarisch [bar'baːrɪʃ] *a* barbaric, barbarous.

Bar- *cpd*: **—bestand** *m* money in hand; **b—fuß** *a* barefoot; **—geld** *nt* cash, ready money; **b—geldlos** *a* non-cash; **b—häuptig** *a* bareheaded; **—hocker** *m* bar stool; **—kauf** *m* cash purchase; **—keeper** ['baːrkiːpər] *m* **-s, -**, **—mann** *m* barman, bartender.

barmherzig [barm'hɛrtsɪç] *a* merciful, compassionate; **B—keit** *f* mercy, compassion.

Barometer [baro'meːtər] *nt* **-s, -** barometer.

Baron [ba'roːn] *m* **-s, -e** baron; **—esse** [baro'nɛsə] *f* **-, -n**, **—in** *f* baroness.

Barren ['barən] *m* **-s, -** parallel bars *pl*; (*Gold—*) ingot.

Barriere [bari'ɛːrə] *f* **-, -n** barrier.

Barrikade [bari'kaːdə] *f* **-, -n** barricade.

Barsch [barʃ] *m* **-(e)s, -e** perch; **b—** [barʃ] *a* brusque, gruff.

Bar- *cpd*: **—schaft** *f* ready money; **—scheck** *m* open *or* uncrossed cheque.

Bart [baːrt] *m* **-(e)s, -e** beard; (*Schlüssel—*) bit.

bärtig ['bɛːrtɪç] *a* bearded.

Barzahlung *f* cash payment.

Base ['baːzə] *f* **-, -n** (*Chem*) base; (*Kusine*) cousin.

basieren [ba'ziːrən] *vt* base; *vi* be based.

Basis ['baːzɪs] *f* **-, Basen** basis.

basisch ['baːzɪʃ] *a* (*Chem*) alkaline.

Baß [bas] *m* **Basses, Bässe** bass; **—schlüssel** *m* bass clef; **—stimme** *f* bass voice.

Bassin [ba'sɛ̃ː] *nt* **-s, -s** pool.

Bassist [ba'sɪst] *m* bass.

Bast [bast] *m* **-(e)s, -e** raffia; **b—eln** *vt* make; *vi* do handicrafts.

Bataillon [batal'joːn] *nt* **-s, -e** battalion.

Batist [ba'tɪst] *m* **-(e)s, -e** batiste.

Batterie [bata'riː] *f* battery.

Bau [bau] *m* **-(e)s** (*Bauen*) building, construction; (*Aufbau*) structure; (*Körper—*) frame; (*Baustelle*) building site; *pl* **-e** (*Tier—*) hole, burrow; (*Min*) working(s); *pl* **-ten** (*Gebäude*) building; **sich im —** befinden be under construction; **—arbeiter** *m* building worker.

Bauch [baux] *m* **-(e)s, Bäuche** belly; (*Anat auch*) stomach, abdomen; **—fell** *nt* peritoneum; **b—ig** *a* bulging; **—muskel** *m* abdominal muscle; **—redner** *m* ventriloquist; **—tanz** *m* belly dance; belly dancing; **—schmerzen** *pl*, **—weh** *nt* stomach-ache.

bauen ['bauən] *vti* build; (*Tech*) construct; *vi* **auf** jdn/etw — depend *or* count upon sb/sth.

Bauer ['bauər] *m* **-n** *or* **-s, -n** farmer; (*Schach*) pawn; *nt or m* **-s, -** (*Vogel—*) cage.

Bäuerin ['bɔyərɪn] *f* farmer; (*Frau des Bauers*) farmer's wife.

bäuerlich *a* rustic.

Bauern- *cpd*: **—brot** *nt* black bread; **—fängerei** *f* deception; **—haus** *nt* farmhouse; **—hof** *m* farm(yard); **—schaft** *f* farming community.

Bau- *cpd*: **b—fällig** *a* dilapidated; **—fälligkeit** *f* dilapidation; **—firma** *f* construction firm; **—führer** *m* site foreman; **—gelände** f building site; **—genehmigung** f building permit; **—herr** m purchaser; **—kasten** m box of bricks; **—kosten** pl construction costs pl; **—land** nt building land; **—leute** pl building workers pl; **b—lich** a structural.

Baum [baum] m **-(e)s, Bäume** tree.

baumeln ['baumeln] vi dangle.

bäumen ['bɔymən] vr rear (up).

Baum- cpd: **—schule** f nursery; **—stamm** m tree trunk; **—stumpf** m tree stump; **—wolle** f cotton.

Bau- cpd: **—plan** m architect's plan; **—platz** m building site.

Bausch [bauʃ] m **-(e)s, Bäusche** (Watte—) ball, wad; in **— und Bogen** (fig) lock, stock and barrel; **b—en** vtir puff out; **b—ig** a baggy, wide.

Bau- cpd: **b—sparen** vi insep save with a building society; **—sparkasse** f building society; **—stein** m building stone, freestone; **—stelle** f building site; **—teil** nt prefabricated part (of building); **—unternehmer** m contractor, builder; **—weise** f (method of) construction; **—werk** nt building; **—zaun** m hoarding.

Bazillus [ba'tsɪlus] m **-, Bazillen** bacillus.

beabsichtigen [bə'apzɪçtɪgən] vt intend.

beachten [bə'axtən] vt take note of; Vorschrift obey; Vorfahrt observe; **—swert** a noteworthy.

beachtlich a considerable.

Beachtung f notice, attention, observation.

Beamte(r) [bə'amtə(r)] m **-n, -n, Beamtin** f official, civil servant; (Bank— etc) employee.

beängstigend [bə'ɛŋstɪgənt] a alarming.

beanspruchen [bə'anʃpruxən] vt claim; Zeit, Platz take up, occupy; Mensch take up sb's time.

beanstanden [bə'anʃtandən] vt complain about, object to.

Beanstandung f complaint.

beantragen [bə'antra:gən] vt apply for, ask for.

beantworten [bə'antvɔrtən] vt answer.

Beantwortung f reply (gen to).

bearbeiten [bə'arbaitən] vt work; Material process; Thema deal with; Land cultivate; (Chem) treat; Buch revise; (col: beeinflussen wollen) work on.

Bearbeitung f processing; treatment; cultivation; revision.

Beatmung [bə'a:tmuŋ] f · respiration.

beaufsichtigen [bə'aufzɪçtɪgən] vt supervise.

Beaufsichtigung f supervision.

beauftragen [bə'auftra:gən] vt instruct; jdn mit etw **—** entrust sb with sth.

bebauen [bə'bauən] vt build on; (Agr) cultivate.

beben ['be:bən] vi tremble, shake; **B—** nt **-s** - earthquake.

bebildern [bə'bɪldərn] vt illustrate.

Becher ['bɛçər] nt **-s,** - mug; (ohne Henkel) tumbler.

Becken ['bɛkən] nt **-s,** - basin; (Mus) cymbal; (Anat) pelvis.

bedacht [bə'daxt] a thoughtful, careful; auf etw (acc) **—** sein be concerned about sth.

bedächtig [bə'dɛçtɪç] a (umsichtig) thoughtful, reflective; (langsam) slow, deliberate.

bedanken [bə'daŋkən] vr say thank you (bei jdm to sb).

Bedarf [bə'darf] m -(e)s need, requirement; (Comm) demand; supply; je nach — according to demand; bei — if necessary; — an etw (dat) haben be in need of sth; —sartikel m requisite; —sfall m case of need; —shaltestelle f request stop.

bedauerlich [bə'dauərliç] a regrettable.

bedauern [bə'dauərn] vt be sorry for; (bemitleiden) pity; B— nt -s regret; —swert a Zustände regrettable; Mensch pitiable, unfortunate.

bedecken [bə'dɛkən] vt cover.

bedeckt a covered; Himmel overcast.

bedenken [bə'dɛŋkən] vt irreg 'think (over), consider; B— nt -s, - (Überlegen) consideration; (Zweifel) doubt; (Skrupel) scruple.

bedenklich a doubtful; (bedrohlich) dangerous, risky.

Bedenkzeit f time for reflection.

bedeuten [bə'dɔytən] vt mean; signify; (wichtig sein) be of importance; —d a important; (beträchtlich) considerable.

Bedeutung f meaning; significance; (Wichtigkeit) importance; b—slos a insignificant, unimportant; b—svoll a momentous, significant.

bedienen [bə'di:nən] vt serve; Maschine work, operate; (v beim Essen) help o.s.; (gebrauchen) make use (gen of).

Bedienung f service; (Kellnerin) waitress; (Verkäuferin) shop assistant; (Zuschlag) service (charge).

bedingen [bə'dıŋən] vt (voraussetzen) demand, involve; (verursachen) cause, occasion.

bedingt a limited, conditional; Reflex conditioned.

Bedingung f condition; (Voraussetzung) stipulation; —sform f (Gram) conditional; b—slos a unconditional.

bedrängen [bə'drɛŋən] vt pester, harass.

Bedrängung f trouble.

bedrohen [bə'dro:ən] vt threaten.

bedrohlich a ominous, threatening.

Bedrohung f threat, menace.

bedrucken [bə'drokən] vt print on.

bedrücken [bə'drʏkən] vt oppress, trouble.

bedürf- [bə'dʏrf-] cpd: —en vi irreg +gen need, require; B—nis nt -ses, -se need; B—nis nach etw haben need sth; B—nisanstalt f public convenience, comfort station (US); —nislos a frugal, modest; —tig a in need (gen of), poor, needy.

beehren [bə'e:rən] vt honour; wir — uns we have pleasure in.

beeilen [bə'ʔaılən] vr hurry.

beeindrucken [bə'ʔaımdrokən] vt impress, make an impression on.

beeinflussen [bə'ʔaınflosən] vt influence.

Beeinflussung f influence.

beeinträchtigen [bə'ʔaımtrɛçtıgən] vt affect adversely; Freiheit infringe upon.

beend(ig)en [bə'ʔend(ıg)ən] vt end, finish, terminate.

Beend(ig)ung f end(ing), finish(ing).

beengen [bə'ʔɛŋən] vt cramp; (fig) hamper, oppress.

beerben [bə'ʔɛrbən] vt inherit from.

beerdigen [bə'ʔe:rdıgən] vt bury.

Beerdigung f funeral, burial; —sunternehmer m undertaker.

Beere ['be:rə] *f* -, **-n** berry; (*Trauben*—) grape.

Beet [be:t] *nt* -(e)s, **-e** bed.

befähigen [bə'fɛ:ɪgən] *vt* enable.

befähigt *a* (*begabt*) talented; (*fähig*) capable (*für* of).

Befähigung *f* capability; (*Begabung*) talent, aptitude.

befahrbar [bə'fa:rba:r] *a* passable; (*Naut*) navigable.

befahren [bə'fa:rən] *vt irreg* use, drive over; (*Naut*) navigate; *a* used.

befallen [bə'falən] *vt irreg* come over.

befangen [bə'faŋən] *a* (*schüchtern*) shy, self-conscious; (*voreingenommen*) biased; **B**—**heit** *f* shyness; bias.

befassen [bə'fasən] *vr* concern o.s.

Befehl [bə'fe:l] *m* -(e)s, **-e** command, order; **b**—**en** *irreg vt* order; **jdm etw b**—**en** order sb to do sth; *vi* give orders; **b**—**igen** *vt* be in command of; —**sempfänger** *m* subordinate; —**sform** *f* (*Gram*) imperative; —**shaber** *m* -s, -commanding officer; —**sverweigerung** *f* insubordination.

befestigen [bə'fɛstɪgən] *vt* fasten (*an* +*dat* to); (*stärken*) strengthen; (*Mil*) fortify.

Befestigung *f* fastening; strengthening; (*Mil*) fortification.

befeuchten [bə'fɔʏçtən] *vt* damp(en), moisten.

befinden [bə'fɪndən] *irreg vr* be; (*sich fühlen*) feel; *vt*: **jdn/etw für** *or* **als etw** — deem sb/sth to be sth; *vi* decide (*über* +*acc* on), adjudicate; **B**— *nt* -s health, condition; (*Meinung*) view, opinion.

befliegen [bə'fli:gən] *vt irreg* fly to.

befolgen [bə'fɔlgən] *vt* comply with, follow.

befördern [bə'fœrdərn] *vt* (*senden*) transport, send; (*beruflich*) promote.

Beförderung *f* transport, conveyance; promotion; —**skosten** *pl* transport costs *pl*.

befragen [bə'fra:gən] *vt* question.

befreien [bə'fraɪən] *vt* set free; (*erlassen*) exempt.

Befreier *m* -s, - liberator.

Befreiung *f* liberation, release; (*Erlassen*) exemption.

befremden [bə'frɛmdən] *vt* surprise, disturb; **B**— *nt* -s surprise, astonishment.

befreunden [bə'frɔʏndən] *vr* make friends; (*mit Idee etc*) acquaint o.s.

befreundet *a* friendly.

befriedigen [bə'fri:dɪgən] *vt* satisfy; —**d** *a* satisfactory.

Befriedigung *f* satisfaction, gratification.

befristet [bə'frɪstət] *a* limited.

befruchten [bə'frʊxtən] *vt* fertilize; (*fig*) stimulate.

Befugnis [bə'fu:knɪs] *f* -, **-se** authorization, powers *pl*.

befugt *a* authorized, entitled.

befühlen [bə'fy:lən] *vt* feel, touch.

Befund [bə'fʊnt] *m* -(e)s, **-e** findings *pl*; (*Med*) diagnosis.

befürchten [bə'fʏrçtən] *vt* fear.

Befürchtung *f* fear, apprehension.

befürwort- [bə'fy:rvɔrt] *cpd*: —**en** *vt* support, speak in favour of; **B**—**er** *m* -s, - supporter, advocate; **B**—**ung** *f* support(ing), favouring.

begabt [bə'ga:pt] *a* gifted.

Begabung [bə'ga:bʊŋ] *f* talent, gift.

begatten [bə'gatən] *vr* mate; *vt* mate *or* pair (with).

begeben [bə'ge:bən] vr irreg (gehen) proceed (zu, nach to); (geschehen) occur; **B—heit** f occurrence.

begegnen [bə'ge:gnən] vi meet (jdm sb); meet with (etw dat sth); (behandeln) treat (jdm sb); Blicke — sich eyes meet.

Begegnung f meeting.

begehen [bə'ge:ən] vt irreg Straftat commit; (abschreiten) cover; Straße etc use, negotiate; Feier celebrate.

begehren [bə'ge:rən] vt desire; **—swert** a desirable.

begehrt a in demand; Junggeselle eligible.

begeistern [bə'gaıstərn] vt fill with enthusiasm, inspire; vr: sich für etw — get enthusiastic about sth.

begeistert a enthusiastic.

Begeisterung f enthusiasm.

Begierde [bə'gi:rdə] f -, -n desire, passion.

begierig [bə'gi:rıç] a eager, keen.

begießen [bə'gi:sən] vt irreg water; (mit Alkohol) drink to.

Beginn [bə'gın] m -(e)s beginning; zu — at the beginning; **b—en** vti irreg start, begin.

beglaubigen [bə'glaubıgən] vt countersign.

Beglaubigung f countersignature; **—sschreiben** nt credentials pl.

begleichen [bə'glaıçən] vt irreg settle, pay.

Begleit- [bə'glaıt] cpd: **b—en** vt accompany; (Mil) escort; **—er** m -s, - companion; (Freund) escort; (Mus) accompanist; **—erscheinung** f concomitant (occurrence); **—musik** f accompaniment; **—schiff** nt escort vessel; **—schreiben** nt covering letter; **—umstände** pl concomit-

ant circumstances pl; **—ung** f company; (Mil) escort; (Mus) accompaniment.

beglücken [bə'glʏkən] vt make happy, delight.

beglückwünschen [bə'glʏkvʏnʃən] vt congratulate (zu on).

Beglückwünschung f congratulation, good wishes pl.

begnadigen [bə'gna:dıgən] vt pardon.

Begnadigung f pardon, amnesty.

begnügen [bə'gny:gən] vr be satisfied, content o.s.

Begonie [bə'go:niə] f begonia.

begraben [bə'gra:bən] vt irreg bury.

Begräbnis [bə'grɛ:pnıs] nt -ses, -se burial, funeral.

begradigen [bə'gra:dıgən] vt straighten (out).

begreifen [bə'graıfən] vt irreg understand, comprehend.

begreiflich [bə'graıflıç] a understandable.

Begrenztheit [bə'grɛntsthaıt] f limitation, restriction; (fig) narrowness.

Begriff [bə'grıf] m -(e)s, -e concept, idea; im — sein, etw zu tun be about to do sth; schwer von — (col) slow, dense; **—sbestimmung** f definition; **b—sstutzig** a dense, slow.

begründ- [bə'grʏnd] cpd: **—en** vt (Gründe geben) justify; **—et** a well-founded, justified; **B—ung** f justification, reason.

begrüßen [bə'gry:sən] vt greet, welcome; **—swert** a welcome.

Begrüßung f greeting, welcome.

begünstigen [bə'gʏnstıgən] vt Person favour; Sache further, promote.

begutachten [bəˈguːtˈaxtən] vt assess.

begütert [bəˈgyːtərt] a wealthy, well-to-do.

behaart [bəˈhaːrt] a hairy.

behäbig [bəˈhɛːbɪç] a (dick) portly, stout; (geruhsam) comfortable.

behaftet [bəˈhaftət] a: mit etw — sein be afflicted by sth.

behagen [bəˈhaːgən] vi: das behagt ihm nicht he does not like it; B—nt -s comfort, ease.

behaglich [bəˈhaːklɪç] a comfortable, cosy; B—keit f comfort, cosiness.

behalten [bəˈhaltən] vt irreg keep, retain; (im Gedächtnis) remember.

Behälter [bəˈhɛltər] m -s, - container, receptacle.

behandeln [bəˈhandəln] vt treat; Thema deal with; Maschine handle.

Behandlung f treatment; (von Maschine) handling.

beharren [bəˈharən] vi: auf etw (dat) — stick or keep to sth.

beharrlich [bəˈharlɪç] a (ausdauernd) steadfast, unwavering; (hartnäckig) tenacious, dogged; B—keit f steadfastness; tenacity.

behaupten [bəˈhauptən] vt claim, assert, maintain; sein Recht defend; vr assert o.s.

Behauptung f claim, assertion.

Behausung [bəˈhauzuŋ] f dwelling, abode; (armselig) hovel.

beheimatet [bəˈhaimatət] a domiciled; Tier, Pflanze with its habitat in.

beheizen [bəˈhaitsən] vt heat.

Behelf [bəˈhɛlf] m -(e)s, -e expedient, makeshift; b—en vr irreg: sich mit etw b—en make do with sth; b—smäßig a improvised,

makeshift; (vorübergehend) temporary.

behelligen [bəˈhɛlɪgən] vt trouble, bother.

Behendigkeit [bəˈhɛndɪçkait] f agility, quickness.

beherbergen [bəˈhɛrbərgən] vt put up, house.

beherrschen [bəˈhɛrʃən] vt Volk rule, govern; Situation control; Sprache, Gefühle master; vr control o.s.

beherrscht a controlled; B—heit f self-control.

Beherrschung f rule; control; mastery.

beherzigen [bəˈhɛrtsɪgən] vt take to heart.

beherzt a spirited, brave.

behilflich [bəˈhɪlflɪç] a helpful; jdm — sein help sb (bei with).

behindern [bəˈhɪndərn] vt hinder, impede.

Behinderte(r) mf disabled person.

Behinderung f hindrance; (Körper—) handicap.

Behörde [bəˈhøːrdə] f -, -n authorities pl.

behördlich [bəˈhøːrtlɪç] a official.

behüten [bəˈhyːtən] vt guard; jdn vor etw (dat) — preserve sb from sth.

behutsam [bəˈhuːtzaːm] a cautious, careful; B—keit f caution, carefulness.

bei [bai] prep + dat (örtlich) near, by; (zeitlich) at, on; (während) during; — uns at our place; — im Friseur or am hairdresser's; — einer Firma arbeiten work for a firm; — Nacht at night; — Nebel in fog; — Regen if it rains; etw — sich haben have sth on one; jdn — sich haben have sb with one;

— Goethe in Goethe; —m Militär in the army; —m Fahren while driving.

beibehalten ['baɪbəhaltən] vt irreg keep, retain.

Beibehaltung f keeping, retaining.

Beiblatt ['baɪblat] nt supplement.

beibringen ['baɪbrɪŋən] vt irreg Beweis, Zeugen bring forward; Gründe adduce; jdm etw — (zufügen) inflict sth on sb; (zu verstehen geben) make sb understand sth; (lehren) teach sb sth.

Beichte ['baɪçtə] f —, -n confession; b—n vt confess; vi go to confession.

Beicht- cpd: —geheimnis nt secret of the confessional; —stuhl m confessional.

beide(s) ['baɪdə(z)] pron, a both; meine —n Brüder my two brothers, both my brothers; die ersten —n the first two; wir — we two; einer von —n one of the two; alles —s both (of them); —mal ad both times; —rlei a of both; —rseitig a mutual, reciprocal; —rseits ad mutually; prep +gen on both sides of.

beidrehen [baɪdre:ən] vi heave to.

beieinander [baɪʔaɪ'nandər] ad together.

Beifahrer ['baɪfa:rər] m passenger; —sitz m passenger seat.

Beifall ['baɪfal] m -(e)s applause; (Zustimmung) approval.

beifällig ['baɪfɛlɪç] a approving; Kommentar favourable.

Beifilm ['baɪfɪlm] m supporting film.

beifügen ['baɪfy:gən] vt enclose.

beige ['bɛːʒə] a beige, fawn.

beigeben ['baɪge:bən] irreg vt (zufügen) add; (mitgeben) give; vi (nachgeben) give in (dat to).

Beigeschmack ['baɪgəʃmak] m aftertaste.

Beihilfe ['baɪhɪlfə] f aid, assistance; (Studien—) grant; (Jur) aiding and abetting.

beikommen ['baɪkomən] vi irreg (+dat) get at; (einem Problem) deal with.

Beil [baɪl] nt -(e)s, -e axe, hatchet.

Beilage [baɪla:gə] f (Buch— etc) supplement; (Cook) vegetables and potatoes pl.

beiläufig ['baɪlɔyfɪç] a casual, incidental; ad casually, by the way.

beilegen ['baɪle:gən] vt (hinzufügen) enclose, add; (beimessen) attribute, ascribe; Streit settle.

beileibe [baɪ'laɪbə] : — nicht ad by no means.

Beileid ['baɪlaɪt] nt condolence, sympathy; herzliches — deepest sympathy.

beiliegend ['baɪli:gənt] a (Comm) enclosed.

beim [baɪm] = bei dem.

beimessen ['baɪmɛsən] vt irreg attribute, ascribe (dat to).

Bein [baɪn] nt -(e)s, -e leg; —bruch m fracture of the leg.

beinah(e) ['baɪna:(ə)] ad almost, nearly.

beinhalten [bə'ʔɪnhaltən] vt contain.

beipflichten ['baɪpflɪçtən] vi: jdm/etw — agree with sb/sth.

Beirat ['baɪra:t] m legal adviser; (Körperschaft) advisory council; (Eltern—) parents' council.

beirren [bə'ʔɪrən] vt confuse, muddle; sich nicht — lassen not let o.s. be confused.

beisammen [baɪ'zamən] ad together; B—sein nt -s get-together.

Beischlaf ['baɪʃla:f] m sexual intercourse.

Beisein ['baizain] nt -s presence.
beiseite [ba'zaitə] ad to one side, aside; stehen on one side, aside; etw — legen (sparen) put sth by; jdn/etw — schaffen put sb/get sth out of the way.
beisetzen ['baizɛtsən] vt bury.
Beisetzung f funeral.
Beisitzer ['baizitsər] m -s, - (bei Prüfung) assessor.
Beispiel ['baiʃpi:l] nt -(e)s, -e example; sich an jdm ein — nehmen take sb as an example; zum — for example; b—haft a exemplary; b—los a unprecedented, unexampled; b—sweise ad for instance or example.
beispringen ['baiʃpriŋən] vi irreg: jdm — come to the aid of sb.
beißen ['baisən] irreg vti bite; (stechen: Rauch, Säure) burn; vr (Farben) clash; —d a biting, caustic; (fig auch) sarcastic.
Beißzange ['bais-tsaŋə] f pliers pl.
Beistand ['baiʃtant] m -(e)s, -e support, help; (Jur) adviser.
beistehen ['baiʃte:ən] vi irreg: jdm — stand by sb.
beisteuern ['baiʃtɔyərn] vt contribute.
beistimmen ['baiʃtimən] vi (+dat) agree with.
Beistrich ['baiʃtriç] m comma.
Beitrag ['baitra:k] m -(e)s, -e contribution; (Zahlung) fee, subscription; (Versicherungs—) premium; b—en ['baitra:gən] vt irreg contribute (zu to); (mithelfen) help (zu with); —szahlende(r) mf fee-paying member.
beitreten ['baitre:tən] vi irreg join (einem Verein a club).
Beitritt ['baitrit] m joining, mem-

bership; —serklärung f declaration of membership.
Beiwagen ['baiva:gən] m (Motorrad—) sidecar; (Straßenbahn—) extra carriage.
beiwohnen ['baivo:nən] vi: einer Sache (dat) — attend or be present at sth.
Beiwort ['baivort] nt adjective.
Beize ['baitsə] f -, -n (Holz—) stain; (Cook) marinade.
beizeiten ['bai'tsaitən] ad in time.
bejahen [bə'ja:ən] vt Frage say yes to, answer in the affirmative; (gutheißen) agree with.
bejahrt [bə'ja:rt] a aged, elderly.
bejammern [bə'jamərn] vt lament, bewail; —swert a lamentable.
bekämpfen [bə'kɛmpfən] vt Gegner fight; Seuche combat; vr fight.
Bekämpfung f fight or struggle against.
bekannt [bə'kant] a (well-)known; (nicht fremd) familiar; mit jdm — sein know sb; jdn mit jdm — machen introduce sb to sb; sich mit etw — machen familiarize o.s. with sth; das ist mir — I know that; es/sie kommt mir — vor it/she seems familiar; durch etw — werden become famous because of sth; B—e(r) mf friend, acquaintance; B—enkreis m circle of friends; B—gabe f announcement; —geben vt irreg announce publicly; —lich ad as is well known, as you know; —machen vt announce; B—machung f publication; announcement; B—schaft f acquaintance.
bekehren [bə'ke:rən] vt convert; vr become converted.
Bekehrung f conversion.
bekennen [bə'kɛnən] vt irreg confess; Glauben profess; Farbe

— (col) show where one stands.

Bekenntnis [bə'kɛntnɪs] nt -ses, -se admission, confession; (Religion) confession, denomination; —schule f denominational school.

beklagen [bə'kla:gən] vt deplore, lament; vr complain; —swert a lamentable, pathetic.

beklatschen [bə'klatʃən] vt applaud, clap.

bekleben [bə'kle:bən] vt: etw mit Bildern — stick pictures onto sth.

bekleiden [bə'klaɪdən] vt clothe; Amt occupy, fill.

Bekleidung f clothing; —sindustrie f clothing industry, rag trade.

beklemmen [bə'klɛmən] vt oppress.

beklommen [bə'klɔmən] a anxious, uneasy; B—heit f anxiety, uneasiness.

bekommen [bə'kɔmən] irreg vt get, receive; Kind have; Zug catch, get; vi: jdm — agree with sb.

bekömmlich [bə'kœmlɪç] a wholesome, easily digestible.

bekräftigen [bə'krɛftɪgən] vt confirm, corroborate.

Bekräftigung f corroboration.

bekreuzigen [bə'krɔYtsɪgən] vr cross o.s.

bekritteln [bə'krɪtəln] vt criticize, pick holes in.

bekümmern [bə'kYmərn] vt worry, trouble.

bekunden [bə'kʊndən] vt (sagen) state; (zeigen) show.

belächeln [bə'lɛçəln] vt laugh at.

beladen [bə'la:dən] vt irreg load.

Belag [bə'la:k] m -(e)s, ⸗e covering, coating; (Brot—) spread; (Zahn—) tartar; (auf Zunge) fur; (Brems—) lining.

belagern [bə'la:gərn] vt besiege.

Belagerung f siege; —szustand m state of siege.

Belang [bə'laŋ] m -(e)s importance; —e pl interests pl, concerns pl; b—en vt (Jur) take to court; b—los a trivial, unimportant; —losigkeit f triviality.

belassen [bə'lasən] vt irreg (in Zustand, Glauben) leave; (in Stellung) retain; es dabei — leave it at that.

belasten [bə'lastən] vt (lit) burden; (fig: bedrücken) trouble, worry; (Comm) Konto debit; (Jur) incriminate; vr weigh o.s. down; (Jur) incriminate o.s.; —d a (Jur) incriminating.

belästigen [bə'lɛstɪgən] vt annoy, pester.

Belästigung f annoyance, pestering.

Belastung [bə'lastʊŋ] f (lit) load; (fig: Sorge etc) weight; (Comm) charge, debit(ing); (Jur) incriminatory evidence; —sprobe f capacity test; (fig) test; —szeuge m witness for prosecution.

belaufen [bə'laʊfən] vr irreg amount (auf +acc to).

belauschen [bə'laʊʃən] vt eavesdrop on.

belebt [bə'le:pt] a Straße crowded.

Beleg [bə'le:k] m -(e)s, -e (Comm) receipt; (Beweis) documentary evidence, proof; (Beispiel) example; b—en [bə'le:gən] vt cover; Kuchen, Brot spread; Platz reserve, book; Kurs, Vorlesung register for; (beweisen) verify, prove; (Mil: mit Bomben) bomb; —schaft f personnel, staff.

belehren [bə'le:rən] vt instruct, teach; jdn eines Besseren — teach sb better.

Belehrung f instruction.

beleibt [bə'laɪpt] a stout, corpulent.

beleidigen [bə'laɪdɪgən] vt insult, offend.

Beleidigung f insult; (Jur) slander, libel.

belesen [bə'leːzən] a well-read.

beleuchten [bə'lɔʏçtən] vt light, illuminate; (fig) throw light on.

Beleuchtung f lighting, illumination.

belichten [bə'lɪçtən] vt expose.

Belichtung f exposure; **—smesser** m exposure meter.

belieben [bə'liːbən] nt: (ganz) nach ~ (just) as you wish.

beliebig [bə'liːbɪç] a any you like, as you like; — viel as many as you like; **ein —es Thema** any subject you like or want.

beliebt [bə'liːpt] a popular; **sich bei jdm —** machen make o.s. popular with sb; **B—heit** f popularity.

beliefern [bə'liːfərn] vt supply.

bellen ['bɛlən] vi bark.

belohnen [bə'loːnən] vt reward.

Belohnung f reward.

belügen [bə'lyːgən] vt irreg lie to, deceive.

belustigen [bə'lʊstɪgən] vt amuse.

Belustigung f amusement.

bemächtigen [bə'mɛçtɪgən] vr: sich einer Sache (gen) — take possession of sth, seize sth.

bemalen [bə'maːlən] vt paint.

bemängeln [bə'mɛŋəln] vt criticize.

bemannen [bə'manən] vt man.

Bemannung f manning; (Naut, Aviat etc) crew.

bemänteln [bə'mɛntəln] vt cloak, hide.

bemerk- [bə'mɛrk] cpd: **—bar** a perceptible, noticeable; **sich —bar machen** (Person) make or get o.s.

noticed; (Unruhe) become noticeable; **—en** vt (wahrnehmen) notice, observe; (sagen) say, mention; **—enswert** a remarkable, noteworthy; **B—ung** f remark; (schriftlich auch) note.

bemitleiden [bə'mɪtlaɪdən] vt pity.

bemühen [bə'myːən] vr take trouble or pains.

Bemühung f trouble, pains pl, effort.

bemuttern [bə'mʊtərn] vt mother.

benachbart [bə'naxbaːrt] a neighbouring.

benachrichtigen [bə'naːxrɪçtɪgən] vt inform.

Benachrichtigung f notification, information.

benachteiligen [bə'naːxtaɪlɪgən] vt (put at a) disadvantage, victimize.

benehmen [bə'neːmən] vr irreg behave; **B—** nt -s behaviour.

beneiden [bə'naɪdən] vt envy; **—swert** a enviable.

benennen [bə'nɛnən] vt irreg name.

Bengel ['bɛŋəl] m -s, - (little) rascal or rogue.

benommen [bə'nɔmən] a dazed.

benötigen [bə'nøːtɪgən] vt need.

benutzen [bə'nʊtsən], **benützen** [bə'nʏtsən] vt use.

Benutzer m -s, - user.

Benutzung f utilization, use.

Benzin [bɛnt'siːn] nt -s, -e (Aut) petrol, gas(oline) (US); **—kanister** m petrol can; **—tank** m petrol tank; **—uhr** f petrol gauge.

beobacht- [bə'oːbaxt] cpd: **—en** vt observe; **B—er** m -s, - observer; (eines Unfalls) witness; (Press, TV) correspondent; **B—ung** f observation.

bepacken [bə'pakən] vt load, pack.

bepflanzen [bə'pflantsən] vt plant.

bequem [bə'kve:m] a comfortable; Ausrede convenient; Person lazy, indolent; —en vr condescend (zu to); B—lichkeit f convenience, comfort; (Faulheit) laziness, indolence.

beraten [bə'ra:tən] irreg vt advise; (besprechen) discuss, debate; vr consult; gut/schlecht — sein be well/ill advised; sich — lassen get advice.

Berater [bə'ra:tɐ] m -s, - adviser.

beratschlagen [bə'ra:t-ʃla:gən] vti deliberate (on), confer (about).

Beratung f advice, consultation; (Besprechung) consultation; —sstelle f advice centre.

berauben [bə'raubən] vt rob.

berechenbar [bə'rɛçənba:r] a calculable.

berechnen [bə'rɛçnən] vt calculate; (Comm: anrechnen) charge; —d a Mensch calculating, scheming; B—ung f calculation; (Comm) charge.

berechtig- [bə'rɛçtɪg] cpd: —en vt entitle, authorize; (fig) justify; —t [bə'rɛçtɪçt] a justifiable, justified; B—ung f authorization; (fig) justification.

bereden [bə're:dən] vtr (besprechen) discuss; (überreden) persuade.

beredt [bə're:t] a eloquent.

Bereich [bə'raiç] m -(e)s, -e (Bezirk) area; (Phys) range; (Ressort, Gebiet) sphere.

bereichern [bə'raiçərn] vt enrich; vr get rich.

Bereifung [bə'raifuŋ] f (set of) tyres pl; (Vorgang) fitting with tyres.

bereinigen [bə'rainigən] vt settle.

bereisen [bə'raizən] vt travel through.

bereit [bə'rait] a ready, prepared; zu etw — sein be ready for sth; sich — erklären declare o.s. willing; —en vt prepare, make ready; Kummer, Freude cause; —halten vt irreg keep in readiness; —legen vt lay out; —machen vtr prepare, get ready; —s ad already; B—schaft f readiness; (Polizei) alert; in B—schaft sein be on the alert or on stand-by; B—schaftsdienst m emergency service; —stehen vt irreg (Person) be prepared; (Ding) be ready; —stellen vt Kisten, Pakete etc put ready; Geld etc make available; Truppen, Maschinen put at the ready; B—ung f preparation; —willig a willing, ready; B—willigkeit f willingness, readiness.

bereuen [bə'rɔyən] vt regret.

Berg [bɛrk] m -(e)s, -e mountain, hill; b—ab ad downhill; b—an, b—auf ad uphill; —arbeiter m miner; —bahn f mountain railway; —bau m mining; b—en ['bɛrgən] irreg (retten) rescue; Ladung salvage; (enthalten) contain; —führer m mountain guide; —gipfel m mountain top, peak; summit; b—ig ['bɛrgɪç] a mountainous, hilly; —kamm m crest, ridge; —kette f mountain range; —mann m, pl —leute miner; —rutsch m landslide; —schuh m walking boot; —steigen nt mountaineering; —steiger(in f) m -s, - mountaineer, climber; —ung ['bɛrguŋ] f (von Menschen) rescue; (von Material) recovery; (Naut) salvage; —wacht f mountain rescue service; —werk nt mine.

Bericht [bə'rɪçt] m -(e)s, -e report, account; b—en vti report; —erstatter m -s, - reporter, (newspaper) correspondent; —erstattung f reporting.

berichtigen [bə'rɪçtɪgən] vt correct.

Berichtigung f correction.

beritten [bə'rɪtən] a mounted.

Bernstein ['bɛrnʃtaɪn] m amber.

bersten ['bɛrstən] vi irreg burst, split.

berüchtigt [bə'rʏçtɪçt] a notorious, infamous.

berücksichtigen [bə'rʏkzɪçtɪgən] vt consider, bear in mind.

Berücksichtigung f consideration.

Beruf [bə'ru:f] m -(e)s, -e occupation, profession; (Gewerbe) trade; b—en irreg vt (in Amt) appoint (in + acc to; zu as); vr: sich auf jdn/etw b—en refer or appeal to sb/sth; b—en a competent, qualified; b—lich a professional; —sausbildung f vocational or professional training; —sberater m careers adviser; —sberatung f vocational guidance; —sbezeichnung f job description; —sgeheimnis nt professional secret; —skrankheit f occupational disease; —sleben nt professional life; b—smäßig a professional; —srisiko nt occupational hazard; —sschule f vocational or trade school; —ssoldat m professional soldier, regular; —ssportler m professional (sportsman); b—stätig a employed; —sverkehr m commuter traffic; —swahl f choice of a job; —ung f vocation, calling; (Ernennung) appointment; (Jur) appeal; —ung einlegen appeal.

beruhen [bə'ru:ən] vi: auf etw (dat) — be based on sth; etw auf sich — lassen leave sth at that.

beruhigen [bə'ru:ɪgən] vt calm, pacify, soothe; vr (Mensch) calm (o.s.) down; (Situation) calm down.

Beruhigung f reassurance; (der Nerven) calming; zu jds — to reassure sb; —smittel nt sedative; —spille f tranquillizer.

berühmt [bə'ry:mt] a famous; B—heit f (Ruf) fame; (Mensch) celebrity.

berühren [bə'ry:rən] vt touch; (gefühlsmäßig bewegen) affect; (flüchtig erwähnen) mention, touch on; vr meet, touch.

Berührung f contact; —spunkt m point of contact.

besagen [bə'za:gən] vt mean.

besagt a Tag etc in question.

besänftig- [bə'zɛnftɪg] cpd: —en vt soothe, calm; —end a soothing; B—ung f soothing, calming.

Besatz [bə'zats] m -es, ⁼e trimming, edging; —ung f garrison; (Naut, Aviat) crew; —ungsmacht f occupying power.

besaufen [bə'zaʊfən] vr irreg (col) get drunk or stoned.

beschädig- [bə'ʃɛ:dɪg] cpd: —en vt damage; B—ung f damage; (Stelle) damaged spot.

beschaffen [bə'ʃafən] vt get, acquire; a constituted; B—heit f constitution, nature.

Beschaffung f acquisition.

beschäftigen [bə'ʃɛftɪgən] vt occupy; (beruflich) employ; vr occupy or concern o.s.

beschäftigt a busy, occupied.

Beschäftigung f (Beruf) employment; (Tätigkeit) occupation; (Befassen) concern.

beschämen [bə'ʃɛ:mən] vt put to shame; —d a shameful; Hilfsbereitschaft shaming.

beschämt a ashamed.

beschatten [bə'ʃatən] vt shade; Verdächtige shadow.

beschaulich [bə'ʃaʊlɪç] a contemplative.

Bescheid [bə'ʃaɪt] m -(e)s, -e information; (Weisung) directions pl; — wissen be well-informed (über + acc about); ich weiß — I know; jdm — geben or sagen let sb know.

bescheiden [bə'ʃaɪdən] vr irreg content o.s.; a modest; B—heit f modesty.

bescheinen [bə'ʃaɪnən] vt irreg shine on.

bescheinigen [bə'ʃaɪnɪgən] vt certify; (bestätigen) acknowledge. **Bescheinigung** f certificate; (Quittung) receipt.

bescheißen [bə'ʃaɪsən] vt irreg (col) cheat.

beschenken [bə'ʃɛŋkən] vt give presents to.

bescheren [bə'ʃeːrən] vt: jdm etw — give sb sth as a present; jdn — give presents to sb. **Bescherung** f giving of presents; (col) mess.

beschildern [bə'ʃɪldərn] vt signpost.

beschimpfen [bə'ʃɪmpfən] vt abuse. **Beschimpfung** f abuse, insult.

Beschiß [bə'ʃɪs] m -sses (col) das ist — that is a swizz or a cheat.

Beschlag [bə'ʃlaːk] m -(e)s, ⸚e (Metallband) fitting; (auf Fenster) condensation; (auf Metall) tarnish; finish; (Hufeisen) horseshoe; jdn/etw in — nehmen or mit — belegen monopolize sb/sth; b—en [bə'ʃlaːgən] irreg vt cover; Pferd shoe; Fenster, Metall cover; b—en

sein be well versed (in or auf + dat in); vir (Fenster etc) mist over; b—nahmen vt seize, confiscate; requisition; —nahmung f confiscation, sequestration.

beschleunigen [bə'ʃlɔʏnɪgən] vt accelerate, speed up; vi (Aut) accelerate. **Beschleunigung** f acceleration.

beschließen [bə'ʃliːsən] vt irreg decide on; (beenden) end, close. **Beschluß** [bə'ʃlʊs] m -sses, -schlüsse decision, conclusion; (Ende) close, end.

beschmutzen [bə'ʃmʊtsən] vt dirty, soil.

beschneiden [bə'ʃnaɪdən] vt irreg cut, prune, trim; (Rel) circumcise.

beschönigen [bə'ʃøːnɪgən] vt gloss over.

beschränken [bə'ʃrɛŋkən] vt limit, restrict (auf + acc to); vr restrict o.s.

beschrankt [bə'ʃraŋkt] a Bahnübergang with barrier.

beschränk- [bə'ʃrɛŋk] cpd: —t a confined, narrow; Mensch limited, narrow-minded; B—theit f narrowness; B—ung f limitation.

beschreiben [bə'ʃraɪbən] vt irreg describe; Papier write on. **Beschreibung** f description.

beschriften [bə'ʃrɪftən] vt mark, label. **Beschriftung** f lettering.

beschuldigen [bə'ʃʊldɪgən] vt accuse. **Beschuldigung** f accusation.

beschummeln [bə'ʃʊməln] vt (col) cheat.

beschütz- [bə'ʃʏts] cpd: —en vt protect (vor + dat from); B—er m -s, - protector B—ung f protection.

Beschwerde [bə'ʃveːrdə] *f* -, -n complaint; (*Mühe*) hardship; (*pl: Leiden*) pain.

beschweren [bə'ʃveːrən] *vt* weight down; (*fig*) burden; *vr* complain.

beschwerlich *a* tiring, exhausting.

beschwichtigen [bə'ʃvɪçtɪgən] *vt* soothe, pacify.

Beschwichtigung *f* soothing, calming.

beschwindeln [bə'ʃvɪndəln] *vt* (*betrügen*) cheat; (*belügen*) fib to.

beschwingt [bə'ʃvɪŋt] *a* cheery, in high spirits.

beschwipst [bə'ʃvɪpst] *a* tipsy.

beschwören [bə'ʃvøːrən] *vt irreg Aussage* swear to; (*anflehen*) implore; *Geister* conjure up.

beseelen [bə'zeːlən] *vt* inspire.

besehen [bə'zeːən] *vt irreg* look at; *genau* — examine closely.

beseitigen [bə'zaɪtɪgən] *vt* remove.

Beseitigung *f* removal.

Besen ['beːzən] *m* -s, - broom; —stiel *m* broomstick.

besessen [bə'zɛsən] *a* possessed.

besetz- [bə'zɛts] *cpd:* —en *vt Haus, Land* occupy; *Platz* take, fill; *Posten* fill; *Rolle* cast; (*mit Edelsteinen*) set; —t *a* full; (*Tel*) engaged, busy; *Platz taken*; *WC engaged*; —tzeichen *nt* engaged tone; **B—ung** *f* occupation; filling; (*von Rolle*) casting; (*die Schauspieler*) cast.

besichtigen [bə'zɪçtɪgən] *vt* visit, look at.

Besichtigung *f* visit.

Besied(e)lung [bə'ziːd(ə)luŋ] *f* population.

besiegeln [bə'ziːgəln] *vt* seal.

besiegen [bə'ziːgən] *vt* defeat, overcome.

Besiegte(r) [bə'ziːgtə(r)] *m* loser.

besinnen [bə'zɪnən] *vr irreg* (*nachdenken*) think, reflect; (*erinnern*) remember; *sich anders* — change one's mind.

besinnlich *a* contemplative.

Besinnung *f* consciousness; *zur — kommen* recover consciousness; (*fig*) come to one's senses; **b—slos** *a* unconscious.

Besitz [bə'zɪts] *m* -es possession; (*Eigentum*) property; **b—anzeigend** *a* (*Gram*) possessive; **b—en** *vt irreg* possess, own; *Eigenschaft* have; —er(in *f*) *m* -s, -, owner, proprietor; —ergreifung *f*, —nahme *f* occupation, seizure.

besoffen [bə'zɔfən] *a* (*col*) drunk, pissed.

besohlen [bə'zoːlən] *vt* sole.

Besoldung [bə'zɔlduŋ] *f* salary, pay.

besondere(r,s) [bə'zɔndərə(r,z)] *a* special; (*eigen*) particular; (*gesondert*) separate; (*eigentümlich*) peculiar.

Besonderheit [bə'zɔndərhaɪt] *f* peculiarity.

besonders [bə'zɔndərs] *ad* especially, particularly; (*getrennt*) separately.

besonnen [bə'zɔnən] *a* sensible, level-headed; **B—heit** *f* prudence.

besorg- [bə'zɔrg] *cpd:* —en *vt* (*beschaffen*) acquire; (*kaufen auch*) purchase; (*erledigen*) *Geschäfte* deal with; (*sich kümmern um*) take care of; *es jdm —en* (*col*) show sb what for; **B—nis** *f* -, -se anxiety, concern; —t [bə'zɔrçt] *a* anxious, worried; **B—theit** *f* anxiety, worry; **B—ung** *f* acquisition; (*Kauf*) purchase.

bespielen [bə'ʃpiːlən] *vt* record.

bespitzeln [bə'ʃpɪtsəln] *vt* spy on.

besprechen [bə'ʃprɛçən] *irreg vt* discuss; *Tonband etc* speak onto; *Buch* review; *vr* discuss, consult.

Besprechung *f* meeting, discussion; (*von Buch*) review.

besser ['bɛsər] *a* better; **nur ein —er ...** just a glorified ...; **—gehen** *vi irreg impers*: **es geht ihm —** he feels better; **—n** *vt* make better, improve; *vr* improve; *Menschen* reform; **B—ung** *f* improvement; **gute B—ung!** get well soon; **B—wisser** *m* **-s, -** know-all.

Bestand [bə'ʃtant] *m* **-(e)s, ⁺e** (*Fortbestehen*) duration, stability; (*Kassen—*) amount, balance; (*Vorrat*) stock; **eiserne(r) —** iron rations *pl*; **— haben, von — sein** last long, endure.

beständig [bə'ʃtɛndiç] *a* (*ausdauernd*) constant (*auch fig*); *Wetter* settled; *Stoffe* resistant; *Klagen etc* continual.

Bestand- *cpd*: **—saufnahme** *f* stocktaking; **—teil** *m* part, component; (*Zutat*) ingredient.

bestärken [bə'ʃtɛrkən] *vt*: **jdn in etw** (*dat*) **—** strengthen *or* confirm sb in sth.

bestätigen [bə'ʃtɛ:tɪgən] *vt* confirm; (*anerkennen, Comm*) acknowledge.

Bestätigung *f* confirmation; acknowledgement.

bestatt- *cpd*: **—en** *vt* bury; **B—er** *m* **-s, -** undertaker; **B—ung** *f* funeral.

bestäuben [bə'ʃtɔybən] *vt* powder, dust; *Pflanze* pollinate.

beste(r,s) ['bɛstə(r,z)] *a* best; **sie singt am —n** she sings best; **so ist es am —n** it's best that way; **am —n gehst du gleich** you'd better go

at once; **jdn zum· —n haben** pull sb's leg; **etw zum —n geben** tell a joke/story *etc*; **aufs —** in the best possible way; **zu· jds B—n** for the benefit of sb.

bestechen [bə'ʃtɛçən] *vt irreg* bribe.

bestechlich *a* corruptible; **B—keit** *f* corruptibility.

Bestechung *f* bribery, corruption.

Besteck [bə'ʃtɛk] *nt* **-(e)s, -e** knife, fork and spoon, cutlery; (*Med*) set of instruments.

bestehen [bə'ʃte:ən] *irreg vi* be; exist; (*andauern*) last; *vt Kampf, Probe, Prüfung* pass; **— auf** (+*dat*) insist on; **— aus** consist of.

bestehlen [bə'ʃte:lən] *vt irreg* rob sb.

besteigen [bə'ʃtaɪgən] *vt irreg* climb, ascend; *Pferd* mount; *Thron* ascend.

Bestell- *cpd*: **—buch** *nt* order book; **b—en** *vt* order; (*kommen lassen*) arrange to see; (*nominieren*) name; *Acker* cultivate; *Grüße, Auftrag* pass on; **—schein** *m* order coupon; **—ung** *f* (*Comm*) order; (*Bestellen*) ordering.

bestenfalls ['bɛstən'fals] *ad* at best.

bestens ['bɛstəns] *ad* very well.

besteuern [bə'ʃtɔyərn] *vt* tax.

Bestie ['bɛstiə] *f* (*lit, fig*) beast.

bestimm- ['bɛʃtɪm] *cpd*: **—en** *vt Regeln* lay down; *Tag, Ort* fix; (*beherrschen*) characterize; (*aussehen*) mean; (*ernennen*) appoint; (*definieren*) define; (*veranlassen*) induce; **—t** *a* (*entschlossen*) firm; (*gewiß*) certain, definite; *Artikel* definite; *ad* (*gewiß*) definitely, for sure; **B—theit** *f* certainty; **B—ung** *f* (*Verordnung*) regulation; (*Festsetzen*) determining; (*Verwendungszweck*) purpose; (*Schicksal*) fate; (*Definition*)

definition; **B—ungsort** ·*m* destination.

Best- *cpd*: **—leistung** *f* best performance; **b—möglich** a best possible.

bestrafen [bə'ʃtraːfən] *vt* punish.

Bestrafung *f* punishment.

bestrahlen [bə'ʃtraːlən] *vt* shine on; (*Med*) treat with X-rays.

Bestrahlung *f* (*Med*) X-ray treatment, radiotherapy.

Bestreben [bə'ʃtreːbən] *nt* **-s**, **Bestrebung** [bə'ʃtreːbʊŋ] *f* endeavour, effort.

bestreichen [bə'ʃtraɪçən] *vt irreg* Brot spread.

bestreiten [bə'ʃtraɪtən] *vt irreg* (*abstreiten*) dispute; (*finanzieren*) pay for, finance.

bestreuen [bə'ʃtrɔyən] *vt* sprinkle, dust; Straße (spread with) grit.

bestürmen [bə'ʃtʏrmən] *vt* (*mit Fragen, Bitten etc*) overwhelm, swamp.

bestürzen [bə'ʃtʏrtsən] *vt* dismay.

bestürzt *a* dismayed.

Bestürzung *f* consternation.

Besuch [bə'zuːx] *m* **-(e)s**, **-e** visit; (*Person*) visitor; **einen — machen bei jdm** pay sb a visit or call; **— haben** have visitors; **bei jdm auf** or **zu — sein** be visiting sb; **b—en** *vt* visit; (*Sch etc*) attend; **gut —t** well-attended; **—er(in** *f*) *m* **-s**, - visitor, guest; **—serlaubnis** *f* permission to visit; **—szeit** *f* visiting hours *pl*.

betagt [bə'taːkt] *a* aged.

betasten [bə'tastən] *vt* touch, feel.

betätigen [bə'tɛːtɪgən] *vt* (*bedienen*) work, operate; *vr* involve o.s.; **sich politisch —** be involved in politics; **sich als etw —** work as sth.

Betätigung *f* activity; (*beruflich*) occupation; (*Tech*) operation.

betäuben [bə'tɔybən] *vt* stun; (*fig*) Gewissen still; (*Med*) anaesthetize.

Betäubungsmittel *nt* anaesthetic.

Bete ['beːtə] *f* **-, -n**: rote — beetroot.

beteiligen [bə'taɪlɪgən] *vr* (*an + dat* in) take part or participate, share; (*an Geschäft: finanziell*) have a share; *vt*: **jdn —** give sb a share or interest (*an + dat* in).

Beteiligung *f* participation; (*Anteil*) share, interest; (*Besucherzahl*) attendance.

beten ['beːtən] *vti* pray.

beteuern [bə'tɔyərn] *vt* assert; Unschuld protest; **jdm etw —** assure sb of sth.

Beteuerung *f* assertion, protest(ation), assurance.

Beton [be'tõ] *m* **-s**, **-s** concrete.

betonen [bə'toːnən] *vt* stress.

betonieren [betoˈniːrən] *vt* concrete.

Betonung *f* stress, emphasis.

betören [bə'tøːrən] *vt* beguile.

Betracht [bə'traxt] *m*: **in — kommen** be concerned or relevant; **nicht in — kommen** be out of the question; **etw in — ziehen** consider sth; **außer — bleiben** not be considered; **b—en** *vt* look at; (*fig auch*) consider; **—er(in** *f*) *m* **-s**, - onlooker.

beträchtlich [bə'trɛçtlɪç] *a* considerable.

Betrachtung *f* (*Ansehen*) examination; (*Erwägung*) consideration.

Betrag [bə'traːk] *m* **-(e)s**, **⁺e** amount; **b—en** [bə'traːgən] *irreg vt* amount to; *vr* behave; **—en** *nt* **-s** behaviour.

betrauen [bə'trauən] *vt*: **jdn mit etw —** entrust sb with sth.

betreffen [bəˈtrɛfən] vt irreg concern, affect; **was mich betrifft** as for me; **—d** a relevant, in question.
betreffs [bəˈtrɛfs]· prep +gen concerning, regarding.
betreiben [bəˈtraɪbən] vt irreg (ausüben) practise; Politik follow; Studien pursue; (vorantreiben) push ahead; (Tech: antreiben) drive.
betreten [bəˈtreːtən] vt irreg enter; Bühne etc step onto; **B— verboten** keep off/out; a embarrassed.
Betrieb [bəˈtriːp] m -(e)s, -e (Firma) firm, concern; (Anlage) plant; (Tätigkeit) operation; (Treiben) traffic; **außer — sein** be out of order; **in — sein** be in operation; **—sausflug** m firm's outing; **b—sfähig** a in working order; **—sferien** pl company holidays pl; **—sklima** nt (working) atmosphere; **—skosten** pl running costs pl; **—srat** m workers' council; **b—ssicher** a safe, reliable; **—sstoff** m fuel; **—sstörung** f breakdown; **—sunfall** m industrial accident; **—swirtschaft** f economics.
betrinken [bəˈtrɪŋkən] vr irreg get drunk.
betroffen [bəˈtrɔfən] a (bestürzt) amazed, perplexed; **von etw — werden** or **sein** be affected by sth.
betrüben [bəˈtryːbən] vt grieve.
betrübt [bəˈtryːpt] a sorrowful, grieved.
Betrug [bəˈtruːk] m -(e)s deception; (Jur) fraud.
betrügen [bəˈtryːgən] irreg vt cheat; (Jur) defraud; Ehepartner be unfaithful to; vr deceive o.s.
Betrüger m -s, - cheat, deceiver; **b—isch** a deceitful; (Jur) fraudulent.

betrunken [bəˈtruŋkən] a drunk.
Bett [bɛt] nt -(e)s, -en bed; **ins** or **zu — gehen** go to bed; **—bezug** m duvet cover; **—decke** f blanket; (Daunen—) quilt; (Überwurf) bedspread.
Bettel- [ˈbɛtəl] cpd: **b—arm** a very poor, destitute; **—ei** [bɛtəˈlaɪ] f begging; **b—n** vi beg.
Bett- cpd: **b—en** vt make a bed for; **b—lägerig** a bedridden; **—laken** nt sheet.
Bettler(in f) [ˈbɛtlər(m)] m -s, - beggar.
Bett- cpd: **—nässer** m -s, - bedwetter; **—vorleger** m bedside rug; **—wäsche** f, **—zeug** nt bedclothes pl, bedding.
beugen [ˈbɔygən] vt bend; (Gram) inflect; vr (sich fügen) bow (dat to).
Beule [ˈbɔylə] f -, -n bump, swelling.
beunruhigen [bəˈʔunruːɪgən] vt disturb, alarm; vr become worried.
Beunruhigung f worry, alarm.
beurkunden [bəˈʔuːrkundən] vt attest, verify.
beurlauben [bəˈʔuːrlaubən] vt give leave or holiday to.
beurteilen [bəˈʔuːrtaɪlən] vt judge; Buch etc review.
Beurteilung f judgement; review; (Note) mark.
Beute [ˈbɔytə] f - booty, loot; **—l** m -s, - bag; (Geld—) purse; (Tabak—) pouch.
bevölkern [bəˈfœlkərn] vt populate.
Bevölkerung f population.
bevollmächtigen [bəˈfɔlmɛçtɪgən] vt authorize.
Bevollmächtigte(r) mf authorized agent.
Bevollmächtigung f authorization.
bevor [bəˈfoːr] cj before; **—munden** vt insep dominate; **—stehen** vi

irreg be in store (*dat* for); **—stehend** a imminent, approaching; **—zugen** *vt insep* prefer; **B—zugung** f preference.

bewachen [bə'vaxən] *vt* watch, guard.

Bewachung f (*Bewachen*) guarding; (*Leute*) guard, watch.

bewaffnen [bə'vafnən] *vt* arm.

Bewaffnung f (*Vorgang*) arming; (*Ausrüstung*) armament, arms *pl*.

bewahren [bə'va:rən] *vt* keep; jdn vor jdm/etw — save sb from sb/sth.

bewähren [bə've:rən] *vr* prove o.s.; (*Maschine*) prove its worth.

bewahrheiten [bə'va:rhaitən] *vr* come true.

bewährt a reliable.

Bewährung f (*Jur*) probation; **—sfrist** f (period of) probation.

bewaldet [bə'valdət] a wooded.

bewältigen [bə'vɛltɪgən] *vt* overcome; *Arbeit* finish; *Portion* manage.

bewandert [bə'vandərt] a expert, knowledgeable.

bewässern [bə'vɛsərn] *vt* irrigate.

Bewässerung f irrigation.

Beweg- [bə've:g] *cpd*: **b—en** *vtr* move; jdn zu etw **b—en** induce sb to (do) sth; **—grund** [bə've:k-] *m* motive; **b—lich** a movable, mobile; (*flink*) quick; **b—t** a Leben eventful; *Meer* rough; (*ergriffen*) touched; **—ung** f movement, motion; (*innere*) emotion; (*körperlich*) exercise; sich (*dat*) **—ung machen** take exercise; **—ungsfreiheit** f freedom of movement or action; **b—ungslos** a motionless.

Beweis [bə'vais] *m* **-es**, **-e** proof; (*Zeichen*) sign; **b—bar** [bə'vaiz-] a provable; **b—en** *vt irreg* prove;

(*zeigen*) show; **—führung** f reasoning; **—kraft** f weight, conclusiveness; **b—kräftig** a convincing, conclusive; **—mittel** *nt* evidence.

bewenden [bə'vɛndən] *vi*: etw dabei — lassen leave sth at that.

Bewerb- [bə'vɛrb] *cpd*: **b—en** *vr irreg* apply (*um* for); **—er(in** f) *m* **-s**, **-** applicant; **—ung** f application.

bewerkstelligen [bə'vɛrkʃtɛlɪgən] *vt* manage, accomplish.

bewerten [bə'vɛrtən] *vt* assess.

bewilligen [bə'vɪlɪgən] *vt* grant, allow.

Bewilligung f granting.

bewirken [bə'vɪrkən] *vt* cause, bring about.

bewirten [bə'vɪrtən] *vt* entertain.

bewirtschaften [bə'vɪrt-ʃaftən] *vt* manage.

Bewirtung f hospitality.

bewohn- [bə'vo:n] *cpd*: **—bar** a inhabitable; **—en** *vt* inhabit, live in; **B—er(in** f) *m* **-s**, **-** inhabitant; (*von Haus*) resident.

bewölkt [bə'vœlkt] a cloudy, overcast.

Bewölkung f clouds *pl*.

Bewunder- [bə'vundər] *cpd*: **—er** *m* **-s**, **-** admirer; **b—n** *vt* admire; **b—nswert** a admirable, wonderful; **—ung** f admiration.

bewußt [bə'vust] a conscious; (*absichtlich*) deliberate; sich (*dat*) einer Sache — sein be aware of sth; **—los** a unconscious; **B—losigkeit** f unconsciousness; **—machen** *vt*: jdm/sich etw **—machen** make sb/o.s. aware of sth; **B—sein** *nt* consciousness; **bei B—sein** conscious.

bezahlen [bə'tsa:lən] *vt* pay (for); es macht sich bezahlt it will pay.

Bezahlung f payment.
bezaubern [bə'tsaubərn] vt enchant, charm.
bezeichnen [bə'tsaiçnən] vt (kennzeichnen) mark; (nennen) call; (beschreiben) describe; (zeigen) show, indicate; **—d · a** characteristic, typical (für of).
Bezeichnung f (Zeichen) mark, sign; (Beschreibung) description.
bezeugen [bə'tsɔygən] vt testify to.
Bezichtigung f accusation.
beziehen [bə'tsiːən] irreg vt (mit Überzug) cover; Bett make; Haus, Position move into; Standpunkt take up; (erhalten) receive; Zeitung subscribe to, take; etw auf jdn/etw — relate sth to sb/sth; vr refer (auf +acc to); (Himmel) cloud over.
Beziehung f (Verbindung) connection; (Zusammenhang) relation; (Verhältnis) relationship; (Hinsicht) respect; **—en** haben (vorteilhaft) have connections or contacts; **b—sweise** ad or; (genauer gesagt auch) that is, or rather.
Bezirk [bə'tsɪrk] m -(e)s, -e district.
Bezug [bə'tsuːk] m -(e)s, ̈e (Hülle) covering; (Comm) ordering; (Gehalt) income, salary; (Beziehung) relationship (zu to); in **b—** (auf +acc) with reference to; — nehmen auf (+acc) refer to.
bezüglich [bə'tsyːklɪç] prep +gen concerning, referring to; a concerning; (Gram) relative.
Bezugs- cpd: **—nahme** f reference (auf +acc to); **—spreis** m retail price; **—squelle** f source of supply.
bezwecken [bə'tsvɛkən] vt aim at.

bezweifeln [bə'tsvaifəln] vt doubt, query.
Bibel ['biːbəl] f -, -n Bible.
Biber ['biːbər] m -s, - beaver.
Biblio- cpd: **—graphie** [biblioɡra'fiː] f bibliography; **—thek** [biblio'teːk] f -, -en library; **—thekar(in** f) [bibliote'kaːr(ɪn)] m -s, - librarian.
biblisch ['biːblɪʃ] a biblical.
bieder ['biːdər] a upright, worthy; Kleid etc plain.
bieg- [biːɡ] cpd: **—bar** a flexible; **—en** irreg vtr bend; vi turn; **—sam** ['biːk-] a supple; **B—ung** f bend, curve.
Biene ['biːnə] f -, -n bee; **—nhonig** m honey; **—nkorb** m beehive; **—nwachs** nt beeswax.
Bier [biːr] nt -(e)s, -e beer; **—brauer** m brewer; **—deckel** m, **—filz** m beer mat; **—krug** m, **—seidel** nt beer mug.
bieten ['biːtən] irreg vt offer; (bei Versteigerung) bid; vr (Gelegenheit) be open (dat to); sich (dat) etw — lassen put up with sth.
Bikini [bi'kiːni] m -s, -s bikini.
Bilanz [bi'lants] f balance; (fig) outcome; — ziehen take stock (aus of).
Bild [bɪlt] nt -(e)s, -er (lit, fig) picture; photo; (Spiegel—) reflection; **—bericht** m pictorial report.
bilden ['bɪldən] vt form; (erziehen) educate; (ausmachen) constitute; vr arise; (erziehen) educate o.s.
Bilder- ['bɪldər] cpd: **—buch** nt picture book; **—rahmen** m picture frame.
Bild- cpd: **—fläche** f screen; (fig) scene; **—hauer** m -s, - sculptor; **b—hübsch** a lovely, pretty as a picture; **b—lich** a figurative; pictorial; **—schirm** m television screen; **b—schön** a lovely; **—ung**

['bɪlduŋ] f formation; (Wissen, Benehmen) education; —ungslücke f gap in one's education; —ungspolitik f educational policy; —weite f (Phot) distance.

Billard ['bɪljart] nt -s, -e billiards; —ball m, —kugel f billiard ball.

billig ['bɪlɪç] a cheap; (gerecht) fair, reasonable; —en ['bɪlɪgən] vt approve of; B—ung f approval.

Billion [bɪ'li:ɔn] f billion, trillion (US).

bimmeln ['bɪməln] vi tinkle.

Binde ['bɪndə] f -, -n bandage; (Arm—) band; (Med) sanitary towel; —glied nt connecting link; b—n vt irreg bind, tie; —strich m hyphen; —wort nt conjunction.

Bind- cpd: —faden m string; —ung f bond, tie; (Ski—) binding.

binnen ['bɪnən] prep +dat or gen within; B—hafen m inland harbour; B—handel m internal trade.

Binse ['bɪnzə] f -, -n rush, reed; —nwahrheit f truism.

Bio- [bio] cpd bio-; —graphie [-gra'fi:] f biography; —loge [-'lo:gə] m -n, -n biologist; —logie [-lo'gi:] f biology; b—logisch [-'lo:gɪʃ] a biological.

Birke ['bɪrkə] f -, -n birch.

Birnbaum m pear tree.

Birne ['bɪrnə] f -, -n pear; (Elec) (light) bulb.

bis [bɪs] ad, prep +acc (räumlich: — zu/an +acc) to, as far as; (zeitlich) till, until; Sie haben — Dienstag Zeit you have until or till Tuesday; — Dienstag muß es fertig sein it must be ready by Tuesday; — hierher this far; — in die Nacht into the night; — auf weiteres until further notice; — bald/gleich see you later/soon; — auf etw (acc) (einschließlich) including sth; (aus-

geschlossen) except sth; — zu up to; cj (mit Zahlen) to; (zeitlich) until, till; von ... — ... from ...to....

Bischof ['bɪʃɔf] m -s, -e bishop.
bischöflich ['bɪʃøːflɪç] a episcopal.

bisher [bɪs'heːr] ad, —ig a till now, hitherto.

Biskuit [bɪs'kviːt] m or nt -(e)s, -s or -e biscuit; —teig m sponge mixture.

bislang [bɪs'laŋ] ad hitherto.

Biß [bɪs] m -sses, -sse bite.
bißchen ['bɪsçən] a, ad bit.

Bissen ['bɪsən] m -s, - bite, morsel.
bissig ['bɪsɪç] a Hund snappy; Bemerkung cutting, biting.

Bistum ['bɪstuːm] nt bishopric.

bisweilen [bɪs'vaɪlən] ad at times, occasionally.

Bitte ['bɪtə] f -, -n request; b— interj please; (wie b—?) (I beg your) pardon; (als Antwort auf Dank) you're welcome; b— schön! it was a pleasure; b—n vti irreg ask (um for); b—nd a pleading, imploring.

bitter ['bɪtər] a bitter; —böse a very angry; B—keit f bitterness; —lich a bitter.

blähen ['blɛːən] vtr swell, blow out.
Blähungen pl (Med) wind.

blam- cpd: —abel [bla'maːbəl] a disgraceful; B—age [bla'maːʒə] f -, -n disgrace; —ieren [bla'miːrən] vr make a fool of o.s., disgrace o.s.; vt let down, disgrace.

blank [blaŋk] a bright; (unbedeckt) bare; (sauber) clean, polished; (col: ohne Geld) broke; (offensichtlich) blatant.

blanko ['blaŋko] ad blank; B—scheck m blank cheque.

Bläschen ['blɛːsçən] *nt* bubble; (*Med*) spot, blister. .

Blase ['blaːzə] *f -, -n* bubble; (*Med*) blister; (*Anat*) bladder; —balg *m* bellows *pl*; b—n *vti* irreg blow.

Blas- *cpd:* —instrument *nt* brass or wind instrument; —kapelle *f* brass band.

blaß [blas] *a* pale.

Blässe ['blɛsə] *f* - paleness, palour.

Blatt [blat] *nt* -(e)s, ˮer leaf; newspaper; (*von Papier*) sheet; (*Cards*) hand; vom — singen/spielen sightread.

blättern ['blɛtərn] *vi:* in etw (*dat*) — leaf through sth.

Blätterteig *m* flaky or puff pastry.

blau [blau] *a* blue; (*col*) drunk, stoned; (*Cook*)˙ boiled; *Auge* black; —er Fleck bruise; Fahrt ins B—e mystery tour; —äugig a blueeyed; B—licht *nt* flashing blue light; —machen *vi* (*col*) skive off work; B—strumpf *m* (*fig*) bluestocking.

Blech [blɛç] *nt* -(e)s, -e tin, sheet metal; (*Back—*) baking tray; —büchse *f*, —dose *f* tin, can; b—en *vti* (*col*) pay; —schaden *m* (*Aut*) damage to bodywork.

Blei [blai] *nt* -(e)s, -e lead; —be *f* -, -n roof over one's head; —ben *vi* irreg stay, remain, b—benlassen *vt* irreg leave (alone).

bleich [blaiç] *a* faded, pale; —en *vt* bleach.

Blei- *cpd:* b—ern a leaden; —stift *m* pencil; —stiftspitzer *m* pencil sharpener.

Blende ['blɛndə] *f -, -n* (*Phot*) aperture; b—n *vt* blind, dazzle; (*fig*) hoodwink; b—nd a (*col*) grand; b—nd aussehen look smashing.

Blick [blik] *m* -(e)s, -e (*kurz*) glance, glimpse; (*Anschauen*) look, ·gaze; (*Aussicht*) view; b—en *vi* look; sich b—en lassen put in an appearance; —fang *m* eye-catching object; —feld *nt* range of vision (*auch fig*).

blind [blint] a blind; *Glas etc* dull; —er Passagier stowaway; B—darm *m* ·appendix; B—darmentzündung ·   *f* appendicitis; B—enschrift ['blindən-] *f* braille; B—heit *f* blindness; —lings ad blindly; B—schleiche *f* slow worm; —schreiben *vt* irreg touch-type.

blink- [blink] *cpd:* —en *vi* twinkle, sparkle; (*Licht*) flash, signal; (*Aut*) indicate; *vt* flash, signal; B—er *m* -s, -, B—licht *nt* (*Aut*) indicator.

blinzeln ['blintsəln] *vi* blink, wink.

Blitz [blits] *m* -es, -e (flash of) lightning; —ableiter *m* lightning conductor; b—en *vi* (*aufleuchten*) glint, shine; es blitzt (*Met*) there's a flash of lightning; —licht *nt* flashlight; b—schnell a, ad as quick as a flash.

Block [blok] *m* -(e)s, ˮe (*lit, fig*) block; (*von Papier*) pad; —ade [blo'kaːdə] *f -, -n* blockade; —flöte *f* recorder; b—frei a (*Pol*) unaligned; b—ieren [blo'kiːrən] *vt* block; *vi* (*Räder*) jam; —schrift *f* block letters *pl*.

blöd [bløːt] a silly, stupid; —eln ['bløːdəln] *vi* (*col*) fool around; B—heit *f* stupidity; B—sinn *m* nonsense; —sinnig a silly, idiotic.

blond [blont] a blond, fair-haired.

bloß [bloːs] a (*unbedeckt*) bare; (*nackt*) naked; (*nur*) mere; ad only, merely; laß das —! just don't do that!

Blöße ['blø:sə] *f* -, -n bareness; nakedness; (*fig*) weakness; sich (*dat*) eine — geben (*fig*) lay o.s. open to attack.

bloß *cpd:* —**legen** *vt* expose; —**stellen** *vt* show up.

blühen ['bly:ən] *vi* (*lit*) bloom, be in bloom; (*fig*) flourish.

Blume ['blu:mə] *f* -, -n flower; (*von Wein*) bouquet; —**nkohl** *m* cauliflower; —**ntopf** *m* flowerpot; —**nzwiebel** *f* bulb.

Bluse ['blu:zə] *f* -, -n blouse.

Blut [blu:t] *nt* -(e)s blood; **b**—**arm** *a* anaemic; (*fig*) penniless; **b**—**befleckt** *a* bloodstained; —**buche** *f* copper beech; —**druck** *m* blood pressure.

Blüte ['bly:tə] *f* -, -n blossom; (*fig*) prime; —**zeit** *f* flowering period; (*fig*) prime.

Blut- *cpd:* —**egel** *m* leech; **b**—**en** *vi* bleed.

Blütenstaub *m* pollen.

Blut- *cpd:* —**er** *m* -s, - (*Med*) haemophiliac; —**erguß** *m* haemorrhage; (*auf Haut*) bruise; —**gruppe** *f* blood group; **b**—**ig** *a* bloody; **b**—**jung** *a* very young; —**probe** *f* blood test; —**schande** *f* incest; —**spender** *m* blood donor; —**übertragung** *f* blood transfusion; —**ung** *f* bleeding, haemorrhage; —**vergiftung** *f* blood poisoning; —**wurst** *f* black pudding.

Bö(e) ['bø:(ə)] *f* -, -en squall.

Bock [bɔk] *m* -(e)s, ⁼e buck, ram; (*Gestell*) trestle, support; (*Sport*) buck.

Boden ['bo:dən] *m* -s, ⁼ ground; (*Fuß*—) floor; (*Meeres*—, *Faß*—) bottom; (*Speicher*) attic; **b**—**los** *a* bottomless; (*col*) incredible; —**satz** *m* dregs *pl*, sediment; —**schätze** *pl* mineral wealth; —**turnen** *nt* floor exercises *pl*.

Bogen ['bo:gən] *m* -s, - (*Biegung*) curve; (*Archit*) arch; (*Waffe*, *Mus*) bow; (*Papier*) sheet; —**gang** *m* arcade; —**schütze** *m* archer.

Bohle ['bo:lə] *f* -, -n plank.

Bohne ['bo:nə] *f* -, -n bean; —**nkaffee** *m* pure coffee; **b**—**rn** *vt* wax, polish; —**rwachs** *nt* floor polish.

Bohr- *cpd:* **b**—**en** *vt* bore; —**er** *m* -s, - drill; —**insel** *f* oil rig; —**maschine** *f* drill; —**turm** *m* derrick.

Boje ['bo:jə] *f* -, -n buoy.

Bolzen ['bɔltsən] *m* -s, - bolt.

Bomb- *cpd:* **b**—**ardieren** [bɔmbar'di:rən] *vt* bombard; (*aus der Luft*) bomb; —**e** ['bɔmbə] *f* -, -n bomb; —**enangriff** *m* bombing raid; —**enerfolg** *m* (*col*) huge success.

Bonbon [bõ'bõ:] *m or nt* -s, -s sweet.

Boot [bo:t] *nt* -(e)s, -e boat.

Bord [bɔrt] *m* -(e)s, -e (*Aviat*, *Naut*) board; **an** — **on** board; *nt* (*Brett*) shelf; —**ell** [bɔr'dɛl] *nt* -s, -e brothel; —**funkanlage** *f* radio; —**stein** *m* kerb(stone).

borgen ['bɔrgən] *vt* borrow; **jdm etw** — lend sb sth.

borniert [bɔr'ni:rt] *a* narrowminded.

Börse ['bø:rzə] *f* -, -n stock exchange; (*Geld*—) purse.

Borste ['bɔrstə] *f* -, -n bristle.

Borte ['bɔrtə] *f* -, -n edging; (*Band*) trimming.

bös [bø:s] *a* bad, evil; (*zornig*) angry; —**artig** ['bø:z-] *a* malicious.

Böschung ['bœʃuŋ] *f* slope; (*Ufer*— *etc*) embankment.

bos- ['bo:s] *cpd:* —**haft** *a* malicious, spiteful; **B**—**heit** *f* malice, spite.

böswillig ['bø:svɪlɪç] a malicious.

Botanik [bo'ta:nɪk] f botany.

botanisch [bo'ta:nɪʃ] a botanical.

Bot- ['bo:t] cpd: **—e** m **-n**, **-n** messenger; **—enjunge** m errand boy; **—schaft** f message, news; (Pol) embassy; **—schafter** m **-s**, **-** ambassador.

Bottich ['bɔtɪç] m **-(e)s**, **-e** vat, tub.

Bouillon [bu'ljɔ:] f **-**, **-s** consommé.

Bowle ['bo:lə] f **-**, **-n** punch.

Box- ['bɔks] cpd: **b—en** vi box; **—er** m **-s**, **-** boxer; **—handschuh** m boxing glove; **—kampf** m boxing match.

boykottieren [bɔykɔ'ti:rən] vt boycott.

Branche ['brã:ʃə] f **-**, **-n** line of business; **—nverzeichnis** nt yellow pages pl.

Brand [brant] m **-(e)s**, **⁼e** fire; (Med) gangrene; **b—en** [brandən] vi surge; (Meer) break; **b—marken** vt brand; (fig) stigmatize; **—salbe** f ointment for burns; **—stifter** m arsonist, fire-raiser; **—stiftung** f arson; **—ung** f surf; **—wunde** f burn.

Branntwein ['brantvaɪn] m brandy.

Brat- [bra:t] cpd: **—apfel** m baked apple; **b—en** vt irreg roast, fry; **—en** m **-s**, **-** roast, joint; **—en m -s**, roast chicken; **—kartoffeln** pl fried or roast potatoes pl; **—pfanne** f frying pan; **—rost** m grill.

Bratsche ['bra:tʃə] f **-**, **-n** viola.

Brat- cpd: **—spieß** m spit; **—wurst** f grilled sausage.

Brauch [braux] m **-(e)s**, **Bräuche** custom; **b—bar** a usable, serviceable; Person capable; **b—en** vt (bedürfen) need; (müssen) have to; (verwenden) use.

Braue ['braoə] f **-**, **-n** brow; **b—n** vt brew; **—'rei** f brewery.

braun [braon] a brown; (von Sonne auch) tanned.

Bräune ['brɔynə] f **-**, **-n** brownness; (Sonnen—) tan; **b—n** vt make brown; (Sonne) tan.

braungebrannt a tanned.

Brause ['braozə] f **-**, **-n** shower bath; (von Gießkanne) rose; (Getränk) lemonade; **b—n** vi roar; (auch vr: duschen) take a shower; **—pulver** nt lemonade powder.

Braut [braot] f **-**, **Bräute** bride; (Verlobte) fiancée.

Bräutigam ['brɔytɪgam] m **-s**, **-e** bridegroom; fiancé.

Braut- cpd: **—jungfer** f bridesmaid; **—paar** nt bride and bridegroom, bridal pair.

brav [bra:f] a (artig) good; (ehrenhaft) worthy, honest.

Brech- ['brɛç] cpd: **—eisen** nt crowbar; **b—en** vti irreg break; Licht refract; (fig) Mensch crush; (speien) vomit; **die Ehe b—en** commit adultery; **—reiz** m nausea, retching.

Brei [braɪ] m **-(e)s**, **-e** (Masse) pulp; (Cook) gruel; (Hafer—) porridge.

breit [braɪt] a wide, broad; **B—e** f **-**, **-n** width; breadth; (Geog) latitude; **—en** vt: etw über etw (acc) **—en** spread sth over sth; **B—engrad** m degree of latitude; **—machen** vr spread o.s. out; **—schult(e)rig** a broad-shouldered; **—treten** vt irreg (col) enlarge upon; **B—wandfilm** m wide-screen film.

Brems- ['brɛmz] cpd: **—belag** m brake lining; **—e** f **-**, **-n** brake; (Zool) horsefly; **b—en** vi brake, apply the brakes; vt Auto brake; (fig) slow down; **—licht** m brake light; **—pedal** nt brake pedal; **—schuh** m brake shoe; **—spur** f tyre marks pl; **—weg** m braking distance.

Brenn- ['brɛn] cpd: **b—bar** a inflammable; **b—en** (irreg v) burn, be on fire; (Licht, Kerze etc) burn; vt Holz etc burn; (Ziegel, Ton fire; Kaffee roast; **darauf b—en, etw zu tun** be dying to do sth; **—material** nt fuel; **—(n)essel** f nettle; **—spiritus** m methylated spirits; **—stoff** m liquid fuel.

brenzlig ['brɛntslɪç] a smelling of burning, burnt; (fig) precarious.

Brett [brɛt] nt -(e)s, -er board, plank; (Bord) shelf; (Spiel—) board; **Schwarze—** ≈ notice board; **—er** pl (Ski) skis pl; (Theat) boards pl; **—erzaun** m wooden fence.

Brezel ['bre:tsəl] f -, -n bretzel, pretzel.

Brief [bri:f] m -(e)s, -e letter; **—beschwerer** m -s, - paperweight; **—kasten** m letterbox; **b—lich** a,ad by letter; **—marke** f postage stamp; **—öffner** m letter opener; **—papier** nt notepaper; **—tasche** f wallet; **—träger** m postman; **—umschlag** m envelope; **—wechsel** m correspondence.

Brikett [bri'kɛt] nt -s, -s briquette.

brillant [brɪl'jant] a (fig) sparkling, brilliant; **B—** m -en, -en brilliant, diamond.

Brille ['brɪlə] f -, -n spectacles pl; (Schutz—) goggles pl; (Toiletten—) (toilet) seat.

bringen ['brɪŋən] vt irreg bring; (mitnehmen, begleiten) take; (einbringen) Profit bring in; (veröffentlichen) publish; (Theat, Cine) show; (Rad, TV) broadcast; (in einen Zustand versetzen) get; (col:

tun können) manage; **jdn dazu —, etw zu tun** make sb do sth; **jdn nach Hause —** take sb home; **jdn um etw —** make sb lose sth; **jdn auf eine Idee —** give sb an idea.

Brise ['bri:zə] f -, -n breeze.

bröckelig ['brœkəlɪç] a crumbly.

Brocken ['brɔkən] m -s, - piece, bit; (Fels—) lump of rock.

brodeln ['bro:dəln] vi bubble.

Brokat [bro'ka:t] m -(e)s, -e brocade.

Brombeere ['brɔmbe:rə] f blackberry, bramble.

bronchial [brɔnçi'a:l] a bronchial.

Bronchien ['brɔnçiən] pl bronchia(l tubes) pl.

Bronze ['brõ:sə] f -, -n bronze.

Brosame ['bro:za:mə] f -, -n crumb.

Brosche ['brɔʃə] f -, -n brooch.

Broschüre [brɔ'ʃy:rə] f -, -n pamphlet.

Brot [bro:t] nt -(e)s, -e bread; (—laib) loaf.

Brötchen ['brø:tçən] nt roll.

brotlos ['bro:tlo:s] a (Person) unemployed; Arbeit etc unprofitable.

Bruch [brux] m -(e)s, ⁼e breakage; (zerbrochene Stelle) break; (fig) split, breach; (Med: Eingeweide—) rupture, hernia; (Bein— etc) fracture; (Math) fraction; **—bude** f (col) shack.

brüchig ['brʏçɪç] a brittle, fragile; Haus dilapidated.

Bruch- cpd: **—landung** f crash landing; **—strich** m (Math) line; **—stück** nt fragment; **—teil** m fraction.

Brücke ['brʏkə] f -, -n bridge; (Teppich) rug.

Bruder ['bru:dər] m -s, ⁼ brother.

Brüder- ['bry:dər] cpd: **b—lich** a brotherly; **—lichkeit** f fraternity;

—schaft f brotherhood, fellowship; **—schaft trinken** fraternize, address each other as 'du.'

Brühe ['bry:ə] f -, -n broth, stock; (pej) muck.

brüllen ['brylən] vi bellow, scream.

Brumm- ['brum] cpd: **—bär** m grumbler; **b—eln** vti mumble; **b—en** vi (Bär, Mensch etc) growl; (Insekt, Radio) buzz; (Motoren) roar; (murren) grumble; vt growl; **jdm brummt der Kopf** sb's head is buzzing.

brünett [bry'nɛt] a brunette, dark-haired.

Brunnen ['brunən] m -s, - fountain; (tief) well; (natürlich) spring; **—kresse** f watercress.

brüsk [brysk] a abrupt, brusque.

Brust [brust] f -, ̈e breast; (Männer—) chest.

brüsten ['brystən] vr boast.

Brust- cpd: **—fellentzündung** f pleurisy; **—kasten** m chest; **—schwimmen** nt breast-stroke; **—warze** f nipple.

Brüstung ['brystuŋ] f parapet.

Brut [bru:t] f -, -en brood; (Brüten) hatching; (pej) **bru'ta:l** a brutal; **—ali'tät** f brutality; **—apparat** m, **—kasten** m incubator.

brüten ['bry:tən] vi hatch, brood (auch fig).

brutto ['bruto] ad gross; **B—ein-kommen** nt, **B—gehalt** nt gross salary; **B—gewicht** nt gross weight; **B—lohn** m gross wages pl.

Bub [bu:p] m -en, -en boy, lad; **—e** [bu:bə] m -n, -n (Schurke) rogue; (Cards) jack; **—ikopf** m bobbed hair, shingle.

Buch [bu:x] nt -(e)s, ̈er book; (Comm) account book; **—binder** m bookbinder; **—drucker** m printer;

—e f -, -n beech tree; **b—en** vt book; Betrag enter.

Bücher- ['by:çər] cpd: **—brett** nt bookshelf; **—ei** ['rai] f library; **—regal** nt bookshelves pl, book-case; **—schrank** m bookcase.

Buch- cpd: **—fink** m chaffinch; **—führung** f book-keeping, accounting; **—halter(in** f) m -s, - book-keeper; **—handel** m book trade; **—händler(in** f) m bookseller; **—handlung** f bookshop.

Büchse ['byksə] f -, -n tin, can; (Holz—) box; (Gewehr) rifle; **—n-fleisch** nt tinned meat; **—nöffner** m tin or can opener.

Buch- cpd: **—stabe** m -ns, -n letter (of the alphabet); **b—stabieren** [bu:xʃta'bi:rən] vt spell; **b—stäb-lich** ['bu:xʃtɛ:plɪç] a literal.

Bucht [buxt] f -, -en bay.

Buchung ['bu:xuŋ] f booking; (Comm) entry.

Buckel ['bukəl] m -s, - hump.

bücken ['bykən] vr bend.

Bückling ['byklıŋ] m (Fisch) kipper; (Verbeugung) bow.

Bude ['bu:də] f -, -n booth, stall; (col) digs pl.

Budget [by'dʒe:] nt -s, -s budget.

Büffel ['byfəl] m -s, - buffalo.

Büf(f)ett [by'fe:] nt -s, -s (An-richte) sideboard; (Geschirr-schrank) dresser; **kaltes —** cold buffet.

Bug [bu:k] m -(e)s, -e (Naut) bow; (Aviat) nose.

Bügel ['by:gəl] m -s, - (Kleider—) hanger; (Steig—) stirrup; (Brillen—) arm; **—brett** nt ironing board; **—eisen** nt iron; **—falte** f crease; **b—n** vti iron.

Bühne ['by:nə] f -, -n stage; **—nbild** nt set, scenery.

Buhruf ['buːruːf] *m* boo.

Bulette [bu'lɛtə] *f* meatball.

Bull- ['bʊl] *cpd:* —**dogge** *f* bulldog; —**dozer** ['bʊldoːzɐr] *m* -s, - bulldozer; —**e** *m* -n, -n bull.

Bummel ['bʊməl] *m* -s, - stroll; *(Schaufenster-)* window-shopping; —**ant** ['-lant] *m* slowcoach; —**ei** ['-'laɪ] *f* wandering; dawdling; skiving; **b~n** *vi* wander, stroll; *(trödeln)* dawdle; *(faulenzen)* skive, loaf around; —**streik** *m* go-slow; —**zug** *m* slow train.

Bummler(in *f)* ['bʊmlɐr(ɪn)] *m* -s, - *(langsamer Mensch)* dawdler; *(Faulenzer)* idler, loafer.

Bund [bʊnt] *m* -(e)s, *=*e *(Freundschafts-* etc) bond; *(Organisation)* union; *(Pol)* confederacy; *(Hosen-, Rock-)* waistband; *nt* -(e)s, -e bunch; *(Stroh-)* bundle.

Bünd- ['bʏnt] *cpd:* —**chen** *nt* ribbing; *(Ärmel-)* cuff; —**el** *nt* -s, -n bundle, bale; **b~eln** *vt* bundle.

Bundes- ['bʊndəs] *in cpds* Federal *(esp* West German); —**bahn** *f* Federal Railways *pl;* —**hauptstadt** *f* Federal capital; —**kanzler** *m* Federal Chancellor; —**land** *nt* Land; —**präsident** *m* Federal President; —**rat** *m* upper house of West German Parliament; —**republik** *f* Federal Republic (of West Germany); —**staat** *m* Federal state; —**straße** *f* Federal Highway, 'A' road; —**tag** *m* West German Parliament; —**verfassungsgericht** *nt* Federal Constitutional Court; —**wehr** *f* West German Armed Forces *pl.*

Bünd- *cpd:* **b~ig** *a (kurz)* concise; —**nis** *nt* -ses, -se alliance.

Bunker ['bʊŋkər] *m* -s, - bunker.

bunt [bʊnt] *a* coloured; *(gemischt)* mixed; **jdm wird es zu — it's**

getting too much for sb; **B~stift** *m* coloured pencil, crayon.

Burg [bʊrk] *f* -, -en castle, fort.

Bürge ['bʏrgə] *m* -n, -n guarantor; **b~n** *vi* vouch; —**r(in** *f)* *m* -s, - citizen; member of the middle class; —**rkrieg** *m* civil war; **b~rlich** *a Rechte* civil; *Klasse* middle-class; *(pej)* bourgeois; **gut b~rliche Küche** good home cooking; —**rmeister** *m* mayor; —**recht** *nt* civil rights *pl;* —**rschaft** *f* population, citizens *pl;* —**rsteig** *m* pavement; —**rtum** *nt* citizens *pl.*

Bürg- *cpd:* —**in** *f see* Bürge; —**schaft** *f* surety; —**schaft leisten** give security.

Büro [by'roː] *nt* -s, -s office; —**angestellte(r)** *mf* office worker; —**klammer** *f* paper clip; —**krat** [byro'kraːt] *m* -en, -en bureaucrat; —**kratie** *f* bureaucracy; **b~kratisch** *a* bureaucratic; —**kratismus** *m* red tape; —**schluß** *m* office closing time.

Bursch(e) [bʊrʃ(ə)] *m* -en, -en lad, fellow; *(Diener)* servant.

Bürste ['bʏrstə] *f* -, -n brush; **b~n** *vt* brush.

Bus [bʊs] *m* -ses, -se bus.

Busch [bʊʃ] *m* -(e)s, *=*e bush, shrub.

Büschel ['bʏʃəl] *nt* -s, - tuft.

buschig *a* bushy.

Busen ['buːzən] *m* -s, - bosom; *(Meer)* inlet, bay; —**freund(in** *f)* *m* bosom friend.

Buße ['buːsə] *f* -, -n atonement, penance; *(Geld)* fine.

büßen ['byːsən] *vti* do penance (for), atone (for).

Büste ['bʏstə] *f* -, -n bust; —**nhalter** *m* bra.

Butter ['bʊtər] *f* - butter; —**blume** *f* buttercup; —**brot** *nt* (piece of) bread and butter; —**brotpapier** *nt* greaseproof paper; —**dose** *f* butter dish; **b**—**weich** *a* soft as butter;

(*fig,col*) soft.
Butzen ['butsən] *m* -s, - core.

C

(*see also under* K *and* Z; CH *under* SCH)

C, c [tse:] *nt* C, c.

Café [ka'fe:] *nt* -s, -s café.

Cafeteria [kafete'ri:a] *f* -, -s cafeteria.

Camp- [kɛmp] *cpd*: **c**—**en** *vi* camp; —**er(in** *f*) *m* -s, - camper; —**ing** *nt* -s camping; —**ingplatz** *m* camp(ing) site.

Caravan ['kɛrəvæn] *m* -s, -s caravan.

Cellist [tʃɛ'lɪst] *m* cellist.

Cello ['tʃɛlo] *nt* -s, -s *or* **Celli** cello.

Chamäleon [ka'mɛːleɔn] *nt* -s, -s chameleon.

Champagner [ʃam'panjər] *m* -s, - champagne.

Champignon ['ʃampɪnjɔ̃] *m* -s, -s button mushroom.

Chance ['ʃãːs(ə)] *f* -, -n chance, opportunity.

Chaos ['ka:ɔs] *nt* -s, - chaos.

chaotisch [ka'o:tiʃ] *a* chaotic.

Charakter [ka'raktər] *m* -s, -e [karak'te:rə] character; **c**—**l'sieren** *vt* characterize; —**istik** [karakte'rɪstɪk] *f* characterization; **c**—**istisch** [karakte'rɪstɪʃ] *a* characteristic, typical (*für* of); **c**—**los** *a* unprincipled; —**losigkeit** *f* lack of principle; —**schwäche** *f* weakness of character; —**stärke** *f* strength of character; —**zug** *m* characteristic, trait.

charmant [ʃar'mant] *a* charming.

Charme [ʃarm] *m* -s charm.

Chassis [ʃa'si:] *nt* -, - chassis.

Chauffeur [ʃo'fø:r] *m* chauffeur.

Chauvinismus [ʃovi'nɪsmus] *m* chauvinism, jingoism.

Chauvinist [ʃovi'nɪst] *m* chauvinist, jingoist.

Chef [ʃɛf] *m* -s, -s head; (*col*) boss; —**arzt** *m* head physician; —**in** *f* (*col*) boss.

Chemie [çe'mi:] *f* - chemistry; —**faser** *f* man-made fibre.

Chemikalie [çemi'ka:liə] *f* -, -n chemical.

Chemiker(in *f*) ['çe:mikər(ɪn)] *m* -s, -(industrial) chemist.

chemisch [çe:mɪʃ] *a* chemical; —**e Reinigung** dry cleaning.

Chiffre ['ʃɪfər] *f* -, -n (*Geheimzeichen*) cipher; (*in Zeitung*) box number.

Chiffriermaschine [ʃɪfri:rma'ʃi:nə] *f* cipher machine.

Chips [tʃɪps] *pl* crisps *pl*, chips *pl* (US).

Chirurg [çi'rʊrk] *m* -en, -en surgeon; —**ie** [-'gi:] *f* surgery; **c**—**isch** *a* surgical.

Chlor [klo:r] *nt* -s chlorine; —**o'form** *nt* -s chloroform; **c**—**ofor'mieren** *vt* chloroform; —**ophyll** [kloro'fyl] *nt* -s chlorophyll.

Cholera ['ko:lera] *f* - cholera.

cholerisch [ko'le:rɪʃ] *a* choleric.

Chor [ko:r] *m* -(e), -e *or* ⁼e choir;
(*Musikstück, Theat*) chorus; **—al**
[ko'ra:l] *m* -s, -äle chorale.
Choreograph [koreo'gra:f] *m* -en,
-en choreographer; **—ie** [-'fi:] *f*
choreography.
Chor- *cpd:* **—gestühl** *nt* choir stalls
pl; **—knabe** *m* choirboy.
Christ [krɪst] *m* -en, -en
Christian; **—baum** *m* Christmas
tree; **—enheit** *f* Christendom;
—entum *nt* Christianity; **—in** *f*
Christian; **—kind** *nt* ≈ Father
Christmas (*Jesus*) baby Jesus;
c—lich a Christian; **—us** *m* Christ.
Chrom [kro:m] *nt* -s (*Chem*)
chromium; chrome; **—osom**
[kromo'zo:m] *nt* -s, -en (*Biol*)
chromosome.
Chron- [kron] *cpd:* **—ik** *f*
chronicle; **c—isch** a chronic;
—ologie [-'lo'gi:] *f* chronology;
c—ologisch [-'lo:gɪʃ] a a chronological.

Chrysantheme [kryzan'te:mə] *f* -,
-n chrysanthemum.
circa ['tsɪrka] *ad* about,
approximately.
Clown [klaun] *m* -s, -s clown.
Computer [kɔm'pju:tər] *m* -s, -
computer.
Conférencier [kõferãsi'e:] *m* -s, -s
compère.
Coupé [ku'pe:] *nt* -s, -s (*Aut*)
coupé, sports version.
Coupon [ku'põ:] *m* -s, -s coupon;
(*Stoff—*) length of cloth.
Cousin [ku'zɛ:] *m* -s, -s cousin; **—e**
[ku'zi:nə] *f* -, -n cousin.
Creme [krɛ:m] *f* -, -s (*lit, fig*)
cream; (*Schuh—*) polish; (*Zahn—*)
paste; (*Cook*) mousse; **c—farben** a
cream(-coloured).
Curry(pulver *nt*) ['kari(pulfər)] *m*
or nt -s curry powder.
Cutter(in *f*) ['katər(ɪn)] *m* -s, -
(*Cine*) editor.

D

D, d [de:] *nt* D, d.
da [da:] *ad* (*dort*) there; (*hier*)
here; (*dann*) then; —, wo where;
cf as; **—behalten** *vt irreg* keep.
dabei [da'bai] *ad* (*räumlich*) close
to it; (*noch dazu*) besides; (*zusammen mit*) with them; (*zeitlich*)
during this; (*obwohl doch*) but,
however; was ist schon —? what
of it?; es ist doch nichts —, wenn
... it doesn't matter if ...; **bleiben
wir** — let's leave it at that; es soll
nicht — bleiben this isn't the end
of it; es bleibt — that's settled;
das Dumme/Schwierige — the
stupid/difficult part of it; er war

gerade —, zu gehen he was just
leaving; —sein *vi irreg* (*anwesend*)
be present; (*beteiligt*) be involved;
—stehen *vi irreg* stand around.
Dach [dax] *nt* -(e)s, ⁼er roof;
—boden *m* attic, loft; **—decker** *m*
-s, - slater, tiler; **—fenster** *nt*,
—luke *f* skylight; **—pappe** *f* roofing
felt; **—rinne** *f* gutter; **—ziegel** *m*
roof tile.
Dachs [daks] *m* -es, -e badger.
Dackel ['dakəl] *m* -s, - dachshund.
dadurch [da'durç] *ad* (*räumlich*)
through it; (*durch diesen
Umstand*) thereby, in that way;

(*deshalb*) because of that, for that reason; *cj*: —, daß because.

dafür [da'fy:r] *ad* for it; (*anstatt*) instead; **er kann nichts** — he can't help it; **er ist bekannt** — he is well-known for that; **was bekomme ich** —? what will I get for it?; **D—halten** *nt* -s: **nach meinem D—halten** in my opinion.

dagegen [da'ge:gən] *ad* against it; (*im Vergleich damit*) in comparison with it; (*bei Tausch*) to it; **ich habe nichts** — I don't mind; **ich war** — I was against it; **— kann man nichts tun** one can't do anything about it; *cj* however; **—halten** *vt irreg* (*vergleichen*) compare with it; (*entgegnen*) object to it.

daheim [da'haim] *ad* at home; **D—** *nt* -s home.

daher [da'he:r] *ad* (*räumlich*) from there; (*Ursache*) from that; **da kommt er auch** that's where he comes from too; *cj* (*deshalb*) that's why; **— die Schwierigkeiten** that's what is causing the difficulties.

dahin [da'hɪn] *ad* (*räumlich*) there; (*zeitlich*) then; (*vergangen*) gone; **das tendiert —** it is tending towards that; **er bringt es noch —, daß ich ...** he'll make me ...; **—gegen** *cj* on the other hand; **—gehend** *ad* on this matter; **—gestellt** *ad*: **—gestellt bleiben** remain to be seen; **—gestellt sein lassen** leave sth open or undecided.

dahinten [da'hɪntən] *ad* over there.

dahinter [da'hɪntər] *ad* behind it; **—kommen** *vi irreg* get to the bottom of sth.

Dahlie [da'li:ə] *f* -, -n dahlia.

dalassen ['da:lasən] *vt irreg* leave (behind).

damalig ['da:ma:lɪç] *a* of that time, then.

damals ['da:ma:ls] *ad* at that time, then.

Damast [da'mast] *m* -(e)s, -e damask.

Dame ['da:mə] *f* -, -n lady; (*Schach, Cards*) queen; (*Spiel*) draughts; **d—nhaft** *a* ladylike; **—nwahl** *f* ladies' excuse-me; **—spiel** *nt* draughts.

damit [da'mɪt] *ad* with it; (*begründend*) by that; **was meint er** —? what does he mean by that?; **genug** —! that's enough; **— basta!** and that's that; **— eilt es nicht** there's no hurry; *cj* in order that or to.

dämlich ['dɛ:mlɪç] *a* (*col*) silly, stupid.

Damm [dam] *m* -(e)s, ⁺e dyke; (*Stau—*) dam; (*Hafen—*) mole; (*Bahn—, Straßen—*) embankment.

Dämm- [dɛm] *cpd*: **d—en** *vt* *Wasser* dam up; *Schmerzen* keep back; **d—erig** *a* dim, faint; **d—ern** *vi* (*Tag*) dawn; (*Abend*) fall; **—erung** *f* twilight; (*Morgen—*) dawn; (*Abend—*) dusk.

Dämon ['dɛ:mɔn] *m* -s, -en [dɛ'mo:nən] demon; **d—isch** [dɛ'mo:nɪʃ] *a* demoniacal.

Dampf [dampf] *m* -(e)s, ⁺e steam; (*Dunst*) vapour; **d—en** *vi* steam.

dämpfen ['dɛmpfən] *vt* (*Cook*) steam; (*bügeln auch*) iron with a damp cloth; (*fig*) dampen, subdue.

Dampf- *cpd*: **—er** *m* -s, - steamer; **—kochtopf** *m* pressure cooker; **—maschine** *f* steam engine; **—schiff** *nt* steamship; **—walze** *f* steamroller.

danach [da'na:x] *ad* after that; (*zeitlich auch*) afterwards; (*gemäß*) accordingly; according to which or that; **er sieht — aus** he looks it.

daneben [da'ne:bən] *ad* beside it; *(im Vergleich)* in comparison; **—benehmen** *vr irreg* misbehave; **—gehen** *vi irreg* miss; *(Plan)* fail.

Dank [daŋk] *m* -(e)s thanks *pl*; vielen *or* schönen — many thanks; jdm — sagen thank sb; **d—** *prep* +*dat or gen* thanks to; **d—bar** *a* grateful; *Aufgabe* rewarding; **—barkeit** *f* gratitude; **d—e** *interj* thank you, thanks; **d—en** *vi* (+*dat*) thank; **d—enswert** *a Arbeit* worthwhile; rewarding; *Bemühung* kind; **d—sagen** *vi* express one's thanks.

dann [dan] *ad* then; — und wann now and then.

daran [da'ran] *ad* on it; *stoßen* against it; es liegt —, daß ... the cause of it is that ...; gut/schlecht — sein be well-/badly off; das Beste/Dümmste — the best/stupidest thing about it; ich war nahe —, zu ... I was on the point of ...; er ist — gestorben he died from *or* of it; **d—gehen** *vi irreg* start; **—setzen** *vt* stake; er hat alles **—gesetzt**, von Glasgow wegzukommen he has done his utmost to get away from Glasgow.

darauf [da'rauf] *ad* (*räumlich*) on it; (*zielgerichtet*) towards it; (*danach*) afterwards; es kommt ganz — **an**, ob ... it depends whether ...; die Tage — the days following *or* thereafter; am Tag — the next day; **—folgend** *a Tag, Jahr* next, following; **—hin** ['-hin] *ad* (*im Hinblick darauf*) in this respect; (*aus diesem Grund*) as a result; **—legen** *vt* lay *or* put on top.

daraus [da'raus] *ad* from it; was ist — geworden? what became of it?; — geht hervor, daß ... this means that ...

Darbietung ['da:rbi:tuŋ] *f* performance.

darin [da'rın] *ad* in (there), in it.

Dar- ['da:r] *cpd*: **d—legen** *vt* explain, expound, set forth; **—legung** *f* explanation; **—leh(e)n** *nt* -s, — loan.

Darm [darm] *m* -(e)s, ⁼e intestine; *(Wurst—)* skin; —saite *f* gut string.

Darstell- ['da:rʃtɛl] *cpd*: **d—en** *vt* (*abbilden, bedeuten*) represent; *(Theat)* act; *(beschreiben)* describe; *vr* appear to be; **—er(in** *f) m* -s, — actor/actress; **—ung** *f* portrayal, depiction.

darüber [da'ry:bər] *ad* (*räumlich*) over/above it; *fahren* over it; (*mehr*) more; (*währenddessen*) meanwhile; *sprechen, streiten* about it; — **geht nichts** there's nothing like it; seine Gedanken — his thoughts about *or* on it.

darum [da'rom] *ad* (*räumlich*) round it; **—herum** round about (it); er bittet — he is pleading for it; es geht —, daß ... the thing is that ...; er würde viel — geben, wenn ... he would give a lot to ...; *cf* that's why; ich tue es —, weil ... I am doing it because ...

darunter [da'rontər] *ad* (*räumlich*) under it; (*dazwischen*) among them; (*weniger*) less; ein Stockwerk — one floor below (it); was verstehen Sie —? what do you understand by that?; **—fallen** *vi irreg* be included; **—mischen** *vt* *Mehl* mix in; *vr* mingle.

das [das] *def* art the; *pron* that; — heißt that is.

Dasein ['da:zaın] *nt* -s (*Leben*) life; (*Anwesenheit*) presence; (*Bestehen*) existence; **d—** *vi irreg* be there.

daß [das] *cj* that.

dasselbe [das'zɛlbə] *art, pron* the same.

dastehen ['da:ʃte:ən] *vi irreg* stand there.

Datenverarbeitung ['da:tən-fɛr'arbaitʊŋ] *f* data processing.

datieren [da'ti:rən] *vt* date.

Dativ ['da:ti:f] *m* -s, -e dative.

Dattel ['datəl] *f* -, -n date.

Datum ['da:tʊm] *nt* -s, Daten date; (*pl* Angaben) data *pl*; das heutige — today's date.

Dauer ['dauər] *f* -, -n duration; (*gewisse Zeitspanne*) length; (*Bestand, Fortbestand*) permanence; es war nur von kurzer — it didn't last long; auf die — in the long run; (*auf längere Zeit*) indefinitely; —auftrag *m* standing order; d—haft *a* lasting, durable; —haftigkeit *f* durability; —karte *f* season ticket; —lauf *m* long-distance run; d—n *vi* last; es hat sehr lang gedauert, bis er ... it took him a long time to ...; d—nd *a* constant; —regen *m* continuous rain; —welle *f* perm(anent wave); —wurst *f* German salami; —zustand *m* permanent condition.

Daumen ['daumən] *m* -s, - thumb; —lutscher *m* thumb-sucker.

Daune ['daunə] *f* -, -n down; —ndecke *f* down duvet *or* quilt.

davon [da'fɔn] *ad* of it; (*räumlich*) away; (*weg von*) from it; (*Grund*) because of it; das kommt —! that's what you get; — abgesehen apart from that; — sprechen/wissen talk/know of *or* about it; was habe ich —? what's the point?; —gehen *vi irreg* leave, go away; —kommen *vi irreg* escape; —laufen *vi irreg* run away; —tragen *vt irreg* carry off; *Verletzung* receive.

davor [da'fo:r] *ad* (*räumlich*) in front of it; (*zeitlich*) before (that); — warnen warn about it.

dazu [da'tsu:] *ad* legen, stellen by it; essen, singen with it; und — noch and in addition; ein Beispiel/seine Gedanken — one example for/his thoughts on this; wie komme ich denn —? why should I?; — fähig sein be capable of it; sich — äußern say sth on it; —gehören *vi* belong to it; —gehörig *a* appropriate; —kommen *vi irreg* (*Ereignisse*) happen too; (*an einen Ort*) come along; —mal [da'tsuma:l] *ad* in those days.

dazwischen [da'tsvɪʃən] *ad* in between; (*räumlich auch*) between (them); (*zusammen mit*) among them; der Unterschied — the difference between them; —kommen *vi irreg* (*hineingeraten*) get caught in it; es ist etwas —gekommen something cropped up; —reden *vi* (*unterbrechen*) interrupt; (*sich einmischen*) interfere; —treten *vi irreg* intervene.

Debatte [de'batə] *f* -, -n debate.

Deck [dɛk] *nt* -(e)s, -s *or* -e deck; an — gehen go on deck; —e *f* -, -n cover; (*Bett—*) blanket; (*Tisch—*) tablecloth; (*Zimmer—*) ceiling; unter einer —e stecken be hand in glove; —el *m* -s, - lid; d—en *vt* cover; *vr* coincide; *vi* lay the table; —mantel *m*: unter dem —mantel von under the guise of; —name *m* assumed name; —ung *f* (*Schützen*) covering; (*Schutz*) cover; (*Sport*) defence; (*Übereinstimmen*) agreement; d—ungsgleich *a* congruent.

Defekt [de'fɛkt] *m* -(e)s, -e fault, defect; d— *a* faulty.

defensiv [defen'si:f] a defensive.

definieren [defi'ni:rən] vt define.

Definition [definitsi'o:n] f definition.

definitiv [defini'ti:f] a definite.

Defizit ['de:fitsit] nt -s, -e deficit.

deftig ['dɛftiç] a Essen large; Witz coarse.

Degen ['de:gən] m -s, - sword.

degenerieren [degene'ri:rən] vi degenerate.

degradieren [degra'di:rən] vt degrade.

Dehn- ['de:n] cpd: d—bar a elastic; (fig) Begriff loose; —barkeit f elasticity; looseness; d—en vtr stretch; —ung f stretching.

Deich [daiç] m -(e)s, -e dyke.

Deichsel ['daiksəl] f -, -n shaft; d—n vt (fig, col) wangle.

dein [dain] pron (D— in Briefen) your; —e(r,s) yours; —er pron gen of du of you; —erseits ad on your part; —esgleichen pron people like you; —etwegen, —etwillen ad (für dich) for your sake; (wegen dir) on your account; —ige pron: der/die/das —ige yours.

dekadent [deka'dɛnt] a decadent.

Dekadenz f decadence.

Dekan [de'ka:n] m -s, -e dean.

Deklination [deklinatsi'o:n] f declension.

deklinieren [dekli'ni:rən] vt decline.

Dekolleté [dekɔl'te:] nt -s, -s low neckline.

Deko- [deko] cpd: —rateur [-ra'tø:r] m window dresser; —ration [-ratsi'o:n] f decoration; (in Laden) window dressing; d—rativ [-ra'ti:f] a decorative; d—rieren [-'ri:rən] vt decorate; Schaufenster dress.

Delegation [delegatsi'o:n] f delegation.

delikat [deli'ka:t] a (zart, heikel) delicate; (köstlich) delicious.

Delikatesse [delika'tɛsə] f -, -n delicacy; (pl: Feinkost) delicatessen pl; —ngeschäft nt delicatessen (shop).

Delikt [de'likt] nt -(e)s, -e (Jur) offence.

Delle ['dɛlə] f -, -n (col) dent.

Delphin [dɛl'fi:n] m -s, -e dolphin.

Delta ['dɛltə] nt -s, -s delta.

dem [de(:)m] art dat of der.

Demagoge [dema'go:gə] m -n, -n demagogue.

Demarkationslinie [demarkatsi'o:nzli:niə] f demarcation line.

dementieren [demɛn'ti:rən] vt deny.

Demo- cpd: —gemäß, —nach ad accordingly; —nächst ad shortly.

Demokrat [demo'kra:t] m -en, -en democrat; —ie [-'ti:] f democracy; d—isch a democratic; d—isieren [-'isi:rən] vt democratize.

demolieren [demo'li:rən] vt demolish.

Demon- [demɔn] cpd: —strant(in f) [-'strant(m)] m demonstrator; —stration [-stratsi'o:n] f demonstration; d—strativ [-stra'ti:f] a demonstrative; Protest pointed; d—strieren [-'stri:rən] vti demonstrate.

Demoskopie [demosko'pi:] f public opinion research.

Demut ['de:mu:t] f -, humility.

demütig ['de:my:tiç] a humble; —en ['de:my:tigən] vt humiliate; D—ung f humiliation.

demzufolge ['de:mtsu'folgə] ad accordingly.

den [de(:)n] art acc of der.

denen [de:nən] pron dat of diese.

Denk- [dɛŋk] cpd: —art f mentality; d—bar a conceivable; d—en

vti irreg think; **—en** *nt* -s thinking;
—er *m* -s, - thinker; **—fähigkeit** *f*
intelligence; **d—faul** *a* lazy;
—fehler *m* logical error; **—mal** *nt*
-s, **-er** monument; **d—würdig** *a*
memorable; **—zettel** *m*: jdm einen
—zettel verpassen teach sb a lesson.
denn [dɛn] *cj* for; *ad* then; (*nach
Komparativ*) than.
dennoch ['dɛnˌnɔx] *cj* nevertheless.
Denunziant [denʊntsiˈant] *m* informer.
deponieren [depoˈniːrən] *vt*
(*Comm*) deposit.
Depot [deˈpoː] *nt* -s, -s warehouse;
(*Bus—*, *Rail*) depot; (*Bank—*)
strongroom.
Depression [deprɛsiˈoːn] *f* depression.
deprimieren [depriˈmiːrən] *vt* depress.
der [de(ː)r] *def art* the; *rel pron*
that, which; (*jemand*) who; *demon
pron* this one; **—art** *ad* so; (*solcher
Art*) such; **—artig** *a* such, this sort
of.
derb [dɛrp] *a* sturdy; *Kost* solid;
(*grob*) coarse; **D—heit** *f* sturdiness; solidity; coarseness.
der— *cpd*: **'—gleichen** *pron* such;
'—jenige *pron* he; she; it; (*rel*) the
one (who); that (which); **'—maßen**
ad to such an extent, so; **—'selbe**
art, pron the same; **'—weil(en)** *ad*
in the meantime; **'—zeitig** *a*
present, current; (*damalig*) then.
des [dɛs] *art gen of* der.
Deserteur [dezɛrˈtøːr] *m* deserter.
desertieren [dezɛrˈtiːrən] *vi* desert.
desgleichen ['dɛsˈglaiçən] *pron* the
same.
deshalb ['dɛsˈhalp] *ad* therefore,
that's why.

Desinfektion [dɛzɪnfɛktsiˈoːn] *f*
disinfection; **—smittel** *nt* dis-
infectant.
desinfizieren [dɛzɪnfiˈtsiːrən] *vt*
disinfect.
dessen ['dɛsən] *pron gen of* der,
das; **—ungeachtet** *ad* nevertheless,
regardless.
Dessert [dɛˈsɛːr] *nt* -s, -s dessert.
Destillation [dɛstilatsiˈoːn] *f* dis-
tillation.
destillieren [dɛstiˈliːrən] *vt* distil.
desto ['dɛsto] *ad* all or so much
the; **— besser** all the better.
deswegen ['dɛsˈveːgən] *cj* therefore, hence.
Detail [deˈtai] *nt* -s, -s detail;
d—lieren [detaˈjiːrən] *vt* specify,
give details of.
Detektiv [detɛkˈtiːf] *m* -s, **-e** detective.
Detektor [deˈtɛktor] *m* (*Tech*) detector.
deut- ['dɔyt] *cpd*: **—en** *vt* interpret,
explain; *vi* point (*auf* + *acc* to or
at); **—lich** *a* clear; *Unterschied*
distinct; **D—lichkeit** *f* clarity;
distinctness; **D—ung** *f* interpretation.
Devise [deˈviːzə] *f* -, **-n** motto,
device; (*pl: Fin*) foreign currency
or exchange.
Dezember [deˈtsɛmbər] *m* -(s), -
December.
dezent [deˈtsɛnt] *a* discreet.
dezimal [detsiˈmaːl] *a* decimal;
D—bruch *m* decimal (fraction);
D—system *nt* decimal system.
Dia ['diːa] *nt* -s, -s *see* Dia-
positiv; **—betes** [diaˈbeːtɛs] *m* -,
- (*Med*) diabetes; **—gnose**
[diaˈgnoːzə] *f* -, **-n** diagnosis;
d—gonal [diagoˈnaːl] *a* diagonal;
—gonale *f* -, **-n** diagonal.

Dialekt [dia'lɛkt] *m* -(e)s, -e
dialect; —ausdruck *m* dialect
expression/word; d—frei a pure,
standard; d—isch a dialectal;
Logik dialectical.

Dialog [dia'loːk] *m* -(e)s, -e
dialogue.

Diamant [dia'mant] *m* diamond.

Diapositiv [diapozi'tiːf] *nt* -s, -e
(*Phot*) slide, transparency.

Diät [di'ɛːt] *f*,- diet; —en *pl* (*Pol*)
allowance. :

dich [dɪç] *pron acc of* **du** you;
yourself.

dicht [dɪçt] a dense; *Nebel* thick;
Gewebe close; (*undurchlässig*)
(water)tight; (*fig*) concise; ad: —
an/bei close to; —bevölkert a
densely or heavily populated; D—e
f -, -n density; thickness; closeness; (water)tightness; (*fig*) conc-
ciseness; —en *vt* (*dicht machen*)
make watertight; seal; (*Naut*)
caulk; *vti* (*Liter*) compose, write;
D—er(in *f*) *m* -s, - poet; (*Autor*)
writer; —erisch a poetical;
—halten *vi irreg* (col) keep mum;
D—ung *f* (*Tech*) washer; (*Aut*)
gasket; (*Gedichte*) poetry; (*Prosa*)
(piece of) writing.

dick [dɪk] a thick; (*fett*) fat; durch
— und dünn through thick and
thin; D—e *f* -, -n thickness;
fatness; —fellig a thickskinned;
—flüssig a viscous; D—icht *nt* -s,
-e thicket; D—kopf *m* mule;
D—milch *f* soured milk.

die [diː] *def art see* **der**.

Dieb(in *f*) [diːp/diːbɪn] *m* -(e)s, -e
thief; d—isch a thieving; (col)
immense; —stahl *m* -(e)s, ⁀e theft.

Diele ['diːlə] *f*-, -n (*Brett*) board;
(*Flur*) hall, lobby; (*Eis—*) ice-
cream parlour; (*Tanz—*) dance hall.

dienen ['diːnən] *vi* serve (*jdm* sb).

Diener *m* -s, - servant; —in *f*
(maid)servant; —schaft *f* servants
pl.

Dienst [diːnst] *m* -(e)s, -e service;
außer — retired; — haben be on
duty; der öffentliche — the civil
service; —ag *m* Tuesday; d—ags
ad on Tuesdays; —bote *m* servant;
d—eifrig a zealous; d—frei a off
duty; —geheimnis *nt* professional
secret; —gespräch *nt* business
call; —grad *m* rank; d—habend a
Arzt on duty; d—lich a official;
—mädchen *nt* domestic servant;
—reise *f* business trip; —stelle *f*
office; d—tuend a on duty;
—vorschrift *f* service regulations
pl; —weg *m* official channels *pl*;
—zeit *f* office hours *pl*; (*Mil*)
period of service.

dies- [diːs] *cpd:* —bezüglich a *Frage*
on⁀this matter; —e(r,s) [diːzə(r,z)]
pron this (one); —elbe [diː'zɛlbə]
pron, art the same; D—elöl *nt*
diesel oil; —ig a drizzly; —jährig
a this year's; —mal *ad* this time;
—seits *prep* +gen on this side;
D—seits *nt* - this life.

Dietrich ['diːtrɪç] *m* -s, -e picklock.

differential [diferɛntsi'aːl] a differential; D—getriebe *nt* differential
gear; D—rechnung *f* differential
calculus.

differenzieren [diferɛn'tsiːrən] *vt*
make differences in; **differenziert**
make differences in; differenziert

Dikt- [dɪkt] *cpd:* —aphon -[a'foːn]
nt dictaphone; —at [-'taːt] *nt* -(e)s,
-e dictation; —ator [-'taːtɔr] *m* dictator; d—atorisch [-a'toːrɪʃ] a dic-
tatorial; —atur [-a'tuːr] *f* dictatorship; d—ieren [-'tiːrən] *vt* dictate.

Dilemma [di'lɛma] *nt* -s, -s *or* -ta
dilemma.

Dilettant [dilɛˈtant] m dilettante, amateur; **d—isch** a amateurisch, dilettante.

Dimension [dimɛnziˈoːn] f dimension.

Ding [dɪŋ] nt -(e)s, -e thing, object; **d—lich** a real, concrete; **—sbums** [ˈdɪŋksbums] nt - (col) thingummybob.

Diözese [diøˈtseːzə] f -, -n diocese.

Diphtherie [dɪfteˈriː] f diphtheria.

Diplom [diˈploːm] nt -(e)s, -e diploma, certificate; **—at** [-ˈmaːt] m -en, -en diplomat; **—atie** [-aˈtiː] f diplomacy; **d—atisch** [-ˈmaːtɪʃ] a diplomatic; **—ingenieur** m qualified engineer.

dir [diːr] pron dat of **du** (to) you.

direkt [diˈrɛkt] a direct; **D—or** m director; (Sch) principal, headmaster; **D—orium** [-ˈtoːrium] nt board of directors; **D—übertragung** f live broadcast.

Dirigent [diriˈgɛnt] m conductor; (Mus) conduct.

dirigieren [diriˈgiːrən] vt direct; (Mus) conduct.

Dirne [ˈdɪrnə] f -, -n prostitute.

Diskont [dɪsˈkɔnt] m -s, -e discount; **—satz** m rate of discount.

Diskothek [dɪskoˈteːk] f -, -en disco(theque).

Diskrepanz [dɪskreˈpants] f discrepancy.

diskret [dɪsˈkreːt] a discreet; **D—ion** [-tsiˈoːn] f discretion.

Diskussion [dɪskusiˈoːn] f discussion; debate; **zur — stehen** be under discussion.

diskutabel [dɪskuˈtaːbəl] a debatable.

diskutieren [dɪskuˈtiːrən] vti discuss; debate.

Dissertation [dɪsɛrtatsiˈoːn] f dissertation, doctoral thesis.

Distanz [dɪsˈtants] f distance.

Distel [ˈdɪstəl] f -, -n thistle.

Disziplin [dɪstsiˈpliːn] f discipline.

divers [diˈvɛrs] a various.

Dividende [diviˈdɛndə] f -, -n dividend.

dividieren [diviˈdiːrən] vt divide (durch by).

doch [dɔx] ad: das ist nicht wahr! **~—!** oh no!; er kam — noch he came after all; cf (aber) but; (trotzdem) all the same.

Docht [dɔxt] m -(e)s, -e wick.

Dock [dɔk] nt -s, -s or -e dock.

Dogge [ˈdɔgə] f -, -n bulldog.

Dogma [ˈdɔgma] nt -s, -men dogma; **d—tisch** [dɔˈgmaːtɪʃ] a dogmatic.

Doktor [ˈdɔktor] m -s, -en [-ˈtoːrən] doctor; **—and** [-ˈrant] m -en, -en candidate for a doctorate; **—arbeit** f doctoral thesis; **—titel** m doctorate.

Dokument [dokuˈmɛnt] nt document; **—arbericht** [-ˈtaːrbərɪçt] m documentary; **—arfilm** m documentary (film); **d—arisch** a documentary.

Dolch [dɔlç] m -(e)s, -e dagger.

dolmetschen [ˈdɔlmɛtʃən] vti interpret.

Dolmetscher(in f) m -s, - interpreter.

Dom [doːm] m -(e)s, -e cathedral.

dominieren [domiˈniːrən] vt dominate; vi predominate.

Dompfaff [ˈdɔmpfaf] m bullfinch.

Dompteur [dɔmpˈtøːr] m, **Dompteuse** [dɔmpˈtøːzə] f (Zirkus) trainer.

Donner [ˈdɔnər] m -s, - thunder; **d—n** vi impers thunder; **—stag** m Thursday; **—wetter** nt thunderstorm; *(fig)* dressing-down; *interj* good heavens!

doof [do:f] *a (col)* daft, stupid.

Doppel ['dɔpəl] *nt* -s, - duplicate; *(Sport)* doubles; —**bett** *nt* double bed; —**fenster** *nt* double glazing; —**gänger** *m* -s, - double; —**punkt** *m* colon; d—**sinnig** *a* ambiguous; —**stecker** *m* two-way adaptor; d—**t** *a* double; **in d—ter Ausführung** in duplicate; —**verdiener** *pl* two-income family; —**zentner** *m* 100 kilograms; —**zimmer** *nt* double room.

Dorf [dɔrf] *nt* -(e)s, ²er village; —**bewohner** *m* villager.

Dorn [dɔrn] *m* -(e)s, -en *(Bot)* thorn; *pl* -e *(Schnallen—)* tongue, pin; d—**ig** *a* thorny; —**röschen** *nt* Sleeping Beauty.

dörren ['dœrən] *vt* dry.

Dörrobst ['dœrəːpst] *nt* dried fruit.

Dorsch [dɔrʃ] *m* -(e)s, -e cod.

dort [dɔrt] *ad* there; — **drüben** over there; — **her** from there; — **hin** *(to)* there; —**ig** *a* of that place; in that town.

Dose ['do:zə] *f* -, -n box; *(Blech—)* tin, can; —**nöffner** *m* tin or can opener.

dösen ['dø:zən] *vi (col)* doze.

Dosis ['do:zɪs] *f* -, **Dosen** dose.

Dotter ['dɔtər] *m* -s, - egg yolk.

Dozent [do'tsɛnt] *m* university lecturer.

Drache ['draxə] *m* -n, -n *(Tier)* dragon; —**n** *m* -, - kite.

Draht [dra:t] *m* -(e)s, ²e wire; **auf — sein** be on the ball; —**gitter** *nt* wire' grating; —**seil** *nt* cable; —**seilbahn** *f* cable railway, funicular; —**zange** *f* pliers *pl*.

drall [dral] *a* strapping; **Frau** buxom.

Drama ['dra:ma] *nt* -s, **Dramen** drama, play; —**tiker** [-'ma:tikər] *m* -s, - dramatist; d—**tisch** [-'ma:tɪʃ] *a* dramatic.

dran [dran] *ad (col)* see **daran.**

Drang [dran] *m* -(e)s, ²e *(Trieb)* impulse, urge, desire *(nach for)*; *(Druck)* pressure.

drängeln ['drɛŋəln] *vti* push, jostle.

drängen ['drɛŋən] *vt (schieben)* push, press; *(antreiben)* urge; *vi (eilig sein)* be urgent; *(Zeit)* press; **auf etw** *(acc)* — press for sth.

drastisch ['drastɪʃ] *a* drastic.

drauf [drauf] *ad (col)* see **darauf;** D—**gänger** *m* -s, - daredevil.

draußen ['drausən] *ad* outside, out-of-doors.

Dreck [drɛk] *m* -(e)s mud, dirt; d—**ig** *a* dirty, filthy.

Dreh- ['dre:] *cpd*: —**achse** *f* axis of rotation; —**arbeiten** *pl (Cine)* shooting; —**bank** *f* lathe; d—**bar** *a* revolving; —**buch** *nt (Cine)* script; d—**en** *vti* turn, rotate; **Zigaretten** roll; *Film* shoot; *vr* turn; *(handeln von)* **be** *(um* about*)*; —**orgel** *f* barrel organ; —**tür** *f* revolving door; —**ung** *f (Rotation)* rotation; *(Um—, Wendung)* turn; —**wurm** *m (col)* **den —wurm haben/bekommen** be/become dizzy; —**zahl** *f* rate of revolutions; —**zahlmesser** *m* rev(olution) counter.

drei [drai] *num* three; **D—eck** *nt* triangle; —**eckig** *a* triangular; —**einhalb** *num* three and a half; **D—einigkeit** ['ˌ'ainɪçkaɪt] *f*, **D—faltigkeit** [-'faltɪçkaɪt] *f* Trinity; —**erlei** *inv* of three kinds; —**fach** *a,ad* triple, treble; —**hundert** *num* three hundred; **D—königsfest** *nt* Epiphany; —**mal** *ad* three times, thrice; —**malig** *a* three times..

dreinreden 82 Duft

dreinreden ['dramre:dən] vi: jdm — (dazwischenreden) interrupt sb.; (sich einmischen) interfere with sb.

dreißig ['draɪsɪç] num thirty.

dreist [draɪst] a bold, audacious; D—igkeit f boldness, audacity.

drei- cpd: —viertel num three-quarters; D—viertelstunde f three-quarters of an hour; —zehn num thirteen.

dreschen ['drɛʃən] vt irreg thresh.

dressieren [drɛ'si:rən] vt train.

Drill- ['drɪl] cpd: —bohrer m light drill; d—en vt (bohren) drill, bore; (Mil) drill; (fig) train; —ing m triplet.

drin [drɪn] ad (col) see darin.

dringen ['drɪŋən] vi irreg (Wasser, Licht, Kälte) penetrate (durch through; in +acc into); auf etw (acc) — insist on sth; in jdn — entreat sb.

dringend ['drɪŋənt], dringlich ['drɪŋlɪç] a urgent.

Dringlichkeit f urgency.

drinnen ['drɪnən] ad inside, indoors.

dritte(r,s) ['drɪtə(r,z)] a third; D—l nt -s, — third; —ns ad thirdly.

droben ['dro:bən] ad above, up there.

Droge ['dro:gə] f -, -n drug; d—nabhängig a addicted to drugs; —rie [-'ri:] f chemist's shop.

Drogist [dro'gɪst] m pharmacist, chemist.

drohen ['dro:ən] vi threaten (jdm sb).

dröhnen ['drø:nən] vi (Motor) roar; (Stimme, Musik) ring, resound.

Drohung ['dro:ʊŋ] f threat.

drollig ['drɔlɪç] a droll.

Droschke ['drɔʃkə] f -, -n cab; —nkutscher m cabman.

Drossel ['drɔsəl] f -, -n thrush.

drüben ['dry:bən] ad over there, on the other side.

drüber ['dry:bər] ad (col) see darüber.

Druck [drʊk] m -(e)s, -e (Phys, Zwang) pressure; (Print) (Vorgang) printing; (Produkt) print; (fig: Belastung) burden, weight; —buchstabe m block letter.

Drück- ['drʏk] cpd: —eberger m -s, - shirker, dodger; d—en vti Knopf, Hand press; (zu eng sein) pinch; (fig) Preise keep down; (fig: belasten) oppress, weigh down; jdm etw in die Hand — en press sth into sb's hand; vr: sich vor etw (dat) d—en get out of (doing) sth; d—end a oppressive; —er m -s, - button; (Tür—) handle; (Gewehr—) trigger.

Druck- cpd: —er m -s, - printer; —erei f printing works, press; —erschwärze f printer's ink; —fehler m misprint; —knopf m press stud, snap fastener; —mittel nt leverage; —sache f printed matter; —schrift f block or printed letters pl.

drunten ['drʊntən] ad below, down there.

Drüse ['dry:zə] f -, -n gland.

Dschungel ['dʒʊŋəl] m -s, - jungle.

du [du:] pron (D— in Briefen) you.

ducken ['dʊkən] vt Kopf, Person duck; (fig) take down a peg or two; vr duck.

Duckmäuser ['dʊkmɔyzər] m -s, - yes-man.

Dudelsack ['du:dəlzak] m bagpipes pl.

Duell [du'ɛl] nt -s, -e duel.

Duett [du'ɛt] nt -(e)s, -e duet.

Duft [dʊft] m -(e)s, =e scent, odour; d—en vi smell, be fragrant;

d—ig a *Stoff, Kleid* delicate, diaphanous; *Muster* fine.

duld- ['dʊld] cpd: **—en** vti suffer; (*zulassen*) tolerate; **—sam** a tolerant.

dumm [dʊm] a stupid; *das wird mir zu —* that's just too much; *der D—e sein* be the loser; **—dreist** a impudent; **—erweise** ad stupidly; **D—heit** f stupidity; (*Tat*) blunder, stupid mistake; **D—kopf** m blockhead.

dumpf [dʊmpf] a *Ton* hollow, dull; *Luft* close; *Erinnerung, Schmerz* vague; **D—heit** f hollowness, dullness; closeness, vagueness; **—ig** a musty.

Düne ['dy:nə] f **—, -n** dune.

Dung [dʊŋ] m **-(e)s** see *Dünger*.

düngen ['dʏŋən] vt manure.

Dünger m **-s, -** dung, manure; (*künstlich*) fertilizer.

dunkel ['dʊŋkəl] a dark; *Stimme* deep; *Ahnung* vague; (*rätselhaft*) obscure; (*verdächtig*) dubious, shady; *im —n tappen* (*fig*) grope in the dark.

Dünkel ['dʏŋkəl] m **-s** self-conceit; **d—haft** a conceited.

Dunkel- cpd: **—heit** f darkness; (*fig*) obscurity; **—kammer** f (*Phot*) dark room; **d—n** vi impers grow dark; **—ziffer** f estimated number of unnotified cases.

dünn [dʏn] a thin; **—flüssig** a watery, thin; **—gesät** a scarce; **D—heit** f thinness.

Dunst [dʊnst] m **-es, ⁻e** vapour; (*Wetter*) haze.

dünsten ['dʏnstən] vt steam.

dunstig ['dʊnstɪç] a vaporous; *Wetter* hazy, misty.

Duplikat [dupli'ka:t] nt **-(e)s, -e** duplicate.

Dur [du:r] nt **-, -** (*Mus*) major.

durch [dʊrç] prep +acc through; (*Mittel, Ursache*) by; (*Zeit*) during; *den Sommer —* during the summer; *8 Uhr —* past 8 o'clock; **— und —** completely; **—arbeiten** vti work through; vr work one's way through; **—aus** ad completely; (*unbedingt*) definitely; **—beißen** irreg vt bite through; vr (*fig*) battle on; **—blättern** vt leaf through.

Durchblick ['dʊrçblɪk] m view; (*fig*) comprehension; **d—en** vi look through; (*cól: verstehen*) understand (*bei etw* sth); *etw d—en lassen* (*fig*) hint at sth.

durch'bohren vt insep bore through, pierce.

durchbrechen ['dʊrçbrɛçən] vti irreg break; [dʊrç'brɛçən] vt irreg insep *Schranken* break through; *Schallmauer* break; *Gewohnheit* break free from.

durch- ['dʊrç] cpd: **—brennen** vi irreg (*Draht, Sicherung*) burn through; (*col*) run away; **—bringen** irreg vt get through; *Geld* squander; vr make a living.

Durchbruch ['dʊrçbrʊx] m (*Öffnung*) breach; (*Mil*) breach; (*von Gefühlen etc*) eruption; (*der Zähne*) cutting; (*fig*) breakthrough; *zum — kommen* break through.

durch- cpd: **—dacht** [dʊrç'daxt] a well thought-out; **—denken** vt irreg insep think out.

durch- ['dʊrç] cpd: **—diskutieren** vt talk over, discuss; **—drängen** vr force one's way through; **—drehen** vt *Fleisch* mince; vi (*col*) crack up.

durchdringen ['dʊrçdrɪŋən] vi irreg penetrate, get through; *mit etw —* get one's way with sth;

[dʊrç'drɪŋən] *vt irreg insep* penetrate.

durcheinander [dʊrç'aɪ'nandər] *ad* in a mess, in confusion; (*col: verwirrt*) confused; — **trinken** mix one's drinks; **D—** *nt* -s (*Verwirrung*) confusion; (*Unordnung*) mess; —**bringen** *vt irreg* mess up; (*verwirren*) confuse; —**reden** *vi* talk at the same time.

durch- ['dʊrç] *cpd*: **D—fahrt** *f* transit; (*Verkehr*) thoroughfare; **D—fall** *m* (*Med*) diarrhoea; —**fallen** *vi irreg* fall through; (*in Prüfung*) fail; —**finden** *vr irreg* find one's way through.

durch'forschen *vt insep* explore.

durch- ['dʊrç] *cpd*: —**fressen** *vt irreg* eat through; —**fragen** *vr* find one's way through by asking.

durchführ- ['dʊrçfy:r] *cpd*: —**bar** *a* feasible, practicable; —**en** *vt* carry out; **D—ung** *f* execution, performance.

Durchgang ['dʊrçgaŋ] *m* passage(way); (*bei Produktion, Versuch*) run; (*Sport*) round; (*bei Wahl*) ballot; — **verboten** no thoroughfare; —**shandel** *m* transit trade; —**slager** *nt* transit camp; —**sstadium** *nt* transitory stage; —**sverkehr** *m* through traffic.

durchgefroren ['dʊrçgəfro:rən] *a* See completely frozen; *Mensch* frozen stiff.

durchgehen ['dʊrçge:ən] *irreg vt* (*behandeln*) go over; *vi* go through; (*ausreißen: Pferd*) break loose; (*Mensch*) run away; **mein Temperament ging mit mir durch** my temper got the better of me; **jdm etw — lassen** let sb get away with sth; —**d** *a Zug* through; *Öffnungszeiten* continuous.

durch- ['dʊrç] *cpd*: —**greifen** *vi irreg* take strong action; —**halten** *irreg vi* last out; *vt* keep up; —**hecheln** *vt* (*col*) gossip about; —**kommen** *vi irreg* get through; (*überleben*) pull through.

durch'kreuzen *vt insep* thwart, frustrate.

durch ['dʊrç] *cpd*: —**lassen** *vt irreg Person* let through; *Wasser* let in; —**lässig** *a* leaky; **D—lauf(wasser)erhitzer** *m* -s, - (hot water) geyser.

durch- *cpd*: —**'leben** *vt insep* live or go through, experience; '—**lesen** *vt irreg* read through; —**leuchten** *vt insep* X-ray; —**löchern** ['-'lœçərn] *vt insep* perforate; (*mit Löchern*) punch holes in; (*mit Kugeln*) riddle; '—**machen** *vt* go through; **die Nacht —machen** make a night of it.

Durch- ['dʊrç] *cpd*: —**marsch** *m* march through; —**messer** *m* -s, - diameter.

durch'nässen *vt insep* soak (through).

durch- ['dʊrç] *cpd*: —**nehmen** *vt irreg* go over; —**numerieren** *vt* number consecutively; —**pausen** *vt* trace; —**peitschen** *vt* (*lit*) whip soundly; (*fig*) *Gesetzentwurf, Reform* force through.

durchqueren [dʊrç'kve:rən] *vt insep* cross.

durch- ['dʊrç] *cpd*: **D—reiche** *f* -, **-n** (*serving*) hatch; **D—reise** *f* transit; **auf der D—reise** passing through; *Güter* in transit; —**ringen** *vr irreg* reach after a long struggle; —**rosten** *vi* rust through.

durchs [dʊrçs] = **durch das**.

Durchsage ['dʊrçza:gə] *f* -, **-n** intercom or radio announcement.

durchschauen ['dʊrçʃauən] *vi* (*lit*) look or see through; [dʊrç'ʃauən]

vt insep Person, Lüge see through.
durchscheinen ['dʊrçʃaɪnən] *vi
irreg* shine through; **—d** a translucent.

Durchschlag ['dʊrçʃlaːk] *m (Doppel)* carbon copy; *(Sieb)* strainer;
d—en *irreg* **vt** *(entzweischlagen)*
split (in two); *(sieben)* sieve; *vi
(zum Vorschein kommen)* emerge,
come out; *vr* get by; **d—end** *a*
resounding.

durch ['dʊrç] *cpd:* **—schlüpfen** *vi*
slip through; **—schneiden** *vt irreg*
cut through.

Durchschnitt ['dʊrçʃnɪt] *m (Mittelwert)* average; *über/unter dem —*
above/below average; *im —* on
average; **d—lich** a average; *ad* on
average; **—geschwindigkeit** *f* average speed; **—smensch** *m* average
man, man in the street; **—swert** *m*
average.

durch- *cpd:* **D—schrift** *f* copy;
—'schwimmen *vt irreg insep* swim
across; **·—'sehen** *vt irreg* look
through.

durchsetzen ['dʊrçzɛtsən] *vt*
enforce; *seinen Kopf —* get one's
own way; *vr (Erfolg haben)*
succeed; *(sich behaupten)* get one's
way; [dʊrç'zɛtsən] *vt insep* mix.

Durchsicht ['dʊrçzɪçt] *f* looking
through, checking; **d—ig** a transparent; **—igkeit** *f* transparence.

durch- *cpd:* **—'sickern** *vi* seep
through; *(fig)* leak out; **'—sieben**
vt sieve; **—'sprechen** *vt irreg* talk
over; **—'stehen** *vt irreg* live
through; **—stöbern** [-'ʃtøːbərn] *vt
insep* ransack, search through;
'—streichen *vt irreg* cross out;
—'suchen *vt insep* search;
D—'suchung *f* search; **—'tränken**
vt insep soak; **—trieben** [-'triːbən]
a cunning, wily; **—'wachsen** a *(lit*

Speck streaky; *(fig: mittelmäßig)*
so-so.

durch- ['dʊrç] *cpd:* **—weg** *ad*
throughout, completely; **—zählen**
vt count; *vi* count through; **—ziehen**
irreg vt Faden draw through; *vi*
pass through.

durch- *cpd:* **—'zucken** *vt insep*
shoot or flash through; **'D—zug** *m
(Luft)* draught; *(von Truppen,
Vögeln)* passage; **'—zwängen** *vtr*
squeeze or force through.

dürfen ['dʏrfən] *vi irreg* be
allowed; *darf ich?* may I?; *es darf
geraucht werden* you may smoke;
was darf es sein? what can I do
for you?; *das darf nicht geschehen*
that must not happen; *das ... Sie
mir glauben* you can believe me;
*es dürfte Ihnen bekannt sein, daß
...* as you will probably know ...

dürftig ['dʏrftɪç] a *(ärmlich)* needy,
poor; *(unzulänglich)* inadequate.

dürr [dʏr] a a dried-up; *Land* arid;
(mager) skinny, gaunt; **D—e** *f* **—,
-n** aridity; *(Zeit)* drought; *(Magerkeit)* skinniness.

Durst [dʊrst] *m* **-(e)s** thirst; **—
haben** be thirsty; **d—ig** a thirsty.

Dusche ['duːʃə] *f* **-, -n** shower;
d—n *vir* have a shower.

Düse ['dyːzə] *f* **-, -n** nozzle;
(Flugzeug—) jet; **—nantrieb** *m* jet
propulsion; **—nflugzeug** *nt* jet
(plane); **—njäger** *m* jet fighter.

Dussel ['dʊsəl] *m* **-s, -** *(col)* twit.

düster ['dyːstər] a dark; *Gedanken,
Zukunft* gloomy; **D—keit** *f* darkness, gloom; gloominess.

Dutzend ['dʊtsənt] *nt* **-s, -e** dozen;
—(e)mal *ad* a dozen times;
—mensch *m* man in the street;
d—weise ad by the dozen.

duzen ['duːtsən] *vtr* use the familiar

form of address or 'du' (jdn to or
with sb).

Dynamik [dy'na:mɪk] *f* (Phys) dy-
namics; (fig: Schwung) momentum; (von Mensch) dynamism.

dynamisch [dy'na:mɪʃ] *a* (lit, fig)
dynamic.

Dynamit [dyna'mi:t] *nt* -s dynamite.

Dynamo [dy'na:mo] *m* -s, -s
dynamo.

D-Zug ['de:tsu:k] *m* through train.

E

E, e [e:] *nt* E, e.

Ebbe ['ɛbə] *f* -, -n low tide.

eben ['e:bən] *a* level; (glatt)
smooth; *ad* just; (bestätigend)
exactly; —deswegen just because
of that; —bürtig *a*: jdm —bürtig
sein be sb's peer; E—e *f* -, -n plain;
—erdig *a* at ground level; —falls
ad likewise; E—heit *f* levelness;
smoothness; —so *ad* just as;
—sogut *ad* just as well; —sooft *ad*
just as often; —soviel *ad* just as
much; —soweit *ad* just as far;
—sowenig *ad* just as little.

Eber ['e:bar] *m* -s, - boar; —esche
f mountain ash, rowan.

ebnen ['e:bnən] *vt* level.

Echo ['ɛço] *nt* -s, -s echo.

echt [ɛçt] *a* genuine; (typisch)
typical; E—heit *f* genuineness.

Eck- ['ɛk] *cpd*: —ball *m* corner
(kick); —e *f* -, -n corner; (Math)
angle; —ig *a* angular; —zahn *m*
eye tooth.

edel ['e:dəl] *a* noble; E—metall *nt*
rare metal; E—stein *m* precious
stone.

Efeu ['e:fɔy] *m* -s ivy.

Effekt- [ɛ'fɛkt] *cpd*: —en *pl* stocks
pl; —enbörse *f* Stock Exchange;
—hasche'rei *f* sensationalism;
e—iv [-'ti:f] *a* effective, actual.

egal [e'ga:l] *a* all the same.

Ego- [ego] *cpd*: —ismus [-'ɪsmus]
m selfishness, egoism; —ist [-'ɪst]
m egoist; e—istisch *a* selfish, ego-
istic; e—zentrisch [-'tsɛntrɪʃ] *a* ego-
centric, self-centred.

Ehe ['e:ə] *f* -, -n marriage; e— *cj*
before; —brecher *m* -s, - adulterer;
—brecherin *f* adulteress; —bruch
m adultery; —frau *f* married
woman; wife; —leute *pl* married
people *pl*; e—lich *a* matrimonial;
Kind legitimate; e—malig *a* former; e—mals *ad* formerly; —mann
m married man; husband; —paar
nt married couple.

eher ['e:ar] *ad* (früher) sooner;
(lieber) rather, sooner; (mehr)
more.

Ehe- *cpd*: —ring *m* wedding ring;
—scheidung *f* divorce; —schließung *f* marriage.

eheste(r,s) ['e:astə(r,z)] *a* (frü-
heste) first, earliest; am —n
(liebsten) soonest; (meist) most;
(wahrscheinlichst) most probably.

Ehr- ['e:r] *cpd*: e—bar *a*
honourable, respectable; —e *f* -, -n
honour; e—en *vt* honour; —engast
m guest of honour; e—enhaft *a*
honourable; —enmann *m* man of
honour; —enmitglied *nt* honorary
member; —enplatz *m* place of
honour; —enrechte *pl* civic rights
pl; e—enrührig *a* defamatory;

—enrunde *f* lap of honour; —ensache *f* point of honour; e—envoll *a* honourable; —enwort *nt* word of honour; e—erbietig *a* respectful; —furcht *f* awe, deep respect; —gefühl *nt* sense of honour; —geiz *m* ambition; e—geizig *a* ambitious; e—lich *a* honest; —lichkeit *f* honesty; e—los *a* dishonourable; —ung *f* honour(ing); e—würdig *a* venerable.

Ei [aɪ] *nt* -(e)s, -er egg; e— *interj* well, well; (*beschwichtigend*) now, now.

Eich- ['aɪç] *cpd:* —amt *nt* Office of Weights and Measures; —e *f* -, -n oak (tree); —el *f* -, -n acorn; (*Cards*) club; e—en *vt* standardize; —hörnchen *nt* squirrel; —maß *nt* standard; —ung *f* standardization.

Eid [aɪt] *m* -(e)s, -e oath; —echse ['aɪdɛksə] *f* -, -n lizard; e—esstattliche Erklärung affidavit; —genosse *m* Swiss; e—lich *a* (sworn) upon oath.

Ei- *cpd:* —dotter *nt* egg yolk; —erbecher *m* eggcup; —erkuchen *m* omelette; pancake; —erschale *f* eggshell; —erstock *m* ovary; —eruhr *f* egg timer.

Eifer ['aɪfər] *m* -s zeal, enthusiasm; —sucht *f* jealousy; e—süchtig *a* jealous (*auf* +*acc* of).

eifrig ['aɪfrɪç] *a* zealous, enthusiastic.

Eigelb ['aɪgɛlp] *nt* -(e)s, -e - egg yolk.

eigen ['aɪgən] *a* own; (—*artig*) peculiar; the der/dem ihm —en ... with that ... peculiar to him; **sich** (*dat*) etw zu — machen make sth one's own; E—art *f* peculiarity; characteristic; —artig *a* peculiar; E—bedarf *m* one's own requirements *pl*; E—gewicht *nt* dead weight; —händig *a* with one's own hand; E—heim *nt* owner-occupied house; E—heit *f* peculiarity; E—lob *nt* self-praise; —mächtig *a* high-handed; E—name *m* proper name; —s *ad* expressly, on purpose; E—schaft *f* quality, property, attribute; E—schaftswort *nt* adjective; E—sinn *m* obstinacy; —sinnig *a* obstinate; —tlich *a* actual, real; *ad* actually, really; E—tor *nt* own goal; E—tum *nt* property; E—tümer(in *f*) *m* -s, - owner, proprietor; —tümlich *a* peculiar; E—tümlichkeit *f* peculiarity; E—tumswohnung *f* freehold flat.

eignen ['aɪgnən] *vr* be suited.

Eignung *f* suitability.

Eil- ['aɪl] *cpd:* —bote *m* courier; —brief *m* express letter; —e *f* haste; **es hat keine —e** there's no hurry; e—en *vi* (*Mensch*) hurry; (*dringend sein*) be urgent; —ends *ad* hastily; e—fertig *a* eager, solicitous; —gut *nt* express goods *pl*, fast freight (*US*); e—ig *a* hasty, hurried; (*dringlich*) urgent; **es e—ig haben** be in a hurry; —zug *m* semi-fast train, limited stop train.

Eimer ['aɪmər] *m* -s, - bucket, pail.

ein(e) [aɪn(ə)] *num* one; *indef art* a, an; *ad:* nicht — noch aus wissen not know what to do; —e(r,s) *pron* one; (*jemand*) someone.

einander [aɪ'nandər] *pron* one another, each other.

einarbeiten ['aɪnarbaɪtən] *vr* familiarize o.s. (*in* +*acc* with).

einarmig ['aɪn'armɪç] *a* one-armed.

einatmen ['aɪna:tmən] *vti* inhale, breathe in.

einäugig ['aɪn'ɔʏgɪç] *a* one-eyed.

Einbahnstraße ['aɪnba:nʃtrasə] *f* one-way street.

Einband ['aɪnbant] *m* binding, cover.

einbändig ['aɪnbɛndɪç] *a* one-volume.

einbau- ['aɪnbaʊ] *cpd:* **—en** *vt* build in; *Motor* install, fit; **E—möbel** *pl* built-in furniture.

einbe- ['aɪnbə] *cpd:* **—griffen** *a* included, inclusive; **—rufen** *vt irreg* convene; *(Mil)* call up; **E—rufung** *f* convocation; call-up.

einbett- ['aɪnbɛt] *cpd:* **—en** *vt* embed; **E—zimmer** *nt* single room.

einbeziehen ['aɪnbətsiːən] *vt irreg* include.

einbiegen ['aɪnbiːgən] *vi irreg* turn.

einbilden ['aɪnbɪldən] *vt:* sich *(dat)* etw — imagine sth.

Einbildung *f* imagination; *(Dünkel)* conceit; **—skraft** *f* imagination.

einbinden ['aɪnbɪndən] *vt irreg* bind (up).

einblenden ['aɪnblɛndən] *vt* fade in.

einbleuen ['aɪnblɔʏən] *vt (col)* jdm etw — hammer sth into sb.

Einblick ['aɪnblɪk] *m* insight.

einbrechen ['aɪnbrɛçən] *vi irreg (in Haus)* break in; *(in Land etc)* invade; *(Nacht)* fall; *(Winter)* set in; *(durchbrechen)* break.

Einbrecher *m* -s, - burglar.

einbringen ['aɪnbrɪŋən] *vt irreg* bring in; *Geld, Vorteil* yield; *(mitbringen)* contribute.

Einbruch ['aɪnbrʊx] *m (Haus—)* break-in, burglary; *(Eindringen)* invasion; *(des Winters)* onset; *(Durchbrechen)* break; *(Met)* approach; *(Mil)* penetration; *— der Nacht* nightfall; **e—ssicher** *a* burglar-proof.

einbürgern ['aɪnbʏrgərn] *vt* naturalize; *vr* become adopted; das hat sich so eingebürgert that's become a custom.

Einbuße ['aɪnbuːsə] *f* loss, forfeiture.

einbüßen ['aɪnbyːsən] *vt* lose, forfeit.

eindecken ['aɪndɛkən] *vr* lay in stocks *(mit* of).

eindeutig ['aɪndɔʏtɪç] *a* unequivocal.

eindring- ['aɪndrɪŋ] *cpd:* **—en** *vi irreg (in +acc)* force one's way in(to); *(in Haus)* break in(to); *(in Land)* invade; *(Gas, Wasser)* penetrate; *(mit Bitten)* pester *(auf jdn* sb); **—lich** *a* forcible, urgent; **E—ling** *m* intruder.

Eindruck ['aɪndrʊk] *m* impression; **e—sfähig** *a* impressionable; **e—svoll** *a* impressive.

eindrücken ['aɪndrʏkən] *vt* press in.

eineiig ['aɪn'aɪɪç] *a* Zwillinge identical.

eineinhalb ['aɪn'aɪn'halp] *num* one and a half.

einengen ['aɪn'ɛŋən] *vt* confine, restrict.

einer- ['aɪnər] *cpd:* **E—'lei** *nt* -s sameness; **—lei** *a (gleichartig)* the same kind of; es ist mir **—lei** it is all the same to me; **—seits** *ad* on one hand.

einfach ['aɪnfax] *a* simple; *(nicht mehrfach)* single; *ad* simply; **E—heit** *f* simplicity.

einfädeln ['aɪnfɛːdəln] *vt* Nadel thread; *(fig)* contrive.

einfahren ['aɪnfaːrən] *irreg vt* bring in; *Barriere* knock down; *Auto* run in; *vi* drive in; *(Zug)* pull in; *(Min)* go down.

Einfahrt *f (Vorgang)* driving in; pulling in; *(Min)* descent; *(Ort)* entrance.

Einfall ['amfal] m (Idee) idea, notion; (Licht—) incidence; (Mil) raid; e—en vi irreg (Licht) fall; (Mil) raid; (einstimmen) join in (in +acc with); (einstürzen) fall in, collapse; etw fällt jdm ein sth ·occurs to sb; das fällt mir gar nicht ein I wouldn't dream of it; sich (dat) etwas e—en lassen have a good idea.

einfältig ['amfɛltɪç] a simple(-minded).

Einfamilienhaus [amfa'mi:liənhaus] nt detached house.

einfangen ['amfaŋən] vt irreg catch.

einfarbig ['amfarbɪç] a all one colour; Stoff etc self-coloured.

einfass- ['amfas] cpd: —en vt set; Beet enclose; Stoff edge, border; Bier barrel; E—ung f setting; enclosure; barrelling.

einfetten ['amfɛtən] vt grease.

einfinden ['amfɪndən] vr irreg come, turn up.

einfliegen ['amfli:gən] vt irreg fly in.

einfließen ['amfli:sən] vi irreg flow in.

einflößen ['amflø:sən] vt: jdm etw — (lit) give sb sth; (fig) instil sth in sb.

Einfluß ['amflus] m influence; —bereich m sphere of influence; e—reich a influential.

einförmig ['amfœrmɪç] a uniform; E—keit f uniformity.

einfrieren ['amfri:rən] irreg vi freeze (in); vt freeze.

einfügen ['amfy:gən] vt fit in; (zusätzlich) add.

Einfuhr ['amfu:r] f - import; —artikel m imported article.

einführ- ['amfy:r] cpd: —en vt bring in; Mensch, Sitten introduce;

Ware import; E—ung f introduction; E—ungspreis m introductory price.

Eingabe ['amga:bə] f petition; (Daten—) input.

Eingang ['amgaŋ] m entrance; (Comm: Ankunft) arrival; (Sendung) post; e—s ad, prep +gen at the outset (of); —sbestätigung f acknowledgement of receipt; —shalle f entrance hall.

eingeben ['amge:bən] vt irreg Arznei give; Daten etc feed; Gedanken inspire.

eingebildet ['amgəbɪldət] a imaginary; (eitel) conceited.

Eingeborene(r) ['amgəbo:rənə(r)] mf native.

Eingebung f inspiration.

einge- ['amgə] cpd: —denk prep +gen bearing in mind; —fallen a Gesicht gaunt; —fleischt a inveterate; —fleischter Junggeselle confirmed bachelor; —froren a frozen.

eingehen ['amge:ən] irreg vi (Aufnahme finden) come in; (verständlich sein) be comprehensible (jdm to sb); (Sendung, Geld) be received; (Tier, Pflanze) die; (Firma) fold; (schrumpfen) shrink; auf etw (acc) — go into sth; auf jdn — respond to sb; vt enter into; Wette make; —d a exhaustive, thorough.

einge- ['amgə] cpd: E—machte(s) nt preserves pl; —meinden vt incorporate; —nommen a (von) fond (of), partial (to); (gegen) prejudiced; —schrieben a registered; —sessen a old-established; —spielt a: aufeinander —spielt sein be in tune with each other; E—ständnis nt -ses, -se admission, confession; —stehen vt irreg confess; —tragen

a (Comm) registered; **E—weide** nt **-s, -** innards pl, intestines pl; **E—weihte(r)** mf initiate; **—wöhnen** vt accustom.

eingießen ['aingi:sən] vt irreg pour (out).

eingleisig ['aınglaızıç] a single-track.

eingraben ['aıngra:bən] irreg vt dig in; vr dig o.s. in.

eingreifen ['aıngraıfən] vi irreg intervene, interfere; (Zahnrad) mesh.

Eingriff ['aıngrıf] m intervention, interference; (Operation) operation.

einhaken ['aınha:kən] vt hook in; vr: sich bei jdm — link arms with sb; vi (sich einmischen) intervene.

Einhalt ['aınhalt] m: — gebieten (+dat) put a stop to; **e—en** irreg vt Regel keep; vi stop.

einhändig ['aınhendıç] a one-handed; **—en** ['-dıgən] vt hand in.

einhängen ['aınhɛŋən] vt hang; Telefon (auch vi) hang up; sich bei jdm — link arms with sb.

einheim- ['aınhaim] cpd: **—isch** a native; **—sen** vt (col) bring home.

Einheit ['aınhaıt] f unity; (Maß, Mil) unit; **e—lich** a uniform; **—spreis** m uniform price.

einheilig ['aınhɛlıç] a,ad unanimous.

einholen ['aınho:lən] vt Tau haul in; Fahne, Segel lower; (Vorsprung aufholen) catch up with; Verspätung make up; Rat, Erlaubnis ask; vi (einkaufen) buy, shop.

Einhorn ['aınhorn] nt unicorn.

einhüllen ['aınhylən] vt wrap up.

einig ['aınıç] a (vereint) united; sich (dat) **— sein** be in agreement; **— werden** agree; **—e** ['aınıgə] pl **some**; (mehrere) several; **—e(r,s)** a some; **—emal** ad a few times;

—en vt unite; vr agree (auf +acc on); **—ermaßen** ad somewhat; (leidlich) reasonably; **—es** pron something; **—gehen** vi irreg agree; **E—keit** f unity; (Übereinstimmung) agreement; **E—ung** f agreement; (Vereinigung) unification.

einimpfen ['aınımpfən] vt inoculate (jdm etw sb with sth); (fig) impress (jdm etw sth upon sb).

einjährig ['aınjɛːrıç] a of or for one year; (Alter) one-year-old; Pflanze annual.

einkalkulieren ['aınkalkuli:rən] vt take into account, allow for.

Einkauf ['aınkauf] m purchase; **e—en** vt buy; vi go shopping; **—sbummel** m shopping spree; **—snetz** nt string bag; **—spreis** m cost price.

einkerben ['aınkɛrbən] vt notch.

einklammern ['aınklamərn] vt put in brackets, bracket.

Einklang ['aınklaŋ] m harmony.

einkleiden ['aınklaıdən] vt clothe; (fig) express.

einklemmen ['aınklɛmən] vt jam.

einknicken ['aınknıkən] vt bend in; Papier fold; vi give way.

einkochen ['aınkɔxən] vt boil down; Obst preserve, bottle.

Einkommen ['aınkomən] nt **-s, -** income; **—(s)steuer** f income tax.

einkreisen ['aınkraızən] vt encircle.

Einkünfte ['aınkynftə] pl income, revenue.

einlad- ['aınla:d] cpd: **—en** vt irreg Person invite; Gegenstände load; jdn ins Kino — take sb to the cinema; **E—ung** f invitation.

Einlage ['aınla:gə] f (Programm—) interlude; (Spar—) deposit; (Schuh—) insole; (Fußstütze) support; (Zahn—) temporary filling; (Cook) noodles pl, vegetables pl etc in soup; e—rn vt store.

Einlaß ['aınlas] m -sses, -lässe admission.

einlassen irreg vt let in; (einsetzen) set in; vr: sich mit jdm/auf etw (acc) — get involved with sb/sth.

Einlauf [aınlauf] m arrival; (von Pferden) finish; (Med) enema; e—en irreg vi arrive, come in; (in Hafen) enter; (Wasser) run in; (Stoff) shrink; vt Schuhe break in; jdm das Haus e—en invade sb's house; vr (Sport) warm up; (Motor, Maschine) run in.

einleben ['aınle:bən] vr settle down.

Einlege- ['aınle:gə] cpd: —arbeit f inlay; e—n vt (einfügen) Blatt, Sohle insert; (Cook) pickle; (in Holz etc) inlay; Geld deposit; Pause have; Protest make; Veto use; Berufung lodge; ein gutes Wort bei jdm e—n put in a good word with sb; —sohle f insole.

einleiten ['aınlaıtən] vt introduce, start; Geburt induce.

Einleitung f introduction; induction.

einleuchten ['aınlɔyçtən] vi be clear or evident (jdm to sb); —d a clear.

einliefern ['aınli:fərn] vt take in (in +acc into).

einlösen ['aınlø:zən] vt Scheck cash; Schuldschein, Pfand redeem; Versprechen keep.

einmachen ['aınmaxən] vt preserve.

einmal ['aınma:l] ad once; (erstens) first; (zukünftig) sometime; nehmen wir — an, just let's suppose; noch — once more; nicht

— not even; auf — all at once; es war — once upon a time there was/were; E—'eins nt multiplication tables pl; —ig a unique; (einmal geschehend) single; (prima) fantastic.

Einmann- [aın'man] cpd: —betrieb m one-man business; —bus m one-man-operated bus.

Einmarsch ['aınmarʃ] m entry; (Mil) invasion; e—ieren vi march in.

einmengen ['aınmɛŋən], **einmischen** ['aınmıʃən] vr interfere (in +acc with).

einmünden ['aınmʏndən] vi run in (in +acc into), join.

einmütig ['aınmy:tıç] a unanimous.

Einnahme ['aınna:mə] f -, -n (Geld) takings pl, revenue; (von Medizin) taking; (Mil) capture, taking; —quelle f source of income.

einnehmen ['aınne:mən] vt irreg take; Stellung, Raum take up; —für/gegen persuade in favour of/against; —d a charming.

einnicken ['aınnıkən] vi nod off.

einnisten ['aınnıstən] vr nest; (fig) settle o.s.

Einöde ['aın'ø:də] f -, -n desert, wilderness.

einordnen ['aın'ɔrdnən] vt arrange, fit in; vr adapt; (Aut) get into lane.

einpacken ['aınpakən] vt pack (up).

einparken ['aınparkən] vt park.

einpendeln ['aınpɛndəln] vr even out.

einperchen ['aınpfɛrçən] vt pen in, coop up.

einpflanzen ['aınpflantsən] vt plant; (Med) implant.

einplanen ['aınpla:nən] vt plan for.

einpräg- ['aınprɛ:g] cpd: —en vt impress, imprint; (beibringen)

impress (jdm oṅ sb); sich (dat) etw
—en memorize sth; (überlassen)
to remember; Melodie catchy.

einrahmen ['amraːmən] vt frame.

einrasten ['amrastən] vi engage.

einräumen ['amrɔʏmən] vt
(ordnend) put away; (überlassen)
Platz give up; (zugestehen) admit,
concede.

einrechnen ['amreçnən] vt
include; (berücksichtigen) take
into account.

einreden ['amreːdən] vt: jdm/sich
etw — talk sb/o.s. into believing
sth.

einreiben ['amraibən] vt irreg rub
in.

einreichen ['amraiçən] vt hand in;
Antrag submit.

Einreise ['amraizə] f entry; —be-
stimmungen pl entry regulations
pl; —erlaubnis f, —genehmigung f
entry permit; e—n vi enter (in ein
Land a country).

einreißen ['amraisən] vt irreg
Papier tear; Gebäude pull down;
vi tear; (Gewohnheit werden)
catch on.

einrichten ['amrıçtən] vt Haus
furnish; (schaffen) establish, set
up; (arrangieren) arrange; (möglich machen) manage; vr (in Haus)
furnish one's house; (sich vorbereiten) prepare o.s. (auf +acc
for); (sich anpassen) adapt (auf
+acc to).

Einrichtung f (Wohnungs—) furn-
ishings pl; (öffentliche Anstalt)
organization; (Dienste) service.

einrosten ['amrostən] vi get rusty.

einrücken ['amrʏkən] vi (Mil)
(Soldat) join up; (in Land) move
in; vt Anzeige insert; Zeile indent.

Eins [ains] f -, -en one; e— num

one'; es ist mir alles e— it's all one
to me.

einsalzen ['amzaltsən] vt salt.

einsam ['amzaːm] a lonely,
solitary; E—keit f loneliness,
solitude.

einsammeln ['amzaməln] vt collect.

Einsatz ['amzats] m (Teil) inset;
(an Kleid) insertion; (Tisch) leaf;
(Verwendung) use, employment;
(Spiel—) stake; (Risiko) risk;
(Mil) operation; (Mus) entry; im
— in action; e—bereit a ready for
action.

einschalten ['amʃaltən] vt (einfügen) insert; Pause make; (Elec)
switch on; (Aut) Gang engage;
Anwalt bring in; vr (dazwischen-
treten) intervene.

einschärfen ['amʃɛrfən] vt impress
(jdm etw sth on sb).

einschätzen ['amʃɛtsən] vt estimate, assess; vr rate o.s.

einschenken ['amʃɛŋkən] vt pour
out.

einschicken ['amʃıkən] vt send in.

einschieben ['amʃiːbən] vt irreg
push in; (zusätzlich) insert.

einschiffen ['amʃıfən] vt take on
board; vr embark, go on board.

einschlafen ['amʃlaːfən] vi irreg
fall asleep, go to sleep.

einschläfernd ['amʃlɛːfərnt] a
(Med) soporific; (langweilig) boring; Stimme lulling.

Einschlag ['amʃlaːk] m impact;
(Aut) lock; (fig: Beimischung)
touch, hint; e—en vt irreg vt knock
in; Fenster smash, break; Zähne,
Schädel smash in; Steuer turn;
(kürzer machen) take up; Ware
pack, wrap up; Weg, Richtung
take; vi hit (in etw (acc) sth, auf
jdn sb); (sich einigen) agree;
(Anklang finden) work, succeed.

einschlägig ['aɪnʃlɛːgɪç] a relevant.

einschleichen ['aɪnʃlaɪçən] vr irreg (in Haus, Fehler) creep in, steal in; (in Vertrauen) worm one's way in.

einschließen ['aɪnʃliːsən] irreg vt Kind lock in; Häftling lock up; Gegenstand lock away; Bergleute cut off; (umgeben) surround; (Mil) encircle; (fig) include, comprise; vr lock o.s. in.

einschließlich ad inclusive; prep + gen inclusive of, including.

einschmeicheln ['aɪnʃmaɪçəln] vr ingratiate o.s. (bei with).

einschnappen ['aɪnʃnapən] vi (Tür) click to; (fig) be touchy; eingeschnappt sein be in a huff.

einschneidend ['aɪnʃnaɪdənt] a incisive.

Einschnitt ['aɪnʃnɪt] m cutting; (Med) incision; (Ereignis) incident.

einschränken ['aɪnʃrɛŋkən] vt limit, restrict; Kosten cut down, reduce; vr cut down (on expenditure); **—d** a restrictive.

Einschränkung f restriction, limitation; reduction; (von Behauptung) qualification.

Einschreib- ['aɪnʃraɪb] cpd: **—(e)brief** m recorded delivery letter; **e—en** irreg vt write in; Post send recorded delivery; (Univ) enrol; **—en** nt recorded delivery letter; **—(e)sendung** f recorded delivery packet.

einschreiten ['aɪnʃraɪtən] vi irreg step in, intervene; **— gegen** take action against.

Einschub ['aɪnʃuːp] m **-s**, **-e** insertion.

einschüchtern ['aɪnʃʏçtərn] vt intimidate.

einsehen ['aɪnzeːən] vt irreg (hineinsehen in) realize; Akten have a look at; (verstehen) see; **E— nt -s**

understanding; **ein E— haben** show understanding.

einseifen ['aɪnzaɪfən] vt soap, lather; (fig) take in, cheat.

einseitig ['aɪnzaɪtɪç] a one-sided; **E—keit** f one-sidedness.

Einsend- ['aɪnzɛnt] cpd: **e—en** vt irreg send in; **—er** m **-s**, **-** sender, contributor; **—ung** f sending in.

einsetzen ['aɪnzɛtsən] vt put (in); (in Amt) appoint, install; Geld stake; (verwenden) use; (Mil) employ; (Mus) enter, come in; vr work hard; **sich für jdn/etw —** support s.o./sth.

Einsicht ['aɪnzɪçt] f insight; (in Akten) inspection; **zu der —kommen, daß ...** come to the conclusion that ...; **e—ig** a Mensch judicious; **—nahme** f **-**, **-n** examination; **e—slos** a unreasonable; **e—svoll** a understanding.

Einsiedler ['aɪnziːdlər] m hermit.

einsilbig ['aɪnzɪlbɪç] a (lit,fig) monosyllabic; **E—keit** f (fig) taciturnity.

einsinken ['aɪnzɪŋkən] vi irreg sink in.

Einsitzer ['aɪnzɪtsər] m **-s**, **-** single-seater.

einspannen ['aɪnʃpanən] vt Werkstück, Papier put (in), insert; Pferde harness; (col) Person rope in.

einsperren ['aɪnʃpɛrən] vt lock up.

einspielen ['aɪnʃpiːlən] vr (Sport) warm up; **sich aufeinander —** become attuned to each other; vt (Film) Geld bring in; Instrument play in; **gut eingespielt** smoothly running.

einspringen ['aɪnʃprɪŋən] vi irreg (aushelfen) help out, step into the breach.

einspritzen ['aɪnʃprɪtsən] vt inject.

Einspruch ['aɪnʃprʊx] m protest, objection; —srecht nt veto.

einspurig ['aɪnʃpuːrɪç] a single-line.

einst [aɪnst] ad once; (zukünftig) one or some day.

Einstand ['aɪnʃtant] m (Tennis) deuce; (Antritt) entrance (to office).

einstechen ['aɪnʃtɛçən] vt irreg stick in.

einstecken ['aɪnʃtɛkən] vt stick in, insert; Brief post; (Elec) Stecker plug in; Geld pocket; (mitnehmen) take; (überlegen sein) put in the shade; (hinnehmen) swallow.

einstehen ['aɪnʃteːən] vi irreg guarantee (für jdn/etw sb/sth); (verantworten) answer (für for).

einsteigen ['aɪnʃtaɪgən] vi irreg get in or on; (in Schiff) go on board; (sich beteiligen) come in; (hineinklettern) climb in.

einstell- ['aɪnʃtɛl] cpd: —bar a adjustable; —en vti (aufhören) stop; Geräte adjust; Kamera etc focus; Sender, Radio tune in; (unterstellen) put; (in Firma) employ, take on; vr (anfangen) set in; (kommen) arrive; sich auf jdn/etw —en adapt to sb/prepare o.s. for sth; E—ung f (Aufhören) suspension, cessation; adjustment; focusing; (von Arbeiter etc) appointment; (Haltung) attitude.

Einstieg ['aɪnʃtiːk] m -(e)s, -e entry; (fig) approach.

einstig ['aɪnstɪç] a former.

einstimm- ['aɪnʃtɪm] cpd: —en vi join in; vt (Mus) tune; (in Stimmung bringen) put in the mood; —ig a unanimous; (Mus) for one voice; E—igkeit f unanimity.

einst- [aɪnst] cpd: —malig a former-er; —mals ad once, formerly.

einstöckig ['aɪnʃtœkɪç] a single-storeyed.

einstudieren ['aɪnʃtudiːrən] vt study, rehearse.

einstündig ['aɪnʃtʏndɪç] a one-hour.

einstürmen ['aɪnʃtʏrmən] vi: auf jdn — rush at sb; (Eindrücke) overwhelm sb.

Einsturz ['aɪnʃtʊrts] m collapse; —gefahr f danger of collapse.

einstürzen ['aɪnʃtʏrtsən] vi fall in, collapse.

einst- [aɪnst] cpd: —weilen ad meanwhile; (vorläufig) temporarily, for the time being; —weilig a temporary.

eintägig ['aɪntɛːgɪç] a one-day.

eintauchen ['aɪntaʊxən] vt immerse, dip in; vi dive.

eintauschen ['aɪntaʊʃən] vt exchange.

eintausend ['aɪntaʊzənt] num one thousand.

einteil- ['aɪntaɪl] cpd: —en vt (in Teile) divide (up); Menschen assign; —ig a one-piece.

eintönig ['aɪntøːnɪç] a monotonous; E—keit f monotony.

Eintopf(gericht nt) ['aɪntɔpf(gərɪçt)] m stew.

Eintracht ['aɪntraxt] f - concord, harmony.

einträchtig ['aɪntrɛçtɪç] a harmonious.

Eintrag ['aɪntraːk] m -(e)s, ̈e entry; amtlicher — entry in the register; e—en irreg vt (in Buch) enter; Profit yield; jdm etw e—en bring sb sth; jdm auf put one's name down.

einträglich ['aɪntrɛːklɪç] a profitable.

eintreffen ['aɪntrɛfən] vi irreg happen; (ankommen) arrive.

eintreten ['aıntre:tən] *irreg vi* occur; *(hineingehen)* enter *(in etw (acc) sth)*; *(sich einsetzen)* intercede; *(in Club, Partei)* join *(in etw (acc) sth)*; *(in Stadium etc)* enter; *vt Tür* kick open.

Eintritt ['aıntrıt] *m (Betreten)* entrance; *(Anfang)* commencement; *(in Club etc)* joining; —**sgeld** *nt*, —**spreis** *m* charge for admission; —**skarte** *f* (admission) ticket.

eintrocknen ['aıntrɔknən] *vi* dry up.

einüben ['aın'y:bən] *vt* practise, drill.

einver- ['aınfɛr-] *cpd*: —**leiben** *vt* incorporate; *Gebiet* annex; **sich** *(dat)* etw —**leiben** *(fig: geistig)* acquire; **E—nehmen** *nt* -s, — agreement, understanding; —**standen** *interj* agreed; **a:** —**standen sein** agree, be agreed; **E—ständnis** *nt* understanding; *(gleiche Meinung)* agreement.

Einwand ['aınvant] *m* -(e)s, **ᵉe** objection; —**erer** ['aınvandərər] *m* immigrant; **e—ern** *vi* immigrate; —**erung** *f* immigration; **e—frei** *a* perfect; *ad* absolutely.

einwärts ['aınvɛrts] *ad* inwards.

einwecken ['aınvɛkən] *vt* bottle, preserve.

Einwegflasche ['aınve:gflaʃə] *f* nodeposit bottle.

einweichen ['aınvaıçən] *vt* soak.

einweih- ['aınvaı-] *cpd*: —**en** *vt Kirche* consecrate; *Brücke* open; *Gebäude* inaugurate; *Person* initiate *(in +acc in)*; **E—ung** *f* consecration; opening; inauguration, initiation.

einweis- ['aınvaız-] *cpd*: —**en** *vt irreg (in Amt)* install; *(in Arbeit)* introduce; *(in Anstalt)* send;

E—ung *f* installation; introduction; sending.

einwenden ['aınvɛndən] *vt irreg* object, oppose *(gegen* to).

einwerfen ['aınvɛrfən] *vt irreg* throw in; *Brief* post; *Geld* put in, insert; *Fenster* smash; *(äußern)* interpose.

einwickeln ['aınvıkəln] *vt* wrap up; *(fig col)* outsmart.

einwillig- ['aınvılıg] *cpd*: —**en** *vi* consent, agree *(in +acc* to); **E—ung** *f* consent.

einwirk- ['aınvırk] *cpd*: —**en** *vi*: **auf jdn/etw** —**en** influence sb/sth; **E—ung** *f* influence.

Einwohner ['aınvo:nər] *m* -s, — inhabitant; —**meldeamt** *nt* registration office; —**schaft** *f* population, inhabitants *pl.*

Einwurf ['aınvurf] *m (Öffnung)* slot; *(Einwand)* objection; *(Sport)* throw-in.

Einzahl ['aıntsa:l] *f* singular; **e—en** *vt* pay in; —**ung** *f* paying in.

einzäunen ['aıntsɔynən] *vt* fence in.

einzeichnen ['aıntsaıçnən] *vt* draw in.

Einzel ['aıntsəl] *nt* -s, — *(Tennis)* singles; *in cpds* individual; single; —**bett** *nt* single bed; —**fall** *m* single instance, individual case; —**haft** *f* solitary confinement; —**heit** *f* particular, detail; **e—n** **a** single; *(vereinzelt)* the odd; *ad* singly; **e—n angeben** specify; **der/die** **e—ne** the individual; **das e—ne** the particular; **ins e—ne gehen** go into detail(s); —**teil** *nt* component (part); —**zimmer** *nt* single room.

einziehen ['aıntsi:ən] *irreg vt* draw in, take in; *Kopf* duck; *Fühler, Antenne, Fahrgestell* retract; *Steuern, Erkundigungen* collect; *(Mil)* draft, call up; *(aus dem Verkehr* ziehen) withdraw; (konfiszieren) confiscate; vi move in(to); (Friede, Ruhe) come; (Flüssigkeit) penetrate.

einzig ['aıntsıç] a only; (ohnegleichen) unique; das —e the only thing; der/die —e the only one; —artig a unique.

Einzug ['aıntsu:k] m entry, moving in.

Eis [aıs] —es, - ice; (Speise—) ice cream; —bahn f ice or skating rink; —bär m polar bear; —becher m sundae; —bein nt pig's trotters pl; —berg m iceberg; —blumen pl ice fern; —decke f sheet of ice; —diele f ice-cream parlour.

Eisen ['aızən] nt -s, - iron; —bahn f railway, railroad (US); —bahner m -s, - railwayman, railway employee, railroader (US); —bahnschaffner m railway guard; —bahnübergang m level crossing, grade crossing (US); —bahnwagen m railway carriage; —erz nt iron ore; —haltig a containing iron.

eisern ['aızərn] a iron; Gesundheit robust; Energie unrelenting; Reserve emergency.

Eis- cpd: e—frei a clear of ice; e—hockey nt ice hockey; e—ig ['aızıç] a icy; e—kalt a icy cold; —kunstlauf m figure skating; —laufen nt ice skating; —läufer(in f) m ice-skater; —pickel m ice-axe; —schießen nt ≈ curling; —schrank m fridge, ice-box (US); —zapfen m icicle; —zeit f ice age.

eitel ['aıtəl] a vain; E—keit f vanity.

Eiter ['aıtər] m -s pus; e—ig a suppurating; e—n vi suppurate.

Ei- [aı] cpd: —weiß nt -es, -e white of an egg; —zelle f ovum.

Ekel ['e:kəl] m -s nausea, disgust; nt -s, - (col: Mensch) nauseating

person; e—erregend, e—haft, ek(e)lig a nauseating, disgusting; e—n vt disgust; es ekelt jdn or jdm sb is disgusted; vr loathe, be disgusted (vor +dat at).

Ekstase [ɛk'sta:zə] f -, -n ecstasy.

Ekzem [ɛk'tse:m] nt -s, -e (Med) eczema.

Elan [e'lã:] m -s elan.

elastisch [e'lastıʃ] a elastic.

Elastizität [elastitsi'tɛ:t] f elasticity.

Elch [ɛlç] m -(e)s, -e elk.

Elefant [ele'fant] m elephant.

elegant [ele'gant] a elegant.

Eleganz [ele'gants] f elegance.

Elek- [e'lek] cpd: —trifizierung [-trifi'tsi:rʊŋ] f electrification; —triker [-trikər] m -s, - electrician; e—trisch [-trıʃ] a electric; e—trisieren [-tri'zi:rən] vt (lit, fig) electrify; Mensch give an electric shock to; vr get an electric shock; —trizität [-tritsi'tɛt] f electricity; —trizitätswerk nt electricity works, power plant.

Elektro- [e'lɛktro] cpd: —de [elɛk'tro:də] f -, -n electrode; —herd m electric cooker; —lyse [-'ly:zə] f -, -n electrolysis; —n [-ɔn] nt -s, -en electron; —nen(ge)hirn [elɛk'tro:nən-] nt electronic brain; —nenrechner m computer; e—nisch a electronic; —rasierer m -s, - electric razor.

Element [ele'mɛnt] nt -s, -e element; (Elec) cell, battery; e—ar [-'ta:r] a elementary; (naturhaft) elemental.

Elend ['e:lɛnt] nt -(e)s misery; e—, a miserable; e—iglich ['elɛnd-] ad miserably; —sviertel nt slum.

elf [ɛlf] num eleven; E— f -, -en (Sport) eleven; E—e f -, -n elf; E—enbein nt ivory; E—meter m (Sport) penalty (kick).

eliminieren [elimi'ni:rən] vt eliminate.

Elite [e'li:tə] f -, -n elite.

Elixier [eli'ksi:r] nt -s, -e elixir.

Ell- cpd: **—e** ['ɛlə] f -, -n ell; (Maß) yard; **—(en)bogen** m elbow; **—ipse** [ɛ'lipsə] f -, -n ellipse.

Elster ['ɛlstər] f -, -n magpie.

Elter- ['ɛltər] cpd: **e—lich** a parental; **—n** pl parents pl; **—nhaus** nt home; **e—nlos** a parentless.

Email [e'ma:j] nt -s, -s enamel; **e—lieren** [ema'ji:rən] vt enamel.

Emanzipation [emantsipatsi'o:n] f emancipation.

emanzi'pieren vt emancipate.

Embryo ['ɛmbryo] m -s, -s or -nen embryo.

Emi- [emi] cpd: **—grant** ['grant] m emigrant; **—gration** [-gratsi'o:n] f emigration; **e—grieren** [-'gri:rən] vi emigrate.

Empfang [ɛm'pfaŋ] m -(e)s, =e reception; (Erhalten) receipt; in **—nehmen** receive; **e—en** irreg vt receive; vi (schwanger werden) conceive.

Empfäng- [ɛm'pfɛŋ] cpd: **—er** m -s, - receiver; (Comm) addressee, consignee; **e—lich** a receptive, susceptible; **—nis** f -, die conception; **—nisverhütung** f contraception.

Empfangs- cpd: **—bestätigung** f acknowledgement; **—dame** f receptionist; **—schein** m receipt; **—zimmer** nt reception room.

empfehlen [ɛm'pfe:lən] irreg vt recommend; vr take one's leave; **—swert** a recommendable.

Empfehlung f recommendation; **—sschreiben** nt letter of recommendation.

empfind- [ɛm'pfɪnt] cpd: **—en** [ɛm'pfɪndən] vt irreg feel; **—lich** a

sensitive; Stelle sore; (reizbar) touchy; E-lichkeit f sensitiveness; (Reizbarkeit) touchiness; **—sam** a sentimental; E—ung f feeling, sentiment; **—ungslos** a unfeeling, insensitive.

empor [ɛm'po:r] ad up, upwards.

empören [ɛm'pø:rən] vt make indignant; shock; vr become indignant; **—d** a outrageous.

empor- cpd: **—kommen** vi irreg rise; succeed; E—kömmling m upstart, parvenu.

Empörung f indignation.

emsig ['ɛmzɪç] a diligent, busy.

End- ['ɛnt] in cpds final; **—auswertung** f final analysis; **—bahnhof** ['ɛnt-] m terminus; **—e** nt -s, -n end; am **—e** at the end; (schließlich) in the end; am **—e** sein be at the end of one's tether; **—e** Dezember at the end of December; zu **—e** sein be finished; **e—en** vi end; e—gültig a final, definite; **e—ivie** [ɛn'di:vie] f endive; e—lich a final, (Math) finite; ad finally; e—lich! at last!; e—los a endless, infinite; **—spiel** nt final(s); **—spurt** m (Sport) final spurt; **—station** f terminus; **—ung** f ending.

Energie [enɛr'gi:] f energy; e—los a lacking in energy, weak; **—wirtschaft** f energy industry.

energisch [e'nɛrgɪʃ] a energetic.

eng [ɛŋ] a narrow; Kleidung tight; (fig) Horizont auch limited; Freundschaft, Verhältnis close; **—an** etw (dat) close to sth.

Engagement [ãgaʒə'mã:] nt -s, -s engagement; (Verpflichtung) commitment.

engagieren [ãga'ʒi:rən] vt engage; ein engagierter Schriftsteller a committed writer; vr commit o.s.

Enge ['ɛŋə] f -, -n (lit,fig) narrowness; (Land—) defile; (Meer—) straits pl; **jdn in die — treiben** drive sb into a corner.

Engel ['ɛŋəl] m -s, - angel; **e—haft** a angelic; **—macher** m -s, - (col) backstreet abortionist.

eng- cpd: **—herzig** a petty; **E—paß** m defile, pass; (fig, Verkehr) bottleneck.

en gros [ã'gro] ad wholesale.

engstirnig ['ɛŋʃtɪrnɪç] a narrowminded.

Enkel ['ɛŋkəl] m -s, - grandson; **—in** f granddaughter; **—kind** nt grandchild.

en masse [ã'mas] ad en masse.

enorm [e'nɔrm] a enormous.

Ensemble [ã'sãbəl] nt -s, -s company, ensemble.

entarten [ɛnt''a:rtən] vi degenerate.

entbehr- [ɛnt'be:r] cpd: **—en** vt do without, dispense with; **—lich** a superfluous; **E—ung** f privation.

entbinden [ɛnt'bɪndən] irreg vt release (gen from); (Med) deliver; vi (Med) give birth.

Entbindung f release; (Med) confinement; **—sheim** nt maternity hospital.

entblößen [ɛnt'blø:sən] vt denude, uncover; (berauben) deprive (gen of).

entdeck- [ɛnt'dɛk] cpd: **—en** vt discover; **jdm etw —en** disclose sth to sb; **E—er** m -s, - discoverer; **E—ung** f discovery.

Ente ['ɛntə] f -, -n duck; (fig) canard, false report.

entehren [ɛnt''e:rən] vt dishonour, disgrace.

enteignen [ɛnt''aɪgnən] vt expropriate; Besitzer dispossess.

enteisen [ɛnt''aɪzən] vt de-ice, defrost.

enterben [ɛnt''ɛrbən] vt disinherit.

entfachen [ɛnt'faxən] vt kindle.

entfallen [ɛnt'falən] vi irreg drop, fall; (wegfallen) be dropped; **jdm — (vergessen)** slip sb's memory; **auf jdn —** be allotted to sb.

entfalten [ɛnt'faltən] vt unfold; Talente develop; vr open; (Mensch) develop one's potential.

Entfaltung f unfolding; (von Talenten) development.

entfern- [ɛnt'fɛrn] cpd: **—en** vt remove; (hinauswerfen) expel; vr go away, retire, withdraw; **—t** a distant; **weit davon —t sein, etw zu tun** be far from doing sth; **E—ung** f distance; (Wegschaffen) removal; **E—ungsmesser** m -s, - (Phot) rangefinder.

entfesseln [ɛnt'fɛsəln] vt (fig) arouse.

entfetten [ɛnt'fɛtən] vt take the fat from.

entfremd- [ɛnt'frɛmd] cpd: **—en** vt estrange, alienate; **E—ung** f alienation, estrangement.

entfrost- [ɛnt'frɔst] cpd: **—en** vt defrost; **E—er** m -s, - (Aut) defroster.

entführ- [ɛnt'fy:r] cpd: **—en** vt carry off, abduct; kidnap; **E—er** m kidnapper; **E—ung** f abduction, kidnapping.

entgegen [ɛnt'ge:gən] prep + dat contrary to, against; ad towards; **—bringen** vt irreg bring; (fig) show (jdm etw sb sth); **—gehen** vi irreg (+ dat) go to meet, go towards; **—gesetzt** a opposite; (widersprechend) opposed; **—halten** vt irreg (fig) object; **—kommen** vi irreg approach; meet (jdm sb); **—kommend** a obliging; (Verkehr) oncoming; **—nehmen** vt irreg receive, accept; **—sehen** vi irreg (+ dat) await; **—setzen** vt oppose (dat to); **—stehen** vi irreg (+ dat) stand in the way of; **—treten** vi irreg (+ dat) step up to; (fig) oppose, counter; **—wirken** vi (+ dat) counteract.

men nt obligingness; —kommend a obliging; —laufen vi irreg (+dat) run towards or to meet; (fig) run counter to; —nehmen vt irreg receive, accept; —sehen vi irreg (+dat) await; —setzen vt oppose (dat to); —treten vi irreg (+dat) (lit) step up to; (fig) oppose, counter; —wirken vi (+dat) counteract.

entgegnen [ent'ge:gnən] vt reply, retort.

Entgegnung f reply, retort.

entgehen [ent'ge:ən] vi irreg (fig) jdm — escape sb's notice; sich (dat) etw — lassen miss sth.

entgeistert [ent'gaistərt] a thunder-struck.

Entgelt [ent'gelt] nt -(e)s, -e compensation, remuneration; e—en vt irreg: jdm etw e—en repay sb for sth.

entgleisen [ent'glaizən] vi (Rail) be derailed; (fig: Person) misbehave; — lassen derail.

Entgleisung f derailment; (fig) faux pas, gaffe.

entgleiten [ent'glaitən] vi irreg slip (jdm from sb's hand).

entgräten [ent'grɛ:tən] vt fillet, bone.

Enthaarungsmittel [ent'ha:rungsmitəl] nt depilatory.

enthalten [ent'haltən] irreg vt contain; vr abstain, refrain (gen from).

enthaltsam [ent'haltza:m] a abstinent, abstemious; E—keit f abstinence.

enthemmen [ent'hɛmən] vt: jdn — free sb from his inhibitions.

enthüllen [ent'hʏlən] vt reveal, unveil.

Enthusiasmus [entuzi'asmus] m enthusiasm.

entkernen [ent'kɛrnən] vt stone; core.

entkommen [ent'kɔmən] vi irreg get away, escape (dat, aus from).

entkorken [ent'kɔrkən] vt uncork.

entkräften [ent'krɛftən] vt weaken, exhaust; Argument refute.

entladen [ent'la:dən] irreg vt unload; (Elec) discharge; vr (Elec, Gewehr) discharge; (Ärger etc) vent itself.

entlang [ent'laŋ] prep +acc or dat, ad along; — dem Fluß, den Fluß — along the river; —gehen vi irreg walk along.

entlarven [ent'larfən] vt unmask, expose.

entlassen [ent'lasən] vt irreg discharge; Arbeiter dismiss.

Entlassung f discharge; dismissal.

entlasten [ent'lastən] vt relieve; Achse relieve the load on; Angeklagte exonerate; Konto clear.

Entlastung f relief; (Comm) crediting; —szeuge m defence witness.

entledigen [ent'le:digən] vr: sich jds/einer Sache —rid o.s. of sb/sth.

entleeren [ent'le:rən] vt empty; evacuate.

entlegen [ent'le:gən] a remote.

entlocken [ent'lɔkən] vt elicit (jdm etw sth from sb).

entlüften [ent'lʏftən] vt ventilate.

entmachten [ent'maxtən] vt deprive of power.

entmenscht [ent'mɛnʃt] a inhuman, bestial.

entmilitarisiert [entmilitari'zi:rt] a demilitarized.

entmündigen [ent'mʏndigən] vt certify.

entmutigen [ent'mu:tigən] vt discourage.

Entnahme [ɛnt'na:mə] *f* -, -n removal, withdrawal.

entnehmen [ɛnt'ne:mən] *vt irreg* (+ *dat*) take out (of), take (from); (*folgern*) infer (from).

entpuppen [ɛnt'pupən] *vr* (*fig*) reveal o.s., turn out (als to be).

entrahmen [ɛnt'ra:mən] *vt* skim.

entreißen [ɛnt'raɪsən] *vt irreg* snatch (away) (jdm etw sth from sb).

entrichten [ɛnt'rɪçtən] *vt* pay.

entrosten [ɛnt'rɔstən] *vt* derust.

entrüst- [ɛnt'ryst] *cpd:* —en *vt* incense, outrage; *vr* be filled with indignation; —et *a* indignant, outraged; E—ung *f* indignation.

entsagen [ɛnt'za:gən] *vi* renounce (*dat* sth).

entschädigen [ɛnt'ʃɛ:dɪgən] *vt* compensate.

Entschädigung *f* compensation.

entschärfen [ɛnt'ʃɛrfən] *vt* defuse; *Kritik* tone down.

Entscheid [ɛnt'ʃaɪt] *m* -(e)s, -e decision; e—en *vtir irreg* decide; e—end *a* decisive; *Stimme* casting; —ung *f* decision; —ungsspiel *nt* play-off.

entschieden [ɛnt'ʃi:dən] *a* decided; (*entschlossen*) resolute; E—heit *f* firmness, determination.

entschließen [ɛnt'ʃli:sən] *vr irreg* decide.

entschlossen [ɛnt'ʃlɔsən] *a* determined, resolute; E—heit *f* determination.

Entschluß [ɛnt'ʃlus] *m* decision; e—freudig *a* decisive; —kraft *f* determination, decisiveness.

entschuld- [ɛnt'ʃold] *cpd:* —bar *a* excusable; —igen *vt* excuse; *vr* apologize; E—igung *f* apology; (*Grund*) excuse; jdn um E—igung

bitten apologize to sb; E—igung! excuse me; (*Verzeihung*) sorry.

entschwinden [ɛnt'ʃvɪndən] *vi irreg* disappear.

entsetz- [ɛnt'zɛts] *cpd:* —en *vt* horrify; (*Mil*) relieve; *vr* be horrified *or* appalled; E—en *nt* -s horror, dismay; —lich *a* dreadful, appalling; —t *a* horrified.

entsichern [ɛnt'zɪçərn] *vt* release the safety catch of.

entsinnen [ɛnt'zɪnən] *vr irreg* remember (*gen* sth).

entspannen [ɛnt'ʃpanən] *vtr Körper* relax; (*Pol*) *Lage* ease.

Entspannung *f* relaxation, rest; (*Pol*) détente; —spolitik *f* policy of détente; —sübungen *pl* relaxation exercises *pl*.

entsprechen [ɛnt'ʃprɛçən] *vi irreg* (+ *dat*) correspond to; *Anforderungen*, *Wünschen* meet, comply with; —d *a* appropriate; *ad* accordingly.

entspringen [ɛnt'ʃprɪŋən] *vi irreg* spring (from).

entstehen [ɛnt'ʃte:ən] *vi irreg* arise, result.

Entstehung *f* genesis, origin.

entstellen [ɛnt'ʃtɛlən] *vt* disfigure; *Wahrheit* distort.

entstören [ɛnt'ʃtø:rən] *vt* (*Rad*) eliminate interference from; (*Aut*) suppress.

enttäuschen [ɛnt'tɔyʃən] *vt* disappoint.

Enttäuschung *f* disappointment.

entwaffnen [ɛnt'vafnən] *vt* (*lit,fig*) disarm.

Entwarnung [ɛnt'varnʊŋ] *f* all clear (signal).

entwässer- [ɛnt'vɛsər] *cpd:* —n *vt* drain; E—ung *f* drainage.

entweder ['ɛntveːdər] *cj* either.

entweichen [ɛnt'vaɪçən] *vi irreg* escape.

entweihen [ɛnt'vaɪən] *vt irreg* desecrate.

entwenden [ɛnt'vɛndən] *vt irreg* purloin, steal.

entwerfen [ɛnt'vɛrfən] *vt irreg Zeichnung* sketch; *Modell* design; *Vortrag, Gesetz etc* draft.

entwerten [ɛnt'veːrtən] *vt* devalue; (*stempeln*) cancel.

entwickeln [ɛnt'vɪkəln] *vtr* develop (*auch Phot*); *Mut, Energie* show, display.

Entwickler *m* -s, - developer.

Entwicklung [ɛnt'vɪkluŋ] *f* development; (*Phot*) developing; —sabschnitt *m* stage of development; —shilfe *f* aid for developing countries; —sjahre *pl* adolescence *sing*; —sland *nt* developing country.

entwirren [ɛnt'vɪrən] *vt* disentangle.

entwischen [ɛnt'vɪʃən] *vi* escape.

entwöhnen [ɛnt'vøːnən] *vt* wean; *Süchtige* cure (*dat, von* of).

Entwöhnung *f* weaning; cure, curing.

entwürdigend [ɛnt'vʏrdɪɡənt] *a* degrading.

Entwurf [ɛnt'vurf] *m* outline, design; (*Vertrags—, Konzept*) draft.

entwurzeln [ɛnt'vurtsəln] *vt* uproot.

entziehen [ɛnt'tsiːən] *irreg vt* withdraw, take away (*dat* from); *Flüssigkeit* draw, extract; *vr* escape (*dat* from); (*jds Kenntnis*) be outside; (*der Pflicht*) shirk.

Entziehung *f* withdrawal; —anstalt *f* drug addiction/alcoholism treatment centre; —skur *f* treatment for drug addiction/alcoholism.

entziffern [ɛnt'tsɪfərn] *vt* decipher; decode.

entzücken [ɛnt'tsʏkən] *vt* delight; E— *nt* -s delight; —d *a* delightful, charming.

entzünden [ɛnt'tsʏndən] *vt* light, set light to; (*fig, Med*) inflame; *Streit* spark off; *vr* (*lit, fig*) catch fire; (*Streit*) start; (*Med*) become inflamed.

Entzündung *f* (*Med*) inflammation.

entzwei [ɛnt'tsvaɪ] *ad* broken; in two; —brechen *vti irreg* break in two; —en *vt* set at odds; *vr* fall out; —gehen *vi irreg* break (in two).

Enzian ['ɛntslaːn] *m* -s, -e gentian.

Enzym [ɛn'tsyːm] *nt* -s, -e enzyme.

Epidemie [epide'miː] *f* epidemic.

Epilepsie [epilɛp'siː] *f* epilepsy.

episch ['eːpɪʃ] *a* epic.

Episode [epi'zoːdə] *f* -, -n episode.

Epoche [e'pɔxə] *f* -, -n epoch; —machend *a* epoch-making.

Epos ['eːpɔs] *nt* -s, Epen epic (poem).

er [eːr] *pron* he; it.

erachten [ɛr'axtən] *vt*: — für *or* als consider (to be); meines E—s in my opinion.

erarbeiten [ɛr'arbaɪtən] *vt* (*auch sich* (*dat*) —) work for, acquire; *Theorie* work out.

erbarmen [ɛr'barmən] *vr* have pity *or* mercy (*gen* on); E— *nt* -s pity.

erbärmlich [ɛr'bɛrmlɪç] *a* wretched, pitiful; E—keit *f* wretchedness.

erbarmungs- [ɛr'barmuŋs] *cpd*: —los *a* pitiless, merciless; —voll *a* compassionate; —würdig *a* pitiable, wretched.

erbau- [ɛr'bau] *cpd*: —en *vt* build, erect; (*fig*) edify; E—er *m* -s, -

builder; **—lich** à edifying; **E—ung** f construction; (fig) edification.

Erbe ['ɛrbə] m **-n, -n** heir; nt **-s** inheritance; (fig) heritage; **e—n** vt inherit.

erbeuten [ɛr'bɔytən] vt carry off; (Mil) capture.

Erb- [ɛrb] cpd: **—faktor** m gene; **—fehler** m hereditary defect; **—folge** f (line of) succession; **—in** f heiress.

erbittern [ɛr'bɪtərn] vt embitter; (erzürnen) incense.

erbittert [ɛr'bɪtərt] a Kampf fierce, bitter.

erblassen [ɛr'blasən] vi, **erbleichen** [ɛr'blaiçən] vi irreg (turn) pale.

erblich ['ɛrplɪç] a hereditary.

Erbmasse ['ɛrbmasə] f estate; (Biol) genotype.

erbosen [ɛr'bo:zən] vt anger; vr grow angry.

erbrechen [ɛr'brɛçən] vtr irreg vomit.

Erb- cpd: **—recht** nt right of succession, hereditary right; law of inheritance; **—schaft** f inheritance, legacy.

Erbse ['ɛrpsə] f **-, -n** pea.

Erb- cpd: **—stück** nt heirloom; **—teil** nt inherited trait; (portion of) inheritance.

Erd- ['e:rd] cpd: **—achse** f earth's axis; **—atmosphäre** f earth's atmosphere; **—bahn** f orbit of the earth; **—beben** nt earthquake; **—beere** f strawberry; **—boden** m ground; **—e** f **-, -n** earth; **zu ebener** at ground level; **e—en** vt (Elec) earth.

erdenkbar [ɛr'dɛŋkba:r], **erdenklich** [-lɪç] a conceivable.

Erd- cpd: **—gas** nt natural gas; **—geschoß** nt ground floor;

—kunde f geography; **—nuß** f peanut; **—oberfläche** f surface of the earth; **—öl** nt (mineral) oil.

erdreisten [ɛr'draistən] vr dare, have the audacity (to do sth).

erdrosseln [ɛr'drɔsəln] vt strangle, throttle.

erdrücken [ɛr'drykən] vt crush.

Erd- cpd: **—rutsch** m landslide; **—teil** m continent.

erdulden [ɛr'dʊldən] vt endure, suffer.

ereifern [ɛr'aifərn] vr get excited.

ereignen [ɛr'aignən] vr happen.

Ereignis [ɛr'aignɪs] nt **-ses, -se** event; **e—reich** a eventful.

erfahren [ɛr'fa:rən] vt irreg learn, find out; (erleben) experience; a experienced.

Erfahrung f experience; **e—sgemäß** ad according to experience.

erfassen [ɛr'fasən] vt seize; (fig) (einbeziehen) include, register; (verstehen) grasp.

erfind- [ɛr'fɪnd] cpd: **—en** vt irreg invent; **E—er** m **-s, -** inventor; **—erisch** a inventive; **E—ung** f invention; **E—ungsgabe** f inventiveness.

Erfolg [ɛr'fɔlk] m **-(e)s, -e** success; (Folge) result; **e—en** vi follow; (sich ergeben) result; (stattfinden) take place; (Zahlung) be effected; **e—los** a unsuccessful; **—losigkeit** f lack of success; **e—reich** a successful; **e—versprechend** a promising.

erforder- [ɛr'fɔrdər] cpd: **—lich** a requisite, necessary; **—n** vt require, demand; **E—nis** nt **-ses, -se** requirement; prerequisite.

erforsch- [ɛr'fɔrʃ] cpd: **—en** vt Land explore; Problem investigate; Gewissen search; **E—er** m **-s, -** explorer; investigator; **E—ung** f exploration; investigation; searching.

erfragen [ɛr'fra:gən] vt inquire after, ascertain.

erfreuen [ɛr'frɔʏən] vr: sich — an (+dat) enjoy; **sich einer Sache** (gen) — enjoy sth; vt delight.

erfreulich [ɛr'frɔʏlɪç] a pleasing, gratifying; **—erweise** ad happily, luckily.

erfrieren [ɛr'fri:rən] vi irreg freeze (to death); (Glieder) get frostbitten; (Pflanzen) be killed by frost.

erfrischen [ɛr'frɪʃən] vt refresh.

Erfrischung f refreshment; —sraum m snack bar, cafeteria.

erfüllen [ɛr'fʏlən] vt Raum etc fill; (fig) Bitte etc fulfil; vr come true.

ergänzen [ɛr'gɛntsən] vt supplement, complete; vr complement one another.

Ergänzung f completion; (Zusatz) supplement.

ergattern [ɛr'gatərn] vt (col) get hold of, hunt up.

ergaunern [ɛr'gaʊnərn] vt (col) sich (dat) etw — get hold of sth by underhand methods.

ergeben [ɛr'ge:bən] vt irreg yield, produce; vr surrender; (sich hingeben) give o.s. up, (add to); (folgen) result; a devoted, humble; (dem Trunk) addicted (to); **E—heit** f devotion, humility.

Ergebnis [ɛr'ge:pnɪs] nt -ses, -se result; **e—los** a without result, fruitless.

ergehen [ɛr'ge:ən] irreg vi be issued, go out; **etw über sich — lassen** put up with sth; vi impers: **es ergeht ihm gut/schlecht** he's faring or getting on well/badly; vr: **sich in etw** (dat) — indulge in sth.

ergiebig [ɛr'gi:bɪç] a productive.

ergötzen [ɛr'gœtsən] vt amuse, delight.

ergreifen [ɛr'graɪfən] vt irreg (lit, fig) seize; Beruf take up; Maßnahmen resort to; (rühren) move; **—d** a moving, affecting.

ergriffen [ɛr'grɪfən] a deeply moved.

Erguß [ɛr'gʊs] m discharge; (fig) outpouring, effusion.

erhaben [ɛr'ha:bən] a (lit) raised, embossed; (fig) exalted, lofty; **über etw** (acc) — sein be above sth.

erhalten [ɛr'haltən] vt irreg receive; (bewahren) preserve, maintain; **gut —** in good condition.

erhältlich [ɛr'hɛltlɪç] a obtainable, available.

Erhaltung f maintenance, preservation.

erhängen [ɛr'hɛŋən] vtr hang.

erhärten [ɛr'hɛrtən] vt harden; **These** substantiate, corroborate.

erhaschen [ɛr'haʃən] vt catch.

erheben [ɛr'he:bən] irreg vt raise; Protest, Forderungen make; Fakten ascertain, establish; vr rise (up); **sich über etw** (acc) — rise above sth.

erheblich [ɛr'he:plɪç] a considerable.

erheitern [ɛr'haɪtərn] vt amuse, cheer (up).

Erheiterung f exhilaration; **zur allgemeinen —** to everybody's amusement.

erhellen [ɛr'hɛlən] vt (lit, fig) illuminate; Geheimnis shed light on; vr brighten, light up.

erhitzen [ɛr'hɪtsən] vt heat; vr heat up; (fig) become heated or aroused.

erhoffen [ɛr'hɔfən] vt hope for.

erhöhen [ɛr'hø:ən] vt raise; (verstärken) increase.

erhol- [ɛr'ho:l] cpd: **—en** vr recover; (entspannen) have a rest; **—sam** a restful; **E—ung** f recovery; relaxation, rest; **—ungsbedürftig** a in need of a rest, rundown; **E—ungsheim** nt convalescent/rest home.

erhören [ɛr'hø:rən] vt Gebet etc hear; Bitte etc yield to.

Erika ['e:rika] ka] f -, **Eriken** heather.

erinnern [ɛr'ɪnɔrn] vt remind (an + acc of); vr remember (an etw (acc) sth).

Erinnerung f memory; (Andenken) reminder; **—stafel** f commemorative plaque.

erkalten [ɛr'kaltən] vi go cold, cool (down).

erkält- [ɛr'kɛlt] cpd: **—en** vr catch cold; **—et** a with a cold; **—et sein** have a cold; **E—ung** f cold.

erkenn- [ɛr'kɛn] cpd: **—bar** a recognizable; **—en** vt irreg recognize; (sehen, verstehen) see; **—tlich** a: sich **—tlich** zeigen show one's appreciation; **E—tlichkeit** f gratitude; (Geschenk) token of one's gratitude; **E—tnis** f -, **-se** knowledge; (das Erkennen) recognition; (Einsicht) insight; zur **E—tnis kommen** realize; **E—ung** f recognition; **E—ungsmarke** f identity disc.

Erker ['ɛrkɔr] m -s, - bay; **—fenster** nt bay window.

erklär- [ɛr'klɛ:r] cpd: **—bar** a explicable; **—en** vt explain; **—lich** a explicable; (verständlich) understandable; **E—ung** f explanation; (Aussage) declaration.

erklecklich [ɛr'klɛklɪç] a considerable.

erklingen [ɛr'klɪŋən] vi irreg resound, ring out.

Erkrankung [ɛr'kraŋkʊŋ] f illness.

erkund- [ɛr'kʊnd] cpd: **—en** vt find out, ascertain; (esp Mil) reconnoitre, scout; **—igen** vr inquire (nach about); **E—igung** f inquiry; **E—ung** f reconnaissance, scouting.

erlahmen [ɛr'la:mən] vi tire; (nachlassen) flag, wane.

erlangen [ɛr'laŋən] vt attain, achieve.

Erlaß [ɛr'las] m **-sses**, **-lässe** decree; (Aufhebung) remission.

erlassen [ɛr'lasən] vt irreg Verfügung issue; Gesetz enact; Strafe remit; jdm etw **—** release sb from sth.

erlauben [ɛr'laubən] vt allow, permit (jdm etw sb to do sth); vr permit o.s., venture.

Erlaubnis [ɛr'laupnɪs] f -, **-se** permission.

erläutern [ɛr'lɔytərn] vt explain.

Erläuterung f explanation.

Erle ['ɛrlə] f -, **-n** alder.

erleben [ɛr'le:bən] vt experience; Zeit live through; (mit—) witness; (noch mit—) live to see.

Erlebnis [ɛr'le:pnɪs] nt **-ses**, **-se** experience.

erledigen [ɛr'le:dɪgən] vt take care of, deal with; Antrag etc process; (col: erschöpfen) wear out; (col: ruinieren) finish; (col: umbringen) do in.

erlegen [ɛr'le:gən] vt kill.

erleichter- [ɛr'laiçtɔr] cpd: **—n** vt make easier; (fig) Last lighten; (lindern, beruhigen) relieve; **—t** a relieved; **E—ung** f facilitation; lightening; relief.

erleiden [ɛr'laidən] vt irreg suffer, endure.

erlernbar a learnable.

erlernen [ɛr'lɛrnən] vt learn, acquire.

erlesen [ɛr'leːzən] a select, choice.

erleuchten [ɛr'lɔyçtən] vt illuminate; (fig) inspire.

Erleuchtung f (Einfall) inspiration.

erlogen [ɛr'loːgən] a untrue, made-up.

Erlös [ɛr'løːs] m -es, -e proceeds pl.

erlöschen [ɛr'lœʃən] vi (Feuer) go out; (Interesse) cease, die; (Vertrag, Recht) expire.

erlösen [ɛr'løːzən] vt redeem, save.

Erlösung f release; (Rel) redemption.

ermächtigen [ɛr'mɛçtɪgən] vt authorize, empower.

Ermächtigung f authorization; authority.

ermahnen [ɛr'maːnən] vt exhort, admonish.

Ermahnung f admonition, exhortation.

ermäßigen [ɛr'mɛsɪgən] vt reduce.

Ermäßigung f reduction.

ermessen [ɛr'mɛsən] vt irreg estimate, gauge; E— nt -s estimation; discretion; in jds E-liegen lie within sb's discretion.

ermitteln [ɛr'mɪtəln] vt determine; Täter trace; vi: gegen jdn — investigate sb.

Ermittlung [ɛr'mɪtlʊŋ] f determination; (Polizei-) investigation.

ermöglichen [ɛr'møːklɪçən] vt make possible (dat for).

ermord- [ɛr'mɔrd] cpd: —en vt murder; E—ung f murder.

ermüden [ɛr'myːdən] vti tire; (Tech) fatigue; —d a tiring; (fig) wearisome.

Ermüdung f fatigue; —serscheinung f sign of fatigue.

ermuntern [ɛr'mʊntɐn] vt rouse; (ermutigen) encourage; (beleben)

liven up; (aufmuntern) cheer up.

ermutigen [ɛr'muːtɪgən] vt encourage.

ernähr- [ɛr'nɛːr] cpd: —en vt feed, nourish; Familie support; vr support o.s., earn a living; sich —en von live on; E—er m -s, - breadwinner; E—ung f nourishment; nutrition; (Unterhalt) maintenance.

ernennen [ɛr'nɛnən] vt irreg appoint.

Ernennung f appointment.

erneu- [ɛr'nɔy] cpd: —ern vt renew; restore; renovate; E—erung f renewal; restoration; renovation; —t a renewed, fresh; ad once more.

erniedrigen [ɛr'niːdrɪgən] vt humiliate, degrade.

Ernst [ɛrnst] m -es seriousness; das ist mein — I'm quite serious; im — in earnest; — machen mit etw put sth into practice; e— a serious; —fall m emergency; e—gemeint a meant in earnest, serious; e—haft a serious; e—haftigkeit f seriousness; e—lich a serious.

Ernte ['ɛrntə] f -, -n harvest; —dankfest nt harvest festival; e—n vt harvest; Lob etc earn.

ernüchtern [ɛr'nyçtɐn] vt sober up; (fig) bring down to earth.

Ernüchterung f sobering up; (fig) disillusionment.

Erober- [ɛr'oːbɐr] cpd: —er m -s, - conqueror; e—n vt conquer; —ung f conquest.

eröffnen [ɛr'œfnən] vt open; jdm etw — disclose sth to sb; vr present itself.

Eröffnung f opening; —sansprache f inaugural or opening address.

erogen [ɛro'ge:n] a erogenous.

erörtern [ɛr''œrtərn] vt discuss.

Erörterung f discussion.

Erotik [e'ro:tık] f eroticism.

erotisch a erotic. .

erpicht [ɛr'pıçt] a eager, keen (auf + acc on).

erpress- [ɛr'prɛs] cpd: **—en** vt Geld etc extort; Mensch blackmail; **E—er** m -s, - blackmailer; **E—ung** f blackmail; extortion.

erproben [ɛr'pro:bən] vt test.

erraten [ɛr'ra:tən] vt irreg guess.

erreg- [ɛr're:k] cpd: **—bar** a excitable; (reizbar) irritable; **E—barkeit** f excitability; irritability; **—en** vt excite; (ärgern) infuriate; (hervorrufen) arouse, provoke; **get excited** or worked up; **E—er** m -s, - causative agent; **E—theit** f excitement; (Beunruhigung) agitation; **E—ung** f excitement.

erreichbar a accessible, within reach.

erreichen [ɛr'raıçən] vt reach; Zweck achieve; Zug catch.

errichten [ɛr'rıçtən] vt erect, put up; (gründen) establish, set up.

erringen [ɛr'rıŋən] vt irreg gain, win.

erröten [ɛr'rø:tən] vi blush, flush.

Errungenschaft [ɛr'rʊŋənʃaft] f achievement; (col: Anschaffung) acquisition.

Ersatz [ɛr'zats] m -es substitute; replacement; (Schaden—) compensation; (Mil) reinforcements pl; **—befriedigung** f vicarious satisfaction; **—dienst** m (Mil) alternative service; **—mann** m replacement; (Sport) substitute; **e—pflichtig** a liable to pay compensation; **—reifen** m (Aut) spare tyre; **—teil** nt spare (part).

ersaufen [ɛr'zaufən] vi irreg (col) drown.

ersäufen [ɛr'zɔyfən] vt drown.

erschaffen [ɛr'ʃafən] vt irreg create.

erscheinen [ɛr'ʃaınən] vi irreg appear.

Erscheinung f appearance; (Geist) apparition; (Gegebenheit) phenomenon; (Gestalt) figure.

erschießen [ɛr'ʃi:sən] vt irreg .shoot (dead).

erschlaffen [ɛr'ʃlafən] vi go limp; (Mensch) become- exhausted.

erschlagen [ɛr'ʃla:gən] vt irreg strike ·dead.

erschleichen [ɛr'ʃlaıçən] vt irreg obtain by stealth or dubious methods.

erschöpf- [ɛr'ʃœpf] cpd: **—en** vt exhaust; **—end** a exhaustive, thorough; **—t** a exhausted; **E—ung** f exhaustion.

erschrecken [ɛr'ʃrɛkən] vt startle, frighten; vi irreg be frightened or startled; **—d** a alarming, frightening.

erschrocken [ɛr'ʃrɔkən] a frightened, startled.

erschüttern [ɛr'ʃytərn] vt shake; (ergreifen) move deeply.

Erschütterung f shaking; shock.

erschweren [ɛr'ʃve:rən] vt complicate.

erschwingen [ɛr'ʃvıŋən] vt irreg afford.

erschwinglich a within one's means.

ersehen [ɛr'ze:ən] vt irreg: aus etw —, daß gather from sth that.

ersetz- [ɛr'zɛts] cpd: **—bar** a replaceable; **—en** vt replace; jdm Unkosten etc **—en** pay sb's expenses etc.

ersichtlich [ɛrˈzɪçtlıç] a evident, obvious.

erspar- [ɛrˈʃpaːr] cpd: **—en** vt Ärger etc spare; Geld save: **E—nis** f -, -se saving.

ersprießlich [ɛrˈʃpriːslıç] a profitable, useful; (angenehm) pleasant.

erst [eːrst] ad (at) first; (nicht früher, nur) only; (nicht bis) not till; **—** einmal first.

erstarren [ɛrˈʃtarən] vi stiffen; (vor Furcht) grow rigid; (Materie) solidify.

erstatten [ɛrˈʃtatən] vt Kosten (re)pay; Anzeige etc — report sb; Bericht — make a report.

Erstaufführung [ˈeːrstaʊffyːrʊŋ] f first performance.

erstaunen [ɛrˈʃtaʊnən] vt astonish; vi be astonished; **E—** nt -s astonishment.

erstaunlich a astonishing.

erst- [ˈeːrst] cpd: E-ausgabe f first edition; **—beste(r,s)** a first that comes along; **—e(r,s)** a first.

erstechen [ɛrˈʃtɛçən] vt irreg stab (to death).

erstehen [ɛrˈʃteːən] vt irreg buy; vi (a)rise.

ersteigen [ɛrˈʃtaɪgən] vt irreg climb, ascend.

erstellen [ɛrˈʃtɛlən] vt erect, build.

erst- cpd: **—emal** ad (the) first time; **—ens** ad firstly, in the first place; **—ere(r,s)** pron (the) former.

ersticken [ɛrˈʃtɪkən] vt (lit, fig) stifle; Mensch suffocate; Flammen smother; vi (Mensch) suffocate; (Feuer) be smothered; in Arbeit — be snowed under with work.

Erstickung f suffocation.

erst- cpd: **—klassig** a first-class; E—kommunion f first communion;

—malig a first; **—mals** ad for the first time.

erstrebenswert [ɛrˈʃtreːbənsveːrt] a desirable, worthwhile.

erstrecken [ɛrˈʃtrɛkən] vr extend, stretch.

Ersttags- [ˈeːrst-taːgz] cpd: **—brief** m first-day cover; **—stempel** m first-day (date) stamp.

ersuchen [ɛrˈzuːxən] vt request.

ertappen [ɛrˈtapən] vt catch, detect.

erteilen [ɛrˈtaɪlən] vt give.

ertönen [ɛrˈtøːnən] vi sound, ring out.

Ertrag [ɛrˈtraːk] m -(e)s, ⁼e yield; (Gewinn) proceeds pl; **e—en** vt irreg bear, stand.

erträglich [ɛrˈtrɛːklıç] a tolerable, bearable.

ertränken [ɛrˈtrɛnkən] vt drown.

erträumen [ɛrˈtrɔymən] vt: sich (dat) etw — dream of sth, imagine sth/

ertrinken [ɛrˈtrɪnkən] vi irreg drown; E— nt -s drowning.

erübrigen [ɛrˈyːbrigən] vt spare; vr be unnecessary.

erwachen [ɛrˈvaxən] vi awake.

erwachsen [ɛrˈvaksən] a grown-up; E—e(r) mf adult; E—enbildung f adult education.

erwägen [ɛrˈvɛːgən] vt irreg consider.

Erwägung f consideration.

erwähn- [ɛrˈvɛːn] cpd: **—en** vt mention; **—enswert** a worth mentioning; E—ung f mention.

erwärmen [ɛrˈvɛrmən] vt warm, heat; vr get warm, warm up; sich — für warm to.

erwarten [ɛrˈvartən] vt expect; (warten auf) wait for; etw kaum — können hardly be able to wait for sth.

Erwartung *f* expectation; **e—s- gemäß** *ad* as expected; **e—svoll** *a* expectant.

erwecken [ɛr'vɛkən] *vt* rouse, awake; **den Anschein —** give the impression.

erwehren [ɛr've:rən] *vr* fend, ward (gen off); (des Lachens etc) refrain (gen from).

erweichen [ɛr'vaiçən] *vt* soften.

Erweis [ɛr'vais] *m* **-es, -e** proof; **e—en** *irreg vt* prove; Ehre, Dienst do (jdm sb); **e—** prove (als to be).

Erwerb [ɛr'vɛrp] *m* **-(e)s, -e** acquisition; (Beruf) trade; **e—en** *vt irreg* acquire; **e—slos** *a* unemployed; **—squelle** *f* source of income; **e—stätig** *a* (gainfully) employed; **e—sunfähig** *a* unemployable.

erwidern ·[ɛr'vi:dərn] *vt* reply; (vergelten) return.

erwiesen [ɛr'vi:zən] *a* proven.

erwischen [ɛr'vɪʃən] *vt* (col) catch, get.

erwünscht [ɛr'vynʃt] *a* desired.

erwürgen [ɛr'vyrgən] *vt* strangle.

Erz [e:rts] *nt* **-es, -e** ore.

erzähl- [ɛr'tsɛ:l] *cpd:* **—en** *vt* tell; **E—er** *m* **-s, -** narrator; **E—ung** *f* story, tale.

Erz- *cpd:* **—bischof** *m* archbishop; **—engel** *m* archangel.

erzeug- [ɛr'tsɔyg] *cpd:* **—en** *vt* produce; (Strom) generate; **E—er- preis** *m* producer's price; **E—nis** *nt* **-ses, -se** product, produce; **E—ung** *f* production; generation.

erziehen [ɛr'tsi:ən] *vt irreg* bring up; (bilden) educate, train.

Erziehung *f* bringing up; (Bildung) education; **—sbeihilfe** *f* educational grant; **—sberechtigte(r)** *mf* parent;

guardian; **—sheim** *nt* approved school.

erzielen [ɛr'tsi:lən] *vt* achieve, obtain; Tor score.

erzwingen [ɛr'tsvɪŋən] *vt irreg* force, obtain by force.

es [ɛs] *pron* nom, acc it.

Esche ['ɛʃə] *f* **-, -n** ash.

Esel ['e:zəl] *m* **-s, -** donkey, ass; **—sohr** *nt* dog-ear.

Eskalation [ɛskalatsi'o:n] *f* escalation.

eßbar ['ɛsba:r] *a* eatable, edible.·

essen ['ɛsən] *vti irreg* eat; **E—** *nt* **-s, -** meal; food; **E—szeit** *f* mealtime; dinner time.

Essig ['ɛsɪç] *m* **-s, -e** vinegar; **—gurke** *f* gherkin.

Eß- ['ɛs] *cpd:* **—kastanie** *f* sweet chestnut; **—löffel** *m* tablespoon; **—tisch** *m* dining table; **—waren** *pl* victuals *pl*, food provisions *pl*; **—zimmer** *nt* dining room.

etablieren [eta'bli:rən] *vr* become established; set up business.

Etage [e'ta:ʒə] *f* **-, -n** floor, storey; **—nbetten** *pl* bunk beds *pl*; **—nwohnung** *f* flat.

Etappe [e'tapə] *f* **-, -n** stage.

Etat [e'ta:] *m* **-s, -s** budget; **—jahr** *nt* financial year; **—posten** *m* budget item.

etepetete [e:tape'te:tə] *a* (col) fussy.

Ethik ['e:tik] *f* ethics sing.

ethisch ['e:tɪʃ] *a* ethical.

Etikett [eti'kɛt] *nt* **-(e)s, -e** label; tag; **—e** *f* etiquette, manners *pl*; **e—ieren** [-'ti:rən] *vt* label; tag.

etliche ['ɛtlɪçə] *pron pl* some, quite a few; **—s** *s* a thing or two.

Etui [ɛt'vi:] *nt* **-s, -s** case.

etwa ['ɛtva] *ad* (ungefähr) about; (vielleicht) perhaps; (beispielsweise) for instance; **nicht —** by no

means; **—ig** ['ɛtva-ɪç] a possible;
—s pron something; anything; (*ein
wenig*) a little; ad a little.
Etymologie [etymolo'giː] f etymology.
euch [ɔʏç] pron acc of **ihr** you;
yourselves; dat of **ihr** (to) you.
euer ['ɔʏər] pron gen of **ihr** of you;
pron your; **—e(r,s)** yours.
Eule ['ɔʏlə] f -, -n owl.
eure(r,s) ['ɔʏrə(r,z)] pron your;
yours; **-rseits** ad on your part;
—sgleichen pron people like you;
—twegen, —twillen ad (*für euch*)
for your sakes; (*wegen euch*) on
your account.
eurige pron: **der/die/das —** yours.
Euro- [ɔʏro] cpd: **—krat** [-'kraːt] m
-en, -en eurocrat; **—pameister**
[ɔʏ'roːpa-] m European champion.
Euter ['ɔʏtər] nt -s, - udder.
evakuieren [evaku'iːrən] vt evacuate.
evangelisch [evaŋ'geːlɪʃ] a Protestant.
Evangelium [evaŋ'geːlium] nt gospel.
Eva(s)kostüm ['eːfa(s)kɔstyːm]
nt: **im —** in one's birthday suit.
eventuell [eventu'ɛl] a possible; ad
possibly, perhaps.
EWG [eː'veː'geː] f - EEC, Common
Market.
ewig ['eːvɪç] a eternal; **E—keit** f
eternity.
exakt [ɛ'ksakt] a exact.
Examen [ɛ'ksaːmən] nt -s, - or
Examina exam(ination).
Exempel [ɛ'ksɛmpəl] nt -s, -
example.
Exemplar [ɛksɛm'plaːr] nt -s, -e
specimen; (*Buch—*) copy; **e—isch**
a exemplary.

exerzieren [ɛksɛr'tsiːrən] vi drill.
Exil [ɛ'ksiːl] nt **-s, -e** exile.
Existenz [ɛksis'tɛnts] f existence;
(*Unterhalt*) livelihood, living; (*pej:
Mensch*) character; **—kampf** m
struggle for existence; **—minimum**
nt **-s** subsistence level.
existieren [ɛksis'tiːrən] vi exist.
exklusiv [ɛksklu'ziːf] a exclusive;
—e [-'ziːvə] a, prep **+gen**
exclusive of, not including.
exorzieren [ɛksɔr'tsiːrən] vt exorcize.
exotisch [ɛ'ksoːtɪʃ] a exotic.
Expansion [ɛkspanzi'oːn] f expansion.
Expedition [ɛkspediitsi'oːn] f expedition; (*Comm*) forwarding department.
Experiment [ɛksperi'mɛnt] nt
experiment; **e—ell** [-'tɛl] a experimental; **e—ieren** [-'tiːrən] vi experiment.
Experte [ɛks'pɛrtə] m -n, -n expert,
specialist.
explo- [ɛksplo] cpd: **—dieren**
[-'diːrən] vi explode; **E—sion**
[ɛksplozi'oːn] f explosion; **—siv**
[-'ziːf] a explosive.
Exponent [ɛkspo'nɛnt] m exponent.
Export [ɛks'pɔrt] m - (e)s, -e
export; **—eur** [-'tøːr] m exporter;
—handel m export trade; **e—ieren**
[-'tiːrən] vt export; **-land** nt
exporting country.
Expreß- [ɛks'prɛs] cpd: **—gut** nt
express goods pl or freight; **—zug**
m express (train).
extra ['ɛkstra] a inv (col:
gesondert) separate; (besondere)
extra; ad (gesondert) separately;
(speziell) specially; (absichtlich)
on purpose; (vor Adjektiven,
zusätzlich) extra; **E—** nt **-s, -s**

extra; E—ausgabe f, E—blatt nt special edition.

Extrakt [eks'trakt] m -(e)s, -e extract.

extrem [eks'tre:m] a extreme; —istisch [-'mɪstɪʃ] a (Pol) extremist; E—itäten [-'tɛːtən] pl

extremities pl.

Exzellenz [ekstsɛ'lɛnts] f excellency.

exzentrisch [eks'tsɛntrɪʃ] a. eccentric.

Exzeß [eks'tsɛs] m -sses, -sse excess.

F

F, f [ef] nt F, f.

Fabel ['faːbəl] f -, -n fable; **f—haft** a fabulous, marvellous.

Fabrik [fa'briːk] f factory; —ant [-'kant] m (Hersteller) manufacturer; (Besitzer) industrialist; —arbeiter m factory worker; —at [-'kaːt] nt -(e)s, -e manufacture, product; —ation [-atsi'oːn] f manufacture, production; —besitzer m factory owner; —gelände nt factory premises pl.

Fach [fax] nt -(e)s, =er compartment; (Sachgebiet) subject; ein Mann vom — an expert; —arbeiter m skilled worker; —arzt m (medical) specialist; —ausdruck m technical term.

Fächer ['fɛçər] m -s, - fan.

Fach- cpd: **f—kundig** a expert, specialist; **f—lich** a professional; expert; **—mann** m, pl -leute specialist; **—schule** f technical college; **f—simpeln** vi talk ˢshop; **—werk** nt timber frame.

Fackel ['fakəl] f -, -n torch; **f—n** vi (col) dither.

fad(e) [faːt, faːdə] a insipid; (langweilig) dull.

Faden ['faːdən] m -s, ⁼ thread; —nudeln pl vermicelli pl; **f—scheinig** a (lit, fig) threadbare.

fähig ['fɛːɪç] a capable (zu, gen of); able; **F—keit** f ability.

Fähnchen ['fɛːnçən] nt pennon, streamer.

fahnden ['faːndən] vi: — nach search for.

Fahndung f search; —sliste f list of wanted criminals, wanted list.

Fahne ['faːnə] f -, -n flag, standard; eine — haben (col) smell of drink; —nflucht f desertion.

Fahrbahn f carriageway (Brit), roadway.

Fähre ['fɛːrə] f -, -n ferry.

fahren ['faːrən] irreg vt drive; Rad ride; (befördern) drive, take; Rennen drive in; vi (sich bewegen) go; (Schiff) sail; (abfahren) leave; mit dem Auto/Zug — go or travel by car/train; mit der Hand — über (+acc) pass one's hand over.

Fahr- cpd: **—er** m -s, - driver; **—erflucht** f hit-and-run; **—gast** m passenger; **—geld** nt fare; **—gestell** nt chassis; (Aviat) undercarriage; **—karte** f. ticket; **—kartenausgabe** f, **—kartenschalter** m ticket office; **f—lässig** a negligent; **f—lässige Tötung** manslaughter; **—lässigkeit** f negligence; **—lehrer** m driving instructor; **—plan** m timetable;

f—planmäßig a (Rail) scheduled; —preis m fare; —prüfung f driving test; —rad nt bicycle; —schein m ticket; —schule f driving school; —schüler(in f) m learner (driver); —stuhl m lift, elevator (US).

Fahrt [fa:rt] f -, -en journey; (kurz) trip; (Aut) drive; (Geschwindigkeit) speed.

Fährte ['fɛːrtə] f -, -n track, trail.

Fahrt- cpd: —kosten pl travelling expenses pl; —richtung f course, direction.

Fahr- cpd: —zeug nt vehicle; —zeughalter m -s, - owner of a vehicle.

Fak- [fak] cpd: f—tisch a actual; —tor m factor; —tum nt -s, -ten fact; —ul'tät f faculty.

Falke ['falkə] m -n, -n falcon.

Fall [fal] m -(e)s, ⁼e (Sturz) fall; (Sachverhalt, Jur, Gram) case; auf jeden —, auf alle ⁼e in any case; (bestimmt) definitely; —e f -, -n trap; f—en vi irreg fall; etw f—en lassen drop sth.

fällen ['fɛlən] vt Baum fell; Urteil pass.

fallenlassen vt irreg Bemerkung make; Plan abandon, drop.

fällig ['fɛlɪç] a due; F—keit f (Comm) maturity.

Fall- cpd: —obst nt fallen fruit, windfall; **f—s** ad in case, if; —schirm m parachute; —schirmjäger pl, —schirmtruppe f paratroops pl; —schirmspringer m parachutist; —tür f trap door.

falsch [falʃ] a false; (unrichtig) wrong.

fälschen ['fɛlʃən] vt forge.

Fälscher m -s, - forger.

Falsch- cpd: —geld nt counterfeit money; —heit f falsity, falseness; (Unrichtigkeit) wrongness.

fälsch- cpd: —lich a false; —licherweise ad mistakenly; F—ung f forgery.

Fältchen ['fɛltçən] nt crease, wrinkle.

Falte ['faltə] f -, -n (Knick) fold, crease; (Haut—) wrinkle; (Rock—) pleat; f—n vt fold; Stirn wrinkle; f—nlos a without folds, without wrinkles.

familiär [famili'ɛːr] a familiar.

Familie [fa'miːliə] f family; —nähnlichkeit f family resemblance; —nkreis m family circle; —nname m surname; —nstand m marital status; —nvater m head of the family.

Fanatiker [fa'naːtikər] m -s, - fanatic.

fanatisch a fanatical.

Fanatismus [fana'tɪsmʊs] m fanaticism.

Fang [faŋ] m -(e)s, ⁼e catch; (Jagen) hunting; (Kralle) talon, claw; f—en irreg vt catch; vr get caught; (Flugzeug) level out; (Mensch: nicht fallen) steady o.s.; (fig) compose o.s.; (in Leistung) get back on form.

Farb- ['farb] cpd: —abzug m coloured print; —aufnahme f colour photograph; —band m typewriter ribbon; —e f -, -n colour; (zum Malen etc) paint; (Stoff—) dye; f—echt a colourfast.

färben ['fɛrbən] vt colour; Stoff, Haar dye.

farben- ['farbən] cpd: —blind a colour-blind; —froh, —prächtig a colourful, gay.

Farb- cpd: —fernsehen nt colour television; —film m colour film; f—ig a coloured; —ige(r) m/f coloured; —kasten m paint-box; f—los a colourless; —photographie

f colour photography; **—stift** *m* coloured pencil; **—stoff** *m* dye; **—ton** *m* hue, tone.

Färbung ['fɛrbʊŋ] *f* colouring; (*Tendenz*) bias.

Farn [farn] *m* **-(e)s, -e, —kraut** *nt* fern; bracken.

Fasan [fa'zaːn] *m* **-(e)s, -e(n)** pheasant.

Fasching ['faʃɪŋ] *m* **-s, -e** *or* **-s** carnival.

Faschismus [fa'ʃɪsmʊs] *m* fascism.

Faschist *m* fascist.

faseln ['faːzəln] *vi* talk nonsense, drivel.

Faser ['faːzər] *f* **-, -n** fibre; **f—n** *vi* fray.

Faß [fas] *nt* **-sses, Fässer** vat, barrel; (*Öl*) drum; **Bier vom —** draught beer; **f—bar** *a* comprehensible; **—bier** *nt* draught beer.

fassen ['fasən] *vt* (*ergreifen*) grasp, take; (*inhaltlich*) hold; (*Entschluß etc*) take; (*verstehen*) understand; **Ring etc** set; (*formulieren*) formulate, phrase; **nicht zu —** unbelievable; *vr* calm down.

faßlich ['faslɪç] *a* intelligible.

Fassung ['fasʊŋ] *f* (*Umrahmung*) mounting; (*Lampen—*) socket; (*Wortlaut*) version; (*Beherrschung*) composure; **jdn aus der — bringen** upset sb; **f—slos** *a* speechless; **—svermögen** *nt* capacity; (*Verständnis*) comprehension.

fast [fast] *ad* almost, nearly.

fasten ['fastən] *vi* fast; **F— -s** fasting; **F—zeit** *f* Lent.

Fastnacht *f* Shrove Tuesday; carnival.

fatal [fa'taːl] *a* fatal; (*peinlich*) embarrassing.

faul [faʊl] *a* rotten; **Person** lazy; **Ausreden** lame; **daran ist etwas —** there's sth fishy about it; **—en** *vi* rot; **—enzen** *vi* idle; **F—enzer** *m* **-s, -** idler, loafer; **F—heit** *f* laziness; **—ig** *a* putrid.

Fäulnis ['fɔylnɪs] *f* **-** decay, putrefaction.

Faust [faʊst] *f* **-, Fäuste** fist; **—handschuh** *m* mitten.

Favorit [favo'riːt] *m* **-en, -en** favourite.

Februar ['feːbruaːr] *m* **-(s), -e** February.

fechten ['fɛçtən] *vi irreg* fence.

Feder ['feːdər] *f* **-, -n** feather; (*Schreib—*) pen nib; (*Tech*) spring; **—ball** *m* shuttlecock; **—ballspiel** *nt* badminton; **—bett** *nt* continental quilt; **—halter** *m* penholder, pen; **f—leicht** *a* light as a feather; **f—n** *vi* (*nachgeben*) be springy; (*sich bewegen*) bounce; *vt* spring; **—ung** *f* suspension; **—vieh** *nt* poultry.

Fee [feː] *f* **-, -n** fairy; **f—nhaft** ['feːən-] *a* fairylike.

Fege- ['feːgə] *cpd:* **—feuer** *nt* purgatory; **f—n** *vt* sweep.

fehl [feːl] **a: — am Platz** *or* **Ort** out of place; **—en** *vi* be wanting *or* missing; (*abwesend sein*) be absent; **etw fehlt jdm** sb lacks sth; **du fehlst mir** I miss you; **was fehlt ihm?** what's wrong with him?; **F—er** *m* **-s, -** mistake, error; (*Mangel, Schwäche*) fault; **—erfrei** *a* faultless; **without any mistakes**; **—erhaft** *a* incorrect; faulty; **F—geburt** *f* miscarriage; **—gehen** *vi irreg* go astray; **F—griff** *m* blunder; **F—konstruktion** *f* badly designed thing; **F—schlag** *m* failure; **—schlagen** *vi irreg* fail; **F—schluß** *m* wrong conclusion;

F—start *m* (Sport) false start; F—tritt *m* false move; (fig) blunder, slip; F—zündung *f* (Aut) misfire, backfire.

Feier ['faɪər] *f* -, -n celebration; —abend *m* time to stop work; —abend machen stop, knock off; was machst du am —abend? what are you doing after work?; jetzt ist —abend! that's enough!; f—lich *a* solemn; —lichkeit *f* solemnity; *pl* festivities *pl*; f—n *vti* celebrate; —tag *m* holiday.

feig(e) ['faɪg(ə)] *a* cowardly; F—e *f* -, -n fig; F—heit *f* cowardice; F—ling *m* coward.

Feil- [faɪl] *cpd*: —e *f* -, -n file; f—en *vti* file; f—schen *vi* haggle.

fein [faɪn] *a* fine; (vornehm) refined; *Gehör etc* keen; —! great! F—e(s) *nt* long-distance call; F—glas *nt* binoculars *pl*; —halten *vtr irreg* keep away; F—lenkung *f* remote control; —liegen *vi irreg*; jdm —liegen be far from sb's mind; F—rohr *nt* telescope; F—schreiber *m* teleprinter; —schriftlich *a* by telex; F—sehapparat *nt* television set; —sehen *vi irreg* watch television; F—sehen *nt* -s television; im F—sehen on television; F—seher *m* television; F—sprecher *m* telephone; F—sprechzelle *f* telephone box or booth (US).

Feind [faɪnt] *m* -(e)s, -e enemy; f—lich *a* hostile; —schaft *f* enmity; f—selig *a* hostile; —seligkeit *f* hostility.

Fein- *cpd*: f—fühlend, f—fühlig *a* sensitive; —gefühl *nt* delicacy, tact; —heit *f* fineness; refinement; keenness; —kostgeschäft *nt* delicatessen (shop); —schmecker *m* -s, - gourmet.

feist [faɪst] *a* fat.

Feld [fɛlt] *nt* -(e)s, -er field; (Schach) square; (Sport) pitch; —blume *f* wild flower; —herr *m* commander; —webel *m* -s, - sergeant; —weg *m* path; —zug *m* (lit, fig) campaign.

Felge ['fɛlgə] *f* -, -n (wheel) rim; —nbremse *f* caliper brake.

Fell [fɛl] *nt* -(e)s, -e fur; coat; (von Schaf) fleece; (von toten Tieren) skin.

Fels [fɛls] *m* -en, -en, **Felsen** ['fɛlzən] *m* -s, - rock; (von Dover etc) cliff; f—enfest *a* firm;

—envorsprung *m* ledge; f—ig *a* rocky; —spalte *f* crevice.

feminin [femi'ni:n] *a* feminine; (pej) effeminate.

Fenster ['fɛnstər] *nt* -s, - window; —brett *nt* windowsill; —laden *m* shutter; —putzer *m* -s, - window cleaner; —scheibe *f* windowpane; —sims *m* windowsill.

Ferien ['fe:riən] *pl* holidays *pl*, vacation (US); — haben be on holiday; —kurs *m* holiday course; —reise *f* holiday trip; —zeit *f* holiday period.

Ferkel ['fɛrkəl] *nt* -s, - piglet.

fern [fɛrn] *a,ad* far-off, distant; von hier a long way (away) from here; F—amt *nt* (Tel) exchange; F—bedienung *f* remote control; F—e *f* -, -n distance; —er *a,ad* further; (weiterhin) in future; F—flug *m* long-distance flight; F—gespräch *nt* trunk call; F—glas *nt* binoculars *pl*; —halten *vtr irreg* keep away; F—lenkung *f* remote control; —liegen *vi irreg*; jdm —liegen be far from sb's mind; F—rohr *nt* telescope; F—schreiber *m* teleprinter; —schriftlich *a* by telex; F—sehapparat *nt* television set; —sehen *vi irreg* watch television; F—sehen *nt* -s television; im F—sehen on television; F—seher *m* television; F—sprecher *m* telephone; F—sprechzelle *f* telephone box or booth (US).

Ferse ['fɛrzə] *f* -, -n heel.

fertig ['fɛrtɪç] *a* (bereit) ready; (beendet) finished; (gebrauchs—) ready-made; F—bau *m* prefab(ricated house); —bringen *vt irreg* (fähig sein) manage, be capable of; (beenden) finish; F—keit *f* skill; —machen *vt* (beenden) finish; (col) Person finish; (körperlich) exhaust; (*moralisch*) get down; *vr* get ready; —stellen *vt* complete; F—ware *f* finished product.

Fessel ['fɛsəl] *f* -, -n fetter; f—n *vt* bind; (*mit Fesseln*) fetter; (*fig*) spellbind; f—nd *a* fascinating, captivating.

fest [fɛst] *a* firm; *Nahrung* solid; *Gehalt* regular; ad schlafen soundly; F— *nt* -(e)s, -e party; festival; —angestellt *a* permanently employed; F—beleuchtung *f* illumination; —binden *vt irreg* tie, fasten; —bleiben *vi irreg* stand firm; F—essen *nt irreg* banquet; —fahren *vr irreg* get stuck; —halten *irreg vt* seize, hold fast; *Ereignis* record; *vr* hold on (an +*dat* to); —igen *vt* strengthen; F—igkeit *f* strength; —klammern *vr* cling on (an +*dat* to); F—land *nt* mainland; —legen *vt* fix; *vr* commit o.s.; —lich *a* festive; —machen *vt* fasten; *Termin etc* fix; F—nahme *f* -, -n capture; —nehmen *vt irreg* capture, arrest; F—rede *f* address; —schnallen *vt* strap down; *vr* fasten one's seat belt; —setzen *vt* fix, settle; F—spiel *nt* festival; —stehen *vi irreg* be certain; —stellen *vt* establish; (*sagen*) remark; F—ung *f* fortress.

Fett [fɛt] *nt* -(e)s, -e fat, grease; f— *a* fat; *Essen etc* greasy; f—arm *a* low fat; f—en *vt* grease; —fleck *m* grease spot or stain; f—gedruckt *a* bold-type; —gehalt *m* fat content; f—ig *a* greasy, fatty; —näpfchen *nt*: ins —näpfchen treten put one's foot in it.

Fetzen ['fɛtsən] *m* -s, - scrap.

feucht [fɔʏçt] *a* damp; *Luft* humid; F—igkeit *f* dampness; humidity.

Feuer ['fɔʏər] *nt* -s, - fire; (*zum Rauchen*) a light; (*fig: Schwung*) spirit; —alarm *m* fire alarm; —eifer *m* zeal; f—fest *a* fireproof; —gefahr *f* danger of fire; f—gefährlich *a* inflammable; —leiter *f* fire escape ladder; —löscher *m* -s, - fire-extinguisher; —melder *m* -s, - fire alarm; f—n *vti* (*lit, fig*) fire; f—sicher *a* fireproof; —stein *m* flint; —wehr *f* -, -en fire brigade; —werk *nt* fireworks *pl*; —zeug *nt* (cigarette) lighter.

Fichte ['fɪçtə] *f* -, -n spruce, pine.

fidel [fi'deːl] *a* jolly.

Fieber ['fiːbər] *nt* -s, - fever, temperature; f—haft *a* feverish; —messer *m*, —thermometer *nt* thermometer.

fies [fiːs] *a* (col) nasty.

Figur [fi'guːr] *f* -, -en figure; (*Schach*) chessman, chess piece.

Filiale [fili'aːlə] *f* -, -n (Comm) branch.

Film [fɪlm] *m* -(e)s, -e film; —aufnahme *f* shooting; f—en *vti* film; —kamera *f* cine-camera; —vorführgerät *nt* cine-projector.

Filter ['fɪltər] *m* -s, - filter; f—n *vt* filter; —mundstück *nt* filter tip; —papier *nt* filter paper; —zigarette *f* tipped cigarette.

Filz [fɪlts] *m* -es, -e felt; f—en *vt* (col) frisk; *vi* (*Wolle*) mat.

Finale [fi'naːlə] *nt* -s, -(s) finale; (Sport) final(s).

Finanz [fi'nants] *f* finance; —amt *nt* Inland Revenue Office; —beamte(r) *m* revenue officer; f—iell [-tsi'ɛl] *a* financial; f—ieren ['tsiːrən] *vt* finance; —minister *m* Chancellor of the Exchequer (Brit), Minister of Finance.

Find- ['find] *cpd:* **f—en** *irreg vt* find; (*meinen*) think; *vr·* be (found); (*sich fassen*) compose o.s.; ich finde nichts dabei, wenn ...; I don't see what's wrong if ...; das wird sich **f—en** things will work out; **—er** *m* -s, - finder; **—erlohn** *m* reward; **f—ig** *a* resourceful.

Finger ['fiŋər] *m* -s, - finger; **—abdruck** *m* fingerprint; **—handschuh** *m* glove; **—hut** *m* thimble; (*Bot*) foxglove; **—ring** *m* ring; **—spitze** *f* fingertip; **—zeig** *m* -(e)s, -e hint, pointer.

fingieren [fiŋ'gi:rən] *vt* feign.

fingiert a made-up, fictitious.

Fink ['fiŋk] *m* -en, -en finch.

finster ['finstər] *a* dark, gloomy; (*verdächtig*) dubious; (*verdrossen*) grim; *Gedanke* dark; **F—nis** *f* -, darkness, gloom.

Finte ['fintə] *f* -, -n feint, trick.

firm [firm] *a* well-up; **F—a** *f* -, -men firm; **F—eninhaber** *m* owner of firm; **F—enschild** *nt* (shop) sign; **F—enzeichen** *nt* registered trademark.

Firnis ['firnis] *m* -ses, -se varnish.

Fisch [fiʃ] *m* -(e)s, -e fish; *pl* (*Astrol*) Pisces; **f—en** *vti* fish; **—er** *m* -s, - fisherman; **—erei** *f* fishing, fishery; **—fang** *m* fishing; **—geschäft** *nt* fishmonger's (shop); **—gräte** *f* fishbone; **—zug** *m* catch or draught of fish.

fix [fiks] *a* fixed; *Person* alert, smart; **— und fertig** finished; (*erschöpft*) done in; **—ieren** [fi'ksi:rən] *vt* fix; (*anstarren*) stare at.

flach [flax] *a* flat; *Gefäß* shallow.

Fläche ['flɛçə] *f* -, -n area; (*Ober—*) surface; **—ninhalt** *m* surface area.

Flach- *cpd:* **—heit** *f* flatness; shallowness; **—land** *nt* lowland.

flackern ['flakərn] *vi* flare, flicker.

Flagge ['flagə] *f* -, -n flag.

flagrant [fla'grant] *a* flagrant; **in —i** red-handed.

Flamme ['flamə] *f* -, -n flame.

Flanell [fla'nɛl] *m* -s, -e flannel.

Flanke ['flaŋkə] *f* -, -n flank; (*Sport: Seite*) wing.

Flasche ['flaʃə] *f* -, -n bottle (*col: Versager*) wash-out; **—nbier** *nt* bottled beer; **—nöffner** *m* bottle opener; **—nzug** *m* pulley.

flatterhaft *a* flighty, fickle.

flattern ['flatərn] *vi* flutter.

flau [flau] *a* weak, listless; *Nachfrage* slack; jdm ist — sb feels queasy.

Flaum [flaum] *m* -(e)s (*Feder*) down; (*Haare*) fluff.

flauschig ['flauʃiç] *a* fluffy.

Flausen ['flauzən] *pl* silly ideas *pl*; (*Ausflüchte*) weak excuses *pl*.

Flaute ['flautə] *f* -, -n calm; (*Comm*) recession.

Flechte ['flɛçtə] *f* -, -n plait; (*Med*) dry scab; (*Bot*) lichen; **f—n** *vt* *irreg* plait; *Kranz* twine.

Fleck [flɛk] *m* -(e)s, -e, **Flecken** *m* -s, - spot; (*Schmutz—*) stain; (*Stoff—*) patch; (*Makel*) blemish; nicht vom — kommen (*lit, fig*) not get any further; vom — weg straight away; **f—enlos** *a* spotless; **—enmittel** *nt*, **—enwasser** *nt* stain remover; **f—ig** *a* spotted; stained.

Fledermaus ['fle:dərmaus] *f* bat.

Flegel ['fle:gəl] *m* -s, - flail; (*Person*) lout; **f—haft** *a* loutish, unmannerly; **—jahre** *pl* adolescence; **f—n** *vr* lounge about.

flehen ['fle:ən] *vi* implore; **—tlich** *a* imploring.

Fleisch ['flaɪʃ] nt -(e)s flesh; (*Essen*) meat; —brühe f beef tea, stock; —er m -s, - butcher; —e'rei f butcher's (shop); f—ig a fleshy; —pastete f meat pie; —wolf m mincer; —wunde f flesh wound.

Fleiß ['flaɪs] m -es diligence, industry; f—ig a diligent, industrious.

flektieren [flɛk'tiːrən] vt inflect.

flennen ['flɛnən] vi (col) cry, blubber.

fletschen ['flɛtʃən] vt Zähne show.

flexibel [flɛ'ksiːbəl] a flexible.

Flicken ['flɪkən] m -s, - patch; f— vt mend.

Flieder ['fliːdər] m -s, - lilac.

Fliege ['fliːgə] f -, -n fly; (*Kleidung*) bow tie; f—n vti irreg fly; auf jdn/etw f—en (col) be mad about sb/sth; —npilz m toadstool; —r m -s, ⊦ flier, airman; —ralarm m air-raid warning.

fliehen ['fliːən] vi irreg flee.

Fliese ['fliːzə] f -, -n tile.

Fließ ['fliːs] cpd: —arbeit f pro-duction-line work; —band nt pro-duction or assembly line; f—en vi irreg flow; f—end a flowing; Rede, Deutsch fluent; Übergänge smooth; —heck nt fastback; —papier nt blotting paper.

flimmern ['flɪmərn] vi glimmer.

flink [flɪŋk] a nimble, lively; F—heit f nimbleness, liveliness.

Flinte ['flɪntə] f -, -n rifle; shotgun.

Flitter ['flɪtər] m -s, - spangle, tinsel; —wochen pl honeymoon.

flitzen ['flɪtsən] vi flit.

Flocke ['flɔkə] f -, -n flake.

flockig a flaky.

Floh [floː] m -(e)s, ⁼e flea.

florieren [flo'riːrən] vi flourish.

Floskel ['flɔskəl] f -, -n empty phrase.

Floß [floːs] nt -es, ⁼e raft, float.

Flosse ['flɔsə] f -, -n fin.

Flöte ['fløːtə] f -, -n flute; (*Block*—) recorder.

Flötist(in f) [fløːtɪst(m)] m flautist.

flott [flɔt] a lively; (*elegant*) smart; (*Naut*) afloat; F—e f -, -n fleet, navy.

Flöz [fløːts] nt -es, -e layer, seam.

Fluch [fluːx] m -(e)s, ⁼e curse; f—en vi curse; swear.

Flucht [fluxt] f -, -en flight; (*Fenster*—) row; (*Reihe*) range; (*Zimmer*—) suite; f—artig a hasty.

flücht- ['flʏçt] cpd: —en vir flee, escape; —ig a fugitive; (Chem) volatile; (*vergänglich*) transitory; (*oberflächlich*) superficial; (*eilig*) fleeting; F—igkeit f transitoriness; volatility; superficiality; F—ig-keitsfehler m careless slip; F—ling m fugitive, refugee.

Flug [fluːk] m -(e)s, ⁼e flight; im — airborne, in flight; —abwehr ['fluːg-] f anti-aircraft defence; —blatt nt pamphlet.

Flügel ['flyːgəl] m -s, - wing; (*Mus*) grand piano.

Fluggast m airline passenger.

flügge ['flyːgə] a (fully-)fledged.

Flug- cpd: —geschwindigkeit f flying or air speed; —gesellschaft f airline (company); —hafen m air-port; —höhe f altitude (of flight); —plan m flight schedule; —platz m airport; (*klein*) airfield; —post f airmail; —s [floːks] ad speedily; —schrift f pamphlet; —strecke f air route; —verkehr m air traffic; —wesen nt aviation; —zeug nt (aero)plane, airplane (*US*); —zeugentführung f hijacking of a

plane; **—zeughalle** f hangar;
—zugträger m aircraft carrier.

Flunder ['flʊndər] f -, -n flounder.

flunkern ['flʊŋkərn] vi fib, tell
stories.

Fluor ['fluːɔr] nt -s fluorine.

Flur [fluːr] m -(e)s, -e hall;
(Treppen—) staircase.

Fluß [flʊs] -sses, -sse river;
(Fließen) flow; im **—** sein (fig) be
in a state of flux.

flüssig ['flʏsɪç] a liquid; **—** machen
vt Geld make available; F—keit f
liquid; (Zustand) liquidity.

flüster- ['flʏstər] cpd: **—n** vti
whisper; F—propaganda f whisper-
ing campaign.

Flut [fluːt] f -, -en (lit, fig) flood;
(Gezeiten) high tide; f—en vti
flood; **—licht** nt floodlight.

Fohlen ['foːlən] nt -s, **-** foal.

Föhn [føːn] m -(e)s, -e foehn,
warm south wind.

Föhre ['føːrə] f -, -n Scots pine.

Folge ['fɔlgə] f -, -n series,
sequence; (Fortsetzung) instalment; (Auswirkung) result; in
rascher **—** in quick succession; etw
zur **—** haben result in sth; **—n**
haben have consequences; einer
Sache **—** leisten comply with sth;
f—n vi follow (jdm sb)
(gehorchen) obey (jdm sb); jdm
f—n können (fig) follow or understand sb; f—nd a following;
f—ndermaßen ad as follows, in the
following way; f—nreich, f—n-
schwer a momentous; f—richtig a
logical; f—rn vt conclude (aus
+dat from); **—rung** f conclusion;
f—widrig a illogical.

folg- cpd: **—lich** ad consequently;
—sam a obedient.

Folie ['foːliə] f -, -n foil.

Folter ['fɔltər] f -, -n torture;
(Gerät) rack; f—n vt torture.

Fön® [føːn] m -(e)s, -e hair-dryer;
f—en vt (blow) dry.

Fontäne [fɔn'tɛːnə] f -, -n fountain.

foppen ['fɔpən] vt tease.

Förder- ['fœrdər] cpd: **—band** nt
conveyor belt; **—korb** m pit cage;
f—lich a beneficial.

fordern ['fɔrdərn] vt demand.

Förder- cpd: f—n vt promote;
(unterstützen) help; Kohle
extract; **—ung** f promotion; help;
extraction.

Forderung ['fɔrdərʊŋ] f demand.

Forelle [fo'rɛlə] f trout.

Form [fɔrm] f -, -en shape;
(Gestaltung) form; (Guß—)
mould; (Back—) baking tin; in **—**
sein be in good form or shape; in
— von in the shape of; f—alisieren
vt formalize; **—alität** f formality;
—at [-'maːt] nt -(e)s, -e format;
(fig) distinction; **—ation** f formation; f—bar a malleable; **—el** f -,
-n formula; f—ell [-'mɛl] a formal;
f—en vt form, shape; **—fehler** m
faux-pas, gaffe; (Jur) irregularity;
f—ieren [-'miːrən] vt form; vr form
up.

förmlich ['fœrmlɪç] a formal; (col)
real; F—keit f formality.

Form- cpd: f—los a shapeless;
Benehmen etc informal; **—ular** nt
-s, -e form; f—ulieren vt formulate.

forsch [fɔrʃ] a energetic, vigorous;
—en vt search (nach for); vi
(wissenschaftlich) (do) research;
—end a searching; F—er m -s, **-**,
research scientist; (Natur—)
explorer.

Forschung ['fɔrʃʊŋ] f research;
—sreise f scientific expedition.

Forst [fɔrst] m -(e)s, -e forest;
—arbeiter m forestry worker;

—wesen nt, —wirtschaft f forestry.
Förster ['fœrstər] m -s, - forester;
(für Wild) gamekeeper.
fort [fɔrt] ad away; (verschwunden) gone; (vorwärts) on;
und so — and so on; in einem —
on and on; —bestehen vi irreg
survive; —bewegen vtr move
away; —bilden vr continue one's
education; —bleiben vi irreg stay
away; —bringen vt irreg take
away; F—dauer f continuance;
—fahren vi irreg depart; (fortsetzen) go on, continue; —führen
vt continue, carry on; —gehen vi
irreg go away; —geschritten a
advance; —kommen vi irreg get
on; (wegkommen) get away;
—können vi irreg be able to get
away;.—müssen vi irreg have to
go; —pflanzen vr reproduce;
F—pflanzung f reproduction;
—schaffen vt remove; —schreiten
vi irreg advance.
Fortschritt ['fɔrt-ʃrɪt] m advance;
—e machen make progress; f—lich
ad progressive.
fort- cpd: —setzen vt continue;
F—setzung f continuation; (folgender Teil) instalment; F—setzung
folgt to be continued; —während
a incessant; continual; —ziehen
irreg vt pull away; vi move on;
(umziehen) move away.
Foto ['fo:to] nt -s, -s photo(graph),
m -s, -s (—apparat) camera;
—graf m photographer; —gra'phie
f photography; (Bild) photograph,
f—gra'phieren vt photograph; vi
take photographs.
Foul nt -s, -s foul.
Fracht [fraxt] f -, -en freight;
(Naut) cargo; (Preis) carriage;
—er m -s, - freighter, cargo boat;
—gut nt freight.

Frack [frak] m -(e)s, =e tails pl.
Frage ['fra:gə] f -, -n question;
etw in — stellen question sth; jdm
eine — stellen ask sb a question,
put a question to sb; nicht in —
kommen be out of the question;
—bogen m questionnaire; f—n vti
ask; —zeichen nt question mark.
frag- cpd: —lich a questionable,
doubtful; —los ad unquestionably.
Fragment [fra'gmɛnt] nt fragment; f—arisch [-'ta:rɪʃ] a fragmentary.
fragwürdig ['fra:kvyrdɪç] a
questionable, dubious.
Fraktion [fraktsi'o:n] f parliamentary party.
frank [frank] a frank, candid;
—ieren [-'ki:rən] vt stamp, frank;
—o ad post-paid; carriage paid.
Franse ['franzə] f -, -n fringe; f—n
vi fray.
Fratze ['fratsə] f -, -n grimace.
Frau [frau] f -, -en woman;
(Ehe—) wife; (Anrede) Mrs; —
Doktor Doctor; —enarzt m
gynaecologist; —enbewegung f
feminist movement; —enzimmer nt
· female, broad (US).
Fräulein ['frɔylaɪn] nt young lady;
(Anrede) Miss.
fraulich ['fraulɪç] a womanly.
frech [frɛç] a cheeky, impudent;
F—dachs m cheeky monkey;
F—heit f cheek, impudence.
Fregatte [fre'gatə] f frigate.
frei [frai] a free; Stelle, Sitzplatz
auch vacant; Mitarbeiter freelance; Geld available; (unbekleidet) bare; sich (dat) einen Tag
— nehmen take a day off; von etw
— sein be free of sth; im F—en
in the open air; —sprechen talk
without notes; F—bad nt open-air
swimming pool; —bekommen a

irreg: jdn/einen Tag —bekommen get sb freed/get a day off; F—er *m* -s, - suitor; —gebig a generous; F—gebigkeit *f* generosity; —halten *vt irreg* keep free; —händig *ad* fahren with no hands; F—heit *f* freedom; —heitlich a liberal; F—heitsstrafe *f* prison sentence; —heraus *ad* frankly; F—karte *f* free ticket; —kommen *vi irreg* get free; —lassen *vt irreg* (set) free; F—lauf *m* freewheeling; —legen *vt* expose; —lich *ad* certainly, admittedly; ja —lich yes of course; F—lichtbühne *f* open-air theatre; —machen *vt* Post frank; Tage —machen take days off; *vr* arrange to be free; —sinnig a liberal; —sprechen *vt irreg* acquit (*von* of); F—spruch *m* acquittal; —stellen *vt:* jdm etw —stellen leave sth (up) to sb; F—stoß *m* free kick; F—tag *m* Friday; —tags *ad* on Fridays; F—übungen *pl* (physical) exercises *pl;* —willig a voluntary; F—willige(r) *mf* volunteer; F—zeit *f* spare or free time; —zügig a liberal, broad-minded; (*mit Geld*) generous.

fremd [frɛmt]* a (*unvertraut*) strange; (*ausländisch*) foreign; (*nicht eigen*) someone else's; etw ist jdm — sth is foreign to sb; —artig a strange; F—e(r) [ˈfrɛmdə(r)] *mf* stranger; (*Ausländer*) foreigner; F—enführer *m* (tourist) guide; F—enlegion *f* foreign legion; F—enverkehr *m* tourism; F—enzimmer *nt* guest room; F—körper *m* foreign body; —ländisch a foreign; F—ling *m* stranger; F—sprache *f* foreign language; —sprachig a foreign-language; F—wort *nt* foreign word.

Frequenz [freˈkvɛnts] *f* (*Rad*) frequency.

fressen [ˈfrɛsən] *vti irreg* eat.

Freude [ˈfrɔydə] *f* -, -n joy, delight.

freudig a joyful, happy.

freudlos a joyless.

freuen [ˈfrɔyən] *vt impers* make happy *or* pleased; *vr* be glad *or* happy; **sich auf etw** (*acc*) — look forward to sth; **sich über etw** (*acc*) — be pleased about sth.

Freund [frɔynt] *m* -(e)s, -e friend; boyfriend; f—in [-dɪn] *f* friend; girlfriend; f—lich a kind, friendly; f—licherweise *ad* kindly; —lichkeit *f* friendliness, kindness; —schaft *f* friendship; f—schaftlich a friendly.

Frevel [ˈfreːfəl] *m* -s, - crime, offence (*an* + *dat* against); f—haft a wicked.

Frieden [ˈfriːdən] *m* -s, - peace; im — in peacetime; —sschluß *m* peace agreement; —sverhandlungen *pl* peace negotiations *pl;* —svertrag *m* peace treaty; —szeit *f* peacetime.

fried- [friːt] *cpd:* —fertig a peaceable; F—hof *m* cemetery; —lich a peaceful.

frieren [ˈfriːrən] *vti irreg* freeze; ich friere, es friert mich I am freezing, I'm cold.

Fries [friːs] *m* -es, -e (*Archit*) frieze.

frigid(e) [friˈgiːt, friˈgiːdə] a frigid.

Frikadelle [frikaˈdɛlə] *f* meatball.

frisch [frɪʃ] a fresh; (*lebhaft*) lively; — gestrichen! wet paint!; sich — machen freshen (o.s.) up; F—e *f* freshness, liveliness.

Friseur [friˈzøːr] *m*, **Friseuse** [friˈzøːzə] *f* hairdresser.

Frisier- [fri'zi:r] cpd: f—en vtr do (one's hair); (fig) Abrechnung fiddle, doctor; —salon m hairdressing salon; —tisch m dressing table.

Frisör [fri'zø:r] m -s, -e hairdresser.

Frist [frɪst] f -, -en period; (Termin) deadline; f—en vt Dasein lead; (kümmerlich) eke out; f—los a Entlassung instant.

Frisur [fri'zu:r] f hairdo, hairstyle.

fritieren [fri'ti:rən] vt deep fry.

frivol [fri'vo:l] a frivolous.

froh [fro:] a happy, cheerful; ich bin —, daß ... I'm glad that ...

fröhlich ['frø:lɪç] a merry, happy; F—keit f merriness, gaiety.

froh- cpd: —'locken vi exult; (pej) gloat; F—sinn m cheerfulness.

fromm [frɔm] a pious, good; Wunsch idle.

Frömm- ['frœm] cpd: —e'lei f false piety; —igkeit f piety.

frönen ['frø:nən] vi indulge (etw (dat) in sth).

Fronleichnam [fro:n'laiçna:m] m -(e)s Corpus Christi.

Front [frɔnt] f -, -en front; f—al [frɔn'ta:l] a frontal.

Frosch [frɔʃ] m -(e)s, -e frog; (Feuerwerk) squib; —mann m frogman; —schenkel m frog's leg.

Frost [frɔst] m -(e)s, -e frost; —beule f chilblain.

frösteln ['frœstəln] vi shiver.

Frost- cpd: f—ig a frosty; —schutzmittel nt anti-freeze.

Frottee [fro'te:] nt or m -(s), -s towelling.

frottieren [fro'ti:rən] vt rub, towel.

Frottier(hand)tuch nt towel.

Frucht [fruxt] f -, -e (lit, fig) fruit; (Getreide) corn; f—bar, f—bringend a fruitful, fertile; —barkeit f fertility; f—en vi be of use; f—los

a fruitless; —saft m fruit juice.

früh [fry:] a, ad early; heute — this morning; F—aufsteher m -s, - early riser; F—e f - early morning; —er a earlier; (ehemalig) former; ad formerly; —er war das anders that used to be different; —estens ad at the earliest; F—geburt f premature birth/baby; F—jahr nt, F—ling m spring; —reif a precocious; F—stück nt breakfast; —stücken vi (have) breakfast; —zeitig a early; (pej) untimely.

frustrieren [frus'tri:rən] vt frustrate.

Fuchs [fuks] m -es, -e fox; f—en (col) vt rile, annoy; vr be annoyed; f—teufelswild a hopping mad.

Füchsin ['fyksɪn] f vixen.

fuchteln ['fuxtəln] vi gesticulate wildly.

Fuge ['fu:gə] f -, -n joint; (Mus) fugue.

fügen ['fy:gən] vt place, join; vr be obedient (in + acc to); (anpassen) adapt oneself (in + acc to); impers happen.

fügsam ['fy:kza:m] a obedient.

fühl- ['fy:l] cpd: —bar a perceptible, noticeable; —en vtir feel; F—er m -s, -feeler.

führen ['fy:rən] vt lead; Geschäft run; Name bear; Buch keep; vi lead; vr behave.

Führer ['fy:rər] m -s, - leader; (Fremden—) guide; —schein m driving licence.

Fuhrmann ['fu:rman] m, pl -leute carter.

Führung ['fy:rʊŋ] f leadership; (eines Unternehmens) management; (Mil) command; (Benehmen) conduct; (Museums—) conducted tour; —szeugnis nt certificate of good conduct.

Fuhrwerk ['fu:rverk] nt cart.
Fülle ['fylə] f - wealth, abundance;
f—n vtr fill; (Cook) stuff; —n nt
-s, - foal; —r m -s, -, Füllfederhalter m fountain pen.
Füllung f filling; (Holz—) panel.
fummeln ['fumɔln] vi (col) fumble.
Fund [funt] m -(e)s, -e find;
—ament [-da'ment] nt foundation;
f—amen'tal a fundamental; —büro
nt lost property office, lost and
found; —grube f (fig) treasure
trove; f—ieren ['di:rən] vt back
up; f—iert a sound.
fünf [fynf] num five; —hundert
num five hundred; —te num fifth;
F—tel nt -s, - fifth; —zehn num
fifteen; —zig num fifty.
fungieren [fuŋ'gi:rən] vi function;
(Person) act.
Funk [fuŋk] m -s radio, wireless;
—e(n) m -ns, -n (lit, fig) spark;
f—eln vi sparkle; f—en vt radio;
—er m -s, - radio operator; —gerät
nt radio set; —haus nt broadcasting centre; —spruch m radio
signal; —station f radio station.
Funktion [fuŋktsi'o:n] f function;
f—ieren ['ni:rən] vi work, function.
für [fy:r] prep +acc for; was —
what kind or sort of; das F— und
Wider the pros and cons pl; Schritt
— Schritt step by step; F—bitte
f intercession.
Furche ['furçə] f -, -n furrow; f—n
vt furrow.
Furcht [furçt] f - fear; f—bar a
terrible, frightful.
fürcht- ['fyrçt] cpd: —en vt be
afraid of, fear; vr be afraid (vor
+dat of); —erlich a awful.

furcht- cpd: —los a fearless;
—sam a timid.
füreinander [fy:r'ai'nandər] ad for
each other.
Furnier [fur'ni:r] nt -s, -e veneer.
fürs [fy:rs] = für das.
Fürsorge ['fy:rzɔrgə] f care;
(Sozial—) welfare; —amt nt
welfare office; —r(in f) m -s, -
welfare worker; —unterstützung f
social security, welfare benefit (US).
Für- cpd: —sprache f recommendation; (um Gnade) intercession;
—sprecher m advocate.
Fürst [fyrst] m -en, -en prince;
—in f princess; —entum nt princi-
pality; f—lich a princely.
Furt [furt] f -, -en ford.
Fürwort ['fy:rvɔrt] nt pronoun.
Fuß [fu:s] m -es, -e foot; (von
Glas, Säule etc) base; (von Möbel)
leg; zu — on foot; —ball m football; —ballspiel nt football match;
—ballspieler m footballer; —boden
m floor; —bremse f (Aut) foot-
brake; f—en vi rest, be based (auf
+dat on); —ende nt foot;
—gänger(in f) m -s, - pedestrian;
—gängerzone f pedestrian precinct; —note f footnote;
—pfleger(in f) m chiropodist;
—spur f footprint; —tritt m kick;
(Spur) footstep; —weg m footpath.
Futter ['futər] nt -s, - fodder, feed;
(Stoff) lining; —al [-'ra:l] nt -s, -e
case.
füttern ['fytərn] vt feed; Kleidung
line.
Futur [fu'tu:r] nt -s, -e future.

G

G, g [ge:] *nt* G, g.
Gabe ['ga:bə] *f* -, -n gift.
Gabel ['ga:bəl] *f* -, -n fork;
—frühstück *nt* mid-morning snack;
—ung *f* fork.
gackern ['gakərn] *vi* cackle.
gaffen ['gafən] *vi* gape.
Gage ['ga:ʒə] *f* -, -n fee; salary.
gähnen ['gɛ:nən] *vi* yawn.
Gala ['gala] *f* - formal dress;
—vorstellung *f* (*Theat*) gala performance.
galant [ga'lant] *a* gallant, courteous.
Galerie [galə'ri:] *f* gallery.
Galgen ['galgən] *m* -s, - gallows
pl; —frist *f* respite; —humor *m*
macabre humour.
Galle ['galə] *f* -, -n gall; (*Organ*)
gall-bladder.
Galopp [ga'lɔp] *m* -s, -s *or* -e
gallop; g—ieren [-'pi:rən] *vi* gallop.
galvanisieren [galvani'zi:rən] *vt*
galvanize.
Gamasche [ga'maʃə] *f* -, -n gaiter;
(*kurz*) spat.
Gammler ['gamlər] *m* -s, - loafer,
layabout.
Gang [gaŋ] *m* -(e)s, ⁼e walk;
(*Boten*—) errand; (—*art*) gait;
(*Abschnitt eines Vorgangs*)
operation; (*Essens*—, *Ablauf*)
course; (*Flur etc*) corridor;
(*Durch*—) passage; (*Tech*) gear; in
— bringen start up; (*fig*) get off
the ground; in — sein be in
operation; (*fig*) be underway;
[gɛ:] f -,-⁏ gang; g— ä: g— und
gäbe usual, normal; g—bar *a*
passable; *Methode* practicable.

Gängel- ['gɛŋəl] *cpd*: —band *nt*:
jdn am —band halten (*fig*) spoonfeed sb; g—n *vt* spoonfeed.
gängig ['gɛŋɪç] *a* common, current;
Ware in demand, selling well.
Ganove [ga'no:və] *m* -s, -n (*col*)
crook.
Gans [gans] *f* -, ⁼e goose.
Gänse- ['gɛnzə] *cpd*: —blümchen *nt*
daisy; —braten *m* roast goose;
—füßchen *pl* (*col*) inverted commas
pl (*Brit*), quotes *pl*; —haut *f* goose
pimples *pl*; —marsch *m*: im
—marsch in single file; —rich *m*
-s, -e gander.
ganz [gants] *a* whole; (*vollständig*)
complete; — Europa all Europe;
sein —es Geld all his money; *ad*
quite; (*völlig*) completely; — und
gar nicht not at all; es sieht — so
aus it really looks like it; aufs G—e
gehen go for the lot.
gänzlich ['gɛntslɪç] *a,ad* complete(ly), entire(ly).
gar [ga:r] *a* cooked, done; *ad* quite;
— nicht/nichts/keiner not/nothing/nobody at all; — nicht schlecht
not bad at all.
Garage [ga'ra:ʒə] *f* -, -n garage.
Garantie [garan'ti:] *f* guarantee;
g—ren *vt* guarantee.
Garbe ['garbə] *f* -, -n sheaf; (*Mil*)
burst of fire.
Garde ['gardə] *f* -, -n guard(s); die
alte — the old guard; —robe *f* -,
-n wardrobe; (*Abgabe*) cloakroom;
—robenfrau *f* cloakroom
attendant; —robenständer *m* hallstand.

Gardine [gar'di:nə] f curtain.

gären ['gɛ:rən] vi irreg ferment.

Garn [garn] nt -(e)s, -e thread; yarn (auch fig).

Garnele [gar'ne:lə] f -, -n shrimp, prawn.

garnieren [gar'ni:rən] vt decorate; Speisen garnish.

Garnison [garni'zo:n] f -, -en garrison.

Garnitur [garni'tu:r] f (Satz) set; (Unterwäsche) set of (matching) underwear; (fig) erste — top rank; zweite — second rate.

garstig ['garstɪç] a nasty, horrid.

Garten ['gartən] m -s, = garden; —arbeit f gardening; —bau m horticulture; —fest nt garden party; —gerät nt gardening tool; —haus nt summerhouse; —kresse f cress; —lokal nt beer garden; —schere f pruning shears pl; —tür f garden gate.

Gärtner(in f) ['gɛrtnər(ɪn)] m -s, - gardener; —ei [-'raɪ] f nursery; (Gemüse-) market garden (Brit), truck farm (US); g—n vi garden.

Gärung ['gɛ:rʊŋ] f fermentation.

Gas [ga:s] nt -es, -e gas; — geben (Aut) accelerate, step on the gas; g—förmig a gaseous; —herd m, —kocher m gas cooker; —leitung f gas pipeline; —maske f gasmask; —pedal nt accelerator, gas pedal.

Gasse ['gasə] f -, -n lane, alley; —njunge m street urchin.

Gast [gast] m -es, -̈e guest; —arbeiter(in f) m foreign worker.

Gästebuch ['gɛstəbu:x] nt visitors' book, guest book.

Gast- cpd: g—freundlich a hospitable; —geber m -s, - host; —geberin f hostess; —haus nt, —hof m hotel, inn; g—ieren [-'ti:rən] vi (Theat) (appear as a) guest; g—lich a hospitable; —lichkeit f hospitality; —rolle f guest role.

gastronomisch [gastro'no:mɪʃ] a gastronomic(al).

Gast- cpd: —spiel nt (Sport) away game; —stätte f restaurant; pub; —wirt m innkeeper; —wirtschaft f hotel, inn; —zimmer nt (guest) room.

Gas- cpd: —vergiftung f gas poisoning; —werk nt gasworks sing or pl; —zähler m gas meter.

Gatte ['gatə] m -n, -n husband, spouse; die —n husband and wife.

Gatter ['gatər] nt -s, - railing, grating; (Eingang) gate.

Gattin f wife; spouse.

Gattung ['gatʊŋ] f genus; kind.

Gaukler ['gaʊklər] m -s, - juggler, conjurer.

Gaul [gaʊl] m -(e)s, Gäule horse; nag.

Gaumen ['gaʊmən] m -s, - palate.

Gauner ['gaʊnər] m -s, - rogue; —ei [-'raɪ] f swindle.

Gaze ['ga:zə] f -, -n gauze.

Gebäck [gə'bɛk] nt -(e)s, -e pastry.

Gebälk [gə'bɛlk] nt -(e)s timberwork.

Gebärde [gə'bɛ:rdə] f -, -n gesture; g—n vr behave.

gebären [gə'bɛ:rən] vt irreg give birth to, bear.

Gebärmutter f uterus, womb.

Gebäude [gə'bɔʏdə] nt -s, - building; —komplex m (building) complex.

Gebein [gə'baɪn] nt -(e)s, -e bones pl.

Gebell [gə'bɛl] nt -(e)s barking.

geben ['ge:bən] irreg vti (jdm etw) give (sb sth or sth to sb); Karten deal; ein Wort gab das andere one angry word led to another; **v impers es gibt there** is/are; there will be; **gegeben** given; **zu gegebener Zeit** in good time; **vr** (*sich verhalten*) behave, act; (*aufhören*) abate; **sich geschlagen —** admit defeat; **das wird sich schon —** that'll soon sort itself out.

Gebet [gə'be:t] *nt* -(e)s, -e prayer.

Gebiet [gə'bi:t] *nt* -(e)s, -e area; (*Hoheits—*) territory; (*fig*) field; **g—en** *vt irreg* command, demand; **—er** *m* -s, - master; (*Herrscher*) ruler; **g—erisch** *a* imperious.

Gebilde [gə'bɪldə] *nt* -s, - object, structure; **g—t** *a* cultured, educated.

Gebimmel [gə'bɪməl] *nt* -s (continual) ringing.

Gebirge [gə'bɪrgə] *nt* -s, - mountain chain.

gebirgig *a* mountainous.

Gebirgszug [gə'bɪrkstsu:k] *m* mountain range.

Gebiß [gə'bɪs] *nt* -sses, -sse teeth *pl*; (*künstlich*) dentures *pl*.

geblümt [gə'bly:mt] *a* flowery.

Geblüt [gə'bly:t] *nt* -(e)s blood, race.

geboren [gə'bo:rən] *a* born; **Frau** née.

geborgen [gə'bɔrgən] *a* secure, safe.

Gebot [gə'bo:t] *nt* -(e)s, -e command(ment *Bibl*); (*bei Auktion*) bid.

Gebräu [gə'brɔy] *nt* -(e)s, -e brew, concoction.

Gebrauch [gə'braux] *m* -(e)s, **Gebräuche** use; (*Sitte*) custom; **g—en** *vt* use.

gebräuchlich [gə'brɔyçlɪç] *a* usual, customary.

Gebrauchs- *cpd*: **—anweisung** *f* directions *pl* for use; **—artikel** *m*

article of everyday use; **g—fertig** *a* ready for use; **—gegenstand** *m* commodity.

gebraucht [gə'brauxt] *a* used; **G—wagen** *m* secondhand *or* used car.

gebrechlich [gə'breçlɪç] *a* frail; **G—keit** *f* frailty.

Gebrüder [gə'bry:dər] *pl* brothers *pl*.

Gebrüll [gə'brʏl] *nt* -(e)s roaring.

Gebühr [gə'by:r] *f* -, -en charge, fee; **nach —** fittingly; **über —** unduly; **g—en** *vi*: **jdm g—en** be sb's due *or* due to sb; *vr* be fitting; **g—end** *a,ad* fitting(ly), appropriate(ly); **—enlaß** *m* remission of fees; **—enermäßigung** *f* reduction of fees; **g—enfrei** *a* free of charge; **g—enpflichtig** *a* subject to charges.

Geburt [gə'bu:rt] *f* -, -en birth; **—enbeschränkung** *f*, **—enkontrolle** *f*, **—enregelung** *f* birth control; **—enziffer** *f* birth-rate.

gebürtig [gə'bʏrtɪç] *a* born in, native of; **—e Schweizerin** native of Switzerland, Swiss-born.

Geburts- *cpd*: **—anzeige** *f* birth notice; **—datum** *nt* date of birth; **—jahr** *nt* year of birth; **—ort** *m* birthplace; **—tag** *m* birthday; **—urkunde** *f* birth certificate.

Gebüsch [gə'bʏʃ] *nt* -(e)s, -e bushes *pl*.

Gedächtnis [gə'dɛçtnɪs] *nt* -ses,-se memory; **—feier** *f* commemoration; **—schwund** *m* loss of memory, failing memory; **—verlust** *m* amnesia.

Gedanke [gə'daŋkə] *m* **-ns, -n** thought; **sich über etw** (*acc*) **—n machen** think about sth; **—naustausch** *m* exchange of ideas; **g—nlos** *a* thoughtless; **—nlosigkeit**

f thoughtlessness; **—nstrich** *m* dash; **—nübertragung** *f* thought transference, telepathy; **g—nverloren** a lost in thought; **g—nvoll** a thoughtful.

Gedärm [gə'dɛrm] *nt* **-(e)s, -e** intestines *pl*, bowels *pl*.

Gedeck [gə'dɛk] *nt* **-(e)s, -e** cover(ing); (*Speisenfolge*) menu; **ein —** auflegen lay a place.

gedeihen [gə'daɪən] *vi irreg* thrive, prosper.

gedenken [gə'dɛŋkən] *vi irreg* (*sich erinnern*) (+gen) remember; (*beabsichtigen*) intend.

Gedenk- *cpd*: **—feier** *f* commemoration; **—minute** *f* minute's silence; **—tag** *m* remembrance day.

Gedicht [gə'dɪçt] *nt* **-(e)s, -e** poem.

gediegen [gə'di:gən] a (a good) quality; *Mensch* reliable, honest; **G—heit** *f* quality; reliability, honesty.

Gedränge [gə'dɛŋkə] *nt* **-s.** crush, crowd; **ins —** kommen (*fig*) get into difficulties.

gedrängt a compressed; **— voll** packed.

gedrungen [gə'drʊŋən] a thickset, stocky.

Geduld [gə'dʊlt] *f* - patience; **g—en** [gə'dʊldən] *vr* be patient; **g—ig** a patient, forbearing; **—sprobe** *f* trial of (one's) patience.

gedunsen [gə'dʊnzən] a bloated.

geeignet [gə''aɪgnət] a suitable.

Gefahr [gə'fa:r] *f* -, **-en** danger; **—** laufen, etw zu tun run the risk of doing sth; **auf eigene —** at one's own risk.

gefährden [gə'fɛ:rdən] *vt* endanger.

Gefahren- *cpd*: **—quelle** *f* source

of danger; **—zulage** *f* danger money.

gefährlich [gə'fɛ:rlɪç] a dangerous.

Gefährte [gə'fɛ:rtə] *m* **-n, -n,** **Gefährtin** *f* companion.

Gefälle [gə'fɛlə] *nt* **-s, -** gradient, incline.

Gefallen [gə'falən] *m* **-s, -** favour; *nt* **-s** pleasure; **an etw** (*dat*) **—** finden derive pleasure from sth; **jdm etw zu —** tun do sth to please sb; **g—** *vi irreg*: **jdm g—** please sb; **er/es gefällt mir** I like him/it; **das gefällt mir an ihm** that's one thing I like about him; **sich** (*dat*) **etw g—** lassen put up with sth; *ptp of* fallen.

gefällig [gə'fɛlɪç] a (*hilfsbereit*) obliging; (*erfreulich*) pleasant; **G—keit** *f* favour; helpfulness; **etw aus G—keit** tun do sth as a favour. **gefälligst** ad kindly.

gefangen [gə'faŋən] a captured; (*fig*) captivated; **G—e(r)** *m* prisoner, captive; **G—enlager** *nt* prisoner-of-war camp; **—halten** *vt irreg* keep prisoner; **G—nahme** *f* -, **-n** capture; **G—schaft** *f* captivity.

Gefängnis [gə'fɛŋnɪs] *nt* **-ses, -se** prison; **—strafe** *f* prison sentence; **—wärter** *m* prison warder.

Gefasel [gə'fa:zəl] *nt* **-s** twaddle, drivel.

Gefäß [gə'fɛ:s] *nt* **-es, -e** vessel (*auch Anat*), container.

gefaßt [gə'fast] a composed, calm; **auf etw** (*acc*) **— sein** be prepared or ready for sth.

Gefecht [gə'fɛçt] *nt* **-(e)s, -e fight;** (*Mil*) engagement.

gefeit [gə'faɪt] a: **gegen etw — sein** be immune to sth.

Gefieder [gə'fi:dər] *nt* **-s, ▪**

plumage, feathers *pl*; **g—t** *a* feathered.

gefleckt [gə'flɛkt] *a* spotted, mottled.

geflissentlich [gə'flɪsəntlɪç] *a,ad* intentional(ly).

Geflügel [gə'fly:gəl] *nt* -s poultry.

Gefolge [gə'fɔlgə] *nt* -s, - retinue.

Gefolg- *cpd*: **—schaft** *f* following; (*Arbeiter*) personnel; **—smann** *m* follower.

gefragt [gə'fra:kt] *a* in demand.

gefräßig [gə'frɛ:sɪç] *a* voracious.

Gefreite(r) [gə'fraɪtə(r)] *m* -n, -n lance corporal; (*Naut*) able seaman; (*Aviat*) aircraftman.

gefrieren [gə'fri:rən] *vi irreg* freeze.

Gefrier- *cpd*: **—fach** *nt* icebox; **—fleisch** *nt* frozen meat; **g—getrocknet** *a* freeze-dried; **—punkt** *m* freezing point; **—schutzmittel** *nt* antifreeze; **—truhe** *f* deep-freeze.

Gefüge [gə'fy:gə] *nt* -s, - structure.

gefügig *a* pliant; *Mensch* obedient.

Gefühl [gə'fy:l] *nt* -(e)s, -e feeling; etw im — haben have a feel for sth; **—los** *a* unfeeling; **g—sbetont** *a* emotional; **—sduselei** [-zdu:zə'laɪ] *f* emotionalism; **g—smäßig** *a* instinctive.

gegebenenfalls [gə'ge:bənənfals] *ad* if need be.

gegen ['ge:gən] *prep +acc* against; (*in Richtung auf, jdn betreffend, kurz vor*) towards; (*im Austausch für*) (in return) for; (*ungefähr*) round about; **G—angriff** *m* counterattack; **G—beweis** *m* counterevidence.

Gegend ['ge:gənt] *f* -, -en area, district.

Gegen- *cpd*: **g—ei'nander** *ad* against one another; **—fahrbahn** *f*

oncoming carriageway; **—frage** *f* counter-question; **—gewicht** *nt* counterbalance; **—gift** *nt* antidote; **—leistung** *f* service in return; **—lichtaufnahme** *f* contre-jour photograph; **—maßnahme** *f* counter-measure; **—probe** *f* crosscheck; **—satz** *m* contrast; **—sätze** überbrücken overcome differences; **g—sätzlich** *a* contrary, opposite; (*widersprüchlich*) contradictory; **—schlag** *m* counter attack; **—seite** *f* opposite side; (*Rückseite*) reverse; **g—seitig** *a* mutual, reciprocal; **sich g—seitig helfen** help each other; **—seitigkeit** *f* reciprocity; **—spieler** *m* opponent; **—stand** *m* object; **g—ständlich** *a* objective, concrete; **—stimme** *f* vote against; **—stoß** *m* counterblow; **—stück** *nt* counterpart; **—teil** *nt* opposite; **im —teil** on the contrary; **ins —teil umschlagen** swing to the other extreme; **g—teilig** *a* opposite, contrary.

gegenüber [ge:gən''y:bar] *prep +dat* opposite; (*zu*) to(wards); (*angesichts*) in the face of; *ad* opposite; **G—** *nt* -s, - person opposite; **—liegen** *vr irreg* face each other; **—stehen** *vr irreg* be opposed (to each other); **—stellen** *vt* confront; (*fig*) contrast; **G—stellung** *f* confrontation; (*fig*) contrast; **—treten** *vi irreg* (*+dat*) face.

Gegen- *cpd*: **—verkehr** *m* oncoming traffic; **—vorschlag** *m* counterproposal; **—wart** *f* present; **g—wärtig** *a* present; **das ist mir nicht mehr g—wärtig** that has slipped my mind; *ad* at present; **—wert** *m* equivalent; **—wind** *m* headwind; **—wirkung** *f* reaction; **g—zeichnen** *vti* countersign; **—zug**

m counter-move; (*Rail*) corresponding train in the other direction.

Gegner ['ge:gnɐr] *m* -s, - opponent; **g—isch** *a* opposing; **—schaft** *f* opposition.

Gehackte(s) [gə'hakta(z)] *nt* mince(d meat).

Gehalt [gə'halt] *m* -(e)s, -e content; *nt* -(e)s, -̈er salary; **—sempfänger** *m* salary earner; **—serhöhung** *f* salary increase; **—szulage** *f* salary increment.

geharnischt [gə'harnɪʃt] *a* (*fig*) forceful, angry.

gehässig [gə'hɛsɪç] *a* spiteful, nasty; **G—keit** *f* spite(fulness).

Gehäuse [gə'hɔyzə] *nt* -s, - case; casing; (*von Apfel etc*) core.

Gehege [gə'he:gə] *nt* -s, - enclosure, preserve; **jdm ins — kommen** (*fig*) poach on sb's preserve.

geheim [gə'haɪm] *a* secret; **G—dienst** *m* secret service, intelligence service; **—halten** *vt irreg* keep secret; **G—nis** *nt* -ses, -se secret; mystery; **G—niskrämer** *m* secretive type; **—nisvoll** *a* mysterious; **G—polizei** *f* secret police; **G—schrift** *f* code, secret writing.

Geheiß [gə'haɪs] *nt* -es command; **auf jds —** at sb's behest.

gehen ['ge:ən] *irreg vti* go; (*zu Fuß —*) walk; **— nach** (*Fenster*) face; *v impers*: **wie geht es (dir)?** how are you or things?; **mir/ihm geht es gut** I'm/he's (doing) fine; **geht das?** is that possible?; **geht's noch?** can you manage?; **es geht** not too bad, O.K.; **das geht nicht** that's not on; **es geht um etw** sth is concerned, it's about sth.

geheuer [gə'hɔyɐr] *a*: **nicht —** eery; (*fragwürdig*) dubious.

Geheul [gə'hɔyl] *nt* -(e)s howling.

Gehilfe [gə'hilfə] *m* -n, -n, **Gehilfin** *f* assistant.

Gehirn [gə'hɪrn] *nt* -(e)s, -e brain; **—erschütterung** *f* concussion; **—wäsche** *f* brainwashing.

Gehör [gə'hø:r] *nt* -(e)s hearing; **musikalisches —** ear; **— gain a hearing; jdm — schenken** give sb a hearing.

gehorchen [gə'hɔrçən] *vi* obey (*jdm* sb).

gehören [gə'hø:rən] *vi* belong; *vr impers* be right or proper.

gehörig *a* proper; **— zu** or **+dat** belonging to; part of.

gehorsam [gə'ho:rza:m] *a* obedient; **G—** *m* -s obedience.

Gehsteig *m*, **Gehweg** *m* ['ge:-] pavement, sidewalk (*US*).

Geier ['gaɪɐr] *m* -s, - vulture.

geifern ['gaɪfɐrn] *vi* salivate; (*fig*) bitch.

Geige ['gaɪgə] *f* -, -n violin; **—r** *m* -s, - violinist; **—rzähler** *m* geiger counter.

geil [gaɪl] *a* randy, horny (*US*).

Geisel ['gaɪzəl] *f* -, -n hostage.

Geißel ['gaɪsəl] *f* -, -n scourge, whip; **g—n** *vt* scourge.

Geist [gaɪst] *m* -(e)s, -er spirit; (*Gespenst*) ghost; (*Verstand*) mind; **g—erhaft** *a* ghostly; **g—esabwesend** *a* absent-minded; **—esblitz** *m* brainwave; **—esgegenwart** *f* presence of mind; **—eshaltung** *f* mental attitude; **g—eskrank** *a* mentally ill; **—eskranke(r)** *mf* mentally ill person; **—eskrankheit** *f* mental illness; **—esstörung** *f* mental disturbance; **—eswissenschaften** *pl* arts (subjects) *pl*; **—eszustand** *m* state of mind; **g—ig** *a* intellectual; mental; *Getränke* alcoholic; **g—ig**

behindert mentally handicapped; **g—lich** a spiritual, religious; clerical; **—liche(r)** m clergyman; **—lichkeit** f clergy; **—los** a uninspired, dull; **g—reich** a clever; witty; **g—tötend** a soul-destroying; **g—voll** a intellectual; (weise) wise.

Geiz [gaits] m -es miserliness, meanness; **g—en** vi be miserly; **—hals** m, **—kragen** m miser; **g—ig** a miserly, mean.

Geklapper [gə'klapər] nt -s rattling.

geknickt [gə'knɪkt] a (fig) dejected.

gekonnt [gə'kɔnt] a skilful.

Gekritzel [gə'krɪtsəl] nt -s scrawl, scribble.

gekünstelt [ge'kynstəlt] a artificial, affected.

Gelächter [gə'lɛçtər] nt -s, - laughter.

geladen [ge'la:dən] a loaded; (Elec) live; (fig) furious.

Gelage [gə'la:gə] nt -s, - feast, banquet.

gelähmt [gə'lɛːmt] a paralysed.

Gelände [gə'lɛndə] nt -s, - land, terrain; (von Fabrik, Sport—) grounds pl; (Bau—) site; **g—gängig** a able to go cross-country; **—lauf** m cross-country race.

Geländer [gə'lɛndər] nt -s, - railing; (Treppen—) banister(s).

gelangen [gə'laŋən] vi (an + acc or zu) reach; (erwerben) attain; **in jds Besitz —** to come into sb's possession.

gelassen [gə'lasən] a calm, composed; **G—heit** f calmness, composure.

Gelatine [ʒela'ti:nə] f gelatine.

geläufig [gə'lɔyfɪç] a (üblich) common; **das ist mir nicht —** I'm

not familiar with that; **G—keit** f commonness; familiarity.

gelaunt [gə'launt] a: schlecht/gut **—** in a bad/good mood; **wie ist er —?** what sort of mood is he in?

Geläut(e) [gə'lɔyt(ə)] nt -(e)s, -(e) ringing; (Läutwerk) chime.

gelb [gɛlp] a yellow; (Ampellicht) amber; **—lich** a yellowish; **G—sucht** f jaundice.

Geld [gɛlt] nt -(e)s, -er money; **etw zu — machen** sell sth off; **—anlage** f investment; **—beutel** m, **—börse** f purse; **—einwurf** m slot; **—geber** m -s, - financial backer; **g—gierig** a avaricious; **—mittel** pl capital, means pl; **—schein** m banknote; **—schrank** m safe, strong-box; **—strafe** f fine; **—stück** nt coin; **—verlegenheit** f: **in —verlegenheit sein/kommen** to be/run short of money; **—verleiher** m -s, - moneylender; **—wechsel** m exchange of money.

Gelee [ʒe'le:] nt or m -s, -s jelly.

gelegen [gə'le:gən] a situated; (passend) convenient, opportune; **etw kommt jdm —** sth is convenient for sb.

Gelegenheit [gə'le:gənhaɪt] f opportunity; (Anlaß) occasion; **bei jeder —** at every opportunity; **—sarbeit** f casual work; **—sarbeiter** m casual worker; **—skauf** m bargain.

gelegentlich [gə'le:gəntlɪç] a occasional; ad occasionally; (bei Gelegenheit) some time (or other); prep + gen on the occasion of.

gelehrig [gə'le:rɪç] a quick to learn, intelligent.

gelehrt a learned; **G—e(r)** mf scholar; **G—heit** f scholarliness.

Geleise [gə'laɪzə] nt -s, - track; see Gleis.

Geleit [gə'laɪt] nt -(e)s, -e escort; **g—en** vt escort; **—schutz** m escort.

Gelenk [gə'lɛŋk] nt -(e)s, -e joint; **g—ig** a supple.

gelernt [gə'lɛrnt] a skilled.

Geliebte(r) [gə'liːptə(r)] mf sweetheart, beloved.

gelind(e) [gə'lɪnt, gə'lɪndə] a mild, light; (fig) Wut fierce; **—e gesagt** to put it mildly.

gelingen [gə'lɪŋən] vi irreg succeed; **die Arbeit gelingt mir nicht** I'm not being very successful with this piece of work; **es ist mir gelungen, etw zu tun** I succeeded in doing sth.

gellen ['gɛlən] vi shrill.

geloben [gə'loːbən] vti vow, swear.

gelten ['gɛltən] irreg vt (wert sein) be worth; **etw gilt bei jdm viel/wenig sb** values sth highly/sb doesn't value sth very highly; **jdm viel/wenig —** mean a lot/not mean much to sb; **was gilt die Wette?** do you want to bet?; vi (gültig sein) be valid; (erlaubt sein) be allowed; **jdm —** (gemünzt sein auf) be meant for or aimed at sb; **etw —lassen** accept sth; **als or für etw —** be considered to be sth; **jdm or für jdn —** (betreffen) apply to or for sb; v impers **es gilt, etw zu tun** it is necessary to do sth; **—d** a prevailing; **etw —d machen** to assert sth; **sich —d machen** make itself/o.s. felt.

Geltung ['gɛltʊŋ] f: **— haben** have validity; **sich/etw** (dat) **verschaffen** establish oneself/sth; **etw zur — bringen** show sth to its best advantage; **zur — kommen** be seen/heard etc to its best advantage; **—sbedürfnis** nt desire for admiration.

Gelübde [gə'lypdə] nt -s, - vow.

gelungen [gə'lʊŋən] a successful.

gemächlich [gə'mɛːçlɪç] a leisurely.

Gemahl [gə'maːl] m -(e)s, -e husband; **—in** f wife.

Gemälde [gə'mɛːldə] nt -s, - picture, painting.

gemäß [gə'mɛːs] prep +dat in accordance with; a appropriate (dat to); **—igt** a moderate; Klima temperate.

gemein [gə'maɪn] a common; (niederträchtig) mean; **etw — haben (mit)** have sth in common (with).

Gemeinde [gə'maɪndə] f -, -n district, community; (Pfarr—) parish; (Kirchen—) congregation; **—steuer** f local rates pl; **—verwaltung** f local administration; **—vorstand** m local council; **—wahl** f local election.

Gemein- cpd: **g—gefährlich** a dangerous to the public; **—gut** nt public property; **—heit** f commonness; mean thing to do/to say; **g—hin** ad generally; **—nutz** m public good; **—platz** m commonplace, platitude; **g—sam** a joint, common (auch Math); **g—same Sache mit jdm machen** be in cahoots with sb; ad together, jointly; **etw g—sam haben** have sth in common; **—samkeit** f community, having in common; **—schaft** f community; **in —schaft mit** jointly or together with; **g—schaftlich** a see g—sam; **—schaftsarbeit** f teamwork; team effort; **—schaftserziehung** f coeducation; **—sinn** m public spirit; **g—verständlich** a generally comprehensible; **—wohl** nt common good.

Gemenge [gə'mɛŋə] nt -s, - mixture; (Hand—) scuffle.

gemessen [gə'mɛsən] à measured.
Gemetzel [gə'mɛtsəl] nt -s, - slaughter, carnage, butchery.
Gemisch [gə'mɪʃ] nt -es, -e mixture; **g—t** a mixed.
Gemse ['gɛmzə] f -, -n chamois.
Gemunkel [gə'muŋkəl] nt -s gossip.
Gemurmel [gə'murməl] nt -s murmur(ing).
Gemüse [gə'my:zə] nt -s, - vegetables pl; **—garten** m vegetable garden; **—händler** m greengrocer.
Gemüt [gə'my:t] nt -(e)s, -er disposition, nature; person; **sich** (dat) **etw zu —e führen** (col) indulge in sth; **die —er erregen** arouse strong feelings; **g—lich** a comfortable, cosy; Person good-natured; **—lichkeit** f comfortableness, cosiness; amiability; **—sbewegung** f emotion; **—smensch** m sentimental person; **—sruhe** f composure; **—szustand** m state of mind; **g—voll** a warm, tender.
genau [gə'nau] a,ad exact(ly), precise(ly); **etw — nehmen** take sth seriously; **—genommen** ad strictly speaking; **G—igkeit** f exactness, accuracy.
genehm [gə'ne:m] a agreeable, acceptable; **—igen** vt approve, authorize; **sich** (dat) **etw —igen** indulge in sth; **G—igung** f approval, authorization.
geneigt [gə'naikt] a well-disposed, willing; **— sein, etw zu tun** be inclined to do sth.
General [gene'ra:l] m -s, -e or =e general; **—direktor** m director general; **—konsulat** nt consulate general; **—probe** f dress rehearsal; **—stabskarte** f ordnance survey map; **—streik** m general strike;

g—überholen vt thoroughly overhaul.
Generation [generatsi'o:n] f generation; **—skonflikt** m generation gap.
Generator [gene'ra:tor] m generator, dynamo.
genesen [gə'ne:zən] vi irreg convalesce, recover, get well; **G—de(r)** mf convalescent.
Genesung f recovery, convalescence.
genetisch [ge'ne:tɪʃ] a genetic.
genial [geni'a:l] a brilliant; **G—ität** f brilliance, genius.
Genick [gə'nɪk] nt -(e)s, -e (back of the) neck; **—starre** f stiff neck.
Genie [ʒe'ni:] nt -s, -s genius.
genieren [ʒe'ni:rən] vt bother; **geniert es Sie, wenn …?** do you mind if …?; vr feel awkward or self-conscious.
genießbar a edible; drinkable.
genießen [gə'ni:sən] vt irreg enjoy; eat; drink.
Genießer m -s, - epicure; pleasure lover; **g—isch** a appreciative; ad with relish.
Genosse [gə'nɔsə] m -n, -n, **Genossin** f comrade (esp Pol), companion; **—nschaft** f cooperative (association).
genug [gə'nu:k] ad enough.
Genüge [gə'ny:gə] f -: **jdm/etw —tun** or **leisten** satisfy sb/sth; **g—n** vi be enough, suffice; (+dat) satisfied; **g—nd** a sufficient.
genügsam [gə'ny:kza:m] a modest, easily satisfied; **G—keit** f moderation.
Genugtuung [gə'nu:ktu:uŋ] f satisfaction.
Genuß [gə'nus] m -sses, =sse pleasure; (Zuschnehmen) con-

sumption; **in den — von etw kommen** receive the benefit of sth; **—mittel** pl (semi-)luxury items pl. **genüßlich** [gə'nyslıç] a with relish.

Geograph [geo'graːf] m -en, -en geographer; **—ie** [-'fiː] f geography; **g—isch** a geographical.

Geologe [geo'loːgə] m -n, -n geologist; **—gie** [-'giː] f geology.

Geometrie [geome'triː] f geometry.

Gepäck [gə'pɛk] nt -(e)s luggage, baggage; **—abfertigung** f, **—annahme** f, **—ausgabe** f luggage desk/office, checkroom (US); **—aufbewahrung** f left-luggage office, checkroom (US); **—netz** nt luggage-rack; **—träger** m porter; (Fahrrad) carrier; **—wagen** m luggage van, baggage car (US).

gepflegt [gə'pfleːkt] a well-groomed; Park etc well looked after.

Gepflogenheit [gə'pfloːgənhaıt] f custom.

Geplapper [gə'plapər] nt -s chatter.

Geplauder [gə'plaudər] nt -s chat(ting).

Gepolter [gə'pɔltər] nt -s din.

gerade [gə'raːdə] a straight; Zahl even; ad (genau) exactly; (örtlich) straight; (eben) just; **warum — ich?** why me?; **— weil** just or precisely because; **nicht — schön** not exactly nice; **das ist es ja —** that's just it; **jetzt — nicht!** not now!; **— noch** just; **— neben** right next to; **G— f -n, -n** straight line; **—aus** ad straight ahead; **—heraus** ad straight out, bluntly; **—so** ad just so; **—so dumm** etc just as stupid etc; **—so wie** just as; **—zu** ad (beinahe) virtually, almost.

geradlinig a rectilinear.

Gerät [gə'rɛːt] nt -(e)s, -e device; (Werkzeug) tool; (Sport)

apparatus; (Zubehör) equipment no pl.

geraten [gə'raːtən] vi irreg (gelingen) turn out well (jdm for sb); ... (gedeihen) thrive; **gut/schlecht — turn** out well/badly; **an jdn —** come across sb; **in etw** (acc) **—** get into sth; **in Angst —** get frightened; **nach jdm —** take after sb.

Geratewohl [gəraːtə'voːl] nt: **aufs — on the off chance**; (bei Wahl) at random.

geraum [gə'raum] a: **seit —er Zeit** for some considerable time.

geräumig [gə'rɔymıç] a roomy.

Geräusch [gə'rɔyʃ] nt -(e)s, -e sound, noise; **g—los** a silent; **g—voll** a noisy.

gerben ['gɛrbən] vt tan.

Gerber m -s, **- tanner**; **—ei** [-'raı] f tannery.

gerecht [gə'rɛçt] a just, fair; **jdm/etw — werden** do justice to sb/sth; **g—igkeit** f justice, fairness.

Gerede [gə'reːdə] nt -s talk, gossip.

gereizt [gə'raıtst] a irritable; **G—heit** f irritation.

Gericht [gə'rıçt] nt -(e)s, -e court; (Essen) dish; **mit jdm ins — gehen** (fig) judge sb harshly; **über jdn zu — sitzen** sit in judgement on sb; **das Letzte — the Last Judgement**; **g—lich** a,ad judicial(ly), legal(ly); **—sbarkeit** f jurisdiction; **—shof** m court (of law); **—skosten** pl (legal) costs pl; **—ssaal** m courtroom; **—sverfahren** nt legal proceedings pl; **—sverhandlung** f court proceedings pl; **—svollzieher** m bailiff.

gerieben [gə'riːbən] a grated; (col: schlau) smart, wily.

gering [gə'rıŋ] a slight, small; (niedrig) low; Zeit short; **—achten** vt think little of; **—fügig** a small,

trivial; —**schätzig** a disparaging;
G—schätzung f disdain; —**ste(r,s)**
a slightest, least; —**stenfalls** ad at
the very least.

gerinnen [gə'rɪnən] vi irreg congeal; (Blut) clot; (Milch) curdle.

Gerinnsel [gə'rɪnzəl] nt -s, - clot.

Gerippe [gə'rɪpə] nt -s, - skeleton.

gerissen [gə'rɪsən] a wily, smart.

gern(e) ['gɛrn(ə)] ad willingly,
gladly; —**haben**, —**mögen** like;
etwas — **tun** like doing something;
G—egroß m -, -e show-off.

Geröll [gə'rœl] nt -(e)s, -e scree.

Gerste ['gɛrstə] f -, -n barley;
—**nkorn** nt (im Auge) stye.

Gerte ['gɛrtə] f -, -n switch, rod;
g—nschlank a willowy.

Geruch [gə'rʊx] m -(e)s, ⁻e smell,
odour; **g—los** a odourless;
g—tilgend a deodorant.

Gerücht [gə'rʏçt] nt -(e)s, -e
rumour.

geruhen [gə'ruːən] vi deign.

Gerümpel [gə'rʏmpəl] nt -s junk.

Gerüst [gə'rʏst] nt -(e)s, -e
(Bau—) scaffold(ing); frame.

gesamt [gə'zamt] a whole, entire;
Kosten total; Werke complete; **im
—en** all in all; **G—ausgabe** f complete edition; —**deutsch** a all-
German; **G—eindruck** m general
impression; **G—heit** f totality,
whole.

Gesandte(r) [gə'zantə(r)] m envoy.

Gesandtschaft [gə'zant-ʃaft] f
legation.

Gesang [gə'zaŋ] m -(e)s, ⁻e song;
(Singen) singing; —**buch** nt (Rel)
hymn book; —**verein** m choral
society.

Gesäß [gə'zɛːs] nt -es, -e seat,
bottom.

Geschäft [gə'ʃɛft] nt -(e)s, -e
business; (Laden) shop;
(—sabschluß) deal; **g—emacher** m
-s, - profiteer; **g—ig** a active, busy;
(pej) officious; **g—lich** a commercial; ad on business;
—**sbericht** m financial report;
—**sführer** m manager; (Klub)
secretary; —**sjahr** nt financial
year; —**slage** f business conditions
pl; —**smann** m businessman;
g—smäßig a businesslike; —**sreise**
f business trip; —**sschluß** m closing
time; —**ssinn** m business sense;
—**sstelle** f office, place of business;
g—stüchtig a efficient; —**sviertel**
nt business quarter; shopping
centre; —**swagen** m company car;
—**szweig** m branch (of a business).

geschehen [gə'ʃeːən] vi irreg
happen; **es war um ihn —** that was
the end of him.

gescheit [gə'ʃait] a clever.

Geschenk [gə'ʃɛŋk] nt -(e)s, -e
present, gift; —**packung** f gift pack.

Geschicht- [gə'ʃɪçt] cpd: —**e** f -,
-n story; (Sache) affair; (Historie)
history; —**enerzähler** m storyteller; **g—lich** a historical;
—**sschreiber** m historian.

Geschick [gə'ʃɪk] nt -(e)s, -e
aptitude; (Schicksal) fate;
—**lichkeit** f skill, dexterity; **g—t** a
skilful.

geschieden [gə'ʃiːdən] a divorced.

Geschirr [gə'ʃɪr] nt -(e)s, -e
crockery; pots and pans pl;
(Pferd) harness; —**spülmaschine** f
dishwashing machine; —**tuch** nt
dish cloth.

Geschlecht [gə'ʃlɛçt] nt -(e)s, -er
sex; (Gram) gender; (Art)
species; family; **g—lich** a sexual;
—**skrankheit** f venereal disease;
—**steil** nt or m genitals pl;

—sverkehr *m* sexual intercourse;
—swort *nt* (*Gram*) article.
Geschmack [gəˈʃmak] *m* -(e)s, ¨e
taste; **nach jds** — to sb's taste;
— **finden an etw** (*dat*) (come to)
like sth; **g—los** a tasteless; (*fig*) in
bad taste; —**(s)sache** *f* matter of
taste; —**sinn** *m* sense of taste;
g—voll a tasteful.
Geschmeide [gəˈʃmaidə] *nt* -s, -
jewellery.
geschmeidig a supple; (*formbar*)
malleable.
Geschmeiß [gəˈʃmais] *nt* vermin *pl.*
Geschmiere [gəˈʃmiːrə] *nt* -s
scrawl; (*Bild*) daub.
Geschöpf [gəˈʃœpf] *nt* -(e)s, -e
creature.
Geschoß [gəˈʃɔs] *nt* -sses, -sse
(*Mil*) projectile, missile; (*Stockwerk*) floor.
geschraubt [gəˈʃraupt] a stilted,
artificial.
Geschrei [gəˈʃrai] *nt* -s cries *pl*,
shouting; (*fig: Aufhebens*) noise,
fuss.
Geschütz [gəˈʃyts] *nt* -es, -e gun,
cannon; **ein schweres — auffahren**
(*fig*) bring out the big guns;
—**feuer** *nt* artillery fire, gunfire;
g—t a protected.
Geschwader [gəˈʃvaːdər] *nt* -s, -
(*Naut*) squadron; (*Aviat*) group.
Geschwafel [gəˈʃvaːfəl] *nt* -s silly
talk.
Geschwätz [gəˈʃvɛts] *nt* -es
chatter, gossip; **g—ig** a talkative;
—**igkeit** *f* talkativeness.
geschweige ad: —
(**denn**) let alone, not to mention.
geschwind [gəˈʃvint] a quick,
swift; **G—igkeit** [-diçkait] *f* speed,
velocity; **G—igkeitsbegrenzung** *f*
speed limit; **G—igkeitsmesser** *m*
(*Aut*) speedometer;

G—igkeitsüberschreitung *f*
exceeding the speed limit.
Geschwister [gəˈʃvistər] *pl*
brothers and sisters *pl.*
geschwollen [gəˈʃvɔlən] a
pompous.
Geschworene(r) [gəˈʃvoːrənə(r)]
mf juror; *pl* jury.
Geschwulst [gəˈʃvulst] *f* -, ¨e
swelling; growth, tumour.
Geschwür [gəˈʃvyːr] *nt* -(e)s, -e
ulcer.
Gesell- [gəˈzɛl] *cpd:* —**e** *m* -n, -n
fellow; (*Handwerk—*) journey-
man; **g—ig** a sociable; —**igkeit** *f*
sociability; —**schaft** *f* society;
(*Begleitung, Comm*) company;
(*Abend—schaft etc*) party;
g—schaftlich a social;
—**schaftsanzug** *m* evening dress;
g—schaftsfähig a socially
acceptable; —**schaftsordnung** *f*
social structure; —**schaftsreise** *f*
group tour; —**schaftsschicht** *f*
social stratum.
Gesetz [gəˈzɛts] *nt* -es, -e law;
—**buch** *nt* statute book; —**entwurf**
m, —**esvorlage** *f* bill; **g—gebend** a
legislative; —**geber** *m* -s, - legislator; —**gebung** *f* legislation; **g—lich**
a legal, lawful; —**lichkeit** *f* legality,
lawfulness; **g—los** a lawless;
g—mäßig a lawful; **g—t** a Mensch
sedate; **g—tenfalls** ad supposing
(that); **g—widrig** a illegal, unlawful.
Gesicht [gəˈziçt] *nt* -(e)s, -er face;
das zweite — second sight; **das ist
mir nie zu** — **gekommen** I've never
laid eyes on that; —**sausdruck** *m*
(facial) expression; —**sfarbe** *f* complexion; —**spunkt** *m* point of view;
—**szüge** *pl* features *pl.*
Gesindel [gəˈzindəl] *nt* -s rabble.
gesinnt [gəˈzint] a disposed,
minded.

Gesinnung [gə'zɪnʊŋ] f disposition; (Ansicht) views pl; —sgenosse m like-minded person; —slosigkeit f lack of conviction; —swandel m change of opinion, volte-face.

gesittet [gə'zɪtət] a well-mannered.

Gespann [gə'ʃpan] nt -(e)s, -e team; (col) couple; g—t a tense, strained; (begierig) eager; ich bin g—t, ob I wonder if or whether; auf etw/jdn g—t sein look forward to sth/meeting sb.

Gespenst [gə'ʃpɛnst] nt -(e)s, -er ghost, spectre; g—erhaft a ghostly.

Gespiele [gə'ʃpiːlə] m -n, -n, **Gespielin** f playmate.

Gespött [gə'ʃpœt] nt -(e)s mockery; zum — werden become a laughing stock.

Gespräch [gə'ʃprɛːç] nt -(e)s, -e conversation; discussion(s); (Anruf) call; zum — werden become a topic of conversation; g—ig a talkative; —igkeit f talkativeness; —sthema nt subject or topic (of conversation).

Gespür [gə'ʃpyːr] nt -s feeling.

Gestalt [gə'ʃtalt] f, -en form, shape; (Person) figure; in — von in the form of; — annehmen take shape; g—en vt (formen) shape, form; (organisieren) arrange, organize; vr turn out (zu to be); —ung f formation; organization.

geständig [gə'ʃtɛndɪç] a: — sein have confessed.

Geständnis [gə'ʃtɛntnɪs] nt -ses, -se confession.

Gestank [gə'ʃtaŋk] m -(e)s stench.

gestatten [gə'ʃtatən] vt permit, allow; — Sie may I?; sich (dat) —, etw zu tun take the liberty of doing sth.

Geste ['gɛstə] f -, -n gesture.

gestehen [gə'ʃteːən] vt irreg confess.

Gestein [gə'ʃtaɪn] nt -(e)s, -e rock.

Gestell [gə'ʃtɛl] nt -(e)s, -e frame; (Regal) rack, stand.

gestern ['gɛstərn] ad yesterday; — abend/morgen yesterday evening/morning.

gestikulieren [gɛstiku'liːrən] vi gesticulate.

Gestirn [gə'ʃtɪrn] nt -(e)s, -e star; (Sternbild) constellation.

Gestöber [gə'ʃtøːbər] nt -s, — flurry, blizzard.

Gesträuch [gə'ʃtrɔʏç] nt -(e)s, -e shrubbery, bushes pl.

gestreift [gə'ʃtraɪft] a striped.

gestrig ['gɛstrɪç] a yesterday's.

Gestrüpp [gə'ʃtryp] nt -(e)s, -e undergrowth.

Gestüt [gə'ʃtyːt] nt -(e)s, -e stud farm.

Gesuch [gə'zuːx] nt -(e)s, -e petition; (Antrag) application; g—t a (Comm) in demand; wanted; (fig) contrived.

gesund [gə'zʊnt] a healthy; wieder — werden get better; G—heit f health(iness) health; G—heit! bless you!; —heitlich a,ad health attr, physical; wie geht es Ihnen —heitlich? how's your health?; —heitsschädlich a unhealthy; G—heitswesen nt health service; G—heitszustand m state of health.

Getöse [gə'tøːzə] nt -s din, racket.

Getränk [gə'trɛŋk] nt -(e)s, -e drink.

getrauen [gə'trauən] vr dare, venture.

Getreide [gə'traɪdə] nt -s, — cereals pl, grain; —speicher m granary.

getrennt [gə'trɛnt] a separate.

getreu [gə'trɔy] a faithful.

Getriebe [gə'triːbə] nt -s, - (Leute) bustle; (Aut) gearbox; —öl nt transmission oil.

getrost [gə'troːst] ad without any bother; — sterben die in peace.

Getue [gə'tuːə] nt -s fuss.

geübt [gəy:pt] a experienced.

Gewächs [gə'vɛks] nt -es, -e growth; (Pflanze) plant.

gewachsen [gə'vaksən] a: jdm/etw — sein is sb's equal/equal to sth.

Gewächshaus nt greenhouse.

gewagt [gə'vaːkt] a daring, risky.

gewählt [gə'vɛːlt] a Sprache refined, elegant.

Gewähr [gə'vɛːr] f - guarantee; keine — übernehmen für accept no responsibility for; g—en vt grant; (geben) provide; g—leisten vt guarantee.

Gewahrsam [gə'vaːrzaːm] m -s, -e safekeeping; (Polizei—) custody.

Gewähr- cpd: —smann m informant, source; —ung f granting.

Gewalt [gə'valt] f -, -en power; (große Kraft) force; (—taten) violence; mit aller — with all one's might; —anwendung f use of force; —herrschaft f tyranny; g—ig a tremendous; Irrtum huge; —marsch m forced march; g—sam a forcible; g—tätig a violent.

Gewand [gə'vant] nt -(e)s, -er garment.

gewandt [gə'vant] a deft, skilful; (erfahren) experienced; G—heit f dexterity, skill.

Gewässer [gə'vɛsər] nt -s, - waters pl.

Gewebe [gə'veːbə] nt -s, - (Stoff) fabric; (Biol) tissue.

Gewehr [gə'veːr] nt -(e)s, -e gun; rifle; —lauf m rifle barrel.

Geweih [gə'vai] nt -(e)s, -e antlers pl.

Gewerb- [gə'vɛrb] cpd: —e nt -s, - trade, occupation; Handel und —e trade and industry; —eschule f technical school; g—etreibend a carrying on a trade; industrial; g—lich a industrial; trade attr; g—smäßig a professional; —szweig m line of trade.

Gewerkschaft [gə'vɛrkʃaft] f trade union; —ler m -s, - trade unionist; g—sbund m trade unions federation.

Gewicht [gə'vɪçt] nt -(e)s, -e weight; (fig) importance; g—ig a weighty.

gewieft [gə'viːft] a, **gewiegt** [gə'viːkt] a shrewd, cunning.

gewillt [gə'vɪlt] a willing, prepared.

Gewimmel [gə'vɪməl] nt -s swarm.

Gewinde [gə'vɪndə] nt -s, - (Kranz) wreath; (von Schraube) thread.

Gewinn [gə'vɪn] m -(e)s, -e profit; (bei Spiel) winnings pl; etw mit — verkaufen sell sth at a profit; —beteiligung f profit-sharing; g—bringend a profitable; g—en vt irreg win; (erwerben) gain; Kohle, Öl extract; vi win; (profitieren) gain; an etw (dat) g—en gain in sth; g—end a winning, attractive; —er(in f) m -s, - winner; —spanne f profit margin; —sucht f love of gain; —(n)ummer f winning number; —ung f winning; gaining; (von Kohle etc) extraction.

Gewirr [gə'vɪr] nt -(e)s, -e tangle; (von Straßen) maze.

gewiß [gə'vɪs] a,ad certain(ly).

Gewissen [gə'vɪsən] nt -s, - conscience; g—haft a conscientious; —haftigkeit f conscientiousness; g—los a unscrupulous; —sbisse pl pangs of conscience pl, qualms pl; —sfrage f matter of conscience; —sfreiheit f freedom of conscience; —skonflikt m moral conflict.

gewissermaßen [gəvɪsər'maːsən] ad more or less, in a way.

Gewiß- cpd: —heit f certainty; g—lich ad surely.

Gewitter [gə'vɪtər] nt -s, - thunderstorm; g—n vi impers: es gewittert there's a thunderstorm; g—schwül a sultry and thundery.

gewitzigt [gə'vɪtsɪçt] a: — sein have learned by experience.

gewitzt [gə'vɪtst] a shrewd, cunning.

gewogen [gə'voːɡən] a well-disposed (+ dat towards).

gewöhnen [gə'vøːnən] vt: jdn an etw (acc) — accustom sb to sth; (erziehen zu) teach sb sth; vr: sich an etw (acc) — get used or accustomed to sth.

Gewohnheit [gə'voːnhart] f habit; (Brauch) custom; aus — from habit; zur — werden become a habit; —s- in cpds habitual; —smensch m creature of habit; —srecht nt common law; —stier nt (col) creature of habit.

gewöhnlich [gə'vøːnlɪç] a usual; ordinary; (pej) common; wie — as usual.

gewohnt [gə'voːnt] a usual; etw — sein be used to sth.

Gewöhnung f getting accustomed (an + acc to sb).

Gewölbe [gə'vœlbə] nt -s, - vault.

Gewühl [gə'vyːl] nt -(e)s throng.

Gewürz [gə'vʏrts] nt -es, -e spice, seasoning; —nelke f clove.

gezähnt [gə'tsɛːnt] a serrated, toothed.

Gezeiten [gə'tsaɪtən] pl tides pl.

Gezeter [gə'tseːtər] nt -s clamour, yelling.

gezielt [gə'tsiːlt] a with a particular aim in mind, purposeful; Kritik pointed.

geziemen [gə'tsiːmən] vr impers be fitting; —d a proper.

geziert [gə'tsiːrt] a affected; G—heit f affectation.

Gezwitscher [gə'tsvɪtʃər] nt -s twitter(ing), chirping.

gezwungen [gə'tsvʊŋən] a forced; —ermaßen of necessity.

Gicht ['ɡɪçt] f - gout; g—isch a gouty.

Giebel ['ɡiːbəl] m -s, - gable; —dach nt gable(d) roof; —fenster nt gable window.

Gier [ɡiːr] f - greed; g—ig a greedy.

Gieß- [ɡiːs] cpd: —bach m torrent; g—en vt irreg pour; Blumen water; Metall cast; Wachs mould; —e'rei f foundry; —kanne f watering can.

Gift [ɡɪft] nt -(e)s, -e poison; g—ig a poisonous; (fig: boshaft) venomous; —zahn m fang.

Gilde ['ɡɪldə] f -, -n guild.

Ginster ['ɡɪnstər] m -s, - broom.

Gipfel ['ɡɪpfəl] m -s, - summit, peak; (fig) height; g—n vi culminate; —treffen nt summit (meeting).

Gips [ɡɪps] m -es, -e plaster; (Med) plaster (of Paris); —abdruck m plaster cast; g—en vt plaster; —figur f plaster figure; —verband m plaster (cast).

Giraffe [ɡi'rafə] f -, -n giraffe.

Girlande [ɡɪr'landə] f -, -n garland.

Giro ['ʒiːro] nt -s, -s giro; —konto nt current account.

girren ['gɪrən] vi coo.

Gischt [gɪʃt] m -(e)s, -e spray, foam.

Gitarre [gi'tarə] f -, -n guitar.

Gitter ['gɪtər] nt -s, - grating, bars pl; (für Pflanzen) trellis; (Zaun) railing(s); —bett nt cot; —fenster nt barred window; —zaun nt railing(s).

Glacéhandschuh [gla'se:hant-ʃu:] m kid glove.

Gladiole [gladi'o:lə] f -, -n gladiolus.

Glanz [glants] m -es shine, lustre; (fig) splendour.

glänzen ['glɛntsən] vi shine (also fig), gleam; vt polish; —d a shining; (fig) brilliant.

Glanz— cpd: —leistung f brilliant achievement; g—los a dull; —zeit f heyday.

Glas [gla:s] nt -es, "er glass; —bläser m -s, - glass blower; —er m -s, - glazier; g—ieren [gla'zi:rən] vt glaze; g—ig a glassy; —scheibe f pane; —ur [gla'zu:r] f glaze; (Cook) icing.

glatt [glat] a smooth; (rutschig) slippery; Absage flat; Lüge downright; G—eis nt (black) ice; jdm aufs G—eis führen (fig) take sb for a ride.

Glätte ['glɛtə] f -, -n smoothness; slipperiness; g—n vt smooth out.

Glatze ['glatsə] f -, -n bald head; eine — bekommen go bald.

glatzköpfig a bald.

Glaube ['glaubə] m -ns, -n faith (an +acc in); belief (an +acc in); g—n vti believe (an +acc in, jdm sb); think; —nsbekenntnis nt creed.

glaubhaft ['glaubhaft] a credible; G—igkeit f credibility.

gläubig ['glɔybɪç] a (Rel) devout; (vertrauensvoll) trustful; G—e(r) mf believer; die G—en the faithful; G—er m -s, - creditor.

glaubwürdig ['glaubvyrdɪç] a credible; Mensch trustworthy; G—keit f credibility; trustworthiness.

gleich [glaɪç] a equal; (identisch) (the) same, identical; es ist mir — it's all the same to me; 2 mal 2 — 4 2 times 2 is or equals 4; ad equally; (sofort) straight away; (bald) in a minute; — groß the same size; — nach/an right after/at; —altrig a of the same age; —artig a similar; —bedeutend a synonymous; —berechtigt a having equal rights; G—berechtigung f equal rights pl; —bleibend a constant; —en vi irreg: jdm/etw be like sb/sth; vr be alike; —ermaßen ad equally; —falls ad likewise; danke —falls! the same to you; G—förmigkeit f uniformity; —gesinnt a likeminded; G—gewicht nt equilibrium, balance; —gültig a indifferent; (unbedeutend) unimportant; G—gültigkeit f indifference; G—heit f equality; —kommen vi irreg +dat be equal to; G—mache'rei f egalitarianism; —mäßig a even, equal; G—mut m equanimity; G—nis nt -ses, -se parable; —sam ad as it were; —sehen vi irreg (jdm) be or look like (sb); G—strom m (Elec) direct current; —tun vi irreg: es jdm —tun match sb; G—ung f equation; —viel ad no matter; —wohl ad nevertheless; —zeitig a simultaneous.

Gleis [glaɪs] nt -es, -e track, rails pl; (Bahnsteig) platform.

Gleit- ['glaɪt] *cpd*: gliding; sliding; **g—en** *vi irreg* glide; (*rutschen*) slide; **—flug** *m* glide; gliding.

Gletscher ['glɛtʃər] *m* -s, - glacier; **—spalte** *f* crevasse.

Glied [gliːt] *nt* **-(e)s, -er** member; (*Arm, Bein*) limb; (*von Kette*) link; (*Mil*) rank(s); **g—ern** *vt* organize, structure; **—erung** *f* structure, organization; **—maßen** *pl* limbs *pl*.

Glimm- ['glɪm] *cpd*: **g—en** *vi irreg* glow, gleam; **—er** *m* -s, - glow, gleam; (*Mineral*) mica; **—stengel** *m* (*col*) fag.

glimpflich ['glɪmpflɪç] *a* mild, lenient; **— davonkommen** get off lightly.

glitzern ['glɪtsərn] *vi* glitter, twinkle.

Globus ['gloːbʊs] *m* - *or* -ses, **Globen** *or* -se globe.

Glöckchen ['glœkçən] *nt* (little) bell.

Glocke ['glɔkə] *f* -, -n bell; etw an die große — hängen (*fig*) shout sth from the rooftops; **—nspiel** *nt* peal of bells; **—nspiel** *nt* chime(s); (*Mus*) glockenspiel.

Glorie ['gloːriə] *f* -, -n glory; (*von Heiligen*) halo.

Glosse ['glɔsə] *f* -, -n comment.

glotzen ['glɔtsən] *vi* (*col*) stare.

Glück [glʏk] *nt* **-(e)s** luck, fortune; (*Freude*) happiness; **— haben** be lucky; **viel —** good luck; **zum —** fortunately; **es glückte ihm**, es bekommen he succeeded in getting it.

gluckern ['glʊkərn] *vi* glug.

Glück- *cpd*: **g—lich** *a* fortunate; (*froh*) happy; **g—licherweise** *ad* fortunately; **—sbringer** *m* -s, - lucky charm; **g—'selig** *a* blissful; **—sfall** *m* stroke of luck; **—skind** *nt* lucky person; **—ssache** *f* matter

of luck; **—sspiel** *nt* game of chance; **—sstern** *m* lucky star; **g—strahlend** *a* radiant (with happiness); **—wunsch** *m* congratulations *pl*, best wishes *pl*.

Glüh- ['glyː] *cpd*: **—birne** *f* light bulb; **g—en** *vi* glow; **—wein** *m* mulled wine; **—würmchen** *nt* glow-worm.

Glut [gluːt] *f* -, -en (*Röte*) glow; (*Feuers—*) fire; (*Hitze*) heat; (*fig*) ardour.

Gnade ['gnaːdə] *f* -, -n (*Gunst*) favour; (*Erbarmen*) mercy; (*Milde*) clemency; **—nfrist** *f* reprieve, respite; **—ngesuch** *nt* petition for clemency; **—nstoß** *m* coup de grâce.

gnädig ['gnɛːdɪç] *a* gracious; (*voll Erbarmen*) merciful.

Gold [gɔlt] *nt* **-(e)s** gold; **g—en** *a* golden; **—fisch** *m* goldfish; **—grube** *f* goldmine; **—regen** *m* laburnum; **—schnitt** *m* gilt edging; **—währung** *f* gold standard.

Golf [gɔlf] *m* **-(e)s, -e** gulf; *m* -s golf; **—platz** *m* golf course; **—schläger** *m* golf club; **—spieler** *m* golfer; **—strom** *m* Gulf Stream.

Gondel ['gɔndəl] *f* -, -n gondola; (*Seilbahn*) cable-car.

gönnen ['gœnən] *vt*: **jdm etw —** not begrudge sb sth; **sich** (*dat*) **etw —** allow oneself sth.

Gönner *m* -s, - patron; **g—haft** *a* patronizing; **—miene** *f* patronizing air.

Gosse ['gɔsə] *f* -, -n gutter.

Gott [gɔt] *m* **-es, ̈-er** god; **um —es Willen!** for heaven's sake!; **— sei Dank!** thank God!; **—esdienst** *m* service; **—eshaus** *nt* place of worship; **—heit** *f* deity.

Gött- [gœt] *cpd*: **—in** *f* goddess; **g—lich** *a* divine.

Gott- cpd: **g—los** a godless; **—vertrauen** nt trust in God.

Götze ['gœtsə] m **-n, -n** idol.

Grab [gra:p] nt **-(e)s, ¨er** grave; **g—en** ['gra:bən] vt irreg dig; **—en** m **-s, ¨** ditch; (Mil) trench; **—rede** f funeral oration; **—stein** m gravestone.

Grad [gra:t] m **-(e)s, -e** degree; **—einteilung** f graduation; **g—weise** ad gradually.

Graf [gra:f] m **-en¨, -en** count, earl; **—schaft** f county.

Gräfin ['grε:fɪn] f countess.

Gram [gra:m] m **-(e)s** grief, sorrow.

grämen ['grε:mən] vr grieve.

Gramm [gram] nt **-s, -e** gram(me); **—atik** ['-'matɪk] f grammar; **g—atisch** a grammatical; **—o'phon** nt **-s, -e** gramophone.

Granat [gra'na:t] m **-(e)s, -e** (Stein) garnet; **—apfel** m pomegranate; **—e** f **-, -n** (Mil) shell; (Hand—) grenade.

Granit [gra'ni:t] m **-s, -e** granite.

graphisch ['gra:fɪʃ] a graphic; **-e Darstellung** graph.

Gras [gra:s] nt **-es, ¨er** grass; **g—en** vi graze; **—halm** m blade of grass; **g—ig** a grassy; **—narbe** f turf.

grassieren [gra'si:rən] vi be rampant, rage.

gräßlich ['grεslɪç] a horrible.

Grat [gra:t] m **-(e)s, -e** ridge.

Gräte ['grε:tə] f **-, -n** fishbone.

gratis ['gra:tɪs] a,ad free (of charge); **G—probe** f free sample.

Gratulation [gratulatsi'o:n] f congratulation(s).

gratulieren [gratu'li:rən] vi: **jdm — (zu etw)** congratulate sb (on sth); **(ich) gratuliere!** congratulations!

grau [grau] a grey; **—en** vi (Tag) dawn; vi impers: **es graut jdm vor etw** sb dreads sth, sb is afraid of sth; vr: **sich —en vor** dread, have a horror of; **G—en** nt **-s** horror; **—enhaft** a horrible; **—haarig** a grey-haired; **—meliert** a grey-flecked.

grausam ['grauza:m] a cruel; **G—keit** f cruelty.

Grausen ['grauzən] nt **-s** horror; **g—** vi impers, vr see grauen.

gravieren [gra'vi:rən] vt engrave; **-d** a grave.

Grazie [gra:tsiə] f **-, -n** grace.

graziös [gratsi'ø:s] a graceful.

greif- [graif] cpd: **—bar** a tangible, concrete; **in —barer Nähe** within reach; **—en** vt irreg seize; grip; **nach etw —en** reach for sth; **um sich —en** (fig) spread; **zu etw —en** (fig) turn to sth.

Greis [grais] m **-es, -e** old man; **—enalter** nt old age; **g—enhaft** a senile.

grell [grεl] a harsh.

Grenz- ['grεnts] cpd: **—beamte(r)** m frontier official; **-e** f **-, -n** boundary; (Staats—) frontier; (Schranke) limit; **g—en** vi border (an +acc on); **g—enlos** a boundless; **—fall** m borderline case; **—linie** f boundary; **—übergang** m frontier crossing.

Greuel ['grɔyəl] m **-s, -** horror, revulsion; **etw ist jdm ein —** sb loathes sth; **—tat** f atrocity.

greulich ['grɔylɪç] a horrible.

griesgrämig ['gri:sgrε:mɪç] a grumpy.

Grieß [gri:s] m **-es, -e** (Cook) semolina.

Griff [grɪf] m **-(e)s, -e** grip; (Vorrichtung) handle; **g—bereit** a handy.

Griffel ['grɪfəl] m -s,- slate pencil; (Bot) style.

Grille ['grɪlə] f -, -n cricket; (fig) whim; g—n vt grill.

Grimasse [grɪ'masə] f -, -n grimace.

Grimm [grɪm] m -(e)s fury; g—ig a furious; (heftig) fierce, severe.

grinsen ['grɪnzən] vi grin.

Grippe ['grɪpə] f-, -n influenza, flu.

grob [gro:p] a coarse, gross; Fehler, Verstoß gross; G—heit f coarseness; (grobe Außerung) G—ian ['gro:bia:n] m -s, -e ruffian; —knochig a large-boned.

Groll [grɔl] m -(e)s resentment; g—en vi bear ill will (+dat or mit towards); (Donner) rumble.

groß [gro:s] a big, large; (hoch) tall; (fig) great; im —en und ganzen on the whole; ad greatly; —artig a great, splendid; G—aufnahme f (Cine) close-up.

Größe ['grø:sə] f -, -n size; (fig) greatness; (Länge) height.

Groß- cpd: —einkauf m bulk purchase; —eltern pl grandparents pl; g—enteils ad mostly.

Größen- cpd: —unterschied m difference in size; —wahn m megalomania.

Groß- cpd: —format nt large size; —handel m wholesale trade; —händler m wholesaler; g—herzig a generous; —macht f great power; —maul m braggart; —mut f - magnanimity; g—mütig a magnanimous; —mutter f grandmother; g—spurig a pompous; —stadt f city, large town.

größte(r,s) ['grø:stə(r,z)] a superl of groß; g—nteils ad for the most part.

Groß- cpd: —tuer m -s, - boaster; g—tun' vi irreg boast; —vater m

grandfather; g—ziehen vt irreg raise; g—zügig a generous; Planung on a large scale.

grotesk [gro'tesk] a grotesque.

Grotte ['grɔtə] f -, -n grotto.

Grübchen ['gry:pçən] nt dimple.

Grube ['gru:bə] f-, -n pit; mine; —narbeiter m miner; —ngas nt firedamp.

grübeln ['gry:bəln] vi brood.

Grübler ['gry:blər] m -s, - brooder; g—isch a brooding, pensive.

Gruft [gruft] f -, -e tomb, vault.

grün [gry:n] a green; G—anlage f park.

Grund [grunt] m ground; (von See, Gefäß) bottom; (fig) reason; im —e genommen basically; —ausbildung f basic training; —bedeutung f basic meaning; —bedingung f fundamental condition; —besitz m land(ed property), real estate; —buch nt land register; g—ehrlich a thoroughly honest.

gründ- [grynd] cpd: —en vt found; —en auf (+acc) base on; vr be based (auf +dat on); g—er m -s, - founder; —lich a thorough; G—ung f foundation.

Grund- cpd: g—falsch a utterly wrong; —gebühr f basic charge; —gedanke m basic idea; —gesetz nt constitution; —lage f foundation; g—legend a fundamental; g—los a groundless; —mauer f foundation wall; —regel f basic rule; —riß m plan; (fig) outline; —satz m principle; g—sätzlich a,ad fundamental(ly); Frage of principle; (prinzipiell) on principle; —schule f elementary school; —stein m foundation stone; —steuer f rates pl; —stück nt estate; plot; g—verschieden a utterly different; —zug *m* characteristic.

Grün- *cpd:* —e *nt* -n: im —en in the open air; —kohl *m* kale; —schnabel *m* greenhorn; —span *m* verdigris; —streifen *m* central reservation.

grunzen ['grʊntsən] *vi* grunt.

Gruppe ['grʊpə] *f* -, -n group; g—nweise *ad* in groups.

gruppieren [grʊ'pi:rən] *vtr* group.

gruselig a creepy.

gruseln ['gru:zəln] *vi impers:* es gruselt jdm vor etw sth gives sb the creeps; *vr* have the creeps.

Gruß [gru:s] *m* -es, ̈-e greeting; (*Mil*) salute; viele ̈-e best wishes; ̈-e an (+*acc*) regards to.

grüßen ['gry:sən] *vt* greet; (*Mil*) salute; jdn von jdm — give sb sb's regards; jdn — lassen send sb one's regards.

gucken ['gʊkən] *vi* look.

Gulasch ['gu:laʃ] *nt* -(e)s, -e goulash.

gültig ['gʏltɪç] a valid; G—keit *f* validity; G—keitsdauer *f* period of validity.

Gummi ['gʊmi] *nt or m* -s, -s rubber; (—harze) gum; (—band *nt*) rubber or elastic band; (*Hosen*—) elastic; g—eren [gʊ'mi:rən] *vt* gum; —knüppel *m* rubber truncheon; —strumpf *m* elastic stocking.

Gunst [gʊnst] *f* - favour.

günstig ['gʏnstɪç] a favourable.

Gurgel ['gʊrgəl] *f* -, -n throat; g—n *vi* gurgle; (*im Mund*) gargle.

Gurke ['gʊrkə] *f* - cucumber; saure — pickled cucumber, gherkin.

Gurt [gʊrt] *m* -(e)s, -e, **Gurte** *f* -n -n belt.

Gürtel ['gʏrtəl] *m* -s, - belt; (*Geog*) zone; —reifen *m* radial tyre.

Guß [gʊs] *m* -sses, **Güsse** casting; (*Regen*—) downpour; (*Cook*) glazing; —eisen *nt* cast iron.

Gut [gu:t] *nt* -(e)s, ̈-er (*Besitz*) possession; (*pl:* Waren) goods *pl*; g— a good; ad well; laß es gut sein that'll do; —achten *nt* -s, - (expert) opinion; —achter *m* -s, - expert; g—artig a good-natured; (*Med*) benign; g—bürgerlich a Küche (good) plain; —dünken *nt:* nach —dünken at one's discretion.

Güte ['gy:tə] *f* - goodness, kindness; (*Qualität*) quality.

Güter- *cpd:* —abfertigung *f* (*Rail*) goods office; —bahnhof *m* goods station; —wagen *m* goods waggon, freight car (*US*); — zug *m* goods train, freight train (*US*).

Gut- *cpd:* g—gehen *v impers irreg* work, come off; es geht jdm g— sb's doing fine; g—gelaunt a good-humoured, in a good mood; g—gemeint a well meant; g—gläubig a trusting; —haben *nt* -s credit; g—heißen *vt irreg* approve (of); g—herzig a kind(-hearted).

gütig ['gy:tɪç] a kind.

gütlich ['gy:tlɪç] a amicable.

Gut- *cpd:* g—mütig a good-natured; —mütigkeit *f* good nature; —sbesitzer *m* landowner; —schein *m* voucher; g—schreiben *vt irreg* credit; —schrift *f* credit; —sherr *m* squire; g—tun *vi irreg:* jdm g—tun do sb good; g—willig a willing.

Gymnasium [gym'na:ziom] *nt* grammar school (*Brit*), high school (*US*).

H

Gymnastik [gym'nastɪk] *f* exercises *pl*, keep fit.

H, h [ha:] *nt* H, h.

Haar [ha:r] *nt* -(e)s, -e hair; um ein — nearly; —bürste *f* hairbrush; **h—en** *vir* lose hair; —esbreite *f*: um —esbreite by a hair's-breadth; **h—genau** *ad* precisely; **h—ig** a hairy; —klemme *f* hair grip; **h—los** a hairless; —nadel *f* hairpin; **h—scharf** ad beobachten very sharply; *daneben* by a hair's breadth; —schnitt *m* haircut; —schopf *m* head of hair; —spalte'rei *f* hair-splitting; —spange *f* hair slide; **h—sträubend** a hair-raising; —teil *nt* hairpiece; —waschmittel *nt* shampoo.

Habe ['ha:bə] *f* - property.

haben ['ha:bən] *vt*, *v aux irreg* have; Hunger/Angst — be hungry/afraid; woher hast du das? where did you get that from?; was hast du denn? what's the matter (with you?); H— *nt* -s, - credit.

Habgier *f* avarice; **h—ig** a avaricious.

Habicht ['ha:bɪçt] *m* -(e)s, -e hawk.

Habseligkeiten *pl* belongings *pl*.

Hachse ['haksə] *f* -, -n (*Cook*) knuckle.

Hacke ['hakə] *f* -, -n hoe; (*Ferse*) heel; **h—n** *vt* hack, chop; *Erde* hoe.

Hackfleisch *nt* mince, minced meat.

Häcksel ['hɛksəl] *m* or *nt* -s chopped straw, chaff.

hadern ['ha:dərn] *vi* quarrel.

Hafen ['ha:fən] *m* -s, ⁼ harbour, port; —arbeiter *m* docker; —damm *m* jetty, mole; —stadt *f* port.

Hafer ['ha:fər] *m* -s, - oats *pl*; —brei *m* porridge; —flocken *pl* porridge oats *pl*; —schleim *m* gruel.

Haft [haft] *f* - custody; **h—bar** a liable, responsible; —befehl *m* warrant (of arrest); **h—en** *vi* stick, cling; **h—en für** be liable or responsible for; **h—enbleiben** *vi irreg* stick (*an* + *dat* to); —pflicht *f* liability; —pflichtversicherung *f* third party insurance; —schalen *pl* contact lenses *pl*; —ung *f* liability.

·**Hage-** ['ha:gə] *cpd*: —butte *f* -, -n rose hip; —dorn *m* hawthorn.

Hagel ['ha:gəl] *m* -s hail; **h—n** *vi impers* hail.

hager ['ha:gər] a gaunt.

Häher ['hɛ:ər] *m* -s, - jay.

Hahn [ha:n] *m* -(e)s, ⁼e cock; (*Wasser-*) tap, faucet (*US*).

Hähnchen ['hɛ:nçən] *nt* cockerel; (*Cook*) chicken.

Hai(fisch) ['haɪ(fɪʃ)] *m* -(e)s, -e shark.

Häkchen ['hɛ:kçən] *nt* small hook.

Häkel- ['hɛ:kəl] *cpd*: —arbeit *f* crochet work; **h—n** *vt* crochet; —nadel *f* crochet hook.

Haken ['ha:kən] *m* -s, - hook; (*fig*) catch; —kreuz *nt* swastika; —nase *f* hooked nose.

halb [halp] a half; — eins half past twelve; ein —es Dutzend half a dozen; H—**dunkel** nt semidarkness..

halber ['halbər] prep +gen (wegen) on account of; (für) for the sake of.

Halb- cpd: —**heit** f half-measure; h—**ieren** vt halve; —**insel** f peninsula; h—**jährlich** a half-yearly; —**kreis** m semicircle; —**kugel** f hemisphere; h—**laut** a in an undertone; —**links** m -, (Sport) inside-left; —**mond** m half-moon; (fig) crescent; h—**offen** a half-open; —**rechts** m -, (Sport) inside-right; —**schuh** m shoe; —**tagsarbeit** f part-time work; h—**wegs** ad half-way; h—**wegs besser** more or less better; —**wüchsige(r)** mf adolescent; —**zeit** f (Sport) half; (Pause) half-time.

Halde ['haldə] f -, -n tip; (Schlacken—) slag heap.

Hälfte ['hɛlftə] -, -n f half.

Halfter ['halftər] f -, -n, or nt -s, - halter; (Pistolen—) holster.

Hall [hal] m -(e)s, -e sound.

Halle ['halə] f -, -n hall; (Aviat) hangar; h—n vi echo, resound; —nbad nt indoor swimming pool.

hallo [ha'lo:] interj hallo.

Halluzination [halutsinatsi'o:n] f hallucination.

Halm [halm] m -(e)s, -e blade, stalk.

Hals [hals] m -es, ⁼e neck; (Kehle) throat; — über Kopf in a rush; —**kette** f necklace; —**krause** f ruff; —**Nasen-Ohren-Arzt** m ear nose and throat specialist; —**schlagader** f carotid artery; —**schmerzen** pl sore throat; h—**starrig** a stubborn, obstinate; —**tuch** nt scarf; —**weh** nt sore throat; —**wirbel** m cervical vertebra.

Halt [halt] m -(e)s, -e stop; (fester —) hold; (innerer —) stability; h—! stop!, halt!; h—**bar** a durable; Lebensmittel non-perishable; (Mil, fig) tenable; —**barkeit** f durability; (non-)perishability; tenability.

halten ['haltən] irreg vt keep; (fest—) hold; — für regard as; — von think of; vi hold; (frisch bleiben) keep; (stoppen) stop; an sich — restrain oneself; vr (frisch bleiben) keep; (sich behaupten) hold out; sich rechts/links — keep to the right/left.

Halt- cpd: —**estelle** f stop; h—**los** a unstable; —**losigkeit** f instability; h—**machen** vi stop; —**ung** f posture; (fig) attitude; (Selbstbeherrschung) composure; —**verbot** nt ban on stopping.

Halunke [ha'luŋkə] m -n, -n rascal.

hämisch ['hɛ:mɪʃ] a malicious.

Hammel ['haməl] m -s, ⁼ or -wether; —**fleisch** nt mutton; —**keule** f leg of mutton.

Hammer ['hamər] m -s, ⁼ hammer.

hämmern ['hɛmərn] vti hammer.

Hampelmann ['hampəlman] m (lit, fig) puppet.

Hamster ['hamstər] m -s, - hamster; —**ei** [-'rai] f hoarding; —**er** m -s, - hoarder; h—**n** vi hoard.

Hand [hant] f -, ⁼e hand; —**arbeit** f manual work; (Nadelarbeit) needlework; —**arbeiter** m manual worker; —**besen** m manual brush; —**bremse** f handbrake; —**buch** nt handbook, manual.

Hände- ['hɛndə] cpd: —**druck** m handshake; —**klatschen** nt clapping, applause.

Handel ['handəl] m -s trade; (Geschäft) transaction; — **haben** quarrel.

handeln ['handəln] vi trade; act; — von be about; vr impers: es — handelt sich um be a question of, be about; H— nt -s action.

Handels- cpd: —bilanz f balance of trade; h—einig a: mit jdm h—einig werden conclude a deal with sb; —kammer f chamber of commerce; —marine f merchant navy; —recht nt commercial law; —reisende(r) m commercial traveller; —schule f business school; —vertreter m sales representative.

Hand- cpd: —feger m -s, - brush; h—fest a hefty; h—gearbeitet a handmade; —gelenk nt wrist; —gemenge nt scuffle; —gepäck nt hand-luggage; h—geschrieben a handwritten; h—greiflich a palpable; h—greiflich werden become violent; —griff m flick of the wrist; h—haben vt irreg insep handle; —karren m handcart; —kuß m kiss on the hand.

Händler ['hɛndlər] m -s, - trader, dealer.

handlich ['handlɪç] a handy.

Handlung ['handluŋ] f -, -en act(ion); (in Buch) plot; (Geschäft) shop; —sbevollmächtige(r) mf authorized agent; —sweise f manner of dealing.

Hand- cpd: —pflege f manicure; —schelle f handcuff; —schlag m handshake; —schrift f handwriting; (Text) manuscript; —schuh m glove; —tasche f handbag; —tuch nt towel; —werk nt trade, craft; —werker m -s - craftsman, artisan; —werkzeug nt tools pl.

Hanf [hanf] m -(e)s hemp.

Hang [haŋ] m -(e)s, -̈e inclination; (Ab-) slope.

Hänge- ['hɛŋə] in cpds hanging; —brücke f suspension bridge; —matte f hammock.

hängen ['hɛŋən] irreg vi hang; — an (fig) be attached to; vt hang (an + acc on(to)); sich — an (+ acc) hang on to, cling to; —bleiben vi irreg be caught (an + dat on); (fig) remain, stick.

Hängeschloß nt padlock.

hänseln ['hɛnzəln] vt tease.

hantieren [han'ti:rən] vi work, be busy; mit etw — handle sth.

hapern ['ha:pərn] vi impers: es hapert an etw (dat) sth leaves something to be desired.

Happen ['hapən] m -s, - mouthful.

Harfe ['harfə] f -, -n harp.

Harke ['harkə] f -, -n rake; h—n vti rake.

harmlos ['harmlo:s] a harmless; H—igkeit f harmlessness.

Harmonie [harmo'ni:] f harmony; h—ren vi harmonize.

Harmonika [har'mo:nika] f -, -s (Zieh—) concertina.

harmonisch [har'mo:nɪʃ] a harmonious.

Harmonium [har'mo:niʊm] nt -s, -nien or -s harmonium.

Harn [harn] m -(e)s, -e urine; —blase f bladder.

Harnisch ['harnɪʃ] m -(e)s, -e armour; jdn in — bringen infuriate sb; in — geraten become angry.

Harpune [har'pu:nə] f -, -n harpoon.

harren ['harən] vi wait (auf + acc for).

hart [hart] a hard; (fig) harsh.

Härte ['hɛrtə] f -, -n hardness; (fig) harshness; h—n vtr harden.

hart- cpd: —gekocht a hard-boiled; —gesotten a tough, hard-boiled;

—herzig a hard-hearted ; **—näckig** a stubborn ; **H—näckigkeit** f stubbornness.

Harz [haːrts] nt -es, -e resin.

Haschee [haˈʃeː] nt -s, -s hash.

haschen [ˈhaʃən] vt catch, snatch ; vi (col) smoke hash.

Haschisch [ˈhaʃɪʃ] nt - hashish.

Hase [ˈhaːzə] m -n, -n hare.

Haselnuß [ˈhaːzəlnus] f hazelnut.

Hasen- cpd : **—fuß** m coward ; **—scharte** f harelip.

Haspe [ˈhaspə] f -, -n hinge ; **—l** f -, -n reel, bobbin ; (Winde) winch.

Haß [has] m -sses hate, hatred.

hassen [ˈhasən] vt hate ; **—enswert** a hateful.

häßlich [ˈhɛslɪç] a ugly ; (gemein) nasty ; **H—keit** f ugliness ; nastiness.

Hast [hast] f - haste ; **h—en** vir rush ; **h—ig** a hasty.

hätscheln [ˈhɛtʃəln] vt pamper ; (zärtlich) cuddle.

Haube [ˈhaubə] f -, -n hood ; (Mütze) cap ; (Aut) bonnet, hood (US).

Hauch [haux] m -(e)s, -e breath ; (Luft—) breeze ; (fig) trace ; **h—en** vi breathe ; **h—fein** a very fine.

Haue [ˈhauə] f -, -n hoe, pick ; (col) hiding ; **h—n** vt irreg hew, cut ; (col) thrash.

Haufen [ˈhaufən] m -s, - heap ; (Leute) crowd ; ein — (x) (col) loads or a lot (of x) ; auf einem — in one heap ; **h—weise** ad in heaps ; in droves ; etw **h—weise** haben have piles of sth.

häufen [ˈhɔyfən] vt pile up ; vr accumulate.

häufig [ˈhɔyfɪç] a,ad frequent(ly) ; **H—keit** f frequency.

Haupt [haupt] nt -(e)s, Häupter head ; (Ober—) chief ; in cpds main ; **—bahnhof** m central station ; **h—beruflich** ad as one's main occupation ; **—buch** nt (Comm) ledger ; **—darsteller(in** f) m leading actor/actress ; **—eingang** m main entrance ; **—fach** nt main subject ; **—film** m main film.

Häuptling [ˈhɔyptlɪŋ] m chief(tain).

Haupt- cpd : **—mann** m, pl **-leute** (Mil) captain ; **—postamt** nt main post office ; **—quartier** nt headquarters pl ; **—rolle** f leading part ; **—sache** f main thing ; **h—sächlich** a,ad chief(ly) ; **—satz** m main clause ; **—schlagader** f aorta ; **—stadt** f capital ; **—straße** f main street ; **—wort** nt noun.

Haus [haus] nt -es, Häuser house ; nach —e home ; zu —e at home ; **—angestellte** f domestic servant ; **—arbeit** f housework ; (Sch) homework ; **—arzt** m family doctor ; **—aufgabe** f (Sch) homework ; **—besitzer(in** f) m, **—eigentümer(in** f) m house-owner.

hausen [ˈhauzən] vi live (in poverty) ; (pej) wreak havoc.

Häuser- [ˈhɔyzər] cpd : **—block** m block (of houses) ; **—makler** m estate agent.

Haus- cpd : **—frau** f housewife ; **—freund** m family friend ; (col) lover ; **h—gemacht** a home-made ; **—halt** m household ; (Pol) budget ; **h—halten** vi irreg keep house ; (sparen) economize ; **—hälterin** f housekeeper ; **—haltsgeld** nt housekeeping (money) ; **—haltsgerät** nt domestic appliance ; **—haltsplan** m budget ; **—haltung** f housekeeping ; **—herr** m host ; (Vermieter) landlord ; **h—hoch** ad : **h—hoch** verlieren lose by a mile.

hausieren [hau'zi:rən] vi hawk, peddle.

Hausierer m -s, - hawker, peddlar.

häuslich ['hɔyslɪç] a domestic; H—keit f domesticity.

Haus- cpd: —**meister** m caretaker, janitor; —**ordnung** f house·rules pl; —**putz** m house cleaning; —**schlüssel** m front-door key; —**schuh** m slipper; —**suchung** f police raid; —**tier** nt domestic animal; —**verwalter** m landlord; —**wirt** m landlord; —**wirtschaft** f domestic science.

Haut [haut] f -, Häute skin; (Tier—) hide.

häuten ['hɔytən] vt skin; vr slough one's skin.

Haut- cpd: h—**eng** a skin-tight; —**farbe** f complexion.

Haxe ['haksə] f -, -n see Hachse.

Hebamme ['he:p'amə] f -, -n midwife.

Hebel ['he:bəl] m -s, - lever.

heben ['he:bən] vt irreg raise, lift.

hecheln ['hɛçəln] vi (Hund) pant.

Hecht [hɛçt] m -(e)s, -e pike.

Heck [hɛk] nt -(e)s, -e stern; (von Auto) rear.

Hecke ['hɛkə] f -, -n hedge; —**nrose** f dog rose; —**schütze** m sniper.

Heer [he:r] nt -(e)s, -e army.

Hefe ['he:fə] f -, -n yeast.

Heft [hɛft] nt -(e)s, -e exercise book; (Zeitschrift) number; (von Messer) haft; h—en vt fasten (an +acc to); (nähen) tack; —er m -s, - folder.

heftig a fierce, violent; H—keit f fierceness, violence.

Heft- cpd: —**klammer** f paper clip; —**maschine** f stapling machine;

—**pflaster** nt sticking plaster; —**zwecke** f drawing pin.

hegen ['he:gən] vt nurse; (fig) harbour, foster.

Hehl [he:l] m or nt: kein(en) — aus etw (dat) machen make no secret of sth; —er m -s, - receiver (of stolen goods), fence.

Heide ['haidə] f -, -n heath, moor; (—kraut) heather; m -n, -n, Heidin f heathen, pagan; —**kraut** nt heather; —**lbeere** f bilberry; h—**nmäßig** a (col) terrific; —**ntum** nt paganism.

heidnisch ['haidnɪʃ] a heathen, pagan.

heikel ['haikəl] a awkward, thorny; (wählerisch) fussy.

Heil [hail] nt -(e)s well-being; (Seelen—) salvation; he— a in one piece, intact; h—interj hail; —and m -(e)s, -e saviour; h—bar a curable; h—en vt cure; vi heal; h—froh a very relieved; —**gymnastin** f physiotherapist.

heilig ['hailɪç] a holy; H—**abend** m Christmas Eve; H—e(r) mf saint; —en vt sanctify, hallow; H—**enschein** m halo; H—**keit** f holiness; —**sprechen** vt irreg canonize; H—**tum** nt shrine; (Gegenstand) relic.

Heil- cpd: h—**los** a unholy; —**mittel** nt remedy; h—**sam** a (fig) salutary; H—**sarmee** f Salvation Army; —**ung** f cure.

Heim [haim] nt -(e), -e home; h—ad home.

Heimat ['haima:t] f -, -en home (town/country etc); —**land** nt homeland; h—**lich** a native, home attr; Gefühle nostalgic; h—**los** a homeless; —**ort** m home town/area; —**vertriebene(r)** mf displaced person.

Heim- cpd: **h—begleiten** vt accompany home; **—elig** a homely; **h—fahren** vi irreg drive/go home; **—fahrt** f journey home; **—gang** m return home; (Tod) decease; **h—gehen** vi irreg go home; (sterben) pass away; **h—isch** a (gebürtig) native; sich **h—isch fühlen** feel at home; **—kehr** f -, -en homecoming; **h—kehren** vi return home; **h—lich** a secret; **—lichkeit** f secrecy; **—reise** f journey home; **h—suchen** vt afflict; (Geist) haunt; **h—tückisch** a malicious; **h—wärts** ad homewards; **—weg** m way home; **—weh** nt homesickness; **—weh haben** be homesick; **h—zahlen** vi; jdm etw **h—zahlen** pay back sb for sth.

Heirat ['haıra:t] f -, -en marriage; **h—en** vti marry; **—santrag** m proposal.

heiser ['haɪzər] a hoarse; **H—keit** f hoarseness.

heiß [haıs] a hot; **—e(r) Draht** hot line; **—blütig** a hot-blooded.

heißen ['haısən] irreg vi be called; (bedeuten) mean; vt command; (nennen) name; v impers it says; it is said.

Heiß- cpd: **h—ersehnt** a longed for; **—hunger** m ravenous hunger; **h—laufen** vir irreg overheat.

heiter ['haɪtər] a cheerful; Wetter bright; **H—keit** f cheerfulness; (Belustigung) amusement.

Heiz- ['haıts] cpd: **h—bar** a heated; Raum with heating; leicht **h—bar** easily heated; **—decke** f electric blanket; **h—en** vt heat; **—er** m -s, - stoker; **—körper** m radiator; **—öl** nt fuel oil; **—sonne** f electric fire; **—ung** f heating; **—ungsanlage** f heating system.

hektisch ['hɛktıʃ] a hectic.

Held [hɛlt] m -en, -en hero; **—in** f heroine.

helfen ['hɛlfən] irreg vi help (jdm sb, bei with); (nützen) be of use; sich (dat) zu — wissen be resourceful; v impers: es hilft nichts, du mußt ... it's no use, you have to ...

Helfer m -s, - helper, assistant; **—shelfer** m accomplice.

hell [hɛl] a clear, bright; Farbe light; **—blau** a light blue; **—blond** a ash-blond; **H—e** f - clearness, brightness; **H—er** m -s, - farthing; **—hörig** a keen of hearing; Wand poorly soundproofed; **H—igkeit** f clearness, brightness; lightness; **H—seher** m clairvoyant; **—wach** a wide-awake.

Helm ['hɛlm] m -(e)s, -e (auf Kopf) helmet.

Hemd [hɛmt] nt -(e)s, -en shirt; (Unter—) vest; **—bluse** f blouse; **—enknopf** m shirt button.

hemmen ['hɛmən] vt check, hold up; gehemmt sein be inhibited.

Hemmung f check; (Psych) inhibition; **h—slos** a unrestrained, without restraint.

Hengst [hɛŋst] m -es, -e stallion.

Henkel ['hɛŋkəl] m -s, - handle; **—krug** m jug.

henken ['hɛŋkən] vt hang.

Henker m -s, - hangman.

Henne ['hɛnə] f -, -n hen.

her [he:r] ad here; (Zeit) ago; **—damit!** hand it over!

herab [hɛ'rap] ad down(ward(s)); **—hängen** vi irreg hang down; **—lassen** irreg vt let down; vr condescend; **H—lassung** f condescension; **—sehen** vi irreg look down (auf +acc on); **—setzen** vt lower, reduce; (fig) belittle,

disparage; **H—setzung** f reduction; disparagement; —würdigen vt belittle, disparage.
heran [hɛˈran] ad: näher —! come up closer!; — zu mir! come up to me!; —bilden vt train; —bringen vt irreg bring up (an +acc to); —fahren vi irreg drive up (an +acc to); —kommen vi irreg (an +acc) approach, come near; —machen vr: sich an jdn —machen make up to sb; —wachsen vi irreg grow up; —ziehen vt irreg pull nearer; (aufziehen) raise; (ausbilden) train; jdn zu etw —ziehen call upon sb to help in sth.
herauf [hɛˈrauf] ad up(ward(s)), up here; —beschwören vt irreg conjure up, evoke; —bringen vt irreg bring up; —ziehen vt irreg draw or pull up; vi approach; (Sturm) gather.
heraus [hɛˈraus] ad out; outside; from; —arbeiten vt work out; —bekommen vt irreg get out; (fig) find or figure out; —bringen vt irreg bring out; Geheimnis elicit; —finden vt irreg find out; —fordern vt challenge; **H—forderung** f challenge; provocation; —geben vt irreg give up, surrender; Geld give back; Buch edit; (veröffentlichen) publish; —geber m -s, - editor; (Verleger) publisher; —gehen vt irreg: aus sich (dat) —gehen come out of one's shell; —halten vr irreg: sich aus etw —halten keep out of sth; —hängen vti irreg hang out; —holen vt get out (aus of); —kommen vi irreg come out; dabei kommt nichts — nothing will come of it; —nehmen vt irreg take out; sich (dat) Freiheiten —nehmen take liberties; —reißen vt irreg tear

out; pull out; —rücken vt Geld fork out, hand over; mit etw —rücken (fig) come out with sth; —rutschen vi slip out; —schlagen vt irreg knock out; (fig) obtain; —stellen vr turn out (als to be); —wachsen vi irreg grow out (aus of); —ziehen vt irreg pull out, extract.
herb [hɛrp] a (slightly) bitter, acid; Wein dry; (fig) (schmerzlich) bitter; (streng) stern, austere.
herbei [hɛrˈbai] ad (over) here; —führen vt bring about; —lassen vr irreg: sich —lassen zu condescend or deign to; —schaffen vt procure.
herbemühen [hɛrbəmyːən] vr take the trouble to come.
Herberge [hɛrˈbɛrgə] f -, -n shelter; hostel, inn.
Herbergsmutter f, **Herbergsvater** m warden.
her- [hɛr] cpd: —bitten vt irreg ask to come (here); —bringen vt irreg bring here.
Herbst [hɛrpst] m -(e)s, -e autumn, fall (US); **h—lich** a autumnal.
Herd [heːrt] m -(e)s, -e cooker; (fig, Med) focus, centre.
Herde [ˈheːrdə] f -, -n herd; (Schaf—) flock.
herein [hɛˈrain] ad in (here), here; —! come in!; —bitten vt irreg ask in; —brechen vi irreg break in; —bringen vt irreg bring in; —dürfen vi irreg have permission to enter; **H—fall** m letdown; —fallen vi irreg be caught, taken in; —fallen auf (+acc) fall for; —kommen vi irreg come in; —lassen vt irreg admit; —legen vt: jdn —legen take sb in; —platzen vi burst in.

Her- 149 hervor

Her- ['hɛr] cpd: **—fahrt** f journey here; **h—fallen** vi irreg: **h—fallen über** fall upon; **—gang** m course of events, circumstances pl; **h—geben** vt irreg give, hand (over); **sich zu etw h—geben** lend one's name to sth; **h—gehen** vi irreg: **hinter jdm h—gehen** follow sb; **es geht hoch h—** there are a lot of goings-on; **h—halten** vt irreg hold out; **h—halten müssen** (col) have to suffer; **h—hören** vi listen; **hör mal h—!** listen here!

Hering ['heːrɪŋ] m **-s, -e** herring.

her- ['hɛr] cpd: **—kommen** vi irreg come; **komm mal h—!** come here!; **—kömmlich** a traditional; **H—kunft** f **-, ¨-künfte** origin; **—laufen** vi irreg; **—laufen hinter** (+dat) run after; **—leiten** vr derive; **—machen** vr: **sich —machen über** (+acc) set about or upon.

Hermelin [hɛrmə'liːn] m or nt **-s, -e** ermine.

hermetisch [hɛr'meːtɪʃ] a,ad hermetic(ally).

her- cpd: **—nach** ad afterwards; **—'nieder** ad down.

heroisch [he'roːɪʃ] a heroic.

Herold ['heːrɔlt] m **-(e)s, -e** herald.

Herr [hɛr] m **-(e)n, -en** master; (Mann) gentleman; (adliger, Rel) Lord; (vor Namen) Mr.; **mein —!** sir!; **meine —en!** gentlemen!; **—enbekanntschaft** f gentleman friend; **—endoppel** nt men's doubles; **—eneinzel** nt men's singles; **—enhaus** nt mansion; **h—enlos** a ownerless.

herrichten ['hɛrrɪçtən] vt prepare.

Herr- cpd: **—in** f mistress; **h—isch** a domineering; **h—lich** a marvellous, splendid; **—lichkeit** f splendour, magnificence; **—schaft**

f power, rule; (Herr und Herrin) master and mistress; **meine —schaften!** ladies and gentlemen!

herrschen ['hɛrʃən] vt rule; (bestehen) prevail.

Herrscher(in f) m **-s, -** ruler.

Herrschsucht f domineering behaviour.

her- ['hɛr] cpd: **—rühren** vi arise, originate; **—sagen** vt recite; **—stammen** vi descend, come from; **—stellen** vt make, manufacture; **H—steller** m **-s, -** manufacturer; **H—stellung** f manufacture; **H—stellungskosten** pl manufacturing costs pl.

herüber [hɛ'ryːbər] ad over (here), across.

herum [hɛ'rʊm] ad about, (a)round; **um etw —** around sth; **—ärgern** vr get annoyed (mit with); **—führen** vt show around; **—gehen** vi irreg walk or go round (um etw sth); walk about; **—irren** vi wander about; **—kriegen** vt bring or talk around; **—lungern** vi lounge about; **—sprechen** vr irreg get around, be spread; **—treiben** vir irreg drift about; **—ziehen** vi irreg wander about.

herunter [hɛ'rʊntər] ad downward(s), down (there); **—gekommen** a run-down; **—hängen** vi irreg hang down; **—holen** vt bring down; **—kommen** vi irreg come down; (fig) come down in the world; **—machen** vt take down; (schimpfen) abuse, criticise severely.

hervor [hɛr'foːr] ad out, forth; **—brechen** vi irreg burst forth, break out; **—bringen** vt irreg produce; Wort utter; **—gehen** vi irreg emerge, result; **—heben** vt irreg stress; (als Kontrast) set off;

—ragend a excellent; (lit) projecting; —rufen vt irreg cause, give rise to; —treten vi irreg come out.

Herz [herts] nt -ens, -en heart; —anfall m heart attack; h—en vt caress, embrace; —enslust f: nach —enslust to one's heart's content; —fehler m heart defect; h—haft a hearty; —infarkt m heart attack; —klopfen nt palpitation; h—lich a cordial; h—lichen Glückwunsch congratulations pl; h—liche Grüße best wishes; —lichkeit f cordiality; h—los a heartless; —losigkeit f heartlessness.

Herzog ['hertso:k] m -(e)s, -e duke; —in f duchess; h—lich a ducal; —tum nt duchy.

Herz- cpd: —schlag m heartbeat, (Med) heart attack; h—zerreißend a heartrending.

heterogen [hetero'ge:n] a heterogeneous.

Hetze ['hetsə] f -, -n (Eile) rush; h—n vt hunt; (verfolgen) chase; jdn/etw auf jdn/etw — set sb/sth on sb/sth; vi (eilen) rush; h—n gegen stir up feeling against; h—n zu agitate for; —rei f agitation; (Eile) rush.

Heu [hɔy] nt -(e)s hay; —boden m hayloft.

Heuchelei [hɔyçə'laɪ] f hypocrisy.

heucheln ['hɔyçəln] vt pretend, feign; vi be hypocritical.

Heuchler(in f) [hɔyçlər(ɪn)] m -s, - hypocrite; h—isch a hypocritical.

Heuer ['hɔyər] f -, -n (Naut) pay; h— ad this year.

Heugabel f pitchfork.

heulen ['hɔylən] vi howl; cry; das —de Elend bekommen get the blues.

heurig ['hɔyrɪç] a this year's.

Heu- cpd: —schnupfen m hay

fever; —schrecke f grasshopper, locust.

heute ['hɔytə] ad today; — abend/früh this evening/morning; das H— today.

heutig ['hɔytɪç] a today's.

heutzutage ['hɔyttsuta:gə] ad nowadays.

Hexe ['hɛksə] f -, -n witch; h—n vi practise witchcraft; ich kann doch nicht h—n I can't work miracles; —nkessel m (lit, fig) cauldron; —nmeister m wizard; —nschuß m lumbago; —rei f witchcraft.

Hieb [hi:p] m -(e)s, -e blow; (Wunde) cut, gash; (Stichelei) cutting remark; —e bekommen get a thrashing.

hier [hi:r] ad here; —auf ad thereupon; (danach) after that; —behalten vt irreg keep here; —bei ad herewith, enclosed; —bleiben vi irreg stay here; —durch ad by this means; (örtlich) through here; —her ad this way, here; —lassen vt irreg leave here; —mit ad hereby; —nach ad hereafter; —von ad about this, hereof; —zulande ad in this country.

hiesig ['hi:zɪç] a of this place, local.

Hilfe ['hɪlfə] f -, -n help; aid; Erste — first aid; —! help!

Hilf- cpd: h—los a helpless; —losigkeit f helplessness; h—reich a helpful; —saktion f relief measures pl; —sarbeiter m labourer; h—sbedürftig a needy; h—sbereit a ready to help; —skraft f assistant, helper; —sschule f school for backward children; —szeitwort nt auxiliary verb.

Himbeere ['hɪmbe:rə] f -, -n raspberry.

Himmel ['hɪml] m -s, - sky; (Rel, liter) heaven; h—angst a: es ist mir

h—angst I'm scared to death;
h—blau a sky-blue; —fahrt f
Ascension; h—schreiend a outrageous; —srichfung f direction.

himmlisch ['hɪmlɪʃ] a heavenly.

hin [hɪn] ad there; — und her to
and fro; bis zur Mauer — up to
the wall; Geld —, Geld her money
or no money; mein Glück ist —
my happiness has gone.

hinab [hɪ'nap] ad down; —gehen vi
irreg go down; —sehen vi irreg
look down.

hinauf [hɪ'nauf] ad up; —arbeiten
vr work one's way up; —steigen
vi irreg climb.

hinaus [hɪ'naus] ad out;
—befördern vt kick/throw out;
—gehen vi irreg go out; —gehen
über (+acc) exceed; —laufen vi
irreg run out; —laufen auf (+acc)
come to, amount to; —schieben vt
irreg put off, postpone; —werfen
vt irreg throw out; —wollen vi
want to .go out; —wollen auf
(+acc) drive at, get at; —ziehen
irreg vt draw out; vr be protracted.

Hinblick ['hɪnblɪk] m: in or im —
auf (+acc) in view of.

hinder- ['hɪndər] cpd: —lich a
awkward; —n vt hinder, hamper;
jdn an etw (dat) —n prevent sb
from doing sth; H—nis nt -ses, -se
obstacle.

hindeuten ['hɪndɔytən] vi point
(auf +acc to).

hindurch [hɪn'durç] ad through;
across; (zeitlich) over.

hinein [hɪ'naɪn] ad in; —fallen vi
irreg fall in; —fallen in (+acc) fall
into; —gehen vi irreg go in;
—gehen in (+acc) go into, enter;
—geraten vi irreg: —geraten in
(+acc) get into; —passen vi fit in;
—passen in (+acc) fit into;

—reden vi: jdm —reden interfere
in sb's affairs; —steigern vr get
worked up; —versetzen vr: sich
—versetzen in (+acc) put oneself
in the position of.

hin- ['hɪn] cpd: —fahren irreg vi go;
drive; vt take; drive; H—fahrt f
journey there; —fallen vi irreg fall
down; —fällig a frail, decrepit;
Regel etc unnecessary, otiose;
H—gabe f devotion; —geben vr
irreg +dat give oneself up to,
devote oneself to; —gehen vi irreg
go; (Zeit) pass; —halten vt irreg
hold out; (warten lassen) put off,
stall.

hinken ['hɪŋkən] vi limp;
(Vergleich) be unconvincing.

hin- ['hɪn] cpd: —legen vt put
down; vr lie down; —nehmen vt
irreg (fig) put up with, take;
—reichen vi be adequate; vt: jdm
etw —reichen hand sb sth;
H—reise f journey out; —reißen vt
irreg carry away, enrapture; sich
—reißen lassen, etw zu tun get
carried away and do sth; —richten
vt execute; H—richtung f
execution; —sichtlich prep +gen
with regard to; H—spiel nt (Sport)
first leg; —stellen vt put (down);
vr place o.s.

hintanstellen [hɪnt'anʃtɛlən] vt
(fig) ignore.

hinten ['hɪntən] ad at the back;
behind; —herum ad round the
back; (fig) secretly.

hinter ['hɪntər] prep +dat or acc
behind; (nach) after; — jdm
hersein be after sb; H—achse f rear
axle; H—bein nt hind leg; sich auf
die H—beine stellen get tough;
H—bliebene(r) mf surviving
relative; —drein ad afterwards;
—e(r,s) a rear, back; —einander ad

one after the other; H—gedanke m ulterior motive; —gehen vt irreg deceive; H—grund m background; H—halt m ambush; —häftig a underhand, sneaky; —her ad afterwards, after; H—hof m backyard; H—kopf m back of one's head; —'lassen vt irreg leave; H—'lassenschaft f (testator's) estate; —'legen vt deposit; H—list f cunning, trickery; (Handlung) trick, dodge; —listig a cunning, crafty; H—mann m, pl —männer person behind; H—rad nt back wheel; H—radantrieb m (Aut) rear wheel drive; —rücks ad from behind; H—teil nt behind; H—treffen nt: ins H—treffen kommen lose ground; —'treiben vt irreg prevent, frustrate; H—tür f back door; (fig: Ausweg) 'escape, loophole; —'ziehen vt irreg Steuern evade (paying).

hinüber [hɪ'ny:bər] ad across, over; —gehen vi irreg go over or across.

hinunter [hɪ'nʊntər] ad down; —bringen vt irreg take down; —schlucken vt (lit, fig) swallow; —steigen vi irreg descend.

hin- ['hɪn] cpd: H—weg m journey out; —'weghelfen vi irreg: jdm über etw (acc) —weghelfen help sb to get over sth; —'wegsetzen vr: sich —wegsetzen über (+acc) disregard; H—weis m -es, -e (Andeutung) hint; (Anweisung) instruction; (Verweis) reference; —weisen vi irreg (auf +acc) (anzeigen) point to; (sagen) point out, refer to; —'werfen vt irreg throw down; —'ziehen vt irreg (fig) drag on; —zielen vi aim (auf +acc at).

hinzu [hɪn'tsu:] ad in addition; —fügen vt add.

Hirn [hɪrn] nt -(e)s, -e brain(s); —gespinst nt -(e)s, -e fantasy; h—verbrannt a half-baked, crazy.
Hirsch [hɪrʃ] m -(e)s, -e stag.
Hirse ['hɪrzə] f -, -n millet.
Hirt [hɪrt] m -en, -en herdsman; (Schaf—, fig) shepherd.
hissen ['hɪsən] vt hoist.
Historiker [hɪs'to:rikər] m -s, — historian.
historisch [hɪs'to:rɪʃ] a historical.
Hitze ['hɪtsə] f - heat; h—beständig a heat-resistant; —welle f heatwave.
hitzig a hot-tempered; Debatte heated.
Hitz- cpd: —kopf m hothead; h—köpfig a fiery, hotheaded; —schlag m heatstroke.
Hobel ['ho:bal] m -s, - plane; —bank f carpenter's bench; h—n vti plane; —späne pl wood shavings pl.
hoch [ho:x] a high; H— nt -s, -s (Ruf) cheer; (Met) anticyclone; —achten vt respect; H—achtung f respect, esteem; —achtungsvoll ad yours faithfully; H—amt nt high mass; —arbeiten vr work one's way up; —begabt a extremely gifted; —betagt a very old, aged; H—betrieb m intense activity; (Comm) peak time; —bringen vt irreg bring up; H—burg f stronghold; H—deutsch nt High German; —dotiert a highly paid; H—druck m high pressure; H—ebene f plateau; —erfreut a highly delighted; —fliegend a (fig) highflown; H—form f top form; —gradig a intense, extreme; —halten vt irreg hold up; (fig) uphold, cherish; H—haus nt multi-storey building; —heben vt irreg lift (up); H—konjunktur f boom;

H—land *nt* highlands *pl*; —leben *vi*: jdn —leben lassen give sb three cheers; H—mut *m* pride; —mütig a proud, haughty; —näsig a stuck-up, snooty; H—ofen *m* blast furnace; —prozentig a *Alkohol* strong; H—rechnung *f* projected result; H—saison *f* high season; H—schätzung *f* high esteem; H—schule *f* college; university; H—sommer *m* middle of summer; H—spannung *f* high tension; H—sprache *f* standard language; —springen *vi irreg* jump up, H—sprung *m* high jump.

höchst [hø:çst] *ad* highly, extremely; —e(r,s) a highest; *(äußerste)* extreme.

Hochstapler ['ho:xsta:plər] *m* -s, - swindler.

Höchst- *cpd*: h—ens *ad* at the most; —geschwindigkeit *f* maximum speed; h—persönlich *ad*. in person; —preis *m* maximum price; h—wahrscheinlich *ad* most probably.

Hoch- *cpd* h—trabend a pompous; —verrat *m* high treason; —wasser *nt* high water; *(Überschwemmung)* floods *pl*; h—wertig a high-class, first-rate; —würden *m* Reverend; —zahl *f (Math)* exponent.

Hochzeit ['hɔxtsait] *f* -, -en wedding; —sreise *f* honeymoon.

hocken ['hɔkən] *vir* squat, crouch.

Hocker *m* -s, - stool.

Höcker ['hœkər] *m* -s, - hump.

Hode ['ho:də] *m* -n, -n testicle.

Hof [ho:f] *m* -(e)s, -̈e *(Hinter—)* yard; *(Bauern—)* farm; *(Königs—)* court.

hoffen ['hɔfən] *vi* hope *(auf +acc* for); —tlich *ad* I hope, hopefully.

Hoffnung ['hɔfnuŋ] *f* hope; h—slos a hopeless; —slosigkeit *f*

hopelessness; —sschimmer *m* glimmer of hope; h—svoll a hopeful.

höflich ['hø:fliç] a polite, courteous; H—keit *f* courtesy, politeness.

hohe(r,s) ['ho:ə(r,z)] a *see* hoch.

Höhe ['hø:ə] *f* -, -n height; *(An—)* hill.

Hoheit ['ho:hait] *f (Pol)* sovereignty; *(Titel)* Highness; —sgebiet *nt* sovereign territory; —sgewässer *nt* territorial waters *pl*; —szeichen *nt* national emblem.

Höhen- ['hø:ən] *cpd*: —angabe *f* altitude reading; *(auf Karte)* height marking; —messer *m* -s, - altimeter; —sonne *f* sun lamp; —unterschied *m* difference in altitude; —zug *m* mountain chain.

Höhepunkt *m* climax.

höher a,*ad* higher.

hohl [ho:l] a hollow.

Höhle ['hø:lə] *f* -, -n cave, hole; *(Mund—)* cavity; *(fig, Zool)* den.

Hohl- *cpd*: —heit *f* hollowness; —maß *nt* measure of volume; —saum *m* hemstitch.

Hohn [ho:n] *m* -(e)s scorn.

höhnen ['hø:nən] *vt* taunt, scoff at.

höhnisch a scornful, taunting.

hold [hɔlt] a charming, sweet.

holen ['ho:lən] *vt* get, fetch; *Atem* take; jdn/etw — lassen send for sb/sth.

Hölle ['hœlə] *f* -, -n hell; —nangst *f*: eine —nangst haben be scared to death.

höllisch ['hœliʃ] a hellish, infernal.

holperig ['hɔlpəriç] a rough, bumpy.

holpern ['hɔlpərn] *vi jolt*.

Holunder [ho'lundər] *m* -s, - elder.

Holz [hɔlts] *nt* -es, -̈er wood.

hölzern ['hœltsərn] a (lit, fig) wooden.

Holz- cpd: **—fäller** m -s, - lumberjack, woodcutter; **h—ig** a woody; **—klotz** m wooden block; **—kohle** f charcoal; **—scheit** nt log; **—schuh** m clog; **—weg** m (fig) wrong track; **—wolle** f fine wood shavings pl; **—wurm** m woodworm.

homosexuell [homozeksu'ɛl] a homosexual.

Honig ['hoːnɪç] m -s, -e honey; **—wabe** f honeycomb.

Honorar [hono'raːr] nt -s, -e fee.

honorieren [hono'riːrən] vt remunerate; Scheck honour.

Hopfen ['hɔpfən] m -s, - hops pl.

hopsen ['hɔpsən] vi hop.

Hör- cpd: **—apparat** m hearing aid; **h—bar** a audible.

horch [hɔrç] interj listen; **—en** vi listen; (pej) eavesdrop; **H—er** m -s, - listener; eavesdropper.

Horde ['hɔrdə] f -, -n horde.

hören ['høːrən] vti hear; **H—sagen** nt: vom **H—sagen** from hearsay.

Hörer m -s, - hearer; (Rad) listener; (Univ) student; (Telefon—) receiver.

Horizont [hori'tsɔnt] m -(e)s, -e horizon; **h—al** [-'taːl] a horizontal.

Hormon [hɔr'moːn] nt -s, -e hormone.

Hörmuschel f (Tel) earpiece.

Horn [hɔrn] nt -(e)s, ⁻er horn; **—haut** f horny skin.

Hornisse [hɔr'nɪsə] f -, -n hornet.

Horoskop [horo'skoːp] nt -s, -e horoscope.

Hör- cpd **—rohr** nt ear trumpet; (Med) stethoscope; **—spiel** nt radio play.

Hort [hɔrt] m -(e)s, -e hoard;

(Sch) nursery school; **h—en** vt hoard.

Hose ['hoːzə] f -, -n trousers pl, pants (US) pl; **—nanzug** m trouser suit; **—nrock** m culottes pl; **—ntasche** f (trouser) pocket; **—nträger** m braces pl, suspenders (US) pl.

Hostie ['hɔstiə] f (Rel) host.

Hotel [ho'tɛl] nt -s, -s hotel; **—ier** [hotɛliˈeː] m -s, -s hotelkeeper, hotelier.

Hub [huːp] m -(e)s, ⁻e lift; (Tech) stroke.

hüben ['hyːbən] ad on this side, over here.

Hubraum m (Aut) cubic capacity.

hübsch [hypʃ] a pretty, nice.

Hubschrauber m -s, - helicopter.

hudeln ['huːdəln] vi be sloppy.

Huf [huːf] m -(e)s, -e hoof; **—eisen** nt horseshoe; **—nagel** m horseshoe nail.

Hüft- ['hyft] cpd: —e f -, -n hip; **—gürtel** m —halter m -s, - girdle.

Hügel ['hyːgəl] m -s, - hill; **h—ig** a hilly.

Huhn [huːn] nt -(e)s, ⁻er hen; (Cook) chicken.

Hühner- ['hyːnər] cpd: **—auge** nt corn; **—brühe** f chicken broth.

Huld [hʊlt] f - favour; **h—igen** ['hʊldɪgən] vi pay homage (jdm to sb); **—igung** f homage.

Hülle ['hylə] f -, -n cover(ing); wrapping; **in —** und Fülle galore; **h—n** vt cover, wrap (in +acc with).

Hülse ['hylzə] f -, -n husk, shell; **—nfrucht** f legume.

human [hu'maːn] a humane; **—itär** a humanitarian; **H—ität** f humanity.

Hummel ['hʊməl] f -, -n bumblebee.

Hummer ['humər] *m* -s, - lobster.
Humor [hu'mo:r] *m* -s, -e humour;
— haben have a sense of humour;
—ist [-'rɪst] *m* humorist; h—istisch
a, h—voll *a* humorous.
humpeln ['humpəln] *vi* hobble.
Humpen ['humpən] *m* -s, - tankard.
Hund [hunt] *m* -(e)s, -e dog;
—ehütte *f* (dog) kennel; —ekuchen
m dog biscuit; h—emüde *a* (col)
dog-tired.
hundert ['hundərt] *num* hundred;
H—'jahrfeier *f* centenary; —
prozentig *a,ad* one hundred per
cent.
Hündin ['hyndɪn] *f* bitch.
Hunger ['huŋər] *m* -s hunger; —
haben be hungry; —lohn *m* starvation wages *pl*; h—n *vi* starve;
—snot *f* famine; —streik *m* hunger
strike.
hungrig ['huŋrɪç] *a* hungry.
Hupe ['hu:pə] *f* -, -n horn, hooter;
h—n *vi* hoot, sound one's horn.
hüpfen ['hypfən] *vi* hop, jump.
Hürde ['hyrdə] *f* -, -n hurdle; (für
Schafe) pen; —nlauf *m* hurdling.
Hure ['hu:rə] *f* -, -n whore.
hurtig ['hurtɪç] *a,ad* brisk(ly),
quick(ly).
huschen ['huʃən] *vi* flit, scurry.
Husten ['hu:stən] *m* -s cough; h—
vi cough; —anfall *m* coughing fit;
—bonbon *m* or *nt* cough drop;

—saft *m* cough mixture.
Hut [hu:t] *m* -(e)s, -̈e hat; *f* - care;
auf der — sein be on one's guard.
hüten ['hy:tən] *vt* guard; *vr* watch•
out; sich —, zu take care not to;
sich — vor beware of.
Hütte ['hytə] *f* -, -n hut, cottage;
(Eisen—) forge; —nwerk *nt*
foundry.
hutzelig ['hutsəlɪç] *a* shrivelled.
Hyäne [hy'ɛ:nə] *f* -, -n hyena.
Hyazinthe [hya'tsɪntə] *f* -, -n
hyacinth.
Hydr- *cpd:* —ant [hy'drant] *m*
hydrant; h—aulisch [hy'draulɪʃ] *a*
hydraulic; —ierung [hy'dri:ruŋ] *f*
hydrogenation.
Hygiene [hygi'e:nə] *f* - hygiene.
hygienisch [hygi'e:nɪʃ] *a* hygienic.
Hymne ['hymnə] *f* -, -n hymn,
anthem.
hyper- ['hypɛr] *pref* hyper-.
Hypno- [hyp'no] *cpd:* —se *f* -, -n
hypnosis; h—tisch *a* hypnotic;
—tiseur [-ti'zø:r] hypnotist; h—
ti'sieren *vt* hypnotize.
Hypothek [hypo'te:k] *f* -, -en
mortgage.
Hypothese [hypo'te:zə] *f* -, -n
hypothesis.
hypothetisch [hypo'te:tɪʃ] *a* hypo-
thetical.
Hysterie [hyste'ri:] *f* hysteria.
hysterisch [hys'te:rɪʃ] *a* hysterical.

I

I, i [i:] *nt* I, i.
ich [ɪç] *pron* I; — bin's! it's me!
I— *nt* -(s), -(s) self; (Psych) ego.
Ideal [ide'a:l] *nt* -s, -e ideal; i— *a*

ideal; —ist [-'lɪst] *m* idealist;
i—istisch [-'lɪstɪʃ] *a* idealistic.
Idee [i'de:] *f* -, -n [i'de:ən] idea;
i—ll [ide'ɛl] *a* ideal.

identi- [i'dɛnti] cpd: **—fizieren** [-fi'tsi:rən] vt identify; **—sch** a identical; **I—tät** ['-'tɛ:t] f identity.

Ideo- [ideo] cpd: **—loge** [-'lo:gə] m -n, -n ideologist; **—logie** [-lo'gi:] f ideology; **i—logisch** [-'lo:giʃ] a ideological.

idiomatisch [idio'ma:tiʃ] a idiomatic.

Idiot [idi'o:t] m -en, -en idiot; **i—isch** a idiotic.

idyllisch [i'dyliʃ] a idyllic.

Igel ['i:gəl] m -s, - hedgehog.

ignorieren [igno'ri:rən] vt ignore.

ihm [i:m] pron dat of er, es (to) him, (to) it.

ihn [i:n] pron acc of er him; it; **—en** pron dat of sie·pl (to) them; **I—en** pron dat of Sie (to) you.

ihr [i:r] pron·nom pl you; dat of sie sing (to) her; **—(e)** poss pron sing her; its; pl their; **I—(e)** poss pron your; **—(e)r,s)** poss pron hers; its; pl theirs; **I—e(r,s)** poss pron yours; **—er** pron gen of sie sing/pl of her/them; **I—er** gen of Sie of you; **—erseits** ad for her/their part; **—esgleichen** pron people like her/them; (von Dingen) others like it; **—etwegen, —etwillen** ad (für sie) for her/its/their sake; (wegen ihr) on her/its/their account; **—ige** pron: der/die/das **—ige** hers; its; theirs.

Ikone [i'ko:nə] f -, -n icon.

illegal ['ilega:l] a illegal.

Illusion [iluzi'o:n] f illusion.

illusorisch [ilu'zo:riʃ] a illusory.

illustrieren [ilus'tri:rən] vt illustrate.

Illustrierte f -n, -n picture magazine.

Iltis ['iltis] m -ses, -se polecat.

im [im] = in dem.

imaginär [imagi'nɛ:r] a imaginary.

Imbiß ['imbis] m -sses, -sse snack; **—halle** f, **—stube** f snack bar.

imitieren [imi'ti:rən] vt imitate.

Imker ['imkər] m -s, - beekeeper.

Immatrikulation [imatrikulat-si'o:n] f (Univ) registration.

immatrikulieren [imatriku'li:rən] vir register.

immer ['imər] ad always; **—wieder** again and again; **—noch** still; **—noch nicht** still not; **für —** forever; **—wenn ich ...** everytime I ...; **—schöner/trauriger** more and more beautiful/sadder and sadder; **was/wer (auch) —** whatever/whoever; **—hin** ad all the same; **—zu** ad all the time.

Immobilien [imo'bi:liən] pl real estate.

immun [i'mu:n] a immune; **I—ität** [-i'tɛ:t] f immunity.

Imperativ ['imperati:f] m -s, -e imperative.

Imperfekt ['imperfɛkt] nt -s, -e imperfect (tense).

Imperialist [imperia'list] imperialist; **I—isch** a imperialistic.

Impf- [impf] cpd: **i—en** vt vaccinate; **—stoff** m vaccine; **—ung** f vaccination; **—zwang** m compulsory vaccination.

implizieren [impli'tsi:rən] vt imply (mit by).

imponieren [impo'ni:rən] vi impress (jdm sb).

Import [im'port] m -(e)s, -e import; **i—ieren** [-'ti:rən] vt import.

imposant [impo'zant] a imposing.

impotent ['impotent] a impotent.

imprägnieren [imprɛ'gni:rən] vt (water)proof.

Improvisation [ɪmproviza'tsi'o:n] f improvization.

improvisieren [ɪmprovi'zi:rən] vti improvize.

Impuls [ɪm'puls] m -es, -e impulse; **i—iv** [-'zi:f] a impulsive.

imstande [ɪm'ʃtandə] a: — sein be in a position; (fähig) be able.

in [ɪn] prep +acc in(to); to; +dat in; — der/die Stadt in/into town; — der/die Schule at/to school.

Inanspruchnahme [ɪn'ʔanʃpru:x-na:mə] f-, -n demands pl (gen on).

Inbegriff ['ɪnbəgrɪf] m embodiment, personification; **i—en** ad included.

inbrünstig ['ɪnbrʏnstɪç] a ardent.

indem [ɪn'de:m] cj while; — man etw macht (dadurch) by doing sth.

indes(sen) [ɪn'dɛs(ən)] ad meanwhile; cj while.

Indianer(in f) [ɪndi'a:nər(ɪn)] m -s, - Red Indian.

indianisch a Red Indian.

indigniert [ɪndi'gni:rt] a indignant.

Indikativ ['ɪndikati:f] m -s, -e indicative.

indirekt ['ɪndirɛkt] a indirect.

indiskret ['ɪndɪskre:t] a indiscreet; **I—ion** [ɪndɪskretsi'o:n] f indiscretion.

indiskutabel ['ɪndɪskuta'be:l] a out of the question.

Individu [ɪndivi'du:] cpd: **—alist** [-a'lɪst] m individualist; **—alität** [-ali'tɛt] f individuality; **i—ell** [-'ɛl] a individual; **—um** [ɪndi'vi:duʊm] nt -s, -en individual.

Indiz [ɪn'di:ts] nt -es, -ien sign (für of); (Jur) clue; **—ienbeweis** m circumstantial evidence.

indoktrinieren [ɪndɔktri'ni:rən] vt indoctrinate.

industrialisieren [ɪndustriali-'zi:rən] vt industrialize.

Industrie [ɪndus'tri:] f industry, in cpds industrial; **—gebiet** nt industrial area; **i—ll** [ɪndustri'ɛl] a industrial; **—zweig** m branch of industry.

ineinander [ɪn'aɪ'nandər] ad in(to) one another or each other.

Infanterie [ɪnfantə'ri:] f infantry.

Infarkt [ɪn'farkt] m -(e)s, -e coronary (thrombosis).

Infektion [ɪnfɛktsi'o:n] f infection; **—skrankheit** f infectious disease.

Infinitiv ['ɪnfiniti:f] m -s, -e infinitive.

infizieren [ɪnfi'tsi:rən] vt infect; vr be infected (bei by).

Inflation [ɪnflatsi'o:n] f inflation.

inflatorisch [ɪnfla'to:rɪʃ] a inflationary.

infolge [ɪn'fɔlgə] prep +gen as a result of, owing to; **—dessen** ['-'dɛsən] ad consequently.

Informatik [ɪnfɔr'ma:tɪk] f information studies pl.

Information [ɪnfɔrmatsi'o:n] f information no pl.

informieren [ɪnfɔr'mi:rən] vt inform; vr find out (über +acc about).

Infusion [ɪnfuzi'o:n] f infusion.

Ingenieur [ɪnʒeni'ø:r] m engineer; **—schule** f school of engineering.

Ingwer ['ɪŋvər] m ginger.

Inhaber(in f) ['ɪnha:bər(ɪn)] m -s, - owner; (Haus—) occupier; (Lizenz—) licensee, holder; (Fin) bearer.

inhaftieren [ɪnhaf'ti:rən] vt take into custody.

inhalieren [ɪnha'li:rən] vti inhale.

Inhalt ['ɪnhalt] m -(e)s, -e contents pl; (eines Buchs etc) content; (Math) area; volume; **i—lich** a as regards content; **—sangabe** f

summary; **l—slos** a empty;
l—(s)reich a full; **—sverzeichnis** nt
table of contents.
inhuman ['ɪnhuːmaːn] a inhuman.
Initiative [ɪnitsiaˈtiːvə] f initiative.
Injektion [ɪnjɛktsiˈoːn] f injection.
inklusive [ɪnkluˈziːvə] prep, ad
inclusive (gen of).
inkognito [ɪnˈkɔgnito] ad incognito.
inkonsequent ['ɪnkɔnzekvɛnt] a
inconsistent.
inkorrekt ['ɪnkɔrɛkt] a incorrect.
Inkrafttreten [ɪnˈkrafttreːtən] nt -s
coming into force.
Inland ['ɪnlant] nt -(e)s (Geog)
inland; (Pol, Comm) home
(country); **—sporto** ad inland
postage.
inmitten [ɪnˈmɪtən] prep +gen in
the middle of; — von among.
innehaben ['ɪnəhaːbən] vt irreg
hold.
innen ['ɪnən] ad inside;
l—aufnahme f indoor photograph;
l—einrichtung f (interior) furnish-
ings pl; **l—minister** m minister of
the interior, Home Secretary
(Brit); **l—politik** f domestic policy;
l—stadt f town/city centre.
inner- ['ɪnər] cpd: **—e(r,s)** a inner;
(im Körper, inländisch) internal;
l—e(s) nt inside; (Mitte) centre;
(fig) heart; **l—eien** ['-raɪən] pl
innards pl; **—halb** ad, prep +gen
within; (räumlich) inside; **—lich** a
internal; (geistig) inward;
l—ste(s) nt heart; **—ste(r,s)** a
innermost.
innig ['ɪnɪç] a profound; Freundschaft intimate.
inoffiziell ['ɪnɔfitsiɛl] a unofficial.
ins [ɪns] = **in das.**
...asse ['ɪnzasə] m -n, -n (Anstalt)
...te; (Aut) passenger.

insbesondere [ɪnsbəˈzɔndərə] ad
(e)specially.
Inschrift ['ɪnʃrɪft] f inscription.
Insekt [ɪnˈzɛkt] nt -(e)s, -en insect.
Insel ['ɪnzəl] f -, -n island.
Inser- cpd: **—at** [ɪnzeˈraːt] nt -(e)s,
-e advertisement; **—ent** [ɪnzeˈrɛnt]
m advertiser; **i—ieren** [ɪnzeˈriːrən]
vti advertise.
insgeheim [ɪnsgəˈhaɪm] ad secretly.
insgesamt [ɪnsgəˈzamt] ad altogether, all in all.
insofern ['ɪnzoˈfɛrn] , **insoweit**
['ɪnzoˈvaɪt] ad in this respect; —
als in so far as; cj if; (deshalb)
(and) so.
Installateur [ɪnstalaˈtøːr] m electrician; plumber.
Instand- [ɪnˈʃtant] cpd: **—haltung**
f maintenance; **—setzung** f overhaul; (eines Gebäudes) restoration.
Instanz [ɪnˈstants] f authority;
(Jur) court; **—enweg** m official
channels pl.
Instinkt [ɪnˈstɪŋkt] m -(e)s, -e
instinct; **i—iv** ['-tiːf] a instinctive.
Institut [ɪnstiˈtuːt] nt -(e)s, -e
institute.
Instrument [ɪnstruˈmɛnt] nt
instrument.
inszenieren [ɪnstseˈniːrən] vt
direct; (fig) stage-manage.
Intell- [ɪntɛl] cpd: **i—ektuell**
[-ɛktuˈɛl] a intellectual; **i—igent**
[-iˈgɛnt] a intelligent; **i—igenz**
[-iˈgɛnts] f intelligence; (Leute)
intelligentsia pl.
Intendant [ɪntɛnˈdant] m director.
intensiv [ɪntɛnˈziːf] a intensive.
Interess- cpd: **i—ant** [ɪntereˈsant] a
interesting; **i—anterweise** ad
interestingly enough; **—e**
[ɪnteˈresə] nt -s, -n interest; **—e**
haben be interested (an +dat in);

—ent [ɪntɛrɛ'sɛnt] *m* interested party; **i—ieren** [ɪntɛrɛ'siːrən] *vt* interest; *vr* be interested (*für* in).

Inter- [ɪntɛr] *cpd:* **—nat** [-'naːt] *nt* -(e)s, -e boarding school; **i—national** [-natsio'naːl] *a* international; **i—nieren** [-'niːrən] *vt* intern; **i—pretieren** [-pre'tiːrən] *vt* interpret; **—punktion** [-pʊŋktsi'oːn] *f* punctuation; **—vall** [-'val] *nt* -s, -e interval; **—view** [-'vjuː] *nt* -s, -s interview; **i—viewen** [-'vjuːəm] *vt* interview.

intim [ɪn'tiːm] *a* intimate; **I—ität** [ɪntimi'tɛːt] *f* intimacy.

intolerant ['ɪntolerant] *a* intolerant.

intransitiv ['ɪntranziːtiːf] *a* (*Gram*) intransitive.

Intrige [ɪn'triːgə] *f* -, -n intrigue, plot.

Invasion [ɪnvazi'oːn] *f* invasion.

Inventar [ɪnvɛn'taːr] *nt* -s, -e inventory.

Inventur [ɪnvɛn'tuːr] *f* stocktaking; **— machen** stocktake.

investieren [ɪnvɛs'tiːrən] *vt* invest.

inwiefern [ɪnviˈfɛrn], **inwieweit** [ɪnviˈvaɪt] *ad* how far, to what extent.

inzwischen [ɪn'tsvɪʃən] *ad* meanwhile.

irdisch ['ɪrdɪʃ] *a* earthly.

irgend ['ɪrgant] *a* at at all; **wann/was/wer —** whenever/whatever/whoever; **— jemand/etwas** somebody/something; **any-** body/anything; **—ein(e,s)** *a* some, any; **—einmal** *ad* sometime or other; (*fragend*) ever; **—wann** *ad* sometime; **—wie** *ad* somehow; **—wo** *ad* somewhere; anywhere.

Ironie [iro'niː] *f* irony.

ironisch [i'roːnɪʃ] *a* ironic(al).

irre ['ɪrə] *a* crazy, mad; **I—(r)** *mf* lunatic; **—führen** *vt* mislead; **—machen** *vt* confuse; **—n** *vir* be mistaken; (*umher—*) wander, stray; **I—nanstalt** *f* lunatic asylum.

irrig ['ɪrɪç] *a* incorrect, wrong.

Irr- *cpd:* **i—sinnig** *a* mad, crazy; (*col*) terrific; **—tum** *m* -s, -tümer mistake, error; **i—tümlich** *a* mistaken.

Isolation [izolatsi'oːn] *f* isolation; (*Elec*) insulation.

Isolator [izo'laːtɔr] *m* insulator.

Isolier- [izo'liːr] *cpd:* **—band** *nt* insulating tape; **i—en** *vt* isolate; (*Elec*) insulate; **—station** *f* (*Med*) isolation ward; **—ung** *f* isolation; (*Elec*) insulation.

J

J, j [jɔt] *nt* J, j.

ja [jaː] *ad* yes; **tu das — nicht!** don't do that!

Jacht [jaxt] *f* -, -en yacht.

Jacke ['jakə] *f* -, -n jacket; (*Woll—*) cardigan.

Jackett [ʒa'kɛt] *nt* -s, -s or -e jacket.

Jagd [jaːkt] *f* -, -en hunt; (*Jagen*) hunting; **—beute** *f* kill; **—flugzeug** *nt* fighter; **—gewehr** *nt* sporting gun.

jagen ['jaːgən] *vi* hunt; (*eilen*) race; *vt* hunt; (*weg—*) drive (off); (*verfolgen*) chase.

Jäger ['jɛːgər] *m* -s, - hunter.

jäh [jɛː] a sudden, abrupt; (*steil*) steep, precipitous; **—lings** *ad* abruptly.

Jahr [jaːr] *nt* **-(e)s, -e** year; **j—elang** *ad* for years; **—esabonnement** *nt* annual subscription; **—esabschluß** *m* end of the year; (*Comm*) annual statement of account; **—esbericht** *m* annual report; **—eswechsel** *m* turn of the year; **—eszahl** f date, year; **—eszeit** f season; **—gang** *m* age group; (*von Wein*) vintage; **—'hundert** *nt* **-s, -e** century; **—'hundertfeier** f centenary.

jährlich ['jɛːrlɪç] a,ad yearly.

Jahr- *cpd:* **—markt** *m* fair; **—'zehnt** *nt* decade.

Jähzorn ['jɛːtsɔrn] *m* sudden anger; hot temper; **j—ig** a hot-tempered.

Jalousie [ʒaluˈziː] f venetian blind.

Jammer ['jamər] *m* **-s** misery; **es ist ein —, daß … it is a crying shame that …**

jämmerlich ['jɛmərlɪç] a wretched, pathetic; **J—keit** f wretchedness.

jammer- *cpd:* **—n** *vi* wail; *vt impers:* **es jammert jdn** it makes sb feel sorry; **—schade** a: **es ist —schade** it is a crying shame.

Januar ['januaːr] *m* **-s, -e** January.

Jargon [ʒarˈgõː] *m* **-s, -s** jargon.

jäten ['jɛːtən] *vt:* **Unkraut —** weed.

jauchzen ['jauxtsən] *vi* rejoice, shout (with joy).

Jauchzer *m* **-s, -** shout of joy.

jaulen ['jaulən] *vi* howl.

ja- *cpd:* **—'wohl** *ad* yes (of course); **J—wort** *nt* consent.

Jazz [dʒɛs] *m* **-** Jazz.

je [jeː] *ad* ever; (*jeweils*) each; **— nach** depending on; **— nachdem** it

depends; **— … desto** or **— the …** the.

jede(r,s) ['jeːdə(r,z)] a every, each; *pron* everybody; (*— einzelne*) each; **ohne — x** without any x; **—nfalls** *ad* in any case; **—rmann** *pron* everone; **—rzeit** *ad* at any time; **—smal** *ad* every time, each time.

jedoch [jeˈdɔx] *ad* however.

jeher ['jeːheːr] *ad:* **von —** all along.

jemals ['jeːmaːls] *ad* ever.

jemand ['jeːmant] *pron* somebody; anybody.

jene(r,s) ['jeːnə(r,z)] a that; *pron* that one.

jenseits ['jɛnzaits] *ad* on the other side; *prep +gen* on the other side of, beyond; **das J—** the hereafter, the beyond.

jetzig ['jɛtsɪç] a present.

jetzt [jɛtst] *ad* now.

je- *cpd:* **—weilig** a respective; **—weils** *ad* **—weils zwei zusammen** two at a time; **zu —weils 5 DM** at 5 marks each; **—weils das erste** the first each time.

Joch [jɔx] *nt* **-(e)s, -e** yoke.

Jockei ['dʒɔkə] *m* **-s, -s** jockey.

Jod [joːt] *nt* **-(e)s** iodine.

jodeln ['joːdəln] *vi* yodel.

Joghurt ['joːgurt] *m or nt* **-s, -s** yogurt.

Johannisbeere [joˈhanisbeːrə] f redcurrant; **schwarze —** blackcurrant.

johlen ['joːlən] *vi* yell.

Jolle ['jɔlə] f **-, -n** dinghy.

jonglieren [ʒõˈgliːrən] *vi* juggle.

Joppe ['jɔpə] f **-, -n** jacket.

Journal- [ʒurˈnaːl] *cpd:* **—ismus** [-ˈɪsmus] *m* journalism; **—ist** (in f) [-ˈlɪst] *m* journalist; **j—istisch** a journalistic.

Jubel ['juːbəl] m -s rejoicing; **j—n** vi rejoice.

Jubiläum [jubiˈlɛːum] nt -s, **Jubiläen** anniversary, jubilee.

jucken ['jukən] vi itch; vt es **juckt mich am Arm** my arm is itching; **das juckt mich** that's itchy.

Juckreiz ['jukraɪts] m itch.

Jude ['juːdə] m -n, -n Jew; **—ntum** nt - Judaism; Jewry; **—nverfolgung** f persecution of the Jews.

Jüd- ['jyːd] cpd: **—in** f Jewess; **j—isch** a Jewish.

Judo ['juːdo] nt -(s) judo.

Jugend ['juːɡənt] f - youth; **—herberge** f youth hostel; **—kriminalität** f juvenile crime; **j—lich** a youthful; **—liche(r)** mf teenager, young person; **—richter** m juvenile court judge.

Juli ['juːli] m -(s), -s July.

jung [jʊŋ] a young; **J—e** m -n, -n boy, lad; **J—e(s)** nt young animal;

(pl) young pl.

Jünger ['jʏŋər] m -s, - disciple; **j—** a younger.

Jung- cpd: **—fer** f -, -n: **alte —fer** old maid; **—fernfahrt** f maiden voyage; **—frau** f virgin; (Astrol) Virgo; **—geselle** m bachelor.

Jüngling ['jʏŋlɪŋ] m youth.

jüngst ['jʏŋst] ad lately, recently; **—e(r,s)** a youngest; (neueste) latest.

Juni ['juːni] m -(s), -s June.

Junior ['juːnior] m -s, -en [-'oːrən] junior.

Jurist [ju'rɪst] m jurist, lawyer; **j—isch** a legal.

Justiz [jus'tiːts] f - justice; **—beamte(r)** m judicial officer; **—irrtum** m miscarriage of justice.

Juwel [ju'veːl] nt or m -s, -en jewel; **—ier** m [-'liːr] m -s, -e jeweller; **—iergeschäft** nt jeweller's (shop).

Jux [jʊks] m -es, -e joke, lark.

K

K, k [kaː] nt K, k.

Kabarett [kaba'rɛt] nt -s, -e or -s cabaret; **—ist** [-'tɪst] m cabaret artiste.

Kabel ['kaːbəl] nt -s, - (Elec) wire; (stark) cable; **—jau** [-jau] m -s, -e or -s' cod; **k—n** vti cable.

Kabine [ka'biːnə] f cabin; (Zelle) cubicle.

Kabinett [kabi'nɛt] nt -s, -e (Pol) cabinet; small room.

Kachel ['kaxəl] f -, -n tile; **k—n** vt tile; **—ofen** m tiled stove.

Kadaver [ka'daːvər] m -s, -

carcass.

Kadett [ka'dɛt] m -en, -en cadet.

Käfer ['kɛːfər] m -s, - beetle.

Kaffee ['kafe] m -s, -s coffee; **—kanne** f coffeepot; **—klatsch** m, **—kränzchen** nt hen party; coffee morning; **—löffel** m coffee spoon; **—mühle** f coffee grinder; **—satz** m coffee grounds pl.

Käfig ['kɛːfɪç] m -s, -e cage.

kahl [kaːl] a bald; **—fressen** vt irreg strip bare; **—geschoren** a shaven, shorn; **K—heit** f baldness; **—köpfig** a bald-headed.

Kahn [ka:n] m -(e)s, ⸚e boat, barge.

Kai [kai] m -s, -e or -s quay.

Kaiser ['kaizər] m -s, - emperor; —in f empress; k—lich a imperial; —reich nt empire; —schnitt m (Med) Caesarian (section).

Kajüte [ka'jy:tə] f -, -n cabin.

Kakao [ka'ka:o] m -s, -s cocoa.

Kaktee [kak'te:(ə)] f -,-n, **Kaktus** ['kaktus] m -, -se cactus.

Kalb [kalp] nt -(e)s, ⸚er calf; k—en ['kalbən] vi calve; —fleisch nt veal; —sleder nt calf(skin).

Kalender [ka'lendər] m -s, - calendar; (Taschen—) diary.

Kali ['ka:li] nt -s, -s potash.

Kaliber [ka'li:bər] nt -s, - (lit, fig) calibre.

Kalk [kalk] m -(e)s, -e lime; (Biol) calcium; —stein m limestone.

Kalkulation [kalkulatsi'o:n] f calculation.

kalkulieren [kalku'li:rən] vt calculate.

Kalorie [kalo'ri:] f calorie.

kalt [kalt] a cold; mir ist (es) — I am cold; —bleiben vi irreg be unmoved; —blütig a cold-blooded; (ruhig) cool; K—blütigkeit f coldbloodedness; coolness.

Kälte ['kɛltə] f - cold; coldness; —grad m degree of frost or below zero; —welle f cold spell.

kalt- cpd: —herzig a cold-hearted; —schnäuzig a cold, unfeeling; —stellen vt chill; (fig) leave out in the cold.

Kamel [ka'me:l] nt -(e)s, -e camel.

Kamera ['kamera] f -, -s camera.

Kamerad [kama'ra:t] m -en, -en comrade, friend; —schaft f comradeship; k—schaftlich a comradely.

Kamera- cpd: —führung f camera work; —mann m cameraman.

Kamille [ka'milə] f -, -n camomile; —ntee m camomile tea.

Kamin [ka'mi:n] m -s, -e (außen) chimney; (innen) fireside, fireplace; —feger, —kehrer m -s, - chimney sweep.

Kamm [kam] m -(e)s, ⸚e comb; (Berg—) ridge; (Hahnen—) crest.

kämmen ['kɛmən] vt comb.

Kammer ['kamər] f -, -n chamber; small bedroom; —diener m valet.

Kampf [kampf] m -(e)s, ⸚e fight, battle; (Wettbewerb) contest; (fig: Anstrengung) struggle; k—bereit a ready for action.

kämpfen ['kɛmpfən] vi fight.

Kämpfer m -s, - fighter, combatant.

Kampfer ['kampfər] m -s camphor.

Kampf- cpd: —handlung f action; k—los a without a fight; k—lustig a pugnacious; —richter m (Sport) referee; (Tennis) umpire.

Kanal [ka'na:l] m -s, Kanäle (Fluß) canal; (Rinne, Ärmel—) channel; (für Abfluß) drain; —isation [-izatsi'o:n] f sewage system; k—isieren [-i'zi:rən] vt provide with a sewage system.

Kanarienvogel [ka'na:rienfo:gəl] m canary.

Kandi- [kandi] cpd: —dat [-'da:t] m -en, -en candidate; —datur [-da'tur] f candidature, candidacy; k—dieren [-'di:rən] vi stand, run.

Kandis(zucker) ['kandıs] m - candy.

Känguruh ['kɛnguru] nt -s, -s kangaroo.

Kaninchen [ka'ni:nçən] nt rabbit.

Kanister [ka'nıstər] m -s, - can, canister.

Kanne ['kanə] f -, -n (*Krug*) jug; (*Kaffee—*) pot; (*Milch—*) churn; (*Gieß—*) can.

Kanon ['ka:nɔn] m -s, -s canon.

Kanone [ka'no:nə] f -, -n gun; (*Hist*) cannon; (*fig: Mensch*) ace.

Kantate [kan'ta:tə] f -, -n cantata.

Kante ['kantə] f -, -n edge.

Kantine [kan'ti:nə] f canteen.

Kantor ['kantɔr] m choirmaster.

Kanu ['ka:nu] nt -s, -s canoe.

Kanzel ['kantsəl] f -, -n pulpit.

Kanzlei [kants'lai] f chancery; (*Büro*) chambers pl.

Kanzler ['kantslər] m -s, - chancellor.

Kap [kap] nt -s, -s cape.

Kapazität [kapatsi'tɛ:t] f capacity; (*Fachmann*) authority.

Kapelle [ka'pelə] f (*Gebäude*) chapel; (*Mus*) band.

Kaper ['ka:pər] f -, -n caper; **k—n** vt capture.

kapieren [ka'pi:rən] vti (*col*) understand.

Kapital [kapi'ta:l] nt -s, -e or -ien capital; **—anlage** f investment; **—ismus** ['-lismus] m capitalism; **—ist** ['-lıst] m capitalist; **k—kräftig** a wealthy; **—markt** m money market.

Kapitän [kapi'tɛ:n] m -s, -e captain.

Kapitel [ka'pɪtəl] nt -s, - chapter.

Kapitulation [kapitulatsi'o:n] f capitulation.

kapitulieren [kapitu'li:rən] vi capitulate.

Kaplan [ka'pla:n] m -s, **Kapläne** chaplain.

Kappe ['kapə] f -, -n cap; (*Kapuze*) hood; **k—n** vt cut.

Kapsel ['kapsəl] f -, -n capsule.

kaputt [ka'put] a (*col*) smashed, broken; *Person* exhausted, finished; **—gehen** vi irreg break; (*Schuhe*) fall apart; (*Firma*) go bust; (*Stoff*) wear out; (*sterben*) cop it; **—lachen** vr laugh o.s. silly; **—machen** vt break; *Mensch* exhaust, wear out.

Kapuze [ka'pu:tsə] f -, -n hood.

Karaffe [ka'rafə] f -, -n caraffe; (*geschliffen*) decanter.

Karambolage [karambo'la:ʒə] f -, -n (*Zusammenstoß*) crash.

Karamel [kara'mɛl] m -s caramel; **—bonbon** m or nt toffee.

Karat [ka'ra:t] nt -(e)s, -e carat; **—e** nt -s karate.

Karawane [kara'va:nə] f -, -n caravan.

Kardinal [kardi'na:l] m -s, **Kardinäle** cardinal; **—zahl** f cardinal number.

Karfreitag [ka:r'fraita:k] m Good Friday.

karg [kark] a scanty, poor; *Mahlzeit auch* meagre; **— mit Worten sein** use few words; **K—heit** f poverty, scantiness; meagreness.

kärglich ['kɛrklıç] a poor, scanty.

kariert [ka'ri:rt] a *Stoff* checked; *Papier* squared.

Karies ['ka:ries] f - caries.

Karikatur [karika'tu:r] f caricature; **—ist** ['-rist] m cartoonist.

karikieren [kari'ki:rən] vt caricature.

Karneval ['karnəval] m -s, -e or -s carnival.

Karo ['ka:ro] nt -s, -s square; (*Cards*) diamonds pl. **—As** nt ace of diamonds.

Karosse [ka'rɔsə] f -, -n coach, carriage; **—rie** [-'ri:] f (Aut) body(work).

Karotte [ka'rɔtə] f -, -n carrot.

Karpfen ['karpfən] m -s, - carp.

Karre ['karə] f -, -n, —n m -s, - cart, barrow; **k—n** vt cart, transport.

Karriere [kari'ɛːrə] f -, -n career; **— machen** vo, get to the top; **—macher** m -s, - careerist.

Karte ['kartə] f -, -n card; (Land—) map; (Speise—) menu; (Eintritts—, Fahr—) ticket; **alles auf eine — setzen** put all one's eggs in one basket.

Kartei [kar'tai] f card index; **—karte** f index card.

Kartell [kar'tɛl] nt -s, -e cartel.

Karten- cpd: **—haus** nt (lit, fig) house of cards; **—spiel** nt card game; pack of cards.

Kartoffel [kar'tɔfəl] f -, -n potato; **—brei** m, **—püree** nt mashed potatoes pl; **—salat** m potato salad.

Karton [kar'tõ] m -s, -s cardboard; (Schachtel) cardboard box; **k—iert** [karto'niːrt] a hardback.

Karussell [karu'sɛl] nt -s, -s roundabout (Brit), merry-go-round.

Karwoche ['kaːrvɔxə] f Holy Week.

Kaschemme [ka'ʃɛmə] f -, -n dive.

Käse ['kɛːzə] m -s, - cheese; **—blatt** nt (col) (local) rag; **—kuchen** m cheesecake.

Kaserne [ka'zɛrnə] f -, -n barracks pl; **—nhof** m parade ground.

Kasino [ka'ziːno] nt -s, -s club; (Mil) officers' mess; (Spiel—) casino.

Kasper ['kaspər] m -s, - Punch; (fig) clown.

Kasse ['kasə] f -, -n (Geldkasten) cashbox; (in Geschäft) till, cash

register; (Kino—, Theater— etc) box office; ticket office; (Kranken—) health insurance; (Spar—) savings bank; **— machen** count the money; **getrennte —führen** pay separately; **an der — (in Geschäft)** at the desk; **gut bei — sein** be in the money; **—narzt** m panel doctor (Brit); **—nbestand** m cash balance; **—npatient** m panel patient (Brit); **—nprüfung** f audit; **—nsturz** m: **—nsturz machen** check one's money; **—nzettel** m receipt.

Kasserolle [kasə'rɔlə] f -, -n casserole.

Kassette [ka'sɛtə] f small box; (Tonband, Phot) cassette; (Bücher—) case; **—nrecorder** m -s, - cassette recorder.

kassieren [ka'siːrən] vt take; vi: **darf ich —?** would you like to pay now?

Kassierer [ka'siːrər] m -s, - cashier; (von Klub) treasurer.

Kastanie [kas'taːniə] f chestnut; **—nbaum** m chestnut tree.

Kästchen ['kɛstçən] nt small box, casket.

Kaste ['kastə] f -, -n caste.

Kasten ['kastən] m -s, ˝ box (Sport auch), case; (Truhe) chest; **—wagen** m van.

kastrieren [kas'triːrən] vt castrate.

Katalog [kata'loːk] m -(e)s, -e catalogue; **k—isieren** [katalogi'ziːrən] vt catalogue.

Katapult [kata'pult] m or nt -(e)s, -e catapult.

Katarrh [ka'tar] m -s, -e catarrh.

katastrophal [katastro'faːl] a catastrophic.

Katastrophe [kata'stroːfə] f -, -n catastrophe, disaster.

Kategorie [katego'ri:] f category.

kategorisch [kate'go:rɪʃ] a categorical.

kategorisieren [kategori'zi:rən] vt categorize.

Kater ['ka:tər] m -s, - tomcat; (col) hangover.

Katheder [ka'te:dər] nt -s, - lecture desk.

Kathedrale [kate'dra:lə] f -, -n cathedral.

Kathode [ka'to:də] f -, -n cathode.

Katholik [kato'li:k] m -en, -en Catholic.

katholisch [ka'to:lɪʃ] a Catholic.

Katholizismus [katoli'tsɪsmʊs] m Catholicism.

Kätzchen ['kɛtsçən] nt kitten.

Katze ['katsə] f -, -n cat; für die Katz (col) in vain, for nothing; —nauge nt cat's eye; (Fahrrad) rear light; —njammer m (col) hangover; —nsprung m (col) stone's throw; short journey; —nwäsche f lick and a promise.

Kauderwelsch ['kaʊdərvɛlʃ] nt -(s) jargon; (col) double Dutch.

kauen ['kaʊən] vti chew.

kauern ['kaʊərn] vi crouch.

Kauf [kaʊf] m -(e)s, Käufe purchase, buy; (Kaufen) buying; ein guter — a bargain; etw in — nehmen put up with sth; k—en vi buy.

Käufer(in f) ['kɔʏfər(ɪn)] m -s, - buyer.

Kauf- cpd: —haus nt department store; —kraft f purchasing power; —laden m shop, store.

käuflich ['kɔʏflɪç] a,ad purchasable, for sale; (pej) venal; — erwerben purchase.

Kauf- cpd: k—lustig a interested in buying; —mann m, pl —leute

businessman; shopkeeper; k—männisch a commercial; —männischer Angestellter clerk.

Kaugummi ['kaʊgʊmi] m chewing gum.

Kaulquappe ['kaʊlkvapə] f -, -n tadpole.

kaum [kaʊm] ad hardly, scarcely.

Kaution [kaʊtsi'o:n] f deposit; (Jur) bail.

Kautschuk ['kaʊtʃʊk] m -s, -e indiarubber.

Kauz [kaʊts] m -es, Käuze owl; (fig) queer fellow.

Kavalier [kava'li:r] m -s, -e gentleman, cavalier; —sdelikt nt peccadillo.

Kavallerie [kavalə'ri:] f cavalry.

Kavallerist [kavalə'rɪst] m trooper, cavalryman.

Kaviar ['ka:viar] m caviar.

keck [kɛk] a daring, bold; K—heit f daring, boldness.

Kegel ['ke:gəl] m -s, - skittle; (Math) cone; —bahn f skittle alley; bowling alley; k—förmig a conical; k—n vi play skittles.

Kehle ['ke:lə] f -, -n throat.

Kehl- cpd: —kopf m larynx; —laut m guttural.

Kehre ['ke:rə] f -, -n turn(ing), bend; k—n vti (wenden) turn; (mit Besen) sweep; sich an etw (dat) nicht k—n not heed sth.

Kehr- cpd: —icht m -s sweepings pl; —maschine f sweeper; —reim m refrain; —seite f reverse, other side; wrong side; bad side; k—tmachen vi turn about, about-turn.

keifen ['kaɪfən] vi scold, nag.

Keil [kaɪl] m -(e)s, -e wedge; (Mil) arrowhead; k—en vt wedge;

vr fight; —e'rei f (col) punch-up;
—riemen m (Aut) fan belt.

Keim [kaɪm] m -(e)s, -e bud;
(Med, fig) germ; etw im —
ersticken nip sth in the bud; k—en
vi germinate; k—frei a sterile;
k—tötend a antiseptic, germicidal;
—zelle f (fig) nucleus.

kein [kaɪn] a no, not any; —e(r,s)
pron no one, nobody; none;
—esfalls ad on no account;
—eswegs ad by no means; —mal
ad not once.

Keks [ke:ks] m or nt -es, -e biscuit.

Kelch [kɛlç] m -(e)s, -e cup,
goblet, chalice.

Kelle ['kɛlə] f -, -n ladle;
(Maurer—) trowel.

Keller ['kɛlər] m -s, - cellar;
—assel f -, -n woodlouse;
—wohnung f basement flat.

Kellner ['kɛlnər] m -s, - waiter;
—in f waitress.

keltern ['kɛltərn] vt press.

kennen ['kɛnən] vt irreg know;
—lernen vt get to know; sich
—lernen get to know each other;
(zum erstenmal) meet.

Kenn- cpd: —er m -s, - connoisseur; —karte f identity card;
k—tlich a distinguishable,
discernible; etw k—tlich machen
mark sth; —tnis f -, -se knowledge
no pl; etw zur —tnis nehmen note
sth; von etw —tnis nehmen take
notice of sth; jdn in —tnis setzen
inform sb; —zeichen nt mark,
characteristic; k—zeichnen vt
insep characterize; k—zeichnender-
weise ad characteristically;
—ziffer f reference number.

kentern ['kɛntərn] vi capsize.

Keramik [ke'ra:mɪk] f -, -en
ceramics pl, pottery.

Kerb- [kɛrb] cpd: —e f -, -n notch,
groove; —el m -s, - chervil; k—en
vt notch; —holz nt: etw auf dem
—holz haben have done sth wrong.

Kerker ['kɛrkər] m -s, - prison.

Kerl [kɛrl] m -s, -e chap, bloke
(Brit), guy.

Kern [kɛrn] m -(e)s, -e (Obst—)
pip, stone; (Nuß—) kernel;
(Atom—) nucleus; (fig) heart,
core; —energie f nuclear energy;
—forschung f nuclear research;
—frage f central issue; —gehäuse
nt core; k—gesund a thoroughly
healthy, fit as a fiddle; k—ig a
robust; Ausspruch pithy; —kraftwerk nt nuclear power station;
k—los a seedless, pipless; —physik
f nuclear physics; —reaktion f
nuclear reaction; —spaltung f
nuclear fission; —waffen pl
nuclear weapons pl.

Kerze ['kɛrtsə] f -, -n candle;
(Zünd—) plug; k—ngerade a
straight as a die; —nständer m
candle holder.

keß [kɛs] a saucy.

Kessel ['kɛsəl] m -s, - kettle; (von
Lokomotive etc) boiler; (Geog)
depression; (Mil) encirclement;
—treiben nt -s, - (fig) witch hunt.

Kette ['kɛtə] f -, -n chain; k—n
vt chain; —nhund m watchdog;
—nladen m chain store;
—nrauchen nt chain smoking;
—nreaktion f chain reaction.

Ketzer ['kɛtsər] m -s, - heretic;
k—isch a heretical.

keuchen ['kɔyçən] vi pant, gasp.

Keuchhusten m whooping cough.

Keule ['kɔylə] f -, -n club; (Cook)
leg.

keusch [kɔyʃ] a chaste; K—heit f
chastity.

Kfz [kɑːˈɛftsɛt] *abbr of*
Kraftfahrzeug.

kichern [ˈkɪçərn] *vi* giggle.

kidnappen [ˈkɪdnɛpən] *vt* kidnap.

Kiebitz [ˈkiːbɪts] *m* -es, -e peewit.

Kiefer [ˈkiːfər] *m* -s, - jaw; *f* -,
-n pine; —zapfen *m* pine cone.

Kiel [kiːl] *m* -(e)s, -e (Feder—)
quill; (Naut) keel; k—holen *vt*
Person keelhaul; Schiff career;
—wasser *nt* wake.

Kieme [ˈkiːmə] *f* -, -n gill.

Kies [kiːs] *m* -es, -e gravel; —el
[ˈkiːzəl] *m* -s, - pebble; —elstein *m*
pebble; —grube *f* gravel pit;
—weg *m* gravel path.

Kilo [ˈkiːlo] kilo; —gramm
[kiloˈgram] *nt* -s, -e kilogram;
—meter [kiloˈmeːtər] *m* kilometre;
—meterzähler *m* ∞ milometer.

Kimme [ˈkɪmə] *f* -, -n notch;
(Gewehr) backsight.

Kind [kɪnt] *nt* -(e)s, -er child; von
— auf from childhood; sich bei jdm
lieb — machen ingratiate o.s. with
sb; —erbett [ˈkɪndərbɛt] *nt* cot;
—erei [kɪndəˈraɪ] *f* childishness;
—ergarten *m* nursery school, play-
group; —ergeld *nt* family allowance; —erlähmung *f* poliomyelitis;
k—erleicht *a* childishly easy;
k—erlos *a* childless; —ermädchen
nt nursemaid; k—erreich *a* with a
lot of children; —erspiel *nt* child's
play; —erstube *f*: eine gute
—erstube haben be well-mannered;
—erwagen *m* pram, baby carriage
(US); —esalter *nt* infancy;
—esbeine *pl*: von —esbeinen an
from early childhood; —heit *f* childhood; k—isch *a* childish; k—lich
a childlike; k—sköpfig *a* childish.

Kinn [kɪn] *nt* -(e)s, -e chin;
—haken *m* (Boxen) uppercut;
—lade *f* jaw.

Kino [ˈkiːno] *nt* -s, -s cinema;
—besucher *m* cinema-goer;
—programm *nt* film programme.

Kiosk [kiˈɔsk] *m* -(e)s, -e kiosk.

Kipp- [ˈkɪp] *cpd*: —e *f* -, -n cigarette
end; (col) fag; auf der —e stehen
(fig) be touch and go; k—en *vi*
topple over, overturn; *vt* tilt.

Kirch- [ˈkɪrç] *cpd*: —e *f* -, -n
church; —endiener *m* church-
warden; —enfest *nt* church
festival; —enlied *nt* hymn;
—gänger *m* -s, - churchgoer; —hof
m churchyard; k—lich *a*
ecclesiastical; —turm *m* church
tower, steeple.

Kirsche [ˈkɪrʃə] *f* -, -n cherry.

Kissen [ˈkɪsən] *nt* -s, - cushion;
(Kopf—) pillow; —bezug *m* pillow-
slip.

Kiste [ˈkɪstə] *f* -, -n box; chest.

Kitsch [kɪtʃ] *m* -(e)s trash; k—ig
a trashy.

Kitt [kɪt] *m* -(e)s, -e putty; —chen
nt (col) clink; —el *m* -s, - overall,
smock; k—en *vt* putty; (fig) Ehe
etc cement.

Kitz [kɪts] *nt* -es, -e kid; (Reh—)
fawn.

kitzel- [ˈkɪtsəl] *cpd*: —ig *a* (lit, fig)
ticklish; k—n *vti* tickle.

klaffen [ˈklafən] *vi* gape.

kläffen [ˈklɛfən] *vi* yelp.

Klage [ˈklaːgə] *f* -, -n complaint;
(Jur) action; k—n *vi* (weh—)
lament, wail; (sich beschweren)
complain; (Jur) take legal action.

Kläger(in *f*) [ˈklɛːgər(ɪn)] *m* -s, -
plaintiff.

kläglich [ˈklɛːklɪç] *a* wretched.

Klamm [klam] *f* -, -en ravine; k—
a Finger numb; (feucht) damp.

Klammer [ˈklamər] *f* -, -n clamp;
(in Text) bracket; (Büro—) clip;

(*Wäsche—*) peg; (*Zahn—*) brace; k—n vr cling (*an +acc* to).

Klang [klaŋ] m -(e)s, -e sound; k—voll a sonorous.

Klappe ['klapə] f -, -n valve; (*Ofen—*) damper; (*col: Mund*) trap; k—n vi (*Geräusch*) click; vti Sitz etc tip; v impers work.

Klapper ['klapər] f -, -n rattle; k—ig a run-down, worn-out; k—n vi clatter, rattle; —schlange f rattlesnake; —storch m stork.

Klapp- cpd: —messer nt jackknife; —rad nt collapsible bicycle; —stuhl m folding chair.

Klaps [klaps] m -es, -e slap; k—en vt slap.

klar [klaːr] a clear; (*Naut*) ready for sea; (*Mil*) ready for action; sich (*dat*) im K—en sein über (*+acc*) be clear about; ins K—e kommen get clear.

Klär- ['klɛːr] cpd: —anlage f purification plant; k—en vt Flüßigkeit purify; Probleme clarify; vr clear (itself) up.

Klar- cpd: —heit f clarity; —inette [klari'nɛtə] f clarinet; k—legen vt clear up, explain; k—machen vt Schiff get ready for sea; jdm etw k—machen make sth clear to sb; k—sehen vi irreg see clearly; —sichtfolie f transparent film; k—stellen vt clarify.

Klärung ['klɛːruŋ] f purification, clarification.

Klasse ['klasə] f -, -n class (Sch auch) form; k— a (col) smashing; —narbeit f test; —nbewußtsein nt class consciousness; —ngesellschaft f class society; —nkampf m class conflict; —nlehrer m form master; k—nlos a classless; —nsprecher(in f) m form prefect; —nzimmer nt classroom.

klassifizieren [klasifi'tsiːrən] vt classify.

Klassifizierung f classification.

Klassik ['klasik] f (*Zeit*) classical period; (*Stil*) classicism; —er m -s, - classic.

klassisch a (*lit, fig*) classical.

Klatsch [klatʃ] m -(e)s, -e smack, crack; (*Gerede*) gossip; —base f gossip, scandalmonger; —e f -, -n (*col*) crib; k—en vi (*Geräusch*) clash; (*reden*) gossip; (*Beifall*) applaud, clap; —mohn m (*corn*) poppy; k—naß a soaking wet; —spalte f gossip column.

klauben ['klaubən] vt pick.

Klaue ['klauə] f -, -n claw; (*col: Schrift*) scrawl; k—n vt claw; (*col*) pinch.

Klause ['klauzə] f -, -n cell; hermitage.

Klausel ['klauzəl] f -, -n clause.

Klausur [klau'zuːr] f seclusion; —arbeit f examination paper.

Klaviatur [klavia'tuːr] f keyboard.

Klavier [kla'viːr] nt -s, -e piano.

Kleb- ['kleːb] cpd: —emittel nt glue; k—en vt stick (*an +acc* to); k—rig a sticky; —stoff m glue; —streifen m adhesive tape.

kleckern ['klɛkərn] vi slobber.

Klecks [klɛks] m -es, -e blot, stain; k—en vi blot; (*pej*) daub.

Klee [kleː] m -s clover; —blatt nt cloverleaf; (*fig*) trio.

Kleid [klait] nt -(e)s, -er garment; (*Frauen—*) dress; pl clothes pl; k—en ['klaidən] vt clothe, dress; (*auch vi*) suit; vr dress; —erbügel m coat hanger; —erbürste f clothes brush; —erschrank m wardrobe; k—sam a becoming; —ung f clothing; —ungsstück nt garment.

Kleie ['klaɪə] f -, -n bran.
klein [klaɪn] a little, small;
K–bürgertum nt petite
bourgeoisie; K–e(r,s) little one;
K–format nt small size; im
K–format small-scale; K–geld nt
small change; —gläubig a of little
faith; —hacken vt chop up, mince;
K–holz nt firewood; K–holz aus
jdm machen make mincemeat of
sb; K–igkeit f trifle; K–kind nt
infant; K–kram f details pl;
—laut a dejected, quiet; —lich a
petty, paltry; K–lichkeit f
pettiness, paltriness; —mütig a
faint-hearted; K–od ['klaɪnoːt] nt
-s, -odien gem, jewel; treasure;
—schneiden vt irreg chop up;
—städtisch a provincial;
—stmöglich a smallest possible.
Kleister ['klaɪstər] m -s, - paste;
k–n vt paste.
Klemme ['klɛmə] f -, -n clip;
(Med) clamp; (fig) jam; k–n vt
(festhalten) jam; (quetschen)
pinch, nip; vr catch o.s.; (sich
hineinzwängen) squeeze o.s.; sich
hinter jdn/etw k–n get on to
sb/get down to sth; vi (Tür) stick,
jam.
Klempner ['klɛmpnər] m -s, -
plumber.
Kleptomanie [klɛptoma'niː] f
kleptomania.
Kleriker ['kleːrikər] m -s, - cleric.
Klerus ['kleːrus] m - clergy.
Klette ['klɛtə] f -, -n burr.
Kletter- ['klɛtər] cpd: —er m -s, -
climber; k–n vi climb; —pflanze
f creeper; —seil nt climbing rope.
klicken ['klɪkən] vi click.
Klient(in f) [kli'ɛnt(in)] m client.
Klima ['kliːma] nt -s, -s or -te
[kli'maːtə] climate; —anlage f air
conditioning; k–tisieren [-i'ziːrən]

vt air-condition; —wechsel m
change of air.
klimpern ['klɪmpərn] vi tinkle; (mit
Gitarre) strum.
Klinge ['klɪŋə] f -, -n blade, sword.
Klingel ['klɪŋəl] f -, -n bell;
—beutel m collection bag; k–n vi
ring.
klingen ['klɪŋən] vi irreg sound;
(Gläser) clink.
Klinik ['kliːnɪk] f hospital, clinic.
klinisch ['kliːnɪʃ] a clinical.
Klinke ['klɪŋkə] f -, -n handle.
Klinker ['klɪŋkər] m -s, - clinker.
Klippe ['klɪpə] f -, -n cliff; (im
Meer) reef; (fig) hurdle; k–nreich
a rocky.
klipp und klar ['klɪp'ʊntklaːr] a
clear and concise.
Klips [klɪps] m -es, -e clip; (Ohr—)
earring.
klirren ['klɪrən] vi clank, jangle;
(Gläser) clink; —de Kälte biting
cold.
Klischee [kli'ʃeː] nt -s, -s (Druck-
platte) plate, block; (fig) cliché;
—vorstellung f stereotyped idea.
Klo [kloː] nt -s, -s (col) loo.
Kloake [klo'aːkə] f -, -n sewer.
klobig ['kloːbɪç] a clumsy.
klopfen ['klɔpfən] vti knock;
(Herz) thump; es klopft sb's
knocking; jdm auf die Schulter —
tap sb on the shoulder; vt beat.
Klopfer m -s, - (Teppich—)
beater; (Tür—) knocker.
Klöppel ['klœpəl] m -s, - (von
Glocke) clapper; k–n vi make lace.
Klops [klɔps] m -es, -e meatball.
Klosett [klo'zɛt] nt -s, -e or -s
lavatory, toilet; —papier nt toilet
paper.
Kloß [kloːs] m -es, ⁻e (Erd—) clod;
(im Hals) lump; (Cook) dumpling.

Kloster ['klo:stər] *nt* -s, ⸗ (Männer—) monastery ; (Frauen—) convent.

klösterlich ['klø:stərlɪç] *a* monastic ; convent.

Klotz [klɔts] *m* -es, ⸗e log ; (Hack—) block ; ein — am Bein (fig) drag, millstone round (sb's) neck.

Klub [klʊp] *m* -s, -s club ; —sessel *m* easy chair.

Kluft [klʊft] *f* -, ⸗e cleft, gap ; (Geol) gorge, chasm.

klug [klu:k] *a* clever, intelligent ; **K—heit** *f* cleverness, intelligence.

Klümpchen ['klʏmpçən] *nt* clot, blob.

Klumpen ['klʊmpən] *m* -s, - (Erd—) clod ; (Blut—) lump, clot ; (Gold—) nugget ; (Cook) lump ; **k—** *vi* go lumpy, clot.

Klumpfuß ['klʊmp-fu:s] *m* club-foot.

knabbern ['knabərn] *vti* nibble.

Knabe ['kna:bə] *m* -n, -n boy ; **k—nhaft** *a* boyish.

Knäckebrot ['knɛkəbro:t] *nt* crisp-bread.

knacken ['knakən] *vti* (lit, fig) crack.

Knall [knal] *m* -(e)s, -e bang ; (Peitschen—) crack ; — und Fall (col) unexpectedly ; —bonbon *m* cracker ; —effekt *m* surprise effect, spectacular effect ; **k—en** *vi* bang ; crack ; **k—rot** *a* bright red.

knapp [knap] *a* tight ; Geld scarce ; Sprache concise ; **K—e** *m* -n, -n (Edelmann) young knight ; **—halten** *vt irreg* stint ; **K—heit** *f* tightness ; scarcity ; conciseness.

knarren ['knarən] *vi* creak.

knattern ['knatərn] *vi* rattle ; (MG) chatter.

Knäuel ['knɔyəl] *m or nt* -s, - (Woll—) ball ; (Menschen—) knot.

Knauf [knauf] *m* -(e)s, **Knäufe** knob ; (Schwert—) pommel.

Knauser ['knauzər] *m* -s, - miser ; **k—ig** *a* miserly ; **k—n** *vi* be mean.

knautschen ['knautʃən] *vti* crumple.

Knebel ['kne:bəl] *m* -s, - gag ; **k—n** *vt* gag ; (Naut) fasten.

Knecht [knɛçt] *m* -(e)s, -e farm labourer ; servant ; **k—en** *vt* enslave ; **K—schaft** *f* servitude.

kneifen ['knaifən] *vi irreg* pinch ; (sich drücken) back out ; vor etw — dodge sth.

Kneipe ['knaipə] *f* -, -n (col) pub.

Knet- [kne:t] *cpd*: **k—en** *vt* knead ; Wachs mould ; **—masse** *f* Plasticine ®.

Knick [knɪk] *m* -(e)s, -e (Sprung) crack ; (Kurve) bend ; (Falte) fold ; **k—en** *vti* (springen) crack ; (brechen) break ; Papier fold ; geknickt sein be downcast.

Knicks [knɪks] *m* -es, -e curtsey ; **k—en** *vi* curtsey.

Knie [kni:] *nt* -s, - knee ; —beuge *f* -, -n knee bend ; **k—n** *vi* kneel ; —fall *m* genuflection ; —gelenk *nt* knee joint ; —kehle *f* back of the knee ; —scheibe *f* kneecap ; —strumpf *m* knee-length sock.

Kniff [knɪf] *m* -(e)s, -e (Zwicken) pinch ; (Falte) fold ; (fig) trick, knack ; **k—elig** *a* tricky.

knipsen ['knɪpsən] *vti* Fahrkarte punch ; (Phot) take a snap (of), snap.

Knirps [knɪrps] *m* -es, -e little chap ; ® (Schirm) telescopic umbrella.

knirschen ['knɪrʃən] *vi* crunch ; mit den Zähnen — grind one's teeth.

knistern ['knɪstərn] vi crackle.

Knitter- ['knɪtər] cpd: **—falte** f crease; **k—frei** a non-crease; **k—n** vi crease.

Knoblauch ['kno:plaux] m -(e)s garlic.

Knöchel ['knœçəl] m -s, - knuckle; (Fuß—) ankle.

Knochen ['knɔxən] m -s, - bone; **—bau** m bone structure; **—bruch** m fracture; **—gerüst** nt skeleton.

knöchern [knœçərn] a bone.

knochig ['knɔxɪç] a bony.

Knödel ['knø:dəl] m -s, - dumpling.

Knolle ['knɔlə] f -, -n bulb.

Knopf [knɔpf] m -(e)s, ꞊e button; (Kragen—) stud; **—loch** nt buttonhole.

knöpfen ['knœpfən] vt button.

Knorpel ['knɔrpəl] m -s, - cartilage, gristle; **k—ig** a gristly.

knorrig ['knɔrɪç] a gnarled, knotted.

Knospe ['knɔspə] f -, -n bud; **k—n** vi bud.

Knoten ['kno:tən] m -s, - knot; (Bot) node; (Med) lump; **k—** vt knot; **—punkt** m junction.

knuffen ['knʊfən] vt (col) cuff.

Knüller ['knʏlər] m -s, - (col) hit; (Reportage) scoop.

knüpfen ['knʏpfən] vt tie; Teppich knot; Freundschaft form.

Knüppel ['knʏpəl] m -s, - cudgel; (Polizei—) baton, truncheon; (Aviat) (joy)stick; **—schaltung** f (Aut) floor-mounted gear change.

knurren ['knʊrən] vi (Hund) snarl, growl; (Magen) rumble; (Mensch) mutter.

knusperig ['knʊspərɪç] a crisp; Keks crunchy.

Koalition [koalitsi'o:n] f coalition.

Kobalt ['ko:balt] nt -s cobalt.

Kobold ['ko:bɔlt] m -(e)s, -e goblin, imp.

Kobra ['ko:bra] f -, -s cobra.

Koch [kɔx] m -(e)s, ꞊e cook; **—buch** nt cookery book; **k—en** vti cook; Wasser boil; **—er** m -s, - stove, cooker.

Köcher ['kœçər] m -s, - quiver.

Kochgelegenheit ['kɔxgəle:gənhaɪt] f cooking facilities pl.

Köchin ['kœçɪn] f cook.

Koch- cpd: **—löffel** m kitchen spoon; **—nische** f kitchenette; **—platte** f boiling ring, hotplate; **—salz** nt cooking salt; **—topf** m saucepan, pot.

Köder ['kø:dər] m -s, - bait, lure; **k—n** vt lure, entice.

Koexistenz [koɛksɪs'tɛnts] f coexistence.

Koffein [kɔfe'i:n] nt -s caffeine; **k—frei** a decaffeinated.

Koffer ['kɔfər] m -s, - suitcase; (Schrank—) trunk; **—radio** nt portable radio; **—raum** m (Aut) boot, trunk (US).

Kognak ['kɔnjak] m -s, -s brandy, cognac.

Kohl [ko:l] m -(e)s, -e cabbage.

Kohle ['ko:lə] f -, -n coal; (Holz—) charcoal; (Chem) carbon; **—hydrat** nt -(e)s, -e carbohydrate; **—ndioxyd** nt -(e)s, -e carbon dioxide; **—ngrube** f coal pit, mine; **—nhändler** m coal merchant, coalman; **—nsäure** f carbon dioxide; **—nstoff** m carbon; **—papier** nt carbon paper; **—stift** m charcoal pencil.

Köhler ['kø:lər] m -s, - charcoal burner.

Kohl- cpd: **—rübe** f turnip; **k—schwarz** a coal-black.

Koje ['koːjə] f -, -n cabin; (*Bett*) bunk.

Kokain [koka'iːn] nt -s cocaine.

kokett [ko'kɛt] a coquettish, flirtatious; **—ieren** [-'tiːrən] vi flirt.

Kokosnuß [ko'kɔsnʊs] f coconut.

Koks [koːks] m -es, -e coke.

Kolben ['kɔlbən] m -s, - (*Gewehr—*) rifle butt; (*Keule*) club; (*Chem*) flask; (*Tech*) piston; (*Mais—*) cob.

Kolchose [kɔl'çoːzə] f -, -n collective farm.

Kolik ['koːlɪk] f colic, gripe.

Kollaps [kɔ'laps] m -es, -e collapse.

Kolleg [kɔ'leːk] nt -s, -s or -ien lecture course; **—e** [kɔ'leːgə] m -n, -n, **—in** f colleague; **—ium** nt board; (*Sch*) staff.

Kollekte [kɔ'lɛktə] f -, -n (*Rel*) collection.

kollektiv [kɔlɛk'tiːf] a collective.

kollidieren [kɔli'diːrən] vi collide; (*zeitlich*) clash.

Kollision [kɔlizi'oːn] f collision; (*zeitlich*) clash.

kolonial [kolo'niaːl] a colonial; **K—warenhändler** m grocer.

Kolonie [kolo'niː] f colony.

kolonisieren [koloni'ziːrən] vt colonize.

Kolonist [kolo'nɪst] m colonist.

Kolonne [ko'lɔnə] f -, -n column; (*von Fahrzeugen*) convoy.

Koloß [ko'lɔs] m -sses, -sse colossus.

kolossal [kolo'saːl] a colossal.

Kombi- ['kɔmbi] cpd: **—nation** [-natsi'oːn] f combination; (*Vermutung*) conjecture; (*Hemdhose*) combinations pl; (*Aviat*) flying suit; **k—nieren** [-'niːrən] vt combine; vi deduce, work out; (*vermuten*) guess;

—wagen m station wagon; **—zange** f (pair of) pliers.

Komet [ko'meːt] m -en, -en comet.

Komfort [kɔm'foːr] m -s luxury.

Komik -, ['koːmɪk] f humour, comedy; **—er** m -s, - comedian.

komisch ['koːmɪʃ] a funny.

Komitee [komi'teː] nt -s, -s committee.

Komma ['kɔma] nt -s, -s or -ta comma.

Kommand- [kɔ'mand] cpd: **—ant** [-'dant] m commander, commanding officer; **—eur** [-'døːr] m commanding officer; **k—ieren** [-'diːrən] vti command; **—o** nt -s, -s command, order; (*Truppe*) detachment, squad; **auf —o** to order.

kommen ['kɔmən] vi irreg come; (*näher —*) approach; (*passieren*) happen; (*gelangen, geraten*) get; (*Blumen, Zähne, Tränen etc*) appear; (*in die Schule, das Zuchthaus etc*) go; **— lassen** send for; **das kommt in den Schrank** that goes in the cupboard; **zu sich —** come round or to; **zu etw —** acquire sth; **um etw — lose** sth; **nichts auf jdn/etw — lassen** have nothing said against sb/sth; **jdm frech — get** cheeky with sb; **auf jeden vierten kommt ein Platz** there's one place to every fourth person; **wer kommt zuerst?** who's first?; **unter ein Auto —** be run over by a car; **wie hoch kommt das?** what does that cost?; **K— nt -s** coming.

Kommentar [kɔmɛn'taːr] m commentary; **kein — no** comment; **k—los** a without comment.

Kommentator [kɔmɛn'taːtor] m (*TV*) commentator.

kommentieren [kɔmɛn'tiːrən] vt comment on.

kommerziell [kɔmɛrtsi'ɛl] a commercial.

Kommilitone [kɔmili'toːnə] m -n, -n fellow student.

Kommiß [kɔ'mɪs] m -sses (life in the) army; —brot nt army bread.

Kommissar [kɔmi'saːr] m police inspector.

Kommission [kɔmisi'oːn] f (Comm) commission; (Ausschuß) committee.

Kommode [kɔ'moːdə] f -, -n (chest of) drawers.

Kommune [kɔ'muːnə] f -, -n commune.

Kommunikation [kɔmunikatsi'oːn] f communication.

Kommunion [kɔmuni'oːn] f communion.

Kommuniqué [kɔmyni'keː] nt -s, -s communiqué.

Kommunismus [kɔmu'nɪsmʊs] m communism.

Kommunist [kɔmu'nɪst] m communist; k—isch a communist.

kommunizieren [kɔmuni'tsiːrən] vi communicate; (Eccl) receive communion.

Komödiant [komødi'ant] m comedian; —in f comedienne.

Komödie [ko'møːdiə] f comedy.

Kompagnon [kɔmpan'jõː] m -s, -s (Comm) partner.

kompakt [kɔm'pakt] a compact.

Kompanie [kɔmpa'niː] f company.

Komparativ ['kɔmparatiːf] m -s, -e comparative.

Kompaß ['kɔmpas] m -sses, -sse compass.

kompetent [kɔmpe'tɛnt] a competent.

Kompetenz [kɔmpe'tɛnts] f competence, authority.

komplett [kɔm'plɛt] a complete.

Komplikation [kɔmplikatsi'oːn] f complication.

Kompliment [kɔmpli'mɛnt] nt compliment.

Komplize [kɔm'pliːtsə] m -n, -n accomplice.

komplizieren [kɔmpli'tsiːrən] vt complicate.

Komplott [kɔm'plɔt] nt -(e)s, -e plot.

komponieren [kɔmpo'niːrən] vt compose.

Komponist [kɔmpo'nɪst] m composer.

Komposition [kɔmpozitsi'oːn] f composition.

Kompost [kɔm'pɔst] m -(e)s, -e compost; —haufen m compost heap.

Kompott [kɔm'pɔt] nt -(e)s, -e stewed fruit.

Kompresse [kɔm'prɛsə] f -, -n compress.

Kompressor [kɔm'prɛsɔr] m compressor.

Kompromiß [kɔmpro'mɪs] m -sses, -sse compromise; k—bereit a willing to compromise; —lösung f compromise solution.

kompromittieren [kɔmprɔmi'tiːrən] vt compromise.

Kondens- [kɔn'dɛns] cpd: —ation [kɔndɛnzatsi'oːn] f condensation; —ator [kɔndɛn'zaːtɔr] m condenser; k—ieren [kɔndɛn'ziːrən] vt condense; —milch f condensed milk; —streifen m vapour trail.

Kondition- [kɔnditsi'oːn] cpd: —alsatz [kɔnditsio'naːlzats] m conditional clause; **—straining** nt fitness training.

Konditor [kɔn'diːtɔr] m pastry-cook; **—ei** [kɔndito'raɪ] f café; cake shop.

kondolieren [kɔndo'liːrən] vi condole (*jdm* with sb).

Kondom [kɔn'doːm] nt **-s, -e** condom.

Konfektion [kɔnfɛktsi'oːn] f production of ready-made clothing; **—skleidung** f ready-made clothing.

Konferenz [kɔnfe'rɛnts] f conference, meeting.

konferieren [kɔnfe'riːrən] vi confer, have a meeting.

Konfession [kɔnfɛsi'oːn] f religion; (*christlich*) denomination; **k—ell** [-'nɛl] a denominational; **k—slos** a non-denominational; **—sschule** f denominational school.

Konfetti [kɔn'fɛti] nt **-(s)** confetti.

Konfirmand [kɔnfir'mant] m candidate for confirmation.

Konfirmation [kɔnfirmatsi'oːn] f (*Eccl*) confirmation.

konfirmieren [kɔnfir'miːrən] vt confirm.

konfiszieren [kɔnfis'tsiːrən] vt confiscate.

Konfitüre [kɔnfi'tyːrə] f **-, -n** jam.

Konflikt [kɔn'flɪkt] m **-(e)s, -e** conflict.

konform [kɔn'fɔrm] a concurring; **— gehen** be in agreement.

konfrontieren [kɔnfrɔn'tiːrən] vt confront.

konfus [kɔn'fuːs] a confused.

Kongreß [kɔn'grɛs] m **-sses, -sse** congress.

Kongruenz [kɔngru'ɛnts] f agreement, congruence.

König ['køːnɪç] m **-(e)s, -e** king; **—in** ['køːnɪgɪn] f queen; **k—lich** a

royal; **—reich** nt kingdom; **—tum** nt **-(e)s, -tümer** kingship.

konisch ['koːnɪʃ] a conical.

Konjugation [kɔnjugatsi'oːn] f conjugation.

konjugieren [kɔnju'giːrən] vt conjugate.

Konjunktion [kɔnjuŋktsi'oːn] f conjunction.

Konjunktiv ['kɔnjunktiːf] m **-s, -e** subjunctive.

Konjunktur [kɔnjunk'tuːr] f economic situation; (*Hoch—*) boom.

konkav [kɔn'kaːf] a concave.

konkret [kɔn'kreːt] a concrete.

Konkurrent(in *f*) [kɔnkʊ'rɛnt(m)] m competitor.

Konkurrenz [kɔnkʊ'rɛnts] f competition; **k—fähig** a competitive; **—kampf** m competition; (*col*) rat race.

konkurrieren [kɔnkʊ'riːrən] vi compete.

Konkurs [kɔn'kurs] m **-es, -e** bankruptcy.

können ['kœnən] vti irreg be able to, can; (*wissen*) know; **—** Sie Deutsch? can you speak German?; ich kann nicht ... I can't or cannot ...; kann ich gehen? can I go?; das kann sein that's possible; ich kann nicht mehr I can't go on; **K—** nt -s ability.

konsequent [kɔnze'kvɛnt] a consistent.

Konsequenz [kɔnze'kvɛnts] f consistency; (*Folgerung*) conclusion.

Konserv- [kɔn'zɛrv] cpd: **k—ativ** [-a'tiːf] a conservative; **—atorium** [-a'toːrium] nt academy of music, conservatory; **—e** f **-, -n** tinned food; **—enbüchse** f tin, can; **k—ieren** [-'viːrən] vt preserve;

—**ierung** f preservation;
—**ierungsmittel** nt preservative.
Konsonant [kɔnzo'nant] m
consonant.
konstant [kɔn'stant] a constant.
Konstitution [kɔnstitutsi'o:n] f
constitution; **k—ell** [-'nɛl] a constitutional.
konstruieren [kɔnstru'i:rən] vt
construct.
Konstrukteur [kɔnstruk'tø:r] m
engineer, designer.
Konstruktion [kɔnstruktsi'o:n] f
construction.
konstruktiv [kɔnstruk'ti:f] a con-
structive.
Konsul ['kɔnzul] m -s, -n consul;
—**at** [-'la:t] nt consulate.
konsultieren [kɔnzul'ti:rən] vt
consult.
Konsum [kɔn'zu:m] m -s
consumption; —**artikel** m consumer article; —**ent** [-'mɛnt] m consumer; **k—ieren** [-'mi:rən] vt
consume.
Kontakt [kɔn'takt] m -(e)s, -e
contact; **k—arm** a unsociable;
k—freudig a sociable; —**linsen** pl
contact lenses pl.
Konterfei ['kɔntərfai] nt -s, -s
picture.
kontern ['kɔntərn] vti counter.
Konterrevolution [kɔntərre-
volutsio:n] f counter-revolution.
Kontinent ['kɔntinɛnt] m continent.
Kontingent [kɔntiŋ'gɛnt] nt -(e)s,
-e quota; (Truppen—) contingent.
kontinuierlich [kɔntinu'i:rlɪç] a
continuous.
Kontinuität [kɔntinui'tɛ:t] f
continuity.
Konto ['kɔnto] nt -s, Konten
account; —**auszug** m statement (of
account); —**inhaber(in** f) m

account holder; —**r** [kɔn'to:r] nt -s,
-e office; —**rist** [-'rɪst] m clerk,
office worker; —**stand** m state of
account.
Kontra ['kɔntra] nt -s, -s (Cards)
double; **jdm — geben** (fig) contradict sb; —**baß** m double bass;
—**hent** [-'hɛnt] m contracting
party; —**punkt** m counterpoint.
Kontrast [kɔn'trast] m -(e)s, -e
contrast.
Kontroll- [kɔn'trɔl] cpd: —**e** f -, -n
control, supervision; (Paß—) passport control; —**eur** [-'lø:r] m
inspector; **k—ieren** [-'li:rən] vt
control, supervise; (nachprüfen)
check.
Kontur [kɔn'tu:r] f contour.
Konvention [kɔnvɛntsi'o:n] f convention; **k—ell** [-'nɛl] a
conventional.
Konversation [kɔnvɛrzatsi'o:n] f
conversation; —**slexikon** nt
encyclopaedia.
konvex [kɔn'vɛks] a convex.
Konvoi ['kɔnvɔy] m -s, -s convoy.
Konzentration [kɔntsɛntratsi'o:n]
f concentration; —**slager** nt concentration camp.
konzentrieren [kɔntsɛn'tri:rən] vtr
concentrate.
konzentriert a concentrated; ad
zuhören, arbeiten intently.
Konzept [kɔn'tsɛpt] nt -(e)s, -e
rough draft; **jdn aus dem —
bringen** confuse sb.
Konzern [kɔn'tsɛrn] m -s, -e
combine.
Konzert [kɔn'tsɛrt] nt -(e)s, -e
concert; (Stück) concerto; —**saal**
m concert hall.
Konzession [kɔntsɛsi'o:n] f
licence; (Zugeständnis)
concession; **k—ieren** [-'ni:rən] vt
license.

Konzil [kɔn'tsiːl] *nt* **-s, -e** or **-ien** council.

konzipieren [kɔntsi'piːrən] *vt* conceive.

Kopf [kɔpf] *m* **-(e)s, ⁼e** head; **—bedeckung** *f* headgear.

köpfen ['kœpfən] *vt* behead; *Baum* lop; *Ei* take the top off; *Ball* head.

Kopf- *cpd*: **—haut** *f* scalp; **—hörer** *m* headphone; **—kissen** *nt* pillow; **k—los** a panic-stricken; **—losigkeit** *f* panic; **k—rechnen** *vi* do mental arithmetic; **—salat** *m* lettuce; **—schmerzen** *pl* headache; **—sprung** *m* header, dive; **—stand** *m* headstand; **—tuch** *nt* headscarf; **k—über** *ad* head over heels; **—weh** *nt* headache; **—zerbrechen** *nt*: jdm **—zerbrechen machen** give sb a lot of headaches.

Kopie [ko'piː] *f* copy; **k—ren** *vt* copy.

Koppel ['kɔpəl] *f* **-, -n** (*Weide*) enclosure; *nt* **-s, -** (*Gürtel*) belt; **k—n** *vt* couple; **—ung** *f* coupling; **—ungsmanöver** *nt* docking manoeuvre.

Koralle [ko'ralə] *f* **-, -n** coral; **—nkette** *f* coral necklace; **—nriff** *nt* coral reef.

Korb [kɔrp] *m* **-(e)s, ⁼e** basket; jdm einen **— geben** (*fig*) turn sb down; **—ball** *m* basketball; **—stuhl** *m* wicker chair.

Kord [kɔrt] *m* **-(e)s, -e** corduroy.

Kordel ['kɔrdəl] *f* **-, -n** cord, string.

Kork [kɔrk] *m* **-(e)s, -e** cork; **—en** *m* **-s, -** stopper, cork; **—enzieher** *m* **-s, -** corkscrew.

Korn [kɔrn] *nt* **-(e)s, ⁼er** corn, grain; (*Gewehr*) sight; **—blume** *f* cornflower; **—kammer** *f* granary.

Körnchen ['kœrnçən] *nt* grain, granule.

Körper ['kœrpər] *m* **-s, -** body; **—bau** *m* build; **k—behindert** a disabled; **—gewicht** *nt* weight; **—größe** *f* height; **—haltung** *f* carriage, deportment; **k—lich** a physical; **—pflege** *f* personal hygiene; **—schaft** *f* corporation; **—teil** *m* part of the body.

Korps [koːr] *nt* **-, -** (*Mil*) corps; students' club.

korpulent [kɔrpu'lɛnt] a corpulent.

korrekt [kɔ'rɛkt] a correct; **K—heit** *f* correctness; **K—or** *m* proofreader; **K—ur** ['-'tuːr] *f* (*eines Textes*) proofreading; (*Text*) proof; (*Sch*) marking, correction.

Korrespondent [kɔrɛspɔn'dɛnt] *cpd*: **—ent(in** *f*) ['dɛnt(ɪn)] *m* correspondent; **—enz** ['dɛnts] *f* correspondence; **k—ieren** ['-'diːrən] *vi* correspond.

Korridor ['kɔridoːr] *m* **-s, -e** corridor.

korrigieren [kɔri'giːrən] *vt* correct.

korrumpieren [kɔrʊm'piːrən] *vt* corrupt.

Korruption [kɔrʊptsi'oːn] *f* corruption.

Korsett [kɔr'zɛt] *nt* **-(e)s, -e** corset.

Kose- ['koːzə] *cpd*: **—form** *f* pet form; **k—n** *vt* caress; *vi* bill and coo; **—name** *m* pet name; **—wort** *nt* term of endearment.

Kosmetik [kɔs'meːtɪk] *f* cosmetics *pl*; **—erin** *f* beautician.

kosmetisch a cosmetic; *Chirurgie* plastic.

kosmisch ['kɔsmɪʃ] a cosmic.

Kosmo- ['kɔsmo] *cpd*: **—naut** ['-'naut] *m* **-en, -en** cosmonaut; **—polit** [-po'liːt] *m* **-en, -en** cosmopolitan; **k—politisch** [-po'liːtɪʃ] a cosmopolitan; **—s** *m* **-** cosmos.

Kost [kɔst] *f* **-** (*Nahrung*) food; (*Verpflegung*) board; **k—bar** a precious; *(teuer)* costly, expensive; —barkeit *f* preciousness; costliness, expensiveness; *(Wertstück)* valuable; —en *pl* cost(s); *(Ausgaben)* expenses *pl*; auf — von at the expense of; k—en *vt* cost; *vti (versuchen)* taste; —enanschlag *m* estimate; k—enlos a free (of charge); —geld *nt* board.

köstlich ['kœstlɪç] *a* precious; *Einfall* delightful; *Essen* delicious; sich — amüsieren have a marvellous time.

Kost- *cpd*: —probe *f* taste; *(fig)* sample; k—spielig *a* expensive.

Kostüm [kɔs'tyːm] *nt* -s, -e costume; *(Damen—)* suit; —fest *nt* fancy-dress party; k—ieren [kɔsty'miːrən] *vtr* dress up; .—verleih *m* costume agency. •

Kot [koːt] *m* -(e)s excrement.

Kotelett [kɔtə'lɛt] *nt* -(e)s, -e *or* -s cutlet, chop; —en *pl* sideboards *pl*.

Köter ['køːtər] *m* -s, - cur.

Kotflügel *m (Aut)* wing.,

Krabbe ['krabə] *f* -, -n shrimp; k—ln *vi* crawl.

Krach [krax] *m* -(e)s, -s *or* -e crash; *(andauernd)* noise; *(col: Streit)* quarrel, row; k—en *vi* crash; *(beim Brechen)* crack; *vr (col)* row, quarrel.

krächzen ['krɛçtsən] *vi* croak.

Kraft [kraft] *f* -, -̈e strength, power, force; *(Arbeits—)* worker; in — treten come into effect; k—... *+gen* by virtue of; —ausdruck *m* swearword; —fahrer *m* motor driver; —fahrzeug *nt* motor vehicle; —fahrzeugbrief *m* logbook; —fahrzeugsteuer *f* ≈ road tax.

kräftig ['krɛftɪç] *a* strong; —en ['krɛftɪgən] *vt* strengthen.

Kraft- *cpd*: k—los *a* weak; powerless; *(Jur)* invalid; —probe *f* trial of strength; —rad *nt* motorcycle; k—voll *a* vigorous; —wagen *m* motor vehicle; —werk *nt* power station.

Kragen ['kraːgən] *m* -s, - collar; —weite *f* collar size.

Krähe ['krɛːə] *f* -, -n crow; k—n *vi* crow.

krakeelen [kra'keːlən] *vi (col)* make a din.

Kralle ['kralə] *f* -, -n claw; *(Vogel—)* talon; k—n *vt* clutch; *(krampfhaft)* claw:

Kram [kraːm] *m* -(e)s stuff, rubbish; k—en *vi* rummage; —laden *m (pej)* small shop.

Krampf [krampf] *m* -(e)s, -̈e cramp; *(zuckend)* spasm; —ader *f* varicose vein; k—haft *a* convulsive; *(fig)* Versuche desperate.

Kran [kraːn] *m* -(e)s, -̈e crane; *(Wasser—)* tap.

Kranich ['kraːnɪç] *m* -s, -e *(Zool)* crane.

krank [krank] *a* ill, sick; K—e(r) *mf* sick person; invalid, patient.

kränkeln ['krɛŋkəln] *vi* be in bad health.

kranken ['krankən] *vi*: an etw *(dat)* — *(fig)* suffer from sth.

kränken ['krɛŋkən] *vt* hurt.

Kranken- *cpd*: —bericht *m* medical report; —geld *nt* sick pay; —haus *nt* hospital; —kasse *f* health insurance; —pfleger *m* nursing orderly; —schwester *f* nurse; —versicherung *f* health insurance; —wagen *m* ambulance.

Krank- *cpd*: k—haft *a* diseased; *Angst etc* morbid; —heit *f* illness, disease; —heitserreger *m* disease-carrying agent.

kränk- ['krɛŋk] *cpd:* **—lich** *a* sickly; **K—ung** *f* insult, offence.

Kranz [krants] *m* -es, ⁻e wreath, garland.

Kränzchen ['krɛntsçən] *nt* small wreath; ladies' party.

Krapfen ['krapfən] *m* -s, - fritter; (*Berliner*) doughnut.

kraß [kras] *a* crass.

Krater ['kra:tər] *m* -s, - crater.

Kratz- ['krats] *cpd:* **—bürste** *f* (*fig*) crosspatch; **k—en** *vti* scratch; **—er** *m* -s, - scratch; (*Werkzeug*) scraper.

Kraul(schwimmen) ['kraʊl(ʃvɪm-en)] *nt* -s crawl; **k—en** *vi* (*schwimmen*) do the crawl; *vt* (*streicheln*) tickle.

kraus [kraʊs] *a* crinkly; *Haar* frizzy; *Stirn* wrinkled; **K—e** ['kraʊzə] *f* -, -n frill, ruffle.

kräuseln ['krɔyzəln] *vt Haar* make frizzy; *Stoff* gather; *Stirn* wrinkle; *vr* (*Haar*) go frizzy; (*Stirn*) wrinkle; (*Wasser*) ripple.

Kraut [kraʊt] *nt* -(e)s, Kräuter plant; (*Gewürz*) herb; (*Gemüse*) cabbage.

Krawall [kra'val] *m* -s, -e row, uproar.

Krawatte [kra'vatə] *f* -, -n tie.

kreativ [krea'ti:f] *a* creative.

Kreatur [krea'tu:r] *f* creature.

Krebs [kre:ps] *m* -es, -e crab; (*Med, Astrol*) cancer.

Kredit [kre'di:t] *m* -(e)s, -e credit.

Kreide ['kraɪdə] *f* -, -n chalk; **k—bleich** *a* as white as a sheet.

Kreis ['kraɪs] *m* -es, -e circle; (*Stadt—* etc) district; **im — gehen** (*lit, fig*) go round in circles.

kreischen ['kraɪʃən] *vi* shriek, screech.

Kreis- *cpd:* **—el** ['kraɪzəl] *m* -s, - top; (*Verkehrs—*) roundabout; **k—en** ['kraɪtsən] *vi* spin; **k—förmig** *a* circular; **—lauf** *m* (*Physiol*) circulation; (*fig: der Natur etc*) cycle; **—säge** *f* circular saw; **—stadt** *f* county town; **—verkehr** *m* roundabout traffic.

Kreißsaal ['kraɪs-za:l] *m* delivery room.

Krem [kre:m] *f* -, -s cream, mousse.

Krematorium [krema'to:rium] *nt* crematorium.

Krempe ['krɛmpə] *f* -, -n brim; **—l** *m* -s (*col*) rubbish.

krepieren [kre'pi:rən] *vi* (*col: sterben*) die, kick the bucket.

Krepp [krɛp] *m* -s, -s *or* -e crepe; **—papier** *nt* crepe paper; **—sohle** *f* crepe sole.

Kresse ['krɛsə] *f* -, -n cress.

Kreuz [krɔyts] *nt* -es, -e cross; (*Anat*) small of the back; (*Cards*) clubs; **k—en** *vtr* cross; *vi* (*Naut*) cruise; **—er** *m* -s, - (*Schiff*) cruiser; **—fahrt** *f* cruise; **—feuer** *nt* (*fig*) **im —feuer stehen** be caught in the crossfire; **—gang** *m* cloisters *pl*; **k—igen** *vt* crucify; **—igung** *f* crucifixion; **—otter** *f* adder; **—ung** *f* (*Verkehrs—*) crossing, junction; (*Züchten*) cross; **—verhör** *nt* cross-examination; **—weg** *m* crossroads; (*Rel*) Way of the Cross; **—worträtsel** *nt* crossword puzzle; **—zeichen** *nt* sign of the cross; **—zug** *m* crusade.

Kriech- ['kri:ç] *cpd:* **k—en** *vi irreg* crawl, creep; (*pej*) grovel, crawl; **—er** *m* -s, - crawler; **—spur** *f* crawler lane; **—tier** *nt* reptile.

Krieg [kri:k] *m* -(e)s, -e war; **k—en** ['kri:gən] *vt* (*col*) get; **—er** *m* -s, - warrior; **k—erisch** *a* warlike; **—führung** *f* warfare;

—sbemalung f war paint;
—serklärung f declaration of war
—sfuß m: mit jdm/etw auf —sfuß
stehen be at loggerheads with
sb/not get on with sth;
—sgefangene(r) m prisoner of war;
—sgefangenschaft f captivity;
—sgericht nt court-martial;
—sschiff nt warship; —sschuld f
war guilt; —sverbrecher m war
criminal; —sversehrte(r) m person
disabled in the war; —szustand m
state of war.

Krimi ['kri:mi] m -s, -s (col)
thriller; **k—nal** ['-na:l] a criminal;
—'nalbeamte(r) m detective;
—nali'tät f criminality;
—'nalpolizei f detective force, CID
(Brit); —'nalroman m detective
story; **k—nell** ['-nɛl] a criminal;
—'nelie(r) m criminal.

Krippe. ['krɪpə] f -, -n manger,
crib; (Kinder—) crèche.

Krise ['kri:zə] f -, -n crisis; **k—ln**
vi: es kriselt there's a crisis;
—nherd m trouble spot.

Kristall [krɪs'tal] m -s, -e crystal;
nt -s (Glas) crystal.

Kriterium-[kri'te:rium] nt criterion.

Kritik [kri'ti:k] f criticism;
(Zeitungs—) review, write-up; —er
['kri:tikər] m -s, - critic; **k—los** a
uncritical.

kritisch ['kri:tɪʃ] a critical.

kritisieren [kriti'zi:rən] vti criticize.

kritteln ['krɪtəln] vi find fault, carp.

kritzeln ['krɪtsəln] vti scribble,
scrawl.

Krokodil [kroko'di:l] nt -s, -e
crocodile.

Krokus ['kro:kus] m -, - or -se
crocus.

Krone ['kro:nə] f -, -n crown;
(Baum—) top.

krönen ['krø:nən] vt crown.

Kron- cpd: —korken m bottle top;
—leuchter m chandelier; —prinz m
crown prince.

Krönung ['krø:nʊŋ] f coronation.

Kropf [krɔpf] m -(e)s, ⁼e (Med)
goitre; (im Vogel) crop.

Kröte ['krø:tə] f -, -n toad.

Krücke ['kryka] f -, -n crutch.

Krug [kru:k] m -(e)s, ⁼e jug;
(Bier—) mug.

Krümel ['kry:məl] m -s, - crumb;
k—n vti crumble.

krumm [krʊm] a (lit, fig) crooked;
(kurvig) curved; —beinig a bandy-
legged.

krümm- ['krʏm] cpd: —en vtr
curve, bend; **K—ung** f bend, curve.

krumm- cpd: —lachen vr (col)
laugh o.s. silly; —nehmen vt irreg
(col) jdm etw —nehmen take sth
amiss.

Krüppel ['krʏpəl] m -s, - cripple.

Kruste ['krustə] f -, -n crust.

Kruzifix [krutsi'fɪks] nt -es, -e
crucifix.

Kübel ['ky:bəl] m -s, - tub; (Eimer)
pail.

Küche ['kʏçə] f -, -n kitchen;
(Kochen) cooking, cuisine.

Kuchen ['ku:xən] m -s, - cake;
—blech nt baking tray; —form f
baking tin; —gabel f pastry fork;
—teig m cake mixture.

Küchen- cpd: —herd m range;
(Gas, Elec) cooker, stove; —schabe
f cockroach; —nschrank m kitchen
cabinet.

Kuckuck ['kʊkʊk] m -s, -e cuckoo.

Kufe ['ku:fə] f -, -n (Faß) vat;
(Schlitten—) runner; (Aviat) skid.

Kugel ['ku:gəl] f -, -n ball; (Math)
sphere; (Mil) bullet; (Erd—)
globe; (Sport) shot; **k—förmig** a

spherical; **—lager** nt ball bearing; **k—n** vt roll; (Sport) bowl; vr (vor Lachen) double up; **k—rund** a (vor Gegenstand round; (col) Person tubby; **—schreiber** m refillable (pen), biro ®; **k—sicher** a bullet-proof; **—stoßen** nt -s shot-put.

Kuh [ku:] f -, -e cow.

kühl [ky:l] a (lit, fig) cool; **K—anlage** f refrigerating plant; **K—e** f coolness; **—en** vt cool; **K—er** m -s, - (Aut) radiator; **K—erhaube** (Aut) bonnet, hood (US); **K—raum** m cold-storage chamber; **K—schrank** m refrigerator; **K—truhe** f freezer; **K—ung** f cooling; **K—wagen** m (Rail) refrigerator van; **K—wasser** nt cooling water.

kühn [ky:n] a bold, daring; **K—heit** f boldness.

Küken ['ky:kən] nt -s, - chicken.

kulant [ku'lant] a obliging.

Kuli ['ku:li] m -s, -s coolie; (col: Kugelschreiber) biro ®.

Kulisse [ku'lɪsə] f -, -n scene.

kullern ['kʊlərn] vi roll.

Kult [kʊlt] m -(e)s, -e worship, cult; **mit etw — treiben** make a cult out of sth; **k—ivieren** [-i'vi:rən] vt cultivate; **k—iviert** a cultivated, refined; **—ur** [kʊl'tu:r] f culture; civilization; (das Boden) cultivation; **k—urell** [kʊl'tʊrɛl] a cultural; **—urfilm** m documentary film.

Kümmel ['kyməl] m -s, - caraway seed; (Branntwein) kümmel.

Kummer ['kʊmər] m -s grief, sorrow.

kümmer- ['kymər] cpd: **—lich** a miserable, wretched; **—n** vr: sich um jdn —n look after sb; sich um etw —n see to sth; vt concern; das kümmert mich nicht that doesn't worry me.

Kumpan [kʊm'pa:n] m -s, -e mate; (pej) accomplice.

Kumpel ['kʊmpəl] m -s, - (col) mate.

kündbar ['kyntba:r] a redeemable, recallable; (Vertrag) terminable.

Kunde ['kʊndə] m -n, -n, **Kundin** f customer; f -, -n (Botschaft) news; **—ndienst** m after-sales service.

Kund- cpd: **—gabe** f announcement; **k—geben** vt irreg announce; **—gebung** f announcement; (Versammlung) rally; **k—ig** a expert, experienced.

Künd- ['kynd] cpd: **k—igen** vi in one's notice; **jdm k—igen** give sb his notice; vt cancel; (jdm) die Stellung/Wohnung — give (sb) notice; **—igung** f notice; **—igungsfrist** f period of notice.

Kundschaft f customers pl, clientele.

künftig ['kynftɪç] a future; ad in future.

Kunst [kʊnst] f -, -e art; (Können) skill; das ist doch keine — it's easy; **—akademie** f academy of art; **—dünger** m artificial manure; **—faser** f synthetic fibre; **—fertigkeit** f skilfulness; **—geschichte** f history of art; **—gewerbe** nt arts and crafts pl; **—griff** m trick, knack; **—händler** m art dealer; **—harz** nt artificial resin.

Künstler(in f) ['kʏnstlər(ɪn)] m -s, - artist; **k—isch** a artistic; **—name** m stagename; pseudonym.

künstlich ['kʏnstlɪç] a artificial.

Kunst- cpd: **—sammler** m -s, - art collector; **—seide** f artificial silk; **—stoff** m synthetic material; **—stopfen** nt -s invisible mending; **—stück** nt trick; **—turnen** nt gymnastics; k—voll a ingenious, artistic; —werk nt work of art.

kunterbunt ['kʊntərbʊnt] a higgledy-piggledy.

Kupfer ['kʊpfər] nt -s, - copper; —geld nt coppers pl; k—n a copper; —stich m copperplate engraving.

Kuppe ['kʊpə] f -, -n (Berg—) top; (Finger—) tip; —l f -, -n cupola, dome; —'lei f (Jur) procuring; k—ln vi (Jur) procure; (Aut) declutch; vt join.

Kupp- ['kʊp] cpd: —ler m -s, - pimp; —lerin f. matchmaker; —lung f coupling; (Aut) clutch.

Kur [ku:r] f -, -en, cure, treatment.

Kür [ky:r] f -, -en (Sport) free skating/exercises pl.

Kurbel ['kʊrbəl] f -, -n crank, winch; (Aut) starting handle; —welle f crankshaft.

Kürbis ['kyrbɪs] m -ses, -se pumpkin; (exotisch) gourd.

Kur- ['ku:r] cpd: —gast m visitor (to a health resort); k—ieren [ku'ri:rən] vt cure; k—ios [kuri'o:s] a curious, odd; —iosität f curiosity; —ort m health resort; —pfuscher m quack.

Kurs [kʊrs] m -es, -e course; (Fin) rate; hoch im — stehen (fig) be highly thought of; —buch nt timetable; k—ieren [kʊr'zi:rən] vi circulate; k—iv ad in italics; —ive [kʊr'zi:və] f -, -n italics pl; —us ['kʊrzʊs] m -, Kurse course; —wagen m (Rail) through carriage.

Kurve ['kʊrvə] f -, -n curve;

(Straßen— auch) bend; k—nreich, kurvig a Straße bendy.

kurz [kʊrts] a short; zu — kommen come off badly; den —eren ziehen get the worst of it; K—arbeit f short-time work; —ärm(e)lig a short-sleeved.

Kürze ['kyrtsə] f -, -n shortness, brevity; k—n vt cut short; (in der Länge) shorten; Gehalt reduce.

kurz- cpd: —erhand ad on the spot; K—fassung f shortened version; —fristig a short-term; —gefaßt a concise; K—geschichte f short story; —halten vt irreg keep short; —lebig a shortlived.

kürzlich ['kyrtslɪç] ad lately, recently.

Kurz- cpd: —schluß m (Elec) short circuit; —schrift f shorthand; k—sichtig a short-sighted; —welle f shortwave.

kuscheln ['kʊʃəln] vr snuggle up.

Kusine [ku'zi:nə] f cousin.

Kuß [kʊs] m -sses, -sse kiss.

küssen ['kʏsən] vtr kiss.

Küste ['kʏstə] f -, -n coast, shore; —nwache f coastguard (station).

Küster ['kʏstər] m -s, - sexton, verger.

Kutsche ['kʊtʃə] f -, -n coach, carriage; —r m -s, - coachman.

Kutte ['kʊtə] f -, -n cowl.

Kuvert [ku'vɛrt] nt -s, -e or -s envelope; cover.

Kybernetik [kybər'ne:tɪk] f cybernetics.

kybernetisch [kybər'ne:tɪʃ] a cybernetic.

L

L, l [ɛl] *nt* L, l.

laben ['la:bən] *vtr* refresh (o.s.).
(*fig*) relish (an *etw* (*dat*) sth.).

Labor [la'bo:r] *nt* -s, -e *or* -s lab;
—ant(in *f*) [labo'rant(ɪn)] *m*
lab(oratory) assistant; —atorium
[labora'to:rium] *nt* laboratory.

Labyrinth [laby'rɪnt] *nt* -s, -e
labyrinth.

Lache ['laxə] *f* -, -n (*Wasser*) pool,
puddle; (*col: Gelächter*) laugh.

lächeln ['lɛçəln] *vi* smile; L— *nt*
-s smile.

lachen ['laxən] *vi* laugh.

lächerlich ['lɛçərlɪç] *a* ridiculous;
L—keit *f* absurdity.

Lach- *cpd:* —gas *nt* laughing gas;
l—haft *a* laughable.

Lachs [laks] *m* -es, -e salmon.

Lack [lak] *m* -(e)s, -e lacquer,
varnish; (*von Auto*) paint; l—ieren
[la'ki:rən] *vt* varnish; *Auto* spray;
—ierer [la'ki:rər] *m* -s, - varnisher;
—leder *nt* patent leather.

Lackmus ['lakmʊs] *m or nt* -
litmus.

Lade ['la:də] *f* -, -n box, chest;
—baum *m* derrick; —fähigkeit *f*
load capacity.

laden ['la:dən] *vt irreg Lasten* load;
(*Jur*) summon; (*einladen*) invite.

Laden ['la:dən] *m* -s, = shop;
(*Fenster—*) shutter; —besitzer *m*
shopkeeper; —dieb *m* shoplifter;
—diebstahl *m* shoplifting; —hüter
m -s, - unsaleable item; —preis *m*
retail price; —schluß *m* closing
time; —tisch *m* counter.

Laderaum *m* (*Naut*) hold.

Ladung ['la:dʊŋ] *f* (*Last*) cargo,
load; (*Beladen*) loading; (*Jur*)
summons; (*Einladung*) invitation;
(*Spreng—*) charge.

Lage ['la:gə] *f* -, -n position, situation; (*Schicht*) layer; in der — sein
be in a position; l—nweise *ad* in
layers.

Lager ['la:gər] *nt* -s, - camp;
(*Comm*) warehouse; (*Schlaf—*)
bed; (*von Tier*) lair; (*Tech*)
bearing; —arbeiter(in *f*) *m* store-
hand; —bestand *m* stocks *pl*;
—geld *nt* storage (charges *pl*);
—haus *nt* warehouse, store.

lagern ['la:gərn] *vi* (*Dinge*) be
stored; (*Menschen*) camp; (*auch
vr: rasten*) lie down; *vt* store;
(*betten*) lay down; *Maschine* bed.

Lager- *cpd:* —schuppen *m* store
shed; —stätte *f* resting place;
—ung *f* storage.

Lagune [la'gu:nə] *f* -, -n lagoon.

lahm [la:m] *a* lame, limp.

lähmen ['lɛ:mən] *vt* paralyse.

lahmlegen *vt* paralyse.

Lähmung *f* paralysis.

Laib [laip] *m* -s, -e loaf.

Laich [laiç] *m* -(e)s, -e spawn;
l—en *vi* spawn.

Laie ['laiə] *m* -n, -n layman;
l—haft *a* amateurish.

Lakai [la'kai] *m* -en, -en lackey.

Laken ['la:kən] *nt* -s, - sheet.

Lakritze [la'krɪtsə] *f* -, -n liquorice.

lallen ['lalən] *vti* slur; (*Baby*)
babble.

Lamelle [la'mɛlə] f lamella; (Elec) lamina; (Tech) plate.

lamentieren [lamɛn'tiːrən] vi lament.

Lametta [la'mɛta] nt -s tinsel.

Lamm [lam] nt -(e)s, ⸚er lamb; —fell nt lambskin; l—fromm a like a lamb; —wolle f lambswool.

Lampe [lampə] f -, -n lamp; —nfieber nt stage fright; —nschirm m lampshade.

Lampion [lãpi'ŏː] m -s, -s Chinese lantern.

Land [lant] nt -(e)s, ⸚er land; (Nation, nicht Stadt) country; (Bundes—) state; auf dem —(e) in the country; —arbeiter m farm or agricultural worker; —besitz m landed property; —besitzer m landowner; —ebahn f runway; l—einwärts ad inland; l—en ['landən] vti land.

Ländereien [lɛndə'raɪən] pl estates pl.

Landes- ['landəs] cpd: —farben pl national colours pl; —innere(s) nt inland region; —tracht f national costume; l—üblich a customary; —verrat m high treason; —verweisung f banishment; —währung f national currency.

Land- cpd: —gut nt estate; —haus nt country house; —karte f map; —kreis m administrative region; l—läufig a customary.

ländlich ['lɛntliç] a rural.

Land- cpd: —schaft f countryside; (Art) landscape; l—schaftlich a scenic; regional; —smann m, —smännin f, pl -sleute compatriot, fellow countryman or countrywoman; —straße f country road; —streicher m -s, - tramp; —strich m region; —tag m (Pol) regional parliament.

Landung ['landʊŋ] f landing; —shoot nt landing craft; —sbrücke f jetty, pier; —sstelle f landing place.

Land- cpd: —vermesser m surveyor; —wirt m farmer; —wirtschaft f agriculture; —zunge f spit.

lang [laŋ] a long; Mensch tall; —atmig a long-winded; —e ad for a long time; dauern, brauchen a long time.

Länge ['lɛŋə] f -, -n length; (Geog) longitude; —ngrad m longitude; —nmaß nt linear measure.

langen ['laŋən] vi (ausreichen) do, suffice; (fassen) reach (nach for); es langt mir I've had enough.

lang- cpd: L—eweile f boredom; —lebig a long-lived.

länglich a longish.

lang- cpd: L—mut f forbearance, patience; —mütig a forbearing.

längs [lɛŋs] prep +gen or dat along; a ad lengthwise.

lang- cpd: —sam a slow; L—samkeit f slowness; L—schläfer(in- f) m late riser; —spielplatte f long-playing record.

längst [lɛŋst] ad das ist — fertig that was finished a long time ago, that has been finished for a long time; —e(r,s) a longest.

lang- cpd: —weilig a boring, tedious; L—welle f long wave; —wierig a lengthy, long-drawn-out.

Lanze ['lantsə] f -, -n lance.

Lanzette [lan'tsɛtə] f lancet.

lapidar [lapi'daːr] a terse, pithy.

Lappalie [la'paːliə] f trifle.

Lappen ['lapən] m -s, - cloth, rag; (Anat) lobe.

läppisch ['lɛpiʃ] a foolish.

Lapsus ['lapsʊs] m -, - slip.

Lärche ['lɛrçə] f -, -n larch.

Lärm [lɛrm] m -(e)s noise; l—en vi be noisy, make a noise.

Larve ['larfə] f -, -n mask; (Biol) larva.

lasch [laʃ] a slack; Geschmack tasteless.

Lasche ['laʃə] f -, -n (Schuh-) tongue; (Rail) fishplate.

Laser ['leizə] m -s, - laser.

lassen ['lasən] vti irreg leave; (erlauben) let; (aufhören mit) stop; (veranlassen) let; etw machen — to have sth done; es läßt sich machen it can be done; es läßt sich öffnen it can be opened, it opens.

lässig ['lɛsɪç] a casual; L—keit f casualness.

läßlich ['lɛslɪç] a pardonable, venial.

Last [last] f -, -en load, burden; (Naut, Aviat) cargo; (usu pl: Gebühr) charge; jdm zur — fallen be a burden to sb; —auto nt lorry, truck; l—en vi (auf + dat) weigh on.

Laster ['lastər] nt -s, - vice.

Lästerer ['lɛstərər] m -s, - mocker; (Gottes—) blasphemer.

lasterhaft a immoral.

lästerlich a scandalous.

lästern ['lɛstərn] vti Gott blaspheme; (schlecht sprechen) mock.

Lästerung f jibe; (Gottes—) blasphemy.

lästig ['lɛstɪç] a troublesome, tiresome.

Last- cpd: —kahn m barge; —kraftwagen m heavy goods vehicle; —schrift f debiting; debit item; —tier nt beast of burden; —träger m porter; —wagen m lorry, truck.

latent [la'tɛnt] a latent.

Laterne [la'tɛrnə] f -, -n lantern; (Straßen—) lamp, light; —npfahl m lamppost.

Latrine [la'tri:nə] f latrine.

Latsche ['latʃə] f -, -n dwarf pine; l—n ['la:tʃən] vi (col) (gehen) wander, go; (lässig) slouch.

Latte ['latə] f -, -n lath; (Sport) goalpost; (quer) crossbar; —nzaun m lattice fence.

Latz [lats] m -es, ²e bib; (Hosen—) flies pl.

Lätzchen ['lɛtsçən] nt bib.

Latzhose f dungarees pl.

lau [lau] a Nacht balmy; Wasser lukewarm.

Laub [laup] nt -(e)s foliage; —baum m deciduous tree; —e ['laubə] f -, -n arbour; —frosch m tree frog; —säge f fretsaw.

Lauch [laux] m -(e)s, -e leek.

Lauer ['lauər] f: auf der — sein or liegen, l—n vi lie in wait; (Gefahr) lurk.

Lauf [lauf] m -(e)s, Läufe run; (Wett—) race; (Entwicklung, Astron) course; (Gewehr) barrel; einer Sache ihren — lassen let sth take its course; —bahn f career; —bursche m errand boy.

laufen ['laufən] vti irreg run; (col: gehen) walk; —d a running; Monat, Ausgaben current; auf dem —den sein/halten be/keep up to date; am —den Band (fig) continuously; — lassen vt irreg leave running; —lassen vt irreg Person let go.

Läufer ['loyfər] m -s, - (Teppich, Sport) runner; (Fußball) halfback; (Schach) bishop.

Lauf- cpd: —kundschaft f passing trade; —masche f run, ladder (Brit); im —schritt at a run;

—stall *m* playpen; —steg *m* dais; —zettel *m* circular.

Lauge ['laugə] *f* -, -n soapy water; (*Chem*) alkaline solution.

Laune ['launə] *f* -, -n mood, humour; (*Einfall*) caprice; (*schlechte*) temper; l—**haft** *a* capricious, changeable.

launisch *a* moody; bad-tempered.

Laus [laus] *f* -, **Läuse** louse; —bub *m* rascal, imp.

lauschen ['lauʃən] *vi* eavesdrop, listen in.

lauschig ['lauʃɪç] *a* snug.

lausen ['lauzən] *vt* delouse.

laut [laut] *a* loud; *ad* loudly; *lesen* aloud; *prep* +*gen or dat* according to; L— *m* -(e)s, -e sound.

Laute ['lautə] *f* -, -n lute.

lauten ['lautən] *vi* say; (*Urteil*) be.

läuten ['lɔytən] *vti* ring, sound.

lauter ['lautər] *a Wasser* clear, pure; *Wahrheit, Charakter* honest; *inv Freude, Dummheit etc* sheer; (*mit pl*) nothing but, only; L—**keit** *f* purity; honesty, integrity.

läutern ['lɔytərn] *vt* purify.

Läuterung *f* purification.

laut- *cpd:* —**hals** *ad* at the top of one's voice; —**los** *a* noiseless, silent; —**malend** *a* onomatopoeic; L—**schrift** *f* phonetics *pl*; L—**sprecher** *m* loudspeaker; L—**sprecherwagen** *m* loudspeaker van; —**stark** *a* vociferous; L—**stärke** *f* (*Rad*) volume.

lauwarm ['lauvarm] *a* (*lit, fig*) lukewarm.

Lava ['la:va] *f* -, **Laven** lava.

Lavendel [la'vɛndəl] *m* -s, - lavender.

Lawine [la'vi:nə] *f* avalanche; —**ngefahr** *f* danger of avalanches.

lax [laks] *a* lax.

Lazarett [latsa'rɛt] *nt* -(e)s, -e (*Mil*) hospital, infirmary.

Lebe- *cpd:* —**hoch** *nt* three cheers *pl*; —**mann** *m, pl* —**männer** man about town.

leben ['le:bən] *vti* live; L— *nt* -s, - *life*; —d *a* living; —dig [le'bɛndɪç] *a* living, alive; (*lebhaft*) lively; L—**digkeit** *f* liveliness.

Lebens- *cpd:* —**alter** *nt* age; —**art** *f* way of life; —**erwartung** *f* life expectancy; l—**fähig** *a* able to live; l—**froh** *a* full of the joys of life; —**gefahr** *f*: —gefahr! danger!; in —gefahr dangerously ill; l—**gefährlich** *a* dangerous; *Verletzung* critical; —**haltungskosten** *pl* cost of living *sing*; —**jahr** *nt* year of life; —**lage** *f* situation in life; —**lauf** *m* curriculum vitae; l—**lustig** *a* cheerful, lively; —**mittel** *pl* food *sing*; —**mittelgeschäft** *nt* grocer's; l—**müde** *a* tired of life; —**retter** *m* lifesaver; —**standard** *m* standard of living; —**stellung** *f* permanent post; —**unterhalt** *m* livelihood; —**versicherung** *f* life insurance; —**wandel** *m* way of life; —**weise** *f* way of life, habits *pl*; —**zeichen** *nt* sign of life; —**zeit** *f* lifetime.

Leber ['le:bər] *f* -, -n liver; —**fleck** *m* mole; —**tran** *m* cod-liver oil; —**wurst** *f* liver sausage.

Lebe- *cpd:* —**wesen** *nt* creature; —**wohl** *nt* farewell, goodbye.

leb- ['le:p] *cpd:* —**haft** *a* lively, vivacious; L—**haftigkeit** *f* liveliness, vivacity; L—**kuchen** *m* gingerbread; —**los** *a* lifeless.

lechzen ['lɛçtsən] *vi:* nach etw — long for sth.

leck [lɛk] *a* leaky, leaking; L— *nt*

-(e)s, -e leak; —en vi (Loch haben) leak; vti (schlecken) lick.

lecker ['lɛkər] a delicious, tasty; l—bissen m dainty morsel; L—maul nt: ein L—maul sein enjoy one's food.

Leder ['le:dər] nt -s, - leather; l—n a leather; —waren pl leather goods pl.

ledig ['le:dɪç] a single; einer Sache — sein be free of sth; —lich ad merely, solely.

leer [le:r] a empty; vacant; L—e f - emptiness; —en vt empty; vr become empty; L—gewicht nt weight when empty; L—lauf m neutral; —stehend a empty; L—ung f emptying; (Post) collection.

legal [le'ga:l] a legal, lawful; —isieren vt legalize; L—ität f legality.

legen ['le:gən] vt lay, put, place; Ei lay; vr lie down; (fig) subside.

Legende [le'gɛndə] f -, -n legend.

leger [le'ʒe:r] a casual.

legieren [le'gi:rən] vt alloy.

Legierung f alloy.

Legislative [legɪsla'ti:və] f legislature.

legitim [legi'ti:m] a legitimate; L—ation [-atsi'o:n] f legitimation; —ieren [-'mi:rən] vt legitimate; vr prove one's identity; L—ität f legitimacy.

Lehm [le:m] m -(e)s, -e loam; l—ig a loamy.

Lehne ['le:nə] f -, -n arm; back; l—n vtr lean.

Lehnstuhl m armchair.

Lehr- cpd: —amt nt teaching profession; —brief m indentures pl; —buch nt textbook.

Lehre ['le:rə] f -, -n teaching, doctrine; (beruflich) apprenticeship; (moralisch) lesson; (Tech) gauge; l—n vt teach; —r(in f) m -s, - teacher.

Lehr- cpd: —gang m course; —jahre pl apprenticeship; —kraft f teacher; —ling m apprentice; —plan m syllabus; —reich a instructive; —satz m proposition; —stelle f apprenticeship; —stuhl m chair; —zeit f apprenticeship.

Leib [laɪp] m -(e)s, -er body; halt ihn mir vom —! keep him away from me; —eserziehung ['laɪbəs-] f physical education; —esübung f physical exercise; l—haftig a personified; Teufel incarnate; l—lich a bodily; Vater etc own; —wache f bodyguard.

Leiche ['laɪçə] f -, -n corpse; —nbeschauer m -s, - doctor who makes out death certificate; —nhemd nt shroud; —nträger m bearer; —nwagen m hearse.

Leichnam ['laɪçna:m] m -(e)s, -e corpse.

leicht [laɪçt] a light; (einfach) easy; L—athletik f athletics sing; —fallen vi irreg: jdm —fallen be easy for sb; —fertig a frivolous; —gläubig a gullible, credulous; L—gläubigkeit f gullibility, credulity; —hin ad lightly; L—igkeit f easiness; mit L—igkeit with ease; —lebig a easy-going; —machen vt: es sich (dat) —machen make things easy for oneself; —nehmen vt irreg take lightly; L—sinn m carelessness; —sinnig a careless.

Leid [laɪt] nt -(e)s grief, sorrow; l— a: etw l— haben or sein be tired of sth; es tut mir/ihm l— I am/he is sorry; er/das tut mir l— I am

6

sorry for him/it; l—en ['laɪdən] *irreg vt* suffer; (*erlauben*) permit; jdn/etw nicht l—en können not be able to stand sb/sth; *vi* suffer; —en *nt* -s, - suffering (*Krankheit*) complaint; —enschaft *f* passion; l—enschaftlich *a* passionate.

leider ['laɪdər] *ad* unfortunately; ja, — yes, I'm afraid so; — nicht I'm afraid not.

leidig ['laɪdɪç] *a* miserable, tiresome.

leidlich *a* tolerable; *ad* tolerably.

Leid- *cpd*: —tragende(r) *mf* bereaved; (*Benachteiligter*) one who suffers; —wesen *nt*: zu jds —wesen to sb's dismay.

Leier ['laɪər] *f* -, -n lyre; (*fig*) old story; —kasten *m* barrel organ; l—n *vti* Kurbel turn; (*col*) Gedicht rattle off.

Leihbibliothek *f* lending library.

leihen ['laɪən] *vt irreg* lend; sich (*dat*) etw — borrow sth.

Leih- *cpd*: —gebühr *f* hire charge; —haus *nt* pawnshop; —schein *m* pawn ticket; (*Buch—*) etc borrowing slip; (*Buch—*) —wagen *m* hired car.

Leim [laɪm] *m* -(e)s, -e glue; l—en *vt* glue.

Leine ['laɪnə] *f* -, -n line, cord; (*Hunde—*) leash, lead; —n *nt* -s, - linen; l—n *a* linen.

Lein- *cpd*: —tuch *nt* (*Bett—*) sheet; linen cloth; —wand *f* (*Art*) canvas; (*Cine*) screen.

leise ['laɪzə] *a* quiet; (*sanft*) soft, gentle.

Leiste ['laɪstə] *f* -, -n ledge; (*Zier—*) strip; (*Anat*) groin.

leisten ['laɪstən] *vt* Arbeit do; Gesellschaft keep; Ersatz wegen; (*vollbringen*) achieve; sich (*dat*) etw — können be able to afford sth.

Leistung *f* performance; (*gute*) achievement; —sdruck *m*

pressure; l—sfähig *a* efficient; —sfähigkeit *f* efficiency; —szulage *f* productivity bonus.

Leit- *cpd*: —artikel *m* leading article; —bild *nt* model.

leiten ['laɪtən] *vt* lead; Firma manage; (*in eine Richtung*) direct; (*Elec*) conduct.

Leiter ['laɪtər] *m* -s, - leader, head; (*Elec*) conductor; *f* -, -n ladder.

Leit- *cpd*: —faden *m* guide; —fähigkeit *f* conductivity; —motiv *nt* leitmotiv; —planke *f* -, -n crash barrier.

Leitung *f* (*Führung*) direction; (*Cine, Theat etc*) production; (*von Firma*) management; directors *pl*; (*Wasser—*) pipe; (*Kabel*) cable; eine lange — haben be slow on the uptake; —sdraht *m* wire; —smast *m* telegraph pole; —srohr *nt* pipe; —swasser *nt* tap water.

Lektion [lɛktsi'oːn] *f* lesson.

Lektor(in *f*) *m* ['lɛktɔr(m)] (*Univ*) lector; (*Verlag*) editor.

Lektüre [lɛk'tyːrə] *f* -, -n (*Lesen*) reading; (*Lesestoff*) reading matter.

Lende ['lɛndə] *f* -, -n loin; —nbraten *m* roast sirloin; —nstück *nt* fillet.

lenk- ['lɛŋk] *cpd*: —bar *a* Fahrzeug steerable; Kind manageable; —en *vt* steer; Kind guide; Blick, Aufmerksamkeit direct (auf + acc at); L—rad *nt* steering wheel; L—stange *f* handlebars *pl*.

Lenz [lɛnts] *m* -es, -e (*liter*) spring.

Leopard [leo'part] *m* -en, -en leopard.

Lepra ['leːpra] *f* - leprosy.

Lerche ['lɛrçə] *f* -, -n lark.

lern- [lɛrn] *cpd*: —begierig *a* eager to learn; —en *vt* learn.

lesbar ['le:sba:r] a legible.

Lesbierin ['lɛsbiərɪn] f lesbian.

lesbisch ['lɛsbɪʃ] a lesbian.

Lese ['le:zə] f -, -n gleaning; (Wein) harvest; —buch nt reading book, reader; l—n vti irreg read; (ernten) gather, pick; —r(in f) m -s, - reader; —rbrief m reader's letter; l—rlich a legible; —saal m reading room; —zeichen nt bookmark.

Lesung ['le:zuŋ] f (Parl) reading; (Eccl) lesson.

letzte(r, s) ['lɛtstə(r,z)] a last; (neueste) latest; zum —nmal ad for the last time; —ns ad lately; —re(r,s) a latter.

Leuchte ['lɔʏçtə] f -, -n lamp, light; l—n vi shine, gleam; —r m -s, - candlestick.

Leucht- cpd: —farbe f fluorescent colour; —feuer nt beacon; —käfer m glow-worm; —kugel f, —rakete f flare; —reklame f neon sign; —röhre f strip light; —turm m lighthouse; —zifferblatt nt luminous dial.

leugnen ['lɔʏgnən] vti deny.

Leugnung f denial.

Leukämie [lɔʏkɛ'mi:] f leukaemia.

Leukoplast® [lɔʏko'plast] nt -(e)s, -e elastoplast ®.

Leumund ['lɔʏmʊnt] m -(e)s, -e reputation; —szeugnis nt character reference.

Leute ['lɔʏtə] pl people pl.

Leutnant ['lɔʏtnant] m -s, -s or -e lieutenant.

leutselig ['lɔʏtze:lɪç] a affable; L—keit f affability.

Lexikon ['lɛksikɔn] nt -s, Lexiken or Lexika dictionary.

Libelle [li'bɛlə] f -, -n dragonfly; (Tech) spirit level.

liberal [libe'ra:l] a liberal; L—ismus [libera'lɪsmʊs] m liberalism.

Libero ['li:bero] m -s, -s (Fußball) sweeper.

Licht [lɪçt] nt -(e)s, -er light; l— a light, bright; —bild nt photograph; (Dia) slide; —blick m cheering prospect; l—empfindlich a sensitive to light; l—en vt clear; Anker weigh; vr clear up; (Haar) thin; l—erloh ad: l—erloh brennen blaze; —hupe f flashing of headlights; —jahr nt light year; —maschine f dynamo; —meß f Candlemas; —schalter m light switch.

Lichtung f clearing, glade.

Lid [li:t] nt -(e)s, -er eyelid; —schatten m eyeshadow.

lieb [li:p] a dear; —äugeln vi insep ogle (mit jdm/etw sb/sth).

Liebe ['li:bə] f -, -n love; l—bedürftig a: l—bedürftig sein need love; —'lei f flirtation; l—n vt love; like; l—nswert a loveable; l—nswürdig a kind; l—nswürdigerweise ad kindly; —nswürdigkeit f kindness.

lieber ['li:bər] ad rather, preferably; ich gehe — nicht I'd rather not go; see gern, lieb.

Liebes- cpd: —brief m love letter; —dienst m good turn; —kummer m: —kummer haben to be lovesick; —paar nt courting couple, lovers pl.

liebevoll a loving.

lieb- ['li:p] cpd: —gewinnen vt irreg get fond of; —haben vt irreg be fond of; L—haber m -s, - lover; L—habe'rei f hobby; —kosen [li:p'ko:zən] vt insep caress; —lich a lovely, charming; L—ling m darling; L—lings- in cpds

favourite; **—los** *a* unloving;
L—schaft *f* love affair.

Lied [li:t] *nt* **-(e)s, -er** song; (*Eccl*)
hymn; **—erbuch** *nt* songbook;
hymn book.

liederlich ['li:dərlıç] *a* slovenly;
Lebenswandel loose, immoral;
L—keit *f* slovenliness; immorality.

Lieferant [lifə'rant] *m* supplier.

liefern ['li:fərn] *vt* deliver;
(*versorgen mit*) supply; *Beweis*
produce.

Liege ['li:gə] *f* **-, -n** bed.

liegen ['li:gən] *vi irreg* lie; (*sich
befinden*) be; **mir liegt nichts/viel
daran** it doesn't matter to me/it
matters a lot to me; **es liegt bei
Ihnen, ob ...** it rests with you
whether ...; **Sprachen — mir nicht**
languages are not my line; **woran
liegt es?** what's the cause?;
—bleiben *vi irreg* (*Person*) stay in
bed; stay lying down; (*Ding*) be
left (behind); **—lassen** *vt irreg*
(*vergessen*) leave behind;
L—schaft *f* real estate.

Liege- *cpd*: **—sitz** *m* (*Aut*) reclining
seat; **—stuhl** *m* deck chair;
—wagen *m* (*Rail*) couchette.

Lift [lıft] *m* **-(e)s, -e** *or* **-s** lift.

Likör [li'kø:r] *m* **-s, -e** liqueur.

lila ['li:la] *a* purple, lilac; **L—** *nt* **-s,
-s** (*Farbe*) purple, lilac.

Lilie ['li:liə] *f* lily.

Limonade [limo'na:də] *f* lemonade.

lind [lınt] *a* gentle, mild; **L—e**
['lındə] *f* **-, -n** lime tree, linden;
—ern *vt* alleviate, soothe;
L—erung *f* alleviation; **—grün** *a*
lime green.

Lineal [line'a:l] *nt* **-s, -e** ruler.

Linie ['li:niə] *f* line; **—nblatt** *nt*
ruled sheet; **—nflug** *m* scheduled
flight; **—nrichter** *m* linesman.

linieren [lini'i:rən] *vt* line.

Linke ['lıŋkə] *f* **-, -n** left side; left
hand; (*Pol*) left; **l—(r,s)** *a* left; **l—**
Masche purl.

linkisch *a* awkward, gauche.

links [lıŋks] *ad* left; to or on the
left; **— von mir** on or to my left;
L—außen [lıŋks'ausņ] *m* **-s, -**
(*Sport*) outside left; **L—händer(in**
f) *m* **-s, -** left-handed person;
L—kurve *f* left-hand bend;
L—verkehr *m* traffic on the left.

Linoleum [li'no:leʊm] *nt* **-s**
lino(leum).

Linse ['lınzə] *f* **-, -n** lentil; (*optisch*)
lens.

Lippe ['lıpə] *f* **-, -n** lip; **—nstift** *m*
lipstick.

liquidieren [likvi'di:rən] *vt*
liquidate.

lispeln ['lıspəln] *vi* lisp.

List [lıst] *f* **-, -en** cunning; trick,
ruse.

Liste ['lıstə] *f* **-, -n** list.

listig ['lıstıç] *a* cunning, sly.

Litanei [lita'nai] *f* litany.

Liter ['li:tər] *nt or m* **-s, -** litre.

literarisch [lite'ra:rɪʃ] *a* literary.

Literatur [litera'tu:r] *f* literature;
—preis *m* award for literature.

Litfaßsäule ['lıtfaszɔylə] *f*
advertising pillar.

Lithographie [litogra'fi:] *f*
lithography.

Liturgie [litur'gi:] *f* liturgy.

liturgisch [li'turgıʃ] *a* liturgical.

Litze ['lıtsə] *f* **-, -n** braid; (*Elec*)
flex.

live [laıf] *ad* (*Rad, TV*) live.

Livree [li'vre:] f -, -n livery.

Lizenz [li'tsɛnts] f licence.

Lkw [ɛlka:'ve:] m = Lastkraftwagen.

Lob [lo:p] nt -(e)s praise; l—en ['lo:bən] vt praise; l—enswert a praiseworthy.

löblich ['lø:plɪç] a praiseworthy, laudable.

Lobrede f eulogy.

Loch [lɔx] nt -(e)s, ᵊer hole; l—en vt punch holes in; —er m -s, - punch.

löcherig ['lœçərɪç] a full of holes.

Loch- cpd: —karte f punch card; —streifen m punch tape.

Locke ['lɔkə] f -, -n lock, curl; l—n vt entice; Haare curl; —nwickler m -s, - curler.

locker ['lɔkər] a loose; —lassen vi irreg: nicht —lassen not let up; —n vt loosen.

lockig ['lɔkɪç] a curly.

Lock- cpd: —ruf m call; —ung f enticement; —vogel m decoy, bait.

Lodenmantel ['lo:dənmantəl] m thick woollen coat.

lodern ['lo:dərn] vi blaze.

Löffel ['lœfəl] m -s, - spoon; l—n vt (eat with a) spoon; l—weise ad by spoonfuls.

Logarithmentafel [loga'rɪt-mənta:fəl] f log(arithm) tables pl.

Logarithmus [loga'rɪtmʊs] m logarithm.

Loge ['lo:ʒə] f -, -n (Theat) box; (Freimaurer) (masonic) lodge; (Pförtner) office.

logieren [lo'ʒi:rən] vi lodge, stay.

Logik ['lo:gɪk] f logic.

logisch ['lo:gɪʃ] a logical.

Lohn [lo:n] m -(e)s, ᵊe reward; (Arbeits—) pay, wages pl; —büro

nt wages office; —empfänger m wage earner.

lohnen ['lo:nən] vt (liter) reward (jdm etw sb for sth); vr impers be worth it; —d a worthwhile.

Lohn- cpd: —steuer f income tax; —streifen m pay slip; —tüte f pay packet.

lokal [lo'ka:l] a local; L— nt -(e)s, -e pub(lic house); l—isieren vt localize; L—isierung f localization.

Lokomotive [lokomo'ti:və] f -, -n locomotive.

Lokomotivführer m engine driver.

Lorbeer ['lɔrbe:r] m -s, -en (lit, fig) laurel; —blatt nt (Cook) bay leaf.

Lore ['lo:rə] f -, -n (Min) truck.

Los [lo:s] nt -es, -e (Schicksal) lot, fate; lottery ticket.

los [lo:s] a loose; —! go on!; etw — sein be rid of sth; was ist —? what's the matter?; dort ist nichts/viel — there's nothing/a lot going on there; etw — haben (col) be clever; —binden vt irreg untie.

löschen ['lœʃən] vt Feuer, Licht put out, extinguish; Durst quench; (Comm) cancel; Tonband erase; Fracht unload; vi (Feuerwehr) put out a fire; (Papier) blot.

Lösch- cpd: —fahrzeug nt fire engine; fire boat; —gerät nt fire extinguisher; —papier nt blotting paper; —ung f extinguishing; (Comm) cancellation; (Fracht) unloading.

lose ['lo:zə] a loose.

Lösegeld nt ransom.

losen ['lo:zən] vi draw lots.

lösen ['lø:zən] vt loosen; Rätsel etc solve; Verlobung up (Chem) dissolve; Partnerschaft break up; Fahrkarte buy; vr (aufgehen) come loose; (Zucker etc) dissolve;

(*Problem, Schwierigkeit*) (re)solve itself.

los- *cpd:* **—fahren** *vi irreg* leave; **—gehen** *vi irreg* set out; (*anfangen*) start; (*Bombe*) go off; **auf jdn —gehen** · go for sb; **—kaufen** *vt Gefangene, Geißeln* pay ransom for; **—kommen** *vi irreg:* **von etw —kommen** get away from sth; **—lassen** *vt irreg Seil* let go of; *Schimpfe* let loose; **—laufen** *vi irreg* run off.

löslich ['lø:slıç] *a* soluble; **L—keit** *f* solubility.

los- *cpd:* **—lösen** *vtr* free; **—machen** *vt* loosen; *Boot* unmoor; *vr* get free; **—sagen** *vr* renounce (*von* jdm/etw sb/sth); **—schrauben** *vt* unscrew; **—sprechen** *vt irreg* absolve.

Losung ['lo:zʊŋ] *f* watchword, slogan.

Lösung ['lø:zʊŋ] *f* (*Lockermachen*) loosening; (*eines Rätsels, Chem*) solution; **—smittel** *nt* solvent.

los- *cpd:* **—werden** *vt irreg* get rid of; **—ziehen** *vi irreg* (*sich aufmachen*) set out; **gegen jdn —ziehen** run sb down.

Lot [lo:t] *nt* **-(e)s, -e** plummet; **im — -** vertical; (*fig*) on an even keel; **l—en** *vti* plumb, sound.

löten ['lø:tən] *vt* solder.

Lötkolben *m* soldering iron.

Lotse ['lo:tsə] *m* **-n, -n** pilot; (*Aviat*) air traffic controller; *see* **Schüler—;** **l—n** *vt* pilot; (*col*) lure.

Lotterie [lɔtə'ri:] *f* lottery.

Löwe ['lø:və] *m* **-n, -n** lion; (*Astrol*) Leo; **—nanteil** *m* lion's share; **—nmaul** *nt* snapdragon; **—nzahn** *m* dandelion.

Löwin ['lø:vɪn] *f* lioness.

loyal [loa'ja:l] *a* loyal; **L—ität** *f* loyalty.

Luchs ['lʊks] *m* **-es, -e** lynx.

Lücke ['lʏkə] *f* **-, -n** gap; **—nbüßer** *m* **-s, -** stopgap; **l—nhaft** *a* defective, full of gaps; **l—nlos** *a* complete.

Luder ['lu:dər] *nt* **-s, -** (*pej: Frau*) hussy; (*bedauernswert*) poor wretch.

Luft [lʊft] *f* **-, =e** air; (*Atem*) breath; **in der — liegen** be in the air; **jdn wie — behandeln** ignore sb; **—angriff** *m* air raid; **—ballon** *m* balloon; **—blase** *f* air bubble; **l—dicht** *a* airtight; **—druck** *m* atmospheric pressure.

lüften ['lʏftən] *vti* air; *Hut* lift, raise.

Luft- *cpd:* **—fahrt** *f* aviation; **l—gekühlt** *a* air-cooled; **l—ig** *a* (*Ort*) breezy; *Raum* airy; *Kleider* summery; **—kissenfahrzeug** *nt* hovercraft; **—krieg** *m* war in the air; aerial warfare; **—kurort** *m* health resort; **l—leer** *a:* **—leerer Raum** vacuum; **—linie** *f:* **in der —linie** as the crow flies; **—loch** *nt* air-hole; (*Aviat*) air-pocket; **—matratze** *f* lilo ®, air mattress; **—pirat** *m* hijacker; **—post** *f* airmail; **—röhre** *f* (*Anat*) wind pipe; **—schlange** *f* streamer; **—schutz** *m* anti-aircraft defence; **—schutzkeller** *m* air-raid shelter; **—sprung** *m:* (*fig*) **einen —sprung machen** jump for joy.

Lüftung ['lʏftʊŋ] *f* ventilation.

Luft- *cpd:* **—verkehr** *m* air traffic; **—waffe** *f* air force; **—zug** *m* draught.

Lüge ['ly:gə] *f* **-, -n** lie; **jdn/etw —n strafen** give the lie to sb/sth; **l—n** *vi irreg* lie.

Lügner(in *f***)** *m* **-s, -** liar.

Luke ['lu:kə] *f* **-, -n** dormer window, hatch.

Lümmel ['lyməl] *m* -s, - 'lout; l—n *vr* lounge (about).

Lump [lump] *m* -en, -en scamp, rascal.

Lumpen ['lumpən] *m* -s, - rag ; **sich nicht l—** lassen not be mean.

lumpig ['lumpiç] *a* shabby.

Lunge ['luŋə] *f* -, -n lung ; **—nentzündung** *f* pneumonia ; **l—nkrank** *a* consumptive.

lungern ['luŋərn] *vi* hang about.

Lunte ['luntə] *f* -, -n fuse ; **— riechen** smell a rat.

Lupe ['lu:pə] *f* -, -n magnifying glass ; **unter die — nehmen** (*fig*) scrutinize.

Lupine [lu'pi:nə] *f* lupin.

Lust [lust] *f* -, ̈e joy, delight ; (*Neigung*) desire ; **— haben zu** *or* **auf etw** (*acc*)/**etw zu tun** feel like sth/doing sth.

lüstern ['lystərn] *a* lustful,
lecherous.

Lustgefühl *nt* pleasurable feeling.

lustig ['lustiç] *a* (*komisch*) amusing, funny ; (*fröhlich*) cheerful.

Lust- *cpd*: **l—los** *a* unenthusiastic ; **—mord** *m* sex(ual) murder ; **—spiel** *nt* comedy ; **l—wandeln** *vi* stroll about.

lutschen ['lutʃən] *vti* suck ; **am Daumen —** suck one's thumb.

Lutscher *m* -s, - lollipop.

luxuriös [luksuri'ø:s] *a* luxurious.

Luxus ['luksus] *m* - luxury ; **—artikel** *pl* luxury goods *pl* ; **—hotel** *nt* luxury hotel ; **—steuer** *f* tax on luxuries.

Lymphe ['lymfə] *f* -, -n lymph.

lynchen ['lynçən] *vt* lynch.

Lyrik ['ly:rik] *f* lyric poetry ; **—er** *m* -s, - lyric poet.

lyrisch ['ly:riʃ] *a* lyrical.

M

M, m [ɛm] *nt* M, m.

Mach- [max] *cpd*: **—art** *f* make ; **m—bar** *a* feasible ; **—e** *f* - (*col*) show, sham ; **m—en** *vt* make ; (*tun*) do ; (*col: reparieren*) fix ; (*betragen*) be ; **das macht nichts** that doesn't matter ; **mach's gut!** good luck! ; *vr* come along (nicely) ; **sich an etw** (*acc*) **m—en** set about sth ; *vi*: **in etw** (*dat*) **m—en** (*Comm*) be *or* deal in sth.

Macht [maxt] *f* -s, ̈e power ; **—haber** *m* -s, - ruler.

mächtig ['mɛçtiç] *a* powerful, mighty ; (*col: ungeheuer*) enormous.

Macht- *cpd*: **m—los** *a* powerless ; **—probe** *f* trial of strength ;

—stellung *f* position of power ; **—wort** *nt*: **ein —wort sprechen** lay down the law.

Machwerk *nt* work ; (*schlechte Arbeit*) botched-up job.

Mädchen ['mɛːtçən] *nt* girl ; **m—haft** *a* girlish ; **—name** *m* maiden name.

Made ['maːdə] *f* -, -n maggot.

madig ['maːdiç] *a* maggoty ; **jdm etw — machen** spoil sth for sb.

Magazin [maga'tsiːn] *nt* -s, -e magazine.

Magd [maːkt] *f* -, ̈e maid(servant).

Magen ['maːgən] *m* -s, - *or* ̈ stomach ; **—schmerzen** *pl* stomach-ache.

mager ['ma:gər] a lean; (dünn) thin; M—keit f leanness; thinness.

Magie [ma'gi:] f magic; —r ['ma:giər] m -s, - magician.

magisch ['ma:gɪʃ] a magical.

Magnet [ma'gne:t] m -s or -en, -en magnet; m—isch a magnetic; m—i'sieren vt magnetize; —nadel f magnetic needle.

Mahagoni [maha'go:ni] nt -s mahogany.

mähen ['mɛ:ən] vti mow.

Mahl [ma:l] nt -(e)s, -e; meal; m—en vt irreg. grind; —stein m grindstone; —zeit f meal; interj enjoy your meal.

Mahnbrief m remainder.

Mähne ['mɛ:nə] f -, -n mane.

Mahn- [ma:n] cpd: m—en vt remind; (warnend) warn; (wegen Schuld) demand payment from; —ung f reminder; admonition, warning.

Mähre ['mɛ:rə] f -, -n mare.

Mai [maɪ] m -(e)s, -e May; —glöckchen nt lily of the valley; —käfer m cockchafer.

Mais [maɪs] m -es, -e maize, corn (US); —kolben m corncob.

Majestät [majɛs'tɛ:t] f majesty; m—isch a majestic.

Major [ma'jo:r] m -s, -e (Mil) major; (Aviat) squadron leader.

Majoran [majo'ra:n] m -·s, -e marjoram.

makaber [ma'ka:bər] a macabre.

Makel ['ma:kəl] m -s, - blemish; (moralisch) stain; m—los a immaculate, spotless.

mäkeln ['mɛ:kəln] vi find fault.

Makkaroni [maka'ro:ni] pl macaroni sing.

Makler ['ma:klər] m -s, - broker.

Makrele [ma'kre:lə] f -, -n mackerel.

Makrone [ma'kro:nə] f -, -n macaroon.

Mal [ma:l] nt -(e)s, -e mark, sign; (Zeitpunkt) time; m—² ad times; (col) see einmal; m— suff -times; m—en vti paint; —er m -s, - painter; —e'rei f painting; m—erisch a picturesque; —kasten m paintbox; m—nehmen vti irreg multiply.

Malz [malts] nt -es malt; —bonbon nt cough drop; —kaffee m malt coffee.

Mama ['mama:] f -, -s, **Mami** ['mami] f -, -s (col) mum(my).

Mammut ['mamut] nt -s, -e or -s mammoth.

man [man] pron one, people pl, you.

manche(r,s) ['mançə(r,z)] a many a; (pl) a number of; pron some; —rlei a inv various; pron a variety of things.

manchmal ad sometimes.

Mandant(in f) [man'dant(ɪn)] m (Jur) client.

Mandarine [manda'ri:nə] f mandarin, tangerine.

Mandat [man'da:t] nt -(e)s, -e mandate.

Mandel ['mandəl] f -, -n almond; (Anat) tonsil.

Manege [ma'nɛ:ʒə] f -, -n ring, arena.

Mangel ['maŋəl] f -, -n mangle; m -s, ² lack; (Knappheit) shortage (an +dat of); (Fehler) defect, fault; —erscheinung f deficiency symptom; m—haft a poor; (fehlerhaft) defective, faulty; m—n vi impers: es mangelt jdm an etw (dat) sb lacks sth; vt Wäsche mangle; m—s prep +gen for lack of.

Manie [ma'ni:] f mania.

Manier [ma'ni:r] f - manner; style; (pej) mannerism; **—en** pl manners pl; m—iert [mani'ri:rt] a mannered, affected; m—lich a well-mannered.

Manifest [mani'fɛst] nt -es, -e manifesto.

Maniküre [mani'ky:rə] f -, -n manicure; m—n vt manicure.

manipulieren [manipu'li:rən] vt manipulate.

Manko ['maŋko] nt -s, -s deficiency; (Comm) deficit.

Mann [man] m -(e)s, ⁼er man; (Ehe—) husband; (Naut) hand; seinen — stehen hold one's own.

Männchen ['mɛnçən] nt little man; (Tier) male.

Mannequin [manə'kɛ̃:] nt -s, -s fashion model.

mannigfaltig ['manɪçfaltɪç] a various, varied; M—keit f variety.

männlich ['mɛnlɪç] a (Biol) male; (fig, Gram) masculine.

Mann- cpd: **—schaft** f (Sport, fig) team; (Naut, Aviat) crew; (Mil other ranks pl; **—sleute** pl (col) menfolk pl; **—weib** nt (pej) mannish woman.

Manöver [ma'nø:vər] nt -s, - manoeuvre.

manövrieren [manø'vri:rən] vti manoeuvre.

Mansarde [man'zardə] f -, -n attic.

Manschette [man'ʃɛtə] f cuff; (Papier—) paper frill; (Tech) collar; sleeve; **—nknopf** m cufflink.

Mantel [mantəl] m -s, ⁼ coat; (Tech) casing, jacket.

Manuskript [manu'skrɪpt] nt -(e)s, -e manuscript.

Mappe ['mapə] f -, -n briefcase; (Akten—) folder.

Märchen ['mɛ:rçən] nt fairy tale; m—haft a fabulous; **—prinz** m prince charming.

Marder ['mardər] m -s, - marten.

Margarine [marga'ri:nə] f. margarine.

Marienkäfer [ma'ri:ənkɛːfər] m ladybird.

Marine [ma'ri:nə] f navy; m—blau a navy-blue.

marinieren [mari'ni:rən] vt marinate.

Marionette [mario'nɛtə] f puppet.

Mark [mark] f -, - (Münze) mark; nt -(e)s (Knochen—) marrow; durch — und Bein gehen go right through sb; m—ant [mar'kant] a striking.

Marke ['markə] f -, -n mark; (Warensorte) brand; (Fabrikat) make; (Rabatt—, Brief—) stamp; (Essens—) ticket; (aus Metall etc) token, disc.

Mark- cpd: m—ieren [mar'ki:rən] vt mark; vi (col) act; **—ierung** f marking; m—ig ['markɪç] a (fig) pithy; **—ise** [mar'ki:zə] f -, -n awning; **—stück** nt one-mark piece.

Markt [markt] m -(e)s, ⁼e market; **—forschung** f market research; **—platz** m market place; **—wirtschaft** f market economy.

Marmelade [marmə'la:də] f -, -n jam.

Marmor ['marmor] m -s, -e marble; m—ieren [-'ri:rən] vt marble; m—n a marble.

Marone [ma'ro:nə] f -, -n or **Maroni** chestnut.

Marotte [ma'rɔtə] f -, -n fad, quirk.

Marsch [marʃ] m -(e)s, ⁼e march; m— interj march; f -, -en marsh; **—befehl** m marching orders pl; m—bereit a ready to move; m—ieren [mar'ʃi:rən] vi march.

Marter ['martər] f -, -n torment; **m—n** vt torture.

Märtyrer(in f) ['mɛrtyrər(ın)] m -s, - martyr.

März [mɛrts] m -(es), -e March.

Marzipan [martsi'paːn] nt -s, -e marzipan.

Masche ['maʃə] f -, -n mesh; (Strick—) stitch; **das ist die neueste** — that's the latest dodge; **—ndraht** m wire mesh; **m—nfest** a runproof.

Maschine [ma'ʃiːnə] f machine; (Motor) engine; **m—ll** [maʃi'nɛl] a machine(-); mechanical; **—nbauer** m mechanical engineer; **—ngewehr** nt machine gun; **—npistole** f submachine gun; **—nschaden** m mechanical fault; **—nschlosser** m fitter; **—nschrift** f typescript; **m—schreiben** vi irreg type.

Maschinist [maʃi'nɪst] m engineer.

Maser ['maːzər] f -, -n grain; speckle; **—n** pl (Med) measles sing; **—ung** f grain(ing).

Maske ['maskə] f -, -n mask; **—nball** m fancy-dress ball; **—rade** ['raːdə] f masquerade.

maskieren [mas'kiːrən] vt mask; (verkleiden) dress up; vr disguise o.s., dress up.

Maß [maːs] nt -es, -e measure; (Mäßigung) moderation; (Grad) degree, extent; f -, -(e) litre of beer.

Massage [ma'saːʒə] f -, -n massage.

Maß- cpd: **—anzug** m made-to-measure suit; **—arbeit** f (fig) neat piece of work.

Masse ['masə] f -, -n mass; **—nartikel** m mass-produced article; **—ngrab** nt mass grave; **m—nhaft** a loads of; **—nmedien** pl mass media pl.

Mass- cpd: **—eur** [ma'søːr] m masseur; **—euse** [ma'søːzə] f masseuse.

maß- cpd: **—gebend** a authoritative; **—halten** vi irreg exercise moderation.

massieren [ma'siːrən] vt massage; (Mil) mass.

massig ['masıç] a massive; (col) massive amount of.

mäßig ['mɛːsıç] a moderate; **—en** ['mɛːsıgən] vt restrain, moderate; **M—keit** f moderation.

massiv [ma'siːf] a solid; (fig) heavy, rough; **M—** nt -s, -e massif.

Maß- cpd: **—krug** m tankard; **m—los** a extreme; **—nahme** f -, -n measure, step; **m—regeln** vt insep reprimand; **—stab** m rule, measure; (fig) standard; (Geog) scale; **m—voll** a moderate.

Mast [mast] m -(e)s, -e(n) mast; (Elec) pylon.

mästen ['mɛstən] vt fatten.

Material [materi'aːl] nt -s, -ien material(s); **—fehler** m material defect; **—ismus** [-'lısmʊs] m materialism; **—ist** [-'lıst] m materialist; **m—istisch** [-'lıstıʃ] a materialistic.

Materie [ma'teːriə] f matter, substance; **m—ll** [materi'ɛl] a material.

Mathematik [matema'tiːk] f mathematics sing; **—er(in** f) [mate'maːtikər(ın)] m -s, - mathematician.

mathematisch [mate'maːtıʃ] a mathematical.

Matratze [ma'tratsə] f -, -n mattress.

Matrize [ma'triːtsə] f -, -n matrix; (zum Abziehen) stencil.

Matrose [ma'troːzə] m -n, -n sailor.

Matsch [matʃ] m -(e)s mud; (Schnee—) slush; **m—ig** a muddy; slushy.

matt [mat] a weak; (glanzlos) dull; (Phot) matt; (Schach) mate.

Matte ['matə] f -, -n mat.

Matt- cpd: **—igkeit** f weakness; dullness; **m—en** vt (col) grumble; (Phot) matt; **—scheibe** f (TV) screen; **—scheibe haben** (col) be not quite with it.

Mauer ['mauər] f -, -n wall; **m—n** vti build; lay bricks; **—werk** nt brickwork; (Stein) masonry.

Maul [maul] nt -(e)s, Mäuler mouth; **m—en** vi (col) grumble; **—esel** m mule; **—korb** m muzzle; **—sperre** f lockjaw; **—tier** nt mule; **—wurf** m mole; **—wurfshaufen** m molehill.

Maurer ['maurər] m -s, - bricklayer.

Maus [maus] f -, Mäuse mouse. **mäuschenstill** ['mɔysçən'ʃtɪl] a very quiet.

Maus- [mauz] cpd: **—efalle** f mousetrap; **m—en** vt (col) flinch; vi catch mice; **m—ern** vr moult; **m—(e)tot** a stone dead.

maximal [maksi'maːl] a maximum.

Maxime [ma'ksiːmə] f -, -n maxim.

Mayonnaise [majɔ'nɛːzə] f -, -n mayonnaise.

Mechan- [me'çaːn] cpd: **—ik** f mechanics sing; (Getriebe) mechanics pl; **—iker** m -s, - mechanic, engineer; **m—isch** a mechanical; **m—i'sieren** vt mechanize; **—i'sierung** f mechanization; **—ismus** [meça'nɪsmus] m mechanism.

meckern ['mɛkərn] vi bleat; (col) moan.

Medaille [me'daljə] f -, -n medal.

Medaillon [medal'jõː] nt -s, -s (Schmuck) locket.

Medikament [medika'mɛnt] nt medicine.

meditieren [medi'tiːrən] vi meditate.

Medizin [medi'tsiːn] f -, -en medicine; **m—isch** a medical.

Meer [meːr] nt -(e)s, -e sea; **—busen** m bay, gulf; **—enge** f straits pl; **—esspiegel** m sea level; **—rettich** m horseradish; **—schweinchen** nt guinea-pig.

Megaphon [mega'foːn] nt -s, -e megaphone.

Mehl [meːl] nt -(e)s, -e flour; **m—ig** a floury.

mehr [meːr] a,ad more; **M—aufwand** m additional expenditure; **—deutig** a ambiguous; **—ere** a several; **—eres** pron several things; **—fach** a multiple; (wiederholt) repeated; **M—heit** f majority; **—malig** a repeated; **—mals** ad repeatedly; **—stimmig** a for several voices; **—stimmig singen** harmonize; **M—wertsteuer** f value added tax, VAT; **M—zahl** f majority; (Gram) plural.

meiden [maɪdən] vt irreg avoid.

Meile ['maɪlə] f -, -n mile; **—nstein** m milestone; **—nweit** a for miles.

mein [maɪn] pron my; **—e(r,s)** mine.

Meineid ['maɪn'aɪt] m perjury.

meinen ['maɪnən] vti think; (sagen) say; (sagen wollen) mean; **das will ich** - I should think so.

mein- cpd: **—er** pron gen of ich of me; **—erseits** ad for my part; **—esgleichen** pron people like me; **—etwegen, —etwillen** ad (für mich) for my sake; (wegen mir) on my account; (von mir aus) as far as I'm concerned; -I don't care or mind; **—ige** pron: der/die/das —ige mine.

Meinung ['maɪnʊŋ] f opinion; **jdm die — sagen** give sb a piece of one's mind; **—saustausch** m exchange of views; **—sumfrage** f opinion poll; **—sverschiedenheit** f difference of opinion.

Meise ['maɪzə] f -, -n tit(mouse).

Meißel ['maɪsəl] m -s, - chisel; **m—n** vt chisel.

meist [maɪst] a,ad most(ly); **—ens** ad generally, usually.

Meister ['maɪstər] m -s, - master; (Sport) champion; **m—haft** a masterly; **m—n** vt master; **—schaft** f mastery; (Sport) championship; **—stück** nt, **—werk** nt masterpiece.

Melancholie [melaŋko'liː] f melancholy.

melancholisch [melaŋ'koːlɪʃ] a melancholy.

Melde- ['mɛldə] cpd: **—frist** f registration period; **m—n** vt report; vr report (bei to); (Sch) put one's hand up; (freiwillig) volunteer; (auf etw, am Telefon) answer; **sich zu Wort m—n** ask to speak; **—pflicht** f obligation to register with the police; **—stelle** f registration office.

Meldung ['mɛldʊŋ] f announcement; (Bericht) report.

meliert [me'liːrt] a mottled, speckled.

melken ['mɛlkən] vt irreg milk.

Melodie [melo'diː] f melody, tune.

melodisch [me'loːdɪʃ] a melodious, tuneful.

Melone [me'loːnə] f -, -n melon; (Hut) bowler (hat).

Membran(e) [mɛm'braːn(ə)] f -, -en (Tech) diaphragm.

Memoiren [memo'aːrən] pl memoirs pl.

Menge ['mɛŋə] f -, -n quantity; (Menschen—) crowd; (große Anzahl) lot (of); **m—n** vt mix; vr: **sich m—n in** (+acc) meddle with; **—nlehre** f (Math) set theory; **—nrabatt** m bulk discount.

Mensch [mɛnʃ] m -en, -en human being, man; person; **kein —** nobody; nt -(e)s, -er hussy; **—enalter** nt generation; **—enfeind** m misanthrope; **m—enfeindlich** a philanthropical; **—enkenner** m -s, - judge of human nature; **—enliebe** f philanthropy; **m—enmöglich** a humanly possible; **—enrecht** nt human rights pl; **m—enscheu** a shy; **m—enunwürdig** a degrading; **—enverstand** m: **gesunder —enverstand** common sense; **—heit** f humanity, mankind; **m—lich** a human; (human) humane; **—lichkeit** f humanity.

Menstruation [mɛnstruatsi'oːn] f menstruation.

Mentalität [mɛntali'tɛːt] f mentality.

Menü [me'nyː] nt -s, -s menu.

Merk- [mɛrk] cpd: **—blatt** nt instruction sheet or leaflet; **m—en** vt notice; **sich** (dat) **etw m—en** remember sth; **m—lich** a noticeable; **—mal** nt sign, characteristic; **m—würdig** a odd.

Meß- [mɛs] cpd: **m—bar** a measurable; **—becher** m measuring cup; **—buch** nt missal.

Messe ['mɛsə] f -, -n fair; (Eccl) mass; (Mil) mess; **m—n** irreg vt measure; vr compete; **—r** nt -s, - knife; **—rspitze** f knife point; (in Rezept) pinch; **—stand** m exhibition stand.

Meß- cpd: —**gerät** nt measuring device, gauge; —**gewand** nt chasuble.

Messing ['mɛsɪŋ] nt -s brass.

Metall [me'tal] nt -s, -e metal; m—en, m—isch a metallic.

Metaphysik [metafy'zi:k] f metaphysics sing.

Metastase [meta'sta:zə] f -, -n (Med) secondary growth.

Meteor [mete'o:r] nt -s, -e meteor.

Meter ['me:tər] nt or m -s, - metre; —**maß** nt tape measure.

Methode [me'to:də] f -, -n method.

methodisch [me'to:dɪʃ] a methodical.

Metropole [metro'po:lə] f -, -n metropolis.

Metzger ['mɛtsgər] m -s, - butcher; —**ei** [-'rai] f butcher's (shop).

Meuchelmord ['mɔʏçəlmɔrt] m assassination.

Meute ['mɔʏtə] f -, -n pack; —**rei** f mutiny; —**rer** m -s, - mutineer; m—**rn** vi mutiny.

miauen ['mi'aʊən] vi mIaow.

mich [mɪç] pron acc of **ich** me; myself.

Miene ['mi:nə] f -, -n look, expression.

mies [mi:s] a (col) lousy.

Miet- ['mi:t] cpd: —**auto** nt hired car; —**e** f -, -n rent; **zur** — **wohnen** live in rented accommodation; m—en vt rent; Auto hire; —**er(in** f) m -s, - tenant.; —**shaus** nt tenement, block of flats; —**vertrag** m tenancy agreement.

Migräne [mi'grɛ:nə] f -, -n migraine.

Mikro- cpd: —**be** [mi'kro:bə] f -, -n microbe; —**fon**, —**phon** [mikro'fo:n] nt -s, -e microphone;

—**skop** [mikro'sko:p] nt -s, -e microscope; m—**skopisch** a microscopic.

Milch [mɪlç] f - milk; (Fisch—) milt, roe; —**glas** nt frosted glass; m—**ig** a milky; —**kaffee** m white coffee; —**pulver** nt powdered milk; —**straße** f Milky Way; —**zahn** m milk tooth.

mild [mɪlt] a mild; Richter lenient; (freundlich) kind, charitable; M—**e** ['mɪldə] f -, -n mildness; leniency; —**ern** vt mitigate, soften; Schmerz alleviate; —**ernde Umstände** extenuating circumstances.

Milieu [mili'ø] nt -s, -s background, environment; m—**ge-schädigt** a maladjusted.

Mili- [mili] cpd: —**tant** [-'tant] a militant; —**tär** [-'tɛ:r] nt -s military, army; —'**tärgericht** nt military court; m—'**tärisch** a military; —**tarismus** [-'tarɪsmʊs] m militarism; m—ta'**ristisch** a militaristic; —'**tärpflicht** f (compulsory) military service.

Milli- ['mili] cpd: —**ardär** [-ar'dɛ:r] m multimillionaire; —**arde** ['ardə] f -, -n milliard; billion (esp US); —**meter** m millimetre; —**on** [-'o:n] f -, -en million; —**onär** [-'o:nɛ:r] m millionaire.

Milz [mɪlts] f -, -en spleen.

Mimik ['mi:mɪk] f mime.

Mimose [mi'mo:zə] f -, -n mimosa; (fig) sensitive person.

minder ['mɪndər] a inferior; ad less; M—**heit** f minority; —**jährig** a minor; M—**jährigkeit** f minority; —**n** vtr decrease, diminish; M—**ung** f decrease; —**wertig** a inferior; M—**wertigkeitsgefühl** nt, M—**wertigkeitskomplex** m inferiority complex.

Mindest- ['mɪndəst] cpd: —**alter** nt minimum age; —**betrag** m minimum amount; **m—e** *a* least; **m—ens, zum —en** *ad* at least; **—lohn** *m* minimum wage; **—maß** *nt* minimum.

Mine ['mi:nə] *f* **-, -n** mine; (*Bleistift—*) lead; (*Kugelschreiber—*) refill; **—nfeld** *nt* minefield.

Mineral [minə'ra:l] *nt* **-s, -e** or **-ien** mineral; **m—isch** *a* mineral; **—wasser** *nt* mineral water.

Miniatur [minia'tu:r] *f* miniature.

minimal [mini'ma:l] *a* minimal.

Minister [mi'nɪstər] *m* **-s, -** minister; **m—iell** [minɪstɛri'ɛl] *a* ministerial; **—ium** [minɪs'te:rium] *nt* ministry; **—präsident** *m* prime minister.

minus ['mi:nus] *ad* minus; **M—** *nt* **-, -** deficit; **M—pol** *m* negative pole; **M—zeichen** *nt* minus sign.

Minute [mi'nu:tə] *f* **-, -n** minute; **—nzeiger** *m* minute hand.

mir [mi:r] *pron dat of* **ich** (to) me; **— nichts, dir nichts** just like that.

Misch- ['mɪʃ] *cpd:* **—ehe** *f* mixed marriage; **m—en** *vt* mix; **—ling** *m* half-caste; **—ung** *f* mixture.

Miß- ['mɪs] *cpd:* **m—achten** *vt insep* disregard; **—'achtung** *f* disregard; **—behagen** *nt* discomfort, uneasiness; **—bildung** *f* deformity; **m—'billigen** *vt insep* disapprove of; **—billigung** *f* disapproval; **—brauch** *m* abuse; (*falscher Gebrauch*) misuse; **m—'brauchen** *vt insep* abuse; misuse (*zu for*); **m—'deuten** *vt insep* misinterpret; **—erfolg** *m* failure.

Misse- ['mɪsə] *cpd:* **—tat** *f* misdeed; **—täter(in** *f*) *m* criminal; (*col*) scoundrel..

Miß- *cpd:* **m—'fallen** *vi irreg insep* displease (*jdm sb*); **—'fallen** *nt* **-s** displeasure; **—geburt** *f* freak; (*fig*)

abortion; **—geschick** *nt* misfortune; **m—glücken** [mɪs'glʏkən] *vi insep* fail; **jdm m—glückt etw** *sb* does not succeed with sth; **—griff** *m* mistake; **—gunst** *f* envy; **m—günstig** *a* envious; **m—handeln** *vt insep* ill-treat; **—'handlung** *f* ill-treatment; **—helligkeit** *f*: **—helligkeiten haben** be at variance.

Mission [mɪsi'o:n] *f* mission; **—ar** [mɪsio'na:r] *m* missionary.

Miß- *cpd:* **—klang** *m* discord; **—kredit** *m* discredit; **m—lingen** [mɪs'lɪŋən] *vi irreg insep* fail; **—'lingen** *nt* **-s** failure; **—mut** *nt* bad temper; **m—mutig** *a* cross; **m—'raten** *vi irreg insep* turn out badly; *a* ill-bred; **—stand** *m* state of affairs; abuse; **—stimmung** *f* ill-humour, discord; **m—'trauen** *vi insep* mistrust; **—'trauen** *nt* **-s** distrust, suspicion (*of*); **—trauensantrag** *m* (*Pol*) motion of no confidence; **—trauensvotum** *nt* **-s, -voten** (*Pol*) vote of no confidence; **m—trauisch** *a* distrustful, suspicious; **—verhältnis** *nt* disproportion; **—verständnis** *nt* misunderstanding; **m—verstehen** *vt irreg insep* misunderstand.

Mist [mɪst] *m* **-(e)s** dung; dirt; (*col*) rubbish; **—el** *f* **-, -n** mistletoe; **—haufen** *m* dungheap.

mit [mɪt] *prep + dat with* ; (*mittels*) by; **— der Bahn** by train; **— 10 Jahren** at the age of 10; *ad* along, too; **wollen Sie —?** do you want to come along?

Mitarbeit ['mit'arbaɪt] *f* cooperation; **m—en** *vi* cooperate, collaborate; **—er(in** *f*) *m* collaborator; co-worker; *pl* staff.

Mit- *cpd:* **—bestimmung** *f* participation in decision-making; (*Pol*) determination; **m—bringen** vt irreg bring along; **—bürger(in** f) m fellow citizen; **m—denken** vi irreg follow; **du hast ja m—gedacht!** good thinking!

miteinander [mɪt'aɪ'nandər] ad together, with one another.

Mit- cpd: **m—erleben** vt see, witness; **—esser** ['mɪt'ɛsər] m, **-** blackhead; **m—geben** vt irreg give; **—gefühl** nt sympathy; **m—gehen** vi irreg go/come along; **m—genommen** a done in, in a bad way; **—gift** f dowry.

Mitglied ['mɪtɡliːt] nt member; **—sbeitrag** m membership fee; **—schaft** f membership.

Mit- cpd: **m—halten** vi irreg keep up; **—hilfe** f help, assistance; **m—hören** vt listen in to; **m—kommen** vi irreg come along; (verstehen) keep up, follow; **—läufer** m hanger-on; (Pol) fellow-traveller.

Mitleid nt sympathy; (Erbarmen) compassion; **—enschaft** f: in **—enschaft ziehen** affect; **m—ig** a sympathetic; **m—slos** a pitiless, merciless.

Mit- cpd: **m—machen** vt join in, take part in; **—mensch** m fellow man; **m—nehmen** vt irreg take along/away; (anstrengen) wear out, exhaust.

mitsamt [mɪt'zamt] prep +dat together with.

Mitschuld f complicity; **m—ig** a also guilty (an +dat of); **—ige(r)** mf accomplice.

Mit- cpd: **—schüler(in** f) m schoolmate; **m—spielen** vi join in, take part; **—spieler(in** f) m partner; **—spracherecht** ['mɪtʃpraːxərɛçt] nt voice, say.

Mittag ['mɪtaːk] m -(e)s, -e midday, lunchtime; (zu) **—** essen have lunch; **m—** ad at lunchtime or noon; **—essen** nt lunch, dinner; **m—s** ad at lunchtime or noon; **—spause** f lunch break; **—sschlaf** m early afternoon nap, siesta.

Mittäter(in f) [mɪttɛːtər(ɪn)] m accomplice.

Mitte ['mɪtə] f -, -n middle; aus unserer **—** from our midst.

mitteil- ['mɪttaɪl] cpd: **—en** vt: jdm etw **—en** inform sb of sth, communicate sth to sb; **—sam** a communicative; **M—ung** f communication.

Mittel ['mɪtəl] nt -s - means; method; (Math) average; (Med) medicine; **ein — zum Zweck** a means to an end; **—alter** nt Middle Ages pl; **m—alterlich** a mediaeval; **m—bar** a indirect; **—ding** nt cross; **m—los** a without means; **m—mäßig** a mediocre, middling; **—mäßigkeit** f mediocrity; **—punkt** m centre; **m—s** prep +gen by means of; **—stand** m middle class; **—streifen** m central reservation; **—stürmer** m centre-forward; **—weg** m middle course; **—welle** f (Rad) medium wave; **—wert** m average value, mean.

mitten ['mɪtən] ad in the middle; **— auf der Straße/in der Nacht** in the middle of the street/night; **—hindurch** ad [-hɪn'dʊrç] through the middle.

Mitternacht ['mɪtərnaxt] f midnight; **m—s** ad at midnight.

mittlere(r,s) ['mɪtlərə(r,z)] a middle; (durchschnittlich) medium, average.

mittlerweile ['mɪtlər'vaɪlə] ad meanwhile.

Mittwoch [mɪtvɔx] m -(e)s, -e
Wednesday; m—s ad on Wednesdays.

mitunter [mɪt'ʊntɐ]. ad
occasionally, sometimes.

Mit- cpd: m—verantwortlich a also
responsible; —verschulden
['mɪtfɐʃʊldən] nt contributory
negligence; m—wirken vi contribute (bei to); (Theat) take part
(bei in); —wirkung f contribution;
participation; —wisser ['mɪtvɪsɐ]
m -s, - sb in the know.

Möbel ['mø:bəl] nt -s, - (piece of)
furniture; —wagen m furniture or
removal van.

mobil [mo'bi:l] a mobile; (Mil)
mobilized; M—iar [mobili'a:r] nt -s,
-e movable assets pl; M—machung
f mobilization.

möblieren [mø'bli:rən] vt furnish;
möbliert wohnen live in furnished
accommodation.

Mode ['mo:də] f -, -n fashion.

Modell [mo'dɛl] nt -s, -e model;
m—ieren [-'li:rən] vt model.

Mode- cpd: —(n)schau f fashion
show; m—rn [mo'dɛrn] a modern;
(modisch) fashionable;
m—rnisieren vt modernize;
—schmuck m fashion jewellery;
—wort nt fashionable word.

modisch ['mo:dɪʃ] a fashionable.

mogeln [mo:gəln] vi (col) cheat.

mögen [mø:gən] vti irreg like; ich
möchte ... I would like ...; das
mag wohl sein that may well be so.

möglich ['mø:klɪç] a possible;
—erweise ad possibly; M—keit f
possibility; nach M—keit if
possible; —st ad as ... as possible.

Mohn [mo:n] m -(e)s, -e (—blume)
poppy; (—samen) poppy seed.

Möhre ['mø:rə] f -, -n, **Mohrrübe**
f carrot.

mokieren [mo'ki:rən] vr make fun
(über +acc of).

Mole ['mo:lə] f -, -n (harbour)
mole; —kül [mole'ky:l] nt -s, -e
molecule.

Molkerei [mɔlkə'raɪ] f dairy.

Moll [mɔl] nt -, - (Mus) minor
(key); m—ig a cosy; (dicklich)
plump.

Moment [mo'mɛnt] m -(e)s, -e
moment; im — at the moment; nt
factor, element; m—an [-'ta:n] a
momentary; ad·at the moment.

Monarch [mo'narç] m -en, -en
monarch; —ie [monar'çi:] f
monarchy.

Monat ['mo:nat] m -(e)s, -e
month; m—elang ad for months;
m—lich a monthly; —skarte f
monthly ticket.

Mönch ['mœnç] m -(e)s, -e monk.

Mond [mo:nt] m -(e)s, -e moon;
—fähre f lunar (excursion) module;
—finsternis f eclipse of the moon;
m—hell a moonlit; —landung f
moon landing; —schein m moon-
light; —sonde f moon probe.

Mono- cpd: in cpds mono; —log
[-'lo:k] m -s, -e monologue; —pol
[-'po:l] nt -s, -e monopoly;
m—polisieren [-poli'zi:rən] vt
monopolize; m—ton [-'to:n] a
monotonous; —tonie [-to'ni:] f
monotony.

Monsun [mɔn'zu:n] m -s, -e
monsoon.

Montag ['mo:nta:k] m -(e)s, -e
Monday; m—s ad on Mondays.

Montage [mɔn'ta:ʒə] f -, -n (Phot
etc) montage; (Tech) assembly;
(Einbauen) fitting.

Monteur [mɔn'tø:r] m fitter,
assembly man.

montieren [mɔn'ti:rən] vt
assemble, set up.

Monument [monu'mɛnt] *nt* monument; **m—al** ['-ta:l] *a* monumental.

Moor [mo:r] *nt* **-(e)s, -e** moor.

Moos [mo:s] *nt* **-es, -e** moss.

Moped ['mo:pɛt] *nt* **-s, -s** moped.

Mops [mɔps] *m* **-es, -̈e** pug.

Moral [mo'ra:l] *f* **-, -en** morality; (*einer Geschichte*) moral; **m—isch** *a* moral.

Moräne [mo'rɛ:nə] *f* **-, -n** moraine.

Morast [mo'rast] *m* **-(e)s, -e** morass, mire; **m—ig** *a* boggy.

Mord [mɔrt] *m* **-(e)s, -e** murder; **—anschlag** *m* murder attempt.

Mörder ['mœrdər] *m* **-s, -** murderer; **—in** *f* murderess.

Mord- *cpd*: **—kommission** *f* murder squad; **—sglück** *nt* (*col*) amazing luck; **m—smäßig** *a* (*col*) terrific, enormous; **—sschreck** *m* (*col*) terrible fright; **—verdacht** *m* suspicion of murder; **—waffe** *f* murder weapon.

morgen ['mɔrgən] *ad*, **M—** *nt* tomorrow; **—** **früh** tomorrow morning; **M—** *m* **-s, -** morning; **M—mantel** *m*, **M—rock** *m* dressing gown; **M—röte** *f* dawn; **—s** *ad* in the morning.

morgig ['mɔrgɪç] *a* tomorrow's; **der —e Tag** tomorrow.

Morphium ['mɔrfium] *nt* morphine.

morsch [mɔrʃ] *a* rotten.

Morse- ['mɔrzə] *cpd*: **—alphabet** *nt* Morse code; **m—n** *vi* send a message by morse code.

Mörtel ['mœrtəl] *m* **-s, -** mortar.

Mosaik [moza'i:k] *nt* **-s, -en** *or* **-e** mosaic.

Moschee [mɔ'ʃe:] *f* **-, -n** [mɔ'ʃe:ən] mosque.

Moskito [mɔs'ki:to] *m* **-s, -s** mosquito.

Most [mɔst] *m* **-(e)s, -e** (unfermented) fruit juice; (*Apfelwein*) cider.

Motel [mo'tɛl] *nt* **-s, -s** motel.

Motiv [mo'ti:f] *nt* **-s, -e** motive; (*Mus*) theme; **m—ieren** [moti'vi:rən] *vt* motivate; **—ierung** *f* motivation.

Motor [mo'to:r] *m* **-s, -en** [mo'to:rən] engine; (*esp Elec*) motor; **—boot** *nt* motorboat; **—enöl** *nt* motor oil; **m—isieren** [motori'zi:rən] *vt* motorize; **—rad** *nt* motorcycle; **—roller** *m* motor scooter; **—schaden** *m* engine trouble *or* failure.

Motte ['mɔtə] *f* **-, -n** moth; **—nkugel** *f*, **—npulver** *nt* mothball(s).

Motto ['mɔto] *nt* **-s, -s** motto.

Möwe ['mø:və] *f* **-, -n** seagull.

Mucke [mukə] *f* **-, -n** (*usu pl*) caprice; (*von Ding*) snag, bug; **seine —n haben** be temperamental.

Mücke ['mʏkə] *f* **-, -n** midge, gnat; **—nstich** *m* midge *or* gnat bite.

mucksen ['muksən] *vr* (*col*) budge; (*Laut geben*) open one's mouth.

müde ['my:də] *a* tired.

Müdigkeit ['my:dɪçkait] *f* tiredness.

Muff [muf] *m* **-(e)s, -e** (*Handwärmer*) muff; **—el** *m* **-s, -** (*col*) killjoy, sourpuss; **m—ig** *a* (*col*) musty.

Mühe ['my:ə] *f* **-, -n** trouble, pains *pl*; **mit Müh und Not** with great difficulty; **sich** (*dat*) — **geben** go to a lot of trouble; **m—los** *a* without trouble, easy.

muhen ['mu:ən] *vi* low, moo.

mühevoll *a* laborious, arduous.

Mühle ['my:lə] *f* **-, -n** mill; (*Kaffee—*) grinder.

Müh- *cpd:* —**sal** *f* -, -**e** hardship, tribulation; **m—sam** *a* arduous, troublesome; **m—selig** *a* arduous, laborious.

Mulatte [mu'latə] *m* -**, -n,**
Mulattin *f* mulatto.

Mulde ['muldə] *f* -**, -n** hollow, depression.

Mull [mul] *m* -(**e)s, -e** thin muslin;
—**binde** *f* gauze bandage.

Müll [myl] *m* -(**e)s** refuse;
—**abfuhr** *f* rubbish disposal;
(*Leute*) dustmen *pl;* —**abladeplatz** *m* rubbish dump; —**eimer** *m* dustbin, garbage can (*US*); —**er** *m* -**s, -** miller; —**haufen** *m* rubbish heap; —**schlucker** *m* -**s, -** garbage disposal unit; —**wagen** *m* dustcart, garbage truck (*US*).

mulmig ['mulmɪç] *a* rotten; (*col*) dodgy; **jdm ist** — **sb** feels funny.

multiplizieren [multipli'tsi:rən] *vt* multiply.

Mumie ['mu:miə] *f* mummy.

Mumm [mum] *m* -**s** (*col*) gumption, nerve.

Mund [munt] *m* -(**e)s, "er** ['myndər] mouth; —**art** *f* dialect.

Mündel ['myndəl] *nt* -**s, -** ward.

münden ['myndən] *vi* flow (*in* + *acc* into).

Mund- *cpd:* **m—faul;** *a* taciturn;
—**fäule** *f* - (*Med*) ulcerative stomatitis; —**geruch** *m* bad breath; —**harmonika** *f* mouth organ.

mündig ['myndɪç] *a* of age;
M—keit *f* majority.

mündlich ['myntlɪç] *a* oral.

Mund- *cpd:* —**stück** *nt* mouthpiece; (*Zigaretten—*) tip; **m—tot** *a:* **jdn m—tot machen** muzzle sb.

Mündung ['myndʊŋ] *f* mouth; (*Gewehr*) muzzle.

Mund- *cpd:* —**wasser** *nt* mouthwash; —**werk** *nt:* **ein großes —werk haben** have a big mouth; —**winkel** *m* corner of the mouth.

Munition [munitsi'o:n] *f* ammunition; —**slager** *nt* ammunition dump.

munkeln ['muŋkəln] *vi* whisper, mutter.

Münster ['mynstər] *nt* -**s, -** minster.

munter ['muntər] *a* lively; **M—keit** *f* liveliness.

Münze ['myntsə] *f* -, -**n** coin; **m—n** *vt* coin, mint; **auf jdn gemünzt sein** be aimed at sb.

Münzfernsprecher ['myntsfɛrn-ʃprɛçər] *m* callbox, pay phone (*US*).

mürb(e) ['myrb(ə)] *a Gestein* crumbly; *Holz* rotten; *Gebäck* crisp; **jdn — machen** wear sb down; **M—(e)teig** *m* shortcrust pastry.

murmeln ['murməln] *vti* murmur, mutter.

Murmeltier ['murməlti:r] *nt* marmot.

murren ['murən] *vi* grumble, grouse.

mürrisch ['myrɪʃ] *a* sullen.

Mus [mu:s] *nt* -**es, -e** puree.

Muschel ['muʃəl] *f* -, -**n** mussel; (—*schale*) shell; (*Telefon—*) receiver.

Muse ['mu:zə] *f* -, -**n** muse.

Museum [mu'ze:um] *nt* -**s,** *pl* **Museen** museum.

Musik [mu'zi:k] *f* music; (*Kapelle*) band; **m—alisch** [-'ka:lɪʃ] *a* musical; —**box** *f* jukebox; —**er** ['mu:zikər] *m* -**s, -** musician; —**hochschule** *f* music school; —**instrument** *nt* musical instrument; —**truhe** *f* radiogram.

musizieren [muzi'tsi:rən] *vi* make music.

Muskat [mʊs'kaːt] *m* -(e)s, -e
nutmeg.

Muskel ['mʊskəl] *m* -s, -n muscle;
—kater *m*: einen —kater haben be
stiff.

Muskulatur [mʊskula'tuːr] *f*
muscular system.

muskulös [mʊsku'løːs] a muscular.

Muß [mʊs] *nt* – necessity, must.

Muße ['muːsə] *f* - leisure.

müssen ['mʏsən] *vi irreg* must,
have to; er hat gehen — he (has)
had to go.

müßig ['myːsɪç] a idle; M—gang *m*
idleness.

Muster ['mʊstər] *nt* -s, - model;
(*Dessin*) pattern; (*Probe*) sample;
— ohne Wert free sample;
m—gültig a exemplary; m—n *vt*
Tapete pattern; (*fig, Mil*) examine;
Truppen inspect; —schüler *m*
model pupil; —ung *f* (*von Stoff*)
pattern; (*Mil*) inspection.

Mut [muːt] *m* courage; nur —!
cheer up!; jdm — machen
encourage sb; m—ig a

courageous; m—los a discouraged,
despondent.

mutmaßlich ['muːtmaːslɪç] a
presumed; *ad* probably.

Mutter ['mʊtər] *f* -, ⸚ mother; *pl*
—n (*Schrauben*—) nut; —land *nt*
mother country.

mütterlich ['mʏtərlɪç] a motherly;
—erseits *ad* on the mother's side.

Mutter- *cpd*: —liebe *f* motherly
love; —mal *nt* birthmark, mole;
—schaft *f* motherhood, maternity;
—schutz *m* maternity regulations;
'm—'seelena'lleın a all alone;
—sprache *f* native language; —tag
m Mother's Day.

mutwillig ['muːtvɪlɪç] a malicious,
deliberate.

Mütze ['mʏtsə] *f* -, -n cap.

mysteriös [mysterɪ'øːs] a
mysterious.

Mystik ['mʏstik] *f* mysticism; —er
m -s, - mystic.

Mythos ['myːtɔs] *m* -, **Mythen**
myth.

N

N, n [ɛn] *nt* N, n.

na [na] *interj* well.

Nabel ['naːbəl] *m* -s, - navel;
—schnur *f* umbilical cord.

nach [naːx] *prep* +*dat* after; (*in
Richtung*) to; (*gemäß*) according
to; — oben/hinten up/back; then
—! after him!; — wie vor still; —
und — gradually; dem Namen —
judging by his name; —äffen *vt*
ape; —ahmen *vt* imitate;
N—ahmung *f* imitation.

Nachbar(in *f*) ['naxbaːr(ɪn)] *m* -s,

—n neighbour; —haus *nt*: im
—haus next door; n—lich a
neighbourly; —schaft *f* neighbourhood; —staat *m* neighbouring state.

nach- *cpd*: —bestellen *vt* order
again; N—bestellung *f* (*Comm*)
repeat order; —bilden *vt* copy;
N—bildung *f* imitation, copy;
—blicken *vi* look or gaze after;
—datieren *vt* postdate.

nachdem [naːx'deːm] *cj* after;
(*weil*) since; je — (**ob**) it depends
(whether).

nach- *cpd:* **—denken** *vi irreg* think (über + *acc* about); **N—denken** *nt* **-s** reflection, meditation; **—denklich** *a* thoughtful, pensive.

Nachdruck ['na:xdruk] *m* emphasis; (*Print*) reprint, reproduction.

nachdrücklich ['na:xdryklɪç] *a* emphatic.

nacheifern ['na:xaɪfərn] *vi* emulate (*jdm* sb).

nacheinander [na:x'aɪ'nandər] *ad* one after the other.

nachempfinden ['na:xɛmpfɪndən] *vt irreg:* jdm etw — feel sth with sb.

Nacherzählung ['na:xɛrtsɛːluŋ] *f* reproduction (of a story).

Nachfahr ['na:xfaːr] *m* **-s, -en** descendant.

Nachfolge ['na:xfɔlgə] *f* succession; **n—n** *vi* (*lit*) follow (*jdm/etw* sb/sth); **—r(in** *f*) *m* **-s, -** successor.

nach- *cpd:* **—forschen** *vti* investigate; **N—forschung** *f* investigation.

Nachfrage ['na:xfraːgə] *f* inquiry; (*Comm*) demand; **n—n** *vi* inquire.

nach- *cpd:* **—fühlen** *vt* see **—empfinden; —füllen** *vt* refill; **—geben** *vi irreg* give way, yield.

Nach- *cpd:* **—gebühr** *f* surcharge; (*Post*) excess postage; **—geburt** *f* afterbirth.

nachgehen ['na:xgeːən] *vi irreg* follow (*jdm* sb); (*erforschen*) inquire (*einer Sache* into sth); (*Uhr*) be slow.

Nachgeschmack ['na:xgəʃmak] *m* aftertaste.

nachgiebig ['na:xgiːbɪç] *a* soft, accommodating; **N—keit** *f* softness.

Nachhall ['na:xhal] *m* resonance; **n—en** *vi* resound.

nachhaltig ['na:xhaltɪç] *a* lasting; Widerstand persistent.

nachhelfen ['na:xhɛlfən] *vi irreg* assist, help (*jdm* sb).

nachher [na:x'heːr] *ad* afterwards.

Nachhilfeunterricht ['na:xhɪlfəʊntərɪçt] *m* extra tuition.

nachholen ['na:xhoːlən] *vt* catch up with; Versäumtes make up for.

Nachkomme ['na:xkɔmə] *m* **-, -n** descendant; **n—n** *vi irreg* follow; einer Verpflichtung fulfil; **—nschaft** *f* descendants *pl.*

Nachkriegs- ['na:xkriːks] *in cpds* postwar; **—zeit** *f* postwar period.

Nach- *cpd:* **—laß** *m* **-lasses, -lässe** (*Comm*) discount, rebate; (*Erbe*) estate; **n—lassen** *irreg vt* Strafe remit; Summe take off; Schulden cancel; *vi* decrease, ease off; (*Sturm auch*) die down; (*schlechter werden*) deteriorate; er hat n—gelassen he has got worse; **n—lässig** *a* negligent, careless; **—lässigkeit** *f* negligence, carelessness.

nachlaufen ['na:xlaʊfən] *vi irreg* run after, chase (*jdm* sb).

nachmachen ['na:xmaxən] *vt* imitate, copy (*jdm etw* sth from sb); (*fälschen*) counterfeit.

Nachmittag ['na:xmɪtaːk] *m* afternoon; am **—, n—s** *ad* in the afternoon.

Nach- *cpd:* **—nahme** *f* **-, -n** cash on delivery; per **—nahme** C.O.D.; **—name** *m* surname; **—porto** *nt* excess postage.

nachprüfen ['na:xpryːfən] *vt* check, verify.

nachrechnen ['na:xrɛçnən] *vt* check.

Nachrede ['na:xreːdə] *f*: üble — libel; slander.

Nachricht ['naːxrɪçt] *f* -, -en (piece of) news; (*Mitteilung*) message; —en *pl* news; —enagentur *f* news agency; —endienst *m* (*Mil*) intelligence service; —ensprecher(in *f*) *m* newsreader; —entechnik *f* telecommunications *sing*.

nachrücken ['naːxrʏkən] *vi* move up.

Nachruf ['naːxruːf] *m* obituary (notice).

nachsagen ['naːxzaːgən] *vt* repeat; jdm etw — say sth of sb.

nachschicken ['naːxʃɪkən] *vt* forward.

Nachschlag- ['naːxʃlaːg] *cpd*: n—en *vt irreg* look up; *vi*: jdm n—en take after sb; —ewerk *nt* reference boook.

Nach- *cpd*: —schlüssel *m* master key; —schub *m* supplies *pl*; (*Truppen*) reinforcements *pl*.

nachsehen ['naːxzeːən] *irreg vt* (*prüfen*) check; jdm etw — forgive sb sth; *vi* look after (jdm sb); (*erforschen*) look and see; das N— ·haben come·off worst.

nachsenden ['naːxzɛndən] *vt irreg* send on, forward.

Nachsicht ['naːxzɪçt] *f* - indulgence, leniency; n—ig *a* indulgent, lenient.

nachsitzen ['naːxzɪtsən] *vi irreg* (*Sch*) be kept in.

Nachspeise ['naːxʃpaɪzə] *f* dessert, sweet, pudding.

Nachspiel ['naːxʃpiːl] *nt* epilogue; (*fig*) sequel.

nachsprechen ['naːxʃprɛçən] *vt irreg* repeat (jdm after sb).

nächst [nɛːçst] *prep* + *dat* (*räumlich*) next to; (*außer*) apart from; —beste(r,s) *a* first that ·comes along; (*zweitbeste*) next best; N—e(r) *mf* neighbour;

—e(r,s) next; (*nächstgelegen*) nearest; N—enliebe *f* love for one's fellow men; —ens *ad* shortly, soon; —liegend *a* (*lit*) nearest; (*fig*) obvious; —möglich *a* next possible.

nachsuchen ['naːxzuːxən] *vi*: um etw — ask *or* apply for sth.

Nacht [naxt] *f* -, ¨e night.

Nachteil ['naːxtaɪl] *m* disadvantage; n—ig *a* disadvantageous.

Nachthemd *nt* nightshirt; nightdress.

Nachtigall ['naxtɪgal] *f* -, -en nightingale.

Nachtisch ['naːxtɪʃ] *m* see **Nachspeise**.

nächtlich ['nɛçtlɪç] *a* nightly.

Nach- *cpd*: —trag *m* -(e)s, -träge supplement; n—tragen *vt irreg* carry (jdm after sb); (*zufügen*) add; jdm etw n—tragen hold sth against sb; n—tragend *a* resentful; n—träglich *a*, *ad* later, subsequent(ly); 'additional(ly); n—trauern *vi*: jdm/etw n—trauern mourn the loss of sb/sth.

Nacht- *cpd*: —ruhe *f* sleep; n—s *ad* by night; —schicht *f* nightshift; n—süber. *ad* during the night; —tarif *m* off-peak tariff; —tisch *m* bedside table; —topf *m* chamberpot; —wächter *m* night watchman.

Nach- *cpd*: —untersuchung *f* checkup; n—wachsen *vi irreg* grow ·again; —wehen *pl* afterpains *pl*; (*fig*) after-effects *pl*.

Nachweis ['naːxvaɪs] *m* -es, -e proof; n—bar *a* provable, demonstrable; n—en ['naːxvaɪzən] *vt irreg* prove; jdm etw n—en point sth out·to sb; n—lich *a* evident, demonstrable.

nach- *cpd*: **—winken** *vi* wave (*jdm* after *sb*); **—wirken** *vi* have after-effects; **N—wirkung** *f* after-effect; **N—wort** *nt* appendix; **N—wuchs** *m* offspring; (*beruflich etc*) new recruits *pl*; **—zahlen** *vti* pay extra; **N—zahlung** *f* additional payment; (*zurückdatiert*) back pay; **—zählen** *vt* count again; **N—zügler** *m* -s, **-** straggler.

Nacken ['nakən] *m* -s, **-** nape of the neck.

nackt [nakt] *a* naked; *Tatsachen* plain, bare; **N—heit** *f* nakedness; **N—kultur** *f* nudism.

Nadel ['na:dəl] *f* -, **-n** needle; (*Steck—*) pin; **—kissen** *nt* pin-cushion; **—öhr** *nt* eye of a needle; **—wald** *m* coniferous forest.

Nagel ['na:gəl] *m* -s, **:** nail; **—feile** *f* nailfile; **—haut** *f* cuticle; **—lack** *m* nail varnish; **n—n** *vti* nail; **n—neu** a brand-new; **—schere** *f* nail scissors *pl*.

nagen ['na:gən] *vti* gnaw.

Nagetier ['na:gəti:r] *nt* rodent.

nah(e) ['na:(ə)] *a,ad* (*räumlich*) near(by); *Verwandte* near; *Freunde* close; (*zeitlich*) near, close; **prep** +*dat* near (to), close to; **N—aufnahme** *f* close-up.

Nähe ['nɛ:ə] *f* - nearness, proximity; (*Umgebung*) vicinity; in der **—** close by; at hand; aus der **—** from close to.

nahe- *cpd*: **—bei** *ad* nearby; **—gehen** *vi irreg* grieve (*jdm* *sb*); **—kommen** *vi irreg* get close (*jdm* to *sb*); **—legen** *vt*: jdm etw **—legen** suggest *sth* to *sb*; **—liegen** *vi irreg* be obvious; **—liegend** a obvious; **—n** *vir* approach, draw near.

Näh- ['nɛ:] *cpd*: **—en** *vti* sew; **n—er** a,ad nearer; *Erklärung, Erkundung* **more** detailed;

—ere(s) *nt* details *pl*, particulars *pl*; **—erei** *f* sewing, needlework; **—erin** *f* seamstress; **n—erkommen** *vir irreg* get closer; **n—ern** *vr* approach; **—erungswert** *m* approximate value.

nahe- *cpd*: **—stehen** *vi irreg* be close (*jdm* to *sb*); einer Sache **—stehen** sympathize with *sth*; **—stehend** a close; **—treten** *vi irreg*: jdm (zu) **—treten** offend *sb*; **—zu** *ad* nearly.

Näh- *cpd*: **—garn** *nt* thread; **—kasten** *m* workbox; **—maschine** *f* sewing machine; **—nadel** *f* needle.

nähren ['nɛ:rən] *vtr* feed.

nahrhaft ['na:rhaft] a nourishing, nutritious.

Nähr- ['nɛ:r] *cpd*: **—gehalt** *m* nutritional value; **—stoffe** *pl* nutrients *pl*.

Nahrung ['na:ruŋ] *f* food; (*fig* *auch*) sustenance; **—smittel** *nt* foodstuffs *pl*; **—smittelindustrie** *f* food industry; **—ssuche** *f* search for food.

Nährwert *m* nutritional value.

Naht [na:t] *f* -, **:e** seam; (*Med*) suture; (*Tech*) join; **n—los** a seamless; **n—los ineinander übergehen** follow without a gap.

Nah- *cpd*: **—verkehr** *m* local traffic; **—verkehrszug** *m* local train; **—ziel** *nt* immediate objective.

naiv [na'i:f] a naive; **N—ität** [naivi'tɛ:t] *f* naivety.

Name ['na:mə] *m* -ns, **-n** name; im **—n** von on behalf of; **n—ns** ad by the name of; **n—ntlich** a by name; ad particularly, especially.

namhaft ['na:mhaft] a (*berühmt*) famed, renowned; (*beträchtlich*) considerable; **— machen** name.

nämlich ['nɛ:mlıç] ad that is to say,

namely; (denn) since; der/die/das
—e the same.

Napf [napf] m -(e)s, ᵉe bowl, dish.

Narbe ['narbə] f -, -n scar.

narbig ['narbiç] a scarred.

Narkose [nar'ko:ze] f -, -n
anaesthetic.

Narr [nar] m -en, -en fool; n—en
vt fool; —heit f foolishness.

Närr- ['nɛr] cpd: —in f. fool;
n—isch a foolish, crazy.

Narzisse [nar'tsɪsə] f -, -n
narcissus; daffodil.

nasch- ['naʃ] cpd: —en vti nibble;
eat secretly; —haft a sweet-
toothed.

Nase ['na:zə] f -, -n nose;
—nbluten nt -s nosebleed; —nloch
nt nostril; —nrücken m bridge of
the nose; —ntropfen pl nose drops
pl; n—weis a pert, cheeky;
(neugierig) nosey.

Nashorn ['na:shɔrn] nt rhinoceros.

naß [nas] a wet.

Nässe ['nɛsə] f - wetness; n—n vt
wet.

Naß- cpd: n—kalt a wet and cold;
—rasur f wet shave.

Nation [natsi'o:n] f nation.

national [natsio'na:l] a national;
—**hymne** f national anthem;
—**isieren** [-'i:zirən] vt nationalize;
—**i'sierung** f nationalization;
—**ismus** [-'lɪsmus] m nationalism;
—**istisch** [-'lɪstiç] a nationalistic;
—**i'tät** f nationality;
N—**mannschaft** f national team;
N—**sozialismus** m national
socialism.

Natron ['na:trɔn] nt -s soda.

Natter ['natər] f -, -n adder.

Natur [na'tu:r] f nature;
(körperlich) constitution; —**alien**
[natu'ra:liən] pl natural produce; in

—alien in kind; —a'lismus m
naturalism; —erscheinung f
natural phenomenon or event;
n—farben a natural coloured;
n—gemäß a natural; —geschichte
f natural history; —gesetz nt law
of nature; —katastrophe f natural
disaster.

natürlich [na'ty:rliç] a natural; ad
naturally; —erweise ad naturally,
of course; N—keit f naturalness.

Natur- cpd: —produkt nt natural
product; n—rein a natural, pure;
—schutzgebiet nt nature reserve;
—wissenschaft f natural science;
—wissenschaftler(in f) m scientist;
—zustand m natural state.

nautisch ['nautiç] a nautical.

Navelorange ['na:vəlorã:ʒə] f
navel orange.

Navigation [navigatsi'o:n] f navigation; —sfehler m navigational
error; —sinstrumente pl navigation
instruments pl.

Nazi ['na:tsi] m -s, -s Nazi.

Nebel ['ne:bəl] m -s, - fog, mist;
n—ig a foggy, misty;
—scheinwerfer m foglamp.

neben ['ne:bən] prep +acc or dat
next to; (außer) apart from,
besides; —an [ne:bən"an] ad next
door; N—anschluß m (Tel)
extension; —bei [ne:bən'bai] ad at
the same time; (außerdem)
additionally; (beiläufig)
incidentally; N—beschäftigung f
sideline; N—buhler(in f) m -s, -
rival; —einander [ne:bən'ai'nandər]
ad side by side; —einanderlegen vt
put next to each other; N—eingang
m side entrance; N—erscheinung f
side effect; N—fach nt subsidiary
subject; N—fluß m tributary;
N—geräusch nt (Rad)
atmospherics pl, interference;

—her [nɛːbənʰeːr] ad (zusätzlich) besides; (gleichzeitig) at the same time; (daneben) alongside; —herfahren vi irreg drive alongside; N—kosten pl extra charges pl, extras pl; N—produkt nt byproduct; N—rolle f minor part; N—sache f trifle, side issue; —sächlich a minor, peripheral; N—straße f side street; N—zimmer nt adjoining room.

Necessaire [nesɛˈsɛːr] nt -s, -s (Näh—) needlework box; (Nagel—) manicure case.

neck- ['nɛk] cpd: —en vt tease; N—e'rei f teasing; —isch a coy; Einfall, Lied amusing.

Neffe ['nɛfə] m -n, -n nephew.

negativ [negaˈtiːf] a negative; N— nt -s, -e (Phot) negative.

Neger ['neːgər] m -s, - negro; —in f negress.

negieren [neˈgiːrən] vt (bestreiten) deny; (verneinen) negate.

nehmen ['neːmən] vt irreg take; jdn zu sich — take sb in; sich ernst — take o.s. seriously; nimm dir noch einmal help yourself.

Neid [naɪt] m -(e)s envy; —er m -s, - envier; n—isch a envious, jealous.

neigen ['naɪgən] vt incline, lean; Kopf bow; vi: zu etw — tend to sth.

Neigung f (des Geländes) slope; (Tendenz) tendency, inclination; (Vorliebe) liking; (Zuneigung) affection; —swinkel m angle of inclination.

nein [naɪn] ad no.

Nelke ['nɛlkə] f -, -n carnation, pink; (Gewürz) clove.

Nenn- ['nɛn] cpd: n—en vt irreg name; (mit Namen) call; n—enswert a worth mentioning;

—er m -s, - denominator; —ung f naming; —wert m nominal value; (Comm) par.

Neon ['neːɔn] nt -s neon; —licht nt neon light; —röhre f neon tube.

Nerv [nɛrf] m -s, -en nerve; jdm auf die —en gehen get on sb's nerves; n—enaufreibend a nerveracking; —enbündel nt bundel of nerves; —enheilanstalt f mental home; n—enkrank a mentally ill; —enschwäche f neurasthenia; —ensystem nt nervous system; —enzusammenbruch m nervous breakdown; n—ös [nɛrˈvøːs] a nervous; —osi'tät f nervousness; n—tötend a nerve-racking; Arbeit soul-destroying.

Nerz [nɛrts] m -es, -e mink.

Nessel ['nɛsəl] f -, -n nettle.

Nest [nɛst] nt -(e)s, -er nest; (col: Ort) dump; n—eln vi fumble or fiddle about (an + dat with).

nett [nɛt] a nice; (freundlich auch) kind; —erweise ad kindly· —o a net.

Netz [nɛts] nt -es, -e net; (Gepäck—) rack; (Einkaufs—) string bag; (Spinnen—) web; (System) network; jdm ins — gehen (fig) fall into sb's trap; —anschluß m mains connection; —haut f retina.

neu [nɔy] a new; Sprache, Geschichte modern; seit —estem (since) recently; — schreiben rewrite, write again; N—anschaffung f new purchase or acquisition; —artig a new kind of; N—auflage f, N—ausgabe f new edition; N—bau m -s, -ten new building; —erdings ad (kürzlich) (since) recently; (von neuem) again; N—erung f innovation, new departure; N—gier f curiosity;

—gierig a curious; N—heit f newness; novelty; N—igkeit f news; N—jahr nt New Year; —lich ad recently, the other day; N—ling m novice; N—mond m new moon.

neun [nɔyn] num nine; —zehn num nineteen; —zig num ninety.

neureich a nouveau riche; N—e(r) mf nouveau riche.

Neur- cpd: —ose [nɔy'ro:zə] f -, -n neurosis; —otiker [nɔy'ro:tikər] m -s, - neurotic; n—otisch a neurotic.

Neutr- cpd: n—al [nɔy'tra:l] a neutral; —alität f neutrality; n—alisieren vt neutralize; —on ['nɔytrɔn] nt -s, -en neutron; —um ['nɔytrʊm] nt -s, -a or -en neuter.

Neu- cpd: —wert m purchase price; —zeit f modern age; n—zeitlich a modern, recent.

nicht [nɪçt] ad not; pref non-; — wahr? isn't it/he?, don't you etc; — doch! don't!; — berühren! do not touch! was du — sagst! the things you say!; N—achtung f disregard; N—angriffspakt m non-aggression pact.

Nichte ['nɪçtə] f -, -n niece.

nichtig ['nɪçtɪç] a (ungültig) null, void; (wertlos) futile; N—keit f nullity, invalidity; (Sinnlosigkeit) futility.

Nicht- cpd: —raucher(in f) m non-smoker; n—rostend a stainless.

nichts [nɪçts] pron nothing; für — und wieder — for nothing at all; N— nt -s nothingness; (pej: Person) nonentity; —destoweniger ad nevertheless; N—nutz m -es, -e good-for-nothing; n—nutzig a worthless, useless; —sagend a meaningless; N—tun nt -s idleness.

Nickel ['nɪkəl] nt -s nickel.

nicken ['nɪkən] vi nod.

Nickerchen ['nɪkərçən] nt nap.

nie [ni:] ad never; — wieder or mehr never again; — und nimmer never ever.

nieder ['ni:dər] low; (gering) inferior; ad down; N—gang m decline; —gehen vi irreg descend; (Aviat) come down; (Regen) fall; (Boxer) go down; —geschlagen a depressed, dejected; N—geschlagenheit f depression, dejection; N—lage f defeat; (Lager) depot; (Filiale) branch; —lassen vr irreg (sich setzen) sit down; (an Ort) settle (down); (Arzt, Rechtsanwalt) set up a practice; N—lassung f settlement; (Comm) branch; —legen vt lay down; Arbeit stop; Amt resign; —machen vt mow down; N—schlag m (Chem) precipitate, sediment; (Met) precipitation; rain-fall; (Boxen) knockdown; —schlagen irreg vt Gegner beat down; Gegenstand knock down; Augen lower; (Jur) Prozeß dismiss; Aufstand put down; vr (Chem) precipitate; N—schrift f transcription; —trächtig a base, mean; N—trächtigkeit f meanness, baseness; outrage; N—ung f (Geog) depression; flats pl.

niedlich ['ni:tlɪç] a sweet, nice, cute.

niedrig ['ni:drɪç] a low; Stand lowly, humble; Gesinnung mean.

niemals ['ni:ma:ls] ad never.

niemand ['ni:mant] pron nobody, no one; N—sland nt no-man's land.

Niere ['ni:rə] f -, -n kidney; —nentzündung f kidney infection.

nieseln ['ni:zəln] vi drizzle.

niesen ['ni:zən] vi sneeze.

Niet [ni:t] m -(e)s, -e, —e f -, -n (Tech) rivet ; (Los) blank ; (Reinfall) flop ; (Mensch) failure ; n—en vt rivet.

Nihil- cpd: —ismus [nihiˈlɪsmʊs] m nihilism ; —ist [nihiˈlɪst] m nihilist ; n—istisch a nihilistic.

Nikotin [nikoˈtiːn] nt -s nicotine.

Nilpferd [ˈniːlpfeːrt] nt hippopotamus.

nimmersatt [ˈnɪmərzat] a insatiable ; N— m -(e)s, -e glutton.

nippen [ˈnɪpən] vti sip.

Nippsachen [ˈnɪpzaxən] pl knickknacks pl.

nirgends [ˈnɪrɡənts], nirgendwo [ˈnɪrɡəntvoː] ad nowhere.

Nische [ˈniːʃə] f -, -n niche.

nisten [ˈnɪstən] vi nest.

Nitrat [niˈtraːt] nt -(e)s, -e nitrate.

Niveau [niˈvoː] nt -s, -s level.

Nixe [ˈnɪksə] f -, -n water nymph.

noch [nɔx] ad still ; (in Zukunft) still, yet ; one day ; (außerdem) else ; cj nor ; — nie never (yet) ; — nicht not yet ; immer — still ; — heute today ; — vor einer Woche only a week ago ; und wenn es — so schwer ist however hard it is ; — einmal again ; — dreimal three more times ; — und — heaps of ; (mit Verb) again and again ; —mal(s) ad again, once more ; —malig a repeated.

Nockenwelle [ˈnɔkənvɛlə] f camshaft.

Nominativ [ˈnoːminatiːf] m -s, -e nominative.

nominell [nomiˈnɛl] a nominal.

Nonne [ˈnɔnə] f -, -n nun ; —nkloster nt convent.

Nord(en) [ˈnɔrd(ən)] m -s north ; n—isch a northern ; —ische

Kombination (Ski) nordic combination.

nördlich [ˈnœrtlɪç] a northerly, northern ; — von, — prep +gen (to the) north of.

Nord- cpd: —pol m North Pole ; n—wärts ad northwards.

Nörg- [ˈnœrɡ] cpd: —elei f grumbling ; n—eln vi grumble ; —ler m -s, - grumbler.

Norm [nɔrm] f -, -en norm ; (Größenvorschrift) standard ; n—al [nɔrˈmaːl] a normal ; n—alerweise ad normally ; n—alisieren vt normalize ; vr return to normal ; n—en vt standardize.

Not [noːt] f -, —e need ; (Mangel) want ; (Mühe) trouble ; (Zwang) necessity ; zur — if necessary ; (gerade noch) just about ; —ar [noˈtaːr] m -s, -e notary ; n—ariell a notarial ; —ausgang m emergency exit ; —behelf m -s, -e makeshift ; —bremse f emergency brake ; n—dürftig a scanty ; (behelfsmäßig) makeshift ; sich n—dürftig verständigen just about understand each other.

Note [ˈnoːtə] f -, -n note ; (Sch) mark ; —nblatt nt sheet of music ; —nschlüssel m clef ; —nständer m music stand.

Not- cpd: —fall m (case of) emergency ; n—falls ad if need be ; n—gedrungen a necessary, unavoidable ; etw n—gedrungen machen be forced to do sth.

notieren [noˈtiːrən] vt note ; (Comm) quote.

Notierung f (Comm) quotation.

nötig [ˈnøːtɪç] a necessary ; etw — haben need sth ; n—en vt compel, force ; —enfalls ad if necessary.

Notiz [noˈtiːts] f -, -en note ; (Zeitungs-) item ; — nehmen take notice; **—buch** nt notebook; **—zettel** m piece of paper.

Not- cpd: **—lage** f crisis, emergency; **n—landen** vi make a forced or emergency landing; **n—leidend** a needy; **—lösung** f temporary solution; **—lüge** f white lie.

notorisch [no'to:rɪʃ] a notorious.

Not- cpd: **—ruf** m emergency call; **—stand** m state of emergency; **—standsgesetz** nt emergency law; **—unterkunft** f emergency accommodation; **—verband** m emergency dressing; **—wehr** f self-defence; **n—wendig** a necessary; **—wendigkeit** f necessity; **—zucht** f rape.

Novelle [ɦo'vɛlə] f -, **-n** short story; (Jur) amendment.

November [no'vɛmbər] m -(s), - November.

Nu [nu:] m: im — in an instant.

Nuance [ny'ã:sə] f -, **-n** nuance.

nüchtern [nʏçtərn] a sober; Magen empty; Urteil prudent; **N—heit** f sobriety.

Nudel ['nu:dəl] f -, **-n** noodle.

Null [nʊl] f -, **-en** nought, zero; (pej: Mensch) washout; **n—** num zero; Fehler no; **n—** Uhr midnight; **n—** und nichtig null and

void; **—punkt** m zero; auf dem **—punkt** at zero.

numerieren [nume'ri:rən] vt number.

numerisch [nu'me:rɪʃ] a numerical.

Nummer ['nʊmər] f -, **-n** number; **—scheibe** f telephone dial; **—nschild** nt (Aut) number or. license (US) plate.

nun [nu:n] ad now; interj well.

nur [nu:r] ad just, only.

Nuß [nʊs] f -, **Nüsse** nut; **—baum** m walnut tree; hazelnut tree; **—knacker** m -s, - nutcracker.

Nüster ['ny:stər] f -, **-n** nostril.

Nutte ['nʊtə] f -, **-n** tart.

nutz [nʊts], **nütze** ['nʏtsə] a: zu nichts — sein to be useless; **—bar** a: **—bar machen** utilize; **N—barmachung** f utilization; **—bringend** a profitable; **—en, nützen** vt use (zu etw for sth); vi be of use; was nützt es? what's the use?, what use is it?; **N—en** m -s usefulness; profit; **von N—en** useful.

nützlich ['nʏtslɪç] a useful; **N—keit** f usefulness.

Nutz- cpd: **n—los** a useless; **—losigkeit** f uselessness; **—nießer** m -s, - beneficiary.

Nymphe ['nʏmfə] f -, **-n** nymph.

O

O, o [o:] nt O, o.

Oase [o'a:zə] f -, **-n** oasis.

ob [ɔp] cj if, whether; — das wohl wahr ist? can that be true?; und **—!** you bet!

Obacht ['o:baxt] f: **—** geben pay attention.

Obdach ['ɔpdax] nt -(e)s shelter, lodging; **o—los** a homeless; **—lose(r)** mf homeless person.

Obduktion [ɔpdʊktsi'o:n] f postmortem.

obduzieren [ɔpdu'tsi:rən] vt do a post mortem on.

O-Beine ['o:bamə] pl bow or bandy legs pl.
oben ['o:bən] ad above; (in Haus) upstairs; — nach — up; von — down; — ohne topless; jdn von — bis unten ansehen look sb up and down; Befehl von — orders from above; —an ad at the top; —auf ad up above, on the top; a (munter) in form; —drein ad into the bargain; —erwähnt, —genannt a above-mentioned; —hin ad cursorily, superficially.
Ober ['o:bər] m -s, - waiter; —arm m upper arm; —arzt m senior physician; —aufsicht f supervision; —befehl m supreme command; —befehlshaber m commander-in-chief; —begriff m generic term; —bekleidung f outer clothing; —'bürgermeister m lord mayor; —deck nt upper or top deck; o—e(r,s) a upper; die —en the bosses; (Eccl) the superiors; —fläche f surface; o—flächlich a superficial; —geschoß nt upper storey; o—halb ad, prep +gen above; —haupt nt head, chief; —haus nt upper house; House of Lords; —hemd nt shirt; —herrschaft f supremacy, sovereignty; —in f matron; (Eccl) Mother Superior; o—irdisch a above ground; Leitung overhead; —kellner m head waiter; —kiefer m upper jaw; —kommando nt supreme command; —körper m trunk, upper part of body; —leitung f direction; (Elec) overhead cable; —licht nt skylight; —lippe f upper lip; —prima f -, -primen final year of secondary school; —schenkel m thigh; —schicht f upper classes pl; —schule f grammar school (Brit),

high school (US); —schwester f (Med) matron; —sekunda f -, -sekunden seventh year of secondary school.
Oberst ['o:bərst] m -en or -s, -en or -e colonel; o—e(r,s) a very top, topmost.
Ober- cpd: —stufe f upper school; —teil nt upper part; —tertia [-tɛrtsia] f -, -tertien fifth year of secondary school; —wasser nt: —wasser haben/bekommen be/get on top (of things); —weite f bust/chest measurement.
obgleich [ɔp'glaiç] cj although.
Obhut ['ɔphu:t] f - care, protection; in jds — sein be in sb's care.
obig ['o:biç] a above.
Objekt [ɔp'jɛkt] nt -(e)s, -e object; —iv [-'ti:f] nt -s, -e lens; o—iv a objective; —ivi'tät f objectivity.
Oblate [o'bla:tə] f -, -n (Gebäck) wafer; (Eccl) host.
obligatorisch [ɔbliga'to:rɪʃ] a compulsory, obligatory.
Oboe [o'bo:ə] f -, -n oboe.
Obrigkeit ['o:brɪçkait] f (Behörden) authorities pl, administration; (Regierung) government.
obschon [ɔp'ʃo:n] cj although.
Observatorium [ɔpzɛrva'to:rium] nt observatory.
obskur [ɔps'ku:r] a obscure; (verdächtig) dubious.
Obst [o:pst] nt -(e)s fruit; —bau m fruit-growing; —baum m fruit tree; —garten m orchard; —händler m fruiterer, fruit merchant; —kuchen m fruit tart.
obszön [ɔps'tsø:n] a obscene; O—i'tät f obscenity.
obwohl [ɔp'vo:l] cj although.

Ochse ['ɔksə] m -n, -n ox; o—n vti (col) cram, swot; —schwanzsuppe f oxtail soup; —nzunge f oxtongue.

öd(e) ['ø:d(ə)] a Land waste, barren; (fig) dull; Ö—e f -, -n desert, waste(land); (fig) tedium.

oder ['o:dər] cj or.

Ofen ['o:fən] m -s, - oven; (Heiz—) fire, heater; (Kohle—) stove; (Hoch—) furnace; (Herd) stove; —rohr nt stovepipe.

offen ['ɔfən] a open; (aufrichtig) frank; Stelle vacant; — gesagt to be honest; —bar a obvious; —baren [ɔfən'ba:rən] vt reveal, manifest; O—'barung f (Rel) revelation; —bleiben vi irreg (Fenster) stay open; (Frage, Entscheidung) remain open; —halten vt irreg keep open; O—heit f candour, frankness; —herzig a candid, frank; Kleid revealing; O—herzigkeit f frankness; —kundig a well-known; (klar) evident; —lassen vt irreg leave open; —sichtlich a evident, obvious; —siv [ɔfən'zi:f] a offensive; O—'sive f -, -n offensive; —stehen vi irreg be open; (Rechnung) be unpaid; es steht Ihnen —, es zu tun you are at liberty to do it.

öffentlich ['œfəntlɪç] a public; Ö—keit f (Leute) public; (einer Versammlung etc) public nature; in aller Ö—keit in public; an die Ö—keit dringen reach the public ear.

offerieren [ɔfe'ri:rən] vt offer.

Offerte [ɔ'fertə] f -, -n offer.

offiziell [ɔfi'tsiɛl] a official.

Offizier [ɔfi'tsi:r] m -s, -e officer; —skasino nt officers' mess.

öffnen ['œfnən] vtr open; jdm die Tür — open the door for sb.

Öffner ['œfnər] m -s, - opener.

Öffnung ['œfnʊŋ] f opening; —szeiten pl opening times pl.

oft [ɔft] ad often.

öfter ['œftər] ad more often or frequently; —s ad often, frequently.

oftmals ad often, frequently.

ohne ['o:nə] prep +acc, cj without; das ist nicht — (col) it's not bad; — weiteres without a second thought; —dies [o:nə'di:s] ad anyway; —einander [o:nə'ar'nandər] ad without each other; —gleichen [o:nə'glaɪçən] a unsurpassed, without equal; —hin [o:nə'hɪn] ad anyway, in any case.

Ohnmacht ['o:nmaxt] f faint; (fig) impotence; in — fallen faint.

ohnmächtig ['o:nmɛçtɪç] a in a faint, unconscious; (fig) weak, impotent; sie ist — she has fainted.

Ohr [o:r] nt -(e)s, -en ear; (Gehör) hearing.

Öhr [ø:r] nt -(e)s, -e eye.

Ohr- cpd: —enarzt m ear specialist; o—enbetäubend a deafening; —enschmalz nt earwax; —enschmerzen pl earache; —enschützer m -s, - earmuff; —feige f slap on the face; box on the ears; o—feigen vt slap sb's face; box sb's ears; —läppchen nt ear lobe; —ringe pl earrings pl; —wurm m earwig; (Mus) catchy tune.

okkupieren [ɔku'pi:rən] vt occupy.

ökonomisch [øko'no:mɪʃ] a economical.

Oktanzahl [ɔk'ta:ntsa:l] f (bei Benzin) octane.

Oktave [ɔk'ta:fə] f -, -n octave.

Oktober [ɔk'to:bər] *m* -·-(s), -
October.

ökumenisch [øku'me:nɪʃ] *a*
ecumenical.

Öl [ø:l] *nt* -(e)s, -e oil; —baum *m*
olive tree; ö—en *vt* oil; (*Tech*)
lubricate; —farbe *f* oil paint;
—feld *nt* oilfield; —film *m* film of
oil; —heizung *f* oil-fired central
heating; ö—ig *a* oily.

oliv [o'li:f] *a* olive-green; O—e
[o'li:və] *f* -, -n olive.

Öl- *cpd*: —meßstab *m* dipstick;
—pest *f* oil pollution; —sardine *f*
sardine; —scheich *m* oil sheik;
—standanzeiger *m* (*Aut*) oil gauge;
—ung *f* lubrication; oiling; (*Eccl*)
anointment; **die Letzte —ung**
Extreme Unction; —wechsel *m* oil
change; —zeug *nt* oilskins *pl*.

Olymp [o'lymp] *cpd*: —iade
[-ja:də] *f* Olympic Games *pl*;
—iasieger(in *f*) [-jazi:gər(ɪn)] *m*
Olympic champion; —iateil-
nehmer(in *f*) *m*, —ionike [-io'ni:kə]
m, —io'nikin *f* Olympic competitor;
o—isch *a* Olympic.

Oma ['o:ma] *f* -, -s (*col*) granny.

Omelett [ɔm(ə)'lɛt] *nt* -(e)s, -s,
Omelette *f* omlet(te).

Omen ['o:mɛn] *nt* -s, - *or* **Omina**
omen.

Omnibus ['ɔmnibʊs] *m* (omni)bus.

Onanie [ona'ni:] *f* masturbation;
o—ren *vi* masturbate.

Onkel ['ɔŋkəl] *m* -s, - uncle.

Opa ['o:pa] *m* -s, -s (*col*) grandpa.

Opal [o'pa:l] *m* -s, -e opal.

Oper ['o:pər] *f* -, -n opera; opera
house; —ation [operatsi'o:n] *f*
operation; —ationssaal *m*
operating theatre; —ette [ope'rɛtə]
f operetta; o—ieren [ope'ri:rən] *vti*
operate; —nglas *nt* opera glasses
pl; —nhaus *nt* opera house;

—nsänger(in *f*) *m* operatic singer.

Opfer ['ɔpfər] *nt* -s, - sacrifice;
(*Mensch*) victim; o—n *vt* sacrifice;
—stock *m* (*Eccl*) offertory box;
—ung *f* sacrifice.

Opium ['o:pium] *nt* -s opium.

opponieren [ɔpo'ni:rən] *vi* oppose
(*gegen jdn/etw* sb/sth).

opportun [ɔpɔr'tu:n] *a* opportune;
O—ismus ['nɪsmus] *m*
opportunism; O—ist ['nɪst] *m*
opportunist.

Opposition [ɔpozitsi'o:n] *f*
opposition; o—ell ['nɛl] *a*
opposing.

Optik ['ɔptɪk] *f* optics *sing*; —er *m*
-s, - optician.

optimal [ɔpti'ma:l] *a* optimal,
optimum.

Optimismus [ɔpti'mɪsmus] *m*
optimism.

Optimist [ɔpti'mɪst] *m* optimist;
o—isch *a* optimistic.

optisch ['ɔptɪʃ] *a* optical.

Orakel [o'ra:kəl] *nt* -s, - oracle.

Orange [o'rã:ʒə] *f* -, -n orange;
o— *a* orange; —ade [orã'ʒa:də] *f*
orangeade; —at [orã'ʒa:t] *nt* -s, -e
candied peel; —nmarmelade *f*
marmelade; —nschale orange peel.

Orchester [ɔr'kɛstər] *nt* -s, -
orchestra.

Orchidee [ɔrçi'de:ə] *f* -, -n orchid.

Orden ['ɔrdən] *m* -s, - (*Eccl*) order;
(*Mil*) decoration; —sschwester *f*
nun.

ordentlich ['ɔrdəntlɪç] *a*
(*anständig*) decent, respectable;
(*geordnet*) tidy, neat; (*col*:
annehmbar) not bad; (*col*: *tüchtig*)
real, proper; —er Professor (full)
professor; *ad* properly; O—keit *f*
respectability; tidiness, neatness.

Ordinalzahl [ɔrdi'naːltsaːl] f ordinal number.

ordinär [ɔrdi'nɛːr] a common, vulgar.

ordnen· ['ɔrdnən] vt order, put in order.

Ordner· m -s, - steward; (Comm) file.

Ordnung f order; (Ordnen) ordering; (Geordnetsein) tidiness; o—sgemäß a proper, according to the rules; o—shalber ad as a matter of form; —sliebe f tidiness, orderliness; —sstrafe f fine; o—swidrig a contrary to the rules, irregular; —szahl f ordinal number.

Organ [ɔr'gaːn] nt -s, -e organ; (Stimme) voice; —isation [-izatsi'oːn] f organisation; —isationstalent nt organizing ability; (Person) good organizer; —isator [-i'zaːtɔr] m organizer; o—isch a organic; o—isieren [-i'ziːrən] vt organize, arrange; (col: beschaffen) acquire; vr organize; —ismus ['-nɪsmʊs] m organism; —ist [-'nɪst] m organist; —verpflanzung f transplantation (of organs).

Orgasmus [ɔr'gasmʊs] m orgasm.

Orgel ['ɔrgəl] f -, -n organ; —pfeife f organ pipe; wie die —pfeifen stehen stand in order of height.

Orgie ['ɔrgiə] f orgy.

Orient ['oːriɛnt] m -s Orient, east; —ale [-'taːlə] m -n, -n Oriental; o—alisch [-'taːlɪʃ] a oriental; o—ieren [-'tiːrən] vt (örtlich) locate; (fig) inform; vr find one's way or bearings; inform oneself; —ierung [-'tiːrʊŋ] f orientation; (fig) information; —ierungssinn m sense of direction.

original [ɔrigi'naːl] a original; O— nt -s, -e original; O—fassung f

original version; O—i'tät f originality.

originell [ɔrigi'nɛl] a original.

Orkan [ɔr'kaːn] m -(e)s, -e hurricane.

Ornament [ɔrna'mɛnt] nt decoration, ornament; o—al [-'taːl] a decorative, ornamental.

Ort [ɔrt] m -(e)s, -e or ̈er place; an — und Stelle on the spot; o—en vt locate.

ortho- [ɔrto] cpd: —dox ['-dɔks] a orthodox; O—graphie [-gra'fiː] f spelling, orthography; —'graphisch a orthographic; O—päde [-'pɛːdə] m -n, -n orthopaedic ̇ specialist, orthopaedist; O—pädie [-pɛ'diː] f orthopaedics sing; —'pädisch a orthopaedic.

örtlich ['œrtlɪç] a local; Ö—keit f locality.

Ort- cpd: —sangabe f (name of the) town; o—sansässig a local; —schaft f village, small town; o—sfremd a non-local; —sfremde(r) mf stranger; —sgespräch nt local (phone)call; —sname m place-name; —snetz nt (Tel) local telephone exchange area; —ssinn m sense of direction; —szeit f local time; —ung f locating.

Öse ['øːzə] f -, -n loop, eye.

Ost- [ɔst] cpd: —block m (Pol) Eastern bloc; —en m -s east; o—entativ [ɔstenta'tiːf] a pointed, ostentatious.

Oster- ['oːstar] cpd: —ei nt Easter egg; —fest nt Easter; —glocke f daffodil; —hase m Easter bunny; —montag m Easter Monday; —n nt -s, - Easter; —sonntag m Easter Day or Sunday.

östlich ['œstlɪç] a eastern, easterly.

Ost- cpd: —see f Baltic Sea; o—wärts ad eastwards; —wind m east wind.

oszillieren [ɔstsi'li:rən] vi oscillate.

Otter ['ɔtər] m -s, - otter; f -, -n (Schlange) adder.

Ouvertüre [uver'ty:rə] f -, -n overture.

oval [o'va:l] a oval.

Ovation [ovatsi'o:n] f ovation.

Ovulation [ovulatsi'o:n] f ovulation.

Oxyd [ɔ'ksy:t] nt -(e)s, -e oxide; o—ieren [ɔksy'di:rən] vti oxidize; —ierung f oxidization.

Ozean ['o:tsea:n] m -s, -e ocean; —dampfer m (ocean-going) liner; o—isch [otse'a:mi] a oceanic.

Ozon [o'tso:n] nt -s ozone.

P

P, p [pe:] nt P, p.

Paar [pa:r] nt -(e)s, -e pair; (Ehe-) couple; ein p— a few; p—en vtr couple; Tiere mate; —lauf m pair skating; p—mal ad: ein p—mal a few times; —ung f combination; mating; p—weise ad in pairs; in couples.

Pacht [paxt] f -, -en lease; p—en vt lease.

Pächter ['pɛçtər] m -s, - leaseholder, tenant.

Pack [pak] m -(e)s, -e or ̈e bundle, pack; nt -(e)s (pej) mob, rabble.

Päckchen ['pɛkçən] nt small package; (Zigaretten) packet; (Post—) small parcel.

Pack- cpd: p—en vt pack; (fassen) grasp, seize; (col: schaffen) manage; (fig: fesseln) grip; —en m -s, - bundle; (fig: Menge) heaps of; —esel m (lit, fig) packhorse; —papier nt brown paper, wrapping paper; —ung f packet; (Pralinen—) box; (Med) compress.

Pädagog- [peda'go:g] cpd: —e m -n, -n teacher; —ik f education; p—isch a educational, pedagogical.

Paddel ['padəl] nt -s, - paddle;

—boot nt canoe; p—n vi paddle.

paffen ['pafən] vti puff.

Page ['pa:ʒə] m -n, -n page; —nkopf m pageboy.

Paillette [paj'jetə] f sequin.

Paket [pa'ke:t] nt -(e)s, -e packet; (Post—) parcel; —karte f dispatch note; —post f parcel post; —schalter m parcels counter.

Pakt [pakt] m -(e)s, -e pact.

Palast [pa'last] m -es, Paläste palace.

Palette [pa'letə] f palette; (Lade—) pallet.

Palme ['palmə] f -, -n palm (tree).

Palmsonntag m Palm Sunday.

Pampelmuse ['pampəlmu:zə] f -, -n grapefruit.

pampig ['pampɪç] a (col: frech) fresh.

panieren [pa'ni:rən] vt (Cook) coat with egg and breadcrumbs.

Paniermehl [pa'ni:rme:l] nt breadcrumbs pl.

Panik ['pa:nɪk] f panic.

panisch ['pa:nɪʃ] a panic-stricken.

Panne [panə] f -, -n (Aut etc) breakdown; (Mißgeschick) slip.

panschen ['panʃən] vi splash about; vt water down.

Pánther ['pantər] m -s, - panther.

Pantóffel [pan'tɔfəl] m -s, -n slipper; —held m (col) henpecked husband.

Pantomime [panto'mi:mə] f -, -n mime.

Panzer ['pantsər] m -s, - armour; (Platte) armour plate; (Fahrzeug) tank; —glas nt bulletproof glass; p—n vtr armour; (fig) arm o.s.; —schrank m strongbox.

Papa [pa'pa:] m -s, -s (col) dad, daddy; —gei [-'gai] m -s, -en parrot.

Papier [pa'pi:r] nt -s, -e paper; (Wert—) share; —fabrik f paper mill; —geld nt paper money; —korb m wastepaper basket; —krieg m red tape; angry correspondence; —tüte f paper bag.

Papp- [pap] cpd: —deckel m, —e f -, -n cardboard; —einband m pasteboard; —el f -, -n poplar; p—en vti (col) stick; —enstiel m (col): keinen —enstiel wert sein not be worth a thing; für einen —enstiel bekommen get for a song; p—erlapapp interj rubbish; p—ig a sticky; —maché [-ma'fe:] nt -s, -s papier-mâché.

Paprika [paprika] m -s, -s (Gewürz) paprika; (—schote) pepper.

Papst [pa:pst] m -(e)s, ᴀe pope. **päpstlich** ['pɛ:pstliç] a papal.

Parabel [pa'ra:bəl] f -, -n parable; (Math) parabola.

Parade [pa'ra:də] f (Mil) parade, review; (Sport) parry; —marsch m march-past; —schritt m goose-step.

Paradies [para'di:s] nt -es, -e paradise; p—isch a heavenly.

paradox [para'dɔks] a paradoxical; P— nt -es, -e paradox.

Paragraph [para'gra:f] m -en, -en paragraph; (Jur) section.

parallel [para'le:l] a parallel; P—e f parallel.

paramilitärisch [paramili'tɛ:rıʃ] a paramilitary.

Paranuß ['pa:ranus] f Brazil nut.

paraphieren [para'fi:rən] vt Vertrag initial.

Parasit [para'zi:t] m -en, -en (lit, fig) parasite.

parat [pa'ra:t] a ready.

Pärchen ['pɛ:rçən] nt couple.

Parfüm [par'fy:m] nt -s, -s or -e perfume; —erie [-ə'ri:] f perfumery; —flasche f scent bottle; p—ieren [-'mi:rən] vt scent, perfume.

parieren [pa'ri:rən] vt parry; vi (col) obey.

Parität [pari'tɛ:t] f parity.

Park [park] m -s, -s park; —anlage f park; (um Gebäude) grounds pl; p—en vti park; —ett [par'kɛt] nt -(e)s, -e parquet (floor); (Theat) stalls pl; —haus nt multi-storey car park; —lücke f parking space; —platz m parking place; car park, parking lot (US); —scheibe f parking disc; —uhr f parking meter; —verbot nt no parking.

Parlament [parla'mɛnt] nt parliament; —arier [-'ta:riər] m -s, - parliamentarian; p—arisch [-'ta:rıʃ] a parliamentary; —sbeschluß m vote of parliament; —smitglied nt member of parliament; —ssitzung f sitting (of parliament).

Parodie [paro'di:] f parody; p—ren vt parody.

Parole [pa'ro:lə] f -, -n password; (Wahlspruch) motto.

Partei [par'tai] f -s, -en party; —ergreifen für jdn take sb's side; —führung f party leadership; —genosse m party member; p—isch a partial, biased; p—los a neutral; —nahme f -, -n support, taking the part of; —tag m party conference.

Parterre [par'tɛr] nt -s, -s ground floor; (Theat) stalls pl.

Partie [par'ti:] f part; (Spiel) game; (Ausflug) outing; (Mann, Frau) catch; (Comm) lot; mit von der — sein join in.

Partikel [par'ti:kəl] f -, -n particle.

Partisan [parti'za:n] m -s or -en, -en partisan.

Partitur [parti'tu:r] f (Mus) score.

Partizip [parti'tsi:p] nt -s, -ien participle.

Partner(in f) ['partnər] m -s, - partner; p—schaftlich a as partners.

Party ['pa:rti] f -, -s or Parties party.

Parzelle [par'tsɛlə] f plot, allotment.

Paß [pas] m -sses, -sse pass; (Ausweis) passport.

Pass- cpd: p—abel [pa'sa:bəl] a passable, reasonable; —age [pa'sa:ʒə] f -, -n passage; —agier [pasa'ʒi:r] m -s, -e passenger; —agierdampfer m passenger steamer; —agierflugzeug nt airliner; —ant [pa'sant] m passer-by.

Paß- cpd: —amt nt passport office; —bild nt passport photograph.

passen ['pasən] vi fit; (Farbe) go (zu with); (auf Frage, Cards, Sport) pass; das paßt mir nicht that doesn't suit me; er paßt nicht zu dir he's not right for you; —d a suitable; (zusammen-) matching; (angebracht) fitting; Zeit convenient.

passier- [pa'si:r] cpd: —bar a passable; —en vt pass; (durch Sieb) strain; vi happen; P—schein m pass, permit.

Passion [pasi'o:n] f passion; p—iert [-'ni:rt] a enthusiastic, passionate; —sspiel nt Passion Play.

passiv ['pasi:f] a passive; P— nt -s, -e passive; P—a pl (Comm) liabilities pl; P—ität f passiveness.

Paste ['pastə] f -, -n paste.

Pastell [pas'tɛl] nt -(e)s, -e pastel.

Pastete [pas'te:tə] f -, -n pie.

pasteurisieren [pastøri'zi:rən] vt pasteurize.

Pastor ['pastor] m vicar; pastor, minister.

Pate ['pa:tə] m -n, -n godfather; —nkind nt godchild.

Patent [pa'tɛnt] nt -(e)s, -e patent; (Mil) commission; p— a clever; —amt nt patent office; p—ieren [-'ti:rən] vt patent; —inhaber m patentee; —schutz m patent right.

Pater ['pa:tər] m -s, - or Patres (Eccl) Father.

pathetisch [pa'te:tɪʃ] a emotional; bombastic.

Pathologe [pato'lo:gə] m -n, -n pathologist.

pathologisch a pathological.

Pathos ['pa:tɔs] nt - emotiveness, emotionalism.

Patient(in f) [patsi'ɛnt(m)] m patient.

Patin ['pa:tɪn] f godmother; —a ['pa:tina] f - patina.

Patriarch [patri'arç] m -en, -en patriarch; p—alisch [-'ça:lɪʃ] a patriarchal.

Patriot [patri'o:t] *m* **-en, -en** patriot; **p—isch** *a* patriotic; **—ismus** [-'tɪsmʊs] *m* patriotism.

Patron [pa'tro:n] *m* **-s, -e** patron; (*pej*) beggar; **—e** *f* -, **-n** cartridge; **—enhülse** *f* cartridge case; **—in** *f* patroness.

Patrouille [pa'trʊljə] *f* -, **-n** patrol.

patrouillieren [patrʊl'ji:rən] *vi* patrol.

patsch [patʃ] *interj* splash; **P—e** *f* -, **-n** (*col: Händchen*) paw; (*Fliegen—*) swat; (*Feuer—*) beater; (*Bedrängnis*) mess, jam; **—en** *vti* smack, slap; (*im Wasser*) splash; **—naß** *a* soaking wet.

patzig ['patsɪç] *a* (*col*) cheeky, saucy.

Pauke ['paʊkə] *f* -, **-n** kettledrum; **auf die —** hauen live it up; **p—n** *vti* (*Sch*) swot, cram; **—r** *m* **-s, -** (*col*) teacher.

pausbäckig ['paʊsbɛkɪç] *a* chubby-cheeked.

pauschal [paʊ'ʃa:l] *a Kosten* inclusive; *Urteil* sweeping; **P—e** *f* -, **-n**, **P—gebühr** *f* flat rate; **P—preis** *m* all-in price; **P—reise** *f* package tour; **P—summe** *f* lump sum.

Pause ['paʊzə] *f* -, **-n** break; (*Theat*) interval; (*Innehalten*) pause; (*Kopie*) tracing; **p—n** *vt* trace; **p—nlos** *a* non-stop; **—nzeichen** *nt* call sign; (*Mus*) rest.

pausieren [paʊ'zi:rən] *vi* make a break.

Pauspapier ['paʊspapi:r] *nt* tracing paper.

Pavian ['pa:via:n] *m* **-s, -e** baboon.

Pazifist [patsi'fɪst] *m* pacifist; **p—isch** *a* pacifistic.

Pech ['pɛç] *nt* **-s, -e** pitch; (*fig*) bad luck; **— haben** be unlucky; **p—schwarz** *a* pitch-black;

—strähne *m* (*col*) unlucky patch; —vogel *m* (*col*) unlucky person.

Pedal [pe'da:l] *nt* **-s, -e** pedal.

Pedant [pe'dant] *m* pedant; **—e'rie** *f* pedantry; **p—isch** *a* pedantic.

Peddigrohr ['pɛdɪçro:r] *nt* cane.

Pegel ['pe:gəl] *m* **-s, -** water gauge; **—stand** *m* water level.

peilen ['paɪlən] *vt* get a fix on.

Pein [paɪn] *f* - agony, pain; **p—igen** *vt* torture; (*plagen*) torment; **p—lich** *a* (*unangenehm*) embarrassing, awkward, painful; (*genau*) painstaking; **P—lichkeit** *f* painfulness, awkwardness; scrupulousness.

Peitsche ['paɪtʃə] *f* -, **-n** whip; **p—n** *vt* whip; (*Regen*) lash.

Pelikan ['pe:lika:n] *m* **-s, -e** pelican.

Pelle ['pɛlə] *f* -, **-n** skin; peel; **p—n** *vt* skin, peel.

Pellkartoffeln *pl* jacket potatoes *pl*.

Pelz [pɛlts] *m* **-es, -e** fur.

Pendel ['pɛndəl] *nt* **-s, -** pendulum; **—verkehr** *m* shuttle traffic; (*für Pendler*) commuter traffic.

Pendler ['pɛndlər] *m* **-s, -** commuter.

penetrant [pene'trant] *a* sharp; *Person* pushing.

Penis ['pe:nɪs] *m* -, **-se** penis.

Pension [penzi'o:n] *f* (*Geld*) pension; (*Ruhestand*) retirement; (*für Gäste*) boarding or guesthouse; **halbe/volle —** half/full board; **—är(in** *f*) [-'nɛ:r(ɪn)] *m* **-s, -e** pensioner; **—at** [-'na:t] *nt* **-(e)s, -e** boarding school; **p—ieren** [-'ni:rən] *vt* pension (off); **p—iert** *a* retired; **—ierung** *f* retirement; **—sgast** *m* boarder, paying guest.

Pensum ['pɛnzʊm] *nt* **-s, Pensen** quota; (*Sch*) curriculum.

per [pɛr] prep +acc by, per; (pro) per; (bis) by.

Perfekt ['pɛrfɛkt] nt -(e)s, -e perfect; p— [-'pɛrfɛkt] a perfect; **—ionismus** [pɛrfɛktsio'nɪsmʊs] m perfectionism.

perforieren [pɛrfo'riːrən] vt perforate.

Pergament [pɛrga'mɛnt] nt parchment; **—papier** nt greaseproof paper.

Periode [peri'oːdə] f -, -n period.

periodisch [peri'oːdɪʃ] a periodic; (dezimal) recurring.

Peripherie [perife'riː] f periphery; (um Stadt) outskirts pl; (Math) circumference.

Perle ['pɛrlə] f -, -n (lit, fig) pearl; p—n vi sparkle; (Tropfen) trickle.

Perlmutt ['pɛrlmʊt] nt -s mother-of-pearl.

perplex [pɛr'plɛks] a dumbfounded.

Persianer [pɛrzi'aːnər] m -s, - Persian lamb.

Person [pɛr'zoːn] f -, -en person; ich für meine — personally I; klein von — of small build; —al [-'naːl] nt -s personnel; (Bedienung) servants pl; —alausweis m identity card; —alien [-'naːliən] pl particulars pl; —alität f personality; —alpronomen nt personal pronoun; —enaufzug m lift, elevator (US); —enkraftwagen m private motorcar; —enkreis m group of people; —enschaden m injury to persons; —enwaage f scales pl; —enzug m stopping train; passenger train; p—ifizieren [-ifi'tsiːrən] vt personify.

persönlich [pɛr'zøːnlɪç] a personal; ad in person; personally; P—keit f personality.

Perspektive [pɛrspɛk'tiːvə] f perspective.

Perücke [pe'rykə] f -, -n wig.

pervers [pɛr'vɛrs] a perverse; P—ität f perversity.

Pessimismus [pɛsi'mɪsmʊs] m pessimism.

Pessimist [pɛsi'mɪst] m pessimist; p—isch a pessimistic.

Pest [pɛst] f -plague.

Petersilie [petɐr'ziːliə] f parsley.

Petroleum [pe'troːleum] nt -s paraffin, kerosene (US).

petzen ['pɛtsən] vi (col) tell tales.

Pfad [pfaːt] m -(e)s, -e path; **—finder** m -s, - boy scout; **—finderin** f girl guide.

Pfahl [pfaːl] m -(e)s, ⁻e post, stake; **—bau** m pile dwelling.

Pfand [pfant] nt -(e)s, ⁻er pledge, security; (Flaschen—) deposit; (im Spiel) forfeit; (fig: der Liebe etc) pledge; **—brief** m bond.

pfänden ['pfɛndən] vt seize, distrain.

Pfänderspiel nt game of forfeits.

Pfand- cpd: **—haus** nt pawnshop; **—leiher** m -s, - pawnbroker; **—schein** m pawn ticket.

Pfändung ['pfɛndʊŋ] f seizure, distraint.

Pfanne ['pfanə] f -, -n (frying) pan.

Pfannkuchen m pancake; (Berliner) doughnut.

Pfarr- ['pfar] cpd: **—ei** [-'raɪ] f parish; **—er** m -s, - priest; (evangelisch) vicar; minister; **—haus** nt vicarage; manse.

Pfau [pfau] m -(e)s, -en peacock; **—enauge** nt peacock butterfly.

Pfeffer ['pfɛfɐr] m -s, - pepper; **—korn** nt peppercorn; **—kuchen** m gingerbread; **—minz** nt -es, -e peppermint; **—mühle** f peppermill; p—n vt pepper; (col: werfen) fling; **gepfefferte Preise/Witze** steep prices/spicy jokes.

Pfeife ['pfaɪfə] f -, -n whistle; (*Tabak-, Orgel-*) pipe; **p—n** vti irreg whistle; **—r** m -s, - piper.

Pfeil [pfaɪl] m -(e)s, -e arrow.

Pfeiler ['pfaɪlər] m -s, - pillar, prop; (*Brücken—*) pier.

Pfennig ['pfɛnɪç] m -(e)s, -e pfennig (*hundredth part of a mark*).

Pferd [pfe:rt] nt -(e)s, -e horse; **—erennen** nt horse-race; **horse-racing**; **—eschwanz** m (*Frisur*) ponytail; **—estall** m stable.

Pfiff [pfɪf] m -(e)s, -e whistle; (*Kniff*) trick; **—erling** ['pfɪfərlɪŋ] m yellow chanterelle; **keinen —erling wert** not worth a thing; **p—ig** a sly, sharp.

Pfingsten ['pfɪŋstən] nt -, -n Whitsun.

Pfingstrose ['pfɪŋstro:zə] f peony.

Pfirsich ['pfɪrzɪç] m -s, -e peach.

Pflanz- ['pflants] cpd: **—e** f -, -n plant; **p—en** vt plant; **—enfett** nt vegetable fat; **—er** m -s, - planter; **—ung** f plantation.

Pflaster ['pflastər] nt -s, - plaster; (*Straße*) pavement; **p—müde** a dead on one's feet; **—n** vt pave; **—stein** m paving stone.

Pflaume ['pflaumə] f -, -n plum.

Pflege ['pfle:gə] f -, -n care; (*von Idee*) cultivation; (*Kranken—*) nursing; **in — sein** (*Kind*) be fostered out; **p—bedürftig** a needing care; **—eltern** pl foster parents pl; **—kind** nt foster child; **p—leicht** a easy-care; **—mutter** f foster mother; **p—n** vt look after; **Kranke** nurse; **Beziehungen** foster; **—r** m -s, - orderly; male nurse; **—rin** f nurse, attendant; **—vater** m foster father.

Pflicht [pflɪçt] f -, -en duty; (*Sport*) compulsory section; **p—bewußt** a conscientious; **—fach** nt (*Sch*) compulsory subject; **—gefühl** nt sense of duty; **p—gemäß** a dutiful; ad as in duty bound; **p—vergessen** a irresponsible; **—versicherung** f compulsory insurance.

Pflock [pflɔk] m -(e)s, ⁼e peg; (*für Tiere*) stake.

pflücken ['pflʏkən] vt pick; **Blumen** auch pluck.

Pflug [pflu:k] m -(e)s, ⁼e plough.

pflügen ['pfly:gən] vt plough.

Pforte ['pfɔrtə] f -, -n gate; door.

Pförtner ['pfœrtnər] m -s, - porter, doorkeeper, doorman.

Pfosten ['pfɔstən] m -s, - post.

Pfote ['pfo:tə] f -, -n paw; (*col: Schrift*) scrawl.

Pfropf [pfrɔpf] m -(e)s, -e (*Flaschen—*) stopper; (*Blut—*) clot; **p—en** vt (*stopfen*) cram; **Baum** graft; **P—en** m -s, -e see Pfropf.

pfui [pfʊɪ] interj ugh; (*na na*) tut tut.

Pfund [pfʊnt] nt -(e)s, -e pound; **p—ig** a (*col*) great; **p—weise** ad by the pound.

pfuschen ['pfʊʃən] vi (*col*) be sloppy; **jdm in etw** (*acc*) **—** interfere in sth.

Pfuscher ['pfʊʃər] m -s, - (*col*) sloppy worker; (*Kur—*) quack; **—ei** ['-'raɪ] f (*col*) sloppy work; (*Kur—*) quackery.

Pfütze ['pfʏtsə] f -, -n puddle.

Phänomen [fɛno'me:n] nt -s, -e phenomenon; **p—al** ['-'na:l] a phenomenal.

Phantasie [fanta'zi:] f imagination; **p—los** a unimaginative;

p—ren *vi* fantasize; -p—voll *a* imaginative.

phantastisch [fan'tastiʃ] *a* fantastic.

Pharisäer [fari'zɛ:ər] *m* -s, - (*lit, fig*) pharisee.

Pharmazeut(in *f*) [farma'tsɔyt(ɪn)] *m* -en, -en pharmacist.

Phase ['fa:zə] *f* -, -n phase.

Philanthrop [filan'tro:p] *m* -en, -en philanthropist; p—isch *a* philanthropic.

Philologe [filo'lo:gə] *m* -n, -n philologist.

Philologie [filolo'gi:] *f* philology.

Philosoph [filo'zo:f] *m* -en, -en philosopher; —ie [-'fi:] *f* philosophy; p—isch *a* philosophical.

Phlegma ['flɛgma] *nt* -s lethargy; p—tisch [flɛ'gma:tɪʃ] *a* lethargic.

Phonet- [fo'ne:t] *cpd*: --ik *f* phonetics *sing*; p—isch *a* phonetic.

Phosphor ['fɔsfɔr] *m* -s phosphorus; —eszieren [fɔsfɔrɛs'tsi:rən] *vt* phosphoresce.

Photo ['fo:to] *nt* -s, -s *etc see* Foto.

Phrase ['fra:zə] *f* -, -n phrase; (*pej*) hollow phrase.

Physik [fy'zi:k] *f* physics *sing*; p—alisch [-'ka:lɪʃ] *a* of physics; —er(in *f*) ['fy:zikər(ɪn)] *m* -s, - physicist.

Physiologe [fyzio'lo:gə] *m* -n, -n physiologist.

Physiologie [fyziolo'gi:] *f* physiology.

physisch ['fy:zɪʃ] *a* physical.

Pianist(in *f*) [pia'nɪst(ɪn)] *m* pianist.

picheln ['pɪçəln] *vi* (*col*) booze.

Pickel ['pɪkəl] *m* -s, - pimple; (*Werkzeug*) pickaxe; (*Berg—*) ice-axe; p—ig *a* pimply.

picken ['pɪkən] *vi* pick, peck.

Picknick ['pɪknɪk] *nt* -s, -e *or* -s picnic; — machen have a picnic.

piepen ['pi:pən], **piepsen** ['pi:psən] *vi* chirp.

piesacken ['pi:zakən] *vt* (*col*) torment.

Pietät [pie'tɛ:t] *f* piety, reverence; p—los *a* impious, irreverent.

Pigment [pɪ'gmɛnt] *nt* pigment.

Pik [pi:k] *nt* -s, -s (*Cards*) spades; einen — auf jdn haben (*col*) have it in for sb; p—ant ['pi:kant] *a* spicy, piquant; (*anzüglich*) suggestive; p—iert [pi'ki:rt] *a* offended.

Pilger ['pɪlgər] *m* -s, - pilgrim; —fahrt *f* pilgrimage.

Pille ['pɪlə] *f* -, -n pill.

Pilot [pi'lo:t] *m* -en, -en pilot.

Pilz [pɪlts] *m* -es, -e fungus; (*eßbar*) mushroom; (*giftig*) toadstool; —krankheit *f* fungal disease.

pingelig ['pɪŋəlɪç] *a* (*col*) fussy.

Pinguin ['pɪŋguˈi:n] *m* -s, -e penguin.

Pinie ['pi:niə] *f* pine.

pinkeln ['pɪŋkəln] *vi* (*col*) pee.

Pinsel ['pɪnzəl] *m* -s, - paintbrush.

Pinzette [pɪn'tsɛtə] *f* tweezers *pl*.

Pionier [pio'ni:r] *m* -s, -e pioneer; (*Mil*) sapper, engineer.

Pirat [pi'ra:t] *m* -en, -en pirate; —ensender *m* pirate radio station.

Pirsch [pɪrʃ] *f* - stalking.

Piste ['pɪstə] *f* -, -n (*Ski*) run, piste; (*Aviat*) runway.

Pistole [pɪs'to:lə] *f* -, -n pistol.

Pizza ['pɪtsa] *f* -, -s pizza.

Pkw [pe:ka:ve:] *m* -(s), -(s) *see* Personenkraftwagen.

Plackerei [plakə'raɪ] *f* drudgery.

plädieren [plɛ'di:rən] *vi* plead.

Plädoyer [plɛdoaˈjeː] nt -s, -s speech for the defence; (fig) plea.

Plage [ˈplaːgə] f -, -n plague; (Mühe) nuisance; —geist m pest, nuisance; p—n vt torment; vr toil, slave.

Plakat [plaˈkaːt] nt -(e)s, -e placard; poster.

Plan [plaːn] -(e)s, ²e plan; (Karte) map; —e f ², -n tarpaulin; p—en vt plan; Mord etc plot; —er m -s, - planner; —et [plaˈneːt] m -en -en planet; —etenbahn f orbit (of a planet); p—gemäß according to schedule or plan; (Rail) on time; p—ieren [plaˈniːrən] vt plane, level; —ierraupe f bulldozer.

Planke [ˈplaŋkə] f -, -n plank.

Plänkelei [plɛŋkəˈlaɪ] f skirmish(ing).

plänkeln [ˈplɛŋkəln] vi skirmish.

Plankton [ˈplaŋktɔn] nt -s plankton.

Plan- cpd: p—los a Vorgehen unsystematic; Umherlaufen aimless; p—mäßig a according to plan; systematic; (Rail) scheduled.

Plansch- [ˈplanʃ] cpd: —becken nt paddling pool; p—en vi splash.

Plan- cpd: —soll nt -s output target; —stelle f post.

Plantage [planˈtaːʒə] f -, -n plantation.

Plan- cpd: —ung f planning; —wagen m covered wagon; —wirtschaft f planned economy.

plappern [ˈplapərn] vi chatter.

plärren [ˈplɛrən] vi (Mensch) cry, whine; (Radio) blare.

Plasma [ˈplasma] nt -s, Plasmen plasma.

Plastik [ˈplastɪk] f sculpture; nt -s (Kunststoff) plastic; —folie f plastic film.

Plastilin [plastiˈliːn] nt -s plasticine.

plastisch [ˈplastɪʃ] a plastic; stell dir das — vor! just picture it!

Platane [plaˈtaːnə] f -, -n plane (tree).

Platin [plaˈtiːn] nt -s platinum.

Platitüde [platiˈtyːdə] f -, -n platitude.

platonisch [plaˈtoːnɪʃ] a platonic.

platsch [platʃ] interj splash; —en vi splash; —naß a drenched.

plätschern [ˈplɛtʃərn] vi babble.

platt [plat] a flat; (col: überrascht) flabbergasted; (fig: geistlos) flat, boring; —deutsch a low German; P—e f -, -n (Speisen—, Phot, Tech) plate; (Stein—) flag; (Kachel) tile; (Schall—) record. -

Plätt- [plɛt] cpd: —eisen nt iron; p—en vti iron.

Platt- cpd: —enspieler m record player; —enteller m turntable; —fuß m flat foot; (Reifen) flat tyre.

Platz [plats] m -es, ²e place; (Sitz—) seat; (Raum) space, room; (in Stadt) square; (Sport—) playing field; jdm — machen make room for sb; —angst f (Med) agoraphobia; (col) claustrophobia; —anweiser(in f) m -s, - usher(ette).

Plätzchen [ˈplɛtsçən] nt spot; (Gebäck) biscuit.

Platz- cpd: p—en vi burst; (Bombe) explode; vor Wut p—en (col) be bursting with anger; —karte f seat reservation; —mangel m lack of space; —patrone f blank cartridge; —regen m downpour; —wunde f cut.

Plauderei [plaudəˈraɪ] f chat, conversation; (Rad) talk.

plaudern [ˈplaudərn] vi chat, talk.

plausibel [plau'zi:bəl] a plausible.
plazieren [pla'tsi:rən] vt place; vr (Sport) be placed; (Tennis) be seeded.
Plebejer [ple'be:jər] m -s, - plebeian.
plebejisch [ple'be:jɪʃ] a plebeian.
pleite ['plaɪtə] a (col) broke; P— f -, -n bankruptcy; (col: Reinfall) flop; P— machen go bust.
Plenum ['ple:nʊm] nt -s plenum.
Pleuelstange ['plɔʏəlʃtaŋə] f connecting rod.
Plissee [plɪ'se:] nt -s, -s pleat.
Plombe ['plɔmbə] f -, -n lead seal; (Zahn—) filling.
plombieren [plɔm'bi:rən] vt seal; Zahn fill.
plötzlich ['plœtslɪç] a sudden; ad suddenly.
plump [plʊmp] a clumsy; Hände coarse; Körper shapeless; —sen vi (col) plump down, fall.
Plunder ['plʊndər] m -s rubbish.
plündern ['plʏndərn] vti plunder; Stadt sack.
Plünderung ['plʏndərʊŋ] f plundering, sack, pillage.
Plural ['plu:ra:l] m -s, -e plural; p—istisch a pluralistic.
Plus [plʊs] nt -, - plus; (Fin) profit; (Vorteil) advantage; p— ad plus.
Plüsch [ply:ʃ] m -(e)s, -e plush.
Plus- cpd: —pol m (Elec) positive pole; —punkt m point; (fig) point in sb's favour; —quamperfekt nt -s, -e pluperfect.
Po [po:] m -s, -s (col) bottom, bum.
Pöbel ['pø:bəl] m -s mob, rabble; —ei [-'laɪ] f vulgarity; p—haft a low, vulgar.
pochen ['pɔxən] vi knock; (Herz) pound; auf etw (acc) — (fig) insist on sth.

Pocken ['pɔkən] pl smallpox.
Podium ['po:dium] nt podium; —sdiskussion f panel discussion.
Poesie [poe'zi:] f poetry.
Poet [po'e:t] m -en, -en poet; p—isch a poetic.
Pointe [po'ɛ̃:tə] f -, -n point.
Pokal [po'ka:l] m -s, -e goblet; (Sport) cup; —spiel nt cup-tie.
Pökel- ['pø:kəl] cpd: —fleisch nt salt meat; p—n vt pickle, salt.
Pol [po:l] m -s, -e pole; p—ar [po'la:r] a polar; —arkreis m arctic circle.
Polemik [po'le:mɪk] f polemics.
polemisch a polemical.
polemisieren [polemi'zi:rən] vi polemicize.
Police [po'li:s(ə)] f -, -n insurance policy.
Polier [po'li:r] m -s, -e foreman; p—en vt polish.
Poliklinik [poli'kli:nɪk] f outpatients.
Politik [poli'ti:k] f politics sing; (eine bestimmte) policy; —er(in f) [po'li:tikər(ɪn)] m -s, - politician.
politisch [po'li:tɪʃ] a political.
politisieren [politi'zi:rən] vi talk politics; vt politicize.
Politur [poli'tu:r] f polish.
Polizei [poli'tsaɪ] f police; —beamte(r) m police officer; p—lich a police; sich p—lich melden register with the police; —revier nt police station; —spitzel m police spy, informer; —staat m police state; —streife f police patrol; —stunde f closing time; p—widrig a illegal.
Polizist [poli'tsɪst] m -en, -en policeman; —in f policewoman.
Pollen ['pɔlən] m -s, - pollen.

Polster ['pɔlstər] nt -s, - cushion;
(*Polsterung*) upholstery; (*in
Kleidung*) padding; (*fig: Geld*)
reserves pl; **—er** m -s, -
upholsterer; **—möbel** pl
upholstered furniture; **p—n** vt
upholster; pad; **—ung** f upholstery.

Polter- ['pɔltər] cpd: **—abend** m
party on eve of wedding; **p—n** vi
(*Krach machen*) crash; (*fig*)
(*schimpfen*) rant.

Polygamie [polyga'mi:] f polygamy.

Polyp [po'ly:p] m -en -en polyp;
(*pl: Med*) adenoids pl; (*col*) cop.

Pomade [po'ma:də] f pomade.

Pommes frites [pɔm'frit] pl chips
pl, French fried potatoes pl.

Pomp [pɔmp] m -(e)s pomp.

Pony ['pɔni] m -s, -s (*Frisur*)
fringe; nt -s, -s (*Pferd*) pony.

Popo [po'po:] m -s, -s bottom, bum.

populär [popu'lɛːr] a popular.

Popularität [populari'tɛːt] f
popularity.

Pore ['po:rə] f -, -n pore.

Pornographie [pɔrnogra'fi:] f
pornography.

porös [po'rø:s] a porous.

Porree ['pɔre] m -s, -s leek.

Portal [pɔr'ta:l] nt -s, -e portal.

Portemonnaie [pɔrtmɔ'ne:] nt -s,
-s purse.

Portier [pɔrti'e:] m -s, -s porter;
see Pförtner.

Portion [pɔrtsi'o:n] f portion,
helping; (*col: Anteil*) amount.

Porto ['pɔrto] nt -s, -s postage;
p—frei a post-free, (postage) prepaid.

Porträt [pɔr'trɛ:] nt -s, -s portrait;
p—ieren [pɔrtrɛ'ti:rən] vt paint,
portray.

Porzellan [pɔrtsɛ'la:n] nt -s, -e
china, porcelain; (*Geschirr*) china.

Posaune [po'zaunə] f -, **-n**
trombone.

Pose ['po:zə] f -, -n pose.

posieren [po'zi:rən] vi pose.

Position [pozitsi'o:n] f position;
—slichter pl (*Aviat*) position lights
pl.

positiv ['pozi:ti:f] a positive; **P—**
nt -s, -e (*Phot*) positive.

Positur [pozi'tu:r] f posture,
attitude.

possessiv ['pɔsesi:f] a possessive;
P—(pronomen) nt -s, -e possessive
pronoun.

possierlich [pɔ'si:rliç] a funny.

Post [pɔst] f -, -en post (office);
(*Briefe*) mail; **—amt** nt post office
—anweisung f postal order, money
order; **—bote** m postman; **—en** m
-s, - post, position; (*Comm*) item;
(*auf Liste*) entry; (*Mil*) sentry;
(*Streik—*) picket; **—fach** nt post-
office box; **—karte** f postcard;
p—lagernd ad poste restante;
—leitzahl f postal code;
—scheckkonto nt postal giro
account; **—sparkasse** f post office
savings bank; **—stempel** m postmark; **p—wendend** ad by return (of
post).

potent [po'tɛnt] a potent; (*fig*) high-
powered.

Potential [potɛntsi'a:l] nt -s, -e
potential.

potentiell [potɛntsi'el] a potential.

Potenz [po'tɛnts] f power; (*eines
Mannes*) potency.

Pracht [praxt] f - splendour,
magnificence.

prächtig ['prɛçtıç] a splendid.

Pracht- cpd: **—stück** nt showpiece; **p—voll** a splendid, magnificent.

Prädikat [prɛdi'ka:t] *nt* -(e)s, -e title; (*Gram*) predicate; (*Zensur*) distinction.

prägen ['prɛ:gən] *vt* stamp; *Münze* mint; *Ausdruck* coin; *Charakter* form.

prägnant [prɛ'gnant] *a* precise, terse.

Prägnanz [prɛ'gnants] *f* conciseness, terseness.

Prägung ['prɛgʊŋ] *f* minting; forming; (*Eigenart*) character, stamp.

prahlen ['pra:lən] *vi* boast, brag.

Prahlerei [pra:lə'rai] *f* boasting.

prahlerisch *a* boastful.

Praktik ['praktɪk] *f* practice; **p—abel** [-'kabəl] *a* practicable; **—ant(in** *f*) [-'kant(m)] *m* trainee; **—um** *nt* -s, Praktika *or* Praktiken practical training.

praktisch ['praktɪʃ] *a* practical, handy; **—er** Arzt general practitioner.

praktizieren [prakti'tsi:rən] *vti* practise.

Praline [pra'li:nə] *f* chocolate.

prall [pral] *a* firmly rounded; *Segel* taut; *Arme* plump; *Sonne* blazing; **—en** *vi* bounce, rebound; (*Sonne*) blaze.

Prämie ['prɛ:miə] *f* premium; (*Belohnung*) award, prize; **p—ren** [prɛ'mi:rən] *vt* give an award to.

Pranger ['praŋər] *m* -s, - (*Hist*) pillory; **jdn an den — stellen** (*fig*) pillory sb.

Präparat [prɛpa'ra:t] *nt* -(e)s, -e (*Biol*) preparation; (*Med*) medicine.

Präposition [prɛpozitsi'o:n] *f* preposition.

Prärie [prɛ'ri:] *f* prairie.

Präsens ['prɛ:zɛns] *nt* - present tense.

präsentieren [prɛzɛn'ti:rən] *vt* present.

Präservativ [prɛzɛrva'ti:f] *nt* -s, -e contraceptive.

Präsident(in *f*) [prɛzi'dɛnt(m)] *m* president; **—schaft** *f* presidency; **—schaftskandidat** *m* presidential candidate.

Präsidium [prɛ'zi:diʊm] *nt* presidency, chair(manship); (*Polizei—*) police headquarters *pl.*

prasseln ['prasəln] *vi* (*Feuer*) crackle; (*Hagel*) drum; (*Wörter*) rain down.

prassen ['prasən] *vi* live it up.

Präteritum [prɛ'te:ritʊm] *nt* -s, Präterita preterite.

Pratze ['pratsə] *f* -, -n paw.

Präventiv- [prɛvɛn'ti:f] *in cpds* preventive.

Praxis ['praksɪs] *f* -, Praxen practice; (*Behandlungsraum*) surgery; (*von Anwalt*) office.

Präzedenzfall [prɛtse'dɛntsfal] *m* precedent.

präzis [prɛ'tsi:s] *a* precise; **P—ion** [prɛtsizi'o:n] *f* precision.

predigen ['pre:digən] *vti* preach.

Prediger *m* -s, - preacher.

Predigt ['pre:dɪçt] *f* -, -en sermon.

Preis [prais] *m* -es, -e price; (*Sieges—*) prize; **um keinen —** not at any price; **—elbeere** *f* cranberry; **p—en** [praizən] *vt irreg* praise; **p—geben** *vt irreg* abandon; (*opfern*) sacrifice; (*zeigen*) expose; **p—gekrönt** *a* prizewinning; **—gericht** *nt* jury; **p—günstig** *a* inexpensive; **—lage** *f* price range; **p—lich** *a* price, in price; **—sturz** *m* slump; **—träger(in** *f*) *m* prizewinner; **p—wert** *a* inexpensive.

prekär [prɛ'kɛ:r] a precarious.

Prell- [prɛl] cpd: **—bock** m buffers pl; **p—en** vt bump; (fig) cheat, swindle; **—ung** f bruise.

Premiere [prəmi'ɛ:rə] f -, -n premiere.

Premierminister [prəmi'e:-minɪstər] m prime minister, premier.

Presse [prɛsə] f -, -n press; **—freiheit** f freedom of the press; **—meldung** f press report; **p—n** vt press.

pressieren [prɛ'si:rən] vi (be in a) hurry.

Preß- [prɛs] cpd: **—luft** f compressed air; **—luftbohrer** . m pneumatic drill.

Prestige [prɛs'ti:ʒə] nt -s prestige.

prickeln [prɪkəln] vti tingle, tickle.

Priester [pri:stər] m -s, - priest.

prima [pri:ma] a first-class, excellent; **P—** f -, Primen sixth form, top class.

primär [pri'mɛ:r] a primary.

Primel [pri:məl] f -, -n primrose.

primitiv [primi'ti:f] a primitive.

Prinz [prɪnts] m -en, -en prince; **—essin** [prɪn'tsɛsɪn] f princess.

Prinzip [prɪn'tsi:p] nt -s, -ien principle; **p—iell** [-i'ɛl] a,ad on principle; **p—ienlos** a unprincipled.

Priorität [priori'tɛ:t] f priority.

Prise [pri:zə] f -, -n pinch.

Prisma [prɪsma] nt -s, Prismen prism.

privat [pri'va:t] a privat; **P—** in cpds private.

pro [pro:] prep +acc per; **P—** nt - pro.

Probe [pro:bə] f -, -n test; (Teststück) sample; (Theat) rehearsal; **jdn auf die — stellen** put sb to the test; **—exemplar** nt specimen copy; **—fahrt** f test drive; **p—n** vt try; (Theat) rehearse; **p—weise** ad on approval; **p—zeit** f probation period.

probieren [pro'bi:rən] vti try; Wein, Speise taste, sample.

Problem [pro'ble:m] nt -s, .-e problem; **—atik** [-'ma:tɪk] f problem; **p—atisch** [-'ma:tɪʃ] a problematic; **p—los** a problem-free.

Produkt [pro'dʊkt] nt -(e)s, -e product; (Agr) produce no pl; **—ion** [produkti'o:n] f production; output; **p—iv** [-'ti:f] a productive; **—ivität** f productivity.

Produzent [produ'tsɛnt] m manufacturer; (Film) producer.

produzieren [produ'tsi:rən] vt produce.

Professor [pro'fɛsor] m professor.

Professur [profɛ'su:r] f chair.

Profil [pro'fi:l] nt -s, -e profile; (fig) image; **p—ieren** [profi'li:rən] vr create an image for o.s.

Profit [pro'fi:t] m -(e)s, -e profit; **p—ieren** [profi'ti:rən] vi profit (von from).

Prognose [pro'gno:zə] f -, -n prediction, prognosis.

Programm [pro'gram] nt -s, -e programme; **p—(mäßig** a according to plan; **p—ieren** [-'mi:rən] vt programme; **—ierer(in** f) m -s, - programmer.

progressiv [progrɛ'si:f] a progressive.

Projekt [pro'jɛkt] nt -(e)s, -e project; **—or** [pro'jɛktor] m projector.

projizieren [proji'tsi:rən] vt project.

proklamieren [prokla'mi:rən] vt proclaim.

Prolet [pro'le:t] m -en, -en prole, pleb; **—ariat** [-ari'a:t] nt -(e)s, -e proletariat; **—arier** [-'tɑːriər] *m* -s, - proletarian.

Prolog [pro'loːk] *m* -(e)s, -e prologue.

Promenade [promə'naːdə] *f* -, -n promenade.

Promille [pro'mɪlə] *nt* -(s), - alcohol level.

prominent [promi'nɛnt] *a* prominent.

Prominenz [promi'nɛnts] *f* VIPs *pl*.

Promotion [promotsi'oːn] *f* - · doctorate, Ph.D.

promovieren [promo'viːrən] *vi* do a doctorate *or* Ph.D.

prompt [prɔmpt] *a* prompt.

Pronomen [pro'noːmən] *nt* -s, - pronoun.

Propaganda [propa'ganda] *f* - propaganda.

Propeller [pro'pɛlər] *m* -s, - propeller.

Prophet [pro'feːt] *m* -en, -en prophet; **—in** *f* prophetess.

prophezeien [profe'tsaɪən] *vt* prophesy.

Prophezeiung *f* prophecy.

Proportion [proportsi'oːn] *f* proportion; **p—al** [-'naːl] *a* proportional.

Prosa ['proːza] *f* - prose; **p—isch** [pro'zaːɪʃ] *a* prosaic.

prosit ['proːzɪt] *interj* cheers.

Prospekt [pro'spɛkt] *m* -(e)s, -e leaflet, brochure.

prost [proːst] *interj* cheers.

Prostituierte [prostitu'iːrtə] *f* -n, -n prostitute.

Prostitution [prostitutsi'oːn] *f* prostitution.

Protest [pro'tɛst] *m* -(e)s, -e protest; **—ant(in** *f)* [protɛs'tant] *m* Protestant; **p—antisch** [protɛs'tantɪʃ] *a* Protestant; **p—ieren** [protɛs'tiːrən] *vi* protest;

—kundgebung *f* (protest) rally.

Prothese [pro'teːzə] *f* -, -n artificial limb; *(Zahn—)* dentures *pl*.

Protokoll [proto'kɔl] *nt* -s, -e register; *(von Sitzung)* minutes *pl*; *(diplomatisch)* protocol; *(Polizei—)* statement; **p—ieren** [-'liːrən] *vt* take down in the minutes.

Proton ['proːtɔn] *nt* -s, -en proton.

Protz ['prɔts] *m* -en, -e(n) swank; **p—en** *vi* show off; **p—ig** *a* ostentatious.

Proviant [provi'ant] *m* -s, -e provisions *pl*, supplies *pl*.

Provinz [pro'vɪnts] *f* -, -en province; **p—iell** *a* provincial.

Provision [provizi'oːn] *f* *(Comm)* commission.

provisorisch [provi'zoːrɪʃ] *a* provisional.

Provokation [provokatsi'oːn] *f* provocation.

provozieren [provo'tsiːrən] *vt* · provoke.

Prozedur [protse'duːr] *f* procedure; *(pej)* carry-on.

Prozent [pro'tsɛnt] *nt* -(e)s, -e per cent, percentage; **—rechnung** *f* percentage calculation; **—satz** *m* percentage; **p—ual** [-u'aːl] *a* percentage; as a percentage.

Prozeß [pro'tsɛs] *m* -sses, -sse trial, case; **—kosten** *pl* (legal) costs *pl*.

prozessieren [protse'siːrən] *vi* bring an action, go to law *(mit* against).

Prozession [protsesi'oːn] *f* · procession.

prüde ['pryːdə] *a* prudish; **P—rie** [-'riː] *f* prudery.

Prüf- ['pryːf] *cpd*: **.p—en** *vt* examine, test; *(nach—)* check;

—er *m* -s, - examiner; —ling *m* examinee; —stein *m* touchstone; —ung *f* examination; checking; —ungsausschuß *m*, —ungskommission *f* examining board.

Prügel ['pryːgəl] *m* -s, - cudgel; *pl* beating; —ei [-'lai] *f* fight; —knabe *m* scapegoat; p—n *vt* beat; *vr* fight; —strafe *f* corporal punishment.

Prunk [prʊŋk] *m* -(e)s pomp, show; p—voll *a* splendid, magnificent.

Psalm [psalm] *m* -s, -en psalm.

pseudo- [psɔydo] *in cpds* pseudo.

Psych— ['psyç] *cpd:* —iater [-i'aːtər] *m* -s, - psychiatrist; p—isch *a* psychological; —oanalyse [-o'analyːzə] *f* psychoanalysis; —ologe [-o'loːgə] *m* -n, -n psychologist; —ologie *f* psychology; p—ologisch *a* psychological.

Pubertät [pubɛr'tɛːt] *f* puberty.

Publikum ['puːblikʊm] *nt* -s audience; (*Sport*) crowd.

publizieren [publi'tsiːrən] *vt* publish, publicize.

Pudding ['pʊdɪŋ] *m* -s, -e *or* -s blancmange.

Pudel ['puːdəl] *m* -s poodle.

Puder ['puːdər] *m* -s, - powder; —dose *f* powder compact; p—n *vt* powder; —zucker *m* icing sugar.

Puff [pʊf] *m* -s, -e (*Wäsche—*) linen basket; (*Sitz—*) pouf; *pl* -e (*col: Stoß*) push; *pl* -s (*col: Bordell*) brothel; —er *m* -s, - buffer; —erstaat *m* buffer state.

Pulli ['pʊli] *m* -s, -s (*col*), **Pullover** [pʊ'loːvər] *m* -s, - pullover, jumper.

Puls [pʊls] *m* -es, -e pulse; —ader *f* artery; p—ieren [pʊl'ziːrən] *vi* throb, pulsate.

Pult [pʊlt] *nt* -(e)s, -e desk.

Pulver ['pʊlfər] *nt* -s, - powder; p—ig *a* powdery; p—isieren [pʊlvɛri'ziːrən] *vt* pulverize; —schnee *m* powdery snow.

pummelig ['pʊməlɪç] *a* chubby.

Pumpe ['pʊmpə] *f* -, -n pump; p—n *vt* pump; (*col*) lend; borrow.

Punkt [pʊŋkt] *m* -(e)s, -e point; (*bei Muster*) dot; (*Satzzeichen*) full stop; p—ieren [-'tiːrən] *vt* dot; (*Med*) aspirate.

pünktlich ['pʏŋktlɪç] *a* punctual; P—keit *f* punctuality.

Punkt— *cpd:* —sieg *m* victory on points; —zahl *f* score.

Punsch [pʊnʃ] *m* -(e)s, -e punch.

Pupille [pu'pilə] *f* -, -n pupil.

Puppe ['pʊpə] *f* -, -n doll; (*Marionette*) puppet; (*Insekten—*) pupa, chrysalis; —nspieler *m* puppeteer; —nstube *f* doll's house.

pur [puːr] *a* pure; (*völlig*) sheer; Whisky neat.

Püree [py're] *nt* -s, -s mashed potatoes *pl*.

Purzel— ['pʊrtsəl] *cpd:* —baum *m* somersault; p—n *vi* tumble.

Puste ['puːstə] *f* - (*col*) puff; (*fig*) steam; —l ['pʊstəl] *f* -, -n pustule; p—n *vi* puff, blow.

Pute ['puːtə] *f* -, -n turkey-hen; —r *m* -s, - turkey-cock.

Putsch [pʊtʃ] *m* -(e)s, -e revolt, putsch; p—en *vi* revolt; —ist [pu'tʃist] *m* rebel.

Putz [pʊts] *m* -es (*Mörtel*) plaster, roughcast; p—en *vt* clean; Nase wipe, blow; *vr* clean oneself; dress oneself up; —frau *f* charwoman; p—ig *a* quaint, funny; —lappen *m* cloth; —tag *m* cleaning day; —zeug *nt* cleaning things *pl*.

Puzzle ['pasəl] *nt* -s, -s jigsaw.
Pyjama [pi'dʒa:ma] *m* -s, -s
pyjamas *pl*.

Pyramide [pyra'mi:də] *f* -, -n
pyramid.

Q

Q, q [ku:] *nt* Q, q.
quabb(e)lig ['kvab(ə)lıç] a wobbly;
Frosch slimy.
Quacksalber ['kvakzalbər] *m* -s,-
quack (doctor).
Quader ['kva:dər] *m* -s, - square
stone; *(Math)* cuboid.
Quadrat [kva'dra:t] *nt* -(e)s, -e
square; **q—isch** a square; **—meter**
m square metre.
quadrieren [kva'dri:rən] *vt* square.
quaken ['kva:kən] *vi* croak; *(Ente)*
quack.
quäken ['kvɛ:kən] *vi* screech; **—d**
a screeching.
Qual [kva:l] *f* -, -en pain, agony;
(seelisch) anguish.
Quäl- [kvɛ:l] *cpd*: **q—en** *vt*
torment; *vr* struggle; *(geistig)*
torment oneself; **—erei** [-ə'raı] *f* torture, torment; **—geist** *m* pest.
qualifizieren [kvalifi'tsi:rən] *vtr*
qualify; *(einstufen)* label.
Qualität [kvali'tɛ:t] *f* quality;
—sware *f* article of high quality.
Qualle ['kvalə] *f* -, -n jellyfish.
Qualm [kvalm] *m* -(e)s thick
smoke; **q—en** *vti* smoke.
qualvoll ['kva:lfɔl] a, excruciating,
painful, agonizing.
Quant- ['kvant] *cpd*: **—entheorie** *f*
quantum theory; **—ität** [-i'tɛ:t] *f*
quantity; **q—itativ** [-ita'ti:f] a
quantitative; **—um** *nt* -s, Quanten
quantity, amount.
Quarantäne [karan'tɛ:nə] *f* -, -n

quarantine.
Quark [kvark] *m* -s curd cheese;
(col) rubbish.
Quarta ['kvarta] *f* -, **Quarten** third
year of secondary school; **—l**
[kvar'ta:l] *nt* -s, -e quarter (year).
Quartier [kvar'ti:r] *nt* -s, -e
accommodation; *(Mil)* quarters *pl*;
(Stadt—) district.
Quarz [kva:rts] *m* -es, -e quartz.
quasseln ['kvasəln] *vi (col)* natter.
Quatsch [kvatʃ] *m* -es rubbish;
q—en *vi* chat, natter.
Quecksilber ['kvɛkzılbər] *nt*
mercury.
Quelle ['kvɛlə] *f* -, -n spring; *(eines
Flusses)* source; **q—n** *vi (hervor—)*
pour or gush forth; *(schwellen)*
swell.
quengel- ['kvɛŋəl] *cpd*: **Q—ei** [-'laı]
f (col) whining; **-ig** a *(col)*
whining; **—n** *vi (col)* whine.
quer [kve:r] *ad* crossways,
diagonally; *(rechtwinklig)* at right
angles; — **auf dem Bett** across the
bed; **Q—balken** *m* crossbeam;
—feldein *ad* across country;

Q—flöte *f* flute; **Q—kopf** *m*
awkward customer; **Q—schiff** *nt*
transept; **Q—schnitt** *m* cross-
section; **—schnittsgelähmt** a
paralysed below the waist;
Q—straße *f* intersecting road;
Q—treiber *m* -s, - obstructionist;
Q—verbindung *f* connection, link; •

quetschen ['kvɛtʃən] vt squash, crush; (Med) bruise.
Quetschung f bruise, contusion.
quieken ['kvi:kən] vi squeak.
quietschen ['kvi:tʃən] vi squeak.
Quint- ['kvɪnt] cpd: **—a** f -, **-en** second form in secondary school; **—essenz** [-'ɛsɛnts] f quintessence; **—ett** [-'tɛt] nt -(e)s, -e quintet.

Quirl [kvɪrl] m -(e)s, -e whisk.
quitt [kvɪt] a quits, even; **Q—e** f -, -n quince; **quittgelb** a sickly yellow; **—ieren** [-'ti:rən] vt give a receipt for; Dienst leave; **Q—ung** f receipt.
Quiz [kvɪs] nt -, - quiz.
Quote ['kvo:tə] f -, -n number, rate.

R

R, r [ɛr] nt R, r.
Rabatt [ra'bat] m -(e)s, -e discount; **—e** f -, -n flowerbed, border; **—marke** f trading stamp.
Rabe ['ra:bə] m -n, -n raven; **—nmutter** f bad mother.
rabiat [rabi'a:t] a furious.
Rache [raxə] f - revenge, vengeance; **—n** m -s, - throat.
rächen ['rɛçən] vt avenge, revenge; vr take (one's) revenge; das wird sich — you'll pay for that.
Rach- [rax] cpd: **—itis** [ra'xi:tɪs] f rickets sing; **—sucht** f vindictiveness; **r—süchtig** a vindictive.
Racker ['rakər] m -s, - rascal, scamp.
Rad [ra:t] nt -(e)s, ⁻er wheel; (Fahr—) bike; **—ar** [ra'da:r] m or nt -s radar; **—arkontrolle** f radar-controlled speed trap; **—au** [ra'dau] m -s (col) row; **—dampfer** m paddle steamer; **r—ebrechen** vt insep: deutsch etc **r—ebrechen** speak broken German etc; **r—eln** vi, **r—fahren** vi irreg cycle; **—fahrer(in** f) m cyclist; **—fahrweg** m cycle track or path.
Radier- [ra'di:r] cpd: **r—en** vt rub out, erase; (Art) etch; **—gummi** m rubber, eraser; **—ung** f etching.

Radieschen [ra'di:sçən] nt radish.
radikal [radi'ka:l] a, **R—e(r)** mf radical.
Radio ['ra:dio] nt -s, -s radio, wireless; **r—aktiv** a radioactive; **—aktivität** f radioactivity; **—apparat** m radio, wireless set.
Radium ['ra:diʊm] nt -s radium.
Radius ['ra:diʊs] m -, **Radien** radius.
Rad- cpd: **—kappe** f (Aut) hub cap; **—ler(in** f) m -s, - cyclist; **—rennbahn** f cycling (track); **—rennen** nt cycle race; cycle racing; **—sport** m cycling.
raff- [raf] cpd: **r—en** vt snatch, pick up; Stoff gather (up); Geld pile up, rake in; **R—inade** [-i'na:də] f refined sugar; **r—inieren** [-i'ni:rən] vt refine; **r—iniert** a crafty, cunning; Zucker refined.
ragen ['ra:gən] vi tower, rise.
Rahm [ra:m] m -s cream; **—en** m -s, - frame(work); im **—en** des Möglichen within the bounds of possibility; **r—en** vt frame; **r—ig** a creamy.
Rakete [ra'ke:tə] f -, -n rocket; **ferngelenkte —** guided missile.

rammen ['ramən] *vt* ram.

Rampe ['rampə] *f* -, -n ramp; —nlicht *vt* (Theat) footlights *pl*.

ramponieren [rampo'ni:rən] *vt* (col) damage.

Ramsch [ramʃ] *m* -(e)s, -e junk.

ran [ran] *ad* (col) = **heran**.

Rand [rant] *m* -(e)s, ⁼er edge; (von Brille, Tasse etc) rim; (Hut—) brim; (auf Papier) margin; (Schmutz—, unter Augen) ring; (fig) verge, brink; außer — und Band wild; am —e bemerkt mentioned in passing; **r**—**alieren** [randa'li:rən] *vi* (go on the) rampage; —**bemerkung** *f* marginal note; (fig) odd comment; —**erscheinung** *f* unimportant side effect, marginal phenomenon.

Rang [raŋ] *m* -(e)s, ⁼e rank; (Stand) standing; (Wert) quality; (Theat) circle; —**abzeichen** *nt* badge of rank; —**älteste(r)** *m* senior officer.

Rangier- [rãʒi:r] *cpd*: —**bahnhof** *m* marshalling yard; **r**—**en** *vt* (Rail) shunt, switch (US); *vi* rank, be classed; —**gleis** *nt* siding.

Rang- *cpd*: —**ordnung** *f* hierarchy; (Mil) rank; —**unterschied** *m* social distinction; (Mil) difference in rank.

Ranke ['raŋkə] *f* -, -n tendril, shoot.

Ränke ['rɛŋkə] *pl* intrigues *pl*; —**schmied** *m* intriguer; **r**—**voll** *a* scheming.

Ranzen ['rantsən] *m* -s, - satchel; (col: Bauch) gut, belly.

ranzig ['rantsiç] *a* rancid.

Rappe ['rapə] *m* -n, -n black horse.

Raps [raps] *m* -es, -e (Bot) rape.

rar [ra:r] *a* rare; sich — machen (col) keep oneself to oneself; **R**—**i'tät** *f* rarity; (Sammelobjekt) curio.

rasant [ra'zant] *a* quick, rapid.

rasch [raʃ] *a* quick; **r**—**eln** *vi* rustle.

Rasen ['ra:zən] *m* -s, - lawn; grass; **r**— *vi* rave; (schnell) race; **r**—**d** *a* furious; **r**—**de** Kopfschmerzen a splitting headache; —**mäher** *m* -s, -, —**mähmaschine** *f* lawnmower; —**platz** *m* lawn.

Raserei [ra:zə'raɪ] *f* raving, ranting; (Schnelle) reckless speeding.

Rasier- [ra'zi:r] *cpd*: —**apparat** *m* shaver; —**creme** *f* shaving cream; **r**—**en** *vtr* shave; —**klinge** *f* razor blade; —**messer** *nt* razor; —**pinsel** *m* shaving brush; —**seife** *f* shaving soap or stick; —**wasser** *nt* shaving lotion.

Rasse ['rasə] *f* -, -n race; (Tier—) breed; —**hund** *m* thoroughbred dog; —**l** *f* -, -n rattle; **r**—**ln** *vi* rattle, clatter; —**nhaß** *m* race or racial hatred; —**ntrennung** *f* racial segregation.

Rast [rast] *f* -, -en rest; **r**—**en** *vi* rest, —**haus** *nt* (Aut) service station; **r**—**los** *a* tireless; (unruhig) restless; —**platz** *m* (Aut) layby.

Rasur [ra'zu:r] *f* shaving; (Radieren) erasure.

Rat [ra:t] *m* -(e)s, —**schläge** (piece of) advice; jdn zu —e ziehen consult sb; keinen — wissen not know what to do; — **e** *f* -, -n instalment; **r**—**en** *vti irreg* guess; (empfehlen) advise (jdm sb); **r**—**enweise** *ad* by instalments; —**enzahlung** *f* hire purchase; —**geber** *m* -s, - adviser; —**haus** *nt* town hall.

ratifizier- [ratifi'tsi:r] *cpd*: —**en** *vt* ratify; **R**—**ung** *f* ratification.

Ration [ratsi'o:n] *f* ration; **r**—**al** ['na:l] *a* rational; **r**—**ali'sieren** *vt*

rationalize; r—ell ['-nɛl] a efficient; r—ieren [-'ni:rən] vt ration.
Rat- cpd: r—los a at a loss, helpless; —losigkeit f helplessness; r—sam a advisable; —schlag m (piece of) advice.

Rätsel ['rɛ:tsəl] nt -s, - puzzle; (Wort—) riddle; r—haft a mysterious; es ist mir r—haft it's a mystery to me.

Rats- cpd: —herr m councillor; —keller m town-hall restaurant.

Ratte ['ratə] f -, -n rat; —nfänger m -s, - ratcatcher.

rattern ['ratərn] vi rattle, clatter.

Raub [raup] m -(e)s robbery; (Beute) loot, booty; —bau m ruthless exploitation; r—en [raubən] vt rob; .Mensch kidnap, abduct.

Räuber ['rɔybər] m -s, - robber; r—isch a thieving.

Raub- cpd: r—gierig a rapacious; —mord m robbery with murder; —tier nt predator; —überfall m robbery with violence; —vogel m bird of prey.

Rauch [raux] m -(e)s smoke; r—en vti smoke; —er m -s, - smoker; —erabteil nt (Rail) smoker.

räuchern ['rɔyçərn] vt smoke, cure.

Rauch- cpd: —fahne f smoke trail; —fleisch nt smoked meat; r—ig a smoky.

räudig ['rɔydɪç] a mangy.

rauf [rauf] ad (col) = herauf;
R—bold m -(e)s, -e rowdy, hooligan; —en vt Haare pull out; vir fight; R—e'rei f brawl, fight; —lustig a spoiling for a fight, rowdy.

rauh [rau] a rough, coarse; Wetter harsh; —haarig a wire-haired; R—reif m hoarfrost.

Raum [raum] m -(e)s, Räume space; (Zimmer, Platz) room; (Gebiet) area; —bild nt 3D picture.

räumen ['rɔymən] vt clear; Wohnung, Platz vacate; (weg-bringen) shift, move; (in Schrank etc) put away.

Raum- cpd: —fahrt f space travel; —inhalt m cubic capacity, volume.

räumlich ['rɔymlɪç] a spatial; R—keiten pl premises pl.

Raum- cpd: —mangel m lack of space; —meter m cubic metre; —pflegerin f cleaner; —schiff nt spaceship; —schiffahrt f space travel; r—sparend a space-saving.

Räumung ['rɔymʊŋ] f vacating, evacuation; clearing (away); —sverkauf m clearance sale.

raunen ['raunən] vti whisper mysteriously.

Raupe ['raupə] f -, -n caterpillar; (—nkette) (caterpillar) track; —nschlepper m caterpillar tractor.

raus [raus] ad (col) = heraus, hinaus.

Rausch [rauʃ] m -(e)s, Räusche intoxication; r—en vi (Wasser) rush; (Baum) rustle; (Radio etc) hiss; (Mensch) sweep, sail; r—end a Beifall thunderous; Fest sumptuous; —gift nt drug; —giftsüchtige(r) mf drug addict.

räuspern ['rɔyspərn] vr clear one's throat.

Raute ['rautə] f -, -n diamond; (Math) rhombus; r—nförmig a rhombic.

Razzia ['ratsia] f -, Razzien raid.

Reagenzglas [rea'gɛntsgla:s] nt test tube.

reagieren [rea'gi:rən] vi react (auf +acc to).

Reakt- cpd: —ion [reaktsi'o:n] f reaction; r—io'när a reactionary;

—ionsgeschwindigkeit f speed of reaction; —or [re'aktɔr] m reactor.

real [re'aːl] a real, material; **R—ismus** [-'lismʊs] m realism; **R—ist** [-'lɪst] m realist; **—istisch** a realistic.

Rebe ['reːbə] f -, -n vine.

Rebell [re'bɛl] m -en, -en rebel; **—i'on** f rebellion; **r—isch** a rebellious.

Reb- cpd: **—ensaft** m grape juice; **—huhn** ['reːphuːn] nt partridge; **—stock** m vine.

Rechen ['rɛçən] m -s, - rake; **r— vti** rake; **—aufgabe** f sum, mathematical problem; **—fehler** m miscalculation; **—maschine** f calculating machine; **—schaft** f account; **—schaftsbericht** m report; **—schieber** m slide rule.

Rech- ['rɛç] cpd: **r—nen** vti calculate; **jdn/etw —nen zu** or **unter** (+acc) count sb/sth among; **r—nen mit** reckon with; **r—nen auf** (+acc) count on; **—ner** m -s, - calculator; **—nung** f calculation(s); (Comm) bill, check (US); **jdm/etw —nung tragen** take sb/sth into account; **—nungsbuch** nt account book; **—nungsjahr** nt financial year; **—nungsprüfer** m auditor; **—nungsprüfung** f audit(ing).

recht [rɛçt] a, ad right; (vor Adjektiv) really, quite; **das ist mir —** that suits me; **jetzt erst —** now more than ever; **— haben** be right; **jdm — geben** agree with sb; **R— nt** -(e)s, -e right; (Jur) law; **R— sprechen** administer justice; **mit R—** rightly, justly; **von R—s wegen** by rights; **R—e** f -n, -n right (hand); (Pol) Right; **—e(r,s)** a right; (Pol) right-wing; **R—e(r)** mf right person; **R—e(s)** nt right thing; **etwas/nichts R—es**

something/nothing proper; **R—eck** nt -s, -e rectangle; **—eckig** a rectangular; **—fertigen** vtr insep justify (o.s.); **R—fertigung** f justification; **—haberisch** a dogmatic; **—lich** a, **—mäßig** a legal, lawful.

rechts [rɛçts] ad on/to the right; **R—anwalt** m, **R—anwältin** f lawyer, barrister; **R—'außen** m -, - (Sport) outside right; **R—beistand** m legal adviser.

Recht- cpd: **r—schaffen** a upright; **—schreibung** f spelling.

Rechts- cpd: **—drehung** f clockwise rotation; **—fall** m (law) case; **—frage** f legal question; **—händer** m -s, - right-handed person; **r—kräftig** a valid, legal; **—kurve** f right-hand bend; **—pflege** f administration of justice; **r—radikal** a (Pol) extreme right-wing; **—spruch** m verdict; **—verkehr** m driving on the right; **r—widrig** a illegal; **—wissenschaft** f jurisprudence.

recht- cpd: **—winklig** a right-angled; **—zeitig** a timely; ad in time.

Reck [rɛk] nt -(e)s, -e horizontal bar; **r—en** vtr stretch.

Redak- cpd: **—teur** [redak'tøːr] m editor; **—tion** [redaktsi'oːn] f editing; (Leute) editorial staff; (Büro) editorial office(s).

Rede ['reːdə] f -, -n speech; (Gespräch) talk; **jdn zur — stellen** take sb to task; **—freiheit** f freedom of speech; **r—gewandt** a eloquent; **r—n** vi talk, speak; vt say; **Unsinn etc** talk; **—n** nt -s talking, speech; **—nsart** f set phrase; **—wendung** f expression, idiom.

red- cpd: **—lich** ['re:tlıç] a honest;
R—lichkeit f honesty; **R—ner** m -s,
- speaker, orator; **—selig**
['re:tze:lıç] a talkative, loquacious;
R—seligkeit f talkativeness.

reduzieren [redu'tsi:rən] vt reduce.

Reede ['re:də] f -, **-n** protected
anchorage; **—r** m -s, **-** shipowner;
—'rei f shipping line or firm.

reell [re'ɛl] a fair, honest; (Math)
real.

Refer- cpd: **—at** [refe'ra:t] nt **-(e)s**,
-e report; (Vortrag) paper;
(Gebiet) section; **—ent** [refe'rɛnt]
m speaker; (Berichterstatter)
reporter; (Sachbearbeiter) expert;
—enz [refe'rɛnts] f reference;
r—ieren [refe'ri:rən] vi: **r—ieren
über** (+acc) speak or talk on.

reflektieren [reflɛk'ti:rən] vti
reflect; **— auf** (+acc) be interested
in.

Reflex [re'flɛks] m **-es**, **-e** reflex;
—bewegung f reflex action; **r—iv**
[-'ksi:f] a (Gram) reflexive.

Reform [re'fɔrm] f -, **-en** reform;
—ati'on f reformation; **- —ator**
[-'ma:tɔr] m reformer; **r—a'torisch**
a reformatory, reforming; **—haus**
nt health food shop; **r—ieren**
[-'mi:rən] vt reform.

Refrain [rə'frɛ:] m **-s**, **-s** refrain,
chorus.

Regal [re'ga:l] nt **-s**, **-e**
(book)shelves pl, bookcase; stand,
rack.

rege ['re:gə] a lively, active;
Geschäft brisk.

Regel ['re:gəl] f -, **-n** rule; (Med)
period; **r—los** a irregular,
unsystematic; **r—mäßig** a regular;
—mäßigkeit f regularity; **r—n** vt
regulate, control; Angelegenheit
settle; vr: sich von selbst **r—n** take
care of itself; **r—recht** a regular,

proper, thorough; **—ung** f
regulation; settlement; **r—widrig** a
irregular, against the rules.

regen ['re:gən] vtr move, stir; **R—**
m **-s**, **-** rain; **R—bogen** m rainbow;
R—bogenhaut f (Anat) iris;
R—guß m downpour; **R—mantel**
m raincoat, mac(kintosh);
R—menge f rainfall; **R—schauer** m
shower (of rain); **R—schirm** m
umbrella.

Regent [re'gɛnt] m regent;
—schaft f regency.

Regen- cpd: **—tag** m rainy day;
—wurm m earthworm; **—zeit** f
rainy season, rains pl.

Regie [re'ʒi:] f (Film etc) direction;
(Theat) production; **r—ren**
[re'gi:rən] vti govern, rule; **—rung**
f government; (Monarchie) reign;
—rungswechsel m change of
government; **—rungszeit** f period
in government; (von König) reign.

Regiment [regi'mɛnt] nt **-s**, **-er**
regiment.

Region [regi'o:n] f region.

Regisseur [reʒı'sø:r] m director;
(Theat) (stage) producer.

Register [re'gıstər] nt **-s**, **-**
register; (in Buch) table of
contents, index.

Registratur [regıstra'tu:r] f
registry, record office.

registrieren [regıs'tri:rən] vt
register.

reg- ['re:g] cpd: **R—ler** m **-s**, **-**
regulator, governor; **—los**
['re:klo:s] a motionless; **—nen** vi
impers rain; **—nerisch** a rainy;
—sam ['re:kza:m] a active.

regulär [regu'lɛ:r] a regular.

regulieren [regu'li:rən] vt regulate;
(Comm) settle.

Regung ['re:gʊŋ] f motion;

(Gefühl) feeling, impulse; r—slos a motionless.

Reh [re:] nt -(e)s, -e deer, roe; —bock m roebuck; —kalb nt, —kitz. nt fawn.

Reib- ['raɪb] cpd: —e f-, -n, —eisen nt grater; r—en vt irreg rub; *(Cook)* grate; —e'rei f friction no pl; —fläche f rough surface; —ung f friction; r—ungslos a smooth.

reich [raɪç] a rich; R— nt -(e)s, -e empire, kingdom; *(fig)* realm; das Dritte R— the Third Reich; —en vi reach; *(genügen)* be enough or sufficient *(jdm* for sb); vt hold out; *(geben)* pass, hand; *(anbieten)* offer; —haltig a ample, rich; —lich a ample, plenty of; R—tum m -s, -tümer wealth; R—weite f range.

reif [raɪf] a ripe; *Mensch, Urteil* mature; R— m -(e)s hoarfrost; -(e)s, -e *(Ring)* ring, hoop; R—e f - ripeness; maturity; —en vi mature; ripen; R—en m -s, - ring, hoop; *(Fahrzeug—)* tyre; R—enschaden m puncture; R—eprüfung f school leaving exam; R—ezeugnis nt school leaving certificate.

Reihe ['raɪə] f -, -n row; *(von Tagen etc, col: Anzahl)* series sing; der — nach in turn; er ist an der — it's his turn; an die — kommen have one's turn; r—n vt set in a row; arrange in series; Perlen string; —nfolge f sequence; alphabetische —nfolge alphabetical order; —nhaus nt terraced house; —r m -s, - heron.

Reim [raɪm] m -(e)s, -e rhyme; r—en vt rhyme.

rein [raɪn] ad *(col)* = herein, hinein; a, ad pure(ly); *(sauber)* clean; etw ins —e schreiben make a fair copy of sth; etw ins —e

bringen clear up sth; R— in cpds *(Comm)* net(t); R—(e)machefrau f charwoman; R—fall m *(col)* letdown; R—gewinn m net profit; R—heit f purity; cleanliness; —igen vt clean; *Wasser* purify; R—igung f cleaning; purification; *(Geschäft)* cleaners; chemische R—igung dry cleaning; dry cleaners; —lich a clean; R—lichkeit f cleanliness; —rassig a pedigree; R—schrift f fair copy; —waschen vr irreg clear oneself.

Reis [raɪs] m -es, -e rice; nt -es, -er twig, sprig.

Reise ['raɪzə] f -, -n journey; *(Schiff—)* voyage; —n pl travels pl; —andenken nt souvenir; —büro nt travel agency; r—fertig a ready to start; —führer m guide(book); *(Mensch)* travel guide; —gepäck nt luggage; —gesellschaft f party of travellers; —kosten pl travelling expenses pl; —leiter m courier; —lektüre f reading matter for the journey; r—n vi travel; go *(nach* to); —nde(r) mf traveller; —paß m passport; —pläne pl plans pl for a journey; —proviant m provisions pl for the journey; —scheck m traveller's cheque; —tasche f travelling bag or case; —verkehr m tourist/holiday traffic; —wetter nt holiday weather; —ziel nt destination.

Reisig ['raɪzɪç] nt -s brushwood.

Reiß- [raɪs] cpd: —aus nehmen run away, flee; —brett nt drawing board; r—en vt/i irreg tear; *(ziehen)* pull, drag; *Witz* crack; etw an sich — snatch sth up; *(fig)* take over sth; sich um etw r—en scramble for sth; r—end a *Fluß* torrential; *(Comm)* rapid;

—er m -s, - (col) thriller; r—erisch a sensationalistic; —leine f (Aviat) ripcord; —nagel m drawing pin, thumbtack· (US); —schiene f drawing rule, square; —verschluß m zip(per), zip fastener; —zeug nt geometry set; —zwecke f = —nagel.

Reit- ['raɪt] cpd: r—en vti irreg ride; —er(in f) m -s, - rider; (Mil) cavalryman, trooper; —e'rei f cavalry; —hose f riding breeches pl; —pferd nt saddle horse; —stiefel m riding boot; —zeug nt riding outfit.

Reiz [raɪts] m -es, -e stimulus; (angenehm) charm; (Verlockung) attraction; r—bar a irritability; —barkeit f irritability; r—en vt stimulate; (unangenehm) irritate; (verlocken) appeal to, attract; r—end a charming; r—los a unattractive; r—voll a attractive; —wäsche f sexy underwear.

rekeln ['re:kəln] vr stretch out; (lümmeln) lounge or loll about.

Reklam- cpd: —ation [reklamatsi'oːn] f complaint; —e [re'klaːmə] f -, -n advertising; advertisement; —e machen für etw advertise sth; r—ieren [rekla'miːrən] vti complain (about); (zurückfordern) reclaim.

rekon- [rekon] cpd: —struieren [struiːrən] vt reconstruct; R—valeszenz [-valɛs'tsɛnts] f convalescence.

Rekord [re'kort] m -(e)s, -e record; —leistung f record performance.

Rekrut [re'kruːt] m -en, -en recruit; r—ieren [-'tiːrən] vt recruit; vr be recruited.

Rektor ['rɛktɔr] m (Univ) rector, vice-chancellor; (Sch) headmaster;

—at [-'rat] nt -(e)s, -e rectorate, vice-chancellorship; headship; (Zimmer) rector's etc office.

Relais [rə'lɛː] nt -, - relay.

relativ [rela'tiːf] a relative; R—ität [relativi'tɛːt] f relativity.

relevant [rele'vant] a relevant.

Relief [reli'ɛf] nt -s, -s relief.

Religion [religi'oːn] f religion; —slehre f, —sunterricht m religious instruction.

religiös [religi'øːs] a religious.

Relikt [re'lɪkt] nt -(e)s, -e relic.

Reling ['reːlɪŋ] f -, -s (Naut) rail.

Reliquie [re'liːkviə] f relic.

Reminiszenz [reminɪs'tsɛnts] f reminiscence, recollection.

Remoulade [remu'laːdə] f remoulade.

Ren [rɛn] nt -s, -s or -e reindeer.

Rendezvous [rãde'vuː] nt -, - rendezvous.

Renn- ['rɛn] cpd: —bahn f race-course; (Aut) circuit, race track; r—en vti irreg run, race; R—en nt -s, - running; (Wettbewerb) race; —fahrer m racing driver; —pferd nt racehorse; —platz m race-course; —wagen m racing car.

renovier- [reno'viːr] cpd: —en vt renovate; R—ung f renovation.

rentabel [rɛn'taːbəl] a profitable, lucrative.

Rentabilität [rɛntabili'tɛːt] f profitability.

Rente ['rɛntə] f -, -n pension; —nempfänger m pensioner.

Rentier ['rɛntiːr] nt reindeer.

rentieren [rɛn'tiːrən] vr pay, be profitable.

Rentner(in f) ['rɛntnər(ɪn)] m -s, - pensioner.

Repar- [repa] cpd: —ation [-atsi'oːn] f reparation; —atur

[-ra'tu:r] f repairing; repair; r—a'turbedürftig a in need of repair; —a'turwerkstatt f repair shop; (Aut) garage; r—ieren ['ri:rən] vt repair.

Repertoire [repɛrto'a:r] nt -s, -s repertoire.

Report- cpd: —age [repɔr'ta:ʒə] f -, -n (on-the-spot) report; (TV, Rad) live commentary or coverage; —er [re'pɔrtər] m -s, - reporter, commentator.

Repräsent- cpd: —ant [reprɛzɛn'tant] m representative; r—a'tiv a representative; Geschenk etc prestigious; r—ieren [reprɛzɛn'ti:rən] vti represent.

Repressalien [reprɛ'sa:liən] pl reprisals pl.

Reproduktion [reproduktsi'o:n] f reproduction.

reproduzieren [reprodu'tsi:rən] vt reproduce.

Reptil [rɛp'ti:l] nt -s, -ien reptile.

Republik [repu'bli:k] f republic; —aner [-'ka:nar] m -s, - republican; r—anisch [-'ka:nɪʃ] a republican.

Reserve- cpd: —at [rezɛr'va:t] nt -(e)s, -e reservation; —e [re'zɛrvə] f -, -n reserve; —erad nt (Aut) spare wheel; —espieler m reserve; —etank m reserve tank; r—ieren [rezɛr'vi:rən] vt reserve; —ist [rezɛr'vɪst] m reservist; —oir [rezɛrvo'a:r] nt -s, -e reservoir.

Residenz [rezi'dɛnts] f residence, seat.

Resignation [rezɪgnatsi'o:n] f resignation.

resignieren [rezɪg'ni:rən] vi resign.

resolut [rezo'lu:t] a resolute; R—ion [rezolutsi'o:n] f resolution.

Resonanz [rezo'nants] f (lit, fig) resonance; —boden m sounding board; —kasten m resonance box.

Resopal ® [rezo'pa:l] nt -s formica ®.

Resozialisierung [rezotsiali'zi:rʊŋ] f rehabilitation.

Respekt [rɛ'spɛkt] m -(e)s respect; r—abel [-'ta:bəl] a respectable; r—ieren [-'ti:rən] vt respect; r—los a disrespectful; —sperson f person commanding respect; r—voll a respectful.

Ressort [rɛ'so:r] nt -s, -s department.

Rest [rɛst] m -(e)s, -e remainder, rest; (Über—) remains pl; —er pl (Comm) remnants pl.

Restaur- cpd: —ant [rɛsto'rã:] nt -s, -s restaurant; —ation [rɛstaʊratsi'o:n] f restoration; r—ieren [rɛstaʊri'ra:rən] vt restore.

Rest- cpd: —betrag m remainder, outstanding sum; r—lich a remaining; r—los a complete.

Resultat [rezʊl'ta:t] nt -(e)s, -e result.

Retorte [re'tɔrtə] f -, -n retort.

retten ['rɛtən] vt save, rescue.

Retter m -s, - rescuer, saviour.

Rettich ['rɛtɪç] m -s, -e radish.

Rettung f rescue; (Hilfe) help; seine letzte — his last hope; —sboot nt lifeboat; —sgürtel m, —sring m lifebelt, life preserver (US); r—slos a hopeless.

retuschieren [retu'ʃi:rən] vt (Phot) retouch.

Reue ['rɔʏə] f - remorse; (Bedauern) regret; r—n vt: es reut ihn he regrets (it) or is sorry (about it).

reuig ['rɔʏɪç] a penitent.

Revanche [re'vã:ʃə] f -, -n revenge; (Sport) return match.

revanchieren [revã'ʃi:rən] vr (sich rächen) get one's own back, have one's revenge; *(erwidern)* reciprocate, return the compliment.

Revers [re've:r] *m or nt* -, - lapel.

revidieren [revi'di:rən] *vt* revise.

Revier [re'vi:r] *nt* -s, -e district; *(Jagd—)* preserve; police station/beat; *(Mil)* sick-bay.

Revision [revizi'o:n] *f* revision; *(Comm)* auditing; *(Jur)* appeal.

Revolte [re'vɔltə] *f* -, -n revolt.

Revolution [revolutsi'o:n] *f* revolution; —**är** ['-'nɛ:r] *m* -s, -e revolutionary; r—**ieren** ['-'ni:rən] *vt* revolutionize.

Revolver [re'vɔlvər] *m* -s, - revolver.

Rezen- [retsen] *cpd:* —**sent** ['-'zɛnt] *m* reviewer, critic; **r—sieren** ['-'zi:rən] *vt* review; —**sion** [-zi'o:n] *f* review, criticism.

Rezept [re'tsɛpt] *nt* -(e)s, -e recipe; *(Med)* prescription; **r—pflichtig** *a* available only on prescription.

rezitieren [retsi'ti:rən] *vt* recite.

Rhabarber [ra'barbər] *m* -s rhubarb.

Rhesusfaktor ['re:zusfaktɔr] *m* rhesus factor.

Rhetorik [re'to:rɪk] *f* rhetoric.

rhetorisch [re'to:rɪʃ] *a* rhetorical.

Rheuma ['rɔyma] *nt* -s, **Rheumatismus** [rɔyma'tɪsmus] *m* rheumatism.

Rhinozeros [ri'no:tserɔs] *nt* - or -ses, -se rhinoceros.

rhyth- ['ryt] *cpd:* —**misch** *a* rythmical; **R—mus** *m* rhythm.

Richt- ['rɪçt] *cpd:* **r—en** *vt* direct *(an + acc* at; *(fig)* to); Waffe aim *(auf + acc* at); *(einstellen)* adjust; *(instand setzen)* repair; *(zurechtmachen)* prepare; *(bestrafen)* pass judgement on; *vr:*

sich r—en nach go by; —**er(in** *f) m* -s, - judge; **r—erlich** *a* judicial; **r—ig** *a* right, correct; *(echt)* proper; *ad (col: sehr)* really; **der/die** —**ige** the right one/person; **das** —**ige** the right thing; —**igkeit** *f* correctness; —**igstellung** *f* correction, rectification; —**preis** *m* recommended price; —**ung** *f* direction; tendency, orientation.

riechen ['ri:çən] *vti irreg* smell *(an etw (dat)* sth; *nach* of); **ich kann das/ihn nicht —** *(col)* I can't stand it/him.

Ried [ri:t] *nt* -(e)s, -e reed; marsh.

Riege ['ri:gə] *f* -, -n team, squad.

Riegel ['ri:gəl] *m* -s, - bolt, bar.

Riemen ['ri:mən] *m* -s, - strap; *(Gürtel, Tech)* belt; *(Naut)* oar.

Riese [ri:zə] *m* -n, -n giant; **r—ln** *vi* trickle; *(Schnee)* fall gently; —**nerfolg** *m* enormous success; **r—ngroß** *a*, **r—nhaft** *a* colossal, gigantic, huge.

ries- ['ri:z] *cpd:* —**ig** *a* enormous, huge, vast; **R—in** *f* giantess.

Riff [rɪf] *nt* -(e)s, -e reef.

Rille ['rɪlə] *f* -, -n groove.

Rind [rɪnt] *nt* -(e)s, -er ox; cow; cattle *pl*; *(Cook)* beef; —**e** f ['rɪndə] -, -n rind; *(Baum—)* bark; *(Brot—)* crust; —**fleisch** *nt* beef; —**sbraten** *m* roast beef; —**vieh** *nt* cattle *pl*; *(col)* blockhead, stupid oaf.

Ring [rɪŋ] *m* -(e)s, -e ring; —**buch** *nt* loose-leaf book; —**elnatter** *f* grass snake; **r—en** *vi irreg* wrestle; —**en** *nt* -s wrestling; —**finger** *m* ring finger; **r—förmig** *a* ring-shaped; —**kampf** *m* wrestling bout; —**richter** *m* referee; **r—s** _um_ *ad* round; **r—sherum** *ad* round about; —**straße** *f* ring road; **r—sum(her)**

ad *(rundherum)* round about; *(überall)* all round.

Rinn- ['rɪn] *cpd:* **—e** f -, -n gutter, drain; **r—en** *vi irreg* run, trickle; **—sal** *nt* -s, -e trickle of water; **—stein** *m* gutter.

Rippchen ['rɪpçən] *nt* small rib; cutlet.

Rippe ['rɪpə] f -, -n rib; **—nfellentzündung** f pleurisy.

Risiko ['riːziko] *nt* -s, -s or **Risiken** risk.

riskant [rɪs'kant] *a* risky, hazardous.

riskieren [rɪs'kiːrən] *vt* risk.

Riß [rɪs] *m* -sses, -sse tear; *(in Mauer, Tasse etc)* crack; *(in Haut)* scratch; *(Tech)* design.

rissig ['rɪsɪç] *a* torn; cracked; scratched.

Ritt [rɪt] *m* -(e)s, -e ride; **—er** *m* -s, - knight; **r—erlich** *a* chivalrous; **—erschlag** *m* knighting; **—ertum** *nt* -s chivalry; **—erzeit** f age of chivalry; **r—lings** *ad* astride.

Ritus ['riːtus] *m* -, **Riten** rite.

Ritze ['rɪtsə] f -, -n crack, chink; **r—n** *vt* scratch.

Rivale [ri'vaːlə] *m* -n, -n rival.

Rivalität [rivali'tɛːt] f rivalry.

Rizinusöl ['riːtsinusøːl] *nt* castor oil.

Robbe ['rɔbə] f -, -n seal.

Robe ['roːbə] f -, -n robe.

Roboter ['rɔbɔtər] *m* -s, - robot.

röcheln ['rœçəln] *vi* wheeze.

Rock [rɔk] *m* -(e)s, ⸚e skirt; *(Jackett)* jacket; *(Uniform—)* tunic.

Rodel ['roːdəl] *m* -s, - toboggan; **—bahn** f toboggan run; **r—n** *vi* toboggan.

roden ['roːdən] *vti* clear.

Rogen ['roːgən] *m* -s, - roe, spawn.

Roggen ['rɔgən] *m* -s, - rye; **—brot** *nt* rye bread, black bread.

roh [roː] *a* raw; *Mensch* coarse, crude; **R—bau** *m* shell of a building; **R—eisen** *nt* pig iron; **R—ling** *m* ruffian; **R—material** *nt* raw material; **R—öl** *nt* crude oil.

Rohr ['roːr] *nt* -(e)s, -e pipe, tube; *(Bot)* cane; *(Schilf)* reed; *(Gewehr—)* barrel; **—bruch** *m* burst pipe.

Röhre ['røːrə] f -, -n tube, pipe; *(Rad etc)* valve; *(Back—)* oven.

Rohr- *cpd:* **—geflecht** *nt* wickerwork; **—leger** *m* -s, - plumber; **—leitung** f pipeline; **—post** f pneumatic post; **—stock** *m* cane; **—stuhl** *m* basket chair; **—zucker** *m* cane sugar.

Roh- *cpd:* **—seide** f raw silk; **—stoff** *m* raw material.

Rokoko ['rokoko] *nt* -s rococo.

Roll- ['rɔl] *cpd:* **—(l)aden** *m* shutter; **—bahn** f, **—feld** *nt* *(Aviat)* runway.

Rolle ['rɔlə] f -, -n roll; *(Theat, soziologisch)* role; *(Garn— etc)* reel, spool; *(Walze)* roller; *(Wäsche—)* mangle; **keine —spielen** not matter; **r—n** *vti* roll; *(Aviat)* taxi; *Wäsche* mangle; **—nbesetzung** f *(Theat)* cast; **—r** *m* -s, - scooter; *(Welle)* roller.

Roll- *cpd:* **—mops** *m* pickled herring; **—schuh** *m* roller skate; **—stuhl** *m* wheelchair; **—treppe** f escalator.

Roman [ro'maːn] *m* -s, -e novel; **—schreiber** *m* **—schriftsteller** *m* novelist; **—tik** [ro'mantɪk] f romanticism; **—tiker** [ro'mantɪkər] *m* -s, - romanticist; **r—tisch** [ro'mantɪʃ] *a* romantic; **—ze** [ro'mantsə] f -, -n romance.

Römer ['røːmər] *m* -s, - wineglass; *(Mensch)* Roman.

röntgen ['rœntgən] vt X-ray; R—aufnahme f, R—bild nt X-ray; R—strahlen pl X-rays pl.
rosa ['ro:za] a pink, rose-(coloured).
Rose ['ro:zə] f -, -n rose; —nkohl m Brussels sprouts pl; —nkranz m rosary; —nmontag m Shrove Monday.
Rosette [ro'zɛtə] f rosette; rose window.
rosig ['ro:zɪç] a rosy.
Rosine [ro'zi:nə] f raisin, currant.
Roß [rɔs] nt -sses, -sse horse, steed; —kastanie f horse chestnut.
Rost [rɔst] m -(e)s, -e rust; (Gitter) grill, gridiron; (Bett—) springs pl; —braten m roast(ed) meat, joint; r—en vi rust.
rösten ['rø:stən] vt roast; toast; grill.
Rost- cpd: r—frei a rust-free; rustproof; stainless; r—ig a rusty; —schutz m rust-proofing.
rot [ro:t] a red; R—ation [rotatsi'o:n] f rotation; —bäckig a red-cheeked; —blond a strawberry blond.
Röte ['rø:tə] f - redness; —ln pl German measles sing; r—n vtr redden.
rot- cpd: —haarig a red-haired; —ieren [ro'ti:rən] vi rotate; R—käppchen nt Little Red Riding Hood; R—kehlchen nt robin; R—stift m red pencil; R—wein m red wine.
Rotz [rɔts] m -es, -e (col) snot.
Roulade [ru'la:də] f (Cook) beef olive.
Route ['ru:tə] f -, -n route.
Routine [ru'ti:nə] f experience; routine.
Rübe ['ry:bə] f -, -n turnip; gelbe

— carrot; rote — beetroot; —nzucker m beet sugar.
Rubin [ru'bi:n] m -s, -e ruby.
Rubrik [ru'bri:k] f heading; (Spalte) column.
Ruck [rʊk] m -(e)s, -e jerk, jolt.
Rück- ['rʏk] cpd: —antwort f reply, answer; r—bezüglich a reflexive; r—blenden vi flash back; r—blickend a retrospective; r—en vti move; —en m -s, - back; (Berg—) ridge; —endeckung f backing; —enlehne f back (of chair); —enmark nt spinal cord; —enschwimmen nt backstroke; —enwind m following wind; r—erstattung f return, restitution; —fahrt f return journey; —fall m relapse; r—fällig a relapsing; r—fällig werden relapse; —flug m return flight; —frage f question; —gabe f return; —gang m decline, recourse; —halt m backing reserve; r—haltlos a unreserved; —kehr f -, -en return; —koppelung f feedback; —lage f f reserve, savings pl; r—läufig a declining, falling; —licht nt back light; r—lings ad from behind; backwards; —nahme f -, -n taking back; —porto nt return postage; —reise f return journey; (Naut) home voyage; —ruf m recall.
Rucksack ['rʊkzak] m rucksack.
Rück- cpd: —schau f reflection; r—schauend a, ad retrospective, in retrospect; —schluß m conclusion; —schritt m retrogression; r—schrittlich a reactionary; retrograde; —seite f back; (von Münze etc) reverse; —sicht f consideration; —sicht nehmen auf

(+acc) show consideration for;
r—sichtslos a inconsiderate;
Fahren reckless; (*unbarmherzig*)
ruthless; r—sichtsvoll a con-
siderate; —sitz m back seat;
—spiegel m (*Aut*) rear-view
mirror; —spiel m return match;
—sprache f further discussion or
talk; —stand m arrears pl;
r—ständig a backward, out-
of-date; *Zahlungen* in arrears;
—stoß m recoil; —strahler m -s,
- rear. reflector; —tritt m
resignation; —trittbremse f pedal
brake; —vergütung f repayment;
(*Comm*) refund; —versicherung f
reinsurance; r—wärtig a rear;
r—wärts ad backward(s), back;
—wärtsgang m (*Aut*) reverse gear;
—weg m return journey, way
back; r—wirkend a retroactive;
—wirkung f reaction; retrospective
effect; —zahlung f repayment;
—zug m retreat.

Rüde ['ry:də] m -n, -n male
dog/fox/wolf; r— a blunt, gruff.
Rudel ['ru:dəl] nt -s, - pack; herd.
Ruder ['ru:dər] nt -s, - oar;
(*Steuer*) rudder; —boot nt rowing
boat; —er m -s, - rower; r—n vti
row.

Ruf [ru:f] m -(e)s, -e call, cry;
(*Ansehen*) reputation; r—en vti
irreg call; cry; —name m usual
(first) name; —nummer f
(tele)phone number; —zeichen nt
(*Rad*) call sign; (*Tel*) ringing tone.
Rüge ['ry:gə] f -, -n reprimand,
rebuke; r—n vti reprimand.
Ruhe ['ru:ə] f - rest;
(*Ungestörtheit*) peace, quiet;
(*Gelassenheit, Stille*) calm;
(*Schweigen*) silence; sich zur —
setzen retire; —! be quiet!,
silence!; r—los a restless; r—n vi

rest; —pause f break; —platz m
resting place; —stand m retirement; letzte —stätte f final resting
place; —störung f breach of the
peace; —tag m closing day.

ruhig ['ru:ɪç] a quiet;
(*bewegungslos*) still; *Hand* steady;
(*gelassen, friedlich*) calm;
Gewissen clear; tu das — feel free
to do that.

Ruhm [ru:m] m -(e)s fame, glory.
rühm- ['ry:m] cpd: —en vt praise;
vr boast; —lich[a] a laudable.

ruhm- cpd: —los a inglorious;
—reich a glorious.

Ruhr ['ru:r] f - dysentery.
Rühr- ['ry:r] cpd: —ei nt scrambled
egg; r—en vt (*lit, fig*) move, stir
(*auch Cook*); vi: r—en von come
or stem from; r—en an (+acc)
touch; (*fig*) touch on; r—end. a
touching, moving; r—ig a active,
lively; r—selig a sentimental,
emotional; —ung f emotion.

Ruin [ru'i:n] m -s, —e f-, -n ruin;
r—ieren [rui'ni:rən] vt ruin.
rülpsen ['rʏlpsən] vi burp, belch.
Rum [rom] m -s, -s rum.
Rummel ['roməl] m -s (col)
hubbub; (*Jahrmarkt*) fair; —platz
m fairground, fair.

rumoren [ru'mo:rən] vi be noisy,
make a noise.
Rumpel- ['rompəl] cpd: —kammer
f junk room; r—n vi rumble;
(*holpern*) jolt.

Rumpf [rompf] m -(e)s, ⁼e trunk,
torso; (*Aviat*) fuselage; (*Naut*)
hull.
rümpfen ['rʏmpfən] vt *Nase* turn
up.

rund [ront] a round; ad (*etwa*)
around; — um etw round sth;
R—bogen m Norman or
Romanesque arch; R—brief m

circular; R—e ['rundə] f -, -n
round; (in Rennen) lap;
(Gesellschaft) circle; —en vt make
round; vr (fig) take shape;
—erneuert a Reifen remoulded;
R—fahrt f (round) trip.

Rundfunk ['runtfuŋk] m -(e)s
broadcasting; (—anstalt) broadcasting service; im — on the radio;
—empfang m reception; —gebühr
f licence; —gerät nt wireless set;
—sendung f broadcast, radio programme.

Rund- cpd: r—heraus ad straight
out, bluntly; r—herum ad round
about; all round; r—lich a plump,
rounded; —reise f round trip;
—schreiben nt (Comm) circular;
—ung f curve, roundness.

runter ['runtər] ad (col) =
herunter, hinunter.

Runzel ['runtsəl] f -, -n wrinkle;
r—ig a wrinkled; r—n vt wrinkle;
die Stirn r—n frown.

Rüpel ['ry:pəl] m -s, - lout; r—haft
a loutish.

rupfen ['rupfən] vt pluck; R— m
-s, - sackcloth.

ruppig ['rupiç] a rough, gruff.

Rüsche ['ry:ʃə] f -, -n frill.

Ruß [ru:s] m -es soot; r—en vi
smoke; (Ofen) be sooty; r—ig a
sooty.

Rüssel ['rysəl] m -s, - snout;
(Elefanten—) trunk.

rüsten ['rystən] vtri prepare; (Mil)
arm.

rüstig ['rystiç] a sprightly,
vigorous; R—keit f sprightliness,
vigour.

Rüstung ['rystuŋ] f preparation;
arming; (Ritter—) armour;
(Waffen etc) armaments pl;
—skontrolle f armaments control.

Rüstzeug nt tools pl; (fig) capacity.

Rute ['ru:tə] f -, -n rod, switch.

Rutsch [rutʃ] m -(e)s, -e slide;
(Erd—) landslide; —bahn f slide;
r—en vi slide; (ausr—en) slip;
r—ig a slippery.

rütteln ['rytəln] vti shake, jolt.

S

S,s [εs] nt S,s.

Saal [za:l] m -(e)s, Säle hall;
room.

Saat [za:t] f -, -en seed; (Pflanzen)
crop; (Säen) sowing.

sabbern ['zabərn] vi (col) dribble.

Säbel ['zɛ:bəl] m -s, - sabre, sword.

Sabotage [zabo'ta:ʒə] f -, -n
sabotage.

sabotieren [zabo'ti:rən] vt
sabotage.

Sach- [zax] cpd: —bearbeiter m
specialist; s—dienlich a relevant,

helpful; —e f -, -n thing;
(Angelegenheit) affair, business;
(Frage) matter; (Pflicht) task; zur
—e to the point; s—gemäß a
appropriate, suitable; s—kundig a
expert; —lage f situation, state of
affairs; s—lich a matter-of-fact,
objective; Irrtum, Angabe factual.

sächlich ['zɛxlıç] a neuter.

Sach- cpd: —schaden m material
damage; s—te ad softly, gently;
—verständige(r) mf expert.

Sack [zak] *m* -(e)s, ⸚e sack; **s—en**
vi sag, sink; **—gasse** *f* cul-de-sac,
dead-end street *(US)*.

Sadismus [za'dɪsmʊs] *m* sadism.

Sadist [za'dɪst] *m* sadist; **—isch** *a*
sadistic.

säen ['zɛːən] *vti* sow.

Saft [zaft] *m* -(e)s, ⸚e juice; *(Bot)*
sap; **s—ig** *a* juicy; **—los** *a* dry.

Sage ['zaːgə] *f* -, -n saga.

Säge ['zɛːgə] *f* -, -n saw; **—mehl**
nt sawdust; **s—n** *vti* saw.

sagen ['zaːgən] *vti* say *(jdm zu sb)*,
tell *(jdm sb)*; **—haft** *a* legendary;
(col) great, smashing.

Sägewerk *nt* sawmill.

Sahne ['zaːnə] *f* - cream.

Saison [zɛ'zõ] *f* -, -s season; **—ar-**
beiter *m* seasonal worker.

Saite ['zaɪtə] *f* -, -n string; **—n-**
instrument *nt* string instrument.

Sakko ['zako] *m or nt* -s, -s jacket.

Sakrament [zakra'mɛnt] *nt*
sacrament.

Sakristei [zakrɪs'taɪ] *f* sacristy.

Salat [za'laːt] *m* -(e)s, -e salad;
(Kopfsalat) lettuce; **—soße** *f* salad
dressing.

Salb- ['zalb] *cpd:* **—e** *f* -, -n ointment; **—ei** [zal'baɪ] *m or f* or -e
- sage; **s—en** *vt* anoint; **—ung** *f*
anointing; **s—ungsvoll** *a* unctuous.

Saldo ['zaldo] *m* -s, **Salden**
balance.

Salmiak [zalmi'ak] *m* -s sal
ammoniac; **—geist** *m* liquid
ammonia.

Salon [za'lõː] *m* -s, -s salon.

salopp [za'lɔp] *a* casual.

Salpeter [zal'peːtər] *m* -s
saltpetre; **—säure** *f* nitric acid.

Salut [za'luːt] *m* -(e)s, -e salute;
s—ieren [-'tiːrən] *vi* salute.

Salve ['zalvə] *f* -, -n salvo.

Salz [zalts] *nt* -es, -e salt; **s—en**
vt irreg salt; **s—ig** *a* salty; **—kar-**
toffeln *pl* boiled potatoes *pl*;
—säure *f* hydrochloric acid.

Samen ['zaːmən] *m* -s, - seed;
(Anat) sperm.

Sammel- ['zaməl] *cpd:* **—band** *m*
anthology; **—becken** *nt* reservoir;
—bestellung *f* collective order;
s—n *vt* collect; *vr* assemble,
gather; *(konzentrieren)* concentrate; **—name** *m* collective term;
—surium ['zuːriʊm] *nt* hotchpotch.

Sammlung ['zamlʊŋ] *f* collection;
assembly, gathering; concentration.

Samstag ['zamstaːk] *m* Saturday;
s—s *ad (on)* Saturdays.

Samt [zamt] *m* -(e)s, -e velvet;
s— *prep* +*dat* (along)- with,
together with; **s— und sonders**
each and every one *(of them)*.

sämtlich ['zɛmtlɪç] *a* all- (the),
entire. .

Sand [zant] *m* -(e)s, -e sand; **—ale**
[zan'daːlə] *f* -, -n sandal; **—bank**
f sandbank; **s—ig** ['zandɪç] *a*
sandy; **—kasten** *m* sandpit;
—kuchen *m* Madeira cake;
—papier *nt* sandpaper; **—stein** *m*
sandstone; **—uhr** *f* hourglass.

sanft [zanft] *a* soft, gentle; **—mütig**
a gentle, meek.

Sänger(in *f)* ['zɛŋər(ɪn)] *m* -s, -
singer.

Sani- *cpd:* **s—eren** [za'niːrən] *vt* re-
develop; *Betrieb* make financially
sound; *vr* line one's pocket;
become financially sound; **—erung**
f redevelopment; making viable;
s—tär [zani'tɛːr] *a* sanitary;
s—täre Anlagen sanitation; **—täter**
[zani'tɛːtər] *m* -s, - first-aid
attendant; *(Mil)* (medical) orderly.

sanktionieren [zaŋktsio'ni:rən] *vt* sanction.

Saphir ['za:fi:r] *m* -s, -e sapphire.

Sardelle [zar'dələ] *f* anchovy.

Sardine [zar'di:nə] *f* sardine.

Sarg [zark] *m* -(e)s, ⁼e coffin.

Sarkasmus [zar'kasmʊs] *m* sarcasm.

sarkastisch [zar'kastıʃ] *a* sarcastic.

Satan ['za:tan] *m* -s, -e Satan; devil.

Satellit [zatɛ'li:t] *m* -en, -en satellite.

Satire [za'ti:rə] *f* -, -n satire.

satirisch [za'ti:rıʃ] *a* satirical.

satt [zat] *a* full; *Farbe* rich, deep; jdn/etw — sein *or* haben be fed up with sb/sth; sich — hören/sehen an (+dat) see/hear enough of; sich — essen eat one's fill; — machen be filling.

Sattel ['zatəl] *m* -s, ⁼ saddle; *(Berg)* ridge; s—fest *a (fig)* proficient; s—n *vt* saddle.

sättigen ['zɛtɪgən] *vt* satisfy; *(Chem)* saturate.

Satz [zats] *m* -es, ⁼e *(Gram)* sentence; *(Neben—, Adverbial—)* clause; *(Theorem)* theorem; *(Mus)* movement; *(Tennis, Briefmarken etc)* set; *(Kaffee)* grounds *pl*; *(Comm)* rate; *(Sprung)* jump; —gegenstand *m (Gram)* subject; —lehre *f* syntax; —teil *m* constituent (of a sentence); —ung *f* statute, rule; s—ungsgemäß *a* statutory; —zeichen *nt* punctuation mark.

Sau [zau] *f* -, Säue sow; *(col)* dirty pig.

sauber ['zaubər] *a* clean; *(ironisch)* fine; —halten, *vt irreg* keep clean; S—keit *f* cleanness; *(einer Person)* cleanliness.

säuber- ['zɔybər] *cpd*: —lich *ad* neatly; —n *vt* clean; *(Pol etc)* purge; S—ung *f* cleaning; purge.

Sauce ['zo:sə] *f* -, -n sauce, gravy.

sauer ['zauər] *a* sour; *(Chem)* acid; *(col)* cross.

Sauerei [zauə'rai] *f (col)* rotten state of affairs; scandal; *(Schmutz etc)* mess; *(Unanständigkeit)* obscenity.

säuerlich ['zɔyərlıç] *a* sourish, tart.

Sauer- *cpd*: —milch *f* sour milk; —stoff *m* oxygen; —stoffgerät *nt* breathing apparatus; —teig *m* leaven.

saufen ['zaufən] *vti irreg (col)* drink, booze.

Säufer ['zɔyfər] *m* -s, - *(col)* boozer.

Sauferei [zaufə'rai] *f* drinking, boozing; booze-up.

saugen ['zaugən] *vti irreg* suck.

säugen ['zɔygən] *vt* suckle.

Sauger ['zaugər] *m* -s, - dummy, comforter (US); *(auf Flasche)* teat; *(Staub—)* vacuum cleaner, hoover ®.

Säug- ['zɔyg] *cpd*: —etier *nt* mammal; —ling *m* infant, baby.

Säule ['zɔylə] *f* -, -n column, pillar; —ngang *m* arcade.

Saum [zaum] *m* -(e)s, Säume hem; *(Naht)* seam.

säumen ['zɔymən] *vt* hem; seam; *vi* delay, hesitate.

Sauna ['zauna] *f* -, -s sauna.

Säure ['zɔyrə] *f* -, -n acid; *(Geschmack)* sourness, acidity; s—beständig *a* acid-proof; s—haltig *a* acidic.

säuseln ['zɔyzəln] *vti* murmur, rustle.

sausen ['zauzən] *vi* blow; *(col: eilen)* rush; *(Ohren)* buzz; etw — lassen *(col)* give sth a miss.

Saustall ['zauʃtal] *m (col)* pigsty.
Saxophon [zakso'foːn] *nt* -s, -e saxophone.
Schabe ['ʃaːbə] *f* -, -n cockroach; **s—n** *vt* scrape; —rnack ['ʃaːbɐnak] *m* -(e)s, -e trick, prank.
schäbig ['ʃɛːbɪç] *a* shabby; **S—keit** *f* shabbiness.
Schablone [ʃaˈbloːnə] *f* -, -n stencil; *(Muster)* pattern; *(fig)* convention; **s—nhaft** *a* stereotyped, conventional.
Schach [ʃax] *nt* -s, -s chess; *(Stellung)* check; —brett *nt* chessboard; —figur *f* chessman; 's—matt a checkmate; —partie *f*, —spiel *nt* game of chess.
Schacht [ʃaxt] *m* -(e)s, ⁀e shaft; —el *f* -, -n box; *(pej: Frau)* bag, cow.
schade ['ʃaːdə] *a* a pity or shame; **sich** *(dat)* **zu — sein** für etw consider oneself too good for sth; *interj* (what a) pity or shame.
Schädel ['ʃɛːdəl] *m* -s, - skull; —bruch *m* fractured skull.
Schaden ['ʃaːdən] *m* -s, ⁀ damage; *(Verletzung)* injury; *(Nachteil)* disadvantage; **s—** *vi* (+*dat*) hurt; **einer Sache s—** damage sth; —ersatz *m* compensation, damages *pl*; **s—ersatzpflichtig** *a* liable for damages; —freude *f* malicious delight; **s—froh** *a* gloating, with malicious delight.
schadhaft ['ʃaːthaft] *a* faulty, damaged.
schäd- ['ʃɛːt] *cpd:* —igen ['ʃɛdɪgən] *vt* damage; *Person* do harm to, harm; **S—igung** *f* damage; harm; —lich *a* harmful (für to); **S—lichkeit** *f* harmfulness; —ling *m* pest; **S—lingsbekämpfungsmittel** *nt* pesticide.

schadlos ['ʃaːtloːs] *a:* **sich — halten an** (+*dat*) take advantage of.
Schaf [ʃaːf] *nt* -(e)s, -e sheep; —bock *m* ram.
Schäfchen ['ʃɛːfçən] *nt* lamb; —wolken *pl* cirrus clouds *pl*.
Schäfer ['ʃɛːfər] *m* -s, -e shepherd; —hund *m* Alsatian; —in *f* shepherdess.
schaffen ['ʃafən] *vt irreg* create; *Platz* make; **sich** *(dat)* **etw —** get o.s. sth; *vt (erreichen)* manage, do; *(erledigen)* finish; *Prüfung* pass; *(transportieren)* take; *vi (col: arbeiten)* work; **sich an etw** *(dat)* **zu — machen** busy oneself with sth; **S—** *nt* -s (creative) activity; **S—sdrang** *m* creative. urge; energy; **S—skraft** *f* creativity.
Schaffner(in *f*) ['ʃafnər(m)] *m* -s, - *(Bus)* conductor/conductress; *(Rail)* guard.
Schaft [ʃaft] *m* -(e)s, ⁀e shaft; *(von Gewehr)* stock; *(von Stiefel)* leg; *(Bot)* stalk; tree trunk; —stiefel *m* high boot.
Schakal [ʃaˈkaːl] *m* -s, -e jackal.
Schäker ['ʃɛːkər] *m* -s, - flirt; joker; **s—n** *vi* flirt; joke.
schal [ʃaːl] *a* flat; *(fig)* insipid; **S—** *m* -s, -e *or* -s scarf.
Schälchen ['ʃɛːlçən] *nt* cup, bowl.
Schale ['ʃaːlə] *f* -, -n skin; *(abgeschält)* peel; *(Nuß—, Muschel—, Ei—)* shell; *(Geschirr)* dish, bowl.
schälen ['ʃɛːlən] *vt* peel; shell; *vr* peel.
Schall [ʃal] *m* -(e)s, -e sound; —dämpfer *m* -s, - *(Aut)* silencer; **s—dicht** *a* soundproof; **s—en** *vi* (re)sound; **s—end** *a* resounding, loud; —mauer *f* sound barrier; —platte *f* (gramophone) record.

Schalt- ['ʃalt] cpd: **—bild** nt circuit diagram; **—brett** nt switchboard; **s—en** vt switch, turn; vi (Aut) change (gear); (col: begreifen) catch on; **s—en und walten** do as one pleases; **—er** m **-s,** - counter; (an Gerät) switch; **—erbeamte(r)** m counter clerk; **—hebel** m switch; (Aut) gear-lever; **—jahr** nt leap year; **—ung** f switching; (Elec) circuit; (Aut) gear change.

Scham [ʃaːm] f - shame; **(—gefühl)** f modesty; (Organe) private parts pl.

schämen ['ʃɛːmən] vr be ashamed.

Scham- cpd: **—haare** pl pubic hair; **s—haft** a modest, bashful; **s—los** a shameless.

Schande ['ʃandə] f - disgrace.

schändlich ['ʃɛntliç] a disgraceful, shameful; **S—keit** f disgracefulness.

Schandtat ['ʃanttaːt] f (col) escapade, shenanigan.

Schändung ['ʃɛnduŋ] f violation, defilement.

Schank- ['ʃaŋk] cpd: **—erlaubnis** f, **—konzession** f (publican's) licence; **—tisch** m bar.

Schanze ['ʃantsə] f **-, -n** (Mil) fieldwork, earthworks pl; (Sprung—) skijump.

Schar [ʃaːr] f **-, -en** band, company; (Vögel) flock; (Menge) crowd; **in —en** in droves; **—ade** [ʃaˈraːdə] f charade; **s—en** vr assemble, rally; **s—enweise** ad in droves.

scharf [ʃarf] a sharp; Essen hot; Munition live; **— nachdenken** think hard; **auf etw** (acc) **— sein** (col) be keen on sth; **S—blick** m (fig) penetration.

Schärf- ['ʃɛrf] cpd: **—e** f **-, -n** sharpness; (Strenge) rigour; **s—en** vt sharpen.

Scharf- cpd: **s—machen** vt (col) stir up; **—richter** m executioner; **—schießen** nt .firing live ammunition; **—schütze** m marksman, sharpshooter; **—sinn** m penetration, astuteness; **s—sinnig** a astute, shrewd.

Scharmützel [ʃarˈmʏtsəl] nt **-s,** - skirmish.

Scharnier [ʃarˈniːr] nt **-s, -e** hinge.

Schärpe ['ʃɛrpə] f **-, -n** sash.

scharren ['ʃarən] vti scrape, scratch.

Scharte ['ʃartə] f **-, -n** notch, nick; (Berg) wind gap.

schartig ['ʃartiç] a jagged.

Schaschlik ['ʃaʃlɪk] m or nt **-s, -s** (shish) kebab.

Schatten ['ʃatən] m **-s,** - shadow; **—bild** nt, **—riß** m silhouette; **—seite** f shady side, dark·side.

schattieren [ʃaˈtiːrən] vti shade.

Schattierung f shading.

schattig ['ʃatiç] a shady.

Schatulle [ʃaˈtulə] f **-, -n** casket; (Geld—) coffer.

Schatz [ʃats] m **-es, ˙-e** treasure; (Person) darling; **—amt** nt treasury.

schätz- ['ʃɛts] cpd: **—bar** a assessable; **S—chen** nt darling, love; **s—en** vt (abschätzen) estimate; Gegenstand value; (würdigen) value, esteem; (vermuten) reckon; **—enlernen** vt learn to appreciate; **S—ung** f estimate; estimation; valuation; **nach meiner S—ung ,,** I reckon that . . . ; **—ungsweise** ad approximately; **it is thought; S—wert** m estimated value.

Schau [ʃau] f **-** show; (Ausstellung) ·display, exhibition; **etw zur — stellen** make a show of sth,. show sth off; **—bild** nt diagram.

Schauder ['ʃaʊdər] *m* **-s, -s** shudder; *(wegen Kälte)* shiver; **s—haft** a horrible; **s—n** *vi* shudder; shiver.

schauen ['ʃaʊən] *vi* look.

Schauer ['ʃaʊər] *m* **-s, -** *(Regen—)* shower; *(Schreck)* shudder; **—geschichte** *f* horror story; **s—lich** a horrific, spine-chilling.

Schaufel ['ʃaʊfəl] *f* **-, -n** shovel; *(Naut)* paddle; *(Tech)* scoop; **s—n** *vt* shovel, scoop.

Schau- *cpd:* **—fenster** *nt* shop window; **—fensterauslage** *f* window display; **—fensterbummel** *m* window-shopping (expedition); **—fensterdekorateur** *m* window dresser; **—geschäft** *nt* show business; **—kasten** *m* showcase.

Schaukel ['ʃaʊkəl] *f* **-, -n** swing; **s—n** *vi* swing, rock; **—pferd** *nt* rocking horse; **—stuhl** *m* rocking chair.

Schaulustige(r) ['ʃaʊlʊstɪgə(r)] *mf* onlooker.

Schaum [ʃaʊm] *m* **-(e)s,** **Schäume** [ʃaʊm] foam; *(Seifen—)* lather.

schäumen ['ʃɔʏmən] *vi* foam.

Schaum- *cpd:* **—gummi** *m* foam (rubber); **s—ig** a frothy, foamy; **—krone** *f* white crest; **—schläger** *m* (fig) windbag; **—wein** *m* sparkling wine.

Schau- *cpd:* **—platz** *m* scene; **s—rig** a horrific, dreadful; **—spiel** *nt* spectacle; *(Theat)* play; **—spieler** *m* actor; **—spielerin** *f* actress; **s—spielern** *vi* insep act.

Scheck [ʃɛk] *m* **-s, -s** cheque; **—buch** *nt* cheque book; **s—ig** a dappled, piebald.

scheel [ʃeːl] a *(col)* dirty; **jdn —ansehen** give sb a dirty look.

scheffeln ['ʃɛfəln] *vt* amass.

Scheibe ['ʃaɪbə] *f* **-, -n** disc; *(Brot etc)* slice; *(Glas—)* pane *(Mil)* target; **—nbremse** *f* (Aut) disc brake; **—nwaschanlage** *f* (Aut) windscreen washers *pl*; **—nwischer** *m* (Aut) windscreen wiper.

Scheich [ʃaɪç] *m* **-s, -e** or **-s** sheik(h).

Scheide ['ʃaɪdə] *f* **-, -n** sheath; *(Grenze)* boundary; *(Anat)* vagina; **s—n** irreg *vt* separate; **Ehe —dissolve; sich s—n lassen** get a divorce; *vi* (de)part.

Scheidung *f* (Ehe—) divorce; **—sgrund** *m* grounds *pl* for divorce; **—sklage** *f* divorce suit.

Schein [ʃaɪn] *m* **-(e)s, -e** light; *(An—)* appearance; *(Geld)* (bank)note; *(Bescheinigung)* certificate; **zum —** in pretence; **s—bar** a apparent; **s—en'** *vi* irreg shine; *(Anschein haben)* seem; **s—heilig** a hypocritical; **—tod** *m* apparent death; **—werfer** *m* **-s, -** floodlight; spotlight; *(Such—)* searchlight; *(Aut)* headlamp.

Scheiß- ['ʃaɪs] *in cpds (col)* bloody; **—e** *f* - *(col)* shit.

Scheit [ʃaɪt] *m* **-(e)s, -e** or **-er** log, billet.

Scheitel ['ʃaɪtəl] *m* **-s, -** top; *(Haar)* parting; **s—n** *vt* part; **—punkt** *m* zenith, apex.

scheitern ['ʃaɪtərn] *vi* fail.

Schelle ['ʃɛlə] *f* **-, -n** small bell; **s—n** *vi* ring.

Schellfisch ['ʃɛlfɪʃ] *m* haddock.

Schelm [ʃɛlm] *m* **-(e)s, -e** rogue; **s—isch** a mischievous, roguish.

Schelte ['ʃɛltə] *f* **-, -n** scolding; **s—n** *vt* irreg scold.

Schema ['ʃeːma] *nt* **-s, -s** or **-ta** scheme, plan; *(Darstellung)* schema; **nach —** quite

mechanically; **s—tisch** [ʃeˈmaːtɪʃ] *a* schematic; *(pej)* mechanical.
Schemel [ˈʃeːməl] *m* -s, - (foot)stool.
Schenkel [ˈʃɛŋkəl] *m* -s, - thigh.
schenken [ˈʃɛŋkən] *vt (lit, fig)* give; *Getränk* pour; **sich** *(dat)* **etw** **—** *(col)* skip sth; **das ist geschenkt!** *(billig)* that's a giveaway!; *(nichts wert)* that's worthless!
Schenkung [ˈʃɛŋkʊŋ] *f* gift; **—surkunde** *f* deed of gift.
Scherbe [ˈʃɛrbə] *f* -, -n broken piece, fragment; *(archäologisch)* potsherd.
Schere [ˈʃeːrə] *f* -, -n scissors *pl*; *(groß)* shears *pl*; **s—n** *vt irreg* cut; *Schaf* shear; *(sich kümmern)* bother; *vr* care; **scher dich (zum Teufel)!** get lost!; **—nschleifer** *m* -s, - knife-grinder; **—rei** *f (col)* bother, trouble.
Scherflein [ˈʃɛrflain] *nt* mite, bit.
Scherz [ʃɛrts] *m* -es, -e joke; fun; **—frage** *f* conundrum; **s—haft** *a* joking, jocular.
scheu [ʃɔy] *a* shy; **S—** *f* - shyness; *(Angst)* fear (*vor* +*dat* of); *(Ehrfurcht)* awe; **S—che** *f* -, -n scarecrow; **—chen** *vt* scare (off); **—en** *vr*: **sich —en vor** (+*dat*) be afraid of, shrink from; *vt* shun; *vi (Pferd)* shy.
Scheuer- [ˈʃɔyər] *cpd*: **—bürste** *f* scrubbing brush; **—lappen** *m* floorcloth; **—leiste** *f* skirting board; **s—n** *vt* scour, scrub.
Scheuklappe *f* blinker.
Scheune [ˈʃɔynə] *f* -, -n barn.
Scheusal [ˈʃɔyzaːl] *nt* -s, -e monster.
scheußlich [ˈʃɔyslɪç] *a* dreadful, frightful; **S—keit** *f* dreadfulness.
Schi [ʃiː] *m see* **Ski.**

Schicht [ʃɪçt] *f* -, -en layer; *(Klasse)* class, level; *(in Fabrik etc)* shift; **—arbeit** *f* shift work; **s—vt** layer, stack.
schick [ʃɪk] *a* stylish, chic; **—en** *vt* send; *vr* resign oneself (*in* +*acc* to); *v impers (anständig sein)* be fitting; **—lich** *a* proper, fitting; **S—sal** *nt* -s, -e fate; **—salsschlag** *m* great misfortune, blow.
Schieb- [ˈʃiːb] *cpd*: **—edach** *nt (Aut)* sunshine roof; **s—en** *vti irreg* push; *Schuld* put (*auf jdn on* sb); **—er** *m* -s, - slide; *(Besteckteil)* pusher; *(Person)* profiteer; **—etür** *f* sliding door; **—lehre** *f (Math)* calliper rule; **—ung** *f* fiddle.
Schieds- [ˈʃiːts] *cpd*: **—gericht** *nt* court of arbitration; **—richter** *m* referee, umpire; *(Schlichter)* arbitrator; **s—richtern** *vti insep* referee, umpire; arbitrate; **—spruch** *m* arbitration award.
schief [ʃiːf] *a* crooked; *Ebene* sloping; *Turm* leaning; *Winkel* oblique; *Blick* funny; *Vergleich* distorted; *ad* crooked(ly); **—ansehen** askance; **etw —** stellen slope sth.
Schiefer [ˈʃiːfər] *m* -s, - slate; **—dach** *nt* slate roof; **—tafel** *f* (child's) slate.
schief- *cpd*: **—gehen** *vi irreg (col)* go wrong; **—lachen** *vr (col)* double up with laughter; **—liegen** *vi irreg (col)* be wrong.
schielen [ˈʃiːlən] *vi* squint; **nach etw —** *(fig)* eye sth.
Schienbein *nt* shinbone.
Schiene [ˈʃiːnə] *f* -, -n rail; *(Med)* splint; **s—n** *vt* put in splints; **—nstrang** *m (Rail etc)* (section of) track.
schier [ʃiːr] *a* pure; *Fleisch* lean and boneless; *(fig)* sheer; *ad* nearly, almost.

Schieß- [ʃiːs] cpd: **—bude** f shooting gallery; **—budenfigur** f (col) clown, ludicrous figure; **s—en** vti irreg shoot (auf +acc at); (Salat etc) run to seed; Ball kick; Geschoß fire; **—e'rei** f shooting incident, shoot-up; **—platz** m firing range; **—pulver** nt gunpowder; **—scharte** f embrasure; **—stand** m rifle or shooting range.

Schiff [ʃif] nt **-(e)s, -e** ship, vessel; (Kirchen—) nave; **s—bar** a navigable; **—bau** m shipbuilding; **—bruch** m shipwreck; **s—brüchig** a shipwrecked; **—chen** nt small boat; (Weben) shuttle; (Mütze) forage cap; **—er** m **-s, -** bargeman, boatman; **—(f)ahrt** f shipping; (Reise) voyage; **—(f)ahrtslinie** f shipping route; **—sjunge** m cabin boy; **—sladung** f cargo, shipload; **—splanke** f gangplank.

Schikane [ʃi'kaːnə] f **-, -n** harassment; dirty trick; mit allen **—n** with all the trimmings.

schikanieren [ʃika'niːrən] vt harass, torment.

Schild [ʃilt] m **-(e)s, -e** shield; (Mützen—) peak, visor; etw im **—e führen** be up to sth; nt **-(e)s, -er** sign; nameplate; (Etikett) label; **—bürger** m duffer, blockhead; **—drüse** f thyroid gland; **s—ern** [ˈʃildərn] vt depict, portray; **—erung** f description, portrayal; **—kröte** f tortoise; (Wasser—) turtle.

Schilf [ʃilf] nt **-(e)s, -e, -rohr** nt (Pflanze) reed; (Material) reeds pl, rushes pl.

schillern [ˈʃilərn] vi shimmer; **s—d** a iridescent.

Schimmel [ˈʃiməl] m **-s, -** mould; (Pferd) white horse; **s—ig** a mouldy; **s—n** vi get mouldy.

Schimmer [ˈʃimər] m **-s** glimmer; **s—n** vi glimmer, shimmer.

Schimpanse [ʃim'panzə] m **-n, -n** chimpanzee.

Schimpf [ʃimpf] m **-(e)s, -e** disgrace; **s—en** vti scold; vi curse, complain; **—wort** nt term of abuse.

Schind- [ˈʃind] cpd: **—el** f **-, -n** shingle; **s—en** irreg vt maltreat, drive too hard; (col) Eindruck **s—en** create an impression; vr sweat and strain, toil away (mit at); **—er** m **-s, -** knacker; (fig) slave driver; **—e'rei** f grind, drudgery; **—luder** nt: **—luder treiben mit** muck or mess about; Vorrecht abuse.

Schinken [ˈʃiŋkən] m **-s, -** ham.

Schippe [ˈʃipə] f **-, -n** shovel; **s—n** vt shovel.

Schirm [ʃirm] m **-(e)s, -e** (Regen—) umbrella; (Sonnen—) parasol, sunshade; (Wand—, Bild—) screen; (Lampen—) (lamp)shade; (Mützen—) peak; (Pilz—) cap; **—bildaufnahme** f X-ray; **—herr** m patron, protector; **—mütze** f peaked cap; **—ständer** m umbrella stand.

schizophren [ʃitso'freːn] a schizophrenic.

Schlacht [ʃlaxt] f **-, -en** battle; **s—en** vt slaughter, kill; **—enbummler** m football supporter; **—er** m **-s, -** butcher; **—feld** nt battlefield; **—haus** nt, **—hof** m slaughterhouse, abattoir; **—plan** m (lit, fig) battle plan; **—ruf** m battle cry, war cry; **—schiff** nt battle ship; **—vieh** nt animals kept for meat; beef cattle.

Schlacke [ˈʃlakə] f **-, -n** slag.

Schlaf [ʃlaːf] m **-(e)s** sleep; **—anzug** m pyjamàs pl.

Schläf- ['ʃlɛːf] cpd: **—chen** nt nap; **—e f** -, -n temple.

schlafen ['ʃaːfən] vi irreg sleep; **S—gehen** nt -s going to bed; **S—szeit f** bedtime.

Schläfer(in f) ['ʃlɛːfər(m)] m -s, - sleeper.

schlaff [ʃlaf] a slack; (energielos) limp; (erschöpft) exhausted; **S—heit f** slackness; limpness; exhaustion.

Schlaf- cpd: **—gelegenheit f** sleeping accommodation; **—lied** nt lullaby; **s—los** a sleepless; **—losigkeit f** sleeplessness, insomnia; **—mittel** nt soporific, sleeping pill.

schläfrig ['ʃlɛːfrɪç] a sleepy.

Schlaf- cpd: **—saal** m dormitory; **—sack** m sleeping bag; **—tablette f** sleeping pill; **s—trunken** a drowsy, half-asleep; **—wagen** m sleeping car, sleeper; **s—wandeln** vi insep sleepwalk; **—zimmer** nt bedroom.

Schlag [ʃlaːk] m -(e)s, ⁼e (lit, fig) blow; stroke (auch Med); (Puls-, Herz-) beat; (pl: Tracht Prügel) beating; (Elec) shock; (Blitz-) bolt, stroke; (Autotür) car door; (col: Portion) helping; (Art) kind, type; mit einem — all at once; — auf — in rapid succession; **—ader f** artery; **—anfall** m stroke; **s—artig** a sudden, without warning; **—baum** m barrier; **s—en** ['ʃlaːgən] irreg vti strike, hit; (wiederholt —, besiegen) beat; (Glocke) ring; Stunde strike; Sahne whip; Schlacht fight; (einwickeln) wrap; nach jdm s—en (fig) take after sb; vr fight; sich gut s—en (fig) do well; s—end a Beweis convincing; s—ende Wetter (Min) firedamp; **—er**

['ʃlaːgər] m -s, - (lit, fig) hit; **—ersänger(in f)** m pop singer.

Schläg- ['ʃlɛːg] cpd: **—er** m -s, - brawler; (Sport) bat; (Tennis etc) racket; (golf) club; hockey stick; (Waffe) rapier; **—erei f** fight, punch-up.

Schlag- cpd: **s—fertig** a quickwitted; **—fertigkeit f** ready wit, quickness of repartee; **—instrument** nt percussion instrument; **—loch** nt pothole; **—rahm** m, **—sahne f** (whipped) cream; **—seite f** (Naut) list; **—wort** nt slogan, catch phrase; **—zeile f** headline; **—zeug** nt percussion; drums pl; **—zeuger** m -s, - drummer.

Schlamassel [ʃlaˈmasəl] m -s, - (col) mess.

Schlamm [ʃlam] m -(e)s, -e mud; **s—ig** a muddy.

Schlamp- ['ʃlamp] cpd: **—e f** -, -n (col) slattern, slut; **s—en** vi (col) be sloppy; **—erei f** (col) disorder, untidiness; sloppy work; **s—ig** a (col) slovenly, sloppy.

Schlange ['ʃlaŋə] f -, -n snake; (Menschen-) queue (Brit), line-up (US); — stehen (form a) queue, line up.

schlängeln ['ʃlɛŋəln] vr twist, wind; (Fluß) meander.

Schlangen- cpd: **—biß** m snake bite; **—ngift** nt snake venom; **—linie f** wavy line.

schlank [ʃlaŋk] a slim, slender; **S—heit f** slimness, slenderness; **S—heitskur f** diet.

schlapp [ʃlap] a limp; (locker) slack; **S—e f** -, -n (col) setback; **S—heit f** limpness; slackness; **S—hut** m slouch hat; **—machen** vi (col) wilt, droop.

Schlaraffenland [ʃlaˈrafənlant] nt land of milk and honey.

schlau [ʃlaʊ] a crafty, cunning.

Schlauch [ʃlaʊx] m -(e)s, .Schläuche hose; (in Reifen) inner 'tube; (col: Anstrengung) grind; —boot nt rubber dinghy; s—en vt (col) tell on, exhaust; s—los a Reifen tubeless.

Schlau- cpd: —heit f, Schläue [ʃlɔʏə] f - cunning; —kopf m clever dick.

schlecht [ʃlɛçt] a bad; — und recht after a fashion; jdm ist — sb feels sick or bad; —gehen vi impers irreg: jdm geht es — sb is in a bad way; S—heit f badness; '—hin ad simply; der Dramatiker —hin THE playwright; S—igkeit f badness; bad deed; —machen vt run down; etw —machen do sth badly; —weg ad simply.

schlecken [ʃlɛkən] vti lick.

Schlegel [ʃle:gəl] m -s, - (drum)stick; (Hammer) mallet, hammer; (Cook) leg.

Schleie [ʃlaɪə] f -, -n tench.

schleichen [ʃlaɪçən] vi irreg creep, crawl; —d a gradual; creeping.

Schleier [ʃlaɪər] m -s, - veil; s—haft a (col) jdm s—haft sein be a mystery to sb.

Schleif- [ʃlaɪf] cpd: —e f -, -n loop; (Band) bow; s—en vt irreg drag; (Mil) Festung raze; vi drag; vt irreg grind; Edelstein cut; (Mil) Soldaten drill; —stein m grindstone.

Schleim [ʃlaɪm] m -(e)s, -e slime; (Med) mucus; (Cook) gruel; s—ig a slimy.

Schlemm- [ʃlɛm] cpd: s—en vi feast; —er m -s, - gourmet; —e'rei f gluttony, feasting.

schlendern [ʃlɛndərn] vi stroll.

Schlendrian [ʃlɛndria:n] m -(e)s sloppy way of working.

schlenkern [ʃlɛŋkərn] vti swing, dangle.

Schlepp- [ʃlɛp] cpd: —e f -, -n train; s—en vt drag; Auto, Schiff tow; (tragen) lug; s—end a dragging, slow; —er m -s, - tractor; (Schiff) tug; —tau nt towrope; jdn ins —tau nehmen (fig) take sb in tow.

Schleuder [ʃlɔʏdər] f -, -n catapult; (Wäsche—) spin-drier; (Butter— etc) centrifuge; s—n vt hurl; Wäsche spin-dry; vi (Aut) skid; —preis m give-away price; —sitz m (Aviat) ejector seat; (fig) hot seat; —ware f cheap or cutprice goods pl.

schleunig [ʃlɔʏnɪç] a quick, prompt; —st ad straight away.

Schleuse [ʃlɔʏzə] f -, -n lock; (—ntor) sluice.

Schlich [ʃlɪç] m -(e)s, -e dodge, trick.

schlicht [ʃlɪçt] a simple, plain; —en vt smooth, dress; Streit settle; S—er m -s, - mediator, arbitrator; S—ung f settlement; arbitration.

Schlick [ʃlɪk] m -(e)s, -e mud; (Öl—) slick.

Schließ- [ʃli:s] cpd: —e f -, -n fastener; s—en irreg vtir close, shut; (beenden) close; Freundschaft, Bündnis, Ehe enter into; (folgern) infer (aus +dat from); etw in sich s—en include sth; —fach nt locker; s—lich ad finally; (— doch) after all.

Schliff [ʃlɪf] m -(e)s, -e cut(ting); (fig) polish.

schlimm [ʃlɪm] a bad; —er a worse; —ste(r,s) a worst; —stenfalls ad at (the) worst.

Schling- [ˈʃlɪŋ] cpd: **—e** f -, -n loop; (esp Henkers—) noose; (Falle) snare; (Méd) sling; **—el** m -s, - rascal; **s—en** irreg vt wind; vti (essen) bolt (one's food), gobble; **s—ern** vt roll.

Schlips [ʃlɪps] m -es, -e tie.

Schlitten [ˈʃlɪtən] m -s, - sledge, sleigh; **—bahn** f toboggan run; **—fahren** nt -s tobogganing.

schlittern [ˈʃlɪtərn] vi slide.

Schlittschuh [ˈʃlɪt-ʃuː] m skate; **— laufen** skate; **—bahn** f skating rink; **—läufer(in** f) m skater.

Schlitz [ʃlɪts] m -es, -e slit; (für Münze) slot; (Hosen—) flies pl; **s—äugig** a slant-eyed; **s—en** vt slit.

schlohweiß [ˈʃloːˈvaɪs] a snow-white.

Schloß [ʃlɔs] nt -sses, ⸚sser lock; (an Schmuck etc) clasp; (Bau) castle; chateau.

Schlosser [ˈʃlɔsər] m -s, - (Auto—) fitter; (für Schlüssel etc) locksmith; **—ei** [-ˈraɪ] f metal (working) shop.

Schlot [ʃloːt] m -(e)s, -e chimney; (Naut) funnel.

schlottern [ˈʃlɔtərn] vi shake, tremble; (Kleidung) be baggy.

Schlucht [ʃlʊxt] f -, -en gorge, ravine.

schluchzen [ˈʃlʊxtsən] vi sob.

Schluck [ʃlʊk] m -(e)s, -e swallow; (Menge) drop; **—auf** m -s, —en m -s, - hiccups pl; **s—en** vti swallow.

schludern [ˈʃluːdərn] vi skimp, do sloppy work.

Schlummer [ˈʃlʊmər] m -s slumber; **s—n** vi slumber.

Schlund [ʃlʊnt] m -(e)s, ⸚e gullet; (fig) jaw.

schlüpfen [ˈʃlʏpfən] vi slip; (Vogel etc) hatch (out).

Schlüpfer [ˈʃlʏpfər] m -s, - panties pl, knickers pl.

Schlupfloch [ˈʃlʊpflɔx] nt hole; hide-out; (fig) loophole.

schlüpfrig [ˈʃlʏpfrɪç] a slippery; (fig) lewd; **S—keit** f slipperiness; (fig) lewdness.

schlurfen [ˈʃlʊrfən] vi shuffle.

schlürfen [ˈʃlʏrfən] vti slurp.

Schluß [ʃlʊs] m -sses, ⸚sse end; (—folgerung) conclusion; **am —** at the end; **— machen mit** finish with.

Schlüssel [ˈʃlʏsəl] m -s, - (lit, fig) key; (Schraub—) spanner, wrench; (Mus) clef; **—bein** nt collarbone; **—blume** f cowslip, primrose; **—bund** m bunch of keys; **—kind** nt latchkey child; **—loch** nt keyhole; **—position** f key position; **—wort** f combination.

schlüssig [ˈʃlʏsɪç] a conclusive.

Schluß- cpd: **—licht** nt taillight; (fig) tailender; **—strich** m (fig) final stroke; **—verkauf** m clearance sale; **—wort** nt concluding words pl.

Schmach [ʃmaːx] f - disgrace, ignominy.

schmachten [ˈʃmaxtən] vi languish; long (nach for).

schmächtig [ˈʃmɛçtɪç] a slight.

schmachvoll a ignominious, humiliating.

schmackhaft [ˈʃmakhaft] a tasty.

schmäh- [ˈʃmɛː] cpd: **—en** vt abuse, revile; **—lich** a ignominious, shameful; **S—ung** f abuse.

schmal [ʃmaːl] a narrow; Person, Buch etc slender, slim; (karg) meagre.

schmälern [ˈʃmɛːlərn] vt diminish; (fig) belittle.

Schmal- *cpd:* —film *m* cine film; —spur *f* narrow gauge.

Schmalz ['ʃmalts] *nt* -es, -e dripping, lard; *(fig)* sentiment, schmaltz; s—ig a *(fig)* schmaltzy, slushy.

schmarotzen [ʃma'rɔtsən] *vi* sponge; *(Bot)* be parasitic.

Schmarotzer *m* -s, - parasite; sponger.

Schmarren ['ʃmarən] *m* -s, - *(Aus)* small piece of pancake; *(fig)* rubbish, tripe.

schmatzen ['ʃmatsən] *vi* smack one's lips; eat noisily.

Schmaus ['ʃmaus] *m* -es, Schmäuse feast; s—en *vi* feast.

schmecken ['ʃmɛkən] *vti* taste; es schmeckt ihm he likes it.

Schmeichel- ['ʃmaɪçəl] *cpd:* —ei [-'laɪ] *f* flattery; s—haft a flattering; s—n *vi* flatter.

schmeißen ['ʃmaɪsən] *vt irreg (col)* throw, chuck.

Schmeißfliege *f* bluebottle.

Schmelz [ʃmɛlts] *m* -es, -e enamel; *(Glasur)* glaze; *(von Stimme)* melodiousness; s—bar a fusible; s—en *vti irreg* melt; Erz smelt; —hütte *f* smelting works *pl*; —punkt *m* melting point; —wasser *nt* melted snow.

Schmerz [ʃmɛrts] *m* -es, -en pain; *(Trauer)* grief; s—empfindlich a sensitive to pain; s—en *vti* hurt; —ensgeld *nt* compensation; s—haft, s—lich a painful; s—los a painless; s—stillend a soothing.

Schmetterling ['ʃmɛtərlɪŋ] *m* butterfly.

schmettern ['ʃmɛtərn] *vt* smash; *Melodie* sing loudly, bellow out; *(Trompete)* blare.

Schmied [ʃmiːt] *m* -(e)s, -e blacksmith; —e ['ʃmiːdə] *f* -, -n smithy,

forge; —eelsen *nt* wrought iron; s—en *vt* forge; *Pläne* devise, concoct.

schmiegen ['ʃmiːgən] *vt* press, nestle; *vr* cling, nestle (up) *(an +acc* to).

schmiegsam ['ʃmiːkzaːm] *a* flexible, pliable.

Schmier- ['ʃmiːr] *cpd:* —e *f* -, -n grease; *(Theat)* greasepaint, make-up; s—en *vt* smear; *(ölen)* lubricate, grease; *(bestechen)* bribe; *vti (schreiben)* scrawl; —fett *nt* grease; —fink *m* messy person; —geld *nt* bribe; s—ig a greasy; —mittel *nt* lubricant; —seife *f* soft soap.

Schminke ['ʃmɪŋkə] *f* -, -n make-up; s—n *vtr* make up.

schmirgel- ['ʃmɪrgəl] *cpd:* —n *vt* sand (down); —papier *nt* emery paper.

Schmöker ['ʃmøːkər] *m* -s, - *(col)* (trashy) old book; s—n *vi (col)* browse.

schmollen ['ʃmɔlən] *vi* sulk, pout; —d a sulky.

Schmor- ['ʃmoːr] *cpd:* —braten *m* stewed or braised meat; s—en *vt* stew, braise.

Schmuck [ʃmʊk] *m* -(e)s, -e jewellery; *(Verzierung)* decoration.

schmücken ['ʃmʏkən] *vt* decorate.

Schmuck- *cpd:* —los a unadorned, plain; —losigkeit *f* simplicity; —sachen *pl* jewels *pl*, jewellery.

Schmuggel ['ʃmʊgəl] *m* -s smuggling; s—n *vti* smuggle.

Schmuggler *m* -s, - smuggler.

schmunzeln ['ʃmʊntsəln] *vi* smile benignly.

Schmutz [ʃmʊts] *m* -es dirt, filth; s—en *vi* get dirty; —fink *m* filthy creature; —fleck m stain; s—ig a dirty.

Schnabel ['ʃnaːbəl] m -s, ⸚ beak, bill; (Ausguß) spout.

Schnake ['ʃnaːkə] f -, -n cranefly; (Stechmücke) gnat.

Schnalle ['ʃnalə] f -, -n buckle, clasp; s—n vt buckle.

schnalzen ['ʃnaltsən] vi snap; (mit Zunge) click.

Schnapp- ['ʃnap] cpd: s—en vt grab, catch; vi snap; —schloß nt spring lock; —schuß m (Phot) snapshot.

Schnaps [ʃnaps] m -es, ⸚e spirits pl; schnapps.

schnarchen ['ʃnarçən] vi snore.

schnattern ['ʃnatərn] vi chatter; (zittern) shiver.

schnauben ['ʃnaubən] vi snort; vr blow one's nose.

schnaufen ['ʃnaufən] vi puff, pant.

Schnauz- ['ʃnauts] cpd: —bart m moustache; —e f -, -n snout, muzzle; (Ausguß) spout; (col) gob.

Schnecke ['ʃnekə] f -, -n snail; —nhaus nt snail's shell.

Schnee [ʃneː] m -s snow; (Ei-) beaten egg white; —ball m snowball; —flocke f snowflake; —gestöber nt snowstorm; —glöckchen nt snowdrop; —kette f (Aut) (snow) chain; —pflug m snowplough; —schmelze f -, -n thaw; —wehe f snowdrift; —wittchen nt Snow White.

Schneid [ʃnaɪt] m -(e)s (col) pluck; —e f ['ʃnaɪdə] f -, -n edge; (Klinge) blade; s—en vtr irreg cut (o.s.); (kreuzen) cross, intersect; s—end a cutting; —er m -s, -, tailor; —erin f dressmaker; s—ern vt make; vi be a tailor; —ezahn m incisor; s—ig a dashing; (mutig) plucky.

schneien ['ʃnaɪən] vi snow.

Schneise ['ʃnaɪzə] f -, -n clearing.

schnell [ʃnɛl] a,ad quick(ly), fast; —en vi shoot, fly; S—hefter m -s, -, loose-leaf binder; S—igkeit f speed; —stens ad as quickly as possible; S—straße f expressway; S—zug m fast or express train.

schneuzen ['ʃnɔʏtsən] vr blow one's nose.

schnippisch ['ʃnɪpɪʃ] a sharp-tongued.

Schnitt [ʃnɪt] m -(e)s, -e cut(ting); (—punkt) intersection; (Quer—) (cross) section; (Durch—) average; (—muster) pattern; (Ernte) crop; (an Buch) edge; (col: Gewinn) profit; —blumen pl cut flowers pl; —e f -, -n slice; (belegt) sandwich; —fläche f section; —lauch m chive; —muster nt pattern; —punkt m (point of) intersection; —wunde f cut.

Schnitz- ['ʃnɪts] cpd: —arbeit f wood carving; —el nt -s, - chip; (Cook) escalope; s—en vt carve; —er m -s, - carver; (col) blunder; —e'rei f carving; carved woodwork.

schnoddrig ['ʃnɔdrɪç] a (col) snotty.

schnöde ['ʃnøːdə] a base, mean.

Schnorchel ['ʃnɔrçəl] m -s, - snorkel.

Schnörkel ['ʃnœrkəl] m -s, - flourish; (Archit) scroll.

schnorren ['ʃnɔrən] vti cadge.

schnüffeln ['ʃnʏfəln] vi sniff.

Schnüffler m -s, - snooper.

Schnuller ['ʃnʊlər] m -s, - dummy, comforter (US).

Schnupfen ['ʃnʊpfən] m -s, - cold.

schnuppern ['ʃnʊpərn] vi sniff.

Schnur [ʃnuːr] *f* -, ⸚e string, cord; (*Elec*) flex; — **gerade** a straight (as a die *or* arrow).

schnüren [ˈʃnyːrən] *vt* tie.

Schnurr- [ˈʃnur] *cpd:* —**bart** *m* moustache; **s—en** *vi* purr; (*Kreisel*) hum.

Schnür- [ˈʃnyː] *cpd:* —**schuh** *m* lace-up (shoe); —**senkel** *m* shoe-lace.

schnurstracks *ad* straight (away).

Schock [ʃɔk] *m* -(e)s, -e shock; **s—ieren** [ʃɔˈkiːrən] *vt* shock, outrage.

Schöffe [ˈʃœfə] *m* -n, -n lay magistrate; —**ngericht** *nt* magistrates' court.

Schöffin *f* lay magistrate.

Schokolade [ʃokoˈlaːdə] *f* -, -n chocolate.

Scholle [ˈʃɔlə] *f* -, -n clod; (*Eis—*) ice floe; (*Fisch*) plaice.

schon [ʃoːn] *ad* already; (*zwar*) certainly; warst du — einmal da? have you ever been there?; ich war — einmal da I've been there before; das ist — immer so that has always been the case; das wird — (noch) gut that'll be OK; wenn ich das — höre . . . I only have to hear that . . . ; — der Gedanke the very thought.

schön [ʃøːn] *a* beautiful; (*nett*) nice; —**e Grüße** best wishes; —**en Dank** (many) thanks.

schonen [ˈʃoːnən] *vt* look after; *vr* take it easy; —**d** a careful, gentle.

Schön- *cpd:* —**geist** *m* cultured person, aesthete; —**heit** *f* beauty; —**heitsfehler** *m* blemish, flaw; —**heitsoperation** *f* cosmetic plastic surgery; **s—machen** *vr* make oneself look nice. .

Schon- *cpd:* —**ung** *f* good care; (*Nachsicht*) consideration; (*Forst*) plantation of young trees; **s—ungslos** a unsparing, harsh; —**zeit** *f* close season.

Schöpf- [ˈʃœpf] *cpd:* **s—en** *vt* scoop, ladle; (*Mut* summon up; *Luft* breath in; —**er** *m* -s, - creator; **s—erisch** a creative; —**kelle** *f* ladle; —**löffel** *m* skimmer, scoop; —**ung** *f* creation.

Schorf [ʃɔrf] *m* -(e)s, -e scab.

Schornstein [ˈʃɔrnʃtain] *m* chimney; (*Naut*) funnel; —**feger** *m* -s, - chimney sweep.

Schoß [ʃoːs] *m* -es, ⸚e lap; (*Rock—*) coat tail; —**hund** *m* pet dog, lapdog.

Schote [ˈʃoːtə] *f* -, -n pod.

Schotter [ˈʃɔtər] *m* -s broken stone, road metal; (*Rail*) ballast.

schraffieren [ʃraˈfiːrən] *vt* hatch.

schräg [ʃrɛːk] a slanting, not straight; **etw** — **stellen** put sth at an angle; — **gegenüber** diagonally opposite; **S—e** *f* -, -n slant; —**schrift** *f* italics *pl*; **S—streifen** *m* bias binding; **S—strich** *m* oblique stroke.

Schramme [ˈʃramə] *f* -, -n scratch; **s—n** *vt* scratch.

Schrank [ʃraŋk] *m* -(e)s, ⸚e cupboard; (*Kleider—*) wardrobe; —**e** *f* -, -n barrier; **s—enlos** a boundless; (*zügellos*) unrestrained; —**enwärter** *m* (*Rail*) level crossing attendant; —**koffer** *m* trunk.

Schraube [ˈʃraubə] *f* -, -n screw; **s—n** *vt* screw; —**nschlüssel** *m* spanner; —**nzieher** *m* -s, - screwdriver.

Schraubstock [ˈʃraupʃtɔk] *m* (*Tech*) vice.

Schrebergarten [ˈʃreːbərgartən] *m* allotment.

Schreck [ʃrɛk] *m* -(e)s, -e, —**en** *m* -s, - terror; fright; **s—en** *vt* frighten, scare; **—gespenst** nt spectre, nightmare; **s—haft** a jumpy, easily frightened; **s—lich** a terrible, dreadful; **—schuß** m shot fired in the air.

Schrei [ʃraɪ] m -(e)s, -e scream; '(Ruf) shout.

Schreib- [ʃraɪb] cpd: **—block** m writing pad; **s—en** irreg vti write; (buchstabieren) spell; **—en** nt -s, - letter, 'communication; **—er** m -s, - writer (Büro—) clerk; **s—faul** a bad about writing letters; **—fehler** m spelling mistake; **—maschine** f typewriter; **—papier** nt notepaper; **—tisch** m desk; **—ung** f spelling; **—waren** pl stationery; **—weise** f spelling; way of writing; **—zeug** nt writing materials pl.

schreien [ʃraɪən] vti irreg scream; (rufen) shout; **—d** a (fig) glaring; Farbe loud.

Schreiner [ʃraɪnər] m -s, - joiner; (Zimmermann) carpenter; (Möbel—) cabinetmaker; **—ei** [-'raɪ] f joiner's workshop.

schreiten [ʃraɪtən] vi irreg stride.

Schrift [ʃrɪft] f -, -en writing; handwriting; (—art) script; (Gedrucktes) pamphlet, work; **—deutsch** nt written German; **—führer** m secretary; **s—lich** a written; ad in writing; **—setzer** m compositor; **—sprache** f written language; **—steller(in** f) m -s, - writer; **—stück** nt document.

schrill [ʃrɪl] a shrill; **—en** vi sound or ring shrilly.

Schritt [ʃrɪt] m -(e)s, -e step; (Gangart) walk; (Tempo) pace; (von Hose) crutch; **—macher** m -s, - pacemaker; **—(t)empo** nt: im **—(t)empo** at a walking pace.

schroff [ʃrɔf] a steep; (zackig)

jagged; (fig) brusque; (ungeduldig) abrupt.

schröpfen [ʃrœpfən] vt (fig) fleece.

Schrot [ʃroːt] m or nt -(e)s, -e (Blei) (small) shot; (Getreide) coarsely ground grain, groats pl; **—flinte** f shotgun.

Schrott [ʃrɔt] m -(e)s, -e scrap metal; **—haufen** m scrap heap; **s—reif** a ready for the scrap heap.

schrubben [ʃrʊbən] vt scrub.

Schrubber m -s, - scrubbing brush.

Schrulle [ʃrʊlə] f -, -n eccentricity, queer idea/habit.

schrumpfen [ʃrʊmpfən] vi shrink; (Äpfel) shrivel.

Schub- [ʃuːb] cpd: **—fach** nt drawer; **—karren** m wheelbarrow; **—lade** f drawer.

schüchtern [ʃʏçtərn] a shy; **S—heit** f shyness.

Schuft [ʃʊft] m -(e)s, -e scoundrel; **s—en** vi (col) graft, slave away.

Schuh [ʃuː] m -(e)s, -e shoe; **—band** nt shoelace; **—creme** f shoe polish; **—löffel** m shoehorn; **—macher** m -s, - shoemaker.

Schul- [ʃuːl] cpd: **—aufgaben** pl homework; **—besuch** m school attendance.

Schuld [ʃʊlt] f -, -en guilt; (Fin) debt; (Verschulden) fault; **s— a:** **s— sein** or **haben be** to blame (an +dat for); er ist or hat **s—** it's his fault; jdm **s—** geben blame sb; **s—en** [ʃʊldən] vt owe; **—enfrei** a free from debt; **—gefühl** nt feeling of guilt; **s—ig** a guilty (an +dat of); (gebührend) due; jdm etw **s—ig** sein owe sb sth; jdm etw **s—ig** bleiben not provide sb with sth; **s—los** a innocent, without guilt; **—ner** m -s, - debtor;

—schein *m* promissory note, IOU ; —spruch *m* verdict of guilty.

Schule ['ʃuːlə] *f* -, -n school ; s—n *vt* train, school.

Schüler(in *f*) ['ʃyːlər(in)] *m* -s, - pupil.

Schul- ['ʃuːl] *cpd*: —ferien *pl* school holidays *pl* ; s—frei *a*: s—freier Tag holiday ; s—frei sein be a holiday ; —funk *m* schools' broadcasts *pl* ; —geld *nt* school fees *pl* ; —hof *m* playground ; —jahr *nt* school year ; —junge *m* schoolboy ; —mädchen *nt* schoolgirl ; s—pflichtig *a* : of school age ; —schiff *nt* (Naut) training ship ; —stunde *f* period, lesson ; —tasche *f* satchel.

Schulter ['ʃultər] *f* -, -n shoulder ; —blatt *nt* shoulder blade ; s—n *vt* shoulder.

Schul- *cpd*: —ung *f* education, schooling ; —wesen *nt* educational system ; —zeugnis *nt* school report.

Schund [ʃunt] *m* -(e)s trash, garbage ; —roman *m* trashy novel.

Schuppe ['ʃupə] *f* -, -n scale ; *pl* (Haar—) dandruff ; s—n *vt* scale ; *vr* peel ; —n *m* -s, - shed.

schuppig ['ʃupiç] *a* scaly.

Schur [ʃuːr] *f* -, -en shearing.

Schür- [ʃyːr] *cpd*: —eisen *nt* poker ; s—en *vt* rake ; (*fig*) stir up ; s—fen ['ʃyrfən] *vti* scrape, scratch ; (*Min*) prospect, dig ; —fung *f* abrasion ; (*Min*) prospecting ; —haken *m* poker.

Schurke ['ʃurkə] *m* -n, -n rogue.

Schurz [ʃurts] *m* -es, -e, **Schürze** ['ʃyrtsə] *f* -, -n apron.

Schuß [ʃus] *m* -sses, ̈sse shot ; (Weben) woof ; —bereich *m* effective range.

Schüssel ['ʃysəl] *f* -, -n bowl.

Schuß- *cpd*: —linie *f* line of fire ; —verletzung *f* bullet wound ;

—waffe *f* firearm ; —weite *f* range (of fire).

Schuster ['ʃuːstər] *m* -s, - cobbler, shoemaker.

Schutt [ʃut] *m* -(e)s rubbish ; (Bau—) rubble ; —abladeplatz *m* refuse dump.

Schütt- [ʃyt] *cpd*: —elfrost *m* shivering ; s—eln *vtr* shake ; s—en *vt* pour ; (Zucker, Kies etc) tip ; (ver—) spill ; *vt impers* pour (down) ; s—er *a* Haare sparse, thin.

Schutt- *cpd*: —halde *f* dump ; —haufen *m* heap of rubble.

Schutz [ʃuts] *m* -es protection ; (Unterschlupf) shelter ; jdn in —nehmen stand up for sb ; —anzug *m* overalls *pl* ; —befohlene(r) *mf* charge ; —blech *nt* mudguard ; —brille *f* goggles *pl*.

Schütze ['ʃytsə] *m* -n, -n gunman ; (Gewehr—) rifleman ; (Scharf-Sport—) marksman ; (Astrol) Sagittarius.

Schutz- *cpd*: —engel *m* guardian angel ; —gebiet *nt* protectorate ; (Natur—) reserve ; —haft *f* protective custody ; —impfung *f* immunisation ; s—los *a* defenceless ; —mann *m*, *pl* -leute or -männer policeman ; —maßnahme *f* precaution ; —patron *m* patron saint ; —umschlag *m* (book) jacket ; —vorrichtung *f* safety device.

schwach [ʃvax] *a* weak, feeble.

Schwäche ['ʃvɛçə] *f* -, -n weakness ; s—n *vt* weaken.

Schwach- *cpd*: —heit *f* weakness ; s—köpfig *a* silly, lame-brained.

Schwäch- *cpd*: s—lich *a* weakly, delicate ; —ling *m* weakling.

Schwach- *cpd*: —sinn *m* imbecility ; s—sinnig *a* mentally deficient; *Idee* idiotic; **—strom** *m* weak current.

Schwächung ['ʃvɛçʊŋ] *f* weakening.

Schwaden ['ʃvɑːdən] *m* -s, - cloud.

schwafeln ['ʃvɑːfəln] *vti* blather, drivel.

Schwager ['ʃvɑːɡər] *m* -s, **≠** brother-in-law.

Schwägerin ['ʃvɛːɡərɪn] *f* sister-law.

Schwalbe ['ʃvalbə] *f* -, -n swallow.

Schwall [ʃval] *m* -(e)s, -e surge; *(Worte)* flood, torrent.

Schwamm [ʃvam] *m* -(e)s, **≠e** sponge; *(Pilz)* fungus; **—ig** *a* spongy; *Gesicht* puffy.

Schwan [ʃvaːn] *m* -(e)s, **≠e** swan; **—en** *vi impers:* jdm schwant etw sb has a foreboding of sth.

schwanger ['ʃvaŋər] *a* pregnant.

schwängern ['ʃvɛŋərn] *vt* make pregnant.

Schwangerschaft *f* pregnancy.

Schwank [ʃvaŋk] *m* -(e)s, **≠e** funny story; **s—en** *vi* sway; *(taumeln)* stagger, reel; *(Preise, Zahlen)* fluctuate; *(zögern)* hesitate, vacillate; **—ung** *f* fluctuation.

Schwanz [ʃvants] *m* -es, **≠e** tail.

schwänzen ['ʃvɛntsən] *(col) vt* skip, cut; *vi* play truant.

Schwänzer ['ʃvɛntsər] *m* -s, - *(col)* truant.

Schwarm [ʃvarm] *m* -(e)s, **≠e** swarm; *(col)* heart-throb, idol.

schwärm- ['ʃvɛrm] *cpd:* **—en** *vi* swarm; **—en für** be mad or wild about; **S—erei** *f* [-ə'raɪ] *f* enthusiasm; **—erisch** *a* impassioned, effusive.

Schwarte ['ʃvartə] *f* -, -n hard skin; *(Speck—)* rind.

schwarz [ʃvarts] *a* black; **ins S—e treffen** *(lit, fig)* hit the bull's eye; **S—arbeit** *f* illicit work, moonlighting; **S—brot** *nt* black bread.

Schwärze ['ʃvɛrtsə] *f* -, -n blackness; *(Farbe)* blacking; *(Drucker—)* printer's ink; **s—n** *vt* blacken.

Schwarz- *cpd:* **s—fahren** *vi irreg* travel without paying; drive without a licence; **—handel** *m* black-market *(trade)*; **s—hören** *vi* listen to the radio without a licence.

schwärzlich ['ʃvɛrtslɪç] *a* blackish, darkish.

Schwarz- *cpd:* **—markt** *m* black market; **s—sehen** *vi irreg (col)* see the gloomy side of things; *(TV)* watch TV without a licence; **—seher** *m* pessimist; *(TV)* viewer without a licence; **s—weiß** *a* black and white.

schwatzen ['ʃvatsən], **schwätzen** ['ʃvɛtsən] *vi* chatter.

Schwätzer ['ʃvɛtsər] *m* -s, - gasbag; **—in** *f* chatterbox, gossip.

schwatzhaft *a* talkative, gossipy.

Schwebe ['ʃveːbə] *f:* in der — *(fig)* in abeyance; **—bahn** *f* overhead railway; **—balken** *m (Sport)* beam; **s—n** *vi* drift, float; *(hoch)* soar; *(unentschieden sein)* be in the balance.

Schwefel ['ʃveːfəl] *m* -s sulphur; **s—ig** *a* sulphurous; **—säure** *f* sulphuric acid.

Schweif [ʃvaɪf] *m* -(e)s, -e tail; **s—en** *vi* wander, roam.

Schweig- ['ʃvaɪg] *cpd:* **—egeld** *nt* hush money; **s—en** *vi irreg* be silent; stop talking; **—en** *nt* -s silence; **s—sam** ['ʃvaɪkzaːm] *a* silent, taciturn; **—samkeit** *f* taciturnity, quietness.

Schwein [ʃvain] *nt* -(e)s; -e pig;
(fig) (good) luck; **—efleisch** *nt*
pork; **—ehund** *m* (col) stinker,
swine; **—erei** [-ə'rai] *f* mess;
(Gemeinheit) dirty trick; **—estall** *m*
pigsty; **s—isch** a filthy; **—sleder** *nt*
pigskin.

Schweiß [ʃvais] *m* -es sweat,
perspiration; **s—en** *vti* weld; **—er**
m -s, - welder; **—füße** *pl* sweaty
feet *pl*; **—naht** *f* weld.

schwelen ['ʃveːlən] *vi* smoulder.

schwelgen ['ʃvɛlgən] *vi* indulge.

Schwelle ['ʃvɛlə] *f* -, -n threshold
(auch fig); doorstep; (Rail)
sleeper; **s—n** *vi irreg* swell.

Schwellung *f* swelling.

Schwengel ['ʃvɛŋəl] *m* -s, - pump
handle; (Glocken-) clapper.

Schwenk- ['ʃvɛŋk] *cpd:* **s—bar** a
swivel-mounted; **s—en** *vt* swing;
Fahne wave; (abspülen) rinse; *vi*
turn, swivel; (Mil) wheel; **—ung** *f*
turn; wheel.

schwer [ʃveːr] a heavy;
(schwierig) difficult, hard;
(schlimm) serious, bad; *ad* (sehr)
very (much); verletzt etc seriously,
badly; **S—arbeiter** *m* manual
worker, labourer; **S—e** *f* -, -n
weight, heaviness; (Phys) gravity;
—elos a weightless; Kammer zero-
G; **S—enöter** *m* -s, - casanova,
ladies' man; **—erziehbar** a difficult
(to bring up); **—fallen** *vi irreg:* jdm
—fallen be difficult for sb; **—fällig**
a ponderous; **S—gewicht** *nt*
heavyweight; (fig) emphasis;
—hörig a hard of hearing;
S—industrie *f* heavy industry;
S—kraft *f* gravity; **S—kranke(r)**
mf person who is seriously ill;
—lich *ad* hardly; **—machen** *vt:*
jdm/sich etw **—machen** make sth
difficult for sb/o.s.; **S—metall** *nt*

heavy metal; **—mütig** a
melancholy; **—nehmen** *vt irreg*
take to heart; **S—punkt** *m* centre
of gravity; (fig) emphasis, crucial
point.

Schwert [ʃveːrt] *nt* -(e)s, -er
sword; **—lilie** *f* iris.

schwer-: **—tun** *vi irreg:* **sich**
(dat or acc) **—tun** have difficulties;
S—verbrecher(in *f*) *m* criminal,
serious offender; **—verdaulich** a
indigestible, heavy; **—verletzt** a
badly injured; **—verwundet** a
seriously wounded; **—wiegend** a
weighty, important.

Schwester ['ʃvɛstər] *f* -, -n sister;
(Med) nurse; **s—lich** a sisterly.

Schwieger- ['ʃviːgər] *cpd:* **—eltern**
pl parents-in-law *pl*; **—mutter** *f*
mother-in-law; **—sohn** *m* son-
in-law; **—tochter** *f* daughter-
in-law; **—vater** *m* father-in-law.

Schwiele ['ʃviːlə] *f* -, -n callus.

schwierig ['ʃviːrɪç] a difficult,
hard; **S—keit** *f* difficulty.

Schwimm- ['ʃvɪm] *cpd:* **—bad** *nt*
swimming baths *pl*; **—becken** *nt*
swimming pool; **s—en** *vi irreg*
swim; (treiben, nicht sinken) float;
(fig: unsicher sein) be all at sea;
—er *m* -s, - swimmer; (Angeln)
float; **—lehrer** *m* swimming
instructor; **—sport** *m* swimming;
—weste *f* life jacket.

Schwindel ['ʃvɪndəl] *m* -s
giddiness; dizzy spell; (Betrug)
swindle, fraud; (Zeug) stuff;
s—frei a free from giddiness; **s—n**
vi (col: lügen) fib; jdm **schwindelt**
es sb feels giddy.

schwinden ['ʃvɪndən] *vi irreg*
disappear; (sich verringern)
decrease; (Kräfte) decline.

Schwind- ['ʃvɪnd] *cpd:* **—ler** *m* -s,
- swindler; (Lügner) liar; **s—lig** a

giddy; **mir ist s̄—lig** I feel giddy.

Schwing- [ʃvɪŋ] *cpd*: **s—en** *vti irreg* swing; *Waffe etc* brandish; *(vibrieren)* vibrate; *(klingen)* sound; **—er** *m* -s, - *(Boxen)* swing; **—tür** *f* swing door(s); **—ung** *f* vibration; *(Phys)* oscillation.

Schwips [ʃvɪps] *m* -es, -e: **einen ~ haben** be tipsy.

schwirren [ʃvɪrən] *vi* buzz.

schwitzen [ʃvɪtsən] *vi* sweat, perspire.

schwören [ʃvøːrən] *vti irreg* swear.

schwul [ʃvuːl] *a* (col) gay, queer.

schwül [ʃvyːl] *a* sultry, close; **S—e** *f* - sultriness, closeness.

Schwulst [ʃvʊlst] *f* -(e)s, ̈e bombast.

schwülstig [ʃvʏlstɪç] *a* pompous.

Schwund [ʃvʊnt] *m* -(e)s loss; *(Schrumpfen)* shrinkage.

Schwung [ʃvʊŋ] *m* -(e)s, ̈e swing; *(Triebkraft)* momentum; *(fig: Energie)* verve, energy; *(col: Menge)* batch; **s—haft** *a* brisk, lively; **—rad** *nt* flywheel; **s—voll** *a* vigorous.

Schwur [ʃvuːr] *m* -(e)s, ̈e oath; **~gericht** *nt* court with a jury.

sechs [zɛks] *num* six; **—hundert** *num* six hundred; **—te(r,s)** *a* sixth; **S—tel** *nt* -s, - sixth.

sechzehn [zɛçtseːn] *num* sixteen.

sechzig [zɛçtsɪç] *num* sixty.

See [zeː] *f* -, -n *m* sea; *m* -s, -n lake; **—bad** *nt* seaside resort; **—fahrt** *f* seafaring; *(Reise)* voyage; **—gang** *m* (motion of the) sea; **—gras** *nt* seaweed; **—hund** *m* seal; **—igel** [zeːʔiːgəl] *m* sea urchin; **s—krank** *a* seasick; **—krankheit** *f* seasickness; **—lachs** *m* rock salmon.

Seel- [zeːl] *cpd*: **—e** *f* -, -n soul; **—enfriede(n)** *m* peace of mind; **s—enruhig** *ad* calmly.

Seeleute [zeːlɔytə] *pl* seamen *pl*.

Seel- *cpd*: **s—isch** *a* mental; **—sorge** *f* pastoral duties *pl*; **—sorger** *m* -s, - clergyman.

See- *cpd*: **—macht** *f* naval power; **—mann** *m*, *pl* **-leute** seaman, sailor; **—meile** *f* nautical mile; **—not** *f* distress; **—pferd(chen)** *nt* sea horse; **—räuber** *m* pirate; **—rose** *f* water lily; **—stern** *m* starfish; **s—tüchtig** *a* seaworthy; **—weg** *m* sea route; **auf dem —weg** by sea; **—zunge** *f* sole.

Segel [zeːgəl] *nt* -s, - sail; **—boot** *nt* yacht; **—fliegen** *nt* -s gliding; **—flieger** *m* glider pilot; **—flugzeug** *nt* glider; **s—n** *vti* sail; **—schiff** *nt* sailing vessel; **—sport** *m* sailing; **—tuch** *nt* canvas.

Segen [zeːgən] *m* -s, - blessing; **s—sreich** *a* beneficial.

Segler [zeːglər] *m* -s, - sailor, yachtsman; *(Boot)* sailing boat.

segnen [zeːgnən] *vt* bless.

Seh- [zeː] *cpd*: **s—en** *vti irreg* see; *(in bestimmte Richtung)* look; **s—enswert** *a* worth seeing; **—enswürdigkeiten** *pl* sights *pl* (of a town); **—er** *m* -s, - seer; **—fehler** *m* sight defect.

Sehn- [zeːn] *cpd*: **—e** *f* -, -n sinew; *(an Bogen)* string; **s—en** *vr* long, yearn *(nach* for*)*; **s—ig** *a* sinewy; **s—lich** *a* ardent; **—sucht** *f* longing; **s—süchtig** *a* longing.

sehr [zeːr] *ad (vor a,ad)* very; *(mit Verben)* a lot, (very) much; **zu —** too much.

seicht [zaɪçt] *a (lit, fig)* shallow.

Seide [zaɪdə] *f* -, -n silk; **—nl** *nt* -s, - tankard, beer mug; **s—n** *a* silk; **—npapier** *nt* tissue paper.

seidig ['zaɪdɪç] a silky.

Seife ['zaɪfə] vt strain, filter. f soapsuds pl; —nlauge dish; —nschale f soap —nschaum m lather.

seifig ['zaɪfɪç] a soapy.

seihen ['zaɪən] vt strain, filter.

Seil [zaɪl] nt -(e)s, -e rope; cable; —bahn f cable railway; —hüpfen nt -s, —springen nt -s skipping; —tänzer(in f) m tightrope walker; —zug m tackle.

sein [zaɪn] vi irreg be; laß das —! leave that!; stop that!; es ist an dir, zu . . . it's up to you to . . .

sein [zaɪn] pron his; its; —e(r,s) his; its; —er pron gen of er of him; —erseits ad for his part; —erzeit ad in those days, formerly; —esgleichen;pron people like him; —etwegen, —etwillen ad (für ihn) for his sake; (wegen ihm) on his account; (von ihm aus) as far as he is concerned; —ige pron: der/die/das — his.

Seismograph [zaɪsmo'gra:f] m -en, -en seismograph.

seit [zaɪt] prep, cj since; er ist — einer Woche hier he has been here for a week; — langem for a long time; —dem [zaɪt'de:m] ad,cj since. Seite ['zaɪtə] f -, -n side; (Buch-) page; (Mil) flank; —nansicht f side view; —nhieb m (fig) passing shot, dig; —nruder nt (Aviat) rudder; s—ns prep +gen on the part of; —nschiff nt aisle; —nsprung m extramarital escapade; —nstechen nt (a) stitch; —nstraße f side road; —nwagen m sidecar; —nzahl f page number; number of pages.

seit- cpd: —her [zaɪt'he:r] ad,cj since (then); —lich a on one or the side; side; —wärts ad sidewards.

Sekretär [zekre'tɛ:r] m secretary; (Möbel) bureau; —in f secretary.

Sekretariat [zekretari'a:t] nt -(e)s, -e secretary's office, secretariat.

Sekt [zɛkt] m -(e)s, -e champagne; —e f -, -n sect.

sekundär [zekun'dɛ:r] a secondary.

Sekunde [ze'kundə] f -, -n second.

selber ['zɛlbər] = selbst.

selbst [zɛlpst] pron myself; itself; themselves etc; von — by itself etc; ad even; S— nt - self; S—achtung f self-respect; —ändig ['zɛlpʃtɛndɪç] a independent; S—ändigkeit f independence; S—auslöser m (Phot) delayed-action shutter release; S—bedienung f self-service; S—befriedigung f masturbation; S—beherrschung f self-control; —bewußt a (self-)confident; S—bewußtsein nt self-confidence; S—erhaltung f self-preservation; S—erkenntnis f self-knowledge; —gefällig a smug, self-satisfied; —gemacht a home-made; S—gespräch nt conversation with oneself; S—kostenpreis m cost price; —los a unselfish, selfless; S—mord m suicide; S—mörder(in f) m suicide; —mörderisch a suicidal; —sicher a self-assured; —süchtig a selfish; —tätig a automatic; —verständlich a obvious; ad naturally;. ich halte das für —verständlich I take that for granted; S—vertrauen nt self-confidence; S—verwaltung f autonomy, self-government; S—zweck m end in itself.

selig ['ze:lɪç] a happy, blissful; (Rel) blessed; (tot) late; S—keit f bliss.

Sellerie ['zɛləri:] m -s, -(s) or f -, -n celery.

selten ['zɛltən] a rare; ad seldom, rarely; **S—heit** f rarity.

Selterswasser ['zɛltərsvasər] nt soda water.

seltsam ['zɛltza:m] a strange, curious; **—erweise** ad curiously, strangely; **S—keit** f strangeness.

Semester [ze'mɛstər] nt -s, - semester.

Semi- [zemi] in cpds semi-; **—kolon** ['ko:lɔn] nt -s, -s semicolon; **—nar** ['-'na:r] nt -s, -e seminary; (Kurs) seminar; (Univ: Ort) department building.

Semmel ['zɛməl] f -, -n roll.

Senat [ze'na:t] m -(e)s, -e senate, council.

Sende- ['zɛndə] cpd: **—bereich** m range of transmission; **—folge** f (Serie) series; **s—n** vt irreg send; yti (Rad, TV) transmit, broadcast; **—r** m -s, - station; (Anlage) transmitter; **—reihe** f series (of broadcasts); **—station** f, **—stelle** f transmitting station.

Sendung ['zɛnduŋ] f consignment; (Aufgabe) mission; (Rad, TV) transmission; (Programm) programme.

Senf [zɛnf] m -(e)s, -e mustard.

sengen ['zɛŋən] vt singe; vi scorch.

Senk- ['zɛŋk] cpd: **—blei** nt plumb; **—e** f -, -n depression; **—el** m -s, - (shoe)lace; **s—en** vt lower; vr sink, drop gradually; **—fuß** m flat foot; **s—recht** a vertical, perpendicular; **—rechte** f -n, -n perpendicular; **—rechtstarter** m (Aviat) vertical take-off plane; (fig) high-flier.

Sensation [zenzatsi'o:n] f sensation; **s—ell** [-'nɛl] a sensational; **—sucht** f sensationalism.

Sense ['zɛnzə] f -, -n scythe.

sensibel [zɛn'zi:bəl] a sensitive.

Sensibilität [zɛnzibili'tɛ:t] f sensitivity.

sentimental [zentimɛn'ta:l] a sentimental; **S—ität** f sentimentality.

separat [zepa'ra:t] a separate.

September [zɛp'ɛmbər] m -(s), - September.

septisch ['zɛptɪʃ] a septic.

Serie ['ze:riə] f series; **—nherstellung** f mass production; **s—nweise** ad in series.

seriös [zeri'ø:s] a serious, bona fide.

Serpentine [zɛrpɛn'ti:n(ə)] f .hairpin (bend).

Serum ['ze:rum] nt -s, Seren serum.

Service [zɛr'vi:s] nt -(s), - set, service; ['zø:rvɪs] m -, -s service.

servieren [zɛr'vi:rən] vti serve.

Serviette [zɛrvi'ɛtə] f napkin, serviette.

Sessel ['zɛsəl] m -s, - armchair; **—lift** m chairlift.

seßhaft ['zɛshaft] a settled; (ansässig) resident.

Sets [zɛts] pl tablemats pl.

setzen ['zɛtsən] vt put, set; Baum etc plant; Segel, (Print) set; vr settle; (person) sit down; vi leap.

Setz- [zɛts] cpd: **—er** m -s, - (Print) compositor; **—e'rei** f caseroom; **—ling** m young plant; **—maschine** f (Print) typesetting machine.

Seuche ['zɔyçə] f -, -n epidemic; **—ngebiet** nt infected area.

seufzen ['zɔyftsən] vti sigh.

Seufzer ['zɔyftsər] m -s, - sigh.

Sex [zɛks] m -(es) sex; **—ualität** [-uali'tɛt] f sex, sexuality; **s—uell** [-u'ɛl] a sexual.

Sexta ['zɛksta] f -, **Sexten** first year of secondary school.

sezieren [ze'tsi:rən] *vt* dissect.

sich [zɪç] *pron* himself; herself; itself; oneself; yourself; yourselves; themselves; each other.

Sichel ['zɪçəl] *f* -, -n sickle; *(Mond—)* crescent.

sicher ['zɪçər] *a* safe *(vor + dat* from); *(gewiß)* certain (+gen of); *(zuverlässig)* secure, reliable, *(selbst—)* confident; **—gehen** *vi irreg* make sure.

Sicherheit ['zɪçərhaɪt] *f* safety; security *(auch Fin)*; *(Gewißheit)* certainty; *(Selbst—)* confidence; **—abstand** *m* safe distance; **—sglas** *nt* safety glass; **s—shalber** *ad* for safety; to be on the safe side; **—snadel** *f* safety pin; **—sschloß** *nt* safety lock; **—sverschluß** *m* safety clasp; **—svorkehrung** *f* safety precaution.

sicher- *cpd*: **—lich** *ad* certainly, surely; **—n** *vt* secure; *(schützen)* protect; *Waffe* put the safety catch on; *jdm/sich etw* **—n** secure sth for sb/(for o.s.); **—stellen** *vt* impound; **S—ung** *f (Sichern)* securing; *(Vorrichtung)* safety device; *(an Waffen)* safety catch; *(Elec)* fuse.

Sicht [zɪçt] *f* - sight; *(Aus—)* view; auf or nach *—* *(Fin)* at sight; auf lange *—* on a long-term basis; **s—bar** *a* visible; **—barkeit** *f* visibility; **s—en** *vt* sight; *(auswählen)* sort out; **s—lich** *a* evident, obvious; **—verhältnisse** *pl* visibility; **—vermerk** *m* visa; **—weite** *f* visibility.

sickern ['zɪkərn] *vi* trickle, seep.

Sie [zi:] *pron* sing, pl, nom, acc you.

sie [zi:] *pron sing nom* she; *acc* her; *pl nom* they; *acc* them.

Sieb [zi:p] *nt* -(e)s, -e sieve; *(Cook)* strainer; **s—en** ['zi:bən] *vt* sift; *Flüssigkeit* strain.

sieben ['zi:bən] *num* seven; **—hundert** *num* seven hundred; **S—sachen** *pl* belongings *pl.*

siebte(r,s) ['zi:ptə(r,z)] *a* seventh; **S—l** *nt* -s, - seventh.

siebzehn ['zi:ptse:n] *num* seventeen.

siebzig ['zi:ptsɪç] *num* seventy.

sied- [zi:d] *cpd*: **—eln** *vi* settle; **—en** *vi* boil, simmer; **S—epunkt** *m* boiling point; **S—ler** *m* -s, - settler; **S—lung** *f* settlement; *(Häuser—)* housing estate.

Sieg [zi:k] *m* -(e)s, -e victory; **—el** ['zi:gəl] *nt* -s, - seal; **—ellack** *m* sealing wax; **—elring** *m* signet ring; **s—en** *vi* be victorious; *(Sport)* win; **—er** *m* -s, - victor; *(Sport etc)* winner; **s—essicher** *a* sure of victory; **—eszug** *m* triumphal procession; **s—reich** *a* victorious.

siehe [zi:ə] *(Imperativ)* see; *(— da)* behold.

siezen ['zi:tsən] *vt* address as 'Sie'.

Signal [zɪ'gna:l] *nt* -s, -e signal.

Signatur [zɪgna'tu:r] *f* signature.

Silbe ['zɪlbə] *f* -, -n syllable.

Silber ['zɪlbər] *nt* -s silver; **—bergwerk** *nt* silver mine; **—blick** *m*: einen **—blick** haben have a slight squint; **s—n** *a* silver; **—papier** *nt* silver paper.

Silhouette [zilu'ɛtə] *f* silhouette.

Silo ['zi:lo] *nt or m* -s, -s silo.

Silvester(abend *m)* [zɪl'vɛstər(a:bənt)] *nt* -s, - New Year's Eve, Hogmanay *(Scot).*

simpel ['zɪmpəl] *a* simple; **S—** *m* -s, - *(col)* simpleton.

Sims [zɪms] *nt or m* -es, -e
(Kamin—) mantelpiece;
(Fenster—) (window)sill.

simulieren [zimu'li:rən] *vti*
simulate; (vortäuschen) feign.

simultan [zimul'ta:n] *a*
simultaneous.

Sinfonie [zɪnfo'ni:] *f* symphony.

singen ['zɪŋən] *vti irreg* sing.

Singular ['zɪŋgula:r] *m* singular.

Singvogel ['zɪŋfo:gəl] *m* songbird.

sinken ['zɪŋkən] *vi irreg* sink;
(Preise etc) fall, go down.

Sinn [zɪn] *m* -(e)s, -e mind;
(Wahrnehmungs—) sense;
(Bedeutung) sense, meaning; — für
etw sense of sth; von —en sein be
out of one's mind; —bild *nt*
symbol; s—bildlich a symbolic;
s—en *vi irreg* ponder; auf etw (*acc*)
s—en contemplate sth;
—enmensch *m* sensualist;
—estäuschung *f* illusion; —gemäß
a faithful; Wiedergabe in one's
own words; —ig a clever; s—lich
a sensual, sensuous;
Wahrnehmung sensory; —lichkeit
f sensuality; s—los a senseless,
meaningless; —losigkeit *f*
senselessness; meaninglessness;
s—voll a meaningful; (vernünftig)
sensible.

Sintflut [zɪntflu:t] *f* Flood.

Sinus ['zi:nus] *m* -, - or -se (Anat)
sinus; (Math) sine.

Siphon [zi'fõ:] *m* -s, -s siphon.

Sippe ['zɪpə] *f* -, -n clan, kin.

Sippschaft ['zɪpʃaft] *f* (pej)
relations *pl*, tribe; (Bande) gang.

Sirene [zi're:nə] *f* -, -n siren.

Sirup ['zi:rup] *m* -s, -e syrup.

Sitt- [zɪt] *cpd*: —e *f* -, -n custom;
pl morals *pl*; —enpolizei *f* vice
squad; s—lich a moral; —lichkeit

f morality; —lichkeitsverbrechen
nt sex offence; s—sam a modest,
demure.

Situation [zituatsi'o:n] *f* situation.

Sitz [zɪts] *m* -es, -e seat; der
Anzug hat einen guten — the suit
is a good fit; s—en *vi irreg* sit;
(Bemerkung, Schlag) strike home,
tell; (Gelerntes) have sunk in;
s—en bleiben remain seated;
s—enbleiben *vi irreg* (Sch) have to
repeat a year; auf etw (dat)
s—enbleiben be lumbered with sth;
s—enbleiben be burdened with sth;
s—end a Tätigkeit sedentary;
s—enlassen *vt irreg* (Sch) make
(sb) repeat a year; Mädchen jilt;
Wartenden stand up; etw auf sich
(dat) s—enlassen take sth lying
down; —gelegenheit *f* place to sit
down; —platz *m* seat; —streik *m*
sit-down strike; —ung *f* meeting.

Skala ['ska:la] *f* -, Skalen scale.

Skalpell [skal'pɛl] *nt* -s, -e scalpel.

Skandal [skan'da:l] *m* -s, -e
scandal; s—ös [skanda'lø:s] *a*
scandalous.

Skelett [ske'lɛt] *nt* -(e)s, -e
skeleton.

Skepsis ['skɛpsɪs] *f* - scepticism.

skeptisch ['skɛptɪʃ] *a* sceptical.

Ski, Schi [ʃi:] *m* -s, -er ski; —
laufen or fahren ski; —fahrer *m*,
—läufer *m* skier; —lehrer *m* ski
instructor; —lift *m* ski-lift; —
springen *nt* ski-jumping.

Skizze ['skɪtsə] *f* -, -n sketch.

skizzieren [skɪ'tsi:rən] *vt* sketch.

Sklave ['skla:və] *m* -n, -n,
Sklavin [—vɪn] *f* slave; —rei *f* slavery.

Skonto ['skɔnto] *m or nt* -s, -s
discount.

Skorpion [skɔrpi'o:n] *m* -s, -e
scorpion; (Astrol) Scorpio.

Skrupel ['skru:pəl] *m* -s, - scruple;
s—los a unscrupulous.

Slalom

Slalom **267** Sonne

Slalom ['slaːlɔm] m -s, -s slalom.

Smaragd [sma'rakt] m -(e)s, -e emerald.

Smoking ['smoːkɪŋ] m -s, -s dinner jacket.

so [zoː] ad so; (auf diese Weise) like this; (etwa) roughly; — ein such a; —, das ist fertig well, that's finished; — etwas! well, well!; —.. wie ... as ... as ...; —, daß so, with the result that; cj so; (vor a) as.

Socke ['zɔkə] f -, -n sock.

Sockel ['zɔkəl] m -s, - pedestal, base.

Sodawasser ['zoːdavasər] nt soda water.

Sodbrennen ['zoːtbrɛnən] nt -s, - heartburn.

soeben [zo'eːbən] ad just (now).

Sofa ['zoːfa] nt -s, -s sofa.

sofern [zo'fɛrn] cj if, provided (that).

sofort [zo'fɔrt] ad immediately, at once; —ig a immediate.

Sog [zoːk] m -(e)s, -e suction.

so- cpd: —gar [-'gaːr] ad even; —genannt ['zoːgənant] a so-called; —gleich [zo'glaɪç] ad straight away, at once.

Sohle ['zoːlə] f -, -n sole; (Tal— etc) bottom; (Min) level.

Sohn [zoːn] m -(e)s, ⁓e son.

solang(e) [zo'laŋ(ə)] cj as or so long as.

Solbad ['zoːlbaːt] nt saltwater bath.

solch [zɔlç] pron such; ein —e(r,s) ... such a ...

Sold [zɔlt] m -(e)s, -e pay; —at [zɔl'daːt] m -en, -en soldier; —atisch a soldierly.

Söldner ['zœldnər] m -s, - mercenary.

solid(e) [zo'liːd(ə)] a solid; Leben, Person staid, respectable; —arisch [zoli'daːrɪʃ] a in/with solidarity; sich —arisch erklären declare one's solidarity.

Solist(in f) [zo'lɪst(ɪn)] m soloist.

Soll [zɔl] nt -(s), -(s) (Fin) debit (side); (Arbeitsmenge) quota, target.

sollen ['zɔlən] vi be supposed to; (Verpflichtung) shall, ought to; du hättest nicht gehen — you shouldn't have gone; soll ich? shall I?; was soll das? what's that supposed to mean?

Solo ['zoːlo] nt -s, -s or Soli solo.

somit [zo'mɪt] cj and so, therefore.

Sommer ['zɔmər] m -s, - summer; s—lich a summery; summer; —sprossen pl freckles pl.

Sonate [zo'naːtə] f -, -n sonata.

Sonde ['zɔndə] f -, -n probe.

Sonder- ['zɔndər] in cpds special; —angebot nt special offer; s—bar a strange, odd; —fahrt f special trip; —fall m special case; s—gleichen a inv without parallel, unparalleled; s—lich a particular; (außergewöhnlich) remarkable; (eigenartig) peculiar; —ling m eccentric; s—n cj but; nicht nur ..., s—n auch not only ..., but also; vt separate; —zug m special train.

sondieren [zɔn'diːrən] vt suss out; Gelände scout out.

Sonett [zo'nɛt] nt -(e)s, -e sonnet.

Sonnabend ['zɔn'aːbənt] m Saturday.

Sonne ['zɔnə] f -, -n sun; s—n vt put out in the sun; vr sun oneself; —naufgang m sunrise; s—nbaden vi sunbathe; —nbrand m sunburn; —nbrille f sunglasses pl; —nfinsternis f solar eclipse;

—nschein *m* sunshine; —nschirm *m* parasol, sunshade; —nstich *m* sunstroke; —nuhr *f* sundial; —nuntergang *m* sunset; —nwende *f* solstice.

sonnig ['zɔnɪç] *a* sunny.

Sonntag ['zɔnta:k] *m* Sunday; s—s *ad* (on) Sundays.

sonst [zɔnst] *ad* otherwise (*auch cj*); (*mit pron, in Fragen*) else; (*zu anderer Zeit*) at other times, normally; — noch etwas? anything else?; — nichts nothing else; —ig *a* other; —jemand *pron* anybody (at all); —wo(hin) *ad* somewhere else; —woher *ad* from somewhere else.

sooft [zo''ɔft] *cj* whenever.

Sopran [zo'pra:n] *m* -s, -e soprano; —istin [zopra'nɪstɪn] *f* soprano.

Sorge ['zɔrgə] *f* -, -n care, worry; s—n *vi*: für jdn s—n look after sb; für etw s—n take care of or see to sth; vr worry (um about); s—nfrei a carefree; —nkind *nt* problem child; s—nvoll a troubled, worried; —recht *nt* custody (of a child).

Sorg- [zɔrk] *cpd*: —falt *f* care(fulness); s—fältig a careful; s—los a careless; (*ohne Sorgen*) carefree; s—sam a careful.

Sorte ['zɔrtə] *f* -, -n sort; (*Waren*—) brand; —n *pl* (*Fin*) foreign currency.

sortieren [zɔr'ti:rən] *vt* sort (out).

Sortiment [zɔrti'mɛnt] *nt* assortment.

sosehr [zo'ze:r] *cj* as much as.

Soße ['zo:sə] *f* -, -n sauce; (*Braten*—) gravy.

Souffleur [zu'flø:r] *m*, **Souffleuse** [zu'flø:zə] *f* prompter.

soufflieren [zu'fli:rən] *vti* prompt, (*überlegen*) superior.

souverän [zuvə'rɛ:n] *a* sovereign.

so- *cpd*: —viel [zo'fi:l] *cj*: as far as; *pron* as much (*wie* as); rede nicht —viel don't talk so much; —weit [zo'vait] *cj* as far as; *a*: —weit sein be ready; —weit wie or als möglich as far as possible; ich bin —weit zufrieden by and large I'm quite satisfied; —wenig [zo've:nɪç] *cj* little as; *pron* as little (*wie* as); —wie [zo'vi:] *cj* (*sobald*) as soon as; (*ebenso*) as well as; —wieso [zovi'zo:] *ad* anyway; —wohl [zo'vo:l] *cj*: —wohl . . . als or wie auch both . . . and.

sozial [zotsi'a:l] *a* social; S—abgaben *pl* national insurance contributions *pl*; S—demokrat *m* social democrat; —isieren *vt* socialize; S—ismus [-'lɪsmʊs] *m* socialism; S—ist [-'lɪst] *m* socialist; —istisch *a* socialist; S—politik *f* social welfare policy; S—produkt *nt* (gross/net) national product; S—staat *m* welfare state.

Sozio- [zotsio] *cpd*: —loge [-'lo:gə] *m* -n, -n sociologist; —logie [-lo:'gi:] *f* sociology; s—logisch [-'lo:gɪʃ] *a* sociological.

Sozius ['zo:tsiʊs] *m* -, -se (*Comm*) partner; (*Motorrad*) pillion rider; —sitz *m* pillion (seat).

sozusagen [zotsu'za:gən] *ad* so to speak.

Spachtel ['ʃpaxtəl] *m* -s, -. spatula.

spähen ['ʃpɛ:ən] *vi* peep, peek.

Spalier [ʃpa'li:r] *nt* -s, -e (*Gerüst*) trellis; (*Leute*) guard of honour.

Spalt [ʃpalt] *m* -(e)s, -e crack; (*Tür*—) chink; (*fig: Kluft*) split; —e *f* -, -n crack, fissure; (*Gletscher*—) crevasse; (*in Text*)

column; s—en vtr (lit, fig) split;
—ung f splitting.
Span [ʃpaːn] m -(e)s, ⁼e shaving;
—ferkel nt sucking-pig.
Spange [ˈʃpaŋə] f -, -n clasp;
(Haar—) hair slide; (Schnalle)
buckle; (Armreif) bangle.
Spann [ʃpan] cpd: —beton m pre-
stressed concrete; —e f -, -n
(Zeit—) space; (Differenz) gap;
s—en vt (straffen) tighten, tauten;
(befestigen) brace; vi be tight;
s—end a exciting, gripping; —kraft
f elasticity; (fig) energy; —ung f
tension; (Elec) voltage; (fig)
suspense; (unangenehm) tension.
Spar- [ˈʃpaːr] cpd: —buch nt
savings book; —büchse f
moneybox; s—en vti save; sich
(dat) etw s—en save oneself sth;
Bemerkung keep sth to oneself; mit
etw (dat) s—en be sparing with
sth; an etw (dat) s—en economize
on sth; —er m -s, - saver.
Spargel [ˈʃpargəl] m -s, -
asparagus.
Spar- cpd: —kasse f savings bank;
—konto nt savings account.
spärlich [ˈʃpɛːrlɪç] a meagre;
Bekleidung scanty.
Spar- cpd: —maßnahme f economy
measure, cut; s—sam a
economical, thrifty; —samkeit f
thrift, economizing; s—schwein nt
piggy bank.
Sparte [ˈʃpartə] f -, -n field; line
of business; (Press) column.
Spaß [ʃpaːs] m -es, ⁼e joke;
(Freude) fun; jdm — machen be
fun (for sb); s—en vi joke; mit ihm
ist nicht zu s—en you can't take
liberties with him; s—eshalber ad
for the fun of it; s—haft, s—ig a
funny, droll; —macher m -s, -

joker, funny man; —verderber m
-s, - spoilsport.
spät [ʃpɛːt] a, ad late; —er a, ad
later; —estens ad at the latest.
Spaten [ˈʃpaːtən] m -s, - spade.
Spatz [ʃpats] m -en, -en sparrow.
spazier- [ʃpaˈtsiːr] cpd: —en vi
stroll, walk; —enfahren vi irreg go
for a drive; —engehen vi irreg go
for a walk; S—gang m walk;
S—stock m walking stick; S—weg
m path, walk.
Specht [ʃpɛçt] m -(e)s, -e
woodpecker.
Speck [ʃpɛk] m -(e)s, -e, bacon.
Spediteur [ʃpediˈtøːr] m carrier;
(Möbel—) furniture remover.
Spedition [ʃpeditsiˈoːn] f carriage;
(—sfirma) road haulage
contractor; removal firm.
Speer [ʃpeːr] m -(e)s, -e spear;
(Sport) javelin.
Speiche [ˈʃpaɪçə] f -, -n spoke.
Speichel [ˈʃpaɪçəl] m -s saliva,
spit(tle).
Speicher [ˈʃpaɪçər] m -s, -
storehouse; (Dach—) attic, loft;
(Korn—) granary; (Wasser—)
tank; (Tech) store; s—n vt store.
speien [ˈʃpaɪən] vti irreg spit;
(erbrechen) vomit; (Vulkan) spew.
Speise [ˈʃpaɪzə] f -, -n food; —eis
['-ʔaɪs] nt ice-cream; —kammer f
larder, pantry; —karte f menu;
s—n vt feed; eat; vi dine; —röhre
f gullet, oesophagus; —saal m
dining room; —wagen m dining
car; —zettel m menu.
Spektakel [ʃpɛkˈtaːkəl] m -s, -
(col) row; nt -s, - spectacle.
Speku- [ʃpeku] cpd: —lant [-ˈlant]
m speculator; —lation [-latsiˈoːn] f
speculation; s—lieren [-ˈliːrən] vi

(fig) . speculate; auf etw *(acc)*
s—lieren have hopes of sth.

Spelunke [ʃpe'luŋka] *f* -, -n dive.

Spende [ʃpɛndə] *f* -, -n donation;
s—n *vt* donate, give; —r *m* -s, -
donor, donator.

spendieren [ʃpɛn'di:rən] *vt* pay
for, buy; jdm etw — treat sb to
sth, stand sb sth.

Sperling [ʃpɛrlŋ] *m* sparrow.

Sperma [ʃpɛrma] *nt* -s, **Spermen**
sperm.

Sperr- [ʃpɛr] *cpd:* s—angelweit
['-aŋəl'vaɪt] a wide open; —e *f* -,
-n barrier; *(Verbot)* ban; s—en *vt*
block; *(Sport)* suspend, ban; *(vom Ball)* obstruct *(einschließen)* lock;
(verbieten) ban; *vr* baulk, jib(e);
—gebiet *nt* prohibited area; —holz
nt plywood; s—ig a bulky; —müll
m bulky refuse; —sitz *m (Theat)*
stalls *pl;* —stunde *f,* —zeit *f*
closing time.

Spesen [ʃpe:zən] *pl* expenses *pl.*

Spezial- [ʃpetsi:a:l] in *cpds* special;
s—i'sieren *vr* specialize;
—i'sierung *f* specialization; —ist
['-lɪst] *m* specialist; —i'tät *f*
speciality.

speziell [ʃpetsi'ɛl] a special.

spezifisch [ʃpe'tsi:fɪʃ] a specific.

Sphäre ['sfɛ:rə] *f* -, -n sphere.

spicken [ʃpɪkən] *vt* lard; *vi (Sch)*
copy, crib.

Spiegel [ʃpi:gəl] *m* -s, - mirror;
(Wasser—) level; *(Mil)* tab; —bild
nt reflection; s—bildlich a
reversed; —ei ['-'aɪ] *nt* fried egg;
—fechterei [-fɛçtə'raɪ] *f* shadow-
boxing, bluff; s—n *vt* mirror,
reflect; *vr* be reflected; *vi* gleam;
(wider—) be reflective; —schrift *f*
mirror-writing; —ung *f* reflection.

Spiel [ʃpi:l] *nt* -(e)s, -e game;
(Schau—) play; *(Tätigkeit)*

play(ing); *(Cards)* deck; *(Tech)*
(free) play; s—en *vti* play; *(um Geld)* gamble; *(Theat)* perform,
act; s—end ad easily; —er *m* -s,
- player; *(um Geld)* gambler;
—e'rei *f* trifling pastime; s—erisch
a playful; *Leichtigkeit* effortless;
s—erisches Können skill as a
player; acting ability; —feld *nt*
pitch, field; —film *m* feature film;
—plan *m (Theat)* programme;
—platz *m* playground; —raum *m*
room to manoeuvre, scope;
—sachen *pl* toys *pl;* —verderber *m*
-s, - spoilsport; —waren *pl,* —zeug
nt toys *pl.*

Spieß [ʃpi:s] *m* -es, -e spear;
(Brat—) spit; —bürger *m,* —er
m -s, - bourgeois; —rutenlaufen *nt*
running the gauntlet.

Spikes [spaɪks] *pl* spikes *pl; (Aut)*
studs *pl.*

Spinat [ʃpi'na:t] *m* -(e)s, -e
spinach.

Spind [ʃpɪnt] *m* or *nt* -(e)s, -e
locker.

Spinn- [ʃpɪn] *cpd:* —e *f* -, -n
spider; s—en *vti irreg* spin; *(col)*
talk rubbish; *(verrückt)* be crazy or
mad; —e'rei *f* spinning mill;
—(en)gewebe *nt* cobweb; —rad *nt*
spinning-wheel; —webe *f* cobweb.

Spion [ʃpi'o:n] *m* -s, -e spy; *(in Tür)* spyhole; —age [ʃpio'na:ʒə] *f*
-, n espionage; s—ieren
[ʃpio'ni:rən] *vi* spy.

Spirale [ʃpi'ra:lə] *f* -, -n spiral.

Spirituosen [ʃpiritu'o:zən] *pl*
spirits *pl.*

Spiritus ['spi:ritus] *m* -, -se
(methylated) spirit.

Spital [ʃpi'ta:l] *nt* -s, ⸚er hospital.

spitz [ʃpɪts] a pointed; *Winkel*
acute; *(fig)* Zunge sharp; *Bemerkung* caustic; S—. *m* -es, -e spitz;

S—bogen m pointed arch; S—bube m rogue; S—e f -, -n point, tip; (Berg—) peak; (Bemerkung) taunt, dig; (erster Platz) lead, top; (usu pl: Gewebe) lace; S—el m -s, - police informer; —en vt sharpen; S—en- in cpds —enleistung f top performance; S—enlohn m top wages pl; S—ensportler m top-class sportsman; —findig a (over)-subtle; —ig a see spitz; S—name m nickname.

Splitter ['ʃplɪtɐ] m -s, - splinter; s—nackt a stark naked.

spontan [ʃpɔn'taːn] a spontaneous.

Sport [ʃpɔrt] m -(e)s, -e sport; (fig) hobby; —lehrer(in f) m games or P.E. teacher; —ler(in f) m -s, - sportsman/woman; —lich a sporting; Mensch sporty; —platz m playing or sports field; —verein m sports club; —wagen m sports car; —zeug nt sports gear.

Spott [ʃpɔt] m -(e)s mockery, ridicule; s—billig a dirt-cheap; s—en vi mock (über +acc at), ridicule.

spöttisch ['ʃpœtɪʃ] a mocking.

Sprach- ['ʃpraːx] cpd: s—begabt a good at languages; —e f -, -n language; —fehler m speech defect; —fertigkeit f fluency; —führer m phrasebook; —gebrauch m (linguistic) usage; —gefühl nt feeling for language; s—lich a linguistic; s—los a speechless; —rohr nt megaphone; (fig) mouthpiece.

Spray [spreː] m or nt -s, -s spray.

Sprech- ['ʃprɛç] cpd: —anlage f intercom; s—en irreg vi speak, talk (mit to); das spricht für ihn that's a point in his favour; vt say; Sprache speak; Person speak to; —er(in f) m -s, - speaker; (für

Gruppe) spokesman; (Rad, TV) announcer; —stunde f consultation (hour); (doctor's) surgery; —stundenhilfe f (doctor's) receptionist; —zimmer nt consulting room, surgery.

spreizen ['ʃpraɪtsən] vt spread; vr put on airs.

Spreng- ['ʃprɛŋ] cpd: —arbeiten pl blasting operations pl; s—en vt sprinkle; (mit Sprengstoff) blow up; Gestein blast; Versammlung break up; —ladung f explosive charge; —stoff m explosive(s).

Spreu [ʃprɔʏ] f - chaff.

Sprich- [ʃprɪç] cpd: —wort nt proverb; s—wörtlich a proverbial.

Spring- ['ʃprɪŋ] cpd: —brunnen m fountain; s—en vi irreg jump; (Glas) crack; (mit Kopfsprung) dive; —er m -s, - jumper; (Schach) knight.

Sprit [ʃprɪt] m -(e)s, -e (col) petrol, fuel.

Spritz- ['ʃprɪts] cpd: —e f -, -n syringe; injection; (an Schlauch) nozzle; s—en vt spray; (Med) inject; vi splash; (heraus—) spurt; (Med) give injections; —pistole f spray gun.

spröde ['ʃprøːdə] a brittle; Person reserved, coy.

Sproß [ʃprɔs] m -sses, -sse shoot; (Kind) scion.

Sprosse ['ʃprɔsə] f -, -n rung.

Sprößling ['ʃprœslɪŋ] m offspring no pl.

Spruch [ʃprux] m -(e)s, -̈e saying, maxim; (Jur) judgement.

Sprudel ['ʃpruːdəl] m -s, - mineral water; lemonade; s—n vi bubble.

Sprüh- ['ʃpryː] cpd: —dose f aerosol (can); s—en vti spray; (fig) sparkle; —regen m drizzle.

Sprung [ʃprʊŋ] m -(e)s, ¨e jump; (Riß) crack; ~brett nt springboard; s~haft a erratic; Aufstieg rapid; ~schanze f skijump.

Spucke ['ʃpʊkə] f - spit; s~n vti spit.

Spuk [ʃpuːk] m -(e)s, -e haunting; (fig) nightmare; s~en vi (Geist) 'walk; hier spukt es this place is haunted.

Spule ['ʃpuːlə] f -, -n spool; (Elec) coil.

Spül- ['ʃpyːl] cpd: —e f -, -n (kitchen) sink; s~en vti rinse; Geschirr wash up; Toilette flush; —maschine f dishwasher; —stein m sink; —ung f rinsing; flush; (Med) irrigation.

Spur [ʃpuːr] f -, -en trace; (Fuß—, Rad—, Tonband—) track; (Fährte) trail; (Fahr—) lane; s~los ad without (a) trace.

spür- ['ʃpyːr] cpd: —bar a noticeable, perceptible; —en vt feel; S~hund m tracker dog; (fig) sleuth.

Spurt [ʃpʊrt] m -(e)s, -s or -e spurt.

sputen ['ʃpuːtən] vr make 'haste.

Staat [ʃtaːt] m -(e)s, -en state; (Prunk) show; (Kleidung) finery; mit etw — machen show off or parade sth; s~enlos a stateless; s~lich a state(-); state-run; —sangehörigkeit f nationality; —sanwalt m public prosecutor; —sbürger m citizen; —sdienst m civil service; s~seigen a stateowned; —sexamen nt (Univ) degree; s~sfeindlich a subversive; —smann m, pl -männer statesman; —ssekretär m secretary of state.

Stab [ʃtaːp] m -(e)s, ¨e rod; (Gitter—) bar; (Menschen) staff; —hochsprubg m pole vault; s~il

[ʃtaˈbiːl] a stable; Möbel sturdy; s~ili'sieren vt stabilize; —reim m alliteration.

Stachel ['ʃtaxəl] m -s, -n spike; (von Tier) spine; (von Insekten) sting; —beere f gooseberry; —draht m barbed wire; s~ig a prickly; —schwein nt porcupine.

Stadion ['ʃtaːdiɔn] nt -s, Stadien stadium.

Stadium ['ʃtaːdiʊm] nt stage, phase.

Stadt [ʃtat] f -, ¨e town.

Städt- ['ʃtɛt] cpd: —chen nt small town; —ebau m town 'planning; —er(in f) m -s, - town dweller; s~isch a municipal; (nicht. ländlich) urban.

Stadt- cpd: —mauer f city wall(s); —plan m street map; —rand m outskirts pl; —teil m district, part of town.

Staffel ['ʃtafəl] f -, -n rung; (Sport) relay (team); (Aviat) squadron; —ei ['-laɪ] f easel; s~n vt graduate; —ung f graduation.

Stahl [ʃtaːl] m -(e)s, ¨e steel; —helm m steel helmet.

Stall [ʃtal] m -(e)s, ¨e stable; (Kaninchen—) hutch; (Schweine—) sty; (Hühner—) henhouse.

Stamm [ʃtam] m -(e)s, ¨e (Baum—) trunk; (Menschen—) tribe; (Gram) stem; —baum m family tree; (von Tier) pedigree; s~eln vti stammer; s~en vi: s~en von or aus come from; —gast m regular (customer); —halter m -s, - son and heir.

stämmig ['ʃtɛmɪç] a sturdy; Mensch stocky; S~keit f sturdiness; stockiness.

stampfen ['ʃtampfən] vti stamp; (stapfen) tramp; (mit Werkzeug) pound.

Stand [ʃtant] *m* -(e)s, ⸚e position; (*Wasser—, Benzin—* etc) level; (*Stehen*) standing position; (*Zustand*) state; (*Spiel—*) score; (*Messe—* etc) stand; (*Klasse*) class; (*Beruf*) profession.

Standard [ˈʃtandart] *m* -s, -s standard.

Ständ- [ˈʃtɛnd] *cpd:* —chen *nt* serenade; —er *m* -s, - stand.

Stand- [ˈʃtand] *cpd:* —esamt *nt* registry office; —esbeamte(r) *m* registrar; —esbewußtsein *nt* status consciousness; s—esgemäß *a,ad* according to one's social position; —esunterschied *m* social difference; s—haft *a* steadfast; —haftigkeit *f* steadfastness; s—halten *vi irreg* stand firm (*jdm/ etw* against sb/sth), resist (*jdm/ etw* sb/sth).

ständig [ˈʃtɛndɪç] *a* permanent; (*ununterbrochen*) constant, continual.

Stand- *cpd:* —licht *nt* sidelights *pl*, parking lights *pl* (US); —ort *m* location; (*Mil*) garrison; —punkt *m* standpoint.

Stange [ˈʃtaŋə] *f* -, -n stick; (*Stab*) pole, bar; rod; (*Zigaretten*) carton; **von der** — (*Comm*) off the peg; **eine** — **Geld** quite a packet.

Stanniol [ʃtaniˈoːl] *nt* -s, -e tinfoil.

Stanze [ˈʃtantsə] *f* -, -n stanza; (*Tech*) stamp; s—n *vt* stamp.

Stapel [ˈʃtaːpəl] *m* -s, - pile; (*Naut*) stocks *pl*; —lauf *m* launch; s—n *vt* pile (up).

Star [ʃtaːr] *m* -(e)s, -e starling; (*Med*) cataract; *m* -s, -s (*Film* etc) star.

stark [ʃtark] *a* strong; (*heftig, groß*) heavy; (*Cook,*

Stärke [ˈʃtɛrkə] *f* -, -n strength; heaviness; thickness; (*Cook,*

Wäsche—) starch; s—n *vt* strengthen; **Wäsche** starch.

Starkstrom *m* heavy current.

Stärkung [ˈʃtɛrkʊŋ] *f* strengthening; (*Essen*) refreshment.

starr [ʃtar] *a* stiff; (*unnachgiebig*) rigid; *Blick* staring; —en *vi* stare; —en vor or von be covered in; **Waffen** be bristling with; **S—heit** *f* rigidity; —köpfig *a* stubborn; **S—sinn** *m* obstinacy.

Start [ʃtart] *m* -(e)s, -e start; (*Aviat*) takeoff; —automatik *f* (*Aut*) automatic choke; —bahn *f* runway; s—en *vti* start; take off; —er *m* -s, - starter; —erlaubnis *f* takeoff clearance; —zeichen *nt* start signal.

Station [ʃtatsiˈoːn] *f* station; hospital ward; s—ieren [-ˈniːrən] *vt* station.

Statist [ʃtaˈtɪst] *m* extra, supernumerary; —ik *f* statistics; —iker *m* -s, - statistician; s—isch *a* statistical.

Stativ [ʃtaˈtiːf] *nt* -s, -e tripod.

statt [ʃtat] *cj, prep* +*gen* or *dat* instead of; **S—** *f* - place.

Stätte [ˈʃtɛtə] *f* -, -n place.

statt- *cpd:* —finden *vi irreg* take place; —haft *a* admissible; —lich *a* imposing, handsome.

Statue [ˈʃtaːtuə] *f* -, **n** statue.

Statur [ʃtaˈtuːr] *f* stature.

Status [ˈʃtaːtʊs] *m* -, - status.

Stau [ʃtau] *m* -(e)s, -e blockage; (*Verkehrs—*) (traffic) jam.

Staub [ʃtaup] *m* -(e)s dust; s—en [ˈʃtaubən] *vi* be dusty; —faden *m* stamen; s—ig *a* dusty; —sauger *m* vacuum cleaner; —tuch *nt* duster.

Staudamm *m* dam.

Staude [ˈʃtaudə] *f* -, -n shrub.

stauen ['ʃtauən] vt Wasser dam up; Blut stop the flow of; vr (Wasser) become dammed up; (Med, Verkehr) become congested; (Menschen) collect together; (Gefühle) build up.

staunen ['ʃtaunən] vi be astonished; S— nt -s amazement.

Stauung ['ʃtauʊŋ] f (von Wasser) damming-up; (von Blut, Verkehr) congestion.

Stech- ['ʃtɛç] cpd: —becken nt bedpan; s—en irreg vi (mit Nadel etc) prick; (mit Messer) stab; (mit Finger) poke; (Biene etc) sting; (Mücke) bite; (Sonne) burn; (Cards) take; (Art) engrave; Torf, Spargel cut; in See s—en put to sea; —en nt -s, - (Sport) play-off; jump-off; s—end a piercing, stabbing; Geruch pungent; —ginster m gorse; —palme f holly; —uhr f time clock.

Steck- ['ʃtɛk] cpd: —brief m 'wanted' poster; —dose f (wall) socket; s—en vt put, insert; Nadel stick; Pflanzen plant; (beim Nähen) pin; vi irreg be put; (festsitzen) be stuck; (Nadeln) stick; s—enbleiben vi irreg get stuck; s—enlassen vt irreg leave in; —enpferd nt hobby-horse; —er m -s, - plug; —nadel f pin; —rübe f swede, turnip; —zwiebel f bulb.

Steg [ʃteːk] m -(e)s, -e small bridge; (Anlege—) landing stage; —reif m: aus dem —reif just like that.

stehen ['ʃteːən] irreg vi stand (zu by); (sich befinden) be; (in Zeitung) say; (still—) have stopped; jdm — suit sb; vi impers: es steht schlecht um things are bad; wie steht's? how are things?; (Sport) what's the score?;

bleiben remain standing; —bleiben vi irreg (Uhr) stop; (Fehler) stay as it is; —lassen vt irreg leave; Bart grow.

stehlen ['ʃteːlən] vt irreg steal.

steif [ʃtaif] a stiff; S—heit f stiffness.

Steig- ['ʃtaik] cpd: —bügel m stirrup; —e f ['ʃtaigə] f-, -n (Straße) steep road; (Kiste) crate; —eisen nt crampon; s—en vi irreg rise; (klettern) climb; s—en in (+acc)/auf (+acc)\ get in/on; s—ern vt raise; (Gram) compare; vi (Auktion) bid; vr increase; —erung f raising; (Gram) comparison; —ung f incline, gradient, rise.

steil [ʃtail] a steep.

Stein [ʃtain] m -(e)s, -e stone; (in Uhr) jewel; s—alt a ancient; —bock m (Astrol) Capricorn; —bruch m quarry; —butt m -s, -e turbot; s—ern a (made of) stone; (fig) stony; —gut nt stoneware; s—hart a hard as stone; s—ig a stony; s—igen vt stone; —kohle f mineral coal; —metz m -es, -e stonemason.

Steiß [ʃtais] m -es, -e rump.

Stell- ['ʃtɛl] cpd: —dichein nt -(s), -(s) rendezvous; —e f -, -n place; (Arbeit) post, job; (Amt) office; s—en vt put; Uhr etc set; (zur Verfügung —) supply; (Dieb) apprehend; vr (sich aufstellen) stand; (sich einfinden) present oneself; (bei Polizei) give oneself up; (vorgeben) pretend (to be); sich zu etw s—en have an opinion of sth; —enangebot nt offer of a post; (Zeitung) vacancies; —engesuch nt application for a post; —ennachweis m, —envermittlung f

employment agency; **—ung** f
position; (Mil) line; **—ung nehmen
zu** comment on; **—ungnahme** f **-,
-n** comment; **s—vertretend** a
-vertreter m
deputy, acting; **—vertreter** m
deputy; **—werk** nt (Rail) signal box.
Stelze [ˈʃtɛltsə] f **-, -n** stilt.
Stemm- [ˈʃtɛm] cpd: **—bogen** m
(Ski) stem turn; **s—en** vt lift (up);
(drücken) press; **sich s—en gegen**
(fig) resist, oppose.
Stempel [ˈʃtɛmpəl] m **-s,** - stamp;
(Bot) pistil; **—kissen** nt inkpad;
s—n vt stamp; Briefmarke cancel;
s—n gehen (col) be/go on the dole.
Stengel [ˈʃtɛŋəl] m **-s,** - stalk.
Steno- [ʃteno] cpd: **- —gramm**
[-ˈgram] nt shorthand report;
—graphie [-graˈfiː] f shorthand;
s—graphieren [-graˈfiːrən] vti write
(in) shorthand; **—typist**(in f)
[-tyˈpɪst(ɪn)] m shorthand typist.
Stepp- [ˈʃtɛp] cpd: **—decke** f quilt;
—e f **-, -n** prairie; steppe; **s—en**
vt stitch; vi tap-dance.
Sterb- [ˈʃtɛrb] cpd: **—ebett** nt
deathbed; **—efall** m death; **s—en**
vi irreg die; **—eurkunde** f death
certificate; **s—lich** [ˈʃtɛrplɪç] a
mortal; **—lichkeit** f mortality;
—lichkeitsziffer f death rate.
stereo- [ˈʃteːreo] in cpds stereo(-);
—typ [ʃtereoˈtyːp] a stereotype.
steril [ʃteˈriːl] a sterile; **—i'sieren**
vt sterilize; **S—i'sierung** f sterilization.
Stern [ʃtɛrn] m **-(e)s, -e** star;
—bild nt constellation; **—chen** nt
asterisk; **—schnuppe** f **-, -n** meteor,
falling star; **—stunde** f historic
moment.
stet [ʃteːt] a steady; **—ig** a
constant, continual; **—s** ad continually, always.

Steuer [ˈʃtɔyər] nt **-s,** - (Naut)
helm; (**—ruder**) rudder; (Aut)
steering wheel; f **-, -n** tax; **—bord**
nt starboard; **—erklärung** f tax
return; **—klasse** f tax group;
—knüppel m control column;
(Aviat) joystick; **—mann** m, pl
—männer or **-leute** helmsman; **s—n**
vti steer; Flugzeug pilot; Entwicklung, Tonstärke control;
s—pflichtig a taxable; Person
liable to pay tax; **—rad** nt steering
wheel; **—ung** f steering (auch
Aut); piloting; control;
(Vorrichtung) controls pl; **—zahler**
m **-s,** - taxpayer; **—zuschlag** m
additional tax.
Steward [ˈstjuːərt] m **-s, -s**
steward; **—eß** [ˈstjuːərdɛs] f **-,
-essen** stewardess; air hostess.
stibitzen [ʃtiˈbɪtsən] vt (col) pilfer,
steal.
Stich [ʃtɪç] m **-(e)s, -e**
(Insekten—) sting; (Messer—)
stab; (beim Nähen) stitch;
(Färbung) tinge; (Cards) trick;
(Art) engraving; **jdn im — lassen**
leave sb in the lurch; **—el** m **-s,**
- engraving tool, style; **—e'lei** f
jibe, taunt; **s—eln** vi (fig) jibe;
s—haltig a sound, tenable; **—probe**
f spot check; **—wahl** f final ballot;
—wort nt cue; (in Wörterbuch)
headword; (für Vortrag) note;
—wortverzeichnis nt index.
Stick- [ʃtɪk] cpd: **s—en** vti
embroider; **—e'rei** f embroidery;
s—ig a stuffy, close; **—stoff** m
nitrogen.
Stiefel [ˈʃtiːfəl] m **-s,** - boot..
Stief- [ˈʃtiːf] in cpds step; **.—kind**
nt stepchild; (fig) Cinderella;
—mutter f stepmother;
—mütterchen nt pansy.

Stiege ['ʃtiːgə] f -, -n staircase.

Stiel [ʃtiːl] m -(e)s, -e handle; (Bot) stalk.

stier [ʃtiːr] a staring, fixed; S— m -(e)s, -e bull; (Astrol) Taurus; —en vi stare.

Stift [ʃtɪft] m -(e)s, -e peg; (Nagel) tack; (Farb—) crayon; (Blei—) pencil; nt -(e)s, -e (charitable) foundation; (Eccl) religious institution; s—en vt found; (Unruhe cause; (spenden) contribute; —er(in f) m -s, - founder; —ung f donation; (Organisation) foundation; —zahn m crown tooth.

Stil [ʃtiːl] m -(e)s, -e style; —blüte f howler.

still [ʃtɪl] a quiet; (unbewegt) still; (heimlich) secret; S—e f -, -n stillness, quietness; in aller S—e quietly; —en vt stop; (befriedigen) satisfy; Säugling breast-feed; —gestanden interj attention; —halten vi irreg keep still; —(le)gen vt close down; —schweigen vi irreg be silent; S—schweigen nt silence; —schweigend a,ad silent(ly); Einverständnis tacit(ly); S—stand m standstill; —stehen vi irreg stand still.

Stimm- ['ʃtɪm] cpd: —abgabe f voting; —bänder pl vocal chords pl; s—berechtigt a entitled to vote; —e f -, -n voice; (Wahl—) vote; s—en vt (Mus) tune; das stimmte ihn traurig that made him feel sad; vi be right; —en für/gegen vote for/against; —enmehrheit f majority (of votes); —enthaltung f abstention; —gabel f tuning fork; s—haft a voiced; —lage f register; s—los a voiceless; —recht nt right to vote; —ung f mood; atmosphere; s—ungsvoll a enjoyable;

full of atmosphere; —zettel m ballot paper.

stinken ['ʃtɪŋkən] vi irreg stink.

Stipendium [ʃti'pɛndɪʊm] nt grant.

Stirn [ʃtɪrn] f -, -en forehead, brow; (Frechheit) impudence; —höhle f sinus; —runzeln nt -s frown(ing).

stöbern ['ʃtøːbərn] vi rummage.

stochern ['ʃtɔxərn] vi poke (about).

Stock [ʃtɔk] m -(e)s, "e stick; (Bot) stock; pl -werke storey; s— in cpds vor a (col) completely; s—en vi stop, pause; s—end a halting; s—finster a (col) pitch-dark; s—taub a stone-deaf; —ung f stoppage; —werk nt storey, floor.

Stoff [ʃtɔf] m -(e)s, -e (Gewebe) material, cloth; (Materie) matter; (von Buch etc) subject (matter); s—lich a material; with regard to subject matter; —wechsel m metabolism.

stöhnen ['ʃtøːnən] vi groan.

stoisch ['ʃtoːɪʃ] a stoical.

Stollen ['ʃtɔlən] m -s, - (Min) gallery; (Cook) cake eaten at Christmas; (von Schuhen) stud.

stolpern ['ʃtɔlpərn] vi stumble, trip.

Stolz [ʃtɔlts] m -es pride; s—a proud; s—ieren [ʃtɔl'tsiːrən] vi strut.

Stopf- ['ʃtɔpf] cpd: s—en vt (hinein—) stuff; (voll—) fill (up); (nähen) darn; vi (Med) cause constipation; —garn nt darning thread.

Stoppel ['ʃtɔpəl] f -, -n stubble.

Stopp- ['ʃtɔp] cpd: s—en vti stop; (mit Uhr) time; —schild nt stop sign; —uhr f stopwatch.

Stöpsel ['ʃtøpsəl] m -s, - plug; (für Flaschen) stopper.

Stör [ʃtøːr] m -(e)s, -e sturgeon.

Storch m -(e)s, ⸚e stork.

Stör- [ʃtøːr] cpd: s—en vt disturb; (behindern, Rad) interfere with; vr sich an etw (dat) s—en let sth bother one; s—end a disturbing, annoying; —enfried m -(e)s, -e troublemaker.

störrig [ˈʃtœrɪç], **störrisch** [ˈʃtœrɪʃ] a stubborn, perverse.

Stör- cpd: —sender m jammer; —ung f disturbance; interference.

Stoß [ʃtoːs] m -es, ⸚e (Schub) push; (Schlag) blow; knock; (mit Schwert) thrust; (mit Fuß) kick; (Erd—) shock; (Haufen) pile; —dämpfer m -s, - shock absorber; s—en irreg vt (mit Druck) shove, push; (mit Schlag) knock, bump; (mit Fuß) kick; Schwert etc thrust; (an—) ˈKopf etc bump; (zerkleinern) pulverize; vr get a knock; sich an etw s—en (+dat) (fig) take exception to; vi: s—en an or auf (+acc) bump into; (finden) come across; (angrenzen) be next to; —stange f (Aut) bumper.

Stotterer [ˈʃtɔtərər] m -s, - stutterer.

stottern [ˈʃtɔtərn] vti stutter.

stracks [ʃtraks] ad straight.

Straf- [ˈʃtraːf] cpd: —anstalt f penal institution; —arbeit f (Sch) punishment; lines pl; —bar a punishable; —barkeit f criminal nature; —e f -, -n punishment; (Jur) penalty; (Gefängnis—) sentence; (Geld—) fine; s—en vt punish.

straff [ʃtraf] a tight; (streng) strict; Stil etc concise; Haltung erect; s—en vt tighten, tauten.

Straf- cpd: —gefangene(r) mf prisoner, convict; —gesetzbuch nt penal code; —kolonie f penal colony.

Sträf- [ˈʃtrɛːf] cpd: s—lich a criminal; —ling m convict.

Straf- cpd: —porto nt excess postage (charge); —predigt f severe lecture; —raum m (Sport) penalty area; —recht nt criminal law; —stoß m (Sport) penalty (kick); —tat f punishable act; —zettel m ticket.

Strahl [ʃtraːl] m -s, -en ray, beam; (Wasser—) jet; s—en vi radiate; (fig) beam; —enbehandlung, —entherapie f radiotherapy; —ung f radiation.

Strähne [ˈʃtrɛːnə] f -, -n strand.

stramm [ʃtram] a tight; Haltung erect; Mensch robust; s—stehen vi irreg (Mil) stand to attention.

strampeln [ˈʃtrampəln] vi kick (about), fidget.

Strand [ʃtrant] m -(e)s, ⸚e shore; (mit Sand) beach; —bad nt open-air swimming pool, lido; s—en [ˈʃtrandən] vi run aground; (fig: Mensch) fail; —gut nt flotsam; —korb m beach chair.

Strang [ʃtraŋ] m -(e)s, ⸚e cord, rope; (Bündel) skein; (Schienen—) track; über die ⸚e schlagen (col) kick over the traces.

Strapaz- cpd: —e f [ʃtraˈpaːtsə] f -n strain, exertion; s—ieren [ʃtrapaˈtsiːrən] vt Material treat roughly, punish; Mensch, Kräfte wear out, exhaust; s—ierfähig a hard-wearing; s—iös [ʃtrapatsiˈøːs] a exhausting, tough.

Straße [ˈʃtraːsə] f -, -n street, road; —nbahn f tram, streetcar (US); —nbeleuchtung f street lighting; —nfeger m, —nkehrer m -s, - roadsweeper; —nsperre f roadblock; —nverkehrsordnung f highway code.

Strateg- ['ftra'te:g] *cpd:* —e m -n, -n strategist; —ie [ftrate'gi:] *f* strategy; s—isch a strategic.

Stratosphäre [ftrato'sfe:rə] *f* - stratosphere.

sträuben ['ftrɔybən] *vt* ruffle; *vr* bristle; *(Mensch)* resist (gegen etw sth).

Strauch [ftraux] *m* -(e)s, Sträucher bush, shrub; s—eln *vi* stumble, stagger.

Strauß [ftraus] *m* -es, Sträuße bunch, bouquet; *pl* -e ostrich.

Streb- ['ftre:b] *cpd:* —e f -, —n strut; —ebalken *m* buttress; s—en *vi* strive *(nach for)*, endeavour; s—en zu *or* nach *(sich bewegen)* make for; —er *m* -s, - *(pej)* pusher, climber; *(Sch)* swot; s—sam a industrious; —samkeit f industry.

Strecke ['ftrekə] *f* -, -n stretch; *(Entfernung)* distance; *(Rail)* line; *(Math)* line; s—n *vt* stretch; *Waffen* lay down; *(Cook)* eke out; *vr* stretch (oneself); *vi (Sch)* put one's hand up.

Streich [ftraiç] *m* -(e)s, -e trick, prank; *(Hieb)* blow; s—eln *vt* stroke; s—en *irreg vt (berühren)* stroke; *(auftragen)* spread; *(anmalen)* paint; *(durch—)* delete; *(nicht genehmigen)* cancel; *vi (berühren)* brush; *(schleichen)* prowl; —holz *nt* match; —instrument *nt* string instrument.

Streif- ['ftraif] *cpd:* —band *nt* wrapper; —e f -, -n patrol; s—en *vt (leicht berühren)* brush against, graze; *(Blick)* skim over; *Thema, Problem* touch on; *(ab—)* take off; *vi (gehen)* roam; —en *m* -s, - *(Linie)* stripe; *(Stück)* strip; *(Film)* film; —endienst *m* patrol duty; —enwagen *m* patrol car; —schuß

m graze, grazing shot; —zug *m* scouting trip.

Streik [ftraik] *m* -(e)s, -s strike; —brecher *m* -s, - blackleg, strikebreaker; s—en *vi* strike; —kasse *f* strike fund; —posten *m* (strike) picket.

Streit [ftrait] *m* -(e)s, -e argument; dispute; s—en *vir irreg* argue; dispute; —frage *f* point at issue; s—ig a: jdm etw s—ig machen dispute sb's right to sth; —igkeiten *pl* quarrel, dispute; —kräfte *pl (Mil)* armed forces *pl*; s—lustig a quarrelsome; —sucht *f* quarrelsomeness.

streng [ftreŋ] a severe; *Lehrer, Maßnahme* strict; *Geruch etc* sharp; S—e f - severity; strictness; —genommen *ad* strictly speaking; —gläubig a orthodox, strict.

Streu [ftrɔy] *f* -, -en litter, bed of straw; s—en *vt* strew, scatter, spread; —ung f dispersion.

Strich [ftriç] *m* -(e)s, -e *(Linie)* line; *(Feder-, Pinsel-)* stroke; *(von Geweben)* nap; *(von Fell)* pile; auf den — gehen *(col)* walk the streets; jdm gegen den — gehen rub sb up the wrong way; einen — machen durch *(lit)* cross out; *(fig)* foil; —einteilung f calibration; —mädchen *nt* streetwalker; —punkt *m* semicolon; s—weise *ad* here and there.

Strick [ftrik] *m* -(e)s, -e rope; *(col: Kind)* rascal; s—en *vti* knit; —jacke f cardigan; —leiter f rope ladder; —nadel f knitting needle; —waren *pl* knitwear.

Strieme ['ftri:mə] f -, -n, **Striemen** ['ftri:mən] *m* -s, - weal.

strikt ['ftrikt] a strict.

strittig [ˈʃtrɪtɪç] a disputed, in dispute.

Stroh [ʃtroː] nt -(e)s straw; —blume f everlasting flower; —dach nt thatched roof; —halm m (drinking) straw; —mann m, pl -männer dummy, straw man; —witwe f grass widow.

Strolch [ʃtrɔlç] m -(e)s, -e layabout, bum.

Strom [ʃtroːm] m -(e)s, -e river; (fig) stream; (Elec) current; s—abwärts [-ˈapvɛrts] ad downstream; s—aufwärts [-ˈaufvɛrts] ad upstream.

strömen [ˈʃtrøːmən] vi stream, pour.

Strom- cpd: —kreis m circuit; s—linienförmig a streamlined; —rechnung f electricity bill; —sperre f power cut; —stärke f amperage.

Strömung [ˈʃtrøːmʊŋ] f current.

Strophe [ˈʃtroːfə] f -, -n verse.

strotzen [ˈʃtrɔtsən] vi: —vor or von abound in, be full of.

Strudel [ˈʃtruːdəl] m -s, - whirlpool, vortex; (Cook) strudel; s—n vi swirl, eddy.

Struktur [ʃtrukˈtuːr] f structure; s—ell [-ˈrɛl] a structural.

Strumpf [ʃtrʊmpf] m -(e)s, -e stocking; —band nt garter; —hose f (pair of) tights.

Strunk [ʃtrʊŋk] m -(e)s, -e stump.

struppig [ˈʃtrʊpɪç] a shaggy, unkempt.

Stube [ˈʃtuːbə] f -, -n room; —narrest m confinement to one's room; (Mil) confinement to quarters; —nhocker m (col) stay-at-home; s—nrein a house-trained.

Stuck [ʃtʊk] m -(e)s stucco.

Stück [ʃtʏk] nt -(e)s, -e piece; (etwas) bit; (Theat) play; —arbeit f piecework; —chen nt little piece; —lohn m piecework wages pl; s—weise ad bit by bit, piecemeal; (Comm) individually; —werk nt bits and pieces pl.

Student(in f) [ʃtuˈdɛnt(ɪn)] m student; s—isch a student, academic.

Studie [ˈʃtuːdiə] f study.

studieren [ʃtuˈdiːrən] vti study.

Studio [ˈʃtuːdio] nt -s, -s studio.

Studium [ˈʃtuːdiʊm] nt studies pl.

Stufe [ˈʃtuːfə] f -, -n step; (Entwicklungs—) stage; —nleiter f (fig) ladder; s—nweise ad gradually.

Stuhl [ʃtuːl] m -(e)s, -e chair; —gang m bowel movement.

stülpen [ˈʃtʏlpən] vt (umdrehen) turn upside down; (bedecken) put.

stumm [ʃtʊm] a silent; (Med) dumb; S—el m -s, - stump; (Zigaretten—) stub; S—film m silent film; S—heit f silence; dumbness.

Stümper [ˈʃtʏmpər] m -s, - incompetent, duffer; s—haft a bungling, incompetent; s—n vi (col) bungle.

stumpf [ʃtʊmpf] a blunt; (teilnahmslos, glanzlos) dull; Winkel obtuse; S— m -(e)s, -e stump; S—heit f bluntness; dullness; S—sinn m tediousness; s—sinnig a dull.

Stunde [ˈʃtʊndə] f -, -n hour; s—n vt: jdm etw s—en give sb time to pay sth; —ngeschwindigkeit f average speed per hour; —nkilometer pl kilometres per hour; s—nlang a for hours; —nlohn m hourly wage; —nplan m timetable; s—nweise a by the hour; every hour.

stündlich ['ʃtʏntlɪç] a hourly.

Stups [ʃtʊps] m -es, -e (col) push; **—nase** f snub nose.

stur [ʃtuːr] a obstinate, pigheaded.

Sturm [ʃtʊrm] m -(e)s, ⁼e storm, gale; (Mil etc) attack, assault.

stürm- ['ʃtʏrm] cpd: **—en** vi (Wind) blow hard, rage; (rennen) storm; ⁺vt (Mil, fig) storm; vr impers **es — t** there's a gale blowing; **S—er** m -s, - (Sport) forward, striker; **—isch** a stormy.

Sturm- cpd: **—warnung** f gale warning; **—wind** m storm, gale.

Sturz [ʃtʊrts] m -es, ⁼e fall; (Pol) overthrow.

stürzen ['ʃtʏrtsən] vt (werfen) hurl; (Pol) overthrow; (umkehren) overturn; vr rush; (hinein—) plunge; vi fall; (Aviat) dive; (rennen) dash.

Sturz- cpd: **—flug** m nose-dive; **—helm** m crash helmet.

Stute ['ʃtuːtə] f -, -n mare.

Stütz- ['ʃtʏts] cpd: **—balken** m brace, joist; **—e** f -, -n support; help; **s—en** vt (lit, fig) support; Ellbogen etc prop up.

stutz- ['ʃtʊts] cpd: **—en** vt trim; Ohr, Schwanz dock; Flügel clip; vi hesitate; become suspicious; **—ig** a perplexed, puzzled; (mißtrauisch) suspicious.

Stütz- cpd: **—mauer** f·supporting wall; **—punkt** m point of support; (von Hebel) fulcrum; (Mil, fig) base.

Styropor ® [ʃtyro'poːr] nt -s polystyrene.

Subjekt [zʊp'jɛkt] nt -(e)s, -e subject; **s—iv** [-'tiːf] a subjective; **—ivi'tät** f subjectivity.

Substantiv [zʊpstan'tiːf] nt -s, -e noun.

Substanz [zʊp'stants] f substance.

subtil [zʊp'tiːl] a subtle.

subtrahieren [zʊptra'hiːrən] vt subtract.

Subvention [zʊpvɛntsi'oːn] f subsidy; **s—ieren** [-'niːrən] vt subsidize.

subversiv [zʊpvɛr'ziːf] a subversive.

Such- ['zuːx] cpd: **—aktion** f search; **—e** f -, -n search; **s—en** vti look (for), seek; (ver—) try; **—er** m -s, - seeker, searcher; (Phot) viewfinder.

Sucht [zʊxt] f -, ⁼e mania; (Med) addiction, craving.

süchtig ['zʏçtɪç] a ·addicted; **S—e(r)** mf addict.

Süd- [zyːt] cpd: **—en** ['zyːdən] m -s south; **—früchte** pl Mediterranean fruit; **s—lich** a southern; **—lich von** (to the) south of; **s—wärts** ad southwards.

süff- cpd: **—ig** ['zʏfɪç] a Wein pleasant to the taste; **—isant** [zʏfi'zant] a smug.

suggerieren [zʊge'riːrən] vt suggest (jdm etw sth to sb).

Sühne ['zyːnə] f -, -n atonement, expiation; **s—n** vt atone for, expiate.

Sulfonamid [zʊlfona'miːt] nt -(e)s, -e (Med) sulphonamide.

Sultan ['zʊltan] m -s, -e sultan; **—ine** [zʊlta'niːnə] f sultana.

Sülze ['zʏltsə] f -, -n brawn.

Summ- [zʊm] cpd: **s—arisch** [zʊ'maːrɪʃ] a summary; **—e** f -, -n sum, total; **s—en** vti hum, buzz; Lied hum; **s—ieren** [zʊ'miːrən] vtr add up (to).

Sumpf [zʊmpf] m -(e)s, ⁼e swamp, marsh; **s—ig** a marshy.

Sünde ['zyndə] *f* -, -n sin; —**nbock** *m* (col) scapegoat; —**nfall** *m* Fall (of man); —**r(in** *f*) *m* -s, - sinner.

Super ['zu:pər] *nt* -s (*Benzin*) four star (petrol); —**lativ** [-lati:f] *m* -s, -e superlative; —**markt** *m* supermarket.

Suppe ['zupə] *f* -, -n soup.

surren ['zurən] *vi* buzz, hum.

Surrogat [zuro'ga:t] *nt* -(e)s, -e substitute, surrogate.

suspekt [zus'pekt] *a* suspect.

süß [zy:s] *a* sweet; **S—e** *f* - sweetness; —**en** *vt* sweeten; **S—igkeit** *f* sweetness; (*Bonbon etc*) sweet, candy (US); —**lich** *a* sweetish; (*fig*) sugary; **S—speise** *f* pudding, sweet; **S—stoff** *m* sweetening agent; **S—wasser** *nt* fresh water.

Sylvester [zyl'vəstər] *nt* -s, - see **Silvester.**

Symbol [zym'bo:l] *nt* -s, -e symbol; **s—isch** *a* symbolic(al).

Symmetrie [zyme'tri:] *f* symmetry; —**achse** *f* symmetric axis.

symmetrisch [zy'me:trɪʃ] *a* symmetrical.

Sympath- *cpd*: —**ie** [zympa'ti:] *f*

liking, sympathy; **s—isch** [zym'pa:tɪʃ] *a* likeable, congenial; **er ist mir s—isch** I like him; **s—i'sieren** *vi* sympathize.

Symptom [zymp'to:m] *nt* -s, -e symptom; **s—atisch** [zympto-'ma:tɪʃ] *a* symptomatic.

Synagoge [zyna'go:gə] *f* -, -n synagogue.

synchron [zyn'kro:n] *a* synchronous; **S—getriebe** *nt* synchromesh (gears *pl*); —**i'sieren** *vt* synchronize; *Film* dub.

Syndikat [zyndi'ka:t] *nt* -(e)s, -e combine, syndicate.

Synonym [zyno'ny:m] *nt* -s, -e synonym; **s—** *a* synonymous.

Syntax ['zyntaks] *f* -, -en syntax.

Synthese [zyn'te:zə] *f* -, -n synthesis.

synthetisch [zyn'te:tɪʃ] *a* synthetic.

Syphilis ['zyfilɪs] *f* - syphilis.

System [zys'te:m] *nt* -s, -e system; **s—atisch** [zyste'ma:tɪʃ] *a* systematic; **s—ati'sieren** *vt* systematize.

Szene ['stse:nə] *f* -, -n scene; —**rie** [stsenə'ri:] *f* scenery.

Szepter ['stsɛptər] *nt* -s, - sceptre.

T

T, t [te:] T, t.

Tabak ['ta:bak] *m* -s, -e tobacco.

Tabell- [ta'bɛl] *cpd*: **t—arisch** [tabɛ'la:rɪʃ] *a* tabular; —**e** *f* table; —**enführer** *m* top of the table, league leader.

Tabernakel [tabɛr'na:kəl] *m* -s, - tabernacle.

Tablette [ta'blɛtə] *f* tablet, pill.

Tachometer [taxo'me:tər] *m* -s, -

.(*Aut*) speedometer.

Tadel ['ta:dəl] *m* -s, - censure, scolding; (*Fehler*) fault, blemish; **t—los** *a* faultless, irreproachable; **t—n** *vt* scold; **t—nswert** *a* blameworthy.

Tafel ['ta:fəl] *f* -, -n table (*auch Math*); (*Anschlag—*) board; (*Wand—*) blackboard; (*Schiefer—*)

slate; *(Gedenk—)* plaque; *(Illustration)* plate; *(Schalt—)* panel; *(Schokolade etc)* bar.

Täfel- ['tɛ:fəl] *cpd:* **t—n** *vt* panel; **—ung** *f* panelling.

Taft [taft] *m* **-(e)s, -e** tafetta.

Tag [ta:k] *m* **-(e)s, -e** day; daylight; **unter/über —** *(Min)* underground/on the surface; **an den — kommen** come to light; **guten —!** good morning/afternoon!; **t—aus, t—ein** day in, day out; **—dienst** *m* day duty; **—ebuch** ['ta:gəbu:x] *nt* diary, journal; **—edieb** *m* idler; **—egeld** *nt* daily allowance; **t—elang** *ad* for days; **t—en** *vi* sit, meet; *v impers:* **es tagt** dawn is breaking; **—esablauf** *m* course of the day; **—esanbruch** *m* dawn; **—eslicht** *nt* daylight; **—esordnung** *f* agenda; **—esatz** *m* daily rate; **—eszeit** *f* time of day; **—eszeitung** *f* daily (paper).

täglich ['tɛ:klɪç] *a,ad* daily.

Tag- *cpd:* **t—süber** *ad* during the day; **—ung** *f* conference.

Taille ['taljə] *f* **-, -n** waist.

Takel ['ta:kəl] *nt* **-s, -** tackle; **t—n** *vt* rig.

Takt [takt] *m* **-(e)s, -e** tact; *(Mus)* time; **—gefühl** *nt* tact; **—ik** *f* tactics *pl*; **t—isch** a tactical; **t—los** a tactless; **—losigkeit** *f* tactlessness; **—stock** *m* (conductor's) baton; **t—voll** a tactful.

Tal [ta:l] *nt* **-(e)s, ⸚er** valley.

Talar [ta'la:r] *m* **-s, -e** *(Jur)* robe; *(Univ)* gown.

Talent [ta'lɛnt] *nt* **-(e)s, -e** talent; **t—iert** [talɛn'ti:rt], **t—voll** a talented, gifted.

Taler ['ta:lər] *m* **-s, -** taler, florin.

Talg [talk] *m* **-(e)s, -e** tallow; **—drüse** *f* sebaceous gland.

Talisman ['ta:lɪsman] *m* **-s, -e** talisman.

Tal- *cpd:* **—sohle** *f* bottom of a valley; **—sperre** *f* dam.

Tamburin [tambu'ri:n] *nt* **-s, -e** tambourine.

Tampon ['tampɔn] *m* **-s, -s** tampon.

Tang [taŋ] *m* **-(e)s, -e** seaweed; **—ente** [taŋ'gɛntə] *f* **-, -n** tangent; **t—ieren** [taŋ'gi:rən] *vt (lit)* be tangent to; *(fig)* affect.

Tank [taŋk] *m* **-s, -s** tank; **t—en** *vi* fill up with petrol or gas *(US)*; *(Aviat)* (re)fuel; **—er** *m* **-s, -**, **—schiff** *nt* tanker; **—stelle** *f* petrol or gas *(US)* station; **—wart** *m* petrol pump or gas *(US)* station attendant.

Tanne ['tanə] *f* **-, -n** fir; **—nbaum** *m* fir tree; **—nzapfen** *m* fir cone.

Tante ['tantə] *f* **-, -n** aunt.

Tanz [tants] *m* **-es, ⸚e** dance.

Tänz- ['tɛnts] *cpd:* **t—eln** *vi* dance along; **—er(in** *f) m* **-s, -** dancer.

Tanz- *cpd:* **t—en** *vti* dance; **—fläche** *f* (dance) floor; **—schule** *f* dancing school.

Tape- *cpd:* **—te** [ta'pe:tə] *f* **-, -n** wallpaper; **—tenwechsel** *m (fig)* change of scenery; **t—zieren** [tape'tsi:rən] *vt* (wall)paper; **—zierer** [tape'tsi:rər] *m* **-s, -** (interior) decorator.

tapfer ['tapfər] a brave; **T—keit** *f* courage, bravery.

tappen ['tapən] *vi* walk uncertainly or clumsily.

täppisch ['tɛpɪʃ] a clumsy.

Tarif [ta'ri:f] *m* **-s, -e** tariff, (scale of) fares/charges; **—lohn** *m* standard wage rate.

Tarn ['tarn] *cpd:* **t—en** *vt* camouflage; **Person, Absicht** disguise;

—farbe f camouflage paint ; —ung f camouflaging ; disguising.

Tasche ['taʃə] f -, -n pocket ; handbag ; —n in cpds pocket ; —nbuch nt paperback ; —ndieb m pickpocket ; —ngeld nt pocket money ; —nlampe f (electric) torch, flashlight (US) ; —nmesser nt penknife ; —nspieler m conjurer ; —ntuch nt handkerchief.

Tasse ['tasə] f -, -n cup.

Tast- ['tast] cpd: —atur [-a'tu:r] f keyboard ; —e f -, -n push-button control ; (an Schreibmaschine) key ; t—en vt feel, touch ; vi feel, grope ; vr feel one's way ; —sinn m sense of touch.

Tat [ta:t] f -, -en act, deed, action ; **in der** — indeed, as a matter of fact ; —bestand m facts pl of the case ; t—enlos a inactive.

Tät- ['tɛ:t] cpd: —er(in f) m -s, - perpetrator, culprit ; —erschaft f guilt ; t—ig a active ; **in einer Firma t—ig sein** work for a firm ; **T—igkeit** f activity ; (Beruf) occupation ; t—lich a violent ; —lichkeit f violence ; pl blows pl.

tätowieren [tɛto'vi:rən] vt tattoo.

Tat- cpd: —sache f fact ; t—sächlich a actual ; ad really.

Tatze ['tatsə] f -, -n paw.

Tau [tau] nt -(e)s, -e rope ; m -(e)s dew.

taub [taup] a deaf ; Nuß hollow ; **T—heit** f deafness ; —stumm a deaf-and-dumb.

Taube ['taubə] f -, -n dove, pigeon ; —nschlag m dovecote.

Tauch- ['taux] cpd: t—en vt dip ; vi dive ; (Naut) submerge ; —er m -s, - diver ; —eranzug m diving suit ; —sieder m -s, - portable immersion heater.

tauen ['tauən] vti, v impers thaw.

Tauf- ['tauf] cpd: —becken nt font ; —e f -, -n baptism ; t—en christen, baptize ; —name m Christian name ; —pate m godfather ; —patin f godmother ; —schein nt certificate of baptism.

Taug- ['taug] cpd: t—en vi be of use ; t—en für do or be good for ; **nicht t—en** be no good or useless ; —enichts m -es, -e good-for-nothing ; t—lich ['tauklɪç] a suitable ; (Mil) fit (for service) ; —lichkeit f suitability ; fitness.

Taumel ['tauməl] m -s dizziness ; (fig) frenzy ; t—ig a giddy, reeling ; t—n vi reel, stagger.

Tausch [tauʃ] m -(e)s, -e exchange ; t—en vt exchange, swap ; —handel m barter.

täuschen ['tɔyʃən] vt deceive ; vi be deceptive ; vr be wrong ; —d a deceptive.

Täuschung f deception ; (optisch) illusion.

tausend ['tauzənt] num (a) thousand ; **T—füßler** m -s, - centipede ; millipede.

Tau- cpd: —tropfen m dew drop ; —wetter nt thaw ; —ziehen nt -s, - tug-of-war.

Taxi ['taksi] nt -(s), -(s) taxi ; —fahrer m taxi driver.

Tech- ['tɛç] cpd: —nik f technology ; (Methode, Kunstfertigkeit) technique ; —niker m -s, - technician ; t—nisch a technical ; —nolo'gie f technology ; t—no'logisch a technological.

Tee [te:] m -s, -s tea ; —kanne f teapot ; —löffel m teaspoon.

Teer [te:r] m -(e)s, -e tar ; t—en vt tar.

Tee- cpd: —sieb nt tea strainer ; —wagen m tea trolley.

Teich [taiç] *m* -(e)s, -e pond.

Teig [taik] *m* -(e)s, -e dough; t—ig *a* doughy; —waren *pl* pasta *sing.*

Teil [tail] *m or nt* -(e)s, -e part; (An—) share; (Bestand—) component; zum — partly; t—bar *a* divisible; —betrag *m* instalment; —chen *nt* (atomic) particle; t—en *vtr* divide; (mit jdm) share; t—haben *vi irreg* share (an +dat in); —haber *m* -s, - partner; —kaskoversicherung *f* third party, fire and theft insurance; —nahme *f* -, -n participation; (Mitleid) sympathy; t—nahmslos *a* disinterested, apathetic; t—nehmen *vi irreg* take part (an +dat in); —nehmer *m* -s, - participant; t—s *ad* partly; —ung *f* division; t—weise *ad* partially, in part; —zahlung *f* payment in instalments.

Teint [tɛ̃:] *m* -s, -s complexion.

Telefon [tele'foːn] *nt* -s, -e telephone; —amt *nt* telephone exchange; —anruf *m*, —at [telefo'naːt] *nt* -(e)s, -e (tele)phone call; —buch *nt* telephone directory; t—ieren [telefo'niːrən] *vi* telephone; t—isch [-ʃ] *a* telephone; Benachrichtigung by telephone; —ist(in *f*) [telefo'nɪst(ɪn)] *m* telephonist; —nummer *f* (tele)phone number; —verbindung *f* telephone connection; —zelle *f* telephone kiosk, callbox; —zentrale *f* telephone exchange.

Telegraf [tele'graːf] *m* -en, -en telegraph; —enleitung *f* telegraph line; —enmast *m* telegraph pole; —ie [-'fiː] *f* telegraphy; t—ieren [-'fiːrən] *vti* telegraph, wire; t—isch *a* telegraphic.

Telegramm [tele'gram] *nt* -s, -e telegram, cable; —adresse *f* tele-

graphic address; —formular *nt* telegram form.

Tele- *cpd:* —graph = —graf; —kolleg ['teleːkɔlek] *nt* university of the air; —objektiv ['teːleʔɔpjɛktiːf] *nt* telephoto lens; —pathie [telepa'tiː] *f* telepathy; t—pathisch [tele'paːtɪʃ] *a* telepathic; —phon = —fon; —skop [tele'skoːp] *nt* -s, -e telescope.

Teller ['tɛlər] *m* -s, - plate.

Tempel ['tɛmpəl] *m* -s, - temple.

Temperafarbe ['tɛmperafarbə] *f* distemper.

Temperament [tɛmpera'mɛnt] *nt* temperament; (Schwung) vivacity, liveliness; t—los *a* spiritless; t—voll *a* high-spirited, lively.

Temperatur [tɛmpera'tuːr] *f* temperature.

Tempo ['tɛmpo] *nt* -s, -s speed, pace; *pl* Tempi (Mus) tempo; —! get a move on!; t—rär [-'rɛːr] *a* temporary; —taschentuch ® *nt* paper handkerchief.

Tendenz [tɛn'dɛnts] *f* tendency; (Absicht) intention; t—iös [-i'øːs] *a* biased, tendentious.

tendieren [tɛn'diːrən] *vi* show a tendency, incline (zu to(wards)).

Tenne ['tɛnə] *f* -, -n threshing floor.

Tennis ['tɛnɪs] *nt* - tennis; —platz *m* tennis court; —schläger *m* tennis racket; —spieler(in *f*) *m* tennis player.

Tenor [te'noːr] *m* -s, -̈e tenor.

Teppich ['tɛpɪç] *m* -s, -e carpet; —boden *m* wall-to-wall carpeting; —kehrmaschine *f* carpet sweeper; —klopfer *m* carpet beater.

Termin [tɛr'miːn] *m* -s, -e (Zeitpunkt) date; (Frist) time limit, deadline; (Arzt— etc) appointment; —kalender *m* diary, appoint-

ments book; —ologie [-olo'gi:] f
terminology.

Termite [tɛr'mi:tə] f -, -n termite.

Terpentin [tɛrpɛn'ti:n] nt -s, -e
turpentine, turps sing.

Terrasse [tɛ'rasə] f -, -n terrace.

Terrine [tɛ'ri:nə] f tureen.

territorial [tɛritori'a:l] a territorial.

Territorium [tɛri'to:rium] nt territory.

Terror ['tɛrɔr] m -s terror; reign
of terror; t—isieren [tɛrori'zi:rən]
vt terrorize; —ismus [-'rɪsmʊs] m
terrorism; —ist [-'rɪst] m terrorist.

Terz [tɛrts] f -, -en (Mus) third;
—ett [tɛr'tsɛt] nt -(e)s, -e trio.

Tesafilm ® ['te:zafɪlm] m sellotape
®.

Testament [tɛsta'mɛnt] nt will,
testament; (Rel) Testament;
t—arisch [-'ta:rɪʃ] a testamentary ;
—svollstrecker m executor (of a
will).

Test- [tɛst] cpd: —at [tɛs'ta:t] nt
-(e)s, -e certificate; —ator
[tɛs'ta:tor] m testator; —bild nt
(TV) test card; t—en vt test.

Tetanus [te:tanʊs] m - tetanus;
—impfung f (anti-)tetanus injection.

teuer ['tɔyər] a dear, expensive;
T—ung f increase in prices;
T—ungszulage f cost of living
bonus.

Teufel ['tɔyfəl] m -s, - devil; —el
[-'laɪ] f devilry ; —saustreibung f
exorcism.

teuflisch ['tɔyflɪʃ] a fiendish,
diabolical.

Text [tɛkst] m -(e)s, -e text;
(Lieder—) words pl; t—en vi write
the words.

textil [tɛks'ti:l] a textile; T—ien pl
textiles pl; T—industrie f textile
industry; —waren pl textiles pl.

Theater [te'a:tər] nt -s, - theatre;
(col) fuss; — spielen (lit, fig) play-
act; —besucher m playgoer;
—kasse f box office; —stück nt
(stage-)play.

theatralisch [tea'tra:lɪʃ] a
theatrical.

Theke ['te:kə] f -, -n (Schanktisch)
bar; (Ladentisch) counter.

Thema ['te:ma] nt -s, Themen or
-ta theme, topic, subject.

Theo- [teo] cpd: —loge [-'lo:gə] m
-n, -n theologian; —logie [-lo'gi:] f
theology; t—logisch [-'lo:gɪʃ] a
theological; —retiker [-'re:tikər] m
-s, - theorist; t—retisch [-'re:tɪʃ] a
theoretical; —rie [-'ri:] f theory.

Thera- [tera] cpd: —peut [-'pɔyt] m
-en, -en therapist; t—peutisch
[-'pɔytɪʃ] a therapeutic; —pie [-'pi:]
f therapy.

Therm- cpd: —albad [tɛrm'a:lba:t]
nt thermal bath; thermal spa;
—ometer [tɛrmo'me:tər] nt -s, -
thermometer; —osflasche
['tɛrmosflaʃə] f Thermos ® flask;
—ostat [tɛrmo'sta:t] m -(e)s or -en,
-e(n) thermostat.

These ['te:zə] f -, -n thesis.

Thrombose [trɔm'bo:zə] f -, -n
thrombosis.

Thron [tro:n] m -(e)s, -e throne;
—besteigung f accession (to the
throne); —erbe m heir to the
throne; —folge f succession (to the
throne).

Thunfisch ['tu:nfɪʃ] m tuna.

Thymian ['ty:mia:n] m -s, -e
thyme.

Tick [tɪk] m -(e)s, -s tic;
(Eigenart) quirk; (Fimmel) craze;
t—en vi tick.

tief [ti:f] a deep; (tiefsinnig) profound; Ausschnitt, Ton low; T—
nt -s, -s (Met) depression;

T—druck *m* low pressure; T—e *f* ~, -n depth; T—ebene *f* plain; T—enpsychologie *f* depth psychology; T—enschärfe *f* (*Phot*) depth of focus; —ernst *a* very grave *or* solemn; T—gang *m* (*Naut*) draught; (*geistig*) depth; —gekühlt *a* frozen; —greifend *a* far-reaching; T—kühlfach *nt* deep-freeze compartment; T—kühltruhe *f* deep-freeze, freezer; T—land *nt* lowlands *pl*; T—punkt *m* low point; (*fig*) low ebb; T—schlag *m* (*Boxen, fig*) blow below the belt; —schürfend *a* profound; T—see *f* deep sea; T—sinn *m* profundity; —sinnig *a* profound; melancholy; T—stand *m* low level; —stapeln *vi* be overmodest; T—start *m* (*Sport*) crouch start; T—stwert *m* minimum *or* lowest value.

Tiegel ['tiːgəl] *m* -s, - saucepan; (*Chem*) crucible.

Tier [tiːr] *nt* -(e)s, -e animal; —arzt *m* vet(erinary surgeon); —garten *m* zoo(logical gardens *pl*); t—isch *a* animal; (*lit, fig*) brutish; (*fig*) Ernst *etc* deadly; —kreis *m* zodiac; —kunde *f* zoology; t—liebend *a* fond of animals; —quälerei [-kvɛːlaˈraɪ] *f* cruelty to animals; —schutzverein *m* society for the prevention of cruelty to animals.

Tiger ['tiːgər] *m* -s, - tiger; —in *f* tigress.

tilgen ['tɪlgən] *vt* erase, expunge; *Sünden* expiate; *Schulden* pay off.

Tilgung *f* erasing, blotting out; expiation; repayment.

Tinktur [tɪŋkˈtuːr] *f* tincture.

Tinte ['tɪntə] *f* ~, -n ink; —nfaß *nt* inkwell; —nfisch *m* cuttlefish; —nfleck *m* ink stain, blot; —nstift *m* copying *or* indelible pencil.

tippen ['tɪpən] *vti* tap, touch; (*col: schreiben*) type; (*col: raten*) tip (*auf jdn sb*); (*im Lotto etc*) bet (on).

Tipp- [tɪp] *cpd:* —fehler *m* (*col*) typing error; —se *f* ~, -n (*col*) typist; t—topp *a* (*col*) tip-top; —zettel *m* (pools) coupon.

Tisch [tɪʃ] *m* -(e)s, -e table; bei — at table; vor/nach — before/after eating; unter den — fallen (*fig*) be dropped; —decke *f* table-cloth; —ler *m* -s, - carpenter, joiner; —lerei *f* joiner's workshop; (*Arbeit*) carpentry, joinery; t—lern *vi* do carpentry *etc*; —rede *f* after-dinner speech; —tennis *nt* table tennis.

Titel ['tiːtəl] *m* -s, - title; —anwärter *m* (*Sport*) challenger; —bild *nt* cover (picture); (*von Buch*) frontispiece; —rolle *f* title role; —seite *f* cover; (*Buch—*) title page; —verteidiger *m* defending champion, title holder.

titulieren [titʊˈliːrən] *vt* entitle; (*anreden*) address.

Toast [toːst] *m* -(e)s, -s *or* -e toast; —er *m* -s, - toaster.

tob- ['toːb] *cpd:* —en *vi* rage; (*Kinder*) romp about; T—sucht *f* raving madness; —süchtig *a* maniacal; —suchtsanfall *m* maniacal fit.

Tochter ['tɔxtər] *f* ~, = daughter.

Tod [toːt] *m* -(e)s, -e death; t—ernst *a* (*col*) deadly serious; *ad* in dead earnest; —esangst ['toːdəsaŋst] *f* mortal fear; —esanzeige *f* obituary (notice); —esfall *m* death; —eskampf *m* throes *pl* of death; —esstoß *m* death-blow; —esstrafe *f* death penalty; —estag *m* anniversary of death; —esursache *f* cause of death; —esurteil *nt* death

sentence; —esverachtung f utter disgust; t—krank a dangerously ill.
tödlich ['tø:tlɪç] a deadly, fatal.
tod- cpd: —müde a dead tired; —schick a (col) smart, classy; —sicher a (col) absolutely or dead certain; T—sünde f deadly sin.
Toilette [toa'lɛtə] f toilet, lavatory; (Frisiertisch) dressing table; (Kleidung) outfit; —nartikel pl toiletries pl, toilet articles pl; —npapier nt toilet paper; —ntisch m dressing table.
toi, toi, toi ['tɔy, 'tɔy, 'tɔy] interj touch wood.
tolerant [tole'rant] a tolerant.
Toleranz [tole'rants] f tolerance.
tolerieren [tole'ri:rən] vt tolerate.
toll [tɔl] a mad; Treiben wild; (col) terrific; —en vi romp; T—heit f madness, wildness; T—kirsche f deadly nightshade; —kühn a daring; T—wut f rabies.
Tölpel ['tœlpəl] m -s, - oaf, clod.
Tomate [to'ma:tə] f -, -n tomato; —nmark nt tomato puree.
Ton [to:n] m -(e)s, -e (Erde) clay; pl -̈e (Laut) sound; (Mus) note; (Redeweise) tone; (Farb—, Nuance) shade; (Betonung) stress; —abnehmer m pick-up; t—angebend a leading; —art f (musical) key; —band nt tape; —bandgerät nt tape recorder.
tönen ['tø:nən] vi sound; vt shade; Haare tint.
tönern ['tø:nərn] a clay.
Ton- cpd: —fall m intonation; —film m sound film; t—haltig a clayey; —höhe f pitch; —la f -, -iken (Mus), —ikum nt -s, -ika (Med) tonic; —künstler m musician; —leiter f (Mus) scale; t—los a soundless.

Tonne ['tɔnə] f -, -n barrel; (Maß) ton.
Ton- cpd: —spur f soundtrack; —taube f clay pigeon; —waren pl pottery, earthenware.
Topf [tɔpf] m -(e)s, -̈e pot; —blume f pot plant.
Töpfer ['tœpfər] m -s, - potter; —ei [-'rai] f piece of pottery; potter's workshop; —scheibe f potter's wheel.
topographisch [topo'gra:fɪʃ] a topographic.
topp [tɔp] interj O.K.
Tor [to:r] m -en, -en fool; nt -(e)s, -e gate; (Sport) goal; —bogen m archway.
Torf [tɔrf] m -(e)s peat; —stechen nt peat-cutting.
Tor- cpd: —heit f foolishness; foolish deed; —hüter m -s, - goalkeeper.
töricht ['tø:rɪçt] a foolish.
torkeln ['tɔrkəln] vi stagger, reel.
torpedieren [tɔrpe'di:rən] vt (lit, fig) torpedo.
Torpedo [tɔr'pe:do] m -s, -s torpedo.
Torte ['tɔrtə] f -, -n cake; (Obst—) flan, tart.
Tortur [tɔr'tu:r] f ordeal.
Tor- cpd: —verhältnis nt goal average; —wart m -(e)s, -e goalkeeper.
tosen ['to:zən] vi roar.
tot [to:t] a dead; einen —en Punkt haben be at one's lowest.
total [to'ta:l] a total; —itär [totali'tɛ:r] a totalitarian; T—schaden m (Aut) complete write-off.
tot- cpd: —arbeiten vr work oneself to death; —ärgern vr (col) be really annoyed.

töten ['tøːtən] *vti* kill.

Tot- *cpd:* —**enbett** *nt* death bed; **t—enblaß** *a* deathly pale, white as a sheet; —**engräber** *m* -s, - grave-digger; —**enhemd** *nt* shroud; —**enkopf** *m* skull; —**enschein** *m* death certificate; —**enstille** *f* deathly silence; —**entanz** *m* danse macabre; —**e(r)** *mf* dead person; **t—fahren** *vt irreg* run over; **t—geboren** *a* stillborn; **t—lachen** *vr (col)* laugh one's head off.

Toto ['toːto] *m or nt* -s, -s pools *pl*; —**schein** *m* pools coupon.

tot- *cpd:* —**sagen** *vt:* **jdn —sagen** say that sb is dead; —**schlagen** *vt irreg (lit, fig)* kill; **T—schläger** *m* killer; *(Waffe)* cosh; —**schweigen** *vt irreg* hush up; —**stellen** *vr* pretend to be dead; —**treten** *vt irreg* trample to death.

Tötung ['tøːtʊŋ] *f* killing.

Toupet [tu'peː] *nt* -s, -s toupee.

toupieren [tu'piːrən] *vt* back-comb.

Tour [tuːr] *f* -, -en tour, trip; *(Umdrehung)* revolution; *(Verhaltensart)* way; **in einer —** incessantly; —**enzahl** *f* number of revolutions; —**enzähler** *m* rev counter; —**ismus** [tu'rɪsmʊs] *m* tourism; —**ist** [tu'rɪst] *m* tourist; —**istenklasse** *f* tourist class; —**nee** [tur'neː] *f* -, -n *(Theat etc)* tour; **auf —nee gehen** go on tour.

Trab [traːp] *m* -(e)s trot; —**ant** [tra'bant] *m* satellite; —**antenstadt** *f* satellite town; **t—en** *vi* trot.

Tracht [traxt] *f* -, -en *(Kleidung)* costume, dress; **eine — Prügel** a sound thrashing; **t—en** *vi* strive *(nach for)*, endeavour; **jdm nach dem Leben t—en** seek to kill sb.

trächtig ['trɛçtɪç] *a Tier* pregnant; *(fig)*. rich, fertile.

Tradition [traditsi'oːn] *f* tradition; **t—ell** [-'nɛl] *a* traditional.

Trag- [traːg] *cpd:* —**bahre** *f* stretcher; **t—bar** *a Gerät* portable; *Kleidung* wearable; *(erträglich)* bearable.

träge ['trɛːgə] *a* sluggish, slow; *(Phys)* inert.

tragen ['traːgən] *irreg vt* carry; *Kleidung,* Brille wear; *Namen, Früchte* bear; *(erdulden)* endure; **sich mit einem Gedanken — have an idea in mind;** *vi (schwanger sein)* be pregnant; *(Eis)* hold; **zum T— kommen** have an effect.

Träger ['trɛːgər] *m* -s, - carrier; wearer; bearer; *(Ordens—)* holder; *(an Kleidung)* (shoulder) strap; *(Körperschaft etc)* sponsor; —**rakete** *f* launch vehicle; —**rock** *m* skirt with shoulder straps.

Trag- ['traːk] *cpd:* —**fähigkeit** *f* load-carrying capacity; —**fläche** *f (Aviat)* wing; —**flügelboot** *nt* hydrofoil.

Trägheit ['trɛːkhaɪt] *f* laziness; *(Phys)* inertia.

Tragi- ['traːgi] *cpd:* —**k** *f* tragedy; **t—komisch** *a* tragi-comic; **t—sch** *a* tragic.

Tragödie [tra'gøːdiə] *f* tragedy.

Trag- ['traːk] *cpd:* —**weite** *f* range; *(fig)* scope; —**werk** *nt* wing assembly.

Train- [trɛːn] *cpd:* —**er** *m* -s, - *(Sport)* trainer, coach; *(Fußball)* manager; **t—ieren** [trɛ'niːrən] *vti* train; *Mensch auch* coach; *Übung* practise; **Fußball t—ieren** do football practice; —**ing** *nt* -s, -s training; —**ingsanzug** *m* track suit.

Traktor ['traktor] *m* tractor.

trällern ['trɛlərn] *vti* trill, sing.

trampeln ['trampəln] *vti* trample, stamp.

trampen ['trampən] *vi* hitch-hike.

Tran [tra:n] *m* -(e)s, -e train oil, blubber.

tranchieren [trã'ʃi:rən] *vt* carve.

Tranchierbesteck [trã'ʃi:rbəʃtɛk] *nt* (pair of) carvers.

Träne ['trɛ:nə] *f* -, -n tear; **t—n** *vi* water; **—ngas** *nt* teargas.

Tränke ['trɛŋkə] *f* -, -n watering place; **t—n** *vt* (naß machen) soak; *Tiere* water.

Trans- *cpd:* **—formator** [transfor'ma:tor] *m* transformer; **—istor** [tran'zistor] *m* transistor; **t—itiv** [tranzi'ti:f] *a* transitive; **t—parent** [transpa'rɛnt] *a* transparent; **—parent** *nt* -(e)s, -e (*Bild*) transparency; (*Spruchband*) banner; **t—pirieren** [transpi'ri:rən] *vi* perspire; **—plantation** [transplantatsi'o:n] *f* transplantation; (*Haut—*) graft(ing); **—port** [trans'pɔrt] *m* -(e)s, -e transport; **t—portieren** [transpɔr'ti:rən] *vt* transport; **—portkosten** *pl* transport charges *pl*, carriage; **—portmittel** *nt* means of transportation; **—portunternehmen** *nt* carrier.

Trapez [tra'pe:ts] *nt* -es, -e trapeze; (*Math*) trapezium.

Traube ['traubə] *f* -, -n grape; bunch (of grapes); **—nlese** *f* vintage; **—nzucker** *m* glucose.

trauen ['trauən] *vi*: jdm/etw *—* trust sb/sth; *vr* dare; *vt* marry.

Trauer ['trauər] *f* - sorrow; (*für Verstorbenen*) mourning; (*—fall* *m* death, bereavement; **—marsch** *m* funeral march; **t—n** *vi* mourn (*um* for); **—rand** *m* black border; **—spiel** *nt* tragedy.

Traufe ['traufə] *f* -, -n eaves *pl*.

träufeln ['trɔyfəln] *vti* drip.

traulich ['traulɪç] *a* cosy, intimate.

Traum [traum] *m* -(e)s, Träume dream; **—a** *nt* -s, -men trauma; **—bild** *nt* vision.

träum- ['trɔym] *cpd:* **t—en** *vti* dream; **T—er** *m* -s, - dreamer; **T—e'rei** *f* dreaming; **—erisch** *a* dreamy.

traumhaft *a* dreamlike; (*fig*) wonderful.

traurig ['traurɪç] *a* sad; **T—keit** *f* sadness.

Trau- ['trau] *cpd:* **—ring** *m* wedding ring; **—schein** *m* marriage certificate; **—ung** *f* wedding ceremony; **—zeuge** *m* witness (to a marriage).

treffen ['trɛfən] *irreg vti* strike, hit; (*Bemerkung*) hurt; (*begegnen*) meet; *Entscheidung* etc make; *Maßnahmen* take; er hat es gut getroffen he did well; **—** *auf* (*+ acc*) come across, meet with; *vr* meet; es traf sich, daß... it so happened that...; es trifft sich gut it's convenient; wie es so trifft as these things happen; **T—** *nt* -s, - meeting; **—d** *a* pertinent, apposite.

Treff- *cpd:* **—er** *m* -s, - hit; (*Tor*) goal; (*Los*) winner; **t—lich** *a* excellent; **—punkt** *m* meeting place.

Treib- ['traib] *cpd:* **—eis** *nt* drift ice; **t—en** *irreg vt* drive; *Studien* etc pursue; *Sport* do, go in for; *Unsinn* **t—en** fool around; *vi* (*Schiff* etc) drift; (*Pflanzen*) sprout; (*Cook: aufgehen*) rise; (*Tee, Kaffee*) be diuretic; **—en** *nt* -s activity; **—haus** *nt* hothouse; **—stoff** *m* fuel.

trenn- ['trɛn] *cpd:* **—bar** *a* separable; **—en** *vt* separate; (*teilen*) divide; *vr* separate; sich **—en von** part with; **T—schärfe** *f* (*Rad*) selectivity; **T—ung** *f* separation; T—wand f partition (wall).

Trepp- ['trεp] cpd: **t—ab** ad down-stairs; **t—auf** ad upstairs; **—e** f -, **-n** stair(case); **—engeländer** nt banister; **—enhaus** nt staircase.

Tresor [tre'zoːr] m -s, -e safe.

treten ['treːtən] irreg vi step; (Tränen, Schweiß) appear; **—** nach kick at; **—** in (+acc) step in(to); in Verbindung **—** get in contact; in Erscheinung **—** appear; vt (mit Fußtritt) kick; (nieder—) tread, trample.

treu [trɔy] a faithful, true; T—e f **-** loyalty, faithfulness; T—händer m -s, **-** trustee; T—handgesellschaft f trust company; **—herzig** a innocent; **—lich** ad faithfully; **—los** a faithless.

Tribüne [tri'byːnə] f -, **-n** grand-stand; (Redner—) platform.

Tribut [tri'buːt] nt -(e)s, -e tribute.

Trichter ['trıçtər] m -s, **-** funnel; (in Boden) crater.

Trick [trık] m -s, -e or -s trick; **—film** m cartoon.

Trieb [triːp] m -(e)s, -e urge, drive; (Neigung) inclination; (an Baum etc) shoot; **—feder** f (fig) motivating force; **t—haft** a impulsive; **—kraft** f (fig) drive; **—täter** m sex offender; **—wagen** m (Rail) diesel railcar; **—werk** nt engine.

triefen ['triːfən] vi drip.

triftig ['trıftıç] a good, convincing.

Trigonometrie [trigonome'triː] f trigonometry.

Trikot [tri'koː] nt -s, -s vest; (Sport) shirt; m -s, -s (Gewebe) tricot.

Triller ['trılər] m -s, **-** (Mus) trill; **t—n** vi trill, warble; **—pfeife** f whistle.

Trimester [tri'mεstər] nt -s, **-** term.

trink- ['trıŋk] cpd: **—bar** a drink-able; **—en** vti irreg drink; T—er m -s, **-** drinker; T—geld nt tip; T—halm m (drinking) straw; T—spruch m toast; T—wasser nt drinking water.

trippeln ['trıpəln] vi toddle.

Tripper ['trıpər] m -s, **-** gonorrhoea.

Tritt [trıt] m -(e)s, -e step; (Fuß—) kick; **—brett** nt (Rail) step; (Aut) running-board.

Triumph [tri'umf] m -(e)s, -e triumph; **—bogen** m triumphal arch; **t—ieren** [-'iːrən] vi triumph; (jubeln) exult.

trivial [trivi'aːl] a trivial.

trocken ['trɔkən] a dry; T—dock nt dry dock; T—element nt dry cell; T—haube f hair-dryer; T—heit f dryness; **—legen** vt Sumpf drain; Kind put a clean nappy on; T—milch f dried milk.

trocknen ['trɔknən] vti dry.

Troddel ['trɔdəl] f -, **-n** tassel.

Trödel ['trøːdəl] m -s (col) junk; **t—n** vi (col) dawdle.

Trödler ['trøːdlər] m -s, **-** second-hand dealer.

Trog [troːk] m -(e)s, *e trough.

Trommel ['trɔməl] f -, **-n** drum; **—fell** nt eardrum; **t—n** vti drum; **—revolver** m revolver; **—waschmaschine** f tumble-action washing machine.

Trommler ['trɔmlər] m -s, **-** drummer.

Trompete [trɔm'peːtə] f -, **-n** trumpet; **—r** m -s, **-** trumpeter.

Tropen ['troːpən] pl tropics pl; **t—beständig** a suitable for the tropics; **—helm** m topee, sun helmet.

Tropf [trɔpf] m -(e)s, ⸚e (col)
rogue; armer — poor devil.

tröpfeln ['trœpfəln] vi drop, trickle.

Tropfen ['trɔpfən] m -s, - drop;
t— vti drip; v impers: es tropft a
few raindrops are falling; t—weise
ad in drops.

Tropfsteinhöhle f stalactite cave.

tropisch ['tro:pɪʃ] a tropical.

Trost [tro:st] m -es consolation,
comfort; t—bedürftig a in need of
consolation.

tröst- ['trø:st] cpd: —en vt console,
comfort; T—er(in f) m -s, -
comfort(er); —lich a comforting.

trost- cpd: —los a bleak;
Verhältnisse wretched; T—preis m
consolation prize; —reich a comforting.

Tröstung ['trø:stʊŋ] f comfort; consolation.

Trott [trɔt] m -(e)s, ⸚e trot;
(Routine) routine; —el m -s, - (col)
fool, dope; t—en vi trot; —oir
[trɔto'a:r] nt -s, -s or e pavement,
sidewalk (US).

Trotz [trɔts] m -es pigheadedness;
etw aus — tun do sth just to show
them; jdm zum — in defiance of
sb; t— prep +gen or dat in spite
of; —alter nt· obstinate phase;
t—dem ad· nevertheless; cj
although; t—ig a defiant, pigheaded; —kopf m obstinate child;
—reaktion f fit of pique.

trüb [try:p] a dull; Flüssigkeit, Glas
cloudy; (fig) gloomy; —en
['try:bən] vt cloud; vr become
clouded; T—heit f dullness; cloudi-
ness; gloom; T—sal f -, -e
distress; —selig a sad,
melancholy; T—sinn m depression; —sinnig a depressed, gloomy.

trudeln ['tru:dəln] vi (Aviat) (go
into a) spin.

Trüffel ['tryfəl] f -, -n truffle.

trüg- ['try:g] cpd: —en vt irreg
deceive; vi be deceptive; —erisch
a deceptive.

Trugschluß ['tru:gʃlʊs] m false
conclusion.

Truhe ['tru:ə] f -, -n chest.

Trümmer ['trʏmər] pl wreckage;
(Bau—) ruins pl; —haufen m heap
of rubble.

Trumpf [trʊmpf] m -(e)s, ⸚e (lit,
fig) trump; t—en vti trump.

Trunk [trʊŋk] m -(e)s, ⸚e drink;
t—en a intoxicated; —enbold m
-(e)s, -e drunkard; —enheit f
intoxication; —enheit am Steuer
drunken driving; —sucht f
alcoholism.

Trupp [trʊp] m -s, -s troop; —e
f -, -n troop; (Waffengattung)
force; (Schauspiel—) troupe; —en
pl troops pl; —enführer m
(military) commander; —enteil m
unit; —enübungsplatz m training
area.

Truthahn ['tru:tha:n] m turkey.

Tube ['tu:bə] f -, -n tube.

Tuberkulose [tubɛrku'lo:zə] f -, -n
tuberculosis.

Tuch [tu:x] nt -(e)s, ⸚er cloth;
(Hals—) scarf; (Kopf—) headscarf; (Hand—) towel.

tüchtig ['tʏçtɪç] a efficient;
(cap)able; (col: kräftig) good,
sound; T—keit f efficiency, ability.

Tücke ['tʏkə] f -, -n (Arglist)
malice; (Trick) trick;
(Schwierigkeit) difficulty, problem;
seine —n haben be temperamental.

tückisch ['tʏkɪʃ] a treacherous;
(böswillig) malicious.

Tugend ['tu:gənt] f -, -en virtue;
t—haft a virtuous.

Tüll [tyl] *m* -s, -e tulle; —e *f* -,
-n spout.

Tulpe ['tʊlpə] *f* -, -n tulip.

tummeln ['tʊməln] *vr* romp,
gambol; *(sich beeilen)* hurry.

Tumor ['tuːmɔr] *m* -s, -e tumour.

Tümpel ['tʏmpəl] *m* -s, - pool,
pond.

Tumult [tu'mʊlt] *m* -(e)s, -e
tumult.

tun [tuːn] *irreg vt (machen)* do;
(legen) put; jdm etw — *(antun)* do
sth to sb; etw tut es auch sth will
do; das t· nichts that doesn't
matter; σ· tut nichts zur Sache
that's neither here nor there; *vi*
act; so —, als ob act as if; *vr:*
es tut sich etwas/viel something/a
lot is happening.

Tünche ['tynçə] *f* -, -n whitewash;
t—n *vt* whitewash.

Tunke ['tʊŋkə] *f* -, -n sauce; t—n
vt dip, dunk.

tunlichst ['tuːnlɪçst] *ad* if at all
possible; — bald as soon as
possible.

Tunnel ['tʊnəl] *m* -s, -s *or* - tunnel.

Tüpfel ['tʏpfəl] *m* -s, - dot, spot;
—chen *nt (small)* dot; t—n *vt* dot,
spot.

tupfen ['tʊpfən] *vti* dab; *(mit
Farbe)* dot; T— *m* -s, - dot, spot.

Tür [tyːr] *f* -, -en door.

Turbine [tʊr'biːnə] *f* turbine.

Türkis [tʏr'kiːs] *m* -es, -e
turquoise; t— *a* turquoise.

Turm [tʊrm] *m* -(e)s, ·e tower;
(Kirch—) steeple; *(Sprung—)* diving platform; *(Schach)* castle, rook.

Türm- ['tʏrm-] *cpd:* —chen *nt*
turret; t—en *vr* tower up; *vt* heap
up; *vi (col)* scarper, bolt.

Turn- ['tʊrn-] *cpd:* t—en *vi* do gym-
nastic exercises; *vt* perform; —en
nt -s gymnastics; *(Sch)* physical
education, P.E.; —er(in *f*) *m* -s, -
gymnast; —halle *f* gym(nasium);
—hose *f* gym shorts *pl*.

Turnier [tʊr'niːr] *nt* -s, -e tournament.

Turnus ['tʊrnʊs] *m* -, -se rota; im
— in rotation.

Turn- *cpd:* —verein *m* gymnastics
club; —zeug *nt* gym things *pl*.

Tusche ['tʊʃə] *f* -, -n Indian ink.

tuscheln ['tʊʃəln] *vti* whisper.

Tuschkasten *m* paintbox.

Tüte ['tyːtə] *f* -, -n bag.

tuten ['tuːtən] *vi (Aut)* hoot.

TÜV [tyf] *m* MOT.

Typ [tyːp] *m* -s, -en type; —e *f*
-, -n *(Print)* type.

Typhus ['tyːfʊs] *m* typhoid (fever).

typisch ['tyːpɪʃ] *a* typical *(für of)*.

Tyrann [ty'ran] *m* -en, -en tyrant;
—ei [-'naɪ] *f* tyranny; t—isch *a*
tyrannical; t—i'sieren *vt* tyrannize.

U

U, u [uː] *nt* U, u.

U-Bahn ['uːbaːn] *f* underground,
tube.

übel ['yːbəl] *a* bad; *(moralisch
auch)* wicked; jdm ist — sb feels
sick; Ü— *nt* -s, - evil; *(Krankheit)*

disease; —gelaunt *a* bad-tempered,
ill-humoured; Ü—keit *f* nausea;
—nehmen *vt irreg:* jdm eine
Bemerkung *etc* —nehmen be
offended at sb's remark *etc*;

Ü—stand *m* bad state of affairs, abuse; —wollend *a* malevolent.

üben ['y:bən] *vti* exercise, practise.

über ['y:bər] *prep* +*dat* or *acc* over; (*hoch* — *auch*) above; (*quer* — *auch*) across; (*Route*) via; (*betreffend*) about; *acc* over; den ganzen Tag — all day long; jdm in etw (*dat*) — sein (*coll*) be superior to sb in sth; — und — all over; —all [y:bər'al] *ad* everywhere.

überanstrengen [y:bər'anʃtrɛŋən] *vtr insep* overexert (o.s.).

überantworten [y:bər'antvɔrtən] *vt insep* hand over, deliver (up).

überarbeiten [y:bər'arbaitən] *vt insep* revise, rework; *vr* overwork (o.s.).

überaus ['y:bər'aus] *ad* exceedingly.

überbelichten ['y:bərbəlɪçtən] *vt* (*Phot*) overexpose.

über'bieten *vt irreg insep* outbid; (*übertreffen*) surpass; Rekord break.

Überbleibsel ['y:bərblaipsəl] *nt* -s, - residue, remainder.

Überblick ['y:bərblɪk] *m* view; (*fig*) (*Darstellung*) survey, overview; (*Fähigkeit*) overall view, grasp (*über* +*acc* of); ü—en ['blɪkən] *vt insep* survey.

überbring- [y:bər'brɪŋ] *cpd:* —en *vt irreg insep* deliver, hand over; Ü—er *m* -s, - bearer; Ü—ung *f* delivery.

überbrücken [y:bər'brʏkən] *vt insep* bridge (over).

über'dauern *vt insep* outlast.

über'denken *vt irreg insep* think over.

überdies [y:bər'di:s] *ad* besides.

überdimensional ['y:bər-dimɛnziona:l] *a* oversize.

Überdruß ['y:bərdrus] *m* -sses weariness; bis zum — ad nauseam.

'überdrüssig ['y:bərdrʏsɪç] *a* tired, sick (*gen* of).

übereifrig ['y:bəraifrɪç] *a* overkeen, overzealous.

übereilen [y:bər'ailən] *vt insep* hurry.

übereilt *a* (over)hasty, premature.

überein- [y:bər'ain] *cpd:* —ander [y:bər'ai'nandər] *ad* one upon the other; *sprechen* about each other; —anderschlagen *vt irreg* fold, cross; —kommen *vi irreg* agree; Ü—kunft *f* -, -künfte agreement; —stimmen *vi* agree; Ü—stimmung *f* agreement.

überempfindlich ['y:bər-ɛmpfɪntlɪç] *a* hypersensitive.

über'fahren [y:bər'fa:rən] *irreg vt* take across; *vi* (go a)cross; [-'fa:rən] *vt insep* (*Aut*) run over; (*fig*) walk all over.

Überfahrt ['y:bərfa:rt] *f* crossing.

Überfall ['y:bərfal] *m* (*Bank—, Mil*) raid; (*auf jdn*) assault; **ü—en** [-'falən] *vt irreg insep* attack; Bank raid; (*besuchen*) surprise.

überfällig ['y:bərfɛlɪç] *a* overdue.

über'fliegen *vt irreg insep* fly over, overfly; Buch skim through.

Überfluß ['y:bərflus] *m* (super)abundance, excess (*an* +*dat* of).

überflüssig ['y:bərflʏsɪç] *a* superfluous.

über'fordern *vt insep* demand too much of; Kräfte etc overtax.

über'führen *vt insep* Leiche etc transport; Täter have convicted (*gen* of).

Überführung *f* transport; conviction; (*Brücke*) bridge, overpass.

Übergabe ['y:bərga:bə] f handing over; (Mil) surrender.

Übergang ['y:bərgaŋ] m crossing; (Wandel, Überleitung) transition; **—serscheinung** f transitory phenomenon; **—slösung** f provisional solution, stopgap; **—sstadium** nt state of transition; **—szeit** f transitional period.

über'geben irreg insep vt hand over; (Mil) surrender; dem Verkehr — open to traffic; vr be sick.

übergehen ['y:bərge:ən] irreg vi (Besitz) pass; (zum Feind etc) go over, defect; (überleiten) go on (zu to); (sich verwandeln) turn (in in +acc into); ['-ge:ən] vt insep pass over, omit.

Übergewicht ['y:bərgəviçt] nt excess weight; (fig) preponderance.

überglücklich ['y:bərglykhç] a overjoyed.

übergroß ['y:bərgro:s] a outsize, huge.

überhaben ['y:bərha:bən] vt irreg (col) be fed up with.

überhandnehmen [y:bər-'hantne:mən] vi irreg gain the ascendancy.

überhängen ['y:bərhɛŋən] vi irreg overhang.

überhaupt [y:bər'haupt] ad at all; (im allgemeinen) in general; (besonders) especially; — nicht not at all.

überheblich [y:bər'he:plıç] a arrogant; Ü—keit f arrogance.

über'holen vt insep overtake; (Tech) overhaul.

überholt a out-of-date, obsolete.

über'hören vt insep not hear; (absichtlich) ignore.

überirdisch ['y:bər'ırdıʃ] a supernatural, unearthly.

überkompensieren ['y:bərk-ɔmpɛnzi:rən] vt insep overcompensate for.

über'laden vt irreg insep overload; a (fig) cluttered.

über'lassen irreg insep vt: jdm etw — leave sth to sb; vr: sich etw (dat) — give o.s. over to sth.

über'lasten vt insep overload; Mensch overtax.

überlaufen ['y:bərlaufən] irreg vi (Flüssigkeit) flow over; (zum Feind etc) go over, defect; ['-laufən] insep vt (Schauer etc) come over; — sein be inundated or besieged.

Überläufer ['y:bərlɔyfər] m -s, - deserter.

über'leben vt insep survive; Ü—de(r) mf survivor.

über'legen vt insep consider; a superior; Ü—heit f superiority.

Überlegung f consideration, deliberation.

über'liefern vt insep hand down, transmit.

Überlieferung f tradition.

überlisten [y:bər'lıstən] vt insep outwit.

überm ['y:bərm] = über dem.

Übermacht ['y:bərmaxt] f superior force, superiority.

übermächtig ['y:bərmɛçtıç] a superior (in strength); Gefühl etc overwhelming.

übermannen [y:bər'manən] vt insep overcome.

Übermaß ['y:bərma:s] nt excess (an +dat of).

übermäßig ['y:bərmɛ:sıç] a excessive.

Übermensch ['y:bərmɛnʃ] m superman; ü—lich a superhuman.

übermitteln [y:bər'mıtəln] vt insep convey.

übermorgen ['y:bərmɔrgən] *ad* the day after tomorrow.

Übermüdung [y:bər'my:duŋ] *f* fatigue, overtiredness.

Übermut [y:bərmu:t] *m* exuberance.

übermütig ['y:bərmy:tɪç] *a* exuberant, high-spirited; — **werden** get overconfident.

übernachten [y:bər'naxtən] *vi insep* spend the night (*bei jdm* at sb's place).

übernächtigt [y:bər'nɛçtɪçt] *a* tired, sleepy.

Übernahme [y:bər'na:mə] *f* -, -n ̄faking over *or* on, acceptance.

über'nehmen *irreg insep* *vt* take on, accept; *Amt, Geschäft* take over; *vr* take on too much.

über'prüfen *vt insep* examine, check.

Überprüfung *f* examination.

überqueren [y:bər'kve:rən] *vt insep* cross.

überragen [y:bər'ra:gən] *vt insep* tower above; *(fig)* surpass; ['y:bərra:gən] *vi* project, stick out.

überraschen [y:bər'raʃən] *vt insep* surprise.

Überraschung *f* surprise.

überreden [y:bər're:dən] *vt insep* persuade.

überreich [y:bər'raɪç] *a* very/too rich; **-en** [-'raɪçən] *vt insep* present, hand over; **-lich** *a, ad* (more than) ample.

überreizt [y:bər'raɪtst] *a* overwrought.

Überreste ['y:bərrɛstə] *pl* remains *pl*, remnants *pl*.

überrumpeln [y:bər'rompəln] *vt insep* take by surprise.

überrunden [y:bər'rundən] *vt insep* lap.

übers ['y:bərs] = **über das**.

übersättigen [y:bər'zɛtɪgən] *vt insep* satiate.

Überschall- ['y:bərʃal] *cpd:* **—flug-zeug** *nt* supersonic jet; **—ge-schwindigkeit** *f* supersonic speed.

über'schätzen *vtr insep* over-estimate.

überschäumen [y:bər'ʃɔʏmən] *vi* froth over; *(fig)* bubble over.

Überschlag ['y:bərʃla:k] *m (Fin)* estimate; *(Sport)* somersault; **ü—en** [-'ʃla:gən] *irreg insep vt (berechnen)* estimate; *(auslassen)* Seite omit; *vr* somersault; *(Stimme)* crack; *(Aviat)* loop the loop; *a* lukewarm, tepid; ['y:bərʃla:gən] *irreg vt Beine* cross; *vi (Wellen)* break over; *(Funken)* flash over.

überschnappen ['y:bərʃnapən] *vi (Stimme)* crack; *(col: Mensch)* flip one's lid.

über'schneiden *vr irreg insep (lit, fig)* overlap; *(Linien)* intersect.

über'schreiben *vt irreg insep* provide with a heading; *jdm etw* **—** transfer *or* make over sth to sb.

über'schreiten *vt irreg insep* cross over; *(fig)* exceed; *(verletzen)* transgress.

Überschrift ['y:bərʃrɪft] *f* heading, title.

Überschuß ['y:bərʃos] *m* surplus (an *+dat* of).

überschüssig ['y:bərʃʏsɪç] *a* sur-plus, excess.

über'schütten *vt insep* jdn/etw mit etw — *(lit)* pour sth over sb/sth; jdn mit etw — *(fig)* shower sb with sth.

Überschwang ['y:bərʃvaŋ] *m* exuberance, excess.

überschwemmen [y:bər'ʃvɛmən] *vt insep* flood.

Überschwemmung f flood.
überschwenglich ['y:bərʃvɛŋlıç] a effusive; **Ü—keit** f effusion.
Übersee ['y:bərze:] f nach/in — overseas; **ü—isch** a overseas.
über'sehen vt irreg insep look (out) over; (fig) Folgen see, get an overall view of; (nicht beachten) overlook.
über'senden vt irreg insep send, forward.
übersetz- cpd **—en** [y:bər'zɛtsən] vt insep translate; ['y:bərzɛtsən] vi cross; **Ü—er(in f)** [-'zɛtsər(ın)] m -s, - translator; **Ü—ung** [-zɛtsuŋ] f translation; (Tech) gear ratio.
Übersicht ['y:bərzıçt] f overall view; (Darstellung) survey; **ü—lich** a clear; Gelände open; **—lichkeit** f clarity, lucidity.
übersiedeln ['y:bərzi:dəln] or [y:bər'zi:dəln] vi sep or insep move.
über'spannen vt insep (zu sehr spannen) overstretch; (über-decken) cover.
überspannt a eccentric; Idee wild, crazy; **Ü—keit** f eccentricity.
überspitzt [y:bər'ʃpıtst] a exaggerated.
über'springen vt irreg insep jump over; (fig) skip.
übersprudeln ['y:bərʃpru:dəln] vi bubble over.
überstehen [y:bər'ʃte:ən] irreg vt insep overcome, get over; Winter etc survive, get through; ['y:bərʃte:ən] vi project.
über'steigen vt irreg insep climb over; (fig) exceed.
über'stimmen vt insep outvote.
Überstunden ['y:bərʃtundən] pl overtime.
über'stürzen insep vt rush; vr

follow (one another) in rapid succession.
überstürzt a (over)hasty.
übertölpeln [y:bər'tœlpəln] vt insep dupe.
über'tönen vt insep drown (out).
Übertrag ['y:bərtra:k] m -(e)s, -träge (Comm) amount brought forward; **ü—bar** [-'tra:kba:r] a transferable; (Med) infectious; **ü—en** [-'tra:gən] irreg vt transfer (auf +acc to); (Rad) broadcast; (übersetzen) render; Krankheit transmit; jdm etw ü—en assign sth to sb; vr spread (auf +acc to); a figurative; **—ung** [-'tra:guŋ] f transfer(ence); (Rad) broadcast; rendering; transmission.
über'treffen vt irreg insep surpass.
über'treiben vt irreg insep exaggerate.
Übertreibung f exaggeration.
übertreten [y:bər'tre:tən] irreg vt insep overstep; Gebot etc break; ['y:bərtre:tən] vi (über Linie, Gebiet) step (over); (Sport) overstep; (in andere Partei) go over (in +acc); (zu anderem Glauben) be converted.
Über'tretung f violation, transgression.
übertrieben [y:bər'tri:bən] a exaggerated, excessive.
übertrumpfen [y:bər'trumpfən] vt insep outdo; (Cards) overtrump.
übervölkert [y:bər'fœlkərt] a overpopulated.
übervoll ['y:bərfɔl] a overfull.
übervorteilen [y:bər'fortailən] vt insep dupe, cheat.
über'wachen vt insep supervise; Verdächtigen keep under surveillance.

Überwachung f supervision; surveillance.

überwältigen [y:bər'vɛltigən] vt insep overpower; **—d** a overwhelming.

überweisen [y:bər'vaɪzən] vt irreg insep transfer.

Überweisung f transfer.

über'wiegen vi irreg insep predominate; **—d** a predominant.

über'winden irreg insep vt overcome; vr make an effort, bring oneself (to do sth).

Überwindung f effort, strength of mind.

Überwurf ['y:bərvʊrf] m wrap, shawl.

Überzahl ['y:bərtsa:l] f superiority, superior numbers pl; **in der — sein** outnumber sb, be numerically superior.

überzählig ['y:bərtse:lɪç] a surplus.

über'zeugen vt insep convince; **—d** a convincing.

Überzeugung f conviction; **—skraft** f power of persuasion.

überziehen ['y:bərtsi:ən] irreg vt put on [-'tsi:ən] vt insep cover; **Konto** overdraw.

Überzug ['y:bərtsu:k] m cover; (Belag) coating.

üblich ['y:plɪç] a usual.

U-Boot ['u:bo:t] nt submarine.

übrig ['y:brɪç] a remaining; **für jdn etwas — haben** (col) be fond of sb; **die —en** ['y:brɪgən] the others; **das —e** the rest; **im —en** besides; **—bleiben** vi irreg remain, be left (over); **—ens** ad besides; (nebenbei bemerkt) by the way; **—lassen** vt irreg leave (over).

Übung ['y:bʊŋ] f practice; (Turn-, Aufgabe etc) exercise; **— macht den Meister** practice makes perfect.

Ufer ['u:fər] nt -s, - bank; (Meeres—) shore; **—befestigung** f embankment.

Uhr [u:r] f -, -en clock; (Armband—) watch; **wieviel — ist es?** what time is it?; **1 —** 1 o'clock; **20 — 8 o'clock**, 20.00 (twenty hundred) hours; **—band** nt watch strap; **—(en)gehäuse** nt clock/watch case; **—kette** f watch chain; **—macher** m -s, - watchmaker; **—werk** nt clockwork; works of a watch; **—zeiger** m hand; **—zeigersinn** m: **im —zeigersinn** clockwise; **entgegen dem —zeigersinn** anticlockwise; **—zeit** f time (of day).

Uhu ['u:hu] m -s, -s eagle owl.

UKW [u:ka:'ve:] abbr VHF.

Ulk [ʊlk] m -s, -e lark; **u—ig** a funny.

Ulme ['ʊlmə] f -, -n elm.

Ultimatum [ʊlti'ma:tʊm] nt -s, **Ultimaten** ultimatum.

Ultra- cpd: **—kurzwellen** [ʊltra'kʊrtsvɛlən] pl very high frequency; **u—violett** ['ʊltra-] a ultraviolet.

um [ʊm] prep +acc (a)round; (zeitlich) at; (mit Größenangabe) by; (für) for; **er schlug — sich hit about him; Stunde — Stunde** hour after hour; **Auge — Auge** an eye for an eye; **— vieles (besser)** (better) by far; **— nichts besser** net in the least better; **— so besser so** much the better; **— ... willen for the sake of; cj** (damit) (in order) **to; zu klug, — zu ... clever to ...; ad** (ungefähr) about.

umadressieren ['ʊmadrɛsi:rən] vt readdress.

umänder- ['ʊm'ɛndər] cpd: **—n vt** alter; **U—ung** f alteration.

umarbeiten ['ʊm'arbaɪtən] vt remodel; *Buch etc* revise, rework.

umarmen [ʊm'armən] vt insep embrace.

Umbau ['ʊmbaʊ] m -(e)s, -e or -ten reconstruction, alteration(s); **u—en** vt rebuild, reconstruct.

umbenennen ['ʊmbənɛnən] vt irreg rename.

umbiegen ['ʊmbi:gən] vt irreg bend (over).

umbilden ['ʊmbɪldən] vt re- organize; *(Pol) Kabinett* reshuffle.

umbinden ['ʊmbɪndən] vt irreg *Krawatte etc* put on; [-'bɪndən] vt irreg insep tie (sth) round.

umblättern ['ʊmblɛtərn] vt turn over.

umblicken ['ʊmblɪkən] vr look around.

umbringen ['ʊmbrɪŋən] vt irreg kill.

Umbruch ['ʊmbrʊx] m radical change; *(Print)* make-up.

umbuchen ['ʊmbu:xən] vti change one's reservation/flight etc.

umdenken ['ʊmdɛŋkən] vi irreg adjust one's views.

umdrängen vt insep crowd round.

umdrehen ['ʊmdre:ən] vtr turn (round); *Hals* wring.

Um'drehung f revolution; rotation.

umeinander [ʊm'aɪ'nandər] ad round one another; *(für einander)* for one another.

umfahren ['ʊmfa:rən] vt irreg run over; ·['fa:rən] insep drive/sail round.

umfallen ['ʊmfalən] vi irreg fall down or over.

Umfang ['ʊmfaŋ] m extent; *(von Buch)* size; *(Reichweite)* range; *(Fläche)* area; *(Math)* circum- ference; **u—reich** a extensive; *Buch etc* voluminous.

um'fassen vt insep embrace; *(umgeben)* surround; *(enthalten)* include; **—d** a comprehensive, extensive.

umform- ['ʊmfɔrm] cpd: **—en** vi transform; **U—er** m -s, - *(Elec)* transformer, converter.

Umfrage ['ʊmfra:gə] f poll.

umfüllen ['ʊmfʏlən] vt transfer; *Wein* decant.

umfunktionieren ['ʊmfʊŋk- tsioni:rən] vt convert, transform.

Umgang ['ʊmgaŋ] m company; *(mit jdm)* dealings pl; *(Behandlung)* way of behaving.

umgänglich ['ʊmgɛŋlɪç] a sociable.

Umgangs- cpd: **—formen** pl manners pl; **—sprache** f colloquial language.

umgeb- [ʊm'ge:b] cpd: **—en** vt irreg insep surround; **U—ung** f surroundings pl; *(Milieu)* environ- ment; *(Personen)* people in one's circle.

umgehen ['ʊmge:ən] irreg vi go (a)round; **im Schlosse —** haunt the castle; **mit jdm grob** etc **—** treat sb roughly etc; **mit Geld sparsam — be** careful with one's money; ['ge:ən] vt insep bypass; *(Mil)* out- flank; *Gesetz etc* circumvent; *(vermeiden)* avoid; **'—d** a immediate.

Um'gehung f bypassing; outflank- ing; circumvention; avoidance; **—sstraße** f bypass.

umgekehrt ['ʊmgəke:rt] a reverse(d); *(gegenteilig)* opposite; ad the other way around; **und —** vice versa.

umgraben ['ʊmgra:bən] vt irreg dig up.

umgruppieren ['ʊmgrʊpi:rən] vt regroup.

Umhang ['ʊmhaŋ] m wrap, cape.
umhängen ['ʊmhɛŋən] vt Bild hang somewhere else; **jdm etw —** put sth on sb.
umhauen ['ʊmhaʊən] vt fell; (fig) bowl over.
umher [ʊm'heːr] ad about, around; **—gehen** vi irreg walk about; **—reisen** vi travel about; **—schweifen** vi roam about; **—ziehen** vi irreg wander from place to place.
umhinkönnen [ʊm'hɪnkœnən] vi irreg ich kann nicht umhin, dass zu tun I can't help doing it.
umhören ['ʊmhøːrən] vr ask around.
Umkehr ['ʊmkeːr] f - turning back; (Änderung) change; **u—en** vi turn back; vt turn round, reverse; Tasche etc turn inside out; Gefäß etc turn upside down.
umkippen ['ʊmkɪpən] vt tip over; vi overturn; (fig: Meinung ändern) change one's mind; (col: Mensch) keel over.
Umkleideraum ['ʊmklaɪdəraʊm] m changing- or dressing room.
umkommen ['ʊmkɔmən] vi irreg die, perish; (Lebensmittel) go bad.
Umkreis ['ʊmkraɪs] m neighbourhood; (Math) circumcircle; **im — von** within a radius of; **u—en** [ʊm'kraɪzən] vt insep circle (round); (Satellit) orbit.
umladen ['ʊmlaːdən] vt irreg transfer, reload.
Umlage ['ʊmlaːgə] f share of the costs.
Umlauf ['ʊmlaʊf] m (Geld-) circulation; (von Gestirn) revolution; (Schreiben) circular; **—bahn** f orbit.
Umlaut ['ʊmlaʊt] m umlaut.
umlegen ['ʊmleːgən] vt put on; (verlegen) move, shift; Kosten

share out; (umkippen) tip over; (col: töten) bump off.
umleiten ['ʊmlaɪtən] vt divert.
Umleitung f diversion.
umlernen ['ʊmlɛrnən] vi learn something new; adjust one's views.
umliegend ['ʊmliːgənt] a surrounding.
Umnachtung [ʊm'naxtʊŋ] f (mental) derangement.
um'rahmen vt insep frame.
um'randen vt insep border, edge.
umrechnen ['ʊmrɛçnən] vt convert.
Umrechnung f conversion; **—skurs** m rate of exchange.
um'reißen vt irreg insep outline, sketch.
um'ringen vt insep surround.
Umriß ['ʊmrɪs] m outline.
umrühren ['ʊmryːrən] vt stir.
ums [ʊms] **= um das.**
umsatteln ['ʊmzatəln] vi (col) change one's occupation; switch.
Umsatz ['ʊmzats] m turnover.
umschalten ['ʊmʃaltən] vt switch.
Umschau ['ʊmʃaʊ] f look(ing) round; — halten nach look around for; **u—en** vr look round.
Umschlag ['ʊmʃlaːk] m cover; (Buch— auch) jacket; (Med) compress; (Brief—) envelope; (Wechsel) change; (von Hose) turn-up; **u—en** ['ʊmʃlaːgən] irreg vi change; (Naut) capsize; vt knock over; Ärmel turn up; Seite turn over; Waren transfer; **—platz** m (Comm) distribution centre.
umschreiben vt irreg ['ʊmʃraɪbən] (neu—) rewrite; (übertragen) transfer (auf +acc to); [-'ʃraɪbən] insep paraphrase; (abgrenzen) circumscribe, define.
umschulen ['ʊmʃuːlən] vt retrain; Kind send to another school.

umschwärmen [um'ʃvɛrmən] vt insep swarm round ; (fig) surround, idolize.

Umschweife ['umʃvaifə] pl: ohne — without beating about the bush, straight out.

Umschwung ['umʃvuŋ] m change (around), revolution.

umsehen ['umze:ən] vr irreg look around or about ; (suchen) look out (nach for).

umseitig ['umzaitıç] ad overleaf.

Umsicht ['umzıçt] f prudence, caution ; u—ig a cautious, prudent.

umsonst [um'zɔnst] ad in vain ; (gratis) for nothing.

umspringen ['umʃpriŋən] vi irreg change ; (Wind auch) veer ; mit jdm — treat sb badly.

Umstand ['umʃtant] m circumstance ; **Umstände** pl (fig: Schwierigkeiten) fuss ; in anderen Umständen sein be pregnant ; Umstände machen go to a lot of trouble ; unter Umständen possibly ; mildernde Umstände (Jur) extenuating circumstances.

umständlich ['umʃtɛntlıç] a ad Methode cumbersome, complicated ; Ausdrucksweise, Erklärung auch long-winded ; Mensch ponderous.

Umstands- cpd: —kleid nt maternity dress ; —wort nt adverb.

Umstehende(n) ['umʃte:əndə(n)] pl bystanders pl.

Umsteig- ['umʃtaig] cpd: —ekarte f transfer ticket ; u—en vi irreg (Rail) change.

umstellen ['umʃtɛlən] vt (an anderen Ort) change round, rearrange ; (Tech) convert ; vr adapt o.s. (auf +acc to) ; [um'ʃtɛlən] vt insep surround.

Umstellung ['umʃtɛluŋ] f change ; (Umgewöhnung) adjustment ; (Tech) conversion.

umstimmen ['umʃtimən] vt (Mus) retune ; jdn — make sb change his mind.

umstoßen ['umʃto:sən] vt irreg (lit) overturn ; Plan etc change, upset.

umstritten [um'ʃtritən] a disputed.

Umsturz ['umʃturts] m overthrow.

umstürzen ['umʃtyrtsən] vt (umwerfen) overturn ; vi collapse, fall down ; Wagen overturn.

umstürzlerisch a revolutionary.

Umtausch ['umtauʃ] m exchange ; u—en vt exchange.

Umtriebe ['umtri:bə] pl machinations pl, intrigues pl.

umtun ['umtu:n] vr irreg see ; sich nach etw — look for sth.

umwandeln ['umvandəln] vt change, convert ; (Elec) transform.

umwechseln ['umvɛksəln] vt change.

Umweg ['umve:k] m detour, roundabout way.

Umwelt ['umvɛlt] f environment ; —verschmutzung f environmental pollution.

umwenden ['umvɛndən] vtr irreg turn (round).

-um'werben vt irreg insep court, woo.

umwerfen ['umvɛrfən] vt irreg (lit) upset, overturn ; Mantel throw on ; (fig: erschüttern) upset, throw.

umziehen ['umtsi:ən] irreg vtr change ; vi move.

umzingeln [um'tsiŋəln] vt insep surround, encircle.

Umzug ['umtsu:k] m procession ; (Wohnungs—) move, removal.

unab- ['un'ap] cpd: —'änderlich a irreversible, unalterable ; —hängig *a* independent; **U—hängigkeit** *f* independence; **—kömmlich** a indispensable; **zur Zeit —kömmlich** not free at the moment; **—lässig** *a* incessant, constant; **—sehbar** *a* immeasurable; *Folgen* unforeseeable; *Kosten* incalculable; **—sichtlich** *a* unintentional; **—'wendbar** *a* inevitable.

unachtsam ['ʊn'axtza:m] *a* careless; **U—keit** *f* carelessness.

unan- ['ʊn'an] *cpd:* **—'fechtbar** a indisputable; **—gebracht** a uncalledfor; **—gemessen** a inadequate; **—genehm** a unpleasant; **U—nehmlichkeit** *f* inconvenience; *pl* trouble; **—sehnlich** a unsightly; **—ständig** a indecent, improper; **U—ständigkeit** *f* indecency, impropriety.

unappetitlich ['ʊn'apeti:tlɪç] *a* unsavoury.

Unart ['ʊn'a:rt] *f* bad manners *pl*; (*Angewohnheit*) bad habit; **u—ig** a naughty, badly behaved.

unauf- ['ʊn'auf] *cpd:* **—fällig** a unobtrusive; *Kleidung* inconspicuous; **—'findbar** a undiscoverable, not to be found; **—gefordert** a unasked; *ad* spontaneously; **—haltsam** a irresistible; **—'hörlich** a incessant, continuous; **—merksam** a inattentive; **—richtig** a insincere.

unaus- ['ʊn'aus] *cpd:* **—'bleiblich** a inevitable, unavoidable; **—geglichen** a volatile; **—'sprechlich** a inexpressible; **—'stehlich** a intolerable; **—'weichlich** a inescapable, ineluctable.

unbändig ['ʊnbɛndɪç] a extreme, excessive.

unbarmherzig ['ʊnbarmhɛrtsɪç] a pitiless, merciless.

unbeabsichtigt ['ʊnbə'apzɪçtɪçt] a unintentional.

unbeachtet ['ʊnbə'axtət] a unnoticed, ignored.

unbedenklich ['ʊnbədɛŋklɪç] a unhesitating; *Plan* unobjectionable; *ad* without hesitation.

unbedeutend ['ʊnbədɔytənt] a insignificant, unimportant; *. Fehler* slight.

unbedingt ['ʊnbədɪŋt] a unconditional; *ad* absolutely; **mußt du — gehen?** do you really have to go?

unbefangen ['ʊnbəfaŋən] a impartial, unprejudiced; (*ohne Hemmungen*) uninhibited; **U—heit** *f* impartiality; uninhibitedness.

unbefriedig- ['ʊnbəfri:dɪg] *cpd:* **—end** a unsatisfactory; **—t** [-dɪçt] a unsatisfied, dissatisfied.

unbefugt ['ʊnbəfu:kt] a unauthorized.

unbegabt ['ʊnbəga:pt] a untalented.

unbegreiflich ['ʊnbə'graɪflɪç] a inconceivable.

unbegrenzt ['ʊnbəgrɛntst] a unlimited.

unbegründet ['ʊnbəgryndət] a unfounded.

Unbehag- ['ʊnbəha:g] *cpd:* **—en** *nt* discomfort; **u—lich** a [-klɪç] a uncomfortable; *Gefühl* uneasy.

unbeholfen ['ʊnbəhɔlfən] a awkward, clumsy; **U—heit** *f* awkwardness, clumsiness.

unbeirrt ['ʊnbə'ɪrt] a imperturbable.

unbekannt ['ʊnbəkant] a unknown.

unbekümmert ['ʊnbəkʏmərt] a unconcerned.

unbeliebt ['ʊnbəli:pt] a unpopular; **U—heit** *f* unpopularity.

unbequem ['ʊnbəkveːm] a *Stuhl* uncomfortable; *Mensch* bothersome; *Regelung* inconvenient.

unberech-   cpd: **—enbar** [ʊnbə'rɛçənbaːr] a incalculable; *Mensch, Verhalten* unpredictable; **—tigt** [ʊnbərɛçtɪçt] a unjustified; (*nicht erlaubt*) unauthorized.

unberufen [ʊnbə'ruːfən] *interj* touch wood.

unberührt ['ʊnbəryːrt] a untouched, intact; **sie ist noch —** she is still a virgin.

unbescheiden ['ʊnbəʃaɪdən] a presumptuous.

unbeschreiblich [ʊnbə'ʃraɪplɪç] a indescribable.

unbesonnen ['ʊnbəzɔnən] a unwise, rash, imprudent.

unbeständig ['ʊnbəʃtɛndɪç] a *Mensch* inconstant; *Wetter* unsettled; *Lage* unstable.

unbestechlich ['ʊnbəʃtɛçlɪç] a incorruptible.

unbestimmt ['ʊnbəʃtɪmt] a indefinite; *Zukunft auch* uncertain; **U—heit** f vagueness.

unbeteiligt [ʊnbə'taɪlɪçt] a unconcerned, indifferent.

unbeugsam ['ʊnbɔʏkzaːm] a inflexible, stubborn; *Wille auch* unbending.

unbewacht ['ʊnbəvaxt] a unguarded, unwatched.

unbeweglich ['ʊnbəveːklɪç] a immovable.

unbewußt ['ʊnbəvʊst] a unconscious.

unbrauchbar ['ʊnbrauxbaːr] a *Arbeit* useless; *Gerät auch* unusable; **U—keit** f uselessness.

und [ʊnt] *cj* and; **— so weiter** and so on.

Undank ['ʊdaŋk] m ingratitude; **u—bar** a ungrateful; **—barkeit** f ingratitude.

undefinierbar [ʊndefi'niːrbaːr] a indefinable.

undenkbar [ʊn'dɛŋkbaːr] a inconceivable.

undeutlich ['ʊndɔʏtlɪç] a indistinct.

undicht ['ʊndɪçt] a leaky.

Unding ['ʊndɪŋ] nt absurdity.

unduldsam ['ʊnduldsaːm] a intolerant.

undurch- ['ʊndʊrç] cpd: **—führbar** ['fyːrbaːr] a impracticable; **—lässig** [-lɛsɪç] a waterproof, impermeable; **—sichtig** [-zɪçtɪç] a opaque; (fig) obscure.

uneben ['ʊn'eːbən] a uneven.

unehelich ['ʊn'eːəlɪç] a illegitimate.

uneigennützig ['ʊn'aɪgənnʏtsɪç] a unselfish.

uneinig ['ʊn'aɪnɪç] a divided; **— sein** disagree; **U—keit** f discord, dissension.

uneins ['ʊn'aɪns] a at variance, at odds.

unempfindlich ['ʊn'ɛmpfɪntlɪç] a insensitive; **U—keit** f insensitivity.

unendlich [ʊn'ɛntlɪç] a infinite; **U—keit** f infinity.

unent- ['ʊn'ɛnt] cpd: **—behrlich** ['beːrlɪç] a indispensable; **—geltlich** [-gɛltlɪç] a free (of charge); **—schieden** [-ʃiːdən] a undecided; **—schieden enden** (Sport) end in a draw; **—schlossen** [-ʃlɔsən] a undecided; irresolute; **—wegt** ['veːkt] a unswerving; (unaufhörlich) incessant.

uner- ['ʊn'eːr] cpd: **—bittlich** [-bɪtlɪç] a unyielding, inexorable; **—fahren** [-faːrən] a inexperienced; **—freulich** [-frɔʏlɪç] a unpleasant; **—gründlich** [-'gryntlɪç] a unfathomable; —heblich [-'he:plɪç] a unimportant; —hört [-hø:rt] a unheard-of; Bitte outrageous; —läßlich [-'lɛslɪç] a indispensable; —laubt [-laupt] a unauthorized; —meßlich [-'mɛslɪç] a immeasurable, immense; —müdlich [-'my:tlɪç] a indefatigable; —sättlich [-'zɛtlɪç] a insatiable; —schöpflich [-'ʃœpflɪç] a inexhaustible; —schütterlich [-'ʃʏtərlɪç] a unshakeable; —schwinglich [-'ʃvɪŋlɪç] a Preis exorbitant; too expensive; —träglich [-'trɛːklɪç] a unbearable; Frechheit insufferable; —wartet [-vartət] a unexpected; —wünscht [-vynʃt] a undesirable, unwelcome; —zogen [-tso:gən] a ill-bred, rude.

unfähig ['unfɛ:ɪç] a incapable (zu of); incompetent; U—keit f incapacity; incompetence.

unfair ['unfɛ:r] a unfair.

Unfall ['unfal] m accident; —flucht f hit-and-run (driving); —stelle f scene of the accident; —versicherung f accident insurance.

unfaßbar [un'fasba:r] a inconceivable. .

unfehlbar [un'fe:lba:r] a infallible; ad inevitably; U—keit f infallibility.

unflätig ['unflɛ:tɪç] a rude.

unfolgsam ['unfɔlkza:m] a disobedient.

unfrankiert ['unfraŋkiːrt] a unfranked.

unfrei ['unfrai] a not free, unfree; —willig a involuntary, against one's will.

unfreundlich ['unfrɔyntlɪç] a unfriendly; U—keit f unfriendliness.

Unfriede(n) ['unfri:də(n)] m dissension, strife.

unfruchtbar ['unfruxtba:r] a infertile; Gespräche unfruitful; U—keit f infertility; unfruitfulness.

Unfug ['unfu:k] m -s (Benehmen) mischief; (Unsinn) nonsense; grober — (Jur) gross misconduct; malicious damage.

ungeachtet ['ungə'axtət] prep +gen notwithstanding.

ungeahnt ['ungə'a:nt] a unsuspected, undreamt-of.

ungebeten ['ungəbe:tən] a uninvited.

ungebildet ['ungəbɪldət] a uneducated; uncultured.

ungebräuchlich ['ungəbrɔyçlɪç] a unusual, uncommon.

ungedeckt ['ungədɛkt] a Scheck uncovered.

Ungeduld ['ungədult] f impatience; u—ig [-dɪç] a impatient.

ungeeignet ['ungə'aɪgnət] a unsuitable.

ungefähr ['ungəfɛ:r] a rough, approximate; das kommt nicht von — that's hardly surprising; —lich a not dangerous, harmless.

ungehalten ['ungəhaltən] a indignant.

ungeheuer ['ungəhɔyər] a huge; ad (col) enormously; U— nt -s, - monster; —lich [-'hɔyərlɪç] a monstrous.

ungehobelt ['ungəhø:bəlt] a (fig) uncouth.

ungehörig ['ungəhø:rɪç] a impertinent, improper; U—keit f impertinence.

ungehorsam ['ungəho:rza:m] a disobedient; U— m disobedience.

ungeklärt ['ungəklɛ:rt] a not cleared up; Rätsel unsolved; Abwasser untreated.

ungeladen ['ungəla:dən] a not loaded; (Elec) uncharged; Gast uninvited.

ungelegen ['ungəle:gən] a inconvenient.

ungelernt ['ungəlɛrnt] a unskilled.

ungelogen ['ungəlo:gən] ad really, honestly.

ungemein ['ungəmaɪn] a uncommon.

ungemütlich ['ungəmy:tlɪç] a uncomfortable; Person disagreeable.

ungenau ['ungənau] a inaccurate; U—igkeit f inaccuracy.

ungeniert ['unʒeni:rt] a free and easy, unceremonious; ad without embarrassment, freely.

ungenießbar ['ungəni:sba:r] a inedible; undrinkable; (col) unbearable.

ungenügend ['ungəny:gənt] a insufficient, inadequate.

ungepflegt ['ungəpfle:kt] a Garten etc untended; Person unkempt; Hände neglected.

ungerade ['ungəra:də] a uneven, odd.

ungerecht ['ungərɛçt] a unjust; —fertigt a unjustified; U—igkeit f injustice, unfairness.

ungern ['ungɛrn] ad unwillingly, reluctantly.

ungeschehen ['ungəʃe:ən] a: — machen undo.

Ungeschick- ['ungəʃɪk] cpd: —lichkeit f clumsiness; u—t a awkward, clumsy.

ungeschminkt ['ungəʃmɪŋkt] a without make-up; (fig) unvarnished.

ungesetzlich ['ungəzɛtslɪç] a illegal.

ungestempelt ['ungəʃtɛmpəlt] a Briefmarke unfranked, uncancelled.

ungestört ['ungəʃtø:rt] a undisturbed.

ungestraft ['ungəʃtra:ft] ad with impunity.

ungestüm ['ungəʃty:m] a impetuous; tempestuous; U— nt -(e)s impetuosity; passion.

ungesund ['ungəzunt] a unhealthy.

ungetrübt ['ungətry:pt] a clear; (fig) untroubled; Freude unalloyed.

Ungetüm ['ungəty:m] nt -(e)s, -e monster.

ungewiß ['ungəvis] a uncertain; U—heit f uncertainty.

ungewöhnlich ['ungəvø:nlɪç] a unusual.

ungewohnt ['ungəvo:nt] a unaccustomed.

Ungeziefer ['ungətsi:fər] nt -s vermin.

ungezogen ['ungətso:gən] a rude, impertinent; U—heit f rudeness, impertinence.

ungezwungen ['ungətsvuŋən] a natural, unconstrained.

ungläubig ['unglɔʏbɪç] a unbelieving; ein —er Thomas a doubting Thomas; die U—en the infidel(s).

unglaub- cpd: —lich [un'glauplɪç] a incredible; —würdig ['unglaupvyrdɪç] a untrustworthy, unreliable; Geschichte improbable.

ungleich ['unglaɪç] a dissimilar; unequal; ad incomparably; —artig a different; U—heit f dissimilarity; inequality.

Unglück ['ungyk] nt -(e)s, -e misfortune; (Pech) bad luck; (—sfall) calamity, disaster; (Verkehrs—) accident; u—lich a unhappy; (erfolglos) unlucky; (unerfreulich) unfortunate; u—licherweise ['waɪzə] ad unfortunately; u—selig a calamitous; Person unfortunate; —sfall m accident, calamity.

ungültig ['ʊngʏltɪç] a invalid; U—keit f invalidity.

ungünstig ['ʊngʏnstɪç] a unfavourable.

ungut ['ʊngu:t] a Gefühl uneasy; nichts für — no offence.

unhaltbar ['ʊnhaltba:r] a untenable.

Unheil ['ʊnhaɪl] nt evil; (Unglück) misfortune; — anrichten cause mischief; u—bar a incurable; u—bringend a fatal, fateful; u—voll a disastrous.

unheimlich ['ʊnhaɪmlɪç] a weird, uncanny; ad (col) tremendously.

unhöflich ['ʊnhø:flɪç] a impolite; U—keit f impoliteness.

unhygienisch ['ʊnhygi'e:nɪʃ] a unhygienic.

Uni ['ʊni] f -, -s university; u— [y'ni:] a self-coloured.

Uniform [uni'fɔrm] f uniform; u—iert [-'mi:rt] a uniformed.

uninteressant ['ʊn'ɪnterɛsant] a uninteresting.

Universität [univɛrzi'tɛ:t] f university.

unkenntlich ['ʊnkɛntlɪç] a unrecognizable.

Unkenntnis ['ʊnkɛntnɪs] f ignorance.

unklar ['ʊnkla:r] a unclear; im —en sein über (+acc) be in the dark about; U—heit f unclarity; (Unentschiedenheit) uncertainty.

unklug ['ʊnklu:k] a unwise.

Unkosten ['ʊnkɔstən] pl expense(s).

Unkraut ['ʊnkraʊt] nt weed; weeds pl.

unlängst ['ʊnlɛŋst] ad not long ago.

unlauter ['ʊnlaʊtər] a unfair.

unleserlich ['ʊnle:zɛrlɪç] a illegible.

unlogisch ['ʊnlo:gɪʃ] a illogical.

unlösbar ['ʊnlø:sbar], unlöslich ['ʊnlø:slɪç] a insoluble.

Unlust ['ʊnlʊst] f lack of enthusiasm; u—ig a unenthusiastic.

unmäßig ['ʊnmɛsɪç] a immoderate.

Unmenge ['ʊnmɛŋə] f tremendous number, hundreds pl.

Unmensch ['ʊnmɛnʃ] m ogre, brute; u—lich a inhuman, brutal; (ungeheuer) awful.

unmerklich ['ʊn'mɛrklɪç] a imperceptible.

unmißverständlich ['ʊnmɪs-fɛrʃtɛntlɪç] a unmistakable.

unmittelbar ['ʊnmɪtəlba:r] a immediate.

unmöbliert ['ʊnmø'bli:rt] a unfurnished.

unmöglich ['ʊnmø:klɪç] a impossible; U—keit f impossibility.

unmoralisch ['ʊnmora:lɪʃ] a immoral.

Unmut ['ʊnmu:t] m ill humour.

unnachgiebig ['ʊnna:xgi:bɪç] a unyielding.

unnahbar ['ʊn'na:ba:r] a unapproachable.

unnötig ['ʊnnø:tɪç] a unnecessary; —erweise ad unnecessarily.

unnütz ['ʊnnʏts] a useless.

unordentlich ['ʊn'ɔrdəntlɪç] a untidy.

Unordnung ['ʊn'ɔrdnʊŋ] f disorder.

unparteiisch ['ʊnpartaɪʃ] a impartial; U—e(r) m umpire; (Fußball) referee.

unpassend ['ʊnpasənt] a inappropriate; Zeit inopportune.

unpäßlich ['ʊnpɛslɪç] a unwell.

unpersönlich ['unpɛrzø:nliç] *a* impersonal.

unpolitisch ['unpoli:tiʃ] *a* apolitical.

unpraktisch ['unpraktiʃ] *a* unpractical.

unproduktiv ['unprodukti:f] *a* unproductive.

unproportioniert ['unproportsioni:rt] *a* out of proportion.

unpünktlich ['unpynktliç] *a* unpunctual.

unrationell ['unratsionɛl] *a* inefficient.

unrecht ['unrɛçt] *a* wrong; **U—** *nt* wrong; **zu U—** wrongly; **U—haben, im U— sein** be wrong; **—mäßig** *a* unlawful, illegal.

unregelmäßig ['unre:gəlmɛsiç] *a* irregular; **U—keit** *f* irregularity.

unreif ['unraif] *a Obst* unripe; *(fig)* immature.

unrentabel ['unrɛnta:bəl] *a* unprofitable.

unrichtig ['unriçtiç] *a* incorrect, wrong.

Unruh ['unru:] *f* -, **-en** *(von Uhr)* balance; **—e** *f* -, **-n** unrest; **—estifter** *m* troublemaker; **u—ig** *a* restless.

uns [uns] *pron acc, dat of* **wir** us; ourselves.

unsachlich ['unzaxliç] *a* not to the point, irrelevant; *(persönlich)* personal.

unsagbar [un'za:kba:r], **unsäglich** [un'zɛ:kliç] *a* indescribable.

unsanft ['unzanft] *a* rough.

unsauber ['unzaubər] *a* unclean, dirty; *(fig)* crooked; *(Mus)* fuzzy.

unschädlich ['unʃɛ:dliç] *a* harmless; **jdn/etw — machen** render sb/sth harmless.

unscharf ['unʃarf] *a* indistinct; *Bild etc* out of focus, blurred.

unscheinbar ['unʃainba:r] *a* insignificant; *Aussehen, Haus etc.* unprepossessing.

unschlagbar [un'ʃla:kba:r] *a* invincible.

unschlüssig ['unʃlysiç] *a* undecided.

Unschuld ['unʃult] *f* innocence; **u—ig** [-diç] *a* innocent.

unselbständig ['unzɛlpʃtɛndiç] *a* dependent, over-reliant on others.

unser ['unzər] *pron* our; *gen of* **wir** of us; **—e(r,s)** ours; **—einer, —eins, —esgleichen** *pron* people like us; **—erseits** *ad* on our part; **—twegen, —twillen** *ad* (für uns) for our sake; *(wegen uns)* on our account; **—ige** *pron:* **der/die/das —ige** ours.

unsicher ['unziçər] *a* uncertain; *Mensch* insecure; **U—heit** *f* uncertainty; insecurity.

unsichtbar ['unziçtba:r] *a* invisible; **U—keit** *f* invisibility.

Unsinn ['unzin] *m* nonsense; **u—ig** *a* nonsensical.

Unsitte ['unzitə] *f* deplorable habit.

unsittlich ['unzitliç] *a* indecent; **U—keit** *f* indecency.

unsportlich ['unʃportliç] *a* not sporty; unfit; *Verhalten* unsporting.

unsre ['unzrə] = **unsere.**

unsrige ['unzrigə] = **unserige.**

unsterblich ['unʃtɛrpliç] *a* immortal; **U—keit** *f* immortality.

Unstimmigkeit ['unʃtimiçkait] *f* inconsistency; *(Streit)* disagreement.

unsympathisch ['unzympa:tiʃ] *a* unpleasant; **er ist mir — I** don't like him.

untätig ['untɛ:tiç] *a* idle.

untauglich ['untauklɪç] a unsuitable; *(Mil)* unfit; **U—keit** f unsuitability; unfitness.

unteilbar [un'tailbaːr] a indivisible.

unten ['untən] ad below; *(im Haus)* downstairs; *(an der Treppe etc)* at the bottom; **nach — down**; — **am Berg** etc at the bottom of the mountain etc; **ich bin bei ihm — durch** *(col)* he's through with me.

unter ['untər] prep +acc or dat under, below; *(bei Menschen)* among; *(während)* during; ad under.

Unter- ['untər] cpd: **—abteilung** f subdivision; **—arm** m forearm.

unterbe- ['untərbə] cpd: **—lichten** vt *(Phot)* underexpose; **U—wußtsein** nt subconscious; **—zahlt** a underpaid.

unterbieten [untər'biːtən] vt irreg insep *(Comm)* undercut; **Rekord** lower, reduce.

unterbinden [untər'bɪndən] vt irreg insep stop, call a halt to.

Unterbodenschutz [untər-'boːdənʃuts] m *(Aut)* underseal.

unterbrech- [untər'brɛç] cpd: **—en** vt irreg insep interrupt; **U—ung** f interruption.

unterbringen ['untərbrɪŋən] vt irreg *(in Koffer)* stow; *(in Zeitung)* place; **Person** *(in Hotel etc)* accommodate, put up; *(beruflich)* fix up *(auf, in with)*.

unterdessen [untər'dɛsən] ad meanwhile.

Unterdruck ['untərdruk] m low pressure.

unterdrücken [untər'drykən] vt insep suppress; **Leute** oppress.

untere(r,s) ['untərə(r,z)] a lower.

untereinander [untər'ai'nandər] ad with each other; among themselves etc.

unterentwickelt ['untər'ɛntvɪkəlt] a underdeveloped.

unterernährt ['untər'ɛrnɛːrt] a undernourished, underfed.

Unterernährung f malnutrition.

Unterführung f subway, underpass.

Untergang ['untərgaŋ] m *(down)*fall, decline; *(Naut)* sinking; *(von Gestirn)* setting.

untergeben a subordinate.

untergehen ['untərgeːən] vi irreg go down; *(Sonne auch)* set; *(Staat)* fall; *(Volk)* perish; *(Welt)* come to an end; *(im Lärm)* be drowned.

Untergeschoß ['untərgəʃɔs] nt basement.

untergliedern vt insep subdivide.

Untergrund ['untərgrunt] m foundation; *(Pol)* underground; **—bahn** f underground, tube, subway *(US)*; **—bewegung** f underground *(movement)*.

unterhalb ['untərhalp] prep +gen, ad below; **— von** below.

Unterhalt ['untərhalt] m maintenance; **u—en** [untər'haltən] irreg insep vt maintain; *(belustigen)* entertain; vr talk; *(sich belustigen)* enjoy o.s.; **u—end** [untər'haltənt] a entertaining; **—ung** f maintenance; *(Belustigung)* entertainment, amusement; *(Gespräch)* talk.

Unterhändler ['untərhɛntlər] m negotiator.

Unterhemd ['untərhɛmt] nt vest, undershirt *(US)*.

Unterhose ['untərhoːzə] f underpants pl.

unterirdisch ['untər'ɪrdɪʃ] a underground.

Unterkiefer ['untərkiːfər] m lower jaw.

unterkommen ['ʊntɐkɔmən] *vi irreg* find shelter; find work; **das ist mir noch nie untergekommen** I've never met with that.

Unterkunft ['ʊntɐkʊnft] *f* -, -künfte accommodation.

Unterlage ['ʊntɐlaːgə] *f* foundation; *(Beleg)* document; *(Schreib- etc)* pad.

unter'lassen *vt irreg insep (versäumen)* fail (to do); *(sich enthalten)* refrain from.

unterlaufen [ʊntɐ'laʊfən] *vi irreg insep* happen; **a: mit Blut —** suffused with blood; *(Augen)* bloodshot.

unterlegen [ʊntɐ'leːgən] *vt* lay or put under; [ʊntɐ'leːgən] *a* inferior *(dat* to); *(besiegt)* defeated.

Unterleib ['ʊntɐlaɪp] *m* abdomen.

unter'liegen *vi irreg insep* be defeated or overcome *(jdm* by sb); *(unterworfen sein)* be subject to.

Untermiete ['ʊntɐmiːtə] *f*: **zur — wohnen** be a subtenant or lodger; **—r(in** *f*) *m* subtenant, lodger.

unter'nehmen *vt irreg insep* undertake; **U— nt -s, -** undertaking, enterprise *(auch Comm)*; **—d** *a* enterprising, daring.

Unternehmer [ʊntɐ'neːmɐ] *m* -s, - entrepreneur, businessman.

Unterprima ['ʊntɐpriːma] *f* -, -primen eighth year of secondary school.

Unterredung [ʊntɐ'reːdʊŋ] *f* discussion, talk.

Unterricht ['ʊntɐrɪçt] *m* -(e)s, -e instruction, lessons *pl*; **u—en** [ʊntɐ'rɪçtən] *insep vt* instruct; *(Sch)* teach; *vr* inform o.s. *(über +acc* about).

Unterrock [ʊntɐrɔk] *m* petticoat, slip.

unter'sagen *vt insep* forbid *(jdm etw sb* to do sth).

unter'schätzen *vt insep* underestimate.

unter'scheiden *irreg insep vt* distinguish; *vr* differ.

Unter'scheidung *f (Unterschied)* distinction; *(Unterscheiden)* differentiation.

Unterschied ['ʊntɐʃiːt] *m* -(e)s, -e difference, distinction; **im — zu** as distinct from; **u—lich** *a* varying, differing; *(diskriminierend)* discriminatory; **u—slos** *ad* indiscriminately.

unter'schlagen *vt irreg insep* embezzle; *(verheimlichen)* suppress.

Unter'schlagung *f* embezzlement.

Unterschlupf ['ʊntɐʃlʊpf] *m* -(e)s, -schlüpfe refuge.

unter'schreiben *vt irreg insep* sign.

Unterschrift ['ʊntɐʃrɪft] *f* signature.

Unterseeboot ['ʊntɐzeːboːt] *nt* submarine.

Untersekunda ['ʊntɐzekʊnda] *f* -, -sekunden sixth year of secondary school.

Untersetzer ['ʊntɐzɛtsɐ] *m* tablemat; *(für Gläser)* coaster.

untersetzt [ʊntɐ'zɛtst] *a* stocky.

unterste(r,s) ['ʊntɐstə(r,z)] *a* lowest, bottom.

unterstehen [ʊntɐ'ʃteːən] *irreg vi insep* be under *(jdm* sb); *vr* dare; [ʊntɐʃteːən] *vi* shelter.

unterstellen [ʊntɐ'ʃtɛlən] *vt insep* subordinate *(dat* to); *(fig)* impute *(jdm etw* sth to sb); ['ʊntɐʃtɛlən] *vt Auto* garage, park; *vr* take shelter.

unter'streichen *vt irreg insep (lit, fig)* underline.

Unterstufe ['untərʃtuːfə] *f* lower grade.

unter'stützen *vt insep* support.

Unter'stützung *f* support, assistance.

unter'suchen *vt insep (Med)* examine; *(Polizei)* investigate.

Unter'suchung *f* examination; investigation, inquiry; —sausschuß *m* committee of inquiry; —shaft *f* imprisonment on remand.

Untertan ['untərtaːn] *m* -s, -en subject.

untertänig ['untərtɛːnɪç] *a* submissive, humble.

Untertasse ['untərtasə] *f* saucer.

untertauchen ['untərtauxən] *vi* dive; *(fig)* disappear, go underground.

Unterteil ['untərtail] *nt or m* lower part, bottom; **u—en** [untər'tailən] *vt insep* divide up.

Untertertia ['untərtɛrtsia] *f* -, **-tertien** fourth year of secondary school.

Unterwäsche ['untərvɛʃə] *f* underwear.

unterwegs [untər'veːks] *ad* on the way.

unter'weisen *vt irreg insep* instruct.

unter'werfen *irreg insep vt* subject; *Volk* subjugate; *vr* submit *(dat* to).

unterwürfig [untər'vyrfɪç] *a* obsequious, servile.

unter'zeichnen *vt insep* sign.

unter'ziehen *irreg insep vt* subject *(dat* to); *vr* undergo *(etw (dat)* sth); *(einer Prüfung)* take.

untreu ['untrɔy] *a* unfaithful; **U—e** *f* unfaithfulness.

untröstlich [un'trøːstlɪç] *a* inconsolable.

Untugend [untuːgənt] *f* vice, failing.

unüber- ['unyːbər] *cpd*: —legt [-leːkt] *a* ill-considered; *ad* without thinking; —sehbar [-'zeːbaːr] *a* incalculable.

unum- [un'um] *cpd*: —gänglich [-ˈɡɛŋlɪç] *a* indispensable, vital; absolutely necessary; —wunden [-'vundən] *a* candid; *ad* straight out.

ununterbrochen [un'untərbrɔxən] *a* uninterrupted.

unver- [unfɛr] *cpd*: —änderlich [-'ɛndərlɪç] *a* unchangeable; —antwortlich [-'antvɔrtlɪç] *a* irresponsible; *(unentschuldbar)* inexcusable; —äußerlich [-'ɔysərlɪç] *a* inalienable; —besserlich [-'bɛsərlɪç] *a* incorrigible; —bindlich [-'bɪntlɪç] *a* not binding; *Antwort* curt; *ad (Comm)* without obligation; —blümt [-'blyːmt] *a,ad* plain(ly), blunt(ly); —daulich [-'daulɪç] *a* indigestible; —dorben [-'dɔrbən] *a* unspoilt; —einbar [-'ambaːr] *a* incompatible; —fänglich [-'fɛŋlɪç] *a* harmless; —froren [-'froːrən] *a* impudent; —hofft [-'hɔft] *a* unexpected; —kennbar [-'kɛnbaːr] *a* unmistakable; —meidlich [-'maitlɪç] *a* unavoidable; —mutet [-'muːtət] *a* unexpected; —nünftig [-'nynftɪç] *a* foolish; —schämt [-'ʃɛːmt] *a* impudent; **U—schämtheit** *f* impudence, insolence; —sehens [-'zeːəns] *ad* all of a sudden; —sehrt [-'zeːrt] *a* uninjured; —söhnlich [-'zøːnlɪç] *a* irreconcilable; —ständlich [-'ʃtɛntlɪç] *a* unintelligible; —träglich [-'trɛːklɪç] *a* quarrelsome; *Meinungen, (Med)* incompatible; —wüstlich [-'vyːstlɪç] *a* indestructible; *Mensch*

irrespressible; —zeihlich ['-tsailiç]
a unpardonable; —züglich
['-tsy:kliç] a immediate.
unvoll- ['unfɔl] cpd: —kommen a
imperfect; —ständig a incomplete.
unvor- ['unfo:r] cpd: —bereitet a
unprepared; —eingenommen a
unbiased; —hergesehen
[-he:rgəze:ən] a unforeseen
[-siçtiç [-zɪçtiç] a careless, imprudent; —stellbar [-'ʃtelba:r] a
inconceivable; —teilhaft [-tailhaft]
a disadvantageous.
unwahr ['unva:r] a untrue;
—haftig a untruthful; —scheinlich
a improbable, unlikely; ad (col)
incredibly; U—scheinlichkeit f
improbability, unlikelihood.
unweigerlich ['un'vaigərliç] a
unquestioning; ad without fail.
Unwesen ['unve:zən] nt nuisance;
(Unfug) mischief; sein — treiben
wreak havoc; u—tlich a
inessential, unimportant; u—tlich
besser marginally better.
Unwetter ['unvetər] nt thunderstorm.
unwichtig ['unviçtiç] a unimportant.
unwider- [unvi:dər] cpd: —legbar
[-'le:kba:r] a irrefutable; —ruflich
[-'ru:fliç] a irrevocable; —stehlich
[-'ʃte:liç] a irresistible.
unwill- ['unvil] cpd: U—e(n) m
indignation; —ig a indignant;
(widerwillig) reluctant; —kürlich
[-ky:rliç] a involuntary; ad
instinctively; lachen involuntarily.
unwirklich ['unvirkliç] a unreal.
unwirsch ['unvirʃ] a cross, surly.
unwirtlich ['unvirtliç] a inhospitable.
unwirtschaftlich ['unvirtʃaftliç]
a uneconomical.

unwissen- ['unvisən] cpd: —d a
ignorant; U—heit f ignorance;
—schaftlich a unscientific.
unwohl ['unvo:l] a unwell, ill;
U—sein nt -s indisposition.
unwürdig ['unvyrdiç] a unworthy
(jds of sb).
unzählig ['un'tse:liç] a innumerable,
countless.
unzer- [untser] cpd: —brechlich
[-'breçliç] a unbreakable; —reißbar
[-'raisba:r] a untearable; —störbar
[-'ʃtø:rba:r] a indestructible;
—trennlich [-'trenliç] a inseparable.
Unzucht ['untsuxt] f sexual offence.
unzüchtig ['untsyçtiç] a immoral,
lewd.
unzu- ['untsu] cpd: —frieden a
dissatisfied; U—friedenheit f
discontent; —länglich ['untsu:len-
liç] a inadequate; —lässig
['untsu:lesiç] a inadmissible;
—rechnungsfähig ['untsu:reç-
nuŋsfe:iç] a irresponsible;
—sammenhängend a disconnected;
Äußerung incoherent; —treffend
['untsu:-] a incorrect; —verlässig
['untsu:-] a unreliable.
unzweideutig ['untsvaideutiç] adj
unambiguous.
üppig ['ʏpiç] adj Frau curvaceous;
Busen full, ample; Essen
sumptuous, lavish; Vegetation
luxuriant, lush.
urait ['ur'alt] a ancient, very old.
Uran [u'ra:n] nt -s uranium.
Ur- ['u:r] in cpds original; —aufführung f first performance; —einwohner m original inhabitant;
—eltern pl ancestors pl; —enkel(in
f) m great-grandchild; —großmutter f great-grandmother;
—großvater m great-grandfather;
—heber m -s, - originator; (Autor)
author.

Urin [u'ri:n] *m* -s, -e urine.

ur- *cpd:* —**komisch** a incredibly funny; **U—kunde** *f* -, -n document, deed; —**kundlich** ['urkuntliç] a documentary; —**laub** n -(e)s, -e holiday(s *pl*), vacation (*US*); —**lauber** *m* -s, - holiday-maker, vacationist (*US*); —**mensch** *m* primitive man.

Urne ['urnə] *f* -, -n vase.

Ursache ['u:rzaxə] *f* cause.

Ursprung ['u:rʃpruŋ] *m* origin, source; *(von Fluß)* source.

ursprünglich [u:rʃpryŋliç] a, ad original(ly).

Urteil ['urtail] *nt* -s, -e opinion; *(Jur)* sentence, judgement; **u—en** *vi* judge; —**sspruch** *m* sentence, verdict.

Ur- *cpd:* —**wald** *m* jungle; —**zeit** *f* prehistoric times *pl.*

usw [u:ɛsve:] *abbr of* **und so weiter** etc.

Utensilien [utɛn'zi:liən] *pl* utensils *pl.*

Utopie [uto'pi:] *f* pipedream.

utopisch [u'to:pɪʃ] a utopian.

V

V, v [fau] *nt* V, v.

vag(e) [va:k, va:gə] a vague.

Vagina [va'gi:na] *f* -, **Vaginen** vagina.

Vakuum ['va:kuum] *nt* -s, **Vakua** or **Vakuen** vacuum.

Vanille [va'nɪljə] *f* - vanilla.

Variation [variatsi'o:n] *f* variation.

variieren [vari'i:rən] *vti* vary.

Vase ['va:zə] *f* -, -n vase.

Vater ['fa:tər] *m* -s, ⁼ father; —**land** *nt* native country; Fatherland; —**landsliebe** *f* patriotism.

väterlich ['fɛ:tərliç] a fatherly; —**erseits** ad on the father's side.

Vater- *cpd:* —**schaft** *f* paternity; —**unser** *nt* -s, - Lord's prayer.

Vegetarier(in *f)* [vege'ta:riər(ɪn)] *m* -s, - vegetarian.

Veilchen ['failçən] *nt* violet.

Vene ['ve:nə] *f* -, -n vein.

Ventil [vɛn'ti:l] *nt* -s, -e valve; —**ator** [vɛnti'la:tər] *m* ventilator.

verab- [fɛr'ap] *cpd:* —**reden** *vt* agree, arrange; *vr* arrange to meet *(mit jdm sb)*; **V—redung** *f* arrange-

ment; *(Treffen)* appointment; —**scheuen** *vt* detest, abhor; —**schieden** *vt Gäste* say goodbye to; *(entlassen)* discharge; *Gesetz* pass; *vr* take one's leave *(von of)*; **V—schiedung** *f* leave-taking; discharge; passing.

ver- *cpd:* —**achten** [-"axtən] *vt* despise; —**ächtlich** [-"ɛçtliç] a contemptuous; *(verachtenswert)* contemptible; **jdn —ächtlich machen** run sb down; **V—achtung** *f* contempt.

verallgemein- [fɛr'algə'main] *cpd:* —**ern** *vt* generalize; **V—erung** *f* generalization.

veralten [fɛr'altən] *vi* become obsolete or out-of-date.

Veranda [ve'randa] *f* -, **Veranden** veranda.

veränder- [fɛr"ɛndər] *cpd:* —**lich** a changeable; **V—lichkeit** *f* variability, instability; —**n** *vtr* change, alter; **V—ung** *f* change, alteration.

veran- [fɛr"an] *cpd:* **—lagt** *a* with a ... nature; **V—lagung** *f* disposition, aptitude; **—lassen** *vt* cause; **Maßnahmen —lassen** take measures; **sich —laßt sehen feel** prompted; **V—lassung** *f* cause; motive; **auf jds V—lassung** (hin) at the instance of sb; **—schaulichen** *vt* illustrate; **—schlagen** *vt* estimate; **—stalten** *vt* organize, arrange; **V—stalter** *m* -s, - organizer; **V—staltung** *f* (Veranstalten) organizing; (Veranstaltetes) event, function.

verantwort- [fɛr"antvort] *cpd:* **—en** *vt* answer for; *vr* justify o.s.; **—lich** *a* responsible; **V—ung** *f* responsibility; **—ungsbewußt** *a* responsible; **—ungslos** *a* irresponsible.

verarbeiten [fɛr"arbaɪtən] *vt* process; (geistig) assimilate; **etw zu etw —** make sth into sth.
Verarbeitung *f* processing; assimilation.

verärgern [fɛr"ɛrgərn] *vt* annoy.

verausgaben [fɛr"ausɡaːbən] *vr* run out of money; (fig) exhaust o.s.

veräußern [fɛr"ɔʏsərn] *vt* dispose of, sell.

Verb [vɛrp] *nt* -s, -en verb.

Verband [fɛr'bant] *m* -(e)s, "e (Med) bandage, dressing; (Bund) association, society; (Mil) unit; **—(s)kasten** *m* medicine chest, first-aid box; **—stoff** *m*, **—zeug** *nt* bandage, dressing material.

verbannen [fɛr'banən] *vt* banish.
Verbannung *f* exile.

verbergen [fɛr'bɛrgən] *vtr irreg* hide (vor +dat from).

verbessern [fɛr'bɛsərn] *vtr* improve; (berichtigen) correct (o.s.).
Verbesserung *f* improvement; correction.

verbeugen [fɛr'bɔʏgən] *vr* bow.
Verbeugung *f* bow.

ver'biegen *vi irreg* bend.

ver'bieten *vt irreg* forbid (jdm etw sb to do sth).

ver'binden *irreg vt* connect; (kombinieren) combine; (Med) bandage; **jdm die Augen —** blindfold sb; *vr* combine (auch Chem), join.

verbindlich [fɛr'bɪntlɪç] *a* binding; (freundlich) friendly; **V—keit** *f* obligation; (Höflichkeit) civility.
Ver'bindung *f* connection; (Zusammensetzung) combination; (Chem) compound; (Univ) club.

verbissen [fɛr'bɪsən] *a* grim, dogged; **V—heit** *f* grimness, doggedness.

ver'bitten *vt irreg:* **sich** (dat) **etw —** not tolerate sth, not stand for sth.

verbittern [fɛr'bɪtərn] *vt* embitter; *vi* get bitter.

verblassen [fɛr'blasən] *vi* fade.

Verbleib [fɛr'blaɪp] *m* -(e)s whereabouts; **v—en** [fɛr'blaɪbən] *vi irreg* remain.

Verblendung [fɛr'blɛndʊŋ] *f* (fig) delusion.

verblöden [fɛr'bløːdən] *vi* get stupid.

verblüffen [fɛr'blʏfən] *vt* stagger, amaze.
Verblüffung *f* stupefaction.

ver'blühen *vi* wither, fade.

ver'bluten *vi* bleed to death.

verborgen [fɛr'bɔrgən] *a* hidden.

Verbot [fɛr'boːt] *nt* -(e)s, -e prohibition, ban; **v—en** *a* forbidden; **Rauchen v—en!** no smoking; **v—enerweise** *ad* though it is forbidden; **—sschild** *nt* prohibitory sign.

Verbrauch [fɛr'braʊx] *m* -(e)s consumption; v—en *vt* use up; —er *m* -s, - consumer; v—t a used up, finished; *Luft* stale; *Mensch* worn-out.

Verbrechen [fɛr'brɛçən] *nt* -s, - crime; v— *vt irreg* perpetrate.

Verbrecher [fɛr'brɛçər] *m* -s, - criminal; v—isch a criminal; —tum *nt* -s criminality.

ver'breiten *vtr* spread; sich über etw (acc) — expound on sth.

verbreitern [fɛr'braɪtərn] *vt* broaden.

Verbreitung *f* spread(ing), propagation.

verbrenn- [fɛr'brɛn] *cpd:* —bar a combustible; —en *vt irreg* burn; *Leiche* cremate; V—ung *f* burning; (*in Motor*) combustion; (*von Leiche*) cremation; V—ungsmotor *m* internal combustion engine.

ver'bringen *vt irreg* spend.

Verbrüderung [fɛr'bry:dərʊŋ] *f* fraternization.

verbrühen [fɛr'bry:ən] *vt* scald.

verbuchen [fɛr'bu:xən] *vt* (*Fin*) register; *Erfolg* enjoy; *Mißerfolg* suffer.

verbunden [fɛr'bʊndən] a connected; jdm — sein be obliged or indebted to sb; falsch — (*Tel*) wrong number; V—heit *f* bond, relationship.

verbünden [fɛr'bʏndən] *vr* ally o.s.

Verbündete(r) [fɛr'bʏndətə(r)] *mf* ally.

ver'bürgen *vr:* sich — für vouch for.

ver'büßen *vt:* eine Strafe — serve a sentence.

verchromt [fɛr'kro:mt] a chromium-plated.

Verdacht [fɛr'daxt] *m* -(e)s suspicion.

verdächtig [fɛr'dɛçtɪç] a suspicious, suspect; —en [fɛr'dɛçtɪgən] *vt* suspect.

verdammen [fɛr'damən] *vt* damn, condemn.

Verdammnis [fɛr'damnɪs] *f* -, -se perdition, damnation.

ver'dampfen *vi* vaporize, evaporate.

ver'danken *vt:* jdm etw — owe sb sth.

verdauen [fɛr'daʊən] *vt* (lit, fig) digest.

verdaulich [fɛr'daʊlɪç] a digestible; das ist schwer — that is hard to digest.

Verdauung *f* digestion.

Verdeck [fɛr'dɛk] *nt* -(e)s, -e (*Aut*) hood; (*Naut*) deck; v—en *vt* cover (up); (*verbergen*) hide.

ver'denken *vt irreg:* jdm etw — blame sb for sth, hold sth against sb.

Verderb- [fɛr'dɛrp] *cpd:* —en [fɛr'dɛrbən] *nt* -s ruin; v—en *vt irreg* spoil; (*schädigen*) ruin; (*moralisch*) corrupt; es mit jdm v—en get into sb's bad books; *vi* (*Essen*) spoil, rot; (*Mensch*) go to the bad; v—lich a (*Einfluß*) pernicious; *Lebensmittel* perishable; v—t a depraved; —theit *f* depravity.

verdeutlichen [fɛr'dɔʏtlɪçən] *vt* make clear.

ver'dichten *vtr* condense.

ver'dienen *vt* earn; (*moralisch*) deserve.

Ver'dienst *m* -(e)s, -e earnings *pl*; *nt* -(e)s, -e merit; (*Leistung*) service (*um* to).

verdient [fɛr'di:nt] a well-earned; *Person* deserving of esteem; **sich um etw — machen** do a lot for sth.

verdoppeln [fɛr'dɔpəln] vt double.

Verdopp(e)lung f doubling.

verdorben [fɛr'dɔrbən] a spoilt; *(geschädigt)* ruined; *(moralisch)* corrupt.

verdrängen [fɛr'drɛŋən] vt oust, displace *(auch Phys)*; *(Psych)* repress.

Verdrängung f displacement; *(Psych)* repression.

ver'drehen vt *(lit, fig)* twist; *Augen* roll; **jdm den Kopf —** *(fig)* turn sb's head.

verdreifachen [fɛr'draifaxən] vt treble.

verdrießlich [fɛr'dri:slɪç] a peevish, annoyed.

verdrossen [fɛr'drɔsən] a cross, sulky.

ver'drücken vt *(col)* put away, eat; vr *(col)* disappear.

Verdruß [fɛr'drʊs] m -sses, -sse annoyance, worry.

ver'duften vi evaporate; vir *(col)* disappear.

verdummen [fɛr'dʊmən] vt make stupid; vi grow stupid.

verdunkeln [fɛr'dʊŋkəln] vtr darken; *(fig)* obscure.

Verdunk(e)lung f blackout; *(fig)* obscuring.

verdünnen [fɛr'dʏnən] vt dilute.

verdunsten [fɛr'dʊnstən] vi evaporate.

verdursten [fɛr'dʊrstən] vi die of thirst.

verdutzt [fɛr'dʊtst] a nonplussed, taken aback.

verehr- [fɛr'e:r] cpd: **—en** vt venerate, worship *(auch Rel)*; **jdm etw — en** present sb with sth;

V—er(in f) m -s, **-** admirer, worshipper *(auch Rel)*; **—t** a esteemed; **V—ung** f respect; *(Rel)* worship.

vereidigen [fɛr'aidɪgən] vt put on oath.

Vereidigung f swearing in.

Verein [fɛr'ain] m -(e)s, -e club, association; **v—bar** a compatible; **v—baren** [-barən] vt agree upon; **—barung** f agreement; **v—fachen** [-faxən] vt simplify; **v—heitlichen** vt standardize; **v—igen** [-igən] vtr unite; **—igung** f union; *(Verein)* association; **v—samen** [-za:mən] vi become lonely; **v—t** a united; **—zelt** a isolated.

vereisen [fɛr'aizən] vi freeze, ice over; vt *(Med)* freeze.

vereiteln [fɛr'aitəln] vt frustrate.

ver'eitern vi suppurate, fester.

verengen [fɛr'ɛŋən] vr narrow.

vererb- [fɛr'ɛrb] cpd: **—en** vt bequeath; *(Biol)* transmit; vr be hereditary; **—lich** [fɛr'ɛrplɪç] a hereditary; **V—ung** f bequeathing; *(Biol)* transmission; *(Lehre)* heredity.

verewigen [fɛr'e:vɪgən] vt immortalize; vr *(col)* leave one's name.

ver'fahren irreg vi act; **— mit** deal with; vr get lost; a tangled; **V—nt -s, -** procedure; *(Tech)* process; *(Jur)* proceedings pl.

Verfall [fɛr'fal] m -(e)s decline; *(von Haus)* dilapidation; *(Fin)* expiry; **v—en** vi irreg decline; *(Haus)* be falling down; *(Fin)* lapse; **v—en in** *(+acc)* lapse into; **v—en auf** *(+acc)* hit upon; **einem Laster — en sein** be addicted to a vice.

verfänglich [fɛr'fɛŋlɪç] a awkward, tricky.

6

ver'färben *vr* change colour.

Verfasser(in *f)* [fɛr'fasər(ɪn)] *m* **-s,** - author, writer.

Verfassung *f* constitution *(auch Pol)*; —**gericht** *nt* constitutional court; **v**—**smäßig** *a* constitutional; **v**—**swidrig** *a* unconstitutional.

ver'faulen *vi* rot.

ver'fechten *vt* *irreg* advocate; defend.

Verfechter [fɛr'fɛçtər] *m* **-s,** - champion; defender.

ver'fehlen *vt* miss; etw für verfehlt halten regard sth as mistaken.

ver'feinern [fɛr'faɪnərn] *vt* refine.

ver'fliegen *vi* *irreg* evaporate; *(Zeit)* pass, fly.

ver'flossen [fɛr'flɔsən] *a* past, former.

ver'fluchen *vt* curse.

verflüchtigen [fɛr'flʏçtɪgən] *vr* vaporize, evaporate; *(Geruch)* fade.

verflüssigen [fɛr'flʏsɪgən] *vt* become liquid.

verfolg- [fɛr'fɔlg] *cpd:* —**en** *vt* pursue; *(gerichtlich)* prosecute; *(grausam, esp Pol)* persecute; **V**—**er** *m* **-s,** - pursuer; **V**—**ung** *f* pursuit; prosecution; persecution; **V**—**ungswahn** *m* persecution mania.

verfremden [fɛr'frɛmdən] *vt* alienate, distance.

verfrüht [fɛr'fry:t] *a* premature.

verfüg- [fɛr'fy:g] *cpd:* —**bar** *a* available; —**en** *vt* direct, order; *vr* proceed; *vi:* —**en über** (*+acc)* have at one's disposal; **V**—**ung** *f* direction, order; **zur V**—**ung** at one's disposal; **jdm zur V**—**ung stehen** be available to sb.

verführ- [fɛr'fy:r] *cpd:* —**en** *vt* tempt; *(sexuell)* seduce; **V**—**er** *m* tempter; seducer; —**erisch** *a* seduc-

---

tive; **V**—**ung** *f* seduction; *(Versuchung)* temptation.

ver'gammeln *vi (col)* go to seed; *(Nahrung)* go off.

vergangen [fɛr'gaŋən] *a* past; **V**—**heit** *f* past.

vergänglich [fɛr'gɛŋlɪç] *a* transitory; **V**—**keit** *f* transitoriness, impermanence.

vergasen [fɛr'ga:zən] *vt* gasify; *(töten)* gas.

Vergaser *m* **-s,** - *(Aut)* carburettor.

vergeb- [fɛr'ge:b] *cpd:* —**en** *vt* *irreg* forgive *(jdm etw sb for sth)*; *(weggeben)* give away; —**en sein** be occupied; *(col: Mädchen)* be spoken-for; —**ens** *ad* in vain; —**lich** [fɛr'ge:plɪç] *ad* in vain; *a* vain, futile; **V**—**bung** *f* forgiveness.

vergegenwärtigen [fɛr'ge:gənvɛrtɪgən] *vr:* **sich** *(dat)* **etw** — recall or visualize sth.

ver'gehen *irreg* *vi* pass by or away; **jdm vergeht etw** sb loses sth; *vr* commit an offence *(gegen etw* against sth); **sich an jdm** — *(sexually)* assault sb; **V**— *nt* **-s,** - offence.

ver'gelten *vt* *irreg* pay back *(jdm etw* sb for sth), repay.

Ver'geltung *f* retaliation, reprisal; —**sschlag** *m (Mil)* reprisal.

vergessen [fɛr'gɛsən] *vt* *irreg* forget; **V**—**heit** *f* oblivion.

vergeßlich [fɛr'gɛslɪç] *a* forgetful; **V**—**heit** *f* forgetfulness.

vergeuden [fɛr'gɔʏdən] *vt* squander, waste.

vergewaltigen [fɛrgə'valtɪgən] *vt* rape; *(fig)* violate.

Vergewaltigung *f* rape.

vergewissern [fɛrgə'vɪsərn] *vr* make sure.

ver'gießen vt irreg shed.

vergiften [fer'gıftən] vt poison.

Vergiftung f poisoning.

Vergißmeinnicht [fer'gısmaınnıçt] nt -(e)s, -e forget-me-not.

verglasen [fer'glɑːzən] vt glaze.

Vergleich [fer'glaıç] m -(e)s, -e comparison; (Jur) settlement; im — mit or zu compared with or to; v~bar a comparable; v~en irreg vt compare; v~weise a comparative.

vergnügen [fer'gnyːgən] vr enjoy or amuse o.s.; V— nt -s, - pleasure; viel V—! enjoy yourself!

vergnügt [fer'gnyːkt] a cheerful.

Vergnügung f pleasure, amusement; —spark m amusement park; v~süchtig a pleasure-loving.

vergolden [fer'gɔldən] vt gild.

ver'gönnen vt grant.

vergöttern [fer'gœtərn] vt idolize.

ver'graben vt bury.

ver'greifen vr irreg: sich an jdm — lay hands on sb; sich an etw — misappropriate sth; sich im Ton — say the wrong thing.

vergriffen [fer'grıfən] a Buch out of print; Ware out of stock.

vergrößern [fer'grøːsərn] vt enlarge; (mengenmäßig) increase; (Lupe) magnify.

Vergrößerung f enlargement; increase; magnification; —sglas nt magnifying glass.

Vergünstigung [fer'gynstıgʊŋ] f concession, privilege.

vergüten [fer'gyːtən] vt: jdm etw — compensate sb for sth.

Vergütung f compensation.

verhaften [fer'haftən] vt arrest.

Verhaftete(r) mf prisoner.

Verhaftung f arrest; —sbefehl m warrant (for arrest).

ver'hallen vi die away.

ver'halten irreg vr be, stand; (sich benehmen) behave; (Math) be in proportion to; vt hold or keep back; Schritt check; V— nt -s behaviour; V~sforschung f behavioural science; V~smaßregel f rule of conduct.

Verhältnis [fer'heltnıs] nt -ses, -se relationship; (Math) proportion, ratio; pl (Umstände) conditions pl; über seine —se leben live beyond one's means; v~mäßig a,ad relative(ly), comparative(ly).

verhandeln [fer'handəln] vi negotiate (über etw (acc) sth); (Jur) hold proceedings; vt discuss; (Jur) hear.

Verhandlung f negotiation; (Jur) proceedings pl.

ver'hängen vt (fig) impose, inflict.

Verhängnis [fer'hɛŋnıs] nt -ses, -se fate, doom; jdm zum — werden be sb's undoing; v~voll a fatal, disastrous.

verharmlosen [fer'harmloːzən] vt make light of, play down.

verharren [fer'harən] vi remain; (hartnäckig) persist.

verhärten [fer'hɛrtən] vr harden.

verhaßt [fer'hast] a odious, hateful.

verheerend [fer'heːrənt] a disastrous, devastating.

verhehlen [fer'heːlən] vt conceal.

ver'heilen vi heal.

verheimlichen [fer'haımlıçən] vt keep secret (jdm from sb).

verheiratet [fer'haıraːtət] a married.

ver'heißen vt irreg: jdm etw — promise sth sth.

ver'helfen vi irreg: jdm — zu help sb to get.

verherrlichen [fɛr'hɛrlɪçən] vt glorify.

ver'hexen vt bewitch; es ist wie verhext it's jinxed.

ver'hindern vt prevent; verhindert sein be unable to make it.

Ver'hinderung f prevention.

verhöhnen [fɛr'hønən] vt mock, sneer at.

Verhör [fɛr'hø:r] nt -(e)s, -e interrogation;   (gerichtlich) (cross-)examination; **v—en** vt interrogate; (cross-)examine; vr misunderstand, mishear.

ver'hungern vi starve, die of hunger.

ver'hüten vt prevent, avert.

Ver'hütung f prevention; —smittel nt contraceptive.

verirren [fɛr'ɪrən] vr go astray.

ver'jagen vt drive away or out.

verjüngen [fɛr'jʏŋən] vt rejuvenate; vr taper.

verkalken [fɛr'kalkən] vi calcify; (col) become senile.

verkalkulieren [fɛrkalku'li:rən] vr miscalculate.

verkannt [fɛr'kant] a unappreciated.

Verkauf [fɛr'kauf] m sale; **v—en** vt sell.

Verkäufer(in f) [fɛr'kɔʏfər(ɪn)] m -s, - seller; salesman; (in Laden) shop assistant.

verkäuflich [fɛr'kɔʏflɪç] a saleable.

Verkehr [fɛr'ke:r] m -s, -e traffic; (Umgang, esp sexuell) intercourse; (Umlauf) circulation; **v—en** vi (Fahrzeug) ply, run; (besuchen) visit regularly (bei jdm sb); **v—en** mit associate with; vtr turn, transform; —sampel f traffic lights pl; —sdelikt nt traffic offence; —sinsel f traffic island;

—sstockung f traffic jam, stoppage; —sunfall m traffic accident; **v—swidrig** a contrary to traffic regulations; —szeichen nt traffic sign; **v—t** a wrong; (umgekehrt) the wrong way round.

ver'kennen vt irreg misjudge, not appreciate.

ver'klagen vt take to court.

verklären [fɛr'klɛ:rən] vt transfigure; verklärt lächeln smile radiantly.

ver'kleben vt glue up, stick; vi stick together.

verkleiden [fɛr'klaɪdən] vtr disguise (o.s.), dress up.

Verkleidung f disguise; (Archit) wainscoting.

verkleinern [fɛr'klaɪnərn] vt make smaller, reduce in size.

verklemmt [fɛr'klɛmt] a- (fig) inhibited.

ver'klingen vi irreg die away.

ver'kneifen vt (col) : sich (dat) etw — Lachen stifle; Schmerz hide; (sich versagen) do without.

verknüpfen [fɛr'knʏpfən] vt tie (up), knot; (fig) connect.

Verknüpfung f connection.

verkohlen [fɛr'ko:lən] vti carbonize; vt (col) fool.

ver'kommen vi irreg deteriorate, decay; (Mensch) go downhill, come down in the world; a (moralisch) dissolute, depraved; **V—heit** f depravity.

verkörpern [fɛr'kœrpərn] vt embody, personify.

verköstigen [fɛr'kœstɪgən] vt feed.

verkraften [fɛr'kraftən] vt cope with.

ver'kriechen vr irreg creep away, creep into a corner.

verkrümmt [fɛr'krʏmt] a crooked.

Verkrümmung f bend, warp; (Anat) curvature.

verkrüppelt [fɛr'krʏpəlt] a crippled.

verkrustet [fɛr'krʊstət] a encrusted.

ver'kühlen vr get a chill.

ver'kümmern vi waste away.

verkünden [fɛr'kʏndən] vt proclaim; Urteil pronounce.

verkürzen [fɛr'kʏrtsən] vt shorten; Wort abbreviate; sich (dat) die Zeit — while away the time.

Verkürzung f shortening; abbreviation.

ver'laden vt irreg load.

Verlag [fɛr'la:k] m -(e)s, -e publishing firm.

verlangen [fɛr'laŋən] vt demand; desire; — Sie Herrn X ask for Mr X; vi — nach ask for, desire; V— nt -s, - desire (nach for); auf jds V— (hin) at sb's request.

verlängern [fɛr'lɛŋərn] vt extend; (länger machen) lengthen.

Verlängerung f extension; (Sport) extra time; —sschnur f extension cable.

verlangsamen [fɛr'laŋza:mən] vtr decelerate, slow down.

Verlaß [fɛr'las] m: auf ihn/das ist kein — he/it cannot be relied upon.

ver'lassen irreg vt leave; vr depend (auf +acc on); a desolate; Mensch abandoned; V—heit f loneliness.

verläßlich [fɛr'lɛslɪç] a reliable.

Verlauf [fɛr'laʊf] m course; v—en irreg vi (zeitlich) pass; (Farben) run; vr get lost; (Menschenmenge) disperse.

ver'lauten vi: etw — lassen disclose sth; wie verlautet as reported.

ver'leben vt spend.

verlebt [fɛr'le:pt] a dissipated, worn out.

ver'legen vt move; (verlieren) mislay; (abspielen lassen) Handlung set (nach in); Buch publish; vr: sich auf etw (acc) — take up or to sth; a embarrassed; nicht — um never at a loss for; V—heit f embarrassment; (Situation) difficulty, scrape.

Verleger [fɛr'le:gər] m -s, - publisher.

Verleih [fɛr'laɪ] m -(e)s, -e hire service; v—en vt irreg lend; Kraft, Anschein confer, bestow; Preis, Medaille award; —ung f lending; bestowal; award.

ver'leiten vt lead astray; — zu talk into, tempt into.

ver'lernen vt forget, unlearn.

ver'lesen irreg vt read out; (aussondern) sort out; vr make a mistake in reading.

verletz- [fɛr'lɛts] cpd: —bar a vulnerable; —en vt (lit, fig) injure, hurt; Gesetz etc violate; —end a (fig) Worte hurtful; —lich a vulnerable, sensitive; V—te(r) mf injured person; V—ung f injury; (Verstoß) violation, infringement.

verleugnen [fɛr'lɔygnən] vt deny; Menschen disown.

Verleugnung f denial.

verleumd- [fɛr'lɔymd] cpd: —en vt slander; —erisch a slanderous; V—ung f slander, libel.

ver'lieben vr fall in love (in jdn with sb).

verliebt [fɛr'li:pt] a in love; V—heit f being in love.

verlieren [fɛr'li:rən] irreg vti lose;

vr get lost; *(verschwinden)* disappear.

verlob- [fɛr'loːb] *cpd:* **—en** *vr* get engaged *(mit* to); **V—te(r)** [fɛr'loːptə(r)] *mf* fiancé(e); **V—ung** *f* engagement.

ver'locken *vt* entice, lure.

Ver'lockung *f* temptation, attraction.

verlogen [fɛr'loːgən] *a* untruthful; **V—heit** *f* untruthfulness.

verloren [fɛr'loːrən] *a* lost; *Eier* poached; *der* **—e** *Sohn* the prodigal son; *etw* **—** *geben* give sth up for lost; **—gehen** *vi irreg* get lost.

verlosen [fɛr'loːzən] *vt* raffle, draw lots for.

Verlosung *f* raffle, lottery.

verlottern [fɛr'lɔtərn], **verludern** [fɛr'luːdərn] *vi (col)* go to the dogs.

Verlust [fɛr'lʊst] *m* **-(e)s, -e** loss; *(Mil)* casualty.

ver'machen *vt* bequeath, leave.

Vermächtnis [fɛr'mɛçtnɪs] *nt* **-ses, -se** legacy.

vermählen [fɛr'mɛːlən] *vr* marry.

Vermählung *f* wedding, marriage.

vermehren [fɛr'meːrən] *vtr* multiply; *(Menge)* increase.

Vermehrung *f* multiplying; increase.

ver'meiden *vt irreg* avoid.

vermeintlich [fɛr'maɪntlɪç] *a* supposed.

vermengen [fɛr'mɛŋən] *vt* mix; *(fig)* mix up, confuse.

Vermerk [fɛr'mɛrk] *m* **-(e)s, -e** note; *(in Ausweis)* endorsement; **v—en** *vt* note.

ver'messen *irreg vt* survey; *vr (falsch messen)* measure incorrectly; *a* presumptuous, bold; **V—heit** *f* presumptuousness; recklessness.

Ver'messung *f* survey(ing).

ver'mieten *vt* let, rent (out); *Auto* hire out, rent.

ver'mieter(in *f) m* **-s,** - landlord/ landlady.

Ver'mietung *f* letting, renting (out); *(von Autos)* hiring (out).

vermindern [fɛr'mɪndərn] *vtr* lessen, decrease; *Preise* reduce.

Verminderung *f* reduction.

ver'mischen *vtr* mix, blend.

ver'missen [fɛr'mɪsən] *vt* miss.

vermißt *(Fähigkeit)* a missing.

vermitteln [fɛr'mɪtəln] *vi* mediate; *vt Gespräch* connect; *jdm etw* **—** help *sb* to obtain sth.

Vermittler [fɛr'mɪtlər] *m* **-s,** - *(Schlichter)* agent, mediator.

Vermittlung *f* procurement; *(Stellen-)* agency; *(Tel)* exchange; *(Schlichtung)* mediation.

ver'mögen *vt irreg* be capable of; **—** *zu* be able to; **V—** *nt* **-s,** - wealth; *(Fähigkeit)* ability; *ein* **V—** *kosten* cost a fortune; **—d** *a* wealthy.

vermuten [fɛr'muːtən] *vt* suppose, guess; *(argwöhnen)* suspect.

vermutlich *a* supposed, presumed; *ad* probably.

Vermutung *f* supposition; suspicion.

vernachlässigen [fɛr'naːxlɛsɪgən] *vt* neglect.

vernarben [fɛr'narbən] *vi* heal up.

ver'nehmen *vt irreg* perceive, hear; *(erfahren)* learn; *(Jur)* (cross-)examine; *dem* **V—** *nach* from what I/we *etc* hear.

vernehmlich [fɛr'neːmlɪç] *a* audible.

Vernehmung *f* (cross-)examination; **v—sfähig** *a* in a condition to be (cross-)examined.

verneigen [fɛr'naɪgən] vr bow.

verneinen [fɛr'naɪnən] vt Frage answer in the negative; (ablehnen) deny; (Gram) negate; **—d** a negative.

Verneinung f negation.

vernichten [fɛr'nɪçtən] vt annihilate, destroy; **—d** a (fig) crushing; Blick withering; Kritik scathing.

Vernichtung f destruction, annihilation.

verniedlichen [fɛr'ni:tlɪçən] vt play down.

Vernunft [fɛr'nʊnft] f - reason, understanding.

vernünftig [fɛr'nynftɪç] a sensible, reasonable.

veröden [fɛr"ø:dən] vi become desolate; vt (Med) remove.

veröffentlichen [fɛr"œfəntlɪçən] vt publish.

Veröffentlichung f publication.

verordnen [fɛr"ɔrdnən] vt (Med) prescribe.

Verordnung f order, decree; (Med) prescription.

ver'pachten vt lease (out).

ver'packen vt pack.

Ver'packung f, **—smaterial** nt packing, wrapping.

ver'passen vt miss; jdm eine Ohrfeige — (col) give sb a clip round the ear.

verpesten [fɛr'pɛstən] vt pollute.

ver'pflanzen vt transplant.

Ver'pflanzung f transplant(ing).

ver'pflegen vt feed, cater for.

Ver'pflegung f feeding, catering; (Kost) food; (in Hotel) board.

verpflichten [fɛr'pflɪçtən] vt oblige, bind; (anstellen) engage; vr undertake; (Mil) sign on; vi carry obligations; jdm zu Dank verpflichtet sein be obliged to sb.

Verpflichtung f obligation, duty.

ver'pfuschen vt (col) bungle, make a mess of.

verplempern [fɛr'plɛmpərn] vt (col) waste.

verpönt [fɛr'pø:nt] a disapproved (of), taboo.

verprassen [fɛr'prasən] vt squander.

ver'prügeln vt (col) beat up, do over.

Verputz [fɛr'pʊts] m plaster, roughcast; **v—en** vt plaster; (col) Essen put away.

verquollen [fɛr'kvɔlən] a swollen; Holz warped.

verrammeln [fɛr'raməln] vt barricade.

Verrat [fɛr'ra:t] m -(e)s treachery; (Pol) treason; **v—en** irreg vt betray; Geheimnis divulge; vr give o.s. away.

Verräter [fɛr'rɛːtər] m -s, - traitor; **—in** f traitress; **v—isch** a treacherous.

ver'rechnen vt: — mit set off against; vr miscalculate.

Verrechnungsscheck [fɛr'rɛçnʊŋsʃɛk] m crossed cheque.

verregnet [fɛr'reːgnət] a spoilt by rain, rainy.

ver'reisen vi go away (on a journey).

ver'reißen vt irreg pull to pieces.

verrenken [fɛr'rɛŋkən] vt contort; (Med) dislocate; sich (dat) den Knöchel — sprain one's ankle.

Verrenkung f contortion; (Med) dislocation, sprain.

ver'richten vt do, perform.

ver'riegeln vt bolt up, lock.

verringern [fɛr'rɪŋərn] vt reduce; vr diminish.

Verringerung f reduction; lessening.

ver'rinnen vi irreg run out or away; (Zeit) elapse.

ver'rosten vi rust.

verrotten [fɛr'rɔtən] vi rot.

ver'rücken vt move, shift.

verrückt [fɛr'rʏkt] a crazy, mad; **V—e(r)** mf lunatic; **V—heit** f madness, lunacy.

Verruf [fɛr'ru:f] m: in — geraten/bringen fall/bring into disrepute; **V—en** a notorious, disreputable.

Vers [fɛrs] m -es, -e verse.

ver'sagen vt: jdm/sich (dat) etw — deny sb/o.s. sth; vi fail; **V—** nt -s failure.

Versager [fɛr'za:gər] m -s, - failure.

ver'salzen vt irreg put too much salt in; (fig) spoil.

ver'sammeln vtr assemble, gather.

Ver'sammlung f meeting, gathering.

Versand [fɛr'zant] m -(e)s forwarding; dispatch; (—abteilung) dispatch department; **—haus** nt mailorder firm.

ver'säumen [fɛr'zɔʏmən] vt miss; (unterlassen) neglect, fail.

Versäumnis f -, -se neglect; omission.

ver'schaffen vt: jdm/sich etw — get or procure sth for sb/o.s.

verschämt [fɛr'ʃɛ:mt] a bashful.

verschandeln [fɛr'ʃandəln] vt (col) spoil.

verschanzen [fɛr'ʃantsən] vr: sich hinter etw (dat) — dig in behind sth; (fig) take refuge behind.

verschärfen [fɛr'ʃɛrfən] vtr intensify; Lage aggravate.

ver'schätzen vr be out in one's reckoning.

ver'schenken vt give away.

verscherzen [fɛr'ʃɛrtsən] vt: sich (dat) etw — lose sth, throw away sth.

verscheuchen [fɛr'ʃɔʏçən] vt frighten away.

ver'schicken vt send off; Sträfling transport, deport.

ver'schieben vt irreg shift; (Rail) shunt; Termin postpone; (Comm) push.

Ver'schiebung f shift, displacement; shunting; postponement.

verschieden [fɛr'ʃi:dən] a different; (pl: mehrere) various; ‚sie sind — groß they are of different sizes; **—e** pl various people/things pl; **—es** pron various things pl; etwas **V—es** something different; **—artig** a various, of different kinds; zwei so **—artige …** two such differing …; **V—heit** f difference; **—tlich** ad several times.

verschlafen [fɛr'ʃla:fən] irreg vt sleep through; (fig: versäumen) miss; vir oversleep; a sleepy.

Verschlag [fɛr'ʃla:k] m shed; **v—en** [fɛr'ʃla:gən] vt irreg board up; (Tennis) hit out of play; Buchseite lose; jdm den Atem **v—en** take sb's breath away; an einen Ort **v—en** werden wind up in a place; a cunning.

verschlampen [fɛr'ʃlampən] vi fall into neglect; vt lose, mislay.

verschlechtern [fɛr'ʃlɛçtərn] vt make worse; vr deteriorate, get worse.

Verschlechterung f deterioration.

Verschleierung [fɛr'ʃlaɪərʊŋ] f veiling; (fig) concealment; (Mil) screening; **—staktik** f smokescreen tactics pl.

Verschleiß [fɛr'ʃlaɪs] *m* -es, -e wear and tear; (Aus) retail trade; **v–en** *irreg vt* wear out; retail; *vir* wear out.

ver'schleppen *vt* carry off, abduct; (zeitlich) drag out, delay.

ver'schleudern *vt* squander; (Comm) sell dirt-cheap.

verschließ- [fɛr'ʃliːs] *cpd:* **–bar** *a* lockable; **–en** *irreg vt* close; lock; *vr sich einer Sache* **–en** close one's mind to sth.

verschlimmern [fɛr'ʃlɪmərn] *vt* make worse, aggravate; *vr* get worse, deteriorate.

Verschlimmerung *f* deterioration.

verschlingen [fɛr'ʃlɪŋən] *vt irreg* devour, swallow up; *Fäden* twist.

verschlossen [fɛr'ʃlɔsən] *a* locked; (fig)· reserved; **V–heit** *f* reserve.

ver'schlucken *vt* swallow; *vr* choke.

Verschluß [fɛr'ʃlʊs] *m* lock; (von Kleid etc) fastener; (Phot) shutter; (Stöpsel) plug; *unter — halten* keep under lock and key.

verschlüsseln [fɛr'ʃlʏsəln] *vt* encode.

verschmähen [fɛr'ʃmɛːən] *vt* disdain, scorn.

ver'schmelzen *vti irreg* merge, blend.

verschmerzen [fɛr'ʃmɛrtsən] *vt* get over.

ver'schmutzen [fɛr'ʃmutsən] *vt* soil; *Umwelt* pollute.

verschneit [fɛr'ʃnaɪt] *a* snowed up, covered in snow.

verschnüren [fɛr'ʃnyːrən] *vt* tie up.

verschollen [fɛr'ʃɔlən] *a* lost, missing.

ver'schonen *vt* spare (jdn mit etw sb sth)

verschönern [fɛr'ʃøːnərn] *vt* decorate; (verbessern) improve.

verschränken [fɛr'ʃrɛŋkən] *vt* cross, fold.

ver'schreiben *irreg vt Papier* use up; (Med) prescribe; *vr* make a mistake (in writing); *sich einer Sache* — devote oneself to sth.

verschrien [fɛr'ʃriːən] *a* notorious.

verschroben [fɛr'ʃroːbən] *a* eccentric, odd.

ver'schrotten [fɛr'ʃrɔtən] *vt* scrap.

verschüchtert -[fɛr'ʃʏçtərt] *a* subdued, intimidated.

verschuld- [fɛr'ʃʊld] *cpd:* **–en** *vt* be guilty of; **V–en** *nt* -s fault, guilt; **–et a** in debt; **V–ung** *f* fault; (Geld) debts *pl.*

ver'schütten *vt* spill; (zuschütten) fill; (unter Trümmern) bury.

ver'schweigen *vt irreg* keep secret; *jdm etw* — keep sth from sb.

verschwend- [fɛr'ʃvɛnd] *cpd:* **–en** *vt* squander; **V–er** *m* -s, - **spend-thrift**; **–erisch** *a* wasteful, extravagant; **V–ung** *f* waste; extravagance.

verschwiegen [fɛr'ʃviːgən] *a* discreet; *Ort* secluded; **V–heit** *f* discretion; seclusion.

ver'schwimmen *vi* · *irreg* grow hazy, become blurred.

ver'schwinden *vi irreg* disappear, vanish; **V–** *nt* -s disappearance.

ver'schwitzen *vt* **stain** with sweat; (col) forget.

verschwommen ·[fɛr'ʃvɔmən] *a* hazy, vague.

verschwör- [fɛr'ʃvøːr] *cpd:* **–en** *vr irreg* plot, conspire; **V–er** *m* -s, - conspirator; **V–ung** *f* conspiracy, plot.

ver'sehen *irreg vt* supply, provide; *Pflicht* carry out; *Amt* fill; *Haushalt* keep; *vr* (*fig*) make a mistake; **ehe er (es) sich — hatte ...** before he knew it ...; **V— nt -s, -** oversight; **aus V—** by mistake; **—tlich** *ad* by mistake.

Versehrte(r) [fɛr'ze:rtə(r)] *mf* disabled person.

ver'senden *vt irreg* forward, dispatch.

ver'senken *vt* sink; *vr* become engrossed (*in* +acc in).

versessen [fɛr'zɛsən] *a:* **— auf** (+acc) mad about.

ver'setzen *vt* transfer; (*verpfänden*) pawn; (*col*) stand up; **jdm einen Tritt/Schlag —** kick/hit sb; **etw mit etw —** mix sth with sth; **jdn in gute Laune —** put sb in a good mood; *vr:* **sich in jdn or in jds Lage —** put o.s. in sb's place.

Ver'setzung *f* transfer.

verseuchen [fɛr'zɔʏçən] *vt* contaminate.

versichern [fɛr'zɪçərn] *vt* assure; (*mit Geld*) insure; *vr* **sich —** (+gen) make sure of.

Versicherung *f* assurance; insurance; **—spolice** *f* insurance policy.

versiegeln [fɛr'zi:gəln] *vt* seal (up).

ver'siegen *vi* dry up.

ver'sinken *vi irreg* sink.

versöhnen [fɛr'zø:nən] *vt* reconcile; *vr* become reconciled.

Versöhnung *f* reconciliation.

ver'sorgen *vt* provide, supply (*mit* with); *Familie etc* look after; *vr* look after o.s.

Ver'sorgung *f* provision, (*Unterhalt*) maintenance; (*Alters—* etc) benefit, assistance.

verspäten [fɛr'ʃpɛ:tən] *vr* be late.

Verspätung *f* delay; **— haben** be late.

ver'sperren *vt* bar, obstruct.

Ver'sperrung *f* barrier.

ver'spielen *vti* lose.

verspielt [fɛr'ʃpi:lt] *a* playful; **bei jdm — haben** be in sb's bad books.

ver'spotten *vt* ridicule, scoff at.

ver'sprechen *irreg vt* promise; **sich** (*dat*) **etw von etw —** expect sth from sth; **V— nt -s, -** promise.

verstaatlichen [fɛr'ʃta:tlɪçən] *vt* nationalize.

Verstand [fɛr'ʃtant] *m* intelligence; mind; **den — verlieren** go out of one's mind; **über jds — gehen** go beyond sb; **v—esmäßig** *a* rational; intellectual.

verständig [fɛr'ʃtɛndɪç] *a* sensible; **—en** [fɛr'ʃtɛndɪgən] *vt* inform; *vr* communicate; (*sich einigen*) come to an understanding; **—keit** *f* good sense; **V—ung** *f* communication; (*Benachrichtigung*) informing; (*Einigung*) agreement.

verständ- [fɛr'ʃtɛnt] *cpd:* **—lich** *a* understandable, comprehensible; **V—lichkeit** *f* clarity, intelligibility; **V—nis** *nt -ses, -se** understanding; **—nislos** *a* uncomprehending; **—nisvoll** *a* understanding, sympathetic.

verstärk- [fɛr'ʃtɛrk] *cpd:* **—en** *vt* strengthen; *Ton* amplify; (*erhöhen*) intensify; *vr* intensify; **V—er** *m -s, -* amplifier; **V—ung** *f* strengthening; (*Hilfe*) reinforcements *pl*; (*von Ton*) amplification.

verstauchen [fɛr'ʃtaʊxən] *vt* sprain.

verstauen [fɛr'ʃtaʊən] *vt* stow away.

Versteck [fɛr'ʃtɛk] *nt -(e)s, -e* hiding (place); **v—en** *vtr* hide;

—spiel nt hide-and-seek; v—t a hidden.

ver'stehen irreg vt understand; vr get on.

versteifen [fɛr'ʃtaɪfən] vt stiffen, brace; vr (fig) insist (auf +acc on).

versteigern [fɛr'ʃtaɪgərn] vt auction.

Versteigerung f auction.

verstell- [fɛr'ʃtɛl] cpd: —bar a adjustable, variable; —en vt move, shift; Uhr adjust; (versperren) block; (fig) disguise; vr pretend, put on an act; V—ung f pretence.

verstiegen [fɛr'ʃtiːgən] a exaggerated.

verstimmt [fɛr'ʃtɪmt] a out of tune; (fig) cross, put out.

verstockt [fɛr'ʃtɔkt] a stubborn; V—heit f stubbornness.

verstohlen [fɛr'ʃtoːlən] a stealthy.

ver'stopfen vt block, stop up; (Med) constipate.

Ver'stopfung f obstruction; (Med) constipation.

verstorben [fɛr'ʃtɔrbən] a deceased, late.

verstört [fɛr'ʃtøːrt] a Mensch distraught.

Verstoß [fɛr'ʃtoːs] m infringement, violation (gegen of); v—en irreg vt disown, reject; vi: v—en gegen offend against.

ver'streichen irreg vt spread; vi elapse.

ver'streuen vt scatter (about).

ver'stricken vt (fig) entangle, ensnare; vr get entangled (in +acc in).

verstümmeln [fɛr'ʃtʏməln] vt maim, mutilate (auch fig).

verstummen [fɛr'ʃtʊmən] vi go silent; (Lärm) die away.

Versuch [fɛr'zuːx] m -(e)s, -e attempt; (Sci) experiment; v—en vt try; (verlocken) tempt; vr: sich an etw (dat) v—en try one's hand at sth; —skaninchen nt guinea-pig; v—sweise ad tentatively; —ung f temptation.

versunken [fɛr'zʊŋkən] a sunken; — sein in (+acc) be absorbed or engrossed in.

versüßen [fɛr'zyːsən] vt: jdm etw — (fig) make sth more pleasant for sb.

vertagen [fɛr'taːgən] vti adjourn.

Vertagung f adjournment.

ver'tauschen vt exchange; (versehentlich) mix up.

verteidig- [fɛr'taɪdɪg] cpd: —en vt defend; V—er m -s, - defender; (Jur) defence counsel; V—ung f defence.

ver'teilen 'vt distribute; Rollen assign; Salbe spread.

Verteilung f distribution, allotment.

verteufelt [fɛr'tɔyfəlt] a,ad (col) awful(ly), devilish(ly).

vertiefen [fɛr'tiːfən] vt deepen; vr: sich in etw (acc) — become engrossed or absorbed in sth.

Vertiefung f depression.

vertikal [vɛrtiˈkaːl] a vertical.

vertilgen [fɛr'tɪlgən] vt exterminate; (col) eat up, consume.

vertippen [fɛr'tɪpən] vr make a typing mistake.

vertonen [fɛr'toːnən] vt set to music.

Vertrag [fɛr'traːk] m -(e)s, -̈e contract, agreement; (Pol) treaty; v—en [fɛr'traːgən] irreg vt tolerate, stand; vr get along; (sich aussöhnen) become reconciled; v—lich a contractual.

verträglich [fɛr'trɛ:klɪç] a good-natured, sociable; *Speisen* easily digested; (*Med*) easily tolerated; **V—keit** f sociability; good nature; digestibility.

Vertrags- cpd: **—bruch** m breach of contract; **v—brüchig** a in breach of contract; **v—mäßig** a,ad stipulated, according to contract; **—partner** m party to a contract; **—spieler** m (*Sport*) contract professional; **v—widrig** a contrary to contract.

vertrauen [fɛr'trauən] vi trust (*jdm sb*); **—auf** (+acc) rely on; **V—nt** -s confidence; **—erweckend** a inspiring trust; **—selig** a too trustful; **—svoll** a trustful; **—swürdig** a trustworthy.

vertraulich [fɛr'traulɪç] a familiar; (*geheim*) confidential; **V—keit** f familiarity; confidentiality.

vertraut [fɛr'traut] a familiar; **V—e(r)** mf confidant, close friend; **V—heit** f familiarity.

vertreiben vt irreg drive away; (*aus Land*) expel; (*Comm*) sell; *Zeit* pass.

Vertreibung f expulsion.

vertret- [fɛr'tre:t] cpd: **—en** vt irreg represent; *Ansicht* hold, advocate; sich (*dat*) die Beine **—en** stretch one's legs; **V—er** m -s, - representative; (*Verfechter*) advocate; **V—ung** f representation; advocacy.

Vertrieb [fɛr'tri:p] m -(e)s, -e marketing.

vertrocknen vi dry up.

vertrödeln vt (col) fritter away.

vertrösten vt put off.

vertun [fɛr'tu:n] irreg vt (col) waste; vr make a mistake.

vertuschen [fɛr'tʊʃən] vt hush or cover up.

verübeln [fɛr'y:bəln] vt: jdm etw — be cross or offended with sb on account of sth.

verüben [fɛr'y:bən] vt commit.

verun- [fɛr'ʊn] cpd: **—glimpfen** [-glɪmpfən] vt disparage; **—glücken** [-glʏkən] vi have an accident; **tödlich —glücken** be killed in an accident; **—reinigen** vt soil; *Umwelt* pollute; **—stalten** [-ʃtaltən] vt disfigure; *Gebäude etc* deface; **—treuen** [-trɔyən] vt embezzle.

verur- [fɛr'u:r] cpd: **—sachen** [-zaxən] vt cause; **—teilen** [-tailən] vt condemn; **V—teilung** f condemnation; (*Jur*) sentence.

verviel- [fɛr'fi:l] cpd: **—fachen** [-faxən] vt multiply; **—fältigen** [-fɛltɪgən] vt duplicate, copy; **V—fältigung** f duplication, copying.

vervoll- [fɛr'fɔl] cpd: **—kommnen** [-kɔmnən] vt perfect; **—ständigen** [-ʃtɛndɪgən] vt complete.

ver'wackeln vt Photo blur.

ver'wählen vr (Tel) dial the wrong number.

verwahr- [fɛr'va:r] cpd: **—en** vt keep, lock away; vr protest; **—losen** [-lo:zən] vi become neglected; (*moralisch*) go to the bad; **—lost** [-lo:st] a neglected; wayward.

verwaist [fɛr'vaist] a orphaned.

verwalt- [fɛr'valt] cpd: **—en** vt manage; administer; **V—er** m -s, - manager; (*Vermögens-*) trustee; **V—ung** f administration; management; **V—ungsbezirk** m administrative district.

ver'wandeln vtr change, transform.

Ver'wandlung f change, transformation.

verwandt [fɛr'vant] a related (*mit* to); **V—e(r)** mf relative, relation;

V—schaft f relationship; (Menschen) relations pl.

ver'warnen vt caution.

Ver'warnung f caution.

ver'waschen a faded; (fig) vague.

verwässern [fɛr'vɛsərn] vt dilute, water down.

ver'wechseln vt confuse (mit with); mistake (mit for); zum V—ähnlich as like as two peas.

Ver'wechslung f confusion, mixing up.

verwegen [fɛr've:gən] a daring, bold; V—heit f daring, audacity, boldness.

Verwehung [fɛr've:ʊŋ] f snow-/sanddrift.

verweichlich- [fɛr'vaiçlɪç] cpd: **—en** vt mollycoddle; **—t** a effeminate, soft.

ver'weigern vt refuse (jdm etw sb sth); den Gehorsam/die Aussage **—** refuse to obey/testify.

Ver'weigerung f refusal.

verweilen [fɛr'vailən] vi stay; (fig) dwell (bei on).

Verweis [fɛr'vais] m -es, -e reprimand, rebuke; (Hinweis) reference; v—en [fɛr'vaizən] vt irreg refer; jdm etw v—en (tadeln) scold sb for sth; jdn von der Schule v—en expel sb (from school); jdn des Landes v—en deport or expel sb; **—ung** f reference; (Tadel) reprimand; (Landes—) deportation.

ver'welken vi fade.

ver'wenden irreg vt use; Mühe, Zeit, Arbeit spend; vr intercede.

Ver'wendung f use.

ver'werfen vt irreg reject.

verwerflich [fɛr'vɛrflɪç] a reprehensible.

ver'werten vt utilize.

Ver'wertung f utilization.

verwesen [fɛr've:zən] vi decay.

Verwesung f decomposition.

ver'wickeln vt tangle (up); (fig) involve (in +acc in); vr get tangled (up); **sich — in** (+acc) (fig) get involved in.

Verwicklung f complication, entanglement.

verwildern [fɛr'vɪldərn] vi run wild.

ver'winden vt irreg get over.

verwirklichen [fɛr'vɪrklɪçən] vt realize, put into effect.

Verwirklichung f realization.

verwirren [fɛr'vɪrən] vt tangle (up); (fig) confuse.

Verwirrung f confusion.

verwittern [fɛr'vɪtərn] vi weather.

verwitwet [fɛr'vɪtvət] a widowed.

verwöhnen [fɛr'vø:nən] vt spoil.

Verwöhnung f spoiling, pampering.

verworfen [fɛr'vɔrfən] a depraved; V—heit f depravity.

verworren [fɛr'vɔrən] a confused.

verwund- cpd: **—bar** [fɛr'vʊntba:r] a vulnerable; **—en** [fɛr'vʊndən] vt wound; **—erlich** [fɛr'vʊndərlɪç] a surprising; V—erung [fɛr'vʊndərʊŋ] f astonishment; V—ete(r) mf injured (person); V—ung f wound, injury.

ver'wünschen vt curse.

verwüsten [fɛr'vy:stən] vt devastate.

Verwüstung f devastation.

verzagen [fɛr'tsa:gən] vi despair.

ver'zählen vr miscount.

verzehren [fɛr'tse:rən] vt consume.

ver'zeichnen vt list; Niederlage, Verlust register.

Verzeichnis [fɛr'tsaiçnɪs] nt -ses, -se list, catalogue; (in Buch) index.

verzeih- [fɛr'tsai] cpd: —en vti irreg forgive (jdm etw sb for sth); —lich a pardonable; V—ung f forgiveness, pardon; V—ung! sorry!, excuse me!

ver'zerren vt distort.

Verzicht [fɛr'tsɪçt] m -(e)s, -e renunciation (auf +acc of); —en vi forgo, give up (auf etw (acc) sth).

ver'ziehen irreg vi move; vt put out of shape; Kind spoil; Pflanzen thin out; das Gesicht — pull a face; vr go out of shape; (Gesicht) contort; (verschwinden) disappear.

verzieren [fɛr'tsiːrən] vt decorate, ornament.

verzinsen [fɛr'tsɪnzən] vt pay interest on.

ver'zögern vt delay.

Ver'zögerung f delay, time-lag; —staktik f delaying tactics pl.

verzollen [fɛr'tsɔlən] vt declare, pay duty on.

verzück- [fɛr'tsyk] cpd: —en vt send into ecstasies, enrapture; —t a enraptured; V—ung f ecstasy.

verzweif- [fɛr'tsvaif] cpd: —eln vi despair; —elt a desperate; V—lung f despair.

verzweigen [fɛr'tsvaigən] vr branch out.

verzwickt [fɛr'tsvɪkt] a (col) awkward, complicated.

Veto ['veːto] nt -s, -s veto.

Vetter ['fɛtər] m -s, -n cousin; —nwirtschaft f nepotism.

vibrieren [viˈbriːrən] vi vibrate.

Vieh [fiː] nt -(e)s cattle pl; v—isch a bestial.

viel [fiːl] a a lot of, much; —e pl a lot of, many; ad a lot, much; — zuwenig much too little; —erlei a a great variety of; —es a a lot; —fach a,ad many times; auf —fachen Wunsch at the request of many people; V—falt f variety; —fältig a varied, many-sided.

vielleicht [fiˈlaiçt] ad perhaps.

viel- cpd: —mal(s) ad many times; danke —mals many thanks; —mehr ad rather, on the contrary; —sagend a significant; —seitig a many-sided; —versprechend a promising.

vier [fiːr] num four; V—eck nt -(e)s, -e four-sided figure; (gleichseitig) square; —eckig a four-sided; square; V—taktmotor m four-stroke engine; —te(r,s) ['fiːrtə(r,z)] a fourth; —teilen vt quarter; V—tel ['fɪrtəl] nt -s, - quarter; —teljährlich a quarterly; V—elnote f crotchet; V—elstunde [fɪrtəl'ʃtundə] f quarter of an hour; —zehn ['fɪrtseːn] num fourteen; in —zehn Tagen in a fortnight; —zehntägig a fortnightly; —zig ['fɪrtsɪç] num forty.

Vikar [viˈkaːr] m -s, -e curate.

Villa ['vɪla] f -, Villen villa.

Villenviertel ['vɪlənfɪrtəl] nt (prosperous) residential area.

violett [vioˈlɛt] a violet.

Violin- [vioˈliːn] cpd: —bogen m violin bow; —e f -, -n violin; —konzert nt violin concerto; —schlüssel m treble clef.

Virus ['viːrus] m or nt -, Viren virus.

Visier [viˈziːr] nt -s, -e gunsight; (am Helm) visor.

Visite [viˈziːtə] f -, -n (Med) visit; —nkarte f visiting card.

visuell [vizuˈɛl] a visual.

Visum ['viːzum] nt -s, Visa or Visen visa.

vital [viˈtaːl] a lively, full of life, vital.

Vitamin [vita'mi:n] *nt* -s, -e vitamin.

Vogel ['fo:gəl] *m* -s, ⁼ bird; einen — haben *(col)* have bats in the belfry; jdm den — zeigen *(col)* tap one's forehead *(to indicate that one thinks sb stupid)*; —bauer *nt* birdcage; —beerbaum *m* rowan tree; —schau *f* bird's-eye view; —scheuche *f* ⁊, -n scarecrow.

Vokab- *cpd:* —el [vo'ka:bəl] *f* ⁊, -n word; —ular [vokabu'la:r] *nt* -s, -e vocabulary.

Vokal [vo'ka:l] *m* -s, -e vowel.

Volk [fɔlk] *nt* -(e)s, ⁼er people; nation.

Völker- ['fœlkər] *cpd:* —bund *m* League of Nations; —recht *nt* international law; v—rechtlich *a* according to international law; —verständigung *f* international understanding; —wanderung *f* migration.

Volks- *cpd:* —abstimmung *f* referendum; —hochschule *f* adult education classes *pl*; —lied *nt* folksong; —republik *f* people's republic; —schule *f* elementary school; —tanz *m* folk dance; v—tümlich ['fɔlksty:mlɪç] *a* popular; —wirtschaft *f* economics.

voll [fɔl] *a* full; — und ganz completely; jdn für — nehmen *(col)* take sb seriously; —auf [fɔl'aʊf] *ad* amply; —blütig a full-blooded; —'bringen *vt irreg insep* accomplish; —'enden *vt insep* finish, complete; —ends ['fɔlɛnts] *ad* completely; V—'endung *f* completion; —er *a* fuller; (+gen) full of; V—eyball ['vɔlibal] *m* volleyball; V—gas *nt:* mit V—gas at full throttle; V—gas geben step on it.

völlig ['fœlɪç] *a,ad* complete(ly).

voll- *cpd:* —jährig *a* of age; V—kaskoversicherung *f* fully comprehensive insurance; —'kommen a perfect; V—'kommenheit *f* perfection; V—kornbrot *nt* wholemeal bread; —machen *vt* fill (up); V—macht *f* ⁊, -en authority, full powers *pl*; V—mond *m* full moon; V—pension *f* full board; —ständig a complete; —'strecken *vt insep* execute; —tanken *vti* fill up; —zählig a complete; in full number; —'ziehen *vt irreg insep* carry out; *vr* happen; V—'zug *m* execution.

Volt [vɔlt] *nt -* or -(e)s, - volt.

Volumen [vo'lu:mən] *nt* -s, - *or* Volumina volume.

vom [fɔm] = von dem.

von [fɔn] *prep +dat* from; *(statt Genitiv, bestehend aus)* of; *(im Passiv)* by; ein Freund — mir a friend of mine; — mir aus *(col)* OK by me; — wegen! no way!; —ei'nander *ad* from each other; —statten [fɔn'ʃtatən] *ad:* —statten gehen proceed, go.

vor [fo:r] *prep +dat or acc* before; *(räumlich)* in front of; — Wut/Liebe with rage/love; — 2 Tagen 2 days ago; — allem above all; V—abend *m* evening before, eve.

voran [fo'ran] *ad* before, ahead; —gehen *vi irreg* go ahead; einer Sache *(dat)* —gehen precede sth.; —gehend a previous; —kommen *vi irreg* come along, make progress.

Vor- [fo:r] *cpd:* —anschlag *m* estimate; —arbeiter *m* foreman.

voraus [fo'raʊs] *ad* ahead; *(zeitlich)* in advance; jdm — sein be ahead of sb; im — in advance; —bezahlen *vt* pay in advance; —gehen *vi irreg* go (on) ahead;

(fig) precede; —haben *vt irreg:* jdm etw —haben have the edge on sb in sth; V—sage *f* -, -n prediction; —sagen *vt* predict; —sehen *vt irreg* foresee; —setzen *vt* assume; —gesetzt, daß . . . provided that . . . , V—setzung *f* requirement, prerequisite; V—sicht *f* foresight; aller V—sicht nach in all probability; in der V—sicht, daß . . . anticipating that . . . ; —sichtlich *ad* probably.

vorbauen ['fo:rbauən] *vt* build up in front; *vi* take precautions *(dat* against).

Vorbehalt ['fo:rbəhalt] *m* -(e)s, -e reservation, proviso; v—en *vt irreg:* sich/jdm etw v—en reserve sth (to o.s.)/to sb; v—los *a,ad* unconditional(ly).

vorbei [fɔr'bai] *ad* by, past; —gehen *vi irreg* pass by, go past.

vorbe- *cpd:* —lastet ['fo:rbəlastət] *a (fig)* handicapped; —reiten ['fo:rbəraitən] *vt* prepare; V—reitung *f* preparation; —straf ['fo:rbəʃtra:ft] *a* previously convicted, with a record.

vorbeugen ['fo:rbɔygən] *vtr* lean forward; *vi* prevent *(einer Sache (dat)* sth); —d *a* preventive.

Vorbeugung *f* prevention; zur — gegen for the prevention of.

Vorbild ['fo:rbɪlt] *nt* model; sich *(dat)* jdn zum — nehmen model o.s. on sb; v—lich *a* model, ideal.

vorbringen ['fo:rbrɪŋən] *vt irreg* advance, state; *(col:* **nach vorne)** bring to the front.

Vorder- ['fɔrdər] *cpd:* —achse *f* front axle; —ansicht *f* front view; v—e(r,s) *a* front; —grund *m* foreground; v—hand *ad* for the present; —mann *m, pl* —männer man in front; jdn auf —mann

bringen *(col)* tell sb to pull his socks up; —seite *f* front (side); v—ste(r,s) *a* front.

vordrängen ['fo:rdrɛŋən] *vt* push to the front.

vorehelich ['fo:r'e:əlɪç] *a* pre-.marital.

voreilig ['fo:r'ailɪç] *a* hasty, rash.

voreingenommen ['fo:r'aingənɔmən] *a* biased; **V—heit** *f* bias.

vorenthalten ['fo:r'ɛnthaltən] *vt irreg:* jdm etw — withhold sth from sb.

vorerst ['fo:r'e:rst] *ad* for the moment or present.

Vorfahr ['fo:rfa:r] *m* -en, -en ancestor; v—en *vi irreg* drive (on) ahead; *(vors Haus etc)* drive up; —t *f (Aut)* right of way; —t achten! give way!; —tsregel *f* right of way; —tsschild *nt* give way sign.

Vorfall ['fo:rfal] *m* incident; v—en *vi irreg* occur.

vorfinden ['fo:rfɪndən] *vt irreg* find.

vorführen ['fo:rfy:rən] *vt* show, display; **dem Gericht —** bring before the court.

Vorgabe ['fo:rga:bə] *f (Sport)* start, handicap.

Vorgang ['fo:rgaŋ] *m* course of events; *(esp Sci)* process; **der — von etw** how sth happens.

Vorgänger(in *f)* ['fo:rgɛŋər(ɪn)] *m* -s, - predecessor.

vorgeben ['fo:rge:bən] *vt irreg* pretend, use as a pretext; *(Sport)* give an advantage *or* a start of.

vorge- ['fo:rgə] *cpd:* —faßt *[-fast]* *a* preconceived; —fertigt *[-fertɪçt]* *a* prefabricated; **V—fühl** *[-fy:l]* *nt* presentiment, anticipation.

vorgehen ['fo:rge:ən] *vi irreg (voraus)* go (on) ahead; *(nach vorn)* go up front; *(handeln)* act, proceed; (Uhr) be fast; (Vorrang haben) take precedence; (passieren) go on; V— nt -s action.

Vorgeschmack ['foːrgəʃmak] m foretaste.

Vorgesetzte(r) ['foːrgəzɛtstə(r)] mf superior.

vorgestern ['foːrgɛstərn] ad the day before yesterday.

vorgreifen ['foːrgraifən] vi irreg anticipate, forestall.

vorhaben ['foːrhaːbən] vt irreg intend; hast du schon was vor? have you got anything on?; V— nt -s, - intention.

vorhalten ['foːrhaltən] irreg vt hold or put up; (fig) reproach (jdm etw sb for sth); vi last.

Vorhaltung f reproach.

vorhanden [foːr'handən] a existing, extant; (erhältlich) available; V—sein nt -s existence, presence.

Vorhang ['foːrhaŋ] m curtain.

Vorhängeschloß ['foːrhɛŋəʃlɔs] nt padlock.

Vorhaut ['foːrhaut] f (Med) foreskin.

vorher [foːr'heːr] ad before(hand); **—bestimmen** vt Schicksal preordain; **—gehen** vi irreg precede; **—ig** [foːr'heːriç] a previous.

Vorherrschaft ['foːrhɛrʃaft] f predominance, supremacy.

vorherrschen ['foːrhɛrʃən] vi predominate.

vorher- [foːr'heːr] cpd: **V—sage** f -, -n forecast; **—sagen** vt forecast, predict; **—sehbar** a predictable; **—sehen** vt irreg foresee.

vorhin [foːr'hɪn] ad not long ago, just now; **—ein** ['foːrhɪnain] ad: im **—ein** beforehand.

vorig ['foːriç] a previous, last.

vorjährig ['foːrjɛːriç] a of the previous year; last year's.

Vorkehrung ['foːrkeːruŋ] f precaution.

vorkommen ['foːrkɔmən] vi come forward; (geschehen, sich finden) occur; (scheinen) seem (to be); sich (dat) dumm etc — feel stupid etc; V— nt -s, - occurrence.

Vorkommnis ['foːrkɔmnɪs] nt -ses, -se occurrence.

Vorkriegs- ['foːrkriːks] in cpds prewar.

Vorladung ['foːrlaːduŋ] f summons.

Vorlage ['foːrlaːgə] f model, pattern; (Gesetzes—) bill; (Sport) pass.

vorlassen ['foːrlasən] vt irreg admit; (vorgehen lassen) allow to go in front.

vorläufig ['foːrlɔyfiç] a temporary, provisional.

vorlaut ['foːrlaut] a impertinent, cheeky.

Vorleg- ['foːrleːg] cpd: v—en vt put in front; (fig) produce, submit; jdm etw v—en put sth before sb; **—er** m -s, - mat.

vorlesen ['foːrleːzən] vt irreg read (out).

Vorlesung f (Univ) lecture.

vorletzte(r, s) ['foːrlɛtstə(r,s)] a last but one.

Vorliebe ['foːrliːbə] f preference, partiality.

vorliebnehmen [foːr'liːpneːmən] vi irreg: — mit make do with.

vorliegen ['foːrliːgən] vi irreg be (here); etw liegt jdm vor sb has sth; **—d** a present, at issue.

vormachen ['foːrmaxən] vt: jdm etw — show sb how to do sth; (fig) fool sb; have sb on.

Vormachtstellung ['fo:rmaxt-ʃtɛlʊŋ] f supremacy, hegemony.

Vormarsch ['fo:rmarʃ] m advance.

vormerken ['fo:rmɛrkən] vt book.

Vormittag ['fo:rmɪta:k] m morning; v—s ad in the morning, before noon.

Vormund ['fo:rmʊnt] m -(e)s, -e or -münder guardian.

vorn(e) ['fɔrn(ə)] ad in front; von — anfangen start at the beginning; nach — to the front.

Vorname ['fo:rna:mə] m first or Christian name.

vornan [fɔrn''an] ad at the front.

vornehm ['fo:rne:m] a distinguished; refined; elegant; —en vt irreg (fig) carry out; sich (dat) etw —en start on sth; (beschließen) decide to do sth; sich (dat) jdn —en tell sb off; —lich ad chiefly, specially.

vornherein ['fɔrnhɛraɪn] ad: von — from the start.

Vorort ['fo:r'ɔrt] m suburb; —zug m commuter train.

Vorrang ['fo:rraŋ] m precedence, priority; v—ig a of prime importance, primary.

Vorrat ['fo:rra:t] m stock, supply; —skammer f pantry.

vorrätig ['fo:rrɛ:tɪç] a in stock.

Vorrecht ['fo:rrɛçt] nt privilege.

Vorrichtung ['fo:rrɪçtʊŋ] f device, contrivance.

vorrücken ['fo:rrʏkən] vi advance; vt move forward.

vorsagen ['fo:rza:gən] vt recite, say out loud; (Sch: zuflüstern) tell secretly, prompt.

Vorsatz ['fo:rzats] m intention; (Jur) intent; einen — fassen make a resolution.

vorsätzlich ['fo:rzɛtslɪç] a,ad intentional(ly); (Jur) premeditated.

Vorschau ['fo:rʃau] f (Rad, TV) (programme) preview; (Film) trailer.

vorschieben ['fo:rʃi:bən] vt irreg push forward; (vor etw) push across; (fig) put forward as an excuse; jdn — use sb as a front.

Vorschlag ['fo:rʃla:k] m suggestion, proposal; v—en vt irreg suggest, propose.

vorschnell ['fo:rʃnɛl] ad hastily, too quickly.

vorschreiben ['fo:rʃraɪbən] vt irreg prescribe, specify.

Vorschrift ['fo:rʃrɪft] f regulation(s); rule(s); (Anweisungen) instruction(s); Dienst nach —, work-to-rule; v—smäßig a as per regulations/instructions.

Vorschuß ['fo:rʃʊs] m advance.

vorschweben ['fo:rʃve:bən] vi: jdm schwebt etw vor sb has sth in mind.

vorsehen ['fo:rze:ən] irreg vt provide for, plan; vr take care, be careful; vi be visible.

Vorsehung f providence.

vorsetzen ['fo:rzɛtsən] vt move forward; (vor etw) put in front; (anbieten) offer.

Vorsicht ['fo:rzɪçt] f caution, care; —! look out!, take care!; (auf Schildern) caution!, danger!; —, Stufe! mind the step!; v—ig a cautious, careful; v—shalber ad just in case.

Vorsilbe ['fo:rzɪlbə] f prefix.

Vorsitz ['fo:rzɪts] m chair(manship); —ende(r) mf chairman/-woman.

Vorsorge ['fo:rzɔrgə] f precaution(s), provision(s); v—n vi treffen provide for; v—en für make provision(s) for.

vorsorglich ['fo:rzɔrklıç] ad as a precaution.

Vorspeise ['fo:rʃpaızə] f hors d'oeuvre, appetizer.

Vorspiel ['fo:rʃpi:l] nt prelude.

vorsprechen ['fo:rʃprɛçən] irreg vt say out loud, recite; vi: bei jdm —; call on sb.

Vorsprung ['fo:rʃprʊŋ] m projection, ledge; (fig) advantage, start.

Vorstadt ['fo:rʃtat] f suburbs pl.

Vorstand ['fo:rʃtant] m executive committee; (Comm) board (of directors); (Person) director, head.

vorstehen ['fo:rʃte:ən] vi irreg project; etw (dat) — (fig) be the head of sth.

vorstell- ['fo:rʃtɛl] cpd: **—bar** a conceivable; **—en** vt put forward; (vor etw) put in front; (bekannt machen) introduce; (darstellen) represent; sich (dat) etw —en imagine sth; **V—ung** f (Bekanntmachen) introduction; (Theat etc) performance; (Gedanke) idea, thought.

Vorstoß ['fo:rʃto:s] m advance; v—en vti irreg push forward.

Vorstrafe ['fo:rʃtra:fə] f previous conviction.

vorstrecken ['fo:rʃtrɛkən] vt stretch out; Geld advance.

Vorstufe ['fo:rʃtu:fə] f.first step(s).

Vortag ['fo:rta:k] m day before (einer Sache sth).

vortäuschen ['fo:rtɔʏʃən] vt feign, pretend.

Vorteil ['fortaıl] m -s, -e advantage (gegenüber over); im — sein have the advantage; v—haft a advantageous.

Vortrag ['fo:rtra:k] m -(e)s, **Vorträge** talk, lecture; (—sart) delivery, rendering; (Comm)

balance carried forward; v—en vt irreg carry forward (auch Comm); (fig) recite; Rede deliver; Lied perform; Meinung etc express.

vortrefflich ['fo:rtrɛflıç] a excellent.

vortreten ['fo:rtre:tən] vi irreg step forward; (Augen etc) protrude.

vorüber ['fo:ry:bər] ad past, over; —gehen vi irreg pass (by); —gehen an (+ dat) (fig) pass over; —gehend a temporary, passing.

Vorurteil ['fo:r'urtaıl] nt prejudice; v—sfrei, v—slos a unprejudiced, open-minded.

Vorverkauf ['fo:rfɛrkauf] m advance booking.

Vorwahl ['fo:rva:l] f preliminary election; (Tel) dialling code.

Vorwand ['fo:rvant] m -(e)s, **Vorwände** pretext.

vorwärts ['fo:rvɛrts] ad forward; V—gang m (Aut etc) forward gear; —gehen vi irreg progress; —kommen vi irreg get on, make progress.

vorweg [fo:r'vɛk] ad in advance; V—nahme f -, -n anticipation; —nehmen vt irreg anticipate.

vorweisen ['fo:rvaızən] vt irreg show, produce.

vorwerfen ['fo:rvɛrfən] vt irreg: jdm etw — reproach sb for sth, accuse sb of sth; sich (dat) nichts vorzuwerfen haben have nothing to reproach o.s. with.

vorwiegend ['fo:rvi:gənt] a,ad predominant(ly).

Vorwitz ['fo:rvıts] m cheek; v—ig a saucy, cheeky.

Vorwort ['fo:rvɔrt] nt -(e)s, -e preface.

Vorwurf ['fo:rvʊrf] m reproach; jdm/sich Vorwürfe machen reproach sb/o.s.; v—svoll a reproachful.

vorzeigen ['fo:rtsaɪɡən] vt show, produce.
vorzeitig ['fo:rtsaɪtıç] a premature.
vorziehen ['fo:rtsi:ən] vt irreg pull forward; Gardinen draw; (lieber haben) prefer.
Vorzug ['fo:rtsu:k] m preference; (gute Eigenschaft) merit, good quality; (Vorteil) advantage; (Rail) relief train.
vorzüglich [fo:r'tsy:klıç] a excellent, first-rate.

vulgär [vʊl'ɡɛ:r] a vulgar.
Vulkan [vʊl'ka:n] m -s, -e volcano; **v-isieren** vt vulcanize.

W

W, w [ve:] nt W, w.
Waage ['va:ɡə] f -, -n scales pl; (Astrol) Libra; **w-recht** a horizontal.
wabb(e)lig ['vab(ə)lıç] a wobbly.
Wabe ['va:bə] f -, -n honeycomb.
wach [vax] a awake; (fig) alert; **W-e** f -, -n guard; **watch**; **w-e halten** keep watch; **W-e stehen** stand guard; **-en** vi be awake; (W-e halten) guard.
Wacholder [va'xɔldər] m -s, - juniper.
Wachs [vaks] nt -es, -e wax.
wachsam ['vaxza:m] a watchful, vigilant, alert; **W-keit** f vigilance.
Wachs- cpd: **w-en** vi irreg grow; vt Skier wax; **-tuch** nt oilcloth; **-tum** nt -s growth.
Wächter ['vɛçtər] m -s, - guard, warder, keeper; (Parkplatz—) attendant.
Wacht- [vaxt] cpd: **-meister** m officer; **-posten** m guard, sentry.
wackel- ['vakəl] cpd: **-ig** a shaky, wobbly; **W-kontakt** m loose connection; **-n** vi shake; (fig: Position) be shaky.
wacker ['vakər] a valiant, stout; ad well, bravely.
Wade ['va:də] f -, -n (Anat) calf.
Waffe ['vafə] f -, -n weapon; **-l** f -, -n waffle; wafer; **-nschein** m gun licence; **-nstillstand** m armistice, truce.
Wagemut ['va:ɡəmu:t] m daring.
wagen ['va:ɡən] vt venture, dare.
Wagen ['va:ɡən] m -s, - vehicle; (Auto) car; (Rail) carriage; (Pferde—) cart; **-führer** m driver; **-heber** m -s, - jack.
Waggon [va'ɡõ] m -s, -s carriage; (Güter—) goods van, freight truck (US).
waghalsig ['va:khalzıç] a foolhardy.
Wagnis ['va:knıs] nt -ses, -se risk.
Wahl [va:l] f -, -en choice; (Pol) election; zweite — seconds pl; **w-berechtigt** a entitled to vote.
wähl- ['vɛ:l] cpd: **-bar** a eligible; **-en** vti choose; (Pol) elect, vote (for); (Tel) dial; **W-er(in** f) m -s, - voter; **-erisch** a fastidious, particular; **W-erschaft** f electorate.
Wahl- cpd: **-fach** nt optional subject; **-gang** m ballot; **-kabine** f polling booth; **-kampf** m election campaign; **-kreis** m constituency; **-liste** f electoral register; **-lokal** nt polling station; **w-los** ad at random; **-recht** nt franchise; **-spruch** m motto; **-urne** f ballot box.

Wahn [va:n] *m* -(e)s delusion; folly; —sinn *m* madness; w—sinnig *a* insane, mad; *ad (col)* incredibly.

wahr [va:r] *a* true; —en *vt* maintain, keep.

währen [vɛːrən] *vi* last; —d *prep* +gen during; *cj* while; —ddessen [vɛːrant'dɛsən] *ad* meanwhile.

wahr- cpd: —haben *vt irreg*: etw nicht —haben wollen refuse to admit sth; —haft *ad* (tatsächlich) truly; —haftig [va:r'haftɪç] a true, real; *ad* really; W—heit *f* truth; —nehmen *vt irreg* perceive, observe; W—nehmung *f* perception; —sagen *vi* prophesy, tell fortunes; W—sager(in *f*) *m* -s, - fortune teller; —scheinlich [va:r'ʃaɪnlɪç] a probable; *ad* probably; W—'scheinlichkeit *f* probability; aller W—scheinlichkeit nach in all probability; W—zeichen *nt* emblem.

Währung [vɛːruŋ] *f* currency.

Waise [vaɪzə] *f* -, -n orphan; —nhaus *nt* orphanage; —nkind *nt* orphan.

Wald [valt] *m* -(e)s, "er wood(s); (groß) forest; w—ig [valdɪç] a wooded.

Wäldchen [vɛltçən] *nt* copse, grove.

Wal(fisch) [va:l(fɪʃ)] *m* -(e)s, -e whale.

Wall [val] *m* -(e)s, "e embankment; (Bollwerk) rampart; w—fahren *vi irreg insep* go on a pilgrimage; —fahrer(in *f*) *m* pilgrim; —fahrt *f* pilgrimage.

Wal- [val] cpd: —nuß *f* walnut; —roß *nt* walrus.

Walze [valtsə] *f* -, -n (Gerät) cylinder; (Fahrzeug) roller; w—n *vt* roll (out).

wälzen [vɛltsən] *vt* roll (over); Bücher hunt through; Probleme deliberate on; *vr* wallow; (vor Schmerzen) roll about; (im Bett) toss and turn.

Walzer [valtsər] *m* -s, - waltz.

Wälzer [vɛltsər] *m* -s, - (col) tome.

Wand [vant] *f* -, "e wall; (Trenn—) partition; (Berg—) precipice.

Wandel [vandəl] *m* -s change; w—bar a changeable, variable; w—n *vtr* change; *vi* (gehen) walk.

Wander- [vandər] cpd: —bühne *f* travelling theatre; —er *m* -s, -, hiker, rambler; w—n *vi* hike; (Blick) wander; (Gedanken) stray; —preis *m* challenge trophy; —schaft *f* travelling; —ung *f* walking tour, hike.

Wand- cpd: —lung *f* change, transformation; (Rel) transubstantiation; —schirm *m* (folding) screen; —schrank *m* cupboard; —teppich *m* tapestry; —verkleidung *f* wainscoting.

Wange [vaŋə] *f* -, -n cheek.

wankelmütig [vaŋkəlmy:tɪç] a vacillating, inconstant.

wanken [vankən] *vi* stagger; (fig) waver.

wann [van] *ad* when.

Wanne [vanə] *f* -, -n tub.

Wanze [vantsə] *f* -, -n bug.

Wappen [vapən] *nt* -s, - coat of arms, crest; —kunde *f* heraldry.

Ware [va:rə] *f* -, -n ware; —nhaus *nt* department store; —nlager *nt* stock, store; —nprobe *f* sample; —nzeichen *nt* trademark.

warm [varm] *a* warm; Essen hot.

Wärm- [vɛrm] cpd: —e *f* -, warmth; w—en *vtr* warm, heat; —flasche *f* hot-water bottle.

warm- *cpd:* **—herzig** *a* warm-hearted; **—laufen** *vi irreg (Aut)* warm up; **W—'wassertank** *m* hot-water tank.

warnen ['varnən] *vt* warn.

Warnung *f* warning.

warten ['vartən] *vi* wait *(auf +acc* for); **auf sich — lassen** take a long time.

Wärter(in *f)* ['vɛrtər(ɪn)] *m -s, -* attendant.

Warte- ['vartə] *cpd:* **—saal** *m (Rail),* **—zimmer** *nt* waiting room.

Wartung *f* servicing, service.

warum [va'rʊm] *ad* why.

Warze [vartsə] *f -, -n* wart.

was [vas] *pron* what; *(col: etwas)* something.

Wasch- ['vaʃ] *cpd:* **w—bar** *a* washable; **—becken** *nt* washbasin; **w—echt** *a* colourfast; *(fig)* genuine.

Wäsche ['vɛʃə] *f -, -n* wash(ing); *(Bett—)* linen; *(Unter—)* underclothing; **—klammer** *f* clothes peg, clothespin *(US);* **—leine** *f* washing line.

waschen ['vaʃən] *irreg vti* wash; *vr* (have a) wash; **sich** *(dat)* **die Hände** — wash one's hands; **— und legen Haare** shampoo and set.

Wäsche- *cpd:* **—rei** *f* laundry; **—schleuder** *f* spin-drier.

Wasch- *cpd:* **—küche** *f* laundry room; **—lappen** *m* face flannel, washcloth *(US);* *(col)* sissy; **—maschine** *f* washing machine; **—mittel** *nt,* **—pulver** *nt* detergent, washing powder; **—tisch** *m* washhand basin.

Wasser ['vasər] *nt -s, -* water; **w—dicht** *a* watertight, waterproof; **—fall** *m* waterfall; **—farbe** *f* watercolour; **w—gekühlt** *a (Aut)* watercooled; **—hahn** *m* tap, faucet *(US).*

wässerig ['vɛsərɪç] *a* watery.

Wasser- *cpd:* **—kraftwerk** *nt* hydroelectric power station; **—leitung** *f* water pipe; **—mann** *m (Astrol)* Aquarius; **w—n** *vi* land on the water.

wässern ['vɛsərn] *vti* water.

Wasser- *cpd:* **w—scheu** *a* afraid of the water; **—schi** *nt* water-skiing; **—stand** *m* water level; **—stoff** *m* hydrogen; **—stoffbombe** *f* hydrogen bomb; **—waage** *f* spirit level; **—welle** *f* shampoo and set; **—zeichen** *nt* watermark.

waten ['va:tən] *vi* wade.

watscheln ['va:tʃəln] *vi* waddle.

Watt [vat] *nt -(e)s, -en* mud flats *pl; nt -s, - (Elec)* watt; **—e** *f -, -n* cotton wool, absorbent cotton *(US);* **w—ieren** [va'ti:rən] *vt* pad.

Web- ['ve:b] *cpd:* **w—en** *vt irreg* weave; **—er** *m -s, -* weaver; **—e'rei** *f (Betrieb)* weaving mill; **—stuhl** *m* loom.

Wechsel ['vɛksəl] *m -s, -* change; *(Comm)* bill of exchange; **—beziehung** *f* correlation; **—geld** *nt* change; **w—haft** *a* Wetter variable; **—jahre** *pl* change of life; **—kurs** *m* rate of exchange; **w—n** *vt* change; *Blicke* exchange; *vi* change; vary; *(Geld —)* have change; **—strom** *m* alternating current; **—wirkung** *f* interaction.

wecken ['vɛkən] *vt* wake (up); call.

Wecker ['vɛkər] *m -s, -* alarm clock.

wedeln ['ve:dəln] *vi (mit Schwanz)* wag; *(mit Fächer)* fan; *(Ski)* wedeln.

weder ['ve:dər] *cj* neither; **— . . . noch . . .** neither . . . nor . . .

weg [vɛk] *ad* away, off; **über etw** *(acc)* **— sein** be over sth; **er war schon — he** had already left;

Finger —! hands off!; W— ['ve:k] *m* -(e)s, -e way; (*Pfad*) path; (*Route*) route; sich auf den W— machen be on one's way; jdm aus dem W— gehen keep out of sb's way; W—bereiter *m* -s, - pioneer; —blasen *vt irreg* blow away; —bleiben *vi irreg* stay away.

wegen ['ve:gən] *prep* +*gen or* (*col*) *dat* because of.

weg- ['vɛk] *cpd*: —fahren *vi irreg* drive away; leave; —fallen *vi irreg* be left out; (*Ferien, Bezahlung*) be cancelled; (*aufhören*) cease; —gehen *vi irreg* go away; leave; —jagen *vt* chase away; —lassen *vt irreg* leave out; —laufen *vi irreg* run away or off; —legen *vt* put aside; —machen *vt* (*col*) get rid of; —müssen *vi irreg* (*col*) have to go; —nehmen *vt irreg* take away; —räumen *vt* clear away; —schaffen *vt* clear away; —schnappen *vt* snatch away (*jdm etw* sth from sb); —tun *vt irreg* put away; —weiser ['ve:gvaɪzər] *m* -s, - road sign, signpost; —werfen *vt irreg* throw away; —werfend *a* disparaging; —ziehen *vi irreg* move away.

weh [ve:] *a* sore; — tun hurt, be sore; jdm/sich — tun hurt sb/o.s.; —(e) *interj*: —(e), wenn du ... woe betide you if ...; o —! oh dear!; W—e *f* -, -n drift; —en *vti* blow; (*Fahnen*) flutter; W—en *pl* (*Med*) labour pains *pl*; —klagen *vi insep* wail; —leidig *a* whiny, whining; W—mut *f* - melancholy; —mütig *a* melancholy.

Wehr [ve:r] *nt* -(e)s, -e weir; *f*: sich zur — setzen defend o.s.; —dienst *m* military service; *vr* defend o.s.; —los *a* defenceless; —macht *f* armed forces *pl*;

—pflicht *f* compulsory military service; w—pflichtig *a* liable for military service.

Weib [vaɪp] *nt* -(e)s, -er woman, female; wife; —chen *nt* female; w—isch ['vaɪbɪʃ] *a* sissyish; —lich *a* feminine.

weich [vaɪç] *a* soft; W—e *f* -, -n (*Rail*) points *pl*; —en *vi irreg* yield, give away; W—ensteller *m* -s, - pointsman; W—heit *f* softness; —lich *a* soft, namby-pamby; W—ling *m* weakling.

Weide ['vaɪdə] *f* -, -n (*Baum*) willow; (*Gras*) pasture; w—n *vi* graze; *vr*: sich an etw (*dat*) w—n delight in sth.

weidlich ['vaɪtlɪç] *ad* thoroughly.

weigern ['vaɪgərn] *vr* refuse.

Weigerung ['vaɪgərʊŋ] *f* refusal.

Weih- ['vaɪ] *cpd*: —e *f* -, -n consecration; (*Priester*—) ordination; w—en *vt* consecrate; ordain; —er *m* -s, - pond; —nacht *f* -, —nachten *nt* - Christmas; w—nachtlich *a* Christmas; —nachtsabend *m* Christmas Eve; —nachtslied *nt* Christmas carol; —nachtsmann *m* Father Christmas, Santa Claus; zweiter —nachtstag *m* Boxing Day; —rauch *m* incense; —wasser *nt* holy water.

weil [vaɪl] *cj* because.

Weile ['vaɪlə] *f* - while, short time.

Wein [vaɪn] *m* -(e)s, -e wine; (*Pflanze*) vine; —bau *m* cultivation of vines; —beere *f* grape; —berg *m* vineyard; —bergschnecke *f* snail; —brand *m* brandy; w—en *vti* cry; das ist zum —en it's enough to make you cry or weep; w—erlich *a* tearful; —geist *m* spirits of wine; —lese *f* vintage; —rebe *f* vine; —stein *m* tartar; —stock *m* vine; —traube *f* grape.

weise ['vaɪzə] a wise; **W—(r)** mf wise old man/woman, sage.

Weise ['vaɪzə] f -, -n manner, way; (Lied) tune; **auf diese —** in this way; **w—n** vt irreg show.

Weisheit ['vaɪshaɪt] f wisdom; **—zahn** m wisdom tooth.

weiß [vaɪs] a white; **W—brot** nt white bread; **—en** vt whitewash; **W—glut** f (Tech) incandescence; **jdn bis zur W—glut bringen** (fig) make sb see red; **W—kohl** m (white) cabbage; **W—wein** m white wine.

Weisung ['vaɪzʊŋ] f instruction.

weit [vaɪt] a wide; Begriff broad; Reise, Wurf long; **wie — ist es . . .?** how far is it . . .?; **in —er Ferne** in the far distance; **das geht zu —** that's going too far; ad far; **—aus** ad by far; **—blickend** a far-seeing; **W—e** f -, -n width; (Raum) space; (von Entfernung) distance; **—en** vtr widen.

weiter ['vaɪtər] a wider; broader; farther (away); (zusätzlich) further; **ohne —es** without further ado; just like that; ad further; **—nichts/niemand** nothing/nobody else; **—arbeiten** vi go on working; **—bilden** vr continue one's studies; **—empfehlen** vt irreg recommend (to others); **W—fahrt** f continuation of the journey; **—gehen** vi irreg go on; **—hin** ad: **etw —hin tun** go on doing sth; **—leiten** vt pass on; **—machen** vti continue; **—reisen** vi continue one's journey.

weit— cpd: **—gehend** a considerable; ad largely; **—läufig** a Gebäude spacious; Erklärung lengthy; Verwandter distant; **—schweifig** a long-winded; **—sichtig** a (lit) long-sighted; (fig)

far-sighted; **W—sprung** m long jump; **—verbreitet** a widespread; **W—winkelobjektiv** nt (Phot) wide-angle lens.

Weizen ['vaɪtsən] m -s, - wheat.

welch [vɛlç] pron: **— ein(e) . . .** what a . . .; **—e** indef pron (col: einige) some; **—e(r,s)** rel pron (für Personen) who; (für Sachen) which; interrog pron (adjektivisch) which; (substantivisch) which one.

welk [vɛlk] a withered; **—en** vi wither.

Well- [vɛl] cpd: **—blech** nt corrugated iron; **—e** f -, -n wave; (Tech) shaft; **—enbereich** m waveband; **—enbrecher** m -s, - breakwater; **—enlänge** f (lit, fig) wavelength; **—enlinie** f wavy line; **—ensittich** m budgerigar; **—pappe** f corrugated cardboard.

Welt [vɛlt] f -, -en world; **—all** nt universe; **—anschauung** f philosophy of life; **w—berühmt** a world-famous; **w—fremd** a unworldly; **—krieg** m world war; **w—lich** a worldly; (nicht kirchlich) secular; **—macht** f world power; **w—männisch** a sophisticated; **—meister** m world champion; **—raum** m space; **—reise** f trip round the world; **—stadt** f metropolis; **w—weit** a world-wide; **—wunder** nt wonder of the world.

wem [veːm] pron (dat) to whom.

wen [veːn] pron (acc) whom.

Wende ['vɛndə] f -, -n turn; (Veränderung) change; **—kreis** m (Geog) tropic; (Aut) turning circle; **—ltreppe** f spiral staircase; **w—n** vtir irreg turn; **sich an jdn w—n** go/come to sb; **—punkt** m turning point.

Wendung f turn; (Rede—) idiom.

wenig ['ve:nɪç] *a,ad* little; **—e** ['ve:nɪgə] *pl* few *pl*; **W—keit** *f* trifle; **meine W—keit** yours truly, little me; **—ste(r,s)** *a* least; **—stens** *ad* at least.

wenn [vɛn] *cj* if; *(zeitlich)* when; **— auch ...;** even if **...;** **— ich doch ...** if only I **...;** **—schon** *ad*: na **—schon** so what?; **—schon, dennschon!** if a thing's worth doing, it's worth doing properly.

wer [ve:r] *pron* who.

Werbe- ['vɛrbə] *cpd*: **—fernsehen** *nt* commercial television; **—kampagne** *f* advertising campaign; **w—n** *irreg vt* win; *(Mitglied)* recruit; *vi* advertise; **um jdn/etw w—n** try to win sb/sth; **für jdn/etw w—n** promote sb/sth.

Werbung *f* advertising; *(von Mitgliedern)* recruitment; *(um jdn/etw)* promotion *(um of)*.

Werdegang ['ve:rdəgaŋ] *m* development; *(beruflich)* career.

werden ['ve:rdən] *vi irreg* become; *v aux (Futur)* shall, will; *(Passiv)* be; **was ist aus ihm/aus der Sache geworden?** what became of him/it?; **es ist nichts/gut geworden** it came to nothing/turned out well; **mir wird kalt** I'm getting cold; **das muß anders —** that will have to change; **zu Eis —** turn to ice.

werfen ['vɛrfən] *vt irreg* throw.

Werft [vɛrft] *f* **-, -en** shipyard, dockyard.

Werk [vɛrk] *nt* **-(e)s, -e** work; *(Tätigkeit)* job; *(Fabrik, Mechanismus)* works *pl*; **ans —gehen** set to work; **—statt** *f* **-, -stätten** workshop; *(Aut)* garage; **—student** *m* self-supporting student; **—tag** *m* working day; **w—tags** *ad* on working days; **w—tägig** *a* working; **—zeug** *nt*

tool; **—zeugschrank** *m* tool chest.

Wermut ['ve:rmu:t] *m* **-(e)s** wormwood; *(Wein)* vermouth.

Wert [ve:rt] *m* **-(e)s, -e** worth; *(Fin)* value; **— legen auf** (+*acc*) attach importance to; **es hat doch keinen —** it's useless; **w— a** worth; *(geschätzt)* dear; worthy; **das ist nichts/viel w—** it's not worth anything/it's worth a lot; **das ist es/er mir w—** it's/he's worth that to me; **—angabe** *f* declaration of value; **w—en** *vt* rate; **—gegenstand** *m* article of value; **w—los** *a* worthless; **—losigkeit** *f* worthlessness; **—papier** *nt* security; **w—voll a** valuable; **—zuwachs** *m* appreciation.

Wesen ['ve:zən] *nt* **-s, -** *(Geschöpf)* being; *(Natur, Character)* nature; **w—tlich** *a* significant; *(beträchtlich)* considerable.

weshalb [vɛs'halp] *ad* why.

Wespe ['vɛspə] *f* **-, -n** wasp.

wessen ['vɛsən] *pron (gen)* whose.

West- [vɛst] *cpd*: **—e** *f* **-, -n** waistcoat, vest *(US)*; *(Woll—)* cardigan; **—en** *m* **-s** west; **w—lich** *a* western; *ad* to the west; **w—wärts** *ad* westwards.

weswegen [vɛs've:gən] *ad* why.

wett [vɛt] *a* even; **W—bewerb** *m* competition; **W—e** *f* **-, -n** bet, wager; **W—eifer** *m* rivalry; **—en** *vti* bet.

Wetter ['vɛtər] *nt* **-s, -** weather; **—bericht** *m* weather report; **—dienst** *m* meteorological service; **—lage** *f* (weather) situation; **—vorhersage** *f* weather forecast; **—warte** *f* **-, -n** weather station; **w—wendisch** *a* capricious.

Wett- *cpd*: **—kampf** *m* contest; **—lauf** *m* race; **w—laufen** *vi irreg* race; w—machen vt make good; —spiel nt match; —streit m contest.

wetzen ['vɛtsən] vt sharpen.

Wicht [vɪçt] m -(e)s, -e titch; (pej) worthless creature; w—ig a important; —igkeit f importance.

wickeln ['vɪkəln] vt wind; Haare set; Kind change; jdn/etw in etw (acc) — wrap sb/sth in sth.

Widder ['vɪdər] m -s, - ram; (Astrol) Aries.

wider ['vi:dər] prep +acc against; —'fahren vi irreg happen (jdm to sb); —'legen vt refute.

widerlich ['vi:dərlɪç] a disgusting, repulsive. W—keit f repulsiveness.

wider- ['vi:dər] cpd: —rechtlich a unlawful; W—rede f contradiction.

Widerruf ['vi:dərru:f] m retraction; countermanding; w—en [vi:dər'ru:fən] vt irreg irreg retract; Anordnung revoke; Befehl countermand.

wider'setzen vr insep oppose (jdm/etw sb/sth).

widerspenstig ['vi:dərʃpɛnstɪç] a wilful; W—keit f wilfulness.

widerspiegeln ['vi:dərʃpi:gəln] vt reflect.

wider'sprechen vi irreg insep contradict (jdm sb); —d a contradictory.

Widerspruch ['vi:dərʃprʊx] m contradiction; w—slos ad without arguing.

Widerstand ['vi:dərʃtant] m resistance; —sbewegung f resistance (movement); w—sfähig a resistant, tough; w—slos a unresisting.

wider'stehen vi irreg insep withstand (jdm/etw sb/sth).

Wider- ['vi:dər] cpd: —streit m conflict; w—wärtig a nasty, horrid;

—wille m aversion (gegen to); w—willig a unwilling, reluctant.

widmen ['vɪtmən] vt dedicate; vr devote (o.s.).

Widmung f dedication.

widrig ['vi:drɪç] a Umstände adverse; Mensch repulsive.

wie [vi:] ad how; cj — ich schon sagte as I said; (so) schön — . . as beautiful as . . .; — du like you; singen — ein . . . sing like a . . .

wieder ['vi:dər] ad again; — da sein be back (again); gehst du schon —? are you off again?; — einmal another . . . ; W—aufbau [-'aufbau] m rebuilding; W—aufnahme [-'aufna:mə] f resumption; —aufnehmen vt irreg resume; —bekommen vt irreg get back; —bringen vt irreg bring back; —erkennen vt irreg recognize; W—erstattung f reimbursement; W—gabe f reproduction; —geben vt irreg (zurückgeben) return; Erzählung etc repeat; Gefühle etc convey; —gutmachen ['-'gu:tmaxən] vt make up for Fehler put right; W—'gutmachung f reparation; —'herstellen vt restore; —'holen vt insep repeat; W—holung f repetition; W—hören nt : auf W—hören (Tel) goodbye; W—kehr f - return; (von Vorfall) repetition, recurrence; W—kunft f -, ¨-e return; —sehen vt irreg see again; auf W—sehen goodbye; —um ad again; (andererseits) on the other hand; —vereinigen vt reunite; W—wahl f re-election.

Wiege ['vi:gə] f -, -n cradle; w—n vt (schaukeln) rock; vti irreg (Gewicht) weigh; —nfest nt birthday.

wiehern ['viːərn] *vi* neigh, whinny.

Wiese ['viːzə] *f* -, -n meadow; —l *nt* -s, - weasel.

wieso [viːˈzoː] *ad* why.

wieviel [viːˈfiːl] *a* how much; — Menschen how many people; —mal *ad* how often; —te(r,s) *a*: zum —ten Mal? how many times?; den W—ten haben wir? what's the date?; an —ter Stelle? in what place?; der —te Besucher war er? how many visitors were there before him?

wieweit [viːˈvait] *ad* to what extent.

wild [vilt] *a* wild; W— *nt* -(e)s game; —ern ['vildərn] *vi* poach; —fremd *a (col)* quite strange *or* unknown; W—heit *f* wildness; W—leder *nt* suede; W—nis *f* -, -se wilderness; W—schwein *nt* (wild) boar.

Wille ['vilə] *m* -ns, -n will; W—n *prep* +gen: um ... w—n for the sake of ...; w—nlos a weak-willed; w—nsstark a strong-willed.

will- *cpd:* —ig a willing; —kommen [vilˈkɔmən] a welcome; jdn —kommen heißen welcome sb; W—kommen *nt* -s, - welcome; —kürlich a arbitrary; Bewegung voluntary.

wimmeln ['vɪməln] *vi* swarm (von with).

wimmern ['vɪmərn] *vi* whimper.

Wimper ['vɪmpər] *f* -, -n eyelash.

Wind [vɪnt] *m* -(e)s, -e wind; —beutel *m* cream puff; (fig) windbag; —e ['vɪndə] *f* -, -n (Tech) winch, windlass; (Bot) bindweed; —el ['vɪndəl] *f* -, -n nappy, diaper (US); w—en ['vɪndən] *vi impers* be windy; *irreg vt* wind; Kranz weave; (ent—) twist; *vr* wind; (Person) writhe; —hose *f* whirlwind; —hund *m* greyhound;

(Mensch) fly-by-night; w—ig ['vɪndɪç] a windy; (fig) dubious; —mühle *f* windmill; —pocken *pl* chickenpox; —schutzscheibe *f* (Aut) windscreen, windshield (US); —stärke *f* wind force; —stille *f* calm; —stoß *m* gust of wind.

Wink [vɪŋk] *m* -(e)s, -e hint; (mit Kopf) nod; (mit Hand) wave.

Winkel ['vɪŋkəl] *m* -s, - (Math) angle; (Gerät) set square; (in Raum) corner.

winken ['vɪŋkən] *vti* wave.

winseln ['vɪnzəln] *vi* whine.

Winter ['vɪntər] *m* -s, - winter; w—lich a wintry; —sport *m* winter sports *pl*.

Winzer ['vɪntsər] *m* -s, - vine grower.

winzig ['vɪntsɪç] a tiny.

Wipfel ['vɪpfəl] *m* -s, - treetop.

wir [viːr] *pron* we; — alle all of us, we all.

Wirbel ['vɪrbəl] *m* -s, - whirl, swirl; (Trubel) hurly-burly; (Aufsehen) fuss; (Anat) vertebra; w—n *vi* whirl, swirl; —säule *f* spine; —tier *nt* vertebrate; —wind *m* whirlwind.

wirken ['vɪrkən] *vi* have an effect; (erfolgreich sein) work; (scheinen) seem; *vt* Wunder work.

wirklich ['vɪrklɪç] a real; W—keit *f* reality.

wirksam ['vɪrkzaːm] a effective; W—keit *f* effectiveness, efficacy.

Wirkung ['vɪrkʊŋ] *f* effect; w—slos a ineffective; w—slos bleiben have no effect; w—svoll a effective.

wirr [vɪr] a confused, wild; W—en *pl* disturbances *pl*; W—warr [-var] *m* -s disorder, chaos.

Wirsing(kohl) ['vɪrzɪŋ(koːl)] *m* **-s** savoy cabbage.

Wirt [vɪrt] *m* **-(e)s, -e** landlord; **—in** *f* landlady; **—schaft** *f* (*Gaststätte*) pub; (*Haushalt*) housekeeping; (*col: Durcheinander*) mess; **w—schaftlich** *a* economical; (*Pol*) economic; **—schaftskrise** *f* economic crisis; **—schaftsprüfer** *m* chartered accountant; **—schaftswunder** *nt* economic miracle; **—shaus** *nt* inn.

Wisch [vɪʃ] *m* **-(e)s, -e** scrap of paper; **w—en** *vt* wipe; **—er** *m* **-s, -** (*Aut*) wiper.

wispern ['vɪspərn] *vti* whisper.

Wißbegier(de) ['vɪsbəɡiːr(də)] *f* thirst for knowledge; **w—ig** *a* inquisitive, eager for knowledge.

wissen ['vɪsən] *vt irreg* know; **W— nt -s** knowledge; **W—schaft** *f* science; **W—schaftler(in** *f*) *m* **-s, -** scientist; **—schaftlich** *a* scientific; **—swert** *a* worth knowing; **—tlich** *a* knowing.

wittern ['vɪtərn] *vt* scent; (*fig*) suspect.

Witterung *f* weather; (*Geruch*) scent.

Witwe ['vɪtvə] *f* **-, -n** widow; **—r** *m* **-s, -** widower.

Witz [vɪts] *m* **-es, -e** joke; **—blatt** *nt* comic (paper); **—bold** *m* **-(e)s, -e** joker, wit; **w—eln** *vi* joke; **w—ig** *a* funny.

wo [voː] *ad* where; (*col: irgendwo*) somewhere; **im Augenblick, — . . .** the moment (that) **. . .;** *cj* (*wenn*) **— . . . the time when . . .;** **—anders** [voː"andərs] *ad* elsewhere; **—bei** [voː'baɪ] *ad* (*rel*) by/with which; (*interrog*) what . . . in/by/with**.**

Woche ['vɔxə] *f* **-, -n** week; **—nende** *nt* weekend; **w—nlang** *a*,*ad* for weeks; **—nschau** *f* newsreel.

wöchentlich ['vœçəntlɪç] *a*,*ad* weekly.

wo- *cpd:* **—durch** [voː'durç] *ad* (*rel*) through which; (*interrog*) what . . . through; **—für** [voː'fyːr] *ad* (*rel*) for which; (*interrog*) what . . . for.

Woge ['voːɡə] *f* **-, -n** wave; **w—n** *vi* heave, surge.

wo- *cpd:* **—gegen** [voː'ɡeːɡən] *ad* (*rel*) against which; (*interrog*) what . . . against; **—her** [voː'heːr] *ad* where . . . from; **—hin** [voː'hɪn] *ad* where . . . to.

wohl [voːl] *ad* well; (*behaglich*) at ease, comfortable; (*vermutlich*) I suppose, probably; (*gewiß*) certainly; **er weiß das —** he knows that perfectly well; **W— nt -(e)s** welfare; **zum W—!** cheers!; **—auf** [voː'"auf] *ad* well; **W—behagen** *nt* comfort; **—behalten** *ad* safe and sound; **W—fahrt** *f* welfare; **—habend** *a* wealthy; **—ig** *a* contented, comfortable; **W—klang** *m* melodious sound; **—schmeckend** *a* delicious; **W—stand** *m* prosperity; **W—standsgesellschaft** *f* affluent society; **W—tat** *f* relief; act of charity; **W—täter(in** *f*) *m* benefactor; **—tätig** *a* charitable; **—tun** *vi irreg* do good (*jdm sb*); **—verdient** *a* well-earned, well-deserved; **—weislich** *ad* prudently; **W—wollen** *nt* **-s** good will; **—wollend** *a* benevolent.

wohn- ['voːn] *cpd:* **—en** *vi* live; **—haft** *a* resident; **—lich** *a* comfortable; **W—ort** *m* domicile; **W—sitz** place of residence; **W—ung** *f* house; (*Etagen—*) flat, apartment (*US*); **W—ungsnot** *f* housing shortage; W—wagen *m* caravan; W—zimmer *nt* living room.

wölben ['vœlbən] *vtr* curve.

Wölbung *f* curve.

Wolf [vɔlf] *m* -(e)s, ʔe wolf.

Wölfin ['vœlfɪn] *f* she-wolf.

Wolke ['vɔlkə] *f* -, -n cloud; —nkratzer *m* skyscraper.

wolkig ['vɔlkɪç] *a* cloudy.

Wolle ['vɔlə] *f* -, -n wool; w—n *a* woollen.

wollen ['vɔlən] *vti* want.

wollüstig ['vɔlʏstɪç] *a* lusty, sensual.

wo- *cpd*: —mit [vo:'mɪt] *ad (rel)* with which; *(interrog)* what . . . with; —möglich [vo:'mø:klɪç] *ad* probably, I suppose; —nach [vo:'na:x] *ad (rel)* after/for which; *(interrog)* what . . . for/after.

Wonne ['vɔnə] *f* -, -n joy, bliss.

wo- *cpd*: —ran [vo:'ran] *ad (rel)* on/at which; *(interrog)* what . . . on/at; —rauf [vo:'rauf] *ad (rel)* on which; *(interrog)* what . . . on; —raus [vo:'raus] *ad (rel)* from/out of which; *(interrog)* what . . . from/out of; —rin [vo:'rɪn] *ad (rel)* in which; *(interrog)* what . . . in.

Wort [vɔrt] *nt* -(e)s, ʔer -e word; jdn beim — nehmen take sb at his word; w—brüchig *a* not true to one's word.

Wörterbuch ['vœrtərbuːx] *nt* dictionary.

Wort- *cpd*: —führer *m* spokesman; w—getreu *a* true to one's word; *Übersetzung* literal; w—karg *a* taciturn; —laut *m* wording.

wörtlich ['vœrtlɪç] *a* literal.

Wort- *cpd*: w—los *a* mute; w—reich *a* wordy, verbose;

—schatz *m* vocabulary; —spiel *nt* play on words, pun; —wechsel *m* dispute.

wo- *cpd*: —rüber [vo:'ry:bər] *ad (rel)* over/about which; *(interrog)* what . . . over/about; —rum [vo:'rum] *ad (rel)* about/round which; *(interrog)* what . . . about/round; —runter [vo:'runtər] *ad (rel)* under which; *(interrog)* what . . . under; —von [vo:'fɔn] *ad (rel)* from which; *(interrog)* what . . . from; —vor [vo:'fo:r] *ad (rel)* in front of/before which; *(interrog)* in front of/before what; of what; —zu [vo:'tsu:] *ad (rel)* to/for which; *(interrog)* what . . . for/to; *(warum)* why.

Wrack [vrak] *nt* -(e)s, -s wreck.

wringen ['vrɪŋən] *vt irreg* wring.

Wucher ['vuːxər] *m* -s profiteering; —er *m* -s, - profiteer; w—isch *a* profiteering; w—n *vi* (*Pflanzen*) grow wild; —ung *f* (*Med*) growth, tumour.

Wuchs [vu:ks] *m* -es (*Wachstum*) growth; (*Statur*) build.

Wucht [vuxt] *f* - force; w—ig *a* solid, massive.

wühlen ['vy:lən] *vi* scrabble; (*Tier*) root; (*Maulwurf*) burrow; (*col: arbeiten*) slave away; *vt* dig.

Wulst [vulst] -es, ʔe bulge; (*an Wunde*) swelling.

wund [vunt] *a* sore, raw; W—e ['vundə] *f* -, -n wound.

Wunder ['vundər] *nt* -s, - miracle; es ist kein — it's no wonder; w—bar *a* wonderful, marvellous; —kind *nt* infant prodigy; w—lich *a* odd, peculiar; w—n *vr* be surprised (*über* + *acc* at); *vt* surprise; w—schön *a* beautiful; w—voll *a* wonderful.

Wundstarrkrampf ['vʊntʃtar-krampf] *m* tetanus, lockjaw.

Wunsch [vʊnʃ] *m* -(e)s, ˸e wish.

wünschen ['vʏnʃən] *vt* wish; **sich** *(dat)* **etw** — want sth, wish for sth; **—swert** *a* desirable.

Würde ['vʏrdə] *f* -, -n dignity; *(Stellung)* honour; **—nträger** *m* dignitary; **w—voll** *a* dignified.

würdig ['vʏrdɪç] *a* worthy; *(würdevoll)* dignified; **—en** ['vʏrdɪgən] *vt* appreciate; **jdn keines Blickes —en** not so much as look at sb.

Wurf [vʊrf] *m* -s, ˸e throw; *(Junge)* litter.

Würfel ['vʏrfəl] *m* -s, - dice; *(Math)* cube; **—becher** *m* (dice) cup; **w—n** *vi* play dice; *vt* dice; **—spiel** *nt* game of dice; **—zucker** *m* lump sugar.

würgen ['vʏrgən] *vti* choke.

Wurm [vʊrm] *m* -(e)s, ˸er worm; **w—en** *vt* *(col)* rile, nettle; **—fortsatz** *m* (Med) appendix; **w—ig** *a* worm-eaten; **—stichig** *a* worm-ridden.

Wurst [vʊrst] *f* -, ˸e sausage; **das ist mir —** *(col)* I don't care, I don't give a damn.

Würze ['vʏrtsə] *f* -, -n seasoning, spice.

Wurzel ['vʊrtsəl] *f* -, -n root.

würz- ['vʏrts] *cpd*: **—en** *vt* season, spice; **—ig** *a* spicy.

wüst [vy:st] *a* untidy, messy; *(ausschweifend)* wild; *(öde)* waste; *(col: heftig)* terrible; **W—e** *f* -, -n desert; **W—ling** *m* rake.

Wut [vu:t] *f* - rage, fury; **—anfall** *m* fit of rage.

wüten ['vy:tən] *vi* rage; **—d** *a* furious, mad.

X

X,x [ɪks] *nt* X,x.

X-Beine ['ɪksbaɪnə] *pl* knock-knees *pl*.

x-beliebig [ɪksbə'li:bɪç] *a* any *(whatever)*.

xerokopieren [kseroko'pi:rən] *vt* xerox, photocopy.

x-mal ['ɪksma:l] *ad* any number of times, n times.

Xylophon [ksylo'fo:n] *nt* -s, -e xylophone.

Y

Y,y ['ʏpsilɔn] *nt* Y,y.

Ypsilon *nt* -(s), -s the letter Y.

Z

Z,z [tsɛt] nt Z,z.
Zacke ['tsakə] f -, -n point;
(Berg—) jagged peak; (Gabel—)
prong; (Kamm—) tooth.
zackig ['tsakɪç] a jagged; (col)
smart; Tempo brisk.
zaghaft ['tsa:khaft] a timid;
Z—igkeit f timidity.
zäh [tsɛ:] a tough; Mensch
tenacious; Flüssigkeit thick;
(schleppend) sluggish; Z—igkeit f
toughness, tenacity.
Zahl [tsa:l] f -, -en number; z—bar
a payable; z—en vti pay; z—en
bitte! the bill please!
zählen ['tsɛ:lən] vti count (auf
+acc on); — zu be numbered
among.
Zahl- cpd: z—enmäßig a numerical; —er m -s, - payer.
Zähler ['tsɛ:lər] m -s, - (Tech)
meter; (Math) numerator.
Zahl- cpd: z—los a countless;
z—reich a numerous; —tag m pay-
day; —ung f payment; z—ungs-
fähig a solvent; —wort nt numeral.
zahm [tsa:m] a tame.
zähmen ['tsɛ:mən] vt tame; (fig)
curb.
Zahn [tsa:n] m -(e)s, ⁻e tooth;
—arzt m dentist; —bürste f tooth-
brush; z—en vi cut teeth; —fäule
f - tooth decay, caries; —fleisch nt
gums pl; —pasta, —paste f toothpaste; —rad nt cog(wheel);
—radbahn f rack railway;
—schmelz m (tooth) enamel;
—schmerzen pl toothache; —stein

m tartar; —stocher m -s, - tooth-
pick.
Zange [tsaŋə] f -, -n pliers pl;
(Zucker— etc) tongs pl; (Beiß—,
Zool) pincers pl; (Med) forceps pl;
—ngeburt f forceps delivery.
Zank- [tsaŋk] cpd: —apfel m bone
of contention; z—en vir quarrel.
zänkisch ['tsɛŋkɪʃ] a quarrelsome.
Zäpfchen ['tsɛpfçən] nt (Anat)
uvula; (Med) suppository.
Zapfen ['tsapfən] m -s, - plug;
(Bot) cone; (Eis—) icicle; z— vt
tap; —streich m (Mil) tattoo.
zappelig ['tsapəlɪç] a wriggly,
(unruhig) fidgety.
zappeln ['tsapəln] vi wriggle,
fidget.
zart [tsart] a (weich, leise) soft;
Braten etc tender; (fein,
schwächlich) delicate; Z—gefühl
nt tact; Z—heit f softness; tenderness; delicacy.
zärtlich ['tsɛ:rtlɪç] a tender,
affectionate; Z—keit f tenderness;
pl caresses pl.
Zauber ['tsaubər] m -s, - magic;
(—bann) spell; —ei [-'rai] f magic;
—er m -s, - magician; conjuror;
z—haft a magical, enchanting;
—künstler m conjuror; z—n vi
conjure, practise magic; —spruch
m (magic) spell.
zaudern ['tsaudərn] vi hesitate.
Zaum [tsaum] m -(e)s, Zäume
bridle; etw im — halten keep sth
in check.
Zaun [tsaun] m -(e)s, Zäune
fence; vom —(e) brechen (fig)

start ; —könig *m* wren ; —pfahl *m*: ein Wink mit dem — pfahl a broad hint.

Zeche ['tsɛçə] *f* -, -n bill; *(Bergbau)* mine.

Zecke ['tsɛkə] *f* -, -n tick.

Zehe [tseːə] *f* -, -n toe; *(Knoblauch—)* clove.

zehn [tseːn] *num* ten; —te(r,s) a tenth; **Z—tel** *nt* -s, - tenth (part).

Zeich- ['tsaɪç] cpd: —en *nt* -s, - sign; z—nen *vti* draw; *(kenn—)* mark; *(unter—)* sign; —ner *m* -s, - artist; technischer —ner draughtsman; —nung *f* drawing; *(Markierung)* markings *pl*.

Zeig- ['tsaɪg] cpd: —efinger *m* index finger; z—en *vt* show; vi point (auf +acc to, at); vr show o.s.; es wird sich z—en time will tell ; es zeigte sich, daß ... it turned out that ... ; —er *m* -s, - pointer ; *(Uhr—)* hand.

Zeile ['tsaɪlə] *f* -, -n line; *(Häuser—)* row ; —nabstand *m* line spacing.

Zeit [tsaɪt] *f* -, -en time; *(Gram)* tense; zur — at the moment; sich *(dat)* — lassen take one's time; von — zu — from time to time; —alter *nt* age; z—gemäß a in keeping with the times; —genosse *m* contemporary; z—ig à early; z—lebens *ad* all one's life; z—lich a temporal; —lupe *f* slow motion; —raffer *m* -s time-lapse photography; z—raubend a time-consuming; —raum *m* period; —rechnung *f* time, era; nach/vor unserer —rechnung A.D./B.C.; —schrift *f* periodical ; —ung *f* newspaper ; —verschwendung *f* waste of time; —vertreib *m* pastime, diversion ; z—weilig a temporary ; z—weise *ad* for a time; —wort *nt*

verb; —zeichen *nt (Rad)* time signal; —zünder *m* time fuse.

Zell- ['tsɛl] cpd: —e *f* -, -n cell; *(Telefon—)* callbox; —kern *m* cell, nucleus; —stoff *m* cellulose; —teilung *f* cell division.

Zelt [tsɛlt] *nt* -(e)s, -e tent; —bahn *f* tarpaulin, groundsheet; z—en *vi* camp.

Zement [tse'mɛnt] *m* -(e)s, -e cement; z—ieren [-'tiːrən] *vt* cement.

zensieren [tsɛn'ziːrən] *vt* censor; *(Sch)* mark.

Zensur [tsɛn'zuːr] *f* censorship; *(Sch)* mark.

Zent- cpd: —imeter [tsɛnti'meːtər] *m* or *nt* centimetre; —ner ['tsɛntnər] *m* -s, - hundredweight.

zentral [tsɛn'traːl] a central; **Z—e** *f* -, -n central office; *(Tel)* exchange; **Z—heizung** *f* central heating; —isieren [tsɛntrali'ziːrən] *vt* centralize.

Zentri- [tsɛntri] cpd: —fugalkraft [-fu'gaːlkraft] *f* centrifugal force; —fuge [-'fuːgə] *f* -, -n centrifuge; *(für Wäsche)* spin-dryer.

Zentrum ['tsɛntrʊm] *nt* -s, **Zentren** centre.

Zepter ['tsɛptər] *nt* -s, - sceptre.

zerbrech- [tsɛr'brɛç] cpd: —en *vti irreg* break; —lich a fragile.

zerbröckeln [tsɛr'brœkəln] *vti* crumble (to pieces).

zer'drücken *vt* squash, crush; *Kartoffeln* mash.

Zeremonie [tseremo'niː] *f* ceremony.

zer'fahren a scatterbrained, distracted.

Zerfall [tsɛr'fal] *m* decay; z—en *vi irreg* disintegrate, decay; *(sich gliedern)* fall (in +acc into).

zerfetzen [tsɛrˈfɛtsən] *vt* tear to pieces.

zer'fließen *vi irreg* dissolve, melt away.

zer'gehen *vi irreg* melt, dissolve.

zerkleinern [tsɛrˈklaɪnərn] *vt* reduce to small pieces.

zerleg- [tsɛrˈleːg] *cpd*: **—bar** *a* able to be dismantled; **—en** *vt* take to pieces; *Fleisch* carve; *Satz* analyse.

zerlumpt [tsɛrˈlʊmpt] *a* ragged.

zermalmen [tsɛrˈmalmən] *vt* crush.

zermürben [tsɛrˈmʏrbən] *vt* wear down.

zer'platzen *vi* burst.

zerquetschen [tsɛrˈkvɛtʃən] *vt* squash.

Zerrbild ['tsɛrbɪlt] *nt* caricature, distorted picture.

zer'reden *vt Problem* flog to death.

zer'reiben *vt irreg* grind down.

zer'reißen *irreg vt* tear to pieces; *vi* tear, rip.

zerren ['tsɛrən] *vt* drag; *vi* tug (*an* + *dat* at).

zer'rinnen *vi irreg* melt away.

zerrissen [tsɛrˈrɪsən] *a* torn, tattered; **Z—heit** *f* tattered state; *(Pol)* disunion, discord; (*innere* **—**) disintegration.

zer'rütten [tsɛrˈrʏtən] *vt* wreck, destroy.

zerrüttet *a* wrecked, shattered.

zer'schießen *vt irreg* shoot to pieces.

zer'schlagen *irreg vt* shatter, smash; *vr* fall through.

zerschleißen [tsɛrˈʃlaɪsən] *vti irreg* wear out.

zer'schneiden *vt irreg* cut up.

zer'setzen *vtr* decompose, dissolve.

zersplittern [tsɛrˈʃplɪtərn] *vti* split (into pieces); *(Glas)* shatter.

zer'springen *vi irreg* shatter, burst.

zerstäub- [tsɛrˈʃtɔʏb] *cpd*: **—en** *vt* spray; **Z—er** *m* -s, - atomizer.

zerstör- [tsɛrˈʃtøːr] *cpd*: **—en** *vt* destroy; **Z—ung** *f* destruction.

zer'stoßen *vt irreg* pound, pulverize.

zer'streiten *vr irreg* fall out, break up.

zerstreu- [tsɛrˈʃtrɔʏ] *cpd*: **—en** *vtr* disperse, scatter; *(unterhalten)* divert; *Zweifel etc* dispel; **—t** *a* scattered; *Mensch* absent-minded; **Z—theit** *f* absent-mindedness; **Z—ung** *f* dispersion; *(Ablenkung)* diversion.

zerstückeln [tsɛrˈʃtʏkəln] *vt* cut into pieces.

zer'teilen *vt* divide into parts.

zer'treten *vt irreg* crush underfoot.

zertrümmern [tsɛrˈtrʏmərn] *vt* shatter; *Gebäude etc* demolish.

Zerwürfnis [tsɛrˈvʏrfnɪs] *nt* -ses, -se dissension, quarrel.

zerzausen [tsɛrˈtsaʊzən] *vt Haare* ruffle up, tousle.

zetern ['tseːtərn] *vi* scold, shriek.

Zettel ['tsɛtəl] *m* -s, - piece of paper, slip; *(Notiz—)* note; *(Formular)* form; **—kasten** *m* card index (box).

Zeug [tsɔʏk] *nt* **-(e)s, -e** *(col)* stuff; *(Ausrüstung)* gear; **dummes —** (stupid) nonsense; **das — haben zu** have the makings of; **sich ins — legen** put one's shoulder to the wheel.

Zeuge ['tsɔʏgə] *m* -n, -n, **Zeugin** ['tsɔʏgɪn] *f* witness; **z—n** *vi* bear witness, testify; **es zeugt von . . .** it testifies to . . . ; *vt Kind* father; **—naussage** *f* evidence; **—nstand** *m* witness box.

Zeugnis ['tsɔʏgnɪs] *nt* -ses, -se certificate; *(Sch)* report; *(Referenz)* reference; *(Aussage)* evidence, testimony; — geben von be evidence of, testify to.

Zeugung ['tsɔʏgʊŋ] *f* procreation; z—sunfähig *a* sterile.

Zickzack ['tsɪktsak] *m* -(e)s, -e zigzag.

Ziege ['tsi:gə] *f* -, -n goat; —nleder *nt* kid.

Ziegel ['tsi:gəl] *m* -s, - brick; *(Dach—)* tile; —ei [-'laɪ] *f* brickworks.

ziehen ['tsi:ən] *irreg vt* draw; *(zerren)* pull; *(Schach etc)* move; *(züchten)* rear; etw nach sich — lead to sth, entail; *vi* draw; *(um—, wandern)* move; *(Rauch, Wolke etc)* drift; *(reißen)* pull; *v impers:* es zieht there is a draught, it's draughty; *vr (Gummi)* stretch; *(Grenze etc)* run; *(Gespräche etc)* be drawn out.

Ziehharmonika ['tsi:harmo:nika] *f* concertina; accordion.

Ziehung ['tsi:ʊŋ] *f (Los—)* drawing.

Ziel [tsi:l] *nt* -(e)s, -e *(einer Reise)* destination; *(Sport)* finish; *(Mil)* target; *(Absicht)* goal, aim; z—en *vi* aim *(auf +acc* at*)*; —fernrohr *nt* telescopic sight; z—los *a* aimless; —scheibe *f* target; z—strebig *a* purposeful.

ziemlich ['tsi:mlɪç] *a* quite a; fair; *ad* rather; quite a bit.

zieren ['tsi:rən] *vr* act coy.

Zier- [tsi:r] *cpd:* z—lich *a* dainty; —lichkeit *f* daintiness; —strauch *m* flowering shrub.

Ziffer [tsɪfər] *f* -, -n figure, digit; —blatt *nt* dial, clock-face.

zig [tsɪk] *a (col)* umpteen.

Zigarette [tsiga'retə] *f* cigarette; —nautomat *m* cigarette machine;

—nschachtel *f* cigarette packet; —nspitze *f* cigarette holder.

Zigarillo [tsiga'rɪlo] *nt* or *m* -s, -s cigarillo.

Zigarre [tsI'garə] *f* -, -n cigar.

Zigeuner(in *f)* [tsi'gɔʏnər(ɪn)] *m* -s, - gipsy.

Zimmer ['tsɪmər] *nt* -s, - room; —antenne *f* indoor aerial; —decke *f* ceiling; —herr *m* lodger; —lautstärke *f* reasonable volume; —mädchen *nt* chambermaid; —mann *m* carpenter; z—n *vt* make, carpenter; —pflanze *f* indoor plant.

zimperlich ['tsɪmpərlɪç] *a* squeamish; *(pingelig)* fussy, finicky.

Zimt [tsɪmt] *m* -(e)s, -e cinnamon; —stange *f* cinnamon stick.

Zink [tsɪŋk] *nt* -(e)s zinc; —e *f* -, -n *(Gabel—)* prong; *(Kamm—)* tooth; z—en *vt* Karten mark; —salbe *f* zinc ointment.

Zinn [tsɪn] *nt* -(e)s *(Element)* tin; *(in —waren)* pewter; z—oberrot [tsɪ'no:bərɔt] *a* vermilion; —soldat *m* tin soldier; —waren *pl* pewter.

Zins [tsɪns] *m* -es, -en interest; —eszins *m* compound interest; —fuß *m*, —satz *m* rate of interest; z—los *a* interest-free.

Zipfel ['tsɪpfəl] *m* -s, - corner; *(spitz)* tip; *(Hemd—)* tail; *(Wurst—)* end; —mütze *f* stocking cap; nightcap.

zirka ['tsɪrka] *ad* (round) about.

Zirkel ['tsɪrkəl] *m* -s, - circle; *(Math)* pair of compasses; —kasten *m* geometry set.

Zirkus ['tsɪrkʊs] *m* -, -se circus.

Zirrhose [tsɪ'ro:zə] *f* -, -n cirrhosis.

zischen ['tsɪʃəln] *vti* whisper.

zischen ['tsɪʃən] *vi* hiss.

Zitat [tsi'ta:t] *nt* -(e)s, -e quotation, quote.

zitieren [tsi'ti:rən] *vt* quote.

Zitronat [tsitro'na:t] *nt* -(e)s, -e candied lemon peel.

Zitrone [tsi'tro:nə] *f* -, -n lemon; —nlimonade *f* lemonade; —nsaft *m* lemon juice; —nscheibe *f* lemon slice.

zittern ['tsitərn] *vi* tremble.

Zitze [tsitsə] *f* -, -n teat, dug.

zivil [tsi'vi:l] *a* civil; Preis moderate; Z— *nt* -s plain clothes *pl*; (Mil) civilian clothing; Z—bevölkerung *f* civilian population; Z—courage *f* courage of one's convictions; Z—isation [tsivilizatsi'o:n] *f* civilization; Z—isationserscheinung *f* phenomenon of civilization; Z—isationskrankheit *f* disease peculiar to civilization; —i'sieren *vt* civilize; Z—ist [tsivi'list] *m* civilian; Z—recht *nt* civil law.

Zölibat [tsøli'ba:t] *nt or m* -(e)s celibacy.

Zoll [tsɔl] *m* -(e)s, -̈e customs *pl*: (Abgabe) duty; —abfertigung *f* customs clearance; —amt *nt* customs office; —beamte(r) *m* customs official; —erklärung *f* customs declaration; z—frei a duty-free; z—pflichtig a liable to duty, dutiable.

Zone ['tso:nə] *f* -, -n zone.

Zoo [tso:] *m* -s, -s zoo; —loge [tsoo'lo:gə] *m* -n, -n zoologist; —lo'gie *f* zoology; z—logisch *a* zoological.

Zopf [tsɔpf] *m* -(e)s, -̈e plait; pigtail; *fig* — antiquated custom.

Zorn [tsɔrn] *m* -(e)s anger; z—ig a angry.

Zote [tso:tə] *f* -, -n smutty joke/remark.

zottig ['tsɔtiç] a shaggy.

zu [tsu:] (mit Infinitiv) to; prep +dat (bei Richtung, Vorgang) to; (bei Orts-, Zeit-, Preisangabe) at; (Zweck) for; —m Fenster herein through the window; — meiner Zeit in my time; ad too; (in Richtung) towards (sb/sth); a (col) shut.

zuallererst [tsu"alər'—] *cpd*: —erst ad first of all; —letzt ad last of all.

Zubehör [tsu:bəhø:r] *nt* -(e)s, -e accessories *pl*.

Zuber ['tsu:bər] *m* -s, - tub.

zubereiten ['tsu:bəraitən] *vt* prepare.

zubilligen ['tsu:biligən] *vt* grant.

zubinden ['tsu:bindən] *vt irreg* tie up.

zubleiben ['tsu:blaibən] *vi irreg* (col) stay shut.

zubringen ['tsu:bringən] *vt irreg* spend; (col) Tür get shut.

Zubringer *m* -s, - (Tech) feeder, conveyor; —straße *f* approach or slip road.

Zucht [tsuxt] *f* -, -en (von Tieren) breed(ing); (von Pflanzen) cultivation; (Rasse) breed; (Erziehung) raising; (Disziplin) discipline.

züchten ['tsyçtən] *vt* Tiere breed; Pflanzen cultivate, grow.

Züchter *m* -s, - breeder; grower.

Zucht- *cpd*: —haus *nt* prison, penitentiary (US); —hengst *m* stallion, stud.

züchtig ['tsyçtiç] a modest, demure; —en ['tsyçtigən] *vt* chastise; Z—ung *f* chastisement.

zucken ['tsukən] *vi* jerk, twitch; (Strahl etc) flicker; *vt* shrug.

zücken ['tsykən] *vt* Schwert draw; Geldbeutel pull out.

Zucker ['tsʊkər] *m* -s, - sugar; *(Med)* diabetes; —**dose** *f* sugar bowl; —**guß** *m* icing; z—**krank** a diabetic; z—**n** *vt* sugar; —**rohr** *nt* sugar cane; —**rübe** *f* sugar beet.

Zuckung ['tsʊkʊŋ] *f* convulsion, spasm; *(leicht)* twitch.

zudecken ['tsuːdɛkən] *vt* cover (up).

zudem [tsuˈdeːm] *ad* in addition to this).

zudrehen ['tsuːdreːən] *vt* turn off.

zudringlich ['tsuːdrɪŋlɪç] a forward, pushing, obtrusive; **Z—keit** *f* forwardness, obtrusiveness.

zudrücken ['tsuːdrʏkən] *vt* close; **ein Auge** — turn a blind eye.

zueinander [tsuʔaɪˈnandər] *ad* to one other; *(in Verbverbindung)* together.

zuerkennen ['tsuːʔɛrkɛnən] *vt irreg* award *(jdm etw* sth to sb, sth sb).

zuerst [tsuˈʔeːrst] *ad* first; *(zu Anfang)* at first; — **einmal** first of all.

Zufahrt ['tsuːfaːrt] *f* approach; —**straße** *f* approach road; *(von Autobahn etc)* slip road.

Zufall ['tsuːfal] *m* chance; *(Ereignis)* coincidence; **durch** — by accident; **so ein** — what a coincidence; **z—en** *vi irreg* close, shut itself; *(Anteil, Aufgabe)* fall *(jdm* to sb).

zufällig ['tsuːfɛlɪç] a chance; *ad* by chance; *(in Frage)* by any chance.

Zuflucht ['tsuːflʊxt] *f* recourse; *(Ort)* refuge.

Zufluß ['tsuːflʊs] *m* *(Zufließen)* inflow, influx; *(Geog)* tributary; *(Comm)* supply.

zufolge [tsuˈfɔlgə] *prep +dat or gen* judging by; *(laut)* according to.

zufrieden [tsuˈfriːdən] a content(ed), satisfied; **Z—heit** *f*

satisfaction, contentedness; —**stellen** *vt* satisfy.

zufrieren ['tsuːfriːrən] *vi irreg* freeze up or over.

zufügen ['tsuːfyːgən], *vt* add *(dat* to); **Leid etc** cause *(jdm etw* sth to sb).

Zufuhr ['tsuːfuːr] *f* -, -en *(Herbeibringen)* supplying; *(Met)* influx; *(Mil)* supplies *pl.*

zuführen ['tsuːfyːrən] *vt (leiten)* bring, conduct; *(transportieren)* convey to; *(versorgen)* supply; *vi:* **auf etw** *(acc)* — lead to sth.

Zug [tsuːk] *m* -(e)s, ̈e *(Eisenbahn)* train; *(Luft—)* draught; *(Ziehen)* pull(ing); *(Gesichts—)* feature; *(Schach etc)* move; *(Klingel—)* pull; *(Schrift—)* stroke; *(Atem—)* breath; *(Charakter—)* trait; *(an Zigarette)* puff, pull, drag; *(Schluck)* gulp; *(Menschengruppe)* procession; *(von Vögeln)* flight; *(Mil)* platoon; **etw in vollen** —**en genießen** enjoy sth to the full.

Zu- *cpd:* —**gabe** *f* extra; *(in Konzert etc)* encore; —**gang** *m* access, approach; z—**gänglich** a accessible; **Mensch** approachable.

Zug- *cpd:* —**abteil** *nt* train compartment; —**brücke** *f* drawbridge.

zugeben ['tsuːgeːbən] *vt irreg (beifügen)* add, throw in; *(zugestehen)* admit; *(erlauben)* permit.

zugehen ['tsuːgeːən] *vi irreg (schließen)* shut; *v impers (sich ereignen)* go on, proceed; **auf jdn/etw** — walk towards sb/sth; **dem Ende** — be finishing.

Zugehörigkeit ['tsuːgəhøːrɪçkaɪt] *f* membership *(zu* of), belonging *(zu* to); —**sgefühl** *nt* feeling of belonging.

zugeknöpft ['tsuːgəknœpft] a (col) reserved, stand-offish.

Zügel ['tsyːgəl] m -s, - rein(s); (fig auch) curb; z—los a unrestrained, licentious; —losigkeit f lack of restraint, licentiousness; z—n vt curb; Pferd auch rein in.

zuge- ['tsuːgə] cpd: —sellen vr join (jdm up with); Z—ständnis nt -ses, -se concession; —stehen vt irreg admit; Rechte concede (jdm to sb).

Zug- cpd: —führer m (Rail) inspector; (Mil) platoon commander; z—ig a draughty.

zügig ['tsyːgɪç] a speedy, swift.

Zug- cpd: —luft f draught; —maschine f traction engine, tractor.

zugreifen ['tsuːgraɪfən] vi irreg seize or grab it; (helfen) help; (beim Essen) help o.s.

zugrunde [tsuˈgrʊndə] ad: — gehen collapse; (Mensch) perish; einer Sache etw — legen base sth on sth; einer Sache — liegen be based on sth; — richten ruin, destroy.

zugunsten [tsuˈgʊnstən] prep +gen or dat in favour of.

zugute [tsuˈguːtə] ad: jdm etw — halten concede sth; jdm — kommen be of assistance to sb.

Zug- cpd: —verbindung f train connection; —vogel m migratory bird.

zuhalten ['tsuːhaltən] irreg vt hold shut; vi: auf jdn/etw — make for sb/sth.

Zuhälter ['tsuːhɛltər] m -s, - pimp.

Zuhause [tsuˈhauzə] nt - home.

Zuhilfenahme [tsuˈhɪlfənaːmə] f: unter — von with the help of.

zuhören ['tsuːhøːrən] vi listen (dat to).

Zuhörer m -s, - listener; —schaft f audience.

zujubeln ['tsuːjuːbəln] vi cheer (jdm sb).

zukleben ['tsuːkleːbən] vt paste up.

zuknöpfen ['tsuːknœpfən] vt button up, fasten.

zukommen ['tsuːkɔmən] vi irreg come up (auf +acc to); (sich gehören) be fitting (jdm for sb); (Recht haben auf) be entitled to; jdm etw — lassen give sb sth; etw auf sich — lassen wait and see.

Zukunft ['tsuːkʊnft] f-, Zukünfte future.

zukünftig [tsuːkynftɪç] a future; mein —er Mann my husband to be; ad in future.

Zukunfts- cpd: —aussichten pl future prospects pl; —musik f (col) wishful thinking; crystal ball gazing; —roman m science-fiction novel.

Zulage ['tsuːlaːgə] f bonus, allowance.

zulassen ['tsuːlasən] vt irreg (hereinlassen) admit; (erlauben) permit; Auto license; (col: nicht öffnen) (keep) shut.

zulässig ['tsuːlɛsɪç] a permissible, permitted.

zulaufen ['tsuːlaufən] vi irreg run (auf +acc towards); (Tier) adopt (jdm sb); spitz — come to a point.

zulegen ['tsuːleːgən] vt add; Geld put in; Tempo accelerate, quicken; (schließen) cover over; sich (dat) etw — (col) get hold of sth.

zuleide [tsuˈlaɪdə] a: jdm etw — tun hurt or harm sb.

zuleiten ['tsuːlaɪtən] vt direct (dat to); (schicken) send.

zuletzt [tsuˈlɛtst] ad finally, at last.

zuliebe [tsu'li:bə] *ad:* **jdm — to** please sb.

zum [tsum] = **zu dem: — dritten Mal** for the third time; **— Scherz** as a joke; **— Trinken** for drinking.

zumachen ['tsu:maxən] *vt* · shut; *Kleidung* do up, fasten; *vi* shut; (col) hurry up.

zumal [tsu'ma:l] *cj* especially (as).

zumeist [tsu'maɪst] *ad* mostly.

zumindest [tsu'mɪndəst] *ad* at least.

zumut- *cpd:* **—bar** [tsu:'mu:tba:r] *a* reasonable; **—e wie ist ihm —e?** how does he feel?; **—en** ['tsu:'mu:tən] *vt* expect, ask (*jdm of* sb); **Z—ung** ['tsu:mu:tʊŋ] *f* unreasonable expectation or demand, impertinence.

zunächst [tsu'nɛ:çst] *ad* first of all; **— einmal** to start with.

zunähen ['tsu:nɛ:ən] *vt* sew up.

Zunahme ['tsu:na:mə] *f* -, **-n** increase.

Zuname ['tsu:na:mə] *m* surname.

Zünd- [tsynd] *cpd:* **z—en** *vi (Feuer)* light, ignite; *(Motor)* fire; *(begeistern)* fire (with enthusiasm) *(bei jdm* sb); **z—end** *a* fiery; **—er** *m* -s, - fuse; *(Mil)* detonator; **—holz** [tsynt-] *nt* match; **—kerze** *f (Aut)* spark(ing) plug; **—schlüssel** *m* ignition key; **—schnur** *f* fuse wire; **—stoff** *m* fuel; *(fig)* dynamite; **—ung** *f* ignition.

zunehmen ['tsu:ne:mən] *vi irreg* increase, grow; *(Mensch)* put on weight.

zuneigen ['tsu:naɪgən] *vi* incline, lean; **sich dem Ende —** draw to a close; **einer Auffassung —** incline towards a view; **jdm zugeneigt sein** be attracted to sb.

Zuneigung *f* affection.

Zunft [tsʊnft] *f* -, **⸚e** guild.

zünftig ['tsynftɪç] *a* proper, real; *Handwerk* decent.

Zunge ['tsʊŋə] *f* -, **-n** tongue; *(Fisch)* sole; **z—nfertig** *a* glib.

zunichte [tsu'nɪçtə] *ad:* **— machen** ruin, destroy; **— werden** come to nothing.

zunutze [tsu'nʊtsə] *ad:* **sich** *(dat)* **etw — machen** make use of sth.

zuoberst [tsu'o:bərst] *ad* at the top.

zupfen ['tsʊpfən] *vt* pull, pick, pluck; *Gitarre* pluck.

zur [tsu:r] = **zu der.**

zurech- ['tsu:rɛç] *cpd:* **—nungsfähig** *a* responsible, accountable; **Z—nungsfähigkeit** *f* responsibility, accountability.

zurecht- [tsu'rɛçt] *cpd:* **—finden** *vr irreg* find one's way (about); **—kommen** *vi irreg* (be able to) deal *(mit* with), manage; **—legen** *vt* get ready; *Ausrede etc* have ready; **—machen** *vt* prepare; *vr* get ready; **—weisen** *vt irreg* reprimand; **Z—weisung** *f* reprimand, rebuff.

zureden ['tsu:re:dən] *vi* persuade, urge (*jdm* sb).

zurichten ['tsu:rɪçtən] *vt Essen* prepare; *(beschädigen)* batter, bash up.

zürnen ['tsyrnən] *vi* be angry (*jdm* with sb).

zurück [tsu'ryk] *ad* back; **—behalten** *vt irreg* keep back; **—bekommen** *vt irreg* get back; **—bezahlen** *vt* repay, pay back; **—bleiben** *vi irreg (Mensch)* remain behind; *(nicht nachkommen)* fall behind, lag; *(Schaden)* remain; **—bringen** *vt irreg* bring back; **—drängen** *vt Gefühle* repress; *Feind* push back; **—drehen** *vt* turn back; **—erobern** *vt* reconquer; **—fahren** *irreg vi* travel back; *(vor*

Schreck) recoil, start; *vt* drive back; *—fallen vi irreg* fall back; *(in Laster)* relapse; *—finden vi irreg* find one's way back; *—fordern vt* demand back; *—führen vt* lead back; *etw auf etw (acc) —führen* trace sth back to sth; *—geben vt irreg* give back; *(antworten)* retort with; *—geblieben a* retarded; *—gehen vi irreg* go back; *(zeitlich)* date back *(auf +acc* to); *(fallen)* go down, fall; *—gezogen a* retired, withdrawn; *—halten irreg vt* hold back; *Mensch* restrain; *(hindern)* prevent; *vr (reserviert sein)* be reserved; *(im Essen)* hold back; *—haltend a* reserved; *Z—haltung f* reserve; *—kehren vi* return; *—kommen vi irreg* come back; *auf etw (acc) —kommen* return to sth; *—lassen vt irreg* leave behind; *—legen vt* put back; *Geld* put by; *(reservieren) Strecke* cover; *—nehmen vt irreg* take back; *—rufen vti irreg* call back; *etw ins Gedächtnis —rufen* recall sth; *—schrecken vi* shrink *(vor +dat* from); *—setzen vt* put back; *(im Preis)* reduce; *(benachteiligen)* put at a disadvantage; *—stecken vt* put back; *vi (fig)* moderate (one's wishes); *—stellen vt* put back, replace; *(aufschieben)* put off, postpone; *(Mil)* turn down; *Interessen* defer; *Ware* keep; *—stoßen vt irreg* repulse; *—treten vi irreg* step back; *(vom Amt)* retire; *gegenüber or hinter etw —treten* diminish in importance in view of sth; *—weisen vt irreg* turn down; *Mensch* reject; *Z—zahlung f* repayment; *—ziehen irreg vt* pull back; *Angebot* withdraw; *vr* retire.

Zuruf ['tsuːruːf] *m* shout, cry.

Zusage ['tsuːzaːgə] *f* -, *-n* promise; *(Annahme)* consent; **z—n** *vt* promise; *vi* accept; *jdm z—n (gefallen)* agree with *or* please sb.

zusammen [tsuˈzamən] *ad* together; **Z—arbeit** *f* cooperation; *—arbeiten vi* cooperate; *—beißen vt irreg Zähne* clench; *—bleiben vi irreg* stay together; *—brechen vi irreg* collapse; *(Mensch auch)* break down; *—bringen vt irreg* bring *or* get together; *Geld* get; *Sätze* put together; **Z—bruch** *m* collapse; *—fahren vi irreg* collide; *(erschrecken)* start; *—fassen vt* summarize; *(vereinigen)* unite; *—fassend a* summarizing; *ad* to summarize; **Z—fassung** *f* summary, résumé; *—finden vir irreg* meet (together); *—fließen vi irreg* flow together, meet; **Z—fluß** *m* confluence; *—fügen vt* join (together), unite; *—gehören vi* belong together; *(Paar)* match; *—gesetzt a* compound, composite; *—halten irreg vt irreg* stick together; **Z—hang** *m* connection; *im/aus dem Z—hang* in/out of context; *—hängen vi* be connected *or* linked; *—hang(s)los a* incoherent, disconnected; *—klappbar a* folding, collapsible; *—kommen vi irreg* meet, assemble; *(sich ereignen)* occur at once *or* together; **Z—kunft** *f* meeting; *—laufen vi irreg* run *or* come together; *(Straßen, Flüsse etc)* converge, meet; *(Farben)* run into one another; *—legen vt* put together; *(stapeln)* pile up; *(falten)* fold; *(verbinden)* combine, unite; *Termine, Fest* amalgamate; *—nehmen irreg vt* summon up; *alles —genommen* all in all; *vr* pull o.s. together; **—passen** vi go well together, match; **—prallen** vi collide; **—schlagen** vt irreg Mensch beat up; Dinge smash up; (falten) fold; Hände clap; Hacken click; **—schließen** vtr irreg join (together); **Z—schluß** m amalgamation; **—schreiben** vt irreg write together; Bericht put together; **—schrumpfen** vi shrink, shrivel up; **Z—sein** nt -s gettogether; **—setzen** vt put together; vr be composed of; **Z—setzung** f composition; **—stellen** vt put together; compile; **Z—stellung** f list; (Vorgang) compilation; **Z—stoß** m collision; **—stoßen** vi irreg collide; **—treffen** vi irreg coincide; Menschen meet; **Z—treffen** nt meeting; coincidence; **—wachsen** vi irreg grow together; **—zählen** vt add up; **—ziehen** irreg vt (verengern) draw together; (vereinigen) bring together; (addieren) add up; vr shrink; (sich bilden) form, develop.

Zusatz ['tsu:zats] m addition; **—antrag** m (Pol) amendment.

zusätzlich ['tsu:zɛtslɪç] a additional.

zuschauen ['tsu:ʃaʊən] vi watch, look on.

Zuschauer m -s, - spectator; pl (Theat) audience.

zuschicken ['tsu:ʃɪkən] vt send, forward (jdm etw sth to sb).

zuschießen ['tsu:ʃi:sən] irreg vt fire (dat at); Geld put in; vi: **—auf** (+acc) rush towards.

Zuschlag ['tsu:ʃla:k] m extra charge, surcharge; **Z—en** ['tsu:ʃla:gən] irreg vt Tür slam; Ball hit (jdm to sb); (bei Auktion) knock down; Steine etc knock into shape; vi (Fenster, Tür) shut;

(Mensch) hit, punch; **—skarte** f (Rail) surcharge ticket; **z—spflichtig** a subject to surcharge.

zuschließen ['tsu:ʃli:sən] vt irreg lock (up).

zuschmeißen ['tsu:ʃmaɪsən] vt irreg (col) slam, bang shut.

zuschneiden ['tsu:ʃnaɪdən] vt irreg cut out or to size.

zuschnüren ['tsu:ʃny:rən] vt tie up.

zuschrauben ['tsu:ʃraʊbən] vt screw down or up.

zuschreiben ['tsu:ʃraɪbən] vt irreg (fig) ascribe, attribute; (Comm) credit.

Zuschrift ['tsu:ʃrɪft] f letter, reply.

zuschulden [tsu:ʃʊldən] ad: sich (dat) etw **—** kommen lassen make o.s. guilty of sth.

Zuschuß ['tsu:ʃʊs] m subsidy, allowance.

zuschütten ['tsu:ʃʏtən] vt fill up.

zusehen ['tsu:ze:ən] vi irreg watch (jdm/etw sb/sth); (dafür sorgen) take care; **—ds** ad visibly.

zusenden ['tsu:zɛndən] vt irreg forward, send on (jdm etw sth to sb).

zusetzen ['tsu:zɛtsən] vt (beifügen) add; Geld lose; vi: jdm **—** harass sb; (Krankheit) take a lot out of sb.

zusichern ['tsu:zɪçərn] vt assure (jdm etw sb of sth).

zusperren ['tsu:ʃpɛrən] vt bar.

zuspielen ['tsu:ʃpi:lən] vti pass (jdm to sb).

zuspitzen ['tsu:ʃpɪtsən] vt sharpen; vr (Lage) become critical.

zusprechen ['tsu:ʃprɛçən] irreg vt (zuerkennen) award (jdm etw sb sth, sth to sb); jdm Trust **—** comfort sb; vi speak (jdm to sb); dem Essen/Alkohol **—** eat/drink a lot.

Zuspruch ['tsu:ʃprʊx] *m* encouragement; (*Anklang*) appreciation, popularity.

Zustand ['tsu:ʃtant] *m* state, condition; z—e bringen *vt irreg* bring about; z—e kommen *vi irreg* come about.

zuständig ['tsu:ʃtɛndɪç] *a* competent, responsible; Z—keit *f* competence, responsibility.

zustehen ['tsu:ʃteːən] *vi irreg*: jdm — be sb's right.

zustellen ['tsu:ʃtɛlən] *vt* (*verstellen*) block; *Post etc* send.

zustimmen ['tsu:ʃtɪmən] *vi* agree (*dat* to).

Zustimmung *f* agreement, consent.

zustoßen ['tsu:ʃtoːsən] *vi irreg* (*fig*) happen (*jdm* to sb).

zutage [tsu'ta:gə] *ad*: — bringen bring to light; — treten come to light.

Zutaten ['tsu:ta:tən] *pl* ingredients *pl*.

zuteilen ['tsu:taɪlən] *vt* allocate, assign.

zutiefst [tsu'ti:fst] *ad* deeply.

zutragen ['tsu:tra:gən] *irreg vt* bring (*jdm etw* sth to sb); *Klatsch* tell; *vr* happen.

zuträglich ['tsu:trɛːklɪç] *a* beneficial.

zutrau- ['tsu:trau] *cpd*: —en *vt* credit (*jdm etw* sb with sth); Z—en *nt* -s trust (*zu* in); —lich *a* trusting, friendly; Z—lichkeit *f* trust.

zutreffen ['tsu:trɛfən] *vi irreg* be correct; ·apply; Z—des bitte unterstreichen please underline where applicable.

zutrinken ['tsu:trɪŋkən] *vi irreg* drink to (*jdm* sb).

Zutritt ['tsu:trɪt] *m* access, admittance.

Zutun ['tsu:tu:n] *nt* -s assistance; *vt irreg* add; (*schließen*) shut.

zuverlässig ['tsu:fɛrlɛsɪç] *a* reliable; Z—keit *f* reliability.

Zuversicht ['tsu:fɛrzɪçt] *f* - confidence; z—lich a confident; —lichkeit *f* confidence, hopefulness.

zuviel [tsu'fi:l] *ad* too much.

zuvor [tsu'foːr] *ad* before, previously; —kommen *vi irreg* anticipate (*jdm* sb), beat (sb) to it; —kommend ·a obliging, courteous.

Zuwachs [tsu'vaks] *m* -es increase, growth; (*col*) addition; z—en *vi irreg* become overgrown; (*Wunde*) heal (up).

zuwandern ['tsu:vandərn] *vi* immigrate.

zuwege [tsu've:gə] *ad*: etw — bringen accomplish sth; mit etw — kommen manage sth; gut — sein be (doing) well.

zuweilen [tsu'vaɪlən] *ad* at times, now and then.

zuweisen ['tsu:vaɪzən] *vt irreg* assign, allocate (*jdm* to sb).

zuwenden ['tsu:vɛndən] *irreg vt* turn (*dat* towards); jdm seine Aufmerksamkeit — give sb one's attention; *vr* devote o.s., turn (*dat* to).

zuwenig ['tsu:ve:nɪç] *ad* too little.

zuwerfen ['tsu:vɛrfən] *vt irreg* throw (*jdm* to sb).

zuwider [tsu'vi:dər] *ad*: etw ist jdm — sb loathes sth, sb finds sth repugnant; *prep* +*dat* contrary to; —handeln *vi* act contrary (*dat* to); einem Gesetz —handeln contravene a law; Z—handlung *f* contravention; —laufen *vi irreg* run counter (*dat* to).

zuziehen ['tsu:tsi:ən] *irreg vt* (*schließen*) Vorhang draw, close; (*herbeirufen*) Experten call in; sich *(dat)* etw – *Krankheit* catch; *Zorn* incur; *vi* move in, come.

zuzüglich ['tsu:tsy:kliç] *prep* +*gen* plus, with the addition of.

Zwang [tsvaŋ] *m* -(e)s, ⁼e compulsion, coercion.

zwängen ['tsvɛŋən] *vtr* squeeze.

Zwang- *cpd:* z—los *a* informal; —losigkeit *f* informality; —sarbeit *f* forced labour; *(Strafe)* hard labour; —sjacke *f* straightjacket; —slage *f* predicament, tight corner; z—släufig *a* necessary, inevitable; —smaßnahme *f* sanction, coercive measure; z—sweise *ad* compulsorily.

zwanzig ['tsvantsiç] *num* twenty.

zwar [tsva:r] *ad* to be sure, indeed; das ist – ..., aber ... that may be ... but ...; und — am Sonntag on Sunday to be precise; und — so schnell, daß ... in fact so quickly that ...

Zweck [tsvɛk] *m* -(e)s, -e purpose, aim; z—dienlich *a* practical, expedient; —e *f* -, -n hobnail; *(Heft—)* drawing pin, thumbtack *(US)*; —entfremdung *f* misuse; z—los *a* pointless; z—mäßig *a* suitable, appropriate; —mäßigkeit *f* suitability; z—widrig *a* unsuitable.

zwei [tsvai] *num* two; —deutig *a* ambiguous; *(unanständig)* suggestive; —erlei *a:* —erlei Stoff two different kinds of material; —erlei Meinung *f* of differing opinions; —erlei zu tun haben have two different things to do; —fach *a* double.

Zweifel ['tsvaifəl] *m* -s, - doubt; z—haft *a* doubtful, dubious; z—los *a* doubtless; z—n *vi* doubt *(an etw (dat)* sth); —sfall *m:* im —sfall in case of doubt.

Zweig [tsvaik] *m* -(e)s, -e branch; —geschäft *nt (Comm)* branch; —stelle *f* branch (office).

zwei- *cpd:* Z—heit *f* duality; —hundert *num* two hundred; Z—kampf *m* duel; —mal *ad* twice; —motorig *a* twin-engined; —reihig *a (Anzug)* double-breasted; —schneidig *a (fig)* two-edged; Z—sitzer *m* -s, - two-seater; —sprachig *a* bilingual; —spurig *a (Aut)* two-lane; —stimmig *a* for two voices; Z—taktmotor *m* two-stroke engine.

zweit- [tsvait] *cpd:* —ens *ad* secondly; —größte(r,s) *a* second largest; —klassig *a* second-class; —letzte(r,s) *a* last but one, penultimate; —rangig *a* second-rate; Z—wagen *m* second car.

Zwerchfell ['tsvɛrçfɛl] *nt* diaphragm.

Zwerg [tsvɛrk] *m* -(e)s, -e dwarf.

Zwetsche ['tsvɛtʃə] *f* -, -n plum.

Zwickel ['tsvikəl] *m* -s, - gusset.

zwicken ['tsvikən] *vt* pinch, nip.

Zwieback ['tsvi:bak] *m* -(e)s, -e rusk.

Zwiebel ['tsvi:bəl] *f* -, -n onion; *(Blumen—)* bulb; z—artig *a* bulbous.

Zwie- ['tsvi:] *cpd:* —gespräch *vt* dialogue; —licht *nt* twilight; z—lichtig *a* shady, dubious; —spalt *m* conflict, split; z—spältig *a* *Gefühle* conflicting; *Charakter* contradictory; —tracht *f* discord, dissension.

Zwilling ['tsviliŋ] *m* -s, -e twin; *pl (Astrol)* Gemini.

zwingen ['tsviŋən] *vt irreg* force; —nd *a* *Grund* etc compelling.

zwinkern ['tsviŋkərn] *vi* blink; *(absichtlich)* wink.

Zwirn [tsvɪrn] *m* -(e)s, -e thread.

zwischen ['tsvɪʃən] *prep* +acc or *dat* between; **Z—bemerkung** *f* (incidental) remark; **—blenden** *vt* (*TV*) insert; **Z—ding** *nt* cross; **—durch** [-'durç] *ad* in between; (*räumlich*) here and there; **Z—ergebnis** *nt* intermediate result; **Z—fall** *m* incident; **Z—frage** *f* question; **Z—gas** *nt*: **Z—gas geben** double-declutch; **Z—handel** *m* middlemen *pl*; middleman's trade; **Z—händler** *m* middleman, agent; **Z—landung** *f* stop, intermediate landing; **—menschlich** *a* interpersonal; **Z—raum** *m* space; **Z—ruf** *m* interjection, interruption; **Z—spiel** *nt* interlude; **—staatlich** *f* interstate; international; **Z—station** *f* intermediate station;

Z—stecker *m* (*Elec*) adaptor; **Z—wand** *f* partition; **Z—zeit** *f* interval; **in der Z—zeit** in the interim, meanwhile.

Zwist [tsvɪst] *m* -es, -e dispute, feud.

zwitschern ['tsvɪtʃərn] *vti* twitter, chirp.

Zwitter ['tsvɪtər] *m* -s, - hermaphrodite.

zwölf [tsvœlf] *num* twelve.

Zyklus ['tsy:klus] *m* -, **Zyklen** cycle.

Zylinder [tsi'lɪndər] *m* -s, - cylinder; (*Hut*) top hat; **z—förmig** *a* cylindrical.

Zyniker ['tsy:nikər] *m* -s, - cynic.

zynisch ['tsy:nɪʃ] *a* cynical.

Zynismus [tsy'nɪsmʊs] *m* cynicism.

Zyste ['tsʏstə] *f* -, -n cyst.

357

Länder, Völker und Sprachen

ich bin Deutscher/Engländer/Albanier I am German/English/Albanian

ein Deutscher/Engländer/Albanier a German/an Englishman/an Albanian;
eine Deutsche/Engländerin/Albanierin a German (woman/girl)/an English
woman/girl/an Albanian (woman/girl)

sprechen Sie Deutsch/Englisch/Albanisch? do you speak German/
English/Albanian?

Adria (die), Adriatische(s) Meer the Adriatic.
Afrika Africa; Afrikaner(in f) m African; afrikanisch a African.
Ägäis (die), Ägäische(s) Meer the Aegean.
Ägypten Egypt; Ägypter(in f) m; ägyptisch a Egyptian.
Albanien Albania; Albanier(in f) m Albanian; albanisch a Albanian.
Algerien Algeria; Algerier(in f) m Algerian; algerisch a Algerian.
Alpen pl (die) the Alps pl.
Amazonas (der) the Amazon.
Amerika America; Amerikaner(in f) m American; amerikanisch a American.
Anden pl (die) the Andes pl.
Antarktis (die) the Antarctic.
Antillen pl (die) the Antilles pl.
Antwerpen Antwerp.
Arabien Arabia; Araber m Arab, Arabian; arabisch a Arab, Arabic, Arabian.
Argentinien Argentina, the Argentine; Argentinier(in f) m Argentinian;
   argentinisch a Argentinian.
Ärmelkanal (der) the English Channel.
Armenien Armenia; Armenier(in f) m Armenian; armenisch a Armenian.
Asien Asia; Asiat(in f) m Asian; asiatisch a Asian, Asiatic.
Athen Athens; Athener(in f) m Athenian; athenisch a Athenian.
Äthiopien Ethiopia; Äthiopier(in f) m Ethiopian; äthiopisch a Ethiopian.
Atlantik (der), Atlantische(r) Ozean the Atlantic (Ocean).
Ätna (der) Mount Etna.
Australien Australia; Australier(in f) m Australian; australisch a Australian.
Azoren pl (die) the Azores pl.
Balkan (der) the Balkans pl.
Basel Basle.
Bayern Bavaria; Bayer(in f) m Bavarian; bayerisch a Bavarian.
Belgien Belgium; Belgier(in f) m Belgian; belgisch a Belgian.

Belgrad Belgrade.
Birma Burma; Birmane *m*, Birmanin *f* Burmese; Birmanisch a Burmese.
Biskaya (die) the Bay of Biscay.
Bodensee (der) Lake Constance.
Böhmen Bohemia; Böhme *m*, Böhmin *f* Bohemian; böhmisch a Bohemian.
Bolivien Bolivia; Bolivianer(in *f*) *m* Bolivian; bolivianisch, bolvisch a Bolivian.
Brasilien Brazil; Brasilianer(in *f*) *m* Brazilian; brasilianisch a Brazilian.
Braunschweig Brunswick.
Brite *m*, Britin *f* Briton; britisch a British.
Brüssel Brussels.
Bulgarien Bulgaria; Bulgare *m*, Bulgarin *f* Bulgarian, Bulgar; bulgarisch a Bulgarian.
Burgund Burgundy; burgundisch, Burgunder a Burgundian.
Calais: Straße von Calais (die) the Straits of Dover *pl.*
Chile Chile; Chilene *m*, Chilenin *f* Chilean; chilenisch a Chilean.
China China; Chinese *m*, Chinesin *f* Chinese; chinesisch a Chinese.
Dänemark Denmark; Däne *m*, Dänin *f* Dane; dänisch a Danish.
Deutsche Demokratische Republik (die) German Democratic Republic, East Germany.
Deutschland Germany; Deutsche(r) *mf* German; deutsch a German.
Dolomiten *pl* (die) the Dolomites *pl.*
Donau (die) the Danube.
Dünkirchen Dunkirk.
Eismeer (das) the Arctic.
Elfenbeinküste (die) the Ivory Coast.
Elsaß (das) Alsace; Elsässer(in *f*) *m* Alsatian; elsässisch a Alsatian.
Engadin (das) the Engadine.
England England; Engländer(in *f*) *m* Englishman/-woman; englisch a English.
Estland Estonia; Este *m*, Estin *f* Estonian; estnisch a Estonian.
Etsch (die) the Adige.
Euphrat (der) the Euphrates.
Eurasien Eurasia.
Europa Europe; Europäer(in *f*) *m* European; europäisch a European.
Ferne(r) Osten (der) the Far East.
Finnland Finland; Finne *m*, Finnin *f* Finn; finnisch a Finnish.
Flandern Flanders; Flame *m*, Flamin *f* Fleming; flämisch a Flemish.
Florenz Florence; Florentiner(in *f*) *m* Florentine; florentinisch a Florentine.
Frankreich France; Franzose *m*, Französin *f* Frenchman/-woman; französisch a French.
Friesland Frisia; Friese *m*, Friesin *f* Frisian; friesisch a Frisian.
Genf Geneva.
Genfer See Lake Geneva.
Genua Genoa; Genuese *m*, Genuesin *f* Genoan; genuesisch a Genoan.
Griechenland Greece; Grieche *m*, Griechin *f* Greek; griechisch a Greek.

Großbritannien Great Britain; **Brite** m, **Britin** f Briton; **britisch, großbritannisch** a British.

Guinea Guinea.

Haag (der), **Den Haag** the Hague.

Hannover Hanover; **Hannoveraner(in** f) m Hanoverian; **Hannoveraner, hannoversch** a Hanoverian.

Hebriden pl (die) the Hebrides pl.

Helgoland Heligoland.

Hessen Hesse; **Hesse** m, **Hessin** f Hessian; **hessisch** a Hessian.

Holland Holland; **Holländer(in** f) m Dutchman/-woman; **holländisch** a Dutch.

Iberische Halbinsel (die) the Iberian Peninsula.

Indien India; **Inder(in** f) m, **Indianer(in** f) m Indian; **indisch, indianisch** a Indian.

Indonesien Indonesia; **Indonesier(in** f) m Indonesian; **indonesisch** a Indonesian.

Irak (auch der) Iraq; **Iraker(in** f) m Iraqi; **irakisch** a Iraqi.

Iran (auch der) Iran; **Iraner(in** f) m Iranian; **iranisch** a Iranian.

Irland Ireland; **Ire** m, **Irin** f Irishman/-woman; **irisch** a Irish.

Island Iceland; **Isländer(in** f) m Icelander; **isländisch** a Icelandic.

Israel Israel; **Israeli** mf Israeli; **israelisch** a Israeli.

Italien Italy; **Italiener(in** f) m Italian; **italienisch** a Italian.

Japan Japan; **Japaner(in** f) m Japanese; **japanisch** a Japanese.

Jemen (auch der) the Yemen; **Jemenit(in** f) m Yemeni; **jemenitisch** a Yemeni.

Jordanien Jordan; **Jordanier(in** f) m Jordanian; **jordanisch** a Jordanian.

Jugoslawien Yugoslavia; **Jugoslawe** m, **Jugoslawin** f Yugoslavian; **jugoslawisch** a Yugoslavian.

Kanada Canada; **Kanadier(in** f) m Canadian; **kanadisch** a Canadian.

Kanalinseln pl (die) the Channel Islands pl.

Kanarische Inseln pl (die) the Canary Islands pl, the Canaries pl.

Kap der Guten Hoffnung (das) the Cape of Good Hope.

Kapstadt Cape Town.

Karibische Inseln pl (die) the Caribbean Islands pl.

Karpaten pl (die) the Carpathians pl.

Kaspische(s) Meer the Caspian Sea.

Kleinasien Asia Minor.

Köln Cologne.

Konstanz Constance.

Kreml (der) the Kremlin.

Kreta Crete; **Kreter(in** f) m Cretan; **kretisch** a Cretan.

Krim (die) the Crimea.

Kroatien Croatia; **Kroate** m, **Kroatin** f Croatian; **kroatisch** a Croatian.

Lappland Lapland; **Lappe** m, **Lappin** f Laplander; **lappisch** a Lapp.

Lateinamerika Latin America.

Lettland Latvia; **Lette** m, **Lettin** f Latvian; **lettisch** a Latvian.

Libanon the Lebanon; **Libanese** *m*, **Libanesin** *f* Lebanese; **libanesisch** a Lebanese.

Libyen Libya; **Libyer(in** *f*) *m* Libyan; **libyisch** a Libyan.

Lissabon Lisbon.

Litauen Lithuania; **Litauer(in** *f*) *m* Lithuanian; **litauisch** a Lithuanian.

Livland Livonia; **Livländer(in** *f*) *m* Livonian; **livländisch** a Livonian.

London London; **Londoner(in** *f*) *m* Londoner; **Londoner** a London.

Lothringen Lorraine.

Lüneburger Heide (die) the Lüneburg Heath.

Luxemburg Luxembourg.

Maas (die) the Meuse.

Mähren Moravia.

Mailand Milan; **Mailänder(in** *f*) *m* Milanese; **mailändisch** a Milanese..

Mallorca Majorca.

Mandschurei (die) Manchuria; **Mandschure** *m*, **Mandschurin** *f* Manchurian; **mandschurisch** a Manchurian.

Marokko Morocco; **Marokkaner(in** *f*) *m* Moroccan; **marokkanisch** a Moroccan.

Mazedonien Macedonia; **Mazedonier(in** *f*) *m* Macedonian; **mazedonisch** a Macedonian.

Mittelamerika Central America.

Mitteleuropa Central Europe.

Mittelmeer (das) the Mediterranean.

Moldau (die) Moldavia.

Mongolei (die) Mongolia; **Mongole** *m*, **Mongolin** *f* Mongol(ian); **mongolisch** a Mongol(ian).

Moskau Moscow; **Moskauer(in** *f*) *m* Muscovite; **moskauisch** a Muscovite.

München Munich.

Nahe(r) Osten (der) the Near East.

Neapel Naples; **Neapolitaner(in** *f*) *m* Neapolitan; **neapolitanisch** a Neapolitan.

Neufundland Newfoundland; **Neufundländer(in** *f*) *m* Newfoundlander; **neufundländisch** a Newfoundland.

Neuguinea New Guinea.

Neuseeland New Zealand; **Neuseeländer(in** *f*) *m* New. Zealander; **neuseeländisch** a New Zealand.

Niederlande *pl* **(die)** the Netherlands; **Niederländer(in** *f*) *m* Dutchman/ -woman; **niederländisch** a Dutch.

Niedersachsen Lower Saxony.

Niederrhein Lower Rhine.

Nil (der) the Nile.

Nordirland Northern Ireland.

Nordsee (die) the North Sea.

Norwegen Norway; **Norweger(in** *f*) *m* Norwegian; **norwegisch** a Norwegian.

Nord-Ostsee-Kanal (der) the Kiel Canal.

Nordrhein-Westfalen North Rhine-Westphalia.

Nürnberg Nuremberg.
Oberbayern Upper Bavaria.
Ostasien Eastern Asia.
Ostende Ostend.
Ostsee (die) the Baltic.
Österreich Austria; Österreicher(in f) m Austrian; österreichisch a Austrian.
Palästina Palestine; Palästinenser(in f) m Palestinian; palästinensisch a Palestinian.
Paris Paris; Pariser(in f) m Parisian; Pariser a Parisian.
Pazifik (der), Pazifische(r) Ozean the Pacific.
Peloponnes (der or die) the Peloponnese.
Persien Persia; Perser(in f) m Persian; persisch a Persian.
Philippinen pl (die) the Philippines pl.
Polen Poland; Pole m, Polin f Pole; polnisch a Polish.
Pommern Pomerania; Pommer(in f) m Pomeranian; pommerisch a Pomeranian.
Portugal Portugal; Portugiese m, Portugiesin f Portuguese; portugiesisch a Portuguese.
Prag Prague.
Preußen Prussia; Preuße m, Preußin f Prussian; preußisch a Prussian.
Pyrenäen pl (die) the Pyrenees pl.
Rhein (der) the Rhine; rheinisch a Rhenish.
Rhodesien Rhodesia; Rhodesier(in f) m Rhodesian; rhodesisch a Rhodesian.
Rhodos Rhodes.
Rom Rome; Römer(in f) m Roman; römisch a Roman.
Rote(s) Meer the Red Sea.
Rumänien Ro(u)mania; Rumäne m, Rumänin f Ro(u)manian; rumänisch a Ro(u)manian.
Rußland Russia; Russe m, Russin f Russian; russisch a Russian.
Saarland the Saar.
Sachsen Saxony; Sachse m, Sächsin f Saxon; sächsisch a Saxon.
Sardinien Sardinia; Sardinier(in f) m, Sarde m, Sardin f Sardinian; sardinisch, sardisch a Sardinian.
Schlesien Silesia; Schlesier(in f) m Silesian; schlesisch a Silesian.
Schottland Scotland; Schotte m, Schottin f Scot, Scotsman/-woman; schottisch a Scottish, Scots, Scotch.
Schwaben Swabia; Schwabe m, Schwäbin f Swabian; schwäbisch a Swabian.
Schwarzwald (der) the Black Forest.
Schweden Sweden; Schwede m, Schwedin f Swede; schwedisch a Swedish.
Schweiz (die) Switzerland; Schweizer(in f) m Swiss; schweizerisch a Swiss.
Serbien Serbia; Serbe m, Serbin f Serbian; serbisch a Serbian.
Sibirien Siberia; sibirisch a Siberian.
Sizilien Sicily; Sizilianer(in f) m, Sizilier(in f) m Sicilian; sizilisch, sizilianisch a Sicilian.

Skandinavien Scandinavia; **Skandinavier**(in f) m Scandinavian; **skandinavisch** a Scandinavian.

Slowakei (die) Slovakia; **Slowake** m, **Slowakin** f Slovak; **slowakisch** a Slovak.

Sowjetunion (die) the Soviet Union; **Sowjetbüger**(in f) m Soviet; **sowjetisch** a Soviet.

Spanien Spain; **Spanier**(in f) m Spaniard; **spanisch** a Spanish.

Steiermark Styria; **Steiermärker**(in f) m, Steirer m, **Steierin** f Styrian; steiermärkisch, steirisch a Styrian.

Stille(r) Ozean the Pacific.

Syrien Syria; **Syrer**(in f) m Syrian; **syrisch** a Syrian.

Teneriffa Tenerife.

Themse (die) the Thames.

Thüringen Thuringia; **Thüringer**(in f) m Thuringian; **thüringisch** a Thuringian.

Tirol the Tyrol; **Tiroler**(in f) m Tyrolean; **tirolisch** a Tyrolean.

Tschechoslowakei (die) Czechoslovakia; **Tscheche** m, **Tschechin** f, **Tschechoslowake** m, **Tschechoslowakin** f Czech, Czechoslovak(ian); tschechisch, tschechoslowakisch a Czech, Czechoslovak(ian).

Toscana (die) Tuscany.

Trient Trent.

Tunesien Tunisia; **Tunesier**(in f) m Tunisian; **tunesisch** a Tunisian.

Türkei (die) Turkey; **Türke** m, **Türkin** f Turk; **türkisch** a Turkish.

Ungarn Hungary; **Ungar**(in f) m Hungarian; **ungarisch** a Hungarian.

Venedig Venice; **Venetianer**(in f) m Venetian; **venetianisch** a Venetian.

Vereinigte Staaten pl (die) the United States pl.

Vesuv (der) Vesuvius.

Vierwaldstättersee (der) Lake Lucerne.

Vogesen pl (die) the Vosges pl.

Volksrepublik China (die) the Peoples's Republic of China.

Vorderasien the Near East.

Warschau Warsaw.

Weichsel (die) the Vistula.

Westfalen Westphalia; **Westfale** m, **Westfälin** f Westphalian; **westfälisch** a Westphalian.

Westindien the West Indies; **westindisch** a West Indian.

Wien Vienna; **Wiener**(in f) m Viennese; Wiener a Viennese.

Zypern Cyprus; **Zyprer**(in f) m, **Zyprier**(in f) m, **Zypriot**(in f) m Cypriot; zyprisch, zypriotisch a Cypriot.

Deutsche Abkürzungen

Abf.	Abfahrt *departure, dep*
Abk.	Abkürzung *abbreviation, abbr*
Abs.	Absatz *paragraph;* Absender *sender*
Abt.	Abteilung *department, dept*
AG	Aktiengesellschaft *(Brit) (public) limited company, Ltd, (US) corporation, inc*
Ank.	Ankunft *arrival, arr*
Anm.	Anmerkung *note*
b.a.w.	bis auf weiteres *until further notice*
Best. Nr.	Bestellnummer *order number*
Betr.	Betreff, betrifft *re*
Bhf.	Bahnhof *station*
BRD	Bundesrepublik Deutschland *Federal Republic of Germany*
b.w.	bitte wenden *please turn over, pto*
bzgl.	bezüglich *with reference to, re*
bzw.	beziehungsweise *(see text)*
ca.	circa, ungefähr *approximately, approx*
Cie., Co.	Kompanie *company, co*
DDR	Deutsche Demokratische Republik *German Democratic Republic, GDR*
d.h.	das heißt *that is, i.e.*
d.J.	dieses Jahres *of this year*
d.M.	dieses Monats *instant, inst*
DM	Deutsche Mark *German Mark, Deutschmark*
EDV	elektronische Datenverarbeitung *electronic data processing, EDP*
einschl.	einschließlich *inclusive, including, incl*
Einw.	Einwohner *inhabitant*
empf.	empfohlen(er Preis) *recommended (price)*
ev.	evangelisch *Protestant*
evtl.	eventuell *perhaps, possibly*
EWG	Europäische Wirtschaftsgemeinschaft *European Economic Community, EEC*
e. Wz.	eingetragenes Warenzeichen *registered trademark*
Expl.	Exemplar *sample, copy*
Fa.	Firma *firm; in Briefen: Messrs*
ff.	folgende Seiten *pages, pp*
Ffm.	Frankfurt am Main
fl. W.	fließendes Wasser *running water*
Forts.	Fortsetzung *continued, cont'd*

geb.	geboren *born;* geborene *née;* gebunden *bound.*
Gebr.	Gebrüder *Brothers, Bros*
ges. gesch.	gesetzlich geschützt *registered*
GmbH	Gesellschaft mit beschränkter Haftung *(Brit) (private) limited company, Ltd, (US) corporation, inc*
Hbf.	Hauptbahnhof *central station*
hl.	heilig *holy*
Hrsg.	Herausgeber *editor, ed*
i.A.	im Auftrag *for;* in Briefen auch: *pp*
Ing.	Ingenieur *engineer*
Inh.	Inhaber *proprietor, prop;* Inhalt *contents*
i.V.	in Vertretung *by proxy, on behalf of;* im Vorjahre *in the last or previous year;* in Vorbereitung *in preparation*
Jh.	Jahrhundert *century, cent*
jr., jun.	junior, der Jüngere *junior, jun, jr*
kath.	katholisch *Catholic, Cath*
kfm.	kaufmännisch *commercial*
Kfz.	*(see text)*
KG	Kommanditgesellschaft *limited partnership*
led.	ledig *single*
Lkw.	*(see text)*
lt.	laut *according to*
m. E.	meines Erachtens *in my opinion*
Mehrw. St.	Mehrwertsteuer *value-added tax, VAT*
Mrd.	Milliarde *thousand millions, (US) billion*
n. Chr.	nach Christus *AD*
Nr.	Numero, Nummer *number, no*
NS	Nachschrift *postscript, PS;* nationalsozialistisch *National Socialist*
OHG	Offene Handelsgesellschaft *general partnership*
PKW, Pkw.	*(see text)*
Pl.	Platz *square*
Postf.	Postfach *post-office box, PO box*
PS	Pferdestärken *horsepower, HP;* Nachschrift *postscript, PS*
S.	Seite *page, p*
s.	siehe *see*
sen.	senior, der Ältere *senior, sen, sr*
s.o.	siehe oben *see above*
St.	Stück *piece;* Sankt *Saint, St*
Std., Stde.	Stunde *hour, hr*
stdl.	stündlich *every hour*
Str.	Straße *street, St*
s.u.	siehe unten *see below*

tägl.	täglich *daily, per day*
Tsd.	Tausend *thousand*
u.	und *and*
u.a.	und andere(s) *and others;* unter anderem/anderen *among other things, inter alia/among others*
U.A.w.g.	Um Antwort wird gebeten *an answer is requested;* auf Einladung: *RSVP*
UdSSR	Union der Sozialistischen Sowjetrepubliken *Union of Soviet Socialist Republics, USSR*
u.E.	unseres Erachtens *in our opinion*
USA	Vereinigte Staaten (von Amerika) *United States (of America), USA.*
usf.	und so fort *and so forth, etc*
usw.	und so weiter *etcetera, etc*
u.U.	unter Umständen *possibly*
v. Chr.	vor Christus *BC*
Verf., Vf.	Verfasser *author*
verh.	verheiratet *married*
Verl.	Verlag *publishing firm;* Verleger *publisher*
vgl.	vergleiche *compare, cf, cp*
v.H.	vom Hundert *per cent*
Wz.	Warenzeichen *registered trademark*
z.B.	zum Beispiel *for example or instance, eg*
z.H(d)	zu Händen *for the attention of*
z.T.	zum Teil *partly*
zw.	zwischen *between; among*
z.Z(t).	zur Zeit *at the time, at present, for the time being*

German irregular verbs
*with 'sein'

infinitive	present indicative (2nd, 3rd sing.)	preterite	past participle
aufschrecken*	schrickst auf, schrickt auf	schrak or schreckte auf	aufgeschreckt
ausbedingen	bedingst aus, bedingt aus	bedang or bedingte aus	ausbedungen
backen	bäckst, bäckt	backte or buk	gebacken
befehlen	befiehlst, befiehlt	befahl	befohlen
beginnen	beginnst, beginnt	begann	begonnen
beißen	beißt, beißt	biß	gebissen
bergen	birgst, birgt	barg	geborgen
bersten*	birst, birst	barst	geborsten
bescheißen*	bescheißt, bescheißt	beschiß	beschissen
bewegen	bewegst, bewegt	bewog	bewogen
biegen	biegst, biegt	bog	gebogen
bieten	bietest, bietet	bot	geboten
binden	bindest, bindet	band	gebunden
bitten	bittest, bittet	bat	gebeten
blasen	bläst, bläst	blies	geblasen
bleiben*	bleibst, bleibt	blieb	geblieben
braten	brätst, brät	briet	gebraten
brechen*	brichst, bricht	brach	gebrochen
brennen	brennst, brennt	brannte	gebrannt
bringen	bringst, bringt	brachte	gebracht
denken	denkst, denkt	dachte	gedacht
dreschen	drisch(e)st, drischt	drasch	gedroschen
dringen*	dringst, dringt	drang	gedrungen
dürfen	darfst, darf	durfte	gedurft
empfehlen	empfiehlst, empfiehlt	empfahl	empfohlen
erbleichen*	erbleichst, erbleicht	erbleichte	erblichen
erlöschen*	erlischst, erlischt	erlosch	erloschen
erschrecken*	erschrickst, erschrickt	erschrak	erschrocken
essen	ißt, ißt	aß	gegessen
fahren*	fährst, fährt	fuhr	gefahren
fallen*	fällst, fällt	fiel	gefallen
fangen	fängst, fängt	fing	gefangen
fechten	fichtst, ficht	focht	gefochten
finden	findest, findet	fand	gefunden

infinitive	present indicative (2nd, 3rd sing.)	preterite	past participle
flechten	flichst, flicht	flocht	geflochten
fliegen*	fliegst, fliegt	flog	geflogen
fliehen*	fliehst, flieht	floh	geflohen
fließen*	fließt, fließt	floß	geflossen
fressen	frißt, frißt	fraß	gefressen
frieren	frierst, friert	fror	gefroren
gären*	gärst, gärt	gor	gegoren
gebären	gebierst, gebiert	gebar	geboren
geben	gibst, gibt	gab	gegeben
gedeihen*	gedeihst, gedeiht	gedieh	gediehen
gehen*	gehst, geht	ging	gegangen
gelingen*	——, gelingt	gelang	gelungen
gelten	giltst, gilt	galt	gegolten
genesen	gene(se)st, genest	genas	genesen
genießen	genießt, genießt	genoß	genossen
geraten*	gerätst, gerät	geriet	geraten
geschehen*	——, geschieht	geschah	geschehen
gewinnen	gewinnst, gewinnt	gewann	gewonnen
gießen	gießt, gießt	goß	gegossen
gleichen	gleichst, gleicht	glich	geglichen
gleiten*	gleitest, gleitet	glitt	geglitten
glimmen	glimmst, glimmt	glomm	geglommen
graben	gräbst, gräbt	grub	gegraben
greifen	greifst, greift	griff	gegriffen
haben	hast, hat	hatte	gehabt
halten	hältst, hält	hielt	gehalten
hängen	hängst, hängt	hing	gehangen
hauen	haust, haut	hieb	gehauen
heben	hebst, hebt	hob	gehoben
heißen	heißt, heißt	hieß	geheißen
helfen	hilfst, hilft	half	geholfen
kennen	kennst, kennt	kannte	gekannt
klimmen*	klimmst, klimmt	klomm	geklommen
klingen	klingst, klingt	klang	geklungen
kneifen	kneifst, kneift	kniff	gekniffen
kommen*	kommst, kommt	kam	gekommen
können	kannst, kann	konnte	gekonnt
kriechen*	kriechst, kriecht	kroch	gekrochen
laden	lädst, lädt	lud	geladen
lassen	läßt, läßt	ließ	gelassen
laufen*	läufst, läuft	lief	gelaufen

infinitive	present indicative (2nd, 3rd sing.)	preterite	past participle
leiden	leidest, leidet	litt	gelitten
leihen	leihst, leiht	lieh	geliehen
lesen	liest, liest	las	gelesen
liegen*	liegst, liegt	lag	gelegen
lügen	lügst, lügt	log	gelogen
mahlen	mahlst, mahlt	mahlte	gemahlen
meiden	meidest, meidet	mied	gemieden
melken	milkst, milkt	molk	gemolken
messen	mißt, mißt	maß	gemessen
mißlingen*	——, mißlingt	mißlang	mißlungen
mögen	magst, mag	mochte	gemocht
müssen	mußt, muß	mußte	gemußt
nehmen	nimmst, nimmt	nahm	genommen
nennen	nennst, nennt	nannte	genannt
pfeifen	pfeifst, pfeift	pfiff	gepfiffen
preisen	preist, preist	pries	gepriesen
quellen*	quillst, quillt	quoll	gequollen
raten	rätst, rät	riet	geraten
reiben	reibst, reibt	rieb	gerieben
reißen*	reißt, reißt	riß	gerissen
reiten*	reitest, reitet	ritt	geritten
rennen*	rennst, rennt	rannte	gerannt
riechen	riechst, riecht	roch	gerochen
ringen	ringst, ringt	rang	gerungen
rinnen*	rinnst, rinnt	rann	geronnen
rufen	rufst, ruft	rief	gerufen
salzen	salzt, salzt	salzte	gesalzen
saufen	säufst, säuft	soff	gesoffen
saugen	saugst, saugt	sog	gesogen
schaffen	schaffst, schafft	schuf	geschaffen
schallen	schallst, schallt	scholl	geschollen
scheiden*	scheidest, scheidet	schied	geschieden
scheinen	scheinst, scheint	schien	geschienen
schelten	schiltst, schilt	schalt	gescholten
scheren	scherst, schert	schor	geschoren
schieben	schiebst, schiebt	schob	geschoben
schießen	schießt, schießt	schoß	geschossen
schinden	schindest, schindet	schund	geschunden
schlafen	schläfst, schläft	schlief	geschlafen
schlagen	schlägst, schlägt	schlug	geschlagen
schleichen*	schleichst, schleicht	schlich	geschlichen

Infinitive	present indicative (2nd, 3rd sing.)	preterite	past participle
schleifen	schleifst, schleift	schliff	geschliffen
schließen	schließt, schließt	schloß	geschlossen
schlingen	schlingst, schlingt	schlang	geschlungen
schmeißen	schmeißt, schmeißt	schmiß	geschmissen
schmelzen*	schmilzt, schmilzt	schmolz	geschmolzen
schneiden	schneidest, schneidet	schnitt	geschnitten
schreiben	schreibst, schreibt	schrieb	geschrieben
schreien	schreist, schreit	schrie	geschrie(e)n
schreiten	schreitest, schreitet	schritt	geschritten
schweigen	schweigst, schweigt	schwieg	geschwiegen
schwellen*	schwillst, schwillt	schwoll	geschwollen
schwimmen*	schwimmst, schwimmt	schwamm	geschwommen
schwinden*	schwindest, schwindet	schwand	geschwunden
schwingen	schwingst, schwingt	schwang	geschwungen
schwören	schwörst, schwört	schwur	geschworen
sehen	siehst, sieht	sah	gesehen
sein*	bist, ist	war	gewesen
senden	sendest, sendet	sandte	gesandt
singen	singst, singt	sang	gesungen
sinken*	sinkst, sinkt	sank	gesunken
sinnen	sinnst, sinnt	sann	gesonnen
sitzen*	sitzt, sitzt	saß	gesessen
sollen	sollst, soll	sollte	gesollt
speien	speist, speit	spie	gespie(e)n
spinnen	spinnst, spinnt	spann	gesponnen
sprechen	sprichst, spricht	sprach	gesprochen
sprießen*	sprießt, sprießt	sproß	gesprossen
springen*	springst, springt	sprang	gesprungen
stechen	stichst, sticht	stach	gestochen
stecken	steckst, steckt	steckte or stak	gesteckt
stehen	stehst, steht	stand	gestanden
stehlen	stiehlst, stiehlt	stahl	gestohlen
steigen*	steigst, steigt	stieg	gestiegen
sterben*	stirbst, stirbt	starb	gestorben
stinken	stinkst, stinkt	stank	gestunken
stoßen	stößt, stößt	stieß	gestoßen
streichen	streichst, streicht	strich	gestrichen
streiten	streitest, streitet	stritt	gestritten
tragen	trägst, trägt	trug	getragen
treffen	triffst, trifft	traf	getroffen
treiben*	treibst, treibt	trieb	getrieben

infinitive	present indicative (2nd, 3rd sing.)	preterite	past participle
treten*	trittst, tritt	trat	getreten
trinken	trinkst, trinkt	trank	getrunken
trügen	trügst, trügt	trog	getrogen
tun	tust, tut	tat	getan
verderben	verdirbst, verdirbt	verdarb	verdorben
verdrießen	verdrießt, verdrießt	verdroß	verdrossen
vergessen	vergißt, vergißt	vergaß	vergessen
verlieren	verlierst, verliert	verlor	verloren
verschleißen	verschleißt, verschleißt	verschliß	verschlissen
wachsen*	wächst, wächst	wuchs	gewachsen
wägen	wägst, wägt	wog	gewogen
waschen	wäschst, wäscht	wusch	gewaschen
weben	webst, webt	wob	gewoben
weichen*	weichst, weicht	wich	gewichen
weisen	weist, weist	wies	gewiesen
wenden	wendest, wendet	wandte	gewandt
werben	wirbst, wirbt	warb	geworben
werden*	wirst, wird	wurde	geworden
werfen	wirfst, wirft	warf	geworfen
wiegen	wiegst, wiegt	wog	gewogen
winden	windest, windet	wand	gewunden
wissen	weißt, weiß	wußte	gewußt
wollen	willst, will	wollte	gewollt
wringen	wringst, wringt	wrang	gewrungen
zeihen	zeihst, zeiht	zieh	geziehen
ziehen*	ziehst, zieht	zog	gezogen
zwingen	zwingst, zwingt	zwang	gezwungen

A

A, a [eɪ] n A nt, a nt.
a, an [eɪ, ə; æn, ən] Indef art
ein/eine/ein. £1 a metre 1£ pro or
das Meter.
aback [ə'bæk] ad: to be taken —
verblüfft sein.
abandon [ə'bændən] vt (give up)
aufgeben; (desert) verlassen; n
Hingabe f.
abashed [ə'bæʃt] a verlegen.
abate [ə'beɪt] vi nachlassen, sich
legen.
abattoir ['æbətwa:*] n Schlacht-
haus nt.
abbey ['æbɪ] n Abtei f.
abbot ['æbət] n Abt m.
abbreviate [ə'bri:vɪeɪt] vt abkürzen.
abbreviation [əbri:vɪ'eɪʃən] n Abkürzung f.
ABC ['eɪbi:'si:] n (lit, fig) Abc nt.
abdicate ['æbdɪkeɪt] vt aufgeben;
vi abdanken.
abdication [æbdɪ'keɪʃən] n Abdankung f; (Amts)niederlegung f.
abdomen ['æbdəmən] n Unterleib
m.
abdominal [æb'dɒmɪnl] a Unter-
leibs-.
abduct [æb'dʌkt] vt entführen;
—ion [æb'dʌkʃən] Entführung f.
aberration [æbə'reɪʃən] n (geistige)
Verwirrung f.
abet [ə'bet] vt see aid vt.
abeyance [ə'beɪəns] n: in — der
Schwebe; (disuse) außer Kraft.

abhor [əb'hɔ:*] vt verabscheuen.
abhorrent [əb'hɒrənt] a verab-
scheuungswürdig.
abide [ə'baɪd] vt vertragen; leiden;
— by vt sich halten an (+acc).
ability [ə'bɪlɪtɪ] n (power) Fähigkeit
f; (skill) Geschicklichkeit f.
abject ['æbdʒekt] a liar übel;
poverty größte(r, s); apology
zerknirscht.
ablaze [ə'bleɪz] a in Flammen; —
with lights hell erleuchtet.
able ['eɪbl] a geschickt, fähig; to be
— to do sth etw tun können; —
bodied a kräftig; seaman Voll-;
(Mil) wehrfähig.
ably ['eɪblɪ] ad geschickt.
abnormal [æb'nɔ:məl] a regel-
widrig, abnorm; —ity
[æbnɔ:'mælɪtɪ] Regelwidrigkeit f;
(Med) krankhafte Erscheinung f.
aboard [ə'bɔ:d] ad, prep an Bord
(+gen).
abode [ə'bəud] n: of no fixed —
ohne festen Wohnsitz.
abolish [ə'bɒlɪʃ] vt abschaffen.
abolition [æbə'lɪʃən] n Abschaffung f.
abominable, abominably ad
[ə'bɒmɪnəbl, -blɪ] scheußlich.
aborigine [æbə'rɪdʒɪni:] n Urein-
wohner m.
abort [ə'bɔ:t] vt abtreiben; fehlge-
bären; —ion [ə'bɔ:ʃən] Abtreibung
f; (miscarriage) Fehlgeburt f;
—ive a mißlungen.

abound [ə'baʊnd] *vi* im Überfluß vorhanden sein; **to —** in Überfluß haben an (+*dat*).

about [ə'baʊt] *ad* (*nearby*) in der Nähe; (*roughly*) ungefähr; (*around*) umher, herum; *prep* (*topic*) über (+*acc*); (*place*) um, um… herum; **to be —** to im Begriff sein zu; **I was —** to go out ich wollte gerade weggehen.

above [ə'bʌv] *ad* oben; *prep* über; *a* obig; **— all** vor allem; **—board** *a* offen, ehrlich.

abrasion [ə'breɪʒən] *n* Abschürfung *f.*

abrasive [ə'breɪzɪv] *n* Schleifmittel *nt*; *a* Schleif-; *personality* zermürbend, aufreibend.

abreast [ə'brest] *ad* nebeneinander; **to keep —** of Schritt halten mit.

abridge [ə'brɪdʒ] *vt* (ab)kürzen.

abroad [ə'brɔːd] *ad* be im Ausland; *go* ins Ausland.

abrupt [ə'brʌpt] *a* (*sudden*) abrupt, jäh; (*curt*) schroff.

abscess ['æbsɪs] *n* Geschwür *nt.*

abscond [æb'skɒnd] *vi* flüchten, sich davonmachen.

absence ['æbsəns] *n* Abwesenheit *f.*

absent ['æbsənt] *a* abwesend, nicht da; (*lost in thought*) geistesabwesend; **—ee** [æbsən'tiː] Abwesende(r) *m*; **—eeism** [æbsən'tiːɪzəm] Fehlen *nt* (am Arbeitsplatz/in der Schule); **—minded** *a* zerstreut.

absolute ['æbsəluːt] *a* absolut; *power* unumschränkt; *rubbish* vollkommen, rein; **—ly** ['æbsəluːtlɪ] *ad* absolut, vollkommen; **—!** ganz bestimmt!

absolve [əb'zɒlv] *vt* entbinden; freisprechen.

absorb [əb'zɔːb] *vt* aufsaugen, absorbieren; (*fig*) ganz in Anspruch

nehmen, fesseln; **—ent** *a* absorbierend; **—ent cotton** (*US*) Verbandwatte *f*; **—ing** *a* aufsaugend; (*fig*) packend.

abstain [əb'steɪn] *vi* (*in vote*) sich enthalten; **to — from** (*keep from*) sich enthalten (+*gen*).

abstemious [əb'stiːmɪəs] *a* mäßig, enthaltsam.

abstention [əb'stenʃən] *n* (*in vote*) (Stimm)enthaltung *f.*

abstinence ['æbstɪnəns] *n* Enthaltsamkeit *f.*

abstract ['æbstrækt] *a* abstrakt; *n* Abriß *m*; [æb'strækt] *vt* abstrahieren, aussondern.

abstruse [æb'struːs] *a* verworren, abstrus.

absurd [əb'sɜːd] *a* absurd; **—ity** Unsinnigkeit *f*, Absurdität *f.*

abundance [ə'bʌndəns] *n* Überfluß *m* (*of an* +*dat*).

abundant [ə'bʌndənt] *a* reichlich.

abuse [ə'bjuːs] *n* (*rude language*) Beschimpfung *f*; (*ill usage*) Mißbrauch *m*; (*bad practice*) (Amts)mißbrauch *m*; [ə'bjuːz] *vt* (*misuse*) mißbrauchen.

abusive [ə'bjuːsɪv] *a* beleidigend, Schimpf-.

abysmal [ə'bɪzməl] *a* scheußlich; *ignorance* bodenlos.

abyss [ə'bɪs] *n* Abgrund *m.*

academic [ækə'demɪk] *a* akademisch; (*theoretical*) theoretisch.

academy [ə'kædəmɪ] *n* (*school*) Hochschule *f*; (*society*) Akademie *f.*

accede [æk'siːd] *vi*: **— to** *office* antreten; *throne* besteigen; *request* zustimmen (+*dat*).

accelerate [æk'seləreɪt] *vi* schneller werden; (*Aut*) Gas geben; *vt* beschleunigen.

acceleration [ækselə'reɪʃən] n Beschleunigung f.

accelerator [ək'seləreɪtə*] n Gas-(pedal) nt.

accent ['æksent] n Akzent m, Tonfall m; (mark) Akzent m; (stress) Betonung f; —uate [æk'sentjueɪt] vt betonen.

accept [ək'sept] vt (take) annehmen; (agree to) akzeptieren; —able a annehmbar; —ance Annahme f.

access ['ækses] n Zugang m; —ible [æk'sesɪbl] a (easy to approach) zugänglich; (within reach) (leicht) erreichbar; —ion [æk'seʃən] (to throne) Besteigung f; (to office) Antritt m.

accessory [æk'sesərɪ] n Zubehörteil nt; accessories pl Zubehör nt; toilet accessories pl Toilettenartikel pl.

accident ['æksɪdənt] n Unfall m; (coincidence) Zufall m; by — zufällig; —al [æksɪ'dentl] a unbeabsichtigt; —ally [æksɪ'dentəlɪ] ad zufällig; to be —-prone zu Unfällen neigen.

acclaim [ə'kleɪm] vt zujubeln (+dat); n Beifall m.

acclimatize [ə'klaɪmətaɪz] vt: to become —d sich gewöhnen (to an + acc), sich akklimatisieren.

accolade ['ækəleɪd] n Auszeichnung f.

accommodate [ə'kɒmədeɪt] vt unterbringen, (hold) Platz haben für; (oblige) (aus)helfen (+ dat).

accommodating [ə'kɒmədeɪtɪŋ] a entgegenkommend.

accommodation [ə'kɒmə'deɪʃən] n Unterkunft f.

accompaniment [ə'kʌmpənɪmənt] n Begleitung f.

accompanist [ə'kʌmpənɪst] n Begleiter m.

accompany [ə'kʌmpənɪ] vt begleiten.

accomplice [ə'kʌmplɪs] n Helfershelfer m, Komplize m.

accomplish [ə'kʌmplɪʃ] vt (fulfil) durchführen; (finish) vollenden; aim erreichen; —ed a vollendet, ausgezeichnet; —ment (skill) Fähigkeit f; (completion) Vollendung f; (feat) Leistung f.

accord [ə'kɔːd] n Übereinstimmung f; of one's own — freiwillig; —ance: in — ance with in Übereinstimmung mit; —ing to nach, laut (+gen); —ingly ad danach, dementsprechend.

accordion [ə'kɔːdɪən] n Ziehharmonika f, Akkordeon nt; —ist Akkordeonspieler m.

accost [ə'kɒst] vt ansprechen.

account [ə'kaʊnt] n (bill) Rechnung f; (narrative) Bericht m; (report) Rechenschaftsbericht m; (in bank) Konto nt; (importance) Geltung f; on — auf Rechnung; of no — ohne Bedeutung; on no — keinesfalls; on — of wegen; to take into — berücksichtigen; — for vt expenditure Rechenschaft ablegen für; how do you — for that? wie erklären Sie (sich) das?; —able a verantwortlich; —ancy Buchhaltung f; —ant Wirtschaftsprüfer(in f) m.

accoutrements [ə'kuːtrəmənts] npl Ausrüstung f.

accredited [ə'kredɪtɪd] a beglaubigt, akkreditiert.

accretion [ə'kriːʃən] n Zunahme f.

accrue [ə'kruː] vi erwachsen, sich ansammeln.

accumulate [ə'kjuːmjuleɪt] vt ansammeln; vi sich ansammeln.

accumulation [əkjuːmjuˈleɪʃən] *n* (*act*) Aufhäufung *f*; (*result*) Ansammlung *f*.

accuracy [ˈækjʊrəsɪ] *n* Genauigkeit *f*.

accurate [ˈækjʊrɪt] *a* genau; **—ly** *ad* genau, richtig.

accursed, accurst [əˈkɜːst] *a* verflucht.

accusation [ækjuːˈzeɪʃən] *n* Anklage *f*, Beschuldigung *f*.

accusative [əˈkjuːzətɪv] *n* Akkusativ *m*, vierte(r) Fall *m*.

accuse [əˈkjuːz] *vt* anklagen, beschuldigen; **—d** Angeklagte(r) *mf*.

accustom [əˈkʌstəm] *vt* gewöhnen (*to* an +*acc*); **—ed** *a* gewohnt.

ace [eɪs] *n* As *nt*; (*col*) As *nt*, Kanone *f*.

ache [eɪk] *n* Schmerz *m*; *vi* (*be sore*) schmerzen, weh tun; **I —** all over mir tut es überall weh.

achieve [əˈtʃiːv] *vt* zustande bringen; *aim* erreichen; **—ment** Leistung *f*; (*act*) Erreichen *nt*.

acid [ˈæsɪd] *n* Säure *f*; *a* sauer, scharf; **—ity** [əˈsɪdɪtɪ] Säuregehalt *m*; **— test** (*fig*) Nagelprobe *f*.

acknowledge [əkˈnɒlɪdʒ] *vt receipt* bestätigen; (*admit*) zugeben; **—ment** Anerkennung *f*; (*letter*) Empfangsbestätigung *f*.

acne [ˈæknɪ] *n* Akne *f*.

acorn [ˈeɪkɔːn] *n* Eichel *f*.

acoustic [əˈkuːstɪk] *a* akustisch; **—s** *pl* Akustik *f*.

acquaint [əˈkweɪnt] *vt* vertraut machen; **—ance** (*person*) Bekannte(r) *m*; (*knowledge*) Kenntnis *f*.

acquiesce [ækwɪˈes] *vi* sich abfinden (*in* mit).

acquire [əˈkwaɪə*] *vt* erwerben.

acquisition [ækwɪˈzɪʃən] *n* Errungenschaft *f*; (*act*) Erwerb *m*.

acquisitive [əˈkwɪzɪtɪv] *a* gewinnsüchtig.

acquit [əˈkwɪt] *vt* (*free*) freisprechen; **to — o.s.** sich bewähren; **—tal** Freispruch *m*.

acre [ˈeɪkə*] *n* Morgen *m*; **—age** Fläche *f*.

acrimonious [ækrɪˈməʊnɪəs] *a* bitter.

acrobat [ˈækrəbæt] *n* Akrobat *m*.

acrobatics [ækrəˈbætɪks] *npl* akrobatische Kunststücke *pl*.

across [əˈkrɒs] *prep* über (+*acc*); **he lives — the river** da wohnt er auf der anderen Seite des Flusses; *ad* hinüber, herüber; **ten metres — zehn Meter breit**; **he lives — from us** er wohnt uns gegenüber; **—the-board** *a* pauschal.

act [ækt] *n* (*deed*) Tat *f*; (*Jur*) Gesetz *nt*; (*Theat*) Akt *m*; (*Theat: turn*) Nummer *f*; *vi* (*take action*) handeln; (*behave*) sich verhalten; (*pretend*) vorgeben; (*Theat*) spielen; *vt* (*in play*) spielen; **—ing** a stellvertretend; *n* Schauspielkunst *f*; (*performance*) Aufführung *f*.

action [ˈækʃən] *n* (*deed*) Tat *f*; Handlung *f*; (*motion*) Bewegung *f*; (*way of working*) Funktionieren *nt*; (*battle*) Einsatz *m*, Gefecht *nt*; (*lawsuit*) Klage *f*, Prozeß *m*; **to take —** etwas unternehmen.

activate [ˈæktɪveɪt] *vt* in Betrieb setzen, aktivieren.

active [ˈæktɪv] *a* (*brisk*) rege, tatkräftig; (*working*) aktiv; (*Gram*) aktiv, Tätigkeits-; **—ly** *ad* aktiv, tätig.

activist [ˈæktɪvɪst] *n* Aktivist *m*.

activity [æk'tɪvɪtɪ] n Aktivität f; (doings) Unternehmungen pl; (occupation) Tätigkeit f.

actor ['æktə*] n Schauspieler m.

actress ['æktrɪs] n Schauspielerin f.

actual ['æktjuəl] a wirklich; —ly ad tatsächlich; —ly no eigentlich nicht.

acumen ['ækjumen] n Scharfsinn m.

acupuncture ['ækjupʌŋktʃə*] n Akupunktur f.

acute [ə'kjuːt] a (severe) heftig, akut; (keen) scharfsinnig; —ly ad akut, scharf.

ad [æd] n abbr of **advertisement**.

adage ['ædɪdʒ] n Sprichwort nt.

Adam ['ædəm] n Adam m; —'s apple Adamsapfel m.

adamant ['ædəmənt] a eisern; hartnäckig.

adapt [ə'dæpt] vt anpassen; vi sich anpassen (to an +acc); —able a anpassungsfähig; —ation [ædæp'teɪʃən] (Theat etc) Bearbeitung f; (adjustment) Anpassung f; —er (Elec) Zwischenstecker m.

add [æd] vt (join) hinzufügen; numbers addieren; — up vi (make sense) stimmen; — up to vt ausmachen.

addendum [ə'dendəm] n Zusatz m.

adder ['ædə*] n Kreuzotter f, Natter f.

addict ['ædɪkt] n Süchtige(r) mf; [ə'dɪktɪd] —ed to -süchtig; —ion [ə'dɪkʃən] Sucht f.

adding machine ['ædɪŋməʃiːn] n Addiermaschine f.

addition [ə'dɪʃən] n Anhang m, Addition f; (Math) Addition f, Zusammenrechnen nt; in — zusätzlich, außerdem; —al a zusätzlich, weiter.

additive ['ædɪtɪv] n Zusatz m.

addled ['ædld] a faul, schlecht; (fig) verwirrt.

address [ə'dres] n Adresse f; (speech) Ansprache f; form of — Anrededorm f; vt letter adressieren; (speak to) ansprechen; (make speech to) eine Ansprache halten an (+acc); —ee [ædre'siː] Empfänger(in f) m, Adressat m.

adenoids ['ædənɔɪdz] npl Polypen pl.

adept ['ædept] a geschickt; **to be** — **at** gut sein in (+dat).

adequacy ['ædɪkwəsɪ] n Angemessenheit f.

adequate ['ædɪkwɪt] a angemessen; —ly ad hinreichend.

adhere [əd'hɪə*] vi: — **to** (lit) haften an (+dat); (fig) festhalten an (+dat).

adhesion [əd'hiːʒən] n Festhaften nt; (Phys) Adhäsion f.

adhesive [əd'hiːzɪv] a klebend; Kleb(e)-; n Klebstoff m.

adieu [ə'djuː] n Adieu nt, Lebewohl nt.

adjacent [ə'dʒeɪsənt] a benachbart.

adjective ['ædʒɪktɪv] n Adjektiv nt, Eigenschaftswort nt.

adjoining [ə'dʒɔɪnɪŋ] a benachbart, Neben-.

adjourn [ə'dʒɜːn] vt vertagen; vi abbrechen.

adjudicate [ə'dʒuːdɪkeɪt] vti entscheiden, ein Urteil fällen.

adjudication [ədʒuːdɪ'keɪʃən] n Entscheidung f.

adjudicator [ə'dʒuːdɪkeɪtə*] n Schiedsrichter m, Preisrichter m.

adjust [ə'dʒʌst] vt (alter) anpassen; (put right) regulieren, richtig stellen; —able a verstellbar; —ment (rearrangement) Anpassung f; (settlement) Schlichtung f.

adjutant ['ædʒətənt] n Adjutant m.

ad-lib [æd'lɪb] vi improvisieren; a Improvisation f; a, ad improvisiert.

administer [æd'mɪnɪstə*] vt (manage) verwalten; (dispense) ausüben; justice sprechen; medicine geben.

administration [ædmɪns'treɪʃən] n Verwaltung f; (Pol) Regierung f.

administrative [æd'mɪnɪstrətɪv] a Verwaltungs-.

administrator [æd'mɪnɪstreɪtə*] n Verwaltungsbeamte(r) m.

admirable ['ædmərəbl] a bewundernswert.

admiral ['ædmərəl] n Admiral m; A—ty Admiralität f.

admiration [ædmɪ'reɪʃən] n Bewunderung f.

admire [æd'maɪə*] vt (respect) bewundern; (love) verehren; —r Bewunderer m.

admission [əd'mɪʃən] n (entrance) Einlaß m; (fee) Eintritt(spreis) m; (confession) Geständnis nt.

admit [əd'mɪt] vt (let in) einlassen; (confess) gestehen; (accept) anerkennen; —tance Zulassung f; —tedly ad zugegebenermaßen.

ado [ə'duː] n: without more — ohne weitere Umstände.

adolescence [ædə'lesns] n Jugendalter m.

adolescent [ædə'lesnt] a heranwachsend, jugendlich; n Jugendliche(r) mf.

adopt [ə'dɒpt] vt child adoptieren; idea übernehmen; —ion [ə'dɒpʃən] (of child) Adoption f; (of idea) Übernahme f.

adorable [ə'dɔːrəbl] a anbetungswürdig; (likeable) entzückend.

adoration [ædɒ'reɪʃən] n Anbetung f; Verehrung f.

adore [ə'dɔː*] vt anbeten; verehren.

adoring [ə'dɔːrɪŋ] a verehrend.

adorn [ə'dɔːn] vt schmücken.

adornment [ə'dɔːnmənt] n Schmuck m, Verzierung f.

adrenalin [ə'drenəlɪn] n Adrenalin nt.

adrift [ə'drɪft] ad Wind und Wellen preisgegeben.

adroit [ə'drɔɪt] a gewandt.

adulation [ædjuː'leɪʃən] n Lobhudelei f.

adult ['ædʌlt] a erwachsen; n Erwachsene(r) mf.

adulterate [ə'dʌltəreɪt] vt verfälschen, mischen.

adultery [ə'dʌltərɪ] n Ehebruch m.

advance [əd'vɑːns] n (progress) Vorrücken nt; (money) Vorschuß m; vt (move forward) vorrücken; money vorschießen; argument vorbringen; vi vorwärtsgehen; in — im voraus; in — of vor (+dat); — booking Vorbestellung f, Vorverkauf m; —d (ahead) vorgerückt; (modern) fortgeschritten; study für Fortgeschrittene; —ment Förderung f; (promotion) Beförderung f.

advantage [əd'vɑːntɪdʒ] n Vorteil m; —ous [ædvən'teɪdʒəs] a vorteilhaft; to have an — over sb jdm gegenüber im Vorteil sein; to be of — von Nutzen sein; to take — of (misuse) ausnutzen; (profit from) Nutzen ziehen aus.

advent ['ædvent] n Ankunft f; A— Advent m.

adventure [əd'ventʃə*] n Abenteuer nt.

adventurous [əd'ventʃərəs] a abenteuerlich, waghalsig.

adverb ['ædvɜ:b] n Adverb nt, Umstandswort nt.

adversary ['ædvəsəri] n Gegner m.

adverse ['ædvɜ:s] a widrig.

adversity [əd'vɜ:sɪtɪ] n Widrigkeit f, Mißgeschick nt.

advert ['ædvɜ:t], **—ise** vt .anzeigen; vi annoncieren; **—isement** [əd'vɜ:tɪsmənt] Anzeige f, Annonce f, Inserat nt; **—ising** Werbung f; **—ising campaign** Werbekampagne f.

advice [əd'vaɪs] n Rat(schlag) m.

advisable [əd'vaɪzəbl] a ratsam.

advise [əd'vaɪz] vt raten (+dat); **—r** Berater m.

advisory [əd'vaɪzərɪ] a beratend, Beratungs-.

advocate ['ædvəkeɪt] vt vertreten.

aegis ['i:dʒɪs] n: under the **—** of unter der Schirmherrschaft von.

aerial ['eərɪəl] n Antenne f; a Luft-.

aero- ['eərəʊ] pref Luft-.

aeroplane ['eərəpleɪn] n Flugzeug nt.

aerosol ['eərəsɒl] n Aerosol nt; Sprühdose f.

aesthetic [ɪs'θetɪk] a ästhetisch; **—s** Ästhetik f.

afar [ə'fɑ:*] ad: from **—** aus der Ferne.

affable ['æfəbl] a umgänglich.

affair [ə'feə*] n (concern) Angelegenheit f; (event) Ereignis nt; (love **—**) (Liebes)verhältnis nt.

affect [ə'fekt] vt (influence) (ein)wirken auf (+acc); (move deeply) bewegen; this change doesn't **—** us diese Änderung betrifft uns nicht; **—ation** [æfek'teɪʃən] Affektiertheit f, Verstellung f; **—ed** a affektiert, gekünstelt; **—ion** [ə'fekʃən] Zuneigung f; **—ionate** [ə'fekʃənɪt] a liebevoll, lieb; **—ionately**

[ə'fekʃənɪtlɪ] ad liebevoll; **—ionately yours** herzlichst Dein.

affiliated [ə'fɪlɪeɪtɪd] a angeschlossen (to dat).

affinity [ə'fɪnɪtɪ] n (attraction) gegenseitige Anziehung f; (relationship) Verwandtschaft f.

affirmation [æfə'meɪʃən] n Behauptung f.

affirmative [ə'fɜ:mətɪv] a bestätigend; n: in the **—** (Gram) nicht verneint; to answer in the **—** mit Ja antworten.

affix [ə'fɪks] vt aufkleben, anheften.

afflict [ə'flɪkt] vt quälen, heimsuchen; **—ion** [ə'flɪkʃən] Kummer m; (illness) Leiden nt.

affluence ['æfluəns] n (wealth) Wohlstand m.

affluent ['æfluənt] a wohlhabend, Wohlstands-.

afford [ə'fɔ:d] vt (sich) leisten, erschwingen; (yield) bieten, einbringen.

affront [ə'frʌnt] n Beleidigung f; **—ed** a beleidigt.

afield [ə'fi:ld] ad: far **—** weit fort.

afloat [ə'fləʊt] a: to be **—** schwimmen.

afoot [ə'fʊt] ad im Gang.

aforesaid [ə'fɔ:sed] a obengenannt.

afraid [ə'freɪd] a ängstlich; to be **—** of Angst haben vor (+dat); to be **—** to sich scheuen; I am **—** I have... ich habe leider...; I'm so/not leider/leider nicht.

afresh [ə'freʃ] ad von neuem.

aft [ɑ:ft] ad achtern.

after ['ɑ:ftə*] prep nach; (following, seeking) hinter ... (dat) ... her; (in imitation) nach, im Stil von; ad: soon **—** bald danach; **—** all letzten Endes; **—effects** pl Nachwirkungen pl; **—life** Leben nt nach dem Tode; —math Auswirkungen pl; —noon Nachmittag m; good —noon! guten Tag!; —shave (lotion) Rasierwasser nt; —thought nachträgliche(r) Einfall m; —wards ad danach, nachher.

again [ə'gen] ad wieder, noch einmal; (besides) außerdem, ferner; — and — immer wieder.

against [ə'genst] prep gegen.

age [eɪdʒ] n (of person) Alter nt; (in history) Zeitalter nt; vi altern, alt werden; — of älter machen; to **come of** — mündig werden; —d a ... Jahre alt, -jährig; ['eɪdʒɪd] (elderly) betagt; **the** —d die Bejahrten pl; — **group** Altersgruppe f, Jahrgang m; —less a zeitlos; — **limit** Altersgrenze f.

agency ['eɪdʒənsɪ] n Agentur f; Vermittlung f; (Chem) Wirkung f.

agenda [ə'dʒendə] n Tagesordnung f.

agent ['eɪdʒənt] n (Comm) Vertreter m; (spy) Agent m.

aggravate ['ægrəveɪt] vt (make worse) verschlimmern; (irritate) reizen.

aggravating ['ægrəveɪtɪŋ] a verschlimmernd; ärgerlich.

aggravation [ægrə'veɪʃən] n Verschlimmerung f, Verärgerung f.

aggregate ['ægrɪgɪt] n Summe f.

aggression [ə'greʃən] n Aggression f.

aggressive a, —**ly** [ə'gresɪv, -lɪ] aggressiv; —**ness** Aggressivität f.

aggrieved [ə'griːvd] a bedrückt, verletzt.

aghast [ə'gɑːst] a entsetzt.

agile ['ædʒaɪl] a flink, agil; mind rege.

agitate ['ædʒɪteɪt] vt rütteln; vi agitieren; —d a aufgeregt.

agitator ['ædʒɪteɪtə*] n Agitator m; (pej) Hetzer m.

agnostic [æg'nɒstɪk] n Agnostiker (in f) m.

ago [ə'gəʊ] ad: two days — vor zwei Tagen; not long — vor kurzem; it's so long — es ist schon so lange her.

agog [ə'gɒg] a, ad gespannt.

agonized ['ægənaɪzd] a gequält.

agonizing ['ægənaɪzɪŋ] a quälend.

agony ['ægənɪ] n Qual f.

agree [ə'griː] vt date vereinbaren; vi (have same opinion, correspond) übereinstimmen (with mit); (consent) zustimmen; (be in harmony) sich vertragen; to — **to do sth** sich bereit erklären, etw zu tun; garlic doesn't — **with me** Knoblauch vertrage ich nicht; **I** — einverstanden, ich stimme zu; to — **on** sth sich auf etw (acc) einigen; —**able** a (pleasing) liebenswürdig; (willing to consent) einverstanden; —**ably** ad angenehm; —d a vereinbart; —**ment** (agreeing) Übereinstimmung f; (contract) Vereinbarung f, Vertrag m.

agricultural [ægrɪ'kʌltʃərəl] a landwirtschaftlich, Landwirtschafts-.

agriculture ['ægrɪkʌltʃə*] n Landwirtschaft f.

aground [ə'graʊnd] a, ad auf Grund.

ahead [ə'hed] ad vorwärts; **to be** — voraus sein.

ahoy [ə'hɔɪ] interj ahoi!

aid [eɪd] n (assistance) Hilfe f, Unterstützung f; (person) Hilfe f; (thing) Hilfsmittel nt; vt unterstützen, helfen (+dat); — **and abet** vti Beihilfe leisten (sb jdm).

aide [eɪd] n (person) Gehilfe m; (Mil) Adjutant m.

ailing ['eɪlɪŋ] a kränkelnd.

ailment ['eɪlmənt] n Leiden nt.

aim [eɪm] vt gun, camera richten auf (+acc); that was —ed at you das war auf dich gemünzt; vi (with gun) zielen; (intend) beabsichtigen; to — at sth etw anstreben; n (intention) Absicht f, Ziel nt; (pointing) Zielen nt, Richten nt; to take — zielen; —less a, —lessly ad zellos.

air [ɛə*] n Luft f, Atmosphäre f; (manner) Miene f, Anschein m; (Mus) Melodie f; vt lüften; (fig) an die Öffentlichkeit bringen; —bed Luftmatratze f; —conditioned a mit Klimaanlage; —conditioning Klimaanlage f; —craft Flugzeug nt, Maschine f; —craft carrier Flugzeugträger m; —force Luftwaffe f; —gun Luftgewehr nt; — hostess Stewardeß f; —ily ad leichtfertig; — letter Luftpost(leicht)brief m; —line Luftverkehrsgesellschaft f; —liner Verkehrsflugzeug nt; —lock Luftblase f; —mail mit Luftpost; —port Flughafen m, Flugplatz m; — raid Luftangriff m; —sick a luftkrank; —strip Landestreifen m; —tight a luftdicht; —y a luftig; manner leichtfertig.

aisle [aɪl] n Gang m.

ajar [ə'dʒɑ:*] ad angelehnt; ein Spalt offen.

alabaster ['æləbɑ:stə*] n Alabaster m.

à la carte [ælæ'kɑ:t] a nach der (Speise)karte, à la carte.

alacrity [ə'lækrɪtɪ] n Bereitwilligkeit f.

alarm [ə'lɑ:m] n (warning) Alarm m; (bell etc) Alarmanlage f; vt erschrecken; — clock Wecker m; —ing a beängstigend; —ist Bangemacher m.

alas [ə'læs] interj ach.

album ['ælbəm] n Album nt.

alcohol ['ælkəhɒl] n Alkohol m; —ic [ælkə'hɒlɪk] a drink alkoholisch; n Alkoholiker(in f) m; —ism Alkoholismus m.

alcove ['ælkəʊv] n Alkoven m.

alderman ['ɔ:ldəmən] n Stadtrat m.

ale [eɪl] n Ale nt.

alert [ə'lɜ:t] a wachsam; n Alarm m; —ness Wachsamkeit f.

algebra ['ældʒɪbrə] n Algebra f.

alias ['eɪlɪəs] ad alias; n Deckname m.

alibi ['ælɪbaɪ] n Alibi nt.

alien ['eɪlɪən] n Ausländer m; (foreign) ausländisch; (strange) fremd; —ate vt entfremden; —ation [eɪlɪə'neɪʃən] Entfremdung f.

alight [ə'laɪt] a, ad brennend; (of building) in Flammen; vi (descend) aussteigen; (bird) sich setzen.

align [ə'laɪn] vt ausrichten; —ment Ausrichtung f; Gruppierung f.

alike [ə'laɪk] a gleich, ähnlich; ad gleich, ebenso.

alimony ['ælɪmənɪ] n Unterhalt m, Alimente pl.

alive [ə'laɪv] a (living) lebend; (lively) lebendig, aufgeweckt; (full of) voll (with von), wimmelnd (with von).

alkali ['ælkəlaɪ] n Alkali nt.

all [ɔ:l] a (every one of) alle; n (the whole) alles, das Ganze; ad (completely) vollkommen, ganz; it's — mine das gehört alles mir; it's — over es ist alles aus or vorbei; — around the edge rund um den Rand; — at once auf einmal; — but alle(s) außer; (almost) fast; — in — alles in allem; — over town in der ganzen Stadt; — right okay, in Ordnung;

not at — ganz und gar nicht ; (*don't mention it*) bitte.

allay [ə'leɪ] vt fears beschwichtigen.

allegation [ælɪ'geɪʃən] n Behauptung f.

allege [ə'ledʒ] vt (*declare*) behaupten ; (*falsely*) vorgeben ; **—dly** [ə'ledʒɪdlɪ] ad angeblich.

allegiance [ə'liːdʒəns] n Treue f, Ergebenheit f.

allegory [æligərɪ] n Allegorie f.

all-embracing ['ɔːlɪm'breɪsɪŋ] a allumfassend.

allergic [ə'lɜːdʒɪk] a allergisch (*to* gegen).

allergy [ælədʒɪ] n Allergie f.

alleviate [ə'liːvɪeɪt] vt erleichtern, lindern.

alleviation [əliːvɪ'eɪʃən] n Erleichterung f.

alley [ælɪ] n Gasse f, Durchgang m.

alliance [ə'laɪəns] n Bund m, Allianz f.

allied [ælaɪd] a vereinigt ; *powers* alliiert ; verwandt (*to* mit).

alligator [ælɪgeɪtə*] n Alligator m.

all-important ['ɔːlɪm'pɔːtənt] a äußerst wichtig.

all-in ['ɔːlɪn] a, ad charge alles inbegriffen, Gesamt- ; (*exhausted*) erledigt, kaputt.

alliteration [əlɪtə'reɪʃən] n Alliteration f, Stabreim m.

all-night ['ɔːl'naɪt] a, café, cinema die ganze Nacht geöffnet, Nacht-.

allocate [æləkeɪt] vt zuweisen, zuteilen.

allocation [ælə'keɪʃən] n Zuteilung f.

allot [ə'lɒt] vt zuteilen ; **—ment** (*share*) Anteil m ; (*plot*) Schrebergarten m.

all-out ['ɔːl'aut] a, ad total.

allow [ə'lau] vt (*permit*) erlauben, gestatten (*sb* jdm) ; (*grant*) bewilligen ; (*deduct*) abziehen ; **— for** vt berücksichtigen, einplanen ; **—ance** Beihilfe f ; to make —ances for berücksichtigen.

alloy [æbɪ] n Metallegierung f.

all-round ['ɔːl'raund] a *sportsman* allseitig, Allround-.

all-rounder ['ɔːl'raundə*] n (*Sport*) vielseitige(r) Sportler ; (*general*) Allerweltskerl m.

all-time ['ɔːl'taɪm] a record, high ... aller Zeiten, Höchst-.

allude [ə'luːd] vi hinweisen, anspielen (*to* auf +acc).

alluring [ə'ljuərɪŋ] a verlockend.

allusion [ə'luːʒən] n Anspielung f, Andeutung f.

alluvium [ə'luːvɪəm] n Schwemmland nt.

ally [ælaɪ] n Verbündete(r) mf ; (*Pol*) Alliierte(r) m.

almanac ['ɔːlmənæk] n Kalender m.

almighty [ɔːl'maɪtɪ] a allmächtig ; the A— der Allmächtige.

almond ['ɑːmənd] n Mandel f.

almost [ɔːlmoust] ad fast, beinahe.

alms [ɑːmz] n Almosen nt.

alone [ə'ləun] a, ad allein.

along [ə'lɒŋ] prep entlang, längs ; ad (*onward*) vorwärts, weiter ; **— with** zusammen mit ; **—side** ad walk nebenher ; come nebendran ; be daneben ; prep (*walk, compared with*) neben (+dat) ; (*come*) neben (+acc) ; (*be*) entlang, neben (+dat) ; (*of ship*) längsseits (+gen) ; **—** the river den Fluß entlang ; I knew all **—** ich wußte die ganze Zeit.

aloof [ə'luːf] a zurückhaltend ; ad fern ; **—ness** Zurückhaltung f, Sich-Fernhalten nt.

aloud [ə'laʊd] ad laut.

alphabet ['ælfəbet] n Alphabet nt; **—ical** [ælfə'betɪkl] a alphabetisch.

alpine ['ælpaɪn] a alpin, Alpen-.

already [ɔ:l'redɪ] ad schon, bereits.

also ['ɔ:lsəʊ] ad auch, außerdem.

altar ['ɔ:ltə*] n Altar m.

alter ['ɔ:ltə*] vti ändern; dress umändern; **—ation** [ɔ:ltə'reɪʃən] Änderung f; Umänderung f; (to building) Umbau m.

alternate [ɒl'tɜ:nɪt] a abwechselnd; [ɒlts:neɪt] vi abwechseln (with mit); **—ly** ad abwechselnd, wechselweise.

alternative [ɒl'tɜ:nətɪv] a andere(r, s); n (Aus)wahl f, Alternative f; what's the —? welche Alternative gibt es?; we have no — uns bleibt keine andere Wahl; **—ly** ad im anderen Falle.

although [ɔ:l'ðəʊ] cj obwohl, wenn auch.

altitude ['æltɪtju:d] n Höhe f.

alto ['æltəʊ] n Alt m.

altogether [ɔ:ltə'geðə*] ad (on the whole) im ganzen genommen; (entirely) ganz und gar.

altruistic [æltru'ɪstɪk] a uneigennützig, altruistisch.

aluminium [ælju'mɪnɪəm], (US) **aluminum** [ə'lu:mɪnəm] n Aluminium nt.

always ['ɔ:lweɪz] ad immer; it was — that way es war schon immer so.

amalgam [ə'mælgəm] n Amalgam nt; (fig) Mischung f.

amalgamate [ə'mælgəmeɪt] vi (combine) sich vereinigen; vt (mix) amalgamieren.

amalgamation [əmælgə'meɪʃən] n Verschmelzung f, Zusammenschluß m.

amass [ə'mæs] vt anhäufen.

amateur ['æmətɜ:*] n Amateur m; (pej) Amateur m, Bastler m, Stümper m; a Amateur-, Bastler-; **—ish** a (pej) dilettantisch, stümperhaft.

amaze [ə'meɪz] vt erstaunen, in Staunen versetzen; **—ment** höchste(s) (Er)staunen nt.

amazing [ə'meɪzɪŋ] a höchst erstaunlich.

ambassador [æm'bæsədə*] n Botschafter m.

amber ['æmbə*] n Bernstein m.

ambidextrous [æmbɪ'dekstrəs] a beidhändig.

ambiguity [æmbɪ'gjʊɪtɪ] n Zweideutigkeit f, Unklarheit f.

ambiguous [æm'bɪgjʊəs] a zweideutig; (not clear) unklar.

ambition [æm'bɪʃən] n Ehrgeiz m.

ambitious [æm'bɪʃəs] a ehrgeizig.

ambivalent [æm'bɪvələnt] n attitude zwiespältig.

amble ['æmbl] vi schlendern.

ambulance ['æmbjʊləns] n Krankenwagen m.

ambush ['æmbʊʃ] n Hinterhalt m; vt aus dem Hinterhalt angreifen, überfallen.

ameliorate [ə'mi:lɪəreɪt] vt verbessern.

amelioration [əmi:lɪə'reɪʃən] n Verbesserung f.

amen ['ɑ:'men] interj amen.

amenable [ə'mi:nəbl] a gefügig; (to reason) zugänglich (to dat); (to flattery) empfänglich (to für); (to law) unterworfen (to dat).

amend [ə'mend] vt law etc abändern, ergänzen; to make **—s** etw wiedergutmachen; **—ment** Abänderung f.

amenity [ə'miːnɪtɪ] n (moderne) Einrichtung f.

Americanize [ə'merɪkənaɪz] vt amerikanisieren.

amethyst ['æmɪθɪst] n Amethyst m.

amiable ['eɪmɪəbl] a liebenswürdig, sympathisch.

amicable ['æmɪkəbl] a freundschaftlich; settlement gütlich.

amid(st) [ə'mɪd(st)] prep mitten in or unter (+dat).

amiss [ə'mɪs] a verkehrt, nicht richtig; ad to take sth — etw übelnehmen.

ammeter ['æmɪtə*] n (Aut) Amperemeter m.

ammunition [æmju'nɪʃən] n Munition f.

amnesia [æm'niːzɪə] n Gedächtnisverlust m.

amnesty ['æmnɪstɪ] n Amnestie f.

amock [ə'mɒk] ad see amuck.

amoeba [ə'miːbə] n Amöbe f.

among(st) [ə'mʌŋ(st)] prep unter.

amoral [æ'mɒrəl] a unmoralisch.

amorous ['æmərəs] a verliebt.

amorphous [ə'mɔːfəs] a formlos, gestaltlos.

amount [ə'maʊnt] n (of money) Betrag m; (of time, energy) Aufwand m (of an +dat); (of water, sand) Menge f; no — of ... kein(e) ...; vi: to — (total) sich belaufen auf (+acc); this —s to treachery das kommt Verrat gleich; it —s to the same es läuft aufs gleiche hinaus; he won't — to much aus ihm wird nie was.

amp [æmp] n, ampere ['æmpɛə*] n Ampere nt.

amphibious [æm'fɪbɪəs] a amphibisch, Amphibien-.

amphitheatre ['æmfɪθɪətə*] n Amphitheater nt.

ample ['æmpl] a portion reichlich; dress weit, groß; — time genügend Zeit.

amplifier ['æmplɪfaɪə*] n Verstärker m.

amply ['æmplɪ] ad reichlich.

amputate ['æmpjuteɪt] vt amputieren, abnehmen.

amuck [ə'mʌk] ad: to run — Amok laufen.

amuse [ə'mjuːz] vt (entertain) unterhalten; (make smile) belustigen; (occupy) unterhalten; I'm not —d das find' ich gar nicht lustig; if that —s you wann es dir Spaß macht; —ment (feeling) Unterhaltung f; (recreation) Zeitvertreib m.

amusing [ə'mjuːzɪŋ] a amüsant, unterhaltend.

an [æn, ən] indef art ein(e).

anaemia [ə'niːmɪə] n Anämie f.

anaemic [ə'niːmɪk] a blutarm.

anaesthetic [ænɪs'θetɪk] n Betäubungsmittel nt; under — in Narkose.

anagram ['ænəgræm] n Anagramm nt.

analgesic [ænæl'dʒiːsɪk] n schmerzlindernde(s) Mittel nt.

analogous [ə'næləgəs] a analog.

analogy [ə'nælədʒɪ] n Analogie f.

analyse ['ænəlaɪz] vt analysieren.

analysis [ə'nælɪsɪs] n Analyse f.

analytic [ænə'lɪtɪk] a analytisch.

anarchist ['ænəkɪst] n Anarchist(in f) m.

anarchy ['ænəkɪ] n Anarchie f.

anathema [ə'næθɪmə] n (fig) Greuel nt.

anatomical [ænə'tɒmɪkəl] a anatomisch.

anatomy [ə'nætəmɪ] n (structure)

anatomische(r) Aufbau *m*; (*study*) Anatomie *f*.

ancestor ['ænsestə*'] *n* Vorfahr *m*.

ancestral [æn'sestrəl] *n* angestammt, Ahnen-.

ancestry ['ænsistri] *n* Abstammung *f*; Vorfahren *pl*.

anchor ['æŋkə*'] *n* Anker *m*; *vi* ankern, vor Anker liegen; *vt* verankern; —age Ankerplatz *m*.

anchovy ['æntʃəvi] *n* Sardelle *f*.

ancient ['einʃənt] *a* alt; *car etc* uralt.

and [ænd, ənd, ən] *cj* und.

anecdote ['ænikdəʊt] *n* Anekdote *f*.

anemia [ə'ni:miə] *n* (*US*) = **anaemia**.

anemone [ə'neməni] *n* Anemone *f*.

anesthetic [ænis'θetik] *n* (*US*) = **anaesthetic**.

anew [ə'nju:] *ad* von neuem.

angel ['eindʒəl] *n* Engel *m*; —**ic** [æn'dʒelik] *a* engelhaft.

anger ['æŋgə*'] *n* Zorn *m*; *vt* ärgern.

angina [æn'dʒainə] *n* Angina *f*, Halsentzündung *f*.

angle ['æŋgl] *n* Winkel *m*; (*point of view*) Standpunkt *m*; *at an* — nicht gerade; *vt* stellen; *to* — *for* aussein auf (+*acc*); —**r** Angler *m*.

Anglican ['æŋglikən] *a* anglikanisch; *n* Anglikaner(in *f*) *m*.

anglicize ['æŋglisaiz] *vt* anglisieren.

angling ['æŋgliŋ] *n* Angeln *nt*.

Anglo- ['æŋgləʊ] *pref* Anglo-.

angrily ['æŋgrili] *ad* ärgerlich, böse.

angry ['æŋgri] *a* ärgerlich, ungehalten, böse; *wound* entzündet.

anguish ['æŋgwiʃ] *n* Qual *f*.

angular ['æŋgjulə*'] *a* eckig, winkelförmig; *face* kantig.

animal ['æniməl] *n* Tier *nt*; (*living creature*) Lebewesen *nt*; *a* tierisch, animalisch.

animate ['ænimeit] *vt* beleben; ['ænimət] *a* lebhaft; —**d** *a* lebendig; *film* Zeichentrick-.

animation [æni'meiʃən] *n* Lebhaftigkeit *f*.

animosity [æni'mɒsiti] *n* Feindseligkeit *f*, Abneigung *f*.

aniseed ['ænisi:d] *n* Anis *m*.

ankle ['æŋkl] *n* (Fuß)knöchel *m*.

annex ['æneks] *n* Anbau *m*; [ə'neks] *vt* anfügen; (*Pol*) annektieren, angliedern.

annihilate [ə'naiəleit] *vt* vernichten.

anniversary [æni'vɜ:səri] *n* Jahrestag *m*.

annotate ['ænəteit] *vt* kommentieren.

announce [ə'naʊns] *vt* ankündigen, anzeigen; —**ment** Ankündigung *f*; (*official*) Bekanntmachung *f*; —**r** Ansager(in *f*) *m*.

annoy [ə'nɔi] *vt* ärgern; —**ance** Ärgernis *nt*, Störung *f*; —**ing** *a* ärgerlich; *person* lästig.

annual ['ænjʊəl] *a* jährlich; *salary* Jahres-; *n* (*plant*) einjährige Pflanze *f*; (*book*) Jahrbuch *nt*; —**ly** *ad* jährlich.

annuity [ə'njʊiti] *n* Jahresrente *f*.

annul [ə'nʌl] *vt* aufheben, annullieren; —**ment** Aufhebung *f*, Annullierung *f*.

anoint [ə'nɔint] *vt* salben.

anomalous [ə'nɒmələs] *a* unregelmäßig, anomal.

anomaly [ə'nɒməli] *n* Abweichung *f* von der Regel.

anon [ə'nɒn] *a* = **anonymous**.

anonymity [ænə'nimiti] *n* Anonymität *f*.

anonymous [ə'nɒniməs] *a* anonym.

anorak ['ænəræk] *n* Anorak *m*, Windjacke *f*.

another [ə'nʌðə*] *a, pron* (*different*) ein(e) andere(r, s); (*additional*) noch eine(r, s).

answer ['ɑːnsə*] *n* Antwort *f*; *vi* antworten; (*on phone*) sich melden; *vt person* antworten (+*dat*); *letter, question* beantworten; *telephone* gehen an (+*acc*), abnehmen; *door* öffnen; **—able** a beantwortbar; (*responsible*) verantwortlich, haftbar; **—back** *vi* frech sein; **to — for sth** für etw verantwortlich sein; **to — to the name of** auf den Namen ... hören.

ant [ænt] *n* Ameise *f*.

antagonism [æn'tægənɪzəm] *n* Antagonismus *m*.

antagonist [æn'tægənɪst] *n* Gegner *m*, Antagonist *m*; **—ic** [æntægə'nɪstɪk] a feindselig.

antagonize [æn'tægənaɪz] *vt* reizen.

anteater ['ænti:tə*] *n* Ameisenbär *m*.

antecedent [æntɪ'si:dənt] *n* Vorhergehende(s) *nt*; **—s** *pl* Vorleben *nt*, Vorgeschichte *f*.

antelope ['æntɪləʊp] *n* Antilope *f*.

antenatal [æntɪ'neɪtl] *a* vor der Geburt.

antenna [æn'tenə] *n* (*Biol*) Fühler *m*; (*Rad*) Antenne *f*.

anteroom ['æntɪrʊm] *n* Vorzimmer *nt*.

anthem ['ænθəm] *n* Hymne *f*.

anthology [æn'θɒlədʒɪ] *n* Gedichtsammlung *f*, Anthologie *f*.

anthropologist [ænθrə'pɒlədʒɪst] *n* Anthropologe *m*.

anthropology [ænθrə'pɒlədʒɪ] *n* Anthropologie *f*.

anti- ['æntɪ] *pref* Gegen-, Anti-

anti-aircraft ['æntɪ'eəkrɑːft] *a* Flugabwehr-

antibiotic ['æntɪbaɪ'ɒtɪk] *n* Antibiotikum *nt*.

anticipate [æn'tɪsɪpeɪt] *vt* (*expect*) trouble, question erwarten, rechnen mit; (*look forward to*) sich freuen auf (+*acc*); (*do first*) vorwegnehmen, (*foresee*) ahnen, vorhersehen.

anticipation [æntɪsɪ'peɪʃən] *n* Erwartung *f*; (*foreshadowing*) Vorwegnahme *f*; **that was good —** das war gut vorausgesehen.

anticlimax ['æntɪ'klaɪmæks] *n* Ernüchterung *f*.

anticlockwise ['æntɪ'klɒkwaɪz] *a* entgegen dem Uhrzeigersinn.

antics ['æntɪks] *npl* Possen *pl*.

anticyclone ['æntɪ'saɪkləʊn] *n* Hoch *nt*, Hochdruckgebiet *nt*.

antidote ['æntɪdəʊt] *n* Gegenmittel *nt*.

antifreeze ['æntɪfri:z] *n* Frostschutzmittel *nt*.

antipathy [æn'tɪpəθɪ] *n* Abneigung *f*, Antipathie *f*.

antiquarian [æntɪ'kweərɪən] a altertümlich; *n* Antiquitätensammler *m*.

antiquated ['æntɪkweɪtɪd] *a* antiquiert.

antique [æn'ti:k] *n* Antiquität *f*; a antik; (*old-fashioned*) altmodisch.

antiquity [æn'tɪkwɪtɪ] *n* Antike *f*, Altertum *nt*.

antiseptic [æntɪ'septɪk] *n* Antiseptikum *nt*; a antiseptisch.

antisocial [æntɪ'səʊʃl] a *person* ungesellig; *law* unsozial.

antithesis [æn'tɪθɪsɪs] *n* Gegensatz *m*, Antithese *f*.

antlers ['æntləz] *npl* Geweih *nt*.

anus ['eɪnəs] *n* After *m*.

anvil ['ænvɪl] *n* Amboß *m*.

anxiety [æŋ'zaɪətɪ] *n* Angst *f*; (*worry*) Sorge *f*.

anxious ['æŋkʃəs] a ängstlich; (*worried*) besorgt; —ly *ad* besorgt; **to be** — to do sth etw unbedingt tun wollen.

any ['enɪ] a: take — one nimm irgendein(e,n,s)!; do you want — apples? willst du Äpfel (haben)?; do you want —? willst du welche?; not — keine; *ad:* — faster schneller; —body *pron* irgend jemand; (*everybody*) jedermann; —how *ad* sowieso, ohnehin; (*carelessly*) einfach so; —one *pron* = —body; —thing *pron* irgend etwas; —time *ad* jederzeit; —way *ad* sowieso, ohnehin; —way, let's stop na ja *or* sei's drum, hören wir auf; —where *ad* irgendwo; (*everywhere*) überall.

apace [ə'peɪs] *ad* rasch.

apart [ə'pɑːt] *ad* (*parted*) auseinander; (*away*) beiseite, abseits; — from außer.

apartheid [ə'pɑːteɪt] *n* Apartheid f.

apartment [ə'pɑːtmənt] *n* (*US*) Wohnung f; —s *pl* (möblierte Miet)wohnung f.

apathetic [æpə'θetɪk] a teilnahmslos, apathisch.

apathy ['æpəθɪ] *n* Teilnahmslosigkeit f, Apathie f.

ape [eɪp] *n* (Menschen)affe *m*; *vt* nachahmen.

aperitif [ə'perɪtɪv] *n* Aperitif *m*.

aperture ['æpətjuə*] *n* Öffnung f; (*Phot*) Blende f.

apex ['eɪpeks] *n* Spitze f, Scheitelpunkt *m*.

aphorism ['æfərɪzəm] *n* Aphorismus *m*.

aphrodisiac [æfrəʊ'dɪzɪæk] *n* Aphrodisiakum *nt*.

apiece [ə'piːs] *ad* pro Stück; (*per person*) pro Kopf.

aplomb [ə'plɒm] *n* selbstbewußte(s) Auftreten *nt*.

apocryphal [ə'pɒkrɪfəl] **a** apokryph, unecht.

apologetic [əpɒlə'dʒetɪk] a entschuldigend; **to be** — sich sehr entschuldigen.

apologize [ə'pɒlədʒaɪz] *vi* sich entschuldigen.

apology [ə'pɒlədʒɪ] *n* Entschuldigung f.

apoplexy ['æpəpleksɪ] *n* Schlaganfall *m*.

apostle [ə'pɒsl] *n* Apostel *m*; (*pioneer*) Vorkämpfer *m*.

apostrophe [ə'pɒstrəfɪ] *n* Apostroph *m*.

appal [ə'pɔːl] *vt* erschrecken; —ling a schrecklich.

apparatus [æpə'reɪtəs] *n* Apparat *m*, Gerät *nt*.

apparent [ə'pærənt] a offenbar; —ly *ad* anscheinend.

apparition [æpə'rɪʃən] *n* (*ghost*) Erscheinung f, Geist *m*; (*appearance*) Erscheinen *nt*.

appeal [ə'piːl] *vi* dringend ersuchen; dringend bitten (*for* um); sich wenden (*to* an +*acc*); (*to public*) appellieren (*to* an +*acc*); (*Jur*) Berufung einlegen; *n* Aufruf *m*; (*Jur*) Berufung f; —ing a ansprechend.

appear [ə'pɪə*] *vi* (*come into sight*) erscheinen; (*be seen*) auftauchen; (*seem*) scheinen; —ance (*coming into sight*) Erscheinen *nt*; (*outward show*) Äußere(s) *nt*; to put in *or* make an —ance sich zeigen.

appease [ə'piːz] *vt* beschwichtigen.

appendage [ə'pendɪdʒ] *n* Anhang *m*, Anhängsel *nt*.

appendicitis [əpendɪ'saɪtɪs] *n* Blinddarmentzündung f.

appendix [ə'pendıks] n (in book) Anhang m; (Med) Blinddarm m.

appetite ['æpıtaıt] n Appetit m; (fig) Lust f.

appetizing ['æpıtaızıŋ] a appetitanregend.

applaud [ə'plɔːd] vti Beifall klatschen (+dat), applaudieren.

applause [ə'plɔːz] n Beifall m, Applaus m.

apple ['æpl] n Apfel m; — tree Apfelbaum m.

appliance [ə'plaıəns] n Gerät nt.

applicable [ə'plıkəbl] a anwendbar; (in forms) zutreffend.

applicant ['æplıkənt] n Bewerber(in f) m.

application [æplı'keıʃən] n (request) Antrag m; (for job) Bewerbung f; (putting into practice) Anwendung f; (hard work) Fleiß m.

applied [ə'plaıd] a angewandt.

apply [ə'plaı] vi (ask) sich wenden (to an +acc), sich melden; (be suitable) zutreffen; vt (place on) auflegen; cream auftragen; (put into practice) anwenden; (devote o.s.) sich widmen (+dat).

appoint [ə'pɔınt] vt (to office) ernennen, berufen; (settle) festsetzen; —ment (meeting) Verabredung f; (at hairdresser etc) Bestellung f; (in business) Termin m; (choice for a position) Ernennung f; (Univ) Berufung f.

apportion [ə'pɔːʃən] vt zuteilen.

appreciable [ə'priːʃəbl] a (perceptible) merklich; (able to be estimated) abschätzbar.

appreciate [ə'priːʃıeıt] vt (value) zu schätzen wissen; (understand) einsehen; vi (increase in value) im Wert steigen.

appreciation [əpriːʃı'eıʃən] n Wertschätzung f; (Comm) Wertzuwachs m.

appreciative [ə'priːʃıətıv] a (showing thanks) dankbar; (showing liking) anerkennend.

apprehend [æprı'hend] vt (arrest) festnehmen; (understand) erfassen.

apprehension [æprı'henʃən] n Angst f.

apprehensive [æprı'hensıv] a furchtsam.

apprentice [ə'prentıs] n Lehrling m; —ship Lehrzeit f.

approach [ə'prəʊtʃ] vi sich nähern; vt herantreten an (+acc); problem herangehen an (+acc); n Annäherung f; (to problem) Ansatz m; (path) Zugang m, Zufahrt f; —able a zugänglich.

approbation [æprə'beıʃən] n Billigung f.

appropriate [ə'prəʊprıeıt] vt (take for o.s.) sich aneignen; (set apart) bereitstellen; [ə'prəʊprıət] a angemessen; remark angebracht; —ly [ə'prəʊprıətlı] ad passend.

approval [ə'pruːvəl] n (show of satisfaction) Beifall m; (permission) Billigung f; (Comm) on — bei Gefallen.

approve [ə'pruːv] vti billigen (of acc); I don't — of it/him ich halte nichts davon/von ihm.

approximate [ə'prɒksımıt] a annähernd, ungefähr; [ə'prɒksımeıt] vt nahekommen (+dat); —ly ad rund, ungefähr.

approximation [əprɒksı'meıʃən] n Annäherung f.

apricot ['eıprıkɒt] n Aprikose f.

April ['eıprəl] n April m.

apron ['eıprən] n Schürze f.

apt [æpt] *a* (*suitable*) passend; (*able*) begabt; (*likely*) geneigt.

aptitude ['æptitju:d] *n* Begabung *f*.

aqualung ['ækwʌlʌŋ] *n* Unterwasseratmungsgerät *nt*.

aquarium [ə'kwɛəriəm] *n* Aquarium *nt*.

Aquarius [ə'kwɛəriəs] *n* Wassermann *m*.

aquatic [ə'kwætik] *a* Wasser-.

aqueduct ['ækwidʌkt] *n* Aquädukt *nt*.

arable ['ærəbl] *a* bebaubar, Kultur-.

arbiter ['a:bitə*] *n* (Schieds)richter *m*.

arbitrary ['a:bitrəri] *a* willkürlich.

arbitrate ['a:bitreit] *vti* schlichten.

arbitration [a:bi'treiʃən] *n* Schlichtung *f*; **to go to —** vor ein Schiedsgericht gehen.

arbitrator ['a:bitreitə*] *n* Schiedsrichter *m*, Schlichter *m*.

arc [a:k]. *n* Bogen *m*.

arcade [a:'keid] *n* Säulengang *m*.

arch [a:tʃ] *n* Bogen *m*; *vt* überwölben; *back* krumm machen; *vi* sich wölben; *a* durchtrieben; **—enemy** Erzfeind *m*.

archaeologist [a:ki'blədʒist] *n* Archäologe *m*.

archaeology [a:ki'blədʒi] *n* Archäologie *f*.

archaic [a:'keiik] *a* altertümlich.

archbishop ['a:tʃ'biʃəp] *n* Erzbischof *m*.

archer ['a:tʃə*] *n* Bogenschütze *m*; **—y** Bogenschießen *n*.

archipelago [a:ki'peligəu] *n* Archipel *m*; (*sea*) Inselmeer *nt*.

architect ['a:kitekt] *n* Architekt(in *f*) *m*; **—ural** [a:ki'tektʃərəl] *a* architektonisch; **—ure** Architektur *f*.

archives ['a:kaivz] *npl* Archiv *nt*.

archivist ['a:kivist] *n* Archivar *m*.

archway [a:tʃwei] *n* Bogen *m*.

ardent ['a:dənt] *a* glühend.

ardour ['a:də*] *n* Eifer *m*.

arduous ['a:djuəs] *a* mühsam.

are [a:*] *see* be.

area ['ɛəriə] *n* Fläche *f*; (*of land*) Gebiet *nt*; (*part of sth*) Teil *m*, Abschnitt *m*.

arena [ə'ri:nə] *n* Arena *f*.

aren't [a:nt] = are not.

arguable ['a:gjuəbl] *a* (*doubtful*) diskutabel; (*possible*) it's — that ... man könnte argumentieren daß

argue ['a:gju:] *vt case* vertreten; *vi* diskutieren; (*angrily*) streiten; **don't —!** keine Widerrede!; **to —** with sb sich mit jdm streiten.

argument ['a:gjumənt] *n* (*theory*) Argument *nt*; (*reasoning*) Argumentation *f*; (*row*) Auseinandersetzung *f*, Streit *m*; **—ative** [a:gju'mentətiv] *a* streitlustig; **to have an —** sich streiten.

aria ['a:riə] *n* Arie *f*.

arid ['ærid] *a* trocken; **—ity** [ə'riditi] *n* Dürre *f*.

Aries ['ɛəri:z] *n* Widder *m*.

arise [ə'raiz] *vi irreg* aufsteigen; (*get up*) aufstehen; (*difficulties etc*) entstehen; (*case*) vorkommen; **to — out of** sth herrühren von etw.

aristocracy [æris'tɒkrəsi] *n* Adel *m*, Aristokratie *f*.

aristocrat ['æristəkræt] *n* Adlige(r) *mf*, Aristokrat(in *f*) *m*; **—ic** [æristə'krætik] *a* adlig, aristokratisch.

arithmetic [ə'riθmətik] *n* Rechnen *nt*, Arithmetik *f*.

ark [a:k] *n*: Noah's A— die Arche Noah.

arm [ɑːm] n Arm m; (branch of military service) Zweig m; vt bewaffnen; —s pl (weapons) Waffen pl; —chair Lehnstuhl m; —ed a forces Streit-, bewaffnet; robbery bewaffnet; —ful Armvoll m.

armistice ['ɑːmɪstɪs] n Waffenstillstand m.

armour ['ɑːmə*]_ n (knight's) Rüstung f; (Mil) Panzerplatte f; —y Waffenlager nt; (factory) Waffenfabrik f.

armpit ['ɑːmpɪt] n Achselhöhle f.

army ['ɑːmɪ] n Armee f, Heer nt; (host) Heer nt.

aroma [ə'rəʊmə] n Duft m, Aroma nt; —tic [ærə'mætɪk] a aromatisch, würzig.

around [ə'raʊnd] ad ringsherum; (almost) ungefähr; prep um ... herum; is he —? ist er hier?

arouse [ə'raʊz] vt wecken.

arrange [ə'reɪndʒ] vt time, meeting festsetzen; holidays festlegen; flowers, hair, objects anordnen; —d to meet him ich habe mit ihm ausgemacht, ihn zu treffen; it's all —d es ist alles arrangiert; —ment (order) Reihenfolge f; (agreement) Übereinkommen nt; (plan) Vereinbarung f.

array [ə'reɪ] n Aufstellung f.

arrears [ə'rɪəz] npl (of debts) Rückstand m; (of work) Unerledigte(s) nt; in — im Rückstand.

arrest [ə'rest] n person verhaften; (stop) aufhalten; n Verhaftung f; under — in Haft; you're under — Sie sind verhaftet.

arrival [ə'raɪvəl] n Ankunft f.

arrive [ə'raɪv] vi ankommen (at in +dat, bei); to — at a decision zu einer Entscheidung kommen.

arrogance ['ærəgəns] n Überheblichkeit f, Arroganz f.

arrogant ['ærəgənt] a anmaßend, arrogant.

arrow ['ærəʊ] n Pfeil m.

arse [ɑːs] n (col) Arsch m.

arsenal ['ɑːsnl] n Waffenlager nt, Zeughaus nt.

arsenic ['ɑːsnɪk] n Arsen nt.

arson ['ɑːsn] n Brandstiftung f.

art [ɑːt] n Kunst f; —s pl Geisteswissenschaften pl; — gallery Kunstgalerie f.

artery ['ɑːtərɪ] n Schlagader f, Arterie f.

artful [ɑːtful] a verschlagen.

arthritis [ɑː'θraɪtɪs] n Arthritis f.

artichoke ['ɑːtɪtʃəʊk] n Artischocke f.

article ['ɑːtɪkl] n (Press, Gram) Artikel m; (thing) Gegenstand m, Artikel m; (clause) Abschnitt m, Paragraph m.

articulate [ɑː'tɪkjʊlɪt] a (able to express o.s.) redegewandt; (speaking clearly) deutlich, verständlich; to be — sich gut ausdrücken können; [ɑː'tɪkjʊleɪt] vt (connect) zusammenfügen, gliedern; —d vehicle Sattelschlepper m.

artifice ['ɑːtɪfɪs] n (skill) Kunstgriff m; (trick) Kniff m, List f.

artificial [ɑːtɪ'fɪʃəl] a künstlich, Kunst-; — respiration künstliche Atmung f.

artillery [ɑː'tɪlərɪ] n Artillerie f.

artisan ['ɑːtɪzæn] n gelernte(r) Handwerker m.

artist ['ɑːtɪst] n Künstler(in f) m; —ic [ɑː'tɪstɪk] a künstlerisch; —ry künstlerische(s) Können nt.

artless ['ɑːtlɪs] a ungekünstelt; character arglos.

arty ['ɑːtɪ] a: to be — auf Kunst machen.

as [æz] *ad, cj (since)* da, weil;
(while) als ; *(like)* wie ; *(in role of)*
als ; — **soon** — **he comes** sobald
er kommt ; — **big** — so groß wie ;
— well auch; — **well** — und auch;
— for him was ihn anbetrifft ; —
if, — though als ob; — **it were**
sozusagen ; **old** — **he** was so alt
er auch war.

asbestos [æz'bestəs] *n* Asbest *m*.

ascend [ə'send] *vi* aufsteigen ; *vt*
besteigen ; —ancy Oberhand *f*.

ascension [ə'senʃən] *n* (Eccl)
Himmelfahrt *f*.

ascent [ə'sent] *n* Aufstieg *m*;
Besteigung *f*.

ascertain [æsə'tem] *vt* feststellen.

ascetic [ə'setik] *a* asketisch.

ascribe [əs'kraib] *vt* zuschreiben
(to dat).

ash [æʃ] *n (dust)* Asche *f*; *(tree)*
Esche *f*.

ashamed [ə'ʃemd] *a* beschämt.

ashen [æʃən] *a (pale)* aschfahl.

ashore [ə'ʃɔ:*] *ad* an Land.

ashtray [æʃtrei] *n* Aschenbecher
m.

aside [ə'said] *ad* beiseite ; — from
(US) abgesehen von; *n* beiseite
gesprochene Worte *pl*.

ask [u:sk] *vti* fragen; *permission*
bitten um; — him his name frage
ihn nach seinem Namen; he —ed
to see you er wollte dich sehen;
'you —ed for that! du hast du selbst
schuld.

askance [əs'kɑːns] *ad*: to look —
at s.o. jdn schief ansehen.

askew [əs'kju:] *ad* schief.

asleep [ə'sliːp] *a, ad*: to be —
schlafen ; to fall — einschlafen.

asp [æsp] *n* Espe *f*.

asparagus [əs'pærəgəs] *n* Spargel
m.

aspect [æspekt] *n (appearance)*
Aussehen *nt*; Aspekt *m*.

asphalt [æsfælt] *n* Asphalt *m*.

asphyxiate [əs'fiksieit] *vt* ersticken.

asphyxiation [əsfiksi'eiʃən] *n*
Erstickung *f*.

aspirate [æspərit] *n* Hauchlaut *m*.

aspiration [æspə'reiʃən] *n*
Trachten *nt*; to have —s towards
sth etw anstreben.

aspire [əs'paiə*] *vi* streben *(to
nach)*.

aspirin [æsprin] *n* Aspirin *nt*.

ass [æs] *n (lit, fig)* Esel *m*.

assailant [ə'seilənt] *n* Angreifer *m*.

assassin [ə'sæsin] *n* Attentäter(in
f) *m*; —ate *vt* ermorden; —ation
[əsæsi'neiʃən] Ermordung *f*.

assault [ə'sɔːlt] *n* Angriff *m*; *vt*
überfallen ; *woman* herfallen über
(+acc).

assemble [ə'sembl] *vt* versammeln; *parts* zusammensetzen; *vi*
sich versammeln.

assembly [ə'sembli] *n (meeting)*
Versammlung *f*; *(construction)*
Zusammensetzung *f*, Montage *f*; —
line Fließband *nt*.

assent [ə'sent] *n* Zustimmung *f*; *vi*
zustimmen *(to dat)*.

assert [ə'sɜːt] *vt* erklären; —ion
[ə'sɜːʃən] Behauptung *f*; —ive *a*
selbstsicher.

assess [ə'ses] *vt* schätzen; —ment
Bewertung *f*, Einschätzung; —or
Steuerberater *m*.

asset [æset] *n* Vorteil *m*, Wert *m*;
—s *pl* Vermögen *nt*; *(estate)*
Nachlaß *m*.

assiduous [ə'sidjʊəs] *a* fleißig, aufmerksam.

assign [ə'sain] *vt* zuweisen.

assignment [ə'sainmənt] *n* Aufgabe *f*, Auftrag *m*.

assimilate [ə'sɪmɪleɪt] *vt* sich aneignen, aufnehmen.

assimilation [əsɪmɪ'leɪʃən] *n* Assimilierung *f*, Aufnahme *f*.

assist [ə'sɪst] *vt* beistehen (+*dat*); **—ance** Unterstützung *f*, Hilfe *f*; **—ant** Assistent(in *f*) *m*, Mitarbeiter(in *f*) *m*; (*in shop*) Verkäufer(in *f*) *m*.

assizes [ə'saɪzɪz] *npl* Landgericht *nt*.

associate [ə'səʊʃɪt] *n* (*partner*) Kollege *m*, Teilhaber *m*; (*member*) außerordentliche(s) Mitglied *nt*; [ə'səʊʃɪeɪt] *vt* verbinden (*with* mit); *vi* (*keep company*) verkehren (*with* mit).

association [əsəʊsɪ'eɪʃən] *n* Verband *m*, Verein *m*; (*Psych*) Assoziation *f*; (*link*) Verbindung *f*; **— football** (*Brit*) Fußball *nt*.

assorted [ə'sɔːtɪd] *a* gemischt, verschieden.

assortment [ə'sɔːtmənt] *n* Sammlung *f*; (*Comm*) Sortiment *nt* (*of* von), Auswahl *f* (*of* an +*dat*).

assume [ə'sjuːm] *vt* (*take for granted*) annehmen; (*put on*) annehmen, sich geben; **—d name** Deckname *m*.

assumption [ə'sʌmpʃən] *n* Annahme *f*.

assurance [ə'ʃʊərəns] *n* (*firm statement*) Versicherung *f*; (*confidence*) Selbstsicherheit *f*; (*Insurance*) (Lebens)versicherung *f*.

assure [ə'ʃʊə*] *vt* (*make sure*) sicherstellen; (*convince*) versichern (+*dat*); *life* versichern.

assuredly [ə'ʃʊərɪdlɪ] *ad* sicherlich.

asterisk ['æstərɪsk] *n* Sternchen *nt*.

astern [əs'tɜːn] *ad* achtern.

asthma ['æsmə] *n* Asthma *nt*; **—tic** [æs'mætɪk] *a* asthmatisch; *n* Asthmatiker(in *f*) *m*.

astir [ə'stɜː*] *ad* in Bewegung.

astonish [əs'tɒnɪʃ] *vt* erstaunen; **—ing** *a* erstaunlich; **—ment** Erstaunen *nt*.

astound [əs'taʊnd] *vt* verblüffen; **—ing** *a* verblüffend.

astray [əs'treɪ] *ad* in die Irre; auf Abwege; *a* irregehend.

astride [əs'traɪd] *ad* rittlings; *prep* rittlings auf.

astringent [əs'trɪndʒənt] *a* (*Med*) zusammenziehend; (*severe*) streng.

astrologer [əs'trɒlədʒə*] *n* Astrologe *m*, Astrologin *f*.

astrology [əs'trɒlədʒɪ] *n* Astrologie *f*.

astronaut ['æstrənɔːt] *n* Astronaut(in *f*) *m*.

astronomer [əs'trɒnəmə*] *n* Astronom *m*.

astronomical [æstrə'nɒmɪkəl] *a* astronomisch; *numbers* astronomisch; *success* riesig.

astronomy [əs'trɒnəmɪ] *n* Astronomie *f*.

astute [əs'tjuːt] *a* scharfsinnig; schlau, gerissen.

asunder [ə'sʌndə*] *ad* entzwei.

asylum [ə'saɪləm] *n* (*home*) Heim *nt*; (*refuge*) Asyl *nt*.

at [æt] *prep* — home zuhause; — John's bei John; — table bei Tisch; — school in der Schule; — Easter an Ostern; — 2 o'clock um 2 Uhr; — (the age of) 16 mit 16; — £5 zu 5 Pfund; — 20 mph mit 20 Meilen pro Stunde; — that darauf, daran.

ate [et, eɪt] *pt of* eat.

atheism ['eɪθɪəzəm] *n* Atheismus *m*.

atheist ['eɪθɪɪst] *n* Atheist(in *f*) *m*.

athlete ['æθliːt] *n* Athlet *m*, Sportler *m*, (*also*).

athletic [æθ'letιk] a sportlich, athletisch; **—s** pl Leichtathletik f.

atlas ['ætləs] n Atlas m.

atmosphere ['ætməsfiə*] n Atmosphäre f.

atoll ['ætɒl] n Atoll nt.

atom ['ætəm] n Atom nt; (fig) bißchen nt; **—ic** [ə'tɒmιk] a atomar, Atom-; **—(ic) bomb** Atombombe f; **—ic power** Atomkraft f; **—izer** Zerstäuber m.

atone [ə'təun] vi sühnen (for acc).

atrocious [ə'trəuʃəs] a gräßlich.

atrocity [ə'trɒsιtι] n Scheußlichkeit f; (deed) Greueltat f.

attach [ə'tætʃ] vt (fasten) befestigen; importance etc legen (to auf +acc), beimessen (to dat); **to be —ed to** sb/sth an jdm/etw hängen; **—é** [ə'tæʃeι] n Attaché m.

attack [ə'tæk] vti angreifen; n Angriff m; (Med) Anfall m.

attain [ə'teιn] vt erreichen; **—ment** Erreichung f; **—ments** pl Kenntnisse pl.

attempt [ə'tempt] n Versuch m; vti versuchen.

attend [ə'tend] vt (go to) teilnehmen (an +dat); lectures besuchen; vi (pay attention) aufmerksam sein; **to — to** needs nachkommen (+dat); person sich kümmern um; **—ance** (presence) Anwesenheit f; (people present) Besucherzahl f; **good —ance** gute Teilnahme f; **—ant** n (companion) Begleiter(in f) m; Gesellschafter(in f) m; (in car park etc) Wächter(in f) m; (servant) Bediente(r) mf; a begleitend; (fig) verbunden mit.

attention [ə'tenʃən] n Aufmerksamkeit f; (care) Fürsorge f; (for machine etc) Pflege f.

attentive a, **—ly** ad [ə'tentιv, -lι] aufmerksam.

attenuate [ə'tenjueιt] vt verdünnen.

attest [ə'test] vt bestätigen; **to — to** sich verbürgen für.

attic ['ætιk] n Dachstube f, Mansarde f.

attire [ə'taιə*] n Gewand nt.

attitude ['ætιtju:d] n (position) Haltung f; (mental) Einstellung f.

attorney [ə'tɜ:nι] n (solicitor) Rechtsanwalt m; (representative) Bevollmächtigte(r) mf; **A— General** Justizminister m.

attract [ə'trækt] vt anziehen; attention erregen; employees anlocken; **—ion** [ə'trækʃən] n Anziehungskraft f; (thing) Attraktion f; **—ive** a attraktiv; **the idea —s me** ich finde die Idee attraktiv.

attribute ['ætrιbju:t] n Eigenschaft f, Attribut nt; [ə'trιbju:t] vt zuschreiben (to dat).

attrition [ə'trιʃən] n Verschleiß m; **war of —** Zermürbungskrieg m.

aubergine ['əubəʒi:n] n Aubergine f.

auburn ['ɔ:bən] a kastanienbraun.

auction ['ɔ:kʃən] n Versteigerung f, Auktion f; vt versteigern; **—eer** [ɔ:kʃə'nιə*] Versteigerer m.

audacious [ɔ:'deιʃəs] a (daring) verwegen; (shameless) unverfroren.

audacity [ɔ:'dæsιtι] n (boldness) Wagemut m; (impudence) Unverfrorenheit f.

audible ['ɔ:dιbl] a hörbar.

audience ['ɔ:dιəns] n Zuhörer pl, Zuschauer pl; (with king etc) Audienz f.

audit ['ɔ:dιt] n Bücherrevision f; vt prüfen.

audition [ɔ:'dιʃən] n Probe f.

auditorium [ɔ:dιtɔ:'rιəm] n Zuschauerraum m.

augment ['ɔ:g'ment] vt vermehren ; vi zunehmen.

augur ['ɔ:gə*] vti bedeuten, voraussagen ; this —s well das ist ein gutes Omen ; **—y** ['ɔ:gjəri] Vorbedeutung f, Omen nt.

August ['ɔ:gəst] n August m.

august [ɔ:'gʌst] a erhaben.

aunt [ɑ:nt] n Tante f; **—y**, **—ie** Tantchen nt.

au pair ['əʊ' pɛə*] n (also — girl) Au-pair-Mädchen nt.

aura ['ɔ:rə] n Nimbus m.

auspices ['ɔ:spisiz] npl: under the — of unter der Schirmherrschaft von.

auspicious [ɔ:s'piʃəs] a günstig ; verheißungsvoll.

austere [ɒs'tiə*] a streng ; room nüchtern.

austerity [ɒs'teriti] n Strenge f; (Pol) wirtschaftliche Einschränkung f.

authentic [ɔ:'θentik] a echt, authentisch ; **—ate** vt beglaubigen ; **—ity** [ɔ:θen'tisiti] n Echtheit f.

author ['ɔ:θə*] n Autor m, Schriftsteller m; (beginner) Urheber m, Schöpfer m.

authoritarian [ɔ:θəri'tɛəriən] a autoritär.

authoritative [ɔ:'θɒritətiv] a account maßgeblich ; manner herrisch.

authority [ɔ:'θɒriti] n (power) Autorität f; (expert) Autorität f, Fachmann m ; **the authorities** pl die Behörden pl.

authorize ['ɔ:θəraiz] vt bevollmächtigen ; (permit) genehmigen.

auto ['ɔ:təʊ] n (US) Auto m, Wagen m.

autobiographical [ɔ:təbaiə'græfikəl] a autobiographisch.

autobiography [ɔ:təbai'ɒgrəfi] n Autobiographie f.

autocracy [ɔ:'tɒkrəsi] n Autokratie f.

autocratic [ɔ:tə'krætik] a autokratisch.

autograph ['ɔ:təgrɑ:f] n (of celebrity) Autogramm nt; vt mit Autogramm versehen.

automate ['ɔ:təmeit] vt automatisieren, auf Automation umstellen.

automatic [ɔ:tə'mætik] a automatisch ; n Selbstladepistole f; (car) Automatik m ; **—ally** ad automatisch.

automation [ɔ:tə'meiʃən] n Automation f.

automaton [ɔ:'tɒmətən] n Automat m, Roboter m.

automobile ['ɔ:təməbi:l] n (US) Auto(mobil) nt.

autonomous [ɔ:'tɒnəməs] a autonom.

autonomy [ɔ:'tɒnəmi] n Autonomie f, Selbstbestimmung f.

autopsy ['ɔ:tɒpsi] n Autopsie f.

autumn ['ɔ:təm] n Herbst m.

auxiliary [ɔ:g'ziliəri] a Hilfs-; Hilfskraft f; (Gram) Hilfsverb nt.

avail [ə'veil] vr: -o.s. of sich einer Sache bedienen ; n: to no — nutzlos ; **—ability** [əveilə'biliti] Erhältlichkeit f, Vorhandensein nt; **—able** erhältlich ; zur Verfügung stehend ; person erreichbar, abkömmlich.

avalanche ['ævəlɑ:nʃ] n Lawine f.

avant-garde ['ævãŋ'gɑ:d] a avant-gardistisch ; n Avantgarde f.

avarice ['ævəris] n Habsucht f, Geiz m.

avaricious [ævə'riʃəs] a geizig, habsüchtig.

avenge [ə'vendʒ] vt rächen, sühnen.

avenue ['ævənju:] n Allee f.

average ['ævərɪdʒ] n Durchschnitt m; a durchschnittlich, Durchschnitts-; vt figures den Durchschnitt nehmen von; (perform) durchschnittlich leisten; (in car etc) im Schnitt fahren; on — durchschnittlich, im Durchschnitt.

averse [ə'vɜːs] a: to be — eine Abneigung haben gegen.

aversion [ə'vɜːʃən] n Abneigung f.

avert [ə'vɜːt] vt (turn away) abkehren; (prevent) abwehren.

aviary ['eɪvɪərɪ] n Vogelhaus nt.

aviation [eɪvɪ'eɪʃən] n Luftfahrt f, Flugwesen nt.

aviator ['eɪvɪeɪtə*] n Flieger m.

avid ['ævɪd] a gierig (for auf + acc); —ly ad gierig.

avocado [ævə'kɑːdəʊ] n (also — pear) Avocado(birne) f.

avoid [ə'vɔɪd] vt vermeiden; —able a vermeidbar; —ance Vermeidung f.

avowal [ə'vaʊəl] n Erklärung f.

await [ə'weɪt] vt erwarten, entgegensehen (+dat).

awake [ə'weɪk] a wach; irreg vi aufwachen; vt (auf)wecken; —ning Erwachen nt.

award [ə'wɔːd] n (judgment) Urteil

nt; (prize) Preis m; vt zuerkennen.

aware [ə'weə*] a bewußt; to be — sich bewußt sein (of gen); —ness Bewußtsein nt.

awash [ə'wɒʃ] a überflutet.

away [ə'weɪ] ad weg, fort.

awe [ɔː] n Ehrfurcht f; —-inspiring, —some a ehrfurchtgebietend; —-struck a von Ehrfurcht ergriffen.

awful ['ɔːful] a (very bad) furchtbar; —ly ad furchtbar, sehr.

awhile [ə'waɪl] ad eine kleine Weile, ein bißchen.

awkward ['ɔːkwəd] a (clumsy) ungeschickt, linkisch; (embarrassing) peinlich; —ness Ungeschicklichkeit f.

awning ['ɔːnɪŋ] n Markise f.

awry [ə'raɪ] ad, a schief; to go — (person) fehlgehen; (plans) schiefgehen.

ax (US), **axe** [æks] n Axt f, Beil nt; vt to end suddenly) streichen.

axiom ['æksɪəm] n Grundsatz m, Axiom nt; —atic [æksɪə'mætɪk] a axiomatisch.

axis ['æksɪs] n Achse f.

axle ['æksl] n Achse f.

ay(e) [aɪ] interj (yes) ja; the —es pl die Jastimmen pl.

azure ['eɪʒə*] a himmelblau.

B

B, b [biː] n B nt, b nt.

babble ['bæbl] vi schwätzen; (stream) murmeln; n Geschwätz nt.

babe [beɪb] n Baby nt.

baboon [bə'buːn] n Pavian m.

baby ['beɪbɪ] n Baby nt, Säugling

m; — carriage (US) Kinderwagen m; —ish a kindisch; —-sit vi irreg Kinder hüten, babysitten; —-sitter Babysitter m.

bachelor ['bætʃələ*] n Junggeselle m; B— of Arts Bakkalaureus m der philosophischen Fakultät; B— of

back   394   balcony

Science Bakkalaureus m der Naturwissenschaften.

back [bæk] n (of person, horse) Rücken m; (of house) Rückseite f; (of train) Ende nt; (Ftbl) Verteidiger m; vt (support) unterstützen; (wager) wetten auf (+acc); car rückwärts fahren; vi (go backwards) rückwärts gehen or fahren; a hinter(e, s); ad zurück; (to the rear) nach hinten; — down vi zurückstecken; kneifen (col); —biting Verleumdung f; —bone Rückgrat nt; (support) Rückhalt m; —cloth Hintergrund m; —er Förderer m; —fire vi (plan) fehlschlagen; (Tech) fehlzünden; —ground Hintergrund m; (information) Hintergrund m, Umstände pl; (person's education) Vorbildung f; —hand (Sport) Rückhand f; a Rückhand-; —handed a shot Rückhand-; compliment zweifelhaft; —ing (support) Unterstützung f; —lash tote(r) Gang m; (fig) Gegenschlag m; —log (of work) Rückstand m; — number (Press) alte Nummer f; — pay (Gehalts-, Lohn)nachzahlung f; —side (col) Hintern m; —stroke Rückenschwimmen nt; —ward a (less developed) zurückgeblieben; (primitive) rückständig; —wardness (of child) Unterentwicklung f; (of country) Rückständigkeit f; —wards ad (in reverse) rückwärts; (towards the past) zurück, rückwärts; —water (fig) Kaff nt; cultural —water tiefste Provinz f; —yard Hinterhof m.

bacon ['beikən] n Schinkenspeck m.

bacteria [bæk'tiəriə] npl Bakterien pl.

bad [bæd] a schlecht, schlimm.

badge [bædʒ] n Abzeichen nt.

badger ['bædʒə*] n Dachs m; vt plagen.

badly ['bædli] ad schlecht, schlimm; — off: he is — off es geht ihm schlecht.

badminton ['bædmintən] n Federballspiel nt.

bad-tempered ['bæd'tempəd] a schlecht gelaunt.

baffle ['bæfl] vt (puzzle) verblüffen.

bag [bæg] n (sack) Beutel m; (paper) Tüte f; (hand—) Tasche f; (suitcase) Koffer m; (booty) Jagdbeute f; (col: old woman) alte Schachtel f; vi sich bauschen; vt (put in sack) in einen Sack stecken; (hunting) erlegen; —ful Sackvoll m; —gage ['bægidʒ] Gepäck nt; —gy a bauschig, sackartig; —pipes pl Dudelsack m.

bail [beil] n (money) Kaution f; vt prisoner gegen Kaution freilassen; (also — out) boat ausschöpfen; see bale.

bailiff ['beilif] n Gerichtsvollzieher(in f) m.

bait [beit] n Köder m; vt mit einem Köder versehen; (fig) ködern.

bake [beik] vti backen; —r Bäcker m; —ry Bäckerei f; —r's dozen dreizehn.

baking ['beikiŋ] n Backen nt; — powder Backpulver nt.

balance ['bæləns] n (scales) Waage f; (equilibrium) Gleichgewicht nt; (Fin: state of account) Saldo m; (difference) Bilanz f; (amount remaining) Restbetrag m; vt (weigh) wägen; (make equal) ausgleichen; —d a ausgeglichen; — sheet Bilanz f, Rechnungsabschluß m.

balcony ['bælkəni] n Balkon m.

bald [bɔːld] *a* kahl; *statement* knapp.

bale [beil] *n* Ballen *m*; **to — or bail out** (*from a plane*) abspringen.

baleful ['beilful] *a* (*sad*) unglückselig; (*evil*) böse.

balk [bɔːk] *vt* (*hinder*) vereiteln; *vi* scheuen (*at* vor +*dat*).

ball [bɔːl] *n* Ball *m*.

ballad ['bæləd] *n* Ballade *f.*

ballast ['bæləst] *n* Ballast *m.*

ball bearing ['bɔːl'beəriŋ] *n* Kugellager *m.*

ballerina [bælə'riːnə] *n* Ballerina *f.*

ballet ['bælei] *n* Ballett *nt.*

ballistics [bə'listiks] *n* Ballistik *f.*

balloon [bə'luːn] *n* (Luft)ballon *m.*

ballot ['bælət] *n* (geheime) Abstimmung *f.*

ball-point (pen) ['bɔːlpɔint('pen)] *n* Kugelschreiber *m.*

ballroom ['bɔːlrum] *n* Tanzsaal *m.*

balmy ['bɑːmi] *a* lindernd; mild.

balsa ['bɔːlsə] *n* (*also* — **wood**) Balsaholz *nt.*

balustrade [bæləs'treid] *n* Brüstung *f.*

bamboo [bæm'buː] *n* Bambus *m.*

bamboozle [bæm'buːzl] *vt* übers Ohr hauen.

ban [bæn] *n* Verbot *nt*; *vt* verbieten.

banal [bə'nɑːl] *a* banal.

banana [bə'nɑːnə] *n* Banane *f.*

band [bænd] *n* Band *nt*; (*group*) Gruppe *f*; (*of criminals*) Bande *f*; (*Mus*) Kapelle *f*, Band *f*; *vi* (+*together*) sich zusammentun; **—age** Verband *m*; (*elastic*) Bandage *f.*

bandit ['bændit] *n* Bandit *m.*

bandy ['bændi] *vt* wechseln; **— legged** *a* o-beinig.

bang [bæŋ] *n* (*explosion*) Knall *m*; (*blow*) Hieb *m*; *vti* knallen.

,bangle ['bæŋgl] *n* Armspange *f.*

banish ['bæniʃ] *vt* verbannen.

banister(s) ['bænistə*(z)] *n*(*pl*) (Treppen)geländer *nt.*

banjo ['bændʒəu] *n* Banjo *nt.*

bank [bæŋk] *n* (*raised ground*) Erd-wall *m*; (*of lake etc*) Ufer *nt*; (*Fin*) Bank *f*; *vt* (*tilt: Aviat*) in die Kurve bringen; *money* einzahlen; **to — on sth** mit etw rechnen; **— account** Bankkonto *nt*; (*employee*) Bank-beamte(r) *m*; **— holiday** gesetzliche(r) Feiertag *m*; **—ing** Bankwesen *nt*, Bankgeschäft *nt*; **—note** Banknote *f*; **—rupt** *n* Zahlungsun-fähige(r) *mf*; *vt* bankrott machen; **to go —rupt** Pleite machen; **—ruptcy** Bankrott *m.*

banner ['bænə*] *n* Banner *nt.*

banns [bænz] *npl* Aufgebot *nt.*

banquet ['bæŋkwit] *n* Bankett *nt*, Festessen *nt.*

banter ['bæntə*] *n* Neckerei *f.*

baptism ['bæptizəm] *n* Taufe *f.*

baptize [bæp'taiz] *vt* taufen.

bar [bɑː*] *n* (*rod*) Stange *f*; (*obstacle*) Hindernis *nt*; (*of chocolate*) Tafel *f*; (*of soap*) Stück *nt*; (*for food, drink*) Buffet *nt*, Bar *f*; (*pub*) Wirtschaft *f*; (*Mus*) Takt-(strich) *m*; *vt* (*fasten*) verriegeln; (*hinder*) versperren; (*exclude*) aus-schließen; **the B—: to be called to the B—** als Anwalt zugelassen werden; **— none** ohne Ausnahme.

barbarian [bɑː'bɛəriən] *n* Barbar(in *f*) *m.*

barbaric [bɑː'bærik] *a* primitiv, un-kultiviert.

barbarity [bɑː'bæriti] *n* Grausam-keit *f.*

barbarous ['bɑːbərəs] *a* grausam, barbarisch.

barbecue ['bɑːbɪkjuː] n Barbecue nt.
barbed wire ['bɑːbd'waɪə*] n Stacheldraht m.
barber ['bɑːbə*] n Herrenfriseur m.
barbiturate [bɑː'bɪtjʊrɪt] n Barbiturat nt, Schlafmittel nt.
bare [bɛə*] a nackt; trees, country kahl; (mere) bloß; vt entblößen; **—back** ad ungesattelt; **—faced** a unverfroren; **—foot** a barfuß; **—headed** a mit bloßem Kopf; **—ly** ad kaum, knapp; **—ness** Nacktheit f; Kahlheit f.
bargain ['bɑːgɪn] n (sth cheap) günstiger Kauf; (agreement) (written) Kaufvertrag m; (oral) Geschäft nt; into the — obendrein; **— for** vt rechnen mit.
barge [bɑːdʒ] n Lastkahn m; **— in** vi hereinplatzen.
baritone ['bærɪtəun] n Bariton m.
bark [bɑːk] n (of tree) Rinde f; (of dog) Bellen nt; vi (dog) bellen.
barley ['bɑːlɪ] n Gerste f.
barmaid ['bɑːmeɪd] n Bardame f.
barman ['bɑːmən] n Barkellner m.
barn [bɑːn] n Scheune f.
barnacle ['bɑːnəkl] n Entenmuschel f.
barometer [bə'rɒmɪtə*] n Barometer nt.
baron ['bærən] n Baron m; **—ess** Baronin f; **—ial** [bə'rəunɪəl] a freiherrlich.
baroque [bə'rɒk] a barock.
barracks ['bærəks] npl Kaserne f.
barrage ['bærɑːʒ] n (gunfire) Sperrfeuer nt; (dam) Staudamm m; Talsperre f.
barrel ['bærəl] n Faß nt; (of gun) Lauf m; **— organ** Drehorgel f.
barren ['bærən] a unfruchtbar.
barricade [bærɪ'keɪd] n Barrikade f; vt verbarrikadieren.

barrier ['bærɪə*] n (obstruction) Hindernis nt; (fence) Schranke f.
barrister ['bærɪstə*] n (Brit) Rechtsanwalt m.
barrow ['bærəu] n (cart) Schubkarren m.
bartender ['bɑːtendə*] n (US) Barmann or -kellner m.
barter ['bɑːtə*] n Tauschhandel m; vi Tauschhandel treiben.
base [beɪs] n (bottom) Boden m, Basis f; (Mil) Stützpunkt m; vt gründen; **to be —d on** basieren auf (+dat); a (low) gemein; **—ball** Baseball m; **—less** a grundlos; **—ment** Kellergeschoß nt.
bash [bæʃ] vt (col) (heftig) schlagen.
bashful ['bæʃful] a schüchtern.
basic ['beɪsɪk] a grundlegend; **—ally** ad im Grunde.
basin ['beɪsn] n (dish) Schüssel f; (for washing, also valley) Becken nt; (dock) (Trocken)becken nt.
basis ['beɪsɪs] n Basis f, Grundlage f.
bask [bɑːsk] vi sich sonnen.
basket ['bɑːskɪt] n Korb m; **—ball** Basketball m.
bass [beɪs] n (Mus, also instrument) Baß m; (voice) Baßstimme f; **— clef** Baßschlüssel m.
bassoon [bə'suːn] n Fagott nt.
bastard ['bɑːstəd] n Bastard m; Arschloch nt.
baste [beɪst] vt meat mit Fett begießen.
bastion ['bæstɪən] n (lit, fig) Bollwerk nt.
bat [bæt] n (Sport) Schlagholz nt; Schläger m; (Zool) Fledermaus f; vt: **he didn't — an eyelid** er hat nicht mit der Wimper gezuckt; **off one's own —** auf eigene Faust.

batch [bætʃ] *n* (*of letters*) Stoß *m*; (*of samples*) Satz *m*.

bated ['beɪtɪd] *a*: with — breath mit verhaltenem Atem.

bath [bɑːθ] *n* Bad *nt*; (*tub*) Badewanne *f*; *vt* baden; **—s** [bɑːðz] *pl* (Schwimm)bad *nt*; **—chair** Rollstuhl *m*.

bathe [beɪð] *vti* baden; **—r** Badende(r) *mf*.

bathing ['beɪðɪŋ] *n* Baden *nt*; **— cap** Badekappe *f*; **— costume** Badeanzug *m*.

bathmat ['bɑːθmæt] *n* Badevorleger *m*.

bathroom ['bɑːθrʊm] *n* Bad(e-zimmer) *nt*.

baths [bɑːðz] *npl* see **bath**.

bath towel ['bɑːθtaʊəl] *n* Badetuch *nt*.

batman ['bætmən] *n* (Offiziers)-bursche *m*.

baton ['bætən] *n* (*of police*) Gummiknüppel *m*; (*Mus*) Taktstock *m*.

battalion [bə'tælɪən] *n* Bataillon *nt*.

batter ['bætə*] *vt* verprügeln; *n* Schlagteig *m*; (*for cake*) Biskuitteig *m*.

battery ['bætərɪ] *n* (Elec) Batterie *f*; (Mil) Geschützbatterie *f*.

battle ['bætl] *n* Schlacht *f* (*small*) Gefecht *nt*; *vi* kämpfen; **—axe** (*col*) Xanthippe *f*; **—field** Schlachtfeld *nt*; **—ments** *pl* Zinnen *pl*; **—ship** Schlachtschiff *nt*.

batty ['bætɪ] *a* (*col*) plemplem.

bauble ['bɔːbl] *n* Spielzeug *nt*.

bawdy ['bɔːdɪ] *a* unflätig.

bawl [bɔːl] *vi* brüllen; **to — sb out** jdn zur Schnecke machen.

bay [beɪ] *n* (*of sea*) Bai *f*; *at* — gestellt, in die Enge getrieben; **to keep at** — unter Kontrolle halten.

bayonet ['beɪənet] *n* Bajonett *nt*.

bay window ['beɪ'wɪndəʊ] *n* Erkerfenster *nt*.

bazaar [bə'zɑː*] *n* Basar *m*.

bazooka [bə'zuːkə] *n* Panzerfaust *f*.

be [biː] *vi irreg* sein; (*become, for passive*) werden; (*be situated*) liegen, sein; **the book is 40p** das Buch kostet 40p; **he wants to — a teacher** er will Lehrer werden; **how long have you been here?** wie lange sind Sie schon da?; **have you been to Rome?** warst du schon einmal in Rom?, bist du schon einmal in Rom gewesen?; **his name is on the list** sein Name steht auf der Liste; **there is/are** es gibt.

beach [biːtʃ] *n* Strand *m*; *vt ship* auf den Strand setzen; **—wear** Strandkleidung *f*.

beacon ['biːkən] *n* (*signal*) Leuchtfeuer *nt*; (*traffic* —)-Bake *f*.

bead [biːd] *n* Perle *f*; (*drop*) Tropfen *m*.

beak [biːk] *n* Schnabel *m*.

beaker ['biːkə*] *n* Becher *m*.

beam [biːm] *n* (*of wood*) Balken *m*; (*of light*) Strahl *m*; (*smile*) strahlende(s) Lächeln *nt*; *vi* strahlen.

bean [biːn] *n* Bohne *f*.

bear [bɛə*] *n* Bär *m*; *vt irreg weight, crops* tragen; (*tolerate*) ertragen; *young* gebären; *vi* Bär *m*; **—able** a erträglich; **to — on** relevant sein für.

beard [bɪəd] *n* Bart *m*; **—ed** *a* bärtig.

bearer ['bɛərə*] *n* Träger *m*.

bearing ['bɛərɪŋ] *n* (*posture*) Haltung *f*; (*relevance*) Relevanz *f*; (*relation*) Bedeutung *f*; (Tech) Kugellager *nt*; **—s** *pl* (*direction*)-Orientierung *f*.

bearskin ['bɛəskɪn] *n* Bärenfellmütze *f*.

beast [biːst] n Tier nt, Vieh nt; (person) Bestie f; (nasty person) Biest nt; **—ly** ad viehisch; (col) scheußlich; **—** of burden Lasttier nt.

beat [biːt] n (stroke) Schlag m; (pulsation) (Herz)schlag m; (police round) Runde f; Revier nt; (Mus) Takt m; Beat m; vt irreg schlagen; **to — about the bush** wie die Katze um den heißen Brei herumgehen; **to — time** den Takt schlagen; **— off** vt abschlagen; **— up** vt zusammenschlagen; **—en track** gebahnte(r) Weg m; (fig) herkömmliche Art und Weise; **off the —en track** abgelegen; **—er** (for eggs, cream) Schneebesen m.

beautiful ['bjuːtɪfʊl] a schön; **—ly** ad ausgezeichnet.

beautify ['bjuːtɪfaɪ] vt verschönern.

beauty ['bjuːtɪ] n Schönheit f.

beaver ['biːvə*] n Bieber m.

becalm [bɪ'kɑːm] vt: **to be —ed** eine Flaute haben.

because [bɪ'kɒz] ad, cj weil; prep: **— of** wegen (+gen or (col) dat).

beckon ['bekən] vti ein Zeichen geben (sb jdm).

become [bɪ'kʌm] vt irreg werden m; (clothes) stehen (+dat).

becoming [bɪ'kʌmɪŋ] a (suitable) schicklich; clothes kleidsam.

bed [bed] n Bett nt; (of river) Flußbett nt; (foundation) Schicht f; (in garden) Beet nt; **— and breakfast** Übernachtung f mit Frühstück; **—clothes** pl Bettwäsche f; **—ding** Bettzeug nt.

bedeck [bɪ'dek] vt schmücken.

bedlam ['bedləm] n (uproar) tolle(s) Durcheinander nt.

bedraggled [bɪ'dræɡld] a ramponiert.

bedridden ['bedrɪdn] a bettlägerig.

bedroom ['bedrʊm] n Schlafzimmer nt.

bedside ['bedsaɪd] n: **at the —** am Bett.

bed-sitter ['bed'sɪtə*] n Einzimmerwohnung f, möblierte(s) Zimmer nt.

bedtime ['bedtaɪm] n Schlafenszeit f.

bee [biː] n Biene f.

beech [biːtʃ] n Buche f.

beef [biːf] n Rindfleisch nt.

beehive ['biːhaɪv] n Bienenstock m.

beeline ['biːlaɪn] n: **to make a — for** schnurstracks zugehen auf (+acc).

beer [bɪə*] n Bier nt.

beetle ['biːtl] n Käfer m.

beetroot ['biːtruːt] n rote Bete f.

befall [bɪ'fɔːl] irreg vi sich ereignen; vt zustoßen (+dat).

befit [bɪ'fɪt] vt sich schicken für.

before [bɪ'fɔː*] prep vor; cj bevor; ad (of time) zuvor; früher; **I've done it —** das hab' ich schon mal getan.

befriend [bɪ'frend] vt sich (jds) annehmen.

beg [beɡ] vti (implore) dringend bitten; alms betteln; **—gar** Bettler(in f) m.

begin [bɪ'ɡɪn] vti irreg anfangen, beginnen; (found) gründen; **to — with** zunächst (einmal); **—ner** Anfänger m; **—ning** Anfang m.

begrudge [bɪ'ɡrʌdʒ] vt (be)neiden; **to — sb sth** jdm etw mißgönnen.

behalf [bɪ'hɑːf] n: **on or in** (US) **— of** im Namen (+gen); **on my —** für mich.

behave [bɪ'heɪv] vi sich benehmen; **—iour,** (US) **behavior** [bɪ'heɪvjə*] n Benehmen nt.

behead [bɪ'hed] vt enthaupten.

behind [br'hamd] *prep* hinter; *ad* (*late*) im Rückstand; (*in the rear*) hinten; *n* (*col*) Hinterteil *nt*.

behold [br'həʊld] *vt irreg* (*old*) erblicken.

beige [beɪʒ] *a* beige.

being ['biːɪŋ] *n* (*existence*) (Da)sein *nt*; (*person*) Wesen *nt*.

belch [belʃ] *n* Rülpsen *nt*; *vi* rülpsen; *vt* smoke ausspeien.

belfry ['belfrɪ] *n* Glockenturm *m*.

belie [br'laɪ] *vt* Lügen strafen (+acc).

belief [br'liːf] *n* Glaube *m* (in an +acc); (*conviction*) Überzeugung *f*.

believable [br'liːvəbl] *a* glaubhaft.

believe [br'liːv] *vt* glauben (+dat); (*think*) glauben, meinen, denken; *vi* (*have faith*) glauben; —**r** Gläubige(r) *mf*.

belittle [br'lɪtl] *vt* herabsetzen.

bell [bel] *n* Glocke *f*.

belligerent [br'lɪdʒərənt] *a person* streitsüchtig; *country* kriegsführend.

bellow ['beləʊ] *vti* brüllen; *n* Gebrüll *nt*.

bellows ['beləʊz] *npl* (*Tech*) Gebläse *nt*; (*for fire*) Blasebalg *m*.

belly ['belɪ] *n* Bauch *m*; *vi* sich ausbauchen.

belong [br'lɒŋ] *vi* gehören (*to* sb jdm); (*to club*) angehören (+dat); it does not — here es gehört nicht hierher; —**ings** *pl* Habe *f*.

beloved [br'lʌvɪd] *a* innig geliebt; *n* Geliebte(r) *mf*.

below [br'ləʊ] *prep* unter; *ad* unten.

belt [belt] *n* (*band*) Riemen *m*; (*round waist*) Gürtel *m*; *vt* (*fasten*) mit Riemen befestigen; (*col: beat*) schlagen; *vi* (*col: go fast*) rasen.

bench [bentʃ] *n* (*seat*) Bank *f*; (*workshop*) Werkbank *f*; (*judge's*

seat) Richterbank *f*; (*judges*) Richterstand *m*.

bend [bend] *vt irreg* (*curve*) biegen; (*stoop*) beugen; *n* Biegung *f*; (*in road*) Kurve *f*.

beneath [br'niːθ] *prep* unter; *ad* darunter.

benefactor ['benɪfæktə*] *n* Wohltäter(in *f*) *m*.

beneficial [benr'fɪʃl] *a* vorteilhaft; (*to health*) heilsam.

beneficiary [benr'fɪʃərɪ] *n* Nutznießer(in *f*) *m*.

benefit ['benɪfɪt] *n* (*advantage*) Nutzen *m*; *vt* fördern; *vi* Nutzen ziehen (*from* aus).

benevolence [br'nevələns] *n* Wohlwollen *nt*.

benevolent [br'nevələnt] *a* wohlwollend.

benign [br'naɪn] *a person* gütig; *climate* mild.

bent [bent] *n* (*inclination*) Neigung *f*; *a* (*col: dishonest*) unehrlich; to be — on versessen sein auf (+acc).

bequeath [br'kwiːð] *vt* vermachen.

bequest [br'kwest] *n* Vermächtnis *nt*.

bereaved [br'riːvd] *n* (*person*) Hinterbliebene(r) *mf*.

bereavement [br'riːvmənt] *n* schmerzliche(r) Verlust *m*.

beret ['beɪ] *n* Baskenmütze *f*.

berry ['berɪ] *n* Beere *f*.

berserk [bə'sɔːk] *a*: to go — wild werden.

berth [bɜːθ] *n* (*for ship*) Ankerplatz *m*; (*in ship*) Koje *f*; (*in train*) Bett *nt*; *vt* am Kai festmachen; *vi* anlegen.

beseech [br'siːtʃ] *vt irreg* anflehen.

beset [br'set] *vt irreg* bedrängen.

beside [br'saɪd] *prep* **neben, bei;**

(except) außer; **to be —** o.s. außer sich sein (with vor +dat).

besides [bɪˈsaɪdz] prep außer, neben; ad zudem, überdies.

besiege [bɪˈsiːdʒ] vt (Mil) belagern; (surround) umlagern, bedrängen.

besmirch [bɪˈsmɜːtʃ] vt besudeln.

bespectacled [bɪˈspektɪkld] a bebrillt.

bespoke tailor [bɪˈspəʊk ˈteɪlə*] n Maßschneider m.

best [best] a beste(r, s); ad am besten; **at —** höchstens; **to make the — of it** das Beste daraus machen; **for the —** zum Besten; **— man** Trauzeuge m.

bestial [ˈbestɪəl] a bestialisch.

bestow [bɪˈstəʊ] vt verleihen.

bestseller [ˈbestˈselə*] n Bestseller m, meistgekaufte(s) Buch nt.

bet [bet] n Wette f; vti irreg wetten.

betray [bɪˈtreɪ] vt verraten; **—al** Verrat m.

better [ˈbetə*] a, ad besser; vt verbessern; n: **to get the — of** jdn überwinden; **he thought — of it er hat sich eines Besseren besonnen; you had — leave Sie gehen jetzt wohl besser; **— off a (richer) wohlhabender.

betting [ˈbetɪŋ] n Wetten nt; **— shop** Wettbüro nt.

between [bɪˈtwiːn] prep zwischen; (among) unter; ad dazwischen.

bevel [ˈbevəl] n Abschrägung f.

beverage [ˈbevərɪdʒ] n Getränk nt.

beware [bɪˈweə*] vt sich hüten vor (+dat); **'— of the dog'** 'Vorsicht, bissiger Hund!'

bewildered [bɪˈwɪldəd] a verwirrt.

bewildering [bɪˈwɪldərɪŋ] a verwirrend.

bewitching [bɪˈwɪtʃɪŋ] a bestrickend.

beyond [bɪˈjɒnd] prep (place) jenseits (+gen); (time) über ... hinaus; (out of reach) außerhalb (+gen); **it's — me** das geht über meinen Horizont; ad darüber hinaus.

bias [ˈbaɪəs] n (slant) Neigung f; (prejudice) Vorurteil nt; **—(s)ed a** voreingenommen.

bib [bɪb] n Latz m.

Bible [ˈbaɪbl] n Bibel f.

biblical [ˈbɪblɪkəl] a biblisch.

bibliography [bɪblɪˈɒɡrəfɪ] n Bibliographie f.

bicentenary [baɪsenˈtiːnərɪ] n Zweihundertjahrfeier f.

biceps [ˈbaɪseps] npl Bizeps m.

bicker [ˈbɪkə*] vi zanken; **—ing** Gezänk nt, Gekeife nt.

bicycle [ˈbaɪsɪkl] n Fahrrad nt.

bid [bɪd] n (offer) Gebot nt; (attempt) Versuch m; vt irreg (offer) bieten; **to — farewell** Lebewohl sagen; **—der** (person) Steigerer m; **—ding** (command) Geheiß nt.

bide [baɪd] vt: **— one's time** abwarten.

big [bɪg] a groß.

bigamy [ˈbɪgəmɪ] n Bigamie f.

bigheaded [ˈbɪgˈhedɪd] a eingebildet.

bigot [ˈbɪgət] n Frömmler m; **—ed** a bigott; **—ry** Bigotterie f.

bigwig [ˈbɪgwɪg] n (col) hohe(s) Tier nt.

bike [baɪk] n Rad nt.

bikini [bɪˈkiːnɪ] n Bikini m.

bilateral [baɪˈlætərəl] a bilateral.

bile [baɪl] n (Biol) Galle(nflüssigkeit) f.

bilge [bɪldʒ] n (water) Bilgenwasser nt.

bilingual   [bar'lɪŋwəl]   a zweisprachig.

bilious ['bɪlɪəs] a (sick) gallenkrank; (peevish) verstimmt.

bill [bɪl] n (account) Rechnung f; (Pol) Gesetzentwurf m; (US Fin) Geldschein m; '— of exchange Wechsel m.

billet ['bɪlɪt] n Quartier nt.

billfold ['bɪlfəʊld] n (US) Geldscheintasche f.

billiards ['bɪlɪədz] n Billard nt.

billion ['bɪlɪən] n Billion f; (US) Milliarde f.

billy goat ['bɪlɪgəʊt] n Ziegenbock m.

bin [bɪn] n Kasten m; (dust—) (Abfall)eimer m.

bind [baind] vt irreg (tie) binden; (tie together) zusammenbinden; (oblige) verpflichten; —ing (Buch)einband m; a verbindlich.

binge [bɪndʒ] n (col) Sauferei f.

bingo ['bɪŋɡəʊ] n Bingo nt.

binoculars [bɪ'nɒkjʊləz] npl Fernglas nt.

biochemistry ['baɪəʊ'kemɪstrɪ] n Biochemie f.

biographer [baɪ'ɒɡrəfə*] n Biograph m.

biographic(al) [baɪəʊ'ɡræfɪk(l)] a biographisch.

biography [baɪ'ɒɡrəfɪ] n Biographie f.

biological [baɪə'lɒdʒɪkəl] a biologisch.

biologist [baɪ'ɒlədʒɪst] n Biologe m.

biology [baɪ'ɒlədʒɪ] n Biologie f.

biped ['baɪped] n Zweifüßler m.

birch [bɜ:tʃ] n Birke f.

bird [bɜ:d] n Vogel m; (col: girl) Mädchen nt; —'s-eye view Vogelschau f.

birth [bɜ:θ] n Geburt f; of good — aus gutem Hause; — certificate Geburtsurkunde f; — control Geburtenkontrolle f; —day Geburtstag m; —place Geburtsort m; — rate Geburtenrate f.

biscuit ['bɪskɪt] n Keks m.

bisect [baɪ'sekt] vt halbieren.

bishop ['bɪʃəp] n Bischof m.

bit [bɪt] n bißchen, Stückchen nt; (horse's) Gebiß nt; a — tired etwas müde.

bitch [bɪtʃ] n (dog) Hündin f; (unpleasant woman) Weibsstück nt.

bite [baɪt] vti irreg beißen; n Biß m; (mouthful) Bissen m; — to eat Happen m.

biting ['baɪtɪŋ] a beißend.

bitter ['bɪtə*] a bitter; memory etc schmerzlich; person verbittert; n (beer) dunkles Bier; to the — end bis zum bitteren Ende; —ness Bitterkeit f; —sweet bittersüß.

bivouac ['bɪvʊæk] n Biwak nt.

bizarre [bɪ'zɑ:*] a bizarr.

blab [blæb] vi klatschen; vt ausplaudern.

black [blæk] a schwarz; night finster; vt schwärzen; shoes wichsen; dry blau schlagen; (industry) boykottieren; — and blue grün und blau; —berry Brombeere f; —bird Amsel f; —board (Wand)tafel f; —currant schwarze Johannisbeere f; —guard Schuft m; —leg Streikbrecher(in f) m; —list schwarze Liste f; —mail Erpressung f; vt erpressen; —mailer Erpresser(in f) m; — market Schwarzmarkt m; —ness Schwärze f; —out Verdunklung f; (Med) to have a —out bewußtlos werden; — sheep schwarze(s) Schaf nt; —smith Schmied m.

bladder ['blædə*] n Blase f.

blade [bleɪd] n (of weapon) Klinge f; (of grass) Halm m; (of oar) Ruderblatt nt.

blame [bleɪm] n Tadel m, Schuld f; vt tadeln, Vorwürfe machen (+ dat) he is to — er ist daran schuld; —less a untadelig.

blanch [blɑːntʃ] vi bleich werden.

blancmange [blə'mɒnʒ] n Pudding m.

bland [blænd] a mild.

blank [blæŋk] a leer, unbeschrieben; look verdutzt; cheque Blanko-; verse Blank-; n (space) Lücke f; Zwischenraum m; (cartridge) Platzpatrone f.

blanket ['blæŋkɪt] n (Woll)decke f.

blankly ['blæŋklɪ] ad leer; look verdutzt.

blare [blɛə*] vti (radio) plärren; (horn) tuten; (Mus) schmettern; n Geplärr nt; Getute nt; Schmettern nt.

blasé ['blɑːzeɪ] a blasiert.

blaspheme [blæs'fiːm] vi (Gott) lästern.

blasphemous ['blæsfɪməs] a lästernd, lästerlich.

blasphemy ['blæsfɪmɪ] n (Gottes)lästerung f, Blasphemie f.

blast [blɑːst] n Explosion f; (of wind) Windstoß m; vt (blow up) sprengen; —! (col) verflixt!; — furnace Hochofen m; —off (Space) (Raketen)abschuß m.

blatant ['bleɪtənt] a offenkundig.

blaze [bleɪz] n (fire) loderndes(s) Feuer nt; vi lodern; vt: — a trail Bahn brechen.

blazer ['bleɪzə*] n Klubjacke f, Blazer m.

bleach [bliːtʃ] n Bleichmittel nt; vt bleichen.

bleak [bliːk] a kahl, rauh; future trostlos.

bleary-eyed ['blɪərɪaɪd] a triefäugig; (on waking up) mit verschlafenen Augen.

bleat [bliːt] n (of sheep) Blöken nt; (of goat) Meckern nt; vi blöken; meckern.

bleed [bliːd] irreg vi bluten; vt (draw blood) Blut abnehmen; to — to death verbluten.

bleeding ['bliːdɪŋ] a blutend.

blemish ['blemɪʃ] n Makel m; vt verunstalten.

blench [blentʃ] vi zurückschrecken; see blanch.

blend [blend] n Mischung f; vt mischen; vi sich mischen.

bless [bles] vt segnen; (give thanks) preisen; (make happy) glücklich machen; — you! Gesundheit!; —ing n Segen m; (at table) Tischgebet nt; (happiness) Wohltat f; Segen m; (good wish) Glück m.

blight [blaɪt] n (Bot) Mehltau m; (fig) schädliche(r) Einfluß m; vt zunichte machen.

blimey ['blaɪmɪ] interj (Brit col) verflucht.

blind [blaɪnd] a blind; corner unübersichtlich; n (for window) Rouleau nt; vt blenden; — alley Sackgasse f; —fold Augenbinde f; a mit verbundenen Augen; vt die Augen verbinden (sb jdm); —ly ad blind; (fig) blindlings; —ness Blindheit f; — spot (Aut) toter Winkel m; (fig) schwache(r) Punkt m.

blink [blɪŋk] vti blinzeln; —ers pl Scheuklappen pl.

bliss [blɪs] n (Glück)seligkeit f; —fully ad glückselig.

blister ['blɪstə*] n Blase f; vt

Blasen werfen auf (+dat); vi Blasen werfen.

blithe [blaɪð] a munter; —ly ad fröhlich.

blitz [blɪts] n Luftkrieg m; vt bombardieren.

blizzard ['blɪzəd] n Schneesturm m.

bloated ['bləʊtɪd] a aufgedunsen; (col: full) nudelsatt.

blob [blɒb] n Klümpchen nt.

bloc [blɒk] n (Pol) Block m.

block [blɒk] n (of wood) Block m, Klotz m; (of houses) Häuserblock m; vt hemmen; —ade [blɒ'keɪd] Blockade f; vt blockieren; —age Verstopfung f.

bloke [bləʊk] n (col) Kerl m, Typ m.

blonde [blɒnd] a blond; n Blondine f.

blood [blʌd] n Blut nt; — donor Blutspender m; — group Blutgruppe f; —less a blutleer; — poisoning Blutvergiftung f; — pressure Blutdruck m; —shed Blutvergießen nt; —shot a blutunterlaufen; —stained a blutbefleckt; —stream Blut m, Blutkreislauf m; —thirsty a blutrünstig; — transfusion Blutübertragung f; —y a (col) verdammt, saumäßig; (lit) blutig; —y-minded a stur.

bloom [blu:m] n Blüte f; (freshness) Glanz m; vi blühen; in — in Blüte.

blossom ['blɒsəm] n Blüte f; vi blühen.

blot [blɒt] n Klecks m; vt beklecksen; ink (ab)löschen; — out vt auslöschen.

blotchy ['blɒtʃɪ] a fleckig.

blotting paper ['blɒtɪŋpeɪpə*] n Löschpapier nt.

blouse [blaʊz] n Bluse f.

blow [bləʊ] n Schlag m; irreg vt blasen; vi (wind) wehen; to — one's top (vor Wut) explodieren; — over vi vorübergehen; — up vi explodieren; vt sprengen; —lamp Lötlampe f; —out (Aut) geplatzte(r) Reifen m; —up (Phot) Vergrößerung f; —y a windig.

blubber ['blʌbə*] n Walfischspeck m.

bludgeon ['blʌdʒən] vt (fig) zwingen.

blue [blu:] a blau; (col: unhappy) niedergeschlagen; (obscene) pornographisch; joke anzüglich; to have the —s traurig sein; —bell Glockenblume f; —blooded a blaublütig; —bottle · Schmeißfliege f; —print (fig) Entwurf m; —s pl (Mus) Blues m.

bluff [blʌf] vt bluffen, täuschen; n (deception) Bluff m; a gutmütig und derb.

bluish ['blu:ɪʃ] a bläulich.

blunder ['blʌndə*] n grobe(r) Fehler m, Schnitzer m; vi einen groben Fehler machen.

blunt [blʌnt] a knife stumpf; talk unverblümt; vt abstumpfen; —ly ad frei heraus; —ness Stumpfheit f; (fig) Plumpheit f.

blur [blɜ:*] n Fleck m; vi verschwimmen; vt verschwommen machen.

blurb [blɜ:b] n Waschzettel m.

blurt [blɜ:t] vt: — out herausplatzen mit.

blush [blʌʃ] vi erröten; n (Scham)-röte f; —ing a errötend.

bluster ['blʌstə*] vi (wind) brausen; (person) darauf lospoltern, schwadronieren; —y a sehr windig.

boa ['bəʊə]. n Boa f.

boar [bɔ:*] n Keiler m, Eber m.

board [bɔ:d] n (of wood) Brett nt; (of card) Pappe f; (committee) Ausschuß m; (of firm) Aufsichtsrat m; (Sch) Direktorium nt; vt train einsteigen in (+acc); ship an Bord gehen (+gen); — and lodging Unterkunft f und Verpflegung; to go by the — flachfallen, über Bord gehen; — up vt mit Brettern vernageln; —er Kostgänger m; (Sch) Internatsschüler(in f) m; —ing house Pension f; — ing school Internat nt; — room Sitzungszimmer nt.

boast [bəʊst] vi prahlen; n Großtuerei f; vt prahlen mit; prahlerisch; —fulness Überheblichkeit f.

boat [bəʊt] n Boot nt; (ship) Schiff nt; —er (hat) Kreissäge f; —ing Bootfahren nt; —swain ['bəʊsn] = bosun; — train Zug m mit Schiffsanschluß.

bob [bɒb] vi sich auf und nieder bewegen.

bobbin ['bɒbɪn] n Spule f.

bobsleigh ['bɒbsleɪ] n Bob m.

bodice ['bɒdɪs] n Mieder nt.

-bodied ['bɒdɪd] a -gebaut.

bodily ['bɒdɪlɪ] a, ad körperlich.

body ['bɒdɪ] n Körper m; (dead) Leiche f; (group) Mannschaft f; (Aut) Karosserie f; (trunk) Rumpf m; in a — in einer Gruppe; the main — of the work der Hauptanteil der Arbeit; —guard Leibwache f; —work Karosserie f.

bog [bɒg] n Sumpf m; vi: to get —ged down sich festfahren.

bogey ['bəʊgɪ] n Schreckgespenst nt.

boggle ['bɒgl] vi stutzen.

bogus ['bəʊgəs] a unecht, Schein-.

boil [bɔɪl] vti kochen; n (Med) Geschwür nt; to come to the — zu kochen anfangen; —er Boiler m; —ing point Siedepunkt m.

boisterous ['bɔɪstərəs] a ungestüm.

bold [bəʊld] a (fearless) unerschrocken; handwriting fest und klar; —ly ad keck; —ness Kühnheit f; (cheekiness) Dreistigkeit f.

bollard ['bɒləd] n (Naut) Poller m; (on road) Pfosten m.

bolster ['bəʊlstə*] n Polster nt; — up vt unterstützen.

bolt [bəʊlt] n Bolzen m; (lock) Riegel m; vt verriegeln; (swallow) verschlingen; vi (horse) durchgehen.

bomb [bɒm] n Bombe f; vt bombardieren; —ard [bɒm'ba:d] vt bombardieren; —ardment [bɒm'ba:dmənt] Beschießung f; —er Bomber m; —ing Bombenangriff m; —shell (fig) Bombe f.

bombastic [bɒm'bæstɪk] a bombastisch.

bona fide ['bəʊnə'faɪd] a echt.

bond [bɒnd] n (link) Band nt; (Fin) Schuldverschreibung f.

bone [bəʊn] n Knochen m; (of fish) Gräte f; (piece of —) Knochensplitter m; — of contention Zankapfel m; vt die Knochen herausnehmen (+dat); fish entgräten; —dry a knochentrocken; —r (US col) Schnitzer m.

bonfire ['bɒnfaɪə*] n Feuer nt im Freien.

bonnet ['bɒnɪt] n Haube f; (for baby) Häubchen nt; (Brit Aut) Motorhaube f.

bonny ['bɒnɪ] a (Scot) hübsch.

bonus ['bəʊnəs] n Bonus m; (annual —) Prämie f.

bony ['bəʊnɪ] a knochig, knochendürr.

boo [buː] vt auspfeifen.

book [bʊk] n Buch nt; vt ticket etc vorbestellen; person verwarnen; —able a im Vorverkauf erhältlich; —case Bücherregal nt, Bücherschrank m; —ing office (Rail) Fahrkartenschalter m; (Theat) Vorverkaufsstelle f; —keeping Buchhaltung f; —let Broschüre f; —maker Buchmacher m; —seller Buchhändler m; —shop Buchhandlung f; —stall Bücherstand m; (Rail) Bahnhofsbuchhandlung f; —worm Bücherwurm m.

boom [buːm] n (noise) Dröhnen nt; (busy period) Hochkonjunktur f; vi dröhnen.

boomerang ['buːməræŋ] n Bumerang m.

boon [buːn] n Wohltat f, Segen m.

boorish ['bʊərɪʃ] a grob.

boost [buːst] n Auftrieb m; (edge) Reklame f; vt Auftrieb geben.

boot [buːt] n Stiefel m; (Brit Aut) Kofferraum m; vt (kick) einen Fußtritt geben; to — (in addition) obendrein.

booty ['buːtɪ] n Beute f.

booze [buːz] n (col) Alkohol m, Schnaps m; vi saufen.

border ['bɔːdə*] n Grenze f; (edge) Kante f; (in garden) (Blumen)rabatte f; — on vt grenzen an (+acc); —line Grenze f.

bore [bɔː*] vt bohren; (weary) langweilen; n (person) langweiliger Mensch m; (thing) langweilige Sache f; (of gun) Kaliber nt; —dom Langeweile f.

boring ['bɔːrɪŋ] a langweilig.

born [bɔːn]: to be — geboren werden.

borough ['bʌrə] n Stadt(gemeinde) f, Stadtbezirk m.

borrow ['bɔrəʊ] vt borgen; —ing (Fin) Anleihe f.

bosom ['bʊzəm] n Busen m.

boss [bɒs] n Chef m, Boß m; vt: — around herumkommandieren; —y a herrisch.

bosun ['bəʊsn] n Bootsmann m.

botanical [bə'tænɪkəl] a botanisch.

botanist ['bɒtənɪst] n Botaniker(in f) m.

botany ['bɒtənɪ] n Botanik f.

botch [bɒtʃ] vt verpfuschen.

both [bəʊθ] a beide(s); — (of) the books beide Bücher; I like them — ich mag (sie) beide; pron beide(s); ad: — X and Y sowohl X wie or als auch Y.

bother ['bɒðə*] vt (pester) quälen; vi (fuss) sich aufregen; (take trouble) sich Mühe machen; n Mühe f, Umstand m.

bottle ['bɒtl] n Flasche f; vt (in Flaschen) abfüllen; —neck (lit, fig) Engpaß m.

bottom ['bɒtəm] n Boden m; (of person) Hintern m; (riverbed) Flußbett nt; at — im Grunde; a unterste(r, s); —less a bodenlos.

bough [baʊ] n Zweig m, Ast m.

boulder ['bəʊldə*] n Felsbrocken m.

bounce [baʊns] vi (ball) hochspringen; (person) herumhüpfen; (cheque) platzen; vt (auf)springen lassen; n (rebound) Aufprall m; —r Rausschmeißer m.

bound [baʊnd] n Grenze f; (leap) Sprung m; vi (spring, leap) (auf)springen; a gebunden, verpflichtet; out of —s Zutritt verboten; to be — to do sth verpflichtet sein, etw zu tun, etw tun müssen; it's — to happen es muß so kommen; to be

— for ... nach ... fahren; —ary Grenze f, Grenzlinie f; —less a grenzenlos.

bouquet [bo'keɪ] n Strauß m; (of wine) Blume f.

bourgeois ['bʊəʒwɑ:] a kleinbürgerlich, bourgeois.

bout [baʊt] n (of illness) Anfall m; (of contest) Kampf m.

bow[1] [baʊ] n (ribbon) Schleife f; (weapon, Mus) Bogen m.

bow[2] [baʊ] vi sich verbeugen; (submit) sich beugen (+dat); n Verbeugung f; (of ship) Bug m.

bowels ['baʊəlz] npl Darm m; (centre) Innere nt.

bowl [baʊl] n (basin) Schüssel f; (of pipe) (Pfeifen)kopf m; (wooden ball) (Holz)kugel f; vti (die Kugel) rollen; —s pl (game) Kegeln nt.

bow-legged ['baʊlegɪd] a o-beinig.

bowler ['baʊlə*] n Werfer m; (hat) Melone f.

bowling ['baʊlɪŋ] n Kegeln nt; — **alley** Kegelbahn f; — **green** Rasen m zum Bowling-Spiel.

bow tie ['baʊ'taɪ] n Fliege f.

box [bʊks] n Schachtel f, (bigger) Kasten m; (Theat) Loge f; vt einpacken; **to** — sb's ears jdm eine Ohrfeige geben; vi boxen; —er Boxer m; — in vt einpferchen; —ing (Sport) Boxen nt; B—ing Day zweiter Weihnachtsfeiertag; —ing ring Boxring m; — office (Theater)kasse f; — room Rumpelkammer f.

boy [bɔɪ] n Junge m; — scout Pfadfinder m.

boycott ['bɔɪkɒt] n Boykott m; vt boykottieren.

boyfriend ['bɔɪfrend] n Freund m.

boyish ['bɔɪʃ] a jungenhaft.

bra [brɑ:] n BH m.

brace [breɪs] n (Tech) Stütze f; (Med) Klammer f; vt stützen; —s pl Hosenträger pl.

bracelet ['breɪslɪt] n Armband nt.

bracing ['breɪsɪŋ] a kräftigend.

bracken ['bræken] n Farnkraut nt.

bracket ['brækɪt] n Halter m, Klammer f; (in punctuation) Klammer f; (group) Gruppe f; vt einklammern; (fig) in diese Gruppe einordnen.

brag [bræg] vi sich rühmen.

braid [breɪd] n (hair) Flechte f; (trim) Borte f.

Braille [breɪl] n Blindenschrift f.

brain [breɪn] n (Anat) Gehirn nt; (intellect) Intelligenz f, Verstand m; (person) kluge(r) Kopf m; —s pl Verstand m; —less a dumm; —**storm** verrückte(r) Einfall m; —**wash** vt Gehirnwäsche f vornehmen bei; —**wave** gute(r) Einfall m, Geistesblitz m; —**y** gescheit.

braise [breɪz] vt schmoren.

brake [breɪk] n Bremse f; vti bremsen.

branch [brɑ:ntʃ] n Ast m; (division) Zweig m; (of road) sich verzweigen.

brand [brænd] n (Comm) Marke f, Sorte f; (on cattle) Brandmal nt; vt brandmarken; (Comm) eine Schutzmarke geben (+dat).

brandish ['brændɪʃ] vt (drohend) schwingen.

brand-new ['brænd'nju:] a funkelnagelneu.

brandy ['brændɪ] n Weinbrand m, Kognak m.

brash [bræʃ] a unverschämt.

brass [brɑ:s] n Messing nt; — **band** Blaskapelle f.

brassière ['bræsɪə*] n Büstenhalter m.

brat [bræt] n ungezogene(s) Kind nt, Gör nt.

bravado [brə'vɑːdəʊ] n Tollkühnheit f.

brave [breɪv] a tapfer; n indianische(r) Krieger m; vt die Stirn bieten (+dat); —ly ad tapfer; —ry ['breɪvərɪ] Tapferkeit f.

bravo ['brɑː'vəʊ] interj bravo!

brawl [brɔːl] n Rauferei f; vi Krawall machen.

brawn [brɔːn] n (Anat) Muskeln pl; (strength) Muskelkraft f; —y a muskulös, stämmig.

bray [breɪ] n Eselsschrei m; vi schreien.

brazen ['breɪzn] a (shameless) unverschämt; vt: — it out sich mit Lügen und Betrügen durchsetzen.

brazier ['breɪzɪə*] n (of workmen) offene(r) Kohlenofen m.

breach [briːtʃ] n (gap) Lücke f; (Mil) Durchbruch m; (of discipline) Verstoß m (gegen die Disziplin); (of faith) Vertrauensbruch m; vt durchbrechen; — of the peace öffentliche Ruhestörung f.

bread [bred] n Brot nt; — and butter Butterbrot nt; —crumbs pl Brotkrumen pl; (Cook) Paniermehl nt; to be on the —line sich gerade so durchschlagen; —winner Ernährer m.

breadth [bretθ] n Breite f.

break [breɪk] irreg vt (destroy) ab- or zer)brechen; promise brechen, nicht einhalten; vi (fall apart) auseinanderbrechen; (collapse) zusammenbrechen; (of dawn) anbrechen; n (gap) Lücke f; (chance) Chance f, Gelegenheit f; (fracture) Bruch m; (rest) Pause f; — down vi (car) eine Panne haben;

(person) zusammenbrechen; to — free or loose sich losreißen; — in vt animal abrichten; horse zureiten; vi (burglar) einbrechen; — out vi ausbrechen; — up vi zerbrechen; (fig) sich zerstreuen; (Sch) in die Ferien gehen; vt brechen; —able a zerbrechlich; —age Bruch m, Beschädigung f; —down (Tech) Panne f; (of nerves) Zusammenbruch m; —er Brecher m; —fast ['brekfəst] Frühstück nt; —through Durchbruch m; —water Wellenbrecher m.

breast [brest] n Brust f; — stroke Brustschwimmen nt.

breath [breθ] n Atem m; out of — außer Atem; under one's — flüsternd.

breathalize ['breθəlaɪz] vt blasen lassen.

breathe [briːð] vti atmen; —r Verschnaufpause f.

breathless ['breθlɪs] a atemlos.

breath-taking ['breθteɪkɪŋ] a atemberaubend.

breed [briːd] irreg vi sich vermehren; vt züchten; n (race) Rasse f, Zucht f; —er (person) Züchter m; —ing Züchtung f; (upbringing) Erziehung f; (education) Bildung f.

breeze [briːz] n Brise f.

breezy ['briːzɪ] a windig; manner munter.

brevity ['brevɪtɪ] n Kürze f.

brew [bruː] vt brauen; plot anzetteln; vi (storm) sich zusammenziehen; —ery Brauerei f.

bribe [braɪb] n Bestechungsgeld nt or -geschenk nt; vt bestechen; —ry ['braɪbərɪ] Bestechung f.

bric-à-brac ['brɪkəbræk] n Nippes pl.

brick [brɪk] n Backstein m; **—layer** Maurer m; **—work** Mauerwerk nt; **—works** Ziegelei f.

bridal ['braɪdl] a Braut-, bräutlich.

bride [braɪd] n Braut f; **—groom** Bräutigam m; **—smaid** Brautjungfer f.

bridge [brɪdʒ] n Brücke f; (Naut) Kommandobrücke f; (Cards) Bridge nt; (Anat) Nasenrücken m; vt eine Brücke schlagen über (+acc); (fig) überbrücken.

bridle ['braɪdl] n Zaum m; vt (fig) zügeln; horse aufzäumen; **—path** Saumpfad m.

brief [briːf] a kurz; n (Jur) Akten pl; vt instruieren; **—s** pl Schlüpfer m, Slip m; **—case** Aktentasche f; **—ing** (genaue) Anweisung f; **—ly** ad kurz; **—ness** Kürze f.

brigade [brɪ'geɪd] n Brigade f.

brigadier [brɪgə'dɪə*] n Brigadegeneral m.

bright [braɪt] a hell; (cheerful) heiter; idea klug; **—en up** vt aufhellen; person aufheitern; vi sich aufheitern; **—ly** ad hell; heiter.

brilliance ['brɪljəns] n Glanz m; (of person) Scharfsinn m.

brilliant a, **—ly** ad ['brɪliənt, -lɪ] glänzend.

brim [brɪm] n Rand m; vi voll sein; **—ful** a übervoll.

brine [braɪn] n Salzwasser nt.

bring [brɪŋ] vt irreg bringen; **— about** vt zustande bringen; **— off** vt davontragen; success erzielen; **— round** or **to** vt wieder zu sich bringen; **— up** vt aufziehen; question zur Sprache bringen.

brisk [brɪsk] a lebhaft.

bristle ['brɪsl] n Borste f; vi sich sträuben; **bristling with** strotzend vor (+dat).

brittle ['brɪtl] a spröde.

broach [brəʊtʃ] vt subject anschneiden.

broad [brɔːd] a breit; hint deutlich; daylight hellicht; (general) allgemein; accent stark; **—cast** n Rundfunkübertragung f; vti irreg übertragen, senden; **—casting** Rundfunk m; **—en** vt erweitern; vi sich erweitern; **—ly** ad allgemein gesagt; **—minded** a tolerant.

brocade [brə'keɪd] n Brokat m.

broccoli ['brɒkəlɪ] n Spargelkohl m, Brokkoli pl.

brochure ['brəʊʃʊə*] n Broschüre f.

broiler ['brɔɪlə*] n Bratrost m.

broke [brəʊk] a (col) pleite.

broken-hearted ['brəʊkən'hɑːtɪd] a untröstlich.

broker ['brəʊkə*] n Makler m.

bronchitis [brɒŋ'kaɪtɪs] n Bronchitis f.

bronze [brɒnz] n Bronze f; **—d** a sonnengebräunt.

brooch [brəʊtʃ] n Brosche f.

brood [bruːd] n Brut f; vi brüten; **—y** a brütend.

brook [brʊk] n Bach m.

broom [bruːm] n Besen m; **—stick** Besenstiel m.

broth [brɒθ] n Suppe f, Fleischbrühe f.

brothel ['brɒθl] n Bordell nt.

brother ['brʌðə*] n Bruder m; **—hood** Bruderschaft f; **—in-law** Schwager m; **—ly** a brüderlich.

brow [braʊ] n (eyebrow) (Augen)braue f; (forehead) Stirn f; (of hill) Bergkuppe f; **—beat** vt irreg einschüchtern.

brown [braʊn] a braun; n Braun nt; vt bräunen; **—ie** Wichtel m; **— paper** Packpapier nt.

browse [brauz] vi (*in books*) blättern; (*in shop*) schmökern, herumschauen.

bruise [bru:z] n Bluterguß m, blaue(r) Fleck m; vti einen blauen Fleck geben/bekommen.

brunette [bru'net] n Brünette f.

brunt [brʌnt] n volle Wucht f.

brush [brʌʃ] n Bürste f; (*for sweeping*) Handbesen m; (*for painting*) Pinsel m; (*fight*) kurze(r) Kampf m; (*Mil*) Scharmützel m; (*fig*) Auseinandersetzung f; vt (*clean*) bürsten; (*sweep*) fegen; (*touch*) streifen; **give sb the ~-off** (col) jdm eine Abfuhr erteilen; **~ aside** vt abtun; **~-wood** Gestrüpp nt.

brusque [bru:sk] a brüsk.

Brussels sprout ['brʌslz'spraʊt] n Rosenkohl m.

brutal ['bru:tl] a brutal; **~ity** [bru'tælɪtɪ] n Brutalität f.

brute [bru:t] n (*person*) Scheusal nt; **~ force** rohe Kraft; (*violence*) nackte Gewalt nt.

brutish ['bru:tɪʃ] a tierisch.

bubble ['bʌbl] n (Luft)blase f; vi sprudeln; (*with joy*) übersprudeln.

buck [bʌk] n Bock m; (US col) Dollar m; vi bocken; **~ up** vi (col) sich zusammenreißen.

bucket ['bʌkɪt] n Eimer m.

buckle ['bʌkl] n Schnalle f; vt (*an- or zusammen*)schnallen; vi (*bend*) sich verziehen.

bud [bʌd] n Knospe f; vi knospen, keimen.

Buddhism ['budɪzəm] n Buddhismus m.

Buddhist ['budɪst] n Buddhist(in f) m; a buddhistisch.

budding ['bʌdɪŋ] a angehend.

buddy ['bʌdɪ] n (col) Kumpel m.

budge [bʌdʒ] vti (sich) von der Stelle rühren.

budgerigar ['bʌdʒərɪga:*] n Wellensittich m.

budget ['bʌdʒɪt] n Budget nt; (*Pol*) Haushalt m; vi haushalten.

budgie ['bʌdʒɪ] n = budgerigar.

buff [bʌf] n colour lederfarben; n (*enthusiast*) Fan m.

buffalo ['bʌfələʊ] n Büffel m.

buffer ['bʌfə*] n Puffer m.

buffet ['bʌfɪt] n (*blow*) Schlag m; ['bʊfeɪ] (*bar*) Imbißraum m, Erfrischungsraum m; (*food*) (kaltes) Büffet nt; vt ['bʌfɪt] (herum)stoßen.

buffoon [bʌ'fu:n] n Hanswurst m.

bug [bʌg] n (*lit, fig*) Wanze f; vt verwanzen; **~bear** Schreckgespenst nt.

bugle ['bju:gl] n Jagd-, Bügelhorn nt.

build [bɪld] vt irreg bauen; n Körperbau m; **~er** n Bauunternehmer m; **~ing** Gebäude nt; **~ing society** Baugenossenschaft f; **~-up** Aufbau m; (*publicity*) Reklame f.

built [bɪlt] well-**~** a person gut gebaut; **~-in** a cupboard eingebaut; **~-up area** Wohngebiet nt.

bulb [bʌlb] n (*Bot*) (Blumen)zwiebel f; (*Elec*) Glühlampe f, Birne f; **~-ous** a knollig.

bulge [bʌldʒ] n (Aus)bauchung f; vi sich (aus)bauchen.

bulk [bʌlk] n Größe f, Masse f; (*greater part*) Großteil m; **~head** Schott nt; **~y** a (sehr) umfangreich; *goods* sperrig.

bull [bʊl] n (*animal*) Bulle m; (*cattle*) Stier m; (*papal*) Bulle f; **~dog** Bulldogge f.

bulldoze ['buldəuz] vt planieren; (fig) durchboxen; —r Planierraupe f, Bulldozer m.

bullet ['bulit] n Kugel f.

bulletin ['bulitin] n Bulletin nt, Bekanntmachung f.

bullfight ['bulfait] n Stierkampf m.

bullion ['buliən] n Barren m.

bullock ['bulək] n Ochse m.

bull's-eye ['bulzai] n das Schwarze nt.

bully ['buli] n Raufbold m; vt einschüchtern.

bum [bʌm] n (col: backside) Hintern m; (tramp) Landstreicher m; (nasty person) fieser Kerl m; — around vi herumgammeln.

bumblebee ['bʌmblbi:] n Hummel f.

bump [bʌmp] n (blow) Stoß m; (swelling) Beule f; vti stoßen, prallen; —er (Brit Aut) Stoßstange f; a edition dick; harvest Rekord-.

bumptious ['bʌmpʃəs] a aufgeblasen.

bumpy ['bʌmpi] a holprig.

bun [bʌn] n Korinthenbrötchen nt.

bunch [bʌntʃ] n (of flowers) Strauß m; (of keys) Bund m; (of people) Haufen m.

bundle ['bʌndl] n Bündel nt; vt bündeln; — off vt fortschicken.

bung [bʌŋ] n Spund m; vt (col: throw) schleudern.

bungalow ['bʌŋgələu] n einstöckige(s) Haus nt, Bungalow m.

bungle ['bʌŋgl] vt verpfuschen.

bunion ['bʌniən] n entzündete(r) Fußballen m.

bunk [bʌŋk] n Schlafkoje f; — bed Etagenbett nt.

bunker ['bʌŋkə*] n (coal store) Kohlenbunker m; (golf) Sandloch nt.

bunny ['bʌni] n Häschen nt.

Bunsen burner ['bʌnsn 'bɜ:nə*] n Bunsenbrenner m.

bunting ['bʌntiŋ] n Fahnentuch nt.

buoy [bɔi] n Boje f; (lifebuoy) Rettungsboje f; —ancy Schwimmkraft f; —ant a (floating) schwimmend; (fig) heiter; — up vt Auftrieb geben (+dat).

burden ['bɜ:dn] n (weight) Ladung f, Last f; (fig) Bürde f; vt belasten.

bureau ['bjuərəu] n (desk) Sekretär m; (for information etc) Büro nt.

bureaucracy [bjuə'rɒkrəsi] n Bürokratie f.

bureaucrat ['bjuərəkræt] n Bürokrat(in f) m; —ic [bjuərə'krætik] a bürokratisch.

burglar ['bɜ:glə*] n Einbrecher m; — alarm Einbruchssicherung f; —ize vt (US) einbrechen in (+acc); —y n Einbruch m.

burgle ['bɜ:gl] vt einbrechen in (+acc).

burial ['beriəl] n Beerdigung f; — ground Friedhof m.

burlesque [bɜ:'lesk] n Burleske f.

burly ['bɜ:li] a stämmig.

burn [bɜ:n] irreg vt verbrennen; vi brennen; n Brandwunde f; to — one's fingers sich die Finger verbrennen; —ing question brennende Frage f.

burnish ['bɜ:niʃ] vt polieren.

burrow ['bʌrəu] n (of fox) Bau m; (of rabbit) Höhle f; vi sich eingraben; vt eingraben.

bursar ['bɜ:sə*] n Kassenverwalter m, Quästor m.

burst [bɜ:st] irreg vt zerbrechen; vi platzen; (into tears) ausbrechen; n Explosion f; (outbreak) Ausbruch m; (in pipe) Bruch(stelle f) m.

bury ['beri] vt vergraben; (in grave) beerdigen; **to — the hatchet** das Kriegsbeil begraben.

bus [bʌs] n (Auto)bus m, Omnibus m.

bush [buʃ] n Busch m.

bushel ['buʃl] n Scheffel m.

bushy ['buʃi] a buschig.

busily ['bizili] ad geschäftig.

business ['biznis] n Geschäft nt; (concern) Angelegenheit f; **it's none of your —** es geht dich nichts an; **to mean —** es ernst meinen; **—man** Geschäftsmann m.

bus-stop ['bʌsstɔp] n Bushaltestelle f.

bust [bʌst] n Büste f; a (broken) kaputt(gegangen); business pleite; **to go —** pleite machen.

bustle ['bʌsl] n Getriebe nt; vi hasten.

bustling ['bʌsliŋ] a geschäftig.

bust-up ['bʌstʌp] n (col) Krach m.

busy ['bizi] a beschäftigt; road belebt; vt: **— o.s.** sich beschäftigen; **—body** Übereifrige(r) mf.

but [bʌt, bət] cj aber; not this — that nicht dies, sondern das; (only) nur; (except) außer.

butane ['bju:tem] n Butan nt.

butcher ['butʃə*] n Metzger m; (murderer) Schlächter m; vt schlachten; (kill) abschlachten.

butler ['bʌtlə*] n Butler m.

butt [bʌt] n (cask) große(s) Faß nt; (target) Zielscheibe f; (thick end) dicke(s) Ende nt; (of gun) Kolben m; (of cigarette) Stummel m; vt (mit dem Kopf) stoßen.

butter ['bʌtə*] n Butter f; vt buttern; **—fly** Schmetterling m.

buttocks ['bʌtəks] npl Gesäß nt.

button ['bʌtn] n Knopf m; vti zuknöpfen; **—hole** Knopfloch nt; Blume f im Knopfloch; vt rankriegen.

buttress ['bʌtris] n Strebepfeiler m; Stützbogen m.

buxom ['bʌksəm] a drall.

buy [bai] vt irreg kaufen; **— up** vt aufkaufen; **—er** Käufer(in f) m.

buzz [bʌz] n Summen nt; vi summen.

buzzard ['bʌzəd] n Bussard m.

buzzer ['bʌzə*] n Summer m.

by [bai] prep (near) bei; (via) über (+acc); (past) an (+dat) ... vorbei; (before) bis; **— day/night** tags/nachts; **— train/bus** mit dem Zug/Bus; **— done —** sb/sth von jdm/durch etw gemacht; **— one-self** allein; **— and large** im großen und ganzen; **—-election** Nachwahl f; **—gone** a vergangen; n: **let —gones be —gones** laß(t) das Vergangene vergangen sein; **—(e)-law** Verordnung f; **—pass** Umgehungsstraße f; **—product** Nebenprodukt nt; **—stander** Zuschauer m; **—word** Inbegriff m.

C

C, c [si:] n C nt, c nt.

cab [kæb] n Taxi nt; (of train) Führerstand m; (of truck) Führersitz m.

cabaret ['kæbərei] n Kabarett nt.

cabbage ['kæbɪdʒ] n Kohl(kopf) m.

cabin ['kæbɪn] n Hütte f; (Naut) Kajüte f; (Aviat) Kabine f; **— cruiser** Motorjacht f.

cabinet ['kæbɪnɪt] n Schrank m; (for china) Vitrine f; (Pol) Kabinett nt; **—maker** Kunsttischler m.

cable ['keɪbl] n Drahtseil nt, Tau nt; (Tel) (Leitungs)kabel nt; (telegram) Kabel nt; vti kabeln, telegraphieren; **—car** Seilbahn f; **—gram** (Übersee)telegramm nt; **— railway** (Draht)seilbahn f.

cache [kæʃ] n Versteck nt; (for ammunition) geheimes Munitionslager nt; (for food) geheimes Proviantlager nt; (supplies of ammunition) Munitionsvorrat m; (supplies of food) Lebensmittelvorrat m.

cackle ['kækl] n Gegacker nt; vi gacken.

cactus ['kæktəs] n Kaktus m, Kaktee f.

caddie ['kædɪ] n Golfjunge m.

caddy ['kædɪ] n Teedose f.

cadence ['keɪdəns] n Tonfall m; (Mus) Kadenz f.

cadet [kə'det] n Kadett m.

cadge [kædʒ] vt schmarotzen, nassauern.

Caesarean [siː'zɛərɪən] a: **— (section)** Kaiserschnitt m.

café ['kæfɪ] n Café nt, Restaurant nt.

cafeteria [kæfɪ'tɪərɪə] n Selbstbedienungsrestaurant nt.

caffein(e) ['kæfiːn] n Koffein nt.

cage [keɪdʒ] n Käfig m; vt einsperren.

cagey ['keɪdʒɪ] a geheimnistuerisch, zurückhaltend.

cajole [kə'dʒəʊl] vt überreden.

cake [keɪk] n Kuchen m; (of soap) Stück nt; **—d** a verkrustet.

calamine ['kæləmaɪn] n Galmei m.

calamitous [kə'læmɪtəs] a katastrophal, unglückselig.

calamity [kə'læmɪtɪ] n Unglück nt, (Schicksals)schlag m.

calcium ['kælsɪəm] n Kalzium nt.

calculate ['kælkjʊleɪt] vt berechnen, kalkulieren.

calculating ['kælkjʊleɪtɪŋ] a berechnend.

calculation [kælkjʊ'leɪʃən] n Berechnung f.

calculator ['kælkjʊleɪtə*] Rechner m.

calculus ['kælkjʊləs] n Rechenart f.

calendar ['kælɪndə*] n Kalender m.

calf [kɑːf] n Kalb nt; (leather) Kalbsleder nt; (Anat) Wade f.

calibre, (US) **caliber** ['kælɪbə*] n Kaliber nt.

call [kɔːl] vt rufen; (summon) herbeirufen; (name) nennen; (meeting) einberufen; (awaken) wecken; (Tel) anrufen; vi (for help) rufen, schreien; (visit) vorbeikommen; n (shout) Schrei m, Ruf m; (visit) Besuch m; (Tel) Anruf m; **on —** in Bereitschaft; **—box** Fernsprechzelle f; **—er** Besucher(in f) m; (Tel) Anrufer m; **— girl** Call-Girl nt; **—ing** (vocation) Berufung f; **to be —ed** heißen; **— for** vt rufen (nach); (fetch) abholen; (fig: require) erfordern, verlangen; **— off** vt meeting absagen; **— on** vt besuchen, aufsuchen; (request) fragen; **— up** vt (Mil) einberufen.

callous a, **—ly** ad ['kæləs, -lɪ] herzlos; **—ness** Herzlosigkeit f.

callow ['kæləʊ] a unerfahren, noch nicht flügge.

calm [kɑːm] n Stille f, Ruhe f; (Naut) Flaute f; vt beruhigen; a

still, ruhig; *person* gelassen; **—ly**
ad ruhig, still; **—ness** Stille *f*, Ruhe
f; *(mental)* Gelassenheit *f*; **—
down** *vi* sich beruhigen; *vt*
beruhigen, besänftigen.

calorie ['kæləri] *n* Kalorie *f*,
Wärmeeinheit *f*.

calve [kɑːv] *vi* kalben.

camber ['kæmbə*] *n* Wölbung *f*.

camel ['kæməl] *n* Kamel *nt*.

cameo ['kæmɪəʊ] *n* Kamee *f*.

camera ['kæmərə] *n* Fotoapparat
m, Kamera *f*; in — unter
Ausschluß der Öffentlichkeit;
—man Kameramann *m*.

camomile ['kæməmaɪl] *n*: — tea
Kamillentee *m*.

camouflage ['kæməflɑːʒ] *n*
Tarnung *f*; *vt* tarnen; *(fig)* verschleiern, bemänteln.

camp [kæmp] *n* Lager *nt*, Camp *nt*;
(Mil) Feldlager *nt*; *(permanent)*
Kaserne *f*; *(camping place)* Zelt-
platz *m*; *vi* zelten, campen.

campaign [kæm'peɪn] *n* Kampagne
f; *(Mil)* Feldzug *m*; *vi* *(Mil)* Krieg
führen; *(participate)* in den Krieg
ziehen; *(fig)* werben, Propaganda
machen; *(Pol)* den Wahlkampf
führen; **electoral —** Wahlkampf *m*.

campbed ['kæmp'bed] *n* Camping-
bett *nt*.

camper ['kæmpə*] *n* Zeltende(r)
mf, Camper *m*.

camping ['kæmpɪŋ] *n*: **to go —**
zelten, Camping machen.

campsite ['kæmpsaɪt] *n* Zeltplatz
m, Campingplatz *m*.

campus ['kæmpəs] *n* *(Sch)*
Schulgelände *nt*; *(Univ)* Univer-
sitätsgelände *nt*, Campus *m*.

can [kæn] *v aux Irreg (be able)*
können, fähig sein; *(be allowed)*
dürfen, können; *n* Büchse *f*, Dose

f; *(for water)* Kanne *f*; *vt* konservieren, in Büchsen einmachen.

canal [kə'næl] *n* Kanal *m*.

canary [kə'nɛərɪ] *n* Kanarienvogel
m; a hellgelb.

cancel ['kænsəl] *vt (delete)* durch-
streichen; *(Math)* kürzen; *arrangement* aufheben; *meeting* absagen;
treaty annullieren; *stamp*
entwerten; **—lation** [kænsə'leɪʃən]
Aufhebung *f*; Absage *f*;
Annullierung *f*; Entwertung *f*.

cancer ['kænsə*] *n* *(also Astrol
C—)* Krebs *m*.

candid ['kændɪd] *a* offen, ehrlich;
—ly *ad* ehrlich.

candidate ['kændɪdeɪt] *n*
Bewerber(in *f*) *m*; *(Pol)*
Kandidat(in *f*) *m*.

candle ['kændl] *n* Kerze *f*; **—light**
Kerzenlicht *nt*; **—stick** Kerzen-
leuchter *m*.

candour ['kændə*] *n* Offenheit *f*.

candy ['kændɪ] *n* Kandis(zucker)
m; *(US)* Bonbons *pl*.

cane [keɪn] *n* *(Bot)* Rohr *nt*; *(for
walking, Sch)* Stock *m*; *vt* schlagen.

canister ['kænɪstə*] *n* Blechdose *f*.

cannabis ['kænəbɪs] *n* Hanf *m*,
Haschisch *nt*.

canned [kænd] *a* Büchsen-, eingemacht.

cannibal ['kænɪbəl] *n* Menschen-
fresser *m*; **—ism** Kannibalismus *m*.

cannon ['kænən] *n* Kanone *f*.

cannot ['kænɒt] = **can not**.

canny ['kænɪ] *a (shrewd)* schlau,
erfahren; *(cautious)* umsichtig, vorsichtig.

canoe [kə'nuː] *n* Paddelboot *nt*,
Kanu *nt*; **—ing** Kanufahren *nt*;
—ist Kanufahrer(in *f*) *m*.

canon ['kænən] *n* Domherr *m*; *(in*

·church law) Kanon m; (standard) Grundsatz m.

canonize ['kænənaiz] vt heiligsprechen.

can opener ['kænəupnə*] n Büchsenöffner m.

canopy ['kænəpi] n Baldachin m.

can't [kænt] = can not.

cantankerous [kæn'tænkərəs] a zänkisch, mürrisch.

canteen [kæn'ti:n] n (in factory) Kantine f; (case of cutlery) Bestecksasten m.

canter ['kæntə*] n Kanter m; kurzer leichter Galopp m; vi in kurzem Galopp reiten.

cantilever ['kæntili:və*] n Träger m, Ausleger m.

canvas ['kænvəs] n Segeltuch nt, Zeltstoff m; (sail) Segel nt; (for painting) Leinwand f; (painting) Ölgemälde nt; under — (people) in Zelten; (boat) unter Segel.

canvass ['kænvəs] vt werben; —er Wahlwerber(in f) m.

canyon ['kænjən] n Felsenschlucht f.

cap [kæp] n Kappe f, Mütze f; (lid) (Verschluß)kappe f, Deckel m; vt verschließen; (surpass) übertreffen.

capability [keipə'biliti] n Fähigkeit f.

capable ['keipəbl] a fähig; to be — of sth zu etw fähig or imstande sein.

capacity [kə'pæsiti] n Fassungsvermögen nt; (ability) Fähigkeit f; (position) Eigenschaft f.

cape [keip] n· (garment) Cape nt, Umhang m; (Geog) Kap nt.

caper ['keipə*] n Kaper f.

capital ['kæpitl] n (— city) Haüptstadt f; (Fin) Kapital nt; (— letter) Großbuchstabe m; —ism Kapitalismus m; —ist a kapitalistisch; .n

Kapitalist(in f) m; — **punishment** Todesstrafe f.

capitulate [kə'pitjuleit] vi kapitulieren.

capitulation [kəpitju'leiʃən] n Kapitulation· f.

capricious [kə'priʃəs] a launisch.

Capricorn ['kæprikɔ:n] n Steinbock m.

capsize [kæp'saiz] vti kentern.

capstan ['kæpstən] n Ankerwinde f, Poller m.

capsule ['kæpsju:l] n Kapsel f.

captain ['kæptin] n Führer m; (Naut) Kapitän m; (Mil) Hauptmann m; (Sport) (Mannschafts)-kapitän m; vt anführen.

caption ['kæpʃən] n Unterschrift f, Text m.

captivate ['kæptiveit] vt· fesseln.

captive ['kæptiv] n Gefangene(r) mf; a gefangen(gehalten).

captivity [kæp'tiviti] n Gefangenschaft f.

·capture ['kæptʃə*] vt fassen, gefangennehmen; n Gefangennahme f.

car [ka:*] n Auto nt, Wagen m.

carafe [kə'ræf] n Karaffe f.

caramel ['kærəmel] n Karamelle f.

carat ['kærət] n Karat nt.

caravan ['kærəvæn] n Wohnwagen m; (in desert) Karawane f.

caraway ['kærəwei] n: — seed Kümmel m.

carbohydrate [ka:bəu'haidreit] n Kohlenhydrat· nt.

carbon ['ka:bən] n Kohlenstoff m; (— paper) Kohlepapier nt; — copy Durchschlag m.

carburettor ['ka:bjuretə*] n Vergaser m.

carcass ['ka:kəs] n Kadaver m.

card [kɑːd] n Karte f; —board Pappe f; —board box Pappschachtel f; — game Kartenspiel nt.

cardiac ['kɑːdɪæk] a Herz-.

cardigan ['kɑːdɪgən] n Strickjacke f.

cardinal ['kɑːdɪnl] a: — number Kardinalzahl f.

care [kɛə*] n Sorge f, Mühe f; (charge) Obhut f, Fürsorge f; vi: I don't — es ist mir egal; to — about sb/sth sich kümmern um jdn/etw; to take — (watch) vorsichtig sein; (take pains) Mühe geben; take — of sorgen für; — for (look after) sorgen für; (like) mögen, gern' haben.

career [kə'rɪə*] n Karriere f, Laufbahn f; vi rasen.

carefree ['kɛəfriː] a sorgenfrei.

careful a, —ly ad ['kɛəful, -fəli] sorgfältig.

careless a, —ly ad ['kɛəlɪs, -lɪ] unvorsichtig; —ness Unachtsamkeit f; (neglect) Nachlässigkeit f.

caress [kə'res] n Liebkosung f; vt liebkosen.

caretaker ['kɛəteɪkə*] n Hausmeister m.

car-ferry ['kɑːferɪ] n Autofähre f.

cargo ['kɑːgəʊ] n Kargo m, Schiffsladung f.

caricature ['kærɪkətjʊə*] n Karikatur f; vt karikieren.

carnage ['kɑːnɪdʒ] n Blutbad nt.

carnal ['kɑːnl] a fleischlich, sinnlich.

carnation [kɑː'neɪʃən] n Nelke f.

carnival ['kɑːnɪvl] n Karneval m, Fastnacht f, Fasching m.

carnivorous [kɑː'nɪvərəs] a fleischfressend.

carol ['kærl] n (Weihnachts)lied nt.

carp [kɑːp] n (fish) Karpfen m; — at vt herumnörgeln an (+dat).

car park ['kɑːpɑːk] n Parkplatz m; Parkhaus nt.

carpenter ['kɑːpɪntə*] n Zimmermann m.

carpentry ['kɑːpɪntrɪ] n Zimmerei f.

carpet ['kɑːpɪt] n Teppich m; vt mit einem Teppich auslegen.

carping ['kɑːpɪŋ] a (critical) krittelnd, Mecker-.

carriage ['kærɪdʒ] n Wagen m; (of goods) Beförderung f; (bearing) Haltung f; —way (on road) Fahrbahn f.

carrier ['kærɪə*] n Träger(in f) m; (Comm) Spediteur m; — bag Tragetasche f; — pigeon Brieftaube f.

carrion ['kærɪən] n Aas nt.

carrot ['kærət] n Möhre f, Mohrrübe f, Karotte f.

carry ['kærɪ] vt tragen; vi weit tragen, reichen; —cot Baby-tragetasche f; to be carried away (fig) hingerissen sein; — on vti fortführen, weitermachen; — out vt orders ausführen.

cart [kɑːt] n Wagen m, Karren m; vt schleppen.

cartilage ['kɑːtɪlɪdʒ] n Knorpel m.

cartographer [kɑː'tɒgrəfə*] n Kartograph(in f) m.

carton ['kɑːtən] n (Papp)karton m; (of cigarettes) Stange f.

cartoon [kɑː'tuːn] n (Press) Karikatur f; (Cine) (Zeichen)trickfilm m.

cartridge ['kɑːtrɪdʒ] n (for gun) Patrone f; (film) Rollfilm m; (of record player) Tonabnehmer m.

carve [kɑːv] vti wood schnitzen; stone meißeln; meat (vor)-schneiden.

carving ['kɑːvɪŋ] n (in wood etc)

Schnitzerei f; — knife Tranchiermesser nt.

car wash ['kɑ:wɒʃ] n Autowäsche f.

cascade [kæs'keɪd] n Wasserfall m; vi kaskadenartig herabfallen.

case [keɪs] n (box) Kasten m, Kiste f; (suit—) Koffer m; (Jur, matter) Fall m; — in — falls, im Falle; in any — jedenfalls, auf jeden Fall.

cash [kæʃ] n (Bar)geld nt; vt einlösen; — desk Kasse f; —ier [kæ'ʃɪə*] Kassierer(in f) m; — on delivery per Nachnahme; —register Registrierkasse f.

cashmere ['kæʃmɪə*] n Kaschmirwolle f.

casing ['keɪsɪŋ] n Gehäuse nt.

casino [kə'si:nəʊ] n Kasino nt.

cask [kɑ:sk] n Faß nt.

casket ['kɑ:skɪt] n Kästchen nt; (US: coffin) Sarg m.

casserole ['kæsərəʊl] n Kasserole f; (food) Auflauf m.

cassock ['kæsək] n Soutane f, Talar m.

cast [kɑ:st] irreg vt werfen; horns etc verlieren; metal gießen; (Theat) besetzen; roles verteilen; n (Theat) Besetzung f; — off vi (Naut) losmachen; —off clothing abgelegte Kleidung.

castanets [kæstə'nets] npl Kastagnetten pl.

castaway ['kɑ:stəweɪ] n Schiffbrüchige(r) mf.

caste [kɑ:st] n Kaste f.

casting ['kɑ:stɪŋ] a: — vote entscheidende Stimme f.

castiron ['kɑ:st'aɪən] n Gußeisen nt; a gußeisern; alibi todsicher.

castle ['kɑ:sl] n Burg f; Schloß nt; (country mansion) Landschloß nt; (chess) Turm m.

castor ['kɑ:stə*] n (wheel) Laufrolle f; — oil Rizinusöl nt; — sugar Streuzucker m.

castrate [kæs'treɪt] vt kastrieren.

casual ['kæʒjʊl] a arrangement beiläufig; attitude nachlässig; dress leger; meeting zufällig; —ly ad dress zwanglos, leger; remark beiläufig.

casualty ['kæʒjʊltɪ] n Verletzte(r) mf; Tote(r) mf; (department in hospital) Unfallstation f.

cat [kæt] n Katze f.

catalog (US), **catalogue** ['kætəlɒg] n Katalog m; vt katalogisieren.

catalyst ['kætəlɪst] n (lit, fig) Katalysator m.

catapult ['kætəpʌlt] n Katapult nt; Schleuder f.

cataract ['kætərækt] n Wasserfall m; (Med) graue(r) Star m.

catarrh [kə'tɑ:*] n Katarrh m.

catastrophe [kə'tæstrəfɪ] n Katastrophe f.

catastrophic [kætəs'trɒfɪk] a katastrophal.

catch [kætʃ] vt irreg fangen; train etc nehmen; erreichen; (surprise) ertappen; (understand) begreifen; n (of lock) Sperrhaken m; (of fish) Fang m; to — a cold sich erkälten.

catching ['kætʃɪŋ] a (Med, fig) ansteckend.

catch phrase ['kætʃfreɪz] n Schlagwort nt, Slogan m.

catchy ['kætʃɪ] a tune eingängig.

catechism ['kætɪkɪzəm] n Katechismus m.

categorical a, **—ly** ad [kætə'gɒrɪkl, -kəlɪ] kategorisch.

categorize ['kætɪgəraɪz] vt kategorisieren.

category ['kætɪgərɪ] *n* Kategorie *f.*

cater ['keɪtə*] *vi* versorgen; **—ing** Gastronomie *f*; Bewirtung *f*; **— for** *vt* (*lit*) party ausrichten; (*fig*) eingestellt sein auf (*+acc*); berücksichtigen.

caterpillar ['kætəpɪlə*] *n* Raupe *f*; **— track** Gleiskette *f.*

cathedral [kə'θiːdrəl] *n* Kathedrale *f*, Dom *m.*

Catholic ['kæθəlɪk] *a* (*Rel*) katholisch; *n* Katholik(in *f*) *m*; **c—** vielseitig.

cattle ['kætl] *npl* Vieh *nt.*

catty ['kætɪ] *a* gehässig.

cauliflower ['kɒlɪflaʊə*] *n* Blumenkohl *m.*

cause [kɔːz] *n* Ursache *f*; Grund *m*; (*purpose*) Sache *f*; **in a good —** zu einem guten Zweck; *vt* verursachen.

causeway ['kɔːzweɪ] *n* Damm *m.*

caustic ['kɔːstɪk] *a* ätzend; (*fig*) bissig.

cauterize ['kɔːtəraɪz] *vt* ätzen, ausbrennen.

caution ['kɔːʃən] *n* Vorsicht *f*; (*warning*) Warnung *f*; (*Jur*) Verwarnung *f*; *vt* (ver)warnen.

cautious *a*, **—ly** *ad* ['kɔːʃəs, -lɪ] vorsichtig.

cavalcade [kævəl'keɪd] *n* Kavalkade *f.*

cavalier [kævə'lɪə*] *a* blasiert.

cavalry ['kævəlrɪ] *npl* Kavallerie *f.*

cave [keɪv] *n* Höhle *f*; **—man** Höhlenmensch *m*; **— in** *vi* einstürzen.

cavern ['kævən] *n* Höhle *f*; **—ous** *a* cheeks hohl; *eyes* tiefliegend.

cavil ['kævɪl] *vi* kritteln (at an *+dat*).

cavity ['kævɪtɪ] *n* Höhlung *f*; (in *tooth*) Loch *nt.*

cavort [kə'vɔːt] *vi* umherspringen.

cease [siːs] *vi* aufhören; *vt* beenden; **—fire** Feuereinstellung *f*; **—less** *a* unaufhörlich.

cedar ['siːdə*] *n* Zeder *f.*

cede [siːd] *vt* abtreten.

ceiling ['siːlɪŋ] *n* Decke *f*; (*fig*) Höchstgrenze *f.*

celebrate ['selɪbreɪt] *vt* feiern; *anniversary* begehen; *vi* feiern; **—d** *a* gefeiert.

celebration [selɪ'breɪʃən] *n* Feier *f.*

celebrity [sɪ'lebrɪtɪ] *n* gefeierte Persönlichkeit *f.*

celery ['selərɪ] *n* Sellerie *m or f.*

celestial [sɪ'lestɪəl] *a* himmlisch.

celibacy ['selɪbəsɪ] *n* Zölibat *nt or m.*

cell [sel] *n* Zelle *f*; (*Elec*) Element *nt.*

cellar ['selə*] *n* Keller *m.*

cellist ['tʃelɪst] *n* Cellist(in *f*) *m.*

cello ['tʃeləʊ] *n* Cello *nt.*

cellophane ® ['seləfeɪn] *n* Cellophan *nt.*

cellular ['seljʊlə*] *a* zellenförmig, zellular.

cellulose ['seljʊləʊs] *n* Zellulose *f.*

cement [sɪ'ment] *n* Zement *m*; *vt* (*lit*) zementieren; (*fig*) festigen.

cemetery ['semɪtrɪ] *n* Friedhof *m.*

cenotaph ['senətɑːf] *n* Ehrenmal *nt*, Zenotaph *m.*

censor ['sensə*] *n* Zensor *m*; **—ship** Zensur *f.*

censure ['senʃə*] *vt* rügen.

census ['sensəs] *n* Volkszählung *f.*

centenary [sen'tiːnərɪ] *n* Jahrhundertfeier *f.*

center ['sentə*] *n* (US) = **centre**.

centigrade ['sentɪgreɪd] *a:* **10 (degrees) —** 10 Grad Celsius.

centilitre, (US) **—liter** ['sentɪliːtə*] *n* Zentiliter *nt or m.*

centimetre, *(US)* **—meter** ['sentımi:tə*] *n* Zentimeter *nt.*

centipede ['sentıpi:d] *n* Tausendfüßler *m.*

central ['sentrəl] *a* zentral; — **heating** Zentralheizung *f*; **—ize** *vt* zentralisieren.

centre ['sentə*] *n* Zentrum *nt*; — **of gravity** Schwerpunkt *m*; **to —on** (sich) konzentrieren auf (+*acc*).

century ['sentjʊrı] *n* Jahrhundert *nt.*

ceramic [sı'ræmık] *a* keramisch.

cereal ['sıərıəl] *n* (*any grain*) Getreide *nt*; (*at breakfast*) Getreideflocken *pl.*

ceremonial [serı'məʊnıəl] *a* zeremoniell.

ceremony ['serımənı] *n* Feierlichkeiten *pl*, Zeremonie *f.*

certain ['sɜ:tən] *a* sicher; (*particular*) gewiß; **for —** ganz bestimmt; **—ly** *ad* sicher, bestimmt; **—ty** Gewißheit *f.*

certificate [sə'tıfıkıt] *n* Bescheinigung *f*; (*Sch etc*) Zeugnis *nt.*

certify ['sɜ:tıfaı] *vti* bescheinigen.

cessation [se'seıʃən] *n* Einstellung *f*, Ende *nt.*

chafe [tʃeıf] *vti* (wund)reiben, scheuern.

chaffinch ['tʃæfıntʃ] *n* Buchfink *m.*

chain [tʃeın] *n* Kette *f*; (*also —up*) anketten; mit Ketten fesseln; **— reaction** Kettenreaktion *f*; **—smoker** Kettenraucher(in *f*) *m*; **—store** Kettenladen *m.*

chair [tʃɛə*] *n* Stuhl *m*; (*arm—*) Sessel *m*; (*Univ*) Lehrstuhl *m*; *vt*: **to —a meeting** in einer Versammlung den Vorsitz führen; **—lift** Sessellift *m*; **—man** Vorsitzende(r) *m*; (*of firm*) Präsident *m.*

chalet ['ʃæleı] *n* Chalet *nt.*

chalice ['tʃælıs] *n* (Abendmahls)kelch *m.*

chalk [tʃɔ:k] *n* Kreide *f.*

challenge ['tʃælındʒ] *n* Herausforderung *f*; *vt* auffordern; (*contest*) bestreiten; **—r** Herausforderer *m.*

challenging ['tʃælındʒıŋ] *a* statement herausfordernd; work anspruchsvoll.

chamber ['tʃeımbə*] *n* Kammer *f*; **— of commerce** Handelskammer *f*; **—maid** Zimmermädchen *nt*; **—music** Kammermusik *f*; **—pot** Nachttopf *m.*

chameleon [kə'mi:lıən] *n* Chamäleon *nt.*

chamois ['ʃæmwɑ:] *n* Gemse *f*; **—leather** ['ʃæmı'leðə*] Sämischleder *nt.*

champagne [ʃæm'peın] *n* Champagner *m*, Sekt *m.*

champion ['tʃæmpıən] *n* (*Sport*) Sieger(in *f*) *m*, Meister *m*; (*of cause*) Verfechter(in *f*) *m*; **—ship** Meisterschaft *f.*

chance [tʃɑ:ns] *n* (*luck, fate*) Zufall *m*; (*possibility*) Möglichkeit *f*; (*opportunity*) Gelegenheit *f*, Chance *f*; (*risk*) Risiko *nt*; *a* zufällig; *vt*: **to — it** es darauf ankommen lassen; **by —** zufällig; **to take a —** ein Risiko eingehen; **no —** keine Chance.

chancel [tʃɑ:nsəl] *n* Altarraum *m*, Chor *m.*

chancellor ['tʃɑ:nsələ*] *n* Kanzler *m*; **C— of the Exchequer** Schatzkanzler *m.*

chancy ['tʃɑ:nsı] *a* (*col*) riskant.

chandelier [ʃændı'lıə*] *n* Kronleuchter *m.*

change [tʃeındʒ] *vt* verändern; money wechseln; *vi* sich verändern; (trains) umsteigen; (colour etc) sich verwandeln; (clothes) sich umziehen; n Veränderung f; (money) Wechselgeld nt; (coins) Kleingeld nt; **—able** a weather unbeständig; **—over** Umstellung f, Wechsel m.

changing ['tʃeɪndʒɪŋ] n veränderlich; **— room** Umkleideraum m.

channel ['tʃænl] n (stream) Bachbett nt; (Naut) Straße f, Meerenge f; (Rad, TV) Kanal m; (fig) Weg m; vt (hindurch)leiten, lenken; through official **—s** durch die Instanzen; the (English) C— der Ärmelkanal; C— Islands Kanalinseln pl.

chant [tʃɑ:nt] n liturgische(r) Gesang m; Sprechgesang m, Sprechchor m; vt intonieren.

chaos ['keɪɔs] n Chaos nt, Durcheinander nt.

chaotic [keɪ'ɔtɪk] a chaotisch.

chap [tʃæp] n (col) Bursche m, Kerl m; vt skin rissig machen; vi (hands etc) aufspringen.

chapel ['tʃæpəl] n Kapelle f.

chaperon ['ʃæpərəʊn] n Anstandsdame f; vt begleiten.

chaplain ['tʃæplɪn] n Geistliche(r) m, Pfarrer m, Kaplan m.

chapter ['tʃæptə*] n Kapitel nt.

char [tʃɑ:*] vt (burn) verkohlen; vi (cleaner) putzen gehen.

character ['kærɪktə*] n Charakter m, Wesen nt; (Liter) Figur f, Gestalt f; (Theat) Person f, Rolle f; (peculiar person) Original nt; (in writing) Schriftzeichen nt; **—istic** [kærɪktə'rɪstɪk] a charakteristisch, bezeichnend (of für); n Kennzeichen nt, Eigenschaft f; **—ize** vt charakterisieren, kennzeichnen.

charade [ʃə'rɑ:d] n Scharade f.

charcoal ['tʃɑ:kəʊl] n Holzkohle f.

charge [tʃɑ:dʒ] n (cost) Preis m; (Jur) Anklage f; (of gun) Ladung f; (attack) Angriff m; vt gun, battery laden; price verlangen; (Mil) angreifen; vi (rush) angreifen, (an)stürmen; to be in **—** of verantwortlich sein für; to take **—** (die Verantwortung) übernehmen.

chariot ['tʃærɪət] n (Streit)wagen m.

charitable ['tʃærɪtəbl] a wohltätig; (lenient) nachsichtig.

charity ['tʃærɪtɪ] n (institution) Wohlfahrtseinrichtung f, Hilfswerk nt; (attitude) Nächstenliebe f, Wohltätigkeit f.

charlady ['tʃɑ:leɪdɪ] n Reinemachefrau f, Putzfrau f.

charlatan ['ʃɑ:lətən] n Scharlatan m, Schwindler m.

charm [tʃɑ:m] n Charme m, gewinnende(s) Wesen nt; (in superstition) Amulett nt; Talisman m; vt bezaubern; **—ing** a reizend, liebenswürdig, charmant.

chart [tʃɑ:t] n Tabelle f; (Naut) Seekarte f.

charter ['tʃɑ:tə*] vt (Naut, Aviat) chartern; n Schutzbrief m; (cost) Schiffsmiete f; **— flight** Charterflug m; **—ed accountant** Wirtschaftsprüfer(in) f) m.

charwoman ['tʃɑ:wʊmən] n Reinemachefrau f, Putzfrau f.

chary ['tʃeərɪ] a zurückhaltend (of sth mit etw).

chase [tʃeɪs] vt jagen, verfolgen; n Jagd f.

chasm ['kæzəm] n Kluft f.

chassis ['ʃæsɪ] n Chassis nt, Fahrgestell nt.

chaste [tʃeɪst] a keusch.

chastity ['tʃæstɪtɪ] *n* Keuschheit *f.*

chat [tʃæt] *vi* plaudern, sich (zwanglos) unterhalten; *n* Plauderei *f.*

chatter ['tʃætə*] *vi* schwatzen; (*teeth*) klappern; *n* Geschwätz *nt*; **—box** Quasselstrippe *f.*

chatty ['tʃætɪ] *a* geschwätzig.

chauffeur ['ʃəʊfə*] *n* Chauffeur *m*, Fahrer *m.*

cheap [tʃiːp] *a* billig; *joke* schlecht; (*of poor quality*) minderwertig; **to** — *o.s.* sich herablassen; **—ly** *ad* billig.

cheat [tʃiːt] *vti* betrügen; (*Sch*) mogeln; *n* Betrüger(in *f*) *m*; **—ing** Betrug *m.*

check [tʃek] *vt* prüfen; (*look up, make sure*) nachsehen; (*control*) kontrollieren; (*restrain*) zügeln; (*stop*) anhalten; *n* (*examination, restraint*) Kontrolle *f*; (*restaurant bill*) Rechnung *f*; (*pattern*) Karo(muster) *nt*; (*US*) = cheque; **—ers** (*US*) Damespiel *nt*; **—list** Kontrollliste *f*; **—mate** Schachmatt *nt*; **—point** Kontrollpunkt *m*; **—up** (Nach)prüfung *f*; (*Med*) (ärztliche) Untersuchung *f.*

cheek [tʃiːk] *n* Backe *f*, Wange *f*; (*fig*) Frechheit *f*, Unverschämtheit *f*; **—bone** Backenknochen *m*; **—y** *a* frech, übermütig.

cheep [tʃiːp] *n* Pieps(er) *nt.*

cheer [tʃɪə*] *n* Beifallsruf *m*, Hochruf *m*; **—s!** Prost!; *vt* zujubeln; (*encourage*) ermuntern, aufmuntern; *vi* jauchzen, Hochrufe ausbringen; **—ful** *a* fröhlich; **—fulness** Fröhlichkeit *f*, Munterkeit *f*; **—ing** Applaus *m*; *a* aufheiternd; **—io** *interj* tschüs!; **—less** *a* prospect trostlos; *person* verdrießlich; — **up** *vt* ermuntern; *vi*: — up! Kopf hoch!

cheese [tʃiːz] *n* Käse *m*; **—board** (gemischte) Käseplatte *f*; **—cake** Käsekuchen *m.*

cheetah ['tʃiːtə] *n* Gepard *m.*

chef [ʃef] *n* Küchenchef *m.*

chemical ['kemɪkəl] *a* chemisch.

chemist ['kemɪst] *n* (*Med*) Apotheker *m*, Drogist *m*; (*Chem*) Chemiker *m*; **—ry** Chemie *f*; **—'s** (shop) (*Med*) Apotheke *f*, Drogerie *f.*

cheque [tʃek] *n* Scheck *m*; **—book** Scheckbuch *nt*; — **card** Scheckkarte *f.*

chequered ['tʃekəd] *a* (*fig*) bewegt.

cherish ['tʃerɪʃ] *vt* person lieben; hope hegen; *memory* bewahren.

cheroot [ʃə'ruːt] *n* Zigarillo *nt* or *m.*

cherry ['tʃerɪ] *n* Kirsche *f.*

chervil ['tʃɜːvɪl] *n* Kerbel *f.*

chess [tʃes] *n* Schach *nt*; **—board** Schachbrett *nt*; **—man** Schachfigur *f*; **—player** Schachspieler(in *f*) *m.*

chest [tʃest] *n* Brust *f*, Brustkasten *m*; (*box*) Kiste *f*, Kasten *m*; **to get sth off one's** — seinem Herzen Luft machen; — **of drawers** Kommode *f.*

chestnut ['tʃesnʌt] *n* Kastanie *f*; — (tree) Kastanienbaum *m.*

chew [tʃuː] *vti* kauen; **—ing gum** Kaugummi *m.*

chic [ʃiːk] *a* schick, elegant.

chicanery [ʃɪ'keɪnərɪ] *n* Schikane *f.*

chick [tʃɪk] *n* Küken *nt*; **—en** Huhn *nt*; (*food: roast*) Hähnchen *nt*; **—enpox** Windpocken *pl*; **—pea** Kichererbse *f.*

chicory ['tʃɪkərɪ] *n* Zichorie *f*; (plant) Chicorée *f.*

chief [tʃiːf] *n* (Ober)haupt *nt*; Anführer *m*; (*Comm*) Chef *m*; *a* höchst, Haupt- ; **—ly** ad hauptsächlich.

chieftain ['tʃiːftən] n Häuptling m.

chilblain ['tʃɪlblem] n Frostbeule f.

child [tʃaɪld] n Kind nt; **—birth** Entbindung f; **—hood** Kindheit f; **—ish** a kindisch; **—like** a kindlich; **—ren** ['tʃɪldrn] npl of child m; **—'s play** (fig) Kinderspiel nt.

chill [tʃɪl] n Kühle f; (Med) Erkältung f; **—y** a kühl, frostig.

chime [tʃaɪm] n Glockenschlag m, Glockenklang m; vi ertönen, (er)klingen.

chimney ['tʃɪmnɪ] n Schornstein m, Kamin m.

chimpanzee [tʃɪmpæn'ziː] n Schimpanse m.

chin [tʃɪn] n Kinn nt.

china ['tʃaɪnə] n Porzellan nt.

chink [tʃɪŋk] n (opening) Ritze f, Spalt m; (noise) Klirren nt.

chintz [tʃɪnts] n Kattun m.

chip [tʃɪp] n (of wood etc) Splitter m; (potato) **—s** pl Pommes frites pl; (US: crisp) Chip m; vt absplittern; **—** in vi Zwischenbemerkungen machen.

chiropodist [kɪ'rɒpədɪst] n Fußpfleger(in f) m.

chirp [tʃɜːp] n Zwitschern nt; vi zwitschern.

chisel ['tʃɪzl] n Meißel m.

chit [tʃɪt] n Notiz f; **—chat** Plauderei f.

chivalrous ['ʃɪvlrəs] a ritterlich.

chivalry ['ʃɪvlrɪ] n Ritterlichkeit f; (honour) Ritterschaft f.

chive [tʃaɪv] n Schnittlauch m.

chloride ['klɔːraɪd] n Chlorid nt.

chlorine ['klɔːriːn] n Chlor nt.

chock [tʃɒk] n Keil m; **—a-block** a vollgepfropft.

chocolate ['tʃɒklɪt] n Schokolade f.

choice [tʃɔɪs] n Wahl f; (of goods) Auswahl f; a auserlesen, Qualitäts-.

choir ['kwaɪə*] n Chor m; **—boy** Chorknabe m.

choke [tʃəʊk] vi ersticken; vt erdrosseln; (block) (ab)drosseln; n (Aut) Starterklappe f.

cholera ['kɒlərə] n Cholera f.

choose [tʃuːz] vt irreg wählen; (decide) beschließen.

chop [tʃɒp] vt (zer)hacken; wood spalten; vt to **—** and change schwanken; n Hieb m; (meat) Kotelett nt; **—py** a bewegt; **—sticks** pl (Eß)stäbchen pl.

choral ['kɔːrəl] a Chor-.

chord [kɔːd] n Akkord m; (string) Saite f.

chore [tʃɔː*] n Pflicht f; harte Arbeit f.

choreographer [kɒrɪ'ɒgrəfə*] n Choreograph(in f) m.

chorister ['kɒrɪstə*] n Chorsänger(in f) m.

chortle ['tʃɔːtl] vi glucksen, tief lachen.

chorus ['kɔːrəs] n Chor m; (in song) Refrain m.

chow [tʃaʊ] n (dog) Chow-Chow m.

Christ [kraɪst] n Christus m.

christen ['krɪsn] vt taufen; **—ing** Taufe f.

Christian ['krɪstɪən] a christlich; **a** Christ(in f) m; **— name** Vorname m; **—ity** [krɪstɪ'ænɪtɪ] Christentum nt.

Christmas ['krɪsməs] n Weihnachten pl; **— card** Weihnachtskarte f; **— tree** Weihnachtsbaum m.

chrome [krəʊm] n = **chromium plating.**

chromium ['krəʊmɪəm] *n* Chrom *nt*; — plating Verchromung *f*.

chronic ['krɒnɪk] *a* (*Med*) chronisch; (*terrible*) scheußlich.

chronicle ['krɒnɪkl] *n* Chronik *f*.

chronological [krɒnə'lɒdʒɪkəl] *a* chronologisch.

chrysalis ['krɪsəlɪs] *n* (Insekten)-puppe *f*.

chrysanthemum [krɪs'ænθɪməm] *n* Chrysantheme *f*.

chubby ['tʃʌbɪ] *a* *child* pausbäckig; *adult* rundlich.

chuck [tʃʌk] *vt* werfen; *n* (*Tech*) Spannvorrichtung *f*.

chuckle ['tʃʌkl] *vi* in sich hinein-lachen.

chum [tʃʌm] *n* (*child*) Spiel-kamerad *m*; (*adult*) Kumpel *m*.

chunk [tʃʌŋk] *n* Klumpen *m*; (*of food*) Brocken *m*.

church [tʃɜːtʃ] *n* Kirche *f*; (*clergy*) Geistlichkeit *f*; —yard Kirchhof *m*.

churlish ['tʃɜːlɪʃ] *a* grob.

churn [tʃɜːn] *n* Butterfaß *nt*; (*for transport*) (große) Milchkanne *f*; — out *vt* (*col*) produzieren.

chute [ʃuːt] *n* Rutsche *f*.

cicada [sɪ'kɑːdə] *n* Zikade *f*.

cider ['saɪdə*] *n* Apfelwein *m*.

cigar [sɪ'gɑː*] *n* Zigarre *f*; —ette [sɪɡə'ret] Zigarette *f*; —ette case Zigarettenetui *nt*; —ette end Zigarettenstummel *m*; —ette holder Zigarettenspitze *f*.

cinch [sɪntʃ] *n* (*col*) klare(r) Fall *m*; (*easy*) Kinderspiel *nt*.

cinder ['sɪndə*] *n* Zinder *m*.

Cinderella [sɪndə'relə] *n* Aschen-brödel *nt*.

cine ['sɪnɪ] *n*: —camera Film-kamera *f*; — film Schmalfilm *m*.

cinema ['sɪnəmə] *n* Kino *nt*.

cine-projector [sɪnɪprə'dʒektə*] *n* Filmvorführapparat *m*.

cinnamon ['sɪnəmən] *n* Zimt *m*.

cipher ['saɪfə*] *n* (*code*) Chiffre *f*; (*numeral*) Ziffer *f*.

circle ['sɜːkl] *n* Kreis *m*; *vi* kreisen; *vt* umkreisen; (*attacking*) umzingeln.

circuit ['sɜːkɪt] *n* Umlauf *m*; (*Elec*) Stromkreis *m*; —ous [sɜː'kjuːɪtəs] *a* weitschweifig.

circular ['sɜːkjʊlə*] *a* (kreis)rund, kreisförmig; *n* Rundschreiben *nt*.

circularize ['sɜːkjʊləraɪz] *vt* (*inform*) benachrichtigen; *letter* herumschicken.

circulate ['sɜːkjʊleɪt] *vi* zirku-lieren; *vt* in Umlauf setzen.

circulation [sɜːkjʊ'leɪʃən] *n* (*of blood*) Kreislauf *m*; (*of newspaper*) Auflage *f*; (*of money*) Umlauf *m*.

circumcise ['sɜːkəmsaɪz] *vt* beschneiden.

circumference [sə'kʌmfərəns] *n* (Kreis)umfang *m*.

circumspect ['sɜːkəmspekt] *a* umsichtig.

circumstances ['sɜːkəmstənsəz] *npl* (*facts connected with sth*) Um-stände *pl*; (*financial condition*) Ver-hältnisse *pl*.

circumvent [sɜːkəm'vent] *vt* umgehen.

circus ['sɜːkəs] *n* Zirkus *m*.

cissy ['sɪsɪ] *n* Weichling *m*.

cistern ['sɪstən] *n* Zisterne *f*; (*of W.C.*) Spülkasten *m*.

citation [saɪ'teɪʃən] *n* Zitat *nt*.

cite [saɪt] *vt* zitieren, anführen.

citizen ['sɪtɪzn] *n* Bürger(in *f*) *m*; (*of nation*) Staatsangehörige(r) *mf*; —ship Staatsangehörigkeit *f*.

citrus ['sɪtrəs] *adj*: — fruit Zitrus-frucht *f*.

city ['sɪtɪ] n Großstadt f; (centre)
Zentrum nt, City f.

civic ['sɪvɪk] a städtisch, Bürger-.

civil ['sɪvɪl] a (of town) Bürger-; (of state) staatsbürgerlich; (not military) zivil; (polite) höflich; — **engineer** Bauingenieur m; — **engineering** Hoch- und Tiefbau m; — **ian** [sɪ'vɪljən] n Zivilperson f; a zivil, Zivil-; — **ization** [sɪvɪlaɪ'zeɪʃən] n Zivilisation f, Kultur f; — **ized** a zivilisiert; Kultur-; — **law** bürgerliche(s) Recht, Zivilrecht nt; — **rights** pl Bürgerrechte pl; — **servant** Staatsbeamte(r) m; — **service** Staatsdienst m; — **war** Bürgerkrieg m.

clad [klæd] a gekleidet; gehüllt in (+acc).

claim [kleɪm] vt beanspruchen; (have opinion) behaupten; n (demand) Forderung f; (right) Anspruch m; Behauptung f; —**ant** Antragsteller(in f) m.

clairvoyant [kleə'vɔɪənt] n Hellseher(in f) m; a hellseherisch.

clam [klæm] n Venusmuschel f.

clamber ['klæmbə*] vi kraxeln.

clammy ['klæmɪ] a feucht(kalt); klamm.

clamorous ['klæmərəs] a lärmend, laut.

clamp ['klæmp] n Schraubzwinge f; vt einspannen.

clan [klæn] n Sippe f, Clan m.

clang [klæŋ] n Klang m; Scheppern nt; vi klingen, scheppern.

clap [klæp] vi klatschen; vt Beifall klatschen (+dat); —**ping** (Beifall)-klatschen nt.

claret ['klærɪt] n rote(r) Bordeaux-(wein) m.

clarification [klærɪfɪ'keɪʃən] n Erklärung f.

clarify ['klærɪfaɪ] vt klären, erklären.

clarinet [klærɪ'net] n Klarinette f.

clarity ['klærɪtɪ] n Klarheit f.

clash [klæʃ] n (fig) Konflikt m, Widerstreit m; (sound) Knall m; vi zusammenprallen; (colours) sich beißen; (argue) sich streiten.

clasp [klɑːsp] n Klammer f, Haken m; (on belt) Schnalle f; vt umklammern.

class [klɑːs] n Klasse f; vt einordnen, einstufen; —**conscious** a klassenbewußt.

classic ['klæsɪk] n Klassiker(in f) m; a (traditional) klassisch; —**al** a klassisch.

classification [klæsɪfɪ'keɪʃən] n Klassifizierung f, Einteilung f.

classify ['klæsɪfaɪ] vt klassifizieren, einteilen.

classroom ['klɑːsrʊm] n Klassenzimmer nt.

classy ['klɑːsɪ] a (col) todschick.

clatter ['klætə*] n Klappern nt, Rasseln nt; (of feet) Getrappel nt; vi klappern, rasseln; (feet) trappeln.

clause [klɔːz] n (Jur) Klausel f; (Gram) Satz(teil) m, Satzglied nt.

claustrophobia [klɒstrə'fəʊbɪə] n Platzangst f, Klaustrophobie f.

claw [klɔː] n Kralle f; vt (zer)-kratzen.

clay [kleɪ] n Lehm m; (for pots) Ton m.

clean [kliːn] a sauber; (fig) schuldlos; shape ebenmäßig; cut glatt; vt saubermachen, reinigen, putzen; —**er** (person) Putzfrau f; (for grease etc) Scheuerpulver nt; —**ers** pl Chemische Reinigung f; —**ing** Reinigen nt, Säubern nt; —**liness** ['klenlɪnɪs] n Sauberkeit f.

Reinlichkeit f; **—ly** ad reinlich; **—se** [klenz] vt reinigen, säubern; **—shaven** a glattrasiert; **—up** Reinigung f; **— out** vt gründlich putzen; **— up** vt aufräumen.

clear ['klɪə*] a water klar; glass durchsichtig; sound deutlich, klar, hell; meaning genau, klar; (certain) klar, sicher; road frei; **to stand — of** sth etw frei halten; vt road etc freimachen; vi (become clear) klarwerden; **—ance** ['klɪərns] (removal) Räumung f; (free space) Lichtung f; (permission) Freigabe f; **—cut** a scharf umrissen; case eindeutig; **—ing** Lichtung f; **—ly** ad klar, deutlich, zweifellos; **—way** (Brit) (Straße f mit) Halteverbot nt; **— up** vi (weather) sich aufklären; vt reinigen, säubern; (solve) aufklären.

clef [klef] n Notenschlüssel m.

clench [klentʃ] vt teeth zusammenbeißen; fist ballen.

clergy ['klɜːdʒɪ] n Geistliche(n) pl; **—man** Geistliche(r) m.

clerical ['klerɪkəl] a (office)Schreib-, Büro-; (Eccl) geistlich, Pfarr(er)-; **— error** Schreibfehler m.

clerk [klɑːk, US klɜːk] n (in office) Büroangestellte(r) mf; (US: salesman) Verkäufer(in f) m.

clever ['klevə*] a, **—ly** ad ['klevə*, -əlɪ] klug, geschickt, gescheit.

cliché ['kliːʃeɪ] n Klischee nt.

click [klɪk] vi klicken; n Klicken nt; (of door) Zuklinken nt.

client ['klaɪənt] n Klient(in f) m; **—ele** [kliːãːn'tel] n Kundschaft f.

cliff [klɪf] n Klippe f.

climate ['klaɪmɪt] n Klima nt.

climatic [klaɪ'mætɪk] a klimatisch.

climax ['klaɪmæks] n Höhepunkt m.

climb [klaɪm] vt besteigen; vi steigen, klettern; n Aufstieg m; **—er** Bergsteiger m, Kletterer m; (fig) Streber m; **—ing** Bergsteigen nt, Klettern nt.

clinch [klɪntʃ] vt (decide) entscheiden; deal festmachen; n (boxing) Clinch m.

cling [klɪŋ] vi irreg anhaften, anhängen.

clinic ['klɪnɪk] n Klinik f; **—al** a klinisch.

clink [klɪŋk] n (of coins) Klimpern nt; (of glasses) Klirren nt; (col: prison) Knast m; vi klimpern; vt klimpern mit; glasses anstoßen.

clip [klɪp] n Spange f; paper — (Büro-, Heft)klammer f; vt papers heften; hair, hedge stutzen; **—pers** pl (instrument) pl (hair) Hecken- schere f; (for hair) Haarschneide- maschine f.

clique [kliːk] n Clique f, Gruppe f.

cloak [kləʊk] n lose(r) Mantel m, Umhang m; **—room** (for coats) Garderobe f; (W.C.) Toilette f.

clobber ['klɒbə*] n (col) Klamotten pl; vt schlagen.

clock [klɒk] n Uhr f; **—wise** ad im Uhrzeigersinn; **—work** Uhrwerk nt; like **—work** wie am Schnürchen.

clog [klɒg] n Holzschuh m; vt verstopfen.

cloister ['klɔɪstə*] n Kreuzgang m.

close [kləʊs] a nahe; march geschlossen; thorough genau, gründ- lich; weather schwül; a knapp; **—ly** ad gedrängt, dicht; **— to** prep in der Nähe (+gen); **I had a — shave** das war knapp; **—up** Nahaufnahme f.

close [kləʊz] vt schließen, abschließen; vi sich schließen; n (end) Ende nt, Schluß m; to ~ with sb jdn angreifen; ~ down vt Geschäft aufgeben; vi eingehen; ~d a road gesperrt; shop etc geschlossen; ~d shop Gewerkschaftszwang m.

closet ['klɒzɪt] n Abstellraum m, Schrank m.

closure ['kləʊʒə*] n Schließung f.

clot [klɒt] n Klumpen m; (of blood) Blutgerinnsel nt; (fool) Blödmann m; vi gerinnen.

cloth [klɒθ] n (material) Stoff m, Tuch nt; (for washing etc) Lappen m, Tuch nt.

clothe [kləʊð] vt kleiden, bekleiden; ~s pl Kleider pl, Kleidung f; see bedclothes; ~s brush Kleiderbürste f; ~s line Wäscheleine f; ~s peg Wäscheklammer f.

clothing ['kləʊðɪŋ] n = clothes.

cloud [klaʊd] n Wolke f; ~burst Wolkenbruch m; ~y a wolkig, bewölkt.

clout [klaʊt] (col) n Schlag m; vt hauen.

clove [kləʊv] n Gewürznelke f; ~ of garlic Knoblauchzehe f.

clover ['kləʊvə*] n Klee m; ~leaf Kleeblatt nt.

clown [klaʊn] n Clown m, Hanswurst m; vi kaspern, sich albern benehmen.

cloy [klɔɪ] vi: it ~s es übersättigt einen.

club [klʌb] n Knüppel m; (society) Klub m; (golf) Golfschläger m; (Cards) Kreuz nt; vt prügeln; ~ together vi (with money etc) zusammenlegen; ~house Klubhaus nt.

cluck [klʌk] vi glucken.

clue [klu:] n Anhaltspunkt m,

Fingerzeig m, Spur f; he hasn't a ~ er hat keine Ahnung.

clump [klʌmp] n Gebüsch nt.

clumsy ['klʌmzɪ] a person ungelenk, unbeholfen; object, shape unförmig.

cluster ['klʌstə*] n Traube f; (of trees etc) Gruppe f; ~ round vi sich scharen um; umschwärmen.

clutch [klʌtʃ] n feste(r) Griff m; (Aut) Kupplung f; vt sich festklammern an (+dat); book an sich klammern.

clutter ['klʌtə*] vt vollpropfen; desk etc übersäen; n Unordnung f.

coach [kəʊtʃ] n Omnibus m, (Überland)bus m; (old) Kutsche f; (Rail) (Personen)wagen m; (trainer) Trainer m; vt (Sch) Nachhilfeunterricht geben (+dat); (Sport) trainieren.

coagulate [kəʊˈægjʊleɪt] vi gerinnen.

coal [kəʊl] n Kohle f.

coalesce [kəʊəˈles] vi: sich verbinden.

coal face ['kəʊlfeɪs] n (Abbau)sohle f, Streb m; at the ~ vor Ort.

coalfield ['kəʊlfiːld] n Kohlengebiet nt.

coalition [kəʊəˈlɪʃən] n Zusammenschluß m, (Pol) Koalition f.

coalmine ['kəʊlmaɪn] n Kohlenbergwerk nt; ~r Bergarbeiter m.

coarse [kɔːs] a (lit) grob; (fig) ordinär.

coast [kəʊst] n Küste f; ~al a Küsten-; ~er Küstenfahrer m; ~guard Küstenwache f; ~line Küste(nlinie) f.

coat [kəʊt] n Mantel m; (on animals) Fell m, Pelz m; (of paint) Schicht f; vt überstreichen; (cover) bedecken; ~ of arms

Wappen *nt*; —hanger Kleiderbügel *m*; —ing Schicht *f*, Überzug *m*; (of paint) Schicht *f*.

coax [kəʊks] *vt* beschwatzen.

cobble(stone)s [ˈkɒbl(stəʊn)z] *npl* Pflastersteine *pl*.

cobra [ˈkəʊbrə] *n* Kobra *f*.

cobweb [ˈkɒbweb] *n* Spinnennetz *nt*.

cocaine [kəˈkeɪn] *n* Kokain *nt*.

cock [kɒk] *n* Hahn *m*; *vt ears* spitzen; *gun* den Hahn spannen; **—erel** junge(r) Hahn *m*; **—eyed** *a* (*fig*) verrückt.

cockle [ˈkɒkl] *n* Herzmuschel *f*.

cockney [ˈkɒknɪ] *n* echte(r) Londoner *m*.

cockpit [ˈkɒkpɪt] *n* (*Aviat*) Pilotenkanzel *f*.

cockroach [ˈkɒkrəʊtʃ] *n* Küchenschabe *f*.

cocktail [ˈkɒkteɪl] *n* Cocktail *m*; **—cabinet** Hausbar *f*; **— party** Cocktailparty *f*; **— shaker** Mixbecher *m*.

cocoa [ˈkəʊkəʊ] *n* Kakao *m*.

coconut [ˈkəʊkənʌt] *n* Kokosnuß *f*.

cocoon [kəˈkuːn] *n* Puppe *f*, Kokon *m*.

cod [kɒd] *n* Kabeljau *m*.

code [kəʊd] *n* Kode *m*; (*Jur*) Kodex *m*; **in —** verschlüsselt, in Kode.

codeine [ˈkəʊdiːn] *n* Kodein *nt*.

codify [ˈkəʊdɪfaɪ] *vt message* verschlüsseln; (*Jur*) kodifizieren.

coeducational [kəʊedjʊˈkeɪʃənl] *a* koedukativ, gemischt.

coerce [kəʊˈɜːs] *vt* nötigen, zwingen.

coercion [kəʊˈɜːʃən] *n* Zwang *m*, Nötigung *f*.

coexistence [ˈkəʊɪgˈzɪstəns] *n* Koexistenz *f*.

coffee [ˈkɒfɪ] *n* Kaffee *m*; **— bar** Kaffeeausschank *m*, Café *nt*.

coffin [ˈkɒfɪn] *n* Sarg *m*.

cog [kɒg] *n* (Rad)zahn *m*.

cogent [ˈkəʊdʒənt] *a* triftig, überzeugend, zwingend.

cognac [ˈkɒnjæk] *n* Kognak *m*.

coherent [kəʊˈhɪərnt] *a* zusammenhängend, einheitlich.

coil [kɔɪl] *n* Rolle *f*; (*Elec*) Spule *f*; *vt* aufrollen, aufwickeln.

coin [kɔɪn] *n* Münze *f*; *vt* prägen; **—age** (*word*) Prägung *f*.

coincide [kəʊɪnˈsaɪd] *vi* (*happen together*) zusammenfallen; (*agree*) übereinstimmen; **—nce** [kəʊˈɪnsɪdəns] Zufall *m*; **by a strange —nce** merkwürdigerweise; **—ntal** [kəʊɪnsɪˈdentl] *a* zufällig.

coke [kəʊk] *n* Koks *m*.

colander [ˈkʌləndə*] *n* Durchschlag *m*.

cold [kəʊld] *a* kalt; **I'm —** mir ist kalt, ich friere; *in* Kälte *f*; (*illness*) Erkältung *f*; **to have — feet** (*fig*) kalte Füße haben, Angst haben; **to give sb the — shoulder** jdm die kalte Schulter zeigen; **—ly** *ad* kalt; (*fig*) gefühllos; **— sore** Erkältungsbläschen *nt*.

coleslaw [ˈkəʊlslɔː] *n* Krautsalat *m*.

colic [ˈkɒlɪk] *n* Kolik *f*.

collaborate [kəˈlæbəreɪt] *vi* zusammenarbeiten.

collaboration [kəlæbəˈreɪʃən] *n* Zusammenarbeit *f*; (*Pol*) Kollaboration *f*.

collaborator [kəˈlæbəreɪtə*] *n* Mitarbeiter *m*; (*Pol*) Kollaborateur *m*.

collage [kɒˈlɑːʒ] *n* Collage *f*.

collapse [kəˈlæps] *vi* (*people*) zusammenbrechen; (*things*) einstürzen; *n* Zusammenbruch *m*, Einsturz *m*.

collapsible [kə'læpsəbl] a zusammenklappbar, Klapp-.

collar ['kɒlə*] n Kragen m; **—bone** Schlüsselbein nt.

collate [kɒ'leɪt] vt zusammenstellen und vergleichen.

colleague ['kɒliːg] n Kollege m, Kollegin f.

collect [kə'lekt] vt sammeln; (fetch) abholen; vi sich sammeln; **— call** (US) R-Gespräch nt; **—ed** a gefaßt; **—ion** [kə'lekʃən] Sammlung f; (Eccl) Kollekte f; **—ive** a gemeinsam; (Pol) kollektiv; **—or** Sammler m; (tax —or) (Steuer)einnehmer m.

college ['kɒlɪdʒ] n (Univ) College nt; (Tech) Fach-, Berufsschule f.

collide [kə'laɪd] vi zusammenstoßen; kollidieren, im Widerspruch stehen (with zu).

collie ['kɒlɪ] n schottische(r) Schäferhund m, Collie m.

colliery ['kɒlɪərɪ] n (Kohlen)bergwerk nt, Zeche f.

collision [kə'lɪʒən] n Zusammenstoß m; (of opinions) Konflikt m.

colloquial [kə'ləʊkwɪəl] a umgangssprachlich.

collusion [kə'luːʒən] n geheime(s) Einverständnis nt, Zusammenspiel nt.

colon ['kəʊlən] n Doppelpunkt m.

colonel ['kɜːnl] n Oberst m.

colonial [kə'ləʊnɪəl] a Kolonial-.

colonize ['kɒlənaɪz] vt kolonisieren.

colonnade [kɒlə'neɪd] n Säulengang m.

colony ['kɒlənɪ] n Kolonie f.

color ['kʌlə*] (US) = colour.

Colorado beetle [kɒlə'rɑːdəʊ 'biːtl] n Kartoffelkäfer m.

colossal [kə'lɒsl] a kolossal, riesig.

colour ['kʌlə*] n Farbe f; off — nicht wohl; vt (lit, fig) färben; vi sich verfärben; **—s** pl Fahne f; **—bar** Rassenschranke f; **—blind** a farbenblind; **—ed** a farbig; **—ed (wo)man** Farbige(r) mf; **— film** Farbfilm m; **—ful** a bunt; **— scheme** Farbgebung f; **— television** Farbfernsehen nt.

colt [kəʊlt] n Fohlen nt.

column ['kɒləm] n Säule f; (Mil) Kolonne f; (of print) Spalte f; **—ist** ['kɒləmnɪst] Kolumnist m.

coma ['kəʊmə] n Koma nt.

comb [kəʊm] n Kamm m; vt kämmen; (search) durchkämmen.

combat ['kɒmbæt] n Kampf m; vt bekämpfen.

combination [kɒmbɪ'neɪʃən] n Verbindung f, Kombination f.

combine [kəm'baɪn] vt verbinden; vi sich vereinigen; ['kɒmbaɪn] n (Comm) Konzern m, Verband m; **— harvester** Mähdrescher m.

combustible [kəm'bʌstɪbl] a brennbar, leicht entzündlich.

combustion [kəm'bʌstʃən] n Verbrennung f.

come [kʌm] irreg vi kommen; (reach) ankommen, gelangen; **— about** vi geschehen; **— across** vt (find) stoßen auf (+acc); **— away** vi (person) weggehen; (handle etc) abgehen; **— by** vi vorbeikommen; vt (find) zu etw kommen; **— down** vi (price) fallen; **— forward** vi (volunteer) sich melden; **— from** vt (result) kommen von; where do you **— from?** wo kommen Sie her?; I **— from London** ich komme aus London; **— in for** vt abkriegen; **— into** vi eintreten in (+acc); (inherit) erben; **— of** vi: what came of it? was ist daraus geworden?;

— off vi (handle) abgeben; (happen) stattfinden; (succeed) klappen; — off it! laß den Quatsch!; — on vi (progress) vorankommen; how's the book coming on? was macht das Buch?; — on! komm! (hurry) beeil dich!; (encouraging) los!; — out vi herauskommen; — out with vt herausrücken mit; — round vi (visit) vorbeikommen; (Med) wieder zu sich kommen; — to vi (Med) wieder zu sich kommen; (bill) sich belaufen auf; — up vi hochkommen; (problem) auftauchen; — upon vt stoßen auf (+acc); — up to vi (approach) zukommen auf (+acc); (water) reichen bis; (expectation) entsprechen (+dat); to — up with sich etw einfallen lassen; —back Wiederauftreten nt, Comeback nt.

comedian [kəˈmiːdiən] n Komiker m.

comedown [ˈkʌmdaun] n Abstieg m.

comedy [ˈkɒmədɪ] n Komödie f.

comet [ˈkɒmɪt] n Komet m.

comfort [ˈkʌmfət] n Bequemlichkeit f; (of body) Behaglichkeit f; (of mind) Trost m; vt trösten; —s pl Annehmlichkeiten pl; —able a bequem, gemütlich; — station (US) öffentliche Toilette f.

comic [ˈkɒmɪk] n Comic(heft) nt; (comedian) Komiker m; a (also —al) komisch, humoristisch.

coming [ˈkʌmɪŋ] n Kommen nt, Ankunft f.

comma [ˈkɒmə] n Komma nt.

command [kəˈmɑːnd] n Befehl m; (control) Führung f; (Mil) Kommando nt, (Ober)befehl m; vt befehlen (+dat); (Mil) komman-

dieren, befehligen; (be able to get) verfügen über (+acc); vi befehlen; —eer [kɒmənˈdɪə*] vt (Mil) requirieren; —er Befehlshaber m, Kommandant m; —ing officer Kommandeur m; —ment Gebot nt; —o (Mitglied einer) Kommandotruppe f.

commemorate [kəˈmeməreɪt] vt gedenken (+gen).

commemoration [kəmeməˈreɪʃən] n: in — of zum Gedächtnis or Andenken an (+acc).

commemorative [kəˈmemərətɪv] a Gedächtnis-; Gedenk-.

commence [kəˈmens] vti beginnen; —ment Beginn m.

commend [kəˈmend] vt (recommend) empfehlen; (praise) loben; —able a empfehlenswert, lobenswert; —ation [kɒmenˈdeɪʃən] Empfehlung f; (Sch) Lob nt.

commensurate [kəˈmensjʊrɪt] a vergleichbar, entsprechend (with dat).

comment [ˈkɒment] n (remark) Bemerkung f; (note) Anmerkung f; (opinion) Stellungnahme f; vi etw sagen (on zu); sich äußern (on zu); —ary [ˈkɒməntrɪ] Kommentar m; Erläuterungen pl; —ator [ˈkɒmənteɪtə*] Kommentator m.

commerce [ˈkɒmɜːs] n Handel m.

commercial [kəˈmɜːʃəl] a kommerziell, geschäftlich; training kaufmännisch; n (TV) Fernsehwerbung f; —ize vt kommerzialisieren; — television Werbefernsehen nt; — vehicle Lieferwagen m.

commiserate [kəˈmɪzəreɪt] vi Mitleid haben.

commission [kəˈmɪʃən] n Auftrag m; (fee) Provision f; (Mil) Offizierspatent nt; (of offence) Begehen nt; (reporting body) Kommission f; vt bevollmächtigen, beauftragen; out of — außer Betrieb; —aire [kəmı'fə'nɛə*] Portier m; —er (Regierungs)bevollmächtigte(r) m.

commit [kə'mɪt] vt crime begehen; (undertake) sich verpflichten; (entrust) übergeben, anvertrauen; I don't want to — myself ich will mich nicht festlegen; —ment Verpflichtung f.

committee [kə'mɪtɪ] n Ausschuß m, Komitee nt.

commodious [kə'məudıəs] a geräumig.

commodity [kə'mɒdıtı] n Ware f; (Handels-, Gebrauchs)artikel m.

commodore ['kɒmədɔ:*] n Flotillenadmiral m.

common ['kɒmən] a cause gemeinsam; (public) öffentlich, allgemein; experience allgemein, alltäglich; (pej) gewöhnlich; (widespread) üblich, häufig, gewöhnlich; n Gemeindeland nt; öffentliche Anlage f; —ly ad im allgemeinen, gewöhnlich; C— Market Gemeinsame(r) Markt m; —place a alltäglich; n Gemeinplatz m; —room Gemeinschaftsraum m; —sense gesunde(r) Menschenverstand m; the C—wealth das Commonwealth.

commotion [kə'məuʃən] n Aufsehen nt, Unruhe f.

communal ['kɒmju:nl] a Gemeinde-; Gemeinschafts-.

commune ['kɒmju:n] n Kommune f; vi sich mitteilen (with dat), vertraulich verkehren.

communicate [kə'mju:nıkeıt] vt (transmit) übertragen; vi (be in touch) in Verbindung stehen; (make self understood) sich verständlich machen.

communication [kəmju:nı'keıʃən] n (message) Mitteilung f; (Rad, TV etc) Kommunikationsmittel nt; (making understood) Kommunikation f; —s pl (transport etc) Verkehrswege pl; — cord Notbremse f.

communion [kə'mju:nıən] n. (group) Gemeinschaft f; (Rel) Religionsgemeinschaft f; (Holy) C— Heilige(s) Abendmahl nt, Kommunion f.

communiqué [kə'mju:nıkeı] n Kommuniqué nt, amtliche Verlautbarung f.

communism ['kɒmjunızəm] n Kommunismus m.

communist ['kɒmjunıst] n Kommunist(in f) m; a kommunistisch.

community [kə'mju:nıtı] n Gemeinschaft f; (public) Gemeinwesen nt; — centre Gemeinschaftszentrum nt; — chest (US) Wohltätigkeitsfonds m.

commutation ticket [kɒmju-'teıʃən'tıkıt] n (US) Zeitkarte f.

commute [kə'mju:t] vi pendeln; —r Pendler m.

compact [kəm'pækt] a kompakt, fest, dicht; ['kɒmpækt] n Pakt m, Vertrag m; (for make-up) Puderdose f.

companion [kəm'pænıən] n Begleiter(in f) m; —ship Gesellschaft f.

company ['kʌmpənı] n Gesellschaft f; (Comm also) Firma f; (Mil) Kompanie f; to keep sb — jdm Gesellschaft leisten.

comparable ['kɒmpərəbl] a vergleichbar.

comparative [kəm'pærətıv] a (relative) verhältnismäßig, relativ; (Gram) steigernd; —ly ad verhältnismäßig.

compare [kəm'pɛə*] vt vergleichen; vi sich vergleichen lassen.

comparison [kəm'pærɪsn] n Vergleich m; (object) Vergleichsgegenstand m; in ~ (with) im Vergleich (mit or zu).

compartment [kəm'pɑ:tmənt] n (Rail) Abteil nt; (in drawer etc) Fach m.

compass ['kʌmpəs] n Kompaß m; ~es pl Zirkel m.

compassion [kəm'pæʃən] n Mitleid nt; ~ate a mitfühlend.

compatible [kəm'pætɪbl] a vereinbar, im Einklang; we're not ~ wir vertragen uns nicht.

compel [kəm'pel] vt zwingen; ~ling a argument zwingend.

compendium [kəm'pendɪəm] n Kompendium n.

compensate ['kɒmpenseɪt] vt entschädigen; to ~ for Ersatz leisten für, kompensieren.

compensation [kɒmpen'seɪʃən] n Entschädigung f; (money) Schadenersatz m; (Jur) Abfindung f; (Psych etc) Kompensation f.

compère ['kɒmpɛə*] n Conférencier m.

compete [kəm'pi:t] vi sich bewerben, konkurrieren, sich messen mit.

competence ['kɒmpɪtəns] n Fähigkeit f; (Jur) Zuständigkeit f.

competent ['kɒmpɪtənt] a kompetent, fähig; (Jur) zuständig.

competition [kɒmpɪ'tɪʃən] n Wettbewerb m; (Comm) Konkurrenz f.

competitive [kəm'petɪtɪv] a Konkurrenz-; (Comm) konkurrenzfähig.

competitor [kəm'petɪtə*] n Mitbewerber(in f) m; (Comm) Konkurrent(in f) m; (Sport) Teilnehmer(in f) m.

compile [kəm'paɪl] vt zusammenstellen.

complacency [kəm'pleɪsnsɪ] n Selbstzufriedenheit f, Gleichgültigkeit f.

complacent [kəm'pleɪsnt] a selbstzufrieden, gleichgültig.

complain [kəm'pleɪn] vi sich beklagen, sich beschweren (about über +acc); ~t Beschwerde f; (Med) Leiden nt.

complement ['kɒmplɪmənt] n Ergänzung f; (ship's crew etc) Bemannung f; ~ary [kɒmplɪ'mentərɪ] a komplementär-, (sich) ergänzend.

complete [kəm'pli:t] a vollständig, vollkommen, ganz; vt vervollständigen; (finish) beenden; ~ly ad vollständig, ganz.

completion [kəm'pli:ʃən] n Vervollständigung f; (of building) Fertigstellung f.

complex ['kɒmpleks] a kompliziert, verwickelt; n Komplex m.

complexion [kəm'plekʃən] n Gesichtsfarbe f, Teint m; (fig) Anstrich m, Aussehen nt.

complexity [kəm'pleksɪtɪ] n Verwicklung f, Kompliziertheit f.

compliance [kəm'plaɪəns] n Fügsamkeit f, Einwilligung f.

complicate ['kɒmplɪkeɪt] vt einbeziehen, verwickeln; ~d a kompliziert, verwickelt.

complication [kɒmplɪ'keɪʃən] a Komplikation f, Erschwerung f.

compliment ['kɒmplɪmənt] n Kompliment nt; ['kɒmplɪment] vt ein Kompliment machen (sb jdm); ~s pl Grüße pl, Empfehlung f; ~ary [kɒmplɪ'mentərɪ] a schmeichelhaft; *(free)* Frei-, Gratis-.

comply [kəm'plaɪ] *vi:* — **with** erfüllen *(+acc)*; entsprechen *(+dat)*.

component [kəm'pəʊnənt] a Teil-; *n* Bestandteil *m*.

compose [kəm'pəʊz] *vt (arrange)* zusammensetzen; *music* komponieren; *poetry* schreiben; *thoughts* sammeln; *features* beherrschen; — **d** ruhig, gefaßt; **to be —d of** bestehen aus; **—r** Komponist(in *f*) *m*.

composite ['kɒmpəzɪt] a zusammengesetzt.

composition [kɒmpə'zɪʃən] *n (Mus)* Komposition *f*; *(Sch)* Aufsatz *m*; *(composing)* Zusammensetzung *f*, Gestaltung *f*; *(structure)* Zusammensetzung *f*, Aufbau *m*.

compositor [kəm'pɒzɪtə*] *n* Schriftsetzer *m*.

compos mentis ['kɒmpɒs'mentɪs] a klar im Kopf.

compost ['kɒmpɒst] *n* Kompost *m*; — **heap** Komposthaufen *m*.

composure [kəm'pəʊʒə*] *n* Gelassenheit *f*, Fassung *f*.

compound ['kɒmpaʊnd] *n (Chem)* Verbindung *f*; *(mixture)* Gemisch *nt*; *(enclosure)* eingezäunte(s) Gelände *nt*; *(Ling)* Kompositum *nt*; a zusammengesetzt; — **fracture** komplizierte(r) Bruch *m*; — **interest** Zinseszinsen *pl*.

comprehend [kɒmprɪ'hend] *vt* begreifen; *(include)* umfassen, einschließen.

comprehension [kɒmprɪ'henʃən] *n* Fassungskraft *f*, Verständnis *nt*.

comprehensive [kɒmprɪ'hensɪv] a umfassend; — **school** Gesamtschule *f*.

compress [kəm'pres] *vt* zusammendrücken, komprimieren; ['kɒmpres] *n (Med)* Kompresse *f*, Umschlag *m*; —**ion** [kəm'preʃən] Komprimieren *nt*.

comprise [kəm'praɪz] *vt (also be —d of)* umfassen, bestehen aus.

compromise ['kɒmprəmaɪz] *n* Kompromiß *m*, Verständigung *f*; *vt reputation* kompromittieren; *vi* einen Kompromiß schließen.

compulsion [kəm'pʌlʃən] *n* Zwang *m*.

compulsive [kəm'pʌlsɪv] a Gewohnheits-.

compulsory [kəm'pʌlsərɪ] a *(obligatory)* obligatorisch, Pflicht-.

computer [kəm'pju:tə*] *n* Computer *m*, Rechner *m*.

comrade ['kɒmrɪd] *n* Kamerad *m*; *(Pol)* Genosse *m*; —**ship** Kameradschaft *f*.

concave ['kɒn'keɪv] a konkav, hohlgeschliffen.

conceal [kən'si:l] *vt secret* verschweigen; **to — o.s.** sich verbergen.

concede [kən'si:d] *vt (grant)* gewähren; *point* zugeben; *vi (admit)* zugeben.

conceit [kən'si:t] *n* Eitelkeit *f*, Einbildung *f*; —**ed** a eitel, eingebildet.

conceivable [kən'si:vəbl] a vorstellbar.

conceive [kən'si:v] *vt idea* ausdenken; *imagine* sich vorstellen; *vti baby* empfangen.

concentrate ['kɒnsəntreɪt] *vi* sich konzentrieren *(on* auf *+acc); vt (gather)* konzentrieren.

concentration [kɒnsən'treɪʃən] *n* Konzentration *f*; — **camp** Konzentrationslager *nt*, KZ *nt*.

concentric [kɒn'sentrɪk] a konzen-
trisch.

concept ['kɒnsept] n Begriff m;
—ion [kən'sepʃən] (idea) Vorstellung f; (Physiol) Empfängnis f.

concern [kən'sɜːn] n (affair)
Angelegenheit f; (Comm) Unternehmen nt, Konzern m; (worry)
Sorge f, Unruhe f; vt (interest)
angehen; (be about) handeln von;
(have connection with) betreffen;
—ed a (anxious) besorgt; **—ing**
prep betreffend, hinsichtlich
(+gen).

concert ['kɒnsət] n Konzert nt; in
— (with) im Einverständnis (mit);
—ed [kən'sɜːtɪd] a gemeinsam; **—**
(Fin) konzertiert; — hall Konzert-
halle f.

concertina [kɒnsə'tiːnə] n Hand-
harmonika f.

concerto [kən'tʃɜːtəu] n Konzert nt.

concession [kən'seʃən] n (yielding)
Zugeständnis nt; (right to do sth)
Genehmigung f.

conciliation [kənsɪlɪ'eɪʃən] n Versöhnung f; (official) Schlichtung f.
conciliatory [kən'sɪlɪətrɪ] a ver-
mittelnd; versöhnlich.

concise [kən'saɪs] a knapp,
gedrängt.

conclave ['kɒnkleɪv] n Konklave nt.

conclude [kən'kluːd] vt (end)
beenden; treaty (ab)schließen;
(decide) schließen, folgern; vi
(finish) schließen.

conclusion [kən'kluːʒən] n (Abschluß m; in — zum Schluß,
schließlich.

conclusive [kən'kluːsɪv] a überzeugend, schlüssig; **—ly** ad
endgültig.

concoct [kən'kɒkt] vt zusammen-
brauen.

concord ['kɒnkɔːd] n Eintracht f.

concourse ['kɒnkɔːs] n (Bahnhofs-
halle f, Vorplatz m.

concrete ['kɒnkriːt] n Beton m; a
konkret.

concur [kən'kɜː] vi übereinstimmen.

concurrently [kən'kʌrəntlɪ] ad
gleichzeitig.

concussion [kən'kʌʃən] n (Gehirn)-
erschütterung f.

condemn [kən'dem] vt
verdammen; (Jur) verurteilen;
building abbruchreif erklären;
—ation [kɒndem'neɪʃən] Verurteilung f; (of object) Verwerfung f.

condensation [kɒndən'seɪʃən] n
Kondensation f.

condense [kən'dens] vi (Chem)
kondensieren; vt (fig) zusammendrängen; **—d** milk Kondensmilch f.

condescend [kɒndɪ'send] vi sich
herablassen; **—ing** a herablassend.

condition [kən'dɪʃən] n (state)
Zustand m, Verfassung f; (presupposition) Bedingung f; vt hair
etc behandeln; (regulate) regeln;
on — that ... unter der Bedingung,
daß ...; — ed gewöhnt an
(+acc); **—ed reflex** bedinger
Reflex; **—s** pl (circumstances,
weather) Verhältnisse pl; **—al** a
bedingt; (Gram) Bedingungs-.

condolences [kən'dəulənsɪz] npl
Beileid nt.

condone [kən'dəun] vt gutheißen.

conducive [kən'djuːsɪv] a dienlich
(to dat).

conduct ['kɒndʌkt] n (behaviour)
Verhalten nt; (management)
Führung f; [kən'dʌkt] vt führen,
leiten; (Mus) dirigieren; **— tour**
Führung f; **—or** [kən'dʌktə] (of
orchestra) Dirigent m; (in bus)

Schaffner *m*; —ress [kən'dʌktrɪs] *f* (*in bus*) Schaffnerin *f*.

conduit ['kɒndɪt] *n* (*water*) Rohrleitung *f*; (*Elec*) Isolierrohr *nt*.

cone [kəʊn] *n* (*Math*) Kegel *m*; (*for ice cream*) (Waffel)tüte *f*; (*fir*) Tannenzapfen *m*.

confectioner [kən'fekʃənə*] *n* Konditor *m*; —'s (*shop*) Konditorei *f*; —y (*cakes*) Konfekt *nt*, Konditorwaren *pl*; (*sweets*) Süßigkeiten *pl*.

confederation [kənfedə'reɪʃən] *n* Bund *m*.

confer [kən'fɜ:*] *vt degree* verleihen; *vi* (*discuss*) konferieren, verhandeln; —ence ['kɒnfərəns] Konferenz *f*.

confess [kən'fes] *vti* gestehen; (*Eccl*) beichten; —ion [kən'feʃən] Geständnis *nt*; (*Eccl*) Beichte *f*; —ional [kən'feʃənl] Beichtstuhl *m*; —or (*Eccl*) Beichtvater *m*.

confetti [kən'fetɪ] *n* Konfetti *nt*.

confide [kən'faɪd] *vi:* — in (sich) anvertrauen (+*dat*); (*trust*) vertrauen (+*dat*); —nce ['kɒnfɪdəns] Vertrauen *nt*; (*assurance*) Selbstvertrauen *nt*; (*secret*) vertrauliche Mitteilung *f*, Geheimnis *nt*; —nce trick ['kɒnfɪdənstrɪk] Schwindel *m*.

confident ['kɒnfɪdənt] *a* (*sure*) überzeugt; sicher; (*self-assured*) selbstsicher; —ial [kɒnfɪ'denʃəl] *a* (*secret*) vertraulich, geheim; (*trusted*) Vertrauens-.

confine [kən'faɪn] *vt* (*limit*) begrenzen, einschränken; (*lock up*) einsperren; —s ['kɒnfaɪnz] *pl* Grenze *f*; —d (*a space eng*, begrenzt; —ment (*of room*) Beengtheit *f*; (*in prison*) Haft *f*; (*Med*) Wochenbett *nt*.

confirm [kən'fɜ:m] *vt* bestätigen; —ation [kɒnfə'meɪʃən] Bestätigung *f*; (*Rel*) Konfirmation *f*; —ed *a*

unverbesserlich, hartnäckig; *bachelor* eingefleischt.

confiscate ['kɒnfɪskeɪt] *vt* beschlagnahmen, konfiszieren.

confiscation [kɒnfɪs'keɪʃən] *n* Beschlagnahme *f*.

conflagration [kɒnflə'greɪʃən] *n* Feuersbrunst *f*.

conflict ['kɒnflɪkt] *n* Kampf *m*; (*of words, opinions*) Konflikt *m*, Streit *m*; [kən'flɪkt] *vi* im Widerspruch stehen; —ing [kən'flɪktɪŋ] *a* gegensätzlich; *testimony* sich widersprechend.

conform [kən'fɔ:m] *vi* sich anpassen (*to dat*); (*to rules*) sich fügen (*to dat*); (*to general trends*) sich richten (*to nach*); —ist Konformist(in *f*) *m*.

confront [kən'frʌnt] *vt enemy* entgegentreten (+*dat*); *sb with sth* konfrontieren; *sb with sth* gegenüberstellen (*with dat*); —ation [kɒnfrən'teɪʃən] Gegenüberstellung *f*; (*quarrel*) Konfrontation *f*.

confuse [kən'fju:z] *vt* verwirren; (*sth with sth*) verwechseln.

confusing [kən'fju:zɪŋ] *a* verwirrend.

confusion [kən'fju:ʒən] *n* (*disorder*) Verwirrung *f*; (*tumult*) Aufruhr *m*; (*embarrassment*) Bestürzung *f*.

congeal [kən'dʒi:l] *vi* (*freeze*) gefrieren; (*clot*) gerinnen.

congenial [kən'dʒi:nɪəl] *a* (*agreeable*) angenehm.

congenital [kən'dʒenɪtəl] *a* angeboren.

conger eel ['kɒŋgər'i:l] *n* Meeraal *m*.

congested [kən'dʒestɪd] *a* überfüllt.

congestion [kən'dʒestʃən] *n* Stauung *f*; Stau *m*.

conglomeration [kənglɒmə-'reɪʃən] n Anhäufung f.

congratulate [kən'grætjuleɪt] vt beglückwünschen (on zu).

congratulations [kən'grætju-'leɪʃənz] npl Glückwünsche pl; —! gratuliere!, herzlichen Glückwunsch!

congregate ['kɒŋgrɪgeɪt] vi sich versammeln.

congregation [kɒŋgrɪ'geɪʃən] n Gemeinde f.

congress ['kɒŋgres] n Kongreß m; —ional [kən'greʃənl] a Kongreß-; —man (US) Mitglied nt des amerikanischen Repräsentantenhauses.

conical ['kɒnɪkəl] a kegelförmig, konisch.

conifer ['kɒnɪfə*] n Nadelbaum m; —ous [kə'nɪfərəs] a zapfentragend.

conjecture [kən'dʒektʃə*] n Vermutung f; vti vermuten.

conjugal ['kɒndʒugəl] a ehelich.

conjunction [kən'dʒʌŋkʃən] n Verbindung f; (Gram) Konjunktion f, Verbindungswort nt.

conjunctivitis [kəndʒʌŋktɪ'vaɪtɪs] n Bindehautentzündung f.

conjure ['kʌndʒə*] vti zaubern; — up vt heraufbeschwören; — r Zauberer m; (entertainer) Zauberkünstler(in f) m.

conjuring ['kʌndʒərɪŋ] n: — trick Zauberkunststück nt.

conk [kɒŋk]: — out vi (col) stehenbleiben, streiken.

connect [kə'nekt] vt verbinden; train koppeln; —ion [kə'nekʃən] Verbindung f; (relation) Zusammenhang m; in —ion with in Verbindung mit.

connexion [kə'nekʃən] n = connection.

connoisseur [kɒnɪ'sə:*] n Kenner m.

connotation [kɒnə'teɪʃən] n Konnotation f.

conquer ['kɒŋkə*] vt (overcome) überwinden, besiegen; (Mil) besiegen; vi siegen; —or Eroberer m.

conquest ['kɒŋkwest] n Eroberung f.

conscience ['kɒnʃəns] n Gewissen nt.

conscientious [kɒnʃɪ'enʃəs] a gewissenhaft; — objector Wehrdienstverweigerer m (aus Gewissensgründen).

conscious ['kɒnʃəs] a bewußt; (Med) bei Bewußtsein; —ness Bewußtsein nt.

conscript ['kɒnskrɪpt] n Wehrpflichtige(r) m; —ion [kən'skrɪpʃən] Wehrpflicht f.

consecrate ['kɒnsɪkreɪt] vt weihen.

consecutive [kən'sekjutɪv] a aufeinanderfolgend.

consensus [kən'sensəs] n allgemeine Übereinstimmung f.

consent [kən'sent] n Zustimmung f; vi zustimmen (to dat).

consequence ['kɒnsɪkwəns] n (importance) Bedeutung f, Konsequenz f; (result, effect) Wirkung f.

consequently ['kɒnsɪkwəntlɪ] ad folglich.

conservation [kɒnsə'veɪʃən] n Erhaltung f, Schutz m.

conservative [kən'sɜ:vətɪv] a konservativ; (cautious) mäßig, vorsichtig; C— a party konservativ; n Konservative(r) mf.

conservatory [kən'sɜ:vətrɪ] n (greenhouse) Gewächshaus nt; (room) Wintergarten m.

conserve [kən'sɜ:v] vt erhalten.

consider [kən'sɪdə*] vt überlegen; (take into account) in Betracht ziehen; (regard) halten für; —able a beträchtlich; —ate a rücksichtsvoll, aufmerksam; —ation [kənsɪdə'reɪʃən] Rücksicht(nahme) f; (thought) Erwägung f; (reward) Entgelt nt; — ing prep in Anbetracht (+gen); cj da; on no —ation unter keinen Umständen.

consign [kən'saɪn] vt übergeben; —ment (of goods) Sendung f, Lieferung f.

consist [kən'sɪst] vi bestehen (of aus).

consistency [kən'sɪstənsɪ] n (of material) Festigkeit f; (of argument) Folgerichtigkeit f; (of person) Konsequenz f.

consistent [kən'sɪstənt] a gleichbleibend, stetig; argument folgerichtig; she's not — sie ist nicht konsequent.

consolation [kənsə'leɪʃən] n Trost m; — prize Trostpreis m.

console [kən'səʊl] vt trösten.

consolidate [kən'sɒlɪdeɪt] vt festigen.

consommé [kən'sɒmeɪ] n Fleischbrühe f.

consonant ['kɒnsənənt] n Konsonant m, Mitlaut m.

consortium [kən'sɔ:tɪəm] n Gruppe f, Konsortium nt.

conspicuous [kən'spɪkjʊəs] a (prominent) auffallend; (visible) deutlich, sichtbar.

conspiracy [kən'spɪrəsɪ] n Verschwörung f, Komplott nt.

conspire [kən'spaɪə*] vi sich verschwören.

constable ['kʌnstəbl] n Polizist(in f) m.

constabulary [kən'stæbjʊlərɪ] n Polizei f.

constancy ['kɒnstənsɪ] n Beständigkeit f, Treue f.

constant ['kɒnstənt] a dauernd; —ly ad (continually) andauernd; (faithfully) treu, unwandelbar.

constellation [kɒnstə'leɪʃən] n (temporary) Konstellation f; (permanent) Sternbild nt.

consternation [kɒnstə'neɪʃən] n (dismay) Bestürzung f.

constipated ['kɒnstɪpeɪtɪd] a verstopft.

constipation [kɒnstɪ'peɪʃən] n Verstopfung f.

constituency [kən'stɪtjʊənsɪ] n Wahlkreis m.

constituent [kən'stɪtjʊənt] n (person) Wähler m; (part) Bestandteil m.

constitute ['kɒnstɪtju:t] vt ausmachen.

constitution [kɒnstɪ'tju:ʃən] n Verfassung f; —al a Verfassungs-; monarchy konstitutionell.

constrain [kən'streɪn] vt zwingen; —t Zwang m; (Psych) Befangenheit f.

constrict [kən'strɪkt] vt zusammenziehen; —ion [kən'strɪkʃən] Zusammenziehung f; (of chest) Zusammenschnürung f, Beklemmung f.

construct [kən'strʌkt] vt bauen; —ion [kən'strʌkʃən] (action) (Er)bauen nt, Konstruktion f; (building) Bau m; under —ion im Bau befindlich; —ive a konstruktiv.

construe [kən'stru:] vt (interpret) deuten.

consul ['kɒnsl] n Konsul m; —ate ['kɒnsjʊlət] Konsulat nt.

consult [kən'sʌlt] vt um Rat fragen; doctor konsultieren; book nachschlagen in (+ dat); **—ant** (Med) Facharzt m; (other specialist) Gutachter m; **—ation** [kɒnsəl'teɪʃən] Beratung f; (Med) Konsultation f; **—ing room** Sprechzimmer nt.

consume [kən'sjuːm] vt verbrauchen; food verzehren, konsumieren; **—r** Verbraucher m.

consummate ['kɒnsʌmeɪt] vt vollenden; marriage vollziehen.

consumption [kən'sʌmpʃən] n Verbrauch m; (of food) Konsum m.

contact ['kɒntækt] n (touch) Berührung f; (connection) Verbindung f; (person) Kontakt m, Beziehung f; vt sich in Verbindung setzen mit; **— lenses** pl Kontaktlinsen pl.

contagious [kən'teɪdʒəs] a ansteckend.

contain [kən'teɪn] vt enthalten; to **— o.s.** sich zügeln; **—er** Behälter m; (transport) Container m.

contaminate [kən'tæmɪneɪt] vt verunreinigen; (germs) infizieren; **contamination** [kəntæmɪ'neɪʃən] n Verunreinigung f.

contemplate ['kɒntəmpleɪt] vt (nachdenklich) betrachten; (think about) überdenken; (plan) vorhaben.

contemplation [kɒntem'pleɪʃən] n Betrachtung f; (Rel) Meditation f.

contemporary [kən'tempərərɪ] a zeitgenössisch; n Zeitgenosse m.

contempt [kən'tempt] n Verachtung f; **—ible** a verächtlich, nichtswürdig; **—uous** a voller Verachtung (of für).

contend [kən'tend] vt (fight) kämpfen (um); (argue) behaupten;

—er (for post) Bewerber(in f) m; (Sport) Wettkämpfer(in f) m.

content [kən'tent] a zufrieden; vt befriedigen; ['kɒntent] n (also **—s**) Inhalt m; **—ed** a zufrieden.

contention [kən'tenʃən] n (dispute) Streit m; (argument) Behauptung f.

contentment [kən'tentmənt] n Zufriedenheit f.

contest ['kɒntest] n (Wett)kampf m; [kən'test] vt (dispute) bestreiten; (Pol) kandidieren (in dat); **—ant** [kən'testənt] Bewerber(in f) m.

context ['kɒntekst] n Zusammenhang m.

continent ['kɒntɪnənt] n Kontinent m, Festland nt; the C— das europäische Festland, der Kontinent; **—al** [kɒntɪ'nentl] a kontinental; n Bewohner(in f) m des Kontinents.

contingency [kən'tɪndʒənsɪ] n Möglichkeit f.

contingent [kən'tɪndʒənt] n (Mil) Kontingent nt; a abhängig (upon von).

continual [kən'tɪnjʊəl] a (endless) fortwährend; (repeated) immer wiederkehrend; **—ly** ad immer wieder.

continuation [kəntɪnjʊ'eɪʃən] n Verlängerung f; Fortsetzung f.

continue [kən'tɪnjuː] vi (go on) anhalten; (last) fortbestehen; shall we —? wollen wir weitermachen?; if this —s wenn das so weitergeht; the rain —d es regnete weiter; vt fortsetzen; to — doing sth fortfahren, etw zu tun.

continuity [kɒntɪ'njuːɪtɪ] n Kontinuität nt; (wholeness) Zusammenhang m.

continuous [kən'tɪnjʊəs] a ununterbrochen.

contort [kən'tɔ:t] vt verdrehen;
—ion [kən'tɔ:ʃən] Verzerrung f;
—ionist [kən'tɔ:ʃənɪst] Schlangen-
mensch m.

contour ['kɒntʊə*] n Umriß m;
(height) Höhenlinie f.

contraband ['kɒntrəbænd] n
Schmuggelware f.

contraception [kɒntrə'sepʃən] n
Empfängnisverhütung f.

contraceptive [kɒntrə'septɪv] n
empfängnisverhütende(s) Mittel
nt; a empfängnisverhütend.

contract ['kɒntrækt] n (agreement) Vertrag m, Kontrakt m;
[kən'trækt] vi (to do sth) sich ver-
traglich verpflichten; (muscle) sich
zusammenziehen; (become
smaller) schrumpfen; **—ion**
[kən'trækʃən] (shortening) Verkürzung f; **—or** [kən'træktə*]
Unternehmer m; (supplier)
Lieferant m.

contradict [kɒntrə'dɪkt] vt widersprechen (+ dat); **—ion**
[kɒntrə'dɪkʃən] Widerspruch m.

contralto [kən'træltəʊ] n (tiefe)
Altstimme f.

contraption [kən'træpʃən] n (col)
komische Konstruktion f,
komische(s) Ding nt.

contrary ['kɒntrərɪ] a entgegengesetzt; wind ungünstig,
Gegen-; (obstinate) widerspenstig,
eigensinnig; n Gegenteil nt; on the
— im Gegenteil.

contrast ['kɒntrɑːst] n Kontrast
m; [kən'trɑːst] vt entgegensetzen;
—ing [kən'trɑːstɪŋ] a Kontrast-.

contravene [kɒntrə'viːn] vt verstoßen gegen.

contribute [kən'trɪbjuːt] vti
beitragen; money spenden.

contribution [kɒntrɪ'bjuːʃən] n
Beitrag m.

contributor [kən'trɪbjʊtə*] n
Beitragende(r) mf.

contrite ['kɒntraɪt] a zerknirscht.

contrivance [kən'traɪvəns] n
Vorrichtung f, Kniff m, Erfindung
f.

contrive [kən'traɪv] vt zustande
bringen; — to do sth es
schaffen, etw zu tun.

control [kən'trəʊl] vt (direct, test)
kontrollieren; n Kontrolle f; (business) Leitung f; —s pl (of vehicle)
Steuerung f; (of engine) Schalttafel
f; — point Kontrollstelle f; out of
— außer Kontrolle; under — unter
Kontrolle.

controversial [kɒntrə'vɜːʃəl] a
umstritten, kontrovers.

controversy ['kɒntrəvɜːsɪ] n
Meinungsstreit m, Kontroverse f.

convalesce [kɒnvə'les] vi gesund
werden; —nce Genesung f; —nt a
auf dem Wege der Besserung; n
Genesende(r) mf.

convector [kən'vektə*] n
Heizlüfter m.

convene [kən'viːn] vt zusam-
menrufen; vi sich versammeln.

convenience [kən'viːnɪəns] n
Annehmlichkeit f; (thing) bequeme
Einrichtung f; see public.

convenient [kən'viːnɪənt] a günstig.

convent ['kɒnvənt] n Kloster nt.

convention [kən'venʃən] n
Versammlung f; (Pol)
Übereinkunft f; (custom) Konvention f; **—al** a herkömmlich, kon-
ventionell.

converge [kən'vɜːdʒ] vi zusammenlaufen.

conversant [kən'vɜːsənt] a

vertraut; (in learning) bewandert (with in + dat).

conversation [kɒnvəˈseɪʃən] n Unterhaltung f; **—al** a Unterhaltungs-.

converse [kənˈvɜːs] vi sich unterhalten; [ˈkɒnvɜːs] a gegenteilig; **—ly** [kɒnˈvɜːslɪ] ad umgekehrt.

conversion [kənˈvɜːʃən] n Umwandlung f; (esp Rel) Bekehrung f; **—** table Umrechnungstabelle f.

convert [kənˈvɜːt] vt (change) umwandeln; (Rel) bekehren; [ˈkɒnvɜːt] n Bekehrte(r) mf; Konvertit(in f) m; **—ible** (Aut) Kabriolett nt; a umwandelbar; (Fin) konvertierbar.

convex [ˈkɒnveks] a konvex.

convey [kənˈveɪ] vt (carry) befördern; feelings vermitteln; **—or belt** Fließband nt.

convict [kənˈvɪkt] vt verurteilen; [ˈkɒnvɪkt] n Häftling m; **—ion** [kənˈvɪkʃən] (verdict) Verurteilung f; (belief) Überzeugung f.

convince [kənˈvɪns] vt überzeugen.

convincing [kənˈvɪnsɪŋ] a überzeugend.

convivial [kənˈvɪvɪəl] a festlich, froh.

convoy [ˈkɒnvɔɪ] n (of vehicles) Kolonne f; (protected) Konvoi m.

convulse [kənˈvʌls] vt zusammenzucken lassen; to be **—d** with laughter sich vor Lachen krümmen.

convulsion [kənˈvʌlʃən] n (esp Med) Zuckung f, Krampf m.

coo [kuː] vi (dove) gurren.

cook [kʊk] vti kochen; n Koch m, Köchin f; **—book** Kochbuch nt; **—er** Herd m; **—ery** Kochkunst f; **—ery book —book**; **—ie** (US) Plätzchen nt; **—ing** Kochen nt.

cool [kuːl] a kühl; vti (ab)kühlen; **— down** vti (fig) (sich) beruhigen; **—ing-tower** Kühlturm m; **—ness** Kühle f; (of temperament) kühle(r) Kopf.

coop [kuːp] n Hühnerstall m; vt: **— up** (fig) einpferchen.

co-op [ˈkuːɒp] n = **cooperative**.

cooperate [kəʊˈɒpəreɪt] vi zusammenarbeiten.

cooperation [kəʊɒpəˈreɪʃən] n Zusammenarbeit f.

cooperative [kəʊˈɒpərətɪv] a hilfsbereit; (Comm) genossenschaftlich; n (of farmers) Genossenschaft f; (— store) Konsumladen m.

coordinate [kəʊˈɔːdɪneɪt] vt koordinieren.

coordination [kəʊɔːdɪˈneɪʃən] n Koordination f.

coot [kuːt] n Wasserhuhn nt.

cop [kɒp] n (col) Polyp m, Bulle m.

cope [kəʊp] vi fertig werden, schaffen (with acc).

co-pilot [ˈkəʊpaɪlət] n Kopilot m.

copious [ˈkəʊpɪəs] a reichhaltig.

copper [ˈkɒpə*] n Kupfer nt; Kupfermünze f; (col: policeman) Polyp m, Bulle m.

coppice [ˈkɒpɪs], **copse** [kɒps] n Unterholz nt.

copulate [ˈkɒpjʊleɪt] vi sich paaren.

copy [ˈkɒpɪ] n (imitation) Nachahmung f; (of book etc) Exemplar nt; (of newspaper) Nummer f; vt kopieren, abschreiben; **—cat** Nachäffer m; **—right** Copyright nt; **—right reserved** alle Rechte vorbehalten, Nachdruck verboten.

coral [ˈkɒrəl] n Koralle f; **— reef** Korallenriff nt.

cord [kɔːd] n Schnur f, Kordel f;
see vocal.

cordial ['kɔːdiəl] a herzlich; n
Fruchtsaft m; —ly ad herzlich.

cordon ['kɔːdn] n Absperrkette f.

corduroy ['kɔːdərɔi] n Kord(samt)
m.

core [kɔː*] n Kern m; vt entkernen.

cork [kɔːk] n (bark) Korkrinde f;
(stopper) Korken m; —age Korken-
geld nt; —screw Korkenzieher m.

corm [kɔːm] n Knolle f.

cormorant ['kɔːmərənt] n
Kormoran m.

corn [kɔːn] n Getreide nt, Korn nt;
(US: maize) Mais m; (on foot)
Hühnerauge nt.

cornea ['kɔːniə] n Hornhaut f.

corned beef ['kɔːnd'biːf] n Corned
Beef nt.

corner ['kɔːnə*] n Ecke f; (nook)
Winkel m; (on road) Kurve f; vt
in die Enge treiben; vi (Aut) in die
Kurve gehen; — flag Eckfahne f;
— kick Eckball m; —stone
Eckstein m.

cornet ['kɔːnɪt] n (Mus) Kornett nt;
(for ice cream) Eistüte f.

cornflour ['kɔːnflauə*] n Maizena
® nt, Maismehl nt.

cornice ['kɔːnis] n Gesims nt.

cornstarch ['kɔːnstɑːtʃ] n (US) =
cornflour.

cornucopia [kɔːnjuːˈkəupiə] n
Füllhorn nt.

corny ['kɔːni] a (joke) blöd(e).

corollary [kəˈrɒləri] n Folgesatz m.

coronary ['kɒrənəri] a (Med)
Koronar-; n Herzinfarkt m; —
thrombosis Koronarthrombose f.

coronation [kɒrəˈneiʃən] n
Krönung f.

coroner ['kɒrənə*] n Unter-

suchungsrichter m und Leichen-
beschauer m.

coronet ['kɒrənɪt] n Adelskrone f.

corporal ['kɔːpərəl] n Oberge-
freite(r) m; a: — **punishment**
Prügelstrafe f.

corporate ['kɔːpərɪt] a gemein-
schaftlich, korporativ.

corporation [kɔːpəˈreiʃən] n
Gemeinde f, Stadt f; (esp business)
Körperschaft f, Aktiengesellschaft f.

corps [kɔː*] n (Armee)korps nt.

corpse [kɔːps] n Leiche f.

corpulent ['kɔːpjulənt] a korpulent.

Corpus Christi ['kɔːpəsˈkristi] n
Fronleichnamsfest nt.

corpuscle ['kɔːpʌsl] n Blut-
körperchen nt.

corral [kəˈrɑːl] n Pferch m, Korral
m.

correct [kəˈrekt] a (accurate)
richtig; (proper) korrekt; vt mistake berichtigen; pupil tadeln;
—ion [kəˈrekʃən] Berichtigung f;
—ly ad richtig, korrekt.

correlate ['kɒrileit] vt aufeinander
beziehen; vi korrelieren.

correlation [kɒriˈleiʃən] n
Wechselbeziehung f.

correspond [kɒrisˈpɒnd] vi
übereinstimmen; (exchange
letters) korrespondieren; —ence
(similarity) Entsprechung f; Brief-
wechsel m, Korrespondenz f;
—ence course Fernkurs m; —ent
(Press) Berichterstatter m; —ing a
entsprechend, gemäß (to dat).

corridor ['kɒridɔː*] n Gang m.

corroborate [kəˈrɒbəreit] vt
bestätigen, erhärten.

corroboration [kərɒbəˈreiʃən] n
Bekräftigung f.

corrode [kəˈrəud] vt zerfressen; vi
rosten.

corrosion [kə'rəʊʒən] n Rost m, Korrosion f.

corrugated ['kɒrəgeɪtɪd] a gewellt; — cardboard Wellpappe f; — iron Wellblech m.

corrupt [kə'rʌpt] a korrupt; vt verderben; (bribe) bestechen; —ion [kə'rʌpʃən] (of society) Verdorbenheit f; (bribery) Bestechung f.

corset ['kɔːsɪt] n Korsett nt.

cortège [kɔː'teːʒ] n Zug m; (of funeral) Leichenzug m.

cortisone ['kɔːtɪzəʊn] n Kortison nt.

cosh [kɒʃ] n Totschläger m; vt über den Schädel hauen.

cosignatory ['kəʊ'sɪgnətərɪ] n Mitunterzeichner(in f) m.

cosine ['kəʊsaɪn] n Kosinus m.

cosiness ['kəʊzɪnɪs] n Gemütlichkeit f.

cosmetic [kɒz'metɪk] n Schönheitsmittel nt, kosmetische(s) Mittel nt; a kosmetisch.

cosmic ['kɒzmɪk] a kosmisch.

cosmonaut ['kɒzmənɔːt] n Kosmonaut(in f) m.

cosmopolitan [kɒzmə'pɒlɪtən] a international; city Welt-.

cosmos ['kɒzmɒs] n Weltall nt, Kosmos m.

cost [kɒst] n Kosten pl, Preis m; vt irreg kosten; it — him his life/job es kostete ihm sein Leben/seine Stelle; at all — s um jeden Preis; — of living Lebenshaltungskosten pl.

co-star ['kəʊstɑː*] n zweite(r) or weitere(r) Hauptdarsteller(in f) m.

costing ['kɒstɪŋ] n Kostenberechnung f.

costly ['kɒstlɪ] a kostspielig.

cost price ['kɒst'praɪs] n Selbstkostenpreis m.

costume ['kɒstjuːm] n Kostüm nt; (fancy dress) Maskenkostüm nt; (for bathing) Badeanzug m; — jewellery Modeschmuck m.

cosy ['kəʊzɪ] a behaglich, gemütlich.

cot [kɒt] n Kinderbett(chen) nt.

cottage ['kɒtɪdʒ] n kleine(s) Haus nt (auf dem Land); — cheese Hüttenkäse m.

cotton ['kɒtn] n (material) Baumwollstoff m; a dress etc Baumwoll-, Kattun-; — wool Watte f.

couch [kaʊtʃ] n Couch f; vt (in Worte) fassen, formulieren.

cougar ['kuːgə*] n Puma m.

cough [kɒf] vi husten; n Husten m; — drop Hustenbonbon nt.

could [kʊd] pt of **can**; —n't = could not.

council ['kaʊnsl] n (of town) Stadtrat m; — estate/house Siedlung f/Haus nt des sozialen Wohnungsbaus; —lor ['kaʊnsɪlə*] Stadtrat m.

counsel ['kaʊnsl] n (barrister) Anwalt m, Rechtsbeistand m; (advice) Rat(schlag) m; —lor Berater m.

count [kaʊnt] vti zählen; vi (be important) zählen, gelten; n (reckoning) Abrechnung f; (nobleman) Graf m; —down Countdown m; — on vt zählen auf (+acc); — up vt zusammenzählen.

counter ['kaʊntə*] n (in shop) Ladentisch m; (in café) Tresen m, Theke f; (in bank, post office) Schalter m; vt entgegnen; ad entgegen; —act [kaʊntə'rækt] vt entgegenwirken (+dat); —attack Gegenangriff m; —balance vt aufwiegen; —clockwise ad entgegen dem Uhrzeigersinn; —espionage Spionageabwehr f; —feit Fälschung f; vt fälschen; a

gefälscht, unecht; —foil (Kontroll)-
abschnitt m; —part (object)
Gegenstück nt; (person)
Gegenüber nt.

countess ['kauntɪs] n Gräfin f.

countless ['kauntlɪs] a zahllos,
unzählig.

countrified ['kʌntrɪfaɪd] a ländlich.

country ['kʌntrɪ] n Land nt; in the
— auf dem Land(e); — dancing
Volkstanztanzen nt; — house Landhaus nt; —man (national) Landsmann m; (rural) Bauer m; —side
Landschaft f.

county ['kauntɪ] n Landkreis m;
(Brit) Grafschaft f; — town Kreis-
stadt f.

coup [ku:] n Coup m; — d'état
Staatsstreich m, Putsch m.

coupé [ku:'peɪ] n (Aut) Coupé n.

couple ['kʌpl] n Paar nt; a — of
ein paar; vt koppeln.

couplet ['kʌplɪt] n Reimpaar nt.

coupling ['kʌplɪŋ] n Kupplung f.

coupon ['ku:pɒn] n Gutschein m.

courage ['kʌrɪdʒ] n Mut m; —ous
[kə'reɪdʒəs] a mutig.

courier ['kurɪə*] n (for holiday)
Reiseleiter m; (messenger) Kurier
m, Eilbote m.

course [kɔːs] n (race) Strecke f,
Bahn f; (of stream) Lauf m; (of
action) Richtung f; (of lectures)
Vortragsreihe f; (of study)
Studiengang m; summer —
Sommerkurs m; (Naut) Kurs m;
(in meal) Gang m; of — natürlich;
in the — of im Laufe (+gen); in
due — zu gegebener Zeit; see golf.

court [kɔːt] n (royal) Hof m; (Jur)
Gericht nt; vt gehen mit; see
tennis.

courteous ['kɜːtɪəs] a höflich,
zuvorkommend.

courtesan [kɔːtɪ'zæn] n Kurtisane
f.

courtesy ['kɜːtəsɪ] n Höflichkeit f.

courthouse ['kɔːthaus] n (US)
Gerichtsgebäude nt.

courtier ['kɔːtɪə*] n Höfling m.

court-martial [kɔːt'mɑːʃəl] n
Kriegsgericht nt; vt vor ein Kriegsgericht stellen.

courtroom ['kɔːtrum] n
Gerichtssaal m.

courtyard ['kɔːtjɑːd] n Hof m.

cousin ['kʌzn] n Cousin m, Vetter
m; Kusine f.

cove [kəuv] n kleine Bucht f.

covenant ['kʌvənənt] n feierliche(s)
Abkommen nt.

cover ['kʌvə*] vt (spread over)
bedecken; (shield) abschirmen;
(include) sich erstrecken über
(+acc); (protect) decken; (lid)
Deckel m; (for bed) Decke f; (Mil)
Bedeckung f; —age ['kʌvrɪdʒ]
(Press) (reports) Berichterstattung
f; (distribution) Verbreitung f; —
charge Bedienungsgeld nt; —ing
Bedeckung f; —ing letter Begleit-
brief m.

covet ['kʌvɪt] vt begehren.

covetous ['kʌvɪtəs] a begehrlich.

cow [kau] n Kuh f.

coward ['kauəd] n Feigling m;
—ice ['kauədɪs] Feigheit f; —ly a
feige.

cowboy ['kaubɔɪ] n Cowboy m.

cower ['kauə*] vi kauern; (movement) sich kauern.

co-worker ['kəu'wɜːkə*] n Mitar-
beiter(in f) m.

cowshed ['kauʃed] n Kuhstall m.

coxswain ['kɒksn] n (abbr cox)
Steuermann m.

coy [kɔɪ] a schüchtern; girl spröde.

coyote [kɔɪ'əʊtɪ] *n* Präriewolf *m*.
crab [kræb] *n* Krebs *m*; —**apple** Holzapfel *m*.
crack [kræk] *n* Riß *m*, Sprung *m*; (*noise*) Knall *m*; *vt* (*break*) springen lassen; *joke* reißen; *vi* (*noise*) krachen, knallen; *a* erstklassig; *troops* Elite-; —**er** (*firework*) Knallkörper *m*, Kracher *m*; (*biscuit*) Keks *m*; (*Christmas* —) Knallbonbon *m*; — **up** *vi* (*fig*) zusammenbrechen.
crackle ['krækl] *vi* knistern; (*fire*) prasseln.
crackling ['kræklɪŋ] *n* Knistern *n*; (*rind*) Kruste *f* (des Schweinebratens).
cradle ['kreɪdl] *n* Wiege *f*.
craft [krɑːft] *n* (*skill*) (Hand- or Kunst)fertigkeit *f*; (*trade*) Handwerk *nt*; (*cunning*) Verschlagenheit *f*; (*Naut*) Fahrzeug *nt*, Schiff *nt*; —**sman** gelernte(r) Handwerker *m*; —**smanship** (*quality*) handwerkliche Ausführung *f*; (*ability*) handwerkliche(s) Können *nt*; —**y** *a* schlau, gerieben.
crag [kræg] *n* Klippe *f*, schroff, felsig.
cram [kræm] *vt* vollstopfen; (*col*) (*teach*) einpauken; *vi* (*learn*) pauken.
cramp [kræmp] *n* Krampf *m*; *vt* (*hinder*) einengen, hemmen.
crampon ['kræmpən] *n* Steigeisen *nt*.
cranberry ['krænbərɪ] *n* Preiselbeere *f*.
crane [kreɪn] *n* (*machine*) Kran *m*; (*bird*) Kranich *m*.
cranium ['kreɪnɪəm] *n* Schädel *m*.
crank [kræŋk] *n* (*lever*) Kurbel *f*; (*person*) Spinner *m*; *vt* ankurbeln; —**shaft** Kurbelwelle *f*.

cranky ['kræŋkɪ] *a* verschroben.
cranny ['krænɪ] *n* Ritze *f*.
crap [kræp] *n* (*col*) Mist *m*, Scheiße *f*.
craps [kræps] *n* (*US*) Würfelspiel *nt*.
crash [kræʃ] *n* (*noise*) Krachen *nt*; (*with cars*) Zusammenstoß *m*; (*with plane*) Absturz *m*; *vi* stürzen; (*cars*) zusammenstoßen; (*plane*) abstürzen; (*economy*) zusammenbrechen; (*noise*) knallen; *a course* Schnell-; —**helmet** Sturzhelm *m*; — **landing** Bruchlandung *f*.
crass [kræs] *a* kraß.
crate [kreɪt] *n* (*lit*, *fig*) Kiste *f*.
crater ['kreɪtə*] *n* Krater *m*.
cravat(e) [krə'væt] *n* Krawatte *f*.
crave [kreɪv] *vi* verlangen (*for* nach).
craving ['kreɪvɪŋ] *n* Verlangen *nt*.
crawl [krɔːl] *vi* kriechen; (*baby*) krabbeln; *n* Kriechen *nt*; (*swim*) Kraul *nt*.
crayon ['kreɪən] *n* Buntstift *m*.
craze [kreɪz] *n* Fimmel *m*.
crazy ['kreɪzɪ] *a* (*foolish*) verrückt; (*insane*) wahnsinnig; (*eager for*) versessen (auf +*acc*); — **paving** Mosaikpflaster *nt*.
creak [kriːk] *n* Knarren *nt*; *vi* quietschen, knarren.
cream [kriːm] *n* (*from milk*) Rahm *m*, Sahne *f*; (*polish, cosmetic*) Creme *f*; (*colour*) Cremefarbe *f*; (*fig: people*) Elite *f*; — **cake** (*small*) Sahnetörtchen *nt*; (*big*) Sahnekuchen *m*; — **cheese** Rahmquark *m*; —**ery** Molkerei *f*; —**y** *a* sahnig.
crease [kriːs] *n* Falte *f*; *vt* falten; (*untidy*) zerknittern.

create [krɪ'eɪt] *vt* erschaffen; (*cause*) verursachen.

creation [krɪ'eɪʃən] *n* Schöpfung *f*.

creative [krɪ'eɪtɪv] *a* schöpferisch, kreativ.

creator [krɪ'eɪtə*] *n* Schöpfer *m*.

creature ['kriːtʃə*] *n* Geschöpf *nt*.

credence ['kriːdəns] *n* Glauben *m*.

credentials [krɪ'denʃəlz] *npl* Beglaubigungsschreiben *nt*.

credibility [kredɪ'bɪltɪ] *n* Glaubwürdigkeit *f*.

credible ['kredɪbl] *a person* glaubwürdig; *story* glaubhaft.

credit [krɪt] *n* (*Comm*) Kredit *m*; Guthaben *nt*; *vt* Glauben schenken (+*dat*); **to sb's** — zu jds Ehre; **—s** *pl* (*of film*) die Mitwirkenden; **—able** *a* rühmlich; **—card** Kreditkarte *m*; **—or** Gläubiger *m*.

credulity [krɪ'djuːlɪtɪ] *n* Leichtgläubigkeit *f*.

creed [kriːd] *n* Glaubensbekenntnis *nt*.

creek [kriːk] *n* (*inlet*) kleine Bucht *f*; (*US: river*) kleine(r) Wasserlauf *m*.

creep [kriːp] *vi irreg* kriechen; **—er** Kletterpflanze *f*; **—y** *a* (*frightening*) gruselig.

cremate [krɪ'meɪt] *vt* einäschern.

cremation [krɪ'meɪʃən] *n* Einäscherung *f*.

crematorium [kremə'tɔːrɪəm] *n* Krematorium *nt*.

creosote ['krɪəsəʊt] *n* Kreosot *nt*.

crepe [kreɪp] *n* Krepp *m*; **— bandage** Elastikbinde *f*.

crescent ['kresnt] *n* (*of moon*) Halbmond *m*.

cress [kres] *n* Kresse *f*.

crest [krest] *n* (*of cock*) Kamm *m*; (*of wave*) Wellenkamm *m*; (*coat of arms*) Wappen *nt*; **—fallen** *a* niedergeschlagen.

cretin ['kretɪn] *n* Idiot *m*.

crevasse [krɪ'væs] *n* Gletscherspalte *f*.

crevice ['krevɪs] *n* Riß *m*; (*in rock*) Felsspalte *f*.

crew [kruː] *n* Besatzung *f*, Mannschaft *f*; **—cut** Bürstenschnitt *m*; **—neck** runde(r) Ausschnitt *m*.

crib [krɪb] *n* (*bed*) Krippe *f*; (*translation*) wortwörtliche Übersetzung *f*, Klatsche *f*.

crick [krɪk] *n* Muskelkrampf *m*.

cricket ['krɪkɪt] *n* (*insect*) Grille *f*; (*game*) Kricket *nt*; **—er** Kricketspieler *m*.

crime [kraɪm] *n* Verbrechen *nt*.

criminal ['krɪmnl] *n* Verbrecher *m*; *a* kriminell, strafbar.

crimp [krɪmp] *vt hair* drehen.

crimson ['krɪmzn] *n* Karmesin *nt*; *a* leuchtend rot.

cringe [krɪndʒ] *vi* sich ducken.

crinkle ['krɪŋkl] *vt* zerknittern; *vi* knittern.

crinkly ['krɪŋklɪ] *a hair* kraus.

cripple ['krɪpl] *n* Krüppel *m*; *vt* lahmlegen; (*Med*) lähmen, verkrüppeln.

crisis ['kraɪsɪs] *n* Krise *f*.

crisp [krɪsp] *a* knusprig; *n* Chip *m*.

criss-cross ['krɪskrɒs] *a* gekreuzt, Kreuz-.

criterion [kraɪ'tɪərɪən] *n* Kriterium *nt*.

critic ['krɪtɪk] *n* Kritiker(in *f*) *m*; **—al** *a* kritisch; **—ally** *ad* kritisch; *ill* gefährdich; **—ally** ['krɪtɪsɪzəm] Kritik *f*; **—ize** ['krɪtɪsaɪz] *vt* kritisieren; (*comment*) beurteilen.

croak [krəʊk] *vi* krächzen; (*frog*) quaken; *n* Krächzen *nt*; Quaken *nt*.

crochet ['krəʊʃeɪ] *n* Häkelei *f*.
crockery ['krɒkərɪ] *n* Geschirr *nt*.
crocodile ['krɒkədaɪl] *n* Krokodil *nt*.
crocus ['krəʊkəs] *n* Krokus *m*.
croft [krɒft] *n* kleine(s) Pachtgut *nt*; **—er** Kleinbauer *m*.
crony ['krəʊnɪ] *n* (col) Kumpel *m*.
crook [krʊk] *n* (criminal) Gauner *m*, Schwindler *m*; (stick) Hirtenstab *m*; **—ed** ['krʊkɪd] a krumm.
crop [krɒp] *n* (harvest) Ernte *f*; (col: series) Haufen *m*; **— up** *vi* auftauchen; (thing) passieren.
croquet ['krəʊkeɪ] *n* Krocket *nt*.
croquette [krə'ket] *n* Krokette *f*.
cross [krɒs] *n* Kreuz *nt*; (Biol) Kreuzung *f*; *vt* road überqueren; legs übereinander legen; (write) einen Querstrich ziehen; (Biol) kreuzen; cheque als Verrechnungsscheck kennzeichnen; a (annoyed) ärgerlich, böse; **—bar** Querstange *f*; **—breed** Kreuzung *f*; **—country (race)** Geländelauf *m*; **—examination** Kreuzverhör *nt*; **—examine** *vt* ins Kreuzverhör nehmen; **—eyed** a: to be **—eyed** schielen; **—ing** (crossroads) (Straßen)kreuzung *f*; (of ship) Überfahrt *f*; (for pedestrians) Fußgängerübergang *m*; **— out** *vt* streichen; **to be at — purposes** von verschiedenen Dingen reden; **—reference** Querverweis *m*; **—roads** Straßenkreuzung *f*; (fig) Scheideweg *m*; **— section** Querschnitt *m*; **—wind** Seitenwind *m*; **—word (puzzle)** Kreuzworträtsel *nt*.
crotch [krɒtʃ] *n* Zwickel *m*; (Anat) Unterleib *m*.
crotchet ['krɒtʃɪt] *n* Viertelnote *f*.
crotchety ['krɒtʃɪtɪ] a person launenhaft.

crouch [kraʊtʃ] *vi* hocken.
crouton ['kru:tɔn] *n* geröstete(r) Brotwürfel *m*.
crow [krəʊ] *n* Krähen *nt*; *vi* krähen.
crowbar ['krəʊbɑ:*] *n* Stemmeisen *nt*.
crowd [kraʊd] *n* Menge *f*, Gedränge *nt*; *vt* (fill) überfüllen; *vi* drängen; **—ed** a überfüllt.
crown [kraʊn] *n* Krone *f*; (of head, hat) Kopf *m*; *vt* krönen; **— jewels** pl Kronjuwelen *pl*; **— prince** Kronprinz *m*.
crow's-nest ['krəʊznest] *n* Krähennest *nt*, Ausguck *m*.
crucial ['kru:ʃəl] a entscheidend.
crucifix ['kru:sɪfɪks] *n* Kruzifix *nt*; **—ion** [kru:sɪ'fɪkʃən] Kreuzigung *f*.
crucify ['kru:sɪfaɪ] *vt* kreuzigen.
crude [kru:d] a (raw) roh; humour, behaviour grob, unfein; **—ly** ad grob; **—ness** Roheit *f*.
crudity ['kru:dɪtɪ] *n* = **crudeness**.
cruel ['krʊəl] a grausam; (distressing) schwer; (hard-hearted) hart, gefühllos; **—ty** Grausamkeit *f*.
cruet ['kru:ɪt] *n* Gewürzständer *m*, Menage *f*.
cruise [kru:z] *n* Kreuzfahrt *f*; *vi* kreuzen; **—r** (Mil) Kreuzer *m*.
cruising-speed ['kru:zɪŋspi:d] *n* Reisegeschwindigkeit *f*.
crumb [krʌm] *n* Krume *f*; (fig) Bröckchen *nt*.
crumble ['krʌmbl] *vti* zerbröckeln.
crumbly ['krʌmblɪ] a krümelig.
crumpet ['krʌmpɪt] *n* Tee(pfann)-kuchen *m*.
crumple ['krʌmpl] *vt* zerknittern.
crunch [krʌntʃ] *n* Knirschen *nt*; (fig) der entscheidende Punkt; *vt* knirschen; **—y** a knusprig.
crusade [kru:'seɪd] *n* Kreuzzug *m*; **—r** Kreuzfahrer *m*.

crush [krʌʃ] n Gedränge nt; vt zerdrücken; (rebellion) unterdrücken, niederwerfen; vi (material) knittern; —ing a überwältigend.

crust [krʌst] n (of bread) Rinde f, Kruste f; (Med) Schorf m.

crutch [krʌtʃ] n Krücke f; see also crotch.

crux [krʌks] n (crucial point) der springende Punkt, Haken m (col).

cry [kraɪ] vi (call) ausrufen; (shout) schreien; (weep) weinen; n (call) Schrei m; —ing a (fig) himmelschreiend; — off vi (plötzlich) absagen.

crypt [krɪpt] n Krypta f.

cryptic ['krɪptɪk] a (secret) geheim; (mysterious) rätselhaft.

crystal ['krɪstl] n Kristall m; (glass) Kristallglas nt; (mineral) Bergkristall m; —clear a kristallklar; —lize vti (lit) kristallisieren; (fig) klären.

cub [kʌb] n Junge(s) nt; (young Boy Scout) Wölfling m.

cubbyhole ['kʌbɪhəʊl] n Eckchen nt.

cube [kjuːb] n Würfel m; (Math) Kubikzahl f.

cubic ['kjuːbɪk] a würfelförmig; centimetre etc Kubik-.

cubicle ['kjuːbɪkl] n Kabine f.

cubism ['kjuːbɪzəm] n Kubismus m.

cuckoo ['kuːkuː] n Kuckuck m; —clock Kuckucksuhr f.

cucumber ['kjuːkʌmbə*] n Gurke f.

cuddle ['kʌdl] vti herzen, drücken (col); n enge Umarmung f.

cuddly ['kʌdlɪ] a anschmiegsam; teddy zum Drücken.

cudgel ['kʌdʒəl] n Knüppel m.

cue [kjuː] n Wink m; (Theat) Stichwort nt; Billardstock m.

cuff [kʌf] n (of shirt, coat etc) Manschette f; Aufschlag m; (US) = turn-up; —link Manschettenknopf m.

cuisine [kwɪ'ziːn] n Kochkunst f, Küche f.

cul-de-sac ['kʌldəsæk] n Sackgasse f.

culinary ['kʌlɪnərɪ] a Koch-.

culminate ['kʌlmɪneɪt] vi gipfeln.

culmination [kʌlmɪ'neɪʃən] n Höhepunkt m.

culpable ['kʌlpəbl] a strafbar, schuldhaft.

culprit ['kʌlprɪt] n Täter m.

cult [kʌlt] n Kult m.

cultivate ['kʌltɪveɪt] vt (Agr) bebauen; mind bilden; —d a (Agr) bebaut; (cultured) kultiviert.

cultivation [kʌltɪ'veɪʃən] n (Agr) Bebauung f; (of person) Bildung f.

cultural ['kʌltʃərəl] a kulturell, Kultur-.

culture ['kʌltʃə*] n (refinement) Kultur f, Bildung f; (of community) Kultur f; —d a gebildet, kultiviert.

cumbersome ['kʌmbəsəm] a task beschwerlich; object schwer zu handhaben.

cummberbund ['kʌməbʌnd] n Kummerbund m.

cumulative ['kjuːmjʊlətɪv] a gehäuft; to be — sich häufen.

cunning ['kʌnɪŋ] n Verschlagenheit f; a schlau.

cup [kʌp] n Tasse f; (prize) Pokal m; —board ['kʌbəd] Schrank m; — final Meisterschaftsspiel nt; —ful Tasse(voll) f.

cupola ['kjuːpələ] n Kuppel f.

curable ['kjʊərəbl] a heilbar.

curator [kjʊ'reɪtə*] n Kustos m.

curb [kɜːb] vt zügeln; n Zaum m; (on spending etc) Einschränkung f.

cure [kjʊə*] n Heilmittel nt; (process) Heilverfahren nt; there's no — for ... es gibt kein Mittel gegen ...; vt heilen.

curfew ['kɜːfjuː] n Ausgangssperre f; Sperrstunde f.

curiosity [kjʊərɪ'ɒsɪtɪ] n Neugier f; (for knowledge) Wißbegierde f; (object) Merkwürdigkeit f.

curious ['kjʊərɪəs] a neugierig; (strange) seltsam; —ly ad besonders.

curl [kɜːl] n Locke f; vti locken; —er Lockenwickler f.

curlew ['kɜːljuː] n Brachvogel m.

curly ['kɜːlɪ] a lockig.

currant ['kʌrənt] n Korinthe f; Johannisbeere f.

currency ['kʌrənsɪ] n Währung f; (of ideas) Geläufigkeit f.

current ['kʌrənt] n Strömung f; a expression gängig, üblich; issue neueste; — account Girokonto nt; — affairs pl Zeitgeschehen nt; —ly ad zur Zeit.

curriculum [kə'rɪkjʊləm] n Lehrplan m; — vitae Lebenslauf m.

curry ['kʌrɪ] n Currygericht nt; — powder Curry(pulver) nt.

curse [kɜːs] vi (swear) fluchen (at auf +acc); vt (insult) verwünschen; n Fluch m.

cursory ['kɜːsərɪ] a flüchtig.

curt [kɜːt] a schroff.

curtail [kɜː'teɪl] vt abkürzen; rights einschränken.

curtain ['kɜːtn] n Vorhang m, Gardine f; (Theat) Vorhang m.

curtsy ['kɜːtsɪ] n Knicks m; vi knicksen.

cushion ['kʊʃən] n Kissen nt; vt polstern.

custard ['kʌstəd] n Vanillesoße f.

custodian [kʌs'təʊdɪən] n Kustos m, Verwalter(in f) m.

custody ['kʌstədɪ] n Aufsicht f; (police) Polizeigewahrsam m.

custom ['kʌstəm] n (tradition) Branch m; (business dealing) Kundschaft f; —s (taxes) Einfuhrzoll m; C—s Zollamt nt; —ary a üblich; —er Kunde m, Kundin f; —made a speziell angefertigt; C—s officer Zollbeamte(r) mf.

cute [kjuːt] a reizend, niedlich.

cuticle ['kjuːtɪkl] n (on nail) Nagelhaut f.

cutlery ['kʌtlərɪ] n Besteck nt.

cutlet ['kʌtlɪt] n (pork) Kotelett nt; (veal) Schnitzel nt.

cutout ['kʌtaʊt] n (Elec) Sicherung f.

cut-price ['kʌtpraɪs] a verbilligt.

cutting ['kʌtɪŋ] a schneidend; n (from paper) Ausschnitt m.

cyanide ['saɪənaɪd] n Zyankali nt.

cybernetics [saɪbə'netɪks] n Kybernetik f.

cyclamen ['sɪkləmən] n Alpenveilchen nt.

cycle ['saɪkl] n Fahrrad nt; (series) Reihe f; (of songs) Zyklus m; vi radfahren.

cycling ['saɪklɪŋ] n Radfahren nt; (Sport) Radsport m.

cyclist ['saɪklɪst] n Radfahrer(in f) m.

cyclone ['saɪkləʊn] n Zyklon m.

cygnet ['sɪgnɪt] n junge(r) Schwan m.

cylinder ['sılındə*] n Zylinder m; (Tech) Walze f; — **block** Zylinderblock m; — **capacity** Zylindervolumen nt, Zylinderinhalt m; — **head** Zylinderkopf m.

cymbals ['sımbəlz] npl Becken nt.

cynic ['sınık] n Zyniker(in f) m; —**al** a zynisch; —**ism** Zynismus m.

cypress ['saıprıs] n Zypresse f.

cyst [sıst] n Zyste f.

czar [zɑː*] n Zar m; —**ina** [zɑ'riːnə] Zarin f.

D

D, d [diː] n D nt, d nt.

dab [dæb] vt wound, paint betupfen; n (little bit) bißchen nt; (of paint) Tupfer m; (smear) Klecks m.

dabble ['dæbl] vi (splash) plätschern; (fig) **to** — **in sth in etw** (dat) machen.

dachshund ['dækshund] n Dackel m.

dad(dy) [dæd, -ı] n Papa m, Vati m; **daddy-long-legs** Weberknecht m.

daffodil ['dæfədıl] n Osterglocke f.

daft [dɑːft] a (col) blöd(e), doof.

dagger ['dægə*] n Dolch m.

dahlia ['deılıə] n Dahlie f.

daily ['deılı] a täglich; n (Press) Tageszeitung f; (woman) Haushaltshilfe f.

dainty ['deıntı] a zierlich; (attractive) reizend.

dairy ['dɛərı] n (shop) Milchgeschäft nt; (on farm) Molkerei f; a Milch-.

daisy ['deızı] n Gänseblümchen nt.

dally ['dælı] vi tändeln.

dam [dæm] n (Stau)damm m; vt stauen.

damage ['dæmıdʒ] n Schaden m; vt beschädigen; —**s** (Jur) Schaden(s)ersatz m.

dame [deım] n Dame f; (col) Weibsbild nt.

damn [dæm] vt verdammen, verwünschen; a (col) verdammt; — it! verflucht!; —**ing** a vernichtend.

damp [dæmp] a feucht; n Feuchtigkeit f; vt (also —**en**) befeuchten; (discourage) dämpfen; —**ness** Feuchtigkeit f.

damson ['dæmzən] n Damaszenerpflaume f.

dance [dɑːns] n Tanz m; (party) Tanz(abend) m; vi tanzen; — **hall** Tanzlokal nt; —**r** Tänzer m.

dancing ['dɑːnsıŋ] n Tanzen nt.

dandelion ['dændılaıən] n Löwenzahn m.

dandruff ['dændrəf] n (Kopf)schuppen pl.

dandy ['dændı] n Dandy m.

danger ['deındʒə*] n Gefahr f; — (sign) Achtung!; **in** — in Gefahr; **on the** —**list** in Lebensgefahr; —**ous** a, —**ously** ad gefährlich.

dangle ['dæŋgl] vi baumeln; vt herabhängen lassen.

dapper ['dæpə*] a elegant.

dare [dɛə*] vt herausfordern; vi: — (to) do sth es wagen, etw zu tun; **I** — **say** ich würde sagen.

daring ['dɛərıŋ] a (audacious) verwegen; (bold) wagemutig; dress gewagt; n Mut m.

dark [dɑːk] a dunkel; (fig) düster, trübe; (deep colour) dunkel-; n Dunkelheit f; after — nach Anbruch der Dunkelheit; D— Ages (finsteres) Mittelalter nt; —en vti verdunkeln; —ness Finsternis nt; — room Dunkelkammer f.

darling [dɑːlɪŋ] n Liebling m; a lieb.

darn [dɑːn] n Gestopfte(s) nt; vt stopfen.

dart [dɑːt] n (leap) Satz m; (weapon) Pfeil m; vi sausen; —s (game) Pfeilwerfen nt; —board Zielscheibe f.

dash [dæʃ] n Sprung m; (mark) (Gedanken)strich m; vt (lit) schmeißen; vi stürzen; —board Armaturenbrett nt; —ing a schneidig.

data [deɪtə] npl Einzelheiten pl, Daten pl; — processing Datenverarbeitung f.

date [deɪt] n Datum nt; (for meeting etc) Termin m; (with person) Verabredung f; (fruit) Dattel f; vt letter etc datieren; person gehen mit; —d a altmodisch; —line Datumsgrenze f.

dative [deɪtɪv] n Dativ m; a Dativ-.

daub [dɔːb] vt beschmieren; paint schmieren.

daughter [dɔːtə*] n Tochter f; —in-law Schwiegertochter f.

daunt [dɔːnt] vt entmutigen.

davenport [dævnpɔːt] n Sekretär m; (US: sofa) Sofa nt.

dawdle [dɔːdl] vi trödeln.

dawn [dɔːn] n Morgendämmerung f; vi dämmern; (fig) dämmern (on dat).

day [deɪ] n Tag m; (daylight) Tageslicht nt; — by — Tag für Tag, täglich; one — eines Tages; —break Tagesanbruch m; —dream n Wachtraum m, Träumerei f; vi

irreg (mit offenen Augen) träumen; —light Tageslicht nt; —time Tageszeit f.

daze [deɪz] vt betäuben; n Betäubung f; —d a benommen.

dazzle [dæzl] vt blenden; n Blenden f.

deacon [diːkən] n Diakon m; Kirchenvorsteher m.

dead [ded] a tot, gestorben; (without feeling) gefühllos; (without movement) leer, verlassen; — centre genau in der Mitte; ad völlig; the — pl die Toten pl; —en vt pain abtöten; sound ersticken; — end Sackgasse f; — heat tote(s) Rennen nt; —line Frist(ablauf) m, Stichtag m; —lock Stillstand m; —ly a tödlich; —pan a undurchdringlich.

deaf [def] a taub; —aid Hörgerät nt; —en vt taub machen; —ening a ohrenbetäubend; —ness Taubheit f; —mute Taubstumme(r) m.

deal [diːl] n Geschäft nt; vti irreg austeilen; a great — of sehr viel; to — with person behandeln; department sich befassen mit; —er (Comm) Händler m; (Cards) Kartengeber m; —ings pl (Fin) Geschäfte pl; (relations) Beziehungen pl, Geschäftsverkehr m.

dean [diːn] n (Protestant) Superintendent m; (Catholic) Dechant m; (Univ) Dekan m.

dear [dɪə*] a lieb; (expensive) teuer; n Liebling m; — me! du liebe Zeit!; D— Sir Sehr geehrter Herr!; D— John Lieber John!; —ly ad love herzlich; pay teuer.

dearth [dɜːθ] n Mangel m (of an + dat).

death [deθ] n Tod m; (end) Ende nt; (statistic) Sterbefall m; —bed

Sterbebett *nt*; — certificate Totenschein *m*; — duties (*Brit*) Erbschaftsteuer *f*; —ly a totenähnlich, Toten-; — penalty Todesstrafe *f*; — rate Sterblichkeitsziffer *f*.

debar [dɪ'bɑː*] *vt* ausschließen.

debase [dɪ'beɪs] *vt* entwerten.

debatable [dɪ'beɪtəbl] *a* anfechtbar.

debate [dɪ'beɪt] *n* Debatte *f*, Diskussion *f*; *vt* debattieren, diskutieren; (*consider*) überlegen.

debauched [dɪ'bɔːtʃt] *a* ausschweifend.

debauchery [dɪ'bɔːtʃərɪ] *n* Ausschweifungen *pl*.

debit ['debɪt] *n* Schuldposten *m*; *vt* belasten.

debris ['debriː] *n* Trümmer *pl*.

debt [det] *n* Schuld *f*; to be in — verschuldet sein; — or Schuldner *m*.

début ['deɪbuː] *n* Debüt *nt*.

decade [dekeɪd] *n* Jahrzehnt *nt*.

decadence ['dekədəns] *n* Verfall *m*, Dekadenz *f*.

decadent ['dekədənt] *a* dekadent.

decanter [dɪ'kæntə*] *n* Karaffe *f*.

decarbonize [diː'kɑːbənaɪz] *vt* entkohlen.

decay [dɪ'keɪ] *n* Verfall *m*; *vi* verfallen; *teeth, meat etc* faulen; *leaves etc* verrotten.

decease [dɪ'siːs] *n* Hinscheiden *nt*; —d verstorben.

deceit [dɪ'siːt] *n* Betrug *m*; —ful *a* falsch.

deceive [dɪ'siːv] *vt* täuschen.

decelerate [diː'seləreɪt] *vti* (sich) verlangsamen, die Geschwindigkeit verringern.

December [dɪ'sembə*] *n* Dezember *m*.

decency ['diːsənsɪ] *n* Anstand *m*.

decent [diːsənt] *a* (*respectable*) anständig; (*pleasant*) annehmbar.

decentralization [diːsentrəlaɪ'zeɪʃən] *n* Dezentralisierung *f*.

deception [dɪ'sepʃən] *n* Betrug *m*.

deceptive [dɪ'septɪv] *a* täuschend, irreführend.

decibel ['desɪbel] *n* Dezibel *nt*.

decide [dɪ'saɪd] *vt* entscheiden; *vi* sich entscheiden; to — on sth etw beschließen; —d a bestimmt, entschieden; —dly *ad* entschieden.

deciduous [dɪ'sɪdjʊəs] *a* jedes Jahr abfallend, Laub-.

decimal ['desɪməl] *a* dezimal; *n* Dezimalzahl *f*; — point Komma *nt* (eines Dezimalbruches); — system Dezimalsystem *nt*.

decimate ['desɪmeɪt] *vt* dezimieren.

decipher [dɪ'saɪfə*] *vt* entziffern.

decision [dɪ'sɪʒən] *n* Entscheidung *f*, Entschluß *m*.

decisive [dɪ'saɪsɪv] *a* entscheidend, ausschlaggebend.

deck [dek] *n* (*Naut*) Deck *nt*; (*of cards*) Pack *m*; —chair Liegestuhl *m*; —hand Matrose *m*.

declaration [deklə'reɪʃən] *n* Erklärung *f*.

declare [dɪ'kleə*] *vt* (*state*) behaupten; *war* erklären; (*Customs*) verzollen.

decline [dɪ'klaɪn] *n* (*decay*) Verfall *m*; (*lessening*) Rückgang *m*, Niedergang *m*; *vt invitation* ausschlagen, ablehnen; *vi* (*of strength*) nachlassen; (*say no*) ablehnen.

declutch [diː'klʌtʃ] *vi* auskuppeln.

decode [diː'kəʊd] *vt* entschlüsseln.

decompose [diːkəm'pəʊz] *vi* (sich) zersetzen.

decomposition [diːkɒmpə'zɪʃən] *n* Zersetzung *f*.

decontaminate [diːkən'tæmɪneɪt] *vt* entgiften.

décor ['deɪkɔ:*] n Ausstattung f.

decorate ['dekəreɪt] vt room tapezieren; streichen; (adorn) (aus)schmücken; cake verzieren; (honour) auszeichnen.

decoration [dekə'reɪʃən] n (of house) (Wand)dekoration f; (medal) Orden m.

decorative ['dekərətɪv] a dekorativ, Schmuck-.

decorator ['dekəreɪtə*] n Maler m, Anstreicher m.

decorum [dɪ'kɔ:rəm] n Anstand m.

decoy ['di:kɔɪ] n (lit, fig) Lockvogel m.

decrease [di:'kri:s] n Abnahme f; vt vermindern; vi abnehmen.

decree [dɪ'kri:] n Verfügung f, Erlaß m.

decrepit [dɪ'krepɪt] a hinfällig.

dedicate ['dedɪkeɪt] vt (to God) weihen; book widmen.

dedication [dedɪ'keɪʃən] n (devotion) Ergebenheit f.

deduce [dɪ'dju:s] vt ableiten, schließen (from aus).

deduct [dɪ'dʌkt] vt abziehen; —ion [dɪ'dʌkʃən] (of money) Abzug m; (conclusion) (Schluß)folgerung f.

deed [di:d] n Tat f; (document) Urkunde f.

deep [di:p] a tief; —en vt vertiefen; —freeze Tiefkühlung f; —seated a tiefsitzend; —set a tiefliegend.

deer [dɪə*] n Reh nt; (with antlers) Hirsch m.

deface [dɪ'feɪs] vt entstellen.

defamation [defə'meɪʃən] n Verleumdung f.

default [dɪ'fɔ:lt] n Versäumnis nt; vi versäumen; by — durch Nichterscheinen nt; —er Schuldner m, Zahlungsunfähige(r) m.

defeat [dɪ'fi:t] n (overthrow) Vernichtung f; (battle) Niederlage f; vt schlagen, zu Fall bringen; —ist ə defätistisch.

defect ['di:fekt] n Defekt m, Fehler m; [dɪ'fekt] vi überlaufen; —ive [dɪ'fektɪv] a fehlerhaft, schadhaft.

defence [dɪ'fens] n (Mil, Sport) Verteidigung f; (excuse) Rechtfertigung f; —less a wehrlos.

defend [dɪ'fend] vt verteidigen; —ant Angeklagte(r) m; —er Verteidiger m.

defensive [dɪ'fensɪv] a defensiv, Schutz-.

defer [dɪ'fə:*] vt verschieben; —ence ['defərəns] Hochachtung f, Rücksichtnahme f; —ential [defə'renʃəl] a ehrerbietig.

defiance [dɪ'faɪəns] n Trotz m, Unnachgiebigkeit f; in — of the order dem Befehl zum Trotz.

defiant [dɪ'faɪənt] a trotzig, unnachgiebig.

deficiency [dɪ'fɪʃənsɪ] n Unzulänglichkeit f, Mangel m.

deficient [dɪ'fɪʃənt] a unzureichend.

deficit ['defɪsɪt] n Defizit nt, Fehlbetrag m.

defile [dɪ'faɪl] vt beschmutzen; n ['di:faɪl] Schlucht f.

define [dɪ'faɪn] vt bestimmen; (explain) definieren.

definite ['defɪnɪt] a bestimmt; (clear) klar, eindeutig; —ly ad bestimmt.

definition [defɪ'nɪʃən] n Definition f; (Phot) Schärfe f.

definitive [dɪ'fɪnɪtɪv] a definitiv, endgültig.

deflate [di:'fleɪt] vt die Luft ablassen aus.

deflation [di:'fleɪʃən] n (Fin) Deflation f.

deflect [dɪ'flekt] vt ablenken.

deform [dɪ'fɔːm] vt deformieren, entstellen; **—ed** a deformiert; **—ity** Verunstaltung f, Mißbildung f.

defraud [dɪ'frɔːd] vt betrügen.

defray [dɪ'freɪ] vt bestreiten.

defrost [diː'frɒst] vt *fridge* abtauen; *food* auftauen.

deft [deft] a geschickt.

defunct [dɪ'fʌŋkt] a verstorben.

defy [dɪ'faɪ] vt (*challenge*) sich widersetzen (+dat); (*resist*) trotzen (+dat), sich stellen gegen.

degenerate [dɪ'dʒenəreɪt] vi degenerieren; [dɪ'dʒenərɪt] a degeneriert.

degradation [degrə'deɪʃən] n Erniedrigung f.

degrading [dɪ'greɪdɪŋ] a erniedrigend.

degree [dɪ'griː] n Grad m; (*Univ*) akademische(r) Grad m; **by —s** allmählich; **to take one's —** sein Examen machen.

dehydrated [diːhaɪ'dreɪtɪd] a getrocknet, Trocken-.

de-ice [diː'aɪs] vt enteisen, auftauen.

deign [deɪn] vi sich herablassen.

deity ['diːɪtɪ] n Gottheit f.

dejected [dɪ'dʒektɪd] a niedergeschlagen.

dejection [dɪ'dʒekʃən] n Niedergeschlagenheit f.

delay [dɪ'leɪ] vt (*hold back*) aufschieben; **the flight was —ed** die Maschine hatte Verspätung, vi (*linger*) sich aufhalten, zögern; n Aufschub m, Verzögerung f; **without —** unverzüglich; **—ed** a action verzögert.

delegate ['delɪgɪt] n Delegierte(r) mf, Abgeordnete(r) mf; ['delɪgeɪt] vt delegieren.

delegation [delɪ'geɪʃən] n Abordnung f; (*foreign*) Delegation f.

delete [dɪ'liːt] vt (aus)streichen.

deliberate [dɪ'lɪbərɪt] a (*intentional*) bewußt, überlegt; (*slow*) bedächtig; [dɪ'lɪbəreɪt] vi (*consider*) überlegen; (*debate*) sich beraten; **—ly** ad vorsätzlich.

deliberation [dɪlɪbə'reɪʃən] n Überlegung f, Beratung f.

delicacy ['delɪkəsɪ] n Zartheit f; (*weakness*) Anfälligkeit f; (*tact*) Zartgefühl nt; (*food*) Delikatesse f.

delicate ['delɪkɪt] a (*fine*) fein; (*fragile*) zart; (*situation*) heikel; (*Med*) empfindlich; **—ly** ad bedenklich.

delicatessen [delɪkə'tesn] n Feinkostgeschäft nt.

delicious [dɪ'lɪʃəs] a köstlich, lecker, delikat.

delight [dɪ'laɪt] n Wonne f; vt entzücken; **—ful** a entzückend, herrlich.

delinquency [dɪ'lɪŋkwənsɪ] n Straffälligkeit f, Delinquenz f.

delinquent [dɪ'lɪŋkwənt] n Straffällige(r) mf; a straffällig.

delirious [dɪ'lɪrɪəs] a irre, im Fieberwahn.

delirium [dɪ'lɪrɪəm] n Fieberwahn m, Delirium nt.

deliver [dɪ'lɪvə*] vt *goods* (ab)liefern; *letter* bringen, zustellen; *verdict* aussprechen; *speech* halten; **—y** (Ab)lieferung f; (*of letter*) Zustellung f; (*of speech*) Vortragsweise f; **—y van** Lieferwagen m.

delouse [diː'laus] vt entlausen.

delta ['deltə] n Delta nt.

delude [dɪ'luːd] vt täuschen.

deluge ['delju:dʒ] n Überschwemmung f; (fig) Flut f; vt (fig) überfluten.

delusion [dɪ'lu:ʒən] n (Selbst)täuschung f.

de luxe [dɪ'lʌks] a Luxus-.

demand [dɪ'mɑ:nd] vt verlangen; n (request) Verlangen nt; (Comm) Nachfrage f; in — begehrt, gesucht; on — auf Verlangen; —ing a anspruchsvoll.

demarcation [di:mɑ:'keɪʃən] n Abgrenzung f.

demeanour [dɪ'mi:nə*] n Benehmen nt.

demented [dɪ'mentɪd] a wahnsinnig.

demi- ['demɪ] pref halb-.

demise [dɪ'maɪz] n Ableben nt.

demobilization ['di:məubɪlaɪ'zeɪʃən] n Demobilisierung f.

democracy [dɪ'mɒkrəsɪ] n Demokratie f.

democrat ['deməkræt] n Demokrat m; —ic a, —ically ad [demə'krætɪk, -lɪ] demokratisch.

demolish [dɪ'mɒlɪʃ] vt (lit) abreißen; (destroy) zerstören; (fig) vernichten.

demolition [demə'lɪʃən] n Abbruch m.

demon ['di:mən] n Dämon m.

demonstrate ['demənstreɪt] vti demonstrieren.

demonstration [demən'streɪʃən] n Demonstration f; (proof) Beweisführung f.

demonstrative [dɪ'mɒnstrətɪv] a demonstrativ.

demonstrator ['demənstreɪtə*] n (Pol) Demonstrant(in f) m.

demoralize [dɪ'mɒrəlaɪz] vt demoralisieren.

demote [dɪ'məut] vt degradieren.

demure [dɪ'mjuə*] a ernst.

den [den] n (of animal) Höhle f, Bau m; Bude f; — of vice Lasterhöhle f.

denationalize [di:'næʃnəlaɪz] vt reprivatisieren.

denial [dɪ'naɪəl] n Leugnung f; official — Dementi nt.

denigrate ['denɪgreɪt] vt verunglimpfen.

denim ['denɪm] a Denim-; —s pl Denim-Jeans.

denomination [dɪnɒmɪ'neɪʃən] n (Eccl) Bekenntnis nt; (type) Klasse f; (Fin) Wert m.

denominator [dɪ'nɒmɪneɪtə*] n Nenner; common — gemeinsame(r) Nenner m.

denote [dɪ'nəut] vt bedeuten.

denounce [dɪ'nauns] vt brandmarken.

dense [dens] a dicht, dick; (stupid) schwer von Begriff; —ly ad dicht.

density ['densɪtɪ] n Dichte f.

dent [dent] n Delle f; vt einbeulen.

dental ['dentl] a Zahn-; — surgeon = dentist.

dentifrice ['dentɪfrɪs] n Zahnputzmittel nt.

dentist ['dentɪst] n Zahnarzt m/-ärztin f; —ry Zahnmedizin f.

denture ['dentʃə*] n künstliche(s) Gebiß nt.

denude [dɪ'nju:d] vt entblößen.

deny [dɪ'naɪ] vt leugnen; rumour widersprechen (+dat); knowledge verleugnen; help abschlagen; to — o.s. sth sich etw versagen.

deodorant [di:'əudərənt] n Desodorans nt.

depart [dɪ'pɑ:t] vi abfahren.

department [dɪ'pɑ:tmənt] n (Comm) Abteilung f, Sparte f;

(*Univ, Sch*) Fachbereich *m*; (*Pol*) Ministerium *nt*, Ressort *nt*; **—al** [di:pɑːˈtməntl] *a* Fach-; **—** **store** Warenhaus *nt*.

departure [dɪˈpɑːtʃə*] *n* (*of person*) Weggang *m*; (*on journey*) Abreise *f*; (*of train*) Abfahrt *f*; (*of plane*) Abflug *m*; **new —** Neuerung *f*.

depend [dɪˈpend] *vi*: **it —s** kommt darauf an; **— on** *vt* abhängen von; *parents etc* angewiesen sein auf (+*acc*); **—able** *a* zuverlässig; **—ence** Abhängigkeit *f*; **—ent** *n* (*person*) Familienangehörige(r) *mf*; *a* bedingt (*on* durch).

depict [dɪˈpɪkt] *vt* schildern.

depleted [dɪˈpliːtd] *a* aufgebraucht.

deplorable [dɪˈplɔːrəbl] *a* bedauerlich.

deplore [dɪˈplɔː*] *vt* mißbilligen.

deploy [dɪˈplɔɪ] *vt* einsetzen.

depopulation [ˈdiːpɒpjʊˈleɪʃən] *n* Entvölkerung *f*.

deport [dɪˈpɔːt] *vt* deportieren; **—ation** [diːpɔːˈteɪʃən] Abschiebung *f*; **—ation order** Ausweisung *f*; **—ment** Betragen *nt*.

depose [dɪˈpəʊz] *vt* absetzen.

deposit [dɪˈpɒzɪt] *n* (*in bank*) Guthaben *nt*; (*down payment*) Anzahlung *f*; (*security*) Kaution *f*; (*Chem*) Niederschlag *m*; *vt* (*in bank*) deponieren; (*put down*) niederlegen; **— account** Sparkonto *nt*; **—or** Kontoinhaber *m*.

depot [ˈdepəʊ] *n* Depot *nt*.

deprave [dɪˈpreɪv] *vt* (*moralisch*) verderben; **—d** *a* verworfen.

depravity [dɪˈprævɪtɪ] *n* Verworfenheit *f*.

deprecate [ˈdeprɪkeɪt] *vt* mißbilligen.

depreciate [dɪˈpriːʃɪeɪt] *vi* im Wert sinken.

depreciation [dɪpriːʃɪˈeɪʃən] *n* Wertminderung *f*.

depress [dɪˈpres] *vt* (*press down*) niederdrücken; (*in mood*) deprimieren; **—ed** *a person* niedergeschlagen, deprimiert; **—ed area** Notstandsgebiet *nt*; **—ing** *a* deprimierend; **—ion** [dɪˈpreʃən] (*mood*) Depression *f*; (*in trade*) Wirtschaftskrise *f*; (*hollow*) Vertiefung *f*; (*Met*) Tief(druckgebiet) *nt*.

deprivation [deprɪˈveɪʃən] *n* Entbehrung *f*, Not *f*.

deprive [dɪˈpraɪv] *vt* berauben (*of* + *gen*); **—d** *a child* sozial benachteiligt; *area* unterentwickelt.

depth [depθ] *n* Tiefe *f*; **in the —s of despair** in tiefster Verzweiflung; **to be out of one's —** den Boden unter den Füßen verloren haben; **— charge** Wasserbombe *f*.

deputation [depjʊˈteɪʃən] *n* Abordnung *f*.

deputize [ˈdepjʊtaɪz] *vi* vertreten (*for* + *acc*).

deputy [ˈdepjʊtɪ] *a* stellvertretend; *n* (Stell)vertreter *m*.

derail [dɪˈreɪl] *vt* entgleisen lassen; **to be —ed** entgleisen; **—ment** Entgleisung *f*.

deranged [dɪˈreɪndʒd] *a* irr, verrückt.

derby [ˈdɑːbɪ] *n* (*US*) Melone *f*.

derelict [ˈderɪlɪkt] *a* verlassen; *building* baufällig.

deride [dɪˈraɪd] *vt* auslachen.

derision [dɪˈrɪʒən] *n* Hohn *m*, Spott *m*.

derisory [dɪˈraɪsərɪ] *a* spöttisch.

derivation [derɪˈveɪʃən] *n* Ableitung *f*.

derivative [dɪ'rɪvətɪv] n Abgeleitete(s) nt; a abgeleitet.

derive [dɪ'raɪv] vt (get) gewinnen; (deduce) ableiten; vi (come from) abstammen.

dermatitis [dɜːmə'taɪtɪs] n Hautentzündung f.

derogatory [dɪ'rɒgətərɪ] a geringschätzig.

derrick [derɪk] n Drehkran m.

desalination [diːsælɪ'neɪʃən] n Entsalzung f.

descend [dɪ'send] vti hinuntersteigen; to — from abstammen von; —ant Nachkomme m.

descent [dɪ'sent] n (coming down) Abstieg m; (origin) Abstammung f.

describe [dɪs'kraɪb] vt beschreiben.

description [dɪs'krɪpʃən] n Beschreibung f; (sort) Art f.

descriptive [dɪs'krɪptɪv] a beschreibend; word anschaulich.

desecrate [desɪkreɪt] vt schänden.

desegregation [diːsegrə'geɪʃən] n Aufhebung f der Rassentrennung.

desert[1] [dezət] n Wüste f.

desert[2] [dɪ'zɜːt] vt verlassen; (temporarily) im Stich lassen; vi (Mil) desertieren; —er Deserteur m; —ion [dɪ'zɜːʃən] (of wife) böswillige(s) Verlassen nt; (Mil) Fahnenflucht f.

deserve [dɪ'zɜːv] vt verdienen.

deserving [dɪ'zɜːvɪŋ] a person würdig; action verdienstvoll.

design [dɪ'zaɪn] n (plan) Entwurf m; (drawing) Zeichnung f; (planning) Gestaltung f, Design nt; vt entwerfen; (intend) bezwecken; to have —s on sb/sth es auf jdn/etw abgesehen haben.

designate [dezɪgneɪt] vt bestimmen; [dezɪgnɪt] a designiert.

designation [dezɪg'neɪʃən] n Bezeichnung f.

designer [dɪ'zaɪnə*] n Designer m; (Theat) Bühnenbildner(in f) m.

desirability [dɪzaɪərə'bɪlɪtɪ] n Erwünschtheit f.

desirable [dɪ'zaɪərəbl] n wünschenswert; woman begehrenswert.

desire [dɪ'zaɪə*] n Wunsch m, Verlangen nt; vt (lust) begehren, wünschen; (ask for) verlangen, wollen.

desirous [dɪ'zaɪərəs] a begierig (of auf + acc).

desist [dɪ'zɪst] vi Abstand nehmen, aufhören.

desk [desk] n Schreibtisch m.

desolate [desəlɪt] a öde; (sad) trostlos.

desolation [desə'leɪʃən] n Trostlosigkeit f.

despair [dɪs'peə*] n Verzweiflung f; vi verzweifeln (of an + dat).

despatch [dɪs'pætʃ] = dispatch.

desperate [despərɪt] a verzweifelt; situation hoffnungslos; to be — for sth etw unbedingt brauchen; —ly ad verzweifelt.

desperation [despə'reɪʃən] n Verzweiflung f.

despicable [dɪs'pɪkəbl] a abscheulich.

despise [dɪs'paɪz] vt verachten.

despite [dɪs'paɪt] prep trotz (+ gen).

despondent [dɪs'pɒndənt] a mutlos.

dessert [dɪ'zɜːt] n Nachtisch m; —spoon Dessertlöffel m.

destination [destɪ'neɪʃən] n (of person) (Reise)ziel nt; (of goods) Bestimmungsort m.

destine [destɪn] vt (set apart) bestimmen.

destiny ['destɪnɪ] n Schicksal nt.

destitute ['destɪtjuːt] a notleidend.

destitution [destɪtjuːʃən] n Elend f.

destroy [dɪs'trɔɪ] vt zerstören; **—er** (Naut) Zerstörer m.

destruction [dɪs'trʌkʃən] n Zerstörung f.

destructive [dɪs'trʌktɪv] a zerstörend.

detach [dɪ'tætʃ] vt loslösen; **—able** a abtrennbar; **—ed** a attitude distanziert, objektiv; house Einzel-; **—ment** (Mil) Abteilung f, Sonderkommando nt; (fig) Abstand m, Unvoreingenommenheit f.

detail ['diːteɪl] n Einzelheit f, Detail nt; (minor part) unwichtige Einzelheit f; vt (relate) ausführlich berichten; (appoint) abkommandieren; **in —** ausführlichst, bis ins kleinste.

detain [dɪ'teɪn] vt aufhalten; (imprison) in Haft halten.

detect [dɪ'tekt] vt entdecken; **—ion** [dɪ'tekʃən] Aufdeckung f; **—ive** Detektiv m; **—ive story** Kriminal(galgeschichte f) m; **—or** Detektor m.

détente [deɪtãːnt] n Entspannung f.

detention [dɪ'tenʃən] n Haft f; (Sch) Nachsitzen nt.

deter [dɪ'tɜː*] vt abschrecken.

detergent [dɪ'tɜːdʒənt] n Waschmittel nt; Reinigungsmittel nt.

deteriorate [dɪ'tɪərɪəreɪt] vi sich verschlechtern.

deterioration [dɪtɪərɪə'reɪʃən] n Verschlechterung f.

determination [dɪtɜːmɪ'neɪʃən] n Entschlossenheit f.

determine [dɪ'tɜːmɪn] vt bestimmen; **—d** a entschlossen.

deterrent [dɪ'terənt] n Abschreckungsmittel nt; a abschreckend.

detest [dɪ'test] vt verabscheuen; **—able** a abscheulich.

dethrone [diː'θrəʊn] vt entthronen.

detonate ['detəneɪt] vt detonieren.

detonator ['detəneɪtə*] n Sprengkapsel f.

detour ['deɪtʊə*] n Umweg m; (on road sign) Umleitung f.

detract [dɪ'trækt] vi schmälern (from acc).

detriment ['detrɪmənt] n: **to the —** of zum Schaden (+gen); **—al** [detrɪ'mentl] a schädlich.

deuce [djuːs] n (tennis) Einstand m.

devaluation [diːvæljʊ'eɪʃən] n Abwertung f.

devalue ['diː'væljuː] vt abwerten.

devastate ['devəsteɪt] vt verwüsten.

devastating ['devəsteɪtɪŋ] a verheerend.

develop [dɪ'veləp] vt entwickeln; resources erschließen; vi sich entwickeln; **—er** (Phot) Entwickler m; (of land) Bauunternehmer m; **—ing** a country Entwicklungs-; **—ment** Entwicklung f.

deviant ['diːvɪənt] a abweichend; n Abweichler m.

deviate ['diːvɪeɪt] vi abweichen.

deviation [diːvɪ'eɪʃən] n Abweichung f.

device [dɪ'vaɪs] n Vorrichtung f, Gerät nt.

devil ['devl] n Teufel m; **·—ish** a teuflisch.

devious ['diːvɪəs] a route gewunden; means krumm; person verschlagen.

devise [dɪ'vaɪz] vt entwickeln.

devoid [dɪ'vɔɪd] a: **— of** ohne, bar (+gen).

devolution [di:vǝ'lu:ʃǝn] *n* Dezentralisierung *f*.

devote [dɪ'vǝʊt] *vt* widmen (*to dat*); **—d** *a* ergeben; **—e** [devǝʊ'ti:] Anhänger(in *f*) *m*, Verehrer(in *f*) *m*.

devotion [dɪ'vǝʊʃǝn] *n* (*piety*) Andacht *f*; (*loyalty*) Ergebenheit *f*, Hingabe *f*.

devour [dɪ'vavǝ*] *vt* verschlingen.

devout [dɪ'vaʊt] *a* andächtig.

dew [dju:] *n* Tau *m*.

dexterity [deks'terɪtɪ] *n* Geschicklichkeit *f*.

diabetes [daɪǝ'bi:ti:z] *n* Zuckerkrankheit *f*.

diabetic [daɪǝ'betɪk] *a* zuckerkrank; *n* Diabetiker *m*.

diagnose ['daɪǝgnǝʊz] *vt* (*Med*) diagnostizieren; feststellen.

diagnosis [daɪǝg'nǝʊsɪs] *n* Diagnose *f*.

diagonal [daɪ'ægǝnl] *a* diagonal, schräg; *n* Diagonale *f*.

diagram ['daɪǝgræm] *n* Diagramm *nt*, Schaubild *nt*.

dial ['daɪǝl] *n* (*Tel*) Wählscheibe *f*; (*of clock*) Zifferblatt *nt*; *vt* wählen; **—ling tone** Amtszeichen *nt*.

dialect ['daɪǝlekt] *n* Dialekt *m*.

dialogue ['daɪǝlɒg] *n* Gespräch *nt*; (*Liter*) Dialog *m*.

diameter [daɪ'æmɪtǝ*] *n* Durchmesser *m*.

diametrically [daɪǝ'metrɪkǝlɪ] *ad*: **— opposed to** genau entgegengesetzt (+*dat*).

diamond ['daɪǝmǝnd] *n* Diamant *m*; (*Cards*) Karo *nt*.

diaper ['daɪǝpǝ*] *n* (*US*) Windel *nt*.

diaphragm ['daɪǝfræm] *n* Zwerchfell *nt*.

diarrhoea [daɪǝ'rɪ:ǝ] *n* Durchfall *m*.

diary ['daɪǝrɪ] *n* Taschenkalender *m*; (*account*) Tagebuch *nt*.

dice [daɪs] *n* Würfel *pl*; *vt* (*Cook*) in Würfel schneiden.

dicey ['daɪsɪ] *a* (*col*) riskant.

dichotomy [dɪ'kɒtǝmɪ] *n* Kluft *f*.

dictate [dɪk'teɪt] *vt* diktieren; (*of circumstances*) gebieten; ['dɪkteɪt] *n* Mahnung *f*, Gebot *nt*.

dictation [dɪk'teɪʃǝn] *n* Diktat *nt*.

dictator [dɪk'teɪtǝ*] *n* Diktator *m*.

dictatorship [dɪk'teɪtǝʃɪp] *n* Diktatur *f*.

diction ['dɪkʃǝn] *n* Ausdrucksweise *f*.

dictionary ['dɪkʃǝnrɪ] *n* Wörterbuch *nt*.

didn't ['dɪdnt] = **did not**.

diddle ['dɪdl] *vt-* (*col*) übers Ohr hauen.

die [daɪ] *vi* sterben; (*end*) aufhören; **— away** *vi* schwächer werden; **— down** *vi* nachlassen; **— out** *vi* aussterben; (*fig*) nachlassen.

diesel ['di:zǝl]: **— engine** Dieselmotor *m*.

diet ['daɪǝt] *n* Nahrung *f*, Kost *f*; (*special food*) Diät *f*; (*slimming*) Abmagerungskur *f*; *vi* eine Abmagerungskur machen.

differ ['dɪfǝ*] *vi* sich unterscheiden; (*disagree*) anderer Meinung sein; **we —** wir sind unterschiedlicher Meinung; **—ence** Unterschied *m*; (*disagreement*) (Meinungs)unterschied *m*; **—ent** *a* verschieden; **that's —ent** das ist anders; **—ently** *ad* verschieden, unterschiedlich; **—ential** [dɪfǝ'renʃǝl] (*Aut*) Differentialgetriebe *nt*; (*in wages*) Lohnstufe *f*; **—entiate** [dɪfǝ'renʃɪeɪt] *vti* unterscheiden.

difficult ['dɪfɪkǝlt] *a* schwierig; **—y**

Schwierigkeit *f*; with —y nur schwer.

diffidence ['dıfıdəns] *n* mangelnde(s) Selbstvertrauen *nt.*

diffident ['dıfıdənt] *a* schüchtern.

diffuse [dı'fjuːs] *a* langatmig; [dı'fjuːz] *vt* verbreiten.

dig [dıg] *vti irreg* hole graben; *garden* (um)graben; *claws* senken; *n (prod)* Stoß *m*; — **in** *vi (Mil)* sich eingraben; *(to food)* sich hermachen über (+*acc*); — **in!** greif zu!; — **up** *vt* ausgraben; *(fig)* aufgabeln.

digest [daı'dʒest] *vt (lit, fig)* verdauen; ['daıdʒest] *n* Auslese *f*; —**ible** *a* verdaulich; —**ion** Verdauung *f.*

digit ['dıdʒıt] *n* einstellige Zahl *f*; *(Anat)* Finger *m*; Zehe *f*; —**al** **computer** Einzahlencomputer *m.*

dignified ['dıgnıfaıd] *a* würdevoll.

dignify ['dıgnıfaı] *vt* Würde verleihen (+*dat*).

dignitary ['dıgnıtərı] *n* Würdenträger *m.*

dignity ['dıgnıtı] *n* Würde *f.*

digress [daı'gres] *vi* abschweifen; —**ion** [daı'greʃən] Abschweifung *f.*

digs [dıgz] *npl (Brit col)* Bude *f.*

dilapidated [dı'læpıdeıtıd] *a* baufällig.

dilate [daı'leıt] *vti* (sich) weiten.

dilatory ['dılətərı] *a* hinhaltend.

dilemma [daı'lemə] *n* Dilemma *nt.*

dilettante [dılı'tæntı] *n* Dilettant *m.*

diligence ['dılıdʒəns] *n* Fleiß *m.*

diligent ['dılıdʒənt] *a* fleißig.

dill [dıl] *n* Dill *m.*

dilly-dally ['dılıdælı] *vi (col)* herumtrödeln.

dilute [daı'luːt] *vt* verdünnen; *a* verdünnt.

dim [dım] *a* trübe, matt; *(stupid)* schwer von Begriff; *(to take a — view of sth* etw mißbilligen; *vt* verdunkeln.

dime [daım] *(US)* Zehncentstück *nt.*

dimension [dı'menʃən] *n* Dimension *f*; —**s** *pl* Maße *pl.*

diminish [dı'mınıʃ] *vti* verringern.

diminutive [dı'mınjutıv] *a* winzig; *n* Verkleinerungsform *f.*

dimly ['dımlı] *ad* trübe.

dimple ['dımpl] *n* Grübchen *nt.*

dim-witted ['dım'wıtıd] *a (col)* dämlich.

din [dın] *n* Getöse *nt.*

dine [daın] *vi* speisen; —**r** Tischgast *m*; *(Rail)* Speisewagen *m.*

dinghy ['dıŋgı] *n* kleine(s) Ruderboot *nt*; Dinghy *nt.*

dingy ['dındʒı] *a* armselig.

dining car ['daıŋkaː*] *n* Speisewagen *m.*

dining room ['daınıŋrum] *n* Eßzimmer *nt*; *(in hotel)* Speisezimmer *nt.*

dinner ['dınə*] *n* Mittagessen *nt*, Abendessen *nt*; *(public)* Festessen *nt*; — **jacket** Smoking *m*; — **party** Tischgesellschaft *f*; — **time** Tischzeit *f.*

dinosaur ['daınəsɔː*] *n* Dinosaurier *m.*

diocese ['daıəsıs] *n* Diözese *f*, Sprengel *m.*

dip [dıp] *n (hollow)* Senkung *f*; *(bathe)* kurze(s) Bad(en) *nt*; *vt* eintauchen; *(Aut)* abblenden; *vi (slope)* sich senken, abfallen.

diphtheria [dıf'θıərıə] *n* Diphterie *f.*

diphthong ['dıfθɒŋ] *n* Diphthong *m.*

diploma [dı'pləumə] *n* Urkunde *f*, Diplom *nt.*

diplomat ['dıpləmæt] *n* Diplomat(in *f*) *m*; —**ic** [dıplə'mætık] *a* diplo-

matisch; —**ic corps** diplomatische(s) Korps *nt.*

dipstick ['dɪpstɪk] *n* Ölmeßstab *m.*

dire [daɪə*] *a* schrecklich.

direct [daɪ'rekt] *a* direkt; *vt* leiten; *film* die Regie führen (+*gen*) *jury* anweisen; *(aim)* richten, lenken; *(tell way)* den Weg erklären (+*dat*); *(order)* anweisen; — **current** Gleichstrom *m;* — **hit** Volltreffer *m;* —**ion** [dɪ'rekʃən] Richtung *f;* *(Cine)* Regie *f;* —**ions** *pl (for use)* Gebrauchsanleitung *f;* *(orders)* Anweisungen *pl;* —**ional** [dɪ'rekʃənl] *a* Richt-; —**ive** Direktive *f;* —**ly** *ad (in straight line)* gerade, direkt; *(at once)* unmittelbar, sofort; —**or** Direktor *m,* Leiter *m;* *(of film)* Regisseur *m;* —**ory** Adreßbuch *nt;* *(Tel)* Telefonbuch *nt.*

dirt [dɜːt] *n* Schmutz *m,* Dreck *m;* — **road** unbefestigte Straße; —**y** *a* schmutzig, dreckig; gemein; *vt* beschmutzen; — **cheap** *a* spottbillig.

disability [dɪsə'bɪlɪtɪ] *n* Körperbehinderung *f.*

disabled [dɪs'eɪbld] *a* körperbehindert.

disabuse [dɪsə'bjuːz] *vt* befreien.

disadvantage [dɪsəd'vɑːntɪdʒ] *n* Nachteil *m;* —**ous** [dɪsædvɑːn'teɪdʒəs] *a* ungünstig.

disagree [dɪsə'griː] *vi* nicht übereinstimmen; *(quarrel)* (sich) streiten; *(food)* nicht bekommen *(with dat)*; —**able** *a person* widerlich; *task* unangenehm; —**ment** *(between persons)* Streit *m;* *(between things)* Widerspruch *m.*

disallow [dɪsə'laʊ] *vt* nicht zulassen.

disappear [dɪsə'pɪə*] *vi* verschwinden; —**ance** Verschwinden *nt.*

disappoint [dɪsə'pɔɪnt] *vt* enttäuschen; —**ing** *a* enttäuschend; —**ment** Enttäuschung *f.*

disapproval [dɪsə'pruːvəl] *n* Mißbilligung *f.*

disapprove [dɪsə'pruːv] *vi* mißbilligen *(of acc)*; **she** —**s** sie mißbilligt es.

disarm [dɪs'ɑːm] *vt* entwaffnen; *(Pol)* abrüsten; —**ament** Abrüstung *f.*

disaster [dɪ'zɑːstə*] *n* Unglück *nt;* Katastrophe *f.*

disastrous [dɪ'zɑːstrəs] *a* verhängnisvoll.

disband [dɪs'bænd] *vt* auflösen.

disbelief ['dɪsbə'liːf] *n* Ungläubigkeit *f.*

disc [dɪsk] *n* Scheibe *f;* *(record)* (Schall)platte *f.*

discard ['dɪskɑːd] *vt* ablegen.

disc brake ['dɪsk breɪk] *n* Scheibenbremse *f.*

discern [dɪ'sɜːn] *vt* unterscheiden (können), erkennen; —**ing** *a* scharfsinnig.

discharge [dɪs'tʃɑːdʒ] *vt ship* entladen; *duties* nachkommen (+*dat*); *(dismiss)* entlassen; *gun* abschießen; *n (of ship)* Entladung *f;* ['dɪstʃɑːdʒ] *(Med)* Ausfluß *m.*

disciple [dɪ'saɪpl] *n* Jünger *m.*

disciplinary ['dɪsɪplɪnərɪ] *a* disziplinarisch.

discipline ['dɪsɪplɪn] *n* Disziplin *f;* *vt (train)* schulen; *(punish)* bestrafen.

disc jockey ['dɪskdʒɒkɪ] *n* Diskjockey *m.*

disclaim [dɪs'kleɪm] *vt* nicht anerkennen; *(Pol)* dementieren.

disclose [dɪs'kləʊz] vt enthüllen.
disclosure [dɪs'kləʊʒə*] n Enthüllung f.
disco ['dɪskəʊ] n abbr of discotheque.
discoloured [dɪs'kʌləd] a verfärbt, verschossen.
discomfort [dɪs'kʌmfət] n Unbehagen nt; (embarrassment) Verlegenheit f.
disconcert [dɪskən'sɜːt] vt aus der Fassung bringen; (puzzle) verstimmen.
disconnect [dɪskə'nekt] vt abtrennen.
discontent [dɪskən'tent] n Unzufriedenheit f; —ed a unzufrieden.
discontinue ['dɪskən'tɪnjuː] vt einstellen; vi aufhören.
discord ['dɪskɔːd] n Zwietracht f; (noise) Dissonanz f; —ant [dɪs'kɔːdənt] a uneinig; noise mißtönend.
discotheque ['dɪskəʊtek] n Diskothek f.
discount ['dɪskaʊnt] n Rabatt m; [dɪs'kaʊnt] vt außer acht lassen.
discourage [dɪs'kʌrɪdʒ] vt entmutigen; (prevent) abraten, abhalten.
discouraging [dɪs'kʌrɪdʒɪŋ] a entmutigend.
discourteous [dɪs'kɜːtɪəs] a unhöflich.
discover [dɪs'kʌvə*] vt entdecken; —y Entdeckung f.
discredit [dɪs'kredɪt] vt in Verruf bringen.
discreet a, —ly ad [dɪs'kriːt, -lɪ] taktvoll, diskret.
discrepancy [dɪs'krepənsɪ] n Unstimmigkeit f, Diskrepanz f.

discretion [dɪs'kreʃən] n Takt m, Diskretion f; (decision) Gutdünken nt; to leave sth to sb's — etw jds Gutdünken überlassen.
discriminate [dɪs'krɪmɪneɪt] vi unterscheiden; to — against diskriminieren.
discriminating [dɪs'krɪmɪneɪtɪŋ] a klug; taste anspruchsvoll.
discrimination [dɪskrɪmɪ'neɪʃən] n Urteilsvermögen nt; (pej) Diskriminierung f.
discus ['dɪskəs] n Diskus m.
discuss [dɪs'kʌs] vt diskutieren, besprechen; —ion [dɪs'kʌʃən] n Diskussion f, Besprechung f.
disdain [dɪs'deɪn] vt verachten, für Verachtung f; —ful a geringschätzig.
disease [dɪ'ziːz] n Krankheit f; —d a erkrankt.
disembark [dɪsɪm'baːk] vt aussteigen lassen; vi von .Bord gehen.
disenchanted ['dɪsɪn'tʃɑːntɪd] a desillusioniert.
disengage [dɪsɪn'geɪdʒ] vt (Aut) auskuppeln.
disentangle [dɪsɪn'tæŋgl] vt entwirren.
disfavour [dɪs'feɪvə*] n Ungunst f.
disfigure [dɪs'fɪgə*] vt entstellen.
disgrace [dɪs'greɪs] n Schande f; (thing) Schandfleck m; vt Schande bringen über (+acc); (less strong) blamieren; —ful a schändlich, unerhört; it's —ful es ist eine Schande.
disgruntled [dɪs'grʌntld] a verärgert.
disguise [dɪs'gaɪz] vt verkleiden; feelings verhehlen; voice ver-

stellen; n Verkleidung f; in — verkleidet, maskiert.

disgust [dɪsˈɡʌst] n Abscheu f; vt anwidern; **—ing** a abscheulich; (terrible) gemein.

dish [dɪʃ] n Schüssel f; (food) Gericht nt; **— up** vt auftischen; **—cloth** Spüllappen m.

dishearten [dɪsˈhɑːtn] vt entmutigen.

dishevelled [dɪˈʃevəld] a hair zerzaust; clothing ungepflegt.

dishonest [dɪsˈɒnɪst] a unehrlich; **—y** Unehrlichkeit f.

dishonour [dɪsˈɒnə*] n Unehre f; vt cheque nicht einlösen; **—able** a unehrenhaft.

dishwasher [ˈdɪʃwɒʃə*] n Geschirrspülmaschine f.

disillusion [dɪsɪˈluːʒn] vt enttäuschen, desillusionieren.

disinfect [dɪsɪnˈfekt] vt desinfizieren; **—ant** Desinfektionsmittel nt.

disingenuous [dɪsɪnˈdʒenjʊəs] a unehrlich.

disinherit [ˈdɪsɪnˈherɪt] vt enterben.

disintegrate [dɪsˈɪntɪɡreɪt] vi sich auflösen.

disinterested [dɪsˈɪntrɪstɪd] a uneigennützig; (col) uninteressiert.

disjointed [dɪsˈdʒɔɪntɪd] a unzusammenhängend.

disk [dɪsk] n = **disc**.

dislike [dɪsˈlaɪk] n Abneigung f; vt nicht leiden können.

dislocate [ˈdɪsləʊkeɪt] vt auskugeln; (upset) in Verwirrung bringen.

dislodge [dɪsˈlɒdʒ] vt verschieben; (Mil) aus der Stellung werfen.

disloyal [ˈdɪsˈlɔɪəl] a treulos.

dismal [ˈdɪzməl] a trostlos, trübe.

dismantle [dɪsˈmæntl] vt demontieren.

dismay [dɪsˈmeɪ] n Bestürzung f; vt bestürzen.

dismiss [dɪsˈmɪs] vt employee entlassen; idea von sich weisen; (send away) wegschicken; (Jur) complaint abweisen; **—al** Entlassung f.

disobedience [dɪsəˈbiːdɪəns] n Ungehorsam m.

disobedient [dɪsəˈbiːdɪənt] a ungehorsam.

disobey [ˈdɪsəˈbeɪ] vt nicht gehorchen (+dat).

disorder [dɪsˈɔːdə*] n (confusion) Verwirrung f; (commotion) Aufruhr m; (Med) Erkrankung f.

disorderly [dɪsˈɔːdəlɪ] a (untidy) unordentlich; (unruly) ordnungswidrig.

disorganized [dɪsˈɔːɡənaɪzd] a unordentlich.

disown [dɪsˈəʊn] vt son verstoßen; I — you ich will nichts mehr mit dir zu tun haben.

disparaging [dɪsˈpærɪdʒɪŋ] a geringschätzig.

disparity [dɪsˈpærɪtɪ] n Verschiedenheit f.

dispassionate [dɪsˈpæʃnɪt] a gelassen, unparteiisch.

dispatch [dɪsˈpætʃ] vt goods abschicken, abfertigen; n Absendung f; (esp Mil) Meldung f.

dispel [dɪsˈpel] vt zerstreuen.

dispensable [dɪsˈpensəbl] a entbehrlich.

dispensary [dɪsˈpensərɪ] n Apotheke f.

dispensation [dɪspenˈseɪʃən] n (Eccl) Befreiung f.

dispense [dɪsˈpens] vt; — with vt verzichten auf (+acc); **—r** (container) Spender m.

dispensing [dɪs'pensɪŋ] a: — chemist Apotheker m.

dispersal [dɪs'pə:sl] n Zerstreuung f.

disperse [dɪs'pə:s] vt zerstreuen; vi sich verteilen.

dispirited [dɪs'pɪrɪtɪd] a niedergeschlagen.

displace [dɪs'pleɪs] vt verschieben; —d a: — person Verschleppte(r) mf.

display [dɪs'pleɪ] n (of goods) Auslage f; (of feeling) Zurschaustellung f; (Mil) Entfaltung f; vt zeigen, entfalten.

displease [dɪs'pli:z] vt mißfallen (+dat).

displeasure [dɪs'pleʒə*] n Mißfallen nt.

disposable [dɪs'pəuzəbl] a container etc Wegwerf-.

disposal [dɪs'pəuzəl] n (of property) Verkauf m; (throwing away) Beseitigung f; to be at one's — einem zur Verfügung stehen.

dispose [dɪs'pəuz]: — of vt loswerden.

disposed [dɪs'pəuzd] a geneigt.

disposition [dɪspə'zɪʃən] n Wesen nt, Natur f.

disproportionate [dɪsprə'pɔ:ʃnɪt] a unverhältnismäßig.

disprove [dɪs'pru:v] vt widerlegen.

dispute [dɪs'pju:t] n Streit m; vt bestreiten.

disqualification [dɪskwɒlɪfɪ-'keɪʃən] n Disqualifizierung f.

disqualify [dɪs'kwɒlɪfaɪ] vt disqualifizieren.

disquiet [dɪs'kwaɪət] n Unruhe f.

disregard [dɪsrɪ'ga:d] vt nicht (be-)achten.

disreputable [dɪs'repjutəbl] a verrufen.

disrepute ['dɪsrɪ'pju:t] n Verruf m.

disrespectful [dɪsrɪs'pektful] a respektlos.

disrupt ['dɪs'rʌpt] vt stören; programme unterbrechen; —ion [dɪs'rʌpʃən] Störung f, Unterbrechung f.

dissatisfaction ['dɪssætɪs'fækʃən] n Unzufriedenheit f.

dissatisfied ['dɪs'sætɪsfaɪd] a unzufrieden.

dissect [dɪ'sekt] vt zerlegen, sezieren.

disseminate [dɪ'semɪneɪt] vt verbreiten.

dissent [dɪ'sent] n abweichende Meinung f; vi nicht übereinstimmen.

dissident ['dɪsɪdənt] a andersdenkend; n Dissident m.

dissimilar ['dɪ'sɪmɪlə*] a unähnlich (to dat).

dissipate ['dɪsɪpeɪt] vt (waste) verschwenden; (scatter) zerstreuen; —d a ausschweifend.

dissipation [dɪsɪ'peɪʃən] n Ausschweifung f.

dissociate [dɪ'səuʃɪeɪt] vt trennen.

dissolute ['dɪsəlu:t] a liederlich.

dissolve [dɪ'zɒlv] vt auflösen; vi sich auflösen.

dissuade [dɪ'sweɪd] vt abraten (+dat).

distance ['dɪstəns] n Entfernung f; in the — in der Ferne.

distant ['dɪstənt] a entfernt, fern; (with time) fern; (formal) distanziert.

distaste ['dɪs'teɪst] n Abneigung f; —ful a widerlich.

distemper [dɪs'tempə*] n (paint) Temperafarbe f; (Med) Staupe f.

distend [dɪs'tend] vti (sich) ausdehnen.

distil [dɪsˈtɪl] *vt* destillieren; **—lery** Brennerei *f.*

distinct [dɪsˈtɪŋkt] *a* (*separate*) getrennt; (*clear*) klar, deutlich; **—ion** [dɪsˈtɪŋkʃən] Unterscheidung *f*; (*eminence*) Berühmtheit *f*; (*in exam*) Auszeichnung *f*; **—ive** a bezeichnend; **—ly** *ad* deutlich.

distinguish [dɪsˈtɪŋgwɪʃ] *vt* unterscheiden; **—ed** a (*eminent*) berühmt; **—ing** a unterscheidend, bezeichnend.

distort [dɪsˈtɔːt] *vt* verdrehen; (*misrepresent*) entstellen; **—ion** [dɪsˈtɔːʃən] Verzerrung *f.*

distract [dɪsˈtrækt] *vt* ablenken; (*bewilder*) verwirren; **—ing** a verwirrend; **—ion** [dɪsˈtrækʃən] Zerstreutheit *f*; (*distress*) Raserei *f*; (*diversion*) Zerstreuung *f.*

distraught [dɪsˈtrɔːt] a bestürzt.

distress [dɪsˈtres] *n* Not *f*; (*suffering*) Qual *f*; *vt* quälen; **—ing** a erschütternd; **— signal** Notsignal *nt.*

distribute [dɪsˈtrɪbjuːt] *vt* verteilen.

distribution [dɪstrɪˈbjuːʃən] *n* Verteilung *f.*

distributor [dɪsˈtrɪbjutə*] *n* Verteiler *m.*

district [ˈdɪstrɪkt] *n* (*of country*) Kreis *m*; (*of town*) Bezirk *m*; **— attorney** (*US*) Oberstaatsanwalt *m*; **— nurse** (*Brit*) Kreiskrankenschwester *f.*

distrust [dɪsˈtrʌst] *n* Mißtrauen *nt*; *vt* mißtrauen (+*dat*).

disturb [dɪsˈtɜːb] *vt* stören; (*agitate*) erregen; **—ance** Störung *f*; **—ing** a beunruhigend.

disuse [ˈdɪsˈjuːs] *n* Nichtgebrauch *m*; **to fall into —** außer Gebrauch kommen.

disused [ˈdɪsˈjuːzd] a. aufgegeben, außer Gebrauch.

ditch [dɪtʃ] *n* Graben *m*; *vt* im Stich lassen.

dither [ˈdɪðə*] *vi* verdattert sein.

ditto [ˈdɪtəu] *n* dito, ebenfalls.

divan [dɪˈvæn] *n* Liegesofa *nt.*

dive [daɪv] *n* (*into water*) Kopfsprung *m*; (*Aviat*) Sturzflug *m*; *vi* tauchen; **—r** Taucher *m.*

diverge [daɪˈvɜːdʒ] *vi* auseinandergehen.

diverse [daɪˈvɜːs] a verschieden.

diversification [daɪvɜːsɪfɪˈkeɪʃən] *n* Verzweigung *f.*

diversify [daɪˈvɜːsɪfaɪ] *vt* (ver)-ändern; *vi* variieren.

diversion [daɪˈvɜːʃən] *n* Ablenkung *f*; (*traffic*) Umleitung *f.*

diversity [daɪˈvɜːsɪtɪ] *n* Verschiedenheit *f*; (*variety*) Mannigfaltigkeit *f.*

divert [daɪˈvɜːt] *vt* ablenken; *traffic* umleiten.

divide [dɪˈvaɪd] *vt* teilen; *vi* sich teilen.

dividend [ˈdɪvɪdend] *n* Dividende *f*; (*fig*) Gewinn *m.*

divine [dɪˈvaɪn] a göttlich; *vt* erraten.

diving board [ˈdaɪvɪŋbɔːd] *n* Sprungbrett *nt.*

divinity [dɪˈvɪnɪtɪ] *n* Gottheit *f*, Gott *m*; (*subject*) Religion *f.*

divisible [dɪˈvɪzəbl] a teilbar.

division [dɪˈvɪʒən] *n* Teilung *f*; (*Math*) Division *f*, Teilung *f*; (*Mil*) Division *f*; (*part*) Teil *m*, Abteilung *f*; (*in opinion*) Uneinigkeit *f.*

divorce [dɪˈvɔːs] *n* (*Ehe*)scheidung *f*; *vt* scheiden; **—d** a geschieden; **to get —d** sich scheiden lassen; **—e** [dɪvɔːˈsiː] Geschiedene(r) *mf.*

divulge [daɪˈvʌldʒ] *vt* preisgeben.

dizziness [ˈdɪzɪnəs] *n* Schwindelgefühl *nt.*

dizzy ['dɪzɪ] a schwindlig.

do [du:] irreg vt tun, machen; vi (proceed) vorangehen; (be suitable) passen; (be enough) genügen; n (party) Party f; how — you —? guten Tag! etc.

docile ['dəʊsaɪl] a gefügig; etc gutmütig.

dock [dɒk] n Dock nt; (Jur) Anklagebank f; vi ins Dock gehen; —er Hafenarbeiter m.

docket ['dɒkɪt] n Inhaltsvermerk m.

dockyard ['dɒkjɑːd] n Werft f.

doctor ['dɒktə*] n Arzt m, Ärztin f; (Univ) Doktor m.

doctrinaire [dɒktrɪ'nɛə*] a doktrinär.

doctrine ['dɒktrɪn] n Doktrin · f.

document ['dɒkjʊmənt] n Dokument nt; —ary [dɒkjʊ'mentərɪ] Dokumentarbericht m; (film) Dokumentarfilm m; a dokumentarisch; —ation [dɒkjʊmen'teɪʃən] dokumentarische(r) Nachweis m.

doddering ['dɒdərɪŋ], doddery ['dɒdərɪ] a zittrig.

dodge [dɒdʒ] n Kniff m; vt umgehen; ausweichen (+dat); —m Boxauto nt.

dodo ['dəʊdəʊ] n Dronte f: as dead as the — von Anno dazumal.

dog [dɒg] n Hund m; — biscuit Hundekuchen m; — collar Hundehalsband nt; (Eccf) Kragen m des Geistlichen; —eared a mit Eselsohren; —fish Hundsfisch m; — food Hundefutter nt.

dogged ['dɒgɪd] a hartnäckig.

dogma ['dɒgmə] n Dogma nt; —tic [dɒg'mætɪk] a dogmatisch.

doings ['duːɪŋz] npl (activities) Treiben nt.

do-it-yourself ['duːɪtjə'self] n Do-it-yourself nt; a zum Selbermachen.

doldrums ['dɒldrəmz] npl: to be in the — Flaute haben; (person) deprimiert sein.

dole [dəʊl] n (Brit) Stempelgeld nt; to be on the — stempeln gehen; — out vt ausgeben, austeilen.

doleful ['dəʊlfʊl] a traurig.

doll [dɒl] n Puppe f; vt: — o.s. up sich aufdonnern.

dollar ['dɒlə*] n Dollar m.

dollop ['dɒləp] n Brocken m.

dolphin ['dɒlfɪn] n Delphin m, Tümmler m.

domain [dəʊ'meɪn] n Sphäre f, Bereich m.

dome [dəʊm] n Kuppel f.

domestic [də'mestɪk] a häuslich; (within country) Innen-, Binnen-; animal Haus-; —ated a person häuslich; animal zahm.

domicile ['dɒmɪsaɪl] n (ständiger) Wohnsitz m.

dominant ['dɒmɪnənt] a vorherrschend.

dominate ['dɒmɪneɪt] vt beherrschen.

domination [dɒmɪ'neɪʃən] n (Vor)herrschaft f.

domineering [dɒmɪ'nɪərɪŋ] a herrisch, überheblich.

dominion [də'mɪnɪən] n (rule) Regierungsgewalt f; (land) Staatsgebiet nt mit Selbstverwaltung.

dominoes ['dɒmɪnəʊz] n Domino-(spiel) nt.

don [dɒn] n akademische(r) Lehrer m.

donate [dəʊ'neɪt] vt (blood, little money) spenden; (lot of money) stiften.

donation [dəʊ'neɪʃən] n Spende f.

donkey ['dɒŋkɪ] n Esel m.

donor ['dəʊnə*] n Spender m.

don't [dəʊnt] = do not.

doom [du:m] *n* böse(s) Geschick *nt*; (*downfall*) Verderben *nt*; *vt*: to be —ed zum Untergang verurteilt sein.

door [dɔ:*] *n* Tür *f*; —bell Türklingel *f*; —handle Türklinke *f*; —man Türsteher *m*; —mat Fußmatte *f*; —step Türstufe *f*; —way Türöffnung *f*.

dope [dəʊp] *n* (*drug*) Aufputschmittel *nt*.

dopey ['dəʊpɪ] *a* (*col*) bekloppt.

dormant ['dɔ:mənt] *a* schlafend, latent.

dormitory ['dɔ:mɪtrɪ] *n* Schlafsaal *m*.

dormouse ['dɔ:maʊs] *n* Haselmaus *f*.

dosage ['dəʊsɪdʒ] *n* Dosierung *f*.

dose [dəʊs] *n* Dosis *f*; *vt* dosieren.

dossier ['dɒsɪeɪ] *n* Dossier *m*, Aktenbündel *nt*.

dot [dɒt] *n* Punkt *m*; on the —pünktlich.

dote [dəʊt]: to — on *vt* vernarrt sein in (+ *acc*).

double ['dʌbl] *a*, *ad* doppelt; *n* Doppelgänger *m*; *vt* verdoppeln; (*fold*) zusammenfalten; *vi* (*in amount*) sich verdoppeln; at the —im Laufschritt; —s (*tennis*) Doppel *nt*; — bass Kontrabaß *m*; —bed Doppelbett *nt*; —breasted *a* zweireihig; —cross *n* Betrug *m*; *vt* hintergehen; —decker Doppeldecker *m*; — room Doppelzimmer *nt*.

doubly ['dʌblɪ] *ad* doppelt.

doubt [daʊt] *n* Zweifel *m*; *vi* zweifeln; *vt* bezweifeln; without — zweifellos; — ful *a* zweifelhaft, fraglich; —less *ad* ohne Zweifel, sicherlich.

dough [dəʊ] *n* Teig *m*; —nut Krapfen *m*, Pfannkuchen *m*.

dove [dʌv] *n* Taube *f*; —tail *n* Schwalbenschwanz *m*, Zinke *f*; *vt* verzahnen, verzinken.

dowdy ['daʊdɪ] *a* unmodern, schlampig.

down [daʊn] *n* (*fluff*) Flaum *m*; (*hill*) Hügel *m*; *ad* unten; (*motion*) herunter; hinunter; *prep* he came — the street er kam die Straße herunter; to go — the street die Straße hinuntergehen; he lives — the street er wohnt unten an der Straße; *vt* niederschlagen; — with X! nieder mit X!; —-and-out *a* abgerissen; *n* Tramp *m*; —-at-heel *a* schäbig; —cast *a* niedergeschlagen; —fall Sturz *m*; —hearted *a* niedergeschlagen, mutlos; —hill *ad* bergab; —pour Platzregen *m*; —right *a* völlig, ausgesprochen; —stairs *ad* unten; (*motion*) nach unten; *a* untere(r, s); —stream *ad* flußabwärts; —town *ad* in die/der Innenstadt; *a* (*US*) im Geschäftsviertel, City-; —ward *a* sinkend, Abwärts-; —wards *ad* abwärts, nach unten.

dowry ['daʊrɪ] *n* Mitgift *f*.

doze [dəʊz] *vi* dösen; *n* Schläfchen *nt*, Nickerchen *nt*.

dozen ['dʌzn] *n* Dutzend *nt*.

drab [dræb] *a* düster, eintönig.

draft [drɑ:ft] *n* Skizze *f*, Entwurf *m*; (*Fin*) Wechsel *m*; (*US Mil*) Einberufung *f*; *vt* skizzieren.

drag [dræg] *vt* schleifen, schleppen; *river* mit einem Schleppnetz absuchen; *vi* sich (dahin)schleppen; *n* (*bore*) etwas Blödes; (*hindrance*) Klotz *m* am Bein; in — als Tunte; — on *vi* sich in die Länge ziehen.

dragon ['drægən] *n* Drache *m*;
—**fly** Libelle *f*.

drain [dreɪn] *n* (*lit*) Abfluß *m*;
(*ditch*) Abflußgraben *m*; (*fig:
burden*) Belastung *f*; *vt* ableiten;
(*exhaust*) erschöpfen; *vi* (*of water*)
abfließen; —**age** Kanalisation *f*;
—**pipe** Abflußrohr *nt*.

drama ['drɑ:mə] *n* (*lit, fig*) Drama
nt; —**tic** [drə'mætɪk] *a* dramatisch;
—**tist** Dramatiker *m*.

drape [dreɪp] *vt* drapieren; *npl:* —**s**
(*US*) Vorhänge *pl*; —**r** Tuch-
händler *m*.

drastic ['dræstɪk] *a* drastisch.

draught [drɑːft] *n* Zug *m*; (*Naut*)
Tiefgang *m*; —**s** Damespiel *nt*;
(*beer*) on — vom Faß; —**board**
Zeichenbrett *nt*; —**sman** tech-
nische(r) Zeichner *m*; —**y** *a* zugig.

draw [drɔː] *irreg vt* ziehen; *crowd*
anlocken; *picture* zeichnen; *money*
abheben; *water* schöpfen; *vi*
(*Sport*) unentschieden spielen; *n*
(*Sport*) Unentschieden *nt*; (*lottery*)
Ziehung *f*; **to —** **to a close** (*speech*)
zu Ende kommen; (*year*) zu Ende
gehen; — **out** *vi* (*train*) ausfahren;
(*lengthen*) sich hinziehen; *vt
money* abheben; — **up** *vi* (*stop*)
halten; *vt document* aufsetzen;
—**back** (*disadvantage*) Nachteil *m*;
(*obstacle*) Haken *m*; —**bridge** Zug-
brücke *f*; —**er** Schublade *f*; —**ing**
Zeichnung *f*; Zeichnen *nt*; —**ing
pin** Reißzwecke *f*; —**ing room**
Salon·*m*.

drawl [drɔːl] *n* schleppende Sprechweise *f*; *vi* gedehnt sprechen.

drawn [drɔːn] *a game* unentschieden; *face* besorgt.

dread [dred] *n* Furcht *f*, Grauen *nt*;
vt fürchten; sich grauen vor
(+*dat*); —**ful** *a* furchtbar.

dream [driːm] *n* Traum *m*; (*fancy*)
Wunschtraum, *vti irreg* träumen
(*about* von); *a house etc* Traum-;
—**er** Träumer *m*; — **world** Traum-
welt *f*; —**y** *a* verträumt.

dreary ['drɪərɪ] *a* trostlos, öde.

dredge [dredʒ] *vt* ausbaggern;
(*with flour etc*) mit Mehl etc
bestreuen; —**r** Baggerschiff *nt*;
(*for flour etc*) (Mehl etc)streuer *m*.

dregs [dregz] *npl* Bodensatz *m*;
(*fig*) Abschaum *m*.

drench [drentʃ] *vt* durchnässen.

dress [dres] *n* Kleidung *f*; (*garment*) Kleid *nt*; *vt* anziehen; (*Med*)
verbinden; (*Agr*) düngen; *food*
anrichten; **to get ·** —**ed** sich
anziehen; — **up** *vi* sich fein
machen; — **circle** erste(r) Rang *m*;
—**er** (*furniture*) Anrichte *f*,
Geschirrschrank *m*; **she's a smart**
—**er** sie zieht sich elegant an; —**ing**
(*Med*) Verband *m*; (*Cook*) Soße *f*;
—**ing gown** Morgenrock *m*; —**ing
room** (*Theat*) Garderobe *f*; (*Sport*)
Umkleideraum *m*; —**ing table**
Toilettentisch *m*; —**maker** Schnei-
derin *f*; —**making** Schneidern *nt*;
— **rehearsal** Generalprobe *f*; —
shirt Frackhemd *nt*.

dribble ['drɪbl] *vi* tröpfeln; *vt*
sabbern.

drift [drɪft] *n* Trift *f*, Strömung *f*;
(*snow*—) Schneewehe *f*; (*fig*)
Richtung *f*; *vi* getrieben werden;
(*aimlessly*) sich treiben lassen;
—**wood** Treibholz *nt*.

drill [drɪl] *n* Bohrer *m*; (*Mil*) Drill
m; *vt* bohren; (*Mil*) ausbilden; *vi*
(*Mil*) exerzieren; bohren (*for*
nach); —**ing** Bohren *nt*; (*hole*)
Bohrloch *nt*; (*Mil*) Exerzieren *nt*.

drink [drɪŋk] *n* Getränk *nt*; (*spirits*)
Drink *m*; *vti irreg* trinken; —**able**

a trinkbar; —**er** Trinker *m*; —**ing water** Trinkwasser *nt*.

drip [drɪp] *n* Tropfen *m*; (*dripping*) Tröpfeln *nt*; *vi* tropfen; —**dry** *a* bügelfrei; —**ping** Bratenfett *nt*; —**ping wet** *a* triefend.

drive [draɪv] *n* Fahrt *f*; (*road*) Einfahrt *f*; (*campaign*) Aktion *f*; (*energy*) Schwung *m*, Tatkraft *f*; (*Sport*) Schlag *m*; *irreg vt* car fahren; *animals* treiben; *nail* einschlagen; *ball* schlagen; (*power*) antreiben; (*force*) treiben; *vi* fahren; — sb mad jdn verrückt machen; what are you driving at? worauf willst du hinaus?; —**in** *a* Drive-in-.

drivel ['drɪvl] *n* Faselei *f*.

driver ['draɪvə*] *n* Fahrer *m*; —'**s license** (*US*) Führerschein *m*.

driving ['draɪvɪŋ] *a rain* stürmisch; — **instructor** Fahrlehrer *m*; — **lesson** Fahrstunde *f*; — **license** (*Brit*) Führerschein *m*; — **school** Fahrschule *f*; — **test** Fahrprüfung *f*.

drizzle ['drɪzl] *n* Nieselregen *m*; *vi* nieseln.

droll [drəʊl] *a* drollig.

dromedary ['drɒmɪdərɪ] *n* Dromedar *nt*.

drone [drəʊn] *n* (*sound*) Brummen *nt*; (*bee*) Drohne *f*.

drool [druːl] *vi* sabbern.

droop [druːp] *vi* (*schlaff*) herabhängen.

drop [drɒp] *n* (*of liquid*) Tropfen *m*; (*fall*) Fall *m*; *vt* fallen lassen; (*lower*) senken; (*abandon*) fallenlassen; *vi* (*fall*) herunterfallen; — **off** *vi* (*sleep*) einschlafen; — **out** *vi* (*withdraw*) aussteigen; —**out** Ausgeflippte(r) *mf*, Drop-out *mf*.

dross [drɒs] *n* Unrat *m*.

drought [draʊt] *n* Dürre *f*.

drove [drəʊv] *n* (*crowd*) Herde *f*.

drown [draʊn] *vt* ertränken; *sound* übertönen; *vi* ertrinken.

drowsy ['draʊzɪ] *a* schläfrig.

drudge [drʌdʒ] *n* Kuli *m*; —**ry** ['drʌdʒərɪ] Plackerei *f*.

drug [drʌg] *n* (*Med*) Arznei *f*; (*narcotic*) Rauschgift *nt*; *vt* betäuben; — **addict** Rauschgiftsüchtige(r) *mf*; —**gist** (*US*) Drogist *m*; —**store** (*US*) Drogerie *f*.

drum [drʌm] *n* Trommel *f*; —**mer** Trommler *m*.

drunk [drʌŋk] *a* betrunken; *n* Betrunkene(r) *m*; Trinker(in *f*) *m*; —**ard** Trunkenbold *m*; —**en** *a* betrunken; —**enness** Betrunkenheit *f*.

dry [draɪ] *a* trocken; *vt* (ab)trocknen; *vi* trocknen, trocken werden; — **up** *vi* austrocknen; (*dishes*) abtrocknen; —**clean** *vt* chemisch reinigen; —**cleaning** chemische Reinigung *f*; —**er** Trockner *m*; —**ness** Trockenheit *f*; — **rot** Hausschwamm *m*.

dual ['djʊəl] *a* doppelt; — **carriageway** zweispurige Fahrbahn *f*; — **nationality** doppelte Staatsangehörigkeit *f*; —**purpose** *a* Mehrzweck-.

dubbed [dʌbd] *a film* synchronisiert.

dubious ['djuːbɪəs] *a* zweifelhaft.

duchess ['dʌtʃɪs] *n* Herzogin *f*.

duck [dʌk] *n* Ente *f*; *vt* (ein)tauchen; *vi* sich ducken; —**ling** Entchen *nt*.

duct [dʌkt] *n* Röhre *f*.

dud [dʌd] *n* Niete *f*; *a* wertlos, miserabel; *cheque* ungedeckt.

due [djuː] *a* fällig; (*fitting*) angemessen; the train is — der

Zug soll ankommen; n Gebühr f; (right) Recht nt; ad south etc genau, gerade; — to infolge (+gen), wegen (+gen).

duel ['djuəl] n Duell nt.

duet [dju:'et] n Duett nt.

duke [dju:k] n Herzog m.

dull [dʌl] a colour, weather trübe; (stupid) schwer von Begriff; (boring) langweilig; vt (soften, weaken) abstumpfen.

duly ['dju:lɪ] ad ordnungsgemäß, richtig; (on time) pünktlich.

dumb [dʌm] a (lit) stumm; (col: stupid) doof, blöde.

dummy ['dʌmɪ] n Schneiderpuppe f; (substitute) Attrappe f; (teat) Schnuller m; a Schein-.

dump [dʌmp] n Abfallhaufen m; (Mil) Stapelplatz m; (col: place) Nest nt; vt abladen, auskippen; —ing (Comm) Schleuderexport m; (of rubbish) Schuttabladen nt.

dumpling ['dʌmplɪŋ] n Kloß m, Knödel m.

dunce [dʌns] n Dummkopf m.

dune [dju:n] n Düne f.

dung [dʌŋ] n Mist m; (Agr) Dünger m.

dungarees [dʌŋgə'ri:z] npl Arbeitsanzug m, Arbeitskleidung pl.

dungeon ['dʌndʒən] n Kerker m.

dupe [dju:p] n Gefoppte(r) m; vt hintergehen, anführen.

duplicate ['dju:plɪkɪt] a doppelt; n Duplikat nt; ['dju:plɪkeɪt] vt verdoppeln; (make copies) kopieren; **in** — in doppelter Ausführung.

duplicator ['dju:plɪkeɪtə*] n Vervielfältigungsapparat m.

durability [djuərə'bɪlɪtɪ] n Haltbarkeit f.

durable ['djuərəbl] a haltbar.

duration [djuə'reɪʃən] n Dauer f.

during ['djuərɪŋ] prep während (+gen).

dusk [dʌsk] n Abenddämmerung f.

dust [dʌst] n Staub m; vt abstauben; (sprinkle) bestäuben; —bin (Brit) Mülleimer m; —er Staubtuch nt; —man (Brit) Müllmann m; — storm Staubsturm m; —y a staubig.

dutiable ['dju:tɪəbl] a zollpflichtig.

duty ['dju:tɪ] n Pflicht f; (job) Aufgabe f; (tax) Einfuhrzoll m; on — im Dienst, diensthabend; —free a zollfrei; —free articles zollfreie Waren pl.

dwarf [dwɔ:f] n Zwerg m.

dwell [dwel] vi irreg wohnen; — on vt verweilen bei; —ing Wohnung f.

dwindle ['dwɪndl] vi schwinden.

dye [daɪ] n Farbstoff m; vt färben.

dying ['daɪŋ] a person sterbend; moments letzt.

dynamic [daɪ'næmɪk] a dynamisch; —s Dynamik f.

dynamite ['daɪnəmaɪt] n Dynamit nt.

dynamo ['daɪnəməu] n Dynamo m.

dynasty ['dɪnəstɪ] n Dynastie f.

dysentery ['dɪsntrɪ] n Ruhr f.

dyspepsia [dɪs'pepsɪə] n Verdauungsstörung f.

E

E, e [i:] *n* E *nt*, e *nt*.

each [i:tʃ] *a* jeder/jede/jedes; *pron* (ein) jeder/(eine) jede/(ein) jedes; — **other** einander, sich.

eager *a*, —**ly** *ad* [i:gə*, -li] eifrig; —**ness** Eifer *m*; Ungeduld *f*.

eagle [i:gl] *n* Adler *m*.

ear [ɪə*] *n* Ohr *nt*; (*of corn*) Ähre *f*; —**ache** Ohrenschmerzen *pl*; —**drum** Trommelfell *nt*.

earl [ɜːl] *n* Graf *m*.

early [ɜ:lɪ] *a, ad* früh; **you're** — du bist früh dran.

earmark [ɪəma:k] *vt* vorsehen.

earn [ɜ:n] *vt* verdienen.

earnest [ɜ:nɪst] *a* ernst; **in** — im Ernst.

earnings [ɜ:nɪŋz] *npl* Verdienst *m*.

earphones [ɪəfəʊnz] *npl* Kopfhörer *pl*.

earplug [ɪəplʌg] *n* Ohropax ® *nt*.

earring [ɪərɪŋ] *n* Ohrring *m*.

earshot [ɪəʃɒt] *n* Hörweite *f*.

earth [ɜ:θ] *n* Erde *f*; (*Elec*) Erdung *f*; *vt* erden; —**enware** Steingut *nt*; —**quake** Erdbeben *nt*.

earthy [ɜ:θɪ] *a* roh; (*sensual*) sinnlich.

earwig [ɪəwɪg] *n* Ohrwurm *m*.

ease [i:z] *n* (*simplicity*) Leichtigkeit *f*; (*social*) Ungezwungenheit *f*; *vt* (*pain*) lindern; *burden* erleichtern; **at** — ungezwungen; (*Mil*) rührt euch!; **to feel at** — sich wohl fühlen; — **off** *or* **up** *vi* nachlassen.

easel [i:zl] *n* Staffelei *f*.

easily [i:zɪlɪ] *ad* leicht.

east [i:st] *n* Osten *m*; *a* östlich; *ad* nach Osten.

Easter [i:stə*] *n* Ostern *nt*.

eastern [i:stən] *a* östlich; orientalisch.

eastward(s) [i:stwəd(z)] *ad* ostwärts.

easy [i:zɪ] *a* (*task*) einfach; *life* bequem; *manner* ungezwungen, natürlich; *ad* leicht.

eat [i:t] *vt irreg* essen; (*animals*) fressen; (*destroy*) (zer)fressen; — **away** *vt* (*corrode*) zerfressen; —**able** *a* genießbar.

eaves [i:vz] *npl* (überstehender) Dachrand *m*.

eavesdrop [i:vzdrɒp] *vi* horchen, lauschen; **to** — **on sb** jdn belauschen.

ebb [eb] *n* Ebbe *f*; *vi* ebben.

ebony [ebənɪ] *n* Ebenholz *nt*.

ebullient [ɪbʌliənt] *a* sprudelnd, temperamentvoll.

eccentric [ɪksentrɪk] *a* exzentrisch, überspannt; *n* exzentrische(r) Mensch *m*.

ecclesiastical [ɪkli:zɪˈæstɪkəl] *a* kirchlich, geistlich.

echo [ekəʊ] *n* Echo *nt*; *vt* zurückwerfen; (*fig*) nachbeten; *vi* widerhallen.

eclipse [ɪklɪps] *n* Verfinsterung *f*, Finsternis *f*; *vt* verfinstern.

ecology [ɪkɒlədʒɪ] *n* Ökologie *f*.

economic [i:kəˈnɒmɪk] *a* (volks)-wirtschaftlich, ökonomisch; —**al** *a* wirtschaftlich; *person* sparsam; —**s** Volkswirtschaft *f*.

economize [ɪ'kɒnəmaɪz] vi sparen (on an +dat).

economy [ɪ'kɒnəmɪ] n (thrift) Sparsamkeit f; (of country) Wirtschaft f.

ecstasy ['ekstəsɪ] n Ekstase f.

ecstatic [eks'tætɪk] a hingerissen.

ecumenical [iːkjuːˈmenɪkəl] a ökumenisch.

eczema ['eksɪmə] n Ekzem nt.

Eden ['iːdn] n (Garten m) Eden nt.

edge [edʒ] n Rand m; (of knife) Schneide f; on — nervös; (nerves) überreizt.

edging ['edʒɪŋ] n Einfassung f.

edgy ['edʒɪ] a nervös.

edible ['edɪbl] a eßbar.

edict ['iːdɪkt] n Erlaß m.

edifice ['edɪfɪs] n Gebäude nt.

edit ['edɪt] vt edieren, redigieren; —ion [ɪ'dɪʃən] Ausgabe f; —or (of newspaper) Redakteur m; (of book) Lektor m; —orial [edɪ'tɔːrɪəl] a Redaktions-; n Leitartikel m.

educate ['edjukeɪt] vt erziehen, (aus)bilden.

education [edjuˈkeɪʃən] n (teaching) Unterricht m; (system) Schulwesen nt; (schooling) Erziehung f; Bildung f; —al a pädagogisch.

eel [iːl] n Aal m.

eerie ['ɪərɪ] a unheimlich.

efface [ɪ'feɪs] vt auslöschen.

effect [ɪ'fekt] n Wirkung f; vt bewirken; in — in der Tat; —s pl (sound, visual) Effekte pl; —ive a wirksam, effektiv.

effeminate [ɪ'femɪnɪt] a weiblich.

effervescent [efəˈvesnt] a (lit, fig) sprudelnd.

efficiency [ɪ'fɪʃənsɪ] n Leistungsfähigkeit f.

efficient a, —ly ad [ɪ'fɪʃənt, -lɪ]

tüchtig; (Tech) leistungsfähig; method wirksam.

effigy ['efɪdʒɪ] n Abbild nt.

effort ['efət] n Anstrengung f; to make an — sich anstrengen; —less a mühelos.

effrontery [ɪ'frʌntərɪ] n Unverfrorenheit f.

egalitarian [ɪgælɪ'tɛərɪən] a Gleichheits-, egalitär.

egg [eg] n Ei nt; — on vt anstacheln; —cup Eierbecher m; —plant Aubergine f; —shell Eierschale f.

ego ['iːgəu] n Ich nt, Selbst nt.

egotism ['egəutɪzəm] n Ichbezogenheit f.

egotist ['egəutɪst] n Egozentriker m.

eiderdown ['aɪdədaun] n Daunendecke f.

eight [eɪt] num acht; —een num achtzehn; —h [eɪtθ] a achte(r,s); n Achtel nt; —y num achtzig.

either ['aɪðə*] cj — ... or entweder ... oder; pron — of the two eine(r,s) von beiden; I don't want — ich will keins von beiden; a on — side auf beiden Seiten; ad I don't — ich auch nicht.

eject [ɪ'dʒekt] vt ausstoßen, vertreiben; — or seat Schleudersitz m.

elaborate [ɪ'læbərɪt] a sorgfältig ausgearbeitet, ausführlich; [ɪ'læbəreɪt] vt sorgfältig ausarbeiten; —ly ad genau, ausführlich.

elaboration [ɪlæbəˈreɪʃən] n Ausarbeitung f.

elapse [ɪ'læps] vi vergehen.

elastic [ɪ'læstɪk] n Gummiband nt; a elastisch; —band Gummiband nt.

elated [ɪ'leɪtɪd] a froh, in gehobener Stimmung.

elation [ɪ'leɪʃən] *n* gehobene Stimmung *f.*

elbow ['elbəʊ] *n* Ellbogen *m.*

elder ['eldə*] *a* älter; *n* Ältere(r) *mf;* **—ly** *a* ältere(r,s).

elect [ɪ'lekt] *vt* wählen; *a* zukünftig; **—ion** Wahl *f;* **—ioneering** [ɪlekʃə'nɪərɪŋ] Wahlpropaganda *f;* **—or** Wähler *m;* **—oral** *a* Wahl-; **—orate** Wähler *pl,* Wählerschaft *f.*

electric [ɪ'lektrɪk] *a* elektrisch, Elektro-; **—al** *a* elektrisch; **— blanket** Heizdecke *f;* **— chair** elektrische(r) Stuhl *m;* **— cooker** Elektroherd *m;* **— current** elektrische(r) Strom *m;* **— fire** elektrische(r) Heizofen *m;* **—ian** [ɪlek'trɪʃən] Elektriker *m;* **—ity** [ɪlek'trɪsɪtɪ] Elektrizität *f.*

electrification [ɪlektrɪfɪ'keɪʃən] *n* Elektrifizierung *f.*

electrify [ɪ'lektrɪfaɪ] *vt* elektrifizieren; *(fig)* elektrisieren.

electro- [ɪ'lektrəʊ] *pref* Elektro-.

electrocute [ɪ'lektrəʊkjuːt] *vt* elektrisieren; durch elektrischen Strom töten.

electrode [ɪ'lektrəʊd] *n* Elektrode *f.*

electron [ɪ'lektrɒn] *n* Elektron *nt.*

electronic [ɪlek'trɒnɪk] *a* elektronisch, Elektronen-; **—s** Elektronik *f.*

elegance ['elɪgəns] *n* Eleganz *f.*

elegant ['elɪgənt] *a* elegant.

elegy ['elɪdʒɪ] *n* Elegie *f.*

element ['elɪmənt] *n* Element *nt; (fig)* Körnchen *nt;* **—ary** [elɪ'mentərɪ] *a* einfach; *(primary)* grundlegend, Anfangs-.

elephant ['elɪfənt] *n* Elefant *m.*

elevate ['elɪveɪt] *vt* emporheben.

elevation [elɪ'veɪʃən] *n (height)* Erhebung *f; (of style)* Niveau *nt; (Archit)* (Quer)schnitt *m.*

elevator ['elɪveɪtə*] *n (US)* Fahrstuhl *m,* Aufzug *m.*

eleven [ɪ'levn] *num* elf; *n (team)* Elf *f.*

elf [elf] *n* Elfe *f.*

elicit [ɪ'lɪsɪt] *vt* herausbekommen.

eligible ['elɪdʒəbl] *a* wählbar; he's not — er kommt nicht in Frage; to be — for a pension/competition pensions-/teilnahmeberechtigt sein; — bachelor gute Partie *f.*

eliminate [ɪ'lɪmɪneɪt] *vt* ausschalten; beseitigen.

elimination [ɪlɪmɪ'neɪʃən] *n* Ausschaltung *f;* Beseitigung *f.*

elite [eɪ'liːt] *n* Elite *f.*

elm [elm] *n* Ulme *f.*

elocution [elə'kjuːʃən] *n* Sprecherziehung *f; (clarity)* Artikulation *f.*

elongated ['iːlɒŋgeɪtɪd] *a* verlängert.

elope [ɪ'ləʊp] *vi* entlaufen; **—ment** Entlaufen *nt.*

eloquence ['eləkwəns] *n* Beredsamkeit *f.*

eloquent *a,* **—ly** *ad* ['eləkwənt, -lɪ] redegewandt.

else [els] *ad* sonst; **—where** *ad* anderswo, woanders; who —? wer sonst?; sb — jd anders; or — sonst.

elucidate [ɪ'luːsɪdeɪt] *vt* erläutern.

elude [ɪ'luːd] *vt* entgehen (+ *dat*).

elusive [ɪ'luːsɪv] *a* schwer faßbar.

emaciated [ɪ'meɪsɪeɪtɪd] *a* abgezehrt.

emanate ['eməneɪt] *vi* ausströmen *(from* aus).

emancipate [ɪ'mænsɪpeɪt] *vt* emanzipieren; *slave* freilassen.

emancipation [ɪmænsɪ'peɪʃən] *n* Emanzipation *f;* Freilassung *f.*

embalm [ɪm'bɑːm] *vt* einbalsamieren.

embankment [ɪmˈbæŋkmənt] n (of river) Uferböschung f; (of road) Straßendamm m.

embargo [ɪmˈbɑːgəʊ] n Embargo nt.

embark [ɪmˈbɑːk] vi sich einschiffen; — on vt unternehmen; —ation [embɑːˈkeɪʃən] Einschiffung f.

embarrass [ɪmˈbærəs] vt in Verlegenheit bringen; —ed a verlegen; —ing a peinlich; —ment Verlegenheit f.

embassy [ˈembəsɪ] n Botschaft f.

embed [ɪmˈbed] vt einbetten.

embellish [ɪmˈbelɪʃ] vt verschönern.

embers [ˈembəz] npl Glut(asche) f.

embezzle [ɪmˈbezl] vt unterschlagen; —ment Unterschlagung f.

embitter [ɪmˈbɪtə*] vt verbittern.

emblem [ˈembləm] n Emblem nt, Abzeichen nt.

embodiment [ɪmˈbɒdɪmənt] n Verkörperung f.

embody [ɪmˈbɒdɪ] vt ideas verkörpern; new features (in sich) vereinigen.

emboss [ɪmˈbɒs] vt prägen.

embrace [ɪmˈbreɪs] vt umarmen; (include) einschließen; n Umarmung f.

embroider [ɪmˈbrɔɪdə*] vt (be)sticken; story ausschmücken; —y Stickerei f.

embryo [ˈembrɪəʊ] n (lit) Embryo m; (fig) Keim m.

emerald [ˈemərəld] n Smaragd nt; a smaragdgrün.

emerge [ɪˈmɜːdʒ] vi auftauchen; (truth) herauskommen; —nce Erscheinen nt; —ncy n Notfall m; a action Not-; —ncy exit Notausgang m.

emery [ˈeməri] nt: — paper Schmirgelpapier nt.

emetic [ɪˈmetɪk] n Brechmittel nt.

emigrant [ˈemɪgrənt] n Auswanderer m, Emigrant m; a Auswanderungs-.

emigrate [ˈemɪgreɪt] vi auswandern, emigrieren.

emigration [emɪˈgreɪʃən] n Auswanderung f, Emigration f.

eminence [ˈemɪnəns] n hohe(r) Rang m; E— Eminenz f.

eminent [ˈemɪnənt] a bedeutend.

emission [ɪˈmɪʃən] n (of gases) Ausströmen nt.

emit [ɪˈmɪt] vt von sich (dat) geben.

emotion [ɪˈməʊʃən] n Emotion f, Gefühl nt; —al a person emotional; scene ergreifend; —ally ad gefühlsmäßig; behave emotional; sing ergreifend.

emotive [ɪˈməʊtɪv] a gefühlsbetont.

emperor [ˈempərə*] n Kaiser m.

emphasis [ˈemfəsɪs] n (Ling) Betonung f; (fig) Nachdruck m.

emphasize [ˈemfəsaɪz] vt betonen.

emphatic a, —ally ad [ɪmˈfætɪk, -əlɪ] nachdrücklich; to be — about sth etw nachdrücklich betonen.

empire [ˈempaɪə*] n Reich nt.

empirical [emˈpɪrɪkəl] a empirisch.

employ [ɪmˈplɔɪ] vt (hire) anstellen; (use) verwenden; —ee [emplɔɪˈiː] Angestellte(r) mf; —er Arbeitgeber(in f) m; —ment Beschäftigung f; in —ment beschäftigt.

empress [ˈempris] n Kaiserin f.

emptiness [ˈemptɪnɪs] n Leere f.

empty [ˈemptɪ] a leer; vt contents leeren; container ausleeren; — handed a mit leeren Händen.

emu [ˈiːmjuː] n Emu m.

emulate [ˈemjʊleɪt] vt nacheifern (+ dat).

enable [ɪ'neɪbl] vt ermöglichen; it —s us to ... das ermöglicht es uns, zu ...

enamel [ɪ'næməl] n Email nt; (of teeth) (Zahn)schmelz m.

enamoured [ɪ'næməd] a verliebt sein (of, in + dat).

encase [ɪn'keɪs] vt einschließen; (Tech) verschalen.

enchant [ɪn'tʃɑ:nt] vt bezaubern; —ing a entzückend.

encircle [ɪn's3:kl] vt umringen.

enclose [ɪn'kləʊz] vt einschließen; (in letter) beilegen (in, with dat); —d (in letter) beiliegend, anbei.

enclosure [ɪn'kləʊʒə*] n Einfriedung f; (in letter) Anlage f.

encore ['ɒŋkɔ:*] n Zugabe f; —! da capo!

encounter [ɪn'kaʊntə*] n Begegnung f; (Mil) Zusammenstoß m; vt treffen; resistance stoßen auf (+ acc).

encourage [ɪn'kʌrɪdʒ] vt ermutigen; —ment Ermutigung f, Förderung f.

encouraging [ɪn'kʌrɪdʒɪŋ] a ermutigend, vielversprechend.

encroach [ɪn'krəʊtʃ] vi eindringen ((up)on in + acc), überschreiten ((up)on acc).

encyclop(a)edia [ensaɪkləʊ'pi:dɪə] n Konversationslexikon nt.

end [end] n Ende nt, Schluß m; (purpose) Zweck m; a End-; vt beenden; vi zu Ende gehen; — up vi landen.

endanger [ɪn'deɪndʒə*] vt gefährden.

endeavour [ɪn'devə*] n Bestrebung f; vi sich bemühen.

ending ['endɪŋ] n Ende nt.

endless ['endlɪs] a endlos; plain unendlich.

endorse [ɪn'dɔ:s] vt unterzeichnen; (approve) unterstützen; —ment Bestätigung f; (of document) Unterzeichnung f; (of licence) Eintrag m.

endow [ɪn'daʊ] vt: — sb with sth jdm etw verleihen; (with money) jdm etw stiften.

end product ['endprɒdʌkt] n Endprodukt nt.

endurable [ɪn'djʊərəbl] a erträglich.

endurance [ɪn'djʊərəns] n Ausdauer f; (suffering) Ertragen nt.

endure [ɪn'djʊə*] vt ertragen; vi (last) (fort)dauern.

enemy ['enɪmɪ] n Feind m; a feindlich.

energetic [enə'dʒetɪk] a tatkräftig.

energy ['enədʒɪ] n (of person) Energie f, Tatkraft f; (Phys) Energie f.

enervating ['en3:veɪtɪŋ] a nervenaufreibend.

enforce [ɪn'fɔ:s] vt durchsetzen; obedience erzwingen.

engage [ɪn'geɪdʒ] vt (employ) einstellen; (in conversation) verwickeln; (Mil) angreifen; (Tech) einrasten lassen, einschalten; —d a verlobt; (Tel, toilet) besetzt; (busy) beschäftigt, unabkömmlich; to get —d sich verloben; —ment (appointment) Verabredung f; (to marry) Verlobung f; (Mil) Gefecht nt; —ment ring Verlobungsring m.

engaging [ɪn'geɪdʒɪŋ] a gewinnend.

engender [ɪn'dʒendə*] vt hervorrufen.

engine ['endʒɪn] n (Aut) Motor m; (Rail) Lokomotive f; —er [endʒɪnɪə*] Ingenieur m; (US Rail) Lokomotivführer m; —ering [endʒɪ'nɪərɪŋ] Technik f; Maschinenbau m; — failure, — trouble Maschinenschaden m; (Aut) Motorschaden m.

engrave [ɪn'greɪv] vt (carve) einschneiden; (fig) tief einprägen; (print) gravieren.

engraving [ɪn'greɪvɪŋ] n Stich m.

engrossed [ɪn'grəʊst] a vertieft.

engulf [ɪn'gʌlf] vt verschlingen.

enhance [ɪn'hɑːns] vt steigern, heben.

enigma [ɪ'nɪgmə] n Rätsel nt; —tic [enɪg'mætɪk] a rätselhaft.

enjoy [ɪn'dʒɔɪ] vt genießen; privilege besitzen; —able a erfreulich; —ment Genuß m, Freude f.

enlarge [ɪn'lɑːdʒ] vt erweitern; (Phot) vergrößern; to — on sth etw weiter ausführen; —ment Vergrößerung f.

enlighten [ɪn'laɪtn] vt aufklären; —ment Aufklärung f.

enlist [ɪn'lɪst] vt gewinnen; vi (Mil) sich melden.

enmity ['enmɪtɪ] n Feindschaft f.

enormity [ɪ'nɔːmɪtɪ] n Ungeheuerlichkeit f.

enormous a, —ly ad [ɪ'nɔːməs, -lɪ] ungeheuer.

enough [ɪ'nʌf] a genug; ad genug, genügend; —! genug!; that's —! das reicht!

enquire [ɪn'kwaɪə*] = inquire.

enrich [ɪn'rɪtʃ] vt bereichern.

enrol [ɪn'rəʊl] vt (Mil) anwerben; vi (register) sich anmelden; —ment (for course) Anmeldung f; (Univ) Einschreibung f.

en route [ɑ:n'ruːt] ad unterwegs.

ensign ['ensaɪn] n (Naut) Flagge f; (Mil) Fähnrich m.

enslave [ɪn'sleɪv] vt versklaven.

ensue [ɪn'sjuː] vi folgen, sich ergeben.

ensuing [ɪn'sjuːɪŋ] a (nach)folgend.

ensure [ɪn'ʃʊə*] vt garantieren.

entail [ɪn'teɪl] vt mit sich bringen.

enter ['entə*] vt eintreten in (+dat), betreten; club beitreten (+dat); (in book) eintragen; vi hereinkommen, hineingehen; — for vt sich beteiligen an (+dat); — into vt agreement eingehen; — argument sich einlassen auf (+acc); — upon vt beginnen.

enterprise ['entəpraɪz] n (in person) Initiative f, Unternehmungsgeist m; (Comm) Unternehmen nt, Betrieb m.

enterprising ['entəpraɪzɪŋ] a unternehmungslustig.

entertain [entə'teɪn] vt guest bewirten; (amuse) unterhalten; —er Unterhaltungskünstler(in f) m; —ing a unterhaltend, amüsant; —ment (amusement) Unterhaltung f; (show) Veranstaltung f.

enthralled [ɪn'θrɔːld] a gefesselt.

enthusiasm [ɪn'θuːzɪæzəm] n Begeisterung f.

enthusiast [ɪn'θuːzɪæst] n Enthusiast m, Schwärmer(in f) m; —ic [ɪnθuːzɪ'æstɪk] a begeistert.

entice [ɪn'taɪs] vt verleiten, locken.

entire [ɪn'taɪə*] a ganz; —ly ad ganz, völlig; —ty [ɪn'taɪərətɪ] n: in its —ty in seiner Gesamtheit.

entitle [ɪn'taɪtl] vt (allow) berechtigen; (name) betiteln.

entity ['entɪtɪ] n Ding nt, Wesen nt.

entrance ['entrəns] n Eingang m; (entering) Eintritt m; [ɪn'trɑːns] vt hinreißen; — examination Aufnahmeprüfung f; — fee Eintrittsgeld nt.

entrancing [ɪn'trɑːnsɪŋ] a bezaubernd.

entrant ['entrənt] n (for exam) Kandidat m; (into job) Anfänger m; (Mil) Rekrut m; (in race) Teilnehmer m.

entreat [ɪn'tri:t] *vt* anflehen, beschwören; —y flehende Bitte *f*, Beschwörung *f*.

entrée ['ɔntreɪ] *n* Zwischengang *m*.

entrenched [ɪn'trentʃt] *a* (*fig*) verwurzelt.

entrust [ɪn'trʌst] *vt* anvertrauen (*sb with sth* jdm etw.).

entry ['entrɪ] *n* Eingang *m*; (*Theat*) Auftritt *m*; (*in account*) Eintragung *f*; (*in dictionary*) Eintrag *m*; 'no —' 'Eintritt verboten'; (*for cars*) 'Einfahrt verboten'; — **form** Anmeldeformular *nt*.

enunciate [ɪ'nʌnsɪeɪt] *vt* (deutlich) aussprechen.

envelop [ɪn'veləp] *vt* einhüllen; —e ['envələup] *n* Umschlag *m*.

enviable ['envɪəbl] *a* beneidenswert.

envious ['envɪəs] *a* neidisch.

environment [ɪn'vaɪərənmənt] *n* Umgebung *f*; (*ecology*) Umwelt *f*; —al [ɪnvaɪərən'mentl] *a* Umwelt-.

envisage [ɪn'vɪzɪdʒ] *vt* sich (*dat*) vorstellen; (*plan*) ins Auge fassen.

envoy ['envɔɪ] *n* Gesandte(r) *mf*.

envy ['envɪ] *n* Neid *m*; (*object*) Gegenstand *m* des Neides; *vt* beneiden (*sb sth* jdn um etw.).

enzyme ['enzaɪm] *n* Enzym *nt*.

ephemeral [ɪ'femərəl] *a* kurzlebig, vorübergehend.

epic ['epɪk] *n* Epos *nt*; (*film*) Großfilm *m*; *a* episch; (*fig*) heldenhaft.

epidemic [epɪ'demɪk] *n* Epidemie *f*.

epigram ['epɪgræm] *n* Epigramm *nt*.

epilepsy ['epɪlepsɪ] *n* Epilepsie *f*.

epileptic [epɪ'leptɪk] *a* epileptisch; *n* Epileptiker(in *f*) *m*.

epilogue ['epɪlɔg] *n* (*of drama*) Epilog *m*; (*of book*) Nachwort *nt*.

episode ['epɪsəud] *n* (*incident*) Vorfall *m*; (*story*) Episode *f*.

epistle [ɪ'pɪsl] *n* Brief *m*.

epitaph ['epɪtɑ:f] *n* Grab(in)schrift *f*.

epitome [ɪ'pɪtəmɪ] *n* Inbegriff *m*.

epitomize [ɪ'pɪtəmaɪz] *vt* verkörpern.

epoch ['i:pɒk] *n* Epoche *f*.

equable ['ekwəbl] *a* ausgeglichen.

equal ['i:kwl] *a* gleich; — **to** the task der Aufgabe gewachsen; *n* Gleichgestellte(r) *mf*; *vt* gleichkommen (+*dat*); **two times two —s** four zwei mal zwei ist (gleich) vier; **without** — ohne seinesgleichen; —**ity** [ɪ'kwɒlɪtɪ] Gleichheit *f*; (*equal rights*) Gleichberechtigung *f*; —**ize** *vt* gleichmachen; *vi* (*Sport*) ausgleichen; —**izer** (*Sport*) Ausgleich(streffer) *m*; —**ly** *ad* gleich; —**s sign** Gleichheitszeichen *nt*.

equanimity [ekwə'nɪmɪtɪ] *n* Gleichmut *m*.

equate [ɪ'kweɪt] *vt* gleichsetzen.

equation [ɪ'kweɪʒən] *n* Gleichung *f*.

equator [ɪ'kweɪtə*] *n* Äquator *m*; —**ial** [ekwə'tɔ:rɪəl] *a* Äquator-.

equilibrium [i:kwɪ'lɪbrɪəm] *n* Gleichgewicht *nt*.

equinox ['i:kwɪnɒks] *n* Tag- und Nachtgleiche *f*.

equip [ɪ'kwɪp] *vt* ausrüsten; —**ment** Ausrüstung *f*; (*Tech*) Gerät *nt*.

equitable ['ekwɪtəbl] *a* gerecht, billig.

equity ['ekwɪtɪ] *n* Billigkeit *f*, Gerechtigkeit *f*.

equivalent [ɪ'kwɪvələnt] *a* gleichwertig (*to dat*), entsprechend (*to dat*); *n* (*amount*) gleiche Menge *f*; (*in money*) Gegenwert *m*; Äquivalent *nt*.

equivocal [ɪ'kwɪvəkəl] *a* zweideutig; (*suspect*) fragwürdig.

era ['ɪərə] n Epoche f, Ära f.

eradicate [ɪ'rædɪkeɪt] vt ausrotten.

erase [ɪ'reɪz] vt ausradieren; *tape* löschen; **—r** Radiergummi m.

erect [ɪ'rekt] a aufrecht; vt errichten; **—ion** Errichtung f; (*Physiol*) Erektion f.

ermine ['ɜ:mɪn] n Hermelin(pelz) m.

erode [ɪ'rəud] vt zerfressen; *land* auswaschen.

erosion [ɪ'rəuʒən] n Auswaschen nt, Erosion f.

erotic [ɪ'rɒtɪk] a erotisch; **—ism** [ɪ'rɒtɪsɪzəm] Erotik f.

err [ɜ:*] vi sich irren.

errand ['erənd] n Besorgung f; **—boy** Laufbursche m.

erratic [ɪ'rætɪk] a sprunghaft; *driving* unausgeglichen.

erroneous [ɪ'rəunɪəs] a irrig, irrtümlich.

error ['erə*] n Fehler m.

erudite ['erudaɪt] a gelehrt.

erudition [eru'dɪʃən] n Gelehrsamkeit f.

erupt [ɪ'rʌpt] vi ausbrechen; **—ion** Ausbruch m.

escalate ['eskəleɪt] vt steigern; vi sich steigern.

escalator ['eskəleɪtə*] n Rolltreppe f.

escapade ['eskəpeɪd] n Eskapade f, Streich m.

escape [ɪs'keɪp] n Flucht f; (*of gas*) Entweichen nt; vti entkommen (+*dat*); (*prisoners*) fliehen; (*leak*) entweichen; **to — notice** unbemerkt bleiben; **the word —s me** das Wort ist mir entfallen.

escapism [ɪs'keɪpɪzəm] n Flucht f (vor der Wirklichkeit).

escort ['eskɔ:t] n (*person accompanying*) Begleiter m; (*guard*)

Eskorte f; [ɪs'kɔ:t] vt *lady* begleiten; (*Mil*) eskortieren.

especially [ɪs'peʃəlɪ] ad besonders.

espionage ['espɪənɑ:ʒ] n Spionage f.

esplanade ['espləneɪd] n Esplanade f, Promenade f.

Esquire [ɪs'kwaɪə*] n (*in address*) J. Brown, Esq Herrn J. Brown.

essay ['eseɪ] n Aufsatz m; (*Liter*) Essay m.

essence ['esəns] n (*quality*) Wesen nt; (*extract*) Essenz f, Extrakt m.

essential [ɪ'senʃəl] a (*necessary*) unentbehrlich; (*basic*) wesentlich; n Hauptbestandteil m, Allernötigste(s) nt; **—ly** ad in der Hauptsache, eigentlich.

establish [ɪs'tæblɪʃ] vt (*set up*) gründen, einrichten; (*prove*) nachweisen; **—ment** (*setting up*) Einrichtung f; (*business*) Unternehmen nt; **the E—ment** das Establishment.

estate [ɪs'teɪt] n Gut nt; (*housing —*) Siedlung f; (*will*) Nachlaß m; **— agent** Grundstücksmakler m; **— car** (*Brit*) Kombiwagen m.

esteem [ɪs'ti:m] n Wertschätzung f.

estimate ['estɪmət] n (*opinion*) Meinung f; (*of price*) (Kosten)voranschlag m; ['estɪmeɪt] vt schätzen.

estimation [estɪ'meɪʃən] n Einschätzung f; (*esteem*) Achtung f.

estuary ['estjuərɪ] n Mündung f.

etching ['etʃɪŋ] n Kupferstich m.

eternal a, **—ly** ad [ɪ'tɜ:nl, -nəlɪ] ewig.

eternity [ɪ'tɜ:nɪtɪ] n Ewigkeit f.

ether ['i:θə*] n (*Med*) Äther m.

ethical ['eθɪkəl] a ethisch.

ethics ['eθɪks] npl Ethik f.

ethnic ['eθnɪk] a Volks-, ethnisch.

etiquette ['etɪket] n Etikette f.

Eucharist ['ju:kərɪst] n heilige(s) Abendmahl nt.

eulogy ['ju:lədʒɪ] n Lobrede f.

eunuch ['ju:nək] n Eunuch m.

euphemism ['ju:fɪmɪzəm] n Euphemismus m.

euphoria [ju:'fɔ:rɪə] n Taumel m, Euphorie f.

euthanasia [ju:θə'neɪzɪə] n Euthanasie f.

evacuate [ɪ'vækjʊeɪt] vt place räumen; people evakuieren; (Med) entleeren.

evacuation [ɪvækju'eɪʃən] n Evakuierung f; Räumung f; Entleerung f.

evade [ɪ'veɪd] vt (escape) entkommen (+dat); (avoid) meiden; duty sich entziehen (+dat).

evaluate [ɪ'væljʊeɪt] vt bewerten; information auswerten.

evangelical [i:væn'dʒelɪkəl] a evangelisch.

evangelist [ɪ'vændʒəlɪst] n Evangelist m.

evaporate [ɪ'væpəreɪt] vi verdampfen; vt verdampfen lassen; —d milk Kondensmilch f.

evaporation [ɪvæpə'reɪʃən] n Verdunstung f.

evasion [ɪ'veɪʒən] n Umgehung f; (excuse) Ausflucht f.

evasive [ɪ'veɪzɪv] a ausweichend.

even ['i:vən] a eben; gleichmäßig; score etc unentschieden; number gerade; vt (ein)ebnen, glätten; ad — you selbst or sogar du; he — said ... er hat sogar gesagt ...; — as he spoke (gerade) da er sprach; — if sogar or selbst wenn, wenn auch; — so dennoch; — out or up vi sich ausgleichen; vt aus-

gleichen; get — sich revanchieren.

evening ['i:vnɪŋ] n Abend m; in the — abends, am Abend; — class Abendschule f; — dress (man's) Gesellschaftsanzug m; (woman's) Abendkleid nt.

evenly ['i:vənlɪ] ad gleichmäßig.

evensong ['i:vənsɒŋ] n (Rel) Abendandacht f.

event [ɪ'vent] n (happening) Ereignis nt; (Sport) Disziplin f; (horses) Rennen nt; the next — der nächste Wettkampf; in the — of im Falle (+gen); —ful a ereignisreich.

eventual [ɪ'ventʃʊəl] a (final) schließlich; —ity [ɪ'ventʃʊ'ælɪtɪ] Möglichkeit f; —ly ad (at last) am Ende; (given time) schließlich.

ever ['evə*] ad (always) immer; (at any time) je(mals); — so big sehr groß; — so many sehr viele; —green a immergrün n Immergrün nt; —lasting a immerwährend.

every ['evrɪ] a jeder/jede/jedes; — day jeden Tag; — other day jeden zweiten Tag; —body pron jeder, alle pl; —day a (daily) täglich; (commonplace) alltäglich, Alltags-; —one = —body; — so often hin und wieder; —thing pron alles; —where ad überall.

evict [ɪ'vɪkt] vt ausweisen; —ion Ausweisung f.

evidence ['evɪdəns] n (sign) Spur f; (proof) Beweis m; (testimony) Aussage f; in — (obvious) zu sehen.

evident ['evɪdənt] a augenscheinlich; —ly ad offensichtlich.

evil ['i:vl] a böse, übel; n Übel nt; Unheil nt; (sin) Böse(s) nt.

evocative [ɪ'vɒkətɪv] a to be — of sth an etw (acc) erinnern.

evoke [ɪ'vəuk] *vt* hervorrufen.

evolution [iːvə'luːʃən] *n* Entwicklung *f*; (*of life*) Evolution *f*.

evolve [ɪ'vɒlv] *vt* entwickeln; *vi* sich entwickeln.

ewe [juː] *n* Mutterschaf *nt*.

ex- [eks] *a* Ex-, Alt-, ehemalig.

exact *a*, **—ly** *ad* [ɪg'zækt, -lɪ] genau; *vt* (*demand*) verlangen; (*compel*) erzwingen; *money, fine* einziehen; *punishment* vollziehen; **—ing** *a* anspruchsvoll; **—itude** Genauigkeit *f*; **—ness** Genauigkeit *f*, Richtigkeit *f*.

exaggerate [ɪg'zædʒəreɪt] *vti* übertreiben; **—d** *a* übertrieben.

exaggeration [ɪgzædʒə'reɪʃən] *n* Übertreibung *f*.

exalt [ɪg'zɔːlt] *vt* (*praise*) verherrlichen.

exam [ɪg'zæm] *n* Prüfung *f*.

examination [ɪgzæmɪ'neɪʃən] *n* Untersuchung *f*; (*Sch, Univ*) Prüfung *f*, Examen *nt*; (*customs*) Kontrolle *f*.

examine [ɪg'zæmɪn] *vt* untersuchen; (*Sch*) prüfen; (*consider*) erwägen; **—r** Prüfer *m*.

example [ɪg'zɑːmpl] *n* Beispiel *nt*; **for —** zum Beispiel.

exasperate [ɪg'zɑːspəreɪt] *vt* zum Verzweifeln bringen.

exasperating [ɪg'zɑːspəreɪtɪŋ] *a* ärgerlich, zum Verzweifeln bringend.

exasperation [ɪgzɑːspə'reɪʃən] *n* Verzweiflung *f*.

excavate ['ekskəveɪt] *vt* (*hollow out*) aushöhlen; (*unearth*) ausgraben.

excavation [ekskə'veɪʃən] *n* Ausgrabung *f*.

excavator ['ekskəveɪtə*] *n* Bagger *m*.

exceed [ɪk'siːd] *vt* überschreiten; *hopes* übertreffen; **—ingly** *ad* in höchstem Maße.

excel [ɪk'sel] *vi* sich auszeichnen; *vt* übertreffen; **—lence** ['eksələns] Vortrefflichkeit *f*; **His E—lency** ['eksələnsɪ] Seine Exzellenz *f*; **—lent** ['eksələnt] *a* ausgezeichnet.

except [ɪk'sept] *prep* (*also* **— for**) außer (+*dat*); *vt* ausnehmen; **—ing** *prep* = except; **—ion** [ɪk'sepʃən] Ausnahme *f*; **to take —ion** to Anstoß nehmen an (+*dat*); **—ional** *a*, **—ionally** *ad* [ɪk'sepʃənl, -nəlɪ] außergewöhnlich.

excerpt ['eksɜːpt] *n* Auszug *m*.

excess [ek'ses] *n* Übermaß *nt* (of an +*dat*); Exzeß *m*; *a money* Nach-; *baggage* Mehr-; **—es** *pl* Ausschweifungen *pl*, Exzesse *pl*; (*violent*) Ausschreitungen *pl*; **—weight** (*of thing*) Mehrgewicht *nt*; (*of person*) Übergewicht *nt*; **—ive** *a*, **—ively** *ad* übermäßig.

exchange [ɪks'tʃeɪndʒ] *n* Austausch *m*; (*Fin*) Wechselstube *f*; (*Tel*) Vermittlung *f*, Zentrale *f*; (*Post Office*) (Fernsprech)amt *nt*; *vt goods* tauschen; *greetings* austauschen; *money, blows* wechseln; *see* rate.

exchequer [ɪks'tʃekə*] *n* Schatzamt *nt*.

excisable ['eksaɪzbl] *a* (verbrauchs)steuerpflichtig.

excise ['eksaɪz] *n* Verbrauchssteuer *f*; [ek'saɪz] *vt* (*Med*) herausschneiden.

excitable [ɪk'saɪtəbl] *a* erregbar, nervös.

excite [ɪk'saɪt] *vt* erregen; **—d** *a* aufgeregt; **to get —d** sich aufregen; **—ment** Aufgeregtheit *f*; (*of interest*) Erregung *f*.

exciting [ɪk'saɪtɪŋ] a aufregend; book, film spannend.

exclaim [ɪks'kleɪm] vi ausrufen.

exclamation [eksklə'meɪʃən] n Ausruf m; — mark Ausrufezeichen nt.

exclude [ɪks'kluːd] vt ausschließen.

exclusion [ɪks'kluːʒən] n Ausschluß m.

exclusive [ɪks'kluːsɪv] a (select) exklusiv; (sole) ausschließlich, Allein-; — of exklusive (+gen); —ly ad nur, ausschließlich.

excommunicate [ekskə'mjuːnɪkeɪt] vt exkommunizieren.

excrement ['ekskrɪmənt] n Kot m.

excruciating [ɪks'kruːʃieɪtɪŋ] a qualvoll.

excursion [ɪks'kɜːʃən] n Ausflug m.

excusable [ɪks'kjuːzəbl] a entschuldbar.

excuse [ɪks'kjuːs] n Entschuldigung f; [ɪks'kjuːz] vt entschuldigen; — me! entschuldigen Sie!

execute ['eksɪkjuːt] vt (carry out) ausführen; (kill) hinrichten.

execution [eksɪ'kjuːʃən] n Ausführung f; (killing) Hinrichtung f; —er Scharfrichter m.

executive [ɪg'zekjutɪv] n (Comm) leitende(r) Angestellte(r) m, Geschäftsführer m; (Pol) Exekutive f; a Exekutiv-, ausführend.

executor [ɪg'zekjutə*] n Testamentsvollstrecker m.

exemplary [ɪg'zemplərɪ] a musterhaft.

exemplify [ɪg'zemplɪfaɪ] vt veranschaulichen.

exempt [ɪg'zempt] a befreit; vt befreien; —ion [ɪg'zempʃən] Befreiung f.

exercise ['eksəsaɪz] n Übung f; vt power ausüben; muscle, patience

üben; dog ausführen; — book (Schul)heft nt.

exert [ɪg'zɜːt] vt influence ausüben; — o.s. sich anstrengen; —ion Anstrengung f.

exhaust [ɪg'zɔːst] n (fumes) Abgase pl; (pipe) Auspuffrohr nt; vt (weary) ermüden; (use up) erschöpfen; —ed a erschöpft; —ing a anstrengend; —ion Erschöpfung f; —ive a erschöpfend.

exhibit [ɪg'zɪbɪt] n (Art) Ausstellungsstück nt; (Jur) Beweisstück nt; vt ausstellen; —ion [eksɪ'bɪʃən] (Art) Ausstellung f; (of temper etc) Zurschaustellung f; —ionist [eksɪ'bɪʃənɪst] Exhibitionist m; —or Aussteller m.

exhilarating [ɪg'zɪləreɪtɪŋ] a erhebend.

exhilaration [ɪgzɪlə'reɪʃən] n erhebende(s) Gefühl nt.

exhort [ɪg'zɔːt] vt ermahnen; beschwören.

exile ['eksaɪl] n Exil nt; (person) im Exil Lebende(r) mf; vt verbannen; in — im Exil.

exist [ɪg'zɪst] vi existieren; (live) leben; —ence Existenz f; (way of life) Leben nt, Existenz f; —ing a vorhanden, bestehend.

exit ['eksɪt] n Ausgang m; (Theat) Abgang m.

exonerate [ɪg'zɒnəreɪt] vt entlasten.

exorbitant [ɪg'zɔːbɪtənt] a übermäßig; price Phantasie-.

exotic [ɪg'zɒtɪk] a exotisch.

expand [ɪks'pænd] vt (spread) ausspannen; operations ausdehnen; vi sich ausdehnen.

expanse [ɪks'pæns] n weite Fläche f, Weite f.

expansion [ɪks'pænʃən] n Erweiterung f.

expatriate [eks'pætrɪeɪt] *a* Exil-; *n* im Exil Lebende(r) *mf*; *vt* ausbürgern.

expect [ɪks'pekt] *vt* erwarten; (*suppose*) annehmen; *vi*: to be —ing ein Kind erwarten; —ant *a* (*hopeful*) erwartungsvoll; *mother* werdend; —ation [ekspek'teɪʃən] (*hope*) Hoffnung *f*; —ations *pl* Erwartungen *pl*; (*prospects*) Aussicht *f*.

expedience [iks'pi:dɪəns], **expediency** [iks'pi:dɪənsɪ] *n* Zweckdienlichkeit *f*.

expedient [iks'pi:dɪənt] *a* zweckdienlich; *n* (Hilfs)mittel *nt*.

expedite ['ekspɪdaɪt] *vt* beschleunigen.

expedition [ekspɪ'dɪʃən] *n* Expedition *f*.

expel [iks'pel] *vt* ausweisen; *student* (ver)weisen.

expend [iks'pend] *vt* *money* ausgeben; *effort* aufwenden; —able *a* entbehrlich; —iture Kosten *pl*, Ausgaben *pl*.

expense [iks'pens] *n* (*cost*) Auslage *f*, Ausgabe *f*; (*high cost*) Aufwand *m*; —s *pl* Spesen *pl*; at the — of auf Kosten von; — account Spesenkonto *nt*.

expensive [iks'pensɪv] *a* teuer.

experience [iks'pɪərɪəns] *n* (*incident*) Erlebnis *nt*; (*practice*) Erfahrung *f*; *vt* erfahren, erleben; *hardship* durchmachen; —d *a* erfahren.

experiment [iks'perɪmənt] *n* Versuch *m*, Experiment *nt*; [iks'perɪment] *vi* experimentieren; —al [eksperɪ'mentl] *a* versuchsweise, experimentell.

expert ['eksp3:t] *n* Fachmann *m*; (*official*) Sachverständige(r) *m*; *a* erfahren; (*practised*) gewandt;

—ise [ekspə'ti:z] Sachkenntnis *f*.

expiration [ekspaɪə'reɪʃən] *n* (*breathing*) Ausatmen *nt*; (*fig*) Ablauf *m*.

expire [iks'paɪə*] *vi* (*end*) ablaufen; (*die*) sterben; (*ticket*) verfallen.

expiry [iks'paɪərɪ] *n* Ablauf *m*.

explain [iks'pleɪn] *vt* (*make clear*) erklären; (*account for*) begründen; — away *vt* wegerklären.

explanation [eksplə'neɪʃən] *n* Erklärung *f*.

explanatory [iks'plænətərɪ] *a* erklärend.

explicable [eks'plɪkəbl] *a* erklärlich.

explicit [iks'plɪsɪt] *a* (*clear*) ausdrücklich; (*outspoken*) deutlich; —ly *ad* deutlich.

explode [iks'pləud] *vi* explodieren; *vt* *bomb* zur Explosion bringen; *theory* platzen lassen.

exploit ['eksplɔɪt] *n* (Helden)tat *f*; [iks'plɔɪt] *vt* ausbeuten; —ation [eksplɔɪ'teɪʃən] Ausbeutung *f*.

exploration [eksplɔ:'reɪʃən] *n* Erforschung *f*.

exploratory [eks'plɔrətərɪ] *a* sondierend, Probe-.

explore [iks'plɔ:*] *vt* (*travel*) erforschen; (*search*) untersuchen; —r Forschungsreisende(r) *mf*, Erforscher(in *f*) *m*.

explosion [iks'pləuʒən] *n* (*lit*) Explosion *f*; (*fig*) Ausbruch *m*.

explosive [iks'pləuzɪv] *a* explosiv, Spreng-; *n* Sprengstoff *m*.

exponent [eks'pəunənt] *n* Exponent *m*.

export [eks'pɔ:t] *vt* exportieren; ['ekspɔ:t] *n* Export *m*; *a* trade Export-; —ation [ekspɔ:'teɪʃən] Ausfuhr *f*; —er Exporteur *m*.

expose [ıks'pəuz] vt (to danger etc) aussetzen (to dat); imposter entlarven; lie aufdecken.

exposé [eks'pəuzeı] n (of scandal) Enthüllung f.

exposed [ıks'pəuzd] a. position exponiert.

exposure [ıks'pəuʒə*] m (Med) Unterkühlung f; (Phot) Belichtung f; — meter Belichtungsmesser m.

expound [ıks'paund] vt entwickeln.

express [ıks'pres] a ausdrücklich; (speedy) Expreß-, Eil-; n (Rail) Zug m; vt ausdrücken; to — o.s. sich ausdrücken; —ion [ıks'preʃən] (phrase) Ausdruck m; (look) (Gesichts)ausdruck m; —ive a ausdrucksvoll; —ly ad ausdrücklich, extra.

expropriate [eks'prəupıeıt] vt enteignen.

expulsion [ıks'pʌlʃən] n Ausweisung f.

exquisite [ıks'kwızıt] a erlesen; —ly ad ausgezeichnet.

extend [ıks'tend] vt visit etc verlängern; (of building) vergrößern, ausbauen; hand ausstrecken; welcome bieten.

extension [ıks'tenʃən] n Erweiterung f; (of building) Anbau m; (Tel) Nebenanschluß m, Apparat m.

extensive [ıks'tensıv] a knowledge umfassend; use weitgehend.

extent [ıks'tent] n Ausdehnung f; (fig) Ausmaß nt.

extenuating [eks'tenjueıtıŋ] a mildernd.

exterior [eks'tıərıə*] a äußere(r,s), Außen-; n Äußere(s) nt.

exterminate [eks'tɜ:mıneıt] vt ausrotten.

extermination [ekstɜ:mı'neıʃən] n Ausrottung f.

external [eks'tɜ:nl] a äußere(r,s), Außen-; —ly ad äußerlich.

extinct [ıks'tıŋkt] a ausgestorben; —ion [ıks'tıŋkʃən] Aussterben nt.

extinguish [ıks'tıŋgwıʃ] vt (aus)löschen; —er Löschgerät nt.

extort [ıks'tɔ:t] vt erpressen (sth from sb jdn um etw); —ion [ıks'tɔ:ʃən] Erpressung f; —ionate [ıks'tɔ:ʃənt] a überhöht, erpresserisch.

extra ['ekstrə] a zusätzlich; ad besonders; n (work) Sonderarbeit f; (benefit) Sonderleistung f; (charge) Zuschlag m; (Theat) Statist m.

extract [ıks'trækt] vt (heraus)ziehen; (select) auswählen; ['ekstrækt] n (from book etc) Auszug m; (Cook) Extrakt m; —ion (Heraus)ziehen nt; (origin) Abstammung f.

extradite ['ekstrədaıt] vt ausliefern.

extradition [ekstrə'dıʃən] n Auslieferung f.

extraneous [eks'treınıəs] a unwesentlich; influence äußere(r,s).

extraordinary [ıks'trɔ:dnrı] a (amazing) außerordentlich; erstaunlich.

extravagance [ıks'trævəgəns] n Verschwendung f; (lack of restraint) Zügellosigkeit f; (an —) Extravaganz f.

extravagant [ıks'trævəgənt] a extravagant.

extreme [ıks'tri:m] a edge äußerste(r,s), hinterste(r,s); cold äußerste(r,s); behaviour außergewöhnlich, übertrieben; n Extrem nt, das Äußerste; —s pl (excesses) Ausschreitungen pl; (opposites)

Extreme pl; **—ly** ad äußerst, höchst.

extremist [iks'tri:mist] a extremistisch; n Extremist(in f) m.

extremity [iks'tremiti] n (end) Spitze f, äußerste(s) Ende nt; (hardship) bitterste Not f; (Anat) Hand f; Fuß m.

extricate ['ekstrikeit] vt losmachen, befreien.

extrovert ['ekstrəuvɜ:t] n Extravertierte(r) mf; a extravertiert.

exuberance [ig'zu:bərəns] n Überschwang m.

exuberant [ig'zu:bərənt] a ausgelassen.

exude [ig'zju:d] vt absondern; vi sich absondern.

exult [ig'zʌlt] vi frohlocken; **—ation** [egzʌl'teiʃən] Jubel m.

eye [ai] n Auge nt; (of needle) Öhr nt; vt betrachten; (up and down) mustern; **to keep an — on** aufpassen auf (+acc); **in the —s of** in den Augen (+gen); **up to the —s** bis zum Hals in; **—ball** Augapfel m; **—bath** Augenbad nt; **—brow** Augenbraue f; **—lash** Augenwimper f; **—lid** Augenlid nt; **that was an —opener** das hat mir die Augen geöffnet; **—shadow** Lidschatten m; **—sight** Sehkraft f; **—sore** Schandfleck m; **—wash** (lit) Augenwasser nt; (fig) Schwindel m; Quatsch m; **— witness** Augenzeuge m.

F

F,f [ef] n F nt, f nt.

fable ['feibl] n Fabel f.

fabric ['fæbrik] n Stoff m, Gewebe nt; (fig) Gefüge nt.

fabricate ['fæbrikeit] vt fabrizieren.

fabulous ['fæbjuləs] a (imaginary) legendär, sagenhaft; (unbelievable) unglaublich; (wonderful) fabelhaft, unglaublich.

façade [fə'sɑ:d] n (lit, fig) Fassade f.

face [feis] n Gesicht nt; (grimace) Grimasse f; (surface) Oberfläche f; (of clock) Zifferblatt nt; vt (point towards) liegen nach; situation, sich gegenübersehen (+dat); difficulty mutig entgegentreten (+dat); **in the — of** angesichts (+gen); **to — up to sth** einer Sache ins Auge sehen; **— cream** Gesichtscreme f;

— powder (Gesichts)puder m.

facet ['fæsit] n Seite f, Aspekt m; (of gem) Kristallfläche f, Schliff m.

facetious [fə'si:ʃəs] a schalkhaft; (humorous) witzig; **—ly** ad spaßhaft, witzig.

face to face [feistə'feis] ad Auge in Auge, direkt.

face value ['feis 'vælju:] n Nennwert m; (fig) **to take sth at its —** etw für bare Münze nehmen.

facial ['feiʃəl] a Gesichts-.

facile ['fæsail] a oberflächlich; (US: easy) leicht.

facilitate [fə'siliteit] vt erleichtern.

facility [fə'siliti] n (ease) Leichtigkeit f; (skill) Gewandtheit f; **facilities** pl Einrichtungen pl.

facing ['feisiŋ] a zugekehrt; prep gegenüber.

facsimile [fæk'smɪlɪ] n Faksimile nt.

fact [fækt] 'n Tatsache f; in — in der Tat.

faction ['fækʃən] n Splittergruppe f.

factor ['fæktə*] n Faktor m.

factory ['fæktərɪ] n Fabrik f.

factual ['fæktjʊəl] a Tatsachen-, sachlich.

faculty ['fækəltɪ] n Fähigkeit f; (Univ) Fakultät f; (US: teaching staff) Lehrpersonal nt.

fade [feɪd] vi (lose colour) verschießen, verblassen; (grow dim) nachlassen, schwinden; (sound, memory) schwächer werden; (wither) verwelken; vt material verblassen lassen; —d a verwelkt; colour verblichen; to — in/out (Cine) ein-/ausblenden.

fag [fæg] n Plackerei f; (col: cigarette) Kippe f; —ged a (exhausted) erschöpft.

Fahrenheit ['færənhaɪt] n Fahrenheit.

fail [feɪl] vt exam nicht bestehen; student durchfallen lassen; (courage) verlassen; (memory) im Stich lassen; vi (supplies) zu Ende gehen; (student) durchfallen; (eyesight) nachlassen; (light) schwächer werden; (crop) fehlschlagen; (remedy) nicht wirken; — to do sth (neglect) es unterlassen, etw zu tun; (be unable) es nicht schaffen, etw zu tun; without — ganz bestimmt, unbedingt; —ing n Fehler m, Schwäche f; prep' in Ermangelung (+gen); —ing this falls nicht, sonst; —ure ['feɪljə*] n (person) Versager m; (act) Versagen nt; (Tech) Defekt m.

faint [feɪnt] a schwach, matt; n Ohnmacht f; vi ohnmächtig wer-

den; —hearted a mutlos, kleinmütig; —ly ad schwach; —ness n Schwäche f; (Med) Schwächegefühl nt.

fair [feə*] a schön; hair blond; skin hell; weather schön, trocken; (just) gerecht, fair; (not very good) leidlich, mittelmäßig; conditions günstig, gut; (sizeable) ansehnlich; ad play ehrlich, fair; n (Comm) Messe f; (fun —) Jahrmarkt m; —ly ad (honestly) gerecht, fair; (rather) ziemlich; —ness n Schönheit f; (of hair) Blondheit f; (of game) Ehrlichkeit f, Fairneß f; —way (Naut) Fahrrinne f.

fairy ['feərɪ] n Fee f; —land Märchenland nt; — tale Märchen nt.

faith [feɪθ] n Glaube m; (trust) Vertrauen nt; (sect) Bekenntnis nt, Religion f; —ful a, —fully ad treu; yours —fully hochachtungsvoll.

fake [feɪk] n (thing) Fälschung f; (person) Schwindler m; a vorgetäuscht; vt fälschen.

falcon ['fɔ:lkən] n Falke m.

fall [fɔ:l] n Fall m, Sturz m; (decrease) Fallen nt; (of snow) (Schnee)fall m; (US: autumn) Herbst m; vi irreg (lit, fig) fallen; (night) hereinbrechen; —s pl (waterfall) Fälle pl; — back on vi in Reserve haben; — down vi (person) hinfallen; (building) einstürzen; — flat vi (lit) platt hinfallen; (joke) nicht ankommen; the plan fell flat es dem Plan wurde nichts; — for vt trick hereinfallen auf (+acc); person sich verknallen in (+acc); — off vi herunterfallen (von); (diminish) sich vermindern; — out vi sich streiten; — through vi (plan) ins Wasser fallen.

fallacy ['fæləsı] n Trugschluß m.

fallible ['fæləbl] a fehlbar.

fallout ['fɔ:laut] n radioaktive(r) Niederschlag m.

fallow ['fæləu] a brach(liegend).

false [fɔ:ls] a falsch; (artificial) gefälscht, künstlich; **under — pretences** unter Vorspiegelung falscher Tatsachen; **—** alarm Fehlalarm m; **—ly** ad fälschlicherweise; **— teeth** pl Gebiß nt.

falter ['fɔ:ltə*] vi schwanken; (in speech) stocken.

fame [feım] n Ruhm m.

familiar [fə'mılıə*] a vertraut, bekannt; (intimate) familiär; **to be — with** vertraut sein mit, gut kennen; **—ity** [fəmılı'ærıtı] Vertrautheit f; **—ize** vt vertraut machen.

family ['fæmılı] n Familie f; (relations) Verwandtschaft f; **— allowance** Kindergeld nt; **— business** Familienunternehmen nt; **— doctor** Hausarzt m; **— life** Familienleben nt; **— planning** Geburtenkontrolle f.

famine ['fæmın] n Hungersnot f.

famished ['fæmıʃt] a ausgehungert.

famous ['feıməs] a berühmt.

fan [fæn] n (folding) Fächer m; (Elec) Ventilator m; (admirer) begeisterte(r) Anhänger m; Fan m; vt fächeln; **— out** vi sich (fächerförmig) ausbreiten.

fanatic [fə'nætık] n Fanatiker(in f) m; **—al** a fanatisch.

fan belt ['fænbelt] n Keilriemen m.

fancied ['fænsıd] a beliebt, populär.

fanciful ['fænsıful] a (odd) seltsam; (imaginative) phantasievoll.

fancy ['fænsı] n (liking) Neigung f; (imagination) Phantasie f, Ein-

bildung f; a schick, ausgefallen; vt (like) gern haben; wollen; (imagine) sich einbilden; (just) — (that)! stellen Sie sich (das nur) vor!; **— dress** Verkleidung f, Maskenkostüm nt; **—dress ball** Maskenball m.

fanfare ['fænfeə*] n Fanfare f.

fang [fæŋ] n Fangzahn m; (snake's) Giftzahn m.

fanlight ['fænlaıt] n Oberlicht nt.

fantastic [fæn'tæstık] a phantastisch.

fantasy ['fæntəzı] n Phantasie f.

far [fɑ:*] a weit; ad weit entfernt; (very much) weitaus, (sehr) viel; **— away, — off** weit weg; **by —** bei weitem; **so — soweit**; bis jetzt; **—away** a weit entfernt; the **F— East** der Ferne Osten.

farce [fɑ:s] n Schwank m, Posse f; (fig) Farce f.

farcical ['fɑ:sıkəl] a possenhaft; (fig) lächerlich.

fare [feə*] n Fahrpreis m; Fahrgeld nt; (food) Kost f; vi: **he is faring well** es ergeht ihm gut; **—well** Abschied(sgruß) m; interj lebe wohl!; a Abschieds-.

far-fetched ['fɑ:'fetʃt] a weit hergeholt.

farm [fɑ:m] n Bauernhof m, Farm f; vt bewirtschaften; vi Landwirt m sein; **—er** Bauer m, Landwirt m; **—hand** Landarbeiter m; **—house** Bauernhaus nt; **—ing** Landwirtschaft f; **—land** Ackerland nt; **—yard** Hof m.

far-reaching ['fɑ:'ri:tʃıŋ] a weitgehend.

far-sighted ['fɑ:'saıtıd] a weitblickend.

fart [fɑ:t] n (col) Furz m; vi (col) furzen.

farther ['fɑːðə*] a, ad weiter.

farthest ['fɑːðɪst] a weiteste(r,s), fernste(r,s); ad am weitesten.

fascinate ['fæsɪneɪt] vt faszinieren, bezaubern.

fascinating ['fæsɪneɪtɪŋ] a faszinierend, spannend.

fascination [fæsɪ'neɪʃən] n Faszination f, Zauber m.

fascism ['fæʃɪzəm] n Faschismus m.

fascist ['fæʃɪst] n Faschist m; a faschistisch.

fashion ['fæʃən] n (of clothes) Mode f; (manner) Art f (und Weise f); vt machen, gestalten; in — in Mode; out of — unmodisch; —able a clothes modern, modisch; place elegant; — show Mode(n)-schau f.

fast [fɑːst] a schnell; (firm) fest; dye waschecht; to be — (clock) vorgehen; ad schnell; (firmly) fest; n Fasten nt; vi fasten.

fasten ['fɑːsn] vt (attach) befestigen; seat belt festmachen; (with rope) zuschnüren; vi sich schließen lassen; —er, —ing Verschluß m.

fastidious [fæs'tɪdɪəs] a wählerisch.

fat [fæt] a dick, fett; n (on person) Fett m, Speck m (col); (on meat) Fett m; (for cooking) (Braten)fett nt.

fatal ['feɪtl] a tödlich; (disastrous) verhängnisvoll; —ism Fatalismus m, Schicksalsglaube m; —ity [fə'tælɪtɪ] (road death etc) Todesopfer nt; —ly ad tödlich.

fate [feɪt] n Schicksal nt; —ful a (prophetic) schicksalsschwer; (important) schicksalhaft.

father ['fɑːðə*] n Vater m; (Rel) Pater m; —-in-law Schwiegervater m; —ly a väterlich.

fathom ['fæðəm] n Klafter m; vt ausloten; (fig) ergründen.

fatigue [fə'tiːg] n Ermüdung f; vt ermüden.

fatness ['fætnɪs] n Dicke f.

fatten ['fætn] vt dick machen; animals mästen; vi dick werden.

fatty ['fætɪ] a food fettig.

fatuous ['fætjʊəs] a albern, einfältig.

faucet ['fɔːsɪt] n (US) Wasserhahn m.

fault [fɔːlt] n (defect) Defekt m; (Elec) Störung f; (blame) Fehler m, Schuld f; (Geog) Verwerfung f; it's your — du bist daran schuld; at — schuldig, im Unrecht; vt: — sth etwas an etw (dat) auszusetzen haben; —less a fehlerfrei, tadellos; —y a fehlerhaft, defekt.

fauna ['fɔːnə] n Fauna f.

favour, (US) **favor** ['feɪvə*] n (approval) Wohlwollen nt; (kindness) Gefallen m; vt (prefer) vorziehen; in — of für; zugunsten (+gen); —able a, —ably ad günstig; —ite ['feɪvərɪt] a Lieblings-; n Günstling m; (child) Liebling m; (Sport) Favorit m; —itism (col) Bevorzugung f; (Pol) Günstlingswirtschaft f.

fawn [fɔːn] a rehbraun; n (colour) Rehbraun nt; (animal) (Reh)kitz nt.

fawning ['fɔːnɪŋ] a kriecherisch.

fear [fɪə*] n Furcht f; vt fürchten; no —! keine Angst!; —ful a (timid) furchtsam; (terrible) fürchterlich; —less a, —lessly ad furchtlos; —lessness Furchtlosigkeit f.

feasibility [fiːzə'bɪlɪtɪ] n Durchführbarkeit f.

feasible ['fiːzəbl] a durchführbar, machbar.

feast [fiːst] n Festmahl nt; (Rel) Kirchenfest nt; vi sich gütlich tun (on an +dat); — day kirchliche(r) Feiertag m.

feat [fi:t] n Leistung f.

feather ['feðə*] n Feder f.

feature ['fi:tʃə*] n (Gesichts)zug m; (important part) Grundzug m; (Cine, Press) Feature nt; vt darstellen; (advertising etc) groß herausbringen; featuring X mit X; vi vorkommen; — film Spielfilm m; —less a nichtssagend.

February ['februəri] n Februar m.

federal ['fedərəl] a Bundes-.

federation [fedə'reiʃən] n (society) Verband m; (of states) Staatenbund m.

fed-up [fed'ʌp] a: to be — with sth etw satt haben; I'm — ich habe die Nase voll.

fee [fi:] n Gebühr f.

feeble ['fi:bl] a (person) schwach; excuse lahm; —minded a geistesschwach.

feed [fi:d] n (for baby) Essen nt; (for animals) Futter nt; vt irreg füttern; (support) ernähren; to — on leben von, fressen; —back (Tech) Rückkopplung f; (information) Feedback nt.

feel [fi:l] n: it has a soft — es fühlt sich weich an; to get the — of sth sich an etw (acc) gewöhnen; irreg vt (sense) fühlen; (touch) anfassen; (think) meinen; vi (person) sich fühlen; (thing) sich anfühlen; I — cold mir ist kalt; I — like a cup of tea ich habe Lust auf eine Tasse Tee; —er Fühler m; —ing Gefühl nt; (opinion) Meinung f.

feet [fi:t] npl of foot.

feign [fein] vt vortäuschen; —ed a vorgetäuscht, Schein-.

feint [feint] n Täuschungsmanöver nt.

feline ['fi:lain] a Katzen-, katzenartig.

fell [fel] vt tree fällen; n (hill) kahle(r) Berg m; a: with one — swoop mit einem Schlag; auf einen Streich.

fellow ['feləu] n (companion) Gefährte m, Kamerad m; (man) Kerl m; — citizen Mitbürger(in f) m; — countryman Landsmann m; — feeling Mitgefühl nt; — men pl Mitmenschen pl; —ship (group) Körperschaft f; (friendliness) Gemeinschaft f, Kameradschaft f; (scholarship) Forschungsstipendium nt; — worker Mitarbeiter(in f) m.

felony ['feləni] n schwere(s) Verbrechen nt.

felt [felt] n Filz m.

female ['fi:meil] n (of animals) Weibchen nt; a weiblich.

feminine ['feminin] a (Gram) weiblich; qualities fraulich.

femininity [femi'niniti] n Weiblichkeit f; (quality) Fraulichkeit f.

feminist ['feminist] n Feminist(in f) m.

fence [fens] n Zaun m; (crook) Hehler m; vi fechten; — in vt einzäunen; — off vt absperren.

fencing ['fensin] n Zaun m; (Sport) Fechten nt.

fend [fend] vi: — for o.s. sich (allein) durchschlagen.

fender ['fendə*] n Kaminvorsetzer m; (US Aut) Kotflügel m.

ferment [fə'ment] vi (Chem) gären; ['fɜ:ment] n (excitement) Unruhe f; —ation [fɜ:men'teiʃən] n Gärung f.

fern [fɜ:n] n Farn m.

ferocious [fə'rəuʃəs] a wild, grausam; —ly ad wild.

ferocity [fə'rɒsɪtɪ] *n* Wildheit *f*, Grimmigkeit *f*.

ferry ['ferɪ] *n* Fähre *f*; *vt* übersetzen.

fertile ['fɜ:taɪl] *a* fruchtbar.

fertility [fə'tɪlɪtɪ] *n* Fruchtbarkeit *f*.

fertilization [fɜːtɪlaɪ'zeɪʃən] *n* Befruchtung *f*.

fertilize ['fɜ:tɪlaɪz] *vt* (*Agr*) düngen; (*Biol*) befruchten; **—r** (*Kunst*)dünger *m*.

fervent ['fɜ:vənt] *a admirer* glühend; *hope* innig.

festival ['festɪvəl] *n* (*Rel etc*) Fest *nt*; (*Art, Mus*) Festspiele *pl*; Festival *nt*.

festive ['festɪv] *a* festlich; the — season (Christmas) die Festzeit *f*.

festivity [fes'tɪvɪtɪ] *n* Festlichkeit *f*.

fetch [fetʃ] *vt* holen; (*in sale*) einbringen, erzielen.

fetching ['fetʃɪŋ] *a* einnehmend, reizend.

fête [feɪt] *n* Fest *nt*.

fetish ['fi:tɪʃ] *n* Fetisch *m*.

fetters ['fetəz] *npl* (*lit, fig*) Fesseln *pl*.

fetus ['fi:təs] *n* (*US*) = foetus.

feud [fju:d] *n* Fehde *f*; *vi* sich befehden; **—al** *a* lehnsherrlich, Feudal-; **—alism** Lehnswesen *nt*, Feudalismus *m*.

fever ['fi:və*] *n* Fieber *nt*; **—ish** *a* (*Med*) fiebrig, Fieber-; (*fig*) fieberhaft; **—ishly** *ad* (*fig*) fieberhaft.

few [fju:] *a* wenig; *pron* wenige; a — a, *pron* einige; **—er** weniger; **—est** wenigste(r,s); a good — ziemlich viele.

fiancé [fɪ'ɑ:nseɪ] *n* Verlobte(r) *m*; **—e** Verlobte *f*.

fiasco [fɪ'æskəʊ] *n* Fiasko *nt*, Reinfall *m*.

fib [fɪb] *n* Flunkerei *f*; *vi* flunkern.

fibre, (*US*) **fiber** ['faɪbə*] *n* Faser *f*, Fiber *f*; (*material*) Faserstoff *m*; **—glass** Glaswolle *f*.

fickle ['fɪkl] *a* unbeständig, wankelmütig; **—ness** Unbeständigkeit *f*, Wankelmut *m*.

fiction ['fɪkʃən] *n* (*novels*) Romanliteratur *f*; (*story*) Erdichtung *f*; **—al** *a* erfunden.

fictitious [fɪk'tɪʃəs] *a* erfunden, fingiert.

fiddle ['fɪdl] *n* Geige *f*, Fiedel *f*; (*trick*) Schwindelei *f*; *vt accounts* frisieren; — with *vi* herumfummeln an (+*dat*); **—r** Geiger *m*.

fidelity [fɪ'delɪtɪ] *n* Treue *f*.

fidget ['fɪdʒɪt] *vi* zappeln; *n* Zappelphilipp *m*; **—y** *a* nervös, zappelig.

field [fi:ld] *n* Feld *nt*; (*range*) Gebiet *nt*; — day (gala) Paradetag *m*; — marshal Feldmarschall *m*; **—work** (*Mil*) Schanze *f*; (*Univ*) Feldforschung *f*.

fiend [fi:nd] *n* Teufel *m*; (*beast*) Unhold *m*; Fanatiker(in *f*) *m*; **—ish** *a* teuflisch.

fierce *a*, **—ly** *ad* [fɪəs, -lɪ] wild; **—ness** Wildheit *f*.

fiery ['faɪərɪ] *a* glühend; (*blazing*) brennend; (*hot-tempered*) hitzig, heftig.

fifteen [fɪf'ti:n] *num* fünfzehn.

fifth [fɪfθ] *a* fünfte(r,s); *n* Fünftel *nt*.

fifty ['fɪftɪ] *num* fünfzig; **———** halbe halbe, fifty fifty (*col*).

fig [fɪg] *n* Feige *f*.

fight [faɪt] *n* Kampf *m*; (*brawl*) Schlägerei *f*; (*argument*) Streit *m*; *irreg vt* kämpfen gegen; sich schlagen mit; (*fig*) bekämpfen; *vi* kämpfen; sich schlagen; streiten; **—er** Kämpfer(in *f*) *m*; (*plane*)

Jagdflugzeug nt; —ing Kämpfen nt; (war) Kampfhandlungen pl.

figment ['figmənt] n — of imagination reine Einbildung f.

figurative ['figərətiv] a bildlich.

figure ['figə*] n Form f; (of person) Figur f; (person) Gestalt f; (illustration) Zeichnung f; (number) Ziffer f; vt (US: imagine) glauben; vi (appear) eine Rolle spielen, erscheinen; (US: make sense) stimmen; — out vt · verstehen, herausbekommen; —head (Naut, fig) Galionsfigur f; — skating Eiskunstlauf m.

filament ['filəmənt] n Faden m; (Elec) Glühfaden m.

file [fail] n (tool) Feile f; (dossier) Akte f; (folder) Aktenordner m; (row) Reihe f; vt metal, nails feilen; papers abheften; claim einreichen; vi: — in/out hintereinander hereinkommen/hinausgehen; in single — einer hinter dem anderen.

filing ['failin] n Feilen nt; —s pl Feilspäne pl; — cabinet Aktenschrank m.

fill [fil] vt füllen; (occupy) ausfüllen; (satisfy) sättigen; n: to eat one's — sich richtig satt essen; to have had one's — genug haben; to — the bill (fig) allen Anforderungen genügen; — in vt hole (auf)füllen; form ausfüllen; — up vt container auffüllen; form ausfüllen.

fillet ['filit] n Filet nt; vt als Filet herrichten.

filling ['filiŋ] n (Cook) Füllung f; (for tooth) (Zahn)plombe f; — station Tankstelle f.

fillip ['filip] n Anstoß m, Auftrieb m.

film [film] n Film m; (layer) Häutchen nt, Film m; vt scene filmen; — star Filmstar m; —strip Filmstreifen m.

filter ['filtə*] · n Filter m; (for traffic) Verkehrsfilter m; vt filtern; vi durchsickern; — tip Filter m, Filtermundstück nt; — tipped cigarette Filterzigarette f.

filth [filθ] n (lit) Dreck m; (fig) Unflat m; —y a dreckig; (behaviour) gemein; weather scheußlich.

fin [fin] n Flosse f.

final ['fainl] a letzte(r,s); (conclusive) endgültig; n (Ftbl etc) Endspiel nt; —s pl (Univ) Abschlußexamen nt; (Sport) Schlußrunde f; —e [fi'na:li] (Theat) Schlußszene f; (Mus) Finale nt; —ist (Sport) Schlußrundenteilnehmer m; —ize vt endgültige Form geben (+dat); abschließen; —ly ad (lastly) zuletzt; (eventually) endlich; (irrevocably) endgültig.

finance [fai'næns] n Finanzwesen nt; —s pl Finanzen pl; (income) Einkünfte pl; vt finanzieren.

financial [fai'nænʃəl] a Finanz-, finanziell; —ly ad finanziell.

financier [fai'nænsiə*] n Finanzier m.

find [faind] irreg vt finden; (realize) erkennen; n Fund m; to — sb guilty· jdn für schuldig erklären; — out herausfinden; to — out heraus finden; —ings pl (Jur) Ermittlungsergebnis nt; (of report) Feststellung f, Befund m.

fine [fain] a fein; (thin) dünn, fein; (good) gut; clothes elegant; weather schön; ad (well) gut; (small) klein; n (Jur) Geldstrafe f; vt (Jur) mit einer Geldstrafe belegen; to cut it — (fig) knapp rechnen; — arts pl die schönen

Künste *pl*; **—ness** *n* Feinheit *f*;
—ry ['faɪnərɪ] Putz *m*; **—sse**
[fi'nes] Finesse *f*.

finger ['fɪŋgə*] *n* Finger *m*; *vt*
befühlen; **—nail** Fingernagel *m*;
—print Fingerabdruck *m*; **—stall**
Fingerling *m*; **—tip** Fingerspitze *f*;
to have sth at one's —tips etw
parat haben.

finicky ['fɪnɪkɪ] *a* pingelig.

finish ['fɪnɪʃ] *n* Ende *nt*; (*Sport*)
Ziel *nt*; (*of object*) Verarbeitung *f*;
(*of paint*) Oberflächenwirkung *f*; *vt*
beenden; *book* zu Ende lesen; **to
be —ed with** sth fertig sein mit
etw; *vi* aufhören; (*Sport*) ans Ziel
kommen; **—ing line** Ziellinie *f*;
—ing school Mädchenpensionat *nt*.

finite ['faɪnaɪt] *a* endlich, begrenzt;
(*Gram*) finit.

fiord [fjɔ:d] *n* Fjord *m*.

fir [fɜ:*] *n* Tanne *f*, Fichte *f*.

fire [faɪə*] *n* (*lit, fig*) Feuer *nt*;
(*damaging*) Brand *m*, Feuer *nt*; **to
set —** **to sth** etw in Brand stecken;
to be on — brennen; *vt* (*Aut*)
zünden; *gun* abfeuern; (*fig*)
imagination entzünden; (*dismiss*)
hinauswerfen; *vi* (*Aut*) zünden; **to
— at sb** auf jdn schießen; **— away!**
schieß los!; **— alarm** Feueralarm
m; **—arm** Schußwaffe *f*; **—
brigade** Feuerwehr *f*; **— engine**
Feuerwehrauto *nt*; **— escape** Feuer-
leiter *f*; **— extinguisher** Löschgerät
nt; **—man** Feuerwehrmann *m*; **—
place** offene(r) Kamin *m*; **—
proof** *a* feuerfest; **—side** Kamin
m; **— station** Feuerwehrwache *f*;
—wood Brennholz *nt*; **—works** *pl*
Feuerwerk *nt*.

firing ['faɪərɪŋ] *n* Schießen *nt*; **—
squad** Exekutionskommando *nt*.

firm *a*, **—ly** *ad* [fɜ:m,-lɪ] fest;
(*determined*) entschlossen; *n*

Firma *f*; **—ness** Festigkeit *f*; Entschlossenheit *f*.

first [fɜ:st] *a* erste(r,s); *ad* zuerst;
arrive als erste(r); *happen* zum
erstenmal; *n* (*person: in race*)
Erste(r) *mf*; (*Univ*) Eins *f*; (*Aut*)
erste(r) Gang *m*; **at —** zuerst,
anfangs; **at all —** zu allererst; **—
aid** Erste Hilfe *f*; **—aid kit**
Verbandskasten *m*; **—-class** *a*
erstklassig; (*travel*) erste(r)
Klasse; **—-hand** *a* aus erster Hand;
— lady (*US*) First Lady *f*; **—ly** *ad*
erstens; **— name** Vorname *m*; **—
night** Premiere *f*, Erstaufführung *f*;
—-rate *a* erstklassig.

fiscal ['fɪskəl] *a* fiskalisch, Finanz-.

fish [fɪʃ] *n* Fisch *m*; *vt* *river* angeln
in (+*dat*); *sea* fischen in (+*dat*);
vi fischen; angeln; **— out** *vt*
herausfischen; **to go —ing** angeln
gehen; (*in sea*) fischen gehen;
—erman Fischer *m*; **—ery** Fisch-
grund *m*; **— finger** Fischstäbchen
nt; **— hook** Angelhaken *m*; **—ing
boat** Fischerboot *nt*; **—ing line**
Angelschnur *f*; **—ing rod** Angel-
(rute) *f*; **—ing tackle** Angelzeug *nt*;
— market Fischmarkt *m*;
—monger Fischhändler *m*; **— slice**
Fischvorlegemesser *nt*; **—y** *a* (*col:
suspicious*) faul.

fission ['fɪʃən] *n* Spaltung *f*.

fissure ['fɪʃə*] *n* Riß *m*.

fist [fɪst] *n* Faust *f*.

fit [fɪt] *a* (*Med*) gesund; (*Sport*) in
Form, fit; (*suitable*) geeignet; *vt*
passen (+*dat*); (*insert, attach*)
einsetzen; *vi* (*correspond*) passen
(zu); (*clothes*) passen; (*in space,
gap*) hineinpassen; *n* (*of clothes*)
Sitz *m*; (*Med, of anger*) Anfall *m*;
(*of laughter*) Krampf *m*; *vi* sich
einfügen; *vt* einpassen; **— out**
vt, **— up** *vt* ausstatten; **—fully, by**

—s and starts move ruckweise; work unregelmäßig; —ment Einrichtungsgegenstand *m*; —ness (suitability) Eignung *f*; (Med) Gesundheit *f*; (Sport) Fitneß *f*; —ter (Tech) Monteur *m*; —ting a passend; *n* (of dress) Anprobe *f*; (piece of equipment) (Ersatz)teil *nt*; —tings pl Zubehör *nt*.

five [faɪv] *num* fünf; —r (Brit) Fünf-Pfund-Note *f*.

fix [fɪks] *vt* befestigen; (settle) festsetzen; (repair) richten, reparieren; drink zurechtmachen; *n*: in a — in der Klemme; —ed a repariert;. time abgemacht; it was —ed (dishonest) das war Schiebung; —ture [ˈfɪkstʃə*] Installationsteil *m*; (Sport) Spiel *nt*.

fizz [fɪz] *n* Sprudeln *nt*; *vi* sprudeln.

fizzle [ˈfɪzl] *vi* zischen; — out *vi* verpuffen.

fizzy [ˈfɪzɪ] *a* Sprudel-, sprudelnd.

fjord [fjɔːd] *n* = fiord.

flabbergasted [ˈflæbəgɑːstɪd] a (col) platt.

flabby [ˈflæbɪ] a wabbelig.

flag [flæg] *n* Fahne *f*; *vi* (strength) nachlassen; (spirit) erlahmen; — down *vt* stoppen, abwinken.

flagon [ˈflægən] *n* bauchige (Wein)-flasche *f*; Krug *m*.

flagpole [ˈflægpəʊl] *n* Fahnenstange *f*.

flagrant [ˈfleɪgrənt] a offenkundig; offence schamlos; violation flagrant.

flagstone [ˈflægstəʊn] *n* Steinplatte *f*.

flair [fleə*] *n* (talent) Talent *nt*; (of style) Schick *m*.

flake [fleɪk] *n* (of snow) Flocke *f*; (of rust) Schuppe *f*; *vi* (also — off) abblättern.

flamboyant [flæmˈbɔɪənt] a extravagant; colours brillant; gesture großartig.

flame [fleɪm] *n* Flamme *f*.

flaming [ˈfleɪmɪŋ] a (col) verdammt; row irre.

flamingo [fləˈmɪŋgəʊ] *n* Flamingo *m*.

flan [flæn] *n* Obsttorte *f*.

flank [flæŋk] *n* Flanke *f*; *vt* flankieren.

flannel [ˈflænl] *n* Flanell *m*; (face —) Waschlappen *m*; (col) Geschwafel *nt*; —s pl Flanellhose *f*.

flap [flæp] *n* Klappe *f*; (col: crisis) (helle) Aufregung *f*; *vt* wings schlagen mit; *vi* lose herabhängen; flattern; (col: panic) sich aufregen.

flare [fleə*] *n* (signal) Leuchtsignal *nt*; (in skirt etc) Weite *f*; — up *vi* aufflammen; (fig) aufbrausen; (revolt) (plötzlich) ausbrechen.

flared [fleəd] a trousers ausgestellt.

flash [flæʃ] *n* Blitz *m*; (news —) Kurzmeldung *f*; (Phot) Blitzlicht *nt*; *vt* aufleuchten lassen; message durchgeben; *vi* aufleuchten; in a — im Nu; to — by or past vorbeirasen; —back Rückblende *f*; —bulb Blitzlichtbirne *f*; —er (Aut) Blinker *m*.

flashy [ˈflæʃɪ] a (pej) knallig.

flask [flɑːsk] *n* Reiseflasche *f*; (Chem) Kolben *m*; (vacuum —) Thermosflasche *f*.

flat [flæt] a flach; (dull) matt; (Mus) erniedrigt; beer schal; tyre platt; A — as; ad (Mus) zu tief; *n* (rooms) Wohnung *f*; (Mus) b *nt*; (Aut) Reifenpanne *f*, Platte(r) *m*; — broke a (col) völlig pleite; —footed a plattfüßig; —ly ad glatt; —ness Flachheit *f*; —ten *vt* (also —ten out) platt machen, (ein)-ebnen.

flatter ['flætə*] vt schmeicheln (+dat); —er Schmeichler(in f) m; —ing a schmeichelhaft; —y Schmeichelei f.

flatulence ['flætjuləns] n Blähungen pl.

flaunt [flɔ:nt] vt prunken mit.

flavour, (US) flavor ['fleɪvə*] n Geschmack m; vt würzen; —ing Würze f.

flaw [flɔ:] n Fehler m; (in argument) schwache(r) Punkt m; —less a einwandfrei.

flax [flæks] n Flachs m; —en a flachsfarben.

flea [fli:] n Floh m.

flee [fli:] irreg vi fliehen; vt fliehen vor (+dat); country fliehen aus.

fleece [fli:s] n Schaffell nt, Vlies nt; vt (col) schröpfen.

fleet [fli:t] n Flotte f.

fleeting ['fli:tɪŋ] a flüchtig.

flesh [fleʃ] n Fleisch nt; (of fruit) Fruchtfleisch nt; — wound Fleisch-wunde f.

flex [fleks] n (Leitungs)kabel nt; vt beugen, biegen; —ibility [fleks'bɪlɪtɪ] Biegsamkeit f; (fig) Flexibilität f; —ible a biegsam; plans flexibel.

flick [flɪk] n Schnippen nt; (blow) leichte(r) Schlag m; vt leicht schlagen; — through vt durch-blättern; to — sth off etw weg-schnippen.

flicker ['flɪkə*] n Flackern nt; (of emotion) Funken m; vi flackern.

flier ['flaɪə*] n Flieger m.

flight [flaɪt] n Fliegen nt; (journey) Flug m; (fleeing) Flucht f; — of stairs Treppe f; to take — die Flucht ergreifen; to put to — in

die Flucht schlagen; — deck Flug-deck nt; —y a flatterhaft.

flimsy ['flɪmzɪ] a nicht stabil, windig; (thin) hauchdünn; excuse fadenscheinig.

flinch [flɪntʃ] vi zurückschrecken (away from vor +dat).

fling [flɪŋ] vt irreg schleudern.

flint [flɪnt] n (in lighter) Feuerstein m.

flip [flɪp] vt werfen; he —ped the lid off er klappte den Deckel auf.

flippancy ['flɪpənsɪ] n Leichtfertig-keit f.

flippant ['flɪpənt] a schnippisch; to be — about sth etw nicht ernst nehmen.

flirt [flɜ:t] vi flirten; n kokette(s) Mädchen nt; he/she is a — er/sie flirtet gern; —ation [flɜ:'teɪʃən] Flirt m.

flit [flɪt] vi flitzen.

float [fləʊt] n (Fishing) Schwimmer m; (esp in procession) Plattform-wagen m; vi schwimmen; (in air) schweben; vt schwimmen lassen; (Comm) gründen; currency floaten; —ing a (lit) schwimmend; (fig) votes unentschieden.

flock [flɒk] n (of sheep, Rel) Herde f; (of birds) Schwarm m; (of people) Schar f.

flog [flɒg] vt prügeln; peitschen; (col: sell) verkaufen.

flood [flʌd] n Überschwemmung f; (fig) Flut f; the F— die Sintflut f; to be in — Hochwasser haben; vt (lit, fig) überschwemmen; —ing Überschwemmung f; —light n Flut-licht nt; vt anstrahlen; —lighting Beleuchtung f.

floor [flɔ:*] n (Fuß)boden m; (storey) Stock m; vt person zu Boden schlagen; ground — (Brit), first — (US) Erdgeschoß nt; first

— (Brit), second — (US) erste(r)
Stock m; —board Diele f; — show
Kabarettvorstellung f; —walker
(Comm) Abteilungsaufseher m.

flop [flɔp] n Plumps m; (failure)
Reinfall m; vi (fail) durchfallen;
the project —ped aus dem Plan
wurde nichts.

floppy ['flɔpɪ] a hängend; — hat
Schlapphut m.

flora ['flɔːrə] n Flora f; —l a
Blumen-.

florid ['flɔrɪd] a style blumig.

florist ['flɔrɪst] n Blumenhändler(in
f) m; —'s (shop) Blumengeschäft
nt.

flotsam ['flɔtsəm] n Strandgut nt.

flounce [flauns] n (on dress) Besatz
m; vi: — in/out hinein-/hinaus-
stürmen.

flounder ['flaundə*] vi herum-
strampeln; (fig) ins Schleudern
kommen.

flour ['flauə*] n Mehl nt.

flourish ['flʌrɪʃ] vi blühen;
gedeihen; vt (wave) schwingen; n
(waving) Schwingen nt; (of
trumpets) Tusch m, Fanfare f;
—ing a blühend.

flout [flaut] vt mißachten, sich hin-
wegsetzen über (+acc).

flow [fləu] n Fließen nt; (of sea)
Flut f; vi fließen.

flower ['flauə*] n Blume f; vi
blühen; — bed Blumenbeet nt;
—pot Blumentopf m; —y a style
blumenreich.

flowing ['fləuɪŋ] a fließend; hair
wallend; style flüssig.

flu [fluː] n Grippe f.

fluctuate ['flʌktjueɪt] vi schwanken.

fluctuation [flʌktjuˈeɪʃən] n
Schwankung f.

fluency ['fluːənsɪ] n Flüssigkeit f;
his — in English seine Fähigkeit,
fließend Englisch zu sprechen.

fluent a —ly ad ['fluːənt,-lɪ] speech
flüssig; to be — in German fließend
Deutsch sprechen.

fluff [flʌf] n Fussel f; —y a
flaumig; pastry flockig.

fluid ['fluːɪd] n Flüssigkeit f; a (lit)
flüssig; (fig) plans veränderbar.

fluke [fluːk] n (col) Dusel m.

fluorescent [fluəˈresnt] a fluores-
zierend, Leucht-.

fluoride ['fluəraɪd] n Fluorid nt.

flurry ['flʌrɪ] n (of activity)
Aufregung f; (of snow) Gestöber nt.

flush [flʌʃ] n Erröten nt; (of excitement) Glühen nt; (Cards) Sequenz
f; vt (aus)spülen; vi erröten; a
glatt; —ed a rot.

fluster ['flʌstə*] n Verwirrung f;
—ed a verwirrt.

flute [fluːt] n Querflöte f.

fluted ['fluːtɪd] a gerillt.

flutter ['flʌtə*] n (of wings)
Flattern nt; (of excitement) Beben
nt; vi flattern; (person) rotieren.

flux [flʌks] n: in a state of — im
Fluß.

fly [flaɪ] n (insect) Fliege f; (on
trousers, also flies) (Hosen)schlitz
m; irreg vt fliegen; vi fliegen;
(flee) fliehen; (flag) wehen; —
open vi auffliegen; let — vti
(shoot) losschießen; (verbally) los-
wettern; insults loslassen; —ing n
Fliegen nt; with —ing colours mit
fliegenden Fahnen; —ing saucer
fliegende Untertasse f; —ing start
gute(r) Start m; —ing visit Stipp-
visite f; —over (Brit) Überführung
f; —paper Fliegenfänger m; —past
Luftparade f; —sheet (for tent)
Regendach nt; —swatter Fliegen-
wedel m; —wheel Schwungrad nt.

foal 492 **foot**

foal [fəʊl] n Fohlen nt.

foam [fəʊm] n Schaum m; (plastic etc) Schaumgummi m; vi schäumen.

fob [fɒb] : — off vt andrehen (sb with sth jdm etw); (with promise) abspeisen.

focal ['fəʊkəl] a im Brennpunkt (stehend), Brennpunkt-.

focus ['fəʊkəs] n Brennpunkt m; (fig) Mittelpunkt m; vt attention konzentrieren; camera scharf einstellen; vi sich konzentrieren (on auf +acc); — sharp eingestellt; out of — unscharf (eingestellt).

fodder ['fɒdə*] n Futter nt.

foe [fəʊ] n (liter) Feind m, Gegner m.

foetus ['fiːtəs] n Fötus m.

fog [fɒg] n Nebel m; vt issue verunklären, verwirren; —gy a neblig, trüb.

foible ['fɔɪbl] n Schwäche f, Faible nt.

foil [fɔɪl] vt vereiteln; n (metal, also fig) Folie f; (fencing) Florett nt.

fold [fəʊld] n (bend, crease) Falte f; (Agr) Pferch m; (for sheep) Pferch m; vt falten; —up vt map etc zusammenfalten; vi (business) eingehen; —er (pamphlet) Broschüre f; (portfolio) Schnellhefter m; —ing a chair etc zusammenklappbar, Klapp-.

foliage ['fəʊlɪdʒ] n Laubwerk nt.

folio ['fəʊlɪəʊ] n Foliant m.

folk [fəʊk] n Volk nt; a Volks-; — s pl Leute pl; —lore (study) Volkskunde f; (tradition) Folklore f; —song Volkslied nt; (modern) Folksong m.

follow ['fɒləʊ] vt folgen (+dat); (obey) befolgen; fashion mitmachen; profession nachgehen (+dat); (understand) folgen können (+dat); vi folgen (result) sich ergeben; — s wie im folgenden; — up vt (weiter) verfolgen; —er Anhänger(in f) m; —ing a folgend; n Folgende(s) nt; (people) Gefolgschaft f.

folly ['fɒlɪ] n Torheit f.

fond [fɒnd] a: to be — of gern haben; —ly ad (with love) liebevoll; (foolishly) törichterweise; —ness Vorliebe f; (for people) Liebe f.

font [fɒnt] n Taufbecken nt.

food [fuːd] n Essen nt, Nahrung f; (for animals) Futter nt; — mixer Küchenmixer m; —poisoning Lebensmittelvergiftung f; —stuffs pl Lebensmittel pl.

fool [fuːl] n Narr m, Närrin f; (jester) (Hof)narr m, Hanswurst m; (food) Mus nt; vt (deceive) hereinlegen; vi (behave like a —) (herum)albern; —hardy a tollkühn; —ish a, —ishly ad dumm; albern; —ishness Dummheit f; —proof a idiotensicher.

foot [fʊt] n Fuß m; (of animal) Pfote f; to put one's — in it ins Fettnäpfchen treten; on — zu Fuß; vt bill bezahlen; —ball Fußball m; —baller Fußballer m; —brake Fußbremse f; —bridge Fußgängerbrücke f; —hills pl Ausläufer pl; —hold Halt m, Stütze f; —ing (lit) Halt m; (fig) Verhältnis nt; to get a —ing in society in der Gesellschaft Fuß fassen; to be on a good —ing with sb mit jdm auf gutem Fuß stehen; —light Rampenlicht nt; —man Bediente(r) m; —and-mouth (disease) Maul- und Klauenseuche f; —note Fußnote f; —path Fußweg m; —rest Fußstütze f; —sore a fußkrank; —step Schritt m; in his father's

—steps in den Fußstapfen seines Vaters; —wear Schuhzeug nt.

fop [fɔp] n Geck m.

for [fɔː*] prep für; cj denn; what —? wozu?

forage ['fɔrɪdʒ] n (Vieh)futter nt; vi nach Nahrung suchen.

foray ['fɔreɪ] n Raubzug m.

forbearing [fɔ'bɛərɪŋ] a geduldig.

forbid [fə'bɪd] vt irreg verbieten; —den a verboten; —ding a einschüchternd, abschreckend.

force [fɔːs] n Kraft f, Stärke f; (compulsion) Zwang m; (Mil) Truppen pl; vt zwingen; lock aufbrechen; plant hochzüchten; in —rule gültig; group in großer Stärke; the F—s pl die Armee; —d a smile gezwungen; landing Not-; —ful a speech kraftvoll; personality resolut.

forceps ['fɔːseps] npl Zange f.

forcible ['fɔːsəbl] a (convincing) wirksam, überzeugend; (violent) gewaltsam.

forcibly ['fɔːsəblɪ] ad unter Zwang, zwangsweise.

ford [fɔːd] n Furt f; vt durchwaten.

fore [fɔː*] a vorder, Vorder-; n: to the — in den Vordergrund.

forearm ['fɔːrɑːm] n Unterarm m.

foreboding [fɔː'bəudɪŋ] n Vorahnung f.

forecast ['fɔːkɑːst] n Vorhersage f; vt irreg voraussagen.

forecourt ['fɔːkɔːt] n (of garage) Vorplatz m.

forefathers ['fɔːfɑːðəz] npl Vorfahren pl.

forefinger ['fɔːfɪŋgə*] n Zeigefinger m.

forefront ['fɔːfrʌnt] n Spitze f.

forego [fɔː'gəu] vt irreg verzichten auf (+acc); —ing a vorangehend;

—ne conclusion ausgemachte Sache.

foreground ['fɔːgraund] n Vordergrund m.

forehead ['fɔrɪd] n Stirn f.

foreign ['fɔrɪn] a Auslands-; country, accent ausländisch; trade Außen-; body Fremd-; —er Ausländer(in f) m; — exchange Devisen pl; — minister Außenminister m.

foreman ['fɔːmən] n Vorarbeiter m.

foremost ['fɔːməust] a erste(r,s).

forensic [fə'rensɪk] a gerichtsmedizinisch.

forerunner ['fɔːrʌnə*] n Vorläufer m.

foresee [fɔː'siː] vt irreg vorhersehen; —able a absehbar.

foreshore ['fɔːʃɔː*] n Küste f, Küstenland nt.

foresight ['fɔːsaɪt] n Voraussicht f.

forest ['fɔrɪst] n Wald m.

forestall [fɔː'stɔːl] vt zuvorkommen (+dat).

forestry ['fɔrɪstrɪ] n Forstwirtschaft f.

foretaste ['fɔːteɪst] n Vorgeschmack m.

foretell [fɔː'tel] vt irreg vorhersagen.

forever [fə'revə*] ad für immer.

forewarn [fɔː'wɔːn] vt vorherwarnen.

foreword ['fɔːwɜːd] n Vorwort nt.

forfeit ['fɔːfɪt] n Einbuße f; vt verwirken.

forge [fɔːdʒ] n Schmiede f; vt fälschen; iron schmieden; — ahead vi Fortschritte machen; —r Fälscher m; —ry Fälschung f.

forget [fə'get] vti irreg vergessen; —ful a vergeßlich; —fulness Vergeßlichkeit f.

forgive [fə'gɪv] vt irreg verzeihen (sb for sth jdm etw).

forgiveness [fə'gɪvnəs] n Verzeihung f.

forgo [fɔː'gəʊ] see forego.

fork [fɔːk] n Gabel f; (in road) Gabelung f; vi (road) sich gabeln; — out vti (col: pay) blechen; —ed a gegabelt; lightning zickzackförmig.

forlorn [fə'lɔːn] a person verlassen; hope vergeblich.

form [fɔːm] n Form f; (type) Art f; (figure) Gestalt f; (Sch) Klasse f; (bench) (Schul)bank f; (document) Formular nt; vt formen; (be part of) bilden.

formal ['fɔːməl] a förmlich, formell; occasion offiziell; —ity [fɔː'mælɪtɪ] Förmlichkeit f; (of occasion) offizieller) Charakter m; —ities pl Formalitäten pl; —ly ad (ceremoniously) formell; (officially) offiziell.

format ['fɔːmæt] n Format nt.

formation [fɔː'meɪʃən] n Bildung f; Gestaltung f; (Aviat) Formation f.

formative ['fɔːmətɪv] a years formend.

former ['fɔːmə*] a früher; (opposite of latter) erstere(r,s); —ly ad früher.

Formica ® [fɔː'maɪkə] n Resopal ® nt.

formidable ['fɔːmɪdəbl] a furchtbar; gewaltig.

formula ['fɔːmjʊlə] n Formel f; —te ['fɔːmjʊleɪt] vt formulieren.

forsake [fə'seɪk] vt irreg im Stich lassen, verlassen; habit aufgeben.

fort [fɔːt] n Feste f, Fort nt.

forte ['fɔːtɪ] n Stärke f, starke Seite f.

forth [fɔːθ] ad: and so — und so weiter; —coming a kommend; character entgegenkommend; —right a offen, gerade heraus.

fortification [fɔːtɪfɪ'keɪʃən] n Befestigung f.

fortify ['fɔːtɪfaɪ] vt (ver)stärken; (protect) befestigen.

fortitude ['fɔːtɪtjuːd] n Seelenstärke f, Mut m.

fortnight ['fɔːtnaɪt] n zwei Wochen pl, vierzehn Tage pl; —ly a zweiwöchentlich; ad alle vierzehn Tage.

fortress ['fɔːtrɪs] n Festung f.

fortuitous [fɔː'tjuːɪtəs] a zufällig.

fortunate ['fɔːtʃənɪt] a glücklich; —ly ad glücklicherweise, zum Glück.

fortune ['fɔːtʃən] n Glück nt; (money) Vermögen nt; —teller Wahrsager(in f) m.

forty ['fɔːtɪ] num vierzig.

forum ['fɔːrəm] n Forum nt.

forward ['fɔːwəd] a vordere(r,s); movement vorwärts; person vorlaut; planning Voraus-; ad vorwärts; n (Sport) Stürmer m; vt (send) schicken; (help) fördern; —s ad vorwärts.

fossil ['fɒsl] n Fossil nt, Versteinerung f.

foster ['fɒstə*] vt talent fördern; — child Pflegekind nt; — mother Pflegemutter f.

foul [faʊl] a schmutzig; language gemein; weather schlecht; n (Sport) Foul nt; vt mechanism blockieren; (Sport) foulen.

found [faʊnd] vt (establish) gründen; —ation [faʊn'deɪʃən] (act) Gründung f; (fig) Fundament nt; —ations pl Fundament nt.

founder ['faʊndə*] n Gründer(in f) m; vi sinken.

foundry ['faʊndrɪ] n Gießerei f, Eisenhütte f.

fount [faʊnt] n (liter) Quell m; —ain (Spring)brunnen m; —ain pen Füllfederhalter m.

four [fɔ:*] num vier; —on all —s auf allen vieren; —some Quartett nt; —teen num vierzehn; —th a vierte(r,s).

fowl [faʊl] n Huhn nt; (food) Geflügel nt.

fox [fɒks] n Fuchs m; —ed a verblüfft; —hunting Fuchsjagd f; —trot Foxtrott m.

foyer ['fɔɪeɪ] n Foyer nt, Vorhalle f.

fracas ['fræka:] n Radau m.

fraction ['frækʃən] n (Math) Bruch m; (part) Bruchteil m.

fracture ['fræktʃə*] n (Med) Bruch m; vt brechen.

fragile ['frædʒaɪl] a zerbrechlich.

fragment ['frægmənt] n 'Bruchstück nt, Fragment nt; (small part) Stück nt, Splitter m; —ary ['fræg'mentərɪ] a bruchstückhaft, fragmentarisch.

fragrance ['freɪgrəns] n Duft m.

fragrant ['freɪgrənt] a duftend.

frail [freɪl] a schwach, gebrechlich.

frame [freɪm] n'Rahmen m; (body) Gestalt f; vt einrahmen; (make) gestalten, machen; (col: incriminate) to — sb jdm etw anhängen; — of mind Verfassung f; —work Rahmen m; (of society) Gefüge nt.

franchise ['fræntʃaɪz] n (aktives) Wahlrecht nt.

frank [fræŋk] a offen; —furter Saitenwürstchen nt; —ly ad offen gesagt; —ness Offenheit f.

frankincense ['fræŋkɪnsens] n Weihrauch m.

frantic ['fræntɪk] a effort verzweifelt; — with worry außer sich vor Sorge; —ally ad außer sich; verzweifelt.

fraternal [frə'tɜ:nl] a brüderlich.

fraternity [frə'tɜ:nɪtɪ] n (club) Vereinigung f; (spirit) Brüderlichkeit f; (US Sch) Studentenverbindung f.

fraternization [frætənaɪ'zeɪʃən] n Verbrüderung f.

fraternize ['frætənaɪz] vi fraternisieren.

fraud [frɔ:d] n (trickery) Betrug m; (trick) Schwindel m, Trick m; (person) Schwindler(in f) m.

fraudulent ['frɔ:djʊlənt] a betrügerisch.

fraught [frɔ:t] a either (with gen).

fray [freɪ] n Rauferei f; vti ausfransen.

freak [fri:k] n Monstrosität f; (crazy person) Irre(r) mf; (storm etc) Ausnahmeerscheinung f; a storm, conditions anormal; animal monströs; — out vi (col) durchdrehen.

freckle ['frekl] n Sommersprosse f; —d a sommersprossig.

free [fri:] a frei; (loose) lose; (liberal) freigebig; to get sth — etw umsonst bekommen; you're — to ... es steht dir frei zu ...; vt (set free) befreien; (unblock) freimachen; —dom Freiheit f; —for-all allgemeine(r) Wettbewerb m; (fight) allgemeine(s) Handgemenge nt; —kick Freistoß m; —lance a frei; artist freischaffend; —ly ad frei; lose; (generously) reichlich; admit offen; —mason Freimaurer m; —masonry Freimaurerei f; —trade Freihandel m; —way (US) Autobahn f; —wheel vi im Freilauf fahren.

freesia ['fri:ʒə] n Freesie f.

freeze [fri:z] irreg vi gefrieren; (feel cold) frieren; vt (lit, fig) einfrieren; n (fig, Fin) Stopp m; ~r Tiefkühltruhe f; (in fridge) Gefrierfach nt.

freezing ['fri:zɪŋ] a eisig; (~ cold) eiskalt; ~ point Gefrierpunkt m.

freight [freɪt] n (goods) Fracht f; (money charged) Fracht(gebühr) f; ~ car (US) Güterwagen m; ~er (Naut) Frachtschiff nt.

French [frentʃ] a: ~ fried potatoes pl Pommes frites pl; ~ window Verandatür f; see appendix.

frenzy ['frenzɪ] n Raserei f, wilde Aufregung f.

frequency ['fri:kwənsɪ] n Häufigkeit f; (Phys) Frequenz f.

frequent a, ~ly ['fri:kwənt,-lɪ] häufig; ['fri:'kwent] vt (regelmäßig) besuchen.

fresco ['freskəʊ] n Fresko nt.

fresh [freʃ] a frisch; (new) neu; (cheeky) frech; ~en (also ~en up) vi (sich) auffrischen; (person) sich frisch machen; vt auffrischen; ~ly ad gerade; ~ness Frische f; ~water a fish Süßwasser-.

fret [fret] vi sich (dat) Sorgen machen (about über + acc).

friar ['fraɪə*] n Klosterbruder m.

friction ['frɪkʃən] n (lit, fig) Reibung f.

Friday ['fraɪdeɪ] n Freitag m; see good.

fridge [frɪdʒ] n Kühlschrank m.

fried [fraɪd] a gebraten.

friend [frend] n Bekannte(r) mf; (more intimate) Freund(in f) m; ~liness Freundlichkeit f; ~ly a freundlich; relations freundschaftlich; ~ship Freundschaft f.

frieze [fri:z] n Fries m.

frigate ['frɪgɪt] n Fregatte f.

fright [fraɪt] n Schrecken m; you look a ~ (col) du siehst unmöglich aus!; ~en vt erschrecken; to be ~ened Angst haben; ~ening a schrecklich; ängstigend; ~ful a, ~fully ad (col) schrecklich, furchtbar.

frigid ['frɪdʒɪd] a kalt, eisig; woman frigide; ~ity [frɪ'dʒɪdɪtɪ] Kälte f; Frigidität f.

frill [frɪl] n Rüsche f.

fringe [frɪndʒ] n Besatz m; (hair) Pony m; (fig) äußere(r) Rand m, Peripherie f.

frisky ['frɪskɪ] a lebendig, ausgelassen.

fritter ['frɪtə*] : ~ away vt vertun, verplempern.

frivolity [frɪ'vɒlɪtɪ] n Leichtfertigkeit f, Frivolität f.

frivolous ['frɪvələs] a frivol, leichtsinnig.

frizzy ['frɪzɪ] a kraus.

fro [frəʊ] see to.

frock [frɒk] n Kleid nt.

frog [frɒg] n Frosch m; ~man Froschmann m.

frolic ['frɒlɪk] n lustige(r) Streich m; vi ausgelassen sein.

from [frɒm] prep von; (place) aus; (judging by) nach; (because of) wegen (+ gen).

front [frʌnt] n Vorderseite f; (of house) Fassade f; (promenade) Strandpromenade f; (Mil, Pol, Met) Front f; (fig: appearances) Fassade f; a (forward) vordere(r,s), Vorder-; (first) vorderste(r,s); page erste(r,s); door Eingangs-, Haus-; in ~ ad vorne; in ~ of prep vor; ~age Vorderfront f; ~al a frontal, Vorder-; ~ier ['frʌntɪə*] Grenze f.

— room (*Brit*) Vorderzimmer *nt*, Wohnzimmer *nt*; —-wheel drive Vorderradantrieb *m*.

frost [frɒst] *n* Frost *m*; —-bite Erfrierung *f*; —ed a glass Milch-; —y a frostig.

froth [frɒθ] *n* Schaum *m*; —y a schaumig.

frown [fraun] *n* Stirnrunzeln *nt*; *vi* die Stirn runzeln.

frozen [frəuzn] a food gefroren; (*Fin*) assets festgelegt.

frugal ['fru:gəl] a sparsam, bescheiden.

fruit [fru:t] *n* (*particular*) Frucht *f*; I like — ich esse gern Obst; —erer Obsthändler *m*; —ful a fruchtbar; —ion [fru:'ɪʃən] Verwirklichung *f*; to come to —ion in Erfüllung gehen; — machine Spielautomat *m*; — salad Obstsalat *m*.

frustrate [frʌs'treit] *vt* vereiteln; —d a gehemmt; (*Psych*) frustriert.

frustration [frʌs'treiʃən] *n* Behinderung *f*; Frustration *f*.

fry [frai] *vt* braten; small — *pl* kleine Leute *pl*; (*children*) Kleine(n) *pl*; —ing pan Bratpfanne *f*.

fuchsia ['fju:ʃə] *n* Fuchsie *f*.

fuddy-duddy ['fʌdɪdʌdɪ] *n* altmodische(r) Kauz *m*.

fudge [fʌdʒ] *n* Karamellen *pl*.

fuel [fjuəl] *n* Treibstoff *m*; (*for heating*) Brennstoff *m*; (*for cigarette lighter*) Benzin *nt*; — oil (*diesel fuel*) Heizöl *nt*; — tank Tank *m*.

fugitive ['fju:dʒɪtɪv] *n* Flüchtling *m*; (*from prison*) Flüchtige(r) *mf*.

fulfil [ful'fil] *vt* duty erfüllen; promise einhalten; —ment Erfüllung *f*; Einhaltung *f*.

full [ful] a box, bottle, price voll; person (*satisfied*) satt; member,

power, employment, moon voll-; (*complete*) vollständig, Voll-; speed höchste(r, s); skirt weit; in — vollständig, ungekürzt; —back Verteidiger *m*; —ness Fülle *f*; — stop Punkt *m*; —-time a job Ganztags-; ad work hauptberuflich; —y ad völlig; —y-fledged a (*lit, fig*) flügge; a —y-fledged teacher ein vollausgebildeter Lehrer.

fumble ['fʌmbl] *vi* herumfummeln (with, at an+dat).

fume [fju:m] *vi* rauchen, qualmen; (*fig*) wütend sein, kochen (*col*); —s *pl* Abgase *pl*; Qualm *m*.

fumigate ['fju:mɪgeit] *vt* ausräuchern.

fun [fʌn] *n* Spaß *m*; to make — of sich lustig machen über (+*acc*).

function ['fʌŋkʃən] *n* Funktion *f*; (*occasion*) Veranstaltung *f*, Feier *f*; *vi* funktionieren; —al a funktionell, praktisch.

fund [fʌnd] *n* (*money*) Geldmittel *pl*, Fonds *m*; (*store*) Schatz *m*, Vorrat *m*.

fundamental [fʌndə'mentl] a fundamental, grundlegend; —s *pl* Grundbegriffe *pl*; —ly ad im Grunde.

funeral ['fju:nərəl] *n* Beerdigung *f*; a Beerdigungs-.

fungus ['fʌŋgəs] *n*, *pl* fungi or funguses Pilz *m*.

funicular [fju:'nɪkjulə*] *n* (Draht-)seilbahn *f*.

funnel ['fʌnl] *n* Trichter *m*; (*Naut*) Schornstein *m*.

funnily ['fʌnɪlɪ] ad komisch; — enough merkwürdigerweise.

funny ['fʌnɪ] a komisch; — bone Musikantenknochen *m*.

fur [fɜ:*] *n* Pelz *m*; — coat Pelzmantel *m*.

furious a, **—ly** ad ['fjuəriəs, -li] wütend; *attempt* heftig.
furlong ['fɜːlɒŋ] n = 220 yards.
furlough ['fɜːləu] n (US) Urlaub m.
furnace ['fɜːnis] n (Brenn)ofen m.
furnish ['fɜːniʃ] vt einrichten, möblieren; (*supply*) versehen; **—ings** pl Einrichtung f.
furniture ['fɜːnitʃə*] n Möbel pl.
furrow ['fʌrəu] n Furche f.
furry ['fɜːri] a pelzartig; *tongue* pelzig; *animal* Pelz-.
further ['fɜːðə*] comp of **far**; a weitere(r,s); ad weiter; vt fördern; **— education** Weiterbildung f; Erwachsenenbildung f; **—more** ad ferner.
furthest ['fɜːðist] superl of **far**.
furtive a, **—ly** ad ['fɜːtiv, -li] verstohlen.
fury ['fjuəri] n Wut f, Zorn m.
fuse [fjuːz] n (Elec) Sicherung f;

(*of bomb*) Zünder m; vt verschmelzen; vi (Elec) durchbrennen; **— box** Sicherungskasten m.
fuselage ['fjuːzəlɑːʒ] n Flugzeugrumpf m.
fusion ['fjuːʒən] n Verschmelzung f.
fuss [fʌs] n Theater nt; **—y** a (*difficult*) heikel; (*attentive to detail*) kleinlich.
futile ['fjuːtail] a zwecklos, sinnlos.
futility [fjuː'tiliti] n Zwecklosigkeit f.
future ['fjuːtʃə*] a zukünftig; n Zukunft f; **in (the) —** in Zukunft, zukünftig.
futuristic [fjuːtʃə'ristik] a futuristisch.
fuze [fjuːz] (US) = **fuse**.
fuzzy ['fʌzi] a (*indistinct*) verschwommen; *hair* kraus.

G

G, g [dʒiː] n G nt, g nt.
gabble ['gæbl] vi plappern.
gable ['geibl] n Giebel m.
gadget ['gædʒit] n Vorrichtung f; **—ry** Kinkerlitzchen pl.
gaffe [gæf] n Fauxpas m.
gag [gæg] n Knebel m; (*Theat*) Gag m; vt knebeln; (*Pol*) mundtot machen.
gaiety ['geiiti] n Fröhlichkeit f.
gaily ['geili] ad lustig, fröhlich.
gain [gein] vt (*obtain*) erhalten; (*win*) gewinnen; vi (*improve*) gewinnen (*in an* + dat); (*make progress*) Vorsprung gewinnen; (*clock*) vorgehen; n Gewinn m; **—ful employment** Erwerbstätigkeit

f.
gala ['gɑːlə] n Fest nt.
galaxy ['gæləksi] n Sternsystem nt.
gale [geil] n Sturm m.
gallant ['gælənt] a tapfer, ritterlich; (*polite*) galant; **—ry** Tapferkeit f, Ritterlichkeit f; Galanterie f.
gall-bladder ['gɔːlblædə*] n Gallenblase f.
gallery ['gæləri] n Galerie f.
galley ['gæli] n (*ship's kitchen*) Kombüse f; (*ship*) Galeere f.
gallon ['gælən] n Gallone f.
gallop ['gæləp] n Galopp m; vi galoppieren.

gallows ['gæləʊz] npl Galgen m.

gallstone ['gɔ:lstəʊn] n Gallenstein m.

gamble ['gæmbl] vi (um Geld) spielen; vt (risk) aufs Spiel setzen; n Risiko nt; —r Spieler(in f) m.

gambling ['gæmblɪŋ] n Glücksspiel nt.

game [geɪm] n Spiel nt; (hunting) Wild nt; a bereit (for zu); (brave) mutig; —keeper Wildhüter m.

gammon ['gæmən] n geräucherte(r) Schinken m.

gander ['gændə*] n Gänserich m.

gang [gæŋ] n (of criminals, youths) Bande f; (of workmen) Kolonne f.

gangrene ['gæŋgri:n] n Brand m.

gangster ['gæŋstə*] n Gangster m.

gangway ['gæŋweɪ] n (Naut) Laufplanke f.

gaol [dʒeɪl] n = jail.

gap [gæp] n (hole) Lücke f; (space) Zwischenraum m.

gape [geɪp] vi glotzen.

gaping ['geɪpɪŋ] a wound klaffend; hole gähnend.

garage ['gærɑ:ʒ] n Garage f; (for repair) (Auto)reparaturwerkstatt f; (for petrol) Tankstelle f; vt einstellen.

garbage ['gɑ:bɪdʒ] n Abfall m; — can (US) Mülltonne f.

garbled ['gɑ:bld] a story verdreht.

garden ['gɑ:dn] n Garten m; vi gärtnern; —er Gärtner(in f) m; —ing Gärtnern nt; — party Gartenfest nt.

gargle ['gɑ:gl] vi gurgeln; n Gurgelmittel nt.

gargoyle ['gɑ:gɔɪl] n Wasserspeier m.

garish ['geərɪʃ] a grell.

garland ['gɑ:lənd] n Girlande f.

garlic ['gɑ:lɪk] n Knoblauch m.

garment ['gɑ:mənt] n Kleidungsstück m.

garnish ['gɑ:nɪʃ] vt food garnieren; n Garnierung f.

garret ['gærɪt] n Dachkammer f, Mansarde f.

garrison ['gærɪsən] n Garnison f; vt besetzen.

garrulous ['gærʊləs] a geschwätzig.

garter ['gɑ:tə*] n Strumpfband nt.

gas [gæs] n Gas nt; (Med) Betäubungsmittel nt; (esp US: petrol) Benzin nt; to step on the — Gas geben; vt vergasen; — cooker Gasherd m; — cylinder Gasflasche f; — fire Gasofen m, Gasheizung f.

gash [gæʃ] n klaffende Wunde f; vt tief verwunden.

gasket ['gæskɪt] n Dichtungsring m.

gasmask ['gæsmɑ:sk] n Gasmaske f.

gas meter ['gæsmi:tə*] n Gaszähler m.

gasoline ['gæsəli:n] n (US) Benzin nt.

gasp [gɑ:sp] vi keuchen; (in astonishment) tief Luft holen; n Keuchen nt.

gas ring ['gæsrɪŋ] n Gasring m.

gas station ['gæssteɪʃən] n (US) Tankstelle f.

gas stove ['gæsstəʊv] n Gaskocher m.

gassy ['gæsɪ] a drink sprudelnd.

gastric ['gæstrɪk] a Magen-; — ulcer Magengeschwür nt.

gastronomy [gæs'trɒnəmɪ] n Kochkunst f.

gate [geɪt] n Tor nt; (barrier) Schranke f; —crash vt party platzen in (+acc); —way Toreingang m.

gather ['gæðə*] vt people versammeln; things sammeln; vi (understand) annehmen; (deduce) schließen (from aus); (assemble) sich versammeln;; —ing Versammlung f.

gauche [gəʊʃ] a linkisch.

gaudy ['gɔ:dɪ] a schreiend.

gauge [geɪdʒ] n Normalmaß nt; (Rail) Spurweite f; (dial) Anzeiger m; (measure) Maß nt; vt (lit) (ab)messen;; (fig) abschätzen.

gaunt [gɔ:nt] a hager.

gauntlet ['gɔ:ntlɪt] n (knight's) Fehdehandschuh m; Handschuh m.

gauze [gɔ:z] n Mull m, Gaze f.

gawk [gɔ:k] vi dumm (an)glotzen (at acc).

gay [geɪ] a lustig; (coloured) bunt; (col) schwul.

gaze [geɪz] n Blick m; vi (an)blicken (at acc).

gazelle [gə'zel] n Gazelle f.

gazetteer [gæzɪ'tɪə*] n geographische(s) Lexikon nt.

gear [gɪə*] n Getriebe nt; (equipment) Ausrüstung f; (Aut) Gang m; to be out of/in — aus-/eingekuppelt sein; —box Getriebe(gehäuse) nt; —lever, —shift (US) Schalthebel m.

geese [gi:s] pl of **goose**.

gelatin(e) ['dʒelətin] n Gelatine f.

gem [dʒem] n Edelstein m; (fig) Juwel nt.

Gemini ['dʒemɪni:] n Zwillinge pl.

gen [dʒen] n (col: information) Infos pl (on über +acc).

gender ['dʒendə*] n (Gram) Geschlecht nt.

gene [dʒi:n] n Gen nt.

general ['dʒenərəl] n General m; a allgemein; — **election** allgemeine Wahlen pl; —**ization** Verall-

gemeinerung f; —**ize** vi verallgemeinern; —**ly** ad allgemein, im allgemeinen.

generate ['dʒenəreɪt] vt erzeugen.

generation [dʒenə'reɪʃən] n Generation f; (act) Erzeugung f.

generator ['dʒenəreɪtə*] n Generator m.

generosity [dʒenə'rɒsɪtɪ] n Großzügigkeit f.

generous a, —**ly** ad ['dʒenərəs, -lɪ] (noble-minded) hochherzig; (giving freely) großzügig.

genetics ['dʒɪ'netɪks] n Genetik f, Vererbungslehre f.

genial ['dʒi:nɪəl] a freundlich, jovial.

genitals ['dʒenɪtlz] npl Geschlechtsteile pl, Genitalien pl.

genitive ['dʒenɪtɪv] n Genitiv m, Wesfall m.

genius ['dʒi:nɪəs] n Genie nt.

genocide ['dʒenəʊsaɪd] n Völkermord m.

genteel [dʒen'ti:l] a (polite) wohlanständig; (affected) affektiert.

gentile ['dʒentaɪl] n Nichtjude m.

gentle ['dʒentl] a sanft, zart; —**man** Herr m; (polite) Gentleman m; —**ness** Zartheit f, Milde f.

gently ['dʒentlɪ] ad zart, sanft.

gentry ['dʒentrɪ] n Landadel m.

gents [dʒents] n: '**G—**' (lavatory) 'Herren'.

genuine ['dʒenjʊɪn] a echt, wahr; —**ly** ad wirklich, echt.

geographer [dʒɪ'ɒgrəfə*] n Geograph(in f) m.

geographical [dʒɪə'græfɪkəl] a geographisch.

geography [dʒɪ'ɒgrəfɪ] n Geographie f, Erdkunde f.

geological [dʒɪəʊ'lɒdʒɪkəl] a geologisch.

geologist [dʒɪˈɒlədʒɪst] *n* Geologe *m*, Geologin *f.*

geology [dʒɪˈɒlədʒɪ] *n* Geologie *f.*

geometric(al) [dʒɪəˈmetrɪk(əl)] *a* geometrisch.

geometry [dʒɪˈɒmɪtrɪ] *n* Geometrie *f.*

geranium [dʒɪˈreɪnɪəm] *n* Geranie *f.*

germ [dʒɜːm] *n* Keim *m*; (*Med*) Bazillus *m.*

germination [dʒɜːmɪˈneɪʃən] *n* Keimen *nt.*

gesticulate [dʒesˈtɪkjʊleɪt] *vi* gestikulieren.

gesticulation [dʒestɪkjʊˈleɪʃən] *n* Gesten *pl*, Gestikulieren *nt.*

gesture [ˈdʒestʃə*] *n* Geste *f.*

get [get] *vt irreg* (*receive*) bekommen, kriegen; (*become*) werden; (*go, travel*) kommen; (*arrive*) ankommen; **to — sb to do sth** jdn dazu bringen, etw zu tun, jdn etw machen lassen; **— along** *vi* (*people*) (*gut*) zurechtkommen; (*depart*) sich (*acc*) auf den Weg machen; **— at** *vt facts* herausbekommen; **to — at sb** (*nag*) an jdm herumnörgeln; **— away** *vi* (*leave*) sich (*acc*) davonmachen; (*escape*) entkommen (*from dat*); **— away with you!** laß den Quatsch!; **— down** *vi* (her)untergehen; *vt* (*depress*) fertigmachen; **— in** *vi* (*train*) ankommen; (*arrive home*) heimkommen; **— off** *vi* (*from train etc*) aussteigen (aus); (*from horse*) absteigen (von); **— on** *vi* (*progress*) vorankommen; (*be friends*) auskommen; (*age*) alt werden; *vt train etc* einsteigen (in + *acc*); *horse* aufsteigen (auf + *acc*); **— out** *vi* (*of house*) herauskommen; (*of vehicle*) aussteigen; *vt* (*take out*) herausholen; **— over** *vt illness* sich (*acc*) erholen von;

surprise verkraften; *news* fassen; *loss* sich abfinden mit; **I couldn't — over her** ich konnte sie nicht vergessen; **— up** *vi* aufstehen; **—away** Flucht *f.*

geyser [ˈgiːzə*] *n* Geiser *m*; (*heater*) Durchlauferhitzer *m.*

ghastly [ˈgɑːstlɪ] *a* (*horrible*) gräßlich; (*pale*) totenbleich.

gherkin [ˈgɜːkɪn] *n* Gewürzgurke *f.*

ghetto [ˈgetəʊ] *n* G(h)etto *nt.*

ghost [gəʊst] *n* Gespenst *nt*, Geist *m*; **—ly** *a* gespenstisch; **— story** Gespenstergeschichte *f.*

giant [ˈdʒaɪənt] *n* Riese *m*; *a* riesig, Riesen-.

gibberish [ˈdʒɪbərɪʃ] *n* dumme(s) Geschwätz *nt.*

gibe [dʒaɪb] *n* spöttische Bemerkung *f.*

giblets [ˈdʒɪblɪts] *npl* Geflügelinnereien *pl.*

giddiness [ˈgɪdɪnəs] *n* Schwindelgefühl *nt.*

giddy [ˈgɪdɪ] *a* schwindlig; (*frivolous*) leichtsinnig.

gift [gɪft] *n* Geschenk *nt*; (*ability*) Begabung *f*; **—ed** *a* begabt.

gigantic [dʒaɪˈgæntɪk] *a* riesenhaft, ungeheuer groß.

giggle [ˈgɪgl] *vi* kichern; *n* Gekicher *nt.*

gild [gɪld] *vt* vergolden.

gill¹ [dʒɪl] *n* (1/4 *pint*) Viertelpinte *f.*

gill² [gɪl] *n* (*of fish*) Kieme *f.*

gilt [gɪlt] *n* Vergoldung *f*; *a* vergoldet.

gimlet [ˈgɪmlɪt] *n* Handbohrer *m.*

gimmick [ˈgɪmɪk] *n* (*for sales, publicity*) Gag *m*; **it's so —y** es ist alles nur ein Gag.

gin [dʒɪn] *n* Gin *m.*

ginger ['dʒɪndʒə*] *n* Ingwer *m*; —ale, — beer Ingwerbier *nt*; —bread Pfefferkuchen *m*; —haired *a* rothaarig.

gingerly ['dʒɪndʒəlɪ] *ad* behutsam.

gipsy ['dʒɪpsɪ] *n* Zigeuner(in *f*) *m*.

giraffe [dʒɪ'rɑːf] *n* Giraffe *f*.

girder ['gɜːdə*] *n* (steel) Eisenträger *m*; (wood) Tragebalken *m*.

girdle ['gɜːdl] *n* (woman's) Hüftgürtel *m*; *vt* umgürten.

girl [gɜːl] *n* Mädchen *nt*; —friend Freundin *f*; —ish *a* mädchenhaft.

girth [gɜːθ] *n* (measure) Umfang *m*; (strap) Sattelgurt *m*.

gist [dʒɪst] *n* Wesentliche(s) *nt*, Quintessenz *f*.

give [gɪv] *irreg vt* geben; *vi* (break) nachgeben; — **away** *vt* (give free) verschenken; (betray) verraten; — **back** *vt* zurückgeben; — **in** *vi* (yield) aufgeben; (agree) nachgeben; *vt* (hand in) abgeben; — **up** *vti* aufgeben; — **way** *vi* (traffic) Vorfahrt lassen; (to feelings) nachgeben (+ *dat*).

glacier ['glæsɪə*] *n* Gletscher *m*.

glad [glæd] *a* froh; **I was — to hear . . .** ich habe mich gefreut, zu hören . . .; —**den** *vt* erfreuen.

gladiator ['glædɪeɪtə*] *n* Gladiator *m*.

gladioli [glædɪ'əʊlaɪ] *npl* Gladiolen *pl*.

gladly ['glædlɪ] *ad* gern(e).

glamorous ['glæmərəs] *a* bezaubernd; *life* reizvoll.

glamour ['glæmə*] *n* Zauber *m*, Reiz *m*.

glance [glɑːns] *n* flüchtige(r) Blick *m*; *vi* schnell (hin)blicken (*at auf* + *acc*); — **off** *vi* (fly off) abprallen von.

glancing ['glɑːnsɪŋ] *a* blow abprallend, Streif-.

gland [glænd] *n* Drüse *f*; —**ular** fever Drüsenentzündung *f*.

glare [glɛə*] *n* (light) grelle(s) Licht *nt*; (stare) wilde(r) Blick *m*; *vi* grell scheinen; (angrily) böse ansehen (*at acc*).

glaring ['glɛərɪŋ] *a* injustice schreiend; mistake kraß.

glass [glɑːs] *n* Glas *nt*; (mirror) Spiegel *m*; —**es** *pl* Brille *f*; —**house** Gewächshaus *nt*; —**ware** Glaswaren *pl*; —**y** *a* glasig.

glaze [gleɪz] *vt* verglasen; (finish with a —) glasieren; *n* Glasur *f*.

glazier ['gleɪzɪə*] *n* Glaser *m*.

gleam [gliːm] *n* Schimmer *m*; *vi* schimmern; —**ing** *a* schimmernd.

glee [gliː] *n* Frohsinn *m*; —**ful** *a* fröhlich.

glen [glen] *n* Bergtal *nt*.

glib [glɪb] *a* (rede)gewandt; (superficial) oberflächlich; —**ly** *ad* glatt.

glide [glaɪd] *vi* gleiten; *n* Gleiten *nt*; (Aviat) Segelflug *m*; —**r** (Aviat) Segelflugzeug *nt*.

gliding ['glaɪdɪŋ] *n* Segelfliegen *nt*.

glimmer ['glɪmə*] *n* Schimmer *m*; — **of hope** Hoffnungsschimmer *m*.

glimpse [glɪmps] *n* flüchtige(r) Blick *m*; *vt* flüchtig erblicken.

glint [glɪnt] *n* Glitzern *nt*; *vi* glitzern.

glisten ['glɪsn] *vi* glänzen.

glitter ['glɪtə*] *vi* funkeln; *n* Funkeln *nt*; —**ing** *a* glitzernd.

gloat over ['gləʊtəʊvə*] *vt* sich weiden an (+ *dat*).

global ['gləʊbl] *a* global.

globe [gləʊb] *n* Erdball *m*; (sphere) Globus *m*; —**trotter** Weltenbummler(in *f*) *m*, Globetrotter(in *f*) *m*.

gloom [glu:m] *n* (*also* —iness) (*darkness*) Dunkel *nt*, Dunkelheit *f*; (*depression*) düstere Stimmung *f*; —ily *ad*, —y a düster.

glorification [glɔːrɪfɪˈkeɪʃən] *n* Verherrlichung *f*.

glorify [ˈglɔːrɪfaɪ] *vt* verherrlichen; **just a glorified cafe** nur ein besseres Café.

glorious [ˈglɔːrɪəs] a glorreich; (*splendid*) prächtig.

glory [ˈglɔːrɪ] *n* Herrlichkeit *f*; (*praise*) Ruhm *m*; **to —** in sich sonnen in (+*dat*).

gloss [glɒs] *n* (*shine*) Glanz *m*; — **paint** Ölfarbe *f*; **— over** *vt* übertünchen.

glossary [ˈglɒsərɪ] *n* Glossar *nt*.

glossy [ˈglɒsɪ] a **surface** glänzend.

glove [glʌv] *n* Handschuh *m*.

glow [gləʊ] *vi* glühen, leuchten; *n* (*heat*) Glühen *nt*; (*colour*) Röte *f*; (*feeling*) Wärme *f*.

glower [ˈglaʊə*] *vi*: **— at** finster anblicken.

glucose [ˈgluːkəʊs] *n* Traubenzucker *m*.

glue [gluː] *n* Klebstoff *m*, Leim *m*; *vt* leimen, kleben.

glum [glʌm] a bedrückt.

glut [glʌt] *n* Überfluß *m*; *vt* überladen.

glutton [ˈglʌtn] *n* Vielfraß *m*; (*fig*) Unersättliche(r) *mf*; **—ous** a gierig; **—y** Völlerei *f*; Unersättlichkeit *f*.

glycerin(e) [ˈglɪsəriːn] *n* Glyzerin *nt*.

gnarled [nɑːld] a knorrig.

gnat [næt] *n* Stechmücke *f*.

gnaw [nɔː] *vt* nagen an (+*dat*).

gnome [nəʊm] *n* Gnom *m*.

go [gəʊ] *vi irreg* gehen; (*travel*) reisen, fahren; (*depart: train*) (ab)fahren; (*money*) ausgehen; (*vision*) verschwinden; (*smell*) verfliegen; (*disappear*) (fort)gehen; (*be sold*) kosten; (*at auction*) weggehen; (*work*) gehen, funktionieren; (*fit, suit*) passen (*with* zu); (*become*) werden; (*break etc*) nachgeben; *n* (*energy*) Schwung *m*; (*attempt*) Versuch *m*; **can I have another —?** darf ich noch mal?; **— ahead** *vi* (*proceed*) weitergehen; **— along with** *vt* (*agree to support*) zustimmen (+*dat*), unterstützen; **— away** *vi* (*depart*) weggehen; **— back** *vi* (*return*) zurückgehen; **— back on** *vt promise* nicht halten; **— by** *vt* (*years, time*) vergehen; **— down** *vi* (*sun*) untergehen; **— for** *vt* (*fetch*) holen (*gehen*); (*like*) mögen; (*attack*) sich stürzen auf (+*acc*); **— in** *vi* hineingehen; **— into** *vt* (*enter*) hineingehen in (+*acc*); (*study*) sich befassen mit; **— off** *vi* (*depart*) weggehen; (*lights*) ausgehen; (*milk etc*) sauer werden; (*explode*) losgehen; *vt* (*dislike*) nicht mehr mögen; **— on** *vi* (*continue*) weitergehen; (*col: complain*) meckern; (*lights*) angehen; **to — on with** sth mit etw weitermachen; **— out** *vi* (*fire, light*) ausgehen; (*of house*) hinausgehen; **— over** *vt* (*examine, check*) durchgehen; **— up** *vi* (*price*) steigen; **— without** *vt* sich behelfen ohne; *food* entbehren.

goad [gəʊd] *vt* anstacheln; *n* Treibstock *m*.

go-ahead [ˈgəʊəhed] a zielstrebig; (*progressive*) fortschrittlich; *n* grünes Licht *nt*.

goal [gəʊl] *n* Ziel *nt*; (*Sport*) Tor *nt*; **—keeper** Torwart *m*; **—post** Torpfosten *m*.

goat [gəut] n Ziege f.

gobble ['gɒbl] vt hinunterschlingen.

go-between ['gəubitwi:n] n Mittelsmann m.

goblet ['gɒblɪt] n Kelch(glas nt) m.

goblin ['gɒblɪn] n Kobold m.

god [gɒd] n Gott m; —child Patenkind nt; —dess Göttin f; —father Pate m; —forsaken a gottverlassen; —mother Patin f; —send Geschenk nt des Himmels.

goggle ['gɒgl] vi (stare) glotzen; to — at anglotzen; —s pl Schutzbrille f.

going ['gəuɪŋ] n (condition of ground) Straßenzustand m; (horseracing) Bahn f; it's hard — es ist schwierig; a rate gängig; concern gutgehend; —s-on pl Vorgänge pl.

gold [gəuld] n Gold nt; —en a golden, Gold-; —fish Goldfisch m; — mine Goldgrube f.

golf [gɒlf] n Golf nt; — club (society) Golfklub m; (stick) Golfschläger m; — course Golfplatz m; —er Golfspieler(in f) m.

gondola ['gɒndələ] n Gondel f.

gong [gɒŋ] n Gong m.

good [gud] n (benefit) Wohl nt; (moral excellence) Güte f; a gut; (suitable) passend; —s pl Ware(n pl) f, Güter pl; a — deal of ziemlich viel; a — many ziemlich viele; —bye! auf Wiedersehen!; G-Friday Karfreitag m; —looking a gutaussehend; — morning! guten Morgen!; —ness Güte f; (virtue) Tugend f; —will (favour) Wohlwollen nt; (Comm) Firmenansehen nt.

goose [gu:s] n Gans f; —berry [guzbəri] Stachelbeere f; —flesh, — pimples pl Gänsehaut f.

gore [gɔ:*] vt durchbohren; aufspießen; n Blut nt.

gorge [gɔ:dʒ] n Schlucht f; vti (sich voll)fressen.

gorgeous ['gɔ:dʒəs] a prächtig; person bildhübsch.

gorilla [gə'rɪlə] n Gorilla m.

gorse [gɔ:s] n Stechginster m.

gory ['gɔ:rɪ] a blutig.

go-slow ['gəu'sləu] n Bummelstreik m.

gospel ['gɒspəl] n Evangelium nt.

gossamer ['gɒsəmə*] n Spinnfäden pl.

gossip ['gɒsɪp] n Klatsch m; (person) Klatschbase f; vi klatschen.

goulash ['gu:læʃ] n Gulasch nt or m.

gout [gaut] n Gicht f.

govern ['gʌvən] vt regieren; verwalten; (Gram) bestimmen; —ess Gouvernante f; —ing a leitend; (fig) bestimmend; —ment Regierung f; a Regierungs-; —or Gouverneur m.

gown [gaun] n Gewand nt; (Univ) Robe f.

grab [græb] vt packen; an sich reißen; n plötzliche(r) Griff m; (crane) Greifer m.

grace [greɪs] n Anmut f; (favour) Güte f, Gefälligkeit f; (blessing) Gnade f; (prayer) Tischgebet nt; (Comm) Zahlungsfrist f; vt (adorn) zieren; (honour) auszeichnen; 5 days' — 5 Tage Aufschub m; —ful a —fully ad anmutig, graziös.

gracious ['greɪʃəs] a gnädig; (kind, courteous) wohlwollend, freundlich.

gradation [grə'deɪʃən] n (Ab-)stufung f.

grade [greɪd] n Grad m; (slope) Gefälle nt; to make the — es schaffen; vt (classify) einstufen; — crossing (US) Bahnübergang m.

gradient ['greidiənt] n Steigung f; Gefälle nt.

gradual a, **—ly** ad ['grædjuəl,-li] allmählich.

graduate ['grædjut] n: to be a — das Staatsexamen haben; ['grædjueit] vi das Staatsexamen machen or bestehen.

graduation [grædju'eiʃən] n Erlangung f eines akademischen Grades.

graft [grɑ:ft] n (on plant) Pfropfreis nt; (hard work) Schufterei f; (Med) Verpflanzung f; (unfair self-advancement) Schiebung f; vt propfen; (fig) aufpfropfen; (Med) verpflanzen.

grain [grein] n Korn nt, Getreide nt; (particle) Körnchen nt, Korn nt; (in wood) Maserung f.

grammar ['græmə*] n Grammatik f.

grammatical [grə'mætikəl] a grammatisch.

gram(me) [græm] n Gramm nt.

gramophone ['græməfəun] n Grammophon nt.

granary ['grænəri] n Kornspeicher m.

grand [grænd] a großartig; **—daughter** Enkelin f; **—eur** ['grændjə*] Erhabenheit f; **—father** Großvater m; **—iose** a (imposing) großartig; (pompous) schwülstig; **—mother** Großmutter f; **— piano** Flügel m; **—son** Enkel m; **—stand** Haupttribüne f; **— total** Gesamtsumme f.

granite ['grænit] n Granit nt.

granny ['græni] n Oma f.

grant [grɑ:nt] vt gewähren; (allow) zugeben; n Unterstützung f; (Univ) Stipendium nt; to take sb/ sth for **—ed** jdn/etw als selbstverständlich (an)nehmen.

granulated ['grænjuleitid] a sugar raffiniert.

granule ['grænju:l] n Körnchen nt.

grape [greip] n (Wein)traube f; **—fruit** Pampelmuse f, Grapefruit f; **— juice** Traubensaft m.

graph [grɑ:f] n Schaubild nt; **—ic** a (descriptive) anschaulich, lebendig; drawing graphisch.

grapple ['græpl] vi sich raufen; — with (lit, fig) kämpfen mit.

grasp [grɑ:sp] vt ergreifen; (understand) begreifen; n Griff m; (possession) Gewalt f; (of subject) Beherrschung f; **—ing** a habgierig.

grass [grɑ:s] n Gras nt; **—hopper** Heuschrecke f; **—land** Weideland nt; **— roots** pl (fig) Basis f; **—snake** Ringelnatter f; **—y** a grasig, Gras-.

grate [greit] n Feuerrost m, Kamin m; vi kratzen; (sound) knirschen; (on nerves) zerren (on an +dat); vt cheese reiben.

grateful a, **—ly** ad ['greitful, -fəli] dankbar.

grater ['greitə*] n (in kitchen) Reibe f.

gratification [grætifi'keiʃən] n Befriedigung f.

gratify ['grætifai] vt befriedigen; **—ing** a erfreulich.

grating ['greitiŋ] n (iron bars) Gitter nt; a noise knirschend.

gratitude ['grætitju:d] n Dankbarkeit f.

gratuitous [grə'tju:itəs] a (uncalled-for) grundlos, überflüssig; (given free) unentgeltlich, gratis.

gratuity [grə'tju:iti] n (Geld)geschenk nt; (Comm) Gratifikation f.

grave [greiv] n Grab nt; a (serious) ernst, schwerwiegend; (solemn) ernst, feierlich; —digger Totengräber m.

gravel ['grævəl] n Kies m.

gravely ['greɪvlɪ] ad schwer, ernstlich.

gravestone ['greɪvstəʊn] n Grabstein m.

graveyard ['greɪvjɑ:d] n Friedhof m.

gravitate ['græviteɪt] vi streben; (fig) tendieren.

gravity ['græviti] n Schwerkraft f; (seriousness) Schwere f, Ernst m.

gravy ['greɪvɪ] n (Braten)soße f.

gray [greɪ] a = grey.

graze [greɪz] vi grasen; vt (touch) streifen; (Med) abschürfen; n (Med) Abschürfung f.

grease [gri:s] n (fat) Fett nt; (lubricant) Schmiere f; vt (ab)schmieren; einfetten; —gun Schmierspritze f; —proof a paper Butterbrot-.

greasy ['gri:sɪ] a fettig.

great [greɪt] a groß; (important) groß, bedeutend; (distinguished) groß, hochstehend; (col: good) prima; —grandfather Urgroßvater m; —grandmother Urgroßmutter f; —ly ad sehr; —ness Größe f.

greed [gri:d] n (also —iness) Gier f (for nach); (meanness) Geiz m; —ily ad gierig; —y a gefräßig, gierig; —y for money geldgierig.

green [gri:n] a grün; n (village —) Dorfwiese f; —grocer Obst- und Gemüsehändler m; —house Gewächshaus nt; —ish a grünlich; —light (lit, fig) grüne(s) Licht nt.

greet [gri:t] vt grüßen; —ing Gruß m, Begrüßung f.

gregarious [grɪ'gɛərɪəs] a gesellig.

grenade [grɪ'neɪd] n Granate f.

grey [greɪ] a grau; —haired a grauhaarig; —hound Windhund m; —ish a gräulich.

grid [grɪd] n Gitter nt; (Elec) Leitungsnetz nt; (on map) Gitternetz nt; —iron Bratrost m.

grief [gri:f] n Gram m, Kummer m.

grievance ['gri:vəns] n Beschwerde f.

grieve [gri:v] vi sich grämen; vt betrüben.

grill [grɪl] n (on cooker) Grill m; vt grillen; (question) in die Mangel nehmen.

grille [grɪl] n (on car etc) (Kühler)gitter nt.

grim [grɪm] a grimmig; situation düster.

grimace [grɪ'meɪs] n Grimasse f; vi Grimassen schneiden.

grime [graɪm] n Schmutz m.

grimly ['grɪmlɪ] ad grimmig, finster.

grimy ['graɪmɪ] a schmutzig.

grin [grɪn] n Grinsen nt; vi grinsen.

grind [graɪnd] vt irreg mahlen; (sharpen) schleifen; teeth knirschen mit; n (bore) Plackerei f.

grip [grɪp] n Griff m; (mastery) Griff m, Gewalt f; (suitcase) kleine(r) Handkoffer m; vt packen.

gripes [graɪps] npl (bowel pains) Bauchschmerzen pl, Bauchweh nt.

gripping ['grɪpɪŋ] a (exciting) spannend.

grisly ['grɪzlɪ] a gräßlich.

gristle ['grɪsl] n Knorpel m.

grit [grɪt] n Splitt m; (courage) Mut m, Mumm m; vt teeth knirschen mit; road (mit Splitt be)streuen.

groan [grəʊn] n Stöhnen nt; vi stöhnen.

grocer ['grəʊsə*] n Lebensmittelhändler m; —ies pl Lebensmittel pl.

grog [grɒg] *n* Grog *m*.

groggy ['grɒgɪ] *a* benommen; (*boxing*) angeschlagen.

groin [grɔɪn] *n* Leistengegend *f*.

groom [gru:m] *n* Bräutigam *m*; (*for horses*) Pferdeknecht *m*; to — o.s. (*of man*) sich zurechtmachen, sich pflegen; (*well*) —ed gepflegt; to — sb for a career jdn auf eine Laufbahn vorbereiten.

groove [gru:v] *n* Rille *f*, Furche *f*.

grope [grəʊp] *vi* tasten.

gross [grəʊs] *a* (*coarse*) dick, plump; (*bad*) grob, schwer; (*Comm*) brutto; Gesamt-; *n* Gros *nt*; —ly *a* höchst, ungeheuerlich.

grotesque [grəʊ'tesk] *a* grotesk.

grotto ['grɒtəʊ] *n* Grotte *f*.

ground [graʊnd] *n* Boden *m*, Erde *f*; (*land*) Grundbesitz *m*; (*reason*) Grund *m*; —s *pl* (*dregs*) Bodensatz *m*; (*around house*) (Garten)anlagen *pl*; *vt* (*run ashore*) auf Strand setzen; aircraft stillegen; (*instruct*) die Anfangsgründe beibringen (+Dat); *vi* (*run ashore*) stranden, auflaufen; — **floor** (*Brit*) Erdgeschoß *nt*, Parterre *nt*; —ing (*instruction*) Anfangsunterricht *m*; —**sheet** Zeltboden *m*; —**work** Grundlage *f*.

group [gru:p] *n* Gruppe *f*; *vti* (sich) gruppieren.

grouse [graʊs] *n* (*bird*) schottische(s) Moorhuhn *nt*; (*complaint*) Nörgelei *f*; *vi* (*complain*) meckern.

grove [grəʊv] *n* Gehölz *nt*, Hain *m*.

grovel ['grɒvl] *vi* auf dem Bauch kriechen; (*fig*) kriechen.

grow [grəʊ] *irreg vi* wachsen, größer werden; (*grass*) wachsen; (*become*) werden; it —s on you man gewöhnt sich daran; *vt* (*raise*) anbauen, ziehen; — **up** *vi* auf-wachsen; (*mature*) erwachsen werden; —er Züchter *m*; —ing *a* wachsend; (*fig*) zunehmend.

growl [graʊl] *vi* knurren; *n* Knurren *nt*.

grown-up ['grəʊn'ʌp] *a* erwachsen *n* Erwachsene(r) *mf*.

growth [grəʊθ] *n* Wachstum *nt*, Wachsen *nt*; (*increase*) Anwachsen *nt*, Zunahme *f*; (*of beard etc*) Wuchs *m*.

grub [grʌb] *n* Made *f*, Larve *f*; (*col: food*) Futter *nt*; —**by** *a* schmutzig, schmuddelig.

grudge [grʌdʒ] *n* Groll *m*; *vt* misgönnen (*sb sth jdm etw*); to bear sb a — einen Groll gegen jdn hegen.

grudging ['grʌdʒɪŋ] *a* neidisch; (*unwilling*) widerwillig.

gruelling ['grʊəlɪŋ] *a* climb, race mörderisch.

gruesome ['gru:səm] *a* grauenhaft.

gruff [grʌf] *a* barsch.

grumble ['grʌmbl] *vi* murren, schimpfen (*sb sth etw*); *n* Brummen *nt*, Murren *nt*.

grumpy ['grʌmpɪ] *a* verdrießlich.

grunt [grʌnt] *vi* grunzen; *n* Grunzen *nt*.

guarantee [gærən'ti:] *n* (*promise to pay*) Gewähr *f*; (*promise to replace*) Garantie *f*; *vt* gewähr-leisten; garantieren.

guarantor [gærən'tɔ:*] *n* Gewährsmann *m*, Bürge *m*.

guard [gɑ:d] *n* (*defence*) Bewachung *f*; (*sentry*) Wache *f*; (*Rail*) Zugbegleiter *m*; to be on — Wache stehen; to be on one's — aufpassen; *vt* bewachen, beschützen; —ed *a* vorsichtig, zurückhaltend; —ian *m* Vormund *m*; (*keeper*) Hüter *m*; —'s **van** (*Brit Rail*) Dienstwagen *m*.

guerrilla [gə'rɪlə] n Guerilla-(kämpfer) m; — warfare Guerillakrieg m.

guess [ges] vti (er)raten, schätzen; n Vermutung f; —work Raterei f; good — gut geraten.

guest [gest] n Gast m; —house Pension f; — room Gastzimmer nt.

guffaw [gʌ'fɔː] n schallende(s) Gelächter nt; vi schallend lachen.

guidance ['gaɪdəns] n (control) Leitung f; (advice) Rat m, Beratung f.

guide [gaɪd] n Führer m; vt führen; girl — Pfadfinderin f; —book Reiseführer m; —d missile Fernlenkgeschoß nt; — lines pl Richtlinien pl.

guild [gɪld] n (Hist) Gilde f; (society) Vereinigung f; —hall (Brit) Stadthalle f.

guile [gaɪl] n Arglist f; —less a arglos.

guillotine [gɪlə'tiːn] n Guillotine f.

guilt [gɪlt] n Schuld -f; —y a schuldig.

guise [gaɪz] n (appearance) Verkleidung f; in the — of (things) in der Form (+gen); (people) gekleidet als.

guitar [gɪ'tɑː*] n Gitarre f; —ist Gitarrist(in f) m.

gulf [gʌlf] n Golf m; (fig) Abgrund m.

gull [gʌl] n Möwe f.

gullet ['gʌlɪt] n Schlund m.

gullible ['gʌlɪbl] a leichtgläubig.

gully ['gʌlɪ] n (Wasser)rinne f; (gorge) Schlucht f.

gulp [gʌlp] vi hinunterschlucken; (gasp) schlucken; n große(r) Schluck m.

gum [gʌm] n (around teeth) Zahnfleisch nt; (glue) Klebstoff m;

(chewing —) Kaugummi m; vt gummieren, kleben; —boots pl Gummistiefel pl.

gumption ['gʌmpʃən] n (col) Mumm m.

gum tree ['gʌmtriː] n Gummibaum m; up a — (col) in der Klemme.

gun [gʌn] n Schußwaffe f; —fire Geschützfeuer nt; —man bewaffnete(r) Verbrecher m; —ner Kanonier m, Artillerist m; —powder Schießpulver nt; —shot Schuß m; — down vt niederknallen.

gurgle ['gɜːgl] n Gluckern nt; vi gluckern.

gush [gʌʃ] n Strom m, Erguß m; vi (rush out) hervorströmen; (fig) schwärmen.

gusset ['gʌsɪt] n Keil m, Zwickel m.

gust [gʌst] n Windstoß m, Bö f.

gusto ['gʌstəʊ] n Genuß m, Lust f.

gut [gʌt] n (Anat) Gedärme pl; (string) Darm m; —s pl (fig) Schneid m.

gutter ['gʌtə*] n Dachrinne f; (in street) Gosse f.

guttural ['gʌtərəl] a guttural, Kehl-.

guy [gaɪ] n (rope) Halteseil m; (man) Typ m, Kerl m.

guzzle ['gʌzl] vti (drink) saufen; (eat) fressen.

gym(nasium) [dʒɪm'neɪzɪəm] n Turnhalle f.

gymnast ['dʒɪmnæst] n Turner(in f) m; —ics [dʒɪm'næstɪks] Turnen nt, Gymnastik f.

gyn(a)ecologist [gaɪn'kɒlədʒɪst] n Frauenarzt m/-ärztin f, Gynäkologe m, Gynäkologin f.

gyn(a)ecology [gaɪn'kɒlədʒɪ] n Gynäkologie f, Frauenheilkunde f.

gypsy ['dʒɪpsɪ] n = **gipsy.**

gyrate [dʒa'reɪt] vi kreisen.

H

H, h [eɪtʃ] n H nt, h nt.
haberdashery [ˈhæbəˈdæʃərɪ] n Kurzwaren pl.
habit [ˈhæbɪt] n (An)gewohnheit f; (monk's) Habit m or m.
habitable [ˈhæbɪtəbl] a bewohnbar.
habitat [ˈhæbɪtæt] n Lebensraum m.
habitation [hæbɪˈteɪʃən] n Bewohnen nt; (place) Wohnung f.
habitual [həˈbɪtjʊəl] a üblich, gewohnheitsmäßig; **—ly** ad gewöhnlich.
hack [hæk] vt hacken; n Hieb m; (writer) Schreiberling m.
hackney cab [ˈhæknɪˈkæb] n Taxi nt.
hackneyed [ˈhæknɪd] a abgedroschen.
haddock [ˈhædək] n Schellfisch m.
hadn't [ˈhædnt] = had not.
haemorrhage, (US) **hemo—** [ˈhemərɪdʒ] n Blutung f.
haemorrhoids, (US) **hemo—** [ˈhemərɔɪdz] Hämorrhoiden pl.
haggard [ˈhægəd] a abgekämpft.
haggle [ˈhægl] vi feilschen.
haggling [ˈhæglɪŋ] n Feilschen nt.
hail [heɪl] n Hagel m; vt umjubeln; **to —** sb as emperor jdn zum Kaiser ausrufen; vi hageln; **—storm** Hagelschauer m.
hair [heə*] n Haar nt, Haare pl; (one —) Haar nt; **—brush** Haarbürste f; **—cut** Haarschnitt m; **to get a —cut** sich (dat) die Haare schneiden lassen; **—do** Frisur f; **—dresser** Friseur m, Friseuse f; **—drier** Trockenhaube f; (hand) Fön m; **—net** Haarnetz nt; **— oil**

Haaröl nt; **—piece** (lady's) Haarteil nt; (man's) Toupet nt; **—pin** (lit) Haarnadel f; (bend) Haarnadelkurve f; **—raising** a haarsträubend; **—'s breadth** Haaresbreite f; **— style** Frisur f; **—y** a haarig.
hake [heɪk] n Seehecht m.
half [hɑːf] n Hälfte f; a halb; ad halb, zur Hälfte; **—back** Läufer m; **—breed**, **—caste** Mischling m; **—hearted** a lustlos, unlustig; **—hour** halbe Stunde f; **—penny** [ˈheɪpnɪ] halbe(r) Penny m; **— price** halbe(r) Preis m; **—time** Halbzeit f; **—way** ad halbwegs, auf halbem Wege.
halibut [ˈhælɪbət] n Heilbutt m.
hall [hɔːl] n Saal m; (entrance —) Hausflur m; (building) Halle f.
hallmark [ˈhɔːlmɑːk] n (lit, fig) Stempel m.
hallo [hʌˈləʊ] see **hello**.
hallucination [həluːsɪˈneɪʃən] n Halluzination f.
halo [ˈheɪləʊ] n (of saint) Heiligenschein m; (of moon) Hof m.
halt [hɔːlt] n Halt m; vti anhalten.
halve [hɑːv] vt halbieren.
ham [hæm] n Schinken m; **— sandwich** Schinkenbrötchen nt; **—burger** Frikadelle f.
hamlet [ˈhæmlɪt] n Weiler m.
hammer [ˈhæmə*] n Hammer m; vt hämmern.
hammock [ˈhæmək] n Hängematte f.
hamper [ˈhæmpə*] vt (be)hindern; n Picknickkorb m; Geschenkkorb m.

hand [hænd] n Hand f; (of clock) (Uhr)zeiger m; (worker) Arbeiter m; vt (pass) geben; **to give sb a** — jdm helfen; **at first** — aus erster Hand; **to** — zur Hand; **in** — (under control) in fester Hand, unter Kontrolle; (being done) im Gange; (extra) übrig; **—bag** Handtasche f; **—ball** Handball m; **—book** Handbuch nt; **—brake** Handbremse f; **— cream** Handcreme f; **—cuffs** pl Handschellen pl;—**ful** Handvoll f; (col: person) Plage f.

handicap ['hændɪkæp] n Handikap nt; vt benachteiligen.

handicraft ['hændɪkrɑːft] n Kunsthandwerk nt.

handkerchief ['hæŋkətʃɪf] n Taschentuch nt.

handle ['hændl] n (of door etc) Klinke f; (of cup etc) Henkel m; (for winding) Kurbel f; vt (touch) anfassen; (deal with) things sich befassen mit; people umgehen mit; **—bars** pl Lenkstange f.

hand-luggage ['hændlʌgɪdʒ] n Handgepäck nt.

handmade ['hændmeɪd] a handgefertigt.

handshake ['hændʃeɪk] n Händedruck m.

handsome ['hænsəm] a gutaussehend; (generous) großzügig.

handwriting ['hændraɪtɪŋ] n Handschrift f.

handy ['hændɪ] a praktisch; shops leicht erreichbar.

handyman ['hændɪmən] n Mädchen nt für alles; (do-it-yourself) Bastler m; (general —) Gelegenheitsarbeiter m.

hang [hæŋ] irreg vt aufhängen; (execute) hängen; **to — sth on sth** etw an etw (acc) hängen; vi

(droop) hängen; — **about** vi sich herumtreiben.

hangar ['hæŋə*] n Hangar m, Flugzeughalle f.

hanger ['hæŋə*] n Kleiderbügel m.

hanger-on ['hæŋər'ɒn] n Anhänger (in f) m.

hangover ['hæŋəʊvə*] n Kater m.

hank [hæŋk] n Strang m.

hanker ['hæŋkə*] vi sich sehnen (for, after nach).

haphazard ['hæp'hæzəd] a wahllos, zufällig.

happen ['hæpən] vi sich ereignen, passieren; **—ing** n Ereignis nt; (Art) Happening nt.

happily ['hæpɪlɪ] ad glücklich; (fortunately) glücklicherweise.

happiness ['hæpɪnɪs] n Glück nt.

happy ['hæpɪ] a glücklich; **—lucky** a sorglos.

harass ['hærəs] vt bedrängen, plagen.

harbour, (US) **harbor** ['hɑːbə*] n Hafen m.

hard [hɑːd] a (firm) hart, fest; (difficult) schwer, schwierig; (physically) schwer; (harsh) hart(herzig), gefühllos; ad work hart; try sehr; push, hit fest; — by (close) dicht or nahe an(+ dat); he **took it** — er hat es schwer genommen, **—back** n kartonierte Ausgabe; **—boiled** a hartgekocht; **—en** vt erhärten; (fig) verhärten; vi hart werden; (fig) sich verhärten; **—hearted** a hartherzig; **—ly** ad kaum; **—ship** Not f; (injustice) Unrecht nt; **—up** a knapp bei Kasse; **—ware** Eisenwaren pl.

hardy ['hɑːdɪ] a (strong) widerstandsfähig; (brave) verwegen.

hare [hεə*] n Hase m.

harem [hɑː'riːm] n Harem m.

harm [hɑːm] n Schaden m; Leid nt;
vt schaden (+ dat); it won't do any
— es kann nicht schaden; **—ful** a
schädlich; **—less** a harmlos,
unschädlich.

harmonica [hɑːˈmɒnɪkə] n Mundharmonika f.

harmonious [hɑːˈməʊnɪəs] a harmonisch.

harmonize [ˈhɑːmənaɪz] vt
abstimmen; vi harmonieren.

harmony [ˈhɑːmənɪ] n Harmonie f;
(fig also) Einklang m.

harness [ˈhɑːnɪs] n Geschirr nt; vt
horse anschirren; (fig) nutzbar
machen.

harp [hɑːp] n Harfe f; to — on
about sth auf etw (dat) herumreiten; **—ist** n Harfenspieler(in f) m.

harpoon [hɑːˈpuːn] n Harpune f.

harrow [ˈhærəʊ] n Egge f; vt eggen.

harrowing [ˈhærəʊɪŋ] a nervenaufreibend.

harsh [hɑːʃ] a (rough) rauh, grob;
(severe) schroff, streng; **—ly** ad
rauh, barsch; **—ness** Härte f.

harvest [ˈhɑːvɪst] n Ernte f; (time)
Erntezeit f; vt ernten.

harvester [ˈhɑːvɪstə*] n Mähbinder
m.

hash [hæʃ] vt kleinhacken; n
(mess) Kuddelmuddel m; (meat
cooked) Haschee nt; (raw)
Gehackte(s) nt.

hashish [ˈhæʃɪʃ] n Haschisch nt.

haste [heɪst] n (speed) Eile f;
(hurry) Hast f; **—n** [ˈheɪsn] vt
beschleunigen; vi eilen, sich
beeilen.

hasty a, **hastily** ad [ˈheɪstɪ, -lɪ]
hastig; (rash) vorschnell.

hat [hæt] n Hut m.

hatbox [ˈhætbɒks] n Hutschachtel
f.

hatch [hætʃ] n (Naut) Luke f; (in
house) Durchreiche f; vi brüten;
(young) ausschlüpfen; vt brood
ausbrüten; plot aushecken.

hatchet [ˈhætʃɪt] n Beil nt.

hate [heɪt] vt hassen; I — queuing
ich stehe nicht gern Schlange; n
Haß m; vt a verhaßt.

hatred [ˈheɪtrɪd] n Haß m; (dislike)
Abneigung f.

hat trick [ˈhættrɪk] n Hattrick m.

haughty a, **haughtily** ad [ˈhɔːtɪ, -lɪ]
hochnäsig, überheblich.

haul [hɔːl] vt ziehen, schleppen; n
(pull) Zug m; (catch) Fang m;
—age Transport m; (Comm)
Spedition f; **—ier** Transportunter-
nehmer m, Spediteur m.

haunch [hɔːntʃ] n Lende f; to sit
on one's **—es** hocken.

haunt [hɔːnt] vt (ghost) spuken in
(+ dat), umgehen in (+ dat);
(memory) verfolgen; pub häufig
besuchen; the castle is **—ed** in dem
Schloß spukt es; n Lieblingsplatz
m.

have [hæv] vt irreg haben; (at
meal) essen; trinken; (col: trick)
hereinlegen; to — sth done etw
machen lassen; to — to do sth etw
tun müssen; to — sb on jdn auf
den Arm nehmen.

haven [ˈheɪvn] n Hafen m; (fig)
Zufluchtsort m.

haversack [ˈhævəsæk] n Rucksack
m.

havoc [ˈhævək] n Verwüstung f.

hawk [hɔːk] n Habicht m.

hay [heɪ] n Heu nt; **— fever**
Heuschnupfen m; **—stack**
Heuschober m.

haywire ['heɪwaɪə*] a (col) durcheinander.

hazard ['hæzəd] n (chance) Zufall m; (danger) Wagnis nt, Risiko nt; vt aufs Spiel setzen; —**ous** a gefährlich, riskant.

haze [heɪz] n Dunst m; (fig) Unklarheit f.

hazelnut ['heɪzlnʌt] n Haselnuß f.

hazy ['heɪzɪ] a (misty) dunstig, diesig; (vague) verschwommen.

he [hiː] pron er.

head [hed] n Kopf m; (top) Spitze f; (leader) Leiter m; a Kopf-; (leading) Ober-; vt (an)führen, leiten; — for Richtung nehmen auf (+acc), zugehen auf (+acc); —**ache** Kopfschmerzen pl, Kopfweh nt; —**ing** Überschrift f; —**lamp** Scheinwerfer m; —**land** Landspitze f; —**light** = —lamp; —**line** Schlagzeile f; —**long** ad kopfüber; —**master** (of primary school) Rektor m; (of secondary school) Direktor m; —**mistress** Rektorin f; Direktorin f; —**on a** Frontal-; —**quarters** pl Zentrale f; (Mil) Hauptquartier nt; —**rest** Kopfstütze f; —**room** (of bridges etc) lichte Höhe f; Platz m für den Kopf; —**s** (on coin) Kopf m, Wappen nt; —**scarf** Kopftuch nt; —**strong a** eigenwillig; —**waiter** Oberkellner m; —**way** Fahrt f (voraus); (fig) Fortschritte pl; —**wind** Gegenwind m; —**y** a (rash) hitzig; (intoxicating) stark, berauschend.

heal [hiːl] vt heilen; vi verheilen.

health [helθ] n Gesundheit f; your —! prost!; —**y** a gesund.

heap [hiːp] n Haufen m; vt häufen.

hear [hɪə*] irreg vt hören; (listen to) anhören; vi hören; —**ing** Gehör nt; (Jur) Verhandlung f; (of wit-

nesses) Vernehmung f; to give sb a —ing jdn anhören; —**ing aid** Hörapparat m; —**say** Hörensagen nt.

hearse [hɜːs] n Leichenwagen m.

heart [hɑːt] n Herz nt; (centre also) Zentrum nt; (courage) Mut m; by — auswendig; the — of the matter der Kern des Problems; — attack Herzanfall m; —beat Herzschlag m; —breaking a herzzerbrechend; —broken a (ganz)gebrochen; —burn Sodbrennen nt; — failure Herzschlag m; —felt a aufrichtig.

hearth [hɑːθ] n Herd m.

heartily ['hɑːtɪlɪ] ad herzlich; eat herzhaft.

heartless ['hɑːtlɪs] a herzlos.

hearty ['hɑːtɪ] a kräftig; (friendly) freundlich.

heat [hiːt] n Hitze f; (of food, water etc) Wärme f; (Sport) Ausscheidungsrunde f; (excitement) Feuer nt; in the — of the moment in der Hitze des Gefechts; vt Wärme heizen; substance heiß machen, erhitzen; — up vi warm werden; vt aufwärmen; —ed a erhitzt; (fig) hitzig; —er (Heiz)ofen m.

heath [hiːθ] n (Brit) Heide f.

heathen ['hiːðən] n Heide m; a heidnisch, Heiden-.

heather ['heðə*] n Heidekraut nt, Erika f.

heating ['hiːtɪŋ] n Heizung f.

heatstroke ['hiːtstrəʊk] n Hitzschlag m.

heatwave ['hiːtweɪv] n Hitzewelle f.

heave [hiːv] vt hochheben; sigh ausstoßen; vi wogen; (breast) sich heben; n Heben nt.

heaven ['hevn] n Himmel m; (bliss) (der siebte) Himmel m; —**ly**

a himmlisch; —ly body Himmels-
körper m.

heavy a, **heavily** ad ['hevɪ, -lɪ]
schwer.

heckle ['hekl] vt unterbrechen; vi
dazwischenrufen, störende Fragen
stellen.

hectic ['hektɪk] a hektisch.

he'd [hi:d] = **he had; he would.**

hedge [hedʒ] n Hecke f; vt
einzäunen; to — one's bets sich
absichern; vi (fig) ausweichen.

hedgehog ['hedʒhɒg] n Igel m.

heed [hi:d] vt beachten; n Beachtung f; —ful a achtsam; —less a
achtlos.

heel [hi:l] n Ferse f; (of shoe)
Absatz m; vt shoes mit Absätzen
versehen.

hefty ['heftɪ] a person stämmig;
portion reichlich; bite kräftig;
weight schwer.

heifer ['hefə*] n Färse f.

height [haɪt] n (of person) Größe
f; (of object) Höhe f; (high place)
Gipfel m; —en vt erhöhen.

heir [ɛə*] n Erbe m; —ess ['ɛərɪs]
Erbin f; —loom Erbstück nt.

helicopter ['helɪkɒptə*] n Hubschrauber m.

hell [hel] n Hölle f; interj verdammt!

he'll [hi:l] = **he will, he shall.**

hellish ['helɪʃ] a höllisch, verteufelt.

hello [hʌ'ləʊ] interj (greeting)
Hallo; (surprise) nein, so.

helm [helm] n Ruder nt, Steuer nt.

helmet ['helmɪt] n Helm m.

helmsman ['helmzmən] n Steuermann m.

help [help] n Hilfe f; vt helfen
(+ dat); **I can't** — it ich kann
nichts dafür; **I couldn't** — laughing ich mußte einfach lachen; —
yourself bedienen Sie sich; —**er**

Helfer m; —**ful** a hilfreich; —**ing**
Portion f; —**less** a hilflos.

hem [hem] n Saum m; — in vt einschließen; (fig) einengen.

hemisphere ['hemɪsfɪə*] n Halb-
kugel f; Hemisphäre f.

hemline ['hemlaɪn] n Rocklänge f.

hemp [hemp] a Hanf m.

hen [hen] n Henne f.

hence [hens] ad von jetzt an;
(therefore) daher.

henchman ['hentʃmən] n
Anhänger m, Gefolgsmann m.

henpecked ['henpekt] a: to be —
unter dem Pantoffel stehen; — husband Pantoffelheld m.

her [hɜ:*] pron (acc) sie; (dat) ihr;
a ihr.

herald ['herəld] n Herold m; (fig)
(Vor)bote m; vt verkünden,
anzeigen.

heraldry ['herəldrɪ] n Wappen-
kunde f.

herb [hɜ:b] n Kraut nt.

herd [hɜ:d] n Herde f.

here [hɪə*] ad hier; (to this place)
hierher; —**after** ad hernach,
künftig; n Jenseits nt; —**by** ad
hiermit.

hereditary [hɪ'redɪtərɪ] a erblich.

heredity [hɪ'redɪtɪ] n Vererbung f.

heresy ['herəsɪ] n Ketzerei f.

heretic ['herətɪk] n Ketzer m; —**al**
[hɪ'retɪkəl] a ketzerisch.

herewith ['hɪə'wɪð] ad hiermit;
(Comm) anbei.

heritage ['herɪtɪdʒ] n Erbe nt.

hermetically [hɜ:'metɪkəlɪ] ad luftdicht, hermetisch.

hermit ['hɜ:mɪt] n Einsiedler m.

hernia ['hɜ:nɪə] n Bruch m.

hero ['hɪərəʊ] n Held m; —**ic**
[hɪ'rəʊɪk] a heroisch.

heroin ['herəʊɪn] *n* Heroin *nt.*

heroine ['herəʊɪn] *n* Heldin *f.*

heroism ['herəʊɪzəm] *n* Heldentum *nt.*

heron ['herən] *n* Reiher *m.*

herring ['herɪŋ] *n* Hering *m.*

hers [hɜːz] *pron* ihre(r,s).

herself [hɜːˈself] *pron* sich (selbst); (*emphatic*) selbst; **she's not** — mit ihr ist etwas los *or* nicht in Ordnung.

he's [hiːz] = **he is, he has.**

hesitant ['hezɪtənt] *a* zögernd; *speech* stockend.

hesitate ['hezɪteɪt] *vi* zögern; (*feel doubtful*) unschlüssig sein.

hesitation [hezɪˈteɪʃən] *n* Zögern *nt,* Schwanken *nt.*

het up [het'ʌp] *a* (*col*) aufgeregt.

hew [hjuː] *vt irreg* hauen, hacken.

hexagon ['heksəgən] *n* Sechseck *nt;* **—al** [hek'sægənəl] *a* sechseckig.

heyday ['heɪdeɪ] *n* Blüte *f,* Höhepunkt *m.*

hi [haɪ] *interj* he, hallo.

hibernate ['haɪbəneɪt] *vi* Winterschlaf halten.

hibernation [haɪbə'neɪʃən] *n* Winterschlaf *m.*

hiccough, hiccup ['hɪkʌp] *vi* den Schluckauf haben; **—s** *pl* Schluckauf *m.*

hide [haɪd] *n* (*skin*) Haut *f,* Fell *nt; irreg vt* verstecken; (*keep secret*) verbergen; *vi* sich verstecken; **—and-seek** Versteckspiel *nt.*

hideous ['hɪdɪəs] *a* abscheulich; **—ly** *ad* scheußlich.

hiding ['haɪdɪŋ] *n* (*beating*) Tracht *f* Prügel; **to be in** — sich versteckt halten; **— place** Versteck *nt.*

hierarchy ['haɪərɑːkɪ] *n* Hierarchie *f.*

high [haɪ] *a* hoch; *importance* groß; *spirits* Hoch-; *wind* stark; *living* extravagant, üppig; *ad* hoch; **—brow** *n* Intellektuelle(r) *mf; a* (*betont*) intellektuell; (*pej*) hochgestochen; **—chair** Hochstuhl *m,* Sitzer *m;* **—handed** *a* eigenmächtig; **—heeled** *a* hochhackig; **—jack** = **hijack; —level** *a meeting* wichtig, Spitzen-; **—light** (*fig*) Höhepunkt *m;* **—ly** *ad* in hohem Maße, höchst; *praise* in hohen Tönen; **—ly strung** *a* überempfindlich, reizbar; **H— Mass** Hochamt *nt;* **—ness** Höhe *f;* **H—ness** Hoheit *f;* **—pitched** *a voice* hoch, schrill, hell; **— school** Oberschule *f;* **—speed** *a* Schnell-; **— tide** Flut *f;* **—way** Landstraße *f.*

hijack ['haɪdʒæk] *vt* hijacken, entführen.

hike [haɪk] *vi* wandern; *n* Wanderung *f;* **—r** Wanderer *m.*

hiking ['haɪkɪŋ] *n* Wandern *nt.*

hilarious [hɪ'lɛərɪəs] *a* lustig; zum Schreien komisch.

hilarity [hɪ'lærɪtɪ] *n* Lustigkeit *f.*

hill [hɪl] *n* Berg *m;* **—side** (Berg)hang *m;* **—top** Bergspitze *f;* **—y** *a* hügelig.

hilt [hɪlt] *n* Heft *nt;* **up to the** — ganz und gar.

him [hɪm] *pron* (*acc*) ihn; (*dat*) ihm.

himself [hɪm'self] *pron* sich (selbst); (*emphatic*) selbst; **he's not** — mit ihm ist etwas los *or* nicht in Ordnung.

hind [haɪnd] *a* hinter, Hinter-; *n* Hirschkuh *f.*

hinder ['hɪndə*] *vt* (*stop*) hindern; (*delay*) behindern.

hindrance ['hɪndrəns] *n* (*delay*) Behinderung *f;* (*obstacle*) Hindernis *nt.*

hinge [hɪndʒ] n Scharnier nt; (on door) Türangel f; vt mit Scharnieren versehen; vi (fig) abhängen (on von).

hint [hɪnt] n Tip m, Andeutung f; (trace) Anflug m; vi andeuten (at acc), anspielen (at auf +acc).

hip [hɪp] n Hüfte f.

hippopotamus [hɪpə'pɒtəməs] n Nilpferd nt.

hire [haɪə*] vt worker anstellen; car mieten; n Miete f; for — taxi frei; to have for — verleihen; — purchase Teilzahlungskauf m.

his [hɪz] poss a sein; poss pron seine(r,s).

hiss [hɪs] vi zischen; n Zischen nt.

historian [hɪs'tɔːrɪən] n Geschichtsschreiber m; Historiker m.

historic [hɪs'tɒrɪk] a historisch.

historical [hɪs'tɒrɪkəl] a historisch, geschichtlich.

history ['hɪstəri] n Geschichte f; (personal) Entwicklung f, Werdegang m.

hit [hɪt] vt irreg schlagen; (injure) treffen, verletzen; n (blow) Schlag m, Stoß m; (success) Erfolg m, Treffer m; (Mus) Hit m.

hitch [hɪtʃ] vt festbinden; (pull up) hochziehen; n (loop) Knoten m; (difficulty) Schwierigkeit f, Haken m.

hitch-hike ['hɪtʃhaɪk] vi trampen, per Anhalter fahren; —r Tramper m.

hitherto ['hɪðə'tuː] ad bislang.

hive [haɪv] n Bienenkorb m.

hoard [hɔːd] n Schatz m; vt horten, hamstern.

hoarding ['hɔːdɪŋ] n Bretterzaun m; (for advertising) Reklamewand f.

hoarfrost ['hɔː'frɒst] n (Rauh)reif m.

hoarse [hɔːs] a heiser, rauh.

hoax [həʊks] n Streich m.

hobble ['hɒbl] vi humpeln.

hobby ['hɒbɪ] n Steckenpferd nt, Hobby nt.

hobo ['həʊbəʊ] n (US) Tippelbruder m.

hock [hɒk] n (wine) weiße(r) Rheinwein m.

hockey ['hɒkɪ] n Hockey nt.

hoe [həʊ] n Hacke f; vt hacken.

hog [hɒg] n Schlachtschwein nt; vt mit Beschlag belegen.

hoist [hɔɪst] n Winde f; vt hochziehen.

hold [həʊld] irreg vt halten; (keep) behalten; (contain) enthalten; (be able to contain) fassen; (keep back) zurück(be)halten; breath anhalten; meeting abhalten; vi (withstand pressure) standhalten, aushalten; n (grasp) Halt m; (claim) Anspruch m; (Naut) Schiffsraum m; — back vt zurückhalten; — down vt niederhalten; job behalten; — out vt hinhalten, bieten; vi aushalten; — up vt (delay) aufhalten; (rob) überfallen; —all Reisetasche f; —er Behälter m; —ing (share) (Aktien)anteil m; —up (in traffic) Stockung f; (robbery) Überfall m.

hole [həʊl] n Loch nt; vt durchlöchern.

holiday ['hɒlədɪ] n (day) Feiertag m; freie(r) Tag m; (vacation) Urlaub m; (Sch) Ferien pl; —maker Feriengast m, Urlauber(in f) m.

holiness ['həʊlɪnɪs] n Heiligkeit f.

hollow ['hɒləʊ] a hohl; (fig) leer; n Vertiefung f; (in rock) Höhle f; — out vt aushöhlen.

holly ['hɒlɪ] *n* Stechpalme *f*.

holster ['həʊlstə*] *n* Pistolenhalfter *m*.

holy ['həʊlɪ] *a* heilig; *(religious)* fromm.

homage ['hɒmɪdʒ] *n* Huldigung *f*; **to pay —** to huldigen (+*dat*).

home [həʊm] *n* Heim *nt*, Zuhause *nt*; *(institution)* Heim *nt*, Anstalt *f*; *a* einheimisch; *(Pol)* inner; *ad* heim, nach Hause; **at —** zu Hause; **—coming** Heimkehr *f*; **—less** *a* obdachlos; **—ly** *a* häuslich; *(US: ugly)* unscheinbar; **—made** *a* selbstgemacht; **—sick** *a*: to be **—sick** Heimweh haben; **—ward(s)** *a* heimwärts; **— work** Hausaufgaben *pl*.

homicide ['hɒmɪsaɪd] *n* *(US)* Totschlag *m*, Mord *m*.

homoeopathy [həʊmɪˈɒpəθɪ] *n* Homöopathie *f*.

homogeneous [hɒməˈdʒiːnɪəs] *a* homogen, gleichartig.

homosexual ['hɒməʊˈseksjʊəl] *a* homosexuell; *n* Homosexuelle(r) *m*.

hone [həʊn] *n* Schleifstein *m*; *vt* feinschleifen.

honest ['ɒnɪst] *a* ehrlich; *(upright)* aufrichtig; **—ly** *ad* ehrlich; **—y** Ehrlichkeit *f*.

honey ['hʌnɪ] *n* Honig *m*; **—comb** Honigwabe *f*; **—moon** Flitterwochen *pl*, Hochzeitsreise *f*.

honk [hɒŋk] *n* *(Aut)* Hupensignal *nt*; *vi* hupen.

honorary ['ɒnərərɪ] *a* Ehren-.

honour, *(US)* **honor** ['ɒnə*] *vt* ehren; *cheque* einlösen; *debts* begleichen; *contract* einhalten; *n* *(respect)* Ehre *f*; *(reputation)* Ansehen *nt*, gute(r) Ruf *m*; *(sense of right)* Ehrgefühl *nt*; **—s** *pl* *(titles)* Auszeichnungen *pl*; **—able**

a ehrenwert, rechtschaffen; *(intention)* ehrenhaft.

hood [hʊd] *n* Kapuze *f*; *(Aut)* Verdeck *nt*; *(US Aut)* Kühlerhaube *f*; **—wink** *vt* reinlegen.

hoof [huːf] *n* Huf *m*.

hook [hʊk] *n* Haken *m*; *vt* einhaken; **—up** Gemeinschaftssendung *f*.

hooligan ['huːlɪgən] *n* Rowdy *m*.

hoop [huːp] *n* Reifen *m*.

hoot [huːt] *vi* *(Aut)* hupen; **to —** **with laughter** schallend lachen; *n* *(shout)* Johlen *nt*; *(Aut)* Hupen *nt*; **—er** *(Naut)* Dampfpfeife *f*; *(Aut)* (Auto)hupe *f*.

hop¹ [hɒp] *vi* hüpfen, hopsen; *n* *(jump)* Hopser *m*.

hop² [hɒp] *n* (Bot) Hopfen *m*.

hope [həʊp] *vi* hoffen; **I — that...** hoffentlich...; *n* Hoffnung *f*; **—ful** *a* hoffnungsvoll; *(promising)* vielversprechend; **—less** *a* hoffnungslos; *(useless)* unmöglich.

horde [hɔːd] *n* Horde *f*.

horizon [həˈraɪzn] *n* Horizont *m*; **—tal** [hɒrɪˈzɒntl] *a* horizontal.

hormone ['hɔːməʊn] *n* Hormon *nt*.

horn [hɔːn] *n* Horn *nt*; *(Aut)* Hupe *f*; **—ed** *a* gehörnt, Horn-.

hornet ['hɔːnɪt] *n* Hornisse *f*.

horny ['hɔːnɪ] *a* schwielig; *(US)* scharf.

horoscope ['hɒrəskəʊp] *n* Horoskop *nt*.

horrible *a*, **horribly** *ad* ['hɒrɪbl, -blɪ] fürchterlich.

horrid *a*, **—ly** *ad* ['hɒrɪd, -lɪ] abscheulich, scheußlich.

horrify ['hɒrɪfaɪ] *vt* entsetzen.

horror ['hɒrə*] *n* Schrecken *m*; *(great dislike)* Abscheu *m* (of vor + *dat*).

hors d'oeuvre [ɔː'dɜːvr] *n* Vorspeise *f.*

horse [hɔːs] *n* Pferd *nt*; on —back beritten; — chestnut Roßkastanie *f*; —drawn *a* von Pferden gezogen, Pferde-; —power Pferdestärke *f*, PS *nt*; —racing Pferderennen *nt*; —shoe Hufeisen *nt.*

horsy ['hɔːsɪ] *a* pferdenärrisch.

horticulture ['hɔːtɪkʌltʃə*] *n* Gartenbau *m.*

hose(pipe) ['həuzpaɪp] *n* Schlauch *m.*

hosiery ['həuzɪərɪ] *n* Strumpfwaren *pl.*

hospitable [hɒs'pɪtəbl] *a* gastfreundlich.

hospital ['hɒspɪtl] *n* Krankenhaus *nt.*

hospitality [hɒspɪ'tælɪtɪ] *n* Gastlichkeit *f,* Gastfreundschaft *f.*

host [həust] *n* Gastgeber *m*; (innkeeper) (Gast)wirt *m*; (large number) Heerschar *f*; (Eccl) Hostie *f.*

hostage ['hɒstɪdʒ] *n* Geisel *f.*

hostel ['hɒstəl] *n* Herberge *f.*

hostess ['həustes] *n* Gastgeberin *f.*

hostile ['hɒstaɪl] *a* feindlich.

hostility [hɒs'tɪlɪtɪ] *n* Feindschaft *f*; hostilities *pl* Feindseligkeiten *pl.*

hot [hɒt] *a* heiß; drink, food, water warm; (spiced) scharf; (angry) hitzig; — air (col) Gewäsch *nt*; —bed (lit) Mistbeet *nt*; (fig) Nährboden *m*; —blooded *a* heißblütig; — dog heiße(s) Würstchen *nt.*

hotel [həu'tel] *n* Hotel *nt*; —ier Hotelier *m.*

hotheaded ['hɒt'hedɪd] *a* hitzig, aufbrausend.

hothouse ['hɒthaus] *n* (lit, fig) Treibhaus *nt.*

hot line ['hɒtlaɪn] *n* (Pol) heiße(r) Draht *m.*

hotly ['hɒtlɪ] *ad* argue hitzig; pursue dicht.

hot news ['hɒt'njuːz] *n* das Neueste vom Neuen.

hotplate ['hɒtpleɪt] *n* Kochplatte *f.*

hot-water bottle [hɒt'wɔː'tɒbtl] *n* Wärmflasche *f.*

hound [haund] *n* Jagdhund *m*; *vt* jagen, hetzen.

hour [auə*] *n* Stunde *f*; (time of day) (Tages)zeit *f*; —ly *a* stündlich.

house [haus] *n* Haus *nt*; [hauz] *vt* (accommodate) unterbringen; (shelter) aufnehmen; —boat Hausboot *nt*; —breaking Einbruch *m*; —hold Haushalt *m*; —keeper Haushälterin *f*; —keeping Haushaltung *f*; —wife Hausfrau *f*; —work Hausarbeit *f.*

housing ['hauzɪŋ] *n* (act) Unterbringung *f*; (houses) Wohnungen *pl*; (Pol) Wohnungsbau *m*; (covering) Gehäuse *nt*; — estate (Wohn)siedlung *f.*

hovel ['hɒvəl] *n* elende Hütte *f*; Loch *nt.*

hover ['hɒvə*] *vi* (bird) schweben; (person) warten herumstehen; —craft Luftkissenfahrzeug *nt.*

how [hau] *ad* wie; — many wie viele; — much wieviel; —ever *ad* (but) (je)doch, aber; —ever you phrase it wie Sie es auch ausdrücken.

howl [haul] *n* Heulen *nt*; *vi* heulen.

howler ['haulə*] *n* grobe(r) Schnitzer *m.*

hub [hʌb] *n* Radnabe *f*; (of the world) Mittelpunkt *m*; (of commerce) Zentrum *nt.*

hubbub ['hʌbʌb] *n* Tumult *m.*

hub cap ['hʌbkæp] n Radkappe f.

huddle ['hʌdl] vi sich zusammendrängen; n Grüppchen nt.

hue [hju:] n Färbung f, Farbton m; — and cry Zetergeschrei nt.

huff [hʌf] n Eingeschnapptsein nt; to go into a — einschnappen.

hug [hʌg] vt umarmen; (fig) sich dicht halten an (+acc); n Umarmung f.

huge [hju:dʒ] a groß, riesig.

hulk [hʌlk] n (ship) abgetakelte(s) Schiff nt; (person) Koloß m; —ing a ungeschlacht.

hull [hʌl] n Schiffsrumpf m.

hullo [hʌ'ləu] see hello.

hum [hʌm] vi summen; (bumblebee) brummen; vt summen; n Summen nt.

human ['hju:mən] a menschlich; n (also — being) Mensch m.

humane [hju:'meɪn] a human.

humanity [hju:'mænɪtɪ] n Menschheit f; (kindliness) Menschlichkeit f.

humble ['hʌmbl] a demütig; (modest) bescheiden; vt demütigen.

humbly ['hʌmblɪ] ad demütig.

humdrum ['hʌmdrʌm] a eintönig, langweilig.

humid ['hju:mɪd] a feucht; —ity [hju:'mɪdɪtɪ] Feuchtigkeit f.

humiliate [hju:'mɪlɪeɪt] vt demütigen.

humiliation [hju:mɪlɪ'eɪʃən] n Demütigung f.

humility [hju:'mɪlɪtɪ] n Demut f.

humorist ['hju:mərɪst] n Humorist m.

humorous ['hju:mərəs] a humorvoll, komisch.

humour, (US) **humor** ['hju:mə*] n (fun) Humor m; (mood) Stimmung

f; vt nachgeben (+dat); bei Stimmung halten.

hump [hʌmp] n Buckel m.

hunch [hʌntʃ] n (presentiment) (Vor)ahnung f; vt shoulders hochziehen; —back Bucklige(r) m.

hundred ['hʌndrɪd] num, a, n hundert; —weight Zentner m.

hunger ['hʌŋgə*] n Hunger m; (fig) Verlangen nt (for nach); vi hungern.

hungry a, **hungrily** ad ['hʌŋgrɪ, -lɪ] hungrig; to be — Hunger haben.

hunt [hʌnt] vt jagen; (search) suchen (for acc); vi jagen; n Jagd f; —er Jäger m; —ing Jagen nt, Jagd f.

hurdle ['hɜ:dl] n (lit, fig) Hürde f.

hurl [hɜ:l] vt schleudern.

hurrah [hu'rɑ:], **hurray** [hu'reɪ] n Hurra nt.

hurricane ['hʌrɪkən] n Orkan m.

hurried ['hʌrɪd] a eilig; (hasty) übereilt; —ly ad übereilt, hastig.

hurry ['hʌrɪ] n Eile f; to be in a — es eilig haben; vi sich beeilen; —! mach schnell!; vt (an)treiben; job übereilen.

hurt [hɜ:t] irreg vt weh tun (+dat); (injure, fig) verletzen; vi weh tun; —ful a schädlich; remark verletzend.

hurtle ['hɜ:tl] vt schleudern; vi sausen.

husband ['hʌzbənd] n (Ehe)mann m, Gatte m.

hush [hʌʃ] n Stille f; vt zur Ruhe bringen; vi still sein; — interj pst, still.

husk [hʌsk] n Spelze f.

husky ['hʌskɪ] a voice rauh; figure stämmig; n Eskimohund m.

hustle ['hʌsl] vt (push) stoßen; (hurry) antreiben, drängen;

(Hoch)betrieb *m*; — and bustle Geschäftigkeit *f*.

hut [hʌt] *n* Hütte *f*.

hutch [hʌtʃ] *n* (Kaninchen)stall *m*.

hyacinth ['haɪəsɪnθ] *n* Hyazinthe *f*.

hybrid ['haɪbrɪd] *n* Kreuzung *f*; *a* Misch-

hydrant ['haɪdrənt] *n* Hydrant *m*.

hydraulic [haɪ'drɔːlɪk] *a* hydraulisch.

hydroelectric ['haɪdrəʊɪ'lektrɪk] *a* hydroelektrisch.

hydrofoil ['haɪdrəʊfɔɪl] *n* Tragflügel *m*; Tragflügelboot *nt*.

hydrogen ['haɪdrɪdʒən] *n* Wasserstoff *m*.

hyena· [haɪ'iːnə] *n* Hyäne *f*.

hygiene ['haɪdʒiːn] *n* Hygiene *f*.

hygienic [haɪ'dʒiːnɪk] *a* hygienisch.

hymn [hɪm] *n* Kirchenlied *nt*.

hyphen ['haɪfən] *n* Bindestrich *m*; Trennungszeichen *nt*.

hypnosis [hɪp'nəʊsɪs] *n* Hypnose *f*.

hypnotism ['hɪpnətɪzəm] *n* Hypnotismus *m*.

hypnotist ['hɪpnətɪst] *n* Hypnotiseur *m*.

hypnotize ['hɪpnətaɪz] *vt* hypnotisieren.

hypochondriac [haɪpəʊ'kɒndrɪæk] *n* eingebildete(r) Kranke(r) *mf*.

hypocrisy [hɪ'pɒkrɪsɪ] *n* Heuchelei *f*, Scheinheiligkeit *f*.

hypocrite ['hɪpəkrɪt] *n* Heuchler *m*, Scheinheilige(r) *m*.

hypocritical [hɪpə'krɪtɪkəl] *a* scheinheilig, heuchlerisch.

hypothesis [haɪ'pɒθɪsɪs] *n* Hypothese *f*.

hypothetic(al) [haɪpəʊ'θetɪk(əl)] *a* hypothetisch.

hysteria [hɪs'tɪərɪə] *n* Hysterie *f*.

hysterical [hɪs'terɪkəl] *a* hysterisch.

hysterics [hɪs'terɪks] *npl* hysterische(r) Anfall *m*.

I

I, i [aɪ] *n* I *nt*, i *nt*; **I** *pron* ich.

ice [aɪs] *n* Eis *nt*; *vt* (*Cook*) mit Zuckerguß überziehen; *vi* (*also* — up) vereisen; **—axe** Eispickel *m*; **—berg** Eisberg *m*; **—box** (*US*) Kühlschrank *m*; **—cream** Eis *nt*; **—cube** Eiswürfel *m*; **—hockey** Eishockey *nt*; **—rink** (Kunst)eisbahn *f*.

icicle ['aɪsɪkl] *n* Eiszapfen *m*.

icing ['aɪsɪŋ] *n* (*on cake*) Zuckerguß *m*; (*on window*) Vereisung *f*.

icon ['aɪkɒn] *n* Ikone *f*.

icy ['aɪsɪ] *a* (*slippery*) vereist; (*cold*) eisig.

I'd [aɪd] ⇒ **I would**; **I had**.

idea [aɪ'dɪə] *n* Idee *f*; **no** — keine Ahnung; **my** — **of a holiday** wie ich mir einen Urlaub vorstelle.

ideal [aɪ'dɪəl] *n* Ideal *nt*; *a* ideal; **—ism** Idealismus *m*; **—ist** Idealist *m*; **—ly** *ad* ideal(erweise).

identical [aɪ'dentɪkəl] *a* identisch; **twins** eineiig.

identification [aɪdentɪfɪ'keɪʃən] *n* Identifizierung *f*.

identify [aɪ'dentɪfaɪ] *vt* identifizieren; (*regard as the same*) gleichsetzen.

identity [aɪ'dentɪtɪ] *n* Identität *f*; **—card** Personalausweis *m*; **— papers** *pl* (Ausweis)papiere *pl*.

ideology [aɪdɪˈɒlədʒɪ] *n* Ideologie *f.*

idiocy [ˈɪdɪəsɪ] *n* Idiotie *f.*

idiom [ˈɪdɪəm] *n* (*expression*) Redewendung *f*; (*dialect*) Idiom *nt.*

idiosyncrasy [ɪdɪəˈsɪŋkrəsɪ] *n* Eigenart *f.*

idiot [ˈɪdɪət] *n* Idiot(in *f*) *m*; **—ic** [ɪdɪˈɒtɪk] *a* idiotisch.

idle [ˈaɪdl] *a* (*doing nothing*) untätig, müßig; (*lazy*) faul; (*useless*) vergeblich, nutzlos; *machine* still(stehend); *threat, talk* leer; **—ness** Müßiggang *m*; Faulheit *f*; **—r** Faulenzer *m.*

idol [ˈaɪdl] *n* Idol *nt*; **—ize** *vt* vergöttern.

idyllic [ɪˈdɪlɪk] *a* idyllisch.

if [ɪf] *cj* wenn, falls; (*whether*) ob; **— only...** wenn... doch nur; **—not** falls nicht.

igloo [ˈɪgluː] *n* Iglu *m* or *nt.*

ignite [ɪgˈnaɪt] *vt* (an)zünden.

ignition [ɪgˈnɪʃən] *n* Zündung *f*; **—key** (Aut) Zündschlüssel *m.*

ignoramus [ɪgnəˈreɪməs] *n* Ignorant *m.*

ignorance [ˈɪgnərəns] *n* Unwissenheit *f*, Ignoranz *f.*

ignorant [ˈɪgnərənt] *a* unwissend.

ignore [ɪgˈnɔː*] *vt* ignorieren.

ikon [ˈaɪkɒn] *n* = icon.

I'll [aɪl] = I will, I shall.

ill [ɪl] *a* krank; (*evil*) schlecht, böse; *n* Übel *nt*; **—advised** *a* schlecht beraten, unklug; **—at-ease** *a* unbehaglich.

illegal *a,* **—ly** *ad* [ɪˈliːgəl, -ɪ] illegal.

illegible [ɪˈledʒəbl] *a* unleserlich.

illegitimate [ɪlɪˈdʒɪtɪmət] *a* unzulässig; *child* unehelich.

ill-fated [ˈɪlˈfeɪtɪd] *a* unselig.

ill-feeling [ˈɪlˈfiːlɪŋ] *n* Verstimmung *f.*

illicit [ɪˈlɪsɪt] *a* verboten.

illiterate [ɪˈlɪtərət] *a* ungebildet.

ill-mannered [ˈɪlˈmænəd] *a* ungebildet.

illness [ˈɪlnəs] *n* Krankheit *f.*

illogical [ɪˈlɒdʒɪkəl] *a* unlogisch.

ill-treat [ˈɪlˈtriːt] *vt* mißhandeln.

illuminate [ɪˈluːmɪneɪt] *vt* beleuchten.

illumination [ɪluːmɪˈneɪʃən] *n* Beleuchtung *f.*

illusion [ɪˈluːʒən] *n* Illusion *f.*

illusive [ɪˈluːsɪv], **illusory** [ɪˈluːsərɪ] *a* illusorisch, trügerisch.

illustrate [ˈɪləstreɪt] *vt book* illustrieren; (*explain*) veranschaulichen.

illustration [ɪləsˈtreɪʃən] *n* Illustration *f*; (*explanation*) Veranschaulichung *f.*

illustrious [ɪˈlʌstrɪəs] *a* berühmt.

ill will [ˈɪlˈwɪl] *n* Groll *m.*

I'm [aɪm] = I am.

image [ˈɪmɪdʒ] *n* Bild *nt*; (*likeness*) Abbild *nt*; (*public* **—**) Image *nt*; **—ry** Symbolik *f.*

imaginable [ɪˈmædʒɪnəbl] *a* vorstellbar.

imaginary [ɪˈmædʒɪnərɪ] *a* eingebildet; *world* Phantasie-.

imagination [ɪmædʒɪˈneɪʃən] *n* Einbildung *f*; (*creative*) Phantasie *f.*

imaginative [ɪˈmædʒɪnətɪv] *a* phantasiereich, einfallsreich.

imagine [ɪˈmædʒɪn] *vt* sich vorstellen; (*wrongly*) sich einbilden.

imbalance [ɪmˈbæləns] *n* Unausgeglichenheit *f.*

imbecile [ˈɪmbəsiːl] *n* Schwachsinnige(r) *mf.*

imbue [ɪmˈbjuː] *vt* durchdringen.

imitate [ˈɪmɪteɪt] *vt* nachmachen, imitieren.

imitation [ɪmɪˈteɪʃən] n Nachahmung f, Imitation f.

imitator [ˈɪmɪteɪtə*] n Nachahmer m.

immaculate [ɪˈmækjʊlɪt] a makellos; dress tadellos; (Eccl) unbefleckt.

immaterial [ɪməˈtɪərɪəl] a unwesentlich.

immature [ɪməˈtjʊə*] a unreif.

immaturity [ɪməˈtjʊərɪtɪ] n Unreife f.

immediate [ɪˈmiːdɪət] a (instant) sofortig; (near) unmittelbar; relatives nächste(r, s); needs dringlich; —ly ad sofort; (in position) unmittelbar.

immense [ɪˈmens] a unermeßlich; —ly ad ungeheuerlich; grateful unheimlich.

immerse [ɪˈmɜːs] vt eintauchen.

immersion heater [ɪˈmɜːʃənhiːtə*] n Heißwassergerät nt.

immigrant [ˈɪmɪgrənt] n Einwanderer m.

immigration [ɪmɪˈgreɪʃən] n Einwanderung f.

imminent [ˈɪmɪnənt] a bevorstehend; danger drohend.

immobilize [ɪˈməʊbɪlaɪz] vt lähmen.

immoderate [ɪˈmɒdərət] a maßlos, übertrieben.

immoral [ɪˈmɒrəl] a unmoralisch; (sexually) unsittlich; —ity [ɪməˈrælɪtɪ] Verderbtheit f.

immortal [ɪˈmɔːtl] a unsterblich; n Unsterbliche(r) mf; —ity [ɪmɔːˈtælɪtɪ] Unsterblichkeit f; (of book etc) Unvergänglichkeit f; —ize vt unsterblich machen.

immune [ɪˈmjuːn] a (secure) geschützt (from gegen), sicher (from vor + dat); (Med) immun.

immunity [ɪˈmjuːnɪtɪ] n (Med, Jur) Immunität f; (fig) Freiheit f.

immunization [ɪmjuːnaɪˈzeɪʃən] n Immunisierung f.

immunize [ˈɪmjʊnaɪz] vt immunisieren.

impact [ˈɪmpækt] n (lit) Aufprall m; (force) Wucht f; (fig) Wirkung f.

impair [ɪmˈpɛə*] vt beeinträchtigen.

impale [ɪmˈpeɪl] vt aufspießen.

impartial [ɪmˈpɑːʃəl] a unparteiisch; —ity [ɪmpɑːʃɪˈælɪtɪ] Unparteilichkeit f.

impassable [ɪmˈpɑːsəbl] a unpassierbar.

impassioned [ɪmˈpæʃnd] a leidenschaftlich.

impatience [ɪmˈpeɪʃəns] n Ungeduld f.

impatient a, —ly ad [ɪmˈpeɪʃənt, -lɪ] ungeduldig; to be — to do sth es nicht erwarten können, etw zu tun.

impeccable [ɪmˈpekəbl] a tadellos.

impede [ɪmˈpiːd] vt (be)hindern.

impediment [ɪmˈpedɪmənt] n Hindernis nt; (in speech) Sprachfehler m.

impending [ɪmˈpendɪŋ] a bevorstehend.

impenetrable [ɪmˈpenɪtrəbl] a (lit, fig) undurchdringlich; forest unwegsam; theory undurchsichtig; mystery unerforschlich.

imperative [ɪmˈperətɪv] a (necessary) unbedingt erforderlich; n (Gram) Imperativ m, Befehlsform f.

imperceptible [ɪmpəˈseptəbl] a nicht wahrnehmbar.

imperfect [ɪmˈpɜːfɪkt] a (faulty) fehlerhaft; (incomplete) unvollständig; —ion [ɪmpəˈfekʃən]

Unvollkommenheit f; (fault) Fehler m; (faultiness) Fehlerhaftigkeit f.

imperial [ɪmˈpɪərɪəl] a kaiserlich; —ism Imperialismus m.

imperil [ɪmˈperɪl] vt gefährden.

impersonal [ɪmˈpɜːsnl] a unpersönlich.

impersonate [ɪmˈpɜːsəneɪt] vt sich ausgeben als; (for amusement) imitieren.

impersonation [ɪmpɜːsəˈneɪʃən] n Verkörperung f; (Theat) Imitation f.

impertinence [ɪmˈpɜːtɪnəns] n Unverschämtheit f.

impertinent [ɪmˈpɜːtɪnənt] a unverschämt, frech.

imperturbable [ɪmpəˈtɜːbəbl] a unerschütterlich, gelassen.

impervious [ɪmˈpɜːvɪəs] a undurchlässig; (fig) unempfänglich (to für).

impetuous [ɪmˈpetjuəs] a heftig, ungestüm.

impetus [ˈɪmpɪtəs] n Triebkraft f; (fig) Auftrieb m.

impinge [ɪmˈpɪndʒ]: — on vt beeinträchtigen; (light) fallen auf (+acc).

implausible [ɪmˈplɔːzəbl] a unglaubwürdig, nicht überzeugend.

implement [ˈɪmplɪmənt] n Werkzeug nt, Gerät nt; [ˈɪmplɪment] vt ausführen.

implicate [ˈɪmplɪkeɪt] vt verwickeln, hineinziehen.

implication [ɪmplɪˈkeɪʃən] n (meaning) Bedeutung f; (effect) Auswirkung f; (hint) Andeutung f; (in crime) Verwicklung f; by —folglich.

implicit [ɪmˈplɪsɪt] a (suggested) unausgesprochen; (utter) vorbehaltlos.

implore [ɪmˈplɔː*] vt anflehen.

imply [ɪmˈplaɪ] vt (hint) andeuten; (be evidence for) schließen lassen auf (+acc); what does that —? was bedeutet das?

impolite [ɪmpəˈlaɪt] a unhöflich.

impolitic [ɪmˈpɒlɪtɪk] a undiplomatisch.

imponderable [ɪmˈpɒndərəbl] a unwägbar.

import [ɪmˈpɔːt] vt einführen, importieren; [ˈɪmpɔːt] n Einfuhr f, Import m; (meaning) Bedeutung f, Tragweite f.

importance [ɪmˈpɔːtəns] n Bedeutung f; (influence) Einfluß m.

important [ɪmˈpɔːtənt] a wichtig; (influential) bedeutend, einflußreich.

import duty [ˈɪmpɔːtˈdjuːtɪ] n Einfuhrzoll m.

imported [ɪmˈpɔːtɪd] a eingeführt, importiert.

importer [ɪmˈpɔːtə*] n Importeur m.

import licence [ˈɪmpɔːtˈlaɪsəns] n Einfuhrgenehmigung f.

impose [ɪmˈpəʊz] vti auferlegen (on dat); penalty, sanctions verhängen (on gegen); to — (o.s.) on sb sich jdm aufdrängen; to — on sb's kindness jds Liebenswürdigkeit ausnützen.

imposing [ɪmˈpəʊzɪŋ] a eindrucksvoll.

imposition [ɪmpəˈzɪʃən] n (of burden, fine) Auferlegung f; (Sch) Strafarbeit f.

impossibility [ɪmpɒsəˈbɪlɪtɪ] n Unmöglichkeit f.

impossible a, **impossibly** ad [ɪmˈpɒsəbl, -blɪ] unmöglich.

impostor [ɪmˈpɒstə*] n Betrüger m; Hochstapler m.

impotence ['ɪmpətəns] Impotenz f.

impotent ['ɪmpətənt] a machtlos; (sexually) impotent.

impound [ɪm'paʊnd] vt beschlagnahmen.

impoverished [ɪm'pɒvərɪʃt] a verarmt.

impracticable [ɪm'præktɪkəbl] a undurchführbar.

impractical [ɪm'præktɪkəl] a unpraktisch.

imprecise [ɪmprə'saɪs] a ungenau.

impregnable [ɪm'pregnəbl] a castle uneinnehmbar.

impregnate ['ɪmpregneɪt] vt (saturate) sättigen; (fertilize) befruchten; (fig) durchdringen.

impresario [ɪmprə'saːrɪəu] n Impresario m.

impress [ɪm'pres] vt (influence) beeindrucken; (imprint) (auf-)drücken; **to — sth on sb** jdm etw einschärfen; **—ion** Eindruck m; (on wax, footprint) Abdruck m; (of stamp) Aufdruck m; (of book) Auflage f; (take-off) Nachahmung f; **I was under the —ion ich hatte den Eindruck; —ionable** a leicht zu beeindrucken(d); —ionist Impressionist m; —ive a eindrucksvoll.

imprison [ɪm'prɪzn] vt ins Gefängnis schicken; **—ment** Inhaftierung f; Gefangenschaft f; **3 years' —ment** eine Gefängnisstrafe von 3 Jahren.

improbable [ɪm'prɒbəbl] a unwahrscheinlich.

impromptu [ɪm'prɒmptju:] a, ad aus dem Stegreif, improvisiert.

improper [ɪm'prɒpə*] a (indecent) unanständig; (wrong) unrichtig, falsch; (unsuitable) unpassend.

impropriety [ɪmprə'praɪətɪ] n Ungehörigkeit f.

improve [ɪm'pru:v] vt verbessern; vi besser werden; **—ment** (Ver-)besserung f; (of appearance) Verschönerung f.

improvisation [ɪmprəvaɪ'zeɪʃən] n Improvisation f.

improvise ['ɪmprəvaɪz] vti improvisieren.

imprudence [ɪm'pru:dəns] n Unklugheit f.

imprudent [ɪm'pru:dənt] a unklug.

impudent ['ɪmpjudənt] a unverschämt.

impulse ['ɪmpʌls] n (desire) Drang m; (driving force) Antrieb m, Impuls m; **my first — was to ...** ich wollte zuerst ...

impulsive [ɪm'pʌlsɪv] a impulsiv.

impunity [ɪm'pju:nɪtɪ] n Straflosigkeit f.

impure [ɪm'pjuə*] a (dirty) unrein; (mixed) gemischt; (bad) schmutzig, unanständig.

impurity [ɪm'pjuərɪtɪ] n Unreinheit f; (Tech) Verunreinigung f.

in [ɪn] prep in; (made of) aus; — **Dickens/a child** bei Dickens/einem Kind; — **him you'll have ...** an ihm hast du ...; — **doing this he has ...** dadurch, daß er das tat, hat er ...; — **saying that I mean ...** indem ich das sage, meine ich ...; **I haven't seen him — years** ich habe ihn seit Jahren nicht mehr gesehen; **15 pence — the £** 15 Pence per Pfund; **blind — the left eye** auf dem linken Auge or links blind; — **itself** an sich; — **that**, — **so** or **as far as** insofern als; ad hinein; **to be — zuhause** sein; (train) da sein; (in fashion) in (Mode) sein; **to have it — for sb** es auf jdn abgesehen haben; **—s and outs** pl Einzelheiten pl; **to**

know the —s and outs sich auskennen.

inability [ɪnə'bɪlɪtɪ] n Unfähigkeit f.

inaccessible [ɪnæk'sesəbl] a
.unzugänglich.

inaccuracy [ɪn'ækjʊrəsɪ] n
Ungenauigkeit f.

inaccurate [ɪn'ækjʊrɪt] a ungenau;
(wrong) unrichtig.

inaction [ɪn'ækʃən] n Untätigkeit f.

inactive [ɪn'æktɪv] a untätig.

inactivity [ɪnæk'tɪvɪtɪ] n Untätigkeit f.

inadequacy [ɪn'ædɪkwəsɪ] n
Unzulänglichkeit f; (of punishment) Unangemessenheit f.

inadequate [ɪn'ædɪkwət] a
unzulänglich; punishment
unangemessen.

inadvertently [ɪnəd'vɜːtəntlɪ] ad
unabsichtlich.

inadvisable [ɪnəd'vaɪzəbl] a nicht
ratsam.

inane [ɪ'neɪn] a dumm, albern.

inanimate [ɪn'ænɪmət] a leblos.

inapplicable [ɪnə'plɪkəbl] a
unzutreffend.

inappropriate [ɪnə'prəʊprɪət] a
clothing ungeeignet; remark
unangebracht.

inapt [ɪn'æpt] a unpassend;
(clumsy) ungeschickt; —itude
Untauglichkeit f.

inarticulate [ɪnɑː'tɪkjʊlət] a
unklar; to be — sich nicht ausdrücken können.

inartistic [ɪnɑː'tɪstɪk] a unkünst-
lerisch.

inasmuch as [ɪnəz'mʌtʃəz] ad da,
weil; (in so far as) soweit.

inattention [ɪnə'tenʃən] n Unauf-
merksamkeit f.

inattentive [ɪnə'tentɪv] a unauf-
merksam.

inaudible [ɪn'ɔːdəbl] a unhörbar.

inaugural [ɪn'ɔːgjʊrəl] a Eröff-
nungs-; (Univ) Antritts-.

inaugurate [ɪn'ɔːgjʊreɪt] vt (open)
einweihen; (admit to office) (feierlich) einführen.

inauguration [ɪnɔːgjʊ'reɪʃən] n
Eröffnung f; (feierliche) Amtsein-
führung f.

inborn ['ɪn'bɔːn] a angeboren.

inbred [ɪn'bred] a quality
angeboren; they are — bei ihnen
herrscht Inzucht.

inbreeding ['ɪn'briːdɪŋ] n Inzucht f.

incalculable [ɪn'kælkjʊləbl] a
person unberechenbar; consequences unabsehbar.

incapability [ɪnkeɪpə'bɪlɪtɪ] n
Unfähigkeit f.

incapable [ɪn'keɪpəbl] a unfähig (of
doing sth etw zu tun); (not able)
nicht einsatzfähig.

incapacitate [ɪnkə'pæsɪteɪt] vt
untauglich machen; —d behindert;
machine nicht gebrauchsfähig.

incapacity [ɪnkə'pæsɪtɪ] n Unfähigkeit f.

incarcerate [ɪn'kɑːsəreɪt] vt
einkerkern.

incarnate [ɪn'kɑːnɪt] a menschge-
worden; (fig) leibhaftig.

incarnation [ɪnkɑː'neɪʃən] n (Eccl)
Menschwerdung f; (fig) Inbegriff
m.

incendiary [ɪn'sendɪərɪ] a brand-
stifterisch, Brand-; (fig) aufrührerisch; n Brandstifter m;
(bomb) Brandbombe f.

incense ['ɪnsens] n Weihrauch m;
[ɪn'sens] vt erzürnen.

incentive [ɪn'sentɪv] n Anreiz m.

incessant a, —ly ad [ɪn'sesnt, -lɪ]
unaufhörlich.

incest ['msest] n Inzest m.

inch [mtʃ] n Zoll m.

incidence ['msidəns] n Auftreten nt; (of crime) Quote f.

incident ['msidənt] n Vorfall m; (disturbance) Zwischenfall m; —al [msɪ'dentl] a music Begleit-; expenses Neben-; (unplanned) zufällig; (unimportant) nebensächlich; remark beiläufig; —al to sth mit etw verbunden; —ally [msɪ'dentəli] ad (by chance) nebenbei; (by the way) nebenbei bemerkt, übrigens.

incinerator [m'smərettə*] n Verbrennungsofen m.

incision [m'sɪʒən] n Einschnitt m.

incisive [m'saɪsɪv] a style treffend; person scharfsinnig.

incite [m'saɪt] vt anstacheln.

inclement [m'klemənt] a weather rauh.

inclination [mklɪ'neɪʃən] n Neigung f.

incline ['mklam] n Abhang m; [m'klam] vt neigen; (fig) veranlassen; to be —d to do sth Lust haben, etw zu tun; (have tendency) dazu neigen, etw zu tun; vi sich neigen.

include [m'kluːd] vt einschließen; (on list, in group) aufnehmen; **including** [m'kluːdɪŋ] prep: — X X inbegriffen.

inclusion [m'kluːʒən] n Aufnahme f, Einbeziehung f.

inclusive [m'kluːsɪv] a einschließlich; (Comm) inklusive.

incognito [mkɒg'niːtəʊ] ad inkognito.

incoherent [mkəʊ'hɪərənt] a zusammenhanglos.

income ['mkʌm] n Einkommen nt; (from business) Einkünfte pl; —

tax Lohnsteuer f; (of self-employed) Einkommensteuer f.

incoming ['mkʌmɪŋ] a ankommend; (succeeding) folgend; mail eingehend; tide steigend.

incomparable [m'kɒmpərəbl] a unvergleichlich.

incompatible [mkəm'pætəbl] a unvereinbar; people unverträglich.

incompetence [m'kɒmpɪtəns] n Unfähigkeit f.

incompetent [m'kɒmpɪtənt] a unfähig; (not qualified) nicht berechtigt.

incomplete [mkəm'pliːt] a unvollständig.

incomprehensible [mkɒmprɪ'hensəbl] a unverständlich.

inconceivable [mkən'siːvəbl] a unvorstellbar.

inconclusive [mkən'kluːsɪv] a nicht schlüssig.

incongruity [mkɒn'gruːɪtɪ] n Seltsamkeit f; (of remark etc) Unangebrachtsein nt.

incongruous [m'kɒngruəs] a seltsam; remark unangebracht.

inconsequential [mkɒnsɪ'kwenʃəl] a belanglos.

inconsiderable [mkən'sɪdərəbl] a unerheblich.

inconsiderate [mkən'sɪdərət] a rücksichtslos; (hasty) unüberlegt.

inconsistency [mkən'sɪstənsɪ] n innere(r) Widerspruch m; (state) Unbeständigkeit f.

inconsistent [mkən'sɪstənt] a unvereinbar; behaviour inkonsequent; action, speech widersprüchlich; person, work unbeständig.

inconspicuous [mkən'spɪkjuəs] a unauffällig.

inconstancy [ɪnˈkɒnstənsɪ] n Unbeständigkeit f.

inconstant [ɪnˈkɒnstənt] a unbeständig.

incontinence [ɪnˈkɒntɪnəns] n (Med) Unfähigkeit f, Stuhl und Harn zurückzuhalten; (fig) Zügellosigkeit f.

incontinent [ɪnˈkɒntɪnənt] a (Med) nicht fähig, Stuhl und Harn zurückzuhalten; (fig) zügellos.

inconvenience [ɪnkənˈviːnɪəns] n Unbequemlichkeit f; (trouble to others) Unannehmlichkeiten pl.

inconvenient [ɪnkənˈviːnɪənt] a ungelegen; journey unbequem.

incorporate [ɪnˈkɔːrpəreɪt] vt (include) aufnehmen; (unite) vereinigen.

incorporated [ɪnˈkɔːrpəreɪtɪd] a eingetragen; (US) GmbH.

incorrect [ɪnkəˈrekt] a unrichtig; behaviour inkorrekt.

incorrigible [ɪnˈkɒrɪdʒəbl] a unverbesserlich.

incorruptible [ɪnkəˈrʌptəbl] a unzerstörbar; person unbestechlich.

increase [ˈɪnkriːs] n Zunahme f, Erhöhung f; (pay —) Gehaltserhöhung f; (in size) Vergrößerung f; [ɪnˈkriːs] vt erhöhen; wealth, rage vermehren; business erweitern; vi zunehmen; (prices) steigen; (in size) größer werden; (in number) sich vermehren.

increasingly [ɪnˈkriːsɪŋlɪ] ad zunehmend.

incredible a, **incredibly** ad [ɪnˈkredəbl, -blɪ] unglaublich.

incredulity [ɪnkrɪˈdjuːlɪtɪ] n Ungläubigkeit f.

incredulous [ɪnˈkredjʊləs] a ungläubig.

increment [ˈɪnkrɪmənt] n Zulage f.

incriminate [ɪnˈkrɪmɪneɪt] vt belasten.

incubation [ɪnkjʊˈbeɪʃən] n Ausbrüten nt; — period Inkubationszeit f.

incubator [ˈɪnkjʊbeɪtə*] n Brutkasten m.

incur [ɪnˈkɔː*] vt sich zuziehen; debts machen.

incurable [ɪnˈkjʊərəbl] a unheilbar; (fig) unverbesserlich.

incursion [ɪnˈkɔːʃən] n (feindlicher) Einfall m.

indebted [ɪnˈdetɪd] a (obliged) verpflichtet (to sb jdm); (owing) verschuldet.

indecency [ɪnˈdiːsnsɪ] n Unanständigkeit f.

indecent [ɪnˈdiːsnt] a unanständig.

indecision [ɪndɪˈsɪʒən] n Unschlüssigkeit f.

indecisive [ɪndɪˈsaɪsɪv] a battle nicht entscheidend; result unentschieden; person unentschlossen.

indeed [ɪnˈdiːd] ad tatsächlich, in der Tat.

indefinable [ɪndɪˈfaɪnəbl] a undefinierbar; (vague) unbestimmt.

indefinite [ɪnˈdefɪnɪt] a unbestimmt; —ly ad auf unbestimmte Zeit; wait unbegrenzt lange.

indelible [ɪnˈdeləbl] a unauslöschlich; — pencil Tintenstift m.

indemnify [ɪnˈdemnɪfaɪ] vt entschädigen; (safeguard) versichern.

indentation [ɪndenˈteɪʃən] n Einbuchtung f; (Print) Einrückung f.

independence [ɪndɪˈpendəns] n Unabhängigkeit f.

independent [ɪndɪˈpendənt] a (free) unabhängig; (unconnected) unabhängig von.

indescribable [ɪndɪs'kraɪbəbl] *a* unbeschreiblich.

index ['ɪndeks] *n* Index *m* (*also* ·Eccl), Verzeichnis *nt*; — **finger** Zeigefinger *m*.

indicate ['ɪndɪkeɪt] *vt* anzeigen; (*hint*) andeuten.

indication [ɪndɪ'keɪʃən] *n* Anzeichen *nt*; (*information*) Angabe *f*.

indicative [ɪn'dɪkətɪv] *n* (*Gram*) Indikativ *m*.

indicator ['ɪndɪkeɪtə*] *n* (*sign*) (An)-zeichen *nt*; (*Aut*) Richtungsanzeiger *m*.

indict [ɪn'daɪt] *vt* anklagen; —**able** *a person* strafrechtlich verfolgbar; *offence* strafbar; —**ment** Anklage *f*.

indifference [ɪn'dɪfrəns] *n* (*lack of interest*) Gleichgültigkeit *f*; (*unimportance*) Unwichtigkeit *f*.

indifferent [ɪn'dɪfrənt] *a* (*not caring*) gleichgültig; (*unimportant*) unwichtig; (*mediocre*) mäßig.

indigenous [ɪn'dɪdʒɪnəs] *a* einheimisch; **a plant — to X** eine in X vorkommende Pflanze.

indigestible [ɪndɪ'dʒestəbl] *a* unverdaulich.

indigestion [ɪndɪ'dʒestʃən] *n* Verdauungsstörung *f*; verdorbene(r) Magen *m*.

indignant [ɪn'dɪgnənt] *a* ungehalten, entrüstet.

indignation [ɪndɪg'neɪʃən] *n* Entrüstung *f*.

indignity [ɪn'dɪgnɪtɪ] *n* Demütigung *f*.

indigo ['ɪndɪgəʊ] *n* Indigo *m or nt*; *a* indigoblau.

indirect *a*, —**ly** *ad* [ɪndɪ'rekt, -lɪ] indirekt; *answer* nicht direkt; **by — means** auf Umwegen.

indiscernible [ɪndɪ'sɜːnəbl] *a* nicht wahrnehmbar.

indiscreet [ɪndɪs'kriːt] *a* (*insensitive*) unbedacht; (*improper*) taktlos; (*telling secrets*) indiskret.

indiscretion [ɪndɪs'kreʃən] *n* Taktlosigkeit *f*; Indiskretion *f*.

indiscriminate [ɪndɪs'krɪmnət] *a* wahllos; kritiklos.

indispensable [ɪndɪs'pensəbl] *a* unentbehrlich.

indisposed [ɪndɪs'pəʊzd] *a* unpäßlich.

indisposition [ɪndɪspə'zɪʃən] *n* Unpäßlichkeit *f*.

indisputable [ɪndɪs'pjuːtəbl] *a* unbestreitbar; *evidence* unanfechtbar.

indistinct [ɪndɪs'tɪŋkt] *a* undeutlich.

indistinguishable [ɪndɪs'tɪŋgwɪʃəbl] *a* nicht unterscheidbar; *difference* unmerklich.

individual [ɪndɪ'vɪdjuəl] *n* Einzelne(r) *mf*, Individuum *nt*; *a* individuell; *case* Einzel-; (*of, for one person*) eigen, individuell; (*characteristic*) eigentümlich; —**ist** Individualist *m*; —**ity** [ɪndɪvɪdju'elɪtɪ] Individualität *f*; —**ly** *ad* einzeln, individuell.

indoctrinate [ɪn'dɒktrɪneɪt] *vt* indoktrinieren.

indoctrination [ɪndɒktrɪ'neɪʃən] *n* Indoktrination *f*.

indolence ['ɪndələns] *n* Trägheit *f*.

indolent ['ɪndələnt] *a* träge.

indoor ['ɪndɔː*] *a* Haus-; Zimmer-; Innen-; (*Sport*) Hallen-; —**s** *ad* drinnen, im Haus; **to go —s hinein** *or* ins Haus gehen.

indubitable [ɪn'djuːbɪtəbl] *a* unzweifelhaft.

indubitably [ɪn'djuːbɪtəblɪ] *ad* zweifellos.

induce [ɪn'djuːs] *vt* dazu bewegen, veranlassen; *reaction* herbeiführen; **—ment** Veranlassung *f*; *(incentive)* Anreiz *m*.

induct [ɪn'dʌkt] *vt* in sein Amt einführen.

indulge [ɪn'dʌldʒ] *vt (give way)* nachgeben (+ *dat*); *(gratify)* frönen (+ *dat*); **to — o.s. in sth** sich (*dat*) etw gönnen; *vi* frönen (*in dat*), sich gönnen (*in acc*); *(enjoyment)* (übermäßiger) Genuß *m*; **—nt** *a* nachsichtig; *(pej)* nachgiebig.

industrial [ɪn'dʌstrɪəl] *a* Industrie-, industriell; *dispute, injury* Arbeits-; **—ist** Industrielle(r) *mf*; **—ize** *vt* industrialisieren.

industrious [ɪn'dʌstrɪəs] *a* fleißig.

industry [ɪndəstrɪ] *n* Industrie *f*; *(diligence)* Fleiß *m*; *hotel —* Hotelgewerbe *nt*.

inebriated [ɪ'niːbrɪeɪtɪd] *a* betrunken, berauscht.

inedible [ɪn'edɪbl] *a* ungenießbar.

ineffective [ɪnɪ'fektɪv], **ineffectual** [ɪnɪ'fektjʊəl] *a* unwirksam, wirkungslos; *person* untauglich.

inefficiency [ɪnɪ'fɪʃənsɪ] *n* Ineffizienz *f*.

inefficient [ɪnɪ'fɪʃənt] *a* ineffizient; *(ineffective)* unwirksam.

inelegant [ɪn'elɪgənt] *a* unelegant.

ineligible [ɪn'elɪdʒəbl] *a* nicht berechtigt; *candidate* nicht wählbar.

ineluctable [ɪnɪ'lʌktəbl] *a* unausweichlich.

inept [ɪ'nept] *a remark* unpassend; *person* ungeeignet.

inequality [ɪnɪ'kwɒlɪtɪ] *n* Ungleichheit *f*.

ineradicable [ɪnɪ'rædɪkəbl] *a* unausrottbar; *mistake* unabänderlich; *guilt* tiefsitzend.

inert [ɪ'nɜːt] *a* träge; *(Chem)* inaktiv; *(motionless)* unbeweglich.

inertia [ɪ'nɜːʃə] *n* Trägheit *f*.

inescapable [ɪnɪs'keɪpəbl] *a* unvermeidbar.

inessential [ɪnɪ'senʃəl] *a* unwesentlich.

inestimable [ɪn'estɪməbl] *a* unschätzbar.

inevitability [ɪnevɪtə'bɪlɪtɪ] *n* Unvermeidlichkeit *f*.

inevitable [ɪn'evɪtəbl] *a* unvermeidlich.

inexact [ɪnɪg'zækt] *a* ungenau.

inexcusable [ɪnɪks'kjuːzəbl] *a* unverzeihlich.

inexhaustible [ɪnɪg'zɔːstəbl] *a* *wealth* unerschöpflich; *talker* unermüdlich; *curiosity* unstillbar.

inexorable [ɪn'eksərəbl] *a* unerbittlich.

inexpensive [ɪnɪks'pensɪv] *a* preiswert.

inexperience [ɪnɪks'pɪərɪəns] *n* Unerfahrenheit *f*; **—d** *a* unerfahren.

inexplicable [ɪnɪks'plɪkəbl] *a* unerklärlich.

inexpressible [ɪnɪks'presəbl] *a* *pain, joy* unbeschreiblich; *thoughts* nicht ausdrückbar.

inextricable [ɪnɪks'trɪkəbl] *a* un(auf)lösbar.

infallibility [ɪnfælə'bɪlɪtɪ] *n* Unfehlbarkeit *f*.

infallible [ɪn'fæləbl] *a* unfehlbar.

infamous ['ɪnfəməs] *a place* verrufen; *deed* schändlich; *person* niederträchtig.

infamy ['ɪnfəmɪ] *n* Verrufenheit *f*; Niedertracht *f*; *(disgrace)* Schande *f*.

infancy ['ɪnfənsɪ] n frühe Kindheit f; (fig) Anfangsstadium nt.

infant ['ɪnfənt] n kleine(s) Kind nt, Säugling m; **—ile** a kindisch, infantil; **— school** Vorschule f.

infantry ['ɪnfəntrɪ] n Infanterie f; **—man** Infanterist m.

infatuated [ɪn'fætjʊeɪtɪd] a vernarrt; **to become — with** sich vernarren in (+acc).

infatuation [ɪnfætju'eɪʃən] n Vernarrtheit f (with in +acc).

infect [ɪn'fekt] vt anstecken (also fig), infizieren; **—ion** Ansteckung f, Infektion f; **—ious** [ɪn'fekʃəs] a ansteckend.

infer [ɪn'fɜ:*] vt schließen; **—ence** ['ɪnfərəns] a Schlußfolgerung f.

inferior [ɪn'fɪərɪə*] a rank untergeordnet, niedriger; quality minderwertig; n Untergebene(r) m; **—ity** [ɪnfɪərɪ'ɒrɪtɪ] Minderwertigkeit f; (in rank) untergeordnete Stellung f; **—ity complex** Minderwertigkeitskomplex m.

infernal [ɪn'fɜ:nl] a höllisch.

inferno [ɪn'fɜ:nəʊ] n Hölle f, Inferno nt.

infertile [ɪn'fɜ:taɪl] a unfruchtbar.

infertility [ɪnfɜ:'tɪlɪtɪ] n Unfruchtbarkeit f.

infest [ɪn'fest] vt plagen, heimsuchen; **to be —ed with** wimmeln von.

infidel ['ɪnfɪdl] n Ungläubige(r) mf.

infidelity [ɪnfɪ'delɪtɪ] n Untreue f.

in-fighting ['ɪnfaɪtɪŋ] n Nahkampf m.

infiltrate ['ɪnfɪltreɪt] vt infiltrieren; spies einschleusen; (liquid) durchdringen; vi (Mil, liquid) einsickern; (Pol) unterwandern (into acc).

infinite ['ɪnfɪnɪt] a unendlich.

infinitive [ɪn'fɪnɪtɪv] n Infinitiv m, Nennform f.

infinity [ɪn'fɪnɪtɪ] n Unendlichkeit f.

infirm [ɪn'fɜ:m] a schwach, gebrechlich; (irresolute) willensschwach.

infirmary [ɪn'fɜ:mərɪ] n Krankenhaus nt.

infirmity [ɪn'fɜ:mɪtɪ] n Schwäche f, Gebrechlichkeit f.

inflame [ɪn'fleɪm] vt (Med) entzünden; person reizen; anger erregen.

inflammable [ɪn'flæməbl] a feuergefährlich.

inflammation [ɪnflə'meɪʃən] n Entzündung f.

inflate [ɪn'fleɪt] vt aufblasen; tyre aufpumpen; prices hochtreiben.

inflation [ɪn'fleɪʃən] n Inflation f; **—ary** a increase inflationistisch; situation inflationär.

inflexible [ɪn'fleksəbl] a person nicht flexibel; opinion starr; thing unbiegsam.

inflict [ɪn'flɪkt] vt zufügen (sth on sb jdm etw); punishment auferlegen (on dat); wound beibringen (on dat); **—ion** [ɪn'flɪkʃən] Zufügung f; Auferlegung f; (suffering) Heimsuchung f.

inflow ['ɪnfləʊ] n Einfließen nt, Zustrom m.

influence ['ɪnflʊəns] n Einfluß m; vt beeinflussen.

influential [ɪnflʊ'enʃəl] a einflußreich.

influenza [ɪnflʊ'enzə] n Grippe f.

influx ['ɪnflʌks] n (of water) Einfluß m; (of people) Zustrom m; (of ideas) Eindringen nt.

inform [ɪn'fɔ:m] vt informieren; **to keep sb —ed** jdn auf dem laufenden halten.

informal [ɪnˈfɔːməl] a zwanglos; —**ity** [ɪnfɔːˈmælɪtɪ] Ungezwungenheit f.

information [ɪnfəˈmeɪʃən] n Auskunft f, Information f.

informative [ɪnˈfɔːmətɪv] a informativ; person mitteilsam.

informer [ɪnˈfɔːmə*] n Denunziant(-in f) m.

infra-red [ˈɪnfrəˈred] a infrarot.

infrequent [ɪnˈfriːkwənt] a selten.

infringe [ɪnˈfrɪndʒ] vt law verstoßen gegen; — upon vt verletzen; —**ment** Verstoß m, Verletzung f.

infuriate [ɪnˈfjʊərɪeɪt] vt wütend machen.

infuriating [ɪnˈfjʊərɪeɪtɪŋ] a ärgerlich.

ingenious [ɪnˈdʒiːnɪəs] a genial; thing raffiniert.

ingenuity [ɪndʒɪˈnjuːɪtɪ] n Findigkeit f, Genialität f; Raffiniertheit f.

ingot [ˈɪŋgət] n Barren m.

ingratiate [ɪnˈgreɪʃɪeɪt] vt einschmeicheln (o.s. with sb sich bei jdm).

ingratitude [ɪnˈgrætɪtjuːd] n Undankbarkeit f.

ingredient [ɪnˈgriːdɪənt] n Bestandteil m; (Cook) Zutat f.

inhabit [ɪnˈhæbɪt] vt bewohnen; —**ant** Bewohner(in f) m; (of island, town) Einwohner(in f) m.

inhale [ɪnˈheɪl] vt einatmen; (Med, cigarettes) inhalieren.

inherent [ɪnˈhɪərənt] a innewohnend (in dat).

inherit [ɪnˈherɪt] vt erben; —**ance** Erbe nt, Erbschaft f.

inhibit [ɪnˈhɪbɪt] vt hemmen; (restrain) hindern; —**ion** [ɪnhɪˈbɪʃən] Hemmung f.

inhospitable [ɪnhɒsˈpɪtəbl] a person ungastlich; country unwirtlich.

inhuman [ɪnˈhjuːmən] a unmenschlich.

inimitable [ɪˈnɪmɪtəbl] a unnachahmlich.

iniquity [ɪˈnɪkwɪtɪ] n Ungerechtigkeit f.

initial [ɪˈnɪʃəl] a anfänglich, Anfangs-; n Anfangsbuchstabe m, Initiale f; vt abzeichnen; (Pol) paraphieren; —**ly** ad anfangs.

initiate [ɪˈnɪʃɪeɪt] vt einführen; negotiations einleiten; (instruct) einweihen.

initiation [ɪnɪʃɪˈeɪʃən] n Einführung f; Einleitung f.

initiative [ɪˈnɪʃɪətɪv] n Initiative f.

inject [ɪnˈdʒekt] vt einspritzen; (fig) einflößen; —**ion** Spritze f, Injektion f.

injure [ˈɪndʒə*] vt verletzen; (fig) schaden (+dat).

injury [ˈɪndʒərɪ] n Verletzung f.

injustice [ɪnˈdʒʌstɪs] n Ungerechtigkeit f.

ink [ɪŋk] n Tinte f.

inkling [ˈɪŋklɪŋ] n (dunkle) Ahnung f.

inlaid [ˈɪnˈleɪd] a eingelegt, Einlege-.

inland [ˈɪnlænd] a Binnen-; (domestic) Inlands-; ad landeinwärts; —**revenue** (Brit) Fiskus m.

in-law [ˈɪnlɔː] n angeheiratete(r) Verwandte(r) mf.

inlet [ˈɪnlet] n Öffnung f, Einlaß m; (bay) kleine Bucht f.

inmate [ˈɪnmeɪt] n Insasse m.

inn [ɪn] n Gasthaus nt, Wirtshaus nt.

innate [ɪˈneɪt] a angeboren, eigen (+dat).

inner ['mə*] a inner, Innen-; (fig) verborgen, innerste(r,s).

innocence ['məsns] n Unschuld f; (ignorance) Unkenntnis f.

innocent ['məsnt] a unschuldig.

innocuous [ɪ'nɒkjuəs] a harmlos.

innovation [məʊ'veɪʃən] n Neuerung f.

innuendo [ɪnjuˈendəʊ] n (versteckte) Anspielung f.

innumerable [ɪ'njuːmərəbl] a unzählig.

inoculation [ɪnɒkjʊ'leɪʃən] n Impfung f.

inopportune [ɪn'ɒpətjuːn] a remark unangebracht; visit ungelegen.

inordinately [ɪ'nɔːdɪnɪtɪ] ad unmäßig.

inorganic [ɪnɔː'gænɪk] a unorganisch; (Chem) anorganisch.

in-patient ['ɪnpeɪʃənt] n stationäre(r) Patient(in f) m.

input ['ɪnput] n (Elec) (Auf)ladung f; (Tech) zugeführte Menge f; (labour) angewandte Arbeitslei-stung f; (money) Investitions-summe f.

inquest , ['ɪnkwest] n gerichtliche Untersuchung f.

inquire [ɪn'kwaɪə*] vi sich erkundigen; vt price sich erkundigen nach; — into vt unter-suchen.

inquiring [ɪn'kwaɪərɪŋ] a mind wissensdurstig.

inquiry [ɪn'kwaɪərɪ] n (question) Erkundigung f, Nachfrage f; (investigation) Untersuchung f; — office Auskunft(sbüro nt) f.

inquisitive [ɪn'kwɪzɪtɪv] a neugierig; look forschend.

inroad ['ɪnrəʊd] n (Mil) Einfall m; (fig) Eingriff m.

insane [ɪn'seɪn] a wahnsinnig; (Med) geisteskrank.

insanitary [ɪn'sænɪtərɪ] a unhygienisch, gesundheitsschädlich.

insanity [ɪn'sænɪtɪ] n Wahnsinn m.

insatiable [ɪn'seɪʃəbl] a unersättlich.

inscription [ɪn'skrɪpʃən] n (on stone) Inschrift f; (in book) Widmung f.

inscrutable [ɪn'skruːtəbl] a unergründlich.

insect ['ɪnsekt] n Insekt nt; —icide [ɪn'sektɪsaɪd] Insektenvertilgungs-mittel nt.

insecure [ɪnsɪ'kjʊə*] a person unsicher; thing nicht fest or sicher.

insecurity [ɪnsɪ'kjʊərɪtɪ] n Unsicherheit f.

insensible [ɪn'sensɪbl] a gefühllos; (unconscious) bewußtlos; (imper-ceptible) unmerklich; — of or to sth unempfänglich für etw.

insensitive [ɪn'sensɪtɪv] a (to pain) unempfindlich; (without feelings) gefühllos.

inseparable [ɪn'sepərəbl] a people unzertrennlich; word untrennbar.

insert [ɪn'sɜːt] vt einfügen; coin einwerfen; (stick into) hinein-stecken; advert aufgeben; ['ɪnsɜːt] n Beifügung f; (in book) Einlage f; (in magazine) Beilage f; —ion Einfügung f; (Press) Inserat nt.

inshore ['ɪnʃɔː*] a Küsten-; [ɪn'ʃɔː*] ad an der Küste.

inside ['ɪn'saɪd] n Innenseite f, Innere(s) nt; a innere(r,s), Innen-; ad (place) innen; (direction) nach innen, hinein; prep (place) in (+dat); (direction) in (+acc) ... hinein; (time) innerhalb (+gen); — forward (Sport) Halbstürmer m; — out ad linksherum; know in-

und auswendig; **—r** Eingeweihte(r) *mf*; (*member*) Mitglied *nt*.

insidious [ɪn'sɪdɪəs] *a* heimtückisch.

insight ['ɪnsaɪt] *n* Einsicht *f*; Einblick *m* (*into* in +acc).

insignificant [ɪnsɪg'nɪfɪkənt] *a* unbedeutend.

insincere [ɪnsɪn'sɪə*] *a* unaufrichtig, falsch.

insincerity [ɪnsɪn'serɪtɪ] *n* Unaufrichtigkeit *f.*

insinuate [ɪn'sɪnjueɪt] *vt* (*hint*) andeuten; (*— o.s. into sth*) sich in etw (*acc*) einschleichen.

insinuation [ɪnsɪnju'eɪʃən] *n* Anspielung *f.*

insipid [ɪn'sɪpɪd] *a* fad(e).

insist [ɪn'sɪst] *vi* bestehen (*on* auf +acc); **—ence** Bestehen *nt*; **—ent** *a* hartnäckig; (*urgent*) dringend.

insolence ['ɪnsələns] *n* Frechheit *f.*

insolent ['ɪnsələnt] *a* frech.

insoluble [ɪn'sɒljubl] *a* unlösbar; (*Chem*) unlöslich.

insolvent [ɪn'sɒlvənt] *a* zahlungs-unfähig.

insomnia [ɪn'sɒmnɪə] *n* Schlaflosig-keit *f.*

inspect [ɪn'spekt] *vt* besichtigen, prüfen; (*officially*) inspizieren; **—ion** Besichtigung *f*, Inspektion *f*; **—or** (*official*) Aufsichtsbeamte(r) *m*, Inspektor *m*; (*police*) Polizeikommissar *m*; (*Rail*) Kontrolleur *m.*

inspiration [ɪnspɪ'reɪʃən] *n* Inspiration *f.*

inspire [ɪn'spaɪə*] *vt* respect ein-flößen (*in* dat); hope wecken (*in* in +dat); person inspirieren; **—** *sb* **to do sth** jdn dazu anregen, etw zu tun; **—d** *a* begabt, einfallsreich.

inspiring [ɪn'spaɪərɪŋ] *a* begeisternd.

instability [ɪnstə'bɪlɪtɪ] *n* Unbeständigkeit *f*, Labilität *f.*

install [ɪn'stɔːl] *vt* (*put in*) einbauen, installieren; *telephone* anschließen; (*establish*) einsetzen; **—ation** [ɪnstə'leɪʃən] (*of person*) (Amts)einsetzung *f*; (*of machinery*) Einbau *m*, Installierung *f*; (*machines etc*) Anlage *f.*

instalment, (*US*) **installment** [ɪn'stɔːlmənt] *n* Rate *f*; (*of story*) Fortsetzung *f*; **to pay in —s** auf Raten zahlen.

instance ['ɪnstəns] *n* Fall *m*; (*example*) Beispiel *nt*; **for —** zum Beispiel.

instant ['ɪnstənt] *n* Augenblick *m*; *a* augenblicklich, sofortig; **—** *coffee* Pulverkaffee *m*; **—ly** *ad* sofort.

instead [ɪn'sted] *ad* stattdessen; **—** *of prep* anstatt (+*gen*).

instigation [ɪnstɪ'geɪʃən] *n* Veran-lassung *f*; (*of crime etc*) Anstiftung *f.*

instil [ɪn'stɪl] *vt* (*fig*) beibringen (*in sb* jdm).

instinct ['ɪnstɪŋkt] *n* Instinkt *m*; **—ive** *a*, **—ively** *ad* [ɪn'stɪŋktɪv, -lɪ] instinktiv.

institute ['ɪnstɪtjuːt] *n* Institut *nt*; (*society also*) Gesellschaft *f*; *vt* ein-führen; *search* einleiten.

institution [ɪnstɪ'tjuːʃən] *n* (*custom*) Einrichtung *f*, Brauch *m*; (*society*) Institution *f*; (*home*) Anstalt *f*; (*beginning*) Einführung *f*; Einleitung *f.*

instruct [ɪn'strʌkt] *vt* anweisen; (*officially*) instruieren; **—ion** [ɪn'strʌkʃən] Unterricht *m*; **—ions** *pl* Anweisungen *pl*; (*for use*) Gebrauchsanweisung *f*; **—ive** *a* lehrreich; **—or** Lehrer *m*; (*Mil*) Ausbilder *m.*

instrument ['ɪnstrʊmənt] n (tool) Instrument nt, Werkzeug nt; (Mus) (Musik)instrument nt; —al [ɪnstrʊ'mentl] a (Mus) Instrumental-; (helpful) behilflich (in bei); —alist [ɪnstrʊ'mentəlɪst] Instrumentalist m; — panel Armaturenbrett nt.

insubordinate [ɪnsə'bɔːdənət] . a aufsässig, widersetzlich.

insubordination ['ɪnsəbɔːdɪ'neɪʃən] n Gehorsamsverweigerung f.

insufferable [ɪn'sʌfərəbl] a unerträglich.

insufficient a, —ly ad [ɪn'səfɪʃənt, -lɪ] ungenügend.

insular ['ɪnsjələ*] a (fig) engstirnig; —ity [ɪnsʊ'lærɪtɪ] (fig) Engstirnigkeit f.

insulate ['ɪnsjʊleɪt] vt (Elec) isolieren; (fig) abschirmen (from vor + dat).

insulating tape ['ɪnsjʊleɪtɪŋteɪp] n Isolierband nt.

insulation [ɪnsjʊ'leɪʃən] n Isolierung f.

insulator ['ɪnsjʊleɪtə*] n Isolator m.

insulin ['ɪnsjʊlɪn] n Insulin nt.

insult ['ɪnsʌlt] n Beleidigung f; [ɪn'sʌlt] vt beleidigen; —ing [ɪn'sʌltɪŋ] a beleidigend.

insuperable [ɪn'suːpərəbl] a unüberwindlich.

insurance [ɪn'ʃʊərəns] n Versicherung f; — agent Versicherungsvertreter m; — policy Versicherungspolice f.

insure [ɪn'ʃʊə*] vt versichern.

insurmountable [ɪnsə'maʊntəbl] a unüberwindlich.

insurrection [ɪnsə'rekʃən] n Aufstand m.

intact [ɪn'tækt] a intakt, unangetastet, ganz.

intake ['ɪnteɪk] n (place) Einlaßöffnung f; (act) Aufnahme f; (amount) aufgenommene Menge f; (Sch) Neuaufnahme f.

intangible [ɪn'tændʒəbl] a unfaßbar; thing nicht greifbar.

integer ['ɪntɪdʒə*] n ganze Zahl f.

integral ['ɪntɪgrəl] a (essential) wesentlich; (complete) vollständig; (Math) Integral-.

integrate ['ɪntɪgreɪt] vt vereinigen; people eingliedern, integrieren.

integration [ɪntɪ'greɪʃən] n Eingliederung f, Integration f.

integrity [ɪn'tegrɪtɪ] n (honesty) Redlichkeit f, Integrität f.

intellect ['ɪntɪlekt] n Intellekt m; —ual [ɪntɪ'lektjʊəl] a geistig, intellektuell n Intellektuelle(r) mf.

intelligence [ɪn'telɪdʒəns] n (understanding) Intelligenz f; (news) Information f; (Mil) Geheimdienst m.

intelligent [ɪn'telɪdʒənt] a intelligent; beings vernunftbegabt; —ly ad klug; write, speak verständlich.

intelligible [ɪn'telɪdʒəbl] a verständlich.

intemperate [ɪn'tempərət] a unmäßig.

intend [ɪn'tend] vt beabsichtigen; that was —ed for you das war für dich gedacht.

intense [ɪn'tens] a stark, intensiv; person ernsthaft; —ly ad äußerst; study intensiv.

intensify [ɪn'tensɪfaɪ] vt verstärken, intensivieren.

intensity [ɪn'tensɪtɪ] n Intensität f, Stärke f.

intensive *a*, **—ly** *ad* [ɪn'tensɪv, -lɪ] intensiv.

intent [ɪn'tent] *n* Absicht *f*; **to all —s and purposes** praktisch; **—ly** *ad* aufmerksam; *look* forschend; **to be — on** doing sth fest entschlossen sein, etw zu tun.

intention [ɪn'tenʃən] *n* Absicht *f*; **with good —s** mit guten Vorsätzen; **—al** *a*, **—ally** *ad* absichtlich.

inter [ɪn'tɜː*] *vt* beerdigen.

inter- [ɪntə*] *pref* zwischen-, Zwischen-.

interact [ɪntər'ækt] *vi* aufeinander einwirken; **—ion** Wechselwirkung *f*.

intercede [ɪntə'siːd] *vi* sich verwenden; *(in argument)* vermitteln.

intercept [ɪntə'sept] *vt* abfangen; **—ion** Abfangen *nt*.

interchange ['ɪntətʃeɪndʒ] *n (exchange)* Austausch *m*; *(on roads)* Verkehrskreuz *nt*; [ɪntə'tʃeɪndʒ] *vt* austauschen; **—able** [ɪntə'tʃeɪndʒəbl] *a* austauschbar.

intercom ['ɪntəkɒm] *n* (Gegen)-sprechanlage *f*.

interconnect [ɪntəkə'nekt] *vt* miteinander verbinden; *vi* miteinander verbunden sein; *(roads)* zusammenführen.

intercontinental ['ɪntəkɒntɪ'nentl] *a* interkontinental.

intercourse ['ɪntəkɔːs] *n (exchange)* Verkehr *m*, Beziehungen *pl*; *(sexual)* Geschlechtsverkehr *m*.

interdependence [ɪntədɪ'pendəns] *n* gegenseitige Abhängigkeit *f*.

interest ['ɪntrɪst] *n* Interesse *nt*; *(Fin)* Zinsen *pl*; *(Comm: share)* Anteil *m*; *(group)* Interessengruppe *f*; **to be of —** von Interesse

sein; *vt* interessieren; **—ed** *a (having claims)* beteiligt; *(attentive)* interessiert; **to be —ed in** sich interessieren für; **—ing** *a* interessant.

interfere [ɪntə'fɪə*] *vi (meddle)* sich einmischen *(with in + acc)* stören *(with acc)*; *(with an object)* sich zu schaffen machen *(with an + dat)*; **—nce** Einmischung *f*; *(TV)* Störung *f*.

interim ['ɪntərɪm] *a* vorläufig; *n*: **in the —** inzwischen.

interior [ɪn'tɪərɪə*] *n* Innere(s) *nt*; *a* innere(r,s), Innen-.

interjection [ɪntə'dʒekʃən] *n* Ausruf *m*; *(Gram)* Interjektion *f*.

interlock [ɪntə'lɒk] *vi* ineinandergreifen; *vt* zusammenschließen, verzahnen.

interloper ['ɪntələupə*] *n* Eindringling *m*.

interlude ['ɪntəluːd] *n* Pause *f*; *(in entertainment)* Zwischenspiel *nt*.

intermarriage [ɪntə'mærɪdʒ] *n* Mischehe *f*.

intermarry [ɪntə'mærɪ] *vi* untereinander heiraten.

intermediary [ɪntə'miːdɪərɪ] *n* Vermittler *m*.

intermediate [ɪntə'miːdɪət] *a* Zwischen-, Mittel-.

interminable [ɪn'tɜːmɪnəbl] *a* endlos.

intermission [ɪntə'mɪʃən] *n* Pause *f*.

intermittent [ɪntə'mɪtənt] *a* periodisch, stoßweise; **—ly** *ad* mit Unterbrechungen.

intern [ɪn'tɜːn] *vt* internieren; ['ɪntɜːn] *n (US)* Assistenzarzt *m/-ärztin f*.

internal [ɪn'tɜːnl] *a (inside)* innere(r,s); *(domestic)* Inlands-;

—ly *ad* innen; (*Med*) innerlich;
intern; — **revenue** (*US*) Sozial-
produkt *nt*.

international [ɪntəˈnæʃnəl] *a* international; *n* (*Sport*) Nationalspieler
m; (*match*) internationale(s) Spiel
nt.

internment [ɪnˈtɜːnmənt] *n*
Internierung *f*.

interplanetary [ɪntəˈplænɪtəri] *a*
interplanetar.

interplay [ˈɪntəpleɪ] *n* Wechselspiel
nt.

Interpol [ˈɪntəpɒl] *n* Interpol *f*.

interpret [ɪnˈtɜːprɪt] *vt* (*explain*)
auslegen, interpretieren; (*translate*) verdolmetschen; (*represent*)
darstellen; —**ation** Deutung *f*, Interpretation *f*; (*translation*) Dolmetschen *nt*; —**er** Dolmetscher(in *f*) *m*.

interrelated [ɪntərɪˈleɪtɪd] *a*
untereinander zusammenhängend.

interrogate [ɪnˈtɛrəgeɪt] *vt*
befragen; (*Jur*) verhören.

interrogation [ɪntɛrəˈgeɪʃən] *n*
Verhör *nt*.

interrogative [ɪntəˈrɒgətɪv] *a*
fragend, Frage-.

interrogator [ɪnˈtɛrəgeɪtə*] *n*
Vernehmungsbeamte(r) *m*.

interrupt [ɪntəˈrʌpt] *vt* unterbrechen; —**ion** Unterbrechung *f*.

intersect [ɪntəˈsɛkt] *vt* (*durch*)-
schneiden; *vi* sich schneiden;
—**ion** (*of roads*) Kreuzung *f*; (*of
lines*) Schnittpunkt *m*.

intersperse [ɪntəˈspɜːs] *vt* (*scatter*)
verstreuen; **to** — **sth with sth** etw
mit etw durchsetzen.

intertwine [ɪntəˈtwaɪn] *vti* (sich)
verflechten.

interval [ˈɪntəvəl] *n* Abstand *m*;
(*break*) Pause *f*; (*Mus*) Intervall

nt; **at** —**s** hier und da; (*time*) dann
und wann.

intervene [ɪntəˈviːn] *vi* dazwischen-
liegen; (*act*) einschreiten (*in
gegen*), eingreifen (*in in* +*acc*).

intervening [ɪntəˈviːnɪŋ] *a*
dazwischenliegend.

intervention [ɪntəˈvɛnʃən] *n*
Eingreifen *nt*, Intervention *f*.

interview [ˈɪntəvjuː] *n* (*Press etc*)
Interview *nt*; (*for job*) Vorstellungs-
gespräch *nt*; *vt* interviewen; —**er**
Interviewer *m*.

intestate [ɪnˈtɛsteɪt] *a* ohne Hinter-
lassung eines Testaments.

intestinal [ɪnˈtɛstɪnl] *a* Darm-.

intestine [ɪnˈtɛstɪn] *n* Darm *m*; —**s**
pl Eingeweide *nt*.

intimacy [ˈɪntɪməsɪ] *n* vertraute(r)
Umgang *m*, Intimität *f*.

intimate [ˈɪntɪmət] *a* (*inmost*)
innerste(r,s); *knowledge*
eingehend; (*familiar*) vertraut;
friends eng; [ˈɪntɪmeɪt] *vt*
andeuten; —**ly** *ad* vertraut, eng.

intimidate [ɪnˈtɪmɪdeɪt] *vt* einschüchtern.

intimidation [ɪntɪmɪˈdeɪʃən] *n* Ein-
.schüchterung *f*.

into [ˈɪntu] *prep* (*motion*) in (+*acc*)
... hinein; **5** — **25** 25 durch 5.

intolerable [ɪnˈtɒlərəbl] *a*
unerträglich.

intolerance [ɪnˈtɒlərəns] *n*
Intoleranz *f*.

intolerant [ɪnˈtɒlərənt] *a* intolerant.

intonation [ɪntəˈneɪʃən] *n* Intonation *f*.

intoxicate [ɪnˈtɒksɪkeɪt] *vt*
betrunken machen; (*fig*)
berauschen; —**d** *a* betrunken; (*fig*)
trunken.

intoxication [ɪntɒksɪˈkeɪʃən] *n*
Rausch *m*.

intractable [ɪn'træktəbl] *a* schwer zu handhaben(d) ; *problem* schwer lösbar.

intransigent [ɪn'trænsɪdʒənt] *a* unnachgiebig.

intransitive [ɪn'trænsɪtɪv] *a* intransitiv.

intravenous [ɪntrə'viːnəs] *a* intravenös.

intrepid [ɪn'trepɪd] *a* unerschrocken.

intricacy ['ɪntrɪkəsɪ] *n* Kompliziertheit *f.*

intricate ['ɪntrɪkət] *a* kompliziert.

intrigue [ɪn'triːg] *n* Intrige *f ; vt* faszinieren.

intriguing [ɪn'triːgɪŋ] *a* faszinierend.

intrinsic [ɪn'trɪnsɪk] *a* innere(r,s) ; *difference* wesentlich.

introduce [ɪntrə'djuːs] *vt* *person* vorstellen (*to sb* jdm) ; *sth new* einführen ; *subject* anschneiden ; *to* ~ *sb to sth* jdn in etw (*acc*) einführen.

introduction [ɪntrə'dʌkʃən] *n* Einführung *f ;* (*to book*) Einleitung *f.*

introductory [ɪntrə'dʌktərɪ] *a* Einführungs-, Vor-.

introspective [ɪntrəʊ'spektɪv] *a* nach innen gekehrt.

introvert ['ɪntrəʊvɜːt] *n* Introvertierte(r) *mf ; a* introvertiert.

intrude [ɪn'truːd] *vi* stören (*on acc*) ; ~**r** Eindringling *m.*

intrusion [ɪn'truːʒən] *n* Störung *f ;* (*coming into*) Eindringen *nt.*

intrusive [ɪn'truːsɪv] *a* aufdringlich.

intuition [ɪn'tjuːɪʃən] *n* Intuition *f.*

intuitive *a,* ~**ly** *ad* [ɪn'tjuːɪtɪv, -lɪ] intuitiv.

inundate ['ɪnʌndeɪt] *vt* (*lit, fig*) überschwemmen.

invade [ɪn'veɪd] *vt* einfallen in (+*acc*) ; ~**r** Eindringling *m.*

invalid ['ɪnvəlɪd] *n* (*disabled*) Kranke(r) *mf ;* Invalide *m ; a* (*ill*) krank ; (*disabled*) invalide ; [ɪn'vælɪd] (*not valid*) ungültig ; ~**ate** [ɪn'vælɪdeɪt] *vt passport* (für) ungültig erklären ; (*fig*) entkräften.

invaluable [ɪn'væljʊəbl] *a* unschätzbar.

invariable [ɪn'veərɪəbl] *a* unveränderlich.

invariably [ɪn'veərɪəblɪ] *ad* ausnahmslos.

invasion [ɪn'veɪʒən] *n* Invasion *f,* Einfall *m.*

invective [ɪn'vektɪv] *n* Beschimpfung *f.*

invent [ɪn'vent] *vt* erfinden ; ~**ion** [ɪn'venʃən] Erfindung *f ;* ~**ive** *a* erfinderisch ; ~**iveness** Erfindungsgabe *f ;* ~**or** Erfinder *m.*

inventory ['ɪnvəntrɪ] *n* (Bestands)verzeichnis *nt,* Inventar *nt.*

inverse ['ɪn'vɜːs] *n* Umkehrung *f ; a,* ~**ly** [ɪn'vɜːs, -lɪ] *ad* umgekehrt.

invert [ɪn'vɜːt] *vt* umdrehen ; ~**ed commas** *pl* Anführungsstriche *pl.*

invertebrate [ɪn'vɜːtɪbrət] *n* wirbellose(s) Tier *nt.*

invest [ɪn'vest] *vt* (*Fin*) anlegen, investieren ; (*endue*) ausstatten.

investigate [ɪn'vestɪgeɪt] *vt* untersuchen.

investigation [ɪnvestɪ'geɪʃən] *n* Untersuchung *f.*

investigator [ɪn'vestɪgeɪtə*] *n* Untersuchungsbeamte(r) *m.*

investiture [ɪn'vestɪtʃə*] *n* Amtseinsetzung *f.*

investment [ɪn'vestmənt] *n* Investition *f.*

investor [ɪn'vestə*] *n* (Geld)anleger *m.*

inveterate [ɪn'vetərət] *a* unverbesserlich.

invigorating [ɪn'vɪgəreɪtɪŋ] *a* stärkend.

invincible [ɪn'vɪnsəbl] *a* unbesiegbar.

inviolate [ɪn'vaɪələt] *a* unverletzt.

invisible [ɪn'vɪzəbl] *a* unsichtbar; *ink* Geheim-.

invitation [ɪnvɪ'teɪʃən] *n* Einladung *f.*

invite [ɪn'vaɪt] *vt* einladen; *criticism, discussion* herausfordern.

inviting [ɪn'vaɪtɪŋ] *a* einladend.

invoice ['ɪnvɔɪs] *n* Rechnung *f,* Lieferschein *m; vt goods* in Rechnung stellen (*sth for sb* jdm etw *acc*).

invoke [ɪn'vəʊk] *vt* anrufen.

involuntary *a,* **involuntarily** *ad* [ɪn'vɒləntərɪ, -lɪ] (*unwilling*) unfreiwillig; (*unintentional*) unabsichtlich.

involve [ɪn'vɒlv] *vt* (*entangle*) verwickeln; (*entail*) mit sich bringen; —*d* a verwickelt; the person —*d* die betreffende Person; —ment Verwicklung *f.*

invulnerable [ɪn'vʌlnərəbl] *a* unverwundbar; (*fig*) unangreifbar.

inward ['ɪnwəd] *a* innere(r,s); *curve* Innen-; —(*s*) *ad* nach innen; —ly *ad* im Innern.

iodine ['aɪədiːn] *n* Jod *nt.*

iota [aɪ'əʊtə] *n* (*fig*) bißchen *nt.*

irascible [ɪ'ræsɪbl] *a* reizbar.

irate [aɪ'reɪt] *a* zornig.

iris ['aɪərɪs] *n* Iris *f.*

irk [ɜːk] *vt* verdrießen.

irksome ['ɜːksəm] *a* lästig.

iron ['aɪən] *n* Eisen *nt;* (*for ironing*) Bügeleisen *nt;* (*golf club*) Golfschläger *m,* Metallschläger *m; a* eisern; *vt* bügeln; —*s* (*chains*) Hand-/Fußschellen *pl;* — *out vt* (*lit, fig*) ausbügeln; *differences* aus-

gleichen; **I—** *Curtain* Eiserne(r) Vorhang *m.*

ironic(al) [aɪ'rɒnɪk(əl)] *a* ironisch; *coincidence etc* witzig; —*ally ad* ironisch; witzigerweise.

ironing ['aɪənɪŋ] *n* Bügeln *nt;* (*laundry*) Bügelwäsche *f;* — *board* Bügelbrett *nt.*

ironmonger ['aɪənmʌŋgə*] *n* Eisenwarenhändler *m;* —'*s* (*shop*) Eisenwarenhandlung *f.*

iron ore ['aɪənɔː*] *n* Eisenerz *nt.*

ironworks ['aɪənwɜːks] *n* Eisenhütte *f.*

irony ['aɪərənɪ] *n* Ironie *f;* the — of it was ... das Witzige daran war ...

irrational [ɪ'ræʃənl] *a* unvernünftig, irrational.

irreconcilable [ɪrekən'saɪləbl] *a* unvereinbar.

irredeemable [ɪrɪ'diːməbl] *a* (*Comm*) money nicht einlösbar; *loan* unkündbar; (*fig*) rettungslos.

irrefutable [ɪrɪ'fjuːtəbl] *a* unwiderlegbar.

irregular [ɪ'regjʊlə*] *a* unregelmäßig; *shape* ungleich-(mäßig); (*fig*) unüblich; *behaviour* ungehörig; —*ity* [ɪregjʊ'lærɪtɪ] Unregelmäßigkeit *f;* Ungleichmäßigkeit *f;* (*fig*) Vergehen *nt.*

irrelevance [ɪ'reləvəns] *n* Belanglosigkeit *f.*

irrelevant [ɪ'reləvənt] *a* belanglos, irrelevant.

irreligious [ɪrɪ'lɪdʒəs] *a* ungläubig.

irreparable [ɪ'repərəbl] *a* nicht, gutzumachen(d).

irreplaceable [ɪrɪ'pleɪsəbl] *a* unersetzlich.

irrepressible [ɪrɪ'presəbl] *a* nicht zu unterdrücken(d); *joy* unbändig.

irreproachable [ɪrɪ'prəutʃəbl] a untadelig.

irresistible [ɪrɪ'zɪstəbl] a unwiderstehlich.

irresolute [ɪ'rezəluːt] a unentschlossen.

irrespective [ɪrɪ'spektɪv] : — of prep ungeachtet (+gen).

irresponsibility ['ɪrɪspɒnsə'bɪlɪtɪ] n Verantwortungslosigkeit f.

irresponsible [ɪrɪs'pɒnsəbl] a verantwortungslos.

irretrievably [ɪrɪ'triːvəblɪ] ad unwiederbringlich; lost unrettbar.

irreverence [ɪ'revərəns] n Mißachtung f.

irreverent [ɪ'revərənt] a respektlos.

irrevocable [ɪ'revəkəbl] a unwiderrufbar.

irrigate ['ɪrɪgeɪt] vt bewässern.

irrigation [ɪrɪ'geɪʃən] n Bewässerung f.

irritability [ɪrɪtə'bɪlɪtɪ] n Reizbarkeit f.

irritable ['ɪrɪtəbl] a reizbar.

irritant ['ɪrɪtənt] n Reizmittel nt.

irritate ['ɪrɪteɪt] vt irritieren, reizen (also Med).

irritating ['ɪrɪteɪtɪŋ] a irritierend, aufreizend.

irritation [ɪrɪ'teɪʃən] n (anger) Ärger m; (Med) Reizung f.

is [ɪz] see be.

Islam ['ɪzlɑːm] n Islam m.

island ['aɪlənd] n Insel f; —er Inselbewohner(in f) m.

isle [aɪl] n (kleine) Insel f.

isn't ['ɪznt] = is not.

isobar ['aɪsəubɑː*] n Isobare f.

isolate ['aɪsəuleɪt] vt isolieren; —d a isoliert; case Einzel-.

isolation [aɪsəu'leɪʃən] n Isolierung f; to treat sth in — etw vereinzelt or isoliert behandeln.

isolationism [aɪsəu'leɪʃənɪzəm] n Isolationismus m.

isotope ['aɪsətəup] n Isotop nt.

issue ['ɪʃuː] n (matter) Problem nt, Frage f; (outcome) Resultat nt, Ausgang m; (of newspaper, shares) Ausgabe f; (offspring) Nachkommenschaft f; (of river) Mündung f; that's not at — das steht nicht zur Debatte; to make an — out of sth ein Theater machen wegen etw (dat); vt ausgeben; warrant erlassen; documents ausstellen; orders erteilen; books herausgeben; verdict aussprechen; to — sb with sth etw (acc) an jdn ausgeben.

isthmus ['ɪsməs] n Landenge f.

it [ɪt] pron (nom, acc) es; (dat) ihm.

italic [ɪ'tælɪk] a kursiv; —s pl Kursivschrift f; in —s kursiv gedruckt.

itch [ɪtʃ] n Juckreiz m; (fig) brennende(s) Verlangen nt; vi jucken; to be —ing to do sth darauf brennen, etw zu tun; —ing Jucken nt; —y a juckend.

it'd ['ɪtd] = it would; it had.

item ['aɪtəm] n Gegenstand m; (on list) Posten m; (in programme) Nummer f; (in agenda) (Programm)punkt m; (in newspaper) (Zeitungs)notiz f; —ize vt verzeichnen.

itinerant [ɪ'tɪnərənt] a person umherreisend.

itinerary [aɪ'tɪnərərɪ] n Reiseroute f; (records) Reisebericht m.

it'll ['ɪtl] = it will, it shall.

its [ɪts] poss a (masculine, neuter) sein; (feminine) ihr; poss pron seine(r,s); ihre(r,s).

it's [ɪts] = it is; it has.

itself [ɪt'self] pron sich (selbst); (emphatic) selbst.

I've [aɪv] = I have.

ivory ['aɪvərɪ] n Elfenbein nt; — ivy ['aɪvɪ] n Efeu nt.

tower (fig) Elfenbeinturm m.

J

J, j [dʒeɪ] n J nt, j nt.

jab [dʒæb] vti (hinein)stechen; n Stich m, Stoß m; (col) Spritze f.

jabber ['dʒæbə*] vi plappern.

jack [dʒæk] n (Wagen)heber m; (Cards) Bube m; — up vt aufbocken.

jackdaw ['dʒækdɔ:] n Dohle f.

jacket ['dʒækɪt] n Jacke f, Jackett nt; (of book) Schutzumschlag m; (Tech) Ummantelung f.

jack-knife ['dʒæknaɪf] n Klappmesser nt; vi (truck) sich zusammenschieben.

jackpot ['dʒækpɒt] n Haupttreffer m.

jade [dʒeɪd] n (stone) Jade m.

jaded ['dʒeɪdɪd] a ermattet.

jagged ['dʒægɪd] a zackig; blade schartig.

jail [dʒeɪl] n Gefängnis nt; vt einsperren; —break Gefängnisausbruch m; —er Gefängniswärter m.

jam [dʒæm] n Marmelade f; (crowd) Gedränge nt; (col: trouble) Klemme f; see traffic; vt people zusammendrängen; (wedge) einklemmen; (cram) hineinzwängen; (obstruct) blockieren; to — on the brakes auf die Bremse treten.

jamboree [dʒæmbə'ri:] n (Pfadfinder)treffen nt.

jangle ['dʒæŋgl] vti klimpern; (bells) bimmeln.

janitor ['dʒænɪtə*] n Hausmeister m.

January ['dʒænjʊərɪ] n Januar m.

jar [dʒɑ:*] n Glas nt; vi kreischen; (colours etc) nicht harmonieren.

jargon ['dʒɑ:gən] n Fachsprache f, Jargon m.

jarring ['dʒɑ:rɪŋ] a sound kreischend; colour unharmonisch.

jasmin(e) ['dʒæzmɪn] n Jasmin m.

jaundice ['dʒɔ:ndɪs] n Gelbsucht f; —d (fig) mißgünstig.

jaunt [dʒɔ:nt] n Spritztour f; —y a (lively) munter; (brisk) flott; attitude unbekümmert.

javelin ['dʒævlɪn] n Speer m.

jaw [dʒɔ:] n Kiefer m; —s pl (fig) Rachen m.

jaywalker ['dʒeɪwɔ:kə*] n unvorsichtige(r) Fußgänger m, Verkehrssünder m.

jazz [dʒæz] n Jazz m; — up vt (Mus) verjazzen; (enliven) aufpolieren; — band Jazzkapelle f; —y a colour schreiend, auffallend.

jealous ['dʒeləs] a (envious) mißgünstig; husband eifersüchtig; (watchful) bedacht (of auf +acc); —ly ad mißgünstig; eifersüchtig; sorgsam; —y Mißgunst f; Eifersucht f.

jeans [dʒi:nz] npl Jeans pl.

jeep [dʒi:p] n Jeep m.

jeer [dʒɪə*] vi höhnisch lachen (at über +acc), verspotten (at sb jdn); n Hohn m; (remark) höhnische Bemerkung f; —ing a höhnisch.

jelly ['dʒelɪ] n Gelee nt; (on meat)

Gallert *nt*; *(dessert)* Grütze *f*;
—**fish** Qualle *f*.

jemmy ['dʒemɪ] *n* Brecheisen *nt*.

jeopardize ['dʒepədaɪz] *vt*
gefährden.

jeopardy ['dʒepədɪ] *n* Gefahr *f*.

jerk [dʒɜːk] *n* Ruck *m*; *(col: idiot)*
Trottel *m*; *vt* ruckartig bewegen;
vi sich ruckartig bewegen;
(muscles) zucken.

jerkin ['dʒɜːkɪn] *n* Wams·*nt*.

jerky ['dʒɜːkɪ] *a* *movement*
ruckartig; *writing* zitterig; *ride*
rüttelnd.

jersey ['dʒɜːzɪ] *n* Pullover *m*.

jest [dʒest] *n* Scherz *m*; in — im
Spaß; *vi* spaßen.

jet [dʒet] *n* *(stream: of water etc)*
Strahl *m*; *(spout)* Düse *f*; *(Aviat)*
Düsenflugzeug *nt*; —**-black** *a*
rabenschwarz; — **engine** Düsen-
motor *m*.

jetsam ['dʒetsəm] *n* Strandgut *nt*.

jettison ['dʒetɪsn] *vt* über Bord
werfen.

jetty ['dʒetɪ] *n* Landesteg *m*, Mole
f.

Jew [dʒuː] *n* Jude *m*.

jewel ['dʒuːəl] *n* *(lit, fig)* Juwel *nt*;
(stone) Edelstein *m*; —**(l)er**
Juwelier *m*; —**(l)er's** *(shop)*
Schmuckwarengeschäft *nt*,
Juwelier *m*; —**(le)ry** Schmuck *m*,
Juwelen *pl*.

Jewess ['dʒuːɪs] *n* Jüdin *f*.

Jewish ['dʒuːɪʃ] *a* jüdisch.

jib [dʒɪb] *n* *(Naut)* Klüver *m*; *vi* sich
scheuen (at vor +*dat*).

jibe [dʒaɪb] *n* spöttische Bemerkung
f.

jiffy ['dʒɪfɪ] *n* *(col)* in a — sofort.

jigsaw (puzzle) ['dʒɪgsɔː(pʌzl)] *n*
Puzzle(spiel) *nt*.

jilt [dʒɪlt] *vt* den Laufpaß geben
(+*dat*).

jingle ['dʒɪŋgl] *n* *(advertisement)*
Werbesong *m*; *(verse)* Reim *m*; *vti*
klimpern; *(bells)* bimmeln.

jinx [dʒɪŋks] *n* Fluch *m*; **to put a**
— **on** sth etw verhexen.

jitters ['dʒɪtəz] *npl* *(col)* **to get the**
— einen Bammel kriegen.

jittery ['dʒɪtərɪ] *a* *(col)* nervös.

jiujitsu [dʒuː'dʒɪtsuː] *n* Jiu-Jitsu *nt*.

job [dʒɒb] *n* *(piece of work)* Arbeit
f; *(occupation)* Stellung *f*, Arbeit *f*;
(duty) Aufgabe *f*; *(difficulty)* Mühe
f; **what's your** — ? was machen
Sie von Beruf?; **it's a good** — **he** ...
es ist ein Glück, daß er ... ; **just
the** — genau das Richtige; —**bing**
a *(in factory)* Akkord-; *(freelance)*
Gelegenheits-; —**less** *a* arbeitslos.

jockey ['dʒɒkɪ] *n* Jockel *m*; *vi*: **to
— for position** sich in einer gute
Position drängeln.

jocular ['dʒɒkjʊlə*] *a* scherzhaft,
witzig.

jodhpurs ['dʒɒdpɜːz] *npl* Reithose
f.

jog [dʒɒg] *vt* *(an)*stoßen; *vi* *(run)*
einen Dauerlauf machen.

john [dʒɒn] *n* *(US col)* Klo *nt*.

join [dʒɔɪn] *vt* *(put together)* verbinden *(to* mit); *club* beitreten
(+*dat*); *person* sich anschließen
(+*dat*); *vi* *(unite)* sich vereinigen;
(bones) zusammenwachsen; *n* Ver-
bindungsstelle *f*, Naht *f*; — **in** *vi*
mitmachen; — **up** *vi* *(Mil)* zur
Armee gehen; —**er** Schreiner *m*;
—**ery** Schreinerei *f*; —**t** *n* *(Tech)*
Fuge *f*; *(of bones)* Gelenk *nt*; *(of
meat)* Braten *m*; *(col: place)* Lokal
nt; *a*, —**tly** *ad* gemeinsam.

joist [dʒɔɪst] *n* Träger *m*.

joke [dʒəʊk] *n* Witz *m*; **it's no** —
es ist nicht zum Lachen; *vi* spaßen,

Witze machen; **you must be joking** das ist doch wohl nicht dein Ernst; —**er** Witzbold *m*; (*Cards*) Joker *m*.

joking ['dʒəʊkɪŋ] a, —**ly** ad zum Spaß; **talk im Spaß,** scherzhaft.

jollity ['dʒɔlɪtɪ] *n* Fröhlichkeit *f.*

jolly ['dʒɔlɪ] a lustig, vergnügt; ad (*col*) ganz schön; — **good!** prima!; **to — sb along** jdn ermuntern.

jolt [dʒəʊlt] *n* (*shock*) Schock *m*; (*jerk*) Stoß *m*, Rütteln *nt*; *vt* (*push*) stoßen; (*shake*) durchschütteln; (*fig*) aufrütteln; *vi* holpern.

jostle ['dʒɔsl] *vt* anrempeln.

jot [dʒɔt] *n*: **not one** — kein Jota *nt*; — **down** *vt* schnell aufschreiben, notieren; —**ter** Notizbuch *nt*; (*Sch*) Schulheft *nt.*

journal ['dʒɜːnl] *n* (*diary*) Tagebuch *nt*; (*magazine*) Zeitschrift *f*; —**ese** [dʒɜːnə'liːz] Zeitungsstil *m*; —**ism** Journalismus *m*; —**ist** Journalist(in *f*) *m.*

journey ['dʒɜːnɪ] *n* Reise *f.*

jovial ['dʒəʊvɪəl] a jovial.

joy [dʒɔɪ] *n* Freude *f*; —**ful** ä freudig; (*gladdening*) erfreulich; —**fully** ad freudig; —**ous** a freudig; — **ride** Schwarzfahrt *f*; —**stick** Steuerknüppel *m.*

jubilant ['dʒuːbɪlənt] a triumphierend.

jubilation [dʒuːbɪ'leɪʃən] *n* Jubel *m.*

jubilee ['dʒuːbɪliː] *n* Jubiläum *nt.*

judge [dʒʌdʒ] *n* Richter *m*; (*fig*) Kenner *m*; *vt* (*Jur*) person die Verhandlung führen über (+acc); *case* verhandeln; (*assess*) beurteilen; (*criticize*) verurteilen; vi ein Urteil abgeben; **as far as I can** — soweit ich das beurteilen kann; **judging by** sth nach etw zu urteilen; —**ment** (*Jur*) Urteil *nt*; (*Eccl*) Gericht *nt*;

(*opinion*) Ansicht *f*; (*ability*) Urteilsvermögen *nt.*

judicial [dʒuː'dɪʃəl] a gerichtlich, Justiz-.

judicious [dʒuː'dɪʃəs] a weis(e).

judo ['dʒuːdəʊ] *n* Judo *nt.*

jug [dʒʌg] *n* Krug *m.*

juggernaut ['dʒʌgənɔːt] *n* (*truck*) Fernlastwagen *m.*

juggle ['dʒʌgl] *vi* jonglieren; *vt facts* verjonglieren; *figures* frisieren; —**r** Jongleur *m.*

jugular ['dʒʌgjʊlə*] a vein Hals-.

juice [dʒuːs] *n* Saft *m.*

juiciness ['dʒuːsɪnɪs] *n* Saftigkeit *f.*

juicy ['dʒuːsɪ] a (lit, fig) saftig; *story* schlüpfrig.

jukebox ['dʒuːkbɒks] *n* Musikautomat *m.*

July [dʒuː'laɪ] *n* Juli *m.*

jumble ['dʒʌmbl] *n* Durcheinander *nt*; *vt* (*also* — up) durcheinanderwerfen; *facts* durcheinanderbringen; — **sale** (*Brit*) Basar *m*, Flohmarkt *m.*

jumbo (jet) ['dʒʌmbəʊ(dʒet)] *n* Jumbo(-Jet) *m.*

jump [dʒʌmp] *vi* springen; (*nervously*) zusammenzucken; **to — to conclusions** voreilige Schlüsse ziehen; *vt* überspringen; **to — the gun** (*fig*) voreilig handeln; **to — the queue** sich vordrängeln; *n* Sprung *m*; **to give sb a —** jdn erschrecken; —**ed-up** a (*col*) eingebildet; —**er** Pullover *m*; —**y** a nervös.

junction ['dʒʌŋkʃən] *n* (*of roads*) (Straßen)kreuzung *f*; (*Rail*) Knotenpunkt *m.*

juncture ['dʒʌŋktʃə*] *n*: **at this —** in diesem Augenblick.

June [dʒuːn] *n* Juni *m.*

jungle ['dʒʌŋgl] *n* Dschungel *m*, Urwald *m.*

junior ['dʒuːnɪə*] *a* (*younger*) jünger; (*after name*) junior; (*Sport*) Junioren-; (*lower position*) untergeordnet; (*for young people*) Junioren- *n* Jüngere(r) *m*.

junk [dʒʌŋk] *n* (*rubbish*) Plunder *m*; (*ship*) Dschunke *f*; **—shop** Ramschladen *m*.

junta ['dʒʌntə] *n* Junta *f*.

jurisdiction [dʒuərɪs'dɪkʃən] *n* Gerichtsbärkeit *f*; (*range of authority*) Zuständigkeit(sbereich *m*) *f*.

jurisprudence [dʒuərɪs'pruːdəns] *n* Rechtswissenschaft *f*, Jura *no art*.

juror ['dʒuərə*] *n* Geschworene(r) *mf*; Schöffe *m*, Schöffin *f*; (*in competition*) Preisrichter *m*.

jury ['dʒuərɪ] *n* (*court*) Geschworene *pl*; (*in competition*) Jury *f*, Preisgericht *nt*; **—man =** juror.

just [dʒʌst] *a* gerecht; *ad* (*recently, now*) gerade, eben; (*barely*) gerade noch; (*exactly*) genau, gerade; (*only*) nur, bloß; (*a small distance*) gleich; (*absolutely*) einfach; **— as** I arrived gerade als ich ankam; **— as** nice genauso nett; **— as well** um so besser; **— about so etwa**; **— now** soeben, gerade, not **— now**

nicht im Moment; **— try versuch** es bloß or mal.

justice ['dʒʌstɪs] *n* (*fairness*) Gerechtigkeit *f*; (*magistrate*) Richter *m*; **— of the peace** Friedensrichter *m*.

justifiable [dʒʌstɪ'faɪəbl] *a* berechtigt.

justifiably [dʒʌstɪ'faɪəblɪ] *ad* berechtigterweise, zu Recht.

justification [dʒʌstɪfɪ'keɪʃən] *n* Rechtfertigung *f*.

justify ['dʒʌstɪfaɪ] *vt* rechtfertigen.

justly ['dʒʌstlɪ] *ad* say mit Recht; condemn gerecht.

justness ['dʒʌstnəs] *n* Gerechtigkeit *f*.

jut [dʒʌt] *vi* (*also* **— out**) herausragen, vorstehen.

juvenile ['dʒuːvənaɪl] *a* (*young*) jugendlich; (*for the young*) Jugend-; *n* Jugendliche(r) *mf*; **— delinquency** Jugendkriminalität *f*; **— delinquent** jugendliche(r) Straftäter(in *f*) *m*.

juxtapose [dʒʌkstə'pəuz] *vt* nebeneinanderstellen.

juxtaposition [dʒʌkstəpə'zɪʃən] *n* Nebeneinanderstellung *f*.

K

K, k [keɪ] *n* K *nt*, k *nt*.

kaleidoscope [kə'laɪdəskəup] *n* Kaleidoskop *nt*.

kangaroo [kæŋgə'ruː] *n* Känguruh *nt*.

kayak ['kaɪæk] *n* Kajak *m or nt*.

keel [kiːl] *n* Kiel *m*; **on an even —** (*fig*) im Lot.

keen [kiːn] *a* eifrig, begeistert; intelligence, wind, blade scharf;

sight, hearing gut; price günstig; **—ly** *ad* leidenschaftlich; (*sharply*) scharf; **—ness** Schärfe *f*; (*eagerness*) Begeisterung *f*.

keep [kiːp] *irreg vt* (*retain*) behalten; (*have*) haben; *animals, one's word* halten; (*support*) versorgen; (*maintain in state*) halten; (*preserve*) aufbewahren; (*restrain*) abhalten; *vi* (*continue in* direction) sich halten; (food) sich halten; (remain: quiet etc) sein, bleiben; **it —s happening** es passiert immer wieder; n Unterhalt m; (tower) Burgfried m; **— back** vt fernhalten; secret verschweigen; **— on** vi: **— on doing sth** etw immer weiter tun; vt anbehalten; hat aufbehalten; **— out** vt draußen lassen, nicht hereinlassen; **'— out!'** 'Eintritt verboten!'; **— up** vi Schritt halten; vt aufrechterhalten; (continue) weitermachen; **—ing** (care) Obhut f; **—in** (with) in Übereinstimmung (mit).

keg [keg] n Faß nt.

kennel ['kenl] n Hundehütte f.

kerb(stone) ['kɜːbstəʊn] n Bordstein m.

kernel ['kɜːnl] n Kern m.

kerosene ['kerəsiːn] n Kerosin nt.

kestrel ['kestrəl] n Turmfalke m.

ketchup ['ketʃəp] n Ketchup nt or m.

kettle ['ketl] n Kessel m; **—drum** Pauke f.

key [kiː] n Schlüssel m; (solution, answers) Schlüssel m, Lösung f; (of piano, typewriter) Taste f; (Mus) Tonart f; (explanatory note) Zeichenerklärung f; a position etc Schlüssel-; **—board** (of piano, typewriter) Tastatur f; **—hole** Schlüsselloch nt; **—note** Grundton m; **—ring** Schlüsselring m.

khaki ['kɑːkɪ] n K(h)aki nt; a k(h)aki(farben).

kick [kɪk] vt einen Fußtritt geben (+dat), treten; vi treten; (baby) strampeln; (horse) ausschlagen; n (Fuß)tritt m; (thrill) Spaß m; **—around** vt person herumstoßen; **—off** vi (Sport) anstoßen; **— up** vt

(col) schlagen; **—off** (Sport) Anstoß m.

kid [kɪd] n (child) Kind nt; (goat) Zicklein nt; (leather) Glacéleder nt; vt auf den Arm nehmen; vi Witze machen.

kidnap ['kɪdnæp] vt entführen, kidnappen; **—per** Kidnapper m, Entführer m; **—ping** Entführung f, Kidnapping nt.

kidney ['kɪdnɪ] n Niere f.

kill [kɪl] vt töten, umbringen; chances ruinieren; vi töten; n Tötung f; (hunting) (Jagd)beute f; **—er** Mörder m.

kiln [kɪln] n Brennofen m.

kilo ['kiːləʊ] n Kilo nt; **—gram(me)** Kilogramm nt; **—metre**, (US) **—meter** Kilometer m; **—watt** Kilowatt nt.

kilt [kɪlt] n Schottenrock m.

kimono [kɪ'məʊnəʊ] n Kimono m.

kin [kɪn] n Verwandtschaft f, Verwandte(n) pl.

kind [kaɪnd] a freundlich, gütig; n Art f; **a — of** eine Art von; (two) **of a —** (zwei) von der gleichen Art; **in —** auf dieselbe Art; (in goods) in Naturalien.

kindergarten ['kɪndəgɑːtn] n Kindergarten m.

kind-hearted ['kaɪnd'hɑːtɪd] a gutherzig.

kindle ['kɪndl] vt (set on fire) anzünden; (rouse) reizen, (er)wecken.

kindliness ['kaɪndlɪnəs] n Freundlichkeit f, Güte f.

kindly ['kaɪndlɪ] a freundlich; ad liebenswürdig(erweise); **would you — ...?** wären Sie so freundlich und ...?

kindness ['kaɪndnəs] n Freundlichkeit f.

kindred ['kɪndrɪd] a verwandt; — **spirit** Gleichgesinnte(r) mf.

kinetic [kɪ'netɪk] a kinetisch.

king [kɪŋ] n König m; —**dom** Königreich nt; —**fisher** Eisvogel m; —**pin** (Tech) Bolzen m; (Aut) Achsschenkelbolzen m; (fig) Stütze f; —**size** a cigarette King-size.

kink [kɪŋk] n Knick m; —**y** a (fig) exzentrisch.

kiosk ['ki:ɒsk] n (Tel) Telefonhäuschen nt.

kipper ['kɪpə*] n Räucherhering m.

kiss [kɪs] n Kuß m; vt küssen; vi: they —ed sie küßten sich.

kit [kɪt] n Ausrüstung f; (tools) Werkzeug nt; —**bag** Seesack m.

kitchen ['kɪtʃɪn] n Küche f; —**garden** Gemüsegarten m; — **sink** Spülbecken nt; —**ware** Küchengeschirr nt.

kite [kaɪt] n Drachen m.

kith [kɪθ] n: — **and kin** Blutsverwandte pl; **with — and kin** mit Kind und Kegel.

kitten ['kɪtn] n Kätzchen nt.

kitty ['kɪtɪ] n (money) (gemeinsame) Kasse f.

kleptomaniac [kleptəʊ'meɪnɪæk] n Kleptomane m, Kleptomanin f.

knack [næk] n Dreh m, Trick m.

knapsack ['næpsæk] n Rucksack m; (Mil) Tornister m.

knave [neɪv] n (old) Schurke m.

knead [ni:d] vt kneten.

knee [ni:] n Knie nt; —**cap** Kniescheibe f; —**deep** a knietief.

kneel [ni:l] vi irreg knien.

knell [nel] n Grabgeläute nt.

knickers ['nɪkəz] npl Schlüpfer m.

knife [naɪf] n Messer nt; vt erstechen.

knight [naɪt] n Ritter m; (chess) Springer m, Pferd nt; —**hood** Ritterwürde f.

knit [nɪt] vti stricken; vi (bones) zusammenwachsen; (people) harmonieren; —**ting** (occupation) Stricken nt; (work) Strickzeug nt; —**ting machine** Strickmaschine f; —**ting needle** Stricknadel f; —**wear** Strickwaren pl.

knob [nɒb] n Knauf m; (on instrument) Knopf m; (of butter etc) kleine(s) Stück nt.

knock [nɒk] vt schlagen; (criticise) heruntermachen; vi klopfen; (knees) zittern; n Schlag m; (on door) Klopfen nt; — **off** vt (do quickly) hinhauen; (col: steal) klauen; vi (finish) Feierabend machen; — **out** vt ausschlagen; (boxing) k.o. schlagen; —**er** (on door) Türklopfer m; —**kneed** a x-beinig; —**out** (lit) k.o.-Schlag m; (fig) Sensation f.

knot [nɒt] n Knoten m; (in wood) Astloch nt; (group) Knäuel nt or m; vt (ver)knoten; —**ted** a verknotet.

knotty ['nɒtɪ] a knorrig; problem kompliziert.

know [nəʊ] vti irreg wissen; (be able to) können; (be acquainted with) kennen; (recognize) erkennen; to — how to do sth wissen, wie man etw macht, etw tun können; you — nicht (wahr); to be well — n bekannt sein; —**how** Kenntnis f, Know-how nt; —**ing** a schlau; look, smile wissend; —**ingly** ad wissend; (intentionally) wissentlich; —**all** Alleswisser m.

knowledge ['nɒlɪdʒ] n Wissen nt, Kenntnis f; —**able** a informiert.

knuckle

545

lament

knuckle ['nʌkl] n Fingerknöchel m.   **kudos** ['kjuːdɒs] n Ehre f.

L

L, l [el] n L nt, l nt.

lab [læb] n (col) Labor nt.

label ['leɪbl] n Etikett nt, Schild nt; vt mit einer Aufschrift versehen, etikettieren.

laboratory [lə'bɒrətərɪ] n Laboratorium nt.

laborious a, **—ly** [lə'bɔːrɪəs, -lɪ] mühsam.

labour, (US) **labor** ['leɪbə*] n Arbeit f; (workmen) Arbeitskräfte pl; (Med) Wehen pl; a (Pol) Labour-; **hard —** Zwangsarbeit f; **—er** Arbeiter m; **—-saving** a arbeitssparend.

laburnum [lə'bɜːnəm] n Goldregen m.

labyrinth ['læbərɪnθ] n (lit, fig) Labyrinth nt.

lace [leɪs] n (fabric) Spitze f; (of shoe) Schnürsenkel m; (braid) Litze f; vt (also — up) (zu)schnüren.

lacerate ['læsəreɪt] vt zerschneiden, tief verwunden.

lack [læk] vt nicht haben; sb **—s** sth jdm fehlt etw (nom); vi: to be **—ing** fehlen; sb is **—ing** in sth es fehlt jdm an etw (dat); n Mangel m; **for — of** aus Mangel an (+dat).

lackadaisical [lækə'deɪzɪkəl] a lasch.

lackey ['lækɪ] n Lakei m.

lacklustre, (US) **lackluster** ['læklʌstə*] a glanzlos, matt.

laconic [lə'kɒnɪk] a lakonisch.

lacquer ['lækə*] n Lack m.

lacrosse [lə'krɒs] n Lacrosse nt.

lacy ['leɪsɪ] a spitzenartig, Spitzen-.

lad [læd] n (boy) Junge m; (young man) Bursche m.

ladder ['lædə*] n (lit) Leiter f; (fig) Stufenleiter f; (Brit: in stocking) Laufmasche f; vt Laufmaschen bekommen in (+dat).

laden ['leɪdn] a beladen, voll.

ladle ['leɪdl] n Schöpfkelle f.

lady ['leɪdɪ] n Dame f; (title) Lady f; 'Ladies' (lavatory) 'Damen'; **—bird,** (US) **—bug** Marienkäfer m; **—-in-waiting** Hofdame f; **—like** a damenhaft, vornehm.

lag [læg] n (delay) Verzug m; (time —) Zeitabstand m; vi (also — behind) zurückbleiben; vt pipes verkleiden.

lager ['lɑːgə*] n Lagerbier nt, helles Bier nt.

lagging ['lægɪŋ] n Isolierung f.

lagoon [lə'guːn] n Lagune f.

laid [leɪd] n: to be — up ans Bett gefesselt sein.

lair [lɛə*] n Lager nt.

laissez-faire ['leɪsɪ'fɛə*] n Laisser-faire nt.

laity ['leɪtɪ] n Laien pl.

lake [leɪk] n See m.

lamb [læm] n Lamm nt; (meat) Lammfleisch nt; **— chop** Lammkotelett nt; **—'s wool** Lammwolle f.

lame [leɪm] a lahm; person also gelähmt; excuse faul.

lament [lə'ment] n Klage f; vt beklagen; **—able** ['læməntəbl] a bedauerlich; (bad) erbärmlich; —ation [læmən'teɪʃən] Wehklage f.

laminated ['læmɪneɪtd] a beschichtet.

lamp [læmp] n Lampe f; (in street) Straßenlaterne f; —post Laternenpfahl m; —shade Lampenschirm m.

lance [lɑːns] n Lanze f; vt (Med) aufschneiden; — corporal Obergefreite(r) m.

lancet ['lɑːnsɪt] n Lanzette f.

land [lænd] n Land nt; vi (from ship) an Land gehen; (Aviat, end up) landen; vt (obtain) gewinnen, kriegen; passengers absetzen; goods abladen; troops, space probe landen; —ed a Land-; —ing Landung f; (on stairs) (Treppen)absatz m; —ing craft Landungsboot nt; —ing stage Landesteg m; —ing strip Landebahn f; —lady (Haus)wirtin f; —locked a landumschlossen, Binnen-; —lord (of house) Hauswirt m, Besitzer m; (of pub) Gastwirt m; (of land) Grundbesitzer m; —lubber Landratte f; —mark Wahrzeichen nt; (fig) Meilenstein m; —owner Grundbesitzer m; —scape Landschaft f; —slide (Geog) Erdrutsch m; (Pol) überwältigende(r) Sieg m.

lane [leɪn] n (in town) Gasse f; (in country) Weg m; Sträßchen nt; (of motorway) Fahrbahn f, Spur f; (Sport) Bahn f.

language ['læŋgwɪdʒ] n Sprache f; (style) Ausdrucksweise f.

languid ['læŋgwɪd] a schlaff, matt.

languish ['læŋgwɪʃ] vi schmachten; (pine) sich sehnen (for nach).

languor ['læŋgə*] n Mattigkeit f.

languorous ['læŋgərəs] a schlaff, träge.

lank [læŋk] a dürr; —y a schlacksig.

lantern ['læntən] n Laterne f.

lanyard ['lænjəd] n (Naut) Taljereep nt; (Mil) Kordel f.

lap [læp] n Schoß m; (Sport) Runde f; vt auflecken; vi (water) plätschern; —dog Schoßhund m.

lapel [lə'pel] n Rockaufschlag m, Revers nt or m.

lapse [læps] n (mistake) Irrtum m; (moral) Fehltritt m; (time) Zeitspanne f.

larceny ['lɑːsənɪ] n Diebstahl m.

lard [lɑːd] n Schweineschmalz nt.

larder ['lɑːdə*] n Speisekammer f.

large [lɑːdʒ] a groß; at — auf freiem Fuß; by and — im großen und ganzen; —ly ad zum größten Teil; —scale a groß angelegt, Groß-; —sse [lɑː'ʒes] Freigebigkeit f.

lark [lɑːk] n (bird) Lerche f; (joke) Jux m; — about vi (col) herumalbern.

larva ['lɑːd] n Larve f.

laryngitis [lærɪn'dʒaɪtɪs] n Kehlkopfentzündung f.

larynx ['lærɪŋks] n Kehlkopf m.

lascivious a, —ly ad [lə'sɪvɪəs, -lɪ] wollüstig.

lash [læʃ] n Peitschenhieb m; vt (beat against) schlagen an (+acc); (rain) schlagen gegen; (whip) peitschen; (bind) festbinden; — out vi (with fists) um sich schlagen; (spend money) sich in Unkosten stürzen; vt money etc springen lassen; —ing (beating) Tracht f Prügel; (tie) Schleife f; —ings of (col) massenhaft.

lass [læs] n Mädchen nt.

lassitude ['læsɪtjuːd] n Abgespanntheit f.

lasso [læ'su:] n Lasso nt; vt mit einem Lasso fangen.

last [lɑ:st] a letzte(r, s); ad zuletzt; (last time) das letztemal; n (person) Letzte(r) mf; (thing) Letzte(s) nt; (for shoe) (Schuh)leisten m; vi (continue) dauern; (remain good) sich halten; (money) ausreichen; at — endlich; — night gestern abend; — ing a dauerhaft, haltbar; shame etc andauernd; —-minute a in letzter Minute.

latch [lætʃ] n Riegel m; —key Hausschlüssel m.

late [leɪt] a spät; zu spät; (recent) jüngste(r, s); (former) frühere(r,s); (dead) verstorben; ad spät; (after proper time) zu spät; to be — zu spät kommen; of — in letzter Zeit; — in the day (lit) spät; (fig) reichlich spät; —comer Nachzügler m; —ly ad in letzter Zeit.

lateness ['leɪtnəs] n (of person) Zuspätkommen nt; (of train) Verspätung f; — of the hour die vorgerückte Stunde.

latent ['leɪtənt] a latent.

lateral ['lætərəl] a seitlich.

latest ['leɪtɪst] n (news) Neu(e)ste(s) nt; at the — spätestens.

latex ['leɪteks] n Milchsaft m.

lath [læθ] n Latte f, Leiste f.

lathe [leɪð] n Drehbank f.

lather ['lɑ:ðə*] n (Seifen)schaum m; vt einschäumen; vi schäumen.

latitude ['lætɪtju:d] n (Geog) Breite f; (freedom) Spielraum m.

latrine [lə'tri:n] n Latrine f.

latter ['lætə*] a (second of two) letztere; (coming at end) letzte(r, s), später; — ly ad in letzter Zeit; —day a modern.

lattice work ['lætɪswɜ:k] n Lattenwerk nt, Gitterwerk nt.

laudable ['lɔ:dəbl] a löblich.

laugh [lɑ:f] n Lachen nt; vi lachen; — at vt lachen über (+acc); — off vt lachend abtun; —able a lachhaft; —ing a lachend; —ing stock Zielscheibe f des Spottes; —ter Lachen nt, Gelächter nt.

launch [lɔ:ntʃ] n (of ship) Stapellauf m; (of rocket) Raketenabschuß m; (boat) Barkasse f; (pleasure boat) Vergnügungsboot nt; vt (set afloat) vom Stapel laufen lassen; rocket (ab)schießen; (set going) in Gang setzen, starten; —ing Stapellauf m; —(ing) pad Abschußrampe f.

launder ['lɔ:ndə*] vt waschen und bügeln; —ette [lɔ:ndə'ret] Waschsalon m.

laundry ['lɔ:ndrɪ] n (place) Wäscherei f; (clothes) Wäsche f.

laureate ['lɔ:rɪət] a see poet.

laurel ['lɒrəl] n Lorbeer m.

lava ['lɑ:və] n Lava f.

lavatory ['lævətrɪ] n Toilette f.

lavender ['lævɪndə*] n Lavendel m.

lavish ['lævɪʃ] a (extravagant) verschwenderisch; (generous) großzügig; vt money verschwenden (on auf +acc); attentions, gifts überschütten mit (on sb jdn); —ly ad verschwenderisch.

law [lɔ:] n Gesetz nt; (system) Recht nt; (of game etc) Regel f; (as studies) Jura no art; —-abiding a gesetzestreu; —breaker Gesetzesübertreter m; — court Gerichtshof m; —ful a gesetzlich, rechtmäßig; —fully ad rechtmäßig; —less a gesetzlos.

lawn [lɔ:n] n Rasen m; —mower Rasenmäher m; — tennis Rasentennis m.

law school ['lɔ:sku:l] n Rechtsakademie f.

law student ['lɔ:stju:dənt] n Jura-student m.

lawsuit ['lɔ:su:t] n Prozeß m.

lawyer ['lɔ:jə*] n Rechtsanwalt m Rechtsanwältin f.

lax [læks] a lax.

laxative ['læksətiv] n Abführmittel nt.

laxity ['læksɪtɪ] n Laxheit f.

lay [leɪ] a Laien-; vt irreg (place) legen; table decken; fire anrichten; egg legen; trap stellen; money wetten; — aside vt zurück-legen; — by vt (set aside) beiseite legen; — down vt hinlegen; rules vorschreiben; arms strecken; — off vt workers (vorübergehend) ent-lassen; — on vt auftragen; concert etc veranstalten; — out vt (her)aus-legen; money ausgeben; corpse aufbahren; — up vt (store) auf-speichern; supplies anlegen; (save) zurücklegen; —about Faulenzer m; —by Parkbucht f; (bigger) Rastplatz m; —er Schicht f; —ette [leɪ'et] Babyausstattung f; —man Laie m; —out Anlage f; (Art) Lay-out nt.

laze [leɪz] vi faulenzen.

lazily ['leɪzɪlɪ] ad träge, faul.

laziness ['leɪzɪnəs] n Faulheit f.

lazy ['leɪzɪ] a faul; (slow-moving) träge.

lead¹ [led] n Blei nt; (of pencil) (Bleistift)mine f; a bleiern, Blei-.

lead² [li:d] n (front position) Führung f; (distance, time ahead) Vorsprung f; (example) Vorbild nt; (clue) Tip m; (of police) Spur f; (Theat) Hauptrolle f; (dog's) Leine f; irreg vt (guide) führen; group etc leiten; vi (be first) führen; — astray vt irreführen; — away vt wegführen; prisoner abführen; — back vi zurückführen; — on vt

anführen; — to vt (street) (hin)führen nach; (result in) führen zu; — up to vt (drive) führen zu; (speaker etc) hinführen auf (+ acc); —er Führer m, Leiter m; (of party) Vorsitzende(r) m; (Press) Leitartikel m; —ership (office) Leitung f; (quality) Führerschaft f; —ing a führend; —ing lady (Theat) Hauptdarstellerin f; —ing light (person) führende(r) Geist m; —ing man (Theat) Hauptdarsteller m.

leaf [li:f] n Blatt nt; (of table) Aus-ziehplatte; —let Blättchen nt; (advertisement) Prospekt m; (pamphlet) Flugblatt nt; (for information) Merkblatt nt; —y a belaubt.

league [li:g] n (union) Bund m, Liga f; (Sport) Liga f, Tabelle f; (measure) 3 englische Meilen.

leak [li:k] n undichte Stelle f; (in ship) Leck nt; vt liquid etc durch-lassen; vi (pipe etc) undicht sein; (liquid etc) auslaufen; — out vi (liquid etc) auslaufen; (informa-tion) durchsickern.

leaky ['li:kɪ] a undicht.

lean [li:n] n mager; vt Magere(s) nt; irreg vi sich neigen; to — against sth an etw (dat) angelehnt sein; sich an etw (acc) anlehnen; vt (an)lehnen; — back vi sich zurück-lehnen; — forward vi sich vorbeugen; — on vi sich stützen auf (+ acc); — over vi sich hinüber-beugen; — towards vt neigen zu; —ing Neigung f; —to Anbau m.

leap [li:p] n Sprung m; vi irreg springen; by —s and bounds schnell; — frog Bockspringen nt; — year Schaltjahr nt.

learn [lɜ:n] vti irreg lernen; (find out) erfahren, hören; —ed [ˈlɜ:nɪd]

a gelehrt; **—er** Anfänger(in *f*) *m*; *(Aut)* Fahrschüler(in *f*) *m*; **—ing** Gelehrsamkeit *f*.

lease [li:s] *n (of property)* Mietvertrag *m*; *(of land)* Pachtvertrag *m*; *vt* mieten; pachten.

leash [li:ʃ] *n* Leine *f*.

least [li:st] *a* kleinste(r, s); *(slightest)* geringste(r, s); *n* Mindeste(s) *nt*; **at** — zumindest; **not in the** —! durchaus nicht!

leather ['leðə*] *n* Leder *nt*; *a* ledern, Leder-; **—y** *a* zäh, ledern.

leave [li:v] *irreg vt* verlassen; *(—behind)* zurücklassen; *(forget)* vergessen; *(allow to remain)* lassen; *(after death)* hinterlassen; *(entrust)* überlassen *(to sb* jdm); **to be left** *(remain)* übrigbleiben; *vi* weggehen, wegfahren; *(for journey)* abreisen; *(bus, train)* abfahren; *n* Erlaubnis *f*; *(Mil)* Urlaub *m*; **on** — auf Urlaub; **to take one's** — **of** Abschied nehmen von; **— off** *vi* aufhören; **— out** *vt* auslassen.

lecherous ['letʃərəs] *a* lüstern.

lectern ['lektз:n] *n* Lesepult *nt*.

lecture ['lektʃə*] *n* Vortrag *m*; *(Univ)* Vorlesung *f*; *vi* einen Vortrag halten; *(Univ)* lesen; **—r** Vortragende(r) *mf*; *(Univ)* Dozent(in *f*) *m*.

ledge [ledʒ] *n* Leiste *f*; *(window* —) Sims *m* or *nt*; *(of mountain)* (Fels)vorsprung *m*.

ledger ['ledʒə*] *n* Hauptbuch *nt*.

lee [li:] *n* Windschatten *m*; *(Naut)* Lee *f*.

leech [li:tʃ] *n* Blutegel *m*.

leek [li:k] *n* Lauch *m*.

leer [lɪə*] *n* schiefe(r) Blick *m*; *vi* schielen *(at* nach).

leeway ['li:wei] *n (fig)* Rückstand *m*; *(freedom)* Spielraum *m*.

left [left] *a* linke(r, s); *ad* links; nach links; *n (side)* linke Seite *f*; **the L—** *(Pol)* die Linke *f*; **—-hand drive** Linkssteuerung *f*; **—-handed** *a* linkshändig; **—-hand side** linke Seite *f*; **—-luggage (office)** Gepäckaufbewahrung *f*; **—-overs** *pl* Reste *pl*, Überbleibsel *pl*; — **wing** linke(r) Flügel *m*; **—-wing** *a* linke(r, s).

leg [leg] *n* Bein *nt*; *(of meat)* Keule *f*; *(stage)* Etappe *f*.

legacy ['legəsɪ] *n* Erbe *nt*, Erbschaft *f*.

legal ['li:gəl] *a* gesetzlich, rechtlich; *(allowed)* legal, rechtsgültig; **to take** — **action** prozessieren; **—ize** *vt* legalisieren; **—ly** *ad* gesetzlich; legal; — **tender** gesetzliche(s) Zahlungsmittel *nt*.

legation [lɪ'geɪʃən] *n* Gesandtschaft *f*.

legend ['ledʒənd] *n* Legende *f*; **—ary** *a* legendär.

-legged ['legɪd] *a* -beinig.

leggings ['legɪŋz] *npl* (hohe) Gamaschen *pl*; *(for baby)* Gamaschenhose *f*.

legibility [ledʒɪ'bɪlɪtɪ] *n* Leserlichkeit *f*.

legible *a*, **legibly** *ad* ['ledʒəbl, -blɪ] leserlich.

legion ['li:dʒən] *n* Legion *f*.

legislate ['ledʒɪsleɪt] *vi* Gesetze geben.

legislation [ledʒɪs'leɪʃən] *n* Gesetzgebung *f.*

legislative ['ledʒɪslətɪv] *a* gesetzgebend.

legislator ['ledʒɪsleɪtə*] *n* Gesetzgeber *m.*

legislature ['ledʒɪslətʃə*] *n* Legislative *f.*

legitimacy [lɪ'dʒɪtɪməsɪ] *n* Recht-

mäßigkeit f; (of birth) Ehelichkeit
f.

legitimate [lɪˈdʒɪtɪmət] a rechtmäßig, legitim; child ehelich.

legroom [ˈlegrʊm] n Platz m für die
Beine.

leisure [ˈleʒə*] n 'Freizeit f; a
Freizeit-; to be at — Zeit haben;
—ly a gemächlich.

lemming [ˈlemɪŋ] n Lemming m.

lemon [ˈlemən] n Zitrone f; (colour)
Zitronengelb nt; —ade [lemə'neɪd]
Limonade f.

lend [lend] vt irreg leihen; to —
sb sth jdm etw leihen; it —s itself
to es eignet sich zu; —er Verleiher
m; —ing library Leihbibliothek f.

length [leŋθ] n Länge f; (section of
road, pipe etc) Strecke f; (of
material) Stück nt; — of time Zeit-
dauer f; at — (lengthily) ausführlich; (at last) schließlich; —en vt
verlängern; vi länger werden;
—ways ad längs; —y a sehr lang;
langatmig.

leniency [ˈliːnɪənsɪ] n Nachsicht f.

lenient [ˈliːnɪənt] a nachsichtig;
—ly ad milde.

lens [lenz] n Linse f; (Phot)
Objektiv nt.

Lent [lent] n Fastenzeit f.

lentil [ˈlentl] n Linse f.

Leo [ˈliːəʊ] n Löwe m.

leopard [ˈlepəd] n Leopard m.

leotard [ˈliːətɑːd] n Trikot nt,
Gymnastikanzug m.

leper [ˈlepə*] n Leprakranke(r) mf.

leprosy [ˈleprəsɪ] n Lepra f.

lesbian [ˈlezbɪən] a lesbisch; n
Lesbierin f.

less [les] a, ad, n weniger.

lessen [ˈlesn] vi abnehmen; vt
verringern, verkleinern.

lesser [ˈlesə*] a kleiner, geringer.

lesson [ˈlesn] n (Sch) Stunde f;
(unit of study) Lektion f; (fig)
Lehre f; (Eccl) Lesung f; —s start
at 9 der Unterricht beginnt um 9.

lest [lest] cj damit ... nicht.

let [let] n: without — or hindrance
völlig unbehindert; vt irreg lassen;
(lease) vermieten; —'s go! gehen
wir!; — down vt hinunterlassen;
(disappoint) enttäuschen; — go vi
loslassen; vt things loslassen;
person gehen lassen; — off vt gun
abfeuern; steam ablassen;
(forgive) laufen lassen; — out vt
herauslassen; scream fahren
lassen; — up vi nachlassen; (stop)
aufhören; —down Enttäuschung f.

lethal [ˈliːθəl] a tödlich.

lethargic [leˈθɑːdʒɪk] a lethargisch,
träge.

lethargy [ˈleθədʒɪ] n Lethargie f,
Teilnahmslosigkeit f.

letter [ˈletə*] n (of alphabet)
Buchstabe m; (message) Brief m;
—s pl (literature) (schöne)
Literatur f; —box Briefkasten m;
—ing n Beschriftung f.

lettuce [ˈletɪs] n (Kopf)salat m.

let-up [ˈletʌp] n (col) Nachlassen nt.

leukaemia, (US) **leukemia**
[luːˈkiːmɪə] n Leukämie f.

level [ˈlevl] a ground eben; (at same
height) auf gleicher Höhe; (equal)
gleich gut; head kühl; to do one's
— best sein möglichstes tun; ad
auf gleicher Höhe; to draw — with
gleichziehen mit; n (instrument)
Wasserwaage f; (altitude) Höhe f;
(flat place) ebene Fläche f;
(position on scale) Niveau nt;
(amount, degree) Grad m; talks on
a high — Gespräche auf hoher
Ebene; profits keep on the same —
Gewinne halten sich auf dem

gleichen Stand; on the moral —
aus moralischer Sicht; on the —
(lit) auf gleicher Höhe; (fig: honest)
ehrlich; vt ground einebnen;
building abreißen; town dem Erdboden gleichmachen; blow
versetzen (at sb jdm); remark
richten (at gegen); — off or out
vi flach or eben werden; (fig) sich
ausgleichen; (plane) horizontal
fliegen; vt ground planieren; differences ausgleichen; — crossing
Bahnübergang m; —headed a
vernünftig.

lever ['li:və*], (US) ['levə*] n Hebel
m; (fig) Druckmittel nt; vt
(hoch)stemmen; —age Hebelkraft
f; (fig) Einfluß m.

levity ['levɪtɪ] n Leichtfertigkeit f.

levy ['levɪ] n (of taxes) Erhebung
f; (tax) Abgaben pl; (Mil) Aushe-
bung f; vt erheben; (Mil) ausheben.

lewd [lu:d] a unzüchtig,
unanständig.

liability [laɪə'bɪlɪtɪ] n (burden)
Belastung f; (duty) Pflicht f; (debt)
Verpflichtung \ f; (proneness)
Anfälligkeit f; (responsibility)
Haftung f.

liable ['laɪəbl] a (responsible) haftbar; (prone) anfällig; to be — for
etw (dat) unterliegen; it's — to
happen es kann leicht vorkommen.

liaison [li:'eɪzɒn] n Verbindung f.

liar ['laɪə*] n Lügner m.

libel ['laɪbl] n Verleumdung f; vt
verleumden; —(l)ous a
verleumderisch.

liberal ['lɪbərəl] a (generous) großzügig; (open-minded) auf-
geschlossen; (Pol) liberal; n liberal
denkende(r) Mensch m; L— (Pol)
Liberale(r) mf; —ly ad (abun-
dantly) reichlich.

liberate ['lɪbəreɪt] vt befreien.

liberation [lɪbə'reɪʃən] n Befreiung
f.

liberty ['lɪbətɪ] n Freiheit f; (permission) Erlaubnis f; to be at —
to do sth etw tun dürfen; to take
liberties with sich (dat) Freiheiten
herausnehmen gegenüber

Libra ['li:brə] n Waage f.

librarian [laɪbrɛərɪən] n Biblio-
thekar(in f) m.

library ['laɪbrərɪ] n Bibliothek f;
(lending —) Bücherei f.

libretto [lɪ'bretəʊ] n Libretto nt.

lice [laɪs] npl of **louse**.

licence, (US) **license** ['laɪsəns] n
(permit) Erlaubnis f, amtliche
Zulassung f; (driving —) Führerschein m; (excess) Zügellosigkeit
f; — plate (US Aut) Nummernschild nt.

license ['laɪsəns] vt genehmigen,
konzessionieren; —e ['laɪsən'si:]
Konzessionsinhaber m.

licentious [laɪ'senʃəs] a ausschweifend.

lichen ['laɪkən] n Flechte f.

lick [lɪk] vt lecken; vi (flames)
züngeln; n Lecken nt; (small
amount) Spur f.

licorice ['lɪkərɪs] n Lakritze f.

lid [lɪd] n Deckel m; (eye—) Lid nt.

lido ['li:dəʊ] n Freibad nt.

lie [laɪ] n Lüge f; vi lügen; irreg
(rest, be situated) liegen; (put o.s.
in position) sich legen; to — idle
stillstehen; — detector Lügen-
detektor m.

lieu [lu:] n: in — of anstatt (+gen).

lieutenant [leftenənt], (US)
[lu:'tenənt] n Leutnant m.

life [laɪf] n Leben nt; (story) Lebens-
geschichte f; (energy) Lebendigkeit
f; — assurance Lebensver-

sicherung f; —belt Rettungsring m; —boat Rettungsboot nt; -guard Badewärter m; Rettungsschwimmer m; —jacket Schwimmweste f; —less a (dead) leblos, tot; (dull) langweilig; —like a lebenswahr, naturgetreu; —line (lit) Rettungsleine f; (fig) Rettungsanker m; —long a lebenslang; —preserver Totschläger m; —raft Rettungsfloß nt; —-sized a in Lebensgröße; — span Lebensspanne f; —time Lebenszeit f.

lift [lɪft] vt hochheben; vi sich heben; n (raising) (Hoch)heben nt; (elevator) Aufzug m, Lift m; to give sb a — jdn mitnehmen; —-off Abheben nt (vom Boden).

ligament ['lɪgəmənt] n Sehne f, Band nt.

light [laɪt] n Licht nt; (lamp) Lampe f; (flame) Feuer nt; —s pl (Aut) Beleuchtung f; in the — of angesichts (+gen); vt irreg beleuchten; lamp anmachen; fire, cigarette anzünden; (brighten) erleuchten, erhellen; a (bright) hell, licht; (pale) hell-; (not heavy, easy) leicht; punishment milde; taxes niedrig; touch leicht; — up vi (lamp) angehen; (face) aufleuchten; vt (illuminate) beleuchten; lights anmachen; —bulb Glühbirne f; —en vi (brighten) hell werden; (lightning) blitzen; vt (give light to) erhellen; hair aufhellen; gloom aufheitern; (make less heavy) leichter machen; (fig) erleichtern; —er (cigarette —) Feuerzeug nt; (boat) Leichter m; —-headed a (thoughtless) leichtsinnig; (giddy) schwindlig; —hearted a leichtherzig, fröhlich; —house Leuchtturm m; —ing Beleuchtung f; —ing-up time Zeit f des Ein-

schaltens der Straßen-/Autobeleuchtung; —ly ad leicht; (irresponsibly) leichtfertig; — meter (Phot) Belichtungsmesser m; —ness (of weight) Leichtigkeit f; (of colour) Helle f; (light) Helligkeit f; —ning Blitz m; —ning conductor Blitzableiter m; —weight a suit leicht; —weight boxer Leichtgewicht nt; —year Lichtjahr nt.

lignite ['lɪgnaɪt] n Lignit m.

like [laɪk] vt mögen, gernhaben; would you —...? hatten Sie gern ...? would you — to ...? möchten Sie gern...? prep wie; what's it/he —? wie ist es/er?; that's just — him das sieht ihm ähnlich; —that/this so; a (similar) ähnlich; (equal) gleich; n Gleiche(s) nt; —able a sympathisch; —lihood Wahrscheinlichkeit f; —ly a (probable) wahrscheinlich; (suitable) geeignet; ad wahrscheinlich; —minded a gleichgesinnt; —n vt vergleichen (to mit); —wise ad ebenfalls.

liking ['laɪkɪŋ] n Zuneigung f; (taste for) Vorliebe f.

lilac ['laɪlək] n Flieder m.

lilting ['lɪltɪŋ] a accent singend; tune munter.

lily ['lɪlɪ] n Lilie f; — of the valley Maiglöckchen nt.

limb [lɪm] n Glied nt.

limber ['lɪmbə*]: — up vi sich auflockern; (fig) sich vorbereiten.

limbo ['lɪmbəʊ] n: to be in — (fig) in der Schwebe sein.

lime [laɪm] n (tree) Linde f; (fruit) Limone f; (substance) Kalk m; —juice Limonensaft m; —light (fig) Rampenlicht nt.

limerick ['lɪmərɪk] n Limerick m.

limestone ['laɪmstəʊn] n Kalkstein m.

limit ['lɪmɪt] n Grenze f; (col) Höhe f; vt begrenzen, einschränken; **—ation** Grenzen pl, Einschränkung f; **—ed** a beschränkt; **—ed company** Gesellschaft f mit beschränkter Haftung, GmbH f.

limousine ['lɪmaziːn] n Limousine f.

limp [lɪmp] n Hinken nt; vi hinken; a (without firmness) schlaff.

limpet ['lɪmpɪt] n (lit) Napfschnecke f; (fig) Klette f.

limpid ['lɪmpɪd] a klar.

limply ['lɪmplɪ] ad schlaff.

line [laɪn] n Linie f; (rope) Leine f, Schnur f; (on face) Falte f; (row) Reihe f; (of hills) Kette f; (US: queue) Schlange f; (company) Linie f, Gesellschaft f; (Rail) Strecke f; (pl) Geleise pl; (Tel) Leitung f; (written) Zeile f; (direction) Richtung f; (fig: business) Branche f; Beruf m; (range of items) Kollektion f; **it's a bad —** (Tel) die Verbindung ist schlecht; **hold the —** bleiben Sie am Apparat; **in —** with in Übereinstimmung mit; vt coat füttern; (border) säumen; **— up** vi sich aufstellen; vt aufstellen; (prepare) sorgen für; support mobilisieren; surprise planen.

linear ['lɪnɪə*] a gerade; (measure) Längen-.

linen ['lɪnɪn] n Leinen nt; (sheets etc) Wäsche f.

liner ['laɪnə*] n Überseedampfer m.

linesman ['laɪnzmən] n (Sport) Linienrichter m.

line-up ['laɪnʌp] n Aufstellung f.

linger ['lɪŋgə*] vi (remain long) verweilen; (taste) (zurück)bleiben; (delay) zögern, verharren.

lingerie ['lænʒərɪ] n Damenunterwäsche f.

lingering ['lɪŋgərɪŋ] a lang; doubt zurückbleibend; disease langwierig; taste nachhaltend; look lang.

lingo ['lɪŋgəʊ] n (col) Sprache f.

linguist ['lɪŋgwɪst] n Sprachkundige(r) mf; (Univ) Sprachwissenschaftler(in f) m.

linguistic [lɪŋ'gwɪstɪc] a sprachlich; sprachwissenschaftlich; **—s** Sprachwissenschaft f, Linguistik f.

liniment ['lɪnɪmənt] n Einreibemittel nt.

lining ['laɪnɪŋ] n (of clothes) Futter nt.

link [lɪŋk] n Glied nt; (connection) Verbindung f; vt verbinden; **—s** Golfplatz m; **—-up** (Tel) Verbindung f; (of spaceships) Kopplung f.

lino ['laɪnəʊ] n, **linoleum** [lɪ'nəʊlɪəm] n Linoleum nt.

linseed oil ['lɪnsiːd'ɔɪl] n Leinöl nt.

lint [lɪnt] n Verbandstoff m.

lintel ['lɪntl] n (Archit) Sturz m.

lion ['laɪən] n Löwe m; **—ess** Löwin f.

lip [lɪp] n Lippe f; (of jug) Tülle f, Schnabel m; **—-read** vi irreg von den Lippen ablesen; **to pay — service (to)** ein Lippenbekenntnis ablegen (zu); **—stick** Lippenstift m.

liquefy ['lɪkwfaɪ] vt verflüssigen.

liqueur [lɪ'kjʊə*] n Likör m.

liquid ['lɪkwɪd] n Flüssigkeit f; a flüssig; **—ate** vt liquidieren; **—ation** Liquidation f.

liquor ['lɪkə*] n Alkohol m, Spirituosen pl.

lisp [lɪsp] n-Lispeln nt; vti lispeln.

list [lɪst] n Liste f, Verzeichnis nt; (of ship) Schlagseite f; vt (write down) eine Liste machen von;

(verbally) aufzählen; *vi (ship)* Schlagseite haben.

listen ['lɪsn] *vi* hören, horchen; — **to** *vt* zuhören (+ *dat*); **-er** (Zu)hörer(in *f*) *m*.

listless *a*, **—ly** *ad* ['lɪstləs, -lɪ] lustlos, teilnahmslos; **—ness** Lustlosigkeit *f*, Teilnahmslosigkeit *f*.

litany ['lɪtəni] *n* Litanei *f*.

literacy ['lɪtərəsɪ] *n* Fähigkeit *f* zu lesen und zu schreiben.

literal ['lɪtərəl] *a* eigentlich, buchstäblich; *translation* wortwörtlich; **—ly** *ad* wörtlich; buchstäblich.

literary ['lɪtərərɪ] *a* literarisch, Literatur-.

literate ['lɪtərət] *a* des Lesens und Schreibens kundig.

literature ['lɪtrətʃə*] *n* Literatur *f*.

lithograph ['lɪθəʊgrɑːf] *n* Lithographie *f*.

litigate ['lɪtɪgeɪt] *vi* prozessieren.

litmus ['lɪtməs] *n* — **paper** Lackmuspapier *nt*.

litre, *(US)* **liter** ['liːtə*] *n* Liter *m*.

litter ['lɪtə*] *n (rubbish)* Abfall *m*; *(of animals)* Wurf *m*; *vt* in Unordnung bringen; **to be —ed with** übersät sein mit.

little ['lɪtl] *a* klein; *(unimportant)* unbedeutend; *ad*, *n* wenig; **a — ein** bißchen; **the — das** wenige.

liturgy ['lɪtədʒɪ] *n* Liturgie *f*.

live[1] [lɪv] *vi* leben; *(last)* fortleben; *(dwell)* wohnen; *vt life* führen; **— down** *vt* Gras wachsen lassen über (+ *acc*); **I'll never — it down das** wird man mir nie vergessen; **— on** *vi* weiterleben; **— on sth von** etw leben; **— up to** *vt standards* gerecht werden (+ *dat*); *principles* anstreben; *hopes* entsprechen (+ *dat*).

live[2] [laɪv] *a* lebendig; *(burning)* glühend; *(Mil)* scharf; *(Elec)* geladen; *broadcast* live.

livelihood ['laɪvlɪhʊd] *n* Lebensunterhalt *m*.

liveliness ['laɪvlɪnəs] *n* Lebendigkeit *f*.

lively ['laɪvlɪ] *a* lebhaft, lebendig.

liver ['lɪvə*] *n (Anat)* Leber *f*; **—ish** *a (bad-tempered)* gallig.

livery ['lɪvərɪ] *n* Livree *f*.

livestock ['laɪvstɒk] *n* Vieh *nt*, Viehbestand *m*.

livid ['lɪvɪd] *a (lit)* bläulich; *(furious)* fuchsteufelswild.

living ['lɪvɪŋ] *n (Lebens)unterhalt *m*; *a* lebendig; *language etc* lebend; *wage* ausreichend; **— room** Wohnzimmer *nt*.

lizard ['lɪzəd] *n* Eidechse *f*.

llama ['lɑːmə] *n* Lama *nt*.

load [ləʊd] *n (burden)* Last *f*; *(amount)* Ladung *f*, Fuhre *f*; **—s of (col)** massenhaft; *vt* (be)laden; *(fig)* überhäufen; *camera* Film einlegen in (+ *acc*); *gun* laden.

loaf [ləʊf] *n* Brot *nt*, Laib *m*; *vi* herumlungern, faulenzen.

loam [ləʊm] *n* Lehmboden *m*.

loan [ləʊn] *n* Leihgabe *f*; *(Fin)* Darlehen *nt*; *vt* leihen; **on —** geliehen.

loathe [ləʊð] *vt* verabscheuen.

loathing ['ləʊðɪŋ] *n* Abscheu *f*.

lobby ['lɒbɪ] *n* Vorhalle *f*; *(Pol)* Lobby *f*; *vt* politisch beeinflussen (wollen).

lobe [ləʊb] *n* Ohrläppchen *nt*.

lobster ['lɒbstə*] *n* Hummer *m*.

local ['ləʊkəl] *a* ortsansässig, hiesig, Orts-; *anaesthetic* örtlich; *n* (pub) Stammwirtschaft *f*; **the —s** *pl* die Ortsansässigen *pl*; **— colour** Lokal-

kolorit nt; **—ity** [ləʊ'kælɪtɪ] Ort m; **—ly** ad örtlich, am Ort.

locate [ləʊ'keɪt] vt ausfindig machen; ·(establish) errichten.

location [ləʊ'keɪʃən] n Platz m, Lage f; **on —** (Cine) auf Außenaufnahme.

loch [lɒx] n (Scot) See m.

lock [lɒk] n Schloß nt; (Naut) Schleuse f; (of hair) Locke f; vt (fasten) (ver)schließen; vi (door etc) sich schließen (lassen); (wheels) blockieren.

locker ['lɒkə*] n Spind m.

locket ['lɒkɪt] n Medaillon nt.

locomotive [ləʊkə'məʊtɪv] n Lokomotive f.

locust ['ləʊkəst] n Heuschrecke f.

lodge [lɒdʒ] n (gatehouse) Pförtnerhaus m; (freemasons') Loge f; vi (in Untermiete) wohnen (with bei); (get stuck) stecken(bleiben); vt protest einreichen; **—r** (Unter)mieter m.

lodgings ['lɒdʒɪŋz] n (Miet)wohnung f; Zimmer nt.

loft [lɒft] n (Dach)boden m.

lofty ['lɒftɪ] a hoch(ragend); (proud) hochmütig.

log [lɒg] n Klotz m; (Naut) Log nt.

logarithm ['lɒgərɪθəm] n Logarithmus m.

logbook ['lɒgbʊk] n Bordbuch nt, Logbuch nt; (for lorry) Fahrtenschreiber m; (Aut) Kraftfahrzeugbrief m.

loggerheads ['lɒgəhedz] n: **to be at —** sich in den Haaren liegen.

logic ['lɒdʒɪk] n Logik f; **—al** a logisch; **—ally** ad logisch(erweise).

logistics [lɒ'dʒɪstɪks] npl Logistik f.

loin [lɔɪn] n Lende f.

loiter ['lɔɪtə*] vi herumstehen, sich herumtreiben.

loll [lɒl] vi sich rekeln.

lollipop ['lɒlɪpɒp] n (Dauer)lutscher m.

lone [ləʊn] a einsam.

loneliness ['ləʊnlɪnəs] n Einsamkeit f.

lonely ['ləʊnlɪ] a einsam.

long [lɒŋ] a lang; distance weit; ad lange; **two-day—** zwei Tage lang; vi sich sehnen (for nach); **—ago** vor langer Zeit; before = bald; **as — as** solange; **in the —run** auf die Dauer; **—distance** a Fern-; **—haired** a langhaarig; **—hand** Langschrift f; **—ing** Verlangen nt, Sehnsucht f; a sehnsüchtig; **—ish** a ziemlich lang; **—itude** Längengrad m; **—jump** Weitsprung m; **—lost** a längst verloren geglaubt; **—playing record** Langspielplatte f; **—range** a Langstrecken-, Fern-; **—sighted** a weitsichtig; **—standing** a alt, seit langer Zeit bestehend; **—suffering** a schwer geprüft; **—term** a langfristig; **— wave** Langwelle f; **—winded** a langatmig.

loo [lu:] n (col) Klo nt.

loofah ['lu:fə*] n (plant) Luffa f; (sponge) Luffa(schwamm) m.

look [lʊk] vi schauen, blicken; (seem) aussehen; (face) liegen nach, gerichtet sein nach; n Blick m; **—s** pl Aussehen nt; **— after** vt (care for) sorgen für; (watch) aufpassen auf (+acc); **— down** vt (fig) herabsehen auf (+acc); **— for** vt (seek) suchen (nach); (expect) erwarten; **— forward to** vt sich freuen auf (+acc); **— out** for vt Ausschau halten nach; (be careful) achtgeben auf (+acc); **— to** vt (take care of) achtgeben auf

(+acc); (rely on) sich verlassen auf (+acc); — up vi aufblicken; (improve) sich bessern; vt word nachschlagen; person besuchen; — up to vt aufsehen zu; —out (watch) Ausschau f; (person) Wachposten m; (place) Ausguck m; (prospect) Aussichten pl.

loom [lu:m] n Webstuhl m; vi sich abzeichnen.

loop [lu:p] n Schlaufe f, Schleife f; vt schlingen; —hole (fig) Hintertürchen nt.

loose [lu:s] a lose, locker; (free) frei; (inexact) unpräzise; vt lösen, losbinden; **to be at a — end** nicht wissen, was man tun soll; —ly ad locker, lose; —ly speaking grob gesagt; —n vt lockern, losmachen; —ness Lockerheit f.

loot [lu:t] n Beute f; vt plündern; —ing Plünderung f.

lop [lop]: — off vt abhacken.

lop-sided ['lop'saidid] a schief.

lord [lo:d] n (ruler) Herr m, Gebieter m; (Brit. title) Lord m; **the L—** (Gott) der Herr m; —ly a vornehm; (proud) stolz.

lore [lo:*] n Überlieferung f.

lorry ['lori] n Lastwagen m.

lose [lu:z] irreg vt verlieren; chance verpassen; — **out on zu kurz kommen bei**; vi verlieren; —r Verlierer m.

losing ['lu:ziŋ] a Verlierer-; (Comm) verlustbringend.

loss [los] n Verlust m; **at a —** (Comm) mit Verlust; (unable) außerstande; **I am at a — for words** mir fehlen die Worte.

lost [lost] a verloren; — cause aussichtslose Sache f; — property Fundsachen pl.

lot [lot] n (quantity) Menge f; (fate, at auction) Los nt; (col: people,

things) Haufen m; **the —** alles; (people) alle; **a —** of viel; pl viele; —s of massenhaft, viel(e).

lotion ['ləuʃən] n Lotion f.

lottery ['lotəri] n Lotterie f.

loud [laud] a laut; (showy) schreiend; ad laut; —ly ad laut; —ness Lautheit f; —speaker Lautsprecher m.

lounge [laundʒ] n (in hotel) Gesellschaftsraum m; (in house) Wohnzimmer nt; (on ship) Salon m; vi sich herumlümmeln; — suit Straßenanzug m.

louse [laus] n Laus f.

lousy ['lauzi] a (lit) verlaust; (fig) lausig, miserabel.

lout [laut] n Lümmel m.

lovable ['lʌvəbl] a liebenswert.

love [lʌv] n Liebe f; (person) Liebling m, Schatz m; (Sport) null; vt person lieben; activity gerne mögen; **to — to do** etw (sehr) gerne tun; **to make —** sich lieben; **to make — to/with sb** jdn lieben; — **affair** (Liebes)verhältnis nt; — **letter** Liebesbrief m; — **life** Liebesleben nt; —ly a schön; person, object also entzückend, reizend; — **making** Liebe f; —r Liebhaber m; Geliebte f; (of books etc) Liebhaber m; **the —rs** die Liebenden, das Liebespaar; —song Liebeslied nt.

loving ['lʌviŋ] a liebend, liebevoll; —ly ad liebevoll.

low [ləu] a niedrig; rank niedere(r, s); level, note, neckline tief; intelligence, density gering; (vulgar) ordinär; (not loud) leise; (depressed) gedrückt; ad (not high) niedrig; (not loudly) leise; n (low point) Tiefstand m; (Met) Tief nt; —cut a dress tiefausgeschnitten.

lower ['ləuə*] vt herunterlassen;

eyes, gun senken; *(reduce)* herabsetzen, senken.

lowly ['ləʊlɪ] *a* bescheiden.

loyal ['lɔɪəl] *a (true)* treu; *(to king)* loyal, treu; **—ly** *ad* treu; loyal; **—ty** Treue *f;* Loyalität *f.*

lozenge ['lɒzɪndʒ] *n* Pastille *f.*

lubricant ['lu:brɪkənt] *n* Schmiermittel *nt.*

lubricate ['lu:brɪkeɪt] *vt* (ab)schmieren, ölen.

lubrication [lu:brɪ'keɪʃən] *n* (Ein- or Ab)schmierung *f.*

lucid ['lu:sɪd] *a* klar; *(sane)* bei klarem Verstand; *moment* licht; **—ity** [lu:'sɪdɪtɪ] Klarheit *f;* **—ly** *ad* klar.

luck [lʌk] *n* Glück *nt; bad* — Pech *nt;* **—ily** *ad* glücklicherweise, zum Glück; **—y** *a* glücklich, Glücks-; to be — Glück haben.

lucrative ['lu:krətɪv] *a* einträglich.

ludicrous ['lu:dɪkrəs] *a* grotesk.

ludo ['lu:dəʊ] *vt* schleppen.
lug [lʌg] Mensch ärgere dich nicht nt.

lug [lʌg] *vt* schleppen.

luggage ['lʌgɪdʒ] *n* Gepäck *nt;* **—rack** Gepäcknetz *nt.*

lugubrious [lu:'gu:brɪəs] *a* traurig.

lukewarm ['lu:kwɔ:m] *a* lauwarm; *(indifferent)* lau.

lull [lʌl] *n* Flaute *f; vt* einlullen; *(calm)* beruhigen; **—aby** ['lʌləbaɪ] Schlaflied *nt.*

lumbago [lʌm'beɪgəʊ] *n* Hexenschuß *m.*

lumber ['lʌmbə*] *n (junk)* Plunder *m; (wood)* Holz *nt;* **—jack** Holzfäller *m.*

luminous ['lu:mɪnəs] *a* leuchtend, Leucht-.

lump [lʌmp] *n* Klumpen *m; (Med)* Schwellung *f; (in breast)* Knoten *m; (of sugar)* Stück *nt; vt*

zusammentun; (judge together) in einen Topf werfen; — **sum** Pauschalsumme *f;* **—y** klumpig; to go **—y** klumpen.

lunacy ['lu:nəsɪ] *n* Irrsinn *m.*

lunar ['lu:nə*] *a* Mond-.

lunatic ['lu:nətɪk] *n* Wahnsinnige(r) *mf; a* wahnsinnig, irr.

lunch [lʌntʃ] *n (also* **—eon** [-ən]) Mittagessen *nt;* — **hour** Mittagspause *f;* **—time** Mittagszeit *f;* **—eon meat** Frühstücksfleisch *nt.*

lung [lʌŋ] *n* Lunge *f;* — **cancer** Lungenkrebs *m.*

lunge [lʌndʒ] *vi* (los)stürzen.

lupin ['lu:pɪn] *n* Lupine *f.*

lurch [lɜ:tʃ] *vi* taumeln; *(Naut)* schlingern; *n* Taumeln *nt; (Naut)* plötzliche(s) Schlingern *nt.*

lure [ljʊə*] *n* Köder *m; (fig)* Lockung *f; vt* (ver)locken.

lurid ['ljʊərɪd] *a (shocking)* grausig, widerlich; *colour* grell.

lurk [lɜ:k] *vi* lauern.

luscious ['lʌʃəs] *a* köstlich; *colour* satt.

lush [lʌʃ] *a* satt; *vegetation* üppig.

lust [lʌst] *n* sinnliche Begierde *f (for* nach); *(sensation)* Wollust *f; (greed)* Gier *f; vi* gieren *(after* nach); **—ful** *a* wollüstig, lüstern.

lustre, *(US)* **luster** ['lʌstə*] *n* Glanz *m.*

lusty ['lʌstɪ] *a* gesund und munter; *old person* rüstig.

lute [lu:t] *a* Laute *f.*

luxuriant [lʌg'zjʊərɪənt] *a* üppig.

luxurious [lʌg'zjʊərɪəs] *a* luxuriös, Luxus-.

luxury ['lʌkʃərɪ] *n* Luxus *m; the little luxuries* die kleinen Genüsse.

lying ['laɪɪŋ] *n* Lügen *nt; a* verlogen.

lynch [lɪntʃ] *vt* lynchen.

lynx [lɪŋks] n Luchs m.
lyre ['laɪə*] n Leier f.
lyric ['lɪrɪk] n Lyrik f; (pl: words
for song) (Lied)text m; a lyrisch;
—al a lyrisch, gefühlvoll.

M

M, m [em] n M nt, m nt.
mac [mæk] n (Brit col) Regenmantel m.
macabre [mə'kɑːbr] a makaber.
macaroni [mækə'rəʊnɪ] n
Makkaroni pl.
mace [meɪs] n Amtsstab m; (spice)
Muskat m.
machine [mə'ʃiːn] n Maschine f; vt
dress etc mit der Maschine nähen;
maschinell herstellen/bearbeiten;
—gun Maschinengewehr nt; —ry
[mə'ʃiːnərɪ] Maschinerie f,
Maschinen pl; — tool Werkzeug-
maschine f.
machinist [mə'ʃiːnɪst] n Machinist
m.
mackerel ['mækrəl] n Makrele f.
mackintosh ['mækɪntɒʃ] n Regenmantel m.
macro- ['mækrəʊ] pref Makro-,
makro-.
mad [mæd] a verrückt; *dog*
tollwütig; (*angry*) wütend; —
about (*fond of*) verrückt nach, versessen auf (+acc).
madam ['mædəm] n gnädige Frau
f.
madden ['mædn] vt verrückt
machen; (*make angry*) ärgern;
—ing a ärgerlich.
made-to-measure ['meɪd-
tə'meʒə*] a Maß-.
made-up ['meɪd.ʌp] a *story*
erfunden.
madly ['mædlɪ] ad wahnsinnig.

madman ['mædmən] n
Verrückte(r) m, Irre(r) m.
madness ['mædnəs] n Wahnsinn m.
Madonna [mə'dɒnə] n Madonna f.
madrigal ['mædrɪgəl] n Madrigal nt.
magazine ['mægəziːn] n Zeitschrift
f; (*in gun*) Magazin m.
maggot ['mægət] n Made f.
magic ['mædʒɪk] n Zauberei f,
Magie f; (*fig*) Zauber m; a
magisch, Zauber-; —al a magisch;
—ian [mə'dʒɪʃən] Zauberer m.
magistrate ['mædʒɪstreɪt] n
(Friedens)richter m.
magnanimity [mægnə'nɪmɪtɪ] n
Großmut f.
magnanimous [mæg'nænɪməs] a
großmütig.
magnate ['mægneɪt] n Magnat m.

magnet ['mægnɪt] n Magnet m;
—ic [mæg'netɪk] a magnetisch;
(*fig*) anziehend, unwiderstehlich;
—ism Magnetismus m; (*fig*) Aus-
strahlungskraft f.
magnification [mægnɪfɪ'keɪʃən] n
Vergrößerung f.
magnificence [mæg'nɪfɪsəns] n
Großartigkeit f.
magnificent a, —ly ad
[mæg'nɪfɪsənt, -lɪ] großartig.
magnify ['mægnɪfaɪ] vt
vergrößern; —ing glass Ver-
größerungsglas nt, Lupe f.

magnitude ['mægnɪtjuːd] n (*size*)
Größe f; (*importance*) Ausmaß nt.

magnolia [mæg'nəʊliə] n Magnolie f.

magpie ['mægpaɪ] n Elster f.

maharajah [mɑːhə'rɑːdʒə] n Maharadscha m.

mahogany [mə'hɒgənɪ] n Mahagoni nt; a Mahagoni-.

maid [meɪd] n Dienstmädchen nt; old — alte Jungfer f; —en (liter) Maid f; a flight, speech Jungfern-; —en name Mädchenname m.

mail [meɪl] n Post f; vt aufgeben; — box (US) Briefkasten m; —ing list Anschreibeliste f; — order Bestellung f durch die Post; — order firm Versandhaus nt.

maim [meɪm] vt verstümmeln.

main [meɪn] a hauptsächlich, Haupt-; n (pipe) Hauptleitung f; in the — im großen und ganzen; —land Festland nt; — road Hauptstraße f; —stay (fig) Hauptstütze f.

maintain [meɪn'teɪn] vt machine, roads instand halten; (support) unterhalten; (keep up) aufrechterhalten; (claim) behaupten; innocence beteuern.

maintenance ['meɪntənəns] n (Tech) Wartung f; (of family) Unterhalt m.

maisonette [meɪzə'net] n kleine(s) Eigenheim nt; Wohnung f.

maize [meɪz] n Mais m.

majestic [mə'dʒestɪk] a majestätisch.

majesty ['mædʒɪstɪ] n Majestät f.

major ['meɪdʒə*] n Major m; a (Mus) Dur-; (more important) Haupt-; (bigger) größer.

majority [mə'dʒɒrɪtɪ] n Mehrheit f; (Jur) Volljährigkeit f.

make [meɪk] vt irreg machen; (appoint) ernennen (zu); (cause to

do sth) veranlassen; (reach) erreichen; (in time) schaffen; (earn) verdienen; to — sth happen etw geschehen lassen; n Marke f, Fabrikat nt; — for vi gehen/fahren nach; — out vi zurechtkommen; vt (write out) ausstellen; (understand) verstehen; (pretend) (so) tun (als ob); — up vt (make) machen, herstellen; face schminken; quarrel beilegen; story erfinden; vi sich versöhnen; — up for vt wiedergutmachen; (Comm) vergüten; —believe n it's —believe es ist nicht wirklich; a Phantasie-, ersonnen; —r (Comm) Hersteller m; —shift a behelfsmäßig, Not-; —up Schminke f, Make-up nt.

making ['meɪkɪŋ] n: in the — im Entstehen; to have the —s of das Zeug haben zu.

maladjusted ['mælə'dʒʌstɪd] a fehlangepaßt, umweltgestört.

malaise [mæ'leɪz] n Unbehagen nt.

malaria [mə'lɛərɪə] n Malaria f.

male [meɪl] n Mann m; (animal) Männchen nt; a männlich.

malevolence [mə'levələns] n Böswilligkeit f.

malevolent [mə'levələnt] a übelwollend.

malfunction [mæl'fʌŋkʃən] vi versagen, nicht funktionieren.

malice ['mælɪs] n Bosheit f.

malicious [mə'lɪʃəs] a; —ly ad böswillig, gehässig.

malign [mə'laɪn] vt verleumden.

malignant [mə'lɪgnənt] a bösartig.

malinger [mə'lɪŋgə*] vi simulieren; —er Drückeberger m, Simulant m.

malleable ['mælɪəbl] a formbar.

mallet ['mælɪt] n Holzhammer m.

malnutrition ['mælnjʊ'trɪʃən] n Unterernährung f.

malpractice ['mæl'præktɪs] n Amtsvergehen nt.

malt [mɔːlt] n Malz nt.

maltreat [mæl'triːt] vt mißhandeln.

mammal ['mæməl] n Säugetier nt.

mammoth ['mæməθ] a Mammut-, Riesen-.

man [mæn] n, pl **men** Mann m; (human race) der Mensch, die Menschen pl; vt bemannen.

manage ['mænɪdʒ] vi zurechtkommen; vt (control) führen, leiten; (cope with) fertigwerden mit; **to — to** do sth etw schaffen; **—able** a person, animal lenksam, fügsam; object handlich; **—ment** (control) Führung f, Leitung f; (directors) Management nt; **—r** Geschäftsführer m, (Betriebs)leiter m; **—ress** ['mænɪdʒə'res] Geschäftsführerin f; **—rial** [mænə'dʒɪərɪəl] a leitend; problem etc Management-.

managing ['mænɪdʒɪŋ] a: **—director** Betriebsleiter m.

mandarin ['mændərɪn] n (fruit) Mandarine f; (Chinese official) Mandarin m.

mandate ['mændeɪt] n Mandat nt.

mandatory ['mændətərɪ] a obligatorisch.

mandolin(e) ['mændəlɪn] n Mandoline f.

mane [meɪn] n Mähne f.

maneuver [mə'nuːvə*] (US) =manoeuvre.

manful a, **—ly** ad ['mænful, -fəlɪ] beherzt; mannhaft.

mangle ['mæŋgl] vt verstümmeln.

mango ['mæŋgəʊ] n Mango(pflaume) f.

mangrove ['mæŋgrəʊv] n Mangrove f.

mangy ['meɪndʒɪ] a dog räudig.

manhandle ['mænhændl] vt grob behandeln.

manhole ['mænhəʊl] n (Straßen)schacht m.

manhood ['mænhʊd] n Mannesalter nt; (manliness) Männlichkeit f.

man-hour ['mæn'aʊə*] n Arbeitsstunde f.

manhunt ['mænhʌnt] n Fahndung f.

mania ['meɪnɪə] n (craze) Sucht f, Manie f; (madness) Wahn(sinn) m; **—c** ['meɪnæk] Wahnsinnige(r) mf, Verrückte(r) mf.

manicure ['mænɪkjʊə*] n Maniküre f; vt maniküren; **— set** Necessaire nt.

manifest ['mænɪfest] vt offenbaren; a offenkundig; **—ation** (showing) Ausdruck m, Bekundung f; (sign) Anzeichen nt; **—ly** ad offenkundig; **—o** [mænɪ'festəʊ] Manifest nt.

manipulate [mə'nɪpjʊleɪt] vt handhaben; (fig) manipulieren.

manipulation [mənɪpjʊ'leɪʃən] n Manipulation f.

mankind [mæn'kaɪnd] n Menschheit f.

manliness ['mænlɪnəs] n Männlichkeit f.

manly ['mænlɪ] a männlich; mannhaft.

man-made ['mæn'meɪd] a fibre künstlich.

manner ['mænə*] n Art f, Weise f; (style) Stil m; **in such a —** so; **in a — of speaking** sozusagen; **—s** pl Manieren pl; **—ism** (of person)

Angewohnheit f; (of style) Manieriertheit f.

manoeuvrable [mə'nu:vrəbl] a manövrierfähig.

manoeuvre [mə'nu:və*] vti manövrieren; n (Mil) Feldzug m; (general) Manöver nt, Schachzug m; —s pl Truppenübungen pl, Manöver nt.

manor ['mænə*] n Landgut nt; — house Herrenhaus nt.

manpower ['mænpauə*] n Arbeitskräfte pl.

manservant ['mænsə:vənt] n Diener m.

mansion ['mænʃən] n Herrenhaus nt, Landhaus nt.

manslaughter ['mænslɔ:tə*] n Totschlag m.

mantelpiece ['mæntlpi:s] n Kaminsims m.

mantle ['mæntl] n (cloak) lange(r) Umhang m.

manual ['mænjuəl] a manuell, Hand-; n Handbuch nt.

manufacture [mænju'fæktʃə*] vt herstellen; n Herstellung f; —r Hersteller m.

manure [mə'njuə*] n Dünger m.

manuscript ['mænjuskript] n Manuskript nt.

many [meni] a viele; as — as 20 sage und schreibe 20; — a good soldier so mancher gute Soldat; —'s the time oft.

map [mæp] n (Land)karte f; (of town) Stadtplan m; of a large scale Karte machen von; — out vt (fig) ausarbeiten.

maple ['meipl] n Ahorn m.

mar [ma:*] vt verderben, beeinträchtigen.

marathon ['mærəθən] n (Sport) Marathonlauf m; (fig) Marathon m.

marauder [mə'rɔ:də*] n Plünderer m.

marble ['ma:bl] n Marmor m; (for game) Murmel f.

March [ma:tʃ] n März m.

march [ma:tʃ] vi marschieren; n Marsch m; —past Vorbeimarsch m.

mare [mɛə*] n Stute f; —'s nest Windei nt.

margarine [ma:dʒə'ri:n] n Margarine f.

margin ['ma:dʒɪn] n Rand m; (extra amount) Spielraum m; (Comm) Spanne f; —al note Rand-; difference etc geringfügig; —ally ad nur wenig.

marigold ['mærigəuld] n Ringelblume f.

marijuana [mæri'hwa:nə] n Marihuana nt.

marina [mə'ri:nə] n Yachthafen m.

marine [mə'ri:n] a Meeres-, See-; n (Mil) Marineinfanterist m; (fleet) Marine f; —r ['mærinə*] Seemann m.

marionette [mæriə'net] n Marionette f.

marital ['mæritl] a ehelich, Ehe-.

maritime ['mæritaim] a See-.

marjoram ['ma:dʒərəm] n Majoran m.

mark [ma:k] n (coin) Mark f; (spot) Fleck m; (scar) Kratzer m; (sign) Zeichen nt; (target) Ziel nt; (Sch) Note f; quick off the — blitzschnell; on your —s auf die Plätze; vt (make mark) Flecken/Kratzer machen auf (+acc); (indicate) markieren, bezeichnen; (note) sich (dat) merken; exam korrigieren; to — time (lit, fig) auf der Stelle treten; — out vt bestimmen; area abstecken; —ed a deutlich; —edly ['ma:kidli] ad merklich; —er (in book) (Lese)zeichen nt; (on road) Schild nt.

market ['mɑːkɪt] n Markt m; (stock —) Börse f; vt (Comm: new product) auf dem Markt bringen; (sell) vertreiben; — day Markttag m; — garden (Brit) Handelsgärtnerei f; —ing Marketing nt; — place Marktplatz m.

marksman ['mɑːksmən] n Scharfschütze m; —ship Treffsicherheit f.

marmalade ['mɑːməleɪd] n Orangenmarmelade f.

maroon [mə'ruːn] vt aussetzen; a (colour) kastanienbraun.

marquee [mɑː'kiː] n große(s) Zelt nt.

marquess, marquis ['mɑːkwɪs] n Marquis m.

marriage ['mærɪdʒ] n Ehe f; (wedding) Heirat f; (fig) Verbindung f.

married ['mærɪd] a person' verheiratet; couple, life Ehe-.

marrow ['mærəʊ] n (Knochen)mark nt; (vegetable) Kürbis m.

marry ['mærɪ] vt (join) trauen; (take as husband, wife) heiraten; vi (also get married) heiraten.

marsh [mɑːʃ] n Marsch f, Sumpfland nt.

marshal ['mɑːʃəl] n (US) Bezirkspolizeichef m; vt (an)ordnen, arrangieren.

marshy ['mɑːʃɪ] a sumpfig.

martial ['mɑːʃəl] a kriegerisch; — law Kriegsrecht nt.

martyr ['mɑːtə*] n (lit, fig) Märtyrer(in f) m; vt zum Märtyrer machen; —dom Martyrium nt.

marvel ['mɑːvəl] n Wunder nt; vi sich wundern (at über +acc); —lous, (US) —ous a, —lously, (US) —ously ad wunderbar.

Marxism ['mɑːksɪzəm] n Marxismus m.

Marxist ['mɑːksɪst] n Marxist(in f) m.

marzipan [mɑːzɪ'pæn] n Marzipan nt.

mascara [mæs'kɑːrə] n Wimperntusche f.

mascot ['mæskət] n Maskottchen nt.

masculine ['mæskjʊlɪn] a männlich; n Maskulinum nt.

masculinity [mæskjʊ'lɪnɪtɪ] n Männlichkeit f.

mashed [mæʃt] a: — potatoes pl Kartoffelbrei m or -püree nt.

mask [mɑːsk] n (lit, fig) Maske f; vt maskieren, verdecken.

masochist ['mæzəʊkɪst] n Masochist(in f) m.

mason ['meɪsn] n (stone—) Steinmetz m; (free—) Freimaurer m; —ic [mə'sɒnɪk] a Freimaurer-; —ry Mauerwerk nt.

masquerade [mæskə'reɪd] n Maskerade f; vi sich maskieren, sich verkleiden; to — as sich ausgeben als.

mass [mæs] n Masse f; (greater part) Mehrheit f; (Rel) Messe f; —es pl massenhaft; vt sammeln, anhäufen; vi sich sammeln.

massacre ['mæsəkə*] n Blutbad nt; vt niedermetzeln, massakrieren.

massage ['mæsɑːʒ] n Massage f; vt massieren.

masseur [mæ'sɜː*] n Masseur m.

masseuse [mæ'sɜːz] n Masseuse f.

massive ['mæsɪv] a gewaltig, massiv.

mass media ['mæs'miːdɪə] npl Massenmedien pl.

mass-produce ['mæsprə'djuːs] vt serienmäßig herstellen.

mass production ['mæsprə'dʌk-ʃən] n Serienproduktion f, Massenproduktion f.

mast [mɑːst] n Mast m.

master ['mɑːstə*] n Herr m; (Naut) Kapitän m; (teacher) Lehrer m; (artist) Meister m; vt meistern; language etc beherrschen; —ly a meisterhaft; —mind n Kapazität f; vt geschickt lenken; M— of Arts Magister Artium m; —piece Meisterstück nt; (Art) Meisterwerk nt; — stroke Glanzstück nt; — Können nt; to gain —y over sb die Oberhand gewinnen über jdn.

masturbate ['mæstəbeɪt] vi masturbieren, onanieren.

masturbation [mæstə'beɪʃən] n Masturbation f, Onanie f.

mat [mæt] n Matte f; (for table) Untersetzer m; vi sich verfilzen; vt verfilzen.

match [mætʃ] n Streichholz nt; (sth corresponding) Pendant nt; (Sport) Wettkampf m; (ball games) Spiel nt; it's a good — es paßt gut (for zu); to be a — for sb sich mit jdm messen können; (sb gewachsen sein; he's a good — er ist eine gute Partie; vt (be alike, suit) passen zu; (equal) gleichkommen (+dat); (Sport) antreten lassen; vi zusammenpassen; —box Streichholzschachtel f; —ing a passend; —less a unvergleichlich; —maker Kuppler(in f) m.

mate [meɪt] n (companion) Kamerad m; (spouse) Lebensgefährte m; (of animal) Weibchen nt/Männchen m; (Naut) Schiffsoffizier m; vi (chess) (schach)matt sein; (animals) sich paaren; vt (chess) matt setzen.

material [mə'tɪərɪəl] n Material nt; (for book, cloth) Material nt, Stoff m; a (important) wesentlich; damage Sach-; comforts etc materiell; —s pl Materialien pl; —istic a materialistisch; —ize vi sich verwirklichen, zustande kommen; —ly ad grundlegend.

maternal [mə'tɜːnl] a mütterlich, Mutter-; — grandmother Großmutter mütterlicherseits.

maternity [mə'tɜːnɪtɪ] a Schwangeren-; dress Umstands-; benefit Wochen-.

matey ['meɪtɪ] a (Brit col) kameradschaftlich.

mathematical a, —ly ad [mæθə'mætɪkəl, -ɪ] mathematisch.

mathematician [mæθəmə'tɪʃən] n Mathematiker m.

mathematics [mæθə'mætɪks] n Mathematik f.

maths [mæθs] n Mathe f.

matinée ['mætɪneɪ] n Matinee f.

mating [meɪtɪŋ] n Paarung f; — call Lockruf m.

matins ['mætɪnz] n (Früh)mette f.

matriarchal [meɪtrɪ'ɑːkl] a matriarchalisch.

matrimonial [mætrɪ'məʊnɪəl] a ehelich, Ehe-.

matrimony ['mætrɪmənɪ] n Ehestand m.

matron ['meɪtrən] n (Med) Oberin f; (Sch) Hausmutter f; —ly a matronenhaft.

matt [mæt] a paint matt.

matter ['mætə*] n (substance) Materie f; (affair) Sache f; (content) Inhalt m; (Med) Eiter m; vi darauf ankommen; it doesn't — es macht nichts; no — how/what egal wie/was; what is the —? was ist los? ; as a — of fact eigentlich ; —-of-fact a sachlich, nüchtern.

mattress ['mætrəs] n Matratze f.

mature [mə'tjʊə*] a reif ; vi reif werden.

maturity [mə'tjʊərɪtɪ] n Reife f.

maudlin ['mɔ:dlɪn] a weinerlich ; gefühlsduselig.

maul [mɔ:l] vt übel zurichten.

mausoleum [mɔ:sə'li:əm] n Mausoleum nt.

mauve [məʊv] a mauve.

mawkish ['mɔ:kɪʃ] a kitschig ; taste süßlich.

maxi ['mæksɪ] pref Maxi-.

maxim ['mæksɪm] n Maxime f.

maximize ['mæksɪmaɪz] vt maximieren.

maximum ['mæksɪməm] a höchste(r, s), Höchst-, Maximal- ; n Höchstgrenze f, Maximum nt.

May [meɪ] n Mai m.

may [meɪ] v aux (be possible) können ; (have permission) dürfen ; I — come ich komme vielleicht, es kann sein, daß ich komme ; we — as well go wir können ruhig gehen ; — you be very happy so I hoffe, ihr seid glücklich ; —be ad vielleicht.

Mayday ['meɪdeɪ] n (message) SOS nt.

mayonnaise [meɪə'neɪz] n Mayonnaise f.

mayor [meə*] n Bürgermeister m ; —ess (wife) (die) Frau f Bürgermeister ; (lady —) Bürgermeisterin f.

maypole ['meɪpəʊl] n Maibaum m.

maze [meɪz] n (lit) Irrgarten m ; (fig) Wirrwarr m ; to be in a — (fig) durcheinander sein.

me [mi:] pron (acc) mich ; (dat) mir ; it's — ich bin's.

meadow ['medəʊ] n Wiese f.

meagre, (US) **meager** ['mi:gə*] a dürftig, spärlich.

meal [mi:l] n Essen nt, Mahlzeit f ; (grain) Schrotmehl nt ; to have a — essen (gehen) ; —time Essenszeit f ; —y-mouthed a: to be —y-mouthed d(a)rum herumreden.

mean [mi:n] a (stingy) geizig ; (spiteful) gemein ; (shabby) armselig, schäbig ; (average) durchschnittlich, Durchschnitts- ; irreg vt (signify) bedeuten ; vi (intend) vorhaben, beabsichtigen ; (be resolved) entschlossen sein ; he —s well er meint es gut ; I — it! ich meine das ernst! ; do you — me? meinen Sie mich? ; it —s nothing to me es sagt mir nichts ; n (average) Durchschnitt m ; —s pl Mittel pl ; (wealth) Vermögen nt ; by —s of durch ; by all —s selbstverständlich ; by no —s keineswegs.

meander [mɪ'ændə*] vi schlängeln.

meaning ['mi:nɪŋ] n Bedeutung f ; (of life) Sinn m ; —ful a bedeutungsvoll ; life sinnvoll ; —less a sinnlos.

meanness ['mi:nnəs] n (stinginess) Geiz m ; (spitefulness) Gemeinheit f ; (shabbiness) Schäbigkeit f.

meantime ['mi:ntaɪm] ad, **meanwhile** ['mi:nwaɪl] ad inzwischen, mittlerweile ; for the — vorerst.

measles ['mi:zlz] n Masern pl ; German — Röteln pl.

measly ['mi:zlɪ] a (col) poplig.

measurable ['meʒərəbl] a meßbar.

measure ['meʒə*] vti messen ; n Maß nt ; (step) Maßnahme f ; to be a — of sth etw erkennen lassen ; —d a (slow) gemessen ; —ment (way of measuring) Messung f ; (amount measured) Maß nt.

meat [mi:t] *n* Fleisch *nt*; **—y** *a* (*lit*) fleischig; (*fig*) gehaltvoll.

mechanic [mɪ'kænɪk] *n* Mechaniker *m*; **—s** Mechanik *f*; **—al** *a* mechanisch.

mechanism ['mekənɪzəm] *n* Mechanismus *m*.

mechanization [mekənaɪ'zeɪʃən] *n* Mechanisierung *f*.

mechanize ['mekənaɪz] *vt* mechanisieren.

medal ['medl] *n* Medaille *f*; (*decoration*) Orden *m*; **—lion** [mɪ'dælɪən] Medaillon *n*; **—list**, (*US*) **—ist** Medaillengewinner(in *f*) *m*.

meddle ['medl] *vi* sich einmischen (*in* in +*acc*); (*tamper*) hantieren (*with* an +*dat*); **—** with sb sich mit jdm einlassen.

media ['mi:dɪə] *npl* Medien *pl*.

mediate ['mi:dɪeɪt] *vi* vermitteln.

mediation [mi:dɪ'eɪʃən] *n* Vermittlung *f*.

mediator ['mi:dɪeɪtə*] *n* Vermittler *m*.

medical ['medɪkəl] *a* medizinisch; Medizin-; ärztlich; *n* (ärztliche) Untersuchung *f*.

medicated ['medɪkeɪtɪd] *a* medizinisch.

medicinal [me'dɪsɪnl] *a* medizinisch, Heil-.

medicine ['medsɪn] *n* Medizin *f*; (*drugs*) Arznei *f*; **—** chest Hausapotheke *f*.

medieval [medɪ'i:vəl] *a* mittelalterlich.

mediocre [mi:dɪ'əʊkə*] *a* mittelmäßig.

mediocrity [mi:dɪ'ɒkrɪtɪ] *n* Mittelmäßigkeit *f*; (*person also*) kleine(r) Geist *m*.

meditate ['medɪteɪt] *vi* nachdenken (*on* über +*acc*); meditieren (*on* über +*acc*).

meditation [medɪ'teɪʃən] *n* Nachsinnen *nt*; Meditation *f*.

medium ['mi:dɪəm] *a* mittlere(r, s), Mittel-, mittel-; *n* Mitte *f*; (*means*) Mittel *nt*; (*person*) Medium *nt*.

medley ['medlɪ] *n* Gemisch *nt*.

meek *a*, **—ly** *ad* [mi:k, -lɪ] sanft(mütig); (*pej*) duckmäuserisch.

meet [mi:t] *irreg vt* (*encounter*) treffen, begegnen (+*dat*); (*by arrangement*) sich treffen mit; (*difficulties* stoßen auf (+*acc*); (*become acquainted with*) kennenlernen; (*fetch*) abholen; (*join*) zusammentreffen mit; (*river*) fließen in (+*acc*); (*satisfy*) entsprechen (+*dat*); *debt* bezahlen; **pleased to — you!** angenehm!; *vi* sich treffen; (*become acquainted*) sich kennenlernen; (*join*) sich treffen; (*rivers*) ineinanderfließen; (*roads*) zusammenlaufen; **— with** *vt problems* stoßen auf (+*acc*); (*US: people*) zusammentreffen mit; **—ing** Treffen *nt*; (*business* —) Besprechung *f*, Konferenz *f*; (*discussion*) Sitzung *f*; (*assembly*) Versammlung *f*; **—ing place** Treffpunkt *m*.

megaphone ['megəfəʊn] *n* Megaphon *nt*.

melancholy ['melənkəlɪ] *n* Melancholie *f*; *a person* melancholisch, schwermütig; *sight, event* traurig.

mellow ['meləʊ] *a* mild, weich; *fruit* reif, weich; (*fig*) gesetzt; *vi* reif werden.

melodious [mɪ'ləʊdɪəs] *a* wohlklingend.

melodrama ['meləʊdrɑːmə] *n* Melodrama *nt*; **—tic** [meləʊdrə'mætɪk] *a* melodramatisch.

melody ['melədı] n Melodie f.

melon ['melən] n Melone f.

melt [melt] vi schmelzen; (anger) verfliegen; vt schmelzen; — away vi dahinschmelzen; — down vt einschmelzen; —ing point Schmelzpunkt m; —ing pot (fig) Schmelztiegel m; to be in the —ing pot in der Schwebe sein.

member ['membə*] n Mitglied nt; (of tribe, species) Angehörige(r) m; (Anat) Glied nt; —ship Mitgliedschaft f.

membrane ['membreın] n Membrane f.

memento [mə'mentəʊ] n Andenken nt.

memo ['meməʊ] n Notiz f; Mitteilung f.

memoirs ['memwɑ:*z] npl Memoiren pl.

memorable ['memərəbl] a denkwürdig.

memorandum [memə'rændəm] n Notiz f; Mitteilung f; (Pol) Memorandum nt.

memorial [mı'mɔ:rıəl] n Denkmal nt; a Gedenk-.

memorize ['meməraız] vt sich einprägen.

memory ['memərı] n Gedächtnis nt; (of computer) Speicher m; (sth recalled) Erinnerung f; in — of zur Erinnerung an (+acc); from — aus dem Kopf.

men [men] npl of man.

menace ['menıs] n Drohung f; Gefahr f; vt bedrohen.

menacing a, —ly ad ['menısıŋ, -lı] drohend.

ménage [me'nɑ:ʒ] n Haushalt m.

menagerie [mı'nædʒərı] n Tierschau f.

mend [mend] vt reparieren, flicken; n ausgebesserte Stelle f; on the — auf dem Wege der Besserung.

menial ['mi:nıəl] a niedrig, untergeordnet.

meningitis [menın'dʒaıtıs] n Hirnhautentzündung f, Meningitis f.

menopause ['menəʊpɔ:z] n Wechseljahre pl, Menopause f.

menstrual ['menstruəl] a Monats-, Menstruations-.

menstruate ['menstruett] vi menstruieren.

menstruation [menstru'eıʃən] n Menstruation f.

mental ['mentl] a geistig, Geistes-; arithmetic Kopf-; hospital Nerven-; cruelty seelisch; (col: abnormal) verrückt; —ity [men'tælıt] Mentalität f; —ly ad geistig; —ly ill geisteskrank.

mentholated ['menθəleıtıd] a Menthol-.

mention ['menʃən] n Erwähnung f; vt erwähnen; names nennen; don't — it! bitte (sehr), gern geschehen.

menu ['menju:] n Speisekarte f; (food) Speisen pl.

mercantile ['mɜ:kəntaıl] a Handels-.

mercenary ['mɜ:sınərı] a person geldgierig; (Mil) Söldner-; n Söldner m.

merchandise ['mɜ:tʃəndaız] n (Handels)ware f.

merchant ['mɜ:tʃənt] n Kaufmann m; a Handels-; — navy Handelsmarine f.

merciful ['mɜ:sıful] a gnädig, barmherzig; —ly ['mɜ:sıfəlı] ad gnädig; (fortunately) glücklicherweise.

merciless a, —ly ad ['mɜ:sıləs, -lı] erbarmungslos.

mercurial [mɜ:'kjʊəriəl] a quecksilbrig, Quecksilber.

mercury ['mɜ:kjʊri] n Quecksilber nt.

mercy ['mɜ:sɪ] n Erbarmen nt; Gnade f; (blessing) Segen m; at the — of ausgeliefert (+dat).

mere a, —ly ad [mɪə*, 'mɪəlɪ] bloß.

merge [mɜ:dʒ] vt verbinden; (Comm) fusionieren; vi verschmelzen; (roads) zusammenlaufen; (Comm) fusionieren; to — into übergehen in (+acc); —r (Comm) Fusion f.

meridian [mə'rɪdiən] n Meridian m.

meringue [mə'ræŋ] n Baiser nt, Schaumgebäck nt.

merit ['merɪt] n Verdienst nt; (advantage) Vorzug m; to judge on — nach Leistung beurteilen; vt verdienen.

mermaid ['mɜ:meɪd] n Wassernixe f, Meerjungfrau f.

merrily ['merɪlɪ] ad lustig.

merriment ['merɪmənt] n Fröhlichkeit f; (laughter) Gelächter nt.

merry ['merɪ] a fröhlich; (col) angeheitert; —go-round Karussell nt.

mesh [meʃ] n Masche f; vi (gears) ineinandergreifen.

mesmerize ['mezmeraɪz] vt hypnotisieren; (fig) faszinieren.

mess [mes] n Unordnung f; (dirt) Schmutz m; (trouble) Schwierigkeiten pl; (Mil) Messe f; to look a — fürchterlich aussehen; to make a — of sth etw verpfuschen; — about vi (tinker with) herummurksen (with an +dat); (play fool) herumalbern; (do nothing in particular) herumgammeln; — up vt verpfuschen; (make untidy) in Unordnung bringen.

message ['mesɪdʒ] n Mitteilung f, Nachricht f; to get the — kapieren.

messenger ['mesɪndʒə*] n Bote m.

messy ['mesɪ] a schmutzig; (untidy) unordentlich.

metabolism [me'tæbəlɪzəm] n Stoffwechsel m.

metal ['metl] n Metall nt; —lic [mɪ'tælɪk] a metallisch; —lurgy [me'tælədʒɪ] Metallurgie f.

metamorphosis [metə'mɔ:fəsɪs] n Metamorphose f.

metaphor ['metəfɔ:*] n Metapher f; —ical [metə'fɒrɪkəl] a bildlich, metaphorisch.

metaphysics [metə'fɪzɪks] n Metaphysik f.

meteor ['mi:tɪə*] n Meteor m; —ic [mi:t'rɪk] a meteorisch, Meteor; —ite Meteorit m; —ological [mi:tɪərə'lɒdʒɪkəl] a meteorologisch; —ology [mi:tɪə'rɒlədʒɪ] Meteorologie f.

meter ['mi:tə*] n Zähler m; (US) = metre.

method ['meθəd] n Methode f; —ical [mɪ'θɒdɪkəl] a methodisch; —ology [meθə'dɒlədʒɪ] Methodik f.

methylated spirit ['meθɪleɪtɪd 'spɪrɪt] n (also meths) (Brenn)spiritus m.

meticulous [mɪ'tɪkjʊləs] a (über)genau.

metre ['mi:tə*] n Meter m or nt; (verse) Metrum nt.

metric ['metrɪk] a (also —al) metrisch; —ation Umstellung f auf das Dezimalsystem; — system Dezimalsystem nt.

metronome ['metrənəʊm] n Metronom nt.

metropolis [me'trɒpəlɪs] n Metropole f.

mettle 568 militate

mettle ['metl] n Mut m.

mezzanine ['mezəni:n] n Hochparterre nt.

miaow [mi:'au] vi miauen.

mice [maɪs] npl of mouse.

mickey ['mɪkɪ] n: to take the — out of sb (col) jdn auf den Arm nehmen.

microbe ['maɪkrəub] n Mikrobe f.

microfilm ['maɪkrəufɪlm] n Mikrofilm m; vt auf Mikrofilm aufnehmen.

microphone ['maɪkrəfəun] n Mikrophon nt.

microscope ['maɪkrəskəup] n Mikroskop nt.

microscopic [maɪkrə'skɒpɪk] a mikroskopisch.

mid [mɪd] a mitten in (+dat); in the — eighties Mitte der achtziger Jahre; in — course mittendrin.

midday ['mɪd'deɪ] n Mittag m.

middle ['mɪdl] n Mitte f; (waist) Taille f; in the — of mitten in (+dat); a mittlere(s, r), Mittel-; —aged of mittleren Alters; the M—Ages pl das Mittelalter; —class Mittelstand m or -klasse f; a Mittelstands-, Mittelklassen-; the M—East der Nahe Osten; —man (Comm) Zwischenhändler m; —name zweiter Vorname m; —of-the-road a gemäßigt.

middling ['mɪdlɪŋ] a mittelmäßig.

midge [mɪdʒ] n Mücke f.

midget ['mɪdʒɪt] n Liliputaner(in f) m; a Kleinst-.

midnight ['mɪdnaɪt] n Mitternacht f.

midriff ['mɪdrɪf] n Taille f.

midst [mɪdst] n in the — of persons mitten unter (+dat); things mitten in (+dat); in our — unter uns.

midsummer ['mɪd'sʌmə*] n Hochsommer m; M—'s Day Sommersonnenwende f.

midway ['mɪd'weɪ] ad auf halbem Wege; a Mittel-.

midweek ['mɪd'wi:k] a, ad in der Mitte der Woche.

midwife ['mɪdwaɪf] n Hebamme f; —ry [mɪdwɪfrɪ] Geburtshilfe f.

midwinter ['mɪd'wɪntə*] n tiefste(r) Winter m.

might [maɪt] n Macht f, Kraft f; pt of may; I — come ich komme vielleicht; —ily ad mächtig; —n't = might not; —y, a, ad mächtig.

migraine ['mi:greɪn] n Migräne f.

migrant ['maɪgrənt] n (bird) Zugvogel m; (worker) Saison- or Wanderarbeiter m; a Wandervogel Zug-.

migrate [maɪ'greɪt] vi (ab)wandern; (birds) (fort)ziehen.

migration [maɪ'greɪʃən] n Wanderung f, Zug m.

mike [maɪk] n = microphone.

mild [maɪld] a mild; medicine, interest leicht; person sanft.

mildew ['mɪldju:] n (on plants) Mehltau m; (on food) Schimmel m.

mildly ['maɪldlɪ] ad leicht; to put it — gelinde gesagt.

mildness ['maɪldnəs] n Milde f.

mile [maɪl] n Meile f; —age Meilenzahl f; —stone (lit, fig) Meilenstein m.

milieu ['mi:ljə:] n Milieu nt.

militant ['mɪlɪtənt] n Militante(r) mf; a militant.

militarism ['mɪlɪtərɪzəm] n Militarismus m.

military ['mɪlɪtərɪ] a militärisch, Militär-, Wehr-; n Militär nt.

militate ['mɪlɪteɪt] vi sprechen; entgegenwirken (against dat).

militia [mɪˈlɪʃə] n Miliz f, Bürgerwehr f.

milk [mɪlk] n Milch f; vt (lit, fig) melken; — **chocolate** Milchschokolade f; —**ing** Melken nt; —**man** Milchmann m; — **shake** Milchmixgetränk nt; **M**—**y Way** Milchstraße f.

mill [mɪl] n Mühle f; (factory) Fabrik f; vt mahlen; vi (move around) umherlaufen; —**ed** a gemahlen.

millennium [mɪˈlenɪəm] n Jahrtausend nt.

miller [ˈmɪlə*] n Müller m.

millet [ˈmɪlɪt] n Hirse f.

milligram(me) [ˈmɪlɪgræm] n Milligramm nt.

millilitre, (US) —**liter** [ˈmɪlɪliːtə*] n Milliliter m.

millimetre, (US) —**meter** [ˈmɪlɪmiːtə*] n Millimeter m.

milliner [ˈmɪlɪnə*] n Hutmacher(in f) m; —**y** (hats) Hüte pl, Modewaren pl; (business) Hutgeschäft nt.

million [ˈmɪljən] n Million f; —**aire** [mɪljəˈnɛə*] n Millionär(in f) m.

millwheel [ˈmɪlwiːl] n Mühlrad nt.

milometer [maɪˈlɒmɪtə*] n Kilometerzähler m.

mime [maɪm] n Pantomime f; (actor) Mime m, Mimin f; vti mimen.

mimic [ˈmɪmɪk] n Mimiker m; vti nachahmen; —**ry** [ˈmɪmɪkrɪ] Nachahmung f; (Biol) Mimikry f..

mince [mɪns] vt (zer)hacken; vi (walk) trippeln; n (meat) Hackfleisch nt; —**meat** süße Pastetenfüllung f; — **pie** gefüllte (süße) Pastete f.

mincing [ˈmɪnsɪŋ] a manner affektiert.

mind [maɪnd] n Verstand m, Geist m; (opinion) Meinung f; **on my** — auf dem Herzen; **to my** — meiner Meinung nach; **to be out of one's** — wahnsinnig sein; **to bear** or **keep in** — bedenken, nicht vergessen; **to change one's** — es sich (dat) anders überlegen; **to make up one's** — sich entschließen; **to have sth in** — an etw (acc) denken; etw beabsichtigen; **to have a good** — **to do sth** große Lust haben, etw zu tun; **to set one's** — **on sth** (object to) etwas haben gegen; vi etwas dagegen haben; **I don't** — the rain der Regen macht mir nichts aus; **do you** — **if I** ... macht es Ihnen etwas aus, wenn ich ...; **do you** —! na hören Sie mal!; **never** —! macht nichts!; — **the step** 'Vorsicht Stufe'; — **your own business** kümmern Sie sich um Ihre eigenen Angelegenheiten; —**ful** a achtsam (of auf +acc); —**less** a achtlos, dumm.

mine [maɪn] poss pron meine(r, s); n (coal—) Bergwerk nt; (Mil) Mine f; (source) Fundgrube f; vt abbauen; (Mil) verminen; vi Bergbau betreiben; **to** — **for sth** etw gewinnen; — **detector** Minensuchgerät nt; —**field** Minenfeld nt; —**er** Bergarbeiter m.

mineral [ˈmɪnərəl] a mineralisch, Mineral-; n Mineral nt; — **water** Mineralwasser nt.

minesweeper [ˈmaɪnswiːpə*] n Minensuchboot nt.

mingle [ˈmɪŋgl] vt vermischen; vi sich mischen (with unter +acc).

mingy [ˈmɪndʒɪ] a (col) knickerig.

mini [ˈmɪnɪ] pref Mini-, Klein-.

miniature [ˈmɪnɪtʃə*] a Miniatur-, Klein-; n Miniatur f; **in** — en miniature.

minibus ['mɪnɪbʌs] n Kleinbus m, Minibus m.

minicab ['mɪnɪkæb] n Kleintaxi nt.

minim ['mɪnɪm] n halbe Note f.

minimal ['mɪnɪml] a kleinste(r, s), minimal, Mindest-.

minimize ['mɪnɪmaɪz] vt auf das Mindestmaß beschränken; (belittle) herabsetzen.

minimum ['mɪnɪməm] n Minimum nt; a Mindest-.

mining ['maɪnɪŋ] n Bergbau m; a Bergbau-, Berg-.

minion ['mɪnjən] n (pej) Trabant m.

miniskirt ['mɪnɪskɜ:t] n Minirock m.

minister ['mɪnɪstə*] n (Pol) Minister m; (Eccl) Geistliche(r) m, Pfarrer m; **—ial** [mɪnɪs'tɪərɪəl] a ministeriell, Minister-.

ministry ['mɪnɪstrɪ] n (government body) Ministerium nt; (Eccl) (office) geistliche(s) Amt nt; (all ministers) Geistlichkeit f.

mink [mɪŋk] n Nerz m.

minnow ['mɪnəʊ] n Elritze f.

minor ['maɪnə*] a kleiner; operation leicht; problem, poet unbedeutend; (Mus) Moll; Smith — Smith der Jüngere; n (Brit: under 18) Minderjährige(r) mf; **—ity** [maɪ'nɒrɪtɪ] Minderheit f.

minster ['mɪnstə*] n Münster nt, Kathedrale f.

minstrel ['mɪnstrəl] n (Hist) Spielmann m, Minnesänger m.

mint [mɪnt] n Minze f; (sweet) Pfefferminzbonbon nt; (place) Münzstätte f; a condition (wie) neu; stamp ungestempelt; — sauce Minzsoße f.

minuet [mɪnjʊ'et] n Menuett nt.

minus ['maɪnəs] n Minuszeichen nt; (amount) Minusbetrag m; prep minus, weniger.

minute [maɪ'nju:t] a winzig, sehr klein; (detailed) minuziös; ['mɪnɪt] n Minute f; (moment) Augenblick m; **—s** pl Protokoll nt; **—ly** [maɪ'nju:tlɪ] ad (in detail) genau.

miracle ['mɪrəkl] n Wunder nt; — play geistliche(s) Drama nt.

miraculous [mɪ'rækjʊləs] a wunderbar; **—ly** ad auf wunderbare Weise.

mirage ['mɪrɑːʒ] n Luftspiegelung f, Fata Morgana f.

mirror ['mɪrə*] n Spiegel m; vt (wider)spiegeln.

mirth [mɜːθ] n Freude f; Heiterkeit f.

misadventure [mɪsəd'ventʃə*] n Mißgeschick nt, Unfall m.

misanthropist [mɪ'zænθrəpɪst] n Menschenfeind m.

misapprehension ['mɪsæprɪ'henʃən] n Mißverständnis nt; to be under the — that . . . irrtümlicherweise annehmen, daß. . .

misappropriate [mɪsə'prəʊprɪeɪt] vt funds veruntreuen.

misappropriation ['mɪsəprəʊprɪ'eɪʃən] n Veruntreuung f.

misbehave ['mɪsbɪ'heɪv] vi sich schlecht benehmen.

miscalculate ['mɪs'kælkjʊleɪt] vt falsch berechnen.

miscalculation ['mɪskælkjʊ'leɪʃən] n Rechenfehler m.

miscarriage ['mɪskærɪdʒ] n (Med) Fehlgeburt f; — of justice Fehlurteil nt.

miscellaneous [mɪsɪ'leɪnɪəs] a verschieden.

miscellany [mɪ'selənɪ] n (bunte) Sammlung f.

mischance [mɪs'tʃɑːns] n Mißgeschick nt.

6

mischief ['mɪstʃɪf] n Unfug m; (harm) Schaden m.

mischievous a, —ly ad ['mɪstʃɪvəs, -lɪ] person durchtrieben; glance verschmitzt; rumour bösartig.

misconception ['mɪskən'sepʃən] n fälschliche Annahme f.

misconduct [mɪs'kɒndʌkt] n Vergehen nt.

misconstrue ['mɪskən'struː] vt mißverstehen.

miscount ['mɪs'kaunt] vt falsch (be)rechnen.

misdemeanour, (US) misdemeanor [mɪsdɪ'miːnə*] n Vergehen nt.

misdirect ['mɪsdɪ'rekt] vt person irreleiten; letter fehlleiten.

miser ['maɪzə*] n Geizhals m.

miserable ['mɪzərəbl] a (unhappy) unglücklich; headache, weather fürchterlich; (poor) elend; (contemptible) erbärmlich.

miserably ['mɪzərəblɪ] ad unglücklich; fail kläglich.

miserly ['maɪzəlɪ] a geizig.

misery ['mɪzərɪ] n Elend nt, Qual f.

misfire ['mɪs'faɪə*] vi (gun) versagen; (engine) fehlzünden; (plan) fehlgehen.

misfit ['mɪsfɪt] n Außenseiter m.

misfortune [mɪs'fɔːtʃən] n Unglück nt.

misgiving [mɪs'gɪvɪŋ] n (often pl) Befürchtung f, Bedenken pl.

misguided ['mɪs'gaɪdɪd] a fehlgeleitet; opinions irrig.

mishandle [mɪs'hændl] vt falsch handhaben.

mishap ['mɪshæp] n Unglück nt; (slight) Panne f.

mishear ['mɪs'hɪə*] vt irreg mißverstehen.

misinform ['mɪsɪn'fɔːm] vt falsch unterrichten.

misinterpret ['mɪsɪn'tɜːprɪt] vt falsch auffassen; —ation ['mɪsɪntɜːprɪ'teɪʃən] falsche Auslegung f.

misjudge ['mɪs'dʒʌdʒ] vt falsch beurteilen.

mislay ['mɪs'leɪ] vt irreg verlegen.

mislead [mɪs'liːd] vt irreg (deceive) irreführen; —ing a irreführend.

mismanage ['mɪs'mænɪdʒ] vt schlecht verwalten; —ment Mißwirtschaft f.

misnomer ['mɪs'nəumə*] n falsche Bezeichnung f.

misogynist [mɪ'sɒdʒɪnɪst] n Weiberfeind m.

misplace ['mɪs'pleɪs] vt verlegen.

misprint ['mɪsprɪnt] n Druckfehler m.

mispronounce ['mɪsprə'nauns] vt falsch aussprechen.

misread ['mɪs'riːd] vt irreg falsch lesen.

misrepresent ['mɪsreprɪ'zent] vt falsch darstellen.

miss [mɪs] vt (fail to hit, catch) verfehlen; (not notice) verpassen; (be too late) versäumen, verpassen; (omit) auslassen; (regret the absence of) vermissen; I — you du fehlst mir; vi fehlen; n (shot) Fehlschuß m; (failure) Fehlschlag m; (title) Fräulein nt.

missal ['mɪsəl] n Meßbuch nt.

misshapen ['mɪs'ʃeɪpən] a mißgestaltet.

missile ['mɪsaɪl] n Geschoß nt, Rakete f.

missing ['mɪsɪŋ] a person vermißt; thing fehlend; to be — fehlen.

mission ['mɪʃən] n (work) Auftrag m, Mission f; (people) Delegation f; (Rel) Mission f; —**ary** Missionar(in f) m.

misspent ['mɪs'spent] a youth vergeudet.

mist [mɪst] n Dunst m, Nebel m; vi (also — over, — up) sich beschlagen.

mistake [mɪs'teɪk] n Fehler m; vt irreg (misunderstand) mißverstehen; (mix up) verwechseln (for mit); —**n a idea** falsch; —**n identity** Verwechslung f; to be —**n** sich irren.

mister ['mɪstə*] n (abbr Mr) Herr m.

mistletoe ['mɪsltəʊ] n Mistel f.

mistranslation ['mɪstræns'leɪʃən] n falsche Übersetzung f.

mistreat [mɪs'triːt] vt schlecht behandeln.

mistress ['mɪstrɪs] n (teacher) Lehrerin f; (in house) Herrin f; (lover) Geliebte f; (abbr Mrs) Frau f.

mistrust [mɪs'trʌst] vt mißtrauen (+dat).

misty ['mɪstɪ] a neblig.

misunderstand ['mɪsʌndə'stænd] vti irreg mißverstehen, falsch verstehen; —**ing** Mißverständnis nt; (disagreement) Meinungsverschiedenheit f.

misunderstood ['mɪsʌndə'stʊd] a person unverstanden.

misuse ['mɪs'juːs] n falsche(r) Gebrauch m; ['mɪs'juːz] vt falsch gebrauchen.

mite [maɪt] n Milbe f; (fig) bißchen nt.

mitigate ['mɪtɪɡeɪt] vt pain lindern; punishment mildern.

mitre, (US) **miter** ['maɪtə*] n (Eccl) Mitra f.

mitt(en) ['mɪt(n)] n Fausthandschuh m.

mix [mɪks] vt (blend) (ver)mischen; vi (liquids) sich (ver)mischen lassen; (people) (get on) sich vertragen; (associate) Kontakt haben; he —**es well** er ist kontaktfreudig; n (mixture) Mischung f; —**ed a** gemischt; —**er** (for food) Mixer m; —**ture** (assortment) Mischung f; (Med) Saft m; —**up** Durcheinander nt, Verwechslung f; — up vt (mix) verwechseln (confuse); to be —**ed up** in sth in etw (dat) verwickelt sein; —**ed-up a** papers, person durcheinander.

moan [məʊn] n Stöhnen nt; (complaint) Klage f; vi stöhnen; (complain) maulen; —**ing** Stöhnen nt; Gemaule nt.

moat [məʊt] n (Burg)graben · m.

mob [mɒb] n Mob m; (the masses) Pöbel m; vt star herfallen über (+acc).

mobile ['məʊbaɪl] a beweglich; library etc fahrbar; n (decoration) Mobile nt; — home Wohnwagen m.

mobility [məʊ'bɪlɪtɪ] n Beweglichkeit f.

moccasin ['mɒkəsɪn] n Mokassin m.

mock [mɒk] vt verspotten; (defy) trotzen (+dat); a Schein-; —**ery** Spott m; (person) Gespött m; —**ing a tone** spöttisch; —**ing bird** Spottdrossel f; —**up** Modell nt.

mode [məʊd] n (Art f und) Weise f.

model ['mɒdl] n Modell nt; (example) Vorbild nt; (in fashion) Mannequin nt; vt (make) formen, modellieren, bilden; (clothes) vorführen; a *railway* Modell-; *(perfect)* Muster-; vorbildlich; **—ling,** (*US*) **—ing** ['mɒdlɪŋ] (*— making*) Basteln *nt*.

moderate ['mɒdərət] *a* gemäßigt; *(fairly good)* mittelmäßig; *n (Pol)* Gemäßigte(r) *mf*; ['mɒdəreɪt] *vi* sich mäßigen; *vt* mäßigen; **—ly** ['mɒdərətlɪ] *ad* mäßig.

moderation [mɒdə'reɪʃən] *n* Mäßigung *f*; **in —** mit Maßen.

modern ['mɒdən] *a* modern; *history, languages* neuere(r, s); *Greek etc* Neu-; **—ity** [mɒ'dɜːnɪtɪ] Modernität *f*; **—ization** [mɒdənaɪ'zeɪʃən] Modernisierung *f*; **—ize** *vt* modernisieren.

modest *a*, **—ly** *ad* ['mɒdɪst, -lɪ] *attitude* bescheiden; *meal, home* einfach; *(chaste)* schamhaft; **—y** Bescheidenheit *f*; *(chastity)* Schamgefühl *nt*.

modicum ['mɒdɪkəm] *n* bißchen *nt*.

modification [mɒdɪfɪ'keɪʃən] *n* (Ab)änderung *f*.

modify ['mɒdɪfaɪ] *vt* abändern; *(Gram)* modifizieren.

modulation [mɒdju'leɪʃən] *n* Modulation *f*.

module ['mɒdjʊl] *n* (Raum)kapsel *f*.

mohair ['məʊheə*] *n* Mohair *m*; *a* Mohair-.

moist [mɔɪst] *a* feucht; **—en** ['mɔɪsn] *vt* befeuchten; **—ure** Feuchtigkeit *f*; **—urizer** Feuchtigkeitscreme *f*.

molar ['məʊlə*] *n* Backenzahn *m*.

molasses [mə'læsɪz] *npl* Melasse *f*.

mold [məʊld] (*US*) **= mould.**

mole [məʊl] *n (spot)* Leberfleck *m*; *(animal)* Maulwurf *m*; *(pier)* Mole *f*.

molecular [mə'lekjʊlə*] *a* molekular, Molekular-.

molecule ['mɒlɪkjuːl] *n* Molekül *nt*.

molest [məʊ'lest] *vt* belästigen.

mollusc ['mɒləsk] *n* Molluske *f*, Weichtier *nt*.

mollycoddle ['mɒlɪkɒdl] *vt* verhätscheln.

molt [məʊlt] (*US*) **= moult.**

molten ['məʊltən] *a* geschmolzen.

moment ['məʊmənt] *n* Moment *m*, Augenblick *m*; *(importance)* Tragweite *f*; **— of truth** Stunde *f* der Wahrheit; **any —** jeden Augenblick; **—arily** ['məʊmən'teərɪlɪ] *ad* momentan; **—ary** *a* kurz; **—ous** [məʊ'mentəs] *a* folgenschwer; **—um** [məʊ'mentəm] Schwung *m*.

monarch ['mɒnək] *n* Herrscher(in *f*) *m*; **—ist** Monarchist(in *f*) *m*; **—y** Monarchie *f*.

monastery ['mɒnəstrɪ] *n* Kloster *nt*.

monastic [mə'næstɪk] *a* klösterlich, Kloster-.

Monday ['mʌndeɪ] *n* Montag *m*.

monetary ['mʌnɪtərɪ] *a* geldlich, Geld-; *(of currency)* Währungs-, monetär.

money ['mʌnɪ] *n* Geld *nt*; **—ed** *a* vermögend; **—lender** Geldverleiher *m*; **—making** *a* einträglich, lukrativ; *n* Gelderwerb *m*; **— order** Postanweisung *f*.

mongol ['mɒŋgəl] *n (Med)* mongoloide(s) Kind *nt*; *a* mongolisch; *(Med)* mongoloid.

mongoose ['mɒŋguːs] *n* Mungo *m*.

mongrel ['mʌŋgrəl] *n* Promenadenmischung *f*; *a* Misch-.

monitor ['mɒnɪtə*] *n (Sch)* Klassenordner *m*; *(television —)* Monitor *m*; *vt broadcasts* abhören; *(control)* überwachen.

monk 574 **more**

monk [mʌŋk] n Mönch m.
monkey ['mʌŋkɪ] n Affe m; — **nut** Erdnuß f; — **wrench** (Tech) Engländer m, Franzose m.
mono- ['mɒnəʊ] pref Mono-.
monochrome ['mɒnəkrəʊm] a schwarz-weiß.
monocle ['mɒnəkl] n Monokel nt.
monogram ['mɒnəgræm] n Monogramm nt.
monolithic [mɒnəʊ'lɪθɪk] a monolithisch.
monologue ['mɒnəlɒg] n Monolog m.
monopolize [mə'nɒpəlaɪz] vt beherrschen.
monopoly [mə'nɒpəlɪ] n Monopol nt.
monorail ['mɒnəʊreɪl] n Einschienenbahn f.
monosyllabic ['mɒnəʊsɪ'læbɪk] a einsilbig.
monotone ['mɒnətəʊn] n gleichbleibende(r) Ton(fall) m.
monotonous [mə'nɒtənəs] a eintönig, monoton.
monotony [mə'nɒtənɪ] n Eintönigkeit f, Monotonie f.
monseigneur [mɒnsen'jɜ:*],
monsignor [mɒn'si:njə*] n Monsignore m.
monsoon [mɒn'su:n] n Monsun m.
monster ['mɒnstə*] n Ungeheuer nt; (person) Scheusal nt; a (col) Riesen-.
monstrosity [mɒns'trɒsɪtɪ] n Ungeheuerlichkeit f; (thing) Monstrosität f.
monstrous ['mɒnstrəs] a (shocking) gräßlich, ungeheuerlich; (huge) riesig.
montage [mɒn'tɑ:ʒ] n Montage f.
month [mʌnθ] n Monat m; —**ly** a monatlich, Monats-; ad einmal im

Monat; n (magazine) Monatsschrift f.
monument ['mɒnjumənt] n Denkmal nt; —**al** [mɒnju'mentl] a (huge) gewaltig; ignorance ungeheuer.
moo [mu:] vi muhen.
mood [mu:d] n Stimmung f, Laune f; to be in the — for aufgelegt sein zu; I am not in the — for laughing mir ist nicht zum Lachen zumute; —**ily** ad launisch; —**iness** Launenhaftigkeit f; —**y** a launisch.
moon [mu:n] n Mond m; —**beam** Mondstrahl m; —**less** a mondlos; —**light** Mondlicht nt; —**lit** a mondhell; —**shot** Mondflug m.
moor [mʊə*] n Heide f, Hochmoor nt; vt ship festmachen, verankern; vi anlegen; —**ings** pl Liegeplatz m; —**land** Heidemoor nt.
moose [mu:s] n Elch m.
moot [mu:t] vt aufwerfen; a: — **point** strittige(r) Punkt m.
mop [mɒp] n Mop m; vt (auf)wischen; — of hair Mähne f.
mope [məʊp] vi Trübsal blasen.
moped ['məʊped] n (Brit) Moped nt.
moping ['məʊpɪŋ] a trübselig.
moquette [mə'ket] n Plüschgewebe nt.
moral ['mɒrəl] a moralisch; values sittlich; (virtuous) tugendhaft; n Moral f; —**s** pl Moral f; —**e** [mɒ'rɑ:l] Moral f, Stimmung f; —**ity** [mə'rælɪtɪ] Sittlichkeit f; —**ly** ad moralisch.
morass [mə'ræs] n Sumpf m.
morbid ['mɔ:bɪd] a morbid, krankhaft; jokes makaber.
more [mɔ:*] a, n, pron, ad mehr; — or less mehr oder weniger; — than ever mehr denn je; a few —

noch ein paar; — beautiful schöner; —over ad überdies.

morgue [mɔːg] n Leichenschauhaus nt.

moribund ['mɒrɪbʌnd] a aussterbend.

morning ['mɔːnɪŋ] n Morgen m; a morgendlich, Morgen-, Früh-; in the — am Morgen; —sickness (Schwangerschafts)erbrechen nt.

moron ['mɔːrɒn] n Schwachsinnige(r) m; —ic [mə'rɒnɪk] a schwachsinnig.

morose [mə'rəʊs] a mürrisch.

morphine ['mɔːfiːn] n Morphium nt.

Morse [mɔːs] n (also — code) Morsealphabet nt.

morsel ['mɔːsl] n Stückchen t, bißchen nt.

mortal ['mɔːtl] a sterblich; (deadly) tödlich; (very great) Todes-; (human being) Sterbliche(r) mf; —ity [mɔː'tælɪtɪ] n Sterblichkeit f; (death rate) Sterblichkeitsziffer f; —ly ad tödlich.

mortar ['mɔːtə*] n (for building) Mörtel m; (bowl) Mörser m; (Mil) Granatwerfer m.

mortgage ['mɔːgɪdʒ] n Hypothek f; vt eine Hypothek aufnehmen (+acc).

mortification [mɔːtɪfɪ'keɪʃən] n Beschämung f.

mortified ['mɔːtɪfaɪd] a: I was — es war mir schrecklich peinlich.

mortuary ['mɔːtjʊərɪ] n Leichenhalle f.

mosaic [məʊ'zeɪk] n Mosaik nt.

mosque [mɒsk] n Moschee f.

mosquito [mɒs'kiːtəʊ] n Moskito m.

moss [mɒs] n Moos nt; —y a bemoost.

most [məʊst] a meiste(r, s); — men die meisten Männer; ad am meisten; (very) höchst; n das meiste, der größte Teil; (people) die meisten; — of the time meistens, die meiste Zeit; — of the winter fast den ganzen Winter über; the — beautiful der/die/das Schönste; at the (very) — allerhöchstens; to make the — of das Beste machen aus; —ly ad größtenteils.

motel ['məʊ'tel] n Motel nt.

moth [mɒθ] n Nachtfalter m; (wool-eating) Motte f; —ball Mottenkugel f; —eaten a mottenzerfressen.

mother ['mʌðə*] n Mutter f; vt bemuttern; a tongue Mutter-; —country Heimat-; —hood Mutterschaft f; —in-law Schwiegermutter f; —ly a mütterlich; —to-be werdende Mutter f.

mothproof ['mɒθpruːf] a mottenfest.

motif [məʊ'tiːf] n Motiv nt.

motion ['məʊʃən] n Bewegung f; (in meeting) Antrag m; vti winken (+dat), zu verstehen geben (+dat); —less a regungslos; —picture Film m.

motivated ['məʊtɪveɪtɪd] a motiviert.

motivation [məʊtɪ'veɪʃən] n Motivierung f.

motive ['məʊtɪv] n Motiv nt, Beweggrund m; a treibend.

motley ['mɒtlɪ] a bunt.

motor ['məʊtə*] n Motor m; (car) Auto nt; vi (im Auto) fahren; a Motor-; —bike Motorrad nt; —boat Motorboot nt; —car Auto nt; —cycle Motorrad nt; —cyclist Motorradfahrer(in f) m; —ing n Autofahren nt; a Auto-; —ist ['məʊtərɪst] Autofahrer(in f) m; —

oil Motorenöl *nt;* — **racing** Autorennen *nt;* — **scooter** Motorroller *m;* — **vehicle** Kraftfahrzeug *nt;* —**way** (Brit) Autobahn *f.*

mottled ['mɒtld] *a* gesprenkelt.

motto ['mɒtəʊ] *n* Motto *nt,* Wahlspruch *m.*

mould [məʊld] *n* Form *f;* (mildew) Schimmel *m; vt* (lit, fig) formen; —**er** *vi* (decay) vermodern; —**ing** Formen *nt;* —**y** *a* schimmelig.

moult [məʊlt] *vi* sich mausern.

mound [maʊnd] *n* (Erd)hügel *m.*

mount [maʊnt] *n* (liter: hill) Berg *m;* (horse) Pferd *nt;* (for jewel etc) Fassung *f; vt* horse steigen auf (+acc); (put in setting) fassen; exhibition veranstalten; attack unternehmen; *vi* (also — **up**) sich häufen; (on horse) aufsitzen; —**ain** ['maʊntɪn] Berg *m;* —**aineer** [maʊntɪ'nɪə*] Bergsteiger(in *f) m;* —**aineering** Bergsteigen *nt;* to go —**aineering** klettern gehen; —**ainous** *a* bergig; —**ainside** Berg(ab)hang *m.*

mourn [mɔːn] *vt* betrauern, beklagen; *vi* trauern (for um); —**er** Trauernde(r) *mf;* —**ful** *a* traurig; —**ing** (grief) Trauer *f;* in —**ing** (period etc) in Trauer; (dress) in Trauerkleidung *f.*

mouse [maʊs] *n, pl* mice Maus *f;* —**trap** Mausefalle *f.*

moustache [məs'tɑːʃ] *n* Schnurrbart *m.*

mousy ['maʊsɪ] *a colour* mausgrau; *person* schüchtern.

mouth [maʊθ] *n* (in man) Mund *m;* (general) Öffnung *f;* (of river) Mündung *f;* (of harbour) Einfahrt *f;* [maʊð] *vt* words affektiert sprechen; **down in the** — niedergeschlagen; —**ful** Mundvoll *m;* — **organ** Mundharmonika *f;* —**piece** (lit) Mund-

stück *nt;* (fig) Sprachrohr *nt;* —**wash** Mundwasser *nt;* —**watering** *a* lecker, appetitlich.

movable ['muːvəbl] *a* beweglich.

move [muːv] *n* (movement) Bewegung *f;* (in game) Zug *m;* (step) Schritt *m;* (of house) Umzug *m; vt* bewegen; object rücken; people transportieren; (in job) versetzen; (emotionally) bewegen, ergreifen; **to** — **sb to do sth** jdn veranlassen, etw zu tun; *vi* sich bewegen; (change place) gehen; (vehicle, ship) fahren; (take action) etwas unternehmen; (go to another house) umziehen; **to get a** — **on** sich beeilen; **on the** — in Bewegung; **to** — **house** umziehen; **to** — **closer to** *or* **towards sth** sich etw (dat) nähern; — **about** *vi* sich hin- und herbewegen; (travel) unterwegs sein; — **away** *vi* weggehen; — **back** *vi* zurückgehen; (to the rear) zurückweichen; — **forward** *vi* vorwärtsgehen, sich vorwärtsbewegen; *vt* vorschieben; time vorverlegen; — **in** *vi* (to house) einziehen; (troops) einrücken; — **on** *vi* weitergehen; *vt* weitergehen lassen; — **out** *vi* (of house) ausziehen; (troops) abziehen; — **up** *vi* aufsteigen; (in job) befördert werden; *vt* nach oben bewegen; (in job) befördern; (Sch) versetzen; —**ment** Bewegung *f;* (Mus) Satz *m;* (of clock) Uhrwerk *nt.*

movie ['muːvɪ] *n* Film *m;* **the** —**s** (the cinema) das Kino; — **camera** Filmkamera *f.*

moving ['muːvɪŋ] *a* beweglich; force treibend; (touching) ergreifend.

mow [məʊ] *vt irreg* mähen; — **down** *vt* (fig) niedermähen; —**er**

(machine) Mähmaschine *f;* *(lawn—)* Rasenmäher *m.*

Mr ['mɪstə*] Herr *m.*

Mrs ['mɪsɪz] Frau *f.*

Ms [mɪz] n Frau *f.*

much [mʌtʃ] *a* viel; *ad* sehr; viel; *n* viel, eine Menge *f;* — better viel besser; — the same size so ziemlich gleich groß; how —? wieviel?; too — zuviel; — to my surprise zu meiner großen Überraschung; — as I should like to so gern ich möchte.

muck [mʌk] *n (lit)* Mist *m; (fig)* Schmutz *m;* — about *(col)* vi herumlungern; *(meddle)* herumalbern *(with an +dat);* vt — sb about mit jdm treiben, was man will; — up vt *(col: ruin)* vermasseln; *(dirty)* dreckig machen; —y *a (dirty)* dreckig.

mucus ['mjuːkəs] *n* Schleim *m.*

mud [mʌd] *n* Schlamm *m; (fig)* Schmutz *m.*

muddle ['mʌdl] *n* Durcheinander *nt;* vt *(also — up)* durcheinanderbringen; — through vi sich durchwursteln.

muddy ['mʌdɪ] *a* schlammig.

mudguard ['mʌdgɑːd] *n* Schutzblech *nt.*

mudpack ['mʌdpæk] *n* Moorpackung *f.*

mud-slinging ['mʌdslɪŋɪŋ] *n (col)* Verleumdung *f.*

muff [mʌf] *n* Muff *m.*

muffin ['mʌfɪn] *n* süße(s) Teilchen *nt.*

muffle ['mʌfl] vt *sound* dämpfen; *(wrap up)* einhüllen.

mufti ['mʌftɪ] *n:* in — in Zivil.

mug [mʌg] *n (cup)* Becher *m; (col: face)* Visage *f; (col: fool)* Trottel

m; vt überfallen und ausrauben; —ging Überfall *m.*

muggy ['mʌgɪ] *a weather* schwül.

mulatto [mjuːˈlætəu] *n* Mulatte *m,* Mulattin *f.*

mule [mjuːl] *n* Maulesel *m.*

mull [mʌl]: — over vt nachdenken über *(+acc).*

mulled [mʌld] *a wine* Glüh-.

multi- ['mʌltɪ] *pref* Multi-, multi-.

multicoloured, (US) **multicolored** ['mʌltɪˈkʌləd] *a* mehrfarbig.

multifarious [mʌltɪˈfɛərɪəs] *a* mannigfaltig.

multilateral ['mʌltɪˈlætərəl] *a* multilateral.

multiple ['mʌltɪpl] *.n* Vielfache(s) *nt; a* mehrfach; *(many)* mehrere; — sclerosis multiple Sklerose *f;* — store Kaufhauskette *f.*

multiplication [mʌltɪplɪˈkeɪʃən] *n* Multiplikation *f.*

multiply ['mʌltɪplaɪ] vt multiplizieren *(by* mit); vi *(Biol)* sich vermehren.

multiracial ['mʌltɪˈreɪʃəl] *a* gemischtrassig; — policy Rassenintegration *f.*

multitude ['mʌltɪtjuːd] *n* Menge *f.*

mum¹ [mʌm] *a:* to keep — den Mund halten *(about* über *+acc).*

mum² [mʌm] *n (col)* Mutti *f.*

mumble ['mʌmbl] vti murmeln; *n* Gemurmel *nt.*

mummy ['mʌmɪ] *n (dead body)* Mumie *f; (col)* Mami *f.*

mumps [mʌmps] *n* Mumps *m.*

munch [mʌntʃ] vti mampfen.

mundane ['mʌnˈdeɪn] *a* weltlich; *(fig)* profan.

municipal [mjuːˈnɪsɪpəl] *a* städtisch, Stadt-; —ity

[mju:nɪsɪ'pælɪtɪ] Stadt f mit Selbstverwaltung.

munificence [mju:'nɪfɪsns] n
Freigebigkeit f.

munitions [mju:'nɪʃənz] npl
Munition f.

mural ['mjʊərəl] n Wandgemälde nt.

murder ['mɜ:də*] n Mord m; it was
— (fig) es war möderisch; **to get
away with** — (fig) sich alles
erlauben können; vt ermorden;
—er Mörder m; **—ess** Mörderin f;
—ous a Mord-; (fig) mörderisch.

murk [mɜ:k] n Dunkelheit f —y a
finster.

murmur ['mɜ:mə*] n Murmeln nt;
(of water, wind) Rauschen nt; **without a** — ohne zu murren; vti
murmeln.

muscle ['mʌsl] n Muskel m.

muscular ['mʌskjʊlə*] a Muskel-;
(strong) muskulös.

muse [mju:z] vi (nach)sinnen; **M—**
Muse f.

museum [mju:'zɪəm] n Museum nt.

mushroom ['mʌʃru:m] n
Champignon m; Pilz m; vi (fig)
emporschießen.

mushy [mʌʃɪ] a breiig; (sentimental) gefühlsduselig.

music ['mju:zɪk] n Musik f;
(printed) Noten pl; **—al** a sound
melodisch; person musikalisch; n
(show) Musical m; **—al box** Spiel-
dose f; **—al instrument** Musik-
instrument nt; **—ally** ad
musikalisch; sing melodisch; **—
hall** (Brit) Varieté nt; **—ian**
[mju:'zɪʃən] Musiker(in f) m.

muslin ['mʌzlɪn] n Musselin m.

mussel ['mʌsl] n Miesmuschel f.

must [mʌst] v aux müssen; (in
negation) dürfen; in Muß nt; **the**

film is a — den Film muß man einfach gesehen haben.

mustache ['mʌstæʃ] (US) =
moustache.

mustard ['mʌstəd] n Senf m.

muster ['mʌstə*] vt (Mil) antreten
lassen; courage zusammennehmen.

mustiness ['mʌstɪnəs] n Muffigkeit
f.

mustn't ['mʌsnt] = must not.

musty ['mʌstɪ] a muffig.

mute [mju:t] a stumm; n (person)
Stumme(r) mf; (Mus) Dämpfer m.

mutilate ['mju:tɪleɪt] vt verstümmeln.

mutilation [mju:tɪ'leɪʃən] n Ver-
stümmelung f.

mutinous ['mju:tɪnəs] a meuterisch.

mutiny ['mju:tɪnɪ] n Meuterei f; vi
meutern.

mutter ['mʌtə*] vti murmeln.

mutton ['mʌtn] n Hammelfleisch nt.

mutual ['mju:tjʊəl] a gegenseitig;
beiderseitig; **—ly** ad gegenseitig;
auf beiden Seiten; für beide Seiten.

muzzle ['mʌzl] n (of animal)
Schnauze f; (for animal) Maulkorb
m; (of gun) Mündung f; vt einen
Maulkorb anlegen (+dat).

my [maɪ] poss a mein.

myopic [maɪ'ɒpɪk] a kurzsichtig.

myrrh [mɜ:*] n Myrrhe f.

myself [maɪ'self] pron mich (acc);
mir (dat); (emphatic) selbst; **I'm
not** — mit mir ist etwas nicht in
Ordnung.

mysterious [mɪs'tɪərɪəs] a
geheimnisvoll, mysteriös; **—ly** ad
auf unerklärliche Weise.

mystery ['mɪstərɪ] n (secret)
Geheimnis nt; (sth difficult) Rätsel
nt; — **play** Mysterienspiel nt.

mystic ['mɪstɪk] n Mystiker m; a

mystisch; **—al** a mystisch; **—ism** ['mɪstɪsɪzəm] Mystizismus m.

mystification [mɪstɪfɪ'keɪʃən] n Verblüffung f.

mystify ['mɪstɪfaɪ] vt ein Rätsel sein (+dat); verblüffen.

mystique [mɪs'tiːk] n geheimnisvolle Natur f.

myth [mɪθ] n Mythos m; (fig) Erfindung f; **—ical** a mythisch, Sagen-; **—ological** [mɪθə'lɒdʒɪkəl] a mythologisch; **—ology** [mɪ'θɒlədʒɪ] Mythologie f.

N

N, n [en] n N nt, n nt.
nab [næb] vt (col) schnappen.
nadir ['neɪdɪə*] n Tiefpunkt m.
nag [næg] n (horse) Gaul m; (person) Nörgler(in f) m; vti herumnörgeln (sb an jdm); **—ging** a doubt nagend; n Nörgelei f.
nail [neɪl] n Nagel m; vt nageln; **— down** vt (lit, fig) festnageln; **—brush** Nagelbürste f; **—file** Nagelfeile f; **— polish** Nagellack m; **— scissors** pl Nagelschere f.
naive a, **—ly** ad [naɪ'iːv, -lɪ] naiv.
naked ['neɪkɪd] a nackt; **—ness** Nacktheit f.
name [neɪm] n Name m; (reputation) Ruf m; vt nennen; (fix new benennen; (appoint) ernennen; what's your —? wie heißen Sie?; **in the — of** im Namen (+gen); (for the sake of) um (+gen) willen; **—dropping:** he's always — dropping er wirft immer mit großen Namen um sich; **—less** a namenlos; **—ly** ad nämlich; **—sake** Namensvetter m.
nanny ['nænɪ] n Kindermädchen nt.
nap [næp] n (sleep) Nickerchen nt; (on cloth) Strich m; **to have a —** ein Nickerchen machen.
napalm ['neɪpɑːm] n Napalm nt.
nape [neɪp] n Nacken m.
napkin ['næpkɪn] n (at table)

Serviette f; (Brit: for baby) Windel f.
nappy ['næpɪ] n (Brit: for baby) Windel f.
narcissism [naː'sɪsɪzəm] n Narzißmus m.
narcotic [naː'kɒtɪk] n Betäubungsmittel nt.
narrate [nə'reɪt] vt erzählen.
narration [nə'reɪʃən] n Erzählung f.
narrative ['nærətɪv] n Erzählung f; a erzählend.
narrator [nə'reɪtə*] n Erzähler(in f) m.
narrow ['nærəʊ] a eng, schmal; (limited) beschränkt; vi sich verengen; **to — sth down to sth** etw auf etw (acc) einschränken; **—ly** ad miss knapp; escape mit knapper Not; **—-minded** a engstirnig; **—-mindedness** Engstirnigkeit f.
nasal ['neɪzəl] a Nasal-.
nastily ['naːstɪlɪ] ad böse, schlimm.
nastiness ['naːstɪnəs] n Ekligkeit f.
nasty ['naːstɪ] a ekelhaft, fies; business, wound schlimm; **to turn —** gemein werden.
nation ['neɪʃən] n Nation f, Volk nt; **—al** ['næʃənl] a national, National-, Landes-; n Staatsangehörige(r) mf; **—al anthem**

Nationalhymne f; —alism
['næʃnəlɪzəm] Nationalismus m;
—alist ['næʃnəlɪst] n Nationalist(in
f) m; a nationalistisch;&—ality
[næʃə'nælɪtɪ] Staatsangehörigkeit f,
Nationalität f; —alization
[næʃnəlaɪ'zeɪʃən] Verstaatlichung
f; —alize ['næʃnəlaɪz] vt verstaatlichen; —ally ['næʃnəlɪ] ad
national, auf Staatsebene; —wide
a, ad allgemein, landesweite.

native ['neɪtɪv] n (born in) Ein-
heimische(r) mf; (original inhabitant) Eingeborene(r) mf; a (coming
from a certain place) einheimisch;
(of the original inhabitants) ein-
geborenen-; (belonging by birth)
heimatlich, Heimat-; (inborn) angeboren, natürlich; a — of Germany
ein gebürtiger Deutscher; — language Muttersprache f.

natter ['nætə*] vi (col: chat)
quatschen; n Gequatsche nt.

natural ['nætʃrəl] a natürlich;
Natur-; (inborn) (an)geboren; —ist
n Naturkundler(in f) m; —ize vt
foreigner einbürgen, naturali-
sieren; plant etc einführen; —ly ad
natürlich; —ness Natürlichkeit f.

nature ['neɪtʃə*] n Natur f; by —
von Natur (aus).

naught [nɔːt] n Null f.

naughtily ['nɔːtɪlɪ] ad unartig.

naughtiness ['nɔːtɪnəs] n Unartig-
keit f.

naughty ['nɔːtɪ] a child unartig, ungezogen; action ungehörig.

nausea ['nɔːsɪə] n (sickness) Übelkeit f; (disgust) Ekel m; —te
['nɔːsɪeɪt] vt anekeln.

nauseating ['nɔːsɪeɪtɪŋ] a ekeler-
regend; job widerlich.

nautical ['nɔːtɪkəl] a nautisch;
See-; expression seemännisch.

naval ['neɪvəl] a Marine-, Flotten-.

nave [neɪv] n Kirchen(haupt)schiff
nt.

navel ['neɪvəl] n Nabel m.

navigable ['nævɪgəbl] a schiffbar.

navigate ['nævɪgeɪt] vt ship etc
steuern; vi (sail) (zu Schiff) fahren.

navigation [nævɪ'geɪʃən] n
Navigation f.

navigator ['nævɪgeɪtə*] n Steuermann m; (explorer) Seefahrer m;
(Aviat) Navigator m; (Aut) Bei-
fahrer(in f) m.

navvy ['nævɪ] n Straßenarbeiter m;
(on railway) Streckenarbeiter m.

navy ['neɪvɪ] n Marine f, Flotte f;
(warships etc) (Kriegs)flotte f; —
blue Marineblau nt; a marineblau.

nay [neɪ] ad (old) (no) nein; (even)
ja sogar.

neap [niːp] a: — tide Nippflut f.

near [nɪə*] a nah; the holidays are
— es sind bald Ferien; ad in der
Nähe; to come —er näher
kommen; (time) näher rücken;
prep (also — to) (space) in der
Nähe (+gen); (time) um (+acc) ...
herum; vi sich nähern (+dat); —
at hand weit weg; —by a
nahe (gelegen); ad in der Nähe;
—ly ad fast; a — miss knapp
daneben; —ness Nähe f; —side
(Aut) Fahrerseite f; a auf der Bei-
fahrerseite; a — thing knapp.

neat a, —ly ad ['niːt, -lɪ] (tidy)
ordentlich; (clever) treffend; solution sauber; (pure) unverdünnt,
rein; —ness Ordentlichkeit f,
Sauberkeit f.

nebulous ['nebjuləs] a nebelhaft,
verschwommen.

necessarily ['nesɪsərɪlɪ] ad
unbedingt; notwendigerweise.

necessary ['nesɪsərɪ] a notwendig,
nötig.

necessitate [nɪ'sesɪteɪt] vt erforderlich machen.

necessity [nɪ'sesɪtɪ] n (need) Not f; (compulsion) Notwendigkeit f; in case of — im Notfall; necessities of life Bedürfnisse pl des Lebens.

neck [nek] n Hals m; — and — Kopf an Kopf; —lace ['neklɪs] Halskette f; —line Ausschnitt m; —tie (US) Krawatte f.

nectar ['nektə*] n Nektar m.

née [neɪ] a geborene.

need [niːd] n Bedarf m no pl (for an +dat); Bedürfnis nt (for für); (want) Mangel m; (necessity) Notwendigkeit f; (poverty) Not f; vt brauchen; to — to do tun müssen; if — be wenn nötig; to be in — of brauchen; there is no — for you to come du brauchst nicht zu kommen; there's no — es ist nicht nötig.

needle ['niːdl] n Nadel f.

needless a, —ly ad ['niːdlɪs, -lɪ] unnötig.

needlework ['niːdlwɜːk] n Handarbeit f.

needy ['niːdɪ] a bedürftig.

negation [nɪ'geɪʃən] n Verneinung f.

negative ['negətɪv] n (Phot) Negativ nt; a negativ; answer abschlägig.

neglect [nɪ'glekt] vt (leave undone) versäumen; (take no care of) vernachlässigen; n Vernachlässigung f.

negligée ['neglɪʒeɪ] n Negligé nt.

negligence ['neglɪdʒəns] n Nachlässigkeit f.

negligent a, —ly ad ['neglɪdʒənt, -lɪ] nachlässig, unachtsam.

negligible ['neglɪdʒəbl] a unbedeutend, geringfügig.

negotiable [nɪ'gəʊʃɪəbl] a cheque übertragbar, einlösbar.

negotiate [nɪ'gəʊʃɪeɪt] vi verhandeln; vt treaty abschließen, aushandeln; difficulty überwinden; corner nehmen.

negotiation [nɪgəʊʃɪ'eɪʃən] n Verhandlung f.

negotiator [nɪ'gəʊʃɪeɪtə*] n Unterhändler m.

Negress ['niːgres] n Negerin f.

Negro ['niːgrəʊ] n Neger m; a Neger-.

neighbour, (US) **neighbor** ['neɪbə*] n Nachbar(in f) m; —hood Nachbarschaft f; Umgebung f; —ing a benachbart, angrenzend; —ly a freundlich.

neither ['naɪðə*] a, pron keine(r, s) (von beiden); cj weder; he can't do it, and — can I er kann es nicht und ich auch nicht.

neo- ['niːəʊ] pref neo-.

neon ['niːɒn] n Neon nt; — light Neonlicht nt.

nephew ['nefjuː] n Neffe m.

nerve [nɜːv] n Nerv m; (courage) Mut m; (impudence) Frechheit f; —racking a nervenaufreibend.

nervous ['nɜːvəs] a (of the nerves) Nerven-; (timid) nervös, ängstlich; — breakdown Nervenzusammenbruch m; —ly ad nervös; —ness Nervosität f.

nest [nest] n Nest nt.

nestle ['nesl] vi sich kuscheln; (village) sich schmiegen.

net [net] n Netz nt; a: —(t) netto, Netto-, Rein-; —ball Netzball m.

netting ['netɪŋ] n Netz(werk) nt, Drahtgeflecht nt.

network ['netwɜːk] n Netz nt.

neurosis [njʊə'rəʊsɪs] n Neurose f.

neurotic [njuəˈrɒtɪk] a neurotisch;
n Neurotiker(in f) m.
neuter [ˈnjuːtə*] a (Biol)
geschlechtslos; (Gram) sächlich; n
(Biol) kastrierte(s) Tier nt; (Gram)
Neutrum nt.
neutral [ˈnjuːtrəl] a neutral; **—ity**
[njuːˈtrælɪtɪ] Neutralität f.
never [ˈnevə*] ad nie(mals); **well I
— na so was!; —ending a endlos;
—theless** [nevəðəˈles] ad trotzdem,
dennoch.
new [njuː] a neu; **they are still —
to the work** die Arbeit ist ihnen
noch neu; **— from** frisch aus or
von; **—born** a neugeboren;
—comer Neuankömmling m; **—ly**
ad frisch, neu; **— moon** Neumond
m; **—ness** Neuheit f.
news [njuːz] n Nachricht f; (Rad,
TV) Nachrichten pl; **—agent**
Zeitungshändler m; **— flash** Kurzmeldung f; **—letter** Rundschreiben
nt; **—paper** Zeitung f; **—reel**
Wochenschau f.
New Year [njuːˈjɪə*] n Neujahr
nt; **—'s Day** Neujahrstag m; **—'s
Eve** Silvester(abend m) nt.
next [nekst] a nächste(r, s); ad
(after) dann, darauf; (next time)
das nächstemal; prep: — to
(gleich) neben (+dat); **— to nothing** so gut wie nichts; **to do sth
— etw als nächstes tun; what — !
was denn noch (alles)?; the — day
am nächsten or folgenden Tag; **—
door** nt nebenan; **— year** nächstes
Jahr; **— of kin** Familienange-
hörige(r) mf.
nib [nɪb] n Spitze f.
nibble [ˈnɪbl] vt knabbern an (+dat).
nice [naɪs] a hübsch, nett, schön;
(subtle) fein; **—looking** a hübsch,
gutaussehend; **—ly** ad gut, fein,
nett.

nick [nɪk] n Einkerbung f; **in the
— of time** gerade rechtzeitig.
nickel [ˈnɪkl] n Nickel nt; (US)
Nickel m (5 cents).
nickname [ˈnɪkneɪm] n Spitzname
m.
nicotine [ˈnɪkətiːn] n Nikotin nt.
niece [niːs] n Nichte f.
niggardly [ˈnɪgədlɪ] a schäbig;
person: geizig.
niggling [ˈnɪglɪŋ] a pedantisch;
doubt, worry: quälend; detail:
kleinlich.
night [naɪt] n Nacht f; (evening)
Abend m; **good —!** gute Nacht!;
at or **by — nachts; abends; —cap**
(drink) Schlummertrunk m; **—club**
Nachtlokal nt; **—dress** Nachthemd
nt; **—fall** Einbruch m der Nacht;
—ie (col) Nachthemd nt; **—ingale**
Nachtigall f; **— life** Nachtleben nt;
—ly a, ad jeden Abend; jede
Nacht; **—mare** Alptraum m; **—
school** Abendschule f; **—time**
Nacht f; **at — time** nachts; **—
watchman** Nachtwächter m.
nil [nɪl] n Nichts nt, Null f (also
Sport).
nimble [ˈnɪmbl] a behend(e), flink;
mind: beweglich.
nimbly [ˈnɪmblɪ] ad flink.
nine [naɪn] a Neun f; a neun;
—teen a Neunzehn f; a neunzehn;
—ty n Neunzig f; a neunzig.
ninth [naɪnθ] a neunte(r, s); n
Neuntel nt.
nip [nɪp] vt kneifen; n Kneifen nt.
nipple [ˈnɪpl] n Brustwarze f.
nippy [ˈnɪpɪ] a (col) person: flink;
car: flott; (cold) frisch.
nit [nɪt] n Nisse f.
nitrogen [ˈnaɪtrədʒən] n Stickstoff
m.

no [nəʊ] a -kein; ad nein; n Nein nt; — further nicht weiter; — more time keine Zeit mehr; in — time schnell.

nobility [nəʊˈbɪlɪtɪ] n Adel m; the — of this deed diese edle Tat.

noble [ˈnəʊbl] a rank adlig; (splendid) nobel, edel; n Adlige(r) mf; —man Edelmann m, Adlige(r) m.

nobly [ˈnəʊblɪ] ad edel, großmütig.

nobody [ˈnəʊbədɪ] pron niemand, keiner; n Niemand m.

nod [nɒd] vi nicken; — off einnicken; n Nicken nt.

noise [nɔɪz] n (sound) Geräusch nt; (unpleasant, loud) Lärm m.

noisily [ˈnɔɪzɪlɪ] ad lärmend, laut.

noisy [ˈnɔɪzɪ] a laut; crowd lärmend.

nomad [ˈnəʊmæd] n Nomade m; —ic [nəʊˈmædɪk] a nomadisch.

no-man's land [ˈnəʊmænzlænd] n (lit, fig) Niemandsland nt.

nominal [ˈnɒmɪnl] a nominell; (Gram) Nominal-.

nominate [ˈnɒmɪneɪt] vt (suggest) vorschlagen; (in election) aufstellen; (appoint) ernennen.

nomination [nɒmɪˈneɪʃən] n (election) Nominierung f; (appointment) Ernennung f.

nominee [nɒmɪˈniː] n Kandidat(in f) m.

non- [nɒn] pref Nicht-, un-; —alcoholic a alkoholfrei.

nonchalant [ˈnɒnʃələnt] a lässig.

nondescript [ˈnɒndɪskrɪpt] a mittelmäßig.

none [nʌn] a, pron kein(e, r, s); ad: — the wiser keineswegs klüger; — of your cheek! sei nicht so frech!

nonentity [nɒˈnentɪtɪ] n Null f (col).

nonetheless [ˈnʌnðəˈles] ad nichtsdestoweniger.

non-fiction [ˈnɒnˈfɪkʃən] n Sachbücher pl.

nonplussed [ˈnɒnˈplʌst] a verdutzt.

nonsense [ˈnɒnsəns] n Unsinn m.

non-stop [ˈnɒnˈstɒp] a pausenlos, Nonstop-.

noodles [ˈnuːdlz] npl Nudeln pl.

nook [nʊk] n Winkel m, Eckchen nt.

noon [nuːn] n (12 Uhr) Mittag m.

no one [ˈnəʊwʌn] pron = **nobody**.

noose [nuːs] n Schlinge f.

norm [nɔːm] n Norm f, Regel f.

normal [ˈnɔːməl] a normal; —ly ad normal; (usually) normalerweise.

north [nɔːθ] n Norden m; a nördlich, Nord-; ad nördlich, nach or im Norden; —east Nordosten m; —ern [ˈnɔːðən] a nördlich, Nord-; —ward(s) ad nach Norden; —west Nordwesten m.

nose [nəʊz] n Nase f; —bleed Nasenbluten nt; —dive Sturzflug m; —y a neugierig.

nostalgia [nɒsˈtældʒɪə] n Sehnsucht f, Nostalgie f.

nostalgic [nɒsˈtældʒɪk] a wehmütig, nostalgisch.

nostril [ˈnɒstrɪl] n Nasenloch nt; (of animal) Nüster f.

not [nɒt] ad nicht; he is — an expert er ist kein Experte; — at all keineswegs; (don't mention it) gern geschehen.

notable [ˈnəʊtəbl] a bemerkenswert.

notably [ˈnəʊtəblɪ] ad (especially) besonders; (noticeably) bemerkenswert.

notch [nɒtʃ] n Kerbe f, Einschnitt m.

note [nəʊt] n (Mus) Note f, Ton m; (short letter) Nachricht f; (Pol) Note f; (comment, attention) Notiz f; (of lecture etc) Aufzeichnung f;

(bank—) Schein *m*; *(fame)* Ruf *m*, Ansehen *nt*; *vt (observe)* bemerken; *(write down)* notieren; **to take —** s of sich Notizen machen über (+*acc*); **—book** Notizbuch *nt*; **—case** Brieftasche *f*; **—d** a bekannt; **—paper** Briefpapier *nt*.

nothing ['nʌθɪŋ] *n* nichts; for — umsonst; it is — **to me** es bedeutet mir nichts.

notice ['nəʊtɪs] *n (announcement)* Anzeige *f*, Bekanntmachung *f*; *(attention)* Beachtung *f*; *(warning)* Ankündigung *f*; *(dismissal)* Kündigung *f*; *vt* bemerken; **to take — of** beachten; **to bring sth to sb's —** jdn auf etw (acc) aufmerksam machen; **take no —!** kümmere dich nicht darum!; **—able** a merklich; **— board** Anschlagtafel *f*.

notification [nəʊtɪfɪ'keɪʃən] *n* Benachrichtigung *f*.

notify ['nəʊtɪfaɪ] *vt* benachrichtigen.

notion ['nəʊʃən] *n (idea)* Vorstellung *f*, Idee *f*; *(fancy)* Lust *f*.

notorious [nəʊ'tɔːrɪəs] a berüchtigt.

notwithstanding [nɒtwɪθ'stændɪŋ] *ad* trotzdem; *prep* trotz.

nougat ['nuːgɑː] *n* weiße(r) Nougat *m*.

nought [nɔːt] *n* Null *f*.

noun [naʊn] *n* Hauptwort *nt*, Substantiv *nt*.

nourish ['nʌrɪʃ] *vt* nähren; **—ing** a nahrhaft; **—ment** Nahrung *f*.

novel ['nɒvəl] *n* Roman *m*; a neu(artig); **—ist** Schriftsteller(in *f*) *m*; **—ty** Neuheit *f*.

November [nəʊ'vembə*] *n* November *m*.

novice ['nɒvɪs] *n* Neuling *m*; *(Eccl)* Novize *m*.

now [naʊ] *ad* jetzt; **right —** jetzt, gerade; **do it right —** tun Sie es sofort; **— and then, — and again**

ab und zu, manchmal; **—, —** na, na; **— ... —** or then bald ... bald, mal ... mal; **—adays** ad heutzutage.

nowhere ['nəʊwɛə*] *ad* nirgends.

nozzle ['nɒzl] *n* Düse *f*.

nuance ['njuːɑːns] *n* Nuance *f*.

nuclear ['njuːklɪə*] a *energy etc* Atom-, Kern-.

nucleus ['njuːklɪəs] *n* Kern *m*.

nude [njuːd] a nackt; *n (person)* Nackte(r) *mf*; *(Art)* Akt *m*; **in the —** nackt.

nudge [nʌdʒ] *vt* leicht anstoßen.

nudist ['njuːdɪst] *n* Nudist(in *f*) *m*.

nudity ['njuːdtɪ] *n* Nacktheit *f*.

nuisance ['njuːsns] *n* Ärgernis *nt*; that's a — das ist ärgerlich; he's a — er geht einem auf die Nerven.

null [nʌl] a: **— and void** null und nichtig; **—ify** *vt* für null und nichtig erklären.

numb [nʌm] a taub, gefühllos; *vt* betäuben.

number ['nʌmbə*] *n* Nummer *f*; *(numeral also)* Zahl *f*; *(quantity)* (An)zahl *f*; *(Gram)* Numerus *m*; *(of magazine also)* Ausgabe *f*; *vt (give a number to)* numerieren; *(amount to)* sein; **his days are —ed** seine Tage sind gezählt; **— plate** *(Brit Aut)* Nummernschild *nt*.

numbness ['nʌmnəs] *n* Gefühllosigkeit *f*.

numbskull ['nʌmskʌl] *n* Idiot *m*.

numeral ['njuːmərəl] *n* Ziffer *f*.

numerical [njuː'merɪkəl] a *order* zahlenmäßig.

numerous ['njuːmərəs] a zahlreich.

nun [nʌn] *n* Nonne *f*.

nurse [nɜːs] *n* Krankenschwester *f*; *(for children)* Kindermädchen *nt*; *vt patient* pflegen; *doubt etc* hegen; **—ry** *(for children)* Kinderzimmer *nt*; *(for plants)* Gärtnerei f; *(for trees)* Baumschule f; **—ry rhyme** Kinderreim m; **—ry school** Kindergarten m.

nursing ['nɜ:sɪŋ] n *(profession)* Krankenpflege f; **— home** Privatklinik f.

nut [nʌt] n Nuß f; *(screw)* Schraubenmutter f; *(col)* Verrückte(r) mf; **—s** a *(col: crazy)* verrückt.

nutcase ['nʌtkeɪs] n *(col)* Verrückte(r) mf.

nutcrackers ['nʌtkrækəz] npl Nußknacker m.

nutmeg ['nʌtmeg] n Muskat(nuß f) m.

nutrient ['nju:trɪənt] n Nährstoff m.

nutrition [nju:'trɪʃən] n Nahrung f.

nutritious [nju:'trɪʃəs] a nahrhaft.

nutshell ['nʌtʃel] n: in a — in aller Kürze.

nylon ['naɪlɒn] n Nylon nt; **a** Nylon-.

O

O, o [əʊ] n O nt, o nt; *(Tel)* Null f; see **oh**.

oaf [əʊf] n Trottel m.

oak [əʊk] n Eiche f; a Eichen(holz)-.

oar [ɔ:*] n Ruder nt.

oasis [əʊ'eɪsɪs] n Oase f.

oath [əʊθ] n *(statement)* Eid m, Schwur m; *(swearword)* Fluch m.

oatmeal ['əʊtmi:l] n Haferschrot m.

oats [əʊts] n pl Hafer m; *(Cook)* Haferflocken pl.

obedience [ə'bi:dɪəns] n Gehorsam m.

obedient [ə'bi:dɪənt] a gehorsam, folgsam.

obelisk ['ɒbɪlɪsk] n Obelisk m.

obesity [əʊ'bi:sɪtɪ] n Korpulenz f, Fettleibigkeit f.

obey [ə'beɪ] vti gehorchen (+dat), folgen (+dat).

obituary [ə'bɪtjʊərɪ] n Nachruf m.

object ['ɒbdʒɪkt] n *(thing)* Gegenstand m, Objekt m; *(of feeling etc)* Gegenstand m; *(purpose)* Ziel nt; *(Gram)* Objekt nt; [əb'dʒekt] vi dagegen sein, Einwände haben *(to gegen)*;

(morally) Anstoß nehmen *(to an +acc)*; **—ion** [əb'dʒekʃən] *(reason against)* Einwand m, Einspruch m; *(dislike)* Abneigung f; **—ionable** [əb'dʒekʃnəbl] a nicht einwandfrei; language anstößig; **—ive** [əb'dʒektɪv] n Ziel nt; a objektiv; **—ively** [əb'dʒektɪvlɪ] ad objektiv; **—ivity** [ɒbdʒɪk'tɪvɪtɪ] Objektivität f; **—or** [əb'dʒektə*] Gegner(in f) m.

obligation [ɒblɪ'geɪʃən] n *(duty)* Pflicht f; *(promise)* Verpflichtung f; no — unverbindlich; be under an — verpflichtet sein.

obligatory [ɒ'blɪgətərɪ] a bindend, obligatorisch; it is — to . . . es ist Pflicht, zu . . .

oblige [ə'blaɪdʒ] vt *(compel)* zwingen; *(do a favour)* einen Gefallen tun *(+dat)*; you are not —d to do it Sie sind nicht verpflichtet, es zu tun; much —d herzlichen Dank.

obliging [ə'blaɪdʒɪŋ] a entgegenkommend.

oblique [ə'bli:k] a schräg, schief; n Schrägstrich m.

obliterate [ə'blɪtəreɪt] vt auslöschen.

oblivion [ə'blɪvɪən] n Vergessenheit f.

oblivious [ə'blɪvɪəs] a nicht bewußt (of gen); he was — of it er hatte es nicht bemerkt.

oblong ['ɒblɒŋ] n Rechteck nt; a länglich.

obnoxious [əb'nɒkʃəs] a abscheulich, widerlich.

oboe ['əʊbəʊ] n Oboe f.

obscene [əb'siːn] a obszön, unanständig.

obscenity [əb'senɪtɪ] n Obszönität f; obscenities Zoten pl.

obscure [əb'skjʊə*] a unklar; (indistinct) undeutlich; (unknown) unbekannt, obskur; (dark) düster; vt verdunkeln; view verbergen; (confuse) verwirren.

obscurity [əb'skjʊərɪtɪ] n Unklarheit f; (being unknown) Verborgenheit f; (darkness) Dunkelheit f.

obsequious [əb'siːkwɪəs] a servil.

observable [əb'zɜːvəbl] a wahrnehmbar, sichtlich.

observance [əb'zɜːvəns] n Befolgung f.

observant [əb'zɜːvənt] a aufmerksam.

observation [ɒbzə'veɪʃən] n (noticing) Beobachtung f; (surveillance) Überwachung f; (remark) Bemerkung f.

observatory [əb'zɜːvətrɪ] n Sternwarte f, Observatorium nt.

observe [əb'zɜːv] vt (notice) bemerken; (watch) beobachten; customs einhalten; —er n Beobachter(in f) m.

obsess [əb'ses] vt verfolgen, quälen; to be —ed with an idea von einem Gedanken besessen sein;

—ion [əb'seʃən] Besessenheit f, Wahn m; —ive a krankhaft.

obsolescence [ɒbsə'lesns] n Veralten nt.

obsolescent [ɒbsə'lesnt] a veraltend.

obsolete ['ɒbsəliːt] a überholt, veraltet.

obstacle ['ɒbstəkl] n Hindernis nt; — race Hindernisrennen nt.

obstetrics [ɒb'stetrɪks] n Geburtshilfe f.

obstinacy ['ɒbstɪnəsɪ] n Hartnäckigkeit f, Sturheit f.

obstinate a, —ly ad ['ɒbstɪnət, -lɪ] hartnäckig, stur.

obstreperous [əb'strepərəs] a aufmüpfig.

obstruct [əb'strʌkt] vt versperren; pipe verstopfen; (hinder) hemmen; —ion [əb'strʌkʃən] Versperrung f; Verstopfung f; (obstacle) Hindernis nt; —ive a hemmend.

obtain [əb'teɪn] vt erhalten, bekommen; result erzielen; —able a erhältlich.

obtrusive [əb'truːsɪv] a aufdringlich.

obtuse [əb'tjuːs] a begriffsstutzig; angle stumpf.

obviate ['ɒbvɪeɪt] vt beseitigen; danger abwenden.

obvious ['ɒbvɪəs] a offenbar, offensichtlich; —ly ad offensichtlich.

occasion [ə'keɪʒən] n Gelegenheit f; (special event) großes Ereignis nt; (reason) Grund m, Anlaß m; on — gelegentlich f; veranlassen; —al a, —ally ad gelegentlich; very —ally sehr selten.

occult [ɒ'kʌlt] n the — der Okkultismus f; a okkult.

occupant ['ɒkjupənt] n Inhaber(in f) m; (of house etc) Bewohner(in f) m.

occupation [ɒkju'peɪʃən] n (employment) Tätigkeit f, Beruf m; (pastime) Beschäftigung f; (of country) Besetzung f, Okkupation f; —al a hazard Berufs-; therapy Beschäftigungs-.

occupier ['ɒkjupaɪə*] n Bewohner(in f) m.

occupy ['ɒkjupaɪ] vt (take possession of) besetzen; seat belegen; (live in) bewohnen; position, office bekleiden; position in sb's life einnehmen; time beanspruchen; mind beschäftigen.

occur [ə'kɜː*] vi (happen) vorkommen, geschehen; (appear) vorkommen; (come to mind) einfallen (to dat); —rence (event) Ereignis nt; (appearing) Auftreten nt.

ocean ['əʊʃən] n Ozean m, Meer nt; —going a Hochsee-.

ochre ['əʊkə*] n Ocker m or nt.

o'clock [ə'klɒk] ad: it is 5 — es ist 5 Uhr.

octagonal [ɒk'tægənl] a achteckig.

octane ['ɒktem] n Oktan nt.

octave ['ɒktɪv] n Oktave f.

October [ɒk'təʊbə*] n Oktober m.

octopus ['ɒktəpəs] n Krake f; (small) Tintenfisch m.

oculist ['ɒkjulɪst] n Augenarzt m/-ärztin f.

odd [ɒd] a (strange) sonderbar; (not even) ungerade; (the other part missing) einzeln; (about) ungefähr; (surplus) übrig; (casual) Gelegenheits-, zeitweilig; —ity (strangeness) Merkwürdigkeit f; (queer person) seltsame(r) Kauz m; (thing) Kuriosität f; —ly ad seltsam; —ly enough merkwürdigerweise; —ment Rest m,

Einzelstück nt; —s pl Chancen pl; (betting) Gewinnchancen pl; it makes no —s es spielt keine Rolle; at —s uneinig; —s and ends pl Reste pl; Krimskrams m.

ode [əʊd] n Ode f.

odious ['əʊdɪəs] a verhaßt; action abscheulich.

odour, (US) **odor** ['əʊdə*] n Geruch m; —less a geruchlos.

of [ɒv, əv] prep von; (indicating material) aus; the first — May der erste Mai; within a month — his death einen Monat nach seinem Tod; a girl — ten ein zehnjähriges Mädchen; fear — God Gottesfurcht f; love — money Liebe f zum Geld; the six — us wir sechs.

off [ɒf] ad (absent) weg, fort; (switch) aus(geschaltet), ab(geschaltet); (milk) sauer; I'm — ich gehe jetzt; the button's — der Knopf ist ab; to be well-/badly — reich/arm sein; prep von; (distant from) ab(gelegen) von; 3% — 3% Nachlaß or Abzug; just — Piccadilly gleich bei Piccadilly; I'm — smoking ich rauche nicht mehr.

offal ['ɒfəl] n Innereien pl.

off-colour ['ɒf'kʌlə*] a nicht wohl.

offence, (US) **offense** ['fens] n (crime) Vergehen nt, Straftat f; (insult) Beleidigung f.

offend [ə'fend] vt beleidigen; —er Gesetzesübertreter m; —ing a verletzend.

offensive [ə'fensɪv] a (unpleasant) übel, abstoßend; weapon Kampf-; remark verletzend; n Angriff m, Offensive f.

offer ['ɒfə*] n Angebot f; on — zum Verkauf angeboten; vt anbieten; reward aussetzen; opinion äußern; resistance leisten;

—ing Gabe *f*; (collection) Kollekte *f*.

offhand ['ɒf'hænd] *a* lässig; *ad* ohne weiteres.

office ['ɒfɪs] *n* Büro *nt*; (position) Amt *nt*; (duty) Aufgabe *f*; (Eccl) Gottesdienst *m*; — **block** Büro(hoch)haus *nt*; — **boy** Laufjunge *m*; —**r** (Mil) Offizier *m*; (public —) Beamte(r) *m* im öffentlichen Dienst; — **work** Büroarbeit *f*; — **worker** Büroangestellte(r) *mf*.

official [ə'fɪʃəl] *a* offiziell, amtlich; *n* Beamte(r) *m*; (Pol) amtliche(r) Sprecher *m* (of club etc) Funktionär *m*, Offizielle(r) *m*; —**ly** *ad* offiziell.

officious [ə'fɪʃəs] *a* aufdringlich.

offing ['ɒfɪŋ] *n*: in the — in (Aus)sicht.

off-licence ['ɒflaɪsəns] *n* Wein- und Spirituosenhandlung *f*.

off-peak ['ɒfpiːk] *a* heating Speicher-; charges verbilligt.

off-season ['ɒfsiːzn] *a* außer Saison.

offset ['ɒfset] *vt irreg* ausgleichen.

offshore ['ɒf'ʃɔː*] *ad* in einiger Entfernung von der Küste; *a* küstennah, Küsten-.

offside ['ɒf'saɪd] *a* (Sport) im Abseits (stehend) *ad* abseits; *n* (Aut) Fahrerseite *f*.

offspring ['ɒfsprɪŋ] *n* Nachkommenschaft *f*; (one) Sprößling *m*.

offstage ['ɒf'steɪdʒ] *ad* hinter den Kulissen.

off-the-cuff ['ɒfðəkʌf] *a* unvorbereitet, aus dem Stegreif.

often ['ɒfən] *ad* oft.

ogle ['əʊgl] *vt* liebäugeln mit.

oh [əʊ] *interj* oh, ach.

oil [ɔɪl] *n* Öl *nt*; *vt* ölen; —**can** Ölkännchen *nt*; —**field** Ölfeld *nt*; —**fired** a Öl-; — **level** Ölstand *m*; — **painting** Ölgemälde *nt*; — **refinery** Ölraffinerie *f*; —**rig** Ölplattform *f*; —**skins** *pl* Ölzeug *nt*; — **tanker** (Öl)tanker *m*; — **well** Ölquelle *f*; —**y** a ölig; (dirty) ölbeschmiert; manners schleimig.

ointment ['ɔɪntmənt] *n* Salbe *f*.

O.K., okay ['əʊ'keɪ] *interj* in Ordnung, O.K.; *a* in Ordnung; that's — with or by me ich bin damit einverstanden; *n* Zustimmung *f*; *vt* genehmigen.

old [əʊld] *a* alt; (former also) ehemalig; in the — days früher; any — thing irgend etwas; — **age** Alter *nt*; —**en** *a* (liter) alt, vergangen; —**fashioned** *a* altmodisch; — **maid** alte Jungfer *f*.

olive ['ɒlɪv] *n* (fruit) Olive *f*; (colour) Olive *nt*; *a* Oliven-; (coloured) olivenfarbig; — **branch** Ölzweig *m*; — **oil** Olivenöl *nt*.

Olympic [əʊ'lɪmpɪk] *a* olympisch; — **Games, —s** *pl* Olympische Spiele *pl*.

omelet(te) ['ɒmlət] *n* Omelett *nt*.

omen ['əʊmən] *n* Zeichen *nt*, Omen *nt*.

ominous ['ɒmɪnəs] *a* bedrohlich.

omission [əʊ'mɪʃən] *n* Auslassung *f*; (neglect) Versäumnis *nt*.

omit [əʊ'mɪt] *vt* auslassen; (fail to do) versäumen.

on [ɒn] *prep* auf; — **TV** im Fernsehen; I have it — me ich habe es bei mir; a ring — his finger ein Ring am Finger; — the main road/the bank of the river an der Hauptstraße/dem Flußufer; — foot zu Fuß; a lecture — Dante eine Vorlesung über Dante; — the left links; — the right rechts; — Sunday am Sonntag; — Sundays sonntags; — hearing this, he left als er das hörte, ging er; ad (dar)auf; she had nothing — sie hatte nichts an; (no plans) sie hatte nichts vor; what's — at the cinema? was läuft im Kino?; move — weitergehen; go — mach weiter; the light is — das Licht ist an; you're — (col) akzeptiert; it's not — (col) das ist nicht drin; — and off hin und wieder.

once [wʌns] ad einmal; cj wenn ... einmal; — you've seen him wenn du ihn erst einmal gesehen hast; — she had seen him sobald sie ihn gesehen hatte; at — sofort; (at the same time) gleichzeitig; all at — plötzlich; — more noch einmal; more than — mehr als einmal; — in a while ab und zu; — and for all ein für allemal; — upon a time es war einmal.

oncoming ['ɒnkʌmɪŋ] a traffic Gegen-, entgegenkommend.

one [wʌn] a ein; (only) einzig; n Eins f; pron eine(r, s); (people, you) man; this —, that — das; dieser/diese/dieses; — day eines Tages; the blue — der/die/das blaue; which — welche(r, s); he is — of us er ist einer von uns; — by — einzeln; — another einander; —man a Einmann-; —self pron sich (selber); —way a street Einbahn-.

ongoing ['ɒngəʊɪŋ] a stattfindend, momentan; (progressing) sich entwickelnd.

onion ['ʌnjən] n Zwiebel f.

onlooker ['ɒnlʊkə*] n Zuschauer(in f) m.

only ['əʊnlɪ] ad nur, bloß; a einzige(r, s); — yesterday erst

gestern; — just arrived gerade erst angekommen.

onset ['ɒnset] n (beginning) Beginn m.

onshore ['ɒnʃɔː*] ad an Land; a Küsten-.

onslaught ['ɒnslɔːt] n Angriff m.

onto ['ɒntu] prep — on to.

onus ['əʊnəs] n Last f, Pflicht f.

onwards ['ɒnwədz] ad (place) voran, vorwärts; from that day — von dem Tag an; from today — ab heute.

onyx ['ɒnɪks] n Onyx m.

ooze [uːz] vi sickern.

opacity [əʊ'pæsɪtɪ] n Undurchsichtigkeit f.

opal ['əʊpəl] n Opal m.

opaque [əʊ'peɪk] a undurchsichtig.

open ['əʊpən] a offen; (public) öffentlich; mind aufgeschlossen; sandwich belegt; in the — (air) im Freien; to keep a day — einen Tag freihalten; vt öffnen, aufmachen; (door, flower) aufgehen; (play) Premiere haben; — out vt ausbreiten; hole, business erweitern; vi (person) aus sich herausgehen; — up vt route erschließen; vi (begin) anfangen; (shop) aufmachen; (door, flower) aufgehen; (play) Premiere haben; — out vt ausbreiten; hole, business erweitern; vi (person) aus sich herausgehen; — up vt route erschließen; —air a Frei(luft)-; —er Öffner m; —ing (hole) Öffnung f, Loch nt; (beginning) Eröffnung f, Anfang m; (good chance) Gelegenheit f; —ly ad offen; (publicly) öffentlich; —minded a aufgeschlossen; —necked a offen-.

opera ['ɒpərə] n Oper f; — glasses pl Opernglas nt; — house Opernhaus nt.

operate ['ɒpəreɪt] vt machine bedienen; brakes, light betätigen; vi (machine) laufen, in Betrieb sein; *(person)* arbeiten; *(Med)* to — on operieren.

operatic [ɔpə'rætik] a Opern-.

operation [ɔpə'reɪʃən] n *(working)* Betrieb m, Tätigkeit f; *(Med)* Operation f; *(undertaking)* Unternehmen m; *(Mil)* Einsatz m; in full — in vollem Gang; to be in — *(Jur)* in Kraft sein; *(machine)* in Betrieb sein; —al a einsatzbereit.

operative ['ɔpərətɪv] a wirksam; *law* rechtsgültig; *(Med)* operativ; n Mechaniker m; Agent m.

operator ['ɔpəreɪtə*] n *(of machine)* Arbeiter m; *(Tel)* Telefonist(in f) m; phone the — rufen Sie die Vermittlung or das Fernamt an.

operetta [ɔpə'retə] n Operette f.

opinion [ə'pɪnjən] n Meinung f; in my — meiner Meinung nach; a matter of — Ansichtssache; —ated a starrsinnig.

opium ['əupjəm] n Opium nt.

opponent [ə'pəunənt] n Gegner m.

opportune ['ɔpətjuːn] a günstig; *remark* passend.

opportunist [ɔpə'tjuːnist] n Opportunist m.

opportunity [ɔpə'tjuːnɪtɪ] n Gelegenheit f, Möglichkeit f.

oppose [ə'pəuz] vt entgegentreten (+dat); *argument, idea* ablehnen; *plan* bekämpfen; —d a: to be —d to sth gegen etw sein; as —d to im Gegensatz zu.

opposing [ə'pəuzɪŋ] a gegnerisch; *points of view* entgegengesetzt.

opposite ['ɔpəzit] a *house* gegenüberliegend; *direction* entgegengesetzt; ad gegenüber; prep gegenüber; — me mir gegenüber; in — Gegenteil nt; — number *(person)* Pendant nt; *(Sport)* Gegenspieler m.

opposition [ɔpə'zɪʃən] n *(resistance)* Widerstand m; *(Pol)* Opposition f; *(contrast)* Gegensatz m.

oppress [ə'pres] vt unterdrücken; *(heat etc)* bedrücken; —ion [ə'preʃən] Unterdrückung f; —ive a *authority, law* ungerecht; *burden, thought* bedrückend; *heat* drückend.

opt [ɔpt] vi: — for sth sich entscheiden für etw; to — to do sth sich entscheiden, etw zu tun; — out vi sich drücken vor (+dat); *(of society)* ausflippen aus (+dat).

optical ['ɔptikəl] a optisch.

optician [ɔp'tɪʃən] n Optiker m.

optimism ['ɔptimɪzəm] n Optimismus m.

optimist ['ɔptimist] n Optimist m; —ic ['ɔpti'mistik] a optimistisch.

optimum ['ɔptiməm] a optimal.

option ['ɔpʃən] n Wahl f; *(Comm)* Vorkaufsrecht nt, Option f; —al a freiwillig; *subject* wahlfrei; —al extras Extras auf Wunsch.

opulence ['ɔpjuləns] n Reichtum m.

opulent ['ɔpjulənt] a sehr reich.

opus ['əupəs] n Werk nt, Opus nt.

or [ɔː*] cj oder; he could not read — write er konnte weder lesen noch schreiben.

oracle ['ɔrəkl] n Orakel nt.

oral ['ɔːrəl] a mündlich; n *(exam)* mündliche Prüfung f, Mündliche(s) nt.

orange ['ɔrɪndʒ] n *(fruit)* Apfelsine f, Orange f; *(colour)* Orange nt; a orange.

orang-outang,   orang-utan [ɔ:'ræŋuːtæŋ] n Orang-Utan m.

oration [ɔː'reɪʃən] n feierliche Rede f.

orator ['ɒrətə*] n Redner(in f) m.

oratorio [ɒrə'tɔːrɪəʊ] n Oratorium nt.

orbit ['ɔːbɪt] n Umlaufbahn f; 2 —s 2 Umkreisungen; **to be in —** (die Erde/den Mond etc) umkreisen; vt umkreisen.

orchard ['ɔːtʃəd] n Obstgarten m.

orchestra ['ɔːkɪstrə] n Orchester nt; —l [ɔː'kestrəl] a Orchester-, orchestral; —te ['ɔːkɪstreɪt] vt orchestrieren.

orchid ['ɔːkɪd] n Orchidee f.

ordain [ɔː'deɪn] vt (Eccl) weihen; (decide) verfügen.

ordeal [ɔː'diːl] n schwere Prüfung f, Qual f.

order ['ɔːdə*] n (sequence) Reihenfolge f; (good arrangement) Ordnung f; (command) Befehl m; (Jur) Anordnung f; (peace) Ordnung f, Ruhe f; (condition) Zustand m; (rank) Klasse f; (Comm) Bestellung f; (Eccl, honour) Orden m; **out of —** außer Betrieb m; **in — to do sth** um etw zu tun; **in — that** damit; **holy —s** Priesterweihe f; vt (arrange) ordnen; (command) befehlen (sth etw acc, sb jdm); (Comm) bestellen; — **form** Bestellschein m; **—ly** n (Mil) Offiziersbursche m; (Mil Med) Sanitäter m; (Med) Pfleger m; a (tidy) ordentlich; (well-behaved) ruhig; **—ly officer** diensthabender Offizier.

ordinal [ɔː'dɪnl] a Ordnungs-, Ordinal-.

ordinarily ['ɔːdnrɪlɪ] ad gewöhnlich.

ordinary ['ɔːdnrɪ] a (usual) gewöhnlich, normal; (commonplace) gewöhnlich, alltäglich.

ordination [ɔːdɪ'neɪʃən] n Priesterweihe f; (Protestant) Ordination f.

ordnance ['ɔːdnəns] n Artillerie f; Munition f; — **factory** Munitionsfabrik f.

ore [ɔː*] n Erz nt.

organ ['ɔːgən] n (Mus) Orgel f; (Biol, fig) Organ nt; —**ic** [ɔː'gænɪk] a organisch; —**ism** ['ɔːgənɪzm] Organismus m; —**ist** Organist(in f) m.

organization [ɔːgənaɪ'zeɪʃən] n Organisation f; (make-up) Struktur f.

organize ['ɔːgənaɪz] vt organisieren; —**r** Organisator m, Veranstalter m.

orgasm ['ɔːgæzm] n Orgasmus m.

orgy ['ɔːdʒɪ] n Orgie f.

Orient ['ɔːrɪənt] n Orient m.

oriental [ɔːrɪ'entəl] a orientalisch; n Orientale m, Orientalin f.

orientate ['ɔːrɪenteɪt] vt orientieren.

orifice ['ɒrɪfɪs] n Öffnung f.

origin ['ɒrɪdʒɪn] n Ursprung m; (of the world) Anfang m, Entstehung f.

original [ə'rɪdʒɪnl] a (first) ursprünglich; painting original; idea originell; n Original nt —**ity** [ərɪdʒɪ'nælɪtɪ] Originalität f —**ly** ad ursprünglich; originell.

originate [ə'rɪdʒɪneɪt] vi entstehen; **to —** from stammen aus; vt ins Leben rufen.

originator [ə'rɪdʒɪneɪtə*] n (of movement) Begründer m; (of invention) Erfinder m.

ornament ['ɔːnəmənt] n Schmuck m; (on mantelpiece) Nippesfigur f; (fig) Zierde f; —**al** [ɔːnə'mentl] a schmückend, Zier-; —**ation** Verzierung f.

ornate [ɔː'neɪt] a reich verziert; style überladen.

ornithologist [ɔːniˈθɒlədʒist] n Ornithologe m, Ornithologin f.

ornithology [ɔːniˈθɒlədʒi] n Vogelkunde f, Ornithologie f.

orphan [ˈɔːfən] n Waise f, Waisenkind nt; vt zur Waise machen; —age Waisenhaus nt.

orthodox [ˈɔːθədɒks] a orthodox.

orthopaedic, (US) **orthopedic** [ɔːθəuˈpiːdik] a orthopädisch.

oscillation [ɒsiˈleiʃən] n Schwingung f, Oszillation f.

ostensible a, **ostensibly** ad [ɒsˈtensəbl, -bli] vorgeblich, angeblich.

ostentation [ɒstenˈteiʃən] n Zurschaustellen nt.

ostentatious [ɒstenˈteiʃəs] a großtuerisch, protzig.

ostracize [ˈɒstrəsaiz] vt ausstoßen.

ostrich [ˈɒstritʃ] n Strauß m.

other [ˈʌðə*] a andere(r, s); the —day neulich; every — day jeden zweiten Tag; any person — than him alle außer ihm; there are 6 da sind noch 6; pron andere(r, s); ad: — than anders als; —wise ad (in a different way) anders; (in other ways) sonst, im übrigen; (or else) sonst.

otter [ˈɒtə*] n Otter m.

ought [ɔːt] v aux sollen; he behaves as he — er benimmt sich, wie es .sich gehört; you — to do that Sie sollten das tun; he — to win er müßte gewinnen; that — to do das müßte or dürfte reichen.

ounce [auns] n Unze f.

our [auə*] poss a unser; **—s** poss pron unsere(r, s); **—selves** pron uns (selbst); (emphatic) (wir) selbst.

oust [aust] vt verdrängen.

out [aut] ad hinaus/heraus; (not indoors) draußen; (not alight) aus; (unconscious) bewußtlos; (results) bekanntgegeben; to eat/go — auswärts essen/ausgehen; that fashion's — das ist nicht mehr Mode; the ball was — der Ball war aus; the flowers are — die Blumen blühen; he was — in his calculations seine Berechnungen waren nicht richtig; to be — for sth auf etw (acc) aus sein; — loud ad laut; — of prep aus; (away from) außerhalb (+gen); to be — of milk etc keine Milch etc mehr haben; made — of wood aus Holz gemacht; — of danger außer Gefahr; — of place fehl am Platz; — of curiosity aus Neugier; nine — of ten neun von zehn; — and — durch und durch; —of-bounds a verboten; —of-date a veraltet; —of-doors ad im Freien; —of-the-way a (off the general route) abgelegen; (unusual) ungewöhnlich.

outback [ˈautbæk] n Hinterland nt.

outboard (motor) [ˈautbɔːd (ˈməutə*)] n Außenbordmotor m.

outbreak [ˈautbreik] n Ausbruch m.

outbuilding [ˈautbildiŋ] n Nebengebäude nt.

outburst [ˈautbəːst] n Ausbruch m.

outcast [ˈautkɑːst] n Ausgestoßene(r) mf.

outclass [autˈklɑːs] vt übertreffen.

outcome [ˈautkʌm] n Ergebnis nt.

outcry [ˈautkrai] n Protest m.

outdated [autˈdeitid] a veraltet, überholt.

outdo [autˈduː] vt irreg übertrumpfen.

outdoor [ˈautdɔː*] a Außen-; (Sport) im Freien.

outdoors [ˈautdɔːz] ad draußen im Freien.

Freien; **to go —** ins Freie *or* nach draußen gehen.

outer ['aʊtə*] *a* äußere(r, s); **— space** Weltraum *m.*

outfit ['aʊtfɪt] *n* Ausrüstung *f;* (*set of clothes*) Kleidung *f;* **—ters** (*for men's clothes*) Herrenausstatter *m.*

outgoings ['aʊtgəʊɪŋz] *npl* Ausgaben *pl.*

outgrow [aʊt'grəʊ] *vt irreg clothes* herauswachsen aus; *habit* ablegen.

outing ['aʊtɪŋ] *n* Ausflug *m.*

outlandish [aʊt'lændɪʃ] *a* eigenartig.

outlaw ['aʊtlɔ:] *n* Geächtete(r) *m;* *vt* ächten; (*thing*) verbieten.

outlay ['aʊtleɪ] *n* Auslage *f.*

outlet ['aʊtlet] *n* Auslaß *m,* Abfluß *m;* (*Comm*) Absatzmarkt *m;* (*for emotions*) Ventil *nt.*

outline ['aʊtlaɪn] *n* Umriß *m.*

outlive [aʊt'lɪv] *vt* überleben.

outlook ['aʊtlʊk] *n* (*lit, fig*) Aussicht *f;* (*attitude*) Einstellung *f.*

outlying ['aʊtlaɪɪŋ] *a* entlegen; *district* Außen-.

outmoded [aʊt'məʊdɪd] *a* veraltet.

outnumber [aʊt'nʌmbə*] *vt* zahlenmäßig überlegen sein (+*dat*).

outpatient ['aʊtpeɪʃənt] *n* ambulante(r) Patient(in *f*) *m.*

outpost ['aʊtpəʊst] *n* (*Mil, fig*) Vorposten *m.*

output ['aʊtpʊt] *n* Leistung *f,* Produktion *f.*

outrage ['aʊtreɪdʒ] *n* (*cruel deed*) Ausschreitung *f,* .Verbrechen *nt;* (*indecency*) Skandal *m; vt morals* verstoßen gegen; *person* empören; **—ous** [aʊt'reɪdʒəs] *a* unerhört, empörend.

outright ['aʊtraɪt] *ad* (*at once*) sofort; (*openly*) ohne Umschweife; **to refuse —** rundweg ablehnen; *a*

denial völlig; *sale* Total-; *winner* unbestritten.

outset ['aʊtset] *n* Beginn *m.*

outside ['aʊt'saɪd] *n* Außenseite *f;* **on the —** außen; **at the very —** höchstens; *a* äußere(r, s), Außen-; *price* Höchst-; *chance* gering; *ad* außen; **to go —** nach draußen *or* hinaus gehen; *prep* außerhalb (+*gen*); **—r** Außenseiter(in *f*) *m.*

outsize ['aʊtsaɪz] *a* übergroß.

outskirts ['aʊtskɜ:ts] *npl* Stadtrand *m.*

outspoken [aʊt'spəʊkən] *a* offen, freimütig.

outstanding [aʊt'stændɪŋ] *a* hervorragend; *debts etc* ausstehend.

outstay [aʊt'steɪ] *vt:* **— one's welcome** länger bleiben als erwünscht.

outstretched [aʊt'stretʃt] *a* ausgestreckt.

outward [aʊt'wəd] *a* äußere(r, s); *journey* Hin-; *freight* ausgehend; *ad* nach außen; **—ly** *ad* äußerlich.

outweigh [aʊt'weɪ] *vt* (*fig*) überwiegen.

outwit [aʊt'wɪt] *vt* überlisten.

outworn [aʊt'wɔ:n] *a expression* abgedroschen.

oval ['əʊvəl] *a* oval; *n* Oval *nt.*

ovary ['əʊvərɪ] *n* Eierstock *m.*

ovation [əʊ'veɪʃən] *n* Beifallssturm *m.* .

oven ['ʌvn] *n* Backofen *m.*

over ['əʊvə*] *ad* (*across*) hinüber/herüber; (*finished*) vorbei; (*left*) übrig; (*again*) wieder, noch einmal; *prep* über; (*in every part of*) in; *pref* (*excessively*) übermäßig; **famous the world —** in der ganzen Welt berühmt; **five times —** fünfmal; **— the weekend** übers Wochenende; **— coffee bei**

einer Tasse Kaffee; — the phone am Telephon; all — (everywhere) überall; (finished) vorbei; — and — immer wieder; — and above darüber hinaus.

over- ['əʊvə*] pref über-.

overact ['əʊvər'ækt] vi übertreiben.

overall ['əʊvərɔːl] n (Brit) (for woman) Kittelschürze f; a situation allgemein; length Gesamt-; ad insgesamt; —s pl (for man) Overall m.

overawe [əʊvər'ɔː] vt (frighten) einschüchtern; (make impression) überwältigen.

overbalance [əʊvə'bæləns] vi Übergewicht bekommen.

overbearing [əʊvə'bɛərɪŋ] a aufdringlich.

overboard ['əʊvəbɔːd] ad über Bord.

overcast ['əʊvəkɑːst] a bedeckt.

overcharge ['əʊvə'tʃɑːdʒ] vt zuviel verlangen von.

overcoat ['əʊvəkəʊt] n Mantel m.

overcome [əʊvə'kʌm] vt irreg überwinden; (sleep, emotion) übermannen; — by the song vom Lied gerührt.

overcrowded [əʊvə'kraʊdɪd] a überfüllt.

overcrowding [əʊvə'kraʊdɪŋ] n Überfüllung f.

overdo [əʊvə'duː] vt irreg (cook too much) .verkochen; (exaggerate) übertreiben.

overdose [əʊvədəʊs] n Überdosis f.

overdraft ['əʊvədrɑːft] n (Konto)überziehung f; to have an — sein Konto überzogen haben.

overdrawn ['əʊvə'drɔːn] a account überzogen.

overdrive ['əʊvədraɪv] n (Aut) Schnellgang m.

overdue ['əʊvə'djuː] a überfällig.

overenthusiastic ['əʊvərɪnɵjuːzɪ'æstɪk] a zu begeistert.

overestimate ['əʊvər'estɪmeɪt] vt überschätzen.

overexcited ['əʊvərɪk'saɪtɪd] a überreizt; children aufgeregt.

overexertion ['əʊvərɪg'zɜːʃən] n Überanstrengung f.

overexpose ['əʊvərɪks'pəʊz] vt (Phot) überbelichten.

overflow [əʊvə'fləʊ] vi überfließen; (person) n (excess) Überschuß m; (outlet) Überlauf m.

overgrown [əʊvə'grəʊn] a garden verwildert.

overhaul [əʊvə'hɔːl] vt car überholen; plans überprüfen; ['əʊvəhɔːl] n Überholung f.

overhead [əʊvəhed] a Hoch-; wire oberirdisch; lighting Decken-; ['əʊvəhed] ad oben; —s pl allgemeine Unkosten pl.

overhear [əʊvə'hɪə*] vt irreg (mit an)hören.

overjoyed [əʊvə'dʒɔɪd] a überglücklich.

overland [əʊvəlænd] a Überland-; [əʊvə'lænd] ad travel über Land.

overlap [əʊvə'læp] vi sich überschneiden; (objects) sich teilweise decken; ['əʊvəlæp] n Überschneidung f.

overload [əʊvə'ləʊd] vt überladen.

overlook [əʊvə'lʊk] vt (view from above) überblicken; (not to notice) übersehen; (pardon) hinwegsehen über (+acc).

overlord ['əʊvəlɔːd] n Lehnsherr m.

overnight ['əʊvə'naɪt] a journey Nacht-; ad über Nacht; — bag

Reisetasche *f;* — stay Übernachtung *f.*

overpass ['əʊvəpɑ:s] *n* Überführung *f.*

overpower [əʊvə'paʊə*] *vt* überwältigen; —ing *a* überwältigend.

overrate ['əʊvə'reɪt] *vt* überschätzen.

override [əʊvə'raɪd] *vt irreg order, decision* aufheben; *objection* übergehen.

overriding [əʊvə'raɪdɪŋ] *a* Haupt-, vorherrschend.

overrule [əʊvə'ru:l] *vt* verwerfen; we were —d unser Vorschlag wurde verworfen.

overseas ['əʊvə'si:z] *ad* nach/in Übersee; *a* überseeisch, Übersee-.

overseer ['əʊvəsɪə*] *n* Aufseher m.

overshadow [əʊvə'ʃædəʊ] *vt* überschatten.

overshoot ['əʊvə'ʃu:t] *vt irreg run-way* hinausschießen über (*+acc*).

oversight ['əʊvəsaɪt] *n* (*mistake*) Versehen *nt.*

oversimplify ['əʊvə'sɪmplɪfaɪ] *vt* zu sehr vereinfachen.

oversleep ['əʊvə'sli:p] *vi irreg* verschlafen.

overspill ['əʊvəspɪl] *n* (Bevölkerungs)überschuß *m.*

overstate [əʊvə'steɪt] *vt* übertreiben; —ment Übertreibung *f.*

overt [əʊ'vɜ:t] *a* offen(kundig).

overtake [əʊvə'teɪk] *vti irreg* überholen.

overthrow [əʊvə'θrəʊ] *vt irreg* (*Pol*) stürzen.

overtime ['əʊvətaɪm] *n* Überstunden *pl.*

overtone ['əʊvətəʊn] *n* (*fig*) Note *f.*

overture ['əʊvətjʊə*] *n* Ouvertüre *f;* —s *pl* (*fig*) Angebot *nt.*

overturn [əʊvə'tɜ:n] *vti* umkippen.

overweight ['əʊvə'weɪt] *a* zu dick, zu schwer.

overwhelm [əʊvə'welm] *vt* überwältigen; —ing *a* überwältigend.

overwork ['əʊvə'wɜ:k] *n* Überarbeitung *f; vt* überlasten; *vi* sich überarbeiten.

overwrought ['əʊvə'rɔ:t] *a* überreizt.

owe [əʊ] *vt* schulden; to — sth to sb *money* jdm etw schulden; *favour etc* jdm etw verdanken.

owing to ['əʊɪŋ'tu:] *prep* wegen (*+gen*).

owl [aʊl] *n* Eule *f.*

own [əʊn] *vt* besitzen; (*admit*) zugeben; who —s that? wem gehört das?; a eigen; I have money of my — ich habe selbst Geld; *n* Eigentum *nt;* all my — mein Eigentum; on one's — allein; up sich zugeben (*to sth etw acc*); —er Besitzer(in *f*) *m,* Eigentümer(in *f*) *m;* .—ership Besitz *m.*

ox [ɒks] *n* Ochse *m.*

oxide ['ɒksaɪd] *n* Oxyd *nt.*

oxtail ['ɒksteɪl] *n:* — soup Ochsenschwanzsuppe *f.*

oxyacetylene ['ɒksɪə'setɪli:n] *a* Azetylensauerstoff-.

oxygen ['ɒksɪdʒən] *n* Sauerstoff *m;* — mask Sauerstoffmaske *f;* — tent Sauerstoffzelt *nt.*

oyster ['ɔɪstə*] *n* Auster *f.*

ozone ['əʊzəʊn] *n* Ozon *nt.*

P

P, p [piː] n P nt, p nt.

pa [pɑː] n (col) Papa m.

pace [peɪs] n Schritt m; (speed) Geschwindigkeit f, Tempo nt; vi schreiten; **to keep — with** Schritt halten mit; **—maker** Schrittmacher m.

pacification [pæsɪfɪ'keɪʃən] n Befriedung f.

pacifism ['pæsɪfɪzəm] n Pazifismus m.

pacifist ['pæsɪfɪst] n Pazifist m.

pacify ['pæsɪfaɪ] vt befrieden; (calm) beruhigen.

pack [pæk] n Packen m; (of wolves) Rudel nt; (of hounds) Meute f; (of cards) Spiel nt; (gang) Bande f; vti case packen; clothes einpacken; **—age** Paket nt; **— tour** Pauschalreise; f; **—et** Päckchen nt; **— horse** Packpferd nt; **— ice** Packeis nt; **—ing** (action) Packen nt; (material) Verpackung f; **—ing case** (Pack)kiste f.

pact [pækt] n Pakt m, Vertrag m.

pad [pæd] n (of paper) (Schreib)block m; (for inking) Stempelkissen nt; (padding) Polster nt; vt polstern.

paddle ['pædl] n Paddel nt; vt boat paddeln; vi (in sea) plantschen.

paddling pool ['pædlɪŋ puːl] n Plantschbecken nt.

paddock ['pædək] n Koppel f.

paddy ['pædɪ] n **— field** Reisfeld nt.

padlock ['pædlɒk] n Vorhängeschloß nt.

padre ['pɑːdrɪ] n Militärgeistliche(r) m.

paediatrics [piːdɪ'ætrɪks] n Kinderheilkunde f.

pagan ['peɪgən] a heidnisch.

page [peɪdʒ] n Seite f; (person) Page m; vt (in hotel etc) ausrufen lassen.

pageant ['pædʒənt] n Festzug m; **—ry** Gepränge nt.

pagoda [pə'gəʊdə] n Pagode f.

pail [peɪl] n Eimer m.

pain [peɪn] n Schmerz m, Schmerzen pl; **—s** pl (efforts) große Mühe f, große Anstrengungen pl; **to be at —s to do sth** sich (dat) Mühe geben, etw zu tun; **—ed** a expression gequält; **—ful** a (physically) schmerzhaft; (embarrassing) peinlich; (difficult) mühsam; **—killing drug** schmerzstillende(s) Mittel nt; **—less** a schmerzlos; **—staking** a gewissenhaft.

paint [peɪnt] n Farbe f; vt anstreichen; picture malen; **—brush** Pinsel m; **—er** Maler m; (decorator) Maler m, Anstreicher m; **—ing** (act) Malen nt; (Art) Malerei f; (picture) Bild nt, Gemälde nt.

pair [peə*] n Paar nt; **— of scissors** Schere f; **— of trousers** Hose f.

pajamas (US) [pə'dʒɑːməz] npl Schlafanzug m.

pal [pæl] n (col) Kumpel m; (woman) (gute) Freundin f.

palace ['pæləs] n Palast m, Schloß nt.

palatable ['pælətəbl] *a* schmackhaft.

palate ['pælɪt] *n* Gaumen *m*; *(taste)* Geschmack *m*.

palaver [pə'lɑːvə*] *n* (col) Theater *nt*.

pale [peɪl] *a* face blaß, bleich; colour hell, blaß; **—ness** Blässe *f*.

palette ['pælɪt] *n* Palette *f*.

palisade [pælɪ'seɪd] *n* Palisade *f*.

pall [pɔːl] *n* Bahr- or Leichentuch *nt*; *(of smoke)* (Rauch)wolke *f*; *vi* jeden Reiz verlieren, verblassen; **—bearer** Sargträger *m*.

pallid ['pælɪd] *a* blaß, bleich.

pally ['pælɪ] *a* (col) befreundet.

palm [pɑːm] *n* (of hand) Handfläche *f*; (also — tree) Palme *f*; **—ist** Handleserin *f*; **P— Sunday** Palmsonntag *m*.

palpable ['pælpəbl] *a* (lit, fig) greifbar.

palpably ['pælpəblɪ] *ad* offensichtlich.

palpitation [pælpɪ'teɪʃən] *n* Herzklopfen *nt*.

paltry ['pɔːltrɪ] *a* armselig.

pamper ['pæmpə*] *vt* verhätscheln.

pamphlet ['pæmflət] *n* Broschüre *f*.

pan [pæn] *n* Pfanne *f*; *vi* (Cine) schwenken.

pan- [pæn] *pref* Pan-, All-.

panacea [pænə'sɪə] *n* (fig) Allheilmittel *nt*.

panache [pə'næʃ] *n* Schwung *m*.

pancake ['pænkeɪk] *n* Pfannkuchen *m*.

panda ['pændə] *n* Panda *m*.

pandemonium ['pændɪ'məʊnɪəm] *n* Hölle *f*; *(noise)* Höllenlärm *m*.

pander ['pændə*] *vi* sich richten (to nach).

pane [peɪn] *n* (Fenster)scheibe *f*.

panel ['pænl] *n* (of wood) Tafel *f*; *(TV)* Diskussionsteilnehmer *pl*; **—ing** (US), **—ling** Täfelung *f*.

pang [pæŋ] *n* Stich *m*, Qual *f*; **—s of conscience** Gewissensbisse *pl*.

panic ['pænɪk] *n* Panik *f*; *a* panisch; *vi* von panischem Schrecken erfaßt werden, durchdrehen; **don't —** (nur) keine Panik; **—ky** *a person* überängstlich.

pannier ['pænɪə*] *n* (Trage)korb *m*; *(on bike)* Satteltasche *f*.

panorama [pænə'rɑːmə] *n* Rundblick *m*, Panorama *nt*.

panoramic [pænə'ræmɪk] *a* Panorama-.

pansy ['pænzɪ] *n* (flower) Stiefmütterchen *nt*; *(col)* Schwule(r) *m*.

pant [pænt] *vi* keuchen; *(dog)* hecheln.

pantechnicon [pæn'teknɪkən] *n* Möbelwagen *m*.

panther ['pænθə*] *n* Panther *m*.

panties ['pæntɪz] *npl* (Damen)slip *m*.

pantomime ['pæntəmaɪm] *n* Märchenkomödie *f* um Weihnachten.

pantry ['pæntrɪ] *n* Vorratskammer *f*.

pants [pænts] *npl* Unterhose *f*; *(trousers)* Hose *f*.

papal ['peɪpəl] *a* päpstlich.

paper ['peɪpə*] *n* Papier *nt*; *(newspaper)* Zeitung *f*; *(essay)* Vortrag *m*, Referat *nt*; *a* Papier-, aus Papier; *vt wall* tapezieren; **—s** *pl* (identity) Ausweis(papiere *pl*) *m*; **—back** Taschenbuch *nt*; **— bag** Tüte *f*; **— clip** Büroklammer *f*; **—weight** Briefbeschwerer *m*; **—work** Schreibarbeit *f*.

papier-mâché ['pæpɪeɪ'mæʃeɪ] *n* Papiermaché *nt*.

paprika ['pæprɪkə] n Paprika m.

papyrus [pə'paɪərəs] n Papyrus m.

par [pɑː*] n (Comm) Nennwert m; (Golf) Par nt; **on a — with** ebenbürtig (+dat); **to be on a — with sb** sich mit jdm messen können; **below —** unter (jds) Niveau.

parable ['pærəbl] n Parabel f; (Rel) Gleichnis nt.

parachute ['pærəʃuːt] n Fallschirm m; vi (mit dem · Fallschirm) abspringen.

parachutist ['pærəʃuːtɪst] n Fallschirmspringer m.

parade [pə'reɪd] n Parade f; vt aufmarschieren lassen; vi paradieren, vorbeimarschieren.

paradise ['pærədaɪs] n Paradies nt.

paradox ['pærədɒks] n Paradox nt; **—ical** [pærə'dɒksɪkəl] a paradox, widersinnig; **—ically** [pærə'dɒksɪkəlɪ] ad paradoxerweise.

paraffin ['pærəfɪn] n Paraffin nt.

paragraph ['pærəgrɑːf] n Absatz m, Paragraph m.

parallel ['pærəlel] a parallel; n Parallele f.

paralysis [pə'rælɪsɪs] n Lähmung f.

paralyze ['pærəlaɪz] vt lähmen.

paramount ['pærəmaʊnt] a höchste(r, s), oberste(r, s).

paranoia [pærə'nɔɪə] n Paranoia f.

parapet ['pærəpɪt] n Brüstung f.

paraphernalia ['pærəfə'neɪlɪə] n Zubehör nt, Utensilien pl.

paraphrase ['pærəfreɪz] vt umschreiben.

paraplegic [pærə'pliːdʒɪk] n Querschnittsgelähmte(r) mf.

parasite ['pærəsaɪt] n (lit, fig) Schmarotzer m, Parasit m.

parasol ['pærəsɒl] n Sonnenschirm m.

paratrooper ['pærətruːpə*] n Fallschirmjäger m.

parcel ['pɑːsl] n Paket nt; vt (also **— up**) einpacken.

parch [pɑːtʃ] vt (aus)dörren; **I'm —ed** ich bin am Verdursten.

parchment ['pɑːtʃmənt] n Pergament nt.

pardon ['pɑːdn] n Verzeihung f; (Jur) begnadigen; **— me!, I beg your —!** verzeihen Sie bitte!; (objection) aber ich bitte Sie!; **— me?** (US), **(I beg your) —?** wie bitte?

parent ['pɛərənt] n Elternteil m; **—al** [pə'rentl] a elterlich, Eltern-; **—hood** Elternschaft f; **—s** pl Eltern pl; **— ship** Mutterschiff nt.

parenthesis [pə'renθɪsɪs] n Klammer f; (sentence) Parenthese f.

parish ['pærɪʃ] n Gemeinde · f; **—ioner** [pə'rɪʃənə*] Gemeindemitglied nt.

parity ['pærɪtɪ] n (Fin) Umrechnungskurs m, Parität f.

park [pɑːk] n Park m; vti parken; **—ing** Parken nt; **'no —ing'** Parken verboten; **—ing lot** (US) Parkplatz m; **—ing meter** Parkuhr f; **—ing place** Parkplatz m.

parliament ['pɑːləmənt] n Parlament nt; **—ary** [pɑːlə'mentərɪ] a parlamentarisch, Parlaments-.

parlour, (US) **parlor** ['pɑːlə*] n Salon m, Wohnzimmer nt.

parlous ['pɑːləs] a state schlimm.

parochial [pə'rəʊkɪəl] a Gemeinde-, gemeindlich; (narrow-minded) eng(stirnig), Provinz-.

parody ['pærədɪ] n Parodie f; · vt parodieren.

parole [pə'rəʊl] n: **on —** (prisoner) auf Bewährung.

parquet ['pɑːkeɪ] *n* Parkett(fußboden *m*) *nt*.

parrot ['pærət] *n* Papagei *m;* —fashion *ad* wie ein Papagei.

parry ['pærɪ] *vt* parieren, abwehren.

parsimonious a, —ly *ad* [pɑːsɪ'məʊnɪəs, -lɪ] knauserig.

parsley ['pɑːslɪ] *n* Petersilie *m*.

parsnip ['pɑːsnɪp] *n* Pastinake *f,* Petersilienwurzel *f.*

parson ['pɑːsn] *n* Pfarrer *m*.

part [pɑːt] *n (piece)* Teil *m,* Stück *nt; (Theat)* Rolle *f; (of machine)* Teil *nt; a* Teil-; *ad* = **partly;** *vt* trennen; *hair* scheiteln, *vi (people)* sich trennen, Abschied nehmen; **for my** — ich für meinen Teil; **for the most** — meistens, größtenteils; — **with** *vt* hergeben; *(renounce)* aufgeben; **in** — **exchange** in Zahlung; —**ial** ['pɑːʃəl] *a (incomplete)* teilweise, Teil-; *(biased)* eingenommen, parteiisch; *eclipse* partiell; **to be** —**ial to** eine (besondere) Vorliebe haben für; —**ially** ['pɑːʃəlɪ] *ad* teilweise, zum Teil.

participate [pɑː'tɪsɪpeɪt] *vi* teilnehmen *(in* an *+dat)*.

participation [pɑːtɪsɪ'peɪʃən] *n* Teilnahme *f; (sharing)* Beteiligung *f.*

participle ['pɑːtɪsɪpl] *n* Partizip *nt,* Mittelwort *nt.*

particular [pətɪkjʊlə*] *a* bestimmt, speziell; *(exact)* genau; *(fussy)* eigen; *n* Einzelheit *f;* —**s** *pl (details)* Einzelheiten *pl;* Personalien *pl;* —**ly** *ad* besonders.

parting ['pɑːtɪŋ] *n (separation)* Abschied *m,* Trennung *f; (of hair)* Scheitel *m; a* Abschieds-.

partisan [pɑːtɪ'zæn] *n* Parteigänger *m; (guerrilla)* Partisan *m; a* Partei-; Partisanen-.

partition [pɑː'tɪʃən] *n (wall)* Trennwand *f; (division)* Teilung *f.*

partly ['pɑːtlɪ] *ad* zum Teil, teilweise.

partner ['pɑːtnə*] *n* Partner *m; (Comm also)* Gesellschafter *m,* Teilhaber *m; vt* der Partner sein von; —**ship** Partnerschaft *f,* Gemeinschaft *f; (Comm)* Teilhaberschaft *f.*

partridge ['pɑːtrɪdʒ] *n* Rebhuhn *nt.*

part-time ['pɑːt'taɪm] *a (half-day only)* halbtägig, Halbtags-; *(part of the week only)* nebenberuflich; *ad* halbtags; nebenberuflich.

party ['pɑːtɪ] *n (Pol, Jur)* Partei *f; (group)* Gesellschaft *f; (celebration)* Party *f; a dress* Gesellschafts-, Party-; *politics* Partei-.

pass [pɑːs] *vt vi* vorbeikommen an *(+dat); (on foot)* vorbeigehen an *(+dat);* vorbeifahren an *(+dat); (surpass)* übersteigen; *(hand on)* weitergeben; *(approve)* gelten lassen, genehmigen; *time* verbringen; *exam* bestehen; *vi (go by)* vorbeigehen, vorbeifahren; *(years)* vergehen; *(be successful)* bestehen; *n (in mountains)* Paß *m; (permission)* Durchgangs- or Passierschein *m; (Sport)* Paß *m,* Abgabe *f; (in exam)* Bestehen *nt;* **to get a** — bestehen; — **away** *vi (euph)* verscheiden; — **by** *vi* vorbeigehen; vorbeifahren; *(years)* vergehen; — **for** *vi* gehalten werden für; — **out** *vi (faint)* ohnmächtig werden; —**able** *a* road passierbar, befahrbar; *(fairly good)* passabel, leidlich; —**ably** *ad* leidlich, ziemlich; —**age** [pæsɪdʒ] *n (corridor)* Gang *m,* Korridor *m; (in book)* (Text)stelle *f; (voyage)* Überfahrt *f;* —**ageway** Passage *f,* Durchgang *m.*

passenger ['pæsɪndʒə*] n Passagier m; (on bus) Fahrgast m; (in aeroplane also) Fluggast m.

passer-by ['pɑːsə'baɪ] n Passant(in f) m.

passing ['pɑːsɪŋ] n (death) Ableben nt; a car vorbeifahrend; thought, affair momentan; in — en passant.

passion ['pæʃən] n Leidenschaft f; —ate a, —ately ad leidenschaftlich.

passive ['pæsɪv] n Passiv nt; a Passiv-, passiv.

Passover ['pɑːsəʊvə*] n Passahfest nt.

passport ['pɑːspɔːt] n (Reise)paß m.

password ['pɑːswɜːd] n Parole f, Kennwort nt, Losung f.

past [pɑːst] n Vergangenheit f; ad vorbei; prep to go — sth an etw (dat) vorbeigehen; to be — 10 (with age) über 10 sein; (with time) nach 10 sein; a years vergangen; president etc ehemalig.

paste [peɪst] n (for pastry) Teig m; (fish — etc) Paste f; (glue) Kleister m; vt kleben; (put — on) mit Kleister bestreichen.

pastel ['pæstəl] a colour Pastell-.

pasteurized ['pæstəraɪzd] a pasteurisiert.

pastille ['pæstɪl] n Pastille f.

pastime ['pɑːstaɪm] n Hobby nt, Zeitvertreib m.

pastor ['pɑːstə*] n Pastor m, Pfarrer m.

pastoral ['pɑːstərəl] a literature Schäfer-, Pastoral-.

pastry ['peɪstrɪ] n Blätterteig m; (tarts etc) Stückchen pl; Tortengebäck nt.

pasture ['pɑːstʃə*] n Weide f.

pasty ['pæstɪ] n (Fleisch)pastete f; ['peɪstɪ] a bläßlich, käsig.

pat [pæt] n leichte(r) Schlag m, Klaps m; vt tätscheln.

patch [pætʃ] n Fleck m; vt flicken; — of fog Nebelfeld nt; a bad — eine Pechsträhne; —work Patchwork nt; —y a (irregular) ungleichmäßig.

pate [peɪt] n Schädel m.

patent ['peɪtənt] n Patent nt; vt patentieren lassen; (by authorities) patentieren; a offenkundig; — leather Lackleder nt; —ly ad offensichtlich; — medicine pharmazeutische(s) Präparat nt.

paternal [pə'tɜːnl] a väterlich; his — grandmother seine Großmutter väterlicherseits; —istic [pətəːnə'lɪstɪk] a väterlich, onkelhaft.

paternity [pə'tɜːnɪtɪ] n Vaterschaft f.

path [pɑːθ] n Pfad m; Weg m; (of the sun) Bahn f.

pathetic [pə'θetɪk] a, —ally ad [pə'θetɪk, -lɪ] (very bad) kläglich; it's — es ist zum Weinen.

pathological [pæθə'lɒdʒɪkəl] a krankhaft, pathologisch.

pathologist [pə'θɒlədʒɪst] n Pathologe m.

pathology [pə'θɒlədʒɪ] n Pathologie f.

pathos ['peɪθɒs] n Rührseligkeit ·f.

pathway ['pɑːθweɪ] n Pfad m, Weg m.

patience ['peɪʃəns] n Geduld f; (Cards) Patience f.

patient ['peɪʃənt] n Patient(in f) m, Kranke(r) mf; a, —ly ad geduldig.

patio ['pætɪəʊ] n Innenhof m; (outside) Terrasse f.

patriotic [pætrɪ'ɒtɪk] a patriotisch.

patriotism ['pætrɪətɪzəm] n Patriotismus m.

patrol [pə'trəul] n Patrouille f; (police) Streife f; vt patrouillieren in (+dat); vi (police) die Runde machen; (Mil) patrouillieren; on — (police) auf Streife; — car Streifenwagen m; —man (US) (Streifen)polizist m.

patron ['peɪtrən] n (in shop) (Stamm)kunde m; (in hotel) (Stamm)gast m; (supporter) Förderer m; —age ['pætrənɪdʒ] Förderung f; Schirmherrschaft f; (Comm) Kundschaft f; —ize also ['pætrənaɪz] vt (support) unterstützen; shop besuchen; ['pætrənaɪz] (treat condescendingly) von oben herab behandeln; —izing a attitude herablassend; — saint Schutzheilige(r) mf, Schutzpatron(in f) m.

patter ['pætə*] n (sound) (of feet) Trappeln nt; (of rain) Prasseln nt; (sales talk) Art f zu reden, Gerede nt; vi (feet) trappeln; (rain) prasseln.

pattern ['pætən] n Muster nt; (sewing) Schnittmuster nt; (knitting) Strickanleitung f; vt — sth on sth etw nach etw bilden.

paunch [pɔːntʃ] n dicke(r) Bauch m, Wanst m.

pauper ['pɔːpə*] n Arme(r) mf.

pause [pɔːz] n Pause f; vi innehalten.

pave [peɪv] vt pflastern; to — the way for den Weg bahnen für; —ment (Brit) Bürgersteig m.

pavilion [pə'vɪlɪən] n Pavillon m; (Sport) Klubhaus nt.

paving ['peɪvɪŋ] n Straßenpflaster nt.

paw [pɔː] n Pfote f; (of big cats) Tatze f, Pranke f; vt (scrape) scharren; (handle) betatschen.

pawn [pɔːn] n Pfand nt; (chess) Bauer m; vt versetzen, verpfänden; —broker Pfandleiher m; —shop Pfandhaus nt.

pay [peɪ] n Bezahlung f, Lohn m; to be in sb's — von jdm bezahlt werden; irreg vt bezahlen; it would — you to ... es würde sich für dich lohnen, zu ...; to — attention achtgeben (to auf +acc); vi zahlen; (be profitable) sich bezahlt machen; it doesn't — es lohnt sich nicht; — for vt bezahlen für; — up vi bezahlen, seine Schulden begleichen; —able a zahlbar, fällig; —day Zahltag m; —ee [peɪ'i:] Zahlungsempfänger m; —ing a einträglich, rentabel; —load Nutzlast f; —ment Bezahlung f; —packet Lohntüte f; —roll Lohnliste f.

pea [pi:] n Erbse f; —souper (col) Suppe f, Waschküche f.

peace [pi:s] n Frieden m; —able a, —ably ad friedlich; —ful a friedlich, ruhig; —keeping a Friedens-; —keeping role Vermittlerrolle f; — offering Friedensangebot nt; —time Friede(n) m.

peach [pi:tʃ] n Pfirsich m.

peacock ['pi:kɒk] n Pfau m.

peak [pi:k] n Spitze f; (of mountain) Gipfel m; (fig) Höhepunkt m; (of cap) (Mützen)schirm m; — period Stoßzeit f, Hauptzeit f.

peal [pi:l] n (Glocken)läuten nt.

peanut ['pi:nʌt] n Erdnuß f; — butter Erdnußbutter f.

pear [peə*] n Birne f.

pearl [pɜːl] n Perle f.

peasant ['pezənt] n Bauer m.

peat [pi:t] n Torf m.

pebble ['pebl] n Kiesel m.

peck [pek] *vti* picken; *n (with beak)* Schnabelhieb *m*; *(kiss)* flüchtige(r) Kuß *m*; —**ish** a *(col)* ein bißchen hungrig.

peculiar [pɪˈkjuːlɪə*] *a (odd)* seltsam; — to charakteristisch für; —**ity** [pɪkjuːlɪˈærɪtɪ] *(singular quality)* Besonderheit *f*; *(strangeness)* Eigenartigkeit *f*; —**ly** *ad* seltsam; *(especially)* besonders.

pecuniary [pɪˈkjuːnɪərɪ] *a* Geld-, finanziell, pekuniär.

pedal [ˈpedl] *n* Pedal *nt*; *vti (cycle)* fahren, radfahren.

pedant [ˈpedənt] *n* Pedant *m*.

pedantic [pɪˈdæntɪk] *a* pedantisch.

pedantry [ˈpedəntrɪ] *n* Pedanterie *f*.

peddle [ˈpedl] *vt* hausieren gehen mit.

pedestal [ˈpedɪstl] *n* Sockel *m*.

pedestrian [pɪˈdestrɪən] *n* Fußgänger *m*; *a* Fußgänger-; *(humdrum)* langweilig; — crossing Fußgängerüberweg *m*; — precinct Fußgängerzone *f*.

pediatrics [piːdɪˈætrɪks] *n (US)* = **paediatrics**.

pedigree [ˈpedɪgriː] *n* Stammbaum *m*; *a* animal reinrassig, Zucht-.

pee [piː] *vi (col)* pissen, pinkeln.

peek [piːk] *n* flüchtige(r) Blick *m*; *vi* gucken.

peel [piːl] *n* Schale *f*; *vt* schälen; *vi (paint etc)* abblättern; *(skin)* sich schälen; —**ings** *pl* Schalen *pl*.

peep [piːp] *n (look)* neugierige(r) Blick *m*; *(sound)* Piepsen *nt*; *vi (look)* neugierig gucken; —**hole** Guckloch *nt*.

peer [pɪə*] *vi* spähen; angestrengt schauen *(at* auf *+acc)*; *(peep)* gucken; *n (nobleman)* Peer *m*; *(equal)* Ebenbürtige(r) *m*; his —s

seinesgleichen; —**age** Peerswürde *f*; —**less** a unvergleichlich.

peeve [piːv] *vt (col)* verärgern; —**d** *a* ärgerlich; *person* sauer.

peevish [ˈpiːvɪʃ] *a* verdrießlich, brummig; —**ness** Verdrießlichkeit *f*.

peg [peg] *n* Stift *m*; *(hook)* Haken *m*; *(stake)* Pflock *m*; *clothes* — Wäscheklammer *f*; off the — von der Stange.

pejorative [pɪˈdʒɒrɪtɪv] *a* pejorativ, herabsetzend.

pekinese [piːkɪˈniːz] *n* Pekinese *m*.

pelican [ˈpelɪkən] *n* Pelikan *m*.

pellet [ˈpelɪt] *n* Kügelchen *nt*.

pelmet [ˈpelmɪt] *n* Blende *f*, Schabracke *f*.

pelt [pelt] *vt* bewerfen; *n* Pelz *m*, Fell *nt*; — **down** *vi* niederprasseln.

pelvis [ˈpelvɪs] *n* Becken *nt*.

pen [pen] *n (fountain —)* Federhalter *m*; *(ball-point)* Kuli *m*; *(for sheep)* Pferch *m*; have you got a —? haben Sie etwas zum Schreiben?

penal [ˈpiːnl] *a* Straf-; —**ize** *vt (make punishable)* unter Strafe stellen; *(punish)* bestrafen; *(disadvantage)* benachteiligen; —**ty** [ˈpenltɪ] Strafe *f*; *(Ftbl)* Elfmeter *m*; —**ty area** Strafraum *m*; —**ty kick** Elfmeter *m*.

penance [ˈpenəns] *n* Buße *f*.

pence [pens] *npl (pl of penny)* Pence *pl*.

penchant [pɑ̃ːŋʃɑ̃ːŋ] *n* Vorliebe *f*, Schwäche *f*.

pencil [ˈpensl] *n* Bleistift *m*; — **sharpener** Bleistiftspitzer *m*.

pendant [ˈpendənt] *n* Anhänger *m*.

pending [ˈpendɪŋ] *prep* bis (zu); *a* unentschieden, noch offen.

pendulum [ˈpendjʊləm] *n* Pendel *nt*.

penetrate ['penitreit] vt durchdringen; (enter into) eindringen in (+acc).

penetrating ['penitreitiŋ] a durchdringend; analysis scharfsinnig.

penetration [peni'treiʃən] n Durchdringen nt; Eindringen nt.

penfriend ['penfrend] n Brieffreund(in f) m.

penguin ['peŋgwin] n Pinguin m.

penicillin [peni'silin] n Penizillin nt.

peninsula [pi'ninsjulə] n Halbinsel f.

penis ['pi:nis] n Penis m, männliche(s) Glied nt.

penitence ['penitəns] n Reue f.

penitent ['penitənt] a reuig; —iary [peni'tenʃəri] (US) Zuchthaus nt.

penknife ['pennaif] n Federmesser nt.

pen name ['pen'neim] n Pseudonym nt.

pennant ['penənt] n Wimpel m; (official —) Stander m.

penniless ['peniləs] a mittellos, ohne einen Pfennig.

penny ['peni] n Penny m.

pension ['penʃən] n Rente f; (for civil servants, executives etc) Ruhegehalt nt, Pension f; —able a person pensionsberechtigt; job mit Renten- or Pensionsanspruch; —er Rentner(in f) m; (civil servant, executive) Pensionär m; — fund Rentenfonds m.

pensive ['pensiv] a nachdenklich.

pentagon ['pentəgən] n Fünfeck nt.

Pentecost ['pentikɔst] n Pfingsten pl or nt.

penthouse ['penthaus] n Dachterrassenwohnung f.

pent-up ['pentʌp] a feelings angestaut.

penultimate [pi'nʌltimət] a vorletzte(r, s).

people ['pi:pl] n (nation) Volk nt; (inhabitants) Bevölkerung f; (persons) Leute pl; — think man glaubt; vt besiedeln.

pep [pep] n (col) Schwung m, Schmiß m; — up vt aufmöbeln.

pepper ['pepə*] n Pfeffer m; (vegetable) Paprika m; vt (pelt) bombardieren; —mint (plant) Pfefferminze f; (sweet) Pfefferminz nt.

peptalk ['peptɔ:k] n (col) Anstachelung f.

per [pɜ:*] prep pro; — annum pro Jahr; — cent Prozent nt.

perceive [pə'si:v] vt (realize) wahrnehmen, spüren; (understand) verstehen.

percentage [pə'sentidʒ] n Prozentsatz m.

perceptible [pə'septəbl] a merklich, wahrnehmbar.

perception [pə'sepʃən] n Wahrnehmung f; (insight) Einsicht f.

perceptive [pə'septiv] a person aufmerksam; analysis tiefgehend.

perch [pɜ:tʃ] n Stange f; (fish) Flußbarsch m; vi sitzen, hocken.

percolator ['pɜ:kəleitə*] n Kaffeemaschine f.

percussion [pə'kʌʃən] n (Mus) Schlagzeug nt.

peremptory [pə'remptəri] a schroff.

perennial [pə'reniəl] a wiederkehrend; (everlasting) unvergänglich; n perennierende Pflanze f.

perfect ['pɜ:fikt] a vollkommen; crime, solution perfekt; (Gram) vollendet; n (Gram) Perfekt nt; [pə'fekt] vt vervollkommnen; —ion [pə'fekʃən] Vollkommenheit f, Perfektion f; —ionist [pə'fekʃənɪst] Perfektionist m; —ly ad vollkommen, perfekt; (quite) ganz, einfach.

perforate ['pɜːfəreɪt] vt durchlöchern; —d a durchlöchert, perforiert.

perforation [pɜːfə'reɪʃən] n Perforation f.

perform [pə'fɔːm] vt (carry out) durch- or ausführen; task verrichten; (Theat) spielen, geben; vi (Theat) auftreten; —ance Durchführung f; (efficiency) Leistung f; (show) Vorstellung f; —er Künstler(in f) m; —ing a animal dressiert.

perfume ['pɜːfjuːm] n Duft m; (lady's) Parfüm nt.

perfunctory [pə'fʌŋktərɪ] a oberflächlich, mechanisch.

perhaps [pə'hæps] ad vielleicht.

peril ['perɪl] n Gefahr f; —ous a, —ously ad gefährlich.

perimeter [pə'rɪmɪtə*] n Peripherie f; (of circle etc) Umfang m.

period ['pɪərɪəd] n Periode f, Zeit f; (Gram) Punkt m; (Med) Periode f; a costume historisch; —ic(al) [pɪərɪ'ɒdɪk(əl)] a periodisch; —ical n Zeitschrift f; —ically [pɪərɪ'ɒdɪkəlɪ] ad periodisch.

peripheral [pə'rɪfərəl] a Rand-, peripher.

periphery [pə'rɪfərɪ] n Peripherie f, Rand m.

periscope ['perɪskəʊp] n Periskop nt, Sehrohr nt.

perish ['perɪʃ] vi umkommen; (material) unbrauchbar werden; (fruit) verderben; — the thought! daran wollen wir nicht denken; —able a fruit leicht verderblich; —ing a (col: cold) eisig.

perjure ['pɜːdʒə*] vr: — o.s. einen Meineid leisten.

perjury ['pɜːdʒərɪ] n Meineid m.

perk [pɜːk] n (col: fringe benefit) Vorteil m, Vergünstigung f; — up vi munter werden; vt ears spitzen; —y a (cheerful) keck.

perm [pɜːm] n Dauerwelle f.

permanence ['pɜːmənəns] n Dauer(haftigkeit) f, Beständigkeit f.

permanent a, —ly ad ['pɜːmənənt, —lɪ] dauernd, ständig.

permissible [pə'mɪsəbl] a zulässig.

permission [pə'mɪʃən] n Erlaubnis f, Genehmigung f.

permissive [pə'mɪsɪv] a nachgiebig; society etc permissiv.

permit ['pɜːmɪt] n Zulassung f, Erlaubnis(schein m) f; [pə'mɪt] vt erlauben, zulassen.

permutation [pɜːmju'teɪʃən] n Veränderung f; (Math) Permutation f.

pernicious [pɜː'nɪʃəs] a schädlich.

perpendicular [pɜːpən'dɪkjʊlə*] a senkrecht.

perpetrate ['pɜːpɪtreɪt] vt begehen, verüben.

perpetual a, —ly ad [pə'petjʊəl, -ɪ] dauernd, ständig.

perpetuate [pə'petjʊeɪt] vt verewigen, bewahren.

perpetuity [pɜːpɪ'tjuːɪtɪ] n Ewigkeit f.

perplex [pə'pleks] vt verblüffen; —ed a verblüfft, perplex; —ing a verblüffend; —ity n Verblüffung f.

persecute ['pɜːsɪkjuːt] vt verfolgen.

persecution [pɜːsɪ'kjuːʃən] n Verfolgung f.

perseverance [pɜːsɪ'vɪərəns] n Ausdauer f.

persevere [pɜːsɪ'vɪə*] vi beharren, durchhalten.

persist [pə'sɪst] *vi (in belief etc)* bleiben *(in bei); (rain, smell)* andauern; *(continue)* nicht aufhören; **—ence** Beharrlichkeit *f*; **—ent** *a*, **—ently** *ad* beharrlich; *(unending)* ständig.

person ['pɜːsn] *n* Person *f*, Mensch *m*; *(Gram)* Person *f*; **on one's —** bei sich; **in —** persönlich; **—able** *a* gut aussehend; **—al** *a* persönlich; *(private)* privat; *(of body)* körperlich, Körper-; **—ality** [pɜːsə'nælɪtɪ] Persönlichkeit *f*; **—ally** *ad* persönlich; **—ification** [pɜːsɒnɪfɪ'keɪʃən] Verkörperung *f*; **—ify** [pɜː'sɒnɪfaɪ] *vt* verkörpern, personifizieren.

personnel [pɜːsə'nel] *n* Personal *nt*; *(in factory)* Belegschaft *f*; **— manager** Personalchef *m*.

perspective [pə'spektɪv] *n* Perspektive *f*.

Perspex ® ['pɜːspeks] *n* Plexiglas ® *nt*.

perspicacity [pɜːspɪ'kæsɪtɪ] *n* Scharfsinn *m*.

perspiration [pɜːspə'reɪʃən] *n* Transpiration *f*.

perspire [pəs'paɪə*] *vi* transpirieren.

persuade [pə'sweɪd] *vt* überreden; *(convince)* überzeugen.

persuasion [pə'sweɪʒən] *n* Überredung *f*; Überzeugung *f*.

persuasive *a*, **—ly** *ad* [pə'sweɪsɪv, -lɪ] überzeugend.

pert [pɜːt] *a* keck.

pertain [pɜː'teɪn] *vi* gehören *(to* zu).

pertaining [pɜː'teɪnɪŋ]: **— to** betreffend *(+acc)*.

pertinent [pɜː'tɪnənt] *a* relevant.

perturb [pə'tɜːb] *vt* beunruhigen.

perusal [pə'ruːzəl] *n* Durchsicht *f*.

peruse [pə'ruːz] *vt* lesen.

pervade [pɜː'veɪd] *vt* erfüllen, durchziehen.

pervasive [pɜː'veɪsɪv] *a* durchdringend; *influence etc* allgegenwärtig.

perverse *a*, **—ly** *ad* [pə'vɜːs, -lɪ] pervers; *(obstinate)* eigensinnig; **—ness** Perversität *f*; Eigensinn *m*.

perversion [pə'vɜːʃən] *n* Perversion *f*; *(of justice)* Verdrehung *f*.

perversity [pə'vɜːsɪtɪ] *n* Perversität *f*.

pervert ['pɜːvɜːt] *n* perverse(r) Mensch *m*; [pə'vɜːt] *vt* verdrehen; *(morally)* verderben.

pessimism ['pesɪmɪzəm] *n* Pessimismus *m*.

pessimist ['pesɪmɪst] *n* Pessimist *m*; **—ic** [pesɪ'mɪstɪk] *a* pessimistisch.

pest [pest] *n* Plage *f*; *(insect)* Schädling *m*; *(fig) (person)* Nervensäge *f*; *(thing)* Plage *f*.

pester ['pestə*] *vt* plagen.

pesticide ['pestɪsaɪd] *n* Insektenvertilgungsmittel *nt*.

pestle ['pesl] *n* Stößel *m*.

pet [pet] *n (animal)* Haustier *nt*; *(person)* Liebling *m*; *vt* liebkosen, streicheln.

petal ['petl] *n* Blütenblatt *nt*.

peter out ['piːtə aʊt] *vi* allmählich zu Ende gehen.

petite [pə'tiːt] *a* zierlich.

petition [pə'tɪʃən] *n* Bittschrift *f*.

petrel ['petrəl] *n* Sturmvogel *m*.

petrified ['petrɪfaɪd] *a* versteinert; *person* starr (vor Schreck).

petrify ['petrɪfaɪ] *vt* versteinern; *person* erstarren lassen.

petrol ['petrəl] *n (Brit)* Benzin *nt*, Kraftstoff *m*; **—engine** Benzinmotor . *m;* —eum [pɪ'trəʊliəm] Petroleum *nt;* — pump *(in car)* Benzinpumpe *f; (at garage)* Zapf-säule *f,* Tanksäule *f;* — station Tankstelle *f;* — tank Benzintank *m.*

petticoat ['petɪkəʊt] *n* Petticoat *m.*

pettifogging ['petɪfɒgɪŋ] *a* kleinlich.

pettiness ['petɪnəs] *n* Gering-fügigkeit *f; (meanness)* Klein-lichkeit *f.*

petty ['petɪ] *a (unimportant)* gering-fügig, unbedeutend; *(mean)* kleinlich; — cash Portokasse *f;* —officer Maat *m.*

petulant ['petjʊlənt] *a* leicht reizbar.

pew [pjuː] *n* Kirchenbank *f.*

pewter ['pjuːtə*] *n* Zinn *nt.*

phallic ['fælɪk] *a* phallisch, Phallus-.

phantom ['fæntəm] *n* Phantom *nt,* Geist *m.*

pharmacist ['fɑːməsɪst] *n* Pharma-zeut *m; (druggist)* Apotheker *m.*

pharmacy ['fɑːməsɪ] *n* Pharmazie *f; (shop)* Apotheke *f.*

phase [feɪz] *n* Phase *f;* — out *vi* langsam abbauen; *model* auslaufen lassen; *person* absetzen.

pheasant ['feznt] *n* Fasan *m.*

phenomenal *a,* —ly *ad* [fɪ'nɒmɪnl, -nəlɪ] phänomenal.

phenomenon [fɪ'nɒmɪnən] *n* Phänomen *nt;* —common — häufige Erscheinung *f.*

phial ['faɪəl] *n* Fläschchen *nt,* Ampulle *f.*

philanderer [fɪ'lændərə*] *n* Schwerenöter *m.*

philanthropic [fɪlən'θrɒpɪk] *a* philanthropisch.

philanthropist [fɪ'lænθrəpɪst] *n* Philanthrop *m,* Menschenfreund *m.*

philatelist [fɪ'lætəlɪst] *n.* Brief-markensammler *m,* Philatelist *m.*

philately [fɪ'lætəlɪ] *n* Briefmarken-sammeln *nt,* Philatelie *f.*

philosopher [fɪ'lɒsəfə*] *n* Philosoph *m.*

philosophical [fɪlə'sɒfɪkəl] *a* philosophisch.

philosophize [fɪlɒsəfaɪz] *vi* philosophieren.

philosophy [fɪ'lɒsəfɪ] *n* Philosophie *f;* Weltanschauung *f.*

phlegm [flem] *n (Med)* Schleim *m; (calmness)* Gelassenheit *f;* —atic [fleg'mætɪk] *a* gelassen.

phobia ['fəʊbɪə] *n* krankhafte Furcht *f,* Phobie *f.*

phoenix ['fiːnɪks] *n.* Phönix *m.*

phone [fəʊn] *(abbr of telephone) n* Telefon *nt; vtf* telefonieren, anrufen.

phonetics [fəʊ'netɪks] *n* Phonetik *f,* Laut(bildungs)lehre *f; pl* Laut-schrift- *f.*

phon(e)y ['fəʊnɪ] *a (col)* unecht; *excuse* faul; *money* gefälscht; *n (person)* Schwindler *m; (thing)* Fälschung *f; (pound note)* Blüte *f.*

phonograph ['fəʊnəgrɑːf] *n (US)* .Grammophon *nt.*

phonology [fəʊ'nɒlədʒɪ] *n* Phonologie *f,* Lautlehre *f.*

phosphate ['fɒsfeɪt] *n* Phosphat *nt.*

phosphorus ['fɒsfərəs] *n* Phosphor *m.*

photo ['fəʊtəʊ] *n (abbr of photograph)* Foto *nt.*

photocopier ['fəʊtəʊ'kɒpɪə*] *n* Kopiergerät *nt.*

photocopy ['fəʊtəʊkɒpɪ] · *n* Fotokopie *f; vt* fotokopieren.

photoelectric ['fəʊtəʊɪ'lektrɪk] *a* fotoelektrisch.

photo finish ['fəʊtəʊ'fɪnɪʃ] n Zielfotografie f.

photogenic [fəʊtəʊ'dʒenɪk] a fotogen.

photograph ['fəʊtəgrɑːf] n Fotografie f, Aufnahme f; vt fotografieren, aufnehmen; —er [fə'tɒgrəfə] Fotograf m; —ic ['fəʊtə'græfɪk] a fotografisch; —y [fə'tɒgrəfɪ] Fotografie f, Fotografieren nt; (of film, book) Aufnahmen pl.

photostat ['fəʊtəʊstæt] n Fotokopie f.

phrase [freɪz] n (kurzer) Satz m; (Gram) Phrase f; (expression) Redewendung f, Ausdruck m; vt ausdrücken, formulieren; — book Sprachführer m.

physical a, **—ly** ad [fɪzɪkəl, -ɪ] physikalisch; (bodily) körperlich, physisch; — training Turnen nt.

physician [fɪ'zɪʃən] n Arzt m.

physicist ['fɪzɪsɪst] n Physiker(in f) m.

physics ['fɪzɪks] n Physik f.

physiology [fɪzɪ'ɒlədʒɪ] n Physiologie f.

physiotherapist [fɪzɪə'θerəpɪst] n Heilgymnast(in f) m.

physiotherapy [fɪzɪə'θerəpɪ] n Heilgymnastik f, Physiotherapie f.

physique [fɪ'ziːk] n Körperbau m; (in health) Konstitution f.

pianist ['pɪənɪst] n Pianist(in f) m.

piano ['pjɑːnəʊ] n Klavier nt, Piano nt; **—accordion** Akkordeon nt.

piccolo ['pɪkələʊ] n Pikkoloflöte f.

pick [pɪk] n (tool) Pickel m; (choice) Auswahl f; the — of die Beste von; vt (gather) (auf)lesen, sammeln; fruit pflücken; (choose) aussuchen; (Mus) zupfen; to — one's nose in der Nase bohren; to

— sb's pocket jdm bestehlen; to — at one's food im Essen herumstochern; — on vt person herumhacken auf (+dat); why — on me? warum ich?; — out vt auswählen; — up vi (improve) sich erholen; (lift up) aufheben; (learn) (schnell) mitbekommen; word aufschnappen; (collect) abholen; girl (sich dat) anlachen; speed gewinnen an (+dat); — axe Pickel m.

picket ['pɪkɪt] n (stake) Pfahl m, Pflock m; (guard) Posten m; (striker) Streikposten m; vt factory (Streik)posten aufstellen vor (+dat); vi (Streik)posten stehen; **—ing** Streikwache f; **— line** Streikpostenlinie f.

pickle ['pɪkl] n (salty mixture) Pökel m; (col) Klemme f; vt (in Essig) einlegen; einpökeln.

pick-me-up ['pɪkmiːʌp] a Schnäpschen nt.

pickpocket ['pɪkpɒkɪt] n Taschendieb m.

pickup ['pɪkʌp] n (on record player) Tonabnehmer m; (small truck) Lieferwagen m.

picnic ['pɪknɪk] n Picknick nt; vi picknicken.

pictorial [pɪk'tɔːrɪəl] a in Bildern; n Illustrierte f.

picture ['pɪktʃə*] n Bild nt; (likeness also) Abbild nt; (in words also) Darstellung f; in the — (fig) im Bild; vt darstellen; (fig: paint) malen; (visualize) sich (dat) vorstellen; **the —s** (Brit) Kino nt; **— book** Bilderbuch nt; **—sque** [pɪktʃə'resk] a malerisch.

piddling ['pɪdlɪŋ] a (col) lumpig; task pingelig.

pidgin ['pɪdʒɪn] a: **— English** Pidgin-Englisch nt.

pie [paɪ] n (meat) Pastete f; (fruit) Torte f.

piebald ['paɪbɔːld] a gescheckt.

piece [piːs] n Stück nt; to go to —s (work, standard) wertlos werden; he's gone to —s er ist vollkommen fertig; in —s entzwei, kaputt; (taken apart) auseinandergenommen; a — of cake (col) ein Kinderspiel nt; —meal ad stückweise, Stück für Stück; —work Akkordarbeit f; — together vt zusammensetzen.

pier [pɪə*] n Pier m, Mole f.

pierce [pɪəs] vt durchstechen, durchbohren (also look); durchdringen (also fig).

piercing ['pɪəsɪŋ] a durchdringend; cry also gellend; look also durchbohrend.

piety ['paɪətɪ] n Frömmigkeit f.

pig [pɪg] n Schwein nt.

pigeon ['pɪdʒən] n Taube f; —hole (compartment) Ablegefach nt; vt ablegen; idea zu den Akten legen.

piggy bank ['pɪgɪbæŋk] n Sparschwein nt.

pigheaded ['pɪg'hedɪd] a dickköpfig.

piglet ['pɪglət] n Ferkel nt, Schweinchen nt.

pigment ['pɪgmənt] n Farbstoff m, Pigment nt (also Biol); —ation [pɪgmən'teɪʃən] Färbung f, Pigmentation f.

pigmy ['pɪgmɪ] n = **pygmy.**

pigskin ['pɪgskɪn] n Schweinsleder nt; a schweinsledern.

pigsty ['pɪgstaɪ] n (lit, fig) Schweinestall m.

pigtail ['pɪgteɪl] n Zopf m.

pike [paɪk] n Pike f; (fish) Hecht m.

pilchard ['pɪltʃəd] n Sardine f.

pile [paɪl] n Haufen m; (of books, wood) Stapel m, Stoß m; (in ground) Pfahl m; (of bridge) Pfeiler m; (on carpet) Flausch m; (also — up) sich anhäufen; vti (also — up) sich anhäufen.

piles [paɪlz] n Hämorrhoiden pl.

pile-up ['paɪlʌp] n (Aut) Massenzusammenstoß m.

pilfer ['pɪlfə*] vt stehlen, klauen; —ing Diebstahl m.

pilgrim ['pɪlgrɪm] n Wallfahrer(in f) m, Pilger(in f) m; —age Wallfahrt f, Pilgerfahrt f.

pill [pɪl] n Tablette f, Pille f; the P— die (Antibaby)pille.

pillage ['pɪlɪdʒ] vt plündern.

pillar ['pɪlə*] n Pfeiler m, Säule f (also fig); — box (Brit) Briefkasten m.

pillion ['pɪljən] n Soziussitz m; — passenger Soziusfahrer m.

pillory ['pɪlərɪ] n Pranger m; vt an den Pranger stellen; (fig) anprangern.

pillow ['pɪləʊ] n Kissen nt; —case Kissenbezug m.

pilot ['paɪlət] n Pilot m; (Naut) Lotse m; a scheme etc Versuchs-; vt führen; ship lotsen; — light Zündflamme f.

pimp [pɪmp] n Zuhälter m.

pimple ['pɪmpl] n Pickel m.

pimply ['pɪmplɪ] a pick(e)lig.

pin [pɪn] n Nadel f; (sewing) Stecknadel f; (Tech) Stift m, Bolzen m; vt stecken, heften (to an +acc); (keep in one position) pressen, drücken; —s and needles Kribbeln nt; I have —s and needles in my leg mein Bein ist (mir) eingeschlafen; — down vt (fig) person festnageln (to auf +acc).

pinafore ['pɪnəfɔː*] n Schürze f; — dress Kleiderrock m.

pincers ['pɪnsəz] npl Kneif- or Beißzange f; (Med) Pinzette f.

pinch [pɪntʃ] n Zwicken, Kneifen nt; (of salt) Prise f; vti zwicken, kneifen; (shoe) drücken; vt (col) (steal) klauen; (arrest) schnappen; at a — notfalls, zur Not; to feel the — die Not or es zu spüren bekommen.

pincushion ['pɪnkuʃən] n Nadelkissen nt.

pine [paɪn] n (also — tree) Kiefer f, Föhre f, Pinie f; vi: — for sich sehnen or verzehren nach; to — away sich zu Tode sehnen.

pineapple ['paɪnæpl] n Ananas f.

ping [pɪŋ] n Peng nt; Kling nt; — pong Pingpong nt.

pink [pɪŋk] n (plant) Nelke f; (colour) Rosa nt; a rosa inv.

pinnacle ['pɪnəkl] n Spitze f.

pinpoint ['pɪnpɔɪnt] vt festlegen.

pinstripe ['pɪnstraɪp] n Nadelstreifen m.

pint [paɪnt] n Pint nt.

pinup ['pɪnʌp] n Pin-up-girl nt.

pioneer [paɪə'nɪə*] n Pionier m; (fig also) Bahnbrecher m.

pious ['paɪəs] a fromm; literature geistlich.

pip [pɪp] n Kern m; (sound) Piepen nt; (on uniform) Stern m; to give sb the — (col) jdn verrückt machen.

pipe [paɪp] n (smoking) Pfeife f; (Mus) Flöte f; (tube) Rohr nt; (in house) (Rohr)leitung f; vti (durch Rohre) leiten; (Mus) blasen; — down vi (be quiet) die Luft anhalten; —dream Luftschloß nt; —line (for oil) Pipeline f; —r Pfeifer m; (bagpipes) Dudelsackbläser m; — tobacco Pfeifentabak m.

piping ['paɪpɪŋ] n Leitungsnetz nt; (on cake) Dekoration f; (uniform) Tresse f; ad: — hot siedend heiß.

piquant ['piːkənt] a pikant.

pique [piːk] n gekränkte(r) Stolz m; —d a pikiert.

piracy ['paɪərəsɪ] n Piraterie f, Seeräuberei f; (plagiarism) Plagiat nt.

pirate ['paɪərɪt] n Pirat m, Seeräuber m; (plagiarist) Plagiator m; — radio Schwarzsender m; (ex-territorial) Piratensender m.

pirouette [pɪru'et] n Pirouette f; vi pirouettieren, eine Pirouette drehen.

Pisces ['paɪsiːz] n Fische pl.

pissed [pɪst] a (col) blau, besoffen.

pistol ['pɪstl] n Pistole f.

piston ['pɪstən] n Kolben m.

pit [pɪt] n Grube f; (Theat) Parterre nt; (orchestra —) Orchestergraben m; vt (mark with scars) zerfressen; (compare) o.s. messen (against mit); sb/sth messen (against an +dat); the — s pl (motor racing) die Boxen.

pitch [pɪtʃ] n Wurf m; (of trader) Stand m; (Sport) (Spiel)feld nt; (slope) Neigung f; (degree) Stufe f; (Mus) Tonlage f; (substance) Pech nt; perfect — absolute(s) Gehör nt; to queer sb's — (col) jdm alles verderben; vt werfen, schleudern; (set up) aufschlagen; song anstimmen; vi (fall) (längelang) hinschlagen; (Naut) rollen; —black a pechschwarz; —ed battle offene Schlacht f.

pitcher ['pɪtʃə*] n Krug m.

pitchfork ['pɪtʃfɔːk] n Heugabel f.

piteous ['pɪtɪəs] a kläglich, erbärmlich.

pitfall ['pɪtfɔːl] n (fig) Falle f.

pith [pɪθ] n Mark nt; (of speech) Kern m.

pithead ['pɪthed] n Schachtkopf m.

pithy ['pɪθɪ] a prägnant.

pitiable ['pɪtɪəbl] a bedauernswert; (contemptible) jämmerlich.

pitiful a, **—ly** ad ['pɪtɪful, -fəlɪ] mitleidig; (deserving pity) bedauernswert; (contemptible) jämmerlich.

pitiless a, **—ly** ad ['pɪtɪləs, -lɪ] erbarmungslos.

pittance ['pɪtəns] n Hungerlohn m.

pity ['pɪtɪ] n (sympathy) Mitleid nt; (shame) Jammer m; to have or take — on sb Mitleid mit jdm haben; for —'s sake um Himmels willen; what a —! wie schade!; it's a — es ist schade; vt Mitleid haben mit; I — you du tust mir leid; **—ing** a mitleidig.

pivot ['pɪvət] n Drehpunkt m; (pin) (Dreh)zapfen m; (fig) Angelpunkt m; vi sich drehen (on um).

pixie ['pɪksɪ] n Elf(e f) m.

placard ['plæka:d] n Plakat nt, Anschlag m; vt anschlagen.

placate [plə'keɪt] vt beschwichtigen, besänftigen.

place [pleɪs] n Platz m; (spot) Stelle f; (town etc) Ort m; vt setzen, stellen, legen; order aufgeben; (Sport) plazieren; (identify) unterbringen; in — am rechten Platz; out of — nicht am rechten Platz; (fig) remark unangebracht; in — of anstelle von; in the first/second etc — erstens/zweitens etc; to give — to Platz machen (+dat); to invite sb to one's — jdn zu sich (nach Hause) einladen; to keep sb in his — jdn in seinen Schranken halten; to put sb in his — jdn in seine Schranken (ver)weisen; — of wor-

ship Stätte f des Gebets; — mat Platzdeckchen nt.

placid ['plæsɪd] a gelassen, ruhig; **—ity** [plə'sɪdɪtɪ] Gelassenheit f, Ruhe f.

plagiarism ['pleɪdʒɪərɪzəm] n Plagiat nt.

plagiarist ['pleɪdʒɪərɪst] n Plagiator m.

plagiarize ['pleɪdʒɪəraɪz] vt abschreiben, plagiieren.

plague [pleɪg] n Pest f; (fig) Plage f; vt plagen.

plaice [pleɪs] n Scholle f.

plaid [plæd] n Plaid nt.

plain a, **—ly** ad [pleɪn, -lɪ] (clear) klar, deutlich; (simple) einfach, schlicht; (not beautiful) einfach, nicht attraktiv; (honest) offen; in Ebene f; in — clothes (police) in Zivil(kleidung); it is — sailing das ist ganz einfach; **—ness** Einfachkeit f.

plaintiff ['pleɪntɪf] n Kläger m.

plait [plæt] n Zopf m; vt flechten.

plan [plæn] n Plan m; vti planen; (intend also) vorhaben; — out vt vorbereiten; according to — planmäßig.

plane [pleɪn] n Ebene f; (Aviat) Flugzeug nt; (tool) Hobel m; (tree) Platane f; a eben, flach; vt hobeln.

planet ['plænɪt] n Planet m.

planetarium [plænɪ'tɛərɪəm] n Planetarium nt.

planetary ['plænɪtərɪ] a planetarisch.

plank [plæŋk] n Planke f, Brett nt; (Pol) Programmpunkt m.

plankton ['plæŋktən] n Plankton nt.

planner ['plænə*] n Planer m.

planning ['plænɪŋ] n Planen nt, Planung f.

plant [plɑ:nt] n Pflanze f; (Tech) (Maschinen)anlage f; (factory) Fabrik f, Werk nt; vt pflanzen; (set firmly) stellen.

plantain ['plæntɪn] n (Mehl)banane f.

plantation [plæn'teɪʃən] n Pflanzung f, Plantage f.

planter ['plɑ:ntə*] n Pflanzer nt.

plaque [plæk] n Gedenktafel f.

plasma ['plæzmə] n Plasma nt.

plaster ['plɑ:stə*] n Gips m; (whole surface) Verputz m; (Med) Pflaster nt; (for fracture: also — of Paris) Gipsverband m; in — (leg etc) in Gips; vt gipsen; hole zugipsen; ceiling verputzen; (fig: with pictures etc) be- or verkleben; —ed a (col) besoffen; —er Gipser m.

plastic ['plæstɪk] n Kunststoff m; a (made of plastic) Kunststoff-, Plastik-; (soft) formbar, plastisch; (Art) plastisch, bildend; p—ine ['plæstɪsi:n] Plastilin nt; — surgery plastische Chirurgie f; Schönheitsoperation f.

plate [pleɪt] n Teller m; (gold/silver) · vergoldete(s)/versilberte(s) Tafelgeschirr nt; (flat sheet) Platte f; (in book) (Bild)tafel f; vt überziehen, plattieren; to — silver/gold— versilbern/vergolden.

plateau ['plætəu] n, pl —x Hochebene f, Plateau nt.

plateful ['pleɪtful] n Teller(voll) m.

plate glass ['pleɪt'glɑ:s] n Tafelglas nt.

platform ['plætfɔ:m] n (at meeting) Plattform f, Podium nt; (stage) Bühne f; (Rail) Bahnsteig m; (Pol) Partieprogramm f; — ticket Bahnsteigkarte f.

platinum ['plætɪnəm] n Platin nt.

platitude ['plætɪtju:d] n Gemeinplatz m, Platitüde f.

platoon [plə'tu:n] n (Mil) Zug m.

platter ['plætə*] n Platte f.

plausibility [plɔ:zə'bɪlɪtɪ] n Plausibilität f.

plausible a, **plausibly** ad ['plɔ:zəbl, -blɪ] plausibel, einleuchtend; liar überzeugend.

play [pleɪ] n Spiel nt (also Tech); (Theat) (Theater)stück nt, Schauspiel nt; vti spielen; another team spielen gegen; (put sb in a team) einsetzen, spielen lassen; to — a joke on sb jdm einen Streich spielen; to — sb off against sb else jdn gegen jdn anders ausspielen; to — a part in —(fig) eine Rolle spielen bei; — down vt bagatellisieren, heruntersplielen; — up vi (cause trouble) frech werden; (bad leg etc) weh tun; vt person plagen; to — up to sb jdm flattieren; —acting n Schauspielerei f; —boy Playboy m; —er Spieler(in f) m; —ful a spielerisch, verspielt; —goer Theaterfreund m; —ground Spielplatz m; —group Kindergarten m; —ing card Spielkarte f; —ing field Sportplatz m; —mate Spielkamerad m; —off (Sport) Entscheidungsspiel nt; —pen Laufstall m; —thing Spielzeug nt; —wright Theaterschriftsteller m.

plea [pli:] n (dringende) Bitte f, Gesuch nt; (Jur) Antwort f des Angeklagten; (excuse) Ausrede f, Vorwand m; (objection) Einrede f; — of guilty Geständnis nt.

plead [pli:d] vt poverty zur Entschuldigung anführen; (Jur) sb's case vertreten; vi (beg) dringend bitten (with sb jdn); (Jur) plädieren; to — guilty schuldig plädieren.

pleasant a, **—ly** ad ['pleznt, .-lı] angenehm; freundlich; **—ness** Angenehme(s) nt; (of person) angenehme(s) Wesen nt, Freundlichkeit f; **—ry** Scherz m.

please [pliːz] vt (be agreeable to) gefallen (+dat); —! bitte! ; — yourself! wie du willst! ; do what you — mach' was du willst; **—d** a zufrieden; (glad) erfreut (with über +acc).

pleasing ['pliːzıŋ] a erfreulich.

pleasurable a, **pleasurably** ad ['pleʒərəbl, -blı] angenehm, erfreulich.

pleasure ['pleʒə*] n Vergnügen nt, Freude f; (old: will) Wünsche pl; it's a — gern geschehen; they take (no/great) — in doing ... haben ihnen (keinen/großen) Spaß zu...; **— ground** Vergnügungspark m; **— seeking** a vergnügungshungrig; **— steamer** Vergnügungsdampfer m.

pleat [pliːt] n Falte f.

plebeian [plɪˈbiːən] n Plebejer(in f) m; a plebejisch.

plebiscite ['plebɪsɪt] n Volksentscheid m, Plebiszit nt.

plebs [plebz] npl Plebs m, Pöbel m.

plectrum ['plektrəm] n Plektron nt.

pledge [pledʒ] n Pfand nt; (promise) Versprechen nt; vt verpfänden; (promise) geloben, versprechen; to take the — dem Alkohol abschwören.

plenipotentiary [plenɪpɒˈtenʃərɪ] m Bevollmächtiger m; a bevollmächtigt; **— power** Vollmacht f.

plentiful ['plentɪful] a reichlich.

plenty ['plentɪ] n Fülle f, Überfluß m; ad (col) ganz schön; — of eine Menge, viel; in — reichlich, massenhaft; to be — genug sein, reichen.

plethora ['pleθərə] n Überfülle f.

pleurisy ['pluərɪsɪ] n Rippenfellentzündung f.

pliability [plaɪəˈbɪlɪtɪ] n Biegsamkeit f; (of person) Beeinflußbarkeit f.

pliable ['plaɪəbl] a biegsam; person beeinflußbar.

pliers ['plaɪəz] npl (Kneif)zange f.

plight [plaɪt] n (Not)lage f; (schrecklicher) Zustand m.

plimsolls ['plɪmsəlz] npl Turnschuhe pl.

plinth [plɪnθ] n Säulenplatte f, Plinthe f.

plod [plɒd] vi (work) sich abplagen; (walk) trotten; **—der** Arbeitstier nt; **—ding** a schwerfällig.

plonk [plɒŋk] n (col: wine) billige(r) Wein m; vt: — sth down etw hinknallen.

plot [plɒt] n Komplott nt, Verschwörung f; (story) Handlung f; (of land) Stück nt Land, Grundstück nt; vt markieren; curve zeichnen; movements nachzeichnen; vi (plan secretly) sich verschwören, ein Komplott schmieden; **—ter** Verschwörer m; **—ting** Intrigen pl.

plough, (US) plow [plau] n Pflug m; vt pflügen; (col) exam candidate durchfallen lassen; — back vt (Comm) wieder in das Geschäft stecken; — through vt water durchpflügen; book sich kämpfen durch; **—ing** Pflügen nt.

ploy [plɔɪ] n Masche f.

pluck [plʌk] vt fruit pflücken; guitar zupfen; goose rupfen; n Mut m; to — up courage all seinen Mut zusammennehmen; **—y** a beherzt.

plug [plʌg] n Stöpsel m; (Elec) Stecker m; (of tobacco) Pfriem m;

(col: publicity) Schleichwerbung *f;*
(Aut) Zündkerze *f; vt* (zu)stopfen;
(col: advertise) Reklame machen
für ; **to — in a lamp** den Stecker
einer Lampe einstecken.

plum [plʌm] *n* Pflaume *f,*
Zwetschge *f; a job etc* Bomben-.

plumage ['pluːmɪdʒ] *n* Gefieder *nt.*

plumb [plʌm] *n* Lot *nt; out of —*
nicht im Lot ; *a* senkrecht ; *ad*
(exactly) genau ; *vt* auslöten ; *(fig)*
.sondieren ; *mystery* ergründen.

plumber ['plʌmə*] *n* Klempner *m,*
Installateur *m.*

plumbing ['plʌmɪŋ] *n (craft)*
Installieren *nt ; (fittings)* Leitungen
pl, Installationen *pl.*

plumbline ['plʌmlaɪn] *n* Senkblei *nt.*

plume [pluːm] *n* Feder *f; (of smoke
etc)* Fahne *f; vt (bird)* putzen.

plummet ['plʌmɪt] *n* Senkblei *nt;
vi* (ab)stürzen.

plump [plʌmp] *a* rundlich, füllig ; *vi*
plumpsen, sich fallen lassen ; *vt*
plumpsen lassen ; **to — for** *(col:
choose)* wählen, sich entscheiden
für ; **—ness** Rundlichkeit *f.*

plunder ['plʌndə*] *n* Plünderung *f;
(loot)* Beute *f; vt* plündern ; *things*
rauben.

plunge [plʌndʒ] *n* Sprung *m,*
Stürzen *nt; vt* stoßen ; *vi* (sich)
stürzen ; *(ship)* eintefen ; **a room —d
into darkness** ein im Dunkeln
getauchtes Zimmer.

plunging ['plʌndʒɪŋ] *a neckline*
offenherzig.

pluperfect ['pluː'pɜːfɪkt] *n*
Plusquamperfekt *nt,* Vorvergangen-
heit *f.*

plural ['plʊərəl] *a* Plural-, Mehr-
zahl- ; *n* Plural *m,* Mehrzahl *f;*
—istic [plʊərə'lɪstɪk] *a* pluralistisch.

plus [plʌs] *prep* plus, und ; *a* Plus-.

plush [plʌʃ] *a* (also **—y:** *col:
luxurious)* feudal ; *n* Plüsch *m.*

ply [plaɪ] *n* as in: **three—** *wood* dreischichtig ; *wool* Dreifach- ; *vt trade*
(be)treiben ; *(with questions)*
zusetzen *(+dat); (ship, taxi)*
befahren ; *vi (ship, taxi)* verkehren ;
—wood Sperrholz *nt.*

pneumatic [njuːˈmætɪk] *a*
pneumatisch ; *(Tech)* Luft- ; **— drill**
Preßlufthammer *m; —* **tyre** Luft-
reifen *m.*

pneumonia [njuːˈməʊnɪə] *n*
Lungenentzündung *f.*

poach [pəʊtʃ] *vt (Cook)* pochieren ;
game stehlen ; *vi (steal)* wildern
(for nach); —ed a egg pochiert,
verloren ; **—er** Wilddieb *m; —ing*
Wildern *nt.*

pocket ['pɒkɪt] *n* Tasche *f; (of ore)*
Ader *f; (of resistance)*
(Widerstands)nest *nt; air —*
Luftloch *nt; vt* einstecken, in die
Tasche stecken ; **to be out of —**
kein Geld haben ; **—book** Taschen-
buch *nt; —ful* Tasche(voll) *f; —
knife* Taschenmesser *nt; —money*
Taschengeld *nt.*

pockmarked ['pɒkmɑːkt] *a face*
pockennarbig.

pod [pɒd] *n* Hülse *f; (of peas also)*
Schote *f.*

podgy ['pɒdʒɪ] *a* pummelig.

poem ['pəʊəm] *n* Gedicht *nt.*

poet ['pəʊɪt] *n* Dichter *m,* Poet *m;*
—ic [pəʊ'etɪk] *a* poetisch,
dichterisch ; *beauty* malerisch,
stimmungsvoll ; **— laureate** Hof-
dichter *m; —ry* Poesie *f; (poems)*
Gedichte *pl.*

poignant *a,* **—ly** *ad* ['pɔɪnjənt, -lɪ]
scharf, stechend ; *(touching)*
ergreifend, quälend.

point [pɔɪnt] *n* Punkt *m (also in
discussion, scoring); (spot also)*

Stelle f; (sharpened tip) Spitze f; (moment) (Zeit)punkt m, Moment m; (purpose) Zweck m; (idea) Argument nt; (decimal) Dezimalstelle f; (personal characteristic) Seite f; vt zeigen mit; gun richten; vi zeigen; —s pl (Rail) Weichen pl; — of view Stand- or Gesichtspunkt m; what's the —? was soll das?; you have a — there da hast du recht; three — two drei Komma zwei; — out vt hinweisen auf (+acc); — to vt zeigen auf (+acc); —blank ad (at close range) aus nächster Entfernung; (bluntly) unverblümt; — duty Verkehrsregelungsdienst m; —ed a, —edly ad spitz, scharf; (fig) gezielt; —er Zeigestock m; (on dial) Zeiger m; —less a, —lessly ad zwecklos, sinnlos; —lessness Zwecklosigkeit f, Sinnlosigkeit f.

poise [pɔɪz] n Haltung f; (fig also) Gelassenheit f; vti balancieren; knife, pen bereithalten; o.s. sich bereitmachen; —d a beherrscht.

poison ['pɔɪzn] n (lit, fig) Gift nt; vt vergiften; —ing Vergiftung f; —ous a giftig, Gift-.

poke [pəʊk] vt stoßen; (put) stecken; fire schüren; hole bohren; n Stoß m; to — one's nose into seine Nase stecken in (+acc); to — fun at sb sich über jdn lustig machen; — about vi herumstochern; herumwühlen; —r Schürhaken m; (Cards) Poker nt; —r-faced a undurchdringlich.

poky ['pəʊki] a eng.

polar ['pəʊlə*] a Polar-, polar; — bear Eisbär m; —ization [pəʊlərai'zeiʃən] n Polarisation f; —ize vt polarisieren; vi sich polarisieren.

pole [pəʊl] n Stange f, Pfosten m; (flag—, telegraph — also) Mast m; (Elec, Geog) Pol m; (Sport) (vaulting —) Stab m; (ski —) Stock m; —s apart durch Welten getrennt; —cat (US) Skunk m; — star Polarstern m; — vault Stabhochsprung m.

polemic [pɒ'lemik] n Polemik f.

police [pə'liːs] n Polizei f; vt polizeilich überwachen; kontrollieren; — car Polizeiwagen m; —man Polizist m; — state Polizeistaat m; — station (Polizei)revier nt, Wache f; —woman Polizistin f.

policy ['pɒlisi] n Politik f; (of business also) Usus m; (insurance) (Versicherungs)police f; (prudence) Klugheit f; (principle) Grundsatz m; — decision/statement Grundsatzentscheidung f/-erklärung f.

polio ['pəʊliəʊ] n (spinale) Kinderlähmung f, Polio f.

polish ['pɒliʃ] n Politur f; (for floor) Wachs nt; (for shoes) Creme f; (nail —) Lack m; (shine) Glanz m; (of furniture) Politur f; (fig) Schliff m; vt polieren; shoes putzen; (fig) den letzten Schliff geben (+dat), aufpolieren; — off vt (col: work) erledigen; food wegputzen; drink hinunterschütten; — up vt essay aufpolieren; knowledge auffrischen; —ed a glänzend (also fig); manners verfeinert.

polite a, —ly ad [pə'lait, -li] höflich; society fein; —ness Höflichkeit f; Feinheit f.

politic ['pɒlitik] a (prudent) diplomatisch; —al a [pə'litikəl, -l] politisch; —al science Politologie f; —ian [pɒli'tiʃən] Politiker m, Staatsmann m; —s pl Politik f.

polka   615   populate

polka ['pɒlkə] *n* Polka *f*; — **dot** Tupfen *m*.

poll [pəʊl] *n* Abstimmung *f*; *(in election)* Wahl *f*; *(votes cast)* Wahlbeteiligung *f*; *(opinion —)* Umfrage *f*; *vt* votes erhalten, auf sich vereinigen.

pollen ['pɒlən] *n* Blütenstaub *m*, Pollen *m*; — **count** Pollenkonzentration *f.*

pollination [pɒlɪ'neɪʃən] *n* Befruchtung *f.*

polling booth ['pəʊlɪŋbuːð] *n* Wahlkabine *f.*

polling day ['pəʊlɪŋ deɪ] *n* Wahltag *m.*

polling station ['pəʊlɪŋ steɪʃən] *n* Wahllokal *nt.*

pollute [pə'luːt] *vt* verschmutzen, verunreinigen.

pollution [pə'luːʃən] *n* Verschmutzung *f.*

polo ['pəʊləʊ] *n* Polo *nt.*

poly- [pɒlɪ] *pref* Poly-.

polygamy [pɒ'lɪgəmɪ] *n* Polygamie *f.*

polytechnic [pɒlɪ'teknɪk] *n* technische Hochschule *f.*

polythene ['pɒlɪθiːn] *n* Plastik *nt*; — **bag** Plastiktüte *f.*

pomegranate ['pɒməgrænɪt] *n* Granatapfel *m.*

pommel ['pʌml] *vt* mit den Fäusten bearbeiten; *n* Sattelknopf *m.*

pomp [pɒmp] *n* Pomp *m*, Prunk *m.*

pompous *a*, **—ly** *ad* ['pɒmpəs, -lɪ] aufgeblasen; *language* geschwollen.

ponce [pɒns] *n (col) (pimp)* Louis *m*; *(queer)* Schwule *m.*

pond [pɒnd] *n* Teich *m*, Weiher *m.*

ponder ['pɒndə*] *vt* nachdenken *or* nachgrübeln über *(+acc)*; **—ous** *a* schwerfällig.

pontiff ['pɒntɪf] *n* Pontifex *m.*

pontificate [pɒn'tɪfɪkeɪt] *vi (fig)* geschwollen reden.

pontoon [pɒn'tuːn] *n* Ponton *m*; *(Cards)* 17-und-4 *nt.*

pony ['pəʊnɪ] *n* Pony *nt*; —**tail** Pferdeschwanz *m.*

poodle ['puːdl] *n* Pudel *m.*

pooh-pooh [puː'puː] *vt* die Nase rümpfen über *(+acc).*

pool [puːl] *n (swimming —)* Schwimmbad *nt*; *(private)* Swimming-pool *m*; *(of spilt liquid, blood)* Lache *f*; *(fund)* (gemeinsame) Kasse *f*; *(billiards)* Poolspiel *nt*; *vt* money etc zusammenlegen.

poor [pʊə*] *a* arm; *(not good)* schlecht, schwach; **the** — *pl* die Armen *pl*; **—ly** *ad* schlecht, schwach; *dressed* ärmlich; *a* schlecht, elend.

pop [pɒp] *n* Knall *m*; *(music)* Popmusik *f*; *(drink)* Limo(nade) *f*; *(US col)* Pa *m*; *vt (put)* stecken; *balloon* platzen lassen; *vi* knallen; — **in/out** *(person)* hereinkommen/hinausgehen; hinein-/hinausspringen; — **concert** Popkonzert *nt*; —**corn** Puffmais *m.*

Pope [pəʊp] *n* Papst *m.*

poplar ['pɒplə*] *n* Pappel *f.*

poplin ['pɒplɪn] *n* Popelin *f.*

poppy ['pɒpɪ] *n* Mohn *m*; —**cock** *(col)* Quatsch *m.*

populace ['pɒpjʊləs] *n* Volk *nt.*

popular ['pɒpjʊlə*] *a* beliebt, populär; *(of the people)* volkstümlich, Populär-; *(widespread)* allgemein; **—ity** [pɒpjʊ'lærɪtɪ] Beliebtheit *f*, Popularität *f*; **—ize** *vt* popularisieren; **—ly** *ad* allgemein, überall.

populate ['pɒpjʊleɪt] *vt* bevölkern; *town* bewohnen.

population [pɒpjʊ'leɪʃən] n Bevölkerung f; (of town) Einwohner pl.

populous ['pɒpjʊləs] a dicht besiedelt.

porcelain ['pɔ:slɪn] n Porzellan nt.

porch [pɔ:tʃ] n Vorbau m, Veranda f; (in church) Vorhalle f.

porcupine ['pɔ:kjʊpaɪn] n Stachelschwein nt.

pore [pɔ:*] n Pore f; — over vt brüten or hocken über (+dat).

pork [pɔ:k] n Schweinefleisch nt.

pornographic a, **—ally** ad [pɔ:nə'græfɪk, -əlɪ] pornographisch.

pornography [pɔ:'mɒgrəfɪ] n Pornographie f.

porous ['pɔ:rəs] a porös; skin porig.

porpoise ['pɔ:pəs] n Tümmler m.

porridge ['pɒrɪdʒ] n Porridge m, Haferbrei m.

port [pɔ:t] n Hafen m; (town) Hafenstadt f; (Naut: left side) Backbord nt; (opening for loads) Luke f; (wine) Portwein m.

portable [pɔ:tabl] a tragbar; radio Koffer-; typewriter Reise-.

portal [pɔ:tl] n Portal nt.

portcullis [pɔ:t'kʌlɪs] n Fallgitter nt.

portend [pɔ:'tend] vt anzeigen, hindeuten auf (+acc).

portent ['pɔ:tent] n schlimme(s) Vorzeichen nt; **—ous** [pɔ:'tentəs] a schlimm, ominös; (amazing) ungeheuer.

porter ['pɔ:tə*] n Pförtner(in f) m; (for luggage) Gepäckträger m.

porthole ['pɔ:thəʊl] n Bullauge nt.

portico ['pɔ:tɪkəʊ] n Säulengang m.

portion ['pɔ:ʃən] n Teil m, Stück nt; (of food) Portion f.

portly ['pɔ:tlɪ] a korpulent, beleibt.

portrait ['pɔ:trɪt] n Porträt nt, Bild(nis) nt.

portray [pɔ:'treɪ] vt darstellen; (describe) schildern; **—al** Darstellung f; Schilderung f.

pose [pəʊz] n Stellung f, Pose f (also affectation); vi posieren, sich in Positur setzen; vt stellen; to — as sich ausgeben als; **—r** knifflige Frage f.

posh [pɒʃ] a (col) (piek)fein.

position [pə'zɪʃən] n Stellung f; (place) Position f, Lage f; (job) Stelle f; (attitude) Standpunkt m, Haltung f; to be in a — to do sth in der Lage sein, etw zu tun; vt aufstellen.

positive a, **—ly** ad ['pɒzɪtɪv, -lɪ] positiv; (convinced) sicher; (definite) eindeutig.

posse ['pɒsɪ] n (US) Aufgebot nt.

possess [pə'zes] vt besitzen; what —ed you to . . .? was ist in dich gefahren, daß...?; **—ed** a besessen; **—ion** [pə'zeʃən] Besitz m; **—ive** a besitzergreifend, eigensüchtig; (Gram) Possessiv-, besitzanzeigend; **—ively** ad besitzergreifend, eigensüchtig; **—or** Besitzer m.

possibility [pɒsə'bɪlɪtɪ] n Möglichkeit f.

possible ['pɒsəbl] a möglich; if — wenn möglich, möglichst; as big as — so groß wie möglich, möglichst groß.

possibly ['pɒsəblɪ] ad möglicherweise, vielleicht; as soon as I — can sobald ich irgendwie kann.

post [pəʊst] n Post f; (pole) Pfosten m, Pfahl m; (place of duty) Posten m; (job) Stelle f; vt notice anschlagen; letters aufgeben; soldiers aufstellen; **—age** Postgebühr f, Porto nt; **—al** a Post-; **—al order** Postanweisung f; **—card** Postkarte f; **—date** vt cheque nachdatieren; **—er Plakat** nt, Poster m; **—e restante** Aufbewahrungsstelle f für postlagernde Sendungen; **to send sth —e restante** etw postlagernd schicken.

posterior [pɒsˈtɪərɪə*] n (col) Hintern m.

posterity [pɒsˈterɪtɪ] n Nachwelt f; (descendants) Nachkommenschaft f.

postgraduate ['pəust'grædjuət] n Weiterstudierender(in f) m.

posthumous ['pɒstjuməs, -lɪ] post(h)um.

postman ['pəustmən] n Briefträger m, Postbote m.

postmark ['pəustmɑːk] n Poststempel m.

postmaster ['pəustmɑːstə*] n Postmeister m; **P— General** Postminister m.

post-mortem ['pəust'mɔːtəm] n Autopsie f.

post office ['pəustɒfɪs] n Postamt nt, Post f (also organization).

postpone [pə'spəun] vt verschieben, aufschieben; **—ment** Verschiebung f, Aufschub m.

postscript ['pəusskrɪpt] n Nachschrift f, Postskript nt; (in book) Nachwort nt.

postulate ['pɒstjuleɪt] vt voraussetzen; (maintain) behaupten.

posture ['pɒstʃə*] n Haltung f; vi posieren.

postwar ['pəust'wɔː*] a Nachkriegs-.

posy ['pəuzɪ] n Blumenstrauß m.

pot [pɒt] n Topf m; (tea—) Kanne f; (col: marijuana) Hasch m; vt plant eintopfen.

---

potash ['pɒtæʃ] n Pottasche f.

potato [pə'teɪtəu] n, pl **-es** Kartoffel f.

potency ['pəutənsɪ] n Stärke f, Potenz f.

potent ['pəutənt] a stark; argument zwingend.

potentate ['pəutənteɪt] n Machthaber m.

potential [pəu'tenʃəl] a potentiell; **he is a —** virtuoso er hat das Zeug zum Virtuosen; n Potential nt; **—ly** ad potentiell.

pothole ['pɒthəul] n Höhle f; (in road) Schlagloch nt; **—r** Höhlenforscher m.

potholing ['pɒthəulɪŋ] n: **to go —** Höhlen erforschen.

potion ['pəuʃən] n Trank m.

potluck ['pɒt'lʌk] n: **to take — with** sth etw auf gut Glück nehmen.

potpourri [pəu'purɪ] n Potpourri nt.

potshot ['pɒtʃɒt] n: **to take a — at** sth auf etw ·(acc) ballern.

potted ['pɒtɪd] a food eingelegt, eingemacht; plant Topf-; (fig: book, version) konzentriert.

potter ['pɒtə*] n Töpfer m; vi herumhantieren, herumwursteln; **—y** Töpferwaren pl, Steingut nt; (place) Töpferei f.

potty ['pɒtɪ] a (col) verrückt; n Töpfchen nt.

pouch [pautʃ] n Beutel m; (under eyes) Tränensack m; (for tobacco) Tabaksbeutel m.

pouffe [puːf] n Sitzkissen nt.

poultice ['pəultɪs] n Packung f.

poultry ['pəultrɪ] n Geflügel nt; **—farm** Geflügelfarm f.

pounce [pauns] vi sich stürzen (on auf +acc); n Sprung m, Satz m.

pound [paund] n (Fin, weight) Pfund nt; (for cars, animals)

Auslösestelle f; (for stray animals) (Tier)asyl nt; vi klopfen, hämmern; vt (zer)stampfen; —ing starke(s) Klopfen nt, Hämmern nt; (Zer)stampfen nt.

pour [pɔː*] vt gießen, schütten; vi gießen; (crowds etc) strömen; — away vt, — off vt abgießen; —ing rain strömende(r) Regen m.

pout [paʊt] n Schnute f, Schmollmund m; vi eine Schnute ziehen, schmollen.

poverty ['pɒvətɪ] n Armut f; — stricken a verarmt, sehr arm.

powder ['paʊdə*] n Pulver nt; (cosmetic) Puder m; vt pulverisieren; (sprinkle) bestreuen; to — one's nose·sich (dat) die Nase pudern; — room Damentoilette f; —y a pulverig, Pulver-.

power [paʊə*] n Macht f (also Pol); (ability) Fähigkeit f; (strength) Stärke f; (authority) Macht f, Befugnis f; (Math) Potenz f; (Elec) Strom m; vt betreiben, antreiben; — cut Stromausfall m; —ful a person mächtig; engine, government stark; —less a machtlos; — line (Haupt)stromleitung f; — point elektrische(r) Anschluß m; — station Elektrizitätswerk nt.

powwow ['paʊwaʊ] n Besprechung f; vi eine Besprechung abhalten.

practicability [præktɪkə'bɪlɪtɪ] n Durchführbarkeit f.

practicable ['præktɪkəbl] a durchführbar.

practical a, —ly ad ['præktɪkəl, -ɪ] praktisch; — joke Streich m.

practice ['præktɪs] n Übung f; (reality) Praxis f; (custom) Brauch m; (in business) Usus m; (doctor's, lawyer's) Praxis f; in — (in reality)

in der Praxis; out of — außer Übung.

practise, (US) **practice** ['præktɪs] vt üben; profession ausüben; to — law/medicine als Rechtsanwalt/Arzt arbeiten; to — (sich) üben; (doctor, lawyer) praktizieren; —d a erfahren.

practising, (US) **practicing** ['præktɪsɪŋ] a praktizierend; Christian etc aktiv.

practitioner [præk'tɪʃənə*] n praktische(r) Arzt m.

pragmatic [præg'mætɪk] a pragmatisch.

pragmatism ['prægmətɪzəm] n Pragmatismus m.

pragmatist ['prægmətɪst] n Pragmatiker m.

prairie ['prɛərɪ] n Prärie f, Steppe f.

praise [preɪz] n Lob nt, Preis m; vt loben; (worship) (lob)preisen, loben; —worthy a lobenswert.

pram [præm] n Kinderwagen m.

prance [prɑːns] vi (horse) tänzeln; (person) stolzieren; (gaily) herumhüpfen.

prank [præŋk] n Streich m.

prattle ['prætl] vi schwatzen, plappern.

prawn [prɔːn] n Garnele f; Krabbe f.

pray [preɪ] vi beten; —er [prɛə*] n Gebet nt; —er book Gebetbuch nt.

pre- [priː] pref prä-, vor(her)-.

preach [priːtʃ] vi predigen; —er n Prediger m.

preamble [priː'æmbl] n Einleitung f.

prearrange ['priːə'reɪndʒ] vt vereinbaren, absprechen; —d a vereinbart; —ment Vereinbarung f, vorherige Absprache f.

precarious *a*, **—ly** *ad* [pri'kɛərıəs, -lı] prekär, unsicher.

precaution [prɪ'kɔːʃən] *n* (Vorsichts)maßnahme *f*, Vorbeugung *f*; **—ary** *a measure* vorbeugend, Vorsichts-.

precede [prɪ'siːd] *vti* vorausgehen (+dat); *(be more important)* an Bedeutung übertreffen; **—nce** ['presɪdəns] Priorität *f*, Vorrang *m*; **to take —nce over** den Vorrang haben vor (+dat); **—nt** ['presɪdənt] Präzedenzfall *m*.

preceding [prɪ'siːdɪŋ] *a* vorhergehend.

precept ['priːsept] *n* Gebot *nt*, Regel *f*.

precinct ['priːsɪŋkt] *n* Gelände *f*; *(district)* Bezirk *m*; *(shopping —)* Einkaufszone *f*.

precious ['preʃəs] *a* kostbar, wertvoll; *(affected)* preziös, geziert.

precipice ['presɪpɪs] *n* Abgrund *m*.

precipitate *a*, **—ly** *ad* [prɪ'sɪpɪtɪt, -lı] überstürzt, übereilt; [prɪ'sɪpɪteɪt] *vt* hinunterstürzen; *events* heraufbeschwören.

precipitation .[prɪsɪpɪ'teɪʃən] *n* Niederschlag *m*.

precipitous *a*, **—ly** *ad* [prɪ'sɪpɪtəs, -lı] abschüssig; *action* überstürzt.

précis ['preɪsiː] *n* (kurze) Übersicht *f*, Zusammenfassung *f*; *(Sch)* Inhaltsangabe *f*.

precise *a*, **—ly** *ad* [prɪ'saɪs, -lı] genau, präzis.

preclude [prɪ'kluːd] *vt* ausschließen; *person* abhalten.

precocious [prɪ'kəʊʃəs] *a* frühreif.

preconceived ['priːkən'siːvd] *a idea* vorgefaßt.

precondition ['priːkən'dɪʃən] *n* Vorbedingung *f*, Voraussetzung *f*.

precursor [priː'kɜːsə*] *n* Vorläufer *m*..

predator ['predətə*] *n* Raubtier *nt*; **—y** *a* Raub-; räuberisch.

predecessor ['priːdɪsesə*] *n* Vorgänger *m*.

predestination [priːdestɪ'neɪʃən] *n* Vorherbestimmung *f*, Prädestination *f*.

predestine [priː'destɪn] *vt* vorherbestimmen.

predetermine ['priːdɪ'tɜːmɪn] *vt* vorherentscheiden, vorherbestimmen.

predicament [prɪ'dɪkəmənt] *n* mißliche Lage *f*; **to be in a —** in der Klemme sitzen.

predicate ['predɪkət] *n* Prädikat *nt*, Satzaussage *f*.

predict [prɪ'dɪkt] *vt* voraussagen; **—ion** [prɪ'dɪkʃən] Voraussage *f*.

predominance [prɪ'dɒmɪnəns] *n (in power)* Vorherrschaft *f*; *(fig)* Vorherrschen *nt*, Überwiegen *nt*.

predominant [prɪ'dɒmɪnənt] *a* vorherrschend; *(fig also)* überwiegend; **—ly** *ad* überwiegend, hauptsächlich.

predominate [prɪ'dɒmɪneɪt] *vi* vorherrschen; *(fig also)* überwiegen.

pre-eminent [priː'emɪnənt] *a* hervorragend, herausragend.

pre-empt [priː'empt] *vt action*, decision vorwegnehmen.

preen [priːn] *vt* putzen; **to — o.s. on sth** sich *(dat)* etwas auf etw *(acc)* einbilden.

prefab ['priːfæb] *n* Fertighaus *nt*.

prefabricated ['priːfæbrɪkeɪtɪd] *a* vorgefertigt, Fertig-.

preface ['prefɪs] *n* Vorwort *nt*, Einleitung *f*.

prefect ['priːfekt] *n* Präfekt *m*; *(Sch)* Aufsichtsschüler(in *f*) *m*.

·prefer [prɪˈfɜː*] vt vorziehen, lieber mögen; to — to do sth etw lieber tun; —able [ˈprefərəbl] a vorzuziehen(d) (to dat); —ably [ˈprefərəblɪ] ad vorzugsweise, am liebsten; —ence [ˈprefərəns] Präferenz f, Vorzug m; —ential [prefəˈrenʃəl] a bevorzugt, Vorzugs-.

prefix [ˈpriːfɪks] n Vorsilbe f, Präfix nt.

pregnancy [ˈpregnənsɪ] n Schwangerschaft f.

pregnant [ˈpregnənt] a schwanger; — with meaning (fig) bedeutungsschwer or -voll.

prehistoric [ˈpriːhɪsˈtɒrɪk] a prähistorisch, vorgeschichtlich.

prehistory [ˈpriːˈhɪstərɪ] n Urgeschichte f.

prejudge [ˈpriːˈdʒʌdʒ] vt vorschnell beurteilen.

prejudice [ˈpredʒudɪs] n Vorurteil nt; Voreingenommenheit f; (harm) Schaden m; vt beeinträchtigen; —d a person voreingenommen.

prelate [ˈprelət] n Prälat m.

preliminary [prɪˈlɪmɪnərɪ] a einleitend, Vor-; the preliminaries pl die vorbereitenden Maßnahmen pl.

prelude [ˈpreljuːd] n Vorspiel nt; (Mus) Präludium nt; (fig also) Auftakt m.

premarital [ˈpriːˈmærɪtl] a vorehelich.

premature [ˈpremətʃuə*] a vorzeitig, verfrüht; birth Frühdecision voreilig; —ly ad vorzeitig; verfrüht; voreilig.

premeditate [priːˈmedɪteɪt] vt im voraus planen; —d a geplant; murder vorsätzlich.

premeditation [priːmedɪˈteɪʃən] n Planung f.

premier [ˈpremɪə*] a erste(r, s), oberste(r, s), höchste(r, s); n Premier m.

premiere [ˈpremɪˈɛə*] n Premiere f; Uraufführung f.

premise [ˈpremɪs] n Voraussetzung f; Prämisse f; —s pl Räumlichkeiten pl; (grounds) Grundstück nt.

premium [ˈpriːmɪəm] n Prämie f; to sell at a — mit Gewinn verkaufen.

premonition [preməˈnɪʃən] n Vorahnung f.

preoccupation [priːɒkjuˈpeɪʃən] n Sorge f.

preoccupied [priːˈɒkjupaɪd] a look geistesabwesend; to be — with sth mit dem Gedanken an etw (acc) beschäftigt sein.

prep [prep] n (Sch: study) Hausaufgabe f.

prepaid [ˈpriːˈpeɪd] a vorausbezahlt; letter frankiert.

preparation [prepəˈreɪʃən] n Vorbereitung f.

preparatory [prɪˈpærətərɪ] a Vor(bereitungs)-.

prepare [prɪˈpɛə*] vt vorbereiten (for auf +acc); vi sich vorbereiten; to be —d to ... bereit sein zu ...

preponderance [prɪˈpɒndərəns] n Übergewicht nt.

preposition [prepəˈzɪʃən] n Präposition f, Verhältniswort nt.

preposterous [prɪˈpɒstərəs] a absurd, widersinnig.

prerequisite [ˈpriːˈrekwɪzɪt] n (unerläßliche) Voraussetzung f.

prerogative [prɪˈrɒɡətɪv] n Vorrecht nt, Privileg nt.

presbytery [ˈprezbɪtərɪ] n (house)

Presbyterium *nt*; *(Catholic)* Pfarrhaus *nt*.
prescribe [prɪs'kraɪb] *vt*
vorschreiben, anordnen; *(Med)*
verschreiben.
prescription [prɪs'krɪpʃən] *n*
Vorschrift *f*; *(Med)* Rezept *nt*.
prescriptive [prɪs'krɪptɪv] *a*
normativ.
presence ['prezns] *n* Gegenwart *f*,
Anwesenheit *f*; — of mind Geistes-
gegenwart *f*.
present ['preznt] *a* anwesend;
(existing) gegenwärtig, augenblicklich; *n* Gegenwart *f*; at — im
Augenblick; Präsens *nt* *(Gram)*;
(gift) Geschenk *nt*; [prɪ'zent] *vt*
vorlegen; *(introduce)* vorstellen;
(show) zeigen; *(give)* überreichen;
to — sb with sth jdm etw überreichen; —able [prɪ'zentəbl] *a*
präsentabel; —ation Überreichung
f; —day *a* heutig, gegenwärtig,
modern; —ly *ad* bald; *(at present)*
im Augenblick; — participle
Partizip *nt* des Präsens, Mittelwort
nt der Gegenwart); — tense
Präsens *nt*, Gegenwart *f*.
preservation [prezə'veɪʃən] *n*
Erhaltung *f*.
preservative [prɪ'zɜːvətɪv] *n*
Konservierungsmittel *nt*.
preserve [prɪ'zɜːv] *vt* erhalten,
schützen; *food* einmachen,
konservieren; *n* *(jam)* Ein-
gemachte(s) *nt*; *(hunting)* Schutzgebiet *nt*.
preside [prɪ'zaɪd] *vi* den Vorsitz
haben.
presidency ['prezɪdənsɪ] *n* *(Pol)*
Präsidentschaft *f*.
president ['prezɪdənt] *n* Präsident
m; —ial [prezɪ'denʃəl] *a*
Präsidenten-; *election* Präsident-
schafts-; *system* Präsidial-.

press [pres] *n* Presse *f*; *(printing
house)* Druckerei *f*; to give the
clothes a — die Kleider bügeln; *vt*
drücken, pressen; *(iron)* bügeln;
(urge) (be)drängen; *vi (push)*
drücken, pressen; to be —ed for
time unter Zeitdruck stehen; to be
—ed for money/space wenig
Geld/Platz haben; to — for sth
drängen auf etw *(acc)*; — on *vi*
vorwärtsdrängen; — agency
Presseagentur *f*; — conference
Pressekonferenz *f*; — cutting
Zeitungsausschnitt *m*; —ing *a*
dringend; —stud Druckknopf *m*.
pressure [preʃə*] *n* Druck *m*; —
cooker Schnellkochtopf *m*; —
gauge Druckmesser *m*; — group
Interessenverband *m*, Pressure
Group *f*.
pressurized ['preʃəraɪzd] *a* Druck-.
prestige [pres'tiːʒ] *n* Ansehen *nt*,
Prestige *nt*.
prestigious [pres'tɪdʒəs] *a*
Prestige-.
presumably [prɪ'zjuːməblɪ] *ad*
vermutlich.
presume [prɪ'zjuːm] *vti* annehmen;
(dare) sich erlauben.
presumption [prɪ'zʌmpʃən] *n*
Annahme *f*; *(impudent behaviour)*
Anmaßung *f*.
presumptuous [prɪ'zʌmptjuəs] *a*
anmaßend.
presuppose [priːsə'pəʊz] *vt* voraussetzen.
presupposition [priːsʌpə'zɪʃən] *n*
Voraussetzung *f*.
pretence [prɪ'tens] *n* Vorgabe *f*,
Vortäuschung *f*; *(false claim)*
Vorwand *m*.
pretend [prɪ'tend] *vt* vorgeben, so
tun als ob ...; *vi* so tun; to — to
sth Anspruch erheben auf etw *(acc)*.

pretense [prɪ'tens] n (US) = pretence.

pretension [prɪ'tenʃən] n Anspruch m; (impudent claim) Anmaßung f.

pretentious [prɪ'tenʃəs] a angeberisch.

pretext ['priːtekst] n Vorwand m.

prettily ['prɪtɪlɪ] ad hübsch, nett.

pretty ['prɪtɪ] a hübsch, nett; ad (col) ganz schön.

prevail [prɪ'veɪl] vi siegen (against, over über +acc); (custom) vorherrschen; to — upon sb to do sth jdn dazu bewegen, etw zu tun; —ing a vorherrschend.

prevalent ['prevələnt] a vorherrschend.

prevarication [prɪværɪ'keɪʃən] n Ausflucht f.

prevent [prɪ'vent] vt (stop) verhindern, verhüten; to — sb from doing sth jdn (daran) hindern, etw zu tun; —able a verhütbar; —ative Vorbeugungsmittel nt; —ion [prɪ'venʃən] Verhütung f, Schutz m (of gegen); —ive a vorbeugend, Schutz-.

preview ['priːvjuː] n private Voraufführung f; (trailer) Vorschau f; vt film privat vorführen.

previous ['priːvɪəs] a früher, vorherig; —ly ad früher.

prewar ['priː'wɔː] a Vorkriegs-.

prey [preɪ] n Beute f; — on vt Jagd machen auf (+acc); mind nagen an (+dat); bird/beast of — Raubvogel m/Raubtier nt.

price [praɪs] n Preis m; (value) Wert m; vt schätzen; (label) auszeichnen; —less a (lit, fig) unbezahlbar; — list Preisliste f; —y a (col) teuer.

prick [prɪk] n Stich m; vti stechen; to — up one's ears die Ohren spitzen.

prickle ['prɪkl] n Stachel m, Dorn m; vi brennen.

prickly ['prɪklɪ] a stachelig; (fig) person reizbar; — heat Hitzebläschen pl; — pear Feigenkaktus m; (fruit) Kaktusfeige f.

pride [praɪd] n Stolz m; (arrogance) Hochmut m; to — o.s. on sth auf etw (acc) stolz sein.

priest [priːst] n Priester m; —ess Priesterin f; —hood Priesteramt nt.

prig [prɪg] n Selbstgefällige(r) mf.

prim [prɪm] a —ly ad [prɪm, -lɪ] prüde.

prima donna ['priːmə 'dɒnə] n Primadonna f.

primarily ['praɪmərɪlɪ] ad vorwiegend, hauptsächlich.

primary ['praɪmərɪ] a Haupt-, Grund-, primär; — colour Grundfarbe f; — education Grundschul(aus)bildung f; — election Vorwahl f; — school Grundschule f, Volksschule f.

primate ['praɪmeɪt] n (Eccl) Primas m; (Biol) Primat m.

prime [praɪm] a oberste(r, s), erste(r, s), wichtigste(r, s); (excellent) erstklassig, prima inv; vt vorbereiten; gun laden; n (of life) beste(s) Alter nt; — minister Premierminister m, Ministerpräsident m; —r Elementarlehrbuch nt, Fibel f.

primeval [praɪ'miːvəl] a vorzeitlich; forests Ur-.

primitive ['prɪmɪtɪv] a primitiv.

primrose ['prɪmrəʊz] n (gelbe) Primel f.

primula ['prɪmjʊlə] n Primel f.

primus (stove) ® ['praɪməs (stəʊv)] n Primuskocher m.

prince [prɪns] n Prinz m; (ruler) Fürst m; —ss [prɪn'ses] Prinzessin f; Fürstin f.

principal ['prɪnsɪpəl] a Haupt-; wichtigste(r, s); n (Sch) (Schul)direktor m, Rektor m; (money) (Grund)kapital nt; —ity [prɪnsɪ'pælɪtɪ] Fürstentum nt; —ly ad hauptsächlich.

principle ['prɪnsəpl] n Grundsatz m, Prinzip nt; in/on — im/aus Prinzip, prinzipiell.

print [prɪnt] n Druck m; (made by feet, fingers) Abdruck m; (Phot) Abzug m; (cotton) Kattun m; vt drucken; name in Druckbuchstaben schreiben; Photo abziehen; —er Drucker m; —ing Drucken nt; (of photos) Abziehen nt; —ing press Druckerpresse f; is the book still in —? wird das Buch noch gedruckt?; out of — vergriffen.

prior ['praɪə*] a früher; — to sth vor etw (dat); — to going abroad, she had ... bevor sie ins Ausland ging, hatte sie ...; n Prior m; —ess Priorin f; —ity [praɪ'ɒrɪtɪ] Vorrang m; Priorität f; —y Kloster nt.

prise [praɪz] vt: — open aufbrechen.

prism ['prɪzəm] n Prisma nt.

prison ['prɪzn] n Gefängnis nt; —er Gefangene(r) mf; —er of war Kriegsgefangene(r) m; to be taken —er in Gefangenschaft geraten.

prissy ['prɪsɪ] a (col) etepetete.

pristine ['prɪstiːn] a makellos.

privacy ['prɪvəsɪ] n Ungestörtheit f, Ruhe f; Privatleben nt.

private ['praɪvɪt] a privat, Privat-; (secret) vertraulich, geheim; soldier einfach; n einfache(r) Soldat m; in — privat, unter vier Augen; — eye Privatdetektiv m; —ly ad privat; vertraulich, geheim.

privet ['prɪvɪt] n Liguster m.

privilege ['prɪvɪlɪdʒ] n Vorrecht nt,

Vergünstigung f, Privileg nt; —d a bevorzugt, privilegiert.

privy ['prɪvɪ] a geheim, privat; — council Geheime(r) Staatsrat m.

prize [praɪz] n Preis m; a example erstklassig; idiot Voll-; vt (hoch)schätzen; — fighting Preisboxen nt; — giving Preisverteilung f; — money Geldpreis m; —winner Preisträger(in f) m; (of money) Gewinner(in f) m.

pro [prəu] pref pro-; n: the —s and cons pl das Für und Wider.

pro [prəu] n (professional) Profi m.

probability [prɒbə'bɪlɪtɪ] n Wahrscheinlichkeit f; in all — aller Wahrscheinlichkeit nach.

probable a, **probably** ad ['prɒbəbl, -blɪ] wahrscheinlich.

probation [prə'beɪʃən] n Probe(zeit) f; (Jur) Bewährung f; on — auf Probe; auf Bewährung; — officer Bewährungshelfer m; —ary a Probe-; —er (nurse) Lernschwester f; Pfleger m in der Ausbildung; (Jur) auf Bewährung freigelassene(r) Gefangene(r) m.

probe [prəub] n Sonde f; (enquiry) Untersuchung f; vti untersuchen, erforschen, sondieren.

probity ['prəubɪtɪ] n Rechtschaffenheit f.

problem ['prɒbləm] n Problem nt; —atic [prɒblɪ'mætɪk] a problematisch.

procedural [prə'siːdjurəl] a verfahrensmäßig, Verfahrens-.

procedure [prə'siːdʒə*] n Verfahren nt, Vorgehen nt.

proceed [prə'siːd] vi (advance) vorrücken; (start) anfangen; (carry on) fortfahren; (set about) vorgehen; (come from) entstehen (from aus); (Jur) gerichtlich vorgehen; —ings pl Verfahren nt;

(record of things) Sitzungsbericht *m*; **—s** ['prəusi:dz] *pl* Erlös *m*, Gewinn *m*.

process ['prəuses] *n* Vorgang *m*, Prozeß *m*; *(method also)* Verfahren *nt*; *vt* bearbeiten; *food* verarbeiten; *film* entwickeln; **—ing** *(Phot)* Entwickeln *nt*.

procession [prə'seʃən] *n* Prozession *f*, Umzug *m*.

proclaim [prə'kleɪm] *vt* verkünden, proklamieren; **to — sb** king zum König ausrufen.

proclamation [prɒklə'meɪʃən] *n* Verkündung *f*, Proklamation *f*; Ausrufung *f*.

procrastination [prəukræstɪ-'neɪʃən] *n* Hinausschieben *nt*.

procreation [prəukrɪ'eɪʃən] *n* (Er)zeugung *f*.

procure [prə'kjuə*] *vt* beschaffen.

prod [prɒd] *vt* stoßen; **to — sb** *(fig)* bohren; *n* Stoß *m*.

prodigal ['prɒdɪgəl] *a* verschwenderisch *(of mit)*; **the — son** der verlorene Sohn.

prodigious [prə'dɪdʒəs] *a* gewaltig, erstaunlich; *(wonderful)* wunderbar.

prodigy ['prɒdɪdʒɪ] *n* Wunder *nt*; **a child —** ein Wunderkind.

produce ['prɒdju:s] *n* *(Agr)* (Boden)produkte *pl*, (Natur)erzeugnis *nt*; [prə'dju:s] *vt* herstellen, produzieren; *(cause)* hervorrufen; *(farmer)* erzeugen; *(yield)* liefern, bringen; *play* inszenieren; **—r** Erzeuger *m*, Hersteller *m*, Produzent *m* *(also Cine)*.

product ['prɒdʌkt] *n* Produkt *nt*, Erzeugnis *nt*; **—ion** [prə'dʌkʃən] Produktion *f*, Herstellung *f*; *(thing)* Erzeugnis *nt*, Produkt *nt*; *(Theat)* Inszenierung *f*; **—ion line** Fließband *nt*; **—ive** *a* produktiv;

(fertile) ertragreich, fruchtbar; **to be —ive of** führe zu, erzeuge.

productivity [prɒdʌk'tɪvɪtɪ] *n* Produktivität *f*; *(Comm)* Leistungsfähigkeit *f*; *(fig)* Fruchtbarkeit *f*.

prof [prɒf] *n* *(col)* Professor *m*.

profane [prə'feɪn] *a* weltlich, profan, Profan-.

profess [prə'fes] *vt* bekennen; *(show)* zeigen; *(claim to be)* vorgeben; **—ion** [prə'feʃən] Beruf *m*; *(declaration)* Bekenntnis *nt*; **—ional** [prə'feʃənl] Fachmann *m*; *(Sport)* Berufsspieler *(in f)* *m*; *a* Berufs-; *(expert)* fachlich; *player* professionell; **—ionalism** *(fachliches)* Können *nt*; Berufssportlertum *nt*; **—or** Professor *m*.

proficiency [prə'fɪʃənsɪ] *n* Fertigkeit *f*, Können *nt*.

proficient [prə'fɪʃənt] *a* fähig.

profile ['prəufaɪl] *n* Profil *nt*; *(fig: report)* Kurzbiographie *f*.

profit ['prɒfɪt] *n* Gewinn *m*, Profit *m*; *vi* profitieren *(by, from von)*, Nutzen *or* Gewinn ziehen *(by, from aus)*; · **—ability** [prɒfɪtə'bɪlɪtɪ] Rentabilität *f*; **—able** *a* einträglich, rentabel; **—ably** *ad* nützlich; **—eering** [prɒfɪ'tɪərɪŋ] Profitmacherei *f*.

profound [prə'faund] *a* tief; *knowledge* profund; *book, thinker* tiefschürfend; **—ly** *ad* zutiefst.

profuse [prə'fju:s] *a* überreich; **to be —in** überschwenglich sein bei; **—ly** *ad* überschwenglich; *sweat* reichlich.

profusion [prə'fju:ʒən] *n* Überfülle *f*, Überfluß *m* *(of an +dat)*.

progeny ['prɒdʒɪnɪ] *n* Nachkommenschaft *f*.

programme, *(US)* **program** ['prəugræm] *n* Programm *nt*; *vt*

planen; *computer* programmieren.
programming, *(US)* **programing**
['prəʊgræmɪŋ] n Programmieren *nt*,
Programmierung *f*.
progress [n 'prəʊgres] n Fortschritte
m; to be in — im Gang sein; to
make — Fortschritte machen;
[prə'gres] *vi* fortschreiten, weitergehen; **—ion** [prə'greʃən] Fortschritt *m*, Progression *f*; *(walking
etc)* Fortbewegung *f*; **—ive**
[prə'gresɪv] a fortschrittlich,
progressiv; **—ively** [prə'gresɪvlɪ] ad
zunehmend.
prohibit [prə'hɪbɪt] *vt* verbieten;
—ion [prəʊɪ'bɪʃən] Verbot *nt*; *(US)*
Alkoholverbot *nt*, Prohibition *f*;
—ive a *price etc* unerschwinglich.
project [n 'prɒdʒekt] n Projekt *nt*;
[prə'dʒekt] *vt* vorausplanen;
(Psych) hineinprojizieren; *film etc*
projizieren; *personality, voice* zum
Tragen bringen; *vi (stick out)*
hervorragen, (her)vorstehen; **—ile**
[prə'dʒektaɪl] Geschoß *nt*, Projektil
nt; **—ion** [prə'dʒekʃən] Projektion
f; *(sth prominent)* Vorsprung *m*;
—or [prə'dʒektə*] Projektor *m*,
Vorführgerät *nt*.
proletarian [prəʊlə'tɛərɪən] a
proletarisch, Proletarier-; n
Proletarier(in *f*) *m*.
proletariat [prəʊlə'tɛərɪət] n
Proletariat *nt*.
proliferate [prə'lɪfəreɪt] *vi* sich
vermehren.
proliferation [prəlɪfə'reɪʃən] n
Vermehrung *f*.
prolific [prə'lɪfɪk] a fruchtbar;
author etc produktiv.
prologue ['prəʊlɒg] n Prolog *m*;
(event) Vorspiel *nt*.
prolong [prə'lɒŋ] *vt* verlängern;
—ed a lang.

prom [prɒm] n abbr of promenade
and promenade concert; *(US:
college ball)* Studentenball *m*.
promenade [prɒmɪ'nɑːd] n
Promenade *f*; **—** concert
Promenadenkonzert *nt*,
Stehkonzert *nt*; **—** deck
Promenadendeck *nt*.
prominence ['prɒmɪnəns] n
(große) Bedeutung *f*, Wichtigkeit *f*;
(sth standing out) vorspringende(r)
Teil *m*.
prominent ['prɒmɪnənt] a
bedeutend; *politician* prominent;
(easily seen) herausragend,
auffallend.
promiscuity [prɒmɪs'kjuːɪtɪ] n
Promiskuität *f*.
promiscuous [prə'mɪskjʊəs] a
lose; *(mixed up)* wild.
promise ['prɒmɪs] n Versprechen
nt; *(hope)* Aussicht *f (of auf +
acc)*; to show — vielversprechend
sein; a writer of — ein vielver-
sprechender Schriftsteller; *vti* versprechen; the **—d** land das Gelobte
Land.
promising ['prɒmɪsɪŋ] a vielversprechend.
promontory ['prɒməntrɪ] n
Vorsprung *m*.
promote [prə'məʊt] *vt* befördern;
(help on) fördern, unterstützen;
—r *(in sport, entertainment)*
Veranstalter *m*; *(for charity etc)*
Organisator *m*.
promotion [prə'məʊʃən] n *(in
rank)* Beförderung *f*; *(furtherance)*
Förderung *f*; *(Comm)* Werbung *f*
(of für).
prompt [prɒmpt] a prompt,
schnell; to be — to do sth etw
sofort tun; ad *(punctually)* genau;
at two o'clock — punkt zwei Uhr;
vt veranlassen; *(Theat)* einsagen

(+dat), soufflieren *(+dat)*; **—er** *(Theat)* Souffleur *m*, Souffleuse *f*; **—ly** ad sofort; **—ness** Schnelligkeit *f*, Promptheit *f*.

promulgate ['prɒməlgeɪt] *vt* (öffentlich) bekanntmachen, verkünden; *beliefs* verbreiten.

prone [prəʊn] *a* hingestreckt; **to be — to sth** zu etw neigen.

prong [prɒŋ] *n* Zinke *f*.

pronoun ['prəʊnaʊn] *n* Pronomen *nt*, Fürwort *nt*.

pronounce [prə'naʊns] *vt* aussprechen; *(Jur)* erklären; *vi (give an opinion)* sich äußern *(on zu)*; **—d** *a* ausgesprochen; **—ment** Erklärung *f*.

pronto ['prɒntəʊ] *ad (col)* fix, pronto.

pronunciation [prənʌnsɪ'eɪʃən] *n* Aussprache *f*.

proof [pru:f] *n* Beweis *m*; *(Print)* Korrekturfahne *f*; *(of alcohol)* Alkoholgehalt *m*; **to put to the —** unter Beweis stellen; **a** sicher; *alcohol* prozentig; *rain—* regendicht.

prop [prɒp] *n* Stütze *f (also fig)*; *(Min)* Stempel *m*; *(Theat)* Requisit *nt*; *vt (also — up)* (ab)stützen.

propaganda [prɒpə'gændə] *n* Propaganda *f*.

propagate ['prɒpəgeɪt] *vt* fortpflanzen; *news* propagieren, verbreiten.

propagation [prɒpə'geɪʃən] *n* Fortpflanzung *f*; *(of knowledge also)* Verbreitung *f*.

propel [prə'pel] *vt* (an)treiben; **—ler** Propeller *m*; **—ling pencil** Drehbleistift *m*.

propensity [prə'pensɪtɪ] *n* Tendenz *f*.

proper ['prɒpə*] *a* richtig; *(seemly)* schicklich; **—ly** ad

richtig; **—ly speaking** genau genommen; **it is not — to . . . es** schickt sich nicht, zu . . .; **— noun** Eigenname *m*.

property ['prɒpətɪ] *n* Eigentum *nt*, Besitz *m*, Gut *nt*; *(quality)* Eigenschaft *f*; *(land)* Grundbesitz *m*; *(Theat)* properties *pl* Requisiten *pl*; **— owner** Grundbesitzer *m*.

prophecy ['prɒfɪsɪ] *n* Prophezeiung *f*.

prophesy ['prɒfɪsaɪ] *vt* prophezeien, vorhersagen.

prophet ['prɒfɪt] *n* Prophet *m*; **—ic** [prə'fetɪk] *a* prophetisch.

proportion [prə'pɔ:ʃən] *n* Verhältnis *nt*, Proportion *f*; *(share)* Teil *m*; *vt* abstimmen *(to auf +acc)*; **—al** *a*, **—ally** ad proportional, verhältnismäßig; **to be —al to** entsprechen *(+dat)*; **—ate** *a*, **—ately** ad verhältnismäßig; **—ed** *a* proportioniert.

proposal [prə'pəʊzl] *n* Vorschlag *m*, Antrag *m*; *(of marriage)* Heiratsantrag *m*.

propose [prə'pəʊz] *vt* vorschlagen; *toast* ausbringen; *vi (offer marriage)* einen Heiratsantrag machen; **—r** Antragsteller *m*.

proposition [prɒpə'zɪʃən] *n* Angebot *nt*; *(Math)* Lehrsatz *m*; *(statement)* Satz *m*.

propound [prə'paʊnd] *vt theory* vorlegen.

proprietary [prə'praɪətərɪ] *a* Eigentums-; *medicine* gesetzlich geschützt.

proprietor [prə'praɪətə*] *n* Besitzer *m*, Eigentümer *m*.

props [prɒps] *npl* Requisiten *pl*.

propulsion [prə'pʌlʃən] *n* Antrieb *m*.

pro-rata [prəʊ'rɑ:tə] ad anteilmäßig,

prosaic [prə'zeɪk] a prosaisch, alltäglich.

prose [prəʊz] n Prosa f.

prosecute ['prɒsɪkjuːt] vt (strafrechtlich) verfolgen.

prosecution [prɒsɪ'kjuːʃən] n Durchführung f; (Jur) strafrechtliche Verfolgung f; (party) Anklage f; Staatsanwaltschaft f.

prosecutor ['prɒsɪkjuːtə*] n Vertreter m der Anklage; Public P— Staatsanwalt m.

prospect ['prɒspekt] n Aussicht f; [prəs'pekt] vi suchen (for nach); —ing [prəs'pektɪŋ] (for minerals) Suche f; —ive [prəs'pektɪv] a möglich; —or [prəs'pektə*] (Gold)sucher m; —us [prəs'pektəs] (Werbe)prospekt m.

prosper ['prɒspə*] vi blühen, gedeihen; (person) erfolgreich sein; —ity [prɒs'perɪtɪ] Wohlstand m; —ous a wohlhabend, reich; business gutgehend, blühend.

prostitute ['prɒstɪtjuːt] n Prostituierte f.

prostrate ['prɒstreɪt] a ausgestreckt (liegend); — with grief/exhaustion von Schmerz/Erschöpfung übermannt.

protagonist [prəʊ'tægənɪst] n Hauptperson f, Held m.

protect [prə'tekt] vt (be)schützen; —ion [prə'tekʃən] Schutz m; —ive a Schutz-, (be)schützend; —or (Be)schützer m.

protégé ['prɒteʒeɪ] n Schützling m.

protein ['prəʊtiːn] n Protein nt, Eiweiß nt.

protest ['prəʊtest] n Protest m; [prə'test] vi protestieren (against gegen); to — that beteuern . . .; P—ant a protestantisch; Protestant(in f) m.

protocol ['prəʊtəkɒl] n Protokoll nt.

prototype ['prəʊtəʊtaɪp] n Prototyp m.

protracted [prə'træktɪd] a sich hinziehend.

protractor [prə'træktə*] n Winkelmesser m.

protrude [prə'truːd] vi (her)vorstehen.

protuberance [prə'tjuːbərəns] n Auswuchs m.

protuberant [prə'tjuːbərənt] a (her)vorstehend.

proud [praʊd] a [praʊd, -lɪ] stolz (of auf +acc).

prove [pruːv] vt beweisen; vi sich herausstellen, sich zeigen.

proverb ['prɒvɜːb] n Sprichwort nt; —ial a, —ially ad [prə'vɜːbɪəl, -ɪ] sprichwörtlich.

provide [prə'vaɪd] vt versehen; (supply) besorgen; person versorgen; — for sorgen für, sich kümmern um; emergency Vorkehrungen treffen für; blankets will be —d Decken werden gestellt; —d (that) cj vorausgesetzt (daß); P—nce ['prɒvɪdəns] die Vorsehung.

providing [prə'vaɪdɪŋ] cj = provided (that).

province ['prɒvɪns] n Provinz f; (division of work) Bereich m; the —s die Provinz.

provincial [prə'vɪnʃəl] a provinziell, Provinz-; n Provinzler(in f) m.

provision [prə'vɪʒən] n Vorkehrung f, Maßnahme f; (condition) Bestimmung f; —s pl (food) Vorräte pl, Proviant m; —al a, —ally ad vorläufig, provisorisch.

proviso [prə'vaɪzəʊ] n Vorbehalt m, Bedingung f.

provocation [prɔvə'keɪʃən] n Provokation f, Herausforderung f.

provocative [prə'vɔkətɪv] a provokativ, herausfordernd.

provoke [prə'vəʊk] vt provozieren; (cause) hervorrufen.

prow [praʊ] n Bug m; —ess überragende(s) Können nt; (valour) Tapferkeit f.

prowl [praʊl] vt streets durchstreifen; vi herumstreichen; (animal) schleichen; n: on the — umherstreifend; (police) auf der Streife; —er Eindringling m.

proximity [prɔk'smɪtɪ] n Nähe f.

proxy ['prɔksɪ] n (Stell)vertreter m, Bevollmächtigte(r) m; (document) Vollmacht f; to vote by — Briefwahl machen.

prudence ['pru:dəns] n Klugheit f, Umsicht f.

prudent a, —ly ad ['pru:dənt, -lɪ] klug, umsichtig.

prudish ['pru:dɪʃ] a prüde; —ness Prüderie f.

prune [pru:n] n Backpflaume f; vt ausputzen; (fig) zurechtstutzen.

pry [praɪ] vi seine Nase stecken (into in +acc).

psalm [sɑ:m] n Psalm m.

pseudo ['sju:dəʊ] a Pseudo-; (false) falsch, unecht; —nym ['sju:dənɪm] Pseudonym nt, Deckname m.

psyche ['saɪkɪ] n Psyche f.

psychiatric [saɪkɪ'ætrɪk] a psychiatrisch.

psychiatrist [saɪ'kaɪətrɪst] n Psychiater m.

psychiatry [saɪ'kaɪətrɪ] n Psychiatrie f.

psychic(al) ['saɪkɪk(əl)] a übersinnlich; person paranormal begabt; you must be — du kannst wohl hellsehen.

psychoanalyse, (US) **psychoanalyze** [saɪkəʊ'ænəlaɪz] vt psychoanalytisch behandeln.

psychoanalysis [saɪkəʊə'nælɪsɪs] n Psychoanalyse f.

psychoanalyst [saɪkəʊ'ænəlɪst] n Psychoanalytiker(in f) m.

psychological a, —ly ad [saɪkə'lɔdʒɪkəl, -ɪ] psychologisch.

psychologist [saɪ'kɔlədʒɪst] n Psychologe m, Psychologin f.

psychology [saɪ'kɔlədʒɪ] n Psychologie f.

psychopath ['saɪkəʊpæθ] n Psychopath(in f) m.

psychosomatic ['saɪkəʊsəʊ'mætɪk] a psychosomatisch.

psychotherapy ['saɪkəʊ'θerəpɪ]. n Psychotherapie f.

psychotic [saɪ'kɔtɪk] a psychotisch; n Psychotiker(in f) m.

pub [pʌb] n Wirtschaft f, Kneipe f.

puberty ['pju:bətɪ] n Pubertät f.

pubic ['pju:bɪk] a Scham-.

public a, —ly ad ['pʌblɪk, -lɪ] öffentlich; n (also general —) Öffentlichkeit f; —an Wirt m; —ation [pʌblɪ'keɪʃən] Publikation f, Veröffentlichung f; — company Aktiengesellschaft f; — convenience öffentliche Toiletten pl; — house Lokal nt, Kneipe f; —ity [pʌb'lɪsɪtɪ] Publicity f, Werbung f; — opinion öffentliche Meinung f; — relations pl Public Relations pl; — school (Brit) Privatschule f, Internatsschule f; —spirited a mit Gemeinschaftssinn; to be —-spirited Gemeinschaftssinn haben..

publish ['pʌblɪʃ] vt veröffentlichen, publizieren; event bekanntgeben; —er Verleger m; —ing Herausgabe f, Verlegen nt; (business) Verlagswesen nt.

puce [pju:s] a violettbraun.

puck [pʌk] n Puck m, Scheibe f.

pucker [ˈpʌkə*] vt face verziehen; lips kräuseln.

pudding [ˈpudɪŋ] n (course) Nachtisch m; Pudding m.

puddle [ˈpʌdl] n Pfütze f.

puerile [ˈpjuəraɪl] a kindisch.

puff [pʌf] n (of wind etc) Stoß m; (cosmetic) Puderquaste f; vt blasen, pusten; pipe paffen; vi keuchen, schnaufen; (smoke) paffen; —ed a (col: out of breath) außer Puste.

puffin [ˈpʌfɪn] n Papageitaucher m.

puff pastry, (US) **puff paste** [ˈpʌfpeɪstrɪ, ˈpʌfpeɪst] n Blätterteig m.

puffy [ˈpʌfɪ] a aufgedunsen.

pull [pul] n Ruck m; Zug m; (influence) Beziehung f; vt ziehen; trigger abdrücken; vi ziehen; to — a face ein Gesicht schneiden; to — sb's leg jdn auf den Arm nehmen; to — to pieces (lit) in Stücke reißen; (fig) verreißen; to — one's weight sich in die Riemen legen; to — o.s. together sich zusammenreißen; — apart vt (break) zerreißen; (dismantle) auseinandernehmen; fighters trennen; — down vt house abreißen; — in vi hineinfahren; (stop) anhalten; (Rail) einfahren; — off vt deal etc abschließen; — out vi (car) herausfahren; (fig: partner) aussteigen; vt herausziehen; — round, — through vi durchkommen; — up vi anhalten.

pulley [ˈpulɪ] n Rolle f, Flaschenzug m.

pullover [ˈpuləuvə*] n Pullover m.

pulp [pʌlp] n Brei m; (of fruit) Fruchtfleisch nt.

pulpit [ˈpulpɪt] n Kanzel f.

pulsate [pʌlˈseɪt] vi pulsieren.

pulse [pʌls] n Puls m.

pulverize [ˈpʌlvəraɪz] vt pulverisieren, in kleine Stücke zerlegen (also fig).

puma [ˈpjuːmə] n Puma m.

pummel [ˈpʌml] vt mit den Fäusten bearbeiten.

pump [pʌmp] n Pumpe f; (shoe) leichter (Tanz)schuh m; vt pumpen; — up vt tyre aufpumpen.

pumpkin [ˈpʌmpkɪn] n Kürbis m.

pun [pʌn] n Wortspiel nt.

punch [pʌntʃ] n (tool) Stanze f; Locher m; (blow) (Faust)schlag m; (drink) Punsch m, Bowle f; vt stanzen; lochen; (strike) schlagen, boxen; —drunk a benommen; — up (col) Keilerei f.

punctual [ˈpʌŋktjuəl] a pünktlich; —ity [pʌŋktjuˈælɪti] Pünktlichkeit f.

punctuate [ˈpʌŋktjueɪt] vt mit Satzzeichen versehen, interpunktieren; (fig) unterbrechen.

punctuation [pʌŋktjuˈeɪʃən] n Zeichensetzung f, Interpunktion f.

puncture [ˈpʌŋktʃə*] n Loch nt; (Aut) Reifenpanne f; vt durchbohren.

pundit [ˈpʌndɪt] n Gelehrte(r) m.

pungent [ˈpʌndʒənt] a scharf.

punish [ˈpʌnɪʃ] vt bestrafen; (in boxing etc) übel zurichten; —able a strafbar; —ment Strafe f; (action) Bestrafung f.

punitive [ˈpjuːnɪtɪv] a strafend.

punt [pʌnt] n Stechkahn m.

punter [ˈpʌntə*] n (better) Wetter m.

puny [ˈpjuːnɪ] a kümmerlich.

pup [pʌp] n = puppy.

pupil ['pju:pl] n Schüler(in f) m; (in eye) Pupille f.

puppet ['pʌpɪt] n Puppe f; Marionette f.

puppy ['pʌpɪ] n junge(r) Hund m.

purchase ['pɜːtʃɪs] n Kauf m, Anschaffung f; (grip) Halt m; vt kaufen, erwerben; ~r Käufer(in f) m.

pure [pjʊə*] a pur; rein (also fig); —ly ['pjʊəlɪ] ad rein; (only) nur; (with a also) rein.

purée ['pjʊəreɪ] n Püree nt.

purgatory ['pɜːgətərɪ] n Fegefeuer nt.

purge [pɜːdʒ] n Säuberung f (also Pol); (medicine) Abführmittel nt; vt reinigen; body entschlacken.

purification [pjʊərɪfɪ'keɪʃən] n Reinigung f.

purify ['pjʊərɪfaɪ] vt reinigen.

purist ['pjʊərɪst] n Purist m.

puritan ['pjʊərɪtən] n Puritaner m; —ical [pjʊərɪ'tænɪkəl] a puritanisch.

purity ['pjʊərɪtɪ] n Reinheit f.

purl [pɜːl] n linke Masche f; vt links stricken.

purple ['pɜːpl] a violett; face dunkelrot; n Violett nt.

purpose ['pɜːpəs] n Zweck m, Ziel nt; (of person) Absicht f; on — absichtlich; —ful a zielbewußt, entschlossen; —ly ad absichtlich.

purr [pɜː*] n Schnurren nt; vi schnurren.

purse [pɜːs] n Portemonnaie nt, Geldbeutel m; vt lips zusammenpressen, schürzen.

purser ['pɜːsə*] n Zahlmeister m.

pursue [pə'sju:] vt verfolgen, nachjagen (+dat); study nachgehen (+dat); ~r Verfolger m.

pursuit [pə'sju:t] n Jagd f (of nach), Verfolgung f; (occupation) Beschäftigung f.

purveyor [pɜː'veɪə*] n Lieferant m.

pus [pʌs] n Eiter m.

push [pʊʃ] n Stoß m, Schub m; (energy) Schwung m; (Mil) Vorstoß m; vt stoßen, schieben; button drücken; idea durchsetzen; vi stoßen, schieben; at a — zur Not; — aside vt beiseiteschieben; — off vi (col) abschieben; — on vi weitermachen; — through vt durchdrücken; policy durchsetzen; — up vt total erhöhen; prices hochtreiben; —chair (Kinder)sportwagen m; —ing a aufdringlich; —over (col) Kinderspiel nt; —y a (col) aufdringlich.

puss [pʊs] n Mieze(katze) f.

put [pʊt] vt irreg setzen, stellen, legen; (express) ausdrücken, sagen; (write) schreiben; — about vi (turn back) wenden; (spread) verbreiten; — across vt (explain) erklären; — away vt weglegen; (store) beiseitelegen; — back vt zurückstellen or -legen; — by vt zurücklegen, sparen; — down vt hinstellen or -legen; (stop) niederschlagen; animal einschläfern; (in writing) niederschreiben; — forward vt idea vorbringen; clock vorstellen; — in vt einlegen, einfügen; — off vt verlegen, verschieben; (discourage) abbringen von; it — me off smoking das hat mir die Lust am Rauchen verdorben; — on vt clothes etc anziehen; light etc anschalten, anmachen; play etc aufführen; brake anziehen; — out vt hand etc (her)ausstrecken; news, rumour verbreiten; light etc ausschalten, ausmachen; — up vt tent aufstellen; building errichten; price

erhöhen; *person* unterbringen; to
— up with sich abfinden mit; I
won't — up with it that laß ich mir
nicht gefallen.

putrid ['pju:trɪd] *a* faul.

putsch [putʃ] *n* Putsch *m*.

putt [pʌt] *vt* (*golf*) putten,
einlochen; *n* (*golf*) Putten *nt*,
leichte(r) Schlag *m*; —er Putter *m*.

putty ['pʌtɪ] *n* Kitt *m*; (*fig*) Wachs
nt.

put-up ['putʌp] a: — job
abgekartete(s) Spiel *nt*.

puzzle ['pʌzl] *n* Rätsel *nt*; (*toy*)
Geduldspiel *nt*; *vt* verwirren; *vi*
sich den Kopf zerbrechen.

puzzling ['pʌzlɪŋ] *a* rätselhaft, verwirrend.

pygmy ['pɪgmɪ] *n* Pygmäe *m*; (*fig*)
Zwerg *m*.

pyjamas [pɪ'dʒɑ:məz] *npl*
Schlafanzug *m*, Pyjama *m*.

pylon ['paɪlən] *n* Mast *m*.

pyramid ['pɪrəmɪd] *n* Pyramide *f*.

python ['paɪθən] *n* Pythonschlange
f.

Q

Q, q [kju:] *n* Q *nt*, q *nt*.

quack [kwæk] *n* Quacken *nt*;
(*doctor*) Quacksalber *m*.

quad [kwɒd] *abbr of* quadrangle,
quadruple, quadruplet.

quadrangle ['kwɒdræŋgl] *n* (*court*)
Hof *m*; (*Math*) Viereck *nt*.

quadruped ['kwɒdruped] *n* Vier-
füßler *m*.

quadruple [kwɒ'dru:pl] *a* vier-
fach; *vi* sich vervierfachen; *vt*
·vervierfachen.

quadruplet [kwɒ'dru:plət] *n*
Vierling *m*.

quagmire ['kwægmaɪə*] *n* Morast
m.

quaint [kweɪnt] *a* kurios;
malerisch; —ly *ad* kurios; —ness
malerischer Anblick *m*; Kuriosität
f.

quake [kweɪk] *vi* beben, zittern;
Q—r Quäker *m*.

qualification [kwɒlɪfɪ'keɪʃən] *n*
Qualifikation *f*; (*sth which limits*)
Einschränkung *f*.

qualified ['kwɒlɪfaɪd] *a* (*compe-*

tent) qualifiziert; (*limited*) bedingt.

qualify ['kwɒlɪfaɪ] *vt* (*prepare*)
befähigen; (*limit*) einschränken; *vi*
sich qualifizieren.

qualitative ['kwɒlɪtətɪv] *a*
qualitativ.

quality ['kwɒlɪtɪ] *n* Qualität *f*;
(*characteristic*) Eigenschaft *f*; *a*
Qualitäts-.

qualm [kwɑ:m] *n* Bedenken *nt*,
Zweifel *m*.

quandary ['kwɒndərɪ] *n*
Verlegenheit *f*; to be in a — in
Verlegenheit sein.

quantitative ['kwɒntɪtətɪv] *a*
quantitativ.

quantity ['kwɒntɪtɪ] *n* Menge *f*,
Quantität *f*.

quarantine ['kwɒrəntiːn] *n*
Quarantäne *f*.

quarrel ['kwɒrəl] *n* Streit *m*; *vi*
sich streiten; —some *a* streitsüchtig.

quarry ['kwɒrɪ] *n* Steinbruch *m*;
(*animal*) Wild *nt*; (*fig*) Opfer *nt*.

quart [kwɔːt] *n* Quart *nt*.

quarter ['kwɔːtə*] *n* Viertel *nt*; *(of year)* Quartal *nt*, Vierteljahr *nt*; *vt (divide)* vierteln, in Viertel teilen; *(Mil)* einquartieren; —s *pl (esp Mil)* Quartier *nt*; — of an hour Viertelstunde *f*; — past three viertel nach drei; — to three dreiviertel drei, viertel vor drei; —deck Achterdeck *nt*; — final Viertelfinale *nt*; —ly a vierteljährlich; —master Quartiermeister *m*.

quartet(te) [kwɔː'tet] *n* Quartett *nt*.

quartz ['kwɔːts] *n* Quarz *m*.

quash [kwɒʃ] *vt verdict* aufheben.

quasi [kwɑːzɪ] *ad* quasi.

quaver ['kweɪvə*] *n (Mus)* Achtelnote *f*; *vi (tremble)* zittern.

quay [kiː] *n* Kai *m*.

queasiness ['kwiːzɪnəs] *n* Übelkeit *f*.

queasy ['kwiːzɪ] *a* übel; he feels — ihm ist übel.

queen [kwiːn] *n* Königin *f*; — mother Königinmutter *f*.

queer [kwɪə*] *a* seltsam, sonderbar, kurios; — fellow komischer Kauz *m*; *n (col: homosexual)* Schwule(r) *m*.

quell [kwel] *vt* unterdrücken.

quench [kwentʃ] *vt thirst* löschen, stillen; *(extinguish)* löschen.

query ['kwɪərɪ] *n (question)* (An)frage *f*; *(question mark)* Fragezeichen *nt*; *vt* in Zweifel ziehen, in Frage stellen.

quest [kwest] *n* Suche *f*.

question ['kwestʃən] *n* Frage *f*; *vt (ask)* (be)fragen; *suspect* verhören; *(doubt)* in Frage stellen, bezweifeln; **beyond** — ohne Frage; **out of the** — ausgeschlossen; —able *a* zweifelhaft; —er Frage

steller *m*; —ing a fragend; — mark Fragezeichen *nt*; —naire Fragebogen *m*; *(enquiry)* Umfrage *f*.

queue [kjuː] *n* Schlange *f*; *vi (also* — up) Schlange stehen.

quibble ['kwɪbl] *n* Spitzfindigkeit *f*; *vi* kleinlich sein.

quick a, ['kwɪk, -lɪ] *a* schnell; *n (of nail)* Nagelhaut *f*; *(old: the living)* die Lebenden; to the — *(fig)* bis ins Innerste; —en *vt (hasten)* beschleunigen; *(stir)* anregen; *vi* sich beschleunigen; —fire *a questions etc* Schnellfeuer-; —ness Schnelligkeit *f*; *(mental)* Scharfsinn *m*; —sand Treibsand *m*; —step Quickstep *m*; —witted *a* schlagfertig, hell.

quid [kwɪd] *n (Brit col: £1)* Pfund *nt*.

quiet ['kwaɪət] *a (without noise)* leise; *(peaceful, calm)* still, ruhig; *n* Stille *f*, Ruhe *f*; —en *(also* —en down) *vi* ruhig werden; *vt* beruhigen; —ly *ad* leise, ruhig; —ness Ruhe *f*, Stille *f*.

quill [kwɪl] *n (of porcupine)* Stachel *m*; *(pen)* Feder *f*.

quilt [kwɪlt] *n* Steppdecke *f*; —ing Füllung *f*, Wattierung *f*.

quin [kwɪn] *abbr of* **quintuplet.**

quince [kwɪns] *n* Quitte *f*.

quinine [kwɪ'niːn] *n* Chinin *nt*.

quinsy ['kwɪnzɪ] *n* Mandelentzündung *f*.

quintet(te) [kwɪn'tet] *n* Quintett *nt*.

quintuplet [kwɪn'tjuːplət] *n* Fünfling *m*.

quip [kwɪp] *n* witzige Bemerkung *f*; *vi* witzeln.

quirk [kwɜːk] *n (oddity)* Eigenart *f*.

quit [kwɪt] *irreg vt* verlassen; *vi* aufhören.

quite [kwaɪt] ad *(completely)* ganz, völlig; *(fairly)* ziemlich; — (so)! richtig!

quits [kwɪts] a quitt.

quiver ['kwɪvə*] vi zittern; n *(for arrows)* Köcher m.

quiz [kwɪz] n *(competition)* Quiz nt; *(series of questions)* Befragung f; vt prüfen; **—zical** a fragend, verdutzt.

quoit [kwɔɪt] n Wurfring m.

quorum ['kwɔːrəm] n beschlußfähige Anzahl f.

quota ['kwəʊtə] n Anteil m; *(Comm)* Quote f.

quotation [kwəʊ'teɪʃən] n Zitat nt; *(price)* Kostenvoranschlag m; **— marks** pl Anführungszeichen pl.

quote [kwəʊt] n see **quotation**; vi *(from book)* zitieren; vt *(from book)* zitieren; *price* angeben.

quotient ['kwəʊʃənt] n Quotient m.

R

R, r [ɑː*] n R nt, r nt.

rabbi ['ræbaɪ] n Rabbiner m; *(title)* Rabbi m.

rabbit ['ræbɪt] n Kaninchen nt; **— hutch** Kaninchenstall m.

rabble ['ræbl] n Pöbel m.

rabies ['reɪbiːz] n Tollwut f.

raccoon [rə'kuːn] n Waschbär m.

race [reɪs] n *(species)* Rasse f; *(competition)* Rennen nt; *(on foot also)* Wettlauf m; *(rush)* Hetze f; vt um die Wette laufen mit; *horses* laufen lassen; vi *(run)* rennen; *(in contest)* am Rennen teilnehmen; **—course** *(for horses)* Rennbahn f; **—horse** Rennpferd nt; **— meeting** *(for horses)* Pferde)rennen nt; **—relations** pl Beziehungen pl zwischen den Rassen; **—track** *(for cars etc)* Rennstrecke f.

racial ['reɪʃəl] a Rassen-; **—discrimination** Rassendiskriminierung f; **—ism** Rassismus m; **—ist** a rassistisch; n Rassist m.

racing ['reɪsɪŋ] n Rennen nt; **— car** Rennwagen m; **— driver** Rennfahrer m.

racism ['reɪsɪzəm] n Rassismus m.

racist ['reɪsɪst] · n Rassist m; a rassistisch.

rack [ræk] n Ständer m, Gestell nt; vt *(zer)*martern; **to go to — and ruin** verfallen.

racket ['rækɪt] n *(din)* Krach m; *(scheme)* (Schwindel)geschäft nt; *(tennis)* (Tennis)schläger m.

racquet ['rækɪt] n = **racket** *(tennis)*.

racy ['reɪsɪ] a gewagt; *style* spritzig.

radar ['reɪdɑː*] n Radar nt or m.

radiance ['reɪdɪəns] n strahlende(r) Glanz m.

radiant ['reɪdɪənt] a *(bright)* strahlend; *(giving out rays)* Strahlungs-.

radiate ['reɪdɪeɪt] vti ausstrahlen; *(roads, lines)* strahlenförmig wegführen.

radiation [reɪdɪ'eɪʃən] n (Aus)strahlung f.

radiator ['reɪdɪeɪtə*] n *(for heating)* Heizkörper m; *(Aut)* Kühler m; **— cap** Kühlerdeckel m.

radical a, **—ly** ad ['rædɪkəl, -ɪ] radikal.

radio ['reɪdɪəu] n Rundfunk m, Radio nt; (set) Radio nt, Radioapparat m; **—active** a radioaktiv; **—activity** Radioaktivität f; **—grapher** [reɪdɪ'ɒgrəfə*] Röntgenassistent(in f) m; **—graphy** [reɪdɪ'ɒgrəfɪ] Radiographie f, Röntgenphotographie f; **—logy** [reɪdɪ'ɒlədʒɪ] Strahlenkunde f; **—station** Rundfunkstation f; **—telephone** Funksprechanlage f; **—telescope** Radioteleskop nt; **—therapist** Radiologieassistent(in f) m.

radish ['rædɪʃ] n (big) Rettich m; (small) Radieschen nt.

radium ['reɪdɪəm] n Radium nt.

radius ['reɪdɪəs] n Radius m, Halbkreis m; (area) Umkreis m.

raffia ['ræfɪə] n (Raffia)bast m.

raffish ['ræfɪʃ] a liederlich; clothes gewagt.

raffle ['ræfl] n Verlosung f, Tombola f.

raft [rɑːft] n Floß nt.

rafter ['rɑːftə*] n Dachsparren m.

rag [ræg] n (cloth) Lumpen m, Lappen m; (col: newspaper) Käseblatt nt; (Univ: for charity) studentische Sammelaktion f; vt auf den Arm nehmen; **—bag** (fig) Sammelsurium nt.

rage [reɪdʒ] n Wut f; (desire) Sucht f; (fashion) große Mode f; **to be in a —** wütend sein; vi wüten, toben.

ragged ['rægɪd] a edge gezackt; clothes zerlumpt.

raging ['reɪdʒɪŋ] a tobend; thirst Heiden-.

raid [reɪd] n Überfall m; (Mil) Angriff m; (by police) Razzia f; vt überfallen; **—er** (person) (Bank)räuber m; (Naut) Kaperschiff nt.

rail [reɪl] n Schiene f, Querstange f; (on stair) Geländer nt; (of ship) Reling f; (Rail) Schiene f; **by —** per Bahn; **—ing(s)** Geländer nt; **—road** (US), **—way** (Brit) Eisenbahn f; **—road** or **—way station** Bahnhof m.

rain [reɪn] n Regen m; vti regnen; **the —s** pl die Regenzeit; **—bow** Regenbogen m; **—coat** Regenmantel m; **—drop** Regentropfen m; **—fall** Niederschlag m; **—storm** heftige(r) Regenguß m; **—y** a region, season Regen-; day regnerisch, verregnet.

raise [reɪz] n (esp US: increase) (Lohn- or Gehalts- or Preis)erhöhung f; vt (lift) (hoch)heben; (increase) erhöhen; question aufwerfen; doubts äußern; funds beschaffen; family großziehen; livestock züchten; (build) errichten.

raisin ['reɪzən] n Rosine f.

rajah ['rɑːdʒə] n Radscha m.

rake [reɪk] n Rechen m, Harke f; (person) Wüstling m; vt rechen, harken; (with gun) (mit Feuer) bestreichen; (search) (durch)suchen; **to — in** or together zusammenscharren.

rally ['rælɪ] n (Pol etc) Kundgebung f; (Aut) Sternfahrt f, Rallye f; (improvement) Erholung f; vt (Mil) sammeln; vi Kräfte sammeln; **—round** vti (sich) scharen um; (help) zu Hilfe kommen (+dat).

ram [ræm] n Widder m; (instrument) Ramme f; vt (strike) rammen; (stuff) hineinstopfen.

ramble ['ræmbl] n Wanderung f, Ausflug m; vi (wander) umherstreifen; (talk) schwafeln; **—r** Wanderer m; (plant) Kletterrose f.

rambling ['ræmblɪŋ] *a plant* Kletter-; *speech* weitschweifig; *town* ausgedehnt.

ramification [ræmɪfɪ'keɪʃən] *n* Verästelung *f*; **—s** *pl* Tragweite *f*.

ramp [ræmp] *n* Rampe *f*.

rampage [ræm'peɪdʒ] *n:* to be on the — (*also* — *vi*) rahdalieren.

rampant ['ræmpənt] *a (heraldry)* aufgerichtet; to be — überhandnehmen.

rampart ['ræmpɑ:t] *n (Schutz)wall m.*

ramshackle ['ræmʃækl] *a* baufällig.

ranch [rɑ:ntʃ] *n* Ranch *f*; **—er** Rancher *m.*

rancid ['rænsɪd] *a* ranzig.

rancour, (*US*) **rancor** ['ræŋkə*] *n* Verbitterung *f*, Groll *m.*

random ['rændəm] *a* ziellos, wahllos; *n:* at — aufs Geratewohl.

randy ['rændɪ] *a (Brit)* geil, scharf.

range [reɪndʒ] *n* Reihe *f*; *(of mountains)* Kette *f*; *(Comm)* Sortiment *nt*; *(selection)* (große) Auswahl *f (of an +dat)*; *(reach)* (Reich)weite *f*; *(of gun)* Schußweite *f (for shooting practice)* Schießplatz *m*; *(stove)* (großer) Herd *m*; *vt (set in row)* anordnen, aufstellen; *(roam)* durchstreifen; *vi (extend)* sich erstrecken; prices ranging from £5 to £10 Preise, die sich zwischen 5£ und 10£ bewegen; **—r** Förster *m.*

rank [ræŋk] *n (row)* Reihe *f*; *(for taxis)* Stand *m*; *(Mil)* Dienstgrad *m*, Rang *m*; *(social position)* Stand *m*; *vt* einschätzen; *vi (have —)* gehören *(among* zu); *a (strongsmelling)* stinkend; *(extreme)* krass; **the —s** *pl (Mil)* die Mannschaften *pl*; **the — and file** *(fig)* die breite Masse.

rankle ['ræŋkl] *vi* nagen.

ransack ['rænsæk] *vt (plunder)* plündern; *(search)* durchwühlen.

ransom ['rænsəm] *n* Lösegeld *nt*; to hold sb to — jdn gegen Lösegeld festhalten.

rant [rænt] *vi* hochtrabend reden; **—ing** Wortschwall *m.*

rap [ræp] *n* Schlag *m*; *vt* klopfen.

rape [reɪp] *n* Vergewaltigung *f*; *vt* vergewaltigen.

rapid ['ræpɪd] *a* rasch, schnell; **—s** *pl* Stromschnellen *pl*; **—ity** [rə'pɪdɪtɪ] Schnelligkeit *f*; **—ly** *ad* schnell.

rapier ['reɪpɪə*] *n* Florett *m.*

rapist ['reɪpɪst] *n* Vergewaltiger *m.*

rapport [ræ'pɔ:*] *n* gute(s) Verhältnis *nt.*

rapprochement [ræ'prɒʃmɑ̃:ŋ] *n* (Wieder)annäherung *f.*

rapt [ræpt] *a* hingerissen.

rapture ['ræptʃə*] *n* Entzücken *nt.*

rapturous ['ræptʃərəs] *a applause* stürmisch; *expression* verzückt.

rare [rɛə*] *a* selten, rar; *(especially good)* vortrefflich; *(underdone)* nicht durchgebraten; **—fied** ['rɛərɪfaɪd] *a* air, atmosphere dünn; **—ly** *ad* selten.

rarity ['rɛərɪtɪ] *n* Seltenheit *f.*

rascal ['rɑ:skəl] *n* Schuft *m*; *(child)* Strick *m.*

rash [ræʃ] *a* übereilt; *(reckless)* unbesonnen; *n (Haut)ausschlag *m.*

rasher ['ræʃə*] *n* Speckscheibe *f.*

rashly ['ræʃlɪ] *ad* vorschnell, unbesonnen.

rashness ['ræʃnəs] *n* Voreiligkeit *f*; *(recklessness)* Unbesonnenheit *f.*

rasp [rɑ:sp] *n* Raspel *f.*

raspberry ['rɑ:zbərɪ] *n* Himbeere *f.*

rasping ['rɑ:spɪŋ] *a noise* kratzend.

rat [ræt] *n (animal)* Ratte *f*; *(person)* Halunke *m.*

ratable ['reɪtəbl] a: — **value** Grundsteuer f.

ratchet ['rætʃɪt] n Sperrad nt.

rate [reɪt] n (proportion) Ziffer f, Rate f; (price) Tarif m, Gebühr f; (speed) Geschwindigkeit f; vt (ein)schätzen; —s pl (Brit) Grundsteuer f, Gemeindeabgaben pl; at any — jedenfalls; (at least) wenigstens; at this — wenn es so weitergeht; — of exchange (Wechsel)kurs m; —payer Steuerzahler(in f) m; see first.

rather ['rɑːðə*] ad (in preference) lieber, eher; (to some extent) ziemlich; —! und ob!

ratification [rætɪfɪ'keɪʃən] n Ratifikation f.

ratify ['rætɪfaɪ] vt bestätigen; (Pol) ratifizieren.

rating ['reɪtɪŋ] n Klasse f; (sailor) Matrose m.

ratio ['reɪʃɪəʊ] n Verhältnis nt.

ration ['ræʃən] n (usually pl) Ration f; vt rationieren.

rational a, **—ly** ad ['ræʃənl, -nəlɪ] rational, vernünftig; **—e** [ræʃə'nɑːl] Grundprinzip nt; **—ization** [ræʃnəlaɪ'zeɪʃən] Rationalisierung f; **—ize** ['ræʃnəlaɪz] vt rationalisieren.

rationing ['ræʃnɪŋ] n Rationierung f.

rat race ['rætreɪs] n Konkurrenzkampf m.

rattle ['rætl] n (sound) Rattern nt, Rasseln nt; (toy) Rassel f; vi rattteln, klappern; **—snake** Klapperschlange f.

raucous a, **—ly** ad ['rɔːkəs, -lɪ] heiser, rauh.

ravage [ræ'vɪdʒ] vt verheeren; —s pl verheerende Wirkungen pl; the —s of time der Zahn der Zeit.

rave [reɪv] vi (talk wildly) phantasieren; (rage) toben.

raven ['reɪvn] n Rabe m.

ravenous ['rævənəs] a heißhungrig; appetite unersättlich.

ravine [rə'viːn] n Schlucht f, Klamm f.

raving ['reɪvɪŋ] a tobend; — **mad** total verrückt.

ravioli [rævɪ'əʊlɪ] n Ravioli pl.

ravish ['rævɪʃ] vt (delight) entzücken; (Jur) woman vergewaltigen; —ing a hinreißend.

raw [rɔː] a roh; (tender) wund(gerieben); wound offen; (inexperienced) unerfahren; — **material** Rohmaterial nt.

ray [reɪ] n (of light) (Licht)strahl m; (gleam) Schimmer m.

rayon ['reɪɒn] n Kunstseide f, Reyon or m.

raze [reɪz] vt dem Erdboden gleichmachen.

razor ['reɪzə*] n Rasierapparat m; — **blade** Rasierklinge f.

re- [riː] pref wieder-.

re [riː] prep (Comm) betreffs (+ gen).

reach [riːtʃ] n Reichweite f; (of river) Flußstrecke f; within — (shops etc) in erreichbarer Weite or Entfernung; vt erreichen; (pass on) reichen, geben; vi (try to get) langen (for nach); (stretch) sich erstrecken; — **out** vi die Hand ausstrecken.

react [riː'ækt] vi reagieren; **—ion** [riː'ækʃən] Reaktion f; **—ionary** [riː'ækʃənrɪ] a reaktionär; **—or** Reaktor m.

read [riːd] vti irreg lesen; (aloud) vorlesen; it — as follows es lautet folgendermaßen; **—able** a leserlich; (worth **—ing**)

lesenswert; -er *(person)* Leser(in f) *m; (book)* Lesebuch *nt; -ership* Leserschaft *f.*

readily ['redɪlɪ] *ad (willingly)* bereitwillig; *(easily)* prompt.

readiness ['redɪnəs] *n (willingness)* Bereitwilligkeit *f; (being ready)* Bereitschaft *f.*

reading ['riːdɪŋ] *n* Lesen *nt; (interpretation)* Deutung *f*, Auffassung *f; —* **lamp** Leselampe *f; — matter** Lesestoff *m*, Lektüre *f; — room** Lesezimmer *nt*, Lesesaal *m.*

readjust [riːə'dʒʌst] *vt* wieder in Ordnung bringen; neu einstellen; **to — (o.s.)** to sth sich wieder anpassen an etw *(acc); —ment* Wiederanpassung *f.*

ready ['redɪ] *a (prepared)* bereit, fertig; *(willing)* bereit, willens; *(in condition to)* reif; *(quick)* schlagfertig; **money** verfügbar, bar; *ad* bereit; *n:* at the **— bereit; —made a** gebrauchsfertig, Fertig-; **clothes** Konfektions-; **— reckoner** Rechentabelle *f.*

real [rɪəl] *a (actual)* wirklich; *(actual)* eigentlich; *(true)* wahr; *(not fake)* echt; **— estate** Grundbesitz *m; —ism** Realismus *m; —ist** Realist *m; —istic a*, **—istically** *ad* realistisch; **—ity** [rɪ'ælɪtɪ] *(real existence)* Wirklichkeit *f*, Realität *f; (facts)* Tatsachen *pl; (understanding)* Erkenntnis *f; (fulfilment)* Verwirklichung *f; —ize vt (understand)* begreifen; *(make real)* verwirklichen; **money** einbringen; **I didn't —ize . . .** ich wußte nicht, . . . ; **—ly** *ad* wirklich.

realm [relm] *n* Reich *nt.*

ream [riːm] *n* Ries *nt.*

reap [riːp] *vt* ·ernten; **—er** Mähmaschine *f.*

reappear ['riːə'pɪə*]· *vi* wieder erscheinen; **—ance** Wiedererscheinen *nt.*

reapply ['riːə'plaɪ] *vi* wiederholt beantragen (for acc); *(for job)* sich erneut bewerben (for um).

reappoint ['riːə'pɔɪnt] *vt* wieder anstellen; wiederernennen.

reappraisal ['riːə'preɪzəl] *n* Neubeurteilung *f.*

rear [rɪə*] *a* hintere(r, s), Rück-; *n* Rückseite *f; (last part)* Schluß *m; vt (bring up)* aufziehen; *(of horse)* sich aufbäumen; **—engined** *a* mit Heckmotor; **—guard** Nachhut *f.*

rearm ['riː'ɑːm] *vt* wieder bewaffnen; *vi* wiederaufrüsten; **—ament** Wiederaufrüstung *f.*

rearrange ['riːə'reɪndʒ] *vt* umordnen; *plans* ändern.

rear-view ['rɪəvjuː] *a:* **— mirror** Rückspiegel *m.*

reason ['riːzn] *n (cause)* Grund *m; (ability to think)* Verstand *m; (sensible thoughts)* Vernunft *f; vi (think)* denken; *(use arguments)* argumentieren; **to — with sb** mit jdm diskutieren; **—able a** vernünftig; **—ably** *ad* vernünftig; *(fairly)* ziemlich; **one could —ably suppose** man könnte doch (mit gutem Grund) annehmen; **—ed a** *argument* durchdacht; **—ing** Urteilen *nt; (argumentation)* Beweisführung *f.*

reassemble ['riːə'sembl] *vt* wieder versammeln; *(Tech)* wieder zusammensetzen, wieder zusammenbauen; *vi* sich wieder versammeln.

reassert ['riːə'sɜːt] *vt* wieder geltend machen.

reassurance ['riːə'ʃʊərəns] *n* Beruhigung *f; (confirmation)* nochmalige Versicherung *f.*

reassure [ˌriːəˈʃʊə*] *vt* beruhigen; *(confirm)* versichern *(sb jdm).*

reassuring [ˌriːəˈʃʊərɪŋ] *a* beruhigend.

reawakening [ˌriːəˈweɪknɪŋ] *n* Wiedererwachen *nt.*

rebate [ˈriːbeɪt] *n* Rabatt *m; (money back)* Rückzahlung *f.*

rebel [ˈrebl] *n* Rebell *m; a* Rebellen—; **—lion** [rɪˈbeljən] rebellion *f,* Aufstand *m;* **—lious** [rɪˈbeljəs] *a* rebellisch; *(fig)* widerspenstig.

rebirth [ˈriːˈbɜːθ] *n* Wiedergeburt *f.*

rebound [rɪˈbaʊnd] *vi* zurückprallen; [ˈriːbaʊnd] *n* Rückprall *m;* **on the —** *(fig)* als Reaktion.

rebuff [rɪˈbʌf] *n* Abfuhr *f; vt* abblitzen lassen.

rebuild [ˈriːˈbɪld] *vt* *Irreg* wiederaufbauen; *(fig)* wiederherstellen; **—ing** Wiederaufbau *m.*

rebuke [rɪˈbjuːk] *n* Tadel *m; vt* tadeln, rügen.

rebut [rɪˈbʌt] *vt* widerlegen.

recalcitrant [rɪˈkælsɪtrənt] *a* widerspenstig.

recall [rɪˈkɔːl] *vt (call back)* zurückrufen; *(remember)* sich erinnern an *(+acc).*

recant [rɪˈkænt] *vi* (öffentlich) widerrufen.

recap [ˈriːkæp] *n* kurze Zusammenfassung *f; vti* *information* wiederholen.

recapture [ˈriːˈkæptʃə*] *vt* wieder (ein)fangen.

recede [rɪˈsiːd] *vi* zurückweichen.

receding [rɪˈsiːdɪŋ] *a:* **— hair** Stirnglatze *f.*

receipt [rɪˈsiːt] *n (document)* Quittung *f; (receiving)* Empfang *m;* **—s** *pl* Einnahmen *pl.*

receive [rɪˈsiːv] *vt* erhalten; *visitors etc* empfangen; **—r** *(Tel)* Hörer *m.*

recent [ˈriːsnt] *a* vor kurzem (geschehen), neuerlich; *(modern)* neu; **—ly** *ad* kürzlich, neulich.

receptacle [rɪˈseptəkl] *n* Behälter *m.*

reception [rɪˈsepʃən] *n* Empfang *m; (welcome)* Aufnahme *f; (in hotel)* Rezeption *f;* **—ist** *(in hotel)* Empfangschef *m/-dame f; (Med)* Sprechstundenhilfe *f.*

receptive [rɪˈseptɪv] *a* aufnahmebereit.

recess [rɪˈses] *n (break)* Ferien *pl; (hollow)* Nische *f;* **—es** *pl* Winkel *m;* **—ion** [rɪˈseʃən] Rezession *f.*

recharge [ˈriːˈtʃɑːdʒ] *vt* battery aufladen.

recipe [ˈresɪpɪ] *n* Rezept *nt.*

recipient [rɪˈsɪpɪənt] *n* Empfänger *m.*

reciprocal [rɪˈsɪprəkəl] *a* gegenseitig; *(mutual)* wechselseitig.

reciprocate [rɪˈsɪprəkeɪt] *vt* erwidern.

recital [rɪˈsaɪtl] *n (Mus)* Konzert *nt,* Vortrag *m.*

recitation [resɪˈteɪʃən] *n* Rezitation *f.*

recite [rɪˈsaɪt] *vt* vortragen, aufsagen; *(give list of also)* aufzählen.

reckless *a,* **—ly** *ad* [ˈrekləs, -lɪ] leichtsinnig; *driving* fahrlässig; **—ness** Rücksichtslosigkeit *f.*

reckon [ˈrekən] *vt (count)* (be- or er)rechnen; *(consider)* halten für; *vi (suppose)* annehmen; **— on** *vt* rechnen mit; **—ing** *(calculation)* Rechnen *nt.*

reclaim [rɪˈkleɪm] *vt* land abgewinnen *(from dat); expenses* zurückverlangen.

reclamation [reklə'meɪʃən] n (of land) Gewinnung f.

recline [rɪ'klaɪn] vi sich zurücklehnen.

reclining [rɪ'klaɪnɪŋ] a verstellbar, Liege-.

recluse [rɪ'kluːs] n Einsiedler m.

recognition [rekəg'nɪʃən] n (recognizing) Erkennen nt; (acknowledgement) Anerkennung f.

recognizable ['rekəgnaɪzəbl] a erkennbar.

recognize ['rekəgnaɪz] vt erkennen; (Pol, approve) anerkennen.

recoil [rɪ'kɔɪl] n Rückstoß m; vi (in horror) zurückschrecken; (rebound) zurückprallen.

recollect [rekə'lekt] vt sich erinnern an (+acc); —ion Erinnerung f.

recommend [rekə'mend] vt empfehlen; —ation Empfehlung f.

recompense ['rekəmpens] n (compensation) Entschädigung f; (reward) Belohnung f; vt entschädigen; belohnen.

reconcilable ['rekənsaɪləbl] a vereinbar.

reconcile ['rekənsaɪl] vt facts vereinbaren, in Einklang bringen; people versöhnen.

reconciliation [rekənsɪlɪ'eɪʃən] n Versöhnung f.

reconditioned [riː'kən'dɪʃənd] a überholt, erneuert.

reconnaissance [rɪ'kɒnɪsəns] n Aufklärung f.

reconnoitre, (US) **reconnoiter** [rekə'nɔɪtə*] vt erkunden; vi aufklären.

reconsider [riː'kən'sɪdə*] vti von neuem erwägen, (es) überdenken.

reconstitute [riː'kɒnstɪtjuːt] vt neu bilden.

reconstruct [riː'kən'strʌkt] vt wiederaufbauen; crime rekonstruieren; —ion [riː'kən'strʌkʃən] Rekonstruktion f.

record [rekɔːd] n Aufzeichnung f; (Mus) Schallplatte f; (best performance) Rekord m; a time Rekord-; [rɪ'kɔːd] vt aufzeichnen; (Mus etc) aufnehmen; — card (in file) Karteikarte f; —ed music Musikaufnahmen pl; —er [rɪ'kɔːdə*] (officer) Protokollführer m; (Mus) Blockflöte f; — holder (Sport) Rekordinhaber m; —ing [rɪ'kɔːdɪŋ] (Mus) Aufnahme f; — library Schallplattenarchiv nt; — player Plattenspieler m.

recount [rɪ'kaʊnt] n Nachzählung f; vt (count again) nachzählen; [rɪ'kaʊnt] (tell) berichten.

recoup [rɪ'kuːp] vt wettmachen.

recourse [rɪ'kɔːs] n Zuflucht f.

recover [rɪ'kʌvə*] vt (get back) zurückerhalten; [riː'kʌvə*] quilt etc neu überziehen; vi sich erholen; —y Wiedererlangung f; (of health) Genesung f.

recreate [riː'krɪ'eɪt] vt wiederherstellen.

recreation [rekrɪ'eɪʃən] n Erholung f; Freizeitbeschäftigung f; —al a Erholungs-.

recrimination [rɪkrɪmɪ'neɪʃən] n Gegenbeschuldigung f.

recruit [rɪ'kruːt] n Rekrut m; vt rekrutieren; —ing office Wehrmeldeamt nt; —ment Rekrutierung f.

rectangle ['rektæŋgl] n Rechteck nt.

rectangular [rek'tæŋgjulə*] a rechteckig, rechtwinklig.

rectify ['rektıfaı] *vt* berichtigen.

rectory ['rektərı] *n* Pfarrhaus *nt*.

recuperate [rı'ku:pəreıt] *vi* sich erholen.

recur [rı'kɔ:*]* *vi* sich wiederholen; —rence Wiederholung *f*; —rent *a* wiederkehrend.

red [red] *n* Rot *nt*; (Pol) Rote(r) *m*; a rot; in the — in den roten Zahlen; R— Cross Rote(s) Kreuz *nt*; —den *vti* (sich) röten; (blush) erröten; —dish *a* rötlich.

redecorate ['ri:dekəreıt] *vt* renovieren.

redecoration [ri:dekə'reıʃən] *n* Renovierung *f*.

redeem [rı'di:m] *vt* (Comm) einlösen; (set free) freikaufen; (compensate) retten; to — sb from sin jdn von seinen Sünden erlösen.

redeeming [rı'di:mıŋ] a virtue, feature rettend.

redeploy [ri:dı'plɔı] *vt* resources umverteilen.

red-haired ['red'heəd] a rothaarig.

red-handed ['red'hændıd] ad auf frischer Tat.

redhead ['redhed] *n* Rothaarige(r) *mf*.

red herring ['red'herıŋ] *n* Ablenkungsmanöver *nt*.

red-hot ['red'hɒt] a rotglühend; (excited) hitzig; tip heiß.

redirect [ri:daı'rekt] *vt* umleiten.

rediscovery ['ri:dıs'kʌvərı] *n* Wiederentdeckung *f*.

redistribute ['ri:dıs'trıbju:t] *vt* neu verteilen.

red-letter day ['red'letədeı] *n* (lit, fig) Festtag *m*.

redness ['rednəs] *n* Röte *f*.

redo ['ri:'du:] *vt* irreg nochmals tun or machen.

redolent ['redəulənt] a: — of riechend nach; (fig) erinnernd an (+acc).

redouble [rı'dʌbl] *vt*. verdoppeln.

red tape ['red'teıp] *n* Bürokratismus *m*.

reduce [rı'dju:s] *vt* price herabsetzen (to auf +acc); speed, temperature vermindern; photo verkleinern; to — sb to tears/silence jdn zum Weinen/Schweigen bringen.

reduction [rı'dʌkʃən] *n* Herabsetzung *f*; Verminderung *f*; Verkleinerung *f*; (amount of money) Nachlaß *m*.

redundancy [rı'dʌndənsı] *n* Überflüssigkeit *f*; (of workers) Entlassung *f*.

redundant [rı'dʌndənt] a überflüssig; workers ohne Arbeitsplatz; to be made — arbeitslos werden.

reed [ri:d] *n* Schilf *nt*; (Mus) Rohrblatt *nt*.

reef [ri:f] *n* Riff *nt*.

reek [ri:k] *vi* stinken (of nach).

reel [ri:l] *n* Spule *f*, Rolle *f*; *vt* (wind) wickeln, spulen; (stagger) taumeln.

re-election ['ri:ı'lekʃən] *n* Wiederwahl *f*.

re-engage ['ri:ın'geıdʒ] *vt* wieder einstellen.

re-enter ['ri:'entə*] *vt* wieder eintreten (in +acc).

re-entry ['ri:'entrı] *n* Wiedereintritt *m*.

re-examine ['ri:ıg'zæmın] *vt* neu überprüfen.

ref [ref] *n* (col) Schiri *m*.

refectory [rı'fektərı] *n* (Univ) Mensa *f*; (Sch) Speisesaal *m*; (Eccl) Refektorium *nt*.

refer [rɪˈfɜ:*] vt: — sb to sb/sth jdn an jdn/etw verweisen; vi: — to hinweisen auf (+acc); (to book) nachschlagen in (+dat); (mention) sich beziehen auf (+acc).

referee [refəˈri:] n Schiedsrichter m; (for job) Referenz f; vt schiedsrichtern.

reference [ˈrefrəns] n (mentioning) Hinweis m; (allusion) Anspielung f; (for job) Referenz f; (in book) Verweis m; (number, code) Aktenzeichen nt; Katalognummer f; with — to in bezug auf (+acc); — book Nachschlagewerk nt.

referendum [refəˈrendəm] n Volksabstimmung f.

refill [ˈriːˈfɪl] vt nachfüllen; [ˈriːfɪl] n Nachfüllung f; (for pen) Ersatzpatrone f; Ersatzmine f.

refine [rɪˈfaɪn] vt (purify) raffinieren, läutern; (fig) bilden, kultivieren; —d a gebildet, kultiviert; —ment Bildung f, Kultiviertheit f; —ry Raffinerie f.

reflect [rɪˈflekt] vt light reflektieren; (fig) (wider)spiegeln, zeigen; vi (meditate) nachdenken (on über +acc); —ion Reflexion f; (image) Spiegelbild nt; (thought) Überlegung f, Gedanke m; —or Reflektor m.

reflex [ˈriːfleks] n Reflex m; —ive [rɪˈfleksɪv] a (Gram) Reflexiv-, rückbezüglich, reflexiv.

reform [rɪˈfɔːm] n Reform f; vt person bessern; the R—ation [refəˈmeɪʃən] die Reformation; —er Reformer m; (Eccl) Reformator m.

refrain [rɪˈfreɪn] vi unterlassen (from acc).

refresh [rɪˈfreʃ] vt erfrischen; —er course Wiederholungskurs m; —ing a erfrischend; —ments pl Erfrischungen pl.

refrigeration [rɪfrɪdʒəˈreɪʃən] n Kühlung f.

refrigerator [rɪˈfrɪdʒəreɪtə*] n Kühlschrank m.

refuel [ˈriːˈfjuəl] vti auftanken; —ling Auftanken nt.

refuge [ˈrefjuːdʒ] n Zuflucht f; —e [refjuˈdʒiː] Flüchtling m.

refund [rɪˈfʌnd] n Rückvergütung f; [rɪˈfʌnd] vt zurückerstatten, rückvergüten.

refurbish [ˈriːˈfɜːbɪʃ] vt aufpolieren.

refurnish [ˈriːˈfɜːnɪʃ] vt neu möblieren.

refusal [rɪˈfjuːzəl] n (Ver)weigerung f; (official) abschlägige Antwort f.

refuse [ˈrefjuːs] n Abfall m, Müll m; [rɪˈfjuːz] vt abschlagen; vi sich weigern.

refute [rɪˈfjuːt] vt widerlegen.

regain [rɪˈgeɪn] vt wiedergewinnen; consciousness wiedererlangen.

regal [ˈriːgəl] a königlich; —ia [rɪˈgeɪlɪə] pl Insignien pl; (of mayor etc) Amtsornat m.

regard [rɪˈgɑːd] n Achtung f; vt ansehen; —s pl Grüße pl; —ing, as —s, with — to bezüglich (+gen), in bezug auf (+acc); —less a ohne Rücksicht (of auf +acc); ad unbekümmert, ohne Rücksicht auf die Folgen.

regatta [rɪˈgætə] n Regatta f.

regency [ˈriːdʒənsɪ] n Regentschaft f.

regent [ˈriːdʒənt] n Regent m.

régime [reɪˈʒiːm] n Regime nt.

regiment [ˈredʒɪmənt] n Regiment nt; —al [redʒɪˈmentl] a Regiments-; —ation Reglementierung f.

region [ˈriːdʒən] n Gegend f, Bereich m; —al a örtlich, regional.

register ['redʒɪstə'] *n* Register *nt*, Verzeichnis *nt*, Liste *f*; *vt* (list) registrieren, eintragen; *emotion* zeigen; (write down) eintragen; *vi* (at hotel) sich eintragen; (with police) sich melden (with bei); (make impression) wirken, ankommen; **—ed** a design eingetragen; *letter* Einschreibe-, eingeschrieben.

registrar [redʒɪs'trɑ:*] *n* Standesbeamte(r) *m*.

registration [redʒɪs'treɪʃən] *n* (act) Erfassung *f*, Registrierung *f*; (number) Autonummer *f*, polizeiliche(s) Kennzeichen *nt*.

registry office ['redʒɪstrɪɒfɪs] *n* Standesamt *nt*.

regret [rɪ'gret] *n* Bedauern *nt*; to have no **—s** nichts bedauern; *vt* bedauern; **—ful** a traurig; to be **—ful** about sth etw bedauern; **—fully** ad mit Bedauern, ungern; **—table** a bedauerlich.

regroup ['ri:gru:p] *vt* umgruppieren; *vi* sich umgruppieren.

regular ['regjulə*] a regelmäßig; (usual) üblich; (fixed by rule) geregelt; (col) regelrecht; *n* (client etc) Stammkunde *m*; (Mil) Berufssoldat *m*; **—ity** [regju'lærɪtɪ] Regelmäßigkeit *f*; **—ly** ad regelmäßig.

regulate ['regjuleɪt] *vt* regeln, regulieren.

regulation [regju'leɪʃən] *n* (rule) Vorschrift *f*; (control) Regulierung *f*; (order) Anordnung *f*, Regelung *f*.

rehabilitation ['ri:həbɪlɪ'teɪʃən] *n* (of criminal) Resozialisierung *f*.

rehash ['ri:'hæʃ] *vt* (col) aufwärmen.

rehearsal [rɪ'hɜ:səl] *n* Probe *f*.

rehearse [rɪ'hɜ:s] *vt* proben.

reign [reɪn] *n* Herrschaft *f*; *vi* herrschen; **—ing** a monarch herrschend; champion gegenwärtig.

reimburse [ri:ɪm'bɜ:s] *vt* entschädigen, zurückzahlen (sb for sth jdm etw).

rein [reɪn] *n* Zügel *m*.

reincarnation ['ri:ɪnkɑ:'neɪʃən] *n* Wiedergeburt *f*.

reindeer ['reɪndɪə*] *n* Ren *nt*.

reinforce [ri:ɪn'fɔ:s] *vt* verstärken; **—d** a verstärkt; concrete Eisen**—ment** Verstärkung *f*; **—ments** pl (Mil) Verstärkungstruppen pl.

reinstate ['ri:ɪn'steɪt] *vt* wiedereinsetzen.

reissue ['ri:'ɪʃu:] *vt* neu herausgeben.

reiterate [ri:'ɪtəreɪt] *vt* wiederholen.

reject ['ri:dʒekt] *n* (Comm) Ausschuß(artikel) *m*; [rɪ'dʒekt] *vt* ablehnen; (throw away) ausrangieren; **—ion** [rɪ'dʒekʃən] Zurückweisung *f*.

rejoice [rɪ'dʒɔɪs] *vi* sich freuen.

rejuvenate [rɪ'dʒu:vɪneɪt] *vt* verjüngen.

rekindle ['ri:'kɪndl] *vt* wieder anfachen.

relapse [rɪ'læps] *n* Rückfall *m*.

relate [rɪ'leɪt] *vt* (tell) berichten, erzählen; (connect) verbinden; **—d** a verwandt (to mit).

relating [rɪ'leɪtɪŋ] prep: **—** to bezüglich (+gen).

relation [rɪ'leɪʃən] *n* Verwandte(r) *mf*; (connection) Beziehung *f*; **—ship** Verhältnis *nt*, Beziehung *f*.

relative ['relətɪv] *n* Verwandte(r) *mf*; *a* relativ, bedingt; **—ly** ad verhältnismäßig; **—** pronoun Verhältniswort *nt*, Relativpronomen *nt*.

relax [rɪˈlæks] vi (slacken) sich lockern; (muscles, person) sich entspannen; (be less strict) freundlicher werden; vt (ease) lockern, entspannen; —! reg' dich nicht auf!; —ation [riːlækˈseɪʃən] Entspannung f; —ed a entspannt, locker; —ing a entspannend.

relay [ˈriːleɪ] n (Sport) Staffel f; vt message weiterleiten; (Rad, TV) übertragen.

release [rɪˈliːs] n (freedom) Entlassung f; (Tech) Auslöser m; vt befreien; prisoner entlassen; report, news verlautbaren, bekanntgeben.

relent [rɪˈlent] vi nachgeben; —less a, —lessly ad unnachgiebig.

relevance [ˈreləvəns] n Bedeutung f, Relevanz f.

relevant [ˈreləvənt] a wichtig, relevant.

reliability [rɪlaɪəˈbɪlɪti] n Zuverlässigkeit f.

reliable a, **reliably** ad [rɪˈlaɪbl, -blɪ] zuverlässig.

reliance [rɪˈlaɪəns] n Abhängigkeit f (on von).

relic [ˈrelɪk] n (from past) Überbleibsel nt; (Rel) Reliquie f.

relief [rɪˈliːf] n Erleichterung f; (help) Hilfe f, Unterstützung f; (person) Ablösung f; (Art) Relief nt; (distinctness) Hervorhebung f.

relieve [rɪˈliːv] vt (ease) erleichtern; (bring help) entlasten; person ablösen; to — sb of sth jdm etw abnehmen.

religion [rɪˈlɪdʒən] n Religion f.

religious [rɪˈlɪdʒəs] a religiös; —ly ad religiös; (conscientiously) gewissenhaft.

reline [riːˈlaɪn] vt brakes neu beschuhen.

relinquish [rɪˈlɪŋkwɪʃ] vt aufgeben.

relish [ˈrelɪʃ] n Würze f, pikante Beigabe f; vt genießen.

relive [ˈriːˈlɪv] vt noch einmal durchleben.

reluctance [rɪˈlʌktəns] n Widerstreben nt, Abneigung f.

reluctant [rɪˈlʌktənt] a widerwillig; —ly ad ungern.

rely [rɪˈlaɪ]: — on vt sich verlassen auf (+acc).

remain [rɪˈmeɪn] vi (be left) übrigbleiben; (stay) bleiben; —der Rest m; —ing a übriggeblieben; —s pl Überreste pl; (dead body) sterbliche Überreste pl.

remand [rɪˈmɑːnd] n: on — in Untersuchungshaft; vt: to — in custody in Untersuchungshaft schicken.

remark [rɪˈmɑːk] n Bemerkung f; vt bemerken; —able a, —ably ad bemerkenswert.

remarry [ˈriːˈmærɪ] vi sich wieder verheiraten.

remedial [rɪˈmiːdɪəl] a Heil-; teaching Hilfsschul-.

remedy [ˈremədɪ] n Mittel nt; vt pain abhelfen (+dat); trouble in Ordnung bringen.

remember [rɪˈmembə*] vt sich erinnern an (+acc); — me to them grüße sie von mir.

remembrance [rɪˈmembrəns] n Erinnerung f; (official) Gedenken nt.

remind [rɪˈmaɪnd] vt erinnern; —er Mahnung f.

reminisce [remɪˈnɪs] vi in Erinnerungen schwelgen; —nces [remɪˈnɪsənsɪz] pl Erinnerungen pl; —nt a erinnernd (of an +acc), Erinnerungen nachrufend (of an +acc).

remit [rɪ'mɪt] *vt money* überweisen *(to* an *+acc);* **—tance** Geldanweisung *f.*

remnant ['remnant] *n* Rest *m.*

remorse [rɪ'mɔːs] *n* Gewissensbisse *pl;* **—ful** a reumütig; **—less** a, **—lessly** ad unbarmherzig.

remote [rɪ'məut] a abgelegen, entfernt; *(slight)* gering; **— control** Fernsteuerung *f;* **—ly** ad entfernt; **—ness** Entlegenheit *f.*

removable [rɪ'muːvəbl] a entfernbar.

removal [rɪ'muːvəl] *n* Beseitigung *f; (of furniture)* Umzug *m; (from office)* Entlassung *f;* **— van** Möbelwagen *m.*

remove [rɪ'muːv] *vt* beseitigen, entfernen; *(dismiss)* entlassen; **—r** *(for paint etc)* Fleckenentferner *m;* **—rs** *pl* Möbelspedition *f.*

remuneration [rɪmjuːnə'reɪʃən] *n* Vergütung *f,* Honorar *nt.*

Renaissance [rə'neɪsɑːns]: the **—** die Renaissance.

rename ['riː'neɪm] *vt* umbenennen.

rend [rend] *vt irreg* zerreißen.

render ['rendə*] *vt* machen; *(translate)* übersetzen; **—ing** *(Mus)* Wiedergabe *f.*

rendezvous ['rɒndɪvuː] *n* Verabredung *f,* Rendezvous *nt.*

renegade ['renɪgeɪd] *n* Überläufer *m.*

renew [rɪ'njuː] *vt* erneuern; *contract, licence* verlängern; *(replace)* ersetzen; **—al** Erneuerung *f;* Verlängerung *f.*

renounce [rɪ'nauns] *vt (give up)* verzichten auf *(+acc); (disown)* verstoßen.

renovate ['renəveɪt] *vt* renovieren; *building* restaurieren.

renovation [renəu'veɪʃən] *n* Renovierung *f;* Restauration *f.*

renown [rɪ'naun] *n* Ruf *m;* **—ed** a namhaft.

rent [rent] *n* Miete *f; (for land)* Pacht *f; vt (hold as tenant)* mieten; pachten; *(let)* vermieten; *.verpachten; car etc* mieten; *(firm)* vermieten; **—al** Miete *f;* Pacht *f,* Pachtgeld *nt.*

renunciation [rɪnʌnsɪ'eɪʃən] *n* Verzicht *m (of* auf *+acc).*

reopen ['riː'əupən] *vt* wiedereröffnen.

reorder ['riː'ɔːdə*] *vt* wieder bestellen.

reorganization ['riːɔːgənaɪ'zeɪʃən] *n* Neugestaltung *f; (Comm etc)* Umbildung *f.*

reorganize ['riː'ɔːgənaɪz] *vt* umgestalten, reorganisieren.

rep [rep] *n (Comm)* Vertreter *m; (Theat)* Repertoire *nt.*

repair [rɪ'peə*] *n* Reparatur *f;* in good **—** in gutem Zustand; *vt* reparieren; *damage* wiedergutmachen; **— kit** Werkzeugkasten *m;* **— man** Mechaniker *m;* **— shop** Reparaturwerkstatt *f.*

repartee [repɑː'tiː] *n* Witzeleien *pl.*

repay [riː'peɪ] *vt irreg* zurückzahlen; *(reward)* vergelten; **—ment** Rückzahlung *f; (fig)* Vergelten *nt.*

repeal [rɪ'piːl] *n* Aufhebung *f; vt* aufheben.

repeat [rɪ'piːt] *n (Rad, TV)* Wiederholung(ssendung) *f; vt* wiederholen; **—edly** ad wiederholt.

repel [rɪ'pel] *vt (drive back)* zurückschlagen; *(disgust)* abstoßen; **—lent** a abstoßend; *n: insect* **—lent** Insektenmittel *nt.*

repent [rɪ'pent] *vti* bereuen; **—ance** Reue *f.*

repercussion [ri:pə'kʌʃən] n Auswirkung f; (of rifle) Rückstoß m.

repertoire ['repətwɑː*] n Repertoire nt.

repertory ['repətəri] n Repertoire nt.

repetition [repə'tiʃən] n Wiederholung f.

repetitive [ri'petitiv] a sich wiederholend.

rephrase [ri:'freiz] vt anders formulieren.

replace [ri'pleis] vt ersetzen; (put back) zurückstellen; —ment Ersatz m.

replenish [ri'pleniʃ] vt (wieder) auffüllen.

replete [ri'pli:t] a (zum Platzen) voll.

replica ['replikə] n Kopie f.

reply [ri'plai] n Antwort f, Erwiderung f; vi antworten, erwidern.

report [ri'pɔːt] n Bericht m; (Sch) Zeugnis nt; (of gun) Knall m; vt (tell) berichten; (give information against) melden; (to police) anzeigen; vi (make report) Bericht erstatten; (present o.s.) sich melden; —er Reporter m.

reprehensible [repri'hensibl] a tadelnswert.

represent [repri'zent] vt darstellen, zeigen; (act) darstellen; (speak for) vertreten; —ation Darstellung f; (being represented) Vertretung f; —ative n (person) Vertreter m; a räpresentativ.

repress [ri'pres] vt unterdrücken; —ion [ri'preʃən] Unterdrückung f; —ive a Unterdrückungs-; (Psych) Hemmungs-.

reprieve [ri'priːv] n Aufschub m; (cancellation) Begnadigung f; (fig) Atempause f; vt Gnadenfrist

gewähren (+dat); begnadigen.

reprimand ['reprimɑːnd] n Verweis m; vt einen Verweis erteilen (+dat).

reprint ['riːprint] n Neudruck m; [riː'print] vt wieder abdrucken.

reprisal [ri'praizəl] n Vergeltung f.

reproach [ri'prəutʃ] n (blame) Vorwurf m, Tadel m; (disgrace) Schande f; beyond — über jeden Vorwurf erhaben; vt Vorwürfe machen (+dat), tadeln; —ful a vorwurfsvoll.

reproduce [riːprə'djuːs] vt reproduzieren; vi (have offspring) sich vermehren.

reproduction [riːprə'dʌkʃən] n Wiedergabe f; (Art, Phot) Reproduktion f; (breeding) Fortpflanzung f.

reproductive [riːprə'dʌktiv] a reproduktiv; (breeding) Fortpflanzungs-.

reprove [ri'pruːv] vt tadeln.

reptile ['reptail] n Reptil nt.

republic [ri'pʌblik] n Republik f; —an a republikanisch; n Republikaner m.

repudiate [ri'pjuːdieit] vt zurückweisen, nicht anerkennen.

repugnance [ri'pʌgnəns] n Widerwille m.

repugnant [ri'pʌgnənt] a widerlich.

repulse [ri'pʌls] n (drive back) zurückschlagen; (reject) abweisen.

repulsion [ri'pʌlʃən] n Abscheu m.

repulsive [ri'pʌlsiv] a abstoßend.

repurchase ['riː'pɜːtʃəs] vt zurückkaufen.

reputable ['repjutəbl] a angesehen.

reputation [repju'teiʃən] n Ruf m.

repute [ri'pjuːt] n hohe(s) Ansehen nt; —d a, —dly ad angeblich.

request [rɪ'kwest] n (asking) Ansuchen nt; (demand) Wunsch m; at sb's — auf jds Wunsch; vt thing erbitten; person ersuchen.

requiem ['rekwɪem] n Requiem nt.

require [rɪ'kwaɪə*] vt (need) brauchen; (wish) wünschen; to be —d to do sth etw tun müssen; —ment (condition) Anforderung f; (need) Bedarf m.

requisite ['rekwɪzɪt] n Erfordernis nt; a erforderlich.

requisition [rekwɪ'zɪʃən] n Anforderung f; vt beschlagnahmen; (order) anfordern.

reroute ['ri:'ru:t] vt umleiten.

rescind [rɪ'sɪnd] vt aufheben.

rescue ['reskju:] n Rettung f; vt retten; — party Rettungsmannschaft f; —r Retter m.

research [rɪ'sɜ:tʃ] n Forschung f; vi Forschungen anstellen (into über +acc); vt erforschen; —er Forscher m; — work Forschungsarbeit f; — worker wissenschaftliche(r) Mitarbeiter(in f) m.

resemblance [rɪ'zembləns] n Ähnlichkeit f.

resemble [rɪ'zembl] vt ähneln (+dat).

resent [rɪ'zent] vt übelnehmen; —ful a nachtragend, empfindlich; —ment Verstimmung f, Unwille m.

reservation [rezə'veɪʃən] n (of seat) Reservierung f; (Theat) Vorbestellung f; (doubt) Vorbehalt m; (land) Reservat nt.

reserve [rɪ'zɜ:v] n (store) Vorrat m, Reserve f; (manner) Zurückhaltung f; (game —) Naturschutzgebiet nt; (native —) Reservat nt; (Sport) Ersatzspieler(in f) m; vt reservieren; judgement sich (dat) vorbehalten; —s pl (Mil) Reserve f; in — in Reserve; —d a

reserviert; all rights —d alle Rechte vorbehalten.

reservist [rɪ'zɜ:vɪst] n Reservist m.

reservoir ['rezəvwa:*] n Reservoir nt.

reshape ['ri:'ʃeɪp] vt umformen.

reshuffle ['ri:'ʃʌfl] vt (Pol) umbilden.

reside [rɪ'zaɪd] vi wohnen, ansässig sein; —nce ['rezɪdəns] (house) Wohnung f, Sitz m; (living) Wohnen nt, Aufenthalt m; —nt ['rezɪdənt] (in house) Bewohner m; (in area) Einwohner m; a wohnhaft, ansässig; —ntial [rezɪ'denʃəl] a Wohn-.

residue ['rezɪdju:] n Rest m; (Chem) Rückstand m; (fig) Bodensatz m.

resign [rɪ'zaɪn] vt office aufgeben, zurücktreten von; to be —ed to sth, to — o.s. to sth sich mit etw abfinden; vi (from office) zurücktreten; —ation [rezɪg'neɪʃən] (resigning) Aufgabe f; (Pol) Rücktritt m; (submission) Resignation f; —ed a resigniert.

resilience [rɪ'zɪlɪəns] n Spannkraft f, Elastizität f; (of person) Unverwüstlichkeit f.

resilient [rɪ'zɪlɪənt] a unverwüstlich.

resin ['rezɪn] n Harz nt.

resist [rɪ'zɪst] vt widerstehen (+dat); —ance Widerstand m; —ant a widerstandsfähig (to gegen); (to stains etc) abstoßend.

resolute a, —ly ad ['rezəlu:t, -lɪ] entschlossen, resolut.

resolution [rezə'lu:ʃən] n (firmness) Entschlossenheit f; (intention) Vorsatz m; (decision) Beschluß m; (personal) Entschluß m.

resolve [rɪ'zɒlv] n Vorsatz m, Entschluß m; vt (decide) beschließen.

it —d itself es löste sich; —d a (fest) entschlossen.

resonant ['rezənənt] a widerhallend; *voice* volltönend.

resort [rɪ'zɔ:t]. n *(holiday place)* Erholungsort m; *(help)* Zuflucht f; vi Zuflucht nehmen *(to* zu); as a last — als letzter Ausweg.

resound [rɪ'zaʊnd] vi widerhallen; —ing a nachhallend; *success* groß.

resource [rɪ'sɔ:s] n Zuflucht f; —s pl *(of energy)* Energiequellen pl; *(of money)* Quellen pl; *(of a country etc)* Bodenschätze pl; —ful a findig; —fulness Findigkeit f.

respect [rɪs'pekt] n Respekt m; *(esteem)* (Hoch)achtung f; vt achten, respektieren; —s pl Grüße pl; with — to in bezug auf *(+acc)*, hinsichtlich *(+gen)*; in — of in bezug auf *(+acc)*; in this — in dieser Hinsicht; —ability [rɪspektə'bɪlɪtɪ] Anständigkeit f; Achtbarkeit f; —able a *(decent)* angesehen, achtbar; *(fairly good)* leidlich; —ed a angesehen; —ful a höflich; —fully ad ehrerbietig; *(in letter)* mit vorzüglicher Hochachtung; —ing prep betreffend; —ive a jeweilig; —ively ad beziehungsweise.

respiration [respɪ'reɪʃən] n Atmung f, Atmen nt.

respiratory [rɪs'pɪrətərɪ] a Atmungs-.

respite ['respaɪt] n Ruhepause f; without — ohne Unterlaß.

resplendent [rɪs'plendənt] a strahlend.

respond [rɪs'pɒnd] vi antworten; *(react)* reagieren *(to* auf *+acc)*.

response [rɪs'pɒns] n Antwort f; Reaktion f; *(to advert etc)* Resonanz f.

responsibility [rɪspɒnsə'bɪlɪtɪ] n Verantwortung f.

responsible [rɪs'pɒnsəbl] a verantwortlich; *(reliable)* verantwortungsvoll.

responsibly [rɪs'pɒnsəblɪ] ad verantwortungsvoll.

responsive [rɪs'pɒnsɪv] a empfänglich.

rest [rest] n Ruhe f; *(break)* Pause f; *(remainder)* Rest m; the — of them die übrigen; vi sich ausruhen; *(be supported)* (auf)liegen; *(remain)* liegen *(with* bei).

restaurant ['restərɔ:ŋ] n Restaurant nt, Gaststätte f; — car Speisewagen m.

rest cure ['restkjʊə*] n Erholung f.

restful ['restful] a erholsam, ruhig.

rest home ['resthəʊm] n Erholungsheim nt.

restitution [restɪ'tju:ʃən] n Rückgabe f, Entschädigung f.

restive ['restɪv] a unruhig; *(disobedient)* störrisch.

restless ['restləs] a unruhig; —ly ad ruhelos; —ness Ruhelosigkeit f.

restock ['ri:'stɒk] vt auffüllen.

restoration [restə'reɪʃən] n Wiederherstellung f; ·Neueinführung f; Wiedereinsetzung f; Rückgabe f; Restauration f; the R— die Restauration.

restore [rɪs'tɔ:*] vt order wiederherstellen; *customs* wieder einführen; *person to position* wiedereinsetzen; *(give back)* zurückgeben; *paintings* restaurieren.

restrain [rɪs'treɪn] vt zurückhalten; *curiosity etc* beherrschen; *a style etc* gedämpft, verhalten; —t *(restraining)* Einschränkung f; *(being restrained)* Beschränkung f; *(self-control)* Zurückhaltung f.

restrict [rɪs'trɪkt] *vt* einschränken; **—ed** a beschränkt; **—ion** [rɪs'trɪkʃən] Einschränkung *f*; **—ive** a einschränkend.

rest room ['restrum] *n (US)* Toilette *f*.

result [rɪ'zʌlt] *n* Resultat *nt*, Folge *f*; *(of exam, game)* Ergebnis *nt*; *vi* zur Folge haben *(in acc)*; **—ant** a (daraus) entstehend *or* resultierend.

resume [rɪ'zjuːm] *vt* fortsetzen; *(occupy again)* wieder einnehmen.

résumé ['rezjuːmeɪ] *n* Zusammenfassung *f*.

resumption [rɪ'zʌmpʃən] *n* Wiederaufnahme *f*.

resurgence [rɪ'sɜːdʒəns] *n* Wiedererwachen *nt*.

resurrection [rezə'rekʃən] *n* Auferstehung *f*.

resuscitate [rɪ'sʌsɪteɪt] *vt* wiederbeleben.

resuscitation [rɪsʌsɪ'teɪʃən] *n* Wiederbelebung *f*.

retail ['riːteɪl] *n* Einzelhandel *m*; a Einzelhandels-, Laden-; ['riːteɪl] *vt* im kleinen verkaufen; *vi* im Einzelhandel kosten; **—er** ['riːteɪlə*] Einzelhändler *m*, Kleinhändler *m*; **— price** Ladenpreis *m*.

retain [rɪ'teɪn] *vt (keep)* (zurück)behalten; *(pay)* unterhalten; **—er** *(servant)* Gefolgsmann *m*; *(fee)* (Honorar)vorschuß *m*.

retaliate [rɪ'tælɪeɪt] *vi* zum Vergeltungsschlag ausholen.

retaliation [rɪtælɪ'eɪʃən] *n* Vergeltung *f*.

retarded [rɪ'tɑːdɪd] a zurückgeblieben.

retention [rɪ'tenʃən] *n* Behalten *nt*.

retentive [rɪ'tentɪv] a *memory* gut.

rethink ['riː'θɪŋk] *vt irreg* nochmals durchdenken.

reticence ['retɪsəns] *n* Schweigsamkeit *f*.

reticent ['retɪsənt] a schweigsam.

retina ['retɪnə] *n* Netzhaut *f*.

retinue ['retɪnjuː] *n* Gefolge *nt*.

retire [rɪ'taɪə*] *vi (from work)* in den Ruhestand treten; *(withdraw)* sich zurückziehen; *(go to bed)* schlafen gehen; **—ant** a person pensioniert, im Ruhestand; **—ment** Ruhestand *m*.

retiring [rɪ'taɪərɪŋ] a zurückhaltend, schüchtern.

retort [rɪ'tɔːt] *n (reply)* Erwiderung *f*; *(Sci)* Retorte *f*; *vi* (scharf) erwidern.

retrace [rɪ'treɪs] *vt* zurückverfolgen.

retract [rɪ'trækt] *vt statement* zurücknehmen; *claws* einziehen; **—able** a *aerial* ausziehbar.

retrain ['riː'treɪn] *vt* umschulen; **—ing** Umschulung *f*.

retreat [rɪ'triːt] *n* Rückzug *m*; *(place)* Zufluchtsort *m*; *vi* sich zurückziehen.

retrial ['riː'traɪəl] *n* Wiederaufnahmeverfahren *nt*.

retribution [retrɪ'bjuːʃən] *n* Strafe *f*.

retrieval [rɪ'triːvəl] *n* Wiedergewinnung *f*.

retrieve [rɪ'triːv] *vt* wiederbekommen; *(rescue)* retten; **—r** Apportierhund *m*.

retroactive [retrəʊ'æktɪv] a rückwirkend.

retrograde ['retrəʊgreɪd] a *step* Rück-; *policy* rückschrittlich.

retrospect ['retrəʊspekt] *n*: **in —** im Rückblick, rückblickend; **—ive** [retrəʊ'spektɪv] a rückwirkend; rückblickend.

return [rɪ'tɜːn] *n* Rückkehr *f*; *(profits)* Ertrag *m*, Gewinn *m*;

(report) amtliche(r) Bericht *m*; *(rail ticket etc)* Rückfahrkarte *f*; *(plane)* Rückflugkarte *f*; *(bus)* Rückfahrschein *m*; **a** **by** ─ **of post** postwendend; *(elect)* wählen; *verdict* aussprechen; ─**able** *a bottle etc* mit Pfand.

reunion [riː'juːnjən] *n* Wiedervereinigung *f*; *(Sch etc)* Treffen *nt*.

reunite ['riːjuːˈnaɪt] *vt* wiedervereinigen.

rev [rev] *n* Drehzahl *f*; *vti (also* ─ **up)** (den Motor) auf Touren bringen.

revamp ['riːˈvæmp] *vt* aufpolieren.

reveal [rɪˈviːl] *vt* enthüllen; ─**ing** *a* aufschlußreich.

reveille [rɪˈvælɪ] *n* Wecken *nt*.

revel ['revl] *vi* genießen *(in acc)*.

revelation [revəˈleɪʃən] *n* Offenbarung *f*.

reveller ['revələ*] *n* Schwelger *m*.

revelry ['revlrɪ] *n* Rummel *m*.

revenge [rɪˈvendʒ] *n* Rache *f*; *vt* rächen; ─**ful** *a* rachsüchtig.

revenue ['revənjuː] *n* Einnahmen *pl*, Staatseinkünfte *pl*.

reverberate [rɪˈvɜːbəreɪt] *vi* widerhallen.

reverberation [rɪvɜːbəˈreɪʃən] *n* Widerhall *m*.

revere [rɪˈvɪə*] *vt* (ver)ehren; ─**nce** ['revərəns] Ehrfurcht *f*; ['revərənd] R─**nd** ... Hochwürden ...; ─**nt** ['revərənt] *a* ehrfurchtsvoll.

reverie ['revərɪ] *n* Träumerei *f*.

reversal [rɪˈvɜːsl] *n* Umkehrung *f*.

reverse [rɪˈvɜːs] *n* Rückseite *f*; *(Aut: gear)* Rückwärtsgang *m*; *a* *order, direction* entgegengesetzt;

vt umkehren; *vi (Aut)* rückwärts fahren.

reversion [rɪˈvɜːʃən] *n* Umkehrung *f*.

revert [rɪˈvɜːt] *vi* zurückkehren.

review [rɪˈvjuː] *n* *(Mil)* Truppenschau *f*; *(of book)* Besprechung *f*, Rezension *f*; *(magazine)* Zeitschrift *f*; **to be under** ─ untersucht werden; *vt* Rückschau halten auf (+*acc*); *(Mil)* mustern; *book* besprechen, rezensieren; *(re-examine)* von neuem untersuchen; ─**er** *(critic)* Rezensent *m*.

revise [rɪˈvaɪz] *vt* durchsehen, verbessern; *book* überarbeiten, *(reconsider)* ändern, revidieren.

revision [rɪˈvɪʒən] *n* Durchsicht *f*, Prüfung *f*; *(Comm)* Revision *f*; *(of book)* verbesserte Ausgabe *f*; *(Sch)* Wiederholung *f*.

revisit ['riːˈvɪzɪt] *vt* wieder besuchen.

revitalize ['riːˈvaɪtəlaɪz] *vt* neu beleben.

revival [rɪˈvaɪvəl] *n* Wiederbelebung *f*; *(Rel)* Erweckung *f*; *(Theat)* Wiederaufnahme *f*.

revive [rɪˈvaɪv] *vt* wiederbeleben; *(fig)* wieder auffrischen; *vi* wiedererwachen; *(fig)* wieder aufleben.

revoke [rɪˈvəʊk] *vt* aufheben.

revolt [rɪˈvəʊlt] *n* Aufstand *m*, Revolte *f*; *vi* sich auflehnen; *vt* entsetzen; ─**ing** *a* widerlich.

revolution [revəˈluːʃən] *n* *(turn)* Umdrehung *f*, *(change)* Umwälzung *f*; *(Pol)* Revolution *f*; ─**ary** *a* revolutionär; *n* Revolutionär *m*; ─**ize** *vt* revolutionieren.

revolve [rɪˈvɒlv] *vi* kreisen; *(on own axis)* sich drehen; ─**r** Revolver *m*.

revue [rɪ'vjuː] *n* Revue *f.*

revulsion [rɪ'vʌlʃən] *n (disgust)* Ekel *m.*

reward [rɪ'wɔːd] *n* Belohnung *f; vt* belohnen; —ing *a* lohnend.

reword · [riː'wɜːd] *vt* anders formulieren.

rewrite [riː'raɪt] *vt irreg* umarbeiten, neu schreiben.

rhapsody [ræpsədɪ] *n* Rhapsodie *f; (fig)* Schwärmerei *f.*

rhetoric [retərɪk] *n* Rhetorik *f,* Redekunst *f;* —al [rɪ'tɒrɪkəl] *a* rhetorisch.

rheumatic [ruː'mætɪk] *a* rheumatisch.

rheumatism [ruːmətɪzəm] *n* Rheumatismus *m,* Rheuma *nt.*

rhinoceros [raɪ'nɒsərəs] *n* Nashorn *nt,* Rhinozeros *nt.*

rhododendron [rəʊdə'dendrən] *n* Rhododendron *m.*

rhubarb [ruːbɑːb] *n* Rhabarber *m.*

rhyme [raɪm] *n* Reim *m.*

rhythm [rɪðəm] *n* Rhythmus *m;* —ic(al) *a,* —ically *ad* [rɪðmɪk(l), -ɪ] rhythmisch.

rib [rɪb] *n* Rippe *f; vt (mock)* hänseln, aufziehen.

ribald [rɪbəld] *a* saftig.

ribbon [rɪbən] *n* Band *nt.*

rice [raɪs] *n* Reis *m;* — pudding Milchreis *m.*

rich [rɪtʃ] *a* reich, wohlhabend; *(fertile)* fruchtbar; *(splendid)* kostbar; food reichhaltig; —es *pl* Reichtum *m,* Reichtümer *pl;* —ly *ad* reich; deserve völlig; —ness *n* Reichtum *m; (of food)* Reichhaltigkeit *f; (of colours)* Sattheit *f.*

rick [rɪk] *n* Schober *m.*

rickets [rɪkɪts] *n* Rachitis *f.*

rickety [rɪkɪtɪ] *a* wack(e)lig.

rickshaw [rɪkʃɔː] *n* Rikscha *f.*

ricochet [rɪkəʃeɪ] *n* Abprallen *nt; (shot)* Querschläger *m; vi* abprallen.

rid [rɪd] *vt irreg* befreien *(of* von*);* to get — of loswerden; good —dance! den/die/das wären wir los!

riddle [rɪdl] *n* Rätsel *nt; vt (esp passive)* durchlöchern.

ride [raɪd] *n (in vehicle)* Fahrt *f; (on horse)* Ritt *m; irreg vt* horse reiten; bicycle fahren; *vi* fahren; reiten; *(ship)* vor Anker liegen; —r Reiter *m; (addition)* Zusatz *m.*

ridge [rɪdʒ] *n (of hills)* Bergkette *f; (top)* Grat *m,* Kamm *m; (of roof)* Dachfirst *m.*

ridicule [rɪdɪkjuːl] *n* Spott *m; vt* lächerlich machen.

ridiculous *a,* —ly *ad* [rɪ'dɪkjuləs, -lɪ] lächerlich.

riding [raɪdɪŋ] *n* Reiten *nt;* to go — reiten gehen; — habit Reitkleid *nt;* — school Reitschule *f.*

rife [raɪf] *a* weit verbreitet.

riffraff [rɪfræf] *n* Gesindel *nt,* Pöbel *m.*

rifle [raɪfl] *n* Gewehr *nt; vt* berauben; — range Schießstand *m.*

rift [rɪft] *n* Ritze *f,* Spalte *f; (fig)* Bruch *m.*

rig [rɪg] *n (outfit)* Takelung *f; (oil)* Aufmachung *f; (oil —)* Bohrinsel *f; vt* election etc manipulieren; —ging Takelage *f;* — out *vt* ausstatten; — up *vt* zusammenbasteln, konstruieren.

right [raɪt] *a (correct, just)* richtig, recht; *(right side)* rechte(r, s); *n* Recht *nt; (not left,* Pol*)* Rechte *f; ad (on 'the right)* rechts; *(to the right)* nach rechts; look, work richtig, recht; *(directly)* gerade; *(exactly)* genau; *vt* in Ordnung bringen, korrigieren; *interj* gut; — away sofort; to be — recht haben; all —! gut!, in Ordnung!, schön! — now in diesem Augenblick, eben; by —s von Rechts wegen; — to the end bis ans Ende; on the — rechts; — angle Rechteck *nt*; —eous ['raɪtʃəs] *a* rechtschaffen; —eousness Rechtschaffenheit *f*; —ful *a* rechtmäßig; —fully *ad* rechtmäßig; (*justifiably*) zu Recht; —hand drive: to have —hand drive das Steuer rechts haben; —handed *a* rechtshändig; —hand man rechte Hand *f*; —hand side rechte Seite *f*; —ly *ad* mit Recht; —minded *a* rechtschaffen; — of way Vorfahrt *f*; —wing rechte(r) Flügel *m*.

rigid ['rɪdʒɪd] *a* (*stiff*) starr, steif; (*strict*) streng; —ity [rɪˈdʒɪdɪtɪ] Starrheit *f*, Steifheit *f*; Strenge *f*; —ly *ad* starr, steif; (*fig*) hart, unbeugsam.

rigmarole ['rɪgmərəʊl] *n* Gewäsch *nt*.

rigor mortis ['rɪgə'mɔ:tɪs] *n* Totenstarre *f*.

rigorous *a*, —ly *ad* ['rɪgərəs, -lɪ] streng.

rigour, (*US*) **rigor** ['rɪgə*] *n* Strenge *f*, Härte *f*.

rig-out ['rɪgaʊt] *n* (*col*) Aufzug *m*.

rile [raɪl] *vt* ärgern.

rim [rɪm] *n* (*edge*) Rand *m*; (*of wheel*) Felge *f*; —less *a* randlos; —med *a* gerändert.

rind [raɪnd] *n* Rinde *f*.

ring [rɪŋ] *n* Ring *m*; (*of people*) Kreis *m*; (*arena*) Ring *m*, Manege *f*; (*of telephone*) Klingeln *nt*, Läuten *nt*; **to give sb a** — jdn anrufen; **it has a familiar** — es klingt bekannt; *vti irreg bell* läuten; (*also* — **up**) anrufen; — **off**

vi aufhängen; — binder Ringbuch *nt*; —leader Anführer *m*, Rädelsführer *m*; —lets *pl* Ringellocken *pl*; — road Umgehungsstraße *f*.

rink [rɪŋk] *n* (*ice*) Eisbahn *f*.

rinse [rɪns] *n* Spülen *nt*; *vt* spülen.

riot ['raɪət] *n* Aufruhr *m*; *vi* randalieren; — er Aufrührer *m*; —ous *a*, —ously *ad* aufrührerisch; (*noisy*) lärmend.

rip [rɪp] *n* Schlitz *m*, Riß *m*; *vti* (zer)reißen.

ripcord ['rɪpkɔ:d] *n* Reißleine *f*.

ripe [raɪp] *a* fruit reif; cheese ausgereift; —n *vti* reifen, reif werden (lassen); —ness Reife *f*.

riposte [rɪˈpɒst] *n* Nachstoß *m*; (*fig*) schlagfertige Antwort *f*.

ripple ['rɪpl] *n* kleine Welle *f*; *vt* kräuseln; *vi* sich kräuseln.

rise [raɪz] *n* (*slope*) Steigung *f*; (*esp in wages*) Erhöhung *f*; (*growth*) Aufstieg *m*; *vi irreg* aufstehen; (*sun*) aufgehen; (*smoke*) aufsteigen; (*mountain*) sich erheben; (*ground*) ansteigen; (*prices*) steigen; (*in revolt*) sich erheben; **to give** — **to** Anlaß geben zu; **to** — **to the occasion** sich der Lage gewachsen zeigen.

risk [rɪsk] *n* Gefahr *f*, Risiko *nt*; *vt* (*venture*) wagen; (*chance loss of*) riskieren, aufs Spiel setzen; —y *a* gewagt, gefährlich, riskant.

risqué ['ri:skeɪ] *a* gewagt.

rissole ['rɪsəʊl] *n* Fleischklößchen *nt*.

rite [raɪt] *n* Ritus *m*; last —s *pl* Letzte Ölung *f*.

ritual ['rɪtjʊəl] *n* Ritual *nt*; *a* ritual, Ritual-; (*fig*) rituell.

rival ['raɪvəl] *n* Rivale *m*, Konkurrent *m*; *a* rivalisierend; *vt* rivalisieren mit; (*Comm*) konkurrieren mit; —ry Rivalität *f*; Konkurrenz *f*.

river ['rɪvə*] *n* Fluß *m*, Strom *m*; —bank Flußufer *nt*; —bed Flußbett *nt*; —side *n* Flußufer *nt*; a am Ufer gelegen, Ufer-.

rivet ['rɪvɪt] *n* Niete *f*; *vt (fasten)* (ver)nieten.

road [rəʊd] *n* Straße *f*; —block Straßensperre *f*; —hog Verkehrsrowdy *m*; —map Straßenkarte *f*; — side *n* Straßenrand *m*; a an der Landstraße (gelegen); — sign Straßenschild *nt*; — user Verkehrsteilnehmer *m*; —way Fahrbahn *f*; —worthy a verkehrssicher.

roam [rəʊm] *vi* (umher)streifen; *vt* durchstreifen.

roar [rɔ:*] *n* Brüllen *nt*, Gebrüll *nt*; *vi* brüllen; —ing *a fire* Bombenprasselnd; *trade* schwunghaft, Bomben-.

roast [rəʊst] *n* Braten *m*; *vt* braten, rösten, schmoren.

rob [rɒb] *vt* bestehlen, berauben; *bank* ausrauben; —ber Räuber *m*; —bery Raub *m*.

robe [rəʊb] *n (dress)* Gewand *nt*; *(US)* Hauskleid *nt*; *(judge's)* Robe *f*; *vt* feierlich ankleiden.

robin ['rɒbɪn] *n* Rotkehlchen *nt*.

robot ['rəʊbɒt] *n* Roboter *m*.

robust [rəʊ'bʌst] *a* stark, robust.

rock [rɒk] *n* Felsen *m*; *(piece)* Stein *m*; *(bigger)* Fels(brocken) *m*; *(sweet)* Zuckerstange *f*; *vti* wiegen, schaukeln; **on the —s** *drink* mit Eis(würfeln); *ship* aufgelaufen; — *marriage* gescheitert; —**bottom** *(fig)* Tiefpunkt *m*; — **climber** (Steil)kletterer *m*; **to go —climbing** (steil)klettern gehen; —**ery** Steingarten *m*.

rocket ['rɒkɪt] *n* Rakete *f*.

rock face ['rɒkfeɪs] *n* Felswand *f*.

rocking chair ['rɒkɪŋtʃeə*] *n* Schaukelstuhl *m*.

rocking horse ['rɒkɪŋhɔ:s] *n* Schaukelpferd *nt*.

rocky ['rɒkɪ] *a* felsig.

rococo [rəʊ'kəʊkəʊ] *a* Rokoko-; *n* Rokoko *nt*.

rod [rɒd] *n (bar)* Stange *f*; *(stick)* Rute *f*.

rodent ['rəʊdənt] *n* Nagetier *nt*.

rodeo ['rəʊdɪəʊ] *n* Rodeo *m* or *nt*.

roe [rəʊ] *n (deer)* Reh *nt*; *(of fish)* Rogen *m*.

rogue [rəʊg] *n* Schurke *m*; *(hum)* Spitzbube *m*.

roguish ['rəʊgɪʃ] *a* schurkisch; *hum* schelmisch.

role [rəʊl] *n* Rolle *f*.

roll [rəʊl] *n (bread)* Brötchen *nt*, Semmel *f*; *(list)* (Namens)liste *f*, Verzeichnis *nt*; *(of drum)* Wirbel *m*; *vt (turn)* rollen, (herum)wälzen; *grass etc* walzen; *vi (swing)* schlingern; *(sound)* (g)rollen; — *by vi (time)* verfließen; — *in vi (mail)* hereinkommen; — *over vi* sich (herum)drehen; — *up vi (arrive)* kommen, auftauchen; *vt carpet* aufrollen; — **call** Namensaufruf *m*; —**ed** *a umbrella* zusammengerollt; —**er** Rolle *f*, Walze *f*; *(road —er)* Straßenwalze *f*; —**er skates** *pl* Rollschuhe *pl*.

rollicking ['rɒlɪkɪŋ] *a* ausgelassen.

rolling ['rəʊlɪŋ] *a landscape* wellig; — **pin** Nudel- or Wellholz *nt*; — **stock** Wagenmaterial *nt*.

Roman ['rəʊmən] *a* römisch; *n* Römer(in *f*) *m*; — **Catholic** · *a* römisch-katholisch; *n* Katholik(in *f*) *m*.

romance [rəʊ'mæns] n Romanze f; (story) (Liebes)roman m; vi aufschneiden, erfinden; **—r** (storyteller) Aufschneider m.

romantic [rəʊ'mæntɪk] a romantisch; **R—ism** [rəʊ'mæntɪsɪzəm] Romantik f.

romp [rɒmp] n Tollen nt; vi (also — about) herumtollen; **—ers** pl Spielanzug m.

rondo ['rɒndəʊ] n (Mus) Rondo nt.

roof [ru:f] n Dach nt; (of mouth) Gaumen nt; vt überdachen, überdecken; **—ing** Deckmaterial nt.

rook [rʊk] n (bird) Saatkrähe f; (chess) Turm m; vt (cheat) betrügen.

room [rʊm] n Zimmer nt, Raum m; (space) Platz m; (fig) Spielraum m; **—s** pl Wohnung f; **—iness** Geräumigkeit f; **—mate** Mitbewohner(in) f m; **— service** Zimmerbedienung f; **—y** a geräumig.

roost [ru:st] n Hühnerstange f; vi auf der Stange hocken.

root [ru:t] n (lit, fig) Wurzel f; vt einwurzeln; **—ed** a (fig) verwurzelt; **—** vi (fig) herumwühlen; **— for** vt Stimmung machen für; **— out** vt ausjäten, (fig) ausrotten.

rope [rəʊp] n Seil nt, Strick m; vt (tie) festschnüren; **to — sb in** jdn gewinnen; **— off** vt absperren; **to know the —s** sich auskennen; **— ladder** Strickleiter f.

rosary ['rəʊzərɪ] n Rosenkranz m.

rose [rəʊz] n Rose f; a Rosen-, rosenrot.

rosé ['rəʊzeɪ] n Rosé m.

rosebed ['rəʊzbed] n Rosenbeet nt.

rosebud ['rəʊzbʌd] n Rosenknospe f.

rosebush ['rəʊzbʊʃ] n Rosenstock m, Rosenstrauch m.

rosemary ['rəʊzmərɪ] n Rosmarin m.

rosette [rəʊ'zet] n Rosette f.

roster ['rɒstə*] n Dienstplan m.

rostrum ['rɒstrəm] n Rednerbühne f.

rosy ['rəʊzɪ] a rosig.

rot [rɒt] n Fäulnis f; (nonsense) Quatsch m, Blödsinn m; vti verfaulen (lassen).

rota ['rəʊtə] n Dienstliste f.

rotary ['rəʊtərɪ] a rotierend, sich drehend.

rotate [rəʊ'teɪt] vt rotieren lassen; (two or more things in order) turnusmäßig wechseln; vi rotieren.

rotating [rəʊ'teɪtɪŋ] a rotierend.

rotation [rəʊ'teɪʃən] n Umdrehung f, Rotation f; **in —** in der Reihe nach, abwechselnd.

rotor ['rəʊtə*] n Rotor m.

rotten ['rɒtn] a faul, verfault; (fig) schlecht, gemein.

rotund [rəʊ'tʌnd] a rund; person rundlich.

rouge [ru:ʒ] n Rouge nt.

rough [rʌf] a (not smooth) rauh; path uneben; (violent) roh, grob; crossing stürmisch; wind rauh; (without comforts) hart, unbequem; (unfinished, makeshift) grob; (approximate) ungefähr; a (grass) unebene(r) Boden m; (person) Rowdy m, Rohling m; **to — it** primitiv leben; **to play —** (Sport) hart spielen; **to sleep —** im Freien schlafen; **— out** vt entwerfen, flüchtig skizzieren; **—en** vt aufrauhen; **—ly** ad grob; (about) ungefähr; **—ness** Rauheit f; (of manner) Ungeschliffenheit f.

roulette [ruːˈlet] *n* Roulette *nt.*

round [raund] *a* rund; *figures* abgerundet, aufgerundet; *ad (in a circle)* rundherum; *prep* um … herum; — Runde *f; (of ammunition)* Magazin *nt; (song)* Kanon *m;* theatre in the — Rundtheater *nt; vt corner* biegen um; — **off** *vt* abrunden; — **up** *vt (end)* abschließen; *figures* aufrunden; — of applause Beifall *m;* —**about** *n (traffic)* Kreisverkehr *m; (merry-go-round)* Karussell *nt;* a **auf** Umwegen; —**ed** a gerundet; —**ly** *ad (fig)* gründlich; —**shouldered** a mit abfallenden Schultern; —**sman** *(general)* Austräger *m; (milk —)* Milchmann *m;* —**up** Zusammentreiben *nt,* Sammeln *nt.*

rouse [rauz] *vt (waken)* (auf)wecken; *(stir up)* erregen.

rousing [ˈrauzɪŋ] *a welcome* stürmisch; *speech* zündend.

rout [raut] *n* wilde Flucht *f;* Überwältigung *f; vt* in die Flucht schlagen.

route [ruːt] *n* Weg *m,* Route *f.*

routine [ruːˈtiːn] *n* Routine *f;* a Routine-.

rover [ˈrəʊvə*] *n* Wanderer *m.*

roving [ˈrəʊvɪŋ] *a reporter* im Außendienst.

row [rəʊ] *n (line)* Reihe *f; vti boat* rudern.

row [rau] *n (noise)* Lärm *m,* Krach *m,* Radau *m; (dispute)* Streit *m; (scolding)* Krach *m; vi* sich streiten.

rowboat [ˈrəʊbəʊt] *n (US)* Ruderboot *nt.*

rowdy [ˈraudɪ] *a* rüpelhaft; *n (person)* Rowdy *m.*

rowing [ˈrəʊɪŋ] *n* Rudern *nt; (Sport)* Rudersport *m;* — **boat** Ruderboot *nt.*

rowlock [ˈrɒlək] *n* Rudergabel *f.*

royal [ˈrɔɪəl] *a* königlich, Königs-; —**ist** *n* Royalist *m;* a königstreu; —**ty** *(family)* königliche Familie *f; (for invention)* Patentgebühr *f; (for book)* Tantieme *f.*

rub [rʌb] *n (problem)* Haken *m;* to give sth a — etw (ab)reiben; *vt* reiben; — **off** *vi (lit, fig)* abfärben *(on auf +acc);* to — it in darauf herumreiten.

rubber [ˈrʌbə*] *n* Gummi *m; (Brit)* Radiergummi *m;* — band Gummiband *nt;* — **plant** Gummibaum *m;* —**y** a gummiartig, wie Gummi.

rubbish [ˈrʌbɪʃ] *n (waste)* Abfall *m; (nonsense)* Blödsinn *m,* Quatsch *m;* — dump Müllabladeplatz *m.*

rubble [ˈrʌbl] *n (Stein)*schutt *m.*

ruby [ˈruːbɪ] *n* Rubin *m;* a rubinrot.

rucksack [ˈrʌksæk] *n* Rucksack *m.*

rudder [ˈrʌdə*] *n* Steuerruder *nt.*

ruddy [ˈrʌdɪ] *a (colour)* rötlich; *(col: bloody)* verdammt.

rude, a, —**ly** *ad* [ruːd, -lɪ] unhöflich, unverschämt; *shock* hart; *awakening* unsanft; *(unrefined, rough)* grob; —**ness** Unhöflichkeit *f,* Unverschämtheit *f;* Grobheit *f.*

rudiment [ˈruːdɪmənt] *n* Grundlage *f;* —**ary** [ruːdɪˈmentərɪ] a rudimentär.

ruff [rʌf] *n* Halskrause *f.*

ruffian [ˈrʌfɪən] *n* Rohling *m.*

ruffle [ˈrʌfl] *vt* kräuseln; durcheinanderbringen.

rug [rʌg] *n* Brücke *f; (in bedroom)* Bettvorleger *m; (for knees)* (Reise)decke *f.*

rugged [ˈrʌgɪd] *a coastline* zerklüftet; *features* markig.

ruin [ˈruːɪn] *n* Ruine *f; (downfall)* Ruin *m; vt* ruinieren; —**s** *pl*

Trümmer *pl*; —ation Zerstörung *f*, Ruinierung *f*; —ous a ruinierend.

rule [ru:l] *n* Regel *f*; (*government*) Herrschaft *f*, Regierung *f*; (*for measuring*) Lineal *nt*; *vti* (*govern*) herrschen über (+*acc*), regieren; (*decide*) anordnen, entscheiden; (*make lines*) linieren; as a — in der Regel; —d a paper liniert; —r Lineal *nt*; Herrscher *m*.

ruling ['ru:lɪŋ] a party Regierungs-; *class* herrschend.

rum [rʌm] *n* Rum *m*; a (*col*) komisch.

rumble ['rʌmbl] *n* Rumpeln *nt*; (*of thunder*) Rollen *nt*; *vi* rumpeln; grollen.

ruminate ['ru:mɪneɪt] *vi* grübeln; (*cows*) wiederkäuen.

rummage ['rʌmɪdʒ] *n* Durch-. suchung *f*; *vi* durchstöbern.

rumour, (US) **rumor** ['ru:mə*] *n* Gerücht *nt*; *vt*: it is —ed that man sagt or man munkelt, daß.

rump [rʌmp] *n* Hinterteil *nt*; (*of fowl*) Bürzel *m*; — **steak** Rumpsteak *nt*.

rumpus ['rʌmpəs] *n* Spektakel *m*, Krach *m*.

run [rʌn] *n* Lauf *m*; (*in car*) (Spazier)fahrt *f*; (*series*) Serie *f*, Reihe *f*; (*of play*) Spielzeit *f*; (*sudden demand*) Ansturm *m*, starke Nachfrage *f*; (*ski* —) (Ski)abfahrt *f*; (*in stocking*) Laufmasche *f*; *vt irreg* (*cause to run*) laufen lassen; *car, train, bus* fahren; (*pay for*) unterhalten; *race, distance* laufen, rennen; (*manage*) leiten, verwalten, führen; *knife* stoßen; (*pass*) *hand, eye* gleiten lassen; *vi* laufen; (*move quickly also*) rennen; (*bus, train*) fahren; (*flow*) fließen, laufen; (*colours*)

(ab)färben; **on the** — auf der Flucht; **in the long** — auf die Dauer; **to** — **a risk** ein Risiko eingehen; **to** — **about** *vi* (*children*) umherspringen; — **across** *vt* (*find*) stoßen auf (+*acc*); — **away** *vi* weglaufen; — **down** *vi* (*clock*) ablaufen; *vt* (*with car*) überfahren; (*talk against*) heruntermachen; **to be** — **down** erschöpft or abgespannt sein; **to** — **for president** für die Präsidentschaft kandidieren; — **off** *vi* fortlaufen; — **out** *vi* (*person*) hinausrennen; (*liquid*) auslaufen; (*lease*) ablaufen; (*money*) ausgehen; **he ran out of money/petrol** mir ging das Geld/Benzin aus; — **over** *vt* (*in accident*) überfahren; (*read quickly*) überfliegen; — **through** *vt instructions* durchgehen; — **up** *vt debt, bill* machen; — **up against** *vt difficulties* stoßen auf (+*acc*); —**about** (*small car*) kleine(r) Flitzer *m*; —**away** *a* **horse** ausgebrochen; *person* flüchtig.

rung [rʌŋ] *n* Sprosse *f*.

runner ['rʌnə*] *n* Läufer(in *f*) *m*; (*messenger*) Bote *m*; (*for sleigh*) Kufe *f*; —**up** Zweite(r) *mf*.

running ['rʌnɪŋ] *n* (*of business*) Leitung *f*; (*of machine*) Laufen *nt*, Betrieb *m*; a **water** fließend; *commentary* laufend; **3 days** — 3 Tage lang or hintereinander.

run-of-the-mill ['rʌnəvðə'mɪl] a gewöhnlich, alltäglich.

runny ['rʌnɪ] a dünn.

runway ['rʌnweɪ] *n* Startbahn *f*, Landebahn *f*, Rollbahn *f*.

rupture ['rʌptʃə*] *n* (*Med*) Bruch *m*; *vt*: —**o.s.** sich (*dat*) einen Bruch zuziehen.

rural ['rʊərəl] a ländlich, Land-.

ruse [ru:z] n Kniff m, List f.
rush [rʌʃ] n Eile f, Hetze f; (Fin) starke Nachfrage f; vt (carry along) auf dem schnellsten Wege schaffen or transportieren; (attack) losstürmen auf (+acc); don't — me dräng mich nicht; vi (hurry) eilen, stürzen; **to —** into sth etw überstürzen; **—es** pl (Bot) Schilf(rohr) nt; **— hour** Hauptverkehrszeit f.
rusk [rʌsk] n Zwieback m.
rust [rʌst] n Rost m; vi rosten.
rustic ['rʌstɪk] a bäuerlich, ländlich, Bauern-.

rustle ['rʌsl] n Rauschen nt, Rascheln nt; vi rauschen, rascheln; vt rascheln lassen; cattle stehlen.
rustproof ['rʌstpru:f] a nicht-rostend, rostfrei.
rusty ['rʌstɪ] a rostig.
rut [rʌt] n (in track) Radspur f; (of deer) Brunst f; (fig) Trott m.
ruthless a, **—ly** ad ['ru:θləs, -lɪ] erbarmungslos; rücksichtslos; **—ness** Unbarmherzigkeit f; Rücksichtslosigkeit f.
rye [raɪ] n Roggen m; **— bread** Roggenbrot nt.

S

S, s [es]; n S nt, s nt.
sabbath ['sæbəθ] n Sabbat m.
sabbatical [sə'bætɪkəl] a: **— year** Beurlaubungs- or Forschungsjahr nt.
sabotage ['sæbətɑ:ʒ] n Sabotage f; vt sabotieren.
sabre, (US) saber ['seɪbə*] n Säbel m.
saccharin(e) ['sækərɪn] n Saccharin nt.
sachet ['sæʃeɪ] n (of shampoo) Briefchen nt, Kissen nt.
sack [sæk] n Sack m; **to give sb the —** (col) jdn hinauswerfen; vt (col) hinauswerfen; (pillage) plündern; **—ful** Sack(voll) m; **—ing** (material) Sackleinen nt; (col) Rausschmiß m.
sacrament ['sækrəmənt] n Sakrament nt.
sacred ['seɪkrɪd] a building, music etc geistlich, Kirchen-; altar, oath heilig.

sacrifice ['sækrɪfaɪs] n Opfer nt; vt (lit, fig) opfern.
sacrilege ['sækrɪlɪdʒ] n Schändung f.
sacrosanct ['sækrəusæŋkt] a sakrosankt.
sad [sæd] a traurig; **—den** vt traurig machen, betrüben.
saddle ['sædl] n Sattel m; vt (burden) aufhalsen (sb with sth jdm etw); **—bag** Satteltasche f.
sadism ['seɪdɪzəm] n Sadismus m.
sadist ['seɪdɪst] n Sadist m; **—ic** [sə'dɪstɪk] a sadistisch.
sadly ['sædlɪ] ad betrübt, beklagenswert; (very) arg.
sadness ['sædnɪs] n Traurigkeit f.
safari [sə'fɑ:rɪ] n Safari f.
safe [seɪf] a (free from danger) sicher; (careful) vorsichtig; it's — to say man kann ruhig behaupten; n Safe m, Tresor m, Geldschrank m; **—guard** n Sicherung f; vt sichern, schützen; **—keeping**

sichere Verwahrung f; —ly ad
sicher; arrive wohlbehalten;
—ness Zuverlässigkeit f; —ty
Sicherheit f; —ty belt Sicherheitsgurt m; —ty curtain eiserne(r)
Vorhang m; —ty first (slogan)
Sicherheit geht vor; —ty pin
Sicherheitsnadel f.

sag [sæg] vi (durch)sacken, sich
senken.

saga ['sɑːgə] n Sage f.

sage [seɪdʒ] n (herb) Salbei m;
(man) Weise(r) m.

Sagittarius [sædʒɪˈtɛərɪəs] n
Schütze m.

sago ['seɪgəu] n Sago m.

said [sed] a besagt.

sail [seɪl] n Segel nt; (trip) Fahrt
f; vi segeln; vt segeln; mit dem
Schiff fahren; (begin voyage)
(person) abfahren; (ship) auslaufen; (fig: cloud etc) dahinsegeln; —boat (US) Segelboot nt;
—ing Segeln nt; to go —ing segeln
gehen; —ing ship Segelschiff nt;
—or Matrose m, Seemann m.

saint [seɪnt] n Heilige(r) mf;
—liness Heiligkeit f; —ly a heilig,
fromm.

sake [seɪk] n: for the — of um
(+gen) willen; for your — um
deinetwillen, deinetwegen, wegen
dir.

salad ['sæləd] n Salat m; — cream
gewürzte Mayonnaise f; —
dressing Salatsoße f; — oil
Speiseöl nt, Salatöl nt.

salami [səˈlɑːmɪ] n Salami f.

salaried ['sælərɪd] a: — staff
Gehaltsempfänger pl.

salary ['sælərɪ] n Gehalt nt.

sale [seɪl] n Verkauf m; (reduced
prices) Schlußverkauf m; —room
Verkaufsraum m; —sman
Verkäufer m; (representative) Ver

treter m; —smanship Geschäftstüchtigkeit f; —swoman Verkäuferin f.

salient ['seɪlɪənt] a hervorspringend, bemerkenswert.

saliva [səˈlaɪvə] n Speichel m.

sallow ['sæləu] a fahl; face bleich.

salmon ['sæmən] n Lachs m.

salon ['sælɔ:ŋ] n Salon m.

saloon [səˈluːn] n (Aut) Limousine
f; (ship's lounge) Salon m.

salt [sɔːlt] n Salz nt; vt (cure) einsalzen; (flavour) salzen; —cellar
Salzfaß nt; — mine Salzbergwerk
nt; —y a salzig.

salubrious [səˈluːbrɪəs] a gesund;
district etc ersprießlich.

salutary ['sæljutərɪ] a gesund,
heilsam.

salute [səˈluːt] n (Mil) Gruß m,
Salut m; (with guns) Salutschüsse
pl; vt (Mil) salutieren.

salvage ['sælvɪdʒ] n (from ship)
Bergung f; (property) Rettung f;
vt bergen; retten.

salvation [sælˈveɪʃən] n Rettung f;
S— Army Heilsarmee f.

salver ['sælvə*] n Tablett nt.

salvo ['sælvəu] n Salve f.

same [seɪm] a (similar) gleiche(r,s)
(identical) derselbe/dieselbe/
dasselbe; all or just the —
trotzdem; it's all the — to me das
ist mir egal; they all look the —
to me für mich sehen sie alle gleich
aus; the — to you gleichfalls; at
the — time zur gleichen Zeit, gleichzeitig; (however) zugleich,
andererseits.

sampan ['sæmpæn] n Sampan m.

sample ['sɑːmpl] n (specimen)
Probe f; (example of sth) Muster
nt, Probe f; vt probieren.

sanatorium [sænə'tɔːrɪəm] *n* Sanatorium *nt*.

sanctify ['sæŋktɪfaɪ] *vt* weihen.

sanctimonious [sæŋktɪ'məʊnɪəs] *a* scheinheilig.

sanction ['sæŋkʃən] *n* Sanktion *f*.

sanctity ['sæŋktɪtɪ] *n* Heiligkeit *f*; (*fig*) Unverletzlichkeit *f*.

sanctuary ['sæŋktjʊərɪ] *n* Heiligtum *nt*; (*for fugitive*) Asyl *nt*; (*refuge*) Zufluchtsort *m*; (*for animals*) Naturpark *m*, Schutzgebiet *nt*.

sand [sænd] *n* Sand *m*; *vt* mit Sand bestreuen; *furniture* schmirgeln; —s *pl* Sand *m*.

sandal ['sændl] *n* Sandale *f*.

sandbag ['sændbæg] *n* Sandsack *m*.

sand dune ['sænddjuːn] *n* (Sand-) düne *f*.

sandpaper ['sændpeɪpə*] *n* Sandpapier *nt*.

sandpit ['sændpɪt] *n* Sandkasten *m*.

sandstone ['sændstəʊn] *n* Sandstein *m*.

sandwich ['sænwɪdʒ] *n* Sandwich *m* or *nt*; *vt* einklemmen.

sandy ['sændɪ] *a* sandig, Sand-; (*colour*) sandfarben; *hair* rotblond.

sane [seɪn] *a* geistig gesund or normal; (*sensible*) vernünftig, gescheit.

sanguine ['sæŋgwɪn] *a* (*hopeful*) zuversichtlich.

sanitarium [sænɪ'tɛərɪəm] *n* (US) = sanatorium.

sanitary ['sænɪtərɪ] *a* hygienisch (einwandfrei); (*against dirt*) hygienisch, Gesundheits-; — napkin (US), — towel (Monats-) binde *f*.

sanitation [sænɪ'teɪʃən] *n* sanitäre Einrichtungen *pl*; Gesundheitswesen *nt*.

sanity ['sænɪtɪ] *n* geistige Gesundheit *f*; (*good sense*) gesunde(r) Verstand *m*, Vernunft *f*.

Santa Claus [sæntə'klɔːz] *n* Nikolaus *m*, Weihnachtsmann *m*.

sap [sæp] *n* (*of plants*) Saft *m*; *vt strength* schwächen; *health* untergraben.

sapling ['sæplɪŋ] *n* junge(r) Baum *m*.

sapphire ['sæfaɪə*] *n* Saphir *m*.

sarcasm ['sɑːkæzəm] *n* Sarkasmus *m*.

sarcastic [sɑː'kæstɪk] *a* sarkastisch.

sarcophagus [sɑː'kɒfəgəs] *n* Sarkophag *m*.

sardine [sɑː'diːn] *n* Sardine *f*.

sardonic [sɑː'dɒnɪk] *a* zynisch.

sari ['sɑːrɪ] *n* Sari *m*.

sash [sæʃ] *n* Schärpe *f*.

Satan ['seɪtn] *n* Satan *m*, Teufel *m*; **s—ic** [sə'tænɪk] *a* satanisch, teuflisch.

satchel ['sætʃəl] *n* (*Sch*) Schulranzen *m*, Schulmappe *f*.

satellite ['sætəlaɪt] *n* Satellit *m*; (*fig*) Trabant *m*; *a* Satelliten-.

satin ['sætɪn] *n* Satin *m*; *a* Satin-.

satire ['sætaɪə*] *n* Satire *f*.

satirical [sə'tɪrɪkəl] *a* satirisch.

satirize ['sætəraɪz] *vt* (durch Satire) verspotten.

satisfaction [sætɪs'fækʃən] *n* Befriedigung *f*, Genugtuung *f*.

satisfactorily [sætɪs'fæktərɪlɪ] *ad* zufriedenstellend.

satisfactory [sætɪs'fæktərɪ] *a* zufriedenstellend, befriedigend.

satisfy ['sætɪsfaɪ] *vt* befriedigen, zufriedenstellen; (*convince*) überzeugen; *conditions* erfüllen; —**ing** *a* befriedigend; *meal* sättigend.

saturate ['sætʃəreɪt] *vt* (durch-) tränken.

saturation 659 scalp

saturation [ˌsætʃəˈreɪʃən] *n* Durchtränkung *f*; (Chem, fig) Sättigung *f*.

Saturday [ˈsætədeɪ] *n* Samstag *m*, Sonnabend *m*.

sauce [sɔːs] *n* Soße *f*, Sauce *f*; —**pan** Kasserolle *f*; —**r** Untertasse *f*.

saucily [ˈsɔːsɪlɪ] *ad* frech.

sauciness [ˈsɔːsməs] *n* Frechheit *f*.

saucy [ˈsɔːsɪ] *a* frech, keck.

sauna [ˈsɔːnə] *n* Sauna *f*.

saunter [ˈsɔːntə*] *vi* schlendern; *n* Schlendern *nt*.

sausage [ˈsɒsɪdʒ] *n* Wurst *f*; —**roll** Wurst *f* im Schlafreck, Wurstpastete *f*.

savage [ˈsævɪdʒ] *a* (fierce) wild, brutal, grausam; (uncivilized) wild, primitiv; *n* Wilde(r) *mf*; *vt* (animals) zerfleischen; —**ly** *ad* grausam; —**ry** Roheit *f*, Grausamkeit *f*.

save [seɪv] *vt* retten; money, electricity etc sparen; strength etc aufsparen; **to** — **you** the trouble um dir Mühe zu ersparen; *n* (Sport) (Ball)abwehr *f*; prep, cj außer, ausgenommen.

saving [ˈseɪvɪŋ] *a* rettend; *n* Sparen *nt*, Ersparnis *f*; —**s** *pl* Ersparnisse *pl*; —**s bank** Sparkasse *f*.

saviour [ˈseɪvjə*] *n* Retter *m*; (Eccl) Heiland *m*, Erlöser *m*.

savoir-faire [ˈsævwɑːˈfɛə*] *n* Gewandtheit *f*.

savour, (US) **savor** [ˈseɪvə*] *n* Wohlgeschmack *m*; *vt* (taste) schmecken; (fig) genießen; *vi* schmecken (of nach), riechen (of nach); —**y** *a* schmackhaft; food pikant, würzig.

savvy [ˈsævɪ] *n* (col) Grips *m*.

saw [sɔː] *n* (tool) Säge *f*; *vti* sägen; —**dust** Sägemehl *nt*; —**mill** Sägewerk *nt*.

saxophone [ˈsæksəfəʊn] *n* Saxophon *nt*.

say [seɪ] *n* Meinung *f*; (right) Mitspracherecht *nt*; **to have no/a** — **in sth** (kein) Mitspracherecht bei etw haben; **let him have his** — laß ihn doch reden; *vti irreg* sagen; **I couldn't** — schwer zu sagen; **how old would you** — **he is?** wie alt schätzt du ihn?; **you don't** —**!** was du nicht sagst!; **don't** — **you forgot** sag bloß nicht, daß du es vergessen hast; **there are,** —, **50** es sind, sagen wir mal, 50...; **that is to** — das heißt; **(more precisely)** beziehungsweise, mit anderen Worten; **to** — **nothing of** ... ganz zu schweigen von...; —**ing** Sprichwort *nt*; —**so** (col) Ja *nt*, Zustimmung *f*.

scab [skæb] *n* Schorf *m*; (of sheep) Räude *f*; (pej) Streikbrecher *m*.

scabby [ˈskæbɪ] *a* sheep räudig; skin schorfig.

scaffold [ˈskæfəʊld] *n* (for execution) Schafott *nt*; —**ing** (Bau)gerüst *nt*.

scald [skɔːld] *n* Verbrühung *f*; *vt* (burn) verbrühen; (clean) (ab)brühen; —**ing** a brühheiß.

scale [skeɪl] *n* (of fish) Schuppe *f*; (Mus) Tonleiter *f*; (dish for measuring) Waagschale *f*; (on map, size) Maßstab *m*; (gradation) Skala *f*; *vt* (climb) erklimmen; —**s** *pl* (balance) Waage *f*; **on a large** — (fig) im großen, in großem Umfang; — **drawing** maßstabgerechte Zeichnung *f*.

scallop [ˈskɒləp] *n* Kammuschel *f*.

scalp [skælp] *n* Kopfhaut *f*; *vt* skalpieren.

scalpel ['skælpəl] n Skalpell nt.

scamp [skæmp] vt schlud(e)rig machen, hinschlampen.

scamper ['skæmpə*] vi huschen.

scan [skæn] vt (examine) genau prüfen; (quickly) überfliegen; horizon absuchen; poetry skandieren.

scandal ['skændl] n (disgrace) Skandal m; (gossip) böswillige(r) Klatsch m; —ize vt schockieren; —ous a skandalös, schockierend.

scant [skænt] a knapp; —ily ad knapp, dürftig; —iness Knappheit f; —y knapp, unzureichend.

scapegoat ['skeɪpgəʊt] n Sündenbock m.

scar [skɑː*] n Narbe f; vt durch Narben entstellen.

scarce [skeəs] a selten, rar; goods knapp; —ly ad kaum; —ness Seltenheit f.

scarcity ['skeəsɪtɪ] n Mangel m, Knappheit f.

scare [skeə*] n Schrecken m, Panik f; vt erschrecken; ängstigen; to be —d Angst haben; —crow Vogelscheuche f; —monger Bangemacher m.

scarf [skɑːf] n Schal m; (on head) Kopftuch nt.

scarlet ['skɑːlət] a scharlachrot; n Scharlachrot nt; — fever Scharlach m.

scarred ['skɑːd] a narbig.

scary ['skeərɪ] a (col) schaurig.

scathing ['skeɪðɪŋ] a scharf, vernichtend.

scatter ['skætə*] n Streuung f; vt (sprinkle) (ver)streuen; (disperse) zerstreuen; vi sich zerstreuen; —brained a flatterhaft, schusselig; —ing (of) ein paar.

scavenger ['skævɪndʒə*] n (animal) Aasfresser m.

scene [siːn] n (of happening) Ort m; (of play, incident) Szene f; (canvas etc) Bühnenbild m; (view) Anblick m; (argument) Szene f; Auftritt m; on the — am Ort, dabei; behind the —s hinter den Kulissen; —ry ['siːnərɪ] (Theat) Bühnenbild nt; (landscape) Landschaft f.

scenic ['siːnɪk] a landschaftlich, Landschafts-.

scent [sent] n Parfüm m; (smell) Duft m; (sense) Geruchsinn m; vt parfümieren.

sceptic ['skeptɪk] n Skeptiker m; —al a skeptisch; —ism ['skeptɪsɪzəm] Skepsis f.

sceptre, (US) scepter ['septə*] n Szepter nt.

schedule ['ʃedjuːl] n (list) Liste f, Tabelle f; (plan) Programm nt; vt: it is —d for 2 es soll um 2 abfahren/stattfinden etc; on — pünktlich, fahrplanmäßig; behind — mit Verspätung.

scheme [skiːm] n Schema nt; (dishonest) Intrige f; (plan of action) Plan m, Programm nt; vt sich verschwören, intrigieren; vt planen.

scheming ['skiːmɪŋ] a intrigierend, ränkevoll.

schism ['skɪzəm] n Spaltung f; (Eccl) Schisma nt, Kirchenspaltung f.

schizophrenic [skɪtsəʊ'frenɪk] a schizophren.

scholar ['skɒlə*] n Gelehrte(r) m; (holding scholarship) Stipendiat m; —ly a gelehrt; —ship Gelehrsamkeit f, Belesenheit f; (grant) Stipendium nt.

school [skuːl] n Schule f; (Univ) Fakultät f; vt schulen; dog

trainieren; **—book** Schulbuch *nt*;
—boy Schüler *m*, Schuljunge *m*;
—days *pl* (alte) Schulzeit *f*; **—girl**
Schülerin *f*, Schulmädchen *nt*; **—**
ing Schulung *f*, Ausbildung *f*;
—master Lehrer *m*; **—mistress**
Lehrerin *f*, **—room** Klassenzimmer
nt; **—teacher** Lehrer(in *f*) *m*.

schooner ['sku:nə*] *n* Schoner *m*;
(glass) große(s) Sherryglas *nt*.

sciatica [saɪ'ætɪkə] *n* Ischias *m* *or*
nt.

science ['saɪəns] *n* Wissenschaft *f*;
(natural —) Naturwissenschaft *f*;
— **fiction** Science-fiction *f*.

scientific [saɪən'tɪfɪk] *a* wissenschaftlich; *(natural sciences)* natur-
wissenschaftlich.

scientist ['saɪəntɪst] *n* Wissen-
schaftler(in *f*) *m*.

scintillating ['sɪntɪleɪtɪŋ] *a*
sprühend.

scissors ['sɪzəz] *npl* Schere *f*; **a**
pair of — eine Schere.

scoff [skɒf] *vt* (eat) fressen; *vi*
(mock) spotten (at über +acc).

scold [skəʊld] *vt* schimpfen.

scone [skɒn] *n* weiche(s) Teege-
bäck *nt*.

scoop [sku:p] *n* Schaufel *f*; *(news)*
sensationelle Erstmeldung *f*; *vt*
(also — out or up) schaufeln.

scooter ['sku:tə*] *n* Motorroller *m*;
(child's) Roller *m*.

scope [skəʊp] *n* Ausmaß *nt*; *(opportunity)* (Spiel)raum *m*, Bewegungs-
freiheit *f*.

scorch [skɔ:tʃ] *n* Brandstelle *f*; *vt*
versengen, verbrennen; **—er** (col)
heiße(r) Tag *m*; **—ing** a brennend,
glühend.

score [skɔ:*] *n* (in game) Punktzahl
f; *(Spiel)*ergebnis *nt*; *(Mus)*
Partitur *f*; *(line)* Kratzer *m*;
(twenty) 20, 20 Stück; **on that —**

in dieser Hinsicht; **what's the —?**
wie steht's?; *vt* **goal** schießen;
points machen; *(mark)* einkerben;
zerkratzen, einritzen; *vi* (keep
record) Punkte zählen; **—board**
Anschreibetafel *f*; **—card** *(Sport)*
Punktliste *f*; **—r** Torschütze *m*;
(recorder) (Auf)schreiber *m*.

scorn ['skɔ:n] *n* Verachtung *f*; *vt*
verhöhnen; **—ful** a, **—fully** ad
höhnisch, verächtlich.

Scorpio ['skɔ:piəʊ] *n* Skorpion *m*.

scorpion ['skɔ:piən] *n* Skorpion *m*.

scotch [skɒtʃ] *vt* (end) unterbinden.

scoundrel ['skaʊndrəl] *n* Schurke
m, Schuft *m*.

scour ['skaʊə*] *vt* (search)
absuchen; *(clean)* schrubben; **—er**
Topfkratzer *m*.

scourge [skɜ:dʒ] *n* (whip) Geißel *f*;
(plague) Qual *f*.

scout [skaʊt] *n* (Mil) Späher *m*,
Aufklärer *m*; *vi* (reconnoitre) auskundschaften; see boy.

scowl [skaʊl] *n* finstere(r) Blick *m*;
vi finster blicken.

scraggy ['skrægɪ] *a* dürr, hager.

scram [skræm] *vi* (col)
verschwinden, abhauen.

scramble ['skræmbl] *n* (climb)
Kletterei *f*; *(struggle)* Kampf *m*; *vi*
klettern; *(fight)* sich schlagen; **—d**
eggs *pl* Rührei *nt*.

scrap [skræp] *n* (bit) Stückchen *nt*;
(fight) Keilerei *f*; a Abfall-; *vt* verwerfen; *vi* (fight) streiten, sich
prügeln; **—book** Einklebealbum
nt; **—s** *pl* (waste) Abfall *m*.

scrape [skreɪp] *n* Kratzen *nt*;
(trouble) Klemme *f*; *vt* kratzen;
car zerkratzen; *(clean)* abkratzen;
vi (make harsh noise) kratzen; **—r**
Kratzer *m*.

scrap heap ['skræphi:p] *n* Abfallhaufen *m*; (*for metal*) Schrotthaufen *m*.

scrap iron ['skræp'æɪən] *n* Schrott *m*.

scrappy ['skræpɪ] *a* zusammengestoppelt.

scratch ['skrætʃ] *n* (*wound*) Kratzer *m*, Schramme *f*; **to start from** — ganz von vorne anfangen; *a* (*improvised*) zusammengewürfelt; *vt* kratzen; **car zerkratzen**; *vi* (*sich*) kratzen.

scrawl [skrɔ:l] *n* Gekritzel *nt*; *vti* kritzeln.

scream [skri:m] *n* Schrei *m*; *vi* schreien.

scree ['skri:] *n* Geröll(halde *f*) *nt*.

screech [skri:tʃ] *n* Schrei *m*; *vi* kreischen.

screen [skri:n] *n* (*protective*) Schutzschirm *m*; (*film*) Leinwand *f*; (*TV*) Bildschirm *m*; (*against insects*) Fliegengitter *nt*; (*Eccl*) Lettner *m*; *vt* (*shelter*) (be)schirmen; **film zeigen, vorführen.**

screw [skru:] *n* Schraube *f*; (*Naut*) Schiffsschraube *f*; *vt* (*fasten*) schrauben; (*vulgar*) bumsen; **to — money out of sb** (*col*) jdm das Geld aus der Tasche ziehen; **—driver** Schraubenzieher *m*; **—y** *a* (*col*) verrückt.

scribble ['skrɪbl] *n* Gekritzel *nt*; *vt* kritzeln.

scribe [skraɪb] *n* Schreiber *m*; (*Jewish*) Schriftgelehrte(r) *m*.

script [skrɪpt] *n* (*handwriting*) Handschrift *f*; (*for film*) Drehbuch *nt*; (*Theat*) Manuskript *nt*, Text *m*.

Scripture ['skrɪptʃə*] *n* Heilige Schrift *f*.

scriptwriter ['skrɪptraɪtə*] *n* Textverfasser *m*.

scroll [skrəʊl] *n* Schriftrolle *f*.

scrounge [skraʊndʒ] *vt* schnorren; *n*: **on the** — beim Schnorren.

scrub [skrʌb] *n* (*clean*) Schrubben *nt*; (*in countryside*) Gestrüpp *nt*; *vt* (*clean*) schrubben; (*reject*) fallenlassen.

scruff [skrʌf] *n* Genick *nt*, Kragen *m*; **—y** *a* unordentlich, vergammelt.

scrum(mage) ['skrʌm(ɪdʒ)] *n* Getümmel *nt*.

scruple ['skru:pl] *n* Skrupel *m*, Bedenken *nt*.

scrupulous *a*, **—ly** *ad* ['skru:pjʊləs, -lɪ] peinlich genau, gewissenhaft.

scrutinize ['skru:tɪnaɪz] *vt* genau prüfen *or* untersuchen.

scrutiny ['skru:tɪnɪ] *n* genaue Untersuchung *f*.

scuff [skʌf] *vt* shoes abstoßen.

scuffle ['skʌfl] *n* Handgemenge *nt*.

scullery ['skʌlərɪ] *n* Spülküche *f*; Abstellraum *m*.

sculptor ['skʌlptə*] *n* Bildhauer *m*.

sculpture ['skʌlptʃə*] *n* (*art*) Bildhauerei *f*; (*statue*) Skulptur *f*.

scum [skʌm] *n* (*lit, fig*) Abschaum *m*.

scurrilous ['skʌrɪləs] *a* unflätig.

scurry ['skʌrɪ] *vi* huschen.

scurvy ['skɜ:vɪ] *n* Skorbut *m*.

scuttle ['skʌtl] *n* Kohleneimer *m*; *vt* **ship** versenken; *vi* (*scamper*) (+ *away*, *off*) sich davonmachen.

scythe [saɪð] *n* Sense *f*.

sea [si:] *n* Meer *nt* (*also fig*), See *f*; **a Meeres-, See-;** — **bird** Meervogel *m*; **—board** Küste *f*; — **breeze** Seewind *m*; **—dog** Seebär *m*; **—farer** Seefahrer *m*; **—faring** *a* seefahrend; **—food** Meeresfrüchte *pl*; — **front** Strandpromenade *f*;

—going *a* seetüchtig, Hochsee-;
—gull Möwe *f.*

seal ['si:l] *n* (*animal*) Robbe *f*, See-
hund *m*; (*stamp, impression*)
Siegel *nt*; *vt* versiegeln.

sea level ['si:levl] *n* Meeresspiegel
m.

sealing wax ['si:liŋwæks] *n*
Siegellack *m.*

sea lion ['si:laiən] *n* Seelöwe *m.*

seam [si:m] *n* Saum *m*; (*edges
joining*) Naht *f*; (*layer*) Schicht *f*;
(*of coal*) Flöz *nt.*

seaman ['si:mən] *n* Seemann *m.*

seamless ['si:mlıs] *a* nahtlos.

seamy ['si:mı] *a* people, café
zwielichtig; *life* anrüchig; — side
of life dunkle Seite *f* des Lebens.

seaport ['si:pɔ:t] *n* Seehafen *m*,
Hafenstadt *f.*

search [sɜ:tʃ] *n* Suche *f* (*for* nach);
vi suchen; *vt* (*examine*) durch-
suchen; —ing a look forschend,
durchdringend; —light Scheinwerfer *m*; — party Suchmann-
schaft *f.*

seashore ['si:ʃɔ:*] *n* Meeresküste *f.*

seasick ['si:sık] *a* seekrank; —ness
Seekrankheit *f.*

seaside ['si:said] *n* Küste *f*; at the
— an der See; to go to the — an
die See fahren.

season ['si:zn] *n* Jahreszeit *f*; (*eg
Christmas*) Zeit *f*, Saison *f*; *vt*
(*flavour*) würzen; —al a Saison-;
—ing Gewürz *nt*,' Würze *f*; —
ticket (*Rail*) Zeitkarte *f*; (*Theat*)
Abonnement *nt.*

seat [si:t] *n* Sitz *m*, Platz *m*; (*in
Parliament*) Sitz *m*; (*part of body*)
Gesäß *nt*; (*part of garment*) Sitz-
fläche *f*, Hosenboden *m*; *vt* (*place*)
setzen; (*have space for*) Sitzplätze
bieten für; — belt Sicherheitsgurt

m; —ing Anweisen *nt* von Sitz-
plätzen.

sea water ['si:wɔ:tə*] *n* Meer-
wasser *nt*, Seewasser *nt.*

seaweed ['si:wi:d] *n* (See)tang *m*,
Alge *f.*

seaworthy ['si:wɜ:ðı] *a* seetüchtig.

secede [sı'si:d] *vi* sich lossagen.

secluded [sı'klu:dıd] *a* abgelegen,
ruhig.

seclusion [sı'klu:ʒən] *n* Zurück-
gezogenheit *f.*

second ['sekənd] *a* zweite(r,s); *ad*
(*in — position*) an zweiter Stelle;
(*Rail*) zweite(r) Klasse; *n* Sekunde
f; (*person*) Zweite(r) *m*; (*Comm:
imperfect*) zweite Wahl *f*; (*Sport*)
Sekundant *m*; *vt* (*support*) unterstützen; —ary a zweitrangig;
'—ary education Sekundarstufe *f*;
—ary school höhere Schule *f*,
Mittelschule *f*; —er Unterstützer
m; —hand a aus zweiter Hand; car
etc gebraucht; —ly ad zweitens;
it is — nature to him es ist ihm
zur zweiten Natur geworden; —
rate a mittelmäßig; to have —
thoughts es sich (*dat*) anders überlegen.

secrecy ['si:krəsı] *n* Geheimhaltung
f.

secret ['si:krət] *n* Geheimnis *nt*; *a*
geheim, heimlich, Geheim-; *in* —
geheim, heimlich.

secretarial [sekrə'teərıəl] *a*
Sekretärs-.

secretariat [sekrə'teərıət] *n* Sekretariat *nt.*

secretary ['sekrətrı] *n* Sekretär(in
f) *m*; (*government*) Staats-
sekretär(in *f*) *m*; Minister *m.*

secretive ['si:krətıv] *a* geheim-
tuerisch.

secretly ['si:krətlı] *ad* heimlich.

sect [sekt] *n* Sekte *f*; **—arian** [sek'tɛəriən] *a* (*belonging to a sect*) Sekten-.

section ['sekʃən] *n* Teil *m*, Ausschnitt *m*; (*department*) Abteilung *f*; (*of document*) Abschnitt *m*, Paragraph *m*; **—al** *a* (*regional*) partikularistisch.

sector ['sektə*] *n* Sektor *m*.

secular ['sekjulə*] *a* weltlich, profan.

secure [sɪ'kjuə*] *a* (*safe*) sicher; (*firmly fixed*) fest; *vt* (*make firm*) befestigen, sichern; (*obtain*) sichern; **—ly** *ad* sicher, fest.

security [sɪ'kjuərɪtɪ] *n* Sicherheit *f*; (*pledge*) Pfand *nt*; (*document*) Sicherheiten *pl*; (*national —*) Staatssicherheit *f*; **— guard** Sicherheitsbeamte(r) *m*; *see* social.

sedate [sɪ'deɪt] *a* (*calm*) gelassen; (*serious*) gesetzt; *vt* (*Med*) ein Beruhigungsmittel geben (+*dat*).

sedation [sɪ'deɪʃən] *n* (*Med*) Einfluß *m* von Beruhigungsmitteln.

sedative ['sedətɪv] *n* Beruhigungsmittel *nt*; *a* beruhigend, einschläfernd.

sedentary ['sedntrɪ] *a job* sitzend.

sediment ['sedɪmənt] *n* (Boden)satz *m*; **—ary** [sedɪ'mentərɪ] *a* (*Geol*) Sediment-.

seduce [sɪ'dju:s] *vt* verführen.

seduction [sɪ'dʌkʃən] *n* Verführung *f*.

seductive [sɪ'dʌktɪv] *a* verführerisch.

see [si:] *irreg vt* sehen; (*understand*) (ein)sehen, erkennen; (*find out*) sehen, herausfinden; (*make sure*) dafür sorgen (daß); (*accompany*) begleiten, bringen; (*visit*) besuchen; **to —** a doctor zum Arzt gehen; *vi* (*be aware*) sehen; (*find out*) nachsehen; **I —**

ach so, ich verstehe; **let me —** warte mal; **we'll — werden** (mal) sehen; *n* (*Eccl*) (*R.C.*) Bistum *nt*; (*Protestant*) Kirchenkreis *m*; **to — sth through** etw durchfechten; **to — through** sb/sth jdn/etw durchschauen; **to — to it** dafür sorgen; **to — sb off** jdn zum Zug *etc* begleiten.

seed [si:d] *n* Samen *m*, (Samen)korn *nt*; *vt* (*Tennis*) plazieren; **—ling** Setzling *m*; **—y** *a* (*ill*) flau, angeschlagen; *clothes* schäbig; *person* zweifelhaft.

seeing [si:ɪŋ] *cj* da.

seek [si:k] *vt irreg* suchen.

seem [si:m] *vi* scheinen; **—ingly** *ad* anscheinend; **—ly** *a* geziemend.

seep [si:p] *vi* sickern.

seer [sɪə*] *n* Seher *m*.

seesaw ['si:sɔ:] *n* Wippe *f*.

seethe [si:ð] *vi* kochen; (*with crowds*) wimmeln von.

see-through ['si:θru:] *a dress* durchsichtig.

segment ['segmənt] *n* Teil *m*; (*of circle*) Ausschnitt *m*.

segregate ['segrɪgeɪt] *vt* trennen, absondern.

segregation [segrɪ'geɪʃən] *n* Rassentrennung *f*.

seismic ['saɪzmɪk] *a* seismisch, Erdbeben-.

seize [si:z] *vt* (*grasp*) (er)greifen, packen; *power* ergreifen; (*take legally*) beschlagnahmen; *point* erfassen, begreifen; **— up** *vi* (*Tech*) sich festfressen.

seizure ['si:ʒə*] *n* (*illness*) Anfall *m*.

seldom ['seldəm] *ad* selten.

select [sɪ'lekt] *vt* ausgewählt; *vt* auswählen; **—ion** [sɪ'lekʃən] *n* Auswahl *f*; **—ive** *a person* wählerisch.

self [self] n Selbst nt, Ich nt; —-adhesive a selbstklebend; —-appointed a selbsternannt; —-assurance Selbstsicherheit f; —-assured a selbstbewußt; —-coloured, (US) —-colored a einfarbig; —-confidence Selbstvertrauen nt, Selbstbewußtsein nt; —-confident a selbstsicher; —-conscious a gehemmt, befangen; —-contained a (complete) (in sich) geschlossen; person verschlossen; —-defeating a: to be —-defeating ein Widerspruch in sich sein; —-defence Selbstverteidigung f; (Jur) Notwehr f; —-employed a frei(schaffend); —-evident a offensichtlich; —-explanatory a für sich (selbst) sprechend; —-indulgent a zügellos; —-interest Eigennutz m; —-ish a, —-ishly ad egoistisch, selbstsüchtig; —-ishness Egoismus m, Selbstsucht f; —-lessly ad selbstlos; —-made a selbstgemacht; —-pity Selbstmitleid nt; —-portrait Selbstbildnis nt; —-propelled a mit Eigenantrieb; —-reliant a unabhängig; —-respect Selbstachtung f; —-respecting a mit Selbstachtung; —-righteous a selbstgerecht; —-satisfied a selbstzufrieden; —-service a Selbstbedienungs-; —-sufficient a selbstgenügsam; —-supporting a (Fin) Eigenfinanzierungs-; person eigenständig.

sell [sel] irreg vt verkaufen; vi verkaufen; (goods) sich verkaufen (lassen); —-er Verkäufer m; —-ing price Verkaufspreis m.

semantic [sɪ'mæntɪk] a semantisch; —-s Semantik f.

semaphore ['seməfɔ:*] n Winkzeichen pl.

semi ['semɪ] n = —-detached house; —-circle Halbkreis m; —-colon Semikolon nt; —-conscious a halbbewußt; —-detached house Zweifamilienhaus nt, Doppelhaus nt; —-final Halbfinale nt.

seminar ['semɪnɑ:*] n Seminar nt.

semiquaver ['semɪkweɪvə*] n Sechzehntel nt.

semiskilled ['semɪ'skɪld] a angelernt.

semitone ['semɪtəʊn] n Halbton m.

semolina [semə'li:nə] n Grieß m.

senate ['senət] n Senat m.

senator ['senətə*] n Senator m.

send [send] vt irreg senden, schicken; (col: inspire) hinreißen; — away to wegschicken; — away for vt holen lassen; — back vt holen zurückschicken; — for vt holen lassen; — off vt goods abschicken; player vom Feld schicken; — out vt invitation aussenden; — up vt hinaufsenden; (col) verulken; —-er Absender m; —-off Verabschiedung f; —-up (col) Verulkung f.

senile ['si:naɪl] a senil, Alters-.

senility [sɪ'nɪlɪtɪ] n Altersschwachheit f.

senior ['si:nɪə*] a (older) älter; (higher rank) Ober-; n (older person) Ältere(r) m; (higher ranking) Rangälteste(r) m; —-ity [si:nɪ'ɒrɪtɪ] (of age) höhere(s) Alter nt; (in rank) höhere(r) Dienstgrad m.

sensation [sen'seɪʃən] n Empfindung f, Gefühl nt; (excitement) Sensation f, Aufsehen nt; —-al a sensationell, Sensations-.

sense [sens] n Sinn m; (understanding) Verstand m, Vernunft f; (meaning) Sinn m, Bedeutung f; (feeling) Gefühl nt; to make —

Sinn ergeben; *vt* fühlen, spüren; —less *a* sinnlos, (*unconscious*) besinnungslos; —lessly *ad* (*stupidly*) sinnlos.

sensibility [sensɪˈbɪlɪtɪ] *n* Empfindsamkeit *f*; (*feeling hurt*) Empfindlichkeit *f*.

sensible *a*, **sensibly** *ad* ['sensəbl, -blɪ] vernünftig.

sensitive [ˈsensɪtɪv] *a* empfindlich (*to* gegen); (*easily hurt*) sensibel, feinfühlig; *film* lichtempfindlich.

sensitivity [sensɪˈtɪvɪtɪ] *n* Empfindlichkeit *f*; (*artistic*) Feingefühl *nt*; (*tact*) Feinfühligkeit *f*.

sensual [ˈsensjʊəl] *a* sinnlich.

sensuous [ˈsensjʊəs] *a* sinnlich, sinnenfreudig.

sentence [ˈsentəns] *n* Satz *m*; (*Jur*) Strafe *f*; Urteil *nt*; *vt* verurteilen.

sentiment [ˈsentɪmənt] *n* Gefühl *nt*; (*thought*) Gedanke *m*, Gesinnung *f*; —al [sentɪˈmentl] *a* sentimental; (*of feelings rather than reason*) gefühlsmäßig; —ality *n* (*artistic*) [sentɪmenˈtælɪtɪ] Sentimentalität *f*.

sentinel [ˈsentɪnl] *n* Wachtposten *m*.

sentry [ˈsentrɪ] *n* (Schild)wache *f*.

separable [ˈsepərəbl] *a* (ab)trennbar.

separate [ˈsepərət] *a* getrennt, separat; [ˈsepəreɪt] *vt* trennen; *vi* sich trennen; —ly *ad* getrennt.

separation [sepəˈreɪʃən] *n* Trennung *f*.

sepia [ˈsiːpɪə] *a* Sepia-.

September [sepˈtembə*] *n* September *m*.

septic [ˈseptɪk] *a* vereitert, septisch.

sequel [ˈsiːkwəl] *n* Folge *f*.

sequence [ˈsiːkwəns] *n* (Reihen)folge *f*.

sequin [ˈsiːkwɪn] *n* Paillette *f*.

serenade [serəˈneɪd] *n* Ständchen *nt*, Serenade *f*; *vt* ein Ständchen bringen (+*dat*).

serene *a*, —ly *ad* [səˈriːn, -lɪ] heiter, gelassen, ruhig.

serenity [sɪˈrenɪtɪ] *n* Heiterkeit *f*, Gelassenheit *f*, Ruhe *f*.

serf [sɜːf] *n* Leibeigene(r) *mf*.

serge [sɜːdʒ] *n* Serge *f*.

sergeant [ˈsɑːdʒənt] *n* Feldwebel *m*; (*police*) (Polizei)wachtmeister *m*.

serial [ˈsɪərɪəl] *n* Fortsetzungsroman *m*; (*TV*) Fernsehserie *f*; —*number* (fort)laufend; —*ize* *vt* in Fortsetzungen veröffentlichen/senden.

series [ˈsɪərɪz] *n* Serie *f*, Reihe *f*.

serious [ˈsɪərɪəs] *a* ernst; *injury* schwer; *development* ernstzunehmend; **I'm —** das meine ich ernst; —ly *ad* ernst(haft); *hurt* schwer; —ness Ernst *m*, Ernsthaftigkeit *f*.

sermon [ˈsɜːmən] *n* Predigt *f*.

serpent [ˈsɜːpənt] *n* Schlange *f*.

serrated [seˈreɪtɪd] *a* gezackt; —*knife* Sägemesser *nt*.

serum [ˈsɪərəm] *n* Serum *nt*.

servant [ˈsɜːvənt] *n* Bedienstete(r) *raf*, Diener(in *f*) *m*; *see* civil.

serve [sɜːv] *vt* dienen (+*dat*); *guest, customer* bedienen; *food* servieren; *writ* zustellen (*on sb* jdm); *vi* dienen, nützen; (*at table*) servieren; (*tennis*) geben, aufschlagen; **it —s him right** das geschieht ihm recht; **that'll — the purpose** das reicht; **that'll — as a table** das geht als Tisch; — **out** *or* **up** *vt* *food* auftragen, servieren.

service [ˈsɜːvɪs] *n* (*help*) Dienst *m*; (*trains etc*) Verkehrsverbindungen *pl*; (*hotel*) Service *m*, Bedienung *f*; (*set of dishes*) Service *nt*; (*Rel*) Gottesdienst *m*; (*Mil*) Waffengattung f; (car) Inspektion f; (for TVs etc) Kundendienst m; (tennis) Aufschlag m; **to be of —** to sb jdm einen großen Dienst erweisen; can **I be of —?** kann ich Ihnen behilflich sein?; vt (Aut, Tech) warten, überholen; **the S—s** pl (armed forces) Streitkräfte pl; **—able** a brauchbar; **— area** (on motorway) Raststätte f; **— charge** Bedienung f; **—man** (soldier etc) Soldat m; **— station** (Groß)tankstelle f.

servicing ['sɜːvɪsɪŋ] n Wartung f.

serviette [sɜːvɪ'et] n Serviette f.

servile ['sɜːvaɪl] a sklavisch, unterwürfig.

session ['seʃən] n Sitzung f; (Pol) Sitzungsperiode f.

set [set] n (collection of things) Satz m, Set nt; (Rad, TV) Apparat m; (tennis) Satz m; (group of people) Kreis m; (Cine) Szene f; (Theat) Bühnenbild nt; a festgelegt; (ready) bereit; **— phrase** feststehende(r) Ausdruck m; **— square** Zeichendreieck nt; irreg vt (place) setzen, stellen, legen; (arrange) (an)ordnen; table decken; time, price festsetzen; alarm, watch stellen; jewels (einfassen; task stellen; exam ausarbeiten; **to — one's hair** die Haare eindrehen; vi (sun) untergehen; (become hard) fest werden; (bone) zusammenwachsen; **to — on fire** anstecken; **to — free** freilassen; **to — sth going** etw in Gang bringen; **to — sail** losfahren; **— about** vt task anpacken; **— aside** vt beseitelegen; **— back** vt zurückwerfen; **— down** vt absetzen; **— off** vi ausbrechen; vt (explode) zur Explosion bringen; alarm losgehen lassen; (show up well) hervorheben; **— out** vi aufbrechen; vt

(arrange) anlegen, arrangieren; (state) darlegen; **— up** vt organization aufziehen; record aufstellen; monument erstellen; **—back** Rückschlag m.

settee [se'tiː] n Sofa nt.

setting ['setɪŋ] n (Mus) Vertonung f; (scenery) Hintergrund m.

settle ['setl] vt beruhigen; (pay) begleichen, bezahlen; (agree) regeln; vi (also — down) sich einleben; (come to rest) sich niederlassen; (sink) sich setzen; (calm down) sich beruhigen; **—ment** Regelung f; (payment) Begleichung f; (colony) Siedlung f, Niederlassung f; **—r** Siedler m.

setup ['setap] n (arrangement) Aufbau m, Gliederung f; (situation) Situation f, Lage f.

seven ['sevn] num sieben; **—teen** num siebzehn; **—th** a siebte(r,s) n Siebtel nt; **—ty** num siebzig.

sever ['sevə*] vt abtrennen.

several ['sevrəl] a mehrere, verschiedene; pron mehrere.

severance ['sevərəns] n Abtrennung f; (fig) Abbruch m.

severe [sɪ'vɪə*] a (strict) streng; (serious) schwer; climate rauh; (plain) streng, schmucklos; **—ly** ad (strictly) streng, strikt; (seriously) schwer, ernstlich.

severity [sɪ'verɪtɪ] n Strenge f; Schwere f; Ernst m.

sew [səʊ] vti irreg nähen; **— up** vt zunähen.

sewage ['sjuːɪdʒ] n Abwässer pl.

sewer ['sjuə*] n (Abwasser)kanal m.

sewing ['səʊɪŋ] n Näharbeit f; **— machine** Nähmaschine f.

sex [seks] n Sex m; (gender) Geschlecht nt; **— act** Geschlechtsakt m.

sextant ['sekstənt] n Sextant m.

sextet [seks'tet] n Sextett nt.

sexual ['seksjʊəl] a sexuell, geschlechtlich, Geschlechts-; —ly ad geschlechtlich, sexuell.

sexy ['seksi] a sexy.

shabbily ['ʃæbili] ad schäbig.

shabbiness ['ʃæbinəs] n Schäbigkeit f.

shabby ['ʃæbi] a (lit, fig) schäbig.

shack [ʃæk] n Hütte f.

shackle ['ʃækl] vt fesseln; —s pl (lit, fig) Fesseln pl, Ketten pl.

shade [ʃeid] n Schatten m; (for lamp) Lampenschirm m; (colour) Farbton m; (small quantity) Spur f, Idee f; vt abschirmen.

shadow ['ʃædəʊ] n Schatten m; vt (follow) beschatten; a: — cabinet (Pol) Schattenkabinett nt; —y a schattig.

shady ['ʃeidi] a schattig; (fig) zwielichtig.

shaft [ʃɑːft] n (of spear etc) Schaft m; (in mine) Schacht m; (Tech) Welle f; (of light) Strahl m.

shaggy ['ʃægi] a struppig.

shake [ʃeik] irreg vt schütteln, rütteln; (shock) erschüttern; to — hands die Hand geben (with dat); they shook hands sie gaben sich die Hand; to — one's head den Kopf schütteln; vi (move) schwanken; (tremble) zittern, beben; a (jerk) Schütteln nt, Rütteln nt; — off vt abschütteln; — up vt (lit) aufschütteln; (fig) aufrütteln; — Aufrüttelung f; (Pol) Umgruppierung f.

shakily ['ʃeikili] ad zitternd, unsicher.

shakiness ['ʃeikinəs] n Wackeligkeit f.

shaky ['ʃeiki] a zittrig; (weak) unsicher.

shale [ʃeil] n Schiefer(ton) m.

shall [ʃæl] v aux irreg werden; (must) sollen.

shallow ['ʃæləʊ] a flach, seicht (also fig); —s pl flache Stellen pl.

sham [ʃæm] n Täuschung f, Trug m, Schein m; a unecht, falsch.

shambles ['ʃæmblz] n sing Durcheinander nt.

shame [ʃeim] n Scham f; (disgrace, pity) Schande f; vt beschämen; what a —! wie schade!; — on you! schäm dich!; —faced a beschämt; —ful a, —fully ad schändlich; —less a schamlos; (immodest) unverschämt.

shampoo [ʃæm'puː] n Schampoo nt; vt schampunieren; — and set Waschen nt und Legen.

shamrock ['ʃæmrɒk] n Kleeblatt nt.

shandy ['ʃændi] n Radlermaß nt.

shan't [ʃɑːnt] = shall not.

shanty ['ʃænti] n (cabin) Hütte f, Baracke f; — town Elendsviertel nt.

shape [ʃeip] n Form f, Gestalt f; vt formen, gestalten; to take — Gestalt annehmen; —less a formlos; —ly a wohlgeformt, wohlproportioniert.

share [ʃɛəˈ] n (An)teil m; (Fin) Aktie f; vt teilen; —holder Aktionär m.

shark [ʃɑːk] n Hai(fisch) m; (swindler) Gauner m.

sharp [ʃɑːp] a scharf; pin spitz; person clever; child aufgeweckt; (unscrupulous) gerissen, raffiniert; (Mus) erhöht; — practices pl Machenschaften pl; n (Mus) Kreuz nt; ad (Mus) zu hoch; nine o'clock — Punkt neun; look —! mach schnell!; —en vt schärfen; pencil spitzen; —ener Spitzer m; —-eyed a scharfsichtig; —ness Schärfe f; —-witted a scharfsinnig, aufgeweckt.

shatter ['ʃætə*] vt zerschmettern; (fig) zerstören; vi zerspringen; —ed a (lit, fig) kaputt; —ing a experience furchtbar.

shave [ʃeɪv] n Rasur f, Rasieren nt; to have a — sich rasieren (lassen); vt rasieren; vi sich rasieren; — a head geschoren; —r (Elec) Rasierapparat m, Rasierer m.

shaving ['ʃeɪvɪŋ] n (action) Rasieren nt; —s pl (of wood etc) Späne pl; — brush Rasierpinsel m; — cream Rasierkrem f; — point Rasiersteckdose f; — soap Rasierseife f.

shawl [ʃɔːl] n Schal m, Umhang m.

she [ʃiː] pron sie; a weiblich; —-bear Bärenweibchen nt.

sheaf [ʃiːf] n Garbe f.

shear [ʃɪə*] vt irreg scheren; — off vt abscheren; —s pl Heckenschere f.

sheath [ʃiːθ] n Scheide f; —e [ʃiːð] vt einstecken; (Tech) verkleiden.

shed [ʃed] n Schuppen m; (for animals) Stall m; vt irreg leaves etc abwerfen, verlieren; tears vergießen.

she'd [ʃiːd] = she had; she would.

sheep [ʃiːp] n Schaf nt; —dog Schäferhund m; —ish a verschämt, betreten; —skin Schaffell nt.

sheer [ʃɪə*] a bloß, rein; (steep) steil, jäh; (transparent) (hauch)dünn, durchsichtig; ad (directly) direkt.

sheet [ʃiːt] n Bettuch nt, Bettlaken nt; (of paper) Blatt nt; (of metal etc) Platte f; (of ice) Fläche f; — lightning Wetterleuchten nt.

sheik(h) [ʃeɪk] n Scheich m.

shelf [ʃelf] n Bord nt, Regal nt.

she'll [ʃiːl] = she will; she shall.

shell [ʃel] n Schale f; (sea—) Muschel f; (explosive) Granate f; (of building) Mauern pl; vt peas schälen; (fire on) beschießen; —fish Schalentier nt; (as food) Meeresfrüchte pl.

shelter ['ʃeltə*] n Schutz m; Bunker m; vt schützen, bedecken; refugees aufnehmen; vi sich unterstellen; —ed a life behütet; spot geschützt.

shelve [ʃelv] vt aufschieben; vi abfallen.

shelving ['ʃelvɪŋ] n Regale pl.

shepherd ['ʃepəd] n Schäfer m; vt treiben, führen; —ess Schäferin f.

sheriff ['ʃerɪf] n Sheriff m.

sherry ['ʃerɪ] n Sherry m.

she's [ʃiːz] = she is; she has.

shield [ʃiːld] n Schild m; (fig) Schirm m, Schutz m; vt (be)schirmen; (Tech) abschirmen.

shift [ʃɪft] n Veränderung f, Verschiebung f; (work) Schicht f; vt (ver)rücken, verschieben; office verlegen; arm wegnehmen; vi sich verschieben; (col) schnell fahren; — work Schichtarbeit f; —y a verschlagen.

shilling ['ʃɪlɪŋ] n (old) Shilling m.

shilly-shally ['ʃɪlɪʃælɪ] vi zögern.

shimmer ['ʃɪmə*] n Schimmer m; vi schimmern.

shin [ʃɪn] n Schienbein nt.

shine [ʃaɪn] n Glanz m, Schein m; irreg vi polieren; to — a torch on sb jdn (mit einer Lampe) anleuchten; vi scheinen; (fig) glänzen.

shingle ['ʃɪŋɡl] n Schindel f; (on

beach) Strandkies *m*; —**s** *pl* (*Med*) Gürtelrose *f.*

shining [ˈʃaɪnɪŋ] *a light* strahlend.

shiny [ˈʃaɪnɪ] *a* glänzend.

ship [ʃɪp] *n* Schiff *nt*; *vt* an Bord bringen, verladen; (*transport as cargo*) verschiffen; —**building** Schiffbau *m*; — *canal* Seekanal *m*; —**ment** Verladung *f*; (*goods shipped*) Schiffsladung *f*; —**per** Verschiffer *m*; —**ping** (*act*) Verschiffung *f*; (*ships*) Schiffahrt *f*; —**shape** *a* in Ordnung; —**wreck** Schiffbruch *m*; (*destroyed ship*) Wrack *nt*; —**yard** Werft *f.*

shirk [ʃɜːk] *vt* ausweichen (+ *dat.*).

shirt [ʃɜːt] *n* (Ober)hemd *nt*; in —**sleeves** in Hemdsärmeln; —**y** *a* (*col*) mürrisch.

shiver [ˈʃɪvə*] *n* Schauer *m*; *vi* frösteln, zittern.

shoal [ʃəʊl] *n* (Fisch)schwarm *m.*

shock [ʃɒk] *n* Stoß *m*, Erschütterung *f*; (*mental*) Schock *m*; (*Elec*) Schlag *m*; *vt* erschüttern; (*offend*) schockieren; — *absorber* Stoßdämpfer *m*; —**ing** *a* unerhört, schockierend; —**proof** *a watch* stoßsicher.

shoddiness [ˈʃɒdɪnəs] *n* Schäbigkeit *f.*

shoddy [ˈʃɒdɪ] *a* schäbig.

shoe [ʃuː] *n* (*branch*) Schuh *m*; (*of horse*) Hufeisen *nt*; *vt irreg horse* beschlagen; —**brush** Schuhbürste *f*; —**horn** Schuhlöffel *m*; —**lace** Schnürsenkel *m.*

shoot [ʃuːt] *n* (*branch*) Schößling *m*; *irreg vt gun* abfeuern; *goal, arrow* schießen; (*kill*) erschießen; *film* drehen, filmen; *shot in the leg* ins Bein getroffen; *vi* (*gun, move quickly*) schießen; *don't* —! nicht schießen!; — *down vt* abschießen;

—**ing** Schießerei *f*; —**ing star** Sternschnuppe *f.*

shop [ʃɒp] *n* Geschäft *nt*, Laden *m*; (*workshop*) Werkstatt *f*; *vi* (*also go* —**ping**) einkaufen gehen; —*assistant* Verkäufer(in *f*) *m*; —**keeper** Geschäftsinhaber *m*; —**lifter** Ladendieb *m*; —**lifting** Ladendiebstahl *m*; —**per** Käufer(in *f*) *m*; —**ping** Einkaufen *nt*, Einkauf *m*; —**ping bag** Einkaufstasche *f*; —**ping centre**, (*US*) —**ping center** Einkaufszentrum *nt*; —**soiled** *a* angeschmutzt; — *steward* Betriebsrat *m*; — *window* Schaufenster *nt*; *see* **talk**.

shore [ʃɔː*] *n* Ufer *nt*; (*of sea*) Strand *m*, Küste *f*; *vt*: — *up* abstützen.

short [ʃɔːt] *a* kurz; *person* klein; (*curt*) kurz angebunden; (*measure*) zu knapp; **to be** — **of** zu wenig ... haben; **two** — zwei zu wenig; *n* (*Elec*: —*circuit*) Kurzschluß *m*; *ad* (*suddenly*) plötzlich; *vi* (*Elec*) einen Kurzschluß haben; **to cut** — abkürzen; **to fall** — **nicht** erreichen; **for** — kurz; —**age** Knappheit *f*, Mangel *m*; —**bread** Mürbegebäck *nt*, Heidesand *m*; —**circuit** Kurzschluß *m*; *vi* einen Kurzschluß haben; —**coming** Fehler *m*, Mangel *m*; — **cut** Abkürzung *f*; —**en** *vt* (ab)kürzen; *clothes* kürzer machen; —**hand** Stenographie *f*, Kurzschrift *f*; —**hand typist** Stenotypistin *f*; —**list** *'*engere Wahl *f*; —**lived** *a* kurzlebig; —**ly** *ad* bald; —**ness** Kürze *f*; —**s** *pl* Shorts *pl*; —**sighted** *a* (*lit, fig*) kurzsichtig; —**sightedness** Kurzsichtigkeit *f*; —**story** Kurzgeschichte *f*; —**tempered** *a* leicht aufbrausend; —

term *a effect* kurzfristig; — *wave*
(Rad) Kurzwelle *f*.

shot [ʃɔt] *n (from gun)* Schuß *m*;
(person) Schütze *m*; *(try)* Versuch
m; *(injection)* Spritze *f*; *(Phot)*
Aufnahme *f*, Schnappschuß *m*; like
a — wie der Blitz; **—gun** Schrot-
flinte *f*.

should [ʃʊd] *v aux*: I — go now
ich sollte jetzt gehen; I — say ich
würde sagen; I — like to sich im
möchte gerne, ich würde gerne.

shoulder [ˈʃəʊldə*] *n* Schulter *f*;
vt rifle schultern; *(fig)* auf sich
nehmen; — **blade** Schulterblatt *nt*.

shouldn't [ˈʃʊdnt] = **should not**.

shout [ʃaʊt] *n* Schrei *m*; *(call)* Ruf
m; *vt* rufen; *vi* schreien, laut
rufen; **to — at** anbrüllen; **—ing**
Geschrei *nt*.

shove [ʃʌv] *n* Schubs *m*, Stoß *m*;
vt schieben, stoßen, schubsen; —
off *vi (Naut)* abstoßen; *(fig col)*
abhauen.

shovel [ˈʃʌvl] *n* Schaufel *f*; *vt*
schaufeln.

show [ʃəʊ] *n (display)* Schau *f*;
(exhibition) Ausstellung *f*; *(Cine,
Theat)* Vorstellung *f*, Show *f*; *irreg
vt* zeigen; *kindness* erweisen; *vi* zu
sehen sein; **to — sb in** jdn herein-
führen; **to — sb out** jdn hinaus-
begleiten; — **off** *vi (pej)* angeben,
protzen; *vt (display)* ausstellen; —
up *vi (stand out)* sich abheben;
(arrive) erscheinen; *vt* aufzeigen;
(unmask) bloßstellen; — **business**
Showbusineß *nt*; **—down** Kraft-
probe *f*, endgültige Auseinandersetzung *f*.

shower [ˈʃaʊə*] *n* Schauer *m*; *(of
stones)* (Stein)hagel *m*; *(of sparks)*
(Funken)regen *m*; (— *bath*)
Dusche *f*; **to have a** — duschen;
vt (fig) überschütten; **—proof** *a*

wasserabstoßend; **—y** *a weather*
regnerisch.

showground [ˈʃəʊɡraʊnd] *n* Aus-
stellungsgelände *nt*.

showing [ˈʃəʊɪŋ] *n (of film)* Vor-
führung *f*.

show jumping [ˈʃəʊdʒʌmpɪŋ] *n*
Turnierreiten *nt*.

showmanship [ˈʃəʊmənʃɪp] *n*
Talent *nt* als Showman.

show-off [ˈʃəʊɔf] *n* Angeber *m*.

showpiece [ˈʃəʊpiːs] *n* Parade-
stück *nt*.

showroom [ˈʃəʊrʊm] *n* Aus-
stellungsraum *m*.

shrapnel [ˈʃræpnl] *n* Schrapnell *nt*.

shred [ʃred] *n* Fetzen *m*; *vt*
zerfetzen; *(Cook)* raspeln; **in —s**
in Fetzen.

shrewd *a*, **—ly** *ad* [ʃruːd, -lɪ]
scharfsinnig, clever; **—ness**
Scharfsinn *m*.

shriek [ʃriːk] *n* Schrei *m*; *vti*
kreischen, schreien.

shrill [ʃrɪl] *a* schrill, gellend.

shrimp [ʃrɪmp] *n* Krabbe *f*, Garnele
f.

shrine [ʃraɪn] *n* Schrein *m*.

shrink [ʃrɪŋk] *irreg vi* schrumpfen,
eingehen; *vt* einschrumpfen
lassen; — Schrumpfung *f*; —
away *vi* zurückschrecken *(from vor
+ dat)*.

shrivel [ˈʃrɪvl] *vti (also — up)*
schrumpfen, schrumpeln.

shroud [ʃraʊd] *n* Leichentuch *nt*;
vt umhüllen, (ein)hüllen.

Shrove Tuesday [ˈʃrəʊvˈtjuːzdeɪ]
n Fastnachtsdienstag *m*.

shrub [ʃrʌb] *n* Busch *m*, Strauch
m; **—bery** Gebüsch *nt*.

shrug [ʃrʌɡ] *n* Achselzucken *nt*; *vti*
die Achseln zucken; — **off** *vt* auf
die leichte Schulter nehmen.

shrunken ['ʃrʌŋkən] *a* eingelaufen.

shudder ['ʃʌdə*] *n* Schauder *m*; *vi* schaudern.

shuffle ['ʃʌfl] *n* (Cards) (Karten-) mischen *nt*; *vt* cards mischen; *vi* (walk) schlurfen.

shun [ʃʌn] *vt* scheuen, (ver)meiden.

shunt [ʃʌnt] *vt* rangieren.

shut [ʃʌt] *irreg vt* schließen, zumachen; *vi* sich schließen (lassen); — **down** *vti* schließen; — **off** *vt supply* abdrehen; — **up** *vi* (keep quiet) den Mund halten; *vt* (close) zuschließen; (silence) zum Schweigen bringen; — up! halt den Mund!; —**ter** Fensterladen *m*, Rolladen *m*; (Phot) Verschluß *m*.

shuttlecock ['ʃʌtlkɒk] *n* Federball *m*; Federballspiel *nt*.

shuttle service ['ʃʌtls3:vɪs] *n* Pendelverkehr *m*.

shy *a*, —**ly** *ad* [ʃaɪ, -lɪ] schüchtern, scheu; —**ness** Schüchternheit *f*, Zurückhaltung *f*.

Siamese [saɪə'mi:z] *a*: — **cat** Siamkatze *f*; — **twins** *pl* siamesische Zwillinge *pl*.

sick [sɪk] *a* krank; **humour** schwarz; joke makaber; **I feel** — mir ist schlecht; **I was** — ich habe gebrochen; **to be** — **of** **sb/sth** jdn/etw satt haben; — **bay** (Schiffs)lazarett *nt*; —**bed** Krankenbett *nt*; —**en** *vt* (disgust) krankmachen; *vi* krank werden; —**ening** *a* (sight) widerlich; (annoying) zum Weinen.

sickle ['sɪkl] *n* Sichel *f*.

sick leave ['sɪkli:v] *n*: **to be on** — krank geschrieben sein.

sick list ['sɪklɪst] *n* Krankenliste *f*.

sickly ['sɪklɪ] *a* kränklich, blaß; (causing nausea) widerlich.

sickness ['sɪknəs] *n* Krankheit *f*; (vomiting) Übelkeit *f*, Erbrechen *nt*.

sick pay ['sɪkpeɪ] *n* Krankengeld *nt*.

side [saɪd] *n* Seite *f*; *a* door, entrance Seiten-, Neben-; **by the** — **of** neben; **on all** —**s** von allen Seiten; **to take** —**s** (with) Partei nehmen (für); *vi*: — **with sb** es halten mit jdm; —**board** Anrichte *f*, Sideboard *nt*; —**boards**, —**burns** *pl* Koteletten *pl*; — **effect** Nebenwirkung *f*; —**light** (Aut) Parkleuchte *f*, Standlicht *nt*; —**line** (Sport) Seitenlinie *f*; (fig: hobby) Nebenbeschäftigung' *f*; — **road** Nebenstraße *f*; — **show** Nebenausstellung *f*; —**track** *vt* (fig) ablenken; —**walk** (US) Bürgersteig *m*; —**ways** *ad* seitwärts.

siding ['saɪdɪŋ] *n* Nebengleis *nt*.

sidle ['saɪdl] *vi*: — **up** sich heranmachen (to an + acc).

siege [si:dʒ] *n* Belagerung *f*.

siesta [sɪ'estə] *n* Siesta *f*.

sieve [sɪv] *n* Sieb *nt*; *vt* sieben.

sift [sɪft] *vt* sieben; (fig) sichten.

sigh [saɪ] *n* Seufzer *m*; *vi* seufzen.

sight [saɪt] *n* (power of seeing) Sehvermögen *nt*, Augenlicht *nt*; (view) (An)blick *m*; (scene) Aussicht *f*, Blick *m*; (of gun) Zielvorrichtung *f*, Korn *nt*; —**s** *pl* (of city etc) Sehenswürdigkeiten *pl*; **in** — in Sicht; **out of** — außer Sicht; *vt* sichten; —**seeing** Besuch *m* von Sehenswürdigkeiten; **to go** —**seeing** Sehenswürdigkeiten besichtigen; —**seer** Tourist *m*.

sign [saɪn] *n* Zeichen *nt*; (notice, road — etc) Schild *nt*; *vt* unterschreiben; — **out** *vi* sich austragen; — **up** *vi* (Mil) sich verpflichten; *vt* verpflichten.

signal ['sɪgnl] *n* Signal *nt*; *vt* ein Zeichen geben (+ dat).

signatory ['sɪgnətrɪ] *n* Signatar *m*.

signature ['sɪgnətʃə*] n Unterschrift f; — **tune** Erkennungsmelodie f.

signet ring ['sɪgnətrɪŋ] n Siegelring m.

significance [sɪg'nɪfɪkəns] n Bedeutung f.

significant [sɪg'nɪfɪkənt] a (meaning sth) bedeutsam; (important) bedeutend, wichtig; —**ly** ad bezeichnenderweise.

signify ['sɪgnɪfaɪ] vt bedeuten; (show) andeuten, zu verstehen geben.

sign language ['saɪnlæŋgwɪdʒ] n Zeichensprache f, Fingersprache f.

signpost ['saɪnpəust] n Wegweiser m, Schild nt.

silence ['saɪləns] n Stille f, Ruhe f; (of person) Schweigen nt; vt zum Schweigen bringen; —**r** (on gun) Schalldämpfer m; (Aut) Auspufftopf m.

silent ['saɪlənt] a still; person schweigsam; —**ly** ad schweigend, still.

silhouette [sɪlu:'et] n Silhouette f, Umriß m; (picture) Schattenbild nt; vt: **to be —d against** sth sich als Silhouette abheben gegen etw.

silk [sɪlk] n Seide f; a seiden, Seiden-; —**y** a seidig.

silliness ['sɪlɪnəs] n Albernheit f, Dummheit f.

silly ['sɪlɪ] a dumm, albern.

silo ['saɪləu] n Silo m.

silt [sɪlt] n Schlamm m, Schlick m.

silver ['sɪlvə*] n Silber nt; a silbern, Silber-; — **paper** Silberpapier nt; —**plate** Silber(geschirr) nt; —**plated** a versilbert; —**smith** Silberschmied m; —**ware** Silber nt; —**y** a silbern.

similar ['sɪmɪlə*] a ähnlich (to dat); —**ity** [sɪmɪ'lærɪtɪ] Ähnlichkeit f; —**ly** ad in ähnlicher Weise.

simile ['sɪmɪlɪ] n Vergleich m.

simmer ['sɪmə*] vti sieden (lassen).

simple ['sɪmpl] a einfach; dress also schlicht; —(-**minded**) a naiv, einfältig.

simplicity [sɪm'plɪsɪtɪ] n Einfachheit f; (of person) Einfältigkeit f.

simplification [sɪmplɪfɪ'keɪʃən] n Vereinfachung f.

simplify ['sɪmplɪfaɪ] vt vereinfachen.

simply ['sɪmplɪ] ad einfach; (only) bloß, nur.

simulate ['sɪmjuleɪt] vt simulieren.

simulation [sɪmju'leɪʃən] n Simulieren nt.

simultaneous [sɪml'teɪnɪəs, -lɪ] a, —**ly** ad gleichzeitig.

sin [sɪn] n Sünde f; vi sündigen.

since [sɪns] ad seither; prep seit, seitdem; cj (time) seit; (because) da, weil.

sincere [sɪn'sɪə*] a aufrichtig, ehrlich, offen; —**ly** aufrichtig; **yours —ly** mit freundlichen Grüßen.

sincerity [sɪn'serɪtɪ] n Aufrichtigkeit f.

sinecure ['saɪnɪkjuə*] n einträgliche(r) Ruheposten m.

sinew ['sɪnju:] n Sehne f; (of animal) Flechse f.

sinful ['sɪnful] a sündig, sündhaft.

sing [sɪŋ] vti irreg singen.

singe [sɪndʒ] vt versengen.

singer ['sɪŋə*] n Sänger(in f) m.

singing ['sɪŋɪŋ] n Singen nt, Gesang m.

single ['sɪŋgl] a (one only) einzig; bed, room Einzel-, einzeln; (unmarried) ledig; ticket einfach; (having one part only) einzeln; n (ticket) einfache Fahrkarte f; **—s** (tennis) Einzel nt; **— out** vi aussuchen, auswählen; **—breasted** a einreihig; **in —** file hintereinander; **—handed** a allein; **—minded** a zielstrebig.

singlet ['sɪŋglət] n Unterhemd nt.

single ['sɪŋgl] ad einzeln, allein.

singular ['sɪŋgjulə*] a (Gram) Singular-; (odd) merkwürdig, seltsam; n (Gram) Einzahl f, Singular m; **—ly** ad besonders, höchst.

sinister ['sɪnɪstə*] a (evil) böse; (ghostly) unheimlich.

sink [sɪŋk] n Spülbecken nt, Ausguß m; irreg vt ship versenken; (dig) einsenken; **— in** vi (news etc) eingehen (+dat); **—ing** a feeling flau.

sinner ['sɪnə*] n Sünder(in f) m.

sinuous ['sɪnjuəs] a gewunden, sich schlängelnd.

sinus ['saɪnəs] n (Anat) Nasenhöhle f, Sinus m.

sip [sɪp] n Schlückchen nt; vt nippen an (+dat).

siphon ['saɪfən] n Siphon(flasche f) m; **— off** vt absaugen; (fig) abschöpfen.

sir [sɜː*] n (respect) Herr m; (knight) Sir m; yes S— ja(wohl, mein Herr).

siren ['saɪərən] n Sirene f.

sirloin ['sɜːlɔɪn] n Lendenstück nt.

sirocco [sɪ'rɒkəu] n Schirokko m.

sissy ['sɪsɪ] n = cissy.

sister ['sɪstə*] n Schwester f; (nurse) Oberschwester f; (nun) Ordensschwester f; **—in-law** n Schwägerin f.

sit [sɪt] irreg. vi sitzen; (hold session) tagen, Sitzung halten; vt exam machen; **to — tight**

abwarten; **— down** vi sich hinsetzen; **— up** vi (after lying) sich aufsetzen; (straight) sich gerade setzen; (at night) aufbleiben.

site [saɪt] n Platz m; vt plazieren, legen.

sit-in ['sɪtɪn] n Sit-in nt.

siting ['saɪtɪŋ] n (location) Platz m, Lage f.

sitting ['sɪtɪŋ] n (meeting) Sitzung f, Tagung f; **— room** Wohnzimmer nt.

situated ['sɪtjueɪtɪd] a: to be — liegen.

situation [sɪtjʊ'eɪʃən] n Situation f, Lage f; (place) Lage f; (employment) Stelle f.

six [sɪks] num sechs; **—teen** num sechzehn; **—th** a sechte(r,s) n Sechstel nt; **—ty** num sechzig.

size [saɪz] n Größe f; (of project) Umfang m; (of glue) Kleister m; **— up** vt (assess) abschätzen, einschätzen; **—able** a ziemlich groß, ansehnlich.

sizzle ['sɪzl] n Zischen nt; vi zischen; (Cook) brutzeln.

skate [skeɪt] n Schlittschuh m; vi Schlittschuh laufen; **—r** Schlittschuhläufer(in f) m.

skating ['skeɪtɪŋ] n Eislauf m; **to go —** Eislaufen gehen; **— rink** Eisbahn f.

skeleton ['skelɪtn] n Skelett nt; (fig) Gerüst nt; **— key** Dietrich m.

skeptic ['skeptɪk] n (US) = sceptic.

sketch [sketʃ] n Skizze f; (Theat) Sketch m; vt skizzieren, eine Skizze machen von; **—book** Skizzenbuch nt; **—ing** Skizzieren nt; **— pad** Skizzenblock m; **—y** a skizzenhaft.

skewer ['skjuə*] n Fleischspieß m.

ski [ski:] n Ski m, Schi m; vi Ski or Schi laufen; — **boot** Skistiefel m.

skid [skɪd] n (Aut) Schleudern nt; vi rutschen; (Aut) schleudern.

skidmark ['skɪdmɑːk] n Rutschspur f.

skier ['skiːə*] n Skiläufer(in f) m.

skiing ['skiːŋ] n: to go — Skilaufen gehen.

ski-jump ['skiːdʒʌmp] . n Sprungschanze f; vi Ski springen.

ski-lift ['skiːlɪft] n Skilift m.

skilful a, —**ly** ad ['skɪlful, -fəlɪ] geschickt.

skill [skɪl] n Können nt, Geschicklichkeit f; —**ed** a geschickt; worker Fach-, gelernt.

skim [skɪm] vt liquid abschöpfen; milk entrahmen; (read) überfliegen; (glide over) gleiten über (+acc).

skimp [skɪmp] vt (do carelessly) oberflächlich tun; —y a work schlecht gemacht; dress knapp.

skin [skɪn] n Haut f; (peel) Schale f; vt abhäuten; schälen; —**deep** a oberflächlich; — **diving** Schwimmtauchen nt; —**ny** a dünn; —**tight** a dress etc hauteng.

skip [skɪp] n Sprung m, Hopser m; vi hüpfen, springen; (with rope) Seil springen; vt (pass over) übergehen.

ski pants ['skiː'pænts] npl Skihosen pl.

skipper ['skɪpə*] n (Naut) Schiffer m, Kapitän m; (Sport) Mannschaftskapitän m; vt führen.

skipping rope ['skɪpɪŋrəʊp] n Hüpfseil nt.

skirmish ['skɜːmɪʃ] n Scharmützel nt.

skirt [skɜːt] n Rock m; vt herumgehen um; (fig) umgehen.

ski run ['skiːrʌn] n Skiabfahrt f.

skit [skɪt] n Parodie f.

ski tow ['skiːtəʊ] n Schlepplift m.

skittle ['skɪtl] n Kegel m; —**s** (game) Kegeln nt.

skive [skaɪv] vi (Brit col) schwänzen.

skulk [skʌlk] vi sich herumdrücken.

skull [skʌl] n Schädel m; — **and crossbones** Totenkopf m.

skunk [skʌŋk] n Stinktier nt.

sky [skaɪ] n Himmel m —**blue** a himmelblau; n Himmelblau nt; —**light** Dachfenster nt, Oberlicht nt; —**scraper** Wolkenkratzer m.

slab [slæb] n (of stone) Platte f; (of chocolate) Tafel f.

slack [slæk] a (loose) lose, schlaff, locker; business flau; (careless) nachlässig, lasch; vi nachlässig sein; n (in rope etc) durchhängende(s) Teil nt; to take up the — straffziehen; —**s** pl Hose(n pl) f; —**en** (also —en off) vi schlaff/locker werden; (become slower) nachlassen, stocken; vt (loosen) lockern; —**ness** Schlaffheit f.

slag [slæg] n Schlacke f; — **heap** Halde f.

slalom ['slɑːləm] n Slalom m.

slam [slæm] n Knall m; vt door zuschlagen, zuknallen; (throw down) knallen; vi zuschlagen.

slander ['slɑːndə*] n Verleumdung f; vt verleumden; —**ous** a verleumderisch.

slang [slæŋ] n Slang m; Jargon m.

slant [slɑːnt] n (lit) Schräge f; (fig) Tendenz f, Einstellung f; vt schräg legen; vi schräg liegen; —**ing a** schräg.

slap 676 slip

slap [slæp] *n* Schlag *m*, Klaps *m*; *vt* schlagen, einen Klaps geben (+*dat*); *ad* (*directly*) geradewegs; —dash a salopp; —stick (*comedy*) Klamauk *m*; —up a meal erstklassig, prima.

slash [slæʃ] *n* Hieb *m*, Schnittwunde *f*; *vt* (auf)schlitzen; expenditure radikal kürzen.

slate [sleit] *n* (*stone*) Schiefer *m*; (*roofing*) Dachziegel *m*; *vt* (*criticize*) verreißen.

slaughter ['slɔːtə*] *n* (*of animals*) Schlachten *nt*; (*of people*) Gemetzel *nt*; *vt* schlachten; people niedermetzeln.

slave [sleiv] *n* Sklave *m* Sklavin *f*; *vi* schuften, sich schinden; —ry Sklaverei *f*; (*work*) Schinderei *f*.

slavish *a*, —ly *ad* ['sleiviʃ, -li] sklavisch.

slay [slei] *vt irreg* ermorden.

sleazy ['sliːzi] *a place* schmierig.

sledge ['sledʒ] *n* Schlitten *m*; —hammer Schmiedehammer *m*.

sleek [sliːk] *a* glatt, glänzend; shape rassig.

sleep [sliːp] *n* Schlaf *m*; *vi irreg* schlafen; to go to — einschlafen; — in *vi* ausschlafen; (*oversleep*) verschlafen; —er *or* (*person*) Schläfer *m*; (*Rail*) Schlafwagen *m*; (*beam*) Schwelle *f*; —ily *ad* schläfrig; —iness Schläfrigkeit *f*; —ing bag Schlafsack *m*; —ing car Schlafwagen *m*; —ing pill Schlaftablette *f*; —less a night schlaflos; —lessness Schlaflosigkeit *f*; —walker Schlafwandler *m*; —y schläfrig.

sleet [sliːt] *n* Schneeregen *m*.

sleeve [sliːv] *n* Ärmel *m*; (*of record*) Umschlag *m*; —less a garment ärmellos.

sleigh [slei] *n* Pferdeschlitten *m*.

sleight [slait] *n*: — of hand Fingerfertigkeit *f*.

slender ['slendə*] *a* schlank; (*fig*) gering.

slice [slais] *n* Scheibe *f*; *vt* in Scheiben schneiden.

slick [slik] *a* (*clever*) raffiniert, aalglatt; *n* Ölteppich *m*.

slide [slaid] *n* Rutschbahn *f* (*Phot*) Dia(positiv) *nt*; (*for hair*) (Haar)spange *f*; (*fall in prices*) (Preis)rutsch *m*; *irreg* *vt* schieben; *vi* (*slip*) gleiten, rutschen; to let things — die Dinge schleifen lassen; — rule Rechenschieber *m*.

sliding ['slaidiŋ] *a door* Schiebe-.

slight [slait] *a* zierlich; (*trivial*) geringfügig; (*small*) leicht, gering; *n* Kränkung *f*; *vt* (*offend*) kränken; —ly *ad* etwas, ein bißchen.

slim [slim] *a* schlank; book dünn; chance gering; *vi* eine Schlankheitskur machen.

slime [slaim] *n* Schlamm *m*; Schleim *m*.

slimming ['slimiŋ] *n* Schlankheitskur *f*.

slimness ['slimnəs] *n* Schlankheit *f*.

slimy ['slaimi] *a* glitschig; (*dirty*) schlammig; person schmierig.

sling [sliŋ] *n* Schlinge *f*; (*weapon*) Schleuder *f*; *vt irreg* werfen; (*hurl*) schleudern.

slip [slip] *n* (*slipping*) Ausgleiten *nt*, Rutschen *nt*; (*mistake*) Flüchtigkeitsfehler *m*; (*petticoat*) Unterrock *m*; (*of paper*) Zettel *m*; to give sb the — jdn entwischen; — of the tongue Versprecher *m*; *vt* (*put*) stecken, schieben; it — ped my mind das ist mir entfallen, ich habe es vergessen; *vi* (*lose balance*) ausrutschen; (*move*) gleiten, rutschen; (*make mistake*) einen Fehler machen; (decline) nachlassen; **to let things** — die Dinge schleifen lassen; — away in sich wegstehlen; — by vi (time) verstreichen; — **in** vt hineingleiten lassen; vi (errors) sich einschleichen; — **out** vi hinausschlüpfen; —**per** Hausschuh m; —**pery** a glatt; (tricky) aalglatt, gerissen; —**road** Auffahrt f/Ausfahrt f; —**shod** a schwungvoll; —**stream** Windschatten m; —**up** Panne f; —**way** Auslaufbahn f.

slit [slɪt] n Schlitz m; vt irreg aufschlitzen.

slither ['slɪðə*] vi schlittern, (snake) sich schlängeln.

slob [slɒb] n (col) Klotz m.

slog [slɒg] n (great effort) Plackerei f; vi (work hard) schuften.

slogan ['sləʊgən] n Schlagwort nt; (Comm) Werbespruch m.

slop [slɒp] vi überschwappen; vt verschütten.

slope [sləʊp] n Neigung f, Schräge f; (of mountains) (Ab)hang m; vi: — down sich senken; — up ansteigen.

sloping ['sləʊpɪŋ] a schräg; shoulders abfallend; ground abschüssig.

sloppily ['slɒpɪlɪ] ad schlampig.

sloppiness ['slɒpməs] n Matschigkeit f; (of work) Nachlässigkeit f.

sloppy ['slɒpɪ] a (wet) matschig; (careless) schlampig; (silly) rührselig.

slot [slɒt] n Schlitz m; vt: — sth in etw einlegen; — machine Automat m.

slouch [slaʊtʃ] vi krumm dasitzen or dastehen.

slovenly ['slʌvnlɪ] a schlampig; speech salopp.

slow [sləʊ] a langsam; to be — (clock) nachgehen; (stupid) begriffsstutzig sein; — down langsamer werden; — down! mach langsam!; vt aufhalten, langsamer machen, verlangsamen; — up vi sich verlangsamen, sich verzögern; vt aufhalten, langsamer machen; —**ly** ad langsam; allmählich; in — motion in Zeitlupe.

sludge [slʌdʒ] n Schlamm m, Matsch m.

slug [slʌg] n Nacktschnecke f; (col: bullet) Kugel f; —**gish** a träge; (Comm) schleppend; —**gishly** ad träge; —**gishness** Langsamkeit f, Trägheit f.

sluice [slu:s] n Schleuse f.

slum [slʌm] n Elendsviertel nt, Slum m.

slumber ['slʌmbə*] n Schlummer m.

slump [slʌmp] n Rückgang m; vi fallen, stürzen.

slur [slɜ:*] n Undeutlichkeit f; (insult) Verleumdung f; vt (also over) hinweggehen über (+acc); —**red** [slɜ:d] a pronunciation undeutlich.

slush [slʌʃ] n (snow) Schneematsch m; (mud) Schlamm m; —**y** a (lit) matschig; (fig: sentimental) schmalzig.

slut [slʌt] n Schlampe f.

sly a, —**ly** [slaɪ, -lɪ] ad schlau, verschlagen; —**ness** Schlauheit f.

smack [smæk] n Klaps m; vt einen Klaps geben (+dat); to — one's lips schmatzen, sich (dat) die Lippen lecken; vi — of riechen nach.

small [smɔ:l] a klein; — change Kleingeld nt; —**holding** Kleinlandbesitz m; — hours pl frühe Morgenstunden pl; —**ish** a ziemlich klein; —**ness** Kleinheit f; —**pox** Pocken *pl;* —**scale** *a* klein, in kleinem Maßstab; — **talk** Konversation *f*, Geplauder *nt*.

smarmy ['smɑːmɪ] *a* (*col*) schmierig.

smart *a*, —**ly** *ad* [smɑːt, -lɪ] (*fashionable*) elegant, schick; (*neat*) adrett; (*clever*) clever; (*quick*) scharf; *vi* brennen, schmerzen; —**en up** *vi* sich in Schale werfen; *vt* herausputzen; —**ness** Gescheitheit *f*; Eleganz *f*.

smash [smæʃ] *n* Zusammenstoß *m*; (*tennis*) Schmetterball *m*; *vt* (*break*) zerschmettern; (*destroy*) vernichten; *vi* (*break*) zersplittern, zerspringen; —**ing** *a* (*col*) toll, großartig.

smattering ['smætərɪŋ] *n* oberflächliche Kenntnis *f*.

smear [smɪə*] *n* Fleck *m*; *vt* beschmieren.

smell [smel] *n* Geruch *m*; (*sense*) Geruchssinn *m*; *vti irreg* riechen (*of* nach); —**y** *a* übelriechend.

smile [smaɪl] *n* Lächeln *nt*; *vi* lächeln.

smirk [smɜːk] *n* blöde(s) Grinsen *nt*; *vi* blöde grinsen.

smith [smɪθ] *n* Schmied *m*; —**y** ['smɪðɪ] Schmiede *f*.

smock [smɒk] *n* Kittel *m*.

smog [smɒg] *n* Smog *m*.

smoke [sməʊk] *n* Rauch *m*; *vt* rauchen; *food* räuchern; *vi* rauchen; — *r* Raucher *m*; (*Rail*) Raucherabteil *nt*; — **screen** Rauchwand *f*.

smoking ['sməʊkɪŋ] *n* Rauchen *nt*; 'no —' 'Rauchen verboten'.

smoky ['sməʊkɪ] *a* rauchig; *room* verraucht; *taste* geräuchert.

smolder ['sməʊldə*] *vi US* = **smoulder.**

smooth [smuːð] *a* glatt; *movement* geschmeidig; *person* glatt, gewandt; *vt* (*also* — out) glätten, glattstreichen; —**ly** *ad* glatt, eben; (*fig*) reibungslos; —**ness** Glätte *f*.

smother ['smʌðə*] *vt* ersticken.

smoulder ['sməʊldə*] *vi* glimmen, schwelen.

smudge [smʌdʒ] *n* Schmutzfleck *m*; *vt* beschmieren.

smug [smʌg] *a* selbstgefällig.

smuggle ['smʌgl] *vt* schmuggeln; — *r* Schmuggler *m*.

smuggling ['smʌglɪŋ] *n* Schmuggel *m*.

smugly ['smʌglɪ] *ad* selbstgefällig.

smugness ['smʌgnəs] *n* Selbstgefälligkeit *f*.

smutty ['smʌtɪ] *a* (*fig: obscene*) obszön, schmutzig.

snack [snæk] *n* Imbiß *m*; — **bar** Imbißstube *f*.

snag [snæg] *n* Haken *m*; (*in stocking*) gezogene(r) Faden *m*.

snail [sneɪl] *n* Schnecke *f*.

snake [sneɪk] *n* Schlange *f*.

snap [snæp] *n* Schnappen *nt*; (*photograph*) Schnappschuß ·*m*; *a decision* schnell; *vt* (*break*) zerbrechen; (*Phot*) knipsen; to — one's fingers mit den Fingern schnipsen; *vi* (*break*) brechen; (*bite*) schnappen; (*speak*) anfauchen; — **out of it!** raff dich auf!; — **off** *vt* (*break*) abbrechen; — **up** *vt* aufschnappen; —**py** *a* flott; —**shot** Schnappschuß *m*.

snare [snɛə*] *n* Schlinge *f*; *vt* mit einer Schlinge fangen.

snarl [snɑːl] *n* Zähnefletschen *nt*; *vi* (*dog*) knurren; (*engine*) brummen, dröhnen.

snatch [snætʃ] *n* (*grab*) Schnappen

nt; (small amount) Bruchteil m; vt schnappen, packen.

sneak [sni:k] vi schleichen.

sneakers ['sni:kaz] npl (US) Freizeitschuhe pl.

sneer [snɪə*] n Hohnlächeln m; vi höhnisch grinsen; spötteln.

sneeze [sni:z] n Niesen nt; vi niesen.

snide [snaɪd] a (col: sarcastic) schneidend.

sniff [snɪf] n Schnüffeln nt; vi schnieben; (smell) schnüffeln; vt schnuppern.

snigger ['snɪgə*] n Kichern nt; vi hämisch kichern.

snip [snɪp] n Schnippel m, Schnipsel m; vt schnippeln.

sniper ['snaɪpə*] n Heckenschütze m.

snippet ['snɪpɪt] n Schnipsel m; (of conversation) Fetzen m.

snivelling ['snɪvlɪŋ] a weinerlich.

snob [snɔb] n Snob m; —bery Snobismus m; —ish a versnobt; —bishness Versnobtheit f, Snobismus m.

snooker ['snu:kə*] n Snooker nt.

snoop [snu:p] vi: — about herumschnüffeln.

snooty ['snu:tɪ] a (col) hochnäsig; restaurant stinkfein.

snooze [snu:z] n Nickerchen nt; vi ein Nickerchen machen, dösen.

snore [snɔ:*] vi schnarchen.

snoring ['snɔ:rɪŋ] n Schnarchen nt.

snorkel ['snɔ:kl] n Schnorchel m.

snort [snɔ:t] n Schnauben nt; vi schnauben.

snotty ['snɔtɪ] a (col) rotzig.

snout [snaut] n Schnauze f; (of pig) Rüssel m.

snow [snəu] n Schnee m; vi schneien; —ball Schneeball m; —

blind a schneeblind; —bound a eingeschneit; —drift Schneewehe f; —drop Schneeglöckchen nt; —fall Schneefall m; —flake Schneeflocke f; —line Schneegrenze f; —man Schneemann m; —plough, (US) —plow Schneepflug m; —storm Schneesturm m.

snub [snʌb] vt schroff abfertigen; n Verweis m, schroffe Abfertigung f; a —nosed stupsnasig.

snuff [snʌf] n Schnupftabak m; —box Schnupftabakdose f.

snug [snʌg] a gemütlich, behaglich.

so [səu] ad so; cj daher, folglich, also; — as to um zu; or — so etwa; — long! (goodbye) tschüß!; — many so viele; — much soviel; — that damit.

soak [səuk] vt durchnässen; (leave in liquid) einweichen; — in sich einsickern in (+acc); —ing Einweichen nt; —ing wet klatschnaß.

soap [səup] n Seife f; —flakes pl Seifenflocken pl; —powder Waschpulver nt; —y a seifig, Seifen-.

soar [sɔ:*] vi aufsteigen; (prices) in die Höhe schnellen.

sob [sɔb] n Schluchzen nt; vi schluchzen.

sober ['səubə*] a (lit, fig) nüchtern; — up vi nüchtern werden; —ly ad nüchtern.

so-called ['səu'kɔ:ld] a sogenannt.

soccer ['sɔkə*] n Fußball m.

sociability [səufə'bɪlɪtɪ] n Umgänglichkeit f.

sociable ['səufəbl] a umgänglich, gesellig.

social ['səufəl] a sozial; (friendly, living with others) gesellig; —ism Sozialismus m; —ist Sozialist(in f) m; a sozialistisch; —ly ad gesellschaftlich, privat; — science Sozialwissenschaft f; — security Sozial-

versicherung f; **— welfare** Fürsorge f; **— work** Sozialarbeit f; **— worker** Sozialarbeiter(in f) m.

society [sə'saɪətɪ] n Gesellschaft f; (fashionable world) die große Welt.

sociological [səʊsɪə'lɒdʒɪkəl] a soziologisch.

sociologist [səʊsɪ'ɒlədʒɪst] n Soziologe m, Soziologin f.

sociology [səʊsɪ'ɒlədʒɪ] n Soziologie f.

sock [sɒk] n Socke f; vt (col) schlagen.

socket [sɒkɪt] n (Elec) Steckdose f; (of eye) Augenhöhle f; (Tech) Rohransatz m.

sod [sɒd] n Rasenstück nt; (col) Saukerl m.

soda ['səʊdə] n Soda f; **— water** Mineralwasser nt, Soda(wasser) nt.

sodden ['sɒdn] a durchweicht.

sofa ['səʊfə] n Sofa nt.

soft [sɒft] a weich; (not loud) leise, gedämpft; (kind) weichherzig, gutmütig; (weak) weich, nachgiebig; **— drink** alkoholfreie(s) Getränk nt; **—en** ['sɒfn] vt weich machen; blow abschwächen, mildern; vi weich werden; **—hearted** a weichherzig; **—ly** ad sanft; leise; **—ness** Weichheit f, (fig) Sanftheit f.

soggy ['sɒgɪ] a ground sumpfig; bread aufgeweicht.

soil [sɔɪl] n Erde f, Boden m; vt beschmutzen; **—ed** a beschmutzt, schmutzig.

solace ['sɒləs] n Trost m.

solar ['səʊlə*] a Sonnen-; **— system** Sonnensystem nt.

solder ['səʊldə*] vt löten; n Lötmetall nt.

soldier ['səʊldʒə*] n Soldat m.

sole [səʊl] n Sohle f; (fish) Seezunge f; a alleinig; **Allein-**; **—ly** ad ausschließlich, nur.

solemn ['sɒləm] a feierlich; (serious) feierlich, ernst.

solicitor [sə'lɪsɪtə*] n Rechtsanwalt m.

solid ['sɒlɪd] a (hard) fest; (of same material) rein, massiv; (not hollow) massiv, stabil; (without break) voll, ganz; (reliable) solide, zuverlässig; (sensible) solide, gut; (united) eins, einig; meal kräftig; n Feste(s) nt; **—arity** [sɒlɪ'dærɪtɪ] Solidarität f, Zusammenhalt m; **—figure** (Math) Körper m; **—ify** [sə'lɪdɪfaɪ] vi fest werden, sich verdichten, erstarren; vt fest machen, verdichten; **—ity** [sə'lɪdɪtɪ] Festigkeit f; **—ly** ad (fig) behind einmütig; work ununterbrochen.

soliloquy [sə'lɪləkwɪ] n Monolog m.

solitaire [sɒlɪ'tɛə*] n (Cards) Patience f; (gem) Solitär m.

solitary ['sɒlɪtərɪ] a einsam, einzeln.

solitude ['sɒlɪtjuːd] n Einsamkeit f.

solo ['səʊləʊ] n Solo nt; **—ist** Soloist(in f) m.

solstice ['sɒlstɪs] n Sonnenwende f.

soluble ['sɒljʊbl] a substance löslich; problem (auf)lösbar.

solution [sə'luːʃən] n (lit, fig) Lösung f; (of mystery) Erklärung f.

solve [sɒlv] vt (auf)lösen.

solvent ['sɒlvənt] a (Fin) zahlungsfähig.

sombre, (US) somber a, **—ly** ad ['sɒmbə*, -rɪ] düster.

some [sʌm] a people etc einige; water etc etwas; (unspecified) (irgend)ein; (remarkable) toll, enorm; that's **— house** das ist vielleicht ein Haus; pron (amount) etwas; (number) einige; **—body**

pron (irgend) jemand; **he is —body** er ist jemand *or* wer; **—day** *ad* irgendwann; **—how** *ad* (*in a certain way*) irgendwie; (*for a certain reason*) aus irgendeinem Grunde; **—one** *pron* = somebody; **—place** *ad* (*US*) = somewhere.

somersault ['sʌməsɔːlt] *n* Purzelbaum *m*; Salto *m*; *vi* Purzelbäume schlagen; einen Salto machen.

something ['sʌmθɪŋ] *pron* (irgend) etwas.

sometime ['sʌmtaɪm] *ad* (irgend) einmal; **—s** *ad* manchmal, gelegentlich.

somewhat ['sʌmwɒt] *ad* etwas, ein wenig, ein bißchen.

somewhere ['sʌmwɛə*] *ad* irgendwo; (*to a place*) irgendwohin.

son [sʌn] *n* Sohn *m*.

sonata [sə'nɑːtə] *n* Sonate *f*.

song [sɒŋ] *n* Lied *nt*; **—writer** Texter *m*.

sonic ['sɒnɪk] *a* Schall-; **— boom** Überschallknall *m*.

son-in-law ['sʌnɪnlɔː] *n* Schwiegersohn *m*.

sonnet ['sɒnɪt] *n* Sonett *nt*.

sonny ['sʌnɪ] *n* (*col*) Kleine(r) *m*.

soon [suːn] *ad* bald; **too —** zu früh; **as — as possible** so bald wie möglich; **—er** *ad* (*time*) eher, früher; (*for preference*) lieber; **no —er** kaum.

soot [sʊt] *n* Ruß *m*.

soothe [suːð] *vt person* beruhigen; *pain* lindern.

soothing ['suːðɪŋ] *a* (*for person*) beruhigend; (*for pain*) lindernd.

sop [sɒp] *n* (*bribe*) Schmiergeld *nt*.

sophisticated [sə'fɪstɪkeɪtɪd] *a person* kultiviert, weltgewandt; *machinery* differenziert, hochentwickelt; *plan* ausgeklügelt.

sophistication [səfɪstɪ'keɪʃən] *n* Weltgewandtheit *f*, Kultiviertheit *f*; (*Tech*) technische Verfeinerung *f*.

sophomore ['sɒfəmɔː*] *n* (*US*) College-Student *m* im 2. Jahr.

soporific [sɒpə'rɪfɪk] *a* einschläfernd, Schlaf-.

sopping ['sɒpɪŋ] *a* (*very wet*) patschnaß, triefend.

soppy ['sɒpɪ] *a* (*col*) schmalzig.

soprano [sə'prɑːnəʊ] *n* Sopran *m*.

sordid ['sɔːdɪd] *a* (*dirty*) schmutzig; (*mean*) niederträchtig.

sore [sɔː*] *a* schmerzend; *point* wund; **to be —** weh tun; (*angry*) böse sein; *n* Wunde *f*; **—ly** *ad tempted* stark, sehr; **—ness** Schmerzhaftigkeit *f*, Empfindlichkeit *f*.

sorrow ['sɒrəʊ] *n* Kummer *m*, Leid *nt*; **—ful** *a* sorgenvoll; **—fully** *ad* traurig, betrübt, kummervoll.

sorry ['sɒrɪ] *a* traurig, erbärmlich; (**I'm**) **—** es tut mir leid; **I feel — for him** er tut mir leid.

sort [sɔːt] *n* Art *f*, Sorte *f*; *vt* (*also* **— out**) *papers* sortieren, sichten; *problems* in Ordnung bringen.

so-so ['səʊ'səʊ] *ad* so(-so) la-la, mäßig.

soufflé ['suːfleɪ] *n* Auflauf *m*, Soufflé *nt*.

soul [səʊl] *n* Seele *f*; (*music*) Soul *m*; **—destroying** *a* trostlos; **—ful** *a* seelenvoll; **—less** *a* seelenlos, gefühllos.

sound [saʊnd] *a* (*healthy*) gesund; (*safe*) sicher, solide; (*sensible*) vernünftig; *theory* stichhaltig; (*thorough*) tüchtig, gehörig; *n* (*noise*) Geräusch *nt*, Laut *m*; (*Geog*) Meerenge *f*, Sund *m*; *vt* erschallen lassen; *alarm* (Alarm) schlagen; (*Med*) abhorchen; **to — one's horn** hupen; *vi* (make a) *sound*) schallen, tönen; (*seem*) klingen; — out *vt opinion* erforschen; *person* auf den Zahn fühlen (+*dat*); — barrier Schallmauer *f*; —ing (*Naut etc*) Lotung *f*; —ly *a* sleep fest, tief; beat tüchtig; —proof *a room* schalldicht; *vt* schalldicht machen; — track Tonstreifen *m*; Filmmusik *f.*

soup [suːp] *n* Suppe *f*; in the — (*col*) in der Tinte; —spoon Suppenlöffel *m.*

sour ['saʊə*] *a* (*lit, fig*) sauer.

source [sɔːs] *n* (*lit, fig*) Quelle *f.*

sourness ['saʊənəs] *n* Säure *f*; (*fig*) Bitterkeit *f.*

south [saʊθ] *n* Süden *m*; *a* Süd-, südlich; *ad* nach Süden, südwärts; —east Südosten *m*; —erly ['sʌðəlɪ] *a* südlich; —ern ['sʌðən] *a* südlich, Süd-; —ward(s) *ad* südwärts, nach Süden; —west Südwesten *m.*

souvenir [suːvə'nɪə*] *n* Andenken *nt*, Souvenir *nt.*

sovereign ['sɒvrɪn] *n* (*ruler*) Herrscher *m*; *a* (*independent*) souverän; —ty Oberhoheit *f*, Souveränität *f.*

sow [saʊ] *n* Sau *f*; [saʊ] *vt irreg* (*lit, fig*) säen.

soya bean ['sɔɪə'biːn] *n* Sojabohne *f.*

spa [spaː] *n* (*spring*) Mineralquelle *f*; (*place*) Kurort *m*, Bad *nt.*

space [speɪs] *n* (*spring*) Platz *m*, Raum *m*; (*universe*) Weltraum *m*, All *nt*; (*length of time*) Abstand *m*; — out *vt* Platz lassen zwischen; (*typing*) gesperrt schreiben; —craft Raumschiff *nt*; —man Raumfahrer *m.*

spacious ['speɪʃəs] *a* geräumig, weit.

spade [speɪd] *n* Spaten *m*; —s

(*Cards*) Pik *nt*, Schippe *f*; —work (*fig*) Vorarbeit *f.*

spaghetti [spə'getɪ] *n* Spaghetti *pl.*

span [spæn] *n* Spanne *f*; Spannweite *f*; *vt* überspannen.

spaniel ['spænjəl] *n* Spaniel *m.*

spank [spæŋk] *vt* verhauen, versohlen.

spanner ['spænə*] *n* Schraubenschlüssel *m.*

spar [spaː*] *n* (*Naut*) Sparren *m*; *vi* (*boxing*) einen Sparring machen.

spare [spɛə*] *a* Ersatz-; *n* — part; *vt lives, feelings* verschonen; *trouble* ersparen; 4 to — 4 übrig; — part Ersatzteil *nt*; — time Freizeit *f.*

spark [spaːk] *n* Funken *m*; —(ing) plug Zündkerze *f.*

sparkle ['spaːkl] *n* Funkeln *nt*, Glitzern *nt*; (*gaiety*) Lebhaftigkeit *f*, Schwung *m*; *vi* funkeln, glitzern.

sparkling ['spaːklɪŋ] *a* funkelnd, sprühend; *wine* Schaum-; *conversation* spritzig, geistreich.

sparrow ['spærəʊ] *n* Spatz *m.*

sparse *a*, —ly *ad* [spaːs, -lɪ] spärlich, dünn.

spasm ['spæzəm] *n* (*Med*) Krampf *m*; (*fig*) Anfall *m*; —odic [spæz'mɒdɪk] *a* krampfartig, spasmodisch; (*fig*) sprunghaft.

spastic ['spæstɪk] *a* spastisch.

spate [speɪt] *n* (*fig*) Flut *f*, Schwall *m*; in — *river* angeschwollen.

spatter ['spætə*] *n* Spritzer *m*; *vt* bespritzen, verspritzen; *vi* spritzen.

spatula ['spætjʊlə] *n* Spatel *m*; (*for building*) Spachtel *f.*

spawn [spɔːn] *vi* laichen.

speak [spiːk] *irreg vt* sprechen, reden; *truth* sagen; *language* sprechen; *vi* sprechen (to *mit* or *zu*); — for *vt* sprechen or eintreten für; — up *vi* lauter sprechen; —er Sprecher *m*, Redner *m*; loud—Lautsprecher *m*; not to be on —ing terms nicht miteinander sprechen.

spear [spɪə*] *n* Speer *m*, Lanze *f*, Spieß *m*; *vt* aufspießen, durchbohren.

spec [spek] *n* (col) on — auf gut Glück.

special ['speʃəl] *a* besondere(r,s); speziell; *n* (Rail) Sonderzug *m*; —ist Spezialist *m* (Tech) Fachmann *m*; (Med) Facharzt *m*; —ity [speʃɪ'ælɪtɪ] Spezialität *f*; (study) Spezialgebiet *nt*; —ize *vi* sich spezialisieren (in auf +acc); —ly *ad* besonders; (explicitly) extra, ausdrücklich.

species ['spi:ʃi:z] *n* Art *f*.

specific [spə'sɪfɪk] *a* spezifisch, eigentümlich, besondere(r,s); —ally *ad* genau, spezifisch; —ations *pl* [spesɪfɪ'keɪʃənz] genaue Angaben *pl*; (Tech) technische Daten *pl*.

specify ['spesɪfaɪ] *vt* genau angeben.

specimen ['spesmɪn] *n* Probe *f*, Muster *nt*.

speck [spek] *n* Fleckchen *nt*; —led *a* gesprenkelt.

specs [speks] *npl* (col) Brille *f*.

spectacle ['spektəkl] *n* Schauspiel *nt*; —s *pl* Brille *f*.

spectacular [spek'tækjulə*] *a* aufsehenerregend, spektakulär.

spectator [spek'teɪtə*] *n* Zuschauer *m*.

spectre, (US) **specter** ['spektə*] *n* Geist *m*, Gespenst *nt*.

spectrum ['spektrəm] *n* Spektrum *nt*.

speculate ['spekjuleɪt] *vi* vermuten, spekulieren (also Fin).

speculation [spekjʊ'leɪʃən] *n* Vermutung *f*, Spekulation *f* (also Fin).

speculative ['spekjulətɪv] *a* spekulativ.

speech [spi:tʃ] *n* Sprache *f*; (address) Rede *f*, Ansprache *f*; (manner of speaking) Sprechweise *f*; — day (Sch) (Jahres)schlußfeier *f*; —less *a* sprachlos; — therapy Sprachheilpflege *f*.

speed [spi:d] *n* Geschwindigkeit *f*; (gear) Gang *m*; *vi* irreg rasen; (Jur) (zu) schnell fahren; — up *vt* beschleunigen; *vi* schneller werden/ fahren; —boat Schnellboot *nt*; —ily *ad* schnell, schleunigst; —ing *vi* zu schnelles Fahren; — limit Geschwindigkeitsbegrenzung *f*; —ometer [spɪ'dɒmɪtə*] Tachometer *m*; —way (bike racing) Motorradrennstrecke *f*; —y *a* schnell, zügig.

spell [spel] *n* (magic) Bann *m*, Zauber *m*; (period of time) Zeit *f*, Zeitlang *f*, Weile *f*; — sunny —s *pl* Aufheiterungen *pl*; rainy —s *pl* vereinzelte Schauer *pl*; *vt* irreg buchstabieren; (imply) bedeuten; how do you — ...? wie schreibt man ...?; —bound *a* (wie) gebannt; —ing Buchstabieren *nt*; English —ing die englische Rechtschreibung.

spend [spend] *vt* irreg money ausgeben; time verbringen; —ing money Taschengeld *nt*.

spent [spent] *a* patience erschöpft.

sperm [spɜ:m] *n* (Biol) Samenflüssigkeit *f*.

spew [spju:] *vt* (er)brechen.

sphere [sfɪə*] *n* (globe) Kugel *f*; (fig) Sphäre *f*, Gebiet *nt*.

spherical ['sferɪkəl] *a* kugelförmig.

sphinx [sfɪŋks] n Sphinx f.

spice [spaɪs] n Gewürz nt; vt würzen.

spiciness ['spaɪsɪnəs] n Würze f.

spick-and-span ['spɪkən'spæn] a blitzblank.

spicy ['spaɪsɪ] a würzig, pikant (also fig).

spider ['spaɪdə*] n Spinne f; —y a writing krakelig.

spike [spaɪk] n Dorn m, Spitze f; —s pl Spikes pl.

spill [spɪl] irreg vt verschütten; vi sich ergießen.

spin [spɪn] n Umdrehung f; (trip in car) Spazierfahrt f; (Aviat) (Ab)trudeln nt; (on ball) Drall m; irreg vt thread spinnen; (like top) schnell drehen, (herum)wirbeln; vi sich drehen; — out vt in die Länge ziehen; story ausmalen.

spinach ['spɪnɪtʃ] n Spinat m.

spinal ['spaɪnl] a spinal, Rückgrat-, Rückenmark-; — cord Rückenmark nt.

spindly ['spɪndlɪ] a spindeldürr.

spin-drier ['spɪn'draɪə*] n Wäscheschleuder f.

spin-dry [spɪn'draɪ] vt schleudern.

spine [spaɪn] n Rückgrat nt; (thorn) Stachel m; —less a (lit, fig) rückgratlos.

spinet [spɪ'net] n Spinett nt.

spinner ['spɪnə*] n (of thread) Spinner m.

spinning ['spɪnɪŋ] n (of thread) (Faden)spinnen nt; — wheel Spinnrad nt.

spinster ['spɪnstə*] n unverheiratete Frau f; (pej) alte Jungfer f.

spiral ['spaɪərəl] n Spirale f; a gewunden, spiralförmig, Spiral-; vi

sich ringeln; — staircase Wendeltreppe f.

spire [spaɪə*] n Turm m.

spirit ['spɪrɪt] n Geist m; (humour, mood) Stimmung f; (courage) Mut m; (verve) Elan m; (alcohol) Alkohol m; —s pl Spirituosen pl; in good —s gut aufgelegt; —ed a beherzt; — level Wasserwaage f; —ual a geistig, seelisch; (Rel) geistlich; n Spiritual nt; —ualism Spiritismus m.

spit [spɪt] n (for roasting) (Brat)spieß m; (saliva) Spucke f; vi irreg spucken; (rain) sprühen; (make a sound) zischen; (cat) fauchen.

spite [spaɪt] n Gehässigkeit f; vt ärgern, kränken; in — of trotz (+gen or dat); —ful a gehässig.

splash [splæʃ] n Spritzer m; (of colour) (Farb)fleck m; vt bespritzen; vi spritzen; —down Wasserlandung f.

spleen [spli:n] n (Anat) Milz f.

splendid a, —ly ad ['splendɪd, -lɪ] glänzend, großartig.

splendour, (US) **splendor** ['splendə*] n Pracht f.

splice [splaɪs] vt spleißen.

splint [splɪnt] n Schiene f.

splinter ['splɪntə*] n Splitter m; vi (zer)splittern.

split [splɪt] n Spalte f; (fig) Spaltung f; (division) Trennung f; irreg vt spalten; vi (divide) reißen; sich spalten; (col: depart) abhauen; — up vi sich trennen; vt aufteilen, teilen; —ting a headache rasend, wahnsinnig.

splutter ['splʌtə*] vi spritzen; (person, engine) stottern.

spoil [spɔɪl] irreg vt (ruin) verderben; child verwöhnen, verziehen; vi (food) verderben; —s pl Beute f; —sport Spielverderber m.

spoke [spəʊk] *n* Speiche *f*; **—sman** Sprecher *m*, Vertreter *m*.

sponge [spʌndʒ] *n* Schwamm *m*; *vt* mit dem Schwamm abwaschen; *vi* auf Kosten leben (*on gen*); **—bag** Kulturbeutel *m*; **— cake** Rührkuchen *m*; **—r** (*col*) Schmarotzer *m*.

spongy ['spʌndʒɪ] *a* schwammig.

sponsor ['spɒnsə*] *n* Bürge *m*; (*in advertising*) Sponsor *m*; *vt* bürgen für; fördern; **—ship** Bürgschaft *f*; (*public*) Schirmherrschaft *f*.

spontaneity [spɒntə'neɪtɪ] *n* Spontanität *f*.

spontaneous *a*, **—ly** *ad* [spɒn'teɪnɪəs, -lɪ] spontan.

spooky ['spu:kɪ] *a* (*col*) gespenstisch.

spool [spu:l] *n* Spule *f*, Rolle *f*.

spoon [spu:n] *n* Löffel *m*; **—feed** *vt irreg* (*lit*) mit dem Löffel füttern; (*fig*) hochpäppeln; **—ful** Löffel(voll) *m*.

sporadic [spə'rædɪk] *a* vereinzelt, sporadisch.

sport [spɔ:t] *n* Sport *m*; (*fun*) Spaß *m*; (*person*) feine(r) Kerl *m*; **—ing** *a* (*fair*) sportlich, fair; **—s car** Sportwagen *m*; **—(s) coat, —(s) jacket** Sportjackett *nt*; **—sman** Sportler *m*; (*fig*) anständige(r) Kerl *m*; **—smanship** Sportlichkeit *f*; (*fig*) Anständigkeit *f*; **—s page** Sportseite *f*; **—swear** Sportkleidung *f*; **—swoman** Sportlerin *f*; **—y** *a* sportlich.

spot [spɒt] *n* Punkt *m*; (*dirty*) Fleck(en) *m*; (*place*) Stelle *f*, Platz *m*; (*Med*) Pickel *m*, Pustel *f*; (*small amount*) Schluck *m*, Tropfen *m*; *vt* erspähen; *mistake* bemerken; **—check** Stichprobe *f*; **—less** *a*, **—ly** *ad* fleckenlos; **—light** Scheinwerferlicht *nt*; (*lamp*) Scheinwerfer *m*;

—ted *a* gefleckt; *dress* gepunktet; **—ty** *a face* pickelig.

spouse [spauz] *n* Gatte *m*/Gattin *f*.

spout [spaut] *n* (*of pot*) Tülle *f*; (*jet*) Wasserstrahl *m*; *vi* speien, spritzen.

sprain [spreɪn] *n* Verrenkung *f*; *vt* verrenken.

sprawl [sprɔ:l] *n* (*of city*) Ausbreitung *f*; *vi* sich strecken.

spray [spreɪ] *n* Spray *m*; (*off sea*) Gischt *f*; (*instrument*) Zerstäuber *m*; Spraydose *f*; (*of flowers*) Zweig *m*; *vt* besprühen, sprayen.

spread [spred] *n* (*extent*) Verbreitung *f*; (*of wings*) Spannweite *f*; (*col: meal*) Schmaus *m*; (*for bread*) Aufstrich *m*; *vt irreg* ausbreiten; (*scatter*) verbreiten; *butter* streichen.

spree [spri:] *n* lustige(r) Abend *m*; (*shopping*) Einkaufsbummel *m*; **to go out on a —** einen draufmachen.

sprig [sprɪg] *n* kleine(r) Zweig *m*.

sprightly ['spraɪtlɪ] *a* munter, lebhaft.

spring [sprɪŋ] *n* (*leap*) Sprung *m*; (*metal*) Feder *f*; (*season*) Frühling *m*; (*water*) Quelle *f*; *vi irreg* (*leap*) springen; **— up** *vi* (*problem*) entstehen, auftauchen; **—board** Sprungbrett *nt*; **—clean** *vt* Frühjahrsputz machen in (+*dat*); **—cleaning** Frühjahrsputz *m*; **—iness** Elastizität *f*; **—time** Frühling *m*; **—y** *a* federnd, elastisch.

sprinkle ['sprɪŋkl] *n* Prise *f*; *vt salt* streuen; *liquid* sprenkeln.

sprinkling ['sprɪŋklɪŋ] *n* Spur *f*, ein bißchen.

sprint [sprɪnt] *n* Kurzstreckenlauf *m*; Sprint *m*; *vi* sprinten; **—er** Sprinter *m*, Kurzstreckenläufer *m*.

sprite [spraɪt] n Elfe f; Kobold m.

sprout [spraʊt] vi sprießen; n see Brussels —.

spruce [spru:s] n Fichte f; a schmuck, adrett.

spry [spraɪ] a flink, rege.

spud [spʌd] n (col) Kartoffel f.

spur [spɜ:ʳ] n Sporn m; (fig) Ansporn m; vt (also — on) (fig) anspornen; **on the — of the moment** spontan.

spurious ['spjʊərɪəs] a falsch, unecht, Pseudo-.

spurn [spɜ:n] vt verschmähen.

spurt [spɜ:t] n (jet) Strahl m; (acceleration) Spurt m; vt spritzen; vi (jet) steigen; (liquid) schießen; (run) spurten.

spy [spaɪ] n Spion m; vi spionieren; vt erspähen; **to — on sb** jdm nachspionieren; **—ing** Spionage f.

squabble ['skwɒbl] n Zank m; vi sich zanken.

squabbling ['skwɒblɪŋ] n Zankerei f.

squad [skwɒd] n (Mil) Abteilung f; (police) Kommando nt.

squadron ['skwɒdrən] n (cavalry) Schwadron f; (Naut) Geschwader nt; (air force) Staffel f.

squalid ['skwɒlɪd] a schmutzig, verkommen.

squall [skwɔ:l] n Bö f, Windstoß m; **—y** a. weather stürmisch; wind böig.

squalor ['skwɒlə*] n Verwahrlosung f, Schmutz m.

squander ['skwɒndə*] vt verschwenden.

square [skwɛə*] n (Math) Quadrat nt; (open space) Platz m; (instrument) Winkel m; (col: person) Spießer m; a viereckig, quad-

ratisch; (fair) ehrlich, reell; (meal) reichlich; (col) ideas, tastes spießig; ad (exactly) direkt, gerade; vt (arrange) ausmachen, aushandeln; (Math) ins Quadrat erheben; (bribe) schmieren; vi (agree) . übereinstimmen; **all — quitt; 2 metres — 2 Meter im Quadrat; 2 — metres 2 Quadratmeter; —ly** ad fest, gerade.

squash [skwɒʃ] n (drink) Saft m; vt zerquetschen.

squat [skwɒt] a untersetzt, gedrungen; vi hocken; **—ter** Squatter m, Siedler m ohne Rechtstitel; Hausbesetzer m.

squaw [skwɔ:] n Squaw f.

squawk [skwɔ:k] n Kreischen nt; vi kreischen.

squeak [skwi:k] n Gequiek(s)e nt; vi quiek(s)en; (spring, door etc) quietschen; **—y** quiek(s)end; quietschend.

squeal [skwi:l] n schrille(r) Schrei m; (of brakes etc) Quietschen nt; vi schrill schreien.

squeamish ['skwi:mɪʃ] a empfindlich; **that made me —** davon wurde mir übel; **—ness** Überempfindlichkeit f.

squeeze [skwi:z] n (lit) Pressen nt; (Pol) Geldknappheit f, wirtschaftliche(r) Engpaß m; vt pressen, drücken; orange auspressen; **— out** vt ausquetschen.

squid [skwɪd] n Tintenfisch m.

squint [skwɪnt] n Schielen nt; vi schielen.

squire [skwaɪə*] n Gutsherr m.

squirm [skwɜ:m] vi sich winden.

squirrel ['skwɪrəl] n Eichhörnchen nt.

squirt [skwɜ:t] n Spritzer m, Strahl m; vti spritzen.

stab [stæb] *n* (*blow*) Stoß *m*, Stich *m*; (*col: try*) Versuch *m*; *vt* erstechen; **—bing** Messerstecherei *f.*

stability [stə'bɪltɪ] *n* Festigkeit *f*, Stabilität *f.*

stabilization [steɪbəlaɪˈzeɪʃən] *n* Festigung *f*, Stabilisierung *f.*

stabilize ['steɪbəlaɪz] *vt* festigen, stabilisieren; **—r** Stabilisator *m.*

stable ['steɪbl] *n* Stall *m*; *vt im* Stall unterbringen; *a* fest, stabil; *person* gefestigt.

staccato [stə'kɑːtəʊ] *a* stakkato.

stack [stæk] *n* Stoß *m*, Stapel *m*; *vt* (*auf*)stapeln.

stadium ['steɪdɪəm] *n* Stadion *nt.*

staff [stɑːf] *n* (*stick, Mil*) Stab *m*; (*personnel*) Personal *nt*; (*Sch*) Lehrkräfte *pl*; *vt* (*with people*) besetzen.

stag [stæg] *n* Hirsch *m.*

stage [steɪdʒ] *n* Bühne *f*; (*of journey*) Etappe *f*; (*degree*) Stufe *f*; (*point*) Stadium *nt*; *vt* (*put on*) aufführen; *play* inszenieren; *demonstration* veranstalten; in **—s** etappenweise; **—coach** Postkutsche *f*; **— door** Bühneneingang *m*; **— manager** Spielleiter *m*, Intendant *m.*

stagger ['stægə*] *vi* wanken, taumeln; *vt* (*amaze*) verblüffen; *hours* staffeln; **—ing** *a* unglaublich.

stagnant ['stægnənt] *a* stagnierend; *water* stehend.

stagnate [stæg'neɪt] *vi* stagnieren.

stagnation [stæg'neɪʃən] *n* Stillstand *m*, Stagnation *f.*

staid [steɪd] *a* gesetzt.

stain [steɪn] *n* Fleck *m*; (*colouring for wood*) Beize *f*; *vt* beflecken, Flecken machen auf (*+acc*); beizen; **—ed glass window** buntes

Glasfenster *nt*; **—less** *a steel* rostfrei, nichtrostend; **—remover** Fleckentferner *m.*

stair [steə*] *n* (*Treppen*)stufe *f*; **—case** Treppenhaus *nt*, Treppe *f*; **—s** *pl* Treppe *f*; **—way** Treppenaufgang *m.*

stake [steɪk] *n* (*post*) Pfahl *m*, Pfosten *m*; (*money*) Einsatz *m*; *vt* (*bet money*) setzen; **to be at —** auf dem Spiel stehen.

stalactite ['stæləktaɪt] *n* Stalaktit *m.*

stalagmite ['stæləgmaɪt] *n* Stalagmit *m.*

stale [steɪl] *a* alt; *beer* schal; *bread* altbacken; **—mate** (*chess*) Patt *nt*; (*fig*) Stillstand *m.*

stalk [stɔːk] *n* Stengel *m*, Stiel *m*; *vt game* sich anpirschen an (*+acc*), jagen; *vi* (*walk*) stolzieren.

stall [stɔːl] *n* (*in stable*) Stand *m*, Box *f*; (*in market*) (Verkaufs)stand *m*; *vt* (*Aut*) (den Motor) abwürgen; *vi* (*Aut*) stehenbleiben; (*avoid*) Ausflüchte machen, ausweichen; **—s** *pl* (*Theat*) Parkett *nt.*

stallion ['stælɪən] *n* Zuchthengst *m.*

stalwart ['stɔːlwət] *a* standhaft; *n* treue(r) Anhänger *m.*

stamina ['stæmɪnə] *n* Durchhaltevermögen *nt*, Zähigkeit *f.*

stammer ['stæmə*] *n* Stottern *nt*; *vti* stottern, stammeln.

stamp [stæmp] *n* Briefmarke *f*; (*with foot*) Stampfen *nt*; (*for document*) Stempel *m*; *vi* stampfen; *vt* (*mark*) stempeln; *mail* frankieren; *foot* stampfen mit; **— album** Briefmarkenalbum *nt*; **— collecting** Briefmarkensammeln *nt.*

stampede [stæm'piːd] *n* panische Flucht *f.*

stance [stæns] *n* (*posture*) Haltung

f, Stellung f; (opinion) Einstellung f.

stand [stænd] n Standort m, Platz m; (for objects) Gestell nt; (seats) Tribüne f; **to make a —** Widerstand leisten; irreg vi stehen; (rise) aufstehen; (decision) feststehen; **to — still** still stehen; vt setzen, stellen; (endure) aushalten; person ausstehen, leiden können; nonsense dulden; **it —s to reason** es ist einleuchtend; **— by** vi (be ready) bereitstehen; vt opinion treu bleiben (+dat); **— for** vt (signify) stehen für; (permit, tolerate) hinnehmen; **— in for** vt einspringen für; **— out** vi (be prominent) hervorstechen; **— up** vi (rise) aufstehen; **— up for** vt sich einsetzen für.

standard ['stændəd] n (measure) Standard m, Norm f; (flag) Standarte f, Fahne f; a size etc Normal-, Durchschnitts-; **—ization** Vereinheitlichung f; **—ize** vt vereinheitlichen, normen; **— lamp** Stehlampe f; **— of living** Lebensstandard m; **— time** Ortszeit f.

stand-by ['stændbaɪ] n Reserve f; **— flight** Standby-Flug m.

stand-in ['stændɪn] n Ersatz(mann) m, Hilfskraft f.

standing ['stændɪŋ] a (erect) stehend; (permanent) ständig, dauernd; **invitation** offen; n (duration) Dauer f; (reputation) Ansehen nt; **— jump** Sprung m aus dem Stand; **— order** (at bank) Dauerauftrag m; **— orders** pl (Mil) Vorschrift f; **— room only** nur Stehplatz.

stand-offish ['stænd'ɔfɪʃ] a zurückhaltend, sehr reserviert.

standpoint ['stændpɔɪnt] n Standpunkt m.

standstill ['stændstɪl] n: **to be at a —** stillstehen; **to come to a —** zum Stillstand kommen.

stanza ['stænzə] n (verse) Strophe f; (poem) Stanze f.

staple ['steɪpl] n (clip) Krampe f; (in paper) Heftklammer f; (article) Haupterzeugnis nt; a Grund-, Haupt-; vt (fest)klammern; **—r** Heftmaschine f.

star [staː*] n Stern m; (person) Star m; vi die Hauptrolle spielen; vt actor in der Hauptrolle zeigen.

starboard ['staːbəd] n Steuerbord nt; a Steuerbord-.

starch [staːtʃ] n Stärke f; vt stärken; **—y** a stärkehaltig; (formal) steif.

stardom ['staːdəm] n Berühmtheit f.

stare [stɛə*] n starre(r) Blick m; vi starren (at auf +acc); **— at** vt anstarren.

starfish ['staːfɪʃ] n Seestern m.

staring ['stɛərɪŋ] a eyes starrend.

stark [staːk] a öde; ad: **— naked** splitternackt.

starless ['staːləs] a sternlos.

starlight ['staːlaɪt] n Sternenlicht nt.

starling ['staːlɪŋ] n Star m.

starlit ['staːlɪt] a sternklar.

starring ['staːrɪŋ] a mit ... in der Hauptrolle.

star-studded ['staːstʌdɪd] a mit Spitzenstars.

starry ['staːrɪ] a Sternen-; **—-eyed** a (innocent) blauäugig.

start [staːt] n Beginn m, Anfang m, Start m; (Sport) Start m; (lead) Vorsprung m; **to give a —** zusammenfahren; **to give sb a —** jdn zusammenfahren lassen; vt in Gang setzen, anfangen; car anlassen; vi anfangen; (car) anspringen; (on journey) aufbrechen; (Sport) starten; — over vi (US) wieder anfangen; — up vi anfangen; (startled) auffahren; vt beginnen; car anlassen; engine starten; —er (Aut) Anlasser m; (for race) Starter m; —ing handle Anlaßkurbel f; —ing point Ausgangspunkt m.

startle ['stɑ:tl] vt erschrecken.

startling ['stɑ:tlɪŋ] a erschreckend.

starvation [stɑ:'veɪʃən] n Verhungern nt; to die of — verhungern.

starve [stɑ:v] vi verhungern; vt verhungern lassen; to be —d of affection unter Mangel an Liebe leiden; — out vt aushungern.

starving ['stɑ:vɪŋ] a (ver)hungernd.

state [steɪt] n (condition) Zustand m; (Pol) Staat m; (col: anxiety) (schreckliche) Verfassung f; vt erklären; facts angeben; — control staatliche Kontrolle f; —d a festgesetzt; —liness Pracht f, Würde f; —ly a würdevoll, erhaben; —ment Aussage f; (Pol) Erklärung f; — secret Staatsgeheimnis nt; —sman Staatsmann m.

static [stætk] n Statik f; a statisch.

station ['steɪʃən] n (Rail etc) Bahnhof m; (police etc) Station f, Wache f; (in society) gesellschaftliche Stellung f; vt aufstellen; to be —ed stationiert sein.

stationary ['steɪʃənərɪ] a stillstehend; car parkend.

stationer ['steɪʃənə*] n Schreibwarenhändler m; —'s (shop) Schreibwarengeschäft nt; —y Schreibwaren pl.

station master ['steɪʃənmɑ:stə*] n Bahnhofsvorsteher m.

station wagon ['steɪʃənwægən] n Kombiwagen m.

statistic [stə'tɪstɪk] n Statistik f; —al a statistisch; —s pl Statistik f.

statue ['stætju:] n Statue f.

statuesque [stætju'esk] a statuenhaft.

statuette ['stætʃo*] n Wuchs m, Statur f; (fig) Größe f.

status ['steɪtəs] n Stellung f, Status m; the — quo der Status quo; — symbol Statussymbol nt.

statute ['stætju:t] n Gesetz nt.

statutory ['stætjutərɪ] a gesetzlich.

staunch a, —ly ad [stɔ:ntʃ, -lɪ] treu, zuverlässig; Catholic standhaft, erz-.

stave [steɪv]: — off vt attack abwehren; threat abwenden.

stay [steɪ] n Aufenthalt m; (support) Stütze f; (for tent) Schnur f; vi bleiben; (reside) wohnen; to — put an Ort und Stelle bleiben; to — with friends bei Freunden untergebracht sein; to — the night übernachten; — behind vi zurückbleiben; — in vi (at home) zu Hause bleiben; — on vi (continue) länger bleiben; — up vi (at night) aufbleiben.

steadfast ['stedfəst] a standhaft, treu.

steadily ['stedɪlɪ] ad stetig, regelmäßig.

steadiness ['stedɪnəs] n Festigkeit f; (fig) Beständigkeit f.

steady ['stedɪ] a (firm) fest, stabil; (regular) gleichmäßig; (reliable) zuverlässig, beständig; hand ruhig; job, boyfriend fest; vt festigen; to — o.s. sich stützen.

steak [steɪk] n Steak nt; (fish) Filet nt.

steal [sti:l] irreg vti stehlen; vi sich stehlen; —th ['stelθ] Heimlichkeit f; —thy ['steθi] a verstohlen, heimlich.

steam [sti:m] n Dampf m; vt (Cook) im Dampfbad erhitzen; vi dampfen; (ship) dampfen, fahren; — **engine** Dampfmaschine f; **-er** Dampfer m; **-roller** Dampfwalze f; **-y** a dampfig.

steel [sti:l] n Stahl m; a Stahl-; (fig) stählern; **-works** Stahlwerke pl.

steep [sti:p] a steil; price gepfeffert; vt einweichen.

steeple ['sti:pl] n Kirchturm m; **-chase** Hindernisrennen nt; **-jack** Turmarbeiter m.

steeply ['sti:plɪ] ad steil.

steepness ['sti:pnəs] n Steilheit f.

steer [stɪə*] n Mastochse m; vti steuern; car etc lenken; **-ing** (Aut) Steuerung f; **-ing column** Lenksäule f; **-ing wheel** Steuer- or Lenkrad nt.

stellar ['stelə*] a Stern(en)-.

stem [stem] n (Biol) Stengel m, Stiel m; (of glass) Stiel m; vt aufhalten; — from vi abstammen von.

stench [stentʃ] n Gestank m.

stencil ['stensl] n Schablone f; (paper) Matrize f; vt (auf)drucken.

stenographer [ste'nɒgrəfə*] n Stenograph(in f) m.

step [step] n Schritt m; (stair) Stufe f; **to take** — s Schritte unternehmen; vi treten, schreiten; **-s** = **-ladder**; — **down** vi (fig) abtreten; — **up** vt steigern; **-brother** Stiefbruder m; **-child** Stiefkind nt; **-father** Stiefvater m; **-ladder** Trittleiter f; **-mother** Stiefmutter f.

steppe [step] n Steppe f.

stepping stone ['stepɪŋstəʊn] Stein m; (fig) Sprungbrett nt.·

stereo ['sterɪəʊ] n Stereoanlage f; **-phonic a** stereophonisch; **-type** n Prototyp m; vt stereotypieren; (fig) stereotyp machen.

sterile ['sterail] a steril, keimfrei; person unfruchtbar; (after operation) steril.

sterility [ste'rɪlɪtɪ] n Unfruchtbarkeit f, Sterilität f.

sterilization [sterɪlaɪ'zeɪʃən] n Sterilisation f.

sterilize ['sterɪlaɪz] vt (make unproductive) unfruchtbar machen; (make germfree) sterilisieren, keimfrei machen.

sterling ['stɜ:lɪŋ] a (Fin) Sterling-; silver von Standardwert; character bewährt, gediegen; £ — Pfund Sterling; — **area** Sterlingblock m.

stern a, **-ly** ad [stɜ:n, -lɪ] streng; n Heck nt, Achterschiff nt; **-ness** Strenge f.

stethoscope ['steθəskəʊp] n Stethoskop nt, Hörrohr nt.

stevedore ['sti:vədɔ:*] n Schauermann m.

stew [stju:] n Eintopf m; vti schmoren.

steward ['stju:əd] n Steward m; (in club) Kellner m; (organizer) Verwalter m; **-ess** Stewardess f.

stick [stɪk] n Stock m, Stecken m; (of chalk etc) Stück nt; irreg vt (stab) stechen; (fix) stecken; (put) stellen; (gum) (an)kleben; (col: tolerate) vertragen; vi (stop) steckenbleiben; (get stuck) klemmen; (hold fast) kleben, haften; — **out** vi (project) hervorstehen aus; — **up** vi (project) in die Höhe stehen; — **up for** vt (defend) eintreten für; **-er** Klebezettel n, Aufkleber m.

stickleback ['stɪklbæk] n Stichling m.

stickler ['stɪklə*] n Pedant m (for in +acc).

stick-up ['stɪkʌp] n (col) (Raub)überfall m.

sticky ['stɪkɪ] a klebrig; *atmosphere* stickig.

stiff [stɪf] a steif; (*difficult*) schwierig, hart; *paste* dick, zäh; *drink* stark; vt versteifen, (ver)stärken; vi sich versteifen; —**ness** Steifheit f.

stifle ['staɪfl] vt *yawn etc* unterdrücken.

stifling ['staɪflɪŋ] a *atmosphere* drückend.

stigma ['stɪgmə] n (*disgrace*) Stigma n.

stile [staɪl] n Steige f.

still [stɪl] a still; ad (immer) noch; (*anyhow*) immerhin; —**born** a totgeboren; — **life** Stilleben nt; —**ness** Stille f.

stilt [stɪlt] n Stelze f.

stilted ['stɪltɪd] a gestelzt.

stimulant ['stɪmjʊlənt] n Anregungsmittel nt, Stimulans nt.

stimulate ['stɪmjʊleɪt] vt anregen, stimulieren.

stimulating ['stɪmjʊleɪtɪŋ] a anregend, stimulierend.

stimulation [stɪmjʊ'leɪʃən] n Anregung f, Stimulation f.

stimulus ['stɪmjʊləs] n Anregung f, Reiz m.

sting [stɪŋ] n Stich m; (*organ*) Stachel m; vti irreg stechen; (*on skin*) brennen.

stingily ['stɪndʒɪlɪ] ad knickerig, geizig.

stinginess ['stɪndʒɪnəs] n Geiz m.

stinging nettle ['stɪŋɪŋnetl] n Brennessel f.

stingy ['stɪndʒɪ] a geizig, knauserig.

stink [stɪŋk] n Gestank m; vi irreg stinken; —**er** (col) (person) gemeine(r) Hund m; (*problem*) böse Sache f; —**ing** a (fig) widerlich; —**ing** rich steinreich.

stint [stɪnt] n Pensum nt; (*period*) Betätigung f; vt einschränken, knapphalten.

stipend ['staɪpend] n Gehalt nt.

stipulate ['stɪpjʊleɪt] vt festsetzen.

stipulation [stɪpjʊ'leɪʃən] n Bedingung f.

stir [stɜ:*] n Bewegung f; (*sensation*) Aufsehen nt; vt (um)rühren; vi sich rühren; — **up** vt mob aufhetzen; fire entfachen; *mixture* umrühren; *dust* aufwirbeln; **to — things up** Ärger machen; —**ring** a ergreifend.

stirrup ['stɪrəp] n Steigbügel m.

stitch [stɪtʃ] n (*with needle*) Stich m; (Med) Faden m; (*of knitting*) Masche f; (*pain*) Stich m, Stechen nt; vt nähen.

stoat [stəʊt] n Wiesel nt.

stock [stɒk] n Vorrat m; (Comm) (Waren)lager nt; (*live—*) Vieh nt; (Cook) Brühe f; (Fin) Grundkapital nt; a stets vorrätig; (*standard*) Normal-; vt versehen, versorgen; (*in shop*) führen; in — auf Vorrat; **to take —** Inventur machen; (fig) Bilanz ziehen; **to — up with** vt Reserven anlegen von; —**ade** [stɒ'keɪd] Palisade f; —**broker** Börsenmakler m; —**exchange** Börse f.

stocking ['stɒkɪŋ] n Strumpf m.

stockist ['stɒkɪst] n Händler m.

stock market ['stɒkmɑːkɪt] n Börse f, Effektenmarkt m.

stockpile ['stɒkpaɪl] n Vorrat m; **nuclear —** Kernwaffenvorräte pl; vt aufstapeln.

stocktaking ['stɒkteıkıŋ] n Inventur f, Bestandsaufnahme f.

stocky ['stɒkı] n untersetzt.

stodgy ['stɒdʒı] a füllend, stopfend; (fig) langweilig, trocken.

stoic ['stəʊık] n Stoiker m; —al a stoisch; —ism ['stəʊısızəm] Stoizismus m; (fig) Gelassenheit f.

stoke [stəʊk] vt schüren; —r Heizer m.

stole [stəʊl] n Stola f; —n a gestohlen.

stolid ['stɒlıd] a schwerfällig; silence stur.

stomach ['stʌmək] n Bauch m, Magen m; I have no — for it das ist nichts für mich; vt vertragen; —ache Magen- or Bauchschmerzen pl.

stone [stəʊn] n Stein m; (seed) Stein m, Kern m; (weight) Gewichtseinheit f = 6.35 kg; a steinern, Stein-; vt entkernen; (kill) steinigen; —cold a eiskalt; — deaf a stocktaub; —mason Steinmetz m; —work Mauerwerk nt.

stony ['stəʊnı] a steinig.

stool [stu:l] n Hocker m.

stoop [stu:p] vi sich bücken.

stop [stɒp] n Halt m; (bus—) Haltestelle f; (punctuation) Punkt m; vt stoppen, anhalten; (bring to end) aufhören (mit), sein lassen; vi aufhören; (clock) stehenbleiben; (remain) bleiben; to — doing sth aufhören, etw zu tun; — it! hör auf (damit)!; — dead vi plötzlich aufhören, innehalten; — in vi (at home) zu Hause bleiben; — off vi kurz haltmachen; — out vi (of house) ausbleiben; — over vi übernachten, für Nacht bleiben; — up vi (at night) aufbleiben, vt hole zustopfen, verstopfen; —lights pl (Aut) Bremslichter pl;

—over (on journey) Zwischenaufenthalt m; —page ['stɒpıdʒ] (An)halten nt; (traffic) Verkehrsstockung f; (strike) Arbeitseinstellung f; —per Propfen m, Stöpsel m; —press letzte Meldung f; —watch Stoppuhr f.

storage ['stɔ:rıdʒ] n Lagerung f.

store [stɔ:*] n Vorrat m; (place) Lager m, Warenhaus nt; (large shop) Kaufhaus nt; vt lagern; — up vt sich eindecken mit; —room Lagerraum m, Vorratsraum m.

storey ['stɔ:rı] n (Brit) Stock m, Stockwerk nt.

stork [stɔ:k] n Storch m.

storm [stɔ:m] n (lit, fig) Sturm m; vti stürmen; to take by — im Sturm nehmen; —cloud Gewitterwolke f; —y a stürmisch.

story ['stɔ:rı] n Geschichte f, Erzählung f; (lie) Märchen nt; (US: storey) Stock m, Stockwerk nt; —book Geschichtenbuch nt; —teller Geschichtenerzähler m.

stout [staʊt] a (bold) mannhaft, tapfer; (too fat) beleibt, korpulent; —ness Festigkeit f; (of body) Korpulenz f.

stove [stəʊv] n (Koch)herd m; (for heating) Ofen m.

stow [stəʊ] vt verstauen; —away blinde(r) Passagier m.

straddle ['strædl] vt horse, fence rittlings sitzen auf (+dat); (fig) überbrücken.

strafe [strɑ:f] vt beschießen, bombardieren.

straggle ['strægl] vi (branches etc) wuchern; (people) nachhinken; —r Nachzügler m.

straight [streıt] a gerade; (honest) offen, ehrlich; (in order) in Ordnung; drink pur, unverdünnt; ad (direct) direkt, geradewegs; (

(*Sport*) Gerade *f*; **—away** *ad* sofort, unverzüglich; **— off** *ad* sofort; direkt nacheinander; **— on** *ad* geradeaus; **—en** vt (*also* **—en out**) (*lit*) gerade machen; (*fig*) in Ordnung bringen, klarstellen; **—forward** *a* einfach, unkompliziert.

strain [streɪn] *n* Belastung *f*; (*streak*, *trace*) Zug *m*; (*of music*) Fetzen *m*; vt überanstrengen; (*stretch*) anspannen; *muscle* zerren; (*filter*) (durch)seihen; **don't — yourself** überanstrenge dich nicht; vi (*make effort*) sich anstrengen; **—ed** *a laugh* gezwungen; *relations* gespannt; **—er** Sieb *nt*.

strait [streɪt] *n* Straße *f*, Meerenge *f*; **—ened** *a circumstances* beschränkt; **—jacket** Zwangsjacke *f*; **—laced** *a* engherzig, streng.

strand [strænd] *n* (*lit*, *fig*) Faden *m*; (*of hair*) Strähne *f*; **to be —ed** (*lit*, *fig*) gestrandet sein.

strange [streɪndʒ] *a* fremd; (*unusual*) merkwürdig, seltsam; **—ly** *ad* merkwürdig; fremd; **—ly enough** merkwürdigerweise; **—ness** Fremdheit *f*; **—r** Fremde(r) *mf*; **I'm a —r here** ich bin hier fremd.

strangle [ˈstræŋgl] vt erdrosseln, erwürgen; **—hold** (*fig*) Unklammerung *f*.

strangulation [stræŋgjʊˈleɪʃən] *n* Erdrosseln *nt*.

strap [stræp] *n* Riemen *m*; (*on clothes*) Träger *m*; vt (*fasten*) festschnallen; **—less** *a dress* trägerlos; **—ping** *a* stramm.

stratagem [ˈstrætədʒəm] *n* (Kriegs)list *f*.

strategic *a*, **—ally** *ad* [strəˈtiːdʒɪk, -əlɪ] strategisch.

strategist [ˈstrætədʒɪst] *n* Stratege *m*.

strategy [ˈstrætədʒɪ] *n* Kriegskunst *f*; (*fig*) Strategie *f*.

stratosphere [ˈstrætəʊsfɪə*] *n* Stratosphäre *f*.

stratum [ˈstrɑːtəm] *n* Schicht *f*.

straw [strɔː] *n* Stroh *nt*; (*single stalk*, *drinking —*) Strohhalm *m*; *a* Stroh-; **—berry** Erdbeere *f*.

stray [streɪ] *n* verirrte(s) Tier *nt*; vi herumstreunen; *a animal* verirrt; *thought* zufällig.

streak [striːk] *n* Streifen *m*; (*in character*) Einschlag *m*; (*in hair*) Strähne *f*; **— of bad luck** Pechsträhne *f*; vt streifen; **—y** *a* gestreift; *bacon* durchwachsen.

stream [striːm] *n* (*brook*) Bach *m*; (*fig*) Strom *m*; (*flow of liquid*) Strom *m*, Flut *f*; vi strömen, fluten; **—er** (*pennon*) Wimpel *m*; (*of paper*) Luftschlange *f*; **—lined** *a* stromlinienförmig; (*effective*) rationell.

street [striːt] *n* Straße *f*; **—car** (*US*) Straßenbahn *f*; **— lamp** Straßenlaterne *f*.

strength [streŋθ] *n* Stärke *f* (*also fig*); Kraft *f*; **—en** vt (ver)stärken.

strenuous [ˈstrenjʊəs] *a* anstrengend; **—ly** *ad* angestrengt.

stress [stres] *n* Druck *m*; (*mental*) Streß *m*; (*Gram*) Betonung *f*; vt betonen.

stretch [stretʃ] *n* Stück *nt*, Strecke *f*; vt ausdehnen, strecken; vi sich erstrecken; (*person*) sich strecken; **at a —** (*continuously*) ununterbrochen; **— out** vi sich ausstrecken; vt ausstrecken; **—er** Tragbahre *f*.

stricken [ˈstrɪkən] *a person* befallen, ergriffen; *city*, *country* heimgesucht.

strict [strɪkt] a (*exact*) genau; (*severe*) streng; **—ly** ad streng, genau; **—ly speaking** streng or genau genommen; **—ness** Strenge f.

stride [straɪd] n lange(r) Schritt m; vi irreg schreiten.

strident ['straɪdənt] a schneidend, durchdringend.

strife [straɪf] n Streit m.

strike [straɪk] n Streik m, Ausstand m; (*discovery*) Fund m; (*attack*) Schlag m; irreg vt (hit) schlagen; treffen; (*collide*) stoßen gegen; (*come to mind*) einfallen (+dat); (*stand out*) auffallen; (*find*) stoßen auf (+acc), finden; vi (*stop work*) streiken; (*attack*) zuschlagen; (*clock*) schlagen; **— down** vt (*lay low*) niederschlagen; **— out** vt (*cross out*) ausstreichen; **— up** vt music anstimmen; friendship schließen; **— pay** Streikgeld nt; **—r** Streikende(r) mf.

striking a, **—ly** ad ['straɪkɪŋ, -lɪ] auffallend, bemerkenswert.

string [strɪŋ] n Schnur f, Kordel f, Bindfaden m; (*row*) Reihe f; (Mus) Saite f; **— bean** grüne Bohne f.

stringency ['strɪndʒənsɪ] n Schärfe f.

stringent ['strɪndʒənt] a streng, scharf.

strip [strɪp] n Streifen m; vt (*uncover*) abstreifen, abziehen; clothes ausziehen; (Tech) auseinandernehmen; vi (*undress*) sich ausziehen; **— cartoon** Bildserie f.

stripe [straɪp] n Streifen m; **—d** a gestreift.

strip light ['strɪplaɪt] n Leuchtröhre f.

stripper ['strɪpə*] n Striptease-tänzerin f.

striptease ['strɪptiːz] n Striptease nt.

strive [straɪv] vi irreg streben (for nach).

stroke [strəʊk] n Schlag m, Hieb m; (swim, row) Stoß m; (Tech) Hub m; (Med) Schlaganfall m; (caress) Streicheln nt; vt streicheln; **at a —** mit einem Schlag; **on the —** of 5 Schlag 5.

stroll [strəʊl] n Spaziergang m; vi spazierengehen, schlendern.

strong [strɒŋ] a stark; (firm) fest; they are 50 — sie sind 50 Mann stark; **—hold** Hochburg f; **—ly** ad stark; **—room** Tresor m.

structural ['strʌktʃərəl] a strukturell.

structure ['strʌktʃə*] n Struktur f, Aufbau m; (building) Gebäude nt, Bau m.

struggle ['strʌgl] n Kampf m, Anstrengung f; vi (fight) kämpfen; **to —** to do sth sich (ab)mühen etw zu tun.

strum [strʌm] vt guitar klimpern auf (+dat).

strung [strʌŋ] see highly.

strut [strʌt] n Strebe f, Stütze f; vi stolzieren.

strychnine ['strɪkniːn] n Strychnin nt.

stub [stʌb] n Stummel m; (of cigarette) Kippe f.

stubble ['stʌbl] n Stoppel f.

stubbly ['stʌblɪ] a stoppelig, Stoppel-.

stubborn a, **—ly** ad ['stʌbən, -lɪ] stur, hartnäckig; **—ness** Sturheit f, Hartnäckigkeit f.

stubby ['stʌbɪ] a untersetzt.

stucco ['stʌkəʊ] n Stuck m.

stuck-up [stʌk'ʌp] a hochnäsig.

stud [stʌd] *n* (*nail*) Beschlagnagel *m*; (*button*) Kragenknopf *m*; (*number of horses*) Stall *m*; (*place*) Gestüt *nt*; —**ded** with übersät mit.

student ['stju:dənt] *n* Student(in *f*) *m*; (*US also*) Schüler(in *f*) *m*; **fellow** — Kommilitone *m*; Kommilitonin *f*.

studied ['stʌdɪd] *a* absichtlich.

studio ['stju:dɪəʊ] *n* Studio *nt*; (*for artist*) Atelier *nt*.

studious *a*, —**ly** *ad* ['stju:dɪəs, -lɪ] lernbegierig.

study ['stʌdɪ] *n* Studium *nt*; (*investigation also*) Untersuchung *f*; (*room*) Arbeitszimmer *nt*; (*essay etc*) Studie *f*; *vt* studieren; *face* erforschen; *evidence* prüfen; *vi* studieren; — **group** Arbeitsgruppe *f*.

stuff [stʌf] *n* Stoff *m*; (*col*) Zeug *nt*; that's hot —! das ist Klasse!; *vt* stopfen, füllen; *animal* ausstopfen; **to** — **o.s.** sich vollstopfen; —**ed full** vollgepfropft; —**iness** Schwüle *f*; Spießigkeit *f*; —**ing** Füllung *f*; —**y** *a room* schwül; *person* spießig.

stumble ['stʌmbl] *vi* stolpern; **to** — **on** zufällig stoßen auf (+*acc*).

stumbling block ['stʌmblɪŋblɒk] *n* Hindernis *nt*, Stein *m* des Anstoßes.

stump [stʌmp] *n* Stumpf *m*; *vt* umwerfen.

stun [stʌn] *vt* betäuben; (*shock*) niederschmettern.

stunning ['stʌnɪŋ] *a* betäubend; *news* überwältigend, umwerfend; —**ly beautiful** traumhaft schön.

stunt [stʌnt] *n* Kunststück *nt*, Trick *m*; *vt* verkümmern lassen; —**ed** *a* verkümmert.

stupefy ['stju:pɪfaɪ] *vt* betäuben; (*by news*) bestürzen; —**ing** *a* betäubend; bestürzend.

stupendous [stju:'pendəs] *a* erstaunlich, enorm.

stupid *a*, —**ly** *ad* ['stju:pɪd, -lɪ] dumm; —**ity** [stju:'pɪdɪtɪ] Dummheit *f*.

stupor ['stju:pə*] *n* Betäubung *f*.

sturdily ['stɜ:dɪlɪ] *ad* kräftig, stabil.

sturdiness [ʃtɜ:dməs] *n* Robustheit *f*.

sturdy ['stɜ:dɪ] *a* kräftig, robust.

stutter ['stʌtə*] *n* Stottern *nt*; *vi* stottern.

sty [staɪ] *n* Schweinestall *m*.

stye [staɪ] *n* Gerstenkorn *nt*.

style [staɪl] *n* Stil *m*; (*fashion*) Mode *f*; *hair* — Frisur *f*; **in** — mit Stil; *vt hair* frisieren.

styling ['staɪlɪŋ] *n* (*of car etc*) Formgebung *f*.

stylish *a*, —**ly** *ad* ['staɪlɪʃ, -lɪ] modisch, schick, flott.

stylized ['staɪlaɪzd] *a* stilisiert.

stylus ['staɪləs] *n* (*Grammophon*)nadel *f*.

styptic ['stɪptɪk] *a*: — **pencil** blutstillende(r) Stift *m*.

suave [swɑ:v] *a* zuvorkommend.

sub- [sʌb] *pref* Unter-.

subconscious ['sʌb'kɒnʃəs] *a* unterbewußt; *n*: **the** — das Unterbewußte.

subdivide ['sʌbdɪ'vaɪd] *vt* unterteilen.

subdivision ['sʌbdɪvɪʒən] *n* Unterteilung *f*; (*department*) Unterabteilung *f*.

subdue [səb'dju:] *vt* unterwerfen; —**d** *a lighting* gedämpft; *person* still.

subject ['sʌbdʒɪkt] *n* (*of kingdom*) Untertan *m*; (*citizen*) Staatsangehörige(r) *mf*; (*topic*) Thema *nt*; (*Sch*) Fach *nt*; (*Gram*) Subjekt *nt*, Satzgegenstand *m*;

[səb'dʒɛkt] vt (subdue) unterwerfen, abhängig machen; (expose) aussetzen; to be — to unterworfen sein (+dat); (exposed) ausgesetzt sein (+dat); —ion [səb'dʒekʃən] (conquering) Unterwerfung f; (being controlled) Abhängigkeit f; —ive a, —ively ad [səb'dʒektɪv, -lɪ] subjektiv; — matter Thema nt.

sub judice [sʌb'dju:dɪsɪ] a in gerichtliche(r) Untersuchung.

subjunctive [səb'dʒʌŋktɪv] n Konjunktiv m, Möglichkeitsform f; a Konjunktiv-, konjunktivisch.

sublet ['sʌb'let] vt irreg untervermieten.

sublime [sə'blaɪm] a erhaben.

submarine [sʌbmə'ri:n] n Unterseeboot nt, U-Boot nt.

submerge [səb'mɜ:dʒ] vt untertauchen; (flood) überschwemmen; vi untertauchen.

submission [səb'mɪʃən] n (obedience) Ergebenheit f, Gehorsam m; (claim) Behauptung f; (of plan) Unterbreitung f.

submit [səb'mɪt] vt behaupten; plan unterbreiten; vi (give in) sich ergeben.

subnormal ['sʌb'nɔ:məl] a minderbegabt.

subordinate [sə'bɔ:dɪnət] a untergeordnet; n Untergebene(r) mf.

subpoena [sə'pi:nə] n Vorladung f; vt vorladen.

subscribe [səb'skraɪb] vi spenden, Geld geben; (to view etc) unterstützen, beipflichten (+dat); (to newspaper) abonnieren (to acc); —r (to periodical) Abonnent m; (Tel) Telefonteilnehmer m.

subscription [səb'skrɪpʃən] n Abonnement nt; (Mitglieds)beitrag m.

subsequent ['sʌbsɪkwənt] a folgend, später; —ly ad später.

subside [səb'saɪd] vi sich senken; —nce [səb'saɪdəns] Senkung f.

subsidiary [səb'sɪdɪərɪ] n Neben-; n (company) Zweig m, Tochtergesellschaft f.

subsidize ['sʌbsɪdaɪz] vt subventionieren.

subsidy ['sʌbsɪdɪ] n Subvention f.

subsistence [səb'sɪstəns] n Unterhalt m; — level Existenzminimum nt.

substance ['sʌbstəns] n Substanz f, Stoff m; (most important part) Hauptbestandteil m.

substandard ['sʌb'stændəd] a unterdurchschnittlich.

substantial [səb'stænʃəl] a (strong) fest, kräftig; (important) wesentlich; —ly ad erheblich.

substantiate [səb'stænʃɪeɪt] vt begründen, belegen.

substation ['sʌbsteɪʃən] n (Elec) Nebenwerk nt.

substitute ['sʌbstɪtju:t] n Ersatz m; vt ersetzen.

substitution [sʌbstɪ'tju:ʃən] n Ersetzung f.

subterfuge ['sʌbtəfju:dʒ] n Vorwand m; Tricks pl.

subterranean [sʌbtə'reɪnɪən] a unterirdisch.

subtitle ['sʌbtaɪtl] n Untertitel m.

subtle ['sʌtl] a fein; (sly) raffiniert; —ty subtile Art f, Raffinesse f.

subtly ['sʌtlɪ] ad fein, raffiniert.

subtract [səb'trækt] vt abziehen, subtrahieren; —ion [səb'trækʃən] Abziehen nt, Subtraktion f.

subtropical ['sʌb'trɒpɪkəl] a subtropisch.

suburb ['sʌbɜ:b] n Vorort m; —an [sə'bɜ:bən] a Vorort(s)-,

Stadtrand-; **—ia** [səˈbɜːbɪə]
Vorstadt f.

subvention [səbˈvenʃən] n (US)
Unterstützung f, Subvention f.

subversive [səbˈvɜːsɪv] a subversiv.

subway [ˈsʌbweɪ] n (US) U-Bahn
f, Untergrundbahn f; (Brit)
Unterführung f.

sub-zero [ˈsʌbˈzɪərəʊ] a unter Null,
unter dem Gefrierpunkt.

succeed [səkˈsiːd] vi gelingen
(+dat), Erfolg haben; he **—ed** es
gelang ihm; vt (nach)folgen
(+dat); **—ing** a (nach)folgend.

success [səkˈses] n Erfolg m; **—ful**
a, **—fully** ad erfolgreich; **—ion**
[səkˈseʃən] (Aufeinander)folge f;
(to throne) Nachfolge f; **—ive** a
[səkˈsesɪv] aufeinanderfolgend;
—or Nachfolger(in f) m.

succinct [səkˈsɪŋkt] a kurz und
bündig, knapp.

succulent [ˈsʌkjulənt] a saftig.

succumb [səˈkʌm] vi zusammenbrechen (to unter +dat); (yield)
nachgeben (die) erliegen.

such [sʌtʃ] a solche(r, s); **—** a so
ein; **—** a lot so viel; **—** is life so
ist das Leben; **—** is my wish das
ist mein Wunsch; **—** as wie; pron
solch; **—** as I have die, die ich
habe; **—like** a derartig; pron
dergleichen.

suck [sʌk] vt saugen; ice cream etc
lecken; toffee etc lutschen; vi
saugen; **—er** (col) Idiot m,
Dummkopf m.

suckle [ˈsʌkl] vt säugen; child
stillen; vi saugen.

suction [ˈsʌkʃən] n Saugen nt,
Saugkraft f.

sudden a **—ly** ad [ˈsʌdn, -lɪ]
plötzlich; all of a **—** ganz plötzlich,
auf einmal; **—ness** Plötzlichkeit f.

sue [suː] vt verklagen.

suède [sweɪd] n Wildleder nt; a
Wildleder-.

suet [suɪt] n Nierenfett nt.

suffer [ˈsʌfə*] vt (er)leiden; (old:
allow) zulassen, dulden; vi leiden;
—er Leidende(r) mf; **—ing**
Leiden nt.

suffice [səˈfaɪs] vi genügen.

sufficient a, **—ly** ad [səˈfɪʃənt, -lɪ]
ausreichend.

suffix [ˈsʌfɪks] n Nachsilbe f.

suffocate [ˈsʌfəkeɪt] vti ersticken.

suffocation [sʌfəˈkeɪʃən] n
Ersticken nt.

suffragette [sʌfrəˈdʒet] n
Suffragette f.

sugar [ˈʃugə*] n Zucker m; vt
zuckern; **—beet** Zuckerrübe f;
—cane Zuckerrohr nt; **—y** a süß.

suggest [səˈdʒest] vt vorschlagen;
(show) schließen lassen auf
(+acc); what does this painting **—**
to you? was drückt das Bild für dich
aus?; **—ion** [səˈdʒestʃən]
Vorschlag m; **—ive** a anregend;
(indecent) zweideutig; to be **—ive**
of sth an etw (acc) erinnern.

suicidal [suɪˈsaɪdl] a
selbstmörderisch; that's **—** das ist
Selbstmord.

suicide [ˈsuɪsaɪd] n Selbstmord m;
to commit **—** Selbstmord begehen.

suit [suːt] n Anzug m; (Cards)
Farbe f; vt passen (+dat); clothes
stehen (+dat); (adapt) anpassen;
— yourself mach doch, was du
willst; **—ability** [suːtəˈbɪlɪtɪ]
Eignung f; **—able** a geeignet,
passend; **—ably** ad angemessen;
—case (Hand)koffer
m.

suite [swiːt] n (of rooms) Zimmer-
flucht f; (of furniture) Einrichtung

f; (*Mus*) Suite f; three-piece — Couchgarnitur f.

sulfur ['sʌlfə*] *n* (*US*) = sulphur.

sulk [sʌlk] *vi* schmollen; **—y** a schmollend.

sullen ['sʌlən] a (*gloomy*) düster; (*bad-tempered*) mürrisch, verdrossen.

sulphur ['sʌlfə*] *n* Schwefel *m*.

sulphuric [sʌl'fjuərɪk] a: — acid Schwefelsäure f.

sultan ['sʌltən] *n* Sultan *m*; **—a** [sʌl'tɑːnə] (*woman*) Sultanin f; (*raisin*) Sultanine f.

sultry ['sʌltrɪ] a schwül.

sum [sʌm] *n* Summe f; (*money also*) Betrag *m*; (*arithmetic*) Rechenaufgabe f; **—s** *pl* Rechnen *nt*; — up *vti* zusammenfassen; —marize *vt* kurz zusammenfassen; —mary Zusammenfassung f; (*of book etc*) Inhaltsangabe f.

summer ['sʌmə*] *n* Sommer *m*; a Sommer—; **—house** (*in garden*) Gartenhaus *nt*; **—time** Sommerzeit f.

summing-up ['sʌmɪŋ'ʌp] *n* Zusammenfassung f.

summit ['sʌmɪt] *n* Gipfel *m*; — conference Gipfelkonferenz f.

summon ['sʌmən] *vt* bestellen, kommen lassen; (*Jur*) vorladen; (*gather up*) aufbieten, aufbringen; **—s** (*Jur*) Vorladung f.

sump [sʌmp] *n* Ölwanne f.

sumptuous ['sʌmptjuəs] a prächtig; **—ness** Pracht f.

sun [sʌn] *n* Sonne f; **—bathe** *vi* sich sonnen; **—bathing** Sonnenbaden *nt*; **—burn** Sonnenbrand *m*; to be **—burnt** einen Sonnenbrand haben.

Sunday ['sʌndeɪ] *n* Sonntag *m*.

sundial ['sʌndaɪəl] *n* Sonnenuhr f.

sundown ['sʌndaun] *n* Sonnenuntergang *m*.

sundry ['sʌndrɪ] a verschieden; *n*: sundries *pl* Verschiedene(s) *nt*; all and — alle.

sunflower ['sʌnflauə*] *n* Sonnenblume f.

sunglasses ['sʌnglɑːsɪz] *npl* Sonnenbrille f.

sunken ['sʌŋkən] a versunken; *eyes* eingesunken.

sunlight ['sʌnlaɪt] *n* Sonnenlicht *nt*.

sunlit ['sʌnlɪt] a sonnenbeschienen.

sunny ['sʌnɪ] a sonnig.

sunrise ['sʌnraɪz] *n* Sonnenaufgang *m*.

sunset ['sʌnset] *n* Sonnenuntergang *m*.

sunshade ['sʌnʃeɪd] *n* Sonnenschirm *m*.

sunshine ['sʌnʃaɪn] *n* Sonnenschein *m*.

sunspot ['sʌnspɒt] *n* Sonnenfleck *m*.

sunstroke ['sʌnstrəuk] *n* Hitzschlag *m*.

sun tan ['sʌntæn] *n* (Sonnen)bräune f; to get a — braun werden.

suntrap ['sʌntræp] *n* sonnige(r) Platz *m*.

sunup ['sʌnʌp] *n* (*col*) Sonnenaufgang *m*.

super ['suːpə*] a (*col*) prima, klasse; Super—, Über—.

superannuation [suːpərænjueɪʃən] *n* Pension f.

superb a, **—ly** ad [suːˈpɜːb, -lɪ] ausgezeichnet, hervorragend.

supercilious [suːpəˈsɪlɪəs] a herablassend.

superficial a, **—ly** ad [suːpəˈfɪʃəl, -ɪ] oberflächlich.

superfluous [suˈpɜːfluəs] a überflüssig.

12

superhuman [su:pə'hju:mən] *a* effort übermenschlich.

superimpose ['su:pərɪm'pəuz] *vt* übereinanderlegen.

superintendent [su:pərɪn'tendənt] *n* Polizeichef *m*.

superior [su'prɪə*] *a* (*higher*) höher(stehend); (*better*) besser; (*proud*) überlegen; *n* Vorgesetzte(r) *mf*; —**ity** [supɪər'ɪrɪtɪ] Überlegenheit *f*.

superlative [su'pə:lətɪv] *a* höchste(r,s); *n* (*Gram*) Superlativ *m*.

superman ['su:pəmæn] *n* Übermensch *m*.

supermarket ['su:pəma:kɪt] *n* Supermarkt *m*.

supernatural [su:pə'nætʃərəl] *a* übernatürlich.

superpower ['su:pəpauə*] *n* Weltmacht *f*.

supersede [su:pə'si:d] *vt* ersetzen.

supersonic ['su:pə'sɒnɪk] *n* Überschall-.

superstition [su:pə'stɪʃən] *n* Aberglaube *m*.

superstitious [su:pə'stɪʃəs] *a* abergläubisch.

supervise ['su:pəvaɪz] *vt* beaufsichtigen, kontrollieren.

supervision [su:pə'vɪʒən] *n* Aufsicht *f*.

supervisor ['su:pəvaɪzə*] *n* Aufsichtsperson *f*; —**y** *a* Aufsichts-.

supper ['sʌpə*] *n* Abendessen *nt*.

supple ['sʌpl] *a* gelenkig, geschmeidig; *wire* biegsam.

supplement ['sʌplɪmənt] *n* Ergänzung *f*; (*in book*) Nachtrag *m*; ['sʌplɪment] *vt* ergänzen; —**ary** ['sʌplɪ'mentərɪ] *a* ergänzend, Ergänzungs-, Zusatz-.

supplier [sə'plaɪə*] *n* Lieferant *m*.

supply [sə'plaɪ] *vt* liefern; *n* Vorrat *m*; (*supplying*) Lieferung *f*; **supplies** *pl* (*food*) Vorräte *pl*; (*Mil*) Nachschub *m*; — and demand Angebot *nt* und Nachfrage.

support [sə'pɔ:t] *n* Unterstützung *f*; (*Tech*) Stütze *f*; *vt* (*hold up*) stützen, tragen; (*provide for*) ernähren; (*speak in favour of*) befürworten, unterstützen; —**er** Anhänger *m*; —**ing** *a* programme Bei-; *role* Neben-.

suppose [sə'pəuz] *vti* annehmen, denken, glauben; I — so ich glaube schon; — he comes ... angenommen, er kommt ...; —**dly** [sə'pəuzɪdlɪ] *ad* angeblich.

supposing [sə'pəuzɪŋ] *cj* angenommen.

supposition [sʌpə'zɪʃən] *n* Voraussetzung *f*.

suppress [sə'pres] *vt* unterdrücken; —**ion** [sə'preʃən] Unterdrückung *f*; —**or** (*Elec*) Entstörungselement *nt*.

supra- ['su:prə] *pref* Über-.

supremacy [su'preməsɪ] *n* Vorherrschaft *f*, Oberhoheit *f*.

supreme *a*, —**ly** *ad* [su'pri:m, -lɪ] oberste(r,s), höchste(r,s).

surcharge ['sɜ:tʃa:dʒ] *n* Zuschlag *m*.

sure [ʃuə*] *a* sicher, gewiß; to be — sicher sein; to be — about sth sich (*dat*) einer Sache sicher sein; we are — to win wir werden ganz sicher gewinnen; *ad* sicher; —! (*of course*) ganz bestimmt!, natürlich!, klar!; to make — of sich vergewissern (+*gen*); —**footed** a sicher (auf den Füßen); —**ly** *ad* (*certainly*) sicherlich, gewiß; —**ly** it's wrong das ist doch wohl falsch!; —**ly not!** das ist doch wohl nicht wahr!; **—ty** Sicherheit *f;* *(person)* Bürge *m.*

surf [sɜ:f] *n* Brandung *f.*

surface ['sɜ:fɪs] *n* Oberfläche *f; vt* roadway teeren; *vi* auftauchen; **— mail** gewöhnliche Post *f,* Post per Bahn *f.*

surfboard ['sɜ:fbɔ:d] *n* Wellenreiterbrett *nt.*

surfeit [sɜ:fɪt] *n* Übermaß *nt.*

surfing [sɜ:fɪŋ] *n* Wellenreiten *nt,* Surfing *nt.*

surge [sɜ:dʒ] *n* Woge *f; vi* wogen.

surgeon ['sɜ:dʒən] *n* Chirurg(in *f) m.*

surgery ['sɜ:dʒərɪ] *n* Praxis *f;* *(room)* Sprechzimmer *nt; (time)* Sprechstunde *f; (treatment)* operative(r) Eingriff *m,* Operation *f;* **he needs** — er muß operiert werden.

surgical ['sɜ:dʒɪkəl] *a* chirurgisch.

surly ['sɜ:lɪ] *a* verdrießlich, grob.

surmise [sɜ:'maɪz] *vt* vermuten.

surmount [sɜ:'maʊnt] *vt* überwinden.

surname ['sɜ:neɪm] *n* Zuname *m.*

surpass [sɜ:'pɑ:s] *vt* übertreffen.

surplus ['sɜ:pləs] *n* Überschuß *m; a* überschüssig, Über(schuß)-.

surprise [sə'praɪz] *n* Überraschung *f; vt* überraschen.

surprising [sə'praɪzɪŋ] *a* überraschend; **—ly** *ad* überraschend(erweise).

surrealism [sə'rɪəlɪzəm] *n* Surrealismus *m.*

surrealist [sə'rɪəlɪst] *a* surrealistisch; *n* Surrealist *m.*

surrender [sə'rendə*] *n* Übergabe *f;* Kapitulation *f; vi* sich ergeben, kapitulieren; *vt* übergeben.

surreptitious *a,* **—ly** *ad.* [sʌrəp'tɪʃəs, -lɪ] verstohlen.

surround [sə'raʊnd] *vt* umgeben; *(come all round)* umringen; **—ed by** umgeben von; **—ing** *a* country-side umliegend; *n:* **—ings** *pl* Umgebung *f; (environment)* Umwelt *f.*

surveillance [sɜ:'veɪləns] *n* Überwachung *f.*

survey ['sɜ:veɪ] *n* Übersicht *f;* [sɜ:'veɪ] *vt* überblicken; *land* vermessen; **—ing** [sə'veɪɪŋ] *(of land)* (Land)vermessung *f;* **—or** [sə'veɪə*] Land(ver)messer *m.*

survival [sə'vaɪvəl] *n* Überleben *nt;* *(sth from earlier times)* Überbleibsel *nt.*

survive [sə'vaɪv] *vti* überleben.

survivor [sə'vaɪvə*] *n* Überlebende(r) *mf.*

susceptible [sə'septəbl] *a* empfindlich *(to* gegen*);* empfänglich *(to* für*).*

suspect ['sʌspekt] *n* Verdächtige(r) *mf; a* verdächtig; [səs'pekt] *vt* verdächtigen; *(think)* vermuten.

suspend [səs'pend] *vt* verschieben; *(from work)* suspendieren; *(hang up)* aufhängen; *(Sport)* sperren; **—ers** *pl* Strumpfhalter *m; (men's)* Sockenhalter *m; (US)* Hosenträger *m.*

suspense [səs'pens] *n* Spannung *f.*

suspension [səs'penʃən] *n* *(hanging)* (Auf)hängen *nt,* Aufhängung *f; (postponing)* Aufschub *m; (from work)* Suspendierung *f; (Sport)* Sperrung *f; (Aut)* Federung *f;* **— bridge** Hängebrücke *f.*

suspicion [səs'pɪʃən] *n* Mißtrauen *nt;* Verdacht *m.*

suspicious *a,* **—ly** *ad* [səs'pɪʃəs, -lɪ] mißtrauisch; *(causing suspicion)* verdächtig; **—ness** Mißtrauen *nt.*

sustain [səs'teɪn] vt (hold up) stützen, tragen; (maintain) aufrechterhalten; (confirm) bestätigen; (Jur) anerkennen; injury davontragen; —ed a effort anhaltend.

sustenance ['sʌstɪməns] n Nahrung f.

swab [swɒb] n (Med) Tupfer m; vt decks schrubben; wound abtupfen.

swagger ['swægə*] vi stolzieren; (behave) prahlen, angeben.

swallow ['swɒləʊ] n (bird) Schwalbe f; (of food etc) Schluck m; vt (ver)schlucken; — up vt verschlingen.

swamp [swɒmp] n Sumpf m; vt überschwemmen; —y a sumpfig.

swan [swɒn] n Schwan m; — song Schwanengesang m.

swap [swɒp] n Tausch m; — (in) tauschen (for gegen); vt tauschen.

swarm [swɔːm] n Schwarm m; vi wimmeln (with von).

swarthy ['swɔːðɪ] a dunkel, braun.

swastika ['swɒstɪkə] n Hakenkreuz nt.

swat [swɒt] vt totschlagen.

sway [sweɪ] vi schwanken; (branches) schaukeln, sich wiegen; vt schwenken; (influence) beeinflussen, umstimmen.

swear [sweə*] vi irreg (promise) schwören; (curse) fluchen; to — to sth schwören auf etw (acc); —word Fluch m.

sweat [swet] n Schweiß m; vi schwitzen; —er Pullover m; —y a verschwitzt.

swede [swiːd] n Steckrübe f.

sweep [swiːp] n (cleaning) Kehren nt; (wide curve) Bogen m; (with arm) schwungvolle Bewegung f;

(chimney —) Schornsteinfeger m; irreg vt fegen, kehren; vi (road) sich dahinziehen; (go quickly) rauschen; — away vt wegfegen; (river) wegspülen; — past vi vorbeisausen; — up vt zusammenkehren; —ing a gesture schwungvoll; statement verallgemeinernd; —stake Toto nt.

sweet [swiːt] n (course) Nachtisch m; (candy) Bonbon nt; a, —ly ad süß; —corn Zuckermais m; —en vt süßen; (fig) versüßen; —heart Liebste(r) mf; —ness Süße f; —pea Gartenwicke f; to have a — tooth ein Leckermaul sein.

swell [swel] n Seegang m; a (col) todschick; irreg vt numbers vermehren; vi (also — up) (an)schwellen; —ing Schwellung f.

sweltering ['sweltərɪŋ] a drückend.

swerve [swɜːv] n Ausschwenken nt; vti ausscheren, zur Seite schwenken.

swift [swɪft] n Mauersegler m; a, —ly ad geschwind, schnell, rasch; —ness Schnelligkeit f.

swig [swɪg] n Zug m.

swill [swɪl] n (for pigs) Schweinefutter nt; vt spülen.

swim [swɪm] n: to go for a — schwimmen gehen; irreg vi schwimmen; my head is —ming mir dreht sich der Kopf; vt (cross) (durch)schwimmen; —mer Schwimmer(in f) m; —ming Schwimmen nt; to go —ming schwimmen gehen; —ming baths pl Schwimmbad nt; —ming cap Badehaube f; Badekappe f; —ming costume Badeanzug m; —ming pool Schwimmbecken nt; (private) Swimming-Pool m; —suit Badeanzug m.

swindle ['swɪndl] n Schwindel m, Betrug m; vt betrügen; —r Schwindler m.

swine [swaɪn] n (lit, fig) Schwein nt.

swing [swɪŋ] n (child's) Schaukel f; (swinging) Schwingen nt, Schwung m; (Mus) Swing m; irreg vt schwingen, (herum)schwenken; vi schwingen, pendeln, schaukeln; (turn quickly) schwenken; in full — in vollem Gange; — bridge Drehbrücke f; — door Schwingtür f.

swipe [swaɪp] n Hieb m; vt (col) (hit) hart schlagen; (steal) klauen.

swirl [swɜːl] n Wirbel m; vi wirbeln.

switch [swɪtʃ] n (Elec) Schalter m; (change) Wechsel m; vti (Elec) schalten; (change) wechseln; — off vt ab- or ausschalten; — on vt an- or einschalten; —back Achterbahn f; —board Vermittlung f, Zentrale f; (board) Schaltbrett nt.

swivel ['swɪvl] vti (also — round) (sich) drehen.

swollen ['swəʊlən] a geschwollen.

swoon [swuːn] vi (old) in Ohnmacht fallen.

swoop [swuːp] n Sturzflug m; (esp by police) Razzia f; vi (also — down) stürzen.

swop [swɒp] = swap.

sword [sɔːd] n Schwert nt; —fish Schwertfisch m; —sman Fechter m.

sworn [swɔːn] a: — enemies pl Todfeinde pl.

sycamore ['sɪkəmɔː*] n (US) Platane f; (Brit) Bergahorn m.

sycophantic [sɪkə'fæntɪk] a schmeichlerisch, kriecherisch.

syllable ['sɪləbl] n Silbe f.

syllabus ['sɪləbəs] n Lehrplan m.

symbol ['sɪmbl] n Symbol nt; —ic(al)· [sɪm'bɒlɪk(əl)]· a

symbolisch; —ism symbolische Bedeutung f; (Art) Symbolismus m; —ize vt versinnbildlichen, symbolisieren.

symmetrical a, —ly ad [sɪ'metrɪkəl, -l] symmetrisch, gleichmäßig.

symmetry ['sɪmɪtrɪ] n Symmetrie f.

sympathetic a, —ally ad [sɪmpə'θetɪk, -əlɪ] mitfühlend.

sympathize ['sɪmpəθaɪz] vi sympathisieren; mitfühlen; —r Mitfühlende(r) mf; (Pol) Sympathisant m.

sympathy ['sɪmpəθɪ] n Mitleid nt, Mitgefühl nt; (condolence) Beileid nt.

symphonic [sɪm'fɒnɪk] a sinfonisch.

symphony ['sɪmfənɪ] n Sinfonie f; — orchestra Sinfonieorchester· nt.

symposium [sɪm'pəʊzɪəm] n Tagung f.

symptom ['sɪmptəm] n Symptom nt, Anzeichen nt; —atic [sɪmptə'mætɪk] a (fig) bezeichnend (of für).

synagogue ['sɪnəgɒg] n Synagoge f.

synchromesh ['sɪŋkrəʊ'meʃ] n Synchronschaltung f.

synchronize ['sɪŋkrənaɪz] vt synchronisieren; vi gleichzeitig sein or ablaufen.

syndicate ['sɪndɪkət] n Konsortium nt, Verband m, Ring m.

syndrome ['sɪndrəʊm] n Syndrom nt.

synonym ['sɪnənɪm] n Synonym nt; —ous [sɪ'nɒnɪməs] a gleichbedeutend.

synopsis [sɪ'nɒpsɪs] n Abriß m, Zusammenfassung f.

syntactic [sɪn'tæktɪk] a syntaktisch.
syntax ['sɪntæks] n Syntax f.
synthesis ['sɪnθəsɪs] n Synthese f.
synthetic a, **—ally** ad [sɪn'θetɪk, -əlɪ] synthetisch, künstlich.
syphilis ['sɪfɪlɪs] n Syphilis f.
syphon ['saɪfən] = **siphon.**

syringe [sɪ'rɪndʒ] n Spritze f.
syrup ['sɪrəp] n Sirup m; (of sugar) Melasse f.
system ['sɪstəm] n System nt; **—atic** a, **—atically** ad [sɪstə'mætɪk, -əlɪ] systematisch, planmäßig.

T

T, t [ti:] n T nt, t nt; **to a —** genau.
ta [tɑ:] interj (Brit col) danke.
tab [tæb] n Schlaufe f, Aufhänger m; (name —) Schild nt.
tabby ['tæbɪ] n (female cat) (weibliche) Katze f; a (black-striped) getigert.
tabernacle ['tæbənækl] n Tabernakel nt or m.
table ['teɪbl] n Tisch m; (list) Tabelle f, Tafel f; **to lay sth on the —** (fig) etw zur Diskussion stellen; vt (Parl: propose) vorlegen, einbringen.
tableau ['tæbləʊ] n lebende(s) Bild nt.
tablecloth ['teɪblklɒθ] n Tischtuch nt, Tischdecke f.
table- d'hôte ['tɑ:bl'dəʊt] n Tagesmenü nt.
tablemat ['teɪblmæt] n Untersatz m.
tablespoon ['teɪblspu:n] n Eßlöffel m; **—ful** Eßlöffel(voll) m.
tablet ['tæblət] n (Med) Tablette f; (for writing) Täfelchen nt; (of paper) Schreibblock m; (of soap) Riegel m.
table talk ['teɪbltɔ:k] n Tischgespräch nt.
table tennis ['teɪbltenɪs] n Tischtennis nt.
table wine ['teɪblwaɪn] n Tafelwein m.

taboo [tə'bu:] n Tabu nt; a tabu.
tabulate ['tæbjʊleɪt] vt tabellarisch ordnen.
tacit a, **—ly** ad ['tæsɪt, -lɪ] stillschweigend; **—urn** a schweigsam, wortkarg.
tack [tæk] n (small nail) Stift m; (US: thumb—) Reißzwecke f; (stitch) Heftstich m; (Naut) Lavieren nt; (course) Kurs m.
tackle ['tækl] n (for lifting) Flaschenzug m; (Naut) Takelage f; (Sport) Tackling nt; vt (deal with) anpacken, in Angriff nehmen; person festhalten; player angehen; **he couldn't — it** er hat es nicht bewältigt.
tacky ['tækɪ] a klebrig.
tact [tækt] n Takt m; **—ful** a, **—fully** ad taktvoll.
tactical ['tæktɪkl] a taktisch.
tactics ['tæktɪks] npl Taktik f.
tactless a, **—ly** ad ['tæktləs, -lɪ] taktlos.
tadpole ['tædpəʊl] n Kaulquappe f.
taffeta ['tæfɪtə] n Taft m.
taffy ['tæfɪ] n (US) Sahnebonbon nt.
tag [tæg] n (label) Schild nt, Anhänger m; (maker's name) Etikett nt; (phrase) Floskel f, Spruch m; **— along** vi mit-

kommen; — **question** Bestätigungsfrage *f.*

tail [teɪl] *n* Schwanz *m;* (*of list*) Schluß *m;* (*of comet*) Schweif *m;* —s (*of coin*) Zahl(seite) *f;* **to** follow (+*dat*); — **off** *vi* abfallen, schwinden; — **end** Schluß *m,* Ende *nt.*

tailor ['teɪlə*]* *n* Schneider *m;* —**ing** Schneidern *nt,* Schneiderarbeit *f;* —**made a** (*lit*) maßgeschneidert; (*fig*) wie auf den Leib geschnitten (*for sb* jdm).

tailwind ['teɪlwɪnd] *n* Rückenwind *m.*

tainted ['teɪntɪd] *a* verdorben.

take [teɪk] *vt irreg* nehmen; *prize* entgegennehmen; *trip, exam* machen; (*capture*) *person* fassen; *town* einnehmen; *disease* bekommen; (*carry to a place*) bringen; (*Math: subtract*) abziehen (*from* von); (*extract*) *quotation* entnehmen (*from dat*); (*get for o.s.*) sich (*dat*) nehmen; (*gain, obtain*) bekommen; (*Fin, Comm*) einnehmen; (*record*) aufnehmen; (*consume*) zu sich nehmen; (*Phot*) aufnehmen, machen; (*put up with*) hinnehmen; (*respond to*) aufnehmen; (*understand, interpret*) auffassen; (*assume*) annehmen; (*contain*) fassen, Platz haben für; (*Gram*) stehen mit; **it** —**s 4 hours** man braucht 4 Stunden; **it** —**s him 4 hours** er braucht 4 Stunden; **to** — **sth from sb** jdm etw wegnehmen; **to** — **part in** teilnehmen an (+*dat*); **to** — **place** stattfinden; — **after** *vt* ähnlich sein (+*dat*); — **back** *vt* (*return*) zurückbringen; (*retract*) zurücknehmen; (*remind*) zurückversetzen (*to* in +*acc*); — **down** *vt* (*pull down*) abreißen; (*write down*) auf-

schreiben; — **in** *vt* (*deceive*) hereinlegen; (*understand*) begreifen; (*include*) einschließen; — **off** *vi* (*plane*) starten; *vt* (*remove*) wegnehmen, abmachen; *clothing* ausziehen; (*imitate*) nachmachen; — **on** *vt* (*undertake*) übernehmen; (*engage*) einstellen; (*opponent*) antreten gegen; — **out** *vt* (*lit, fig*) ausführen; (*extract*) herausnehmen; *insurance* abschließen; *licence* sich (*dat*) geben lassen; *book* ausleihen; (*remove*) entfernen; **to** — **sth out on sb** etw an jdm auslassen; — **over** *vt* übernehmen; *vi* ablösen (*from acc*); — **to** *vt* (*like*) mögen; (*adopt as practice*) sich (*dat*) angewöhnen; — **up** *vt* (*raise*) aufnehmen; *hem* kürzer machen; (*occupy*) in Anspruch nehmen; (*absorb*) aufsaugen; (*engage in*) sich befassen mit; **to** — **sb up on sth** jdn beim Wort nehmen; **to be** —**n with** begeistert sein von; —**off** (*Aviat*) Abflug *m,* Start *m;* (*imitation*) Nachahmung *f;* —**over** (*Comm*) Übernahme *f;* —**over bid** Übernahmeangebot *nt.*

takings ['teɪkɪŋz] *npl,* (*Comm*) Einnahmen *pl.*

talc [tælk] *n* (*also* —**um powder**) Talkumpuder *m.*

tale [teɪl] *n* Geschichte *f,* Erzählung *f.*

talent ['tælənt] *n* Talent *nt,* Begabung *f;* —**ed a** talentiert, begabt.

talk [tɔ:k] *n* (*conversation*) Gespräch *nt;* (*rumour*) Gerede *nt;* (*speech*) Vortrag *m; vi* sprechen, reden; (*gossip*) klatschen, reden; —**ing of ... da wir gerade von ...** sprechen; — **about** impertinence! so eine Frechheit!; **to** — **sb into**

doing sth jdn überreden, etw zu tun; to — shop fachsimpeln; — over vt besprechen; —ative a redselig, gesprächig; —er Schwätzer m.

tall [tɔːl] a groß; building hoch; —boy Kommode f; —ness Größe f; Höhe f; — story übertriebene Geschichte f.

tally ['tælɪ] n Abrechnung f; vi übereinstimmen.

talon ['tælən] n Kralle f.

tambourine [tæmbə'riːn] n Tamburin nt.

tame [teɪm] a zahm; (fig) fade, langweilig; vt zähmen; —ness Zahmheit f; (fig) Langweiligkeit f.

tamper ['tæmpə*]: — with vt herumpfuschen an (+dat); documents fälschen.

tampon ['tæmpɔn] n Tampon m.

tan [tæn] n (on skin) (Sonnen)bräune f; (colour) Gelbbraun nt; a (colour) (gelb)braun.

tandem ['tændəm] n Tandem nt.

tang [tæŋ] n Schärfe f, scharfe(r) Geschmack m or Geruch m.

tangent ['tændʒənt] n Tangente f.

tangerine [tændʒə'riːn] n Mandarine f.

tangible ['tændʒəbl] a (lit) greifbar; (real) handgreiflich.

tangle ['tæŋgl] n Durcheinander nt; (trouble) Schwierigkeiten pl; vt verwirren.

tango ['tæŋgəʊ] n Tango m.

tank [tæŋk] n (container) Tank m, Behälter m; (Mil) Panzer m.

tankard ['tæŋkəd] n Seidel nt, Deckelkrug m.

tanker ['tæŋkə*] n (ship) Tanker m; (vehicle) Tankwagen m.

tankful ['tæŋkfʊl] n volle(r) Tank m.

tanned [tænd] a skin gebräunt, sonnenverbrannt.

tantalizing ['tæntəlaɪzɪŋ] a verlockend; (annoying) quälend.

tantamount ['tæntəmaʊnt] a gleichbedeutend (to mit).

tantrum ['tæntrəm] n Wutanfall m.

tap [tæp] n Hahn m; (gentle blow) leichte(r) Schlag m, Klopfen nt; vt (strike) klopfen; supply anzapfen.

tap-dance ['tæpdɑːns] vi steppen.

tape [teɪp] n Band nt; (magnetic) (Ton)band nt; (adhesive) Klebstreifen m; vt (record) (auf Band) aufnehmen; — measure Maßband nt.

taper ['teɪpə*] n (dünne) Wachskerze f; vi spitz zulaufen.

tape recorder ['teɪprɪkɔːdə*] n Tonbandgerät nt.

tapered ['teɪpəd], **tapering** ['teɪpərɪŋ] a spitz zulaufend.

tapestry ['tæpɪstrɪ]. n Wandteppich m, Gobelin m.

tapioca [tæpɪ'əʊkə] n Tapioka f.

tappet ['tæpɪt] n (Aut) Nocke f.

tar [tɑː*] n Teer m.

tarantula [tə'ræntjʊlə] n Tarantel f.

tardy ['tɑːdɪ] a langsam, spät.

target ['tɑːgɪt] n Ziel nt; (board) Zielscheibe f.

tariff ['tærɪf] n (duty paid) Zoll m; (list) Tarif m.

tarmac ['tɑːmæk] n (Aviat) Rollfeld nt.

tarn [tɑːn] n Gebirgssee m.

tarnish ['tɑːnɪʃ] vt (lit) matt machen; (fig) beflecken.

tarpaulin [tɑː'pɔːlɪn] n Plane f, Persenning f.

tarry ['tærɪ] vi (liter) bleiben; (delay) säumen.

tart [tɑːt] n (Obst)torte f; (col)

Nutte f; a scharf, sauer; remark scharf, spitz.

tartan ['tɑːtən] n schottischkarierte(r) Stoff m; Schottenkaro nt.

tartar ['tɑːtə*] n Zahnstein m; —(e) sauce Remouladensoße f.

tartly ['tɑːtlɪ] ad spitz.

task [tɑːsk] n Aufgabe f; (duty) Pflicht f; — force Sondertrupp m.

tassel ['tæsəl] n Quaste f.

taste [teɪst] n Geschmack m; (sense) Geschmackssinn m; (small quantity) Kostprobe f; (liking) Vorliebe f; vt schmecken; (try) versuchen; vi schmecken (of nach); —ful a, —fully ad geschmackvoll; —less a (insipid) ohne Geschmack, fade; (in bade taste) geschmacklos; —lessly ad geschmacklos.

tastily ['teɪstɪlɪ] ad schmackhaft.

tastiness ['teɪstɪnəs] n Schmackhaftigkeit f.

tasty ['teɪstɪ] a schmackhaft.

tata ['tæ'tɑː] interj (Brit col) tschüß.

tattered ['tætəd] a zerrissen, zerlumpt.

tatters ['tætəz] npl: in — in Fetzen.

tattoo [tə'tuː] n (Mil) Zapfenstreich m; (on skin) Tätowierung f; vt tätowieren.

tatty ['tætɪ] a (col) schäbig.

taunt [tɔːnt] n höhnische Bemerkung f; vt verhöhnen.

Taurus ['tɔːrəs] n Stier m.

taut [tɔːt] a straff.

tavern ['tævən] n Taverne f.

tawdry ['tɔːdrɪ] a (bunt und) billig.

tawny ['tɔːnɪ] a gelbbraun.

tax [tæks] n Steuer f; vt besteuern; (strain) strapazieren; strength angreifen; —ation [tæk'seɪʃən] Besteuerung f; — collector

Steuereinnehmer m; —-free a steuerfrei.

taxi ['tæksɪ] n Taxi nt; vi (plane) rollen.

taxidermist ['tæksɪdɔːmɪst] n Tierausstopfer m.

taxi driver ['tæksɪ draɪvə*] n Taxifahrer m.

taxi rank ['tæksɪræŋk] n Taxistand m.

taxpayer ['tækspeɪə*] n Steuerzahler m.

tax return ['tæksrɪ'tɜːn] n Steuererklärung f.

tea [tiː] n Tee m; (meal) (frühes) Abendessen nt; — bag Tee(aufguß)beutel m; — break Teepause f; — cake Rosinenbrötchen nt.

teach [tiːtʃ] vti irreg lehren; (Sch also) unterrichten; (show) zeigen, beibringen (sb sth jdm etw); that'll — him! das hat er nun davon!; —er Lehrer(in f) m; —in Teach-in nt; —ing (teacher's work) Unterricht m, Lehren nt; (doctrine) Lehre f.

tea cosy ['tiːkəʊzɪ] n Teewärmer m.

teacup ['tiːkʌp] n Teetasse f.

teak [tiːk] n Teakbaum m; a Teak-(holz)-.

tea leaves ['tiːliːvz] npl Teeblätter pl.

team [tiːm] n (workers) Team nt; (Sport) Mannschaft f; (animals) Gespann nt; — spirit Gemeinschaftsgeist m; (Sport) Mannschaftsgeist m; —work Zusammenarbeit f, Teamwork nt.

tea party ['tiːpɑːtɪ] n Kaffeeklatsch m.

teapot ['tiːpɒt] n Teekanne f.

tear [tɛə*] n Riß m; irreg vt zerreißen; muscle zerren; I am torn between ... ich schwanke

zwischen ...; *vt* (zer)reißen;
(*rush*) rasen, sausen.

tear [tɪə*] *n* Träne *f*; in —s in
Tränen (aufgelöst); —ful *a*
weinend; *voice* weinerlich; — gas
Tränengas *nt*.

tearing ['tɛərɪŋ] *a*: to be in a —
hurry es schrecklich eilig haben.

tearoom ['tɪrʊm] *n* Teestube *f*.

tease [ti:z] *n* Hänsler *m*; *vt* necken,
aufziehen; *animal* quälen; I was
only teasing ich habe nur Spaß
gemacht.

tea set ['ti:set] *n* Teeservice *nt*.

teashop ['ti:ʃɒp] *n* Café *nt*.

teaspoon ['ti:spu:n] *n* Teelöffel *m*;
—ful Teelöffel(voll) *m*.

tea strainer ['ti:streɪnə*] *n* Teesieb
nt.

teat [ti:t] *n* (*of woman*) Brustwarze
f; (*of animal*) Zitze *f*; (*of bottle*)
Sauger *m*.

tea towel ['ti:taʊəl] *n* Küchen-
handtuch *nt*.

tea urn ['ti:ɜ:n] *n* Teemaschine *f*.

technical ['teknɪkəl] *a* technisch;
knowledge, *terms* Fach-; —ity
[teknɪ'kælɪtɪ] technische Einzelheit
f; (*Jur*) Formsache *f*; —ly *ad*
technisch; *speak* spezialisiert; *(fig)* genau genommen.

technician [tek'nɪʃən] *n* Techniker
m.

technique [tek'ni:k] *n* Technik *f*.

technological [teknə'lɒdʒɪkəl] *a*
technologisch.

technologist [tek'nɒlədʒɪst] *n*
Technologe *m*.

technology [tek'nɒlədʒɪ] *n* Techno-
logie *f*.

teddy (bear) ['tedɪ(bɛə*)] *n* Teddy-
bär *m*.

tedious *a*, —ly *ad* ['ti:dɪəs, -lɪ] langweilig, ermüdend.

tedium ['ti:dɪəm] *n* Langweiligkeit
f.

tee [ti:] *n* (*golf*) Abschlagstelle *f*;
(*object*) Tee *nt*.

teem [ti:m] *vi* (*swarm*) wimmeln
(*with von*); (*pour*) gießen.

teenage ['ti:neɪdʒ] *a fashions etc*
Teenager-, jugendlich; —r Teenager *m*, Jugendliche(r) *mf*.

teens [ti:nz] *npl* Jugendjahre *pl*.

teeter ['ti:tə*] *vi* schwanken.

teeth [ti:θ] *npl of* tooth.

teethe [ti:ð] *vi* zahnen.

teething ring ['ti:ðɪŋrɪŋ] *n* Beißring
m.

teetotal ['ti:'təʊtl] *a* abstinent;
—ler, (*US*) —er Antialkoholiker *m*,
Abstinenzler *m*.

telecommunications ['telɪ-
kəmju:nɪ'keɪʃənz] *npl* Fernmelde-
wesen *nt*.

telegram ['telɪgræm] *n* Telegramm
nt.

telegraph ['telɪgrɑ:f] *n* Telegraph
m; —ic [telɪ'græfɪk] *a address* Tele-
gramm-; — pole Telegraphenmast
m.

telepathic [telɪ'pæθɪk] *a* tele-
pathisch.

telepathy [tə'lepəθɪ] *n* Telepathie *f*,
Gedankenübertragung *f*.

telephone ['telɪfəʊn] *n* Telefon *nt*,
Fernsprecher *m*; *vi* telefonieren; *vt*
anrufen; *message* telefonisch
mitteilen; — booth, — box Telefonhäuschen *nt*, Fernsprechzelle *f*;
— call Telefongespräch *nt*, Anruf
m; — directory Telefonbuch *nt*; —
exchange Telefonvermittlung *f*,
Telefonzentrale *f*; — number
Telefonnummer *f*.

telephonist [tə'lefənɪst] *n* Tele-
fonist(in *f*) *m*.

telephoto lens ['telɪ'fəʊtəʊ'lenz] n Teleobjektiv nt.

teleprinter ['telɪprɪntə*] n Fernschreiber m.

telescope ['telɪskəʊp] n Teleskop nt, Fernrohr nt; vt ineinanderschieben.

telescopic [telɪs'kɒpɪk] a teleskopisch; aerial etc ausziehbar.

televiewer ['telɪvjuːə*] n Fernsehteilnehmer(in f) m.

televise ['telɪvaɪz] vt durch das Fernsehen übertragen.

television ['telɪvɪʒən] n Fernsehen nt; to watch — fernsehen; — (set) Fernsehapparat m, Fernseher m; on — im Fernsehen.

telex ['teleks] n Telex nt.

tell [tel] irreg vt story erzählen; secret ausplaudern; (say, make known) sagen (sth to sb jdm etw); (distinguish) erkennen (sb by sth jdn an etw dat); (be sure) wissen; (order) sagen, befehlen (sb jdm); to — a lie lügen; to — sb about sth jdm von etw erzählen; vi (be sure) wissen; (divulge) es verraten; (have effect) sich auswirken; — off vt schimpfen; — on vt verraten, verpetzen; —er Kassenbeamte(r) mf; —ing verräterisch; blow hart; moment der Wahrheit; —tale a verräterisch.

telly ['telɪ] n (col) Fernseher m.

temerity [tɪ'merɪtɪ] n (Toll)kühnheit f.

temper ['tempə*] n (disposition) Temperament nt, Gemütsart f; (anger) Gereiztheit f, Zorn m; to be in a (bad) — wütend or gereizt sein; vt (tone down) mildern; metal härten; quick —ed jähzornig, aufbrausend; —ament Temperament nt, Veranlagung f; —amental [tempərə'mentl] a (moody) launisch.

temperance ['tempərəns] n Mäßigung f; (abstinence) Enthaltsamkeit f; — hotel alkoholfreie(s) Hotel nt.

temperate ['tempərət] a gemäßigt.

temperature ['temprɪtʃə*] n Temperatur f; (Med: high —) Fieber nt.

tempered ['tempəd] a steel gehärtet.

tempest ['tempɪst] n (wilder) Sturm m; —uous [tem'pestjʊəs] a stürmisch; (fig) ungestüm.

template ['templət] n Schablone f.

temple ['templ] n Tempel m; (Anat) Schläfe f.

tempo ['tempəʊ] n Tempo nt.

temporal ['tempərəl] a (of time) zeitlich; (worldly) irdisch, weltlich.

temporarily ['tempərərɪlɪ] ad zeitweilig, vorübergehend.

temporary ['tempərərɪ] a vorläufig; road, building provisorisch.

tempt [tempt] vt (persuade) verleiten, in Versuchung führen; (attract) reizen, (ver)locken; —ation [temp'teɪʃən] n Versuchung f; —ing a person verführerisch; object, situation verlockend.

ten [ten] num zehn.

tenable ['tenəbl] a haltbar; to be — (post) vergeben werden.

tenacious [tə'neɪʃəs, -lɪ] a zäh, hartnäckig.

tenacity [tə'næsɪtɪ] n Zähigkeit f, Hartnäckigkeit f.

tenancy ['tenənsɪ] n Mietverhältnis nt; Pachtverhältnis nt.

tenant ['tenənt] n Mieter m; (of larger property) Pächter m.

tend [tend] vt (look after) sich kümmern um; vi neigen, tendieren (to zu); to — to do sth (things) etw gewöhnlich tun; **—ency** Tendenz f; (of person also) Neigung f.

tender ['tendə*] a (soft) weich, zart; (delicate) zart; (loving) liebevoll, zärtlich; n (Comm: offer) Kostenanschlag m; **—ize** vt weich machen; **—ly** ad liebevoll; (touch also) zart; **—ness** Zartheit f; (being loving) Zärtlichkeit f.

tendon ['tendən] n Sehne f.

tenement ['tenəmənt] n Mietshaus nt.

tenet ['tenət] n Lehre f.

tennis ['tenɪs] n Tennis nt; **— ball** Tennisball m; **— court** Tennisplatz m; **— racket** Tennisschläger m.

tenor ['tenə*] n (voice) Tenor(stimme f) m; (singer) Tenor m; (meaning) Sinn m, wesentliche(r) Inhalt m.

tense [tens] a angespannt; (stretched tight) gespannt, straff; n Zeitform f; **—ly** ad (an)gespannt; **—ness** Spannung f; (strain) Angespanntheit f.

tension ['tenʃən] n Spannung f; (strain) Angespanntheit f.

tent [tent] n Zelt nt.

tentacle ['tentəkl] n Fühler m; (of sea animals) Fangarm m.

tentative ['tentətɪv] a movement unsicher; offer Probe-; arrangement vorläufig; suggestion unverbindlich; **—ly** ad versuchsweise, try, move vorsichtig.

tenterhooks ['tentəhuks] npl: to be on — auf die Folter gespannt sein.

tenth [tenθ] a zehnte(r,s); n Zehntel nt.

tent peg ['tentpeg] n Hering m.

tent pole ['tentpəul] n Zeltstange f.

tenuous ['tenjuəs] a fein; air dünn; connection, argument schwach.

tenure ['tenjuə*] n (of land) Besitz m; (of office) Amtszeit f.

tepid ['tepɪd] a lauwarm.

term [tɜːm] n (period of time) Zeit(raum m) f; (limit) Frist f; (Sch) Quartal nt; (Univ) Trimester nt; (expression) Ausdruck m; vt (be)nennen; **—s** pl (conditions) Bedingungen pl; (relationship) Beziehungen pl; **to be on good —s with sb** mit jdm gut auskommen; **—inal** (Rail, bus —inal; also —inus) Endstation f; (Aviat) Terminal m; a Schluß-; (Med) unheilbar; inal cancer Krebs m im Endstadium; **—inate** [-eɪt] vt beenden; vi enden, aufhören (in auf + dat); **—ination** [tɜːmɪ'neɪʃən] Ende nt; (act) Beendigung f; **—inology** [tɜːmɪ'nɒlədʒɪ] Terminologie f.

termite ['tɜːmaɪt] n Termite f.

terrace ['terəs] n (of houses) Häuserreihe f; (in garden etc) Terrasse f; **—d** a garden terrassenförmig angelegt; house Reihen-.

terracotta ['terə'kɒtə] n Terrakotta f.

terrain [te'reɪn] n Gelände nt, Terrain m.

terrible ['terəbl] a schrecklich, entsetzlich, fürchterlich.

terribly ['terəblɪ] ad fürchterlich.

terrier ['terɪə*] n Terrier m.

terrific a, **—ally** ad [tə'rɪfɪk, -lɪ] unwahrscheinlich; **—!** klasse!

terrify ['terɪfaɪ] vt erschrecken; **—ing** a erschreckend, grauenvoll.

territorial [terɪ'tɔːrɪəl] a Gebiets-, territorial; **— waters** pl Hoheitsgewässer pl.

territory ['terɪtərɪ] n Gebiet nt.

terror ['terə*] n Schrecken m; (Pol) Terror m; **—ism** n Terrorismus m; **—ist** Terrorist(in f) m; **—ize** vt terrorisieren.

terse [tɜːs] a knapp, kurz, bündig.

Terylene ® ['terəliːn] n Terylen(e) nt.

test [test] n Probe f; (examination) Prüfung f; (Psych, Tech) Test m; vt prüfen; (Psych) testen.

testament ['testəmənt] n Testament nt.

test card ['testkɑːd] n (TV) Testbild nt.

test case ['testkeɪs] n (Jur) Präzedenzfall m; (fig) Musterbeispiel nt.

test flight ['testflaɪt] n Probeflug m.

testicle ['testɪkl] n Hoden m.

testify ['testɪfaɪ] vi aussagen; bezeugen (to acc).

testimonial [testɪ'məʊnɪəl] n (of character) Referenz f.

testimony ['testɪmənɪ] n (Jur) Zeugenaussage f; (fig) Zeugnis nt.

test match ['testmætʃ] n (Sport) Länderkampf m.

test paper ['testpeɪpə*] n schriftliche (Klassen)arbeit f.

test pilot ['testpaɪlət] n Testpilot m.

test tube ['testtjuːb] n Reagenzglas nt.

testy ['testɪ] a gereizt; reizbar.

tetanus ['tetənəs] n Wundstarrkrampf m, Tetanus m.

tether ['teðə*] vt anbinden; to be at the end of one's — völlig am Ende sein.

text [tekst] n Text m; (of document) Wortlaut m; **—book** Lehrbuch nt.

textile ['tekstaɪl] n Gewebe nt; **—s** pl Textilien pl.

texture ['tekstʃə*] n Beschaffenheit f, Struktur f.

than [ðæn] prep, cj als.

thank [θæŋk] vt danken (+dat); you've him to — for your success Sie haben Ihren Erfolg ihm zu verdanken; **—ful** a dankbar; **—fully** ad (luckily) zum Glück; **—less** a undankbar; **—s** pl Dank m; **—s** to dank (+gen); — you, **—s** interj danke, dankeschön; T—sgiving (US) (Ernte)dankfest nt.

that [ðæt] a der/die/das, jene(r,s); pron das; cj daß; and **—'s** — und damit Schluß; — is das heißt; after — danach; at — dazu noch; — big so groß.

thatched [θætʃt] a strohgedeckt.

thaw [θɔː] n Tauwetter nt; vi tauen; (frozen foods, fig: people) auftauen; vt (auf)tauen lassen.

the [ðiː, ðə] def art der/die/das; to play — piano Klavier spielen; — sooner — better je eher desto besser.

theatre, (US) **theater** ['θɪətə*] n Theater nt; (for lectures etc) Saal m; (Med) Operationssaal m; **—goer** Theaterbesucher(in f) m.

theatrical [θɪ'ætrɪkl] a Theater-; career Schauspieler-; (showy) theatralisch.

theft [θeft] n Diebstahl m.

their [ðɛə*] poss a ihr; **—s** poss pron ihre(r,s).

them [ðem, ðəm] pron (acc) sie; (dat) ihnen.

theme [θiːm] n Thema nt; (Mus) Motiv nt; — song Titelmusik f.

themselves [ðəm'selvz] pl pron (reflexive) sich (selbst); (emphatic) selbst.

then [ðen] ad (at that time) damals; (next) dann; cj also, folglich; (furthermore) ferner; a

theologian [θɪəˈləʊdʒən] n Theologe m, Theologin f.

theological [θɪəˈlɒdʒɪkəl] a theologisch.

theology [θɪˈɒlədʒɪ] n Theologie f.

theorem [ˈθɪərəm] n Grundsatz m, Theorem nt.

theoretical a, **—ly** ad [θɪəˈretɪkəl, -l] theoretisch.

theorize [ˈθɪəraɪz] vi theoretisieren.

theory [ˈθɪərɪ] n Theorie f.

therapeutic(al) [θerəˈpjuːtɪk(əl)] a (Med) therapeutisch; erholsam.

therapist [ˈθerəpɪst] n Therapeut(in f) m.

therapy [ˈθerəpɪ] n Therapie f, Behandlung f.

there [ðeə*] ad dort; (to a place) dorthin; interj (see) na also; (to child) (sei) ruhig, na na; — is =es gibt; — are es sind, es gibt; **—abouts** ad so ungefähr; **—after** [ðeərˈɑːftə*] ad danach, später; **—by** ad dadurch; **—fore** ad daher, deshalb; **—'s** = there is.

thermal [ˈθɜːml] a springs Thermal-; (Phys) thermisch.

thermodynamics [ˈθɜːməʊdaɪˈnæmɪks] n Thermodynamik f.

thermometer [θəˈmɒmɪtə*] n Thermometer nt.

thermonuclear [ˈθɜːməʊˈnjuːklɪə*] a thermonuklear.

Thermos ® [ˈθɜːməs] n Thermosflasche f.

thermostat [ˈθɜːməstæt] n Thermostat m.

thesaurus [θɪˈsɔːrəs] n Synonymwörterbuch nt.

these [ðiːz] pl pron, a diese.

thesis [ˈθiːsɪs] n (for discussion) These f; (Univ) Dissertation f, Doktorarbeit f.

they [ðeɪ] pl pron sie; (people in general) man; **—'d** = they had; they would; **—'ll** = they shall, they will; **—'re** = they are; **—'ve** = they have.

thick [θɪk] a dick; forest dicht; liquid dickflüssig; (slow, stupid) dumm, schwer von Begriff; n: in the — of mitten in (+dat); **—en** vi (fog) dichter werden; vt sauce etc verdicken; **—ness** (of object) Dicke f; Dichte f; Dickflüssigkeit f; (of person) Dummheit f; **—set** a untersetzt; **—skinned** a dickhäutig.

thief [θiːf] n Dieb(in f) m.

thieving [ˈθiːvɪŋ] n Stehlen nt; a diebisch.

thigh [θaɪ] n Oberschenkel m; **—bone** Oberschenkelknochen m.

thimble [ˈθɪmbl] n Fingerhut m.

thin [θɪn] a dünn; person also mager; (not abundant) spärlich; fog, rain leicht; excuse schwach.

thing [θɪŋ] n Ding nt; (affair) Sache f; my **—s** pl meine Sachen pl.

think [θɪŋk] vti irreg denken; (believe) meinen, denken; to — of doing sth vorhaben or beabsichtigen, etw zu tun; — over vt überdenken; — up vt sich (dat) ausdenken; **—ing** a denkend.

thinly [ˈθɪnlɪ] ad dünn; disguised kaum.

thinness [ˈθɪnnəs] n Dünnheit f; Magerkeit f; Spärlichkeit f.

third [θɜːd] a dritte(r,s); n (person) Dritte(r) mf; (part) Drittel nt; **—ly** ad drittens; **— party insurance** Haftpflichtversicherung f; **—rate** a minderwertig.

thirst [θɜːst] n (lit, fig) Durst m; (fig) Verlangen nt; —y a person durstig; work durstig machend; to be —y Durst haben.

thirteen [ˈθɜːˈtiːn] num dreizehn.

thirty [ˈθɜːtɪ] num dreißig.

this [ðɪs] a diese(r,s); pron dies/das; it was — long es war so lang.

thistle [ˈθɪsl] n Distel f.

thong [θɒŋ] n (Leder)riemen m.

thorn [θɔːn] n Dorn m, Stachel m; (plant) Dornbusch m; —y a dornig; problem schwierig.

thorough [ˈθʌrə] a gründlich; contempt bei—; —bred Vollblut nt; a reinrassig, Vollblut-; —fare Straße f; —ly ad gründlich; (extremely) vollkommen, äußerst; —ness Gründlichkeit f.

those [ðəʊz] pl pron die (da), jene; a die, jene; — who diejenigen, die.

though [ðəʊ] cj obwohl; ad trotzdem; as — als ob.

thought [θɔːt] n (idea) Gedanke m; (opinion) Auffassung f, (thinking) Denken nt, Denkvermögen nt; —ful a (thinking) gedankenvoll, nachdenklich; (kind) rücksichtsvoll, aufmerksam; —less a gedankenlos, unbesonnen; (unkind) rücksichtslos.

thousand [ˈθaʊzənd] num tausend.

thrash [θræʃ] vt (lit) verdreschen; (fig) vernichtend) schlagen.

thread [θred] n Faden m, Garn nt; (on screw) Gewinde nt; (in story) Faden m, Zusammenhang m; vt needle einfädeln; vi: — one's way sich hindurchschlängeln; —bare a (lit, fig) fadenscheinig.

threat [θret] n Drohung f; (danger) Bedrohung f, Gefahr f; —en vt bedrohen; vi drohen; to — sb with sth jdm etw androhen;

—ening a drohend; letter Droh-.

three [θriː] num drei; —dimensional a dreidimensional; —fold a dreifach; —piece suit dreiteilige(r) Anzug m; —piece suite dreiteilige Polstergarnitur f; —ply a wool dreifach; wood dreischichtig; —quarter [θriːˈkwɔːtə*] a dreiviertel; —wheeler Dreiradwagen m.

thresh [θreʃ] vti dreschen; —ing machine Dreschmaschine f.

threshold [ˈθreʃhəʊld] n Schwelle f.

thrift [θrɪft] n Sparsamkeit f; —y a sparsam.

thrill [θrɪl] n Reiz m, Erregung f; it gave me quite a — to ... es war ein Erlebnis für mich, zu ...; vt begeistern, packen; vi beben, zittern; —er Krimi m; —ing a spannend, packend; news aufregend.

thrive [θraɪv] vi gedeihen (on bei). **thriving** [ˈθraɪvɪŋ] a blühend, gut gedeihend.

throat [θrəʊt] n Hals m, Kehle f.

throb [θrɒb] n Pochen nt, Schlagen nt; (Puls)schlag m; vi klopfen, pochen.

throes [θrəʊz] npl: in the — of mitten in (+dat).

thrombosis [θrɒmˈbəʊsɪs] n Thrombose f.

throne [θrəʊn] n Thron m; (Eccl) Stuhl m.

throttle [ˈθrɒtl] n Gashebel m; to open the — Gas geben; vt erdrosseln.

through [θruː] prep durch; (time) während (+gen); (because of) aus, durch; ad durch; to go — jdn verbinden (to mit); a ticket, train durchgehend; (finished) fertig; —out [θruːˈaʊt] prep (place) überall in (+*dat*); (*time*) während (+*gen*); *ad* überall; die ganze Zeit; we're — es ist aus zwischen uns.

throw [θrəʊ] *n* Wurf *m*; *vt irreg* werfen; **— out** *vt* hinauswerfen; *rubbish* wegwerfen; *plan* verwerfen; **— up** *vti* (*vomit*) speien; **—away** *a* (*disposable*) Wegwerf-; *bottle* Einweg-; **—in** Einwurf *m*.

thru [θru:] (*US*) = **through**.

thrush [θrʌʃ] *n* Drossel *f*.

thrust [θrʌst] *n* (*Tech*) Schubkraft *f*; *vti irreg* (*push*) stoßen; (*fig*) sich drängen; **to —** oneself on sb sich jdm aufdrängen; **—ing** *a person* aufdringlich, unverfroren.

thud [θʌd] *n* dumpfe(r) (Auf)schlag *m*.

thug [θʌg] *n* Schlägertyp *m*.

thumb [θʌm] *n* Daumen *m*; *vt book* durchblättern; **to — a** well-ed book ein abgegriffenes Buch; **to — a** lift per Anhalter fahren (wollen); **— index** Daumenregister *nt*; **—nail** Daumennagel *m*; **—tack** (*US*) Reißzwecke *f*.

thump [θʌmp] *n* (*blow*) Schlag *m*; (*noise*) Bums *m*; *vi* hämmern, pochen; *vt* schlagen auf (+*acc*).

thunder [ˈθʌndə*] *n* Donner *m*; *vi* donnern; *vt* brüllen; **—ous** *a* stürmisch; **—storm** Gewitter *nt*, Unwetter *nt*; **—struck** *a* wie vom Donner gerührt; **—y** *a* gewitterschwül.

Thursday [ˈθɜːzdei] *n* Donnerstag *m*.

thus [ðʌs] *ad* (*in this way*) so; (*therefore*) somit, also, folglich.

thwart [θwɔːt] *vt* vereiteln, durchkreuzen; *person* hindern.

thyme [taim] *n* Thymian *m*.

thyroid [ˈθairɔid] *n* Schilddrüse *f*.

tiara [tiˈɑːrə] *n* Diadem *nt*; (*pope's*) Tiara *f*.

tic [tik] *n* Tick *m*.

tick [tik] *n* (*sound*) Ticken *nt*; (*mark*) Häkchen *nt*; **in a —** (*col*) sofort; *vi* ticken; *vt* abhaken.

ticket [ˈtikit] *n* (*for travel*) Fahrkarte *f*; (*for entrance*) (Eintritts)karte *f*; (*price —*) Preisschild *nt*; (*luggage —*) (Gepäck)schein *m*; (*raffle —*) Los *nt*; (*parking —*) Strafzettel *m*; (*permission*) Parkschein *m*; **— collector** Fahrkartenkontrolleur *m*; **— holder** Karteninhaber *m*; **— office** (*Rail etc*) Fahrkartenschalter *m*; (*Theat etc*) Kasse *f*.

ticking-off [ˈtikiŋˈɒf] *n* (*col*) Anschnauzer *m*.

tickle [ˈtikl] *n* Kitzeln *nt*; *vt* kitzeln; (*amuse*) amüsieren; **that —d her** fancy das gefiel ihr.

ticklish [ˈtikliʃ] *a* (*lit, fig*) kitzlig.

tidal [ˈtaidl] *a* Flut-, Tide-.

tidbit [ˈtidbit] *n* (*US*) Leckerbissen *m*.

tiddlywinks [ˈtidliwiŋks] *n* Floh(hüpf)spiel *nt*.

tide [taid] *n* Gezeiten *pl*, Ebbe *f* und Flut; **the —** is in/out es ist Flut/Ebbe.

tidily [ˈtaidili] *ad* sauber, ordentlich.

tidiness [ˈtaidinəs] *n* Ordnung *f*.

tidy [ˈtaidi] *a* ordentlich; *vt* aufräumen, in Ordnung bringen.

tie [tai] *n* (*necktie*) Kravatte *f*, Schlips *m*; (*sth connecting*) Band *nt*; (*Sport*) Unentschieden *nt*; *vt* (*fasten, restrict*) binden; *knot* schnüren, festbinden; *vi* (*Sport*) unentschieden spielen; (*in competition*) punktgleich sein; **— down** *vt* (*lit*) festbinden; (*fig*) binden; **— up** *vt dog* anbinden;

parcel verschnüren; *boat* festmachen; *person* fesseln; **I am —d up** right now ich bin im Moment beschäftigt.

tier [tɪə*] *n* Reihe *f*, Rang *m*; (*of cake*) Etage *f*.

tiff [tɪf] *n* kleine Meinungsverschiedenheit *f*.

tiger ['taɪgə*] *n* Tiger *m*.

tight [taɪt] *a* (*close*) eng, knapp; *schedule* gedrängt; (*firm*) fest, dicht; *screw* festsitzend; *control* streng; (*stretched*) stramm, (an)gespannt; (*col*) blau, stramm; **—s** *pl* Strumpfhose *f*; **—en** *vt* anziehen, anspannen; *restrictions* verschärfen; (*screw*) sich spannen; **—fisted** *a* knauserig; **—ly** *ad* eng; fest, dicht; **stretched** straff; **—ness** Enge *f*; Festigkeit *f*; Straffheit *f*; (*of money*) Knappheit *f*; **,—rope** Seil *nt*.

tile [taɪl] *n* (*in roof*) Dachziegel *m*; (*on wall or floor*) Fliese *f*; **—d** *a roof* gedeckt, Ziegel-; *floor, wall* mit Fliesen belegt.

till [tɪl] *n* Kasse *f*; *vt* bestellen; *prep,cj* bis; not — (*in future*) nicht vor; (*in past*) erst.

tiller ['tɪlə*] *n* Ruderpinne *f*.

tilt [tɪlt] *vt* kippen, neigen; *vi* sich neigen.

timber ['tɪmbə*] *n* Holz *nt*; (*trees*) Baumbestand *m*.

time [taɪm] *n* Zeit *f*; (*occasion*) Mal *nt*; (*rhythm*) Takt *m*; *vt* zur rechten Zeit tun, zeitlich einrichten; (*Sport*) stoppen; **I have no — for people** like him für Leute wie ihn habe ich nichts übrig; **in 2 weeks' —** in 2 Wochen; **for the —being** vorläufig; **at all —s** immer; **at one —** früher; **at no —** nie; **at —s** manchmal; **by the —** bis; **this — diesmal**, dieses Mal; **to have a**

good — viel Spaß haben, sich amüsieren; **in —** (*soon enough*) rechtzeitig; (*after some time*) mit der Zeit; (*Mus*) im Takt; **on —** pünktlich, rechtzeitig; **five — fünfmal**; *local* — Ortszeit *f*; **what — is it?** wieviel Uhr ist es?, wie spät ist es?; **—keeper** Zeitnehmer *m*; **—lag** (*in travel*) Verzögerung *f*; (*difference*) Zeitunterschied *m*; **—less** *a beauty* zeitlos; **— limit** Frist *f*; **—ly** *a* rechtzeitig; günstig; **—saving** *a* zeitsparend; **— switch** Zeitschalter *m*; **—table** Fahrplan *m*; (*Sch*) Stundenplan *m*; **— zone** Zeitzone *f*.

timid ['tɪmɪd] *a* ängstlich, schüchtern; **—ity** [tɪ'mɪdɪtɪ] Ängstlichkeit *f*; **—ly** *ad* ängstlich.

timing ['taɪmɪŋ] *n* Wahl *f* des richtigen Zeitpunkts, Timing *nt*; (*Aut*) Einstellung *f*.

timpani ['tɪmpənɪ] *npl* Kesselpauken *pl*.

tin [tɪn] *n* (*metal*) Blech *nt*; (*container*) Büchse *f*, Dose *f*; **—foil** Staniolpapier *nt*.

tinge [tɪndʒ] *n* (*colour*) Färbung *f*; (*fig*) Anflug *m*; *vt* färben, einen Anstrich geben (+*dat*).

tingle ['tɪŋgl] *n* Prickeln *nt*; *vi* prickeln.

tinker ['tɪŋkə*] *n* Kesselflicker *m*; **— with** *vt* herumpfuschen an (+*dat*).

tinkle ['tɪŋkl] *n* Klingeln *nt*; *vi* klingeln.

tinned [tɪnd] *a food* Dosen-, Büchsen-.

tinny ['tɪnɪ] *a* Blech-, blechern.

tin opener ['tɪnəʊpnə*] *n* Dosen- or Büchsenöffner *m*.

tinsel ['tɪnsəl] *n* Rauschgold *nt*; Lametta *nt*.

tint [tɪnt] n Farbton m; (slight colour) Anflug m; (hair) Tönung f.

tiny ['taɪnɪ] a winzig.

tip [tɪp] n (pointed end) Spitze f; (money) Trinkgeld nt; (hint) Wink m, Tip m; it's on the — of my tongue es liegt mir auf der Zunge; vt (slant) kippen; hat antippen; (— over) umkippen; waiter ein Trinkgeld geben (+dat); —off Hinweis m, Tip m; —ped a cigarette Filter-.

tipple ['tɪpl] n (drink) Schnäpschen nt.

tipsy ['tɪpsɪ] a beschwipst.

tiptoe ['tɪptəʊ] n: on — auf Zehenspitzen.

tiptop ['tɪp'tɒp] a: in — condition tipptopp, erstklassig.

tire ['taɪə*] n (US) = **tyre**; vti ermüden, müde machen/werden; —d a müde; to be —d of sth etw satt haben; —dness Müdigkeit f; —less a, —lessly ad unermüdlich; —some a lästig.

tiring ['taɪərɪŋ] a ermüdend.

tissue ['tɪʃuː] n Gewebe nt; (paper handkerchief) Papiertaschentuch nt; — paper Seidenpapier nt.

tit [tɪt] n (bird) Meise f; (col: breast) Titte f; — for tat wie du mir, so ich dir.

titbit ['tɪtbɪt] n Leckerbissen m.

titillate ['tɪtɪleɪt] vt kitzeln.

titillation [tɪtɪ'leɪʃən] n Kitzeln nt.

titivate ['tɪtɪveɪt] vt schniegeln.

title ['taɪtl] n Titel m; (in law) Rechtstitel m, Eigentumsrecht nt; — deed Eigentumsurkunde f; — role Hauptrolle f.

tittle-tattle ['tɪtltætl] n Klatsch m.

titter ['tɪtə*] vi kichern.

titular ['tɪtjʊlə*] a Titular-, nominell; possessions Titel-.

to [tuː, tə] prep (towards) zu; (with countries, towns) nach; (indir obj) dat; (as far as) bis; (next to) an (+dat); (per); cj (in order to) um... zu; ad — and fro hin und her; to go — school/the theatre/bed in die Schule/ins Theater/ins Bett gehen; I have never been — Germany ich war noch nie in Deutschland; to give sth — sb jdm etw geben; this day bis auf den heutigen Tag; 20 (minutes) — 4 20 (Minuten) vor 4; superior — sth besser als etw; they tied him — a tree sie banden ihn an einen Baum.

toad [təʊd] n Kröte f; —stool Giftpilz m; —y Speichellecker m, Kriecher m; vi kriechen (to vor +dat).

toast [təʊst] n (bread) Toast m; (drinking) Trinkspruch m; vt trinken auf (+acc); bread toasten; (warm) wärmen; —er Toaster m; —master Zeremonienmeister m; —rack Toastständer m.

tobacco [tə'bækəʊ] n Tabak m; —nist [tə'bækənɪst] Tabakhändler m; —nist's (shop) Tabakladen m.

toboggan [tə'bɒgən] n (Rodel)-schlitten m.

today [tə'deɪ] ad heute; (at the present time) heutzutage; n (day) heutige(r) Tag m; (time) Heute nt, heutige Zeit f.

toddle ['tɒdl] vi watscheln.

toddler ['tɒdlə*] n Kleinkind nt.

toddy ['tɒdɪ] n (Whisky)grog m.

to-do [tə'duː] n Aufheben nt, Theater nt.

toe [təʊ] n Zehe f; (of sock, shoe) Spitze f; vt: — the line (fig) sich einfügen; — hold Halt m für die Fußspitzen; —nail Zehennagel m.

toffee ['tɒfɪ] n Sahnebonbon nt; — apple kandierte(r) Apfel m.

toga ['təʊgə] n Toga f.

together [tə'geðə*] ad zusammen; (at the same time) gleichzeitig; —ness (company) Beisammensein nt; (feeling) Zusammengehörigkeitsgefühl nt.

toil [tɔɪl] n harte Arbeit f, Plackerei f; vi sich abmühen, sich plagen.

toilet ['tɔɪlət] n Toilette f; a Toiletten-; — bag Waschbeutel m; — paper Toilettenpapier nt; —ries ['tɔɪlətrɪz] pl Toilettenartikel pl; — roll Rolle f Toilettenpapier; — soap Toilettenseife f; — water Toilettenwasser nt.

token ['təʊkən] n Zeichen nt; (gift —) Gutschein m.

tolerable ['tɒlərəbl] a (bearable) erträglich; (fairly good) leidlich.

tolerably ['tɒlərəblɪ] ad ziemlich, leidlich.

tolerance ['tɒlərəns] n Toleranz f.

tolerant a, —ly ad ['tɒlərənt, -lɪ] tolerant; (patient) geduldig.

tolerate ['tɒləreɪt] vt dulden; noise ertragen.

toleration [tɒlə'reɪʃən] n Toleranz f.

toll [təʊl] n Gebühr f; it took a heavy — of human life es forderte or kostete viele Menschenleben; vi (bell) läuten; —bridge gebührenpflichtige Brücke f; — road gebührenpflichtige Autostraße f.

tomato [tə'mɑːtəʊ] n, pl -es Tomate f.

tomb [tuːm] n Grab(mal) nt.

tombola [tɒm'bəʊlə] n Tombola f.

tomboy ['tɒmbɔɪ] n Wildfang m; she's a — sie ist sehr burschikos.

tombstone ['tuːmstəʊn] n Grabstein m.

tomcat ['tɒmkæt] n Kater m.

tome [təʊm] n (volume) Band m; (big book) Wälzer m.

tomorrow [tə'mɒrəʊ] n Morgen nt; ad morgen.

ton [tʌn] n Tonne f; —s of (col) eine Unmenge von.

tonal ['təʊnl] a tonal; Klang-.

tone [təʊn] n Ton m; vi (harmonize) passen (zu), harmonisieren (mit); vt eine Färbung geben (+dat); — down vt criticism, demands mäßigen; colours abtonen; —deaf a ohne musikalisches Gehör.

tongs [tɒŋz] npl Zange f; (curling —) Lockenstab m.

tongue [tʌŋ] n Zunge f; (language) Sprache f; with — in cheek ironisch, scherzhaft; —tied a stumm, sprachlos; —twister Zungenbrecher m.

tonic ['tɒnɪk] n (Med) Stärkungsmittel nt; (Mus) Grundton m, Tonika f; — water Tonic(water) nt.

tonight [tə'naɪt] n heutige(r) Abend m; diese Nacht f; ad heute abend; heute nacht.

tonnage ['tʌnɪdʒ] n Tonnage f.

tonsil ['tɒnsl] n Mandel f; —itis [tɒnsɪ'laɪtɪs] Mandelentzündung f.

too [tuː] ad zu; (also) auch.

tool [tuːl] n (lit, fig) Werkzeug nt; —box Werkzeugkasten m; —kit Werkzeug nt.

toot [tuːt] n Hupen nt; vi tuten; (Aut) hupen.

tooth [tuːθ] n, pl teeth Zahn m; —ache Zahnschmerzen pl, Zahnweh nt; —brush Zahnbürste f; —paste Zahnpasta f; —pick

Zahnstocher m; **— powder** Zahnpulver nt.

top [tɒp] n Spitze f; (of mountain) Gipfel m; (of tree) Wipfel m; (toy) Kreisel m; (— gear) vierte(r) Gang m; a oberste(r,s); vt list an erster Stelle stehen auf (+dat); to — it all, he said ... und er setzte dem noch die Krone auf, indem er sagte ...; from — to toe von Kopf bis Fuß; **—coat** Mantel m; **—flight** a erstklassig, prima; **— hat** Zylinder m; **—heavy** a oben schwerer als unten, kopflastig.

topic ['tɒpɪk] n Thema nt, Gesprächsgegenstand m; **—al** a aktuell.

topless ['tɒpləs] a dress oben ohne.

top-level ['tɒp'levl] a auf höchster Ebene.

topmost ['tɒpməʊst] a oberste(r,s), höchste(r,s).

topple ['tɒpl] vti stürzen, kippen.

top-secret ['tɒp'si:krət] a streng geheim.

topsy-turvy ['tɒpsi'tɜ:vi] ad durcheinander; a auf den Kopf gestellt.

torch [tɔ:tʃ] n (Elec) Taschenlampe f; (with flame) Fackel f.

torment ['tɔ:ment] n Qual f; [tɔ:'ment] vt (annoy) plagen; (distress) quälen.

torn [tɔ:n] a hin- und hergerissen.

tornado [tɔ:'neɪdəʊ] n Tornado m, Wirbelsturm m.

torpedo [tɔ:'pi:dəʊ] n Torpedo m.

torpor ['tɔ:pə*] n Erstarrung f.

torrent ['tɒrənt] n Sturzbach m; **—ial** [tə'renʃəl] a wolkenbruchartig.

torso ['tɔ:səʊ] n Torso m.

tortoise ['tɔ:təs] n Schildkröte f.

tortuous ['tɔ:tjʊəs] a (winding) gewunden; (deceitful) krumm, unehrlich.

torture ['tɔ:tʃə*] n Folter f; vt foltern.

Tory ['tɔ:rɪ] n Tory m; a Tory-, konservativ.

toss [tɒs] vt werfen, schleudern; n (of coin) Hochwerfen nt; to — a coin, to — up for sth etw mit einer Münze entscheiden.

tot [tɒt] n (small quantity) bißchen nt; (small child) Knirps m.

total ['təʊtl] n Gesamtheit f, Ganze(s) nt; a ganz, gesamt, total; vt (add up) zusammenzählen; (amount to) sich belaufen auf; **—itarian** [təʊtælɪ'teərɪən] a totalitär; **—ity** [təʊ'tælɪtɪ] Gesamtheit f; **—ly** ad gänzlich, total.

totem pole ['təʊtəmpəʊl] n Totempfahl m.

totter ['tɒtə*] vi wanken, schwanken, wackeln.

touch [tʌtʃ] n Berührung f; (sense of feeling) Tastsinn m; (small amount) Spur f; (style) Stil m; vt (feel) berühren; (come against) leicht anstoßen; (emotionally) bewegen, rühren; in — with in Verbindung mit; — on vt topic berühren, erwähnen; — up vt paint auffrischen; —and-go a riskant, knapp; **—down** Landen nt, Niedergehen nt; **—iness** Empfindlichkeit f; **—ing** a rührend, ergreifend; **—line** Seitenlinie f; **—y** a empfindlich, reizbar.

tough [tʌf] a (strong) zäh, widerstandsfähig; (difficult) schwierig, hart; meat zäh; — luck Pech nt; n Schläger(typ) m; — up vt zäh machen; (make strong) abhärten; vi zäh werden; **—ness** Zähigkeit f; Härte f.

toupée ['tu:peɪ] n Toupet nt.

tour ['tuə*] n Reise f, Tour f, Fahrt f; vi umherreisen; (Theat) auf Tour sein/gehen; —ing Umherreisen nt; (Theat) Tournee f; —ism Fremdenverkehr m, Tourismus m; —ist Tourist(in f); a (class) Touristen-; ad Touristenklasse; —ist office Verkehrsamt nt.

tournament ['tuənəmənt] n Turnier nt.

tousled ['tauzld] a zerzaust.

tow [tou] n Schleppen nt; vt (ab)schleppen.

toward(s) [tə'wo:d(z)] prep (with time) gegen; (in direction of) nach; he walked — me/the town er kam auf mich zu/er ging auf die Stadt zu; my feelings — him meine Gefühle ihm gegenüber.

towel ['tauəl] n Handtuch nt.

tower ['tauə*] n Turm m; — over vi (lit, fig) überragen; —ing a hochragend; rage rasend.

town [taun] n Stadt f; — clerk Stadtdirektor m; — hall Rathaus nt; — planner Stadtplaner m.

towpath ['təupɑ:θ] n Leinpfad m.

towrope ['təurəup] n Abschlepptau nt.

toxic ['tɒksik] a giftig, Gift-.

toy [tɔi] n Spielzeug nt; — with vt spielen mit; —shop Spielwarengeschäft nt.

trace [treis] n Spur f; vt (follow a course) nachspüren (+dat); (find out) aufspüren; (copy) zeichnen, durchpausen.

track [træk] n (mark) Spur f; (path) Weg m, Pfad m; (race—) Rennbahn f; (Rail) Gleis nt; vt verfolgen; to keep — of sb jdn im Auge behalten; to keep — of an argument einer Argumentation folgen können; to keep — of the situation die Lage verfolgen; to

make —s (for) gehen (nach); — down vt aufspüren; —er dog Spürhund m; —less a pfadlos.

tract [trækt] n (of land) Gebiet nt; (booklet) Abhandlung f, Traktat nt.

tractor ['træktə*] n Traktor m.

trade [treid] n (commerce) Handel m; (business) Geschäft nt, Gewerbe nt; (people) Geschäftsleute pl; (skilled manual work) Handwerk nt; vi handeln (in nt); vt tauschen; — in vt in Zahlung geben; —mark Warenzeichen nt; — name Handelsbezeichnung f; —r Händler m; —sman (shopkeeper) Geschäftsmann m; (workman) Handwerker m; (delivery man) Lieferant m; — union Gewerkschaft f; — unionist Gewerkschaftler(in f) m.

trading ['treidiŋ] n Handel m; — estate Industriegelände nt; — stamp Rabattmarke f.

tradition [trə'diʃən] n Tradition f; —al a traditionell, herkömmlich; —ally ad üblicherweise, schon immer.

traffic ['træfik] n Verkehr m; (esp in drugs) Handel m (in mit); vt esp drugs handeln; — circle (US) Kreisverkehr m; — jam Verkehrsstauung f; — lights pl Verkehrsampeln pl.

tragedy ['trædʒədi] n (lit, fig) Tragödie f.

tragic ['trædʒik] a tragisch; —ally ad tragisch, auf tragische Weise.

trail [treil] n (track) Spur f, Fährte f; (of meteor) Schweif m; (of smoke) Rauchfahne f; (of dust) Staubwolke f; (road) Pfad m, Weg m; vt animal verfolgen; person folgen (+dat); (drag) schleppen; vi (hang loosely) schleifen; (plants) sich ranken; (be behind) hinter-

herhinken; (*Sport*) weit zurück-
liegen; (*walk*) zuckeln; on the —
auf der Spur; — behind *vi* zurückbleiben; —er Anhänger *m*; (*US*:
caravan) Wohnwagen *m*; (*for film*)
Vorschau *f*.

train [trein] *n* Zug *m*; (*of dress*)
Schleppe *f*; (*series*) Folge *f*, Kette
f; *vt* (*teach*) person ausbilden;
animal abrichten; mind schulen;
(*Sport*) trainieren; (*aim*) richten
(*on* auf +*acc*); plant wachsen
lassen, ziehen; *vi* (*exercise*)
trainieren; (*study*) ausgebildet
werden; —ed a eye geschult;
person, voice ausgebildet; —ee
Anlernling *m*; Lehrling *m*;
Praktikant(in *f*) *m*; —er (*Sport*)
Trainer *m*; Ausbilder *m*; —ing (*for
occupation*) Ausbildung *f*; (*Sport*)
Training *nt*; in —ing im Training;
—ing college Pädagogische Hochschule *f*, Lehrerseminar *nt*; (*for
priests*) Priesterseminar *nt*.

traipse [treips] *vi* latschen.

trait [trei(t)] *n* Zug *m*, Merkmal *nt*.

traitor ['treitə*] *n* Verräter *m*.

trajectory [trə'dʒektəri] *n*
Flugbahn *f*.

tram(car) ['træm(kɑ:*)] *n*
Straßenbahn *f*; —line Straßenbahn-
schiene *f*; (*route*) Straßenbahnlinie
f.

tramp [træmp] *n* Landstreicher *m*;
vi (*walk heavily*) stampfen,
stapfen; (*travel on foot*) wandern; —le ['træmpl] *vt* (*nieder*)trampeln;
vi (*herum*)trampeln; —oline
Trampolin *nt*.

trance [trɑ:ns] *n* Trance *f*.

tranquil ['træŋkwil] *a* ruhig, fried-
lich; —ity [træŋ'kwiliti] Ruhe *f*; —izer Beruhigungsmittel *nt*.

trans- [trænz] *pref* Trans-.

transact [træn'zækt] *vt* (*durch*)-
führen, abwickeln; —ion Durchführung *f*, Abwicklung *f*; (*piece of
business*) Geschäft *nt*, Transaktion
f.

transatlantic ['trænzət'læntik] a
transatlantisch.

transcend [træn'send] *vt*
übersteigen.

transcendent [træn'sendənt] a
transzendent.

transcript ['trænskript] *n* Abschrift
f, Kopie *f*; (*Jur*) Protokoll *nt*; —ion
[træn'skripʃən] Transkription *f*;
(*product*) Abschrift *f*.

transept ['trænsept] *n* Querschiff
nt.

transfer ['trænsfə*] *n* (*trans-
ferring*) Übertragung *f*; (*of
business*) Umzug *m*; (*being trans-
ferred*) Versetzung *f*; (*design*)
Abziehbild *nt*; (*Sport*) Transfer *m*;
(*player*) Transferspieler *m*;
[træns'fə:*] *vt* business verlegen;
person versetzen; prisoner über-
führen; drawing übertragen;
money überweisen; —able
[træns'fə:rəbl] a übertragbar.

transform [træns'fɔ:m] *vt*
umwandeln, verändern; —ation
[trænsfə'meiʃən] Umwandlung *f*,
Veränderung *f*, Verwandlung *f*; —er (*Elec*) Transformator *m*.

transfusion [træns'fju:ʒən] *n*
Blutübertragung *f*, Transfusion *f*.

transient ['trænziənt] a kurz(lebig).

transistor [træn'zistə*] *n* (*Elec*)
Transistor *m*; (*radio*) Transistor-
radio *nt*.

transit ['trænzit] *n*: in —
unterwegs, auf dem Transport.

transition [træn'ziʃən] *n* Übergang
m; —al a Übergangs-.

transitive a, —ly ad ['trænzitiv,
-li] transitiv.

transitory ['trænzıtərı] *a* vorübergehend.

translate [trænz'leıt] *vtl* übersetzen.

translation [trænz'leıʃən] *n* Übersetzung *f.*

translator [trænz'leıtə*] *n* Übersetzer(in *f*) *m.*

transmission [trænz'mıʃən] *n* (*of information*) Übermittlung *f*; (*Elec, Med, TV*) Übertragung *f*; (*Aut*) Getriebe *nt*; (*process*) Übersetzung *f.*

transmit [trænz'mıt] *vt message* übermitteln; (*Elec, Med, TV*) übertragen; **—ter** Sender *m.*

transparency [træns'pεərənsı] *n* Durchsichtigkeit *f*, Transparenz *f*; (*Phot also* ['-pærənsı]) Dia(positiv) *nt.*

transparent [træns'pærənt] *a* (*lit*) durchsichtig; (*fig*) offenkundig.

transplant [træns'plɑ:nt] *vt* umpflanzen; (*Med*) verpflanzen; (*fig*) *person* verpflanzen; ['trænsplɑ:nt] *n* (*Med*) Transplantation *f*; (*organ*) Transplantat *nt.*

transport ['trænspɔ:t] *n* Transport *m*, Beförderung *f*; (*vehicle*) fahrbare(r) Untersatz *m*; means of — Transportmittel *nt*; [træns'pɔ:t] *vt* befördern, transportieren; **—able** [træns'pɔ:təbl] *a* transportabel; **—ation** [trænspɔ:'teıʃən] Transport *m*, Beförderung *f*; (*means*) Beförderungsmittel *nt*; (*cost*) Transportkosten *pl.*

transverse ['trænzvɜ:s] *a* Quer-; *position* **·**horizontal; *engine* querliegend.

transvestite [trænz'vestaıt] *n* Transvestit *m.*

trap [træp] *n* Falle *f*; (*carriage*) zweirädrige(r) Einspänner *m*; (*col: mouth*) Klappe *f*; *vt* fangen;

person in eine Falle locken; the miners were —ed die Bergleute waren eingeschlossen; **—door** Falltür *f.*

trapeze [trə'pi:z] *n* Trapez *nt.*

trapper ['træpə*] *n* Fallensteller *m*, Trapper *m.*

trappings ['træpıŋz] *npl* Aufmachung *f.*

trash [træʃ] *n* (*rubbish*) wertlose(s) Zeug *nt*, Plunder *m*; (*nonsense*) Mist *m*, Blech *nt*; — **can** (*US*) Mülleimer *m*; **—y** *a* wertlos; *novel etc* Schund-.

trauma ['trɔ:mə] *n* Trauma *nt*; **—tic** [trɔ:'mætɪk] *a* traumatisch.

travel ['trævl] *n* Reisen *nt*; *vi* reisen, eine Reise machen; *vt distance* zurücklegen; *country* bereisen; **—ler**, (*US*) **—er** Reisende(r) *mf*; (*salesman*) Handlungsreisende(r) *m*; **—ler's cheque**, (*US*) **—er's check** Reisescheck *m*; **—ling**, (*US*) **—ing** Reisen *nt*; **—ling bag** Reisetasche *f*; — **sickness** Reisekrankheit *f.*

traverse [træ'vɜ:s] *vt* (*cross*) durchqueren; (*lie across*) überspannen.

travesty ['trævəstı] *n* Zerrbild *nt*, Travestie *f*; a — *of justice* ein Hohn *ni* auf die Gerechtigkeit.

trawler ['trɔ:lə*] *n* Fischdampfer *m*, Trawler *m.*

tray [treı] *n* (*tea* —) Tablett *nt*; (*receptacle*) Schale *f*; (*for mail*) Ablage *f.*

treacherous ['tretʃərəs] *a* verräterisch; *memory* unzuverlässig; *road* tückisch.

treachery ['tretʃərı] *n* Verrat *m*; (*of road*) tückische(r) Zustand *m.*

treacle ['tri:kl] *n* Sirup *m*, Melasse *f.*

tread [tred] *n* Schritt *m*, Tritt *m*; (*of stair*) Stufe *f*; (*on tyre*) Profil *nt*; *vi irreg* treten; (*walk*) gehen; — on *vt* treten auf (+acc).

treason ['tri:zn] *n* Verrat *m* (to an +dat).

treasure ['treʒə*] *n* Schatz *m*; *vt* schätzen; — hunt Schatzsuche *f*; —r Kassenverwalter *m*, Schatzmeister *m*.

treasury ['treʒərɪ] *n* (Pol) Finanzministerium *nt*.

treat [tri:t] *n* besondere Freude *f*; (*school* — etc) Fest *nt*; (*outing*) Ausflug *m*; *vt* (*deal with*) behandeln; (*entertain*) bewirten; to — sb to sth jdn zu etw einladen, jdm etw spendieren.

treatise ['tri:tɪz] *n* Abhandlung *f*.

treatment ['tri:tmənt] *n* Behandlung *f*.

treaty ['tri:tɪ] *n* Vertrag *m*.

treble ['trebl] *a* dreifach; *vt* verdreifachen; *n* (*voice*) Sopran *m*; (*music*) Diskant *m*; — clef Violinschlüssel *m*.

tree [tri:]. *n* Baum *m*; —lined *a* baumbestanden; — trunk Baumstamm *m*.

trek [trek] *n* Treck *m*, Zug *m*; *vi* trecken.

trellis ['trelɪs] *n* Gitter *nt*; (*for gardening*) Spalier *nt*.

tremble ['trembl] *vi* zittern; (*ground*) beben.

trembling ['tremblɪŋ] *n* Zittern *nt*; *a* zitternd.

tremendous [trə'mendəs] *a* gewaltig, kolossal; (*col: very good*) prima; —ly *ad* ungeheuer, enorm; (*col*) unheimlich.

tremor ['tremə*] *n* Zittern *nt*; (*of earth*) Beben *nt*.

trench [trentʃ] *n* Graben *m*; (Mil) Schützengraben *m*.

trend [trend] *n* Richtung *f*, Tendenz *f*; *vi* sich neigen, tendieren; —y *a* (*col*) modisch.

trepidation [trepɪ'deɪʃən] *n* Beklommenheit *f*.

trespass ['trespəs] *vi* widerrechtlich betreten (on acc); '—ers will be prosecuted' 'Betreten verboten.'

tress [tres] *n* Locke *f*.

trestle ['tresl] *n* Bock *m*; — table Klapptisch *m*.

tri- [traɪ] *pref* Drei-, drei-.

trial ['traɪəl] *n* (Jur) Prozeß *m*, Verfahren *nt*; (*test*) Versuch *m*, Probe *f*; (*hardship*) Prüfung *f*; by — and error durch Ausprobieren.

triangle ['traɪæŋgl] *n* Dreieck *nt*; (Mus) Triangel *m*.

triangular [traɪ'æŋgjulə*] *a* dreieckig.

tribal ['traɪbəl] *a* Stammes-.

tribe [traɪb] *n* Stamm *m*; —sman Stammesangehörige(r) *m*.

tribulation [trɪbju'leɪʃən] *n* Not *f*, Mühsal *f*.

tribunal [traɪ'bju:nl] *n* Gericht *nt*; (*inquiry*) Untersuchungsausschuß *m*.

tributary ['trɪbjutərɪ] *n* Nebenfluß *m*.

tribute ['trɪbju:t] *n* (*admiration*) Zeichen *nt* der Hochachtung.

trice [traɪs] *n*: in a — im Nu.

trick [trɪk] *n* Trick *m*; (*mischief*) Streich *m*; (*habit*) Angewohnheit *f*; (*Cards*) Stich *m*; *vt* überlisten, beschwindeln; —ery Betrügerei *f*, Tricks *pl*.

trickle ['trɪkl] *n* Tröpfeln *nt*; (*small river*) Rinnsal *nt*; *vi* tröpfeln; (*seep*) sickern.

tricky ['trɪkɪ] *a problem* schwierig; *situation* kitzlig.

tricycle ['traisikl] *n* Dreirad *nt.*

tried [traid] *a* erprobt, bewährt.

trier ['traiə*] *n*: to be a — sich (*dat*) ernsthaft Mühe geben.

trifle ['traifl] *n* Kleinigkeit *f*; (*Cook*) Trifle *m*; *ad*: **a** — ein bißchen.

trifling ['traiflɪŋ] *a* geringfügig.

trigger ['trɪgə*] *n* Drücker *m*; — **off** *vt* auslösen.

trigonometry [trɪgə'nɒmətrɪ] *n* Trigonometrie *f.*

trilby ['trɪlbɪ] *n* weiche(r) Filzhut *m.*

trill [trɪl] *n* (*Mus*) Triller *m.*

trilogy ['trɪlədʒɪ] *n* Trilogie *f.*

trim [trɪm] *a* ordentlich, gepflegt; *figure* schlank; *n* (gute) Verfassung *f*; (*embellishment, on car*) Verzierung *f*; **to give sb's hair a** — jdm die Haare etwas schneiden; *vt* (*clip*) schneiden; *trees* stutzen; (*decorate*) besetzen; *sails* trimmen; —**mings** *pl* (*decorations*) Verzierung(en *pl*) *f*; (*extras*) Zubehör *nt.*

Trinity ['trɪnɪtɪ] *n*: **the** — die Dreieinigkeit.

trinket ['trɪŋkɪt] *n* kleine(s) Schmuckstück *nt.*

trio ['trɪəʊ] *n* Trio *nt.*

trip [trɪp] *n* (kurze) Reise *f*; (*outing*) Ausflug *m*; (*stumble*) Stolpern *nt*; *vi* (*walk quickly*) trippeln; (*stumble*) stolpern; — **over** *vt* stolpern über (+*acc*); — **up** *vi* stolpern; (*fig also*) einen Fehler machen; *vt* zu Fall bringen; (*fig*) hereinlegen.

tripe [traip] *n* (*food*) Kutteln *pl*; (*rubbish*) Mist *m.*

triple ['trɪpl] *a* dreifach; —**ts** ['trɪplɪts] *pl* Drillinge *pl.*

triplicate ['trɪplɪkət] *n*: **in** — **in** dreifacher Ausfertigung.

tripod ['traipɒd] *n* Dreifuß *m*; (*Phot*) Stativ *nt.*

tripper ['trɪpə*] *n* Ausflügler(in *f*) *m.*

trite [trait] *a* banal.

triumph ['traiʌmf] *n* Triumph · *m*; *vi* triumphieren; —**al** [traiʌmfəl] *a* triumphal, Sieges-; —**ant** [trai'ʌmfənt] *a* triumphierend; (*victorious*) siegreich; —**antly** *ad* triumphierend; siegreich.

trivial ['trɪvɪəl] *a* gering(fügig), trivial; —**lity** [trɪvɪ'ælɪtɪ] *n* Trivialität *f*, Nebensächlichkeit *f.*

trolley ['trɒlɪ] *n* Handwagen *m*; (*in shop*) Einkaufswagen *m*; (*for luggage*) Kofferkuli *m*; (*table*) Teewagen *m*; — **bus** O(berleitungs)bus *m.*

trollop ['trɒləp] *n* Hure *f*; (*slut*) Schlampe *f.*

trombone [trɒm'bəʊn] *n* Posaune *f.*

troop [truːp] *n* Schar *f*; (*Mil*) Trupp *m*; —**s** *pl* Truppen *pl*; — **in/out** *vi* hinein-/hinausströmen; —**er** *n* Kavallerist *m*; —**ship** Truppentransporter *m.*

trophy ['trəʊfɪ] *n* Trophäe *f.*

tropic ['trɒpɪk] *n* Wendekreis *m*; **the** —**s** *pl* die Tropen *pl*; —**al** *a* tropisch.

trot [trɒt] *n* Trott *m*; *vi* trotten.

trouble ['trʌbl] *n* (*worry*) Sorge *f*, Kummer *m*; (*in country, industry*) Unruhen *pl*; (*effort*) Umstand *m*, Mühe *f*; (*disturb*) beunruhigen, stören, belästigen; **to** — **to do sth** sich bemühen, etw zu tun; **to make** — Schwierigkeiten *or* Unannehmlichkeiten machen; **to have** — **with** Ärger haben mit; **to be in** — Probleme *or* Ärger haben; —**d** *a person* beunruhigt; *country* geplagt; —**free** *a* sorglos

—maker Unruhestifter m;
—shooter Vermittler m; —some a
lästig, unangenehm; child
schwierig.

trough [trɒf] n (vessel) Trog m;
(channel) Rinne f, Kanal m; (Met)
Tief nt.

trounce [trauns] vt (esp Sport)
vernichtend schlagen.

troupe [tru:p] n Truppe f.

trousers ['trauzəz] npl (lange)
Hose f, Hosen pl.

trousseau ['tru:səu] n Aussteuer f.

trout [traut] n Forelle f.

trowel ['trauəl] n Kelle f.

truant ['tru:ənt] n: to play — (die
Schule) schwänzen.

truce [tru:s] n Waffenstillstand m.

truck [trʌk] n Lastwagen m,
Lastauto nt; (Rail) offener(r) Güterwagen m; (barrow) Gepäckkarren
m; to have no — with sb nichts
zu tun haben wollen mit jdm; —
driver Lastwagenfahrer m; — farm
(US) Gemüsegärtnerei f.

truculent ['trʌkjulənt] a trotzig.

trudge [trʌdʒ] vi sich (mühselig)
dahinschleppen.

true [tru:] a (exact) wahr;
(genuine) echt; friend treu.

truffle ['trʌfl] n Trüffel f.

truly ['tru:lɪ] ad (really) wirklich;
(exactly) genau; (faithfully) treu;
yours — Ihr sehr ergebener.

trump [trʌmp] n (Cards) Trumpf
m; —ed-up a erfunden.

trumpet ['trʌmpɪt] n Trompete f;
vt ausposaunen; vi trompeten.

truncated [trʌŋ'keɪtɪd] a
verstümmelt.

truncheon ['trʌntʃən] n
Gummiknüppel m.

trundle ['trʌndl] vt schieben; vi: —

along (person) dahinschlendern;
(vehicle) entlangrollen.

trunk [trʌŋk] n (of tree) (Baum)-
stamm m, Rumpf m; (box)
Truhe f, Überseekoffer m; (of
elephant) Rüssel m; —s pl
Badehose f; — call Ferngespräch
nt.

truss [trʌs] n (Med) Bruchband nt.

trust [trʌst] n (confidence)
Vertrauen nt; (for property etc)
Treuhandvermögen nt; vt (rely on)
vertrauen (+dat), sich verlassen
auf (+acc); (hope) hoffen; — him
to break it! er muß es natürlich
kaputt machen, typisch!; to — sth
to sb jdm etw anvertrauen; —ed
a treu; —ee [trʌs'ti:] Vermögens-
verwalter m; —ful a, —ing a vertrauensvoll; —worthy a vertrauens-
würdig; account glaubwürdig; —y
a treu, zuverlässig.

truth [tru:θ] n Wahrheit f; —ful a
ehrlich; ad
wahrheitsgemäß; —fulness Ehrlichkeit f; (of statement) Wahrheit f.

try [traɪ] n Versuch m; to have a
— es versuchen; vt (attempt)
versuchen; (test) (aus)probieren;
(Jur) person unter Anklage stellen;
case verhandeln; (strain)
anstrengen; courage, patience auf
die Probe stellen; vi (make effort)
versuchen, sich bemühen; — on vt
dress anprobieren; hat auf-
probieren; — out vt ausprobieren;
—ing a schwierig; —ing for
anstrengend für.

tsar [zɑ:*] n Zar m.

T-shirt ['ti:ʃɜ:t] n T-shirt nt.

T-square ['ti:skwɛə*] n
Reißschiene f.

tub [tʌb] n Wanne f, Kübel m; (for
margarine etc) Becher m.

tuba ['tju:bə] *n* Tuba *f.*

tubby ['tʌbɪ] *a* rundlich, klein und dick.

tube [tju:b] *n* (*pipe*) Röhre *f*, Rohr *nt*; (*for toothpaste etc*) Tube *f*; (*in London*) U-Bahn *f*; (*Aut: for tyre*) Schlauch *m*; **—less** *a* (*Aut*) schlauchlos.

tuber ['tju:bə*] *n* Knolle *f.*

tuberculosis [tjubɜ:kju'ləʊsɪs] *n* Tuberkulose *f.*

tube station ['tju:bsteɪʃən] *n* U-Bahnstation *f.*

tubular ['tju:bjʊlə*] *a* röhrenförmig.

tuck [tʌk] *n* (*fold*) Falte *f*, Einschlag *m*; *vt* (*put*) stecken; (*gather*) fälteln, einschlagen; **—** *in vt* hineinstecken; *blanket etc* feststecken; *person* zudecken; *vi* (*eat*) hineinhauen, zulangen; **— up** *vt child warm* zudecken; **— shop** *n* Süßwarenladen *m.*

Tuesday ['tju:zdeɪ] *n* Dienstag *m.*

tuft [tʌft] *n* Büschel *m.*

tug [tʌg] *n* (*jerk*) Zerren *nt*, Ruck *m*; (*Naut*) Schleppdampfer *m*; *vti* zerren, ziehen; *boat* schleppen; **—of-war** Tauziehen *nt.*

tuition [tju'ɪʃən] *n* Unterricht *m.*

tulip ['tju:lɪp] *n* Tulpe *f.*

tumble ['tʌmbl] *n*. (*fall*) Sturz *m*; *vi* (*fall*) fallen, stürzen; **—** *to vt* kapieren; **—down** *a* baufällig; **—r** (*glass*) Trinkglas *nt*, Wasserglas *nt*; (*for drying*) Trockenautomat *m.* .

tummy ['tʌmɪ] *n* (*col*) Bauch *m.*

tumour ['tju:mə*] *n* Tumor *m*, Geschwulst *f.*

tumult ['tju:mʌlt] *n* Tumult *m*; **—uous** [tju:'mʌltjʊəs] *a* lärmend, turbulent.

tumulus ['tju:mjʊləs] *n* Grabhügel *m.*

tuna ['tju:nə] *n* Thunfisch *m.*

tundra ['tʌndrə] *n* Tundra *f.*

tune [tju:n] *n* Melodie *f*; *vt* (*put in tune*) stimmen; (*Aut*) richtig einstellen; **to sing in —/out of —** richtig/falsch singen; **to be out of —** with nicht harmonieren mit; **—** *in vi* einstellen (*to acc*); **— up** *vi* (*Mus*) stimmen; **—er** (*person*) (Instrumenten)stimmer *m*; (*radio set*) Empfangsgerät *nt*, Steuergerät *nt*; (*part*) Tuner *m*, Kanalwähler *m*; **—ful** *a* melodisch.

tungsten ['tʌŋstən] *n* Wolfram *nt.*

tunic ['tju:nɪk] *n* Waffenrock *m*; (*loose garment*) lange Bluse *f.*

tuning ['tju:nɪŋ] *n* (*Rad, Aut*) Einstellen *nt*; (*Mus*) Stimmen *nt.*

tunnel ['tʌnl] *n* Tunnel *m*, Unterführung *f*; *vi* einen Tunnel anlegen.

tunny ['tʌnɪ] *n* Thunfisch *m.*

turban ['tɜ:bən] *n* Turban *m.*

turbid ['tɜ:bɪd] *a* trübe; (*fig*) verworren.

turbine ['tɜ:baɪn] *n* Turbine *f.*

turbot ['tɜ:bət] *n* Steinbutt *m.*

turbulence ['tɜ:bjʊləns] *n* (*Aviat*) Turbulenz *f.*

turbulent ['tɜ:bjʊlənt] *a* stürmisch.

tureen [tjʊri:n] *n* Terrine *f.*

turf [tɜ:f] *n* Rasen *m*; (*piece*) Sode *f.*

turgid ['tɜ:dʒɪd] *a* geschwollen.

turkey ['tɜ:kɪ] *n* Puter *m*, Truthahn *m.*

turmoil ['tɜ:mɔɪl] *n* Aufruhr *m*, Tumult *m.*

turn [tɜ:n] *n* (*rotation*) (Um)drehung *f*; (*performance*) (Programm)nummer *f*; (*Med*) Schock *m*; *vt* (*rotate*) drehen; (*change position of*) umdrehen, wenden; *page* umblättern; (*transform*) verwandeln; (*direct*) zuwenden; *vi* (rotate) sich drehen; (change direction) (in car) abbiegen; (wind) drehen; (—round) umdrehen, wenden; (become) werden; (leaves) sich verfärben; (milk) sauer werden; (weather) umschlagen; (become) werden; to make a — to the left nach links abbiegen; the — of the tide der Gezeitenwechsel; the — of the century die Jahrhundertwende; to take a — for the worse sich zum Schlechten wenden; it's your — du bist dran or an der Reihe; in —, by —s abwechselnd; to take —s sich abwechseln; to do sb a good/bad — jdm einen guten/schlechten Dienst erweisen; it gave me quite a — das hat mich schön erschreckt; to — sb loose jdn los- or freilassen; — back *vt* umdrehen; *person* zurückschicken; *clock* zurückstellen; *vi* umkehren; — down *vt* (refuse) ablehnen; (fold down) umschlagen; — in (go to bed) ins Bett gehen; *vt* (fold inwards) einwärts biegen; — into *vi* sich verwandeln in (+acc); — off *vi* abbiegen; *vt* ausschalten; *tap* zudrehen; *machine, electricity* abstellen; — on *vt* (light) anschalten, einschalten; *tap* aufdrehen; *machine* anstellen; — out *vi* (prove to be) sich herausstellen, sich erweisen; (people) sich entwickeln; how did the cake — out? wie ist der Kuchen geworden?; *vt light* ausschalten; *gas* abstellen; (produce) produzieren; — to *vt* sich zuwenden (+dat); — up *vi* auftauchen; (happen) passieren, sich ereignen; *vt collar* hochklappen, hochstellen; *nose*

rümpfen; (increase) *radio* lauter stellen; *heat* höher drehen; —about Kehrtwendung *f*; —ed-up *a nose* Stups-; —ing (in road) Abzweigung *f*; —ing point Wendepunkt *m*.

turnip ['tɜːnɪp] *n* Steckrübe *f*.

turnout ['tɜːnaʊt] *n* (Besucher)zahl *f*; (Comm) Produktion *f*.

turnover ['tɜːnəʊvə*] *n* Umsatz *m*; (of staff) Wechsel *m*; (Cook) Tasche *f*.

turnpike ['tɜːnpaɪk] *n* (US) gebührenpflichtige Straße *f*.

turnstile ['tɜːnstaɪl] *n* Drehkreuz *nt*.

turntable ['tɜːnteɪbl] *n* (of record-player) Plattenteller · *m*; (Rail) Drehscheibe *f*.

turn-up ['tɜːnʌp] *n* (on trousers) Aufschlag *m*.

turpentine ['tɜːpəntaɪn] *n* Terpentin *nt*.

turquoise ['tɜːkwɔɪz] *n* (gem) Türkis *m*; (colour) Türkis *nt*; *a* türkisfarben.

turret ['tʌrɪt] *n* Turm *m*.

turtle ['tɜːtl] *n* Schildkröte *f*.

tusk [tʌsk] *n* Stoßzahn *m*.

tussle [tʌsl] *n* Balgerei *f*.

tutor ['tjuːtə*] *n* (teacher) Privatlehrer *m*; (college instructor) Tutor *m*; —ial [tjuː'tɔːrɪəl] (Univ) Kolloquium *nt*, Seminarübung *f*.

tuxedo [tʌk'siːdəu] *n* (US) Smoking *m*.

TV ['tiː'viː] *n* Fernseher *m*; *a* Fernseh-.

twaddle ['twɒdl] *n* (col) Gewäsch *nt*.

twang [twæŋ] *n* scharfe(r) Ton *m*; (of voice) Näseln *nt*; *vt* zupfen; *vi* klingen; (talk) näseln.

tweed [twiːd] *n* Tweed *m*.

tweezers ['twi:zəz] *npl* Pinzette *f.*

twelfth [twelfθ] *a* zwölfte(r,s); T— Night Dreikönigsabend *m.*

twelve [twelv] *num a* zwölf.

twenty ['twenti] *num a* zwanzig.

twerp [twɜ:p] *n* (*col*) Knülch *m.*

twice [twais] *ad* zweimal; — as much doppelt soviel; — my age doppelt so alt wie ich.

twig [twig] *n* dünne(r) Zweig *m*; *vt* (*col*) kapieren, merken.

twilight ['twailait] *n* Dämmerung *f*, Zwielicht *nt.*

twill [twil] *n* Köper *m.*

twin [twin] *n* Zwilling *m*; Zwillings-; (*very similar*) Doppel-.

twine [twain] *n* Bindfaden *m*; *vi* binden.

twinge [twind̠ʒ] *n* stechende(r) Schmerz *m*, Stechen *nt.*

twinkle ['twiŋkl] *n* Funkeln *nt*, Blitzen *nt*; *vi* funkeln.

twin town ['twintaun] *n* Partnerstadt *f.*

twirl [twɜ:l] *n* Wirbel *m*; *vti* (herum)wirbeln.

twist [twist] *n* (*twisting*) Biegen *nt*, Drehung *f*; (*bend*) Kurve *f*; *vt* (*turn*) drehen; (*make crooked*) verbiegen; (*distort*) verdrehen; *vi* (*wind*) sich drehen; (*curve*) sich winden.

twit [twit] *n* (*col*) Idiot *m.*

twitch [twitʃ] *n* Zucken *nt*; *vi* zucken.

two [tu:] *num a* zwei; to break in — in zwei Teile brechen; — by — zu zweit; to be in — minds nicht genau wissen; to put — and — together seine Schlüsse ziehen; — door a zweitürig; —faced a falsch; —fold a, ad zweifach, doppelt; —piece a zweiteilig; — seater (*plane, car*) Zweisitzer *m*; —some Paar *nt*; —way a traffic Gegen-.

tycoon [tai'ku:n] *n* (Industrie)-magnat *m.*

type [taip] *n* Typ *m*, Art *f*; (*Print*) Type *f*; *vti* maschineschreiben, tippen; —cast a (*Theat, TV*) auf eine Rolle festgelegt; —script maschinegeschriebene(r) Text *m*; —writer Schreibmaschine *f*; —written a maschinegeschrieben.

typhoid ['taifɔid] *n* Typhus *m.*

typhoon [tai'fu:n] *n* Taifun *m.*

typhus ['taifəs] *n* Flecktyphus *m.*

typical a, —ly ad ['tipikəl, -kli] typisch (of für).

typify ['tipifai] *vt* typisch sein für.

typing ['taipiŋ] *n* Maschineschreiben *nt.*

typist ['taipist] *n* Maschinenschreiber(in *f*) *m*, Tippse *f* (*col*).

tyranny ['tirəni] *n* Tyrannei *f*, Gewaltherrschaft *f.*

tyrant ['taiərənt] *n* Tyrann *m.*

tyre [taiə*] *n* Reifen *m.*

U

U, u [ju:] *n* U *nt*, u *nt.*

ugh [ɜ:h] *interj* hu.

ubiquitous [ju:'bikwitəs] *adj* überall zu finden(d); allgegenwärtig.

ugliness ['ʌglinəs] *n* Hässlichkeit *f.*

udder ['ʌdə*] *n* Euter *nt.*

ugly ['ʌgli] a häßlich; (*bad*) böse, schlimm.

ukulele [ju:kə'leɪlɪ] *n* Ukulele *f*.

ulcer ['Alsə*] *n* Geschwür *nt*.

ulterior [Al'tɪərɪə*] *a*: — motive Hintergedanke *m*.

ultimate ['Altɪmət] *a* äußerste(r,s), allerletzte(r,s) ; **—ly** *ad* schließlich, letzten Endes.

ultimatum [Altɪ'meɪtəm] *n* Ultimatum *nt*.

ultra- ['Altrə] *pref* ultra-.

ultraviolet ['Altrə'vaɪələt] *a* ultraviolett.

umbilical cord [Am'bɪlɪkl kɔ:d] *n* Nabelschnur *f*.

umbrage ['Ambrɪdʒ] *n*: to take — Anstoß nehmen (*at* an +*dat*).

umbrella [Am'brelə] *n* Schirm *m*.

umpire ['Ampaɪə*] *n* Schiedsrichter *m* ; *vti* schiedsrichtern.

umpteen ['Amptiːn] *num* (col) zig.

un- [An] *pref* un-.

unabashed [Anə'bæʃt] *a* unerschrocken.

unabated [Anə'beɪtɪd] *a* unvermindert.

unable ['An'eɪbl] *a* außerstande; to be — to do sth etw nicht tun können.

unaccompanied [Anə'kAmpənɪd] *a* ohne Begleitung.

unaccountably [Anə'kaʊntəblɪ] *ad* unerklärlich.

unaccustomed [Anə'kAstəmd] *a* nicht gewöhnt (*to* an +*acc*); (*unusual*) ungewohnt.

unadulterated [Anə'dAltəreɪtəd] *a* rein, unverfälscht.

unaided ['An'eɪdɪd] *a* selbständig, ohne Hilfe.

unanimity [ju:nə'nɪmɪtɪ] *n* Einstimmigkeit *f*.

unanimous *a*, **—ly** *ad* [ju:'nænɪməs, -lɪ] einmütig; *vote* einstimmig.

unattached [Anə'tætʃt] *a* ungebunden.

unattended [Anə'tendɪd] *a person* unbeaufsichtigt; *thing* unbewacht.

unattractive [Anə'træktɪv] *a* unattraktiv.

unauthorized [An'ɔ:θəraɪzd] *a* unbefugt.

unavoidable *a*, **unavoidably** *ad* [Anə'vɔɪdəbl, -blɪ] unvermeidlich.

unaware [Anə'weə*] *a*: to be — of sth sich (*dat*) einer Sache nicht bewußt sein; **—s** *ad* unversehens.

unbalanced [An'bælənst] *a* unausgeglichen; (*mentally*) gestört.

unbearable [An'beərəbl] *a* unerträglich.

unbeatable [An'bi:təbl] *a* unschlagbar.

unbeaten [An'bi:tn] *a* ungeschlagen.

unbecoming [Anbɪ'kAmɪŋ] *a dress* unkleidsam; *behaviour* unpassend, unschicklich.

unbeknown [Anbɪ'nəʊn] *ad* ohne jedes Wissen (*to* gen).

unbelief [Anbɪ'li:f] *n* Unglaube *m*.

unbelievable [Anbɪ'li:vəbl] *a* unglaublich.

unbend [An'bend] *irreg vt* geradebiegen, gerademachen; *vi* aus sich herausgehen.

unbounded [An'baʊndɪd] *a* unbegrenzt.

unbreakable [An'breɪkəbl] *a* unzerbrechlich.

unbridled [An'braɪdld] *a* ungezügelt.

unbroken [An'brəʊkən] *a period* ununterbrochen; *spirit* ungebrochen; *record* unübertroffen.

unburden [An'bɜ:dn] *vt*: — o.s. (jdm) sein Herz ausschütten.

unbutton [An'bAtn] *vt* aufknöpfen.

uncalled-for [ʌn'kɔːldfɔ:*] a unnötig.

uncanny [ʌn'kænɪ] a unheimlich.

unceasing [ʌn'siːsɪŋ] a unaufhörlich.

uncertain [ʌn'sɜːtn] a unsicher; (doubtful) ungewiß; (unreliable) unbeständig; (vague) undeutlich, vage; **—ty** Ungewißheit f.

unchanged [ʌn'tʃeɪndʒd] a unverändert.

uncharitable [ʌn'tʃærɪtəbl] a hartherzig; remark unfreundlich.

uncharted [ʌn'tʃɑːtɪd] a nicht verzeichnet.

unchecked ['ʌn'tʃekt] a ungeprüft; (not stopped) advance ungehindert.

uncivil [ʌn'sɪvɪl] a unhöflich, grob.

uncle [ʌŋkl] n Onkel m.

uncomfortable [ʌn'kʌmfətəbl] a unbequem, ungemütlich.

uncompromising [ʌn'kɒmprəmaɪzɪŋ] a kompromißlos, unnachgiebig.

unconditional ['ʌnkən'dɪʃənl] a bedingungslos.

uncongenial ['ʌnkən'dʒiːnɪəl] a unangenehm.

unconscious [ʌn'kɒnʃəs] a (Med) bewußtlos; (not aware) nicht bewußt; (not meant) unbeabsichtigt; **the** Unbewußte; **—ly** ad unwissentlich, unbewußt; **—ness** Bewußtlosigkeit f.

uncontrollable ['ʌnkən'trəuləbl] a unkontrollierbar, unbändig.

uncork ['ʌn'kɔːk] vt entkorken.

uncouth [ʌn'kuːθ] a grob, ungehobelt.

uncover [ʌn'kʌvə*] vt aufdecken.

unctuous [ʌŋktjuəs] a salbungsvoll.

undaunted [ʌn'dɔːntɪd] a unerschrocken.

undecided ['ʌndɪ'saɪdɪd] a unschlüssig.

undeniable [ʌndɪ'naɪəbl] a unleugbar.

undeniably [ʌndɪ'naɪəblɪ] ad unbestreitbar.

under ['ʌndə*] prep unter; ad darunter; **— repair** in Reparatur; **—age** a minderjährig.

undercarriage ['ʌndəkærɪdʒ] n Fahrgestell nt.

underclothes ['ʌndəkləuðz] npl Unterwäsche f.

undercoat ['ʌndəkəut] n (paint) Grundierung f.

undercover ['ʌndəkʌvə*] a Geheim-.

undercurrent ['ʌndəkʌrənt] n Unterströmung f.

undercut [ʌndə'kʌt] vt irreg unterbieten.

underdeveloped ['ʌndədɪ'veləpt] a Entwicklungs-, unterentwickelt.

underdog ['ʌndədɒg] n Unterlegene(r) mf.

underdone ['ʌndə'dʌn] a (Cook) nicht gar, nicht durchgebraten.

underestimate ['ʌndər'estɪmeɪt] vt unterschätzen.

underexposed ['ʌndərɪks'pəuzd] a unterbelichtet.

underfed ['ʌndə'fed] a unterernährt.

underfoot ['ʌndə'fut] ad unter den Füßen.

undergo ['ʌndə'gəu] vt irreg experience durchmachen; operation, test sich unterziehen (+ dat).

undergraduate ['ʌndə'grædjuət] n Student(in f) m.

underground ['ʌndəgraund] n

Untergrundbahn f, U-Bahn f; a press etc Untergrund-.

undergrowth ['ʌndəgrəʊθ] n Gestrüpp nt, Unterholz nt.

underhand ['ʌndəhænd] a hinterhältig.

underlie [ʌndə'laɪ] vt irreg (form the basis of) zugrundeliegen (+dat).

underline [ʌndə'laɪn] vt unterstreichen; (emphasize) betonen.

underling ['ʌndəlɪŋ] n Handlanger m.

undermine [ʌndə'maɪn] vt unterhöhlen; (fig) unterminieren, untergraben.

underneath [ʌndə'niːθ] ad darunter; prep unter.

underpaid [ʌndə'peɪd] a unterbezahlt.

underpants ['ʌndəpænts] npl Unterhose f.

underpass ['ʌndəpɑːs] n Unterführung f.

underplay [ʌndə'pleɪ] vt herunterspielen.

underprice [ʌndə'praɪs] vt zu niedrig ansetzen.

underprivileged [ʌndə'prɪvɪlɪdʒd] a benachteiligt, unterprivilegiert.

underrate [ʌndə'reɪt] vt unterschätzen.

undershirt ['ʌndəʃɜːt] n (US) Unterhemd nt.

undershorts ['ʌndəʃɔːts] npl (US) Unterhose f.

underside ['ʌndəsaɪd] n Unterseite f.

underskirt ['ʌndəskɜːt] n Unterrock m.

understand [ʌndə'stænd] vt irreg verstehen; I — that ... ich habe gehört, daß ...; am I to — that ...? soll das (etwa) heißen, daß

...?; what do you — by that? was verstehen Sie darunter?; it is understood that ... es wurde verstanden, daß ...; to make o.s. understood sich verständlich machen; is that understood? is das klar?; —able a verständlich; —ing Verständnis nt; a verständnisvoll.

understatement [ʌndə'steɪtmənt] n Untertreibung f, Understatement nt.

understudy ['ʌndəstʌdɪ] n Ersatz(schau)spieler(in f) m.

undertake [ʌndə'teɪk] irreg vt unternehmen; vi (promise) sich verpflichten; —r Leichenbestatter m; —r's Beerdigungsinstitut nt.

undertaking [ʌndə'teɪkɪŋ] n (enterprise) Unternehmen nt; (promise) Verpflichtung f.

underwater [ʌndə'wɔːtə*] ad unter Wasser; a Unterwasser-.

underwear ['ʌndəwɛə*] n Unterwäsche f.

underweight [ʌndə'weɪt] a: to be — Untergewicht haben.

underworld ['ʌndəwɜːld] n (of crime) Unterwelt f.

underwriter ['ʌndəraɪtə*] n Assekurant m.

undesirable [ʌndɪ'zaɪərəbl] a unerwünscht.

undies ['ʌndɪz] npl (col) (Damen)unterwäsche f.

undiscovered [ʌndɪs'kʌvəd] a unentdeckt.

undisputed [ʌndɪs'pjuːtɪd] a unbestritten.

undistinguished [ʌndɪs'tɪŋwɪʃt] a unbekannt, nicht ausgezeichnet.

undo ['ʌn'duː] vt irreg (unfasten) öffnen, aufmachen; work zunichte machen; —ing Verderben nt.

undoubted [ʌn'dautɪd] *a* unbezweifelt; **—ly** *ad* zweifellos, ohne Zweifel.

undress [ʌn'dres] *vtl* (sich) ausziehen.

undue [ʌndju:] *a* übermäßig.

undulating [ʌndjʊleɪtɪŋ] *a* wellenförmig; *country* wellig.

unduly [ʌn'dju:lɪ] *ad* übermäßig.

unearth [ʌn'ɜ:θ] *vt* (*dig up*) ausgraben; (*discover*) ans Licht bringen; **—ly** *a* schauerlich.

unease [ʌn'i:z] *n* Unbehagen *nt*; (*public*) Unruhe *f.*

uneasy [ʌn'i:zɪ] *a* (*worried*) unruhig; *feeling* ungut; (*embarrassed*) unbequem'; **I feel —** about it mir ist nicht wohl dabei.

uneconomic(al) [ʌni:kə'nɒmɪk(əl)] *a* unwirtschaftlich.

uneducated [ʌn'edjʊkeɪtɪd] *a* ungebildet.

unemployed [ʌnɪm'plɔɪd] *a* arbeitslos; **the —** die Arbeitslosen *pl.*

unemployment [ʌnɪm'plɔɪmənt] *n* Arbeitslosigkeit *f.*

unending [ʌn'endɪŋ] *a* endlos.

unenviable [ʌn'envɪəbl] *a* wenig beneidenswert.

unerring [ʌn'ɜ:rɪŋ] *a* unfehlbar.

uneven [ʌn'i:vən] *a* *surface* uneben; *quality* ungleichmäßig.

unexpected [ʌnɪks'pektɪd] *a* nicht explodiert.

unfailing [ʌn'feɪlɪŋ] *a* nie versagend.

unfair *a*, **—ly** *ad* [ʌn'feə*, -əlɪ] ungerecht, unfair.

unfaithful [ʌn'feɪθfʊl] *a* untreu.

unfasten [ʌn'fa:sn] *vt* öffnen, aufmachen.

unfavourable, (*US*) **unfavorable** [ʌn'feɪvərəbl] *a* ungünstig.

unfeeling [ʌn'fi:lɪŋ] *a* gefühllos, kalt.

unfinished [ʌn'fɪnɪʃt] *a* unvollendet.

unfit [ʌn'fɪt] *a* ungeeignet (*for* zu, für); (*in bad health*) nicht fit.

unflagging [ʌn'flægɪŋ] *a* unermüdlich.

unflappable [ʌn'flæpəbl] *a* unerschütterlich.

unflinching [ʌn'flɪntʃɪŋ] *a* unerschrocken.

unfold [ʌn'fəʊld] *vt* entfalten; *paper* auseinanderfalten; *vi* (*develop*) sich entfalten.

unforeseen [ʌnfɔ:'si:n] *a* unvorhergesehen.

unforgivable [ʌnfə'gɪvəbl] *a* unverzeihlich.

unfortunate [ʌn'fɔ:tʃnət] *a* unglücklich, bedauerlich; **—ly** *ad* leider.

unfounded [ʌn'faʊndɪd] *a* unbegründet.

unfriendly [ʌn'frendlɪ] *a* unfreundlich.

unfurnished [ʌn'fɜ:nɪʃt] *a* unmöbliert.

ungainly [ʌn'geɪnlɪ] *a* linkisch.

ungodly [ʌn'gɒdlɪ] *a* *hour* nachtschlafend; *row* heillos.

unguarded [ʌn'gɑ:dɪd] *a* *moment* unbewacht.

unhappiness [ʌn'hæpɪnəs] *n* Unglück *nt*, Unglückseligkeit *f.*

unhappy [ʌn'hæpɪ] *a* unglücklich.

unharmed [ʌn'hɑ:md] *a* wohlbehalten, unversehrt.

unhealthy [ʌn'helθɪ] *a* ungesund.

unheard-of [ʌn'hɜ:dɒv] *a* unerhört.

unhurt [ʌn'hɜ:t] *a* unverletzt.

unicorn ['ju:nɪkɔ:n] *n* Einhorn *nt.*

unidentified [ʌnaɪ'dentɪfaɪd] *a* unbekannt, nicht identifiziert.

unification [juːnɪfɪˈkeɪʃən] n Vereinigung f.

uniform [ˈjuːnɪfɔːm] n Uniform f; a einheitlich; **-ity** [juːnɪˈfɔːmɪtɪ] n Einheitlichkeit f.

unify [ˈjuːnɪfaɪ] vt vereinigen.

unilateral [juːnɪˈlætərəl] a einseitig.

unimaginable [ʌnɪˈmædʒɪnəbl] a unvorstellbar.

uninjured [ˈʌnˈɪndʒəd] a unverletzt.

unintentional [ˈʌnɪnˈtenʃənl] a unabsichtlich.

union [ˈjuːnjən] n (uniting) Vereinigung f; (alliance) Bund m, Union f; (trade —) Gewerkschaft f; U— Jack Union Jack m.

unique [juːˈniːk] a einzig(artig).

unison [ˈjuːnɪzn] n Einstimmigkeit f; in — einstimmig.

unit [ˈjuːnɪt] n Einheit f.

unite [juːˈnaɪt] vt vereinigen; vi sich vereinigen; **—d** a vereinigt; (together) vereint; U—d Nations Vereinte Nationen pl.

unit trust [ˈjuːnɪtˈtrʌst] n (Brit) Treuhandgesellschaft f.

unity [ˈjuːnɪtɪ] n Einheit f; (agreement) Einigkeit f.

universal a, **—ly** ad [juːnɪˈvɜːsəl, -ɪ] allgemein.

universe [ˈjuːnɪvɜːs] n (Welt)all nt, Universum nt.

university [juːnɪˈvɜːsɪtɪ] n Universität f.

unjust [ˈʌnˈdʒʌst] a ungerecht.

unjustifiable [ʌnˈdʒʌstɪfaɪəbl] a ungerechtfertigt.

unkempt [ʌnˈkempt] a ungepflegt, verwahrlost.

unkind [ʌnˈkaɪnd] a unfreundlich.

unknown [ˈʌnˈnəun] a unbekannt (to also).

unladen [ʌnˈleɪdn] a weight Leer-, unbeladen.

unleash [ʌnˈliːʃ] vt entfesseln.

unleavened [ʌnˈlevnd] a ungesäuert.

unless [ənˈles] cj wenn nicht, es sei denn ...

unlicensed [ˈʌnˈlaɪsənst] a (to sell alcohol) unkonzessioniert.

unlike [ʌnˈlaɪk] a unähnlich; prep im Gegensatz zu.

unlimited [ʌnˈlɪmɪtɪd] a unbegrenzt.

unload [ʌnˈləud] vt entladen.

unlock [ʌnˈlɔk] vt aufschließen.

unmannerly [ʌnˈmænəlɪ] a unmanierlich.

unmarried [ˈʌnˈmærɪd] a unverheiratet, ledig.

unmask [ˈʌnˈmɑːsk] vt demaskieren; (fig) entlarven.

unmistakable [ˈʌnmɪsˈteɪkəbl] a unverkennbar.

unmistakably [ˈʌnmɪsˈteɪkəblɪ] ad unverwechselbar, unverkennbar.

unmitigated [ʌnˈmɪtɪgeɪtɪd] a ungemildert, ganz.

unnecessary [ʌnˈnesəsərɪ] a unnötig.

unobtainable [ʌnəbˈteɪnəbl] a: this number is — kein Anschluß unter dieser Nummer.

unoccupied [ˈʌnˈɔkjupaɪd] a seat frei.

unopened [ˈʌnˈəupənd] a ungeöffnet.

unorthodox [ˈʌnˈɔːθədɔks] a unorthodox.

unpack [ˈʌnˈpæk] vti auspacken.

unpalatable [ʌnˈpælətəbl] a truth bitter.

unparalleled [ʌnˈpærəleld] a beispiellos.

unpleasant [ʌnˈpleznt] a unangenehm.

unplug [ʌnˈplʌg] vt den Stecker herausziehen von.

unpopular [ˈʌnˈpɒpjulə*] *a* unbeliebt, unpopulär.

unprecedented [ʌnˈpresɪdəntɪd] *a* noch nie dagewesen; beispiellos.

unqualified [ˈʌnˈkwɒlɪfaɪd] *a success* uneingeschränkt, voll; *person* unqualifiziert.

unravel [ʌnˈrævəl] *vt* (*disentangle*) auffasern, entwirren; (*solve*) lösen.

unreal [ˈʌnˈrɪəl] *a* unwirklich.

unreasonable [ʌnˈriːznəbl] *a* unvernünftig; *demand* übertrieben; that's — das ist zuviel verlangt.

unrelenting [ˈʌnrɪˈlentɪŋ] *a* unerbittlich.

unrelieved [ˈʌnrɪˈliːvd] *a monotony* ungemildert.

unrepeatable [ˈʌnrɪˈpiːtəbl] *a* nicht zu wiederholen(d).

unrest [ʌnˈrest] *n* (*discontent*) Unruhe *f*; (*fighting*) Unruhen *pl*.

unroll [ˈʌnˈrəʊl] *vt* aufrollen.

unruly [ʌnˈruːlɪ] *a child* undiszipliniert; schwer lenkbar.

unsafe [ʌnˈseɪf] *a* nicht sicher.

unsaid [ʌnˈsed] *a*: to leave sth — etw ungesagt sein lassen.

unsatisfactory [ˈʌnsætɪsˈfæktərɪ] *a* unbefriedigend; unzulänglich.

unsavoury, (*US*) **unsavory** [ˈʌnˈseɪvərɪ] *a* (*fig*) widerwärtig.

unscrew [ˈʌnˈskruː] *vt* aufschrauben.

unscrupulous [ʌnˈskruːpjuləs] *a* skrupellos.

unselfish [ˈʌnˈselfɪ] *a* selbstlos, uneigennützig.

unsettled [ˈʌnˈsetld] *a* unstet; *person* rastlos; *weather* wechselhaft; *dispute* nicht beigelegt.

unshaven [ˈʌnˈʃevn] *a* unrasiert.

unsightly [ʌnˈsaɪtlɪ] *a* unansehnlich.

unskilled [ˈʌnˈskɪld] *a* ungelernt.

unsophisticated [ˈʌnsəˈfɪstɪkeɪtɪd] *a* einfach, natürlich.

unsound [ˈʌnˈsaʊnd] *a ideas* anfechtbar.

unspeakable [ʌnˈspiːkəbl] *a joy* unsagbar; *crime* scheußlich.

unstuck [ˈʌnˈstʌk] *a*: to come — (*lit*) sich lösen; (*fig*) ins Wasser fallen.

unsuccessful [ˈʌnsəkˈsesful] *a* erfolglos.

unsuitable [ˈʌnˈsuːtəbl] *a* unpassend.

unsuspecting [ˈʌnsəsˈpektɪŋ] *a* nichtsahnend.

unswerving [ʌnˈswɜːvɪŋ] *a loyalty* unerschütterlich.

untangle [ˈʌnˈtæŋgl] *vt* entwirren.

untapped [ˈʌnˈtæpt] *a resources* ungenützt.

unthinkable [ʌnˈθɪŋkəbl] *a* unvorstellbar.

untidy [ʌnˈtaɪdɪ] *a* unordentlich.

untie [ˈʌnˈtaɪ] *vt* aufmachen, aufschnüren.

until [ənˈtɪl] *prep, cj* bis.

untimely [ʌnˈtaɪmlɪ] *a death* vorzeitig.

untold [ˈʌnˈtəʊld] *a* unermeßlich.

untoward [ʌntəˈwɔːd] *a* widrig, ungünstig.

untranslatable [ˈʌntrænsˈleɪtəbl] *a* unübersetzbar.

untried [ˈʌnˈtraɪd] *a plan* noch nicht ausprobiert.

unused [ˈʌnˈjuːzd] *a* unbenutzt.

unusual *a*, **—ly** *ad* [ʌnˈjuːʒuəl, -ɪ] ungewöhnlich.

unveil [ʌnˈveɪl] *vt* enthüllen.

unwary [ʌnˈwɛərɪ] *a* unbedacht(sam).

unwavering [ʌnˈweɪvərɪŋ] *a* standhaft, unerschütterlich.

unwell ['ʌn'wel] *a* unpäßlich.

unwieldy [ʌn'wi:ldɪ] *a* unhandlich, sperrig.

unwilling ['ʌn'wɪlɪŋ] *a* unwillig.

unwind ['ʌn'waɪnd] *irreg vt · (lit)* abwickeln; *vi (relax)* sich entspannen.

unwitting [ʌn'wɪtɪŋ] *a* unwissentlich.

unwrap ['ʌn'ræp] *vt* aufwickeln, auspacken.

unwritten ['ʌn'rɪtn] *a* ungeschrieben.

up [ʌp] *prep* auf; *ad* nach oben, hinauf; *(out of bed)* auf; it is — to you es liegt bei Ihnen; what is he — to? was hat er vor?; he is not — to it er kann es nicht (tun); what's —? was ist los?; — to *(temporally)* bis; —and-coming *a* im Aufstieg; the —s and downs der Auf und Ab.

upbringing ['ʌpbrɪŋɪŋ] *n* Erziehung *f.*

update [ʌp'deɪt] *vt* auf den neuesten Stand bringen.

upend [ʌp'end] *vt* auf Kante stellen.

upgrade [ʌp'greɪd] *vt* höher einstufen.

upheaval [ʌp'hi:vəl] *n* Umbruch *m.*

uphill ['ʌp'hɪl] *a* ansteigend; *(fig)* mühsam; *ad* bergauf.

uphold [ʌp'həʊld] *vt irreg* unterstützen.

upholstery [ʌp'həʊlstərɪ] *n* Polster *nt;* Polsterung *f.*

upkeep ['ʌpki:p] *n* Instandhaltung *f.*

upon [ə'pɒn] *prep* auf.

upper ['ʌpə*] *n (on shoe)* Oberleder *nt;* *a* obere(r,s), höhere(r,s); the — class die Oberschicht; —class *a* vornehm; —most *a* oberste(r,s), höchste(r,s).

upright ['ʌpraɪt] *a (erect)* aufrecht; *(honest)* aufrecht, rechtschaffen; *n* Pfosten *m.*

uprising [ʌp'raɪzɪŋ] *n* Aufstand *m.*

uproar ['ʌprɔ:*] *n* Aufruhr *m.*

uproot [ʌp'ru:t] *vt* ausreißen; *tree* entwurzeln.

upset ['ʌpset] *n* Aufregung *f;* [ʌp'set] *vt irreg (overturn)* umwerfen; *(disturb)* aufregen, bestürzen; *plans* durcheinanderbringen; —ting *a* bestürzend.

upshot ['ʌpʃɒt] *n* (End)ergebnis *nt,* Ausgang *m.*

upside-down [ʌpsaɪd'daʊn] *ad* verkehrt herum; *(fig)* drunter und drüber.

upstairs ['ʌp'stɛəz] *ad* oben, im oberen Stockwerk; *go* nach oben; *a room* obere(r,s), Ober-; *n* obere(s) Stockwerk *nt.*

upstart ['ʌpstɑ:t] *n* Emporkömmling *m.*

upstream ['ʌp'stri:m] *ad* stromaufwärts.

uptake ['ʌpteɪk] *n:* to be quick on the — schnell begreifen; to be slow on the — schwer von Begriff sein.

uptight ['ʌp'taɪt] *a (col) (nervous)* nervös; *(inhibited)* verklemmt.

up-to-date ['ʌptə'deɪt] *a; clothes* modisch, modern; *information* neueste(r,s); to bring sth up to date etw auf den neuesten Stand bringen.

upturn ['ʌptɜ:n] *n (in luck)* Aufschwung *m.*

upward ['ʌpwəd] *a* nach oben gerichtet; —(s) *ad* aufwärts.

uranium [jʊə'reɪnɪəm] *n* Uran *nt.*

urban ['ɜ:bən] *a* städtisch, Stadt-.

urbane [ɜ:'beɪn] *a* höflich, weltgewandt.

urchin ['ɜ:tʃɪn] *n (boy)* Schlingel *m;* *(sea —)* Seeigel *m.*

urge ['ɜːdʒ] n Drang m; vt drängen, dringen in (+acc); — on vt antreiben.

urgency ['ɜːdʒənsɪ] n Dringlichkeit f.

urgent a, —ly ad ['ɜːdʒənt, -lɪ] dringend.

urinal ['jʊərɪnl] n (Med) Urinflasche f; (public) Pissoir nt.

urinate ['jʊərɪneɪt] vi urinieren, Wasser lassen.

urine ['jʊərɪn] n Urin m, Harn m.

urn [ɜːn] n Urne f; (tea —) Teemaschine f.

us [ʌs] pron uns.

usage ['juːzɪdʒ] n Gebrauch m; (esp Ling) Sprachgebrauch m.

use [juːs] n Verwendung f; (custom) Brauch m, Gewohnheit f; (employment) Gebrauch m; (point) Zweck m; in — in Gebrauch; out of — außer Gebrauch; it's no — es hat keinen Zweck; what's the —? was soll's?; [juːz] vt gebrauchen; —d to [juːst] gewöhnt an (+acc); she —d to live here sie hat früher mal hier gewohnt; — up [juːz] vt aufbrauchen, verbrauchen; —d [juːzd] a car Gebraucht—; —ful a nützlich; —fulness Nützlichkeit f; —less a nutzlos, unnütz; —lessly ad

nutzlos; —lessness Nutzlosigkeit f; —r ['juːzə*] Benutzer m.

usher ['ʌʃə*] n Platzanweiser m; —ette [ʌʃə'ret] Platzanweiserin f.

usual ['juːʒʊəl] a gewöhnlich, üblich; —ly ad gewöhnlich.

usurp [juː'zɜːp] vt an sich reißen; —er Usurpator m.

usury ['juːʒʊrɪ] n Wucher m.

utensil [juː'tensl] n Gerät nt, Utensil n.

uterus ['juːtərəs] n Gebärmutter f, Uterus m.

utilitarian [juːtɪlɪ'tɛərɪən] a Nützlichkeits-.

utility [juː'tɪlɪtɪ] n (usefulness) Nützlichkeit f; (also public —) öffentliche(r) Versorgungsbetrieb m.

utilization [juːtɪlaɪ'zeɪʃən] n Nutzbarmachung f; Benutzung f.

utilize ['juːtɪlaɪz] vt nutzbar machen; benützen.

utmost ['ʌtməʊst] a äußerste(r,s); n: to do one's — sein möglichstes tun.

utter ['ʌtə*] a äußerste(r,s) höchste(r,s), völlig; vt äußern, aussprechen; —ance Äußerung f; —ly ad äußerst, absolut, völlig.

U-turn ['juː'tɜːn] n (Aut) Kehrtwendung f.

V

V, v [viː] n V nt, v nt.

vacancy ['veɪkənsɪ] n (job) offene Stelle f; (room) freies Zimmer nt.

vacant ['veɪkənt] a leer; (un-occupied) frei; house leerstehend, unbewohnt; (stupid) (gedanken)

leer; '—' (on door) 'frei'.

vacate [və'keɪt] vt seat frei machen; room räumen.

vacation [və'keɪʃən] n Ferien pl, Urlaub m; —ist (US) Ferienreisende(r) mf.

vaccinate ['væksneıt] vt impfen.

vaccination [væksı'neıʃən] n Impfung f.

vaccine ['væksi:n] n Impfstoff m.

vacuum ['vækjum] n luftleere(r) Raum m, Vakuum nt; — **bottle** (US), — **flask** (Brit) Thermosflasche f; — **cleaner** Staubsauger m.

vagary ['veıgərı] n Laune f.

vagina ' [və'dʒaınə] n Scheide f, Vagina f.

vagrant ['veıgrənt] n Landstreicher m.

vague [veıg] a unbestimmt, vage; outline verschwommen; (absentminded) geistesabwesend; —**ly** ad unbestimmt, vage; understand, correct ungefähr; —**ness** Unbestimmtheit f; Verschwommenheit f.

vain [veın] a (worthless) eitel, nichtig; attempt vergeblich; (conceited) eitel, eingebildet; in — vergebens, umsonst; —**ly** ad vergebens, vergeblich; eitel, eingebildet.

valentine ['væləntaın] n Valentinsgruß m.

valiant a, —**ly** ad ['væliənt, -lı] tapfer.

valid ['vælıd] a gültig; argument stichhaltig; objection berechtigt; —**ity** [və'lıdıtı] Gültigkeit f; Stichhaltigkeit f.

valise [və'li:z] n Reisetasche f.

valley ['vælı] n Tal nt.

valuable ['væljuəbl] a wertvoll; time kostbar; —**s** pl Wertsachen pl.

valuation [vælju'eıʃən] n (Fin) Schätzung f, Beurteilung f.

value ['vælju:] n Wert m; (usefulness) Nutzen m; vt (prize) (hoch)-schätzen, werthalten; (estimate)

schätzen; —**d** a (hoch)geschätzt; —**less** a wertlos; —**r** Schätzer m.

valve [vælv] n Ventil nt; (Biol) Klappe f; (Rad) Röhre f.

vampire ['væmpaıə*] n Vampir m.

van [væn] n Lieferwagen m; Kombiwagen m.

vandal ['vændəl] n Vandale m; —**ism** mutwillige Beschädigung f, Vandalismus m.

vanilla [və'nılə] n Vanille f.

vanish ['vænıʃ] vi verschwinden.

vanity ['vænıtı] n Eitelkeit f, Einbildung f; — **case** Schminkkoffer m.

vantage ['va:ntıdʒ] n: — **point** gute(r) Aussichtspunkt m.

vapour, (US) **vapor** ['veıpə*] n (mist) Dunst m; (gas) Dampf m.

variable ['vɛərıəbl] a wechselhaft, veränderlich; speed, height regulierbar.

variance ['vɛərıəns] n: **to be at** — uneinig sein.

variant ['vɛərıənt] n Variante f.

variation [vɛərı'eıʃən] n Variation f, Veränderung f; (of temperature, prices) Schwankung f.

varicose ['værıkəus] a: — **veins** Krampfadern pl.

varied ['vɛərıd] a verschieden, unterschiedlich; life abwechslungsreich.

variety [və'raıətı] n (difference) Abwechslung f; (varied collection) Vielfalt f; (Comm) Auswahl f; (sorte) Sorte f, Art f; — **show** Varieté nt.

various ['vɛərıəs] a verschieden; (several) mehrere.

varnish ['va:nıʃ] n Lack m; (on pottery) Glasur f; vt lackieren; truth beschönigen.

vary ['vɛərɪ] vt (alter) verändern; (give variety to) abwechslungsreicher gestalten; vi sich (ver)ändern; (prices) schwanken; (weather) unterschiedlich sein; to — from sth sich von etw unterscheiden; —ing a unterschiedlich; veränderlich.

vase [vɑːz] n Vase f.

vast [vɑːst] a weit, groß, riesig; —ly ad wesentlich; grateful, amused äußerst; —ness Unermeßlichkeit f, Weite f.

vat [væt] n große(s) Faß nt.

Vatican ['vætɪkən] n: the — der Vatikan.

vaudeville ['vəʊdəvɪl] n (US) Varieté nt.

vault [vɔːlt] n (of roof) Gewölbe nt; (tomb) Gruft f; (in bank) Tresorraum m; (leap) Sprung m; vt überspringen.

vaunted ['vɔːntɪd] a gerühmt, gepriesen.

veal [viːl] n Kalbfleisch nt.

veer [vɪə*] vi sich drehen; (of car) ausscheren.

vegetable ['vedʒətəbl] n Gemüse nt; (plant) Pflanze f.

vegetarian [vedʒɪ'tɛərɪən] n Vegetarier(in f) m; a vegetarisch.

vegetate ['vedʒɪteɪt] vi (dahin)vegetieren.

vegetation [vedʒɪ'teɪʃən] n Vegetation f.

vehemence ['viːɪməns] n Heftigkeit f.

vehement ['viːɪmənt] a heftig; feelings leidenschaftlich.

vehicle ['viːɪkl] n Fahrzeug nt; (fig) Mittel nt.

vehicular [vɪ'hɪkjʊlə*] a Fahrzeug-; traffic Kraft-.

veil [veɪl] n (lit, fig) Schleier m; vt verschleiern.

vein [veɪn] n Ader f; (Anat) Vene f; (mood) Stimmung f.

velocity [vɪ'lɒsɪtɪ] n Geschwindigkeit f.

velvet ['velvɪt] n Samt m.

vendetta [ven'detə] n Fehde f; (in family) Blutrache f.

vending machine ['vendɪŋməʃiːn] n Automat m.

vendor ['vendɔː*] n Verkäufer m.

veneer [və'nɪə*] n (lit) Furnier(holz) nt; (fig) äußere(r) Anstrich m.

venerable ['venərəbl] a ehrwürdig.

venereal [vɪ'nɪərɪəl] a disease Geschlechts-.

venetian [vɪ'niːʃən] a: — blind Jalousie f.

vengeance ['vendʒəns] n Rache f; with a — gewaltig.

venison ['venɪsn] n Reh(fleisch) nt.

venom ['venəm] n Gift nt; —ous a, —ously ad giftig, gehässig.

vent [vent] n Öffnung f; (in coat) Schlitz m; (fig) Ventil nt; vt emotion abreagieren.

ventilate ['ventɪleɪt] vt belüften; question erörtern.

ventilation [ventɪ'leɪʃən] n (Be)lüftung f, Ventilation f.

ventilator ['ventɪleɪtə*] n Ventilator m.

ventriloquist [ven'trɪləkwɪst] n Bauchredner m.

venture ['ventʃə*] n Unternehmung f, Projekt nt; vt wagen; life aufs Spiel setzen; vi sich wagen.

venue ['venjuː] n Schauplatz m; Treffpunkt m.

veranda(h) [və'rændə] n Veranda f.

verb [vɜːb] n Zeitwort nt, Verb nt; —al a (spoken) mündlich; trans-

lation wörtlich; (*of a verb*) verbal, Verbal-; —**ally** *ad* mündlich; (*as a verb*) verbal; —**atim** [vɜ:'beɪtɪm] *ad* Wort für Wort; ,a wortwörtlich.

verbose [vɜ:'bəʊs] *a* wortreich.

verdict ['vɜ:dɪkt] *n* Urteil *nt*.

verge [vɜ:dʒ] *n* Rand *m*; **on the —** **of doing sth** im Begriff, etw zu tun; *vi*: **— on** grenzen an (+acc).

verger ['vɜ:dʒə*] *n* Kirchendiener *m*, Küster *m*.

verification [verɪfɪ'keɪʃən] *n* Bestätigung *f*; (*checking*) Überprüfung *f*; (*proof*) Beleg *m*.

verify ['verɪfaɪ] *vt* (über)prüfen; (*confirm*) bestätigen; *theory* beweisen.

vermin ['vɜ:mɪn] *npl* Ungeziefer *nt*.

vermouth ['vɜ:məθ] *n* Wermut *m*.

vernacular [və'nækjʊlə*] *n* Landessprache *f*; (*dialect*) Dialekt *m*, Mundart *f*; (*jargon*) Fachsprache *f*.

versatile ['vɜ:sətaɪl] *a* vielseitig.

versatility [vɜ:sə'tɪlɪt] *n* Vielseitigkeit *f*.

verse [vɜ:s] *n* (*poetry*) Poesie *f*; (*stanza*) Strophe *f*; (*of Bible*) Vers *m*; **in —** in Versform; —**d** *a*: —**d** **in** bewandert in (+dat), beschlagen in (+dat).

version ['vɜ:ʃən] *n* Version *f*; (*of car*) Modell *nt*.

versus ['vɜ:səs] *prep* gegen.

vertebra ['vɜ:tɪbrə] *n* (Rücken-) wirbel *m*.

vertebrate ['vɜ:tɪbrət] *a animal* Wirbel-.

vertical ['vɜ:tɪkəl] *a* senkrecht, vertikal; —**ly** *ad* senkrecht, vertikal.

vertigo ['vɜ:tɪgəʊ] *n* Schwindel *m*, Schwindelgefühl *nt*.

verve [vɜ:v] *n* Schwung *m*.

very ['verɪ] *ad* sehr; *a* (*extreme*) äußerste(r,s) *the* — **book** genau das Buch; **at that** **— moment** gerade or genau in dem Augenblick; · **at the — latest** allerspätestens; **the — same day** noch am selben Tag; **the — thought der** Gedanke allein, der bloße Gedanke.

vespers ['vespəz] *npl* Vesper *f*.

vessel ['vesl] *n* (*ship*) Schiff *nt*; (*container*) Gefäß *nt*.

vest [vest] *n* Unterhemd *nt*; (*US: waistcoat*) Weste *f*; *vt*: **— sb with** **sth** or **sth in sb** jdm etw verleihen; —**ed** *a*: —**ed interests** *pl* finanzielle Beteiligung *f*; (*people*) finanziell Beteiligte *pl*; (*fig*) persönliche(s) Interesse *nt*.

vestibule ['vestɪbju:l] *n* Vorhalle *f*.

vestige ['vestɪdʒ] *n* Spur *f*.

vestry ['vestrɪ] *n* Sakristei *f*.

vet [vet] *n* Tierarzt *m*/-ärztin *f*; *vt* genau prüfen.

veteran ['vetərən] *n* Veteran *m*; *a* altgedient.'

veterinary ['vetɪnərɪ] *a* Veterinär-; — **surgeon** Tierarzt *m*/-ärztin *f*.

veto ['vi:təʊ] *n* Veto *nt*; *power of* — Vetorecht *nt*; *vt* sein Veto einlegen gegen.

vex [veks] *vt* ärgern; —**ed** *a* verärgert; —**ed question** umstrittene Frage *f*; —**ing** *a* ärgerlich.

via ['vaɪə] *prep* über (+acc).

viability [vaɪə'bɪlɪtɪ] *n* (*of plan,* *scheme*) Durchführbarkeit *f*; (*of* *company*) Rentabilität *f*; (*of life* *forms*) Lebensfähigkeit *f*.

viable ['vaɪəbl] *a plan* durchführbar; *company* rentabel; *plant,* *economy* lebensfähig.

viaduct ['vaɪədʌkt] *n* Viadukt *m*.

vibrate [vaɪ'breɪt] *vi* zittern, beben; (*machine, string*) schwingen; (*notes*) schwingen.

vibration [vaɪ'breɪʃən] *n* Schwingung *f*; (*of machine*) Vibrieren ·*nt*; (*of voice, ground*) Beben *nt*.

vicar ['vɪkə*] *n* Pfarrer *m*; —age Pfarrhaus *nt*

vice [vaɪs] *n* (*evil*) Laster *nt*; (*Tech*) Schraubstock *m*; pref: —chairman stellvertretende(r) Vorsitzende(r) *m*; —president Vizepräsident *m*; —versa *ad* umgekehrt.

vicinity [vɪ'sɪnɪtɪ] *n* Umgebung *f*; (*closeness*) Nähe *f*.

vicious [vɪʃəs] *a* gemein, böse; —circle Teufelskreis *m*; —ness Bösartigkeit *f*, Gemeinheit *f*.

vicissitudes [vɪ'sɪsɪtjuːdz] *npl* Wechselfälle *pl*.

victim ['vɪktɪm] *n* Opfer *nt*; —ization [vɪktɪmaɪ'zeɪʃən] Benachteiligung *f*; —ize *vt* benachteiligen.

victor ['vɪktə*] *n* Sieger *m*.

Victorian [vɪk'tɔːrɪən] *a* viktorianisch; (*fig*) (sitten)streng.

victorious [vɪk'tɔːrɪəs] *a* siegreich.

victory ['vɪktərɪ] *n* Sieg *m*.

video ['vɪdɪəʊ] *a* Fernseh-, Bild-.

vie [vaɪ] *vi* wetteifern.

view [vjuː] *n* (*sight*) Sicht *f*, Blick *m*; (*scene*) Aussicht *f*; (*opinion*) Ansicht *f*, Meinung *f*; (*intention*) Absicht *f*; **to have sth in —** etw beabsichtigen; **in — of** wegen (+gen), angesichts (+gen); *vt* (*situation*) betrachten; (*house*) besichtigen; **—er** (*viewfinder*) Sucher *m*; (*Phot: small projector*) Gucki *m*; (*TV*) Fernsehteilnehmer·(in *f*) *m*; **—finder** Sucher *m*; **—point** Standpunkt *m*.

vigil ['vɪdʒɪl] *n* (Nacht)wache *f*; —ance Wachsamkeit *f*; —ant *a* wachsam; —antly *ad* aufmerksam.

vigorous *a*, **—ly** *ad* ['vɪgərəs, -lɪ] kräftig; *protest* energisch, heftig.

vigour, (*US*) **vigor** ['vɪgə*] *n* Kraft *f*, Vitalität *f*; (*of protest*) Heftigkeit *f*.

vile [vaɪl] *a* (*mean*) gemein; (*foul*) abscheulich.

vilify ['vɪlɪfaɪ] *vt* verleumden.

villa ['vɪlə] *n* Villa *f*.

village ['vɪlɪdʒ] *n* Dorf *nt*; —r Dorfbewohner·(in *f*) *m*.

villain ['vɪlən] *n* Schurke *m*, Bösewicht *m*. ·

vindicate ['vɪndɪkeɪt] *vt* rechtfertigen; (*clear*) rehabilitieren.

vindication [vɪndɪ'keɪʃən] *n* Rechtfertigung *f*; Rehabilitation *f*.

vindictive [vɪn'dɪktɪv] *a* nachtragend, rachsüchtig.

vine [vaɪn] *n* Rebstock *m*, Rebe·*f*.

vinegar ['vɪnɪgə*] *n* Essig *m*.

vineyard ['vɪnjəd] *n* Weinberg *m*.

vintage ['vɪntɪdʒ] *n* (*of wine*) Jahrgang *m*; **— car** Vorkriegsmodell *nt*; **— wine** edle(r) Wein *m*; **— year** besondere(s) Jahr *nt*.

viola [vɪ'əʊlə] *n* Bratsche *f*.

violate ['vaɪəleɪt] *vt* *promise* brechen; *law* übertreten; *rights, rule, neutrality* verletzen; *sanctity, woman* schänden.

violation [vaɪə'leɪʃən] *n* Verletzung *f*; Übertretung *f*.

violence ['vaɪələns] *n* (*force*) Heftigkeit *f*; (*brutality*) Gewalttätigkeit *f*.

violent *a*, **—ly** *ad* ['vaɪələnt, -lɪ] (*strong*) heftig; (*brutal*) gewalttätig, brutal; *contrast* kraß; *death* gewaltsam.

violet ['vaɪələt] *n* Veilchen *nt*; *a* veilchenblau, violett.

violin [vaɪə'lɪn] n Geige f, Violine f.

viper ['vaɪpə*] n Viper· f; (fig) Schlange f.

virgin ['vɜ:dʒɪn] n Jungfrau f; a jungfräulich, unberührt; —ity [vɜ:'dʒɪnɪtɪ] Unschuld f.

Virgo ['vɜ:gəʊ] n Jungfrau f.

virile ['vɪraɪl] a männlich; (fig) kraftvoll.

virility [vɪ'rɪlɪtɪ] n Männlichkeit f.

virtual ['vɜ:tjʊəl] a eigentlich; it was a — disaster es war geradezu eine Katastrophe; —ly ad praktisch, fast.

virtue ['vɜ:tju:] n (moral goodness) Tugend f; (good quality) Vorteil m, Vorzug m; by — of aufgrund (+gen).

virtuoso [vɜ:tjʊ'əʊzəʊ] n Virtuose m.

virtuous ['vɜ:tjʊəs] a tugendhaft.

virulence ['vɪrjʊləns] n Bösartigkeit f.

virulent ['vɪrjʊlənt] a (poisonous) bösartig; (bitter) scharf, geharnischt.

virus ['vaɪərəs] n Virus m.

visa ['vi:zə] n Visum nt, Sichtvermerk m.

vis-à-vis ['vi:zəvi:] prep gegenüber.

visibility [vɪzɪ'bɪlɪtɪ] n Sichtbarkeit f; (Met) Sicht(weite) f.

visible ['vɪzəbl] a sichtbar.

visibly ['vɪzəblɪ] ad sichtlich.

vision ['vɪʒən] n (ability) Sehvermögen nt; (foresight) Weitblick m; (in dream, image) Vision f; —ary Hellseher m; (dreamer) Phantast m; a phantastisch.

visit ['vɪzɪt] n Besuch m; vt besuchen; town, country fahren nach; —ing a professor Gast-; —ing card Visitenkarte f; —or (in house) Besucher(in f) m; (in hotel) Gast m; —or's book Gästebuch nt.

visor ['vaɪzə*] n Visier nt; (on cap) Schirm m; (Aut) Blende f.

vista ['vɪstə] n Aussicht f.

visual ['vɪzjʊəl] a Seh-, visuell; — aid Anschauungsmaterial nt; —ize vt (imagine) sich (dat) vorstellen; (expect) erwarten; —ly ad visuell.

vital ['vaɪtl] a (important) unerläßlich; (necessary for life) Lebens-, lebenswichtig; (lively) vital; —ity [vaɪ'tælɪtɪ] Vitalität f, Lebendigkeit f; —ly ad äußerst, ungeheuer.

vitamin ['vɪtəmɪn] n Vitamin nt.

vitiate ['vɪʃɪeɪt] vt verunreinigen; theory etc ungültig machen.

vivacious [vɪ'veɪʃəs] a lebhaft.

vivacity [vɪ'væsɪtɪ] n Lebhaftigkeit f, Lebendigkeit f.

vivid a, —ly ad ['vɪvɪd, -lɪ] (graphic) lebendig, deutlich; memory lebhaft; (bright) leuchtend.

vivisection [vɪvɪ'sekʃən] n Vivisektion f.

vocabulary [vəʊ'kæbjʊlərɪ] n Wortschatz m, Vokabular nt.

vocal ['vəʊkəl] a Vokal-, Gesang-; (fig) lautstark; — cord Stimmband nt; —ist Sänger(in f) m.

vocation [vəʊ'keɪʃən] n (calling) Berufung f; —al a Berufs-.

vociferous a, —ly ad [vəʊ'sɪfərəs, -lɪ] lautstark.

vodka ['vɒdkə] n Wodka m.

vogue [vəʊg] n Mode f.

voice [vɔɪs] n (lit) Stimme f; (fig) Mitspracherecht nt; (Gram) Aktionsart f; active/passive — Aktiv nt/Passiv nt; with one — einstimmig; vt äußern; —d consonant stimmhafte(r) Konsonant m.

void [vɔɪd] n Leere f; a (empty) leer; (lacking) ohne (of acc), bar (of gen); (Jur) ungültig; see null.

volatile ['vɒlətaɪl] a gas flüchtig; person impulsiv; situation brisant.

volcanic [vɒl'kænɪk] a vulkanisch, Vulkan-.

volcano [vɒl'keɪnəʊ] n Vulkan m.

volition [və'lɪʃən] n Wille m; of one's own — aus freiem Willen.

volley ['vɒlɪ] n (of guns) Salve f; (of stones) Hagel m; (of words) Schwall m; (tennis) Flugball m; —ball Volleyball m.

volt [vəʊlt] n Volt nt; —age (Volt)-spannung f.

volte-face ['vɒlt'fɑːs] n (Kehrt)-wendung f.

voluble ['vɒljubl] a redselig.

volume ['vɒljuːm] n (book) Band m; (size) Umfang m; (space) Rauminhalt m, Volumen nt; (of sound) Lautstärke f.

voluntary a, **voluntarily** ad ['vɒləntəri, -lɪ] freiwillig.

volunteer [vɒlən'tɪə*] n Freiwillige(r) mf; vi sich freiwillig melden; vt anbieten.

voluptuous [və'lʌptjʊəs] a sinnlich,

wollüstig.

vomit ['vɒmɪt] n Erbrochene(s) nt; (act) Erbrechen nt; vt speien; vi sich übergeben.

vote [vəʊt] n Stimme f; (ballot) Wahl f, Abstimmung f; (result) Wahl- or Abstimmungsergebnis nt; (right to vote) Wahlrecht nt; vti wählen; —r Wähler(in f) m.

voting ['vəʊtɪŋ] n Wahl f; low — geringe Wahlbeteiligung f.

vouch [vaʊtʃ]: — for vt bürgen für.

voucher ['vaʊtʃə*] n Gutschein m.

vow [vaʊ] n Versprechen nt; (Rel) Gelübde nt; vt geloben; vengeance schwören.

vowel ['vaʊəl] n Vokal m, Selbstlaut m.

voyage ['vɔɪdʒ] n Reise f.

vulgar ['vʌlgə*] a (rude) vulgär; (of common people) allgemein, Volks-; —ity [vʌl'gærɪtɪ] Gewöhnlichkeit f, Vulgarität f.

vulnerability [vʌlnərə'bɪlɪtɪ] n Verletzlichkeit f.

vulnerable ['vʌlnərəbl] a (easily injured) verwundbar; (sensitive) verletzlich.

vulture ['vʌltʃə*] n Geier m.

W

W, w ['dʌblju:] n W nt, w nt.

wad [wɒd] n (bundle) Bündel nt; (of paper) Stoß m; (of money) Packen m.

wade [weɪd] vi waten.

wafer ['weɪfə*] n Waffel f; (Eccl) Hostie f.

waffle ['wɒfl] n Waffel f; (col: empty talk) Geschwafel nt; vi (col) schwafeln.

waft [wɑːft] vti wehen.

wag [wæg] vt tail wedeln mit; vi (tail) wedeln; her tongue never stops—ging ihr Mund steht nie still.

wage [weɪdʒ] n (Arbeits)lohn m; vt führen; —s pl Lohn m; — claim Lohnforderung f; — earner Lohnempfänger(in f) m; — freeze Lohnstopp m.

wager ['weɪdʒə*] n Wette f; vti wetten.

waggle ['wægl] vt tail wedeln mit; vi wedeln.

wag(g)on ['wægən] n (horse-drawn) Fuhrwerk nt; (US Aut) Wagen m; (Brit Rail) Waggon m.

wail [weɪl] n Wehgeschrei nt; vi wehklagen, jammern.

waist [weɪst] n Taille f; —coat Weste f; —line Taille f.

wait [weɪt] n Wartezeit f; vi warten (for auf +acc); to — for sb to do sth darauf warten, daß jd etw tut; — and see! abwarten!; to — at table servieren; —er Kellner m; (as address) Herr Ober m; —ing list Warteliste f; —ing room (Med) Wartezimmer nt; (Rail) Wartesaal m; —ress Kellnerin f; (as address) Fräulein nt.

waive [weɪv] vt verzichten auf (+acc).

wake [weɪk] irreg vt wecken; vi aufwachen; to — up to (fig) sich bewußt werden (+gen); n (Naut) Kielwasser nt; (for dead) Totenwache f; in the — of unmittelbar nach; —n vt aufwecken.

walk [wɔːk] n Spaziergang m; (way of walking) Gang m; (route) Weg m; —s of life pl Sphären pl; to take sb for a — mit jdm einen Spaziergang machen; a 10-minute — 10 Minuten zu Fuß; vi gehen; (stroll) spazierengehen; (longer) wandern; —er Spaziergänger m; (hiker) Wanderer m; —ie-talkie tragbare(s) Sprechfunkgerät nt; —ing n Gehen nt; Spazieren-(gehen) nt; Wandern nt; a Wander-; —ing stick Spazierstock m; —out Streik m; —over (col) leichter Sieg m.

wall [wɔːl] n (inside) Wand f; (outside) Mauer f; —ed a von Mauern umgeben.

wallet ['wɒlɪt] n Brieftasche f.

wallow ['wɒləʊ] vi sich wälzen or suhlen.

wallpaper ['wɔːlpeɪpə*] n Tapete f.

walnut ['wɔːlnʌt] n Walnuß f; (tree) Walnußbaum m; (wood) Nußbaumholz nt.

walrus ['wɔːlrəs] n Walroß nt.

waltz [wɔːlts] n Walzer m; vi Walzer tanzen.

wan [wɒn] a bleich.

wand [wɒnd] n Stab m.

wander ['wɒndə*] vi (roam) (herum)wandern; (fig) abschweifen; —er Wanderer m; —ing a umherziehend; thoughts abschweifend.

wane [weɪn] vi abnehmen; (fig) schwinden.

want [wɒnt] n (lack) Mangel m (of an +dat); (need) Bedürfnis nt; for — of aus Mangel an (+dat); mangels (+gen); vt (need) brauchen; (desire) wollen; (lack) nicht haben; I — to do sth will gehen; he —s confidence ihm fehlt das Selbstvertrauen.

wanton ['wɒntən] a mutwillig, zügellos.

war [wɔː*] n Krieg m.

ward [wɔːd] n (in hospital) Station f; (child) Mündel nt; (of city) Bezirk m; to — off abwenden, abwehren.

warden ['wɔːdən] n (guard) Wächter m, Aufseher m; (in youth hostel) Herbergsvater m; (Univ) Heimleiter m.

warder ['wɔːdə*] n Gefängniswärter m.

wardrobe ['wɔ:drəub] *n* Kleider-
schrank *m*; (*clothes*) Garderobe *f.*
ware [wɛə*] *n* Ware *f*; **—house**
Lagerhaus *nt.*
warfare ['wɔ:fɛə*] *n* Krieg *m*;
Kriegsführung *f.*
warhead ['wɔ:hed] *n* Sprengkopf *m.*
warily ['wɛərɪlɪ] *ad* vorsichtig.
warlike ['wɔ:laɪk] *a* kriegerisch.
warm [wɔ:m] *a* warm; *welcome*
herzlich; *vti* wärmen; — **up** *vt* aufwärmen; *vi* warm werden; **—-
hearted** *a* warmherzig; **—ly** *ad*
warm; herzlich; **—th** Wärme *f*;
Herzlichkeit *f.*
warn [wɔ:n] *vt* warnen (*of, against*
vor +*dat*); **—ing** Warnung *f*;
without **—ing** unerwartet; **—ing
light** Warnlicht *nt.*
warp [wɔ:p] *vt* verziehen; **—ed** *a*
(*lit*) wellig; (*fig*) pervers.
warrant ['wɔrənt] *n* Haftbefehl *m.*
warranty ['wɔrəntɪ] *n* Garantie *f.*
warrior ['wɔrɪə*] *n* Krieger *m.*
warship ['wɔ:ʃɪp] *n* Kriegsschiff *m.*
wart [wɔ:t] *n* Warze *f.*
wartime ['wɔ:taɪm] *n* Kriegszeit *f,*
Krieg *m.*
wary ['wɛərɪ] *a* vorsichtig;
mißtrauisch.
was [wɒz, wəz] *pt of* be.
wash [wɒʃ] *n* Wäsche *f*; **to give
sth a —** etw waschen; **to have a
—** sich waschen; *vt* waschen;
dishes abwaschen; *vi* sich
waschen; (*do washing*) waschen;
— away *vt* abwaschen, wegspülen;
—able *a* waschbar; **—basin** Wasch-
becken *nt*; **—er** (*Tech*)
Dichtungsring *m*; (*machine*)
Wasch- or Spülmaschine *f*; **—ing**
Wäsche *f*; **—ing machine** Waschmaschine *f*; **—ing powder** Waschpulver *nt*; **—ing-up** Abwasch *m*;

— leather Waschleder *nt*; **—out**
(*col*) (*event*) Reinfall *m*; (*person*)
Niete *f*; **—room** Waschraum *m.*
wasn't ['wɒznt] = **was not.**
wasp [wɒsp] *n* Wespe *f.*
wastage ['weɪstɪdʒ] *n* Verlust *m*;
natural — Verschleiß *m.*
waste [weɪst] *n* (*wasting*) Verschwendung *f*; (*what is wasted*)
Abfall *m*; **—s** *pl* Einöde *f*; *a*
(*useless*) überschüssig, Abfall-; *vt*
object verschwenden; *time, life*
vergeuden; *vi:* **— away** verfallen;
—ful *a*, **—fully** *ad* verschwenderisch; *process* aufwendig; **—land** Ödland *nt*; **—paper
basket** Papierkorb *m.*
watch [wɒtʃ] *n* Wache *f*; (*for
time*) Uhr *f*; **to be on the —** (*for
sth*) (auf etw *acc*) aufpassen; *vt*
ansehen; (*observe*) beobachten;
(*be careful of*) aufpassen auf
(+*acc*); (*guard*) bewachen; **to —
TV** fernsehen; **to — sb** doing sth
jdm bei etw zuschauen; **— it!** paß
bloß auf!; *vi* zusehen; (*guard*)
Wache halten; **to — for** sb/sth
nach jdm/etw Ausschau halten; **—
out!** paß auf!; **—dog** (*lit*)
Wachthund *m*; (*fig*) Wächter *m*;
—ful *a* wachsam; **—maker**
Uhrmacher *m*; **—man** (Nacht)-
wächter *m*; **—strap** Uhrarmband
nt.
water ['wɔ:tə*] *n* Wasser *nt*; **—s**
pl Gewässer *nt*; *vt* (be)gießen;
(*river*) bewässern; *horses* tränken;
vi (*eye*) tränen; **my mouth is —ing**
mir läuft das Wasser im Mund
zusammen; **— down** *vt* verwässern; **— closet** Wasserklosett
nt; **—colour,** (*US*) **—color**
(*painting*) Aquarell *nt*; (*paint*)
Wasserfarbe *f*; **—cress**
(Brunnen)kresse *f*; **—fall** Wasser-

fall *m*; — hole Wasserloch *nt*; —ing can Gießkanne *f*; — level Wasserstand *m*; —lily Seerose *f*; —line Wasserlinie *f*; —logged *a* ground voll Wasser; wood mit Wasser vollgesogen; —melon Wassermelone *f*; — polo Wasserball(spiel) *nt*; —proof *a* wasserdicht; —shed Wasserscheide *f*; —skiing Wasserschilaufen *nt*; to go —skiing Wasserschilaufen gehen; —tight *a* wasserdicht; —works *pl* Wasserwerk *nt*; —y *a* wäss(e)rig.

watt [wɔt] *n* Watt *nt*.

wave [weɪv] *n* Welle *f*; (with hand) Winken *nt*; *vt* (move to and fro) schwenken; hand, flag winken mit; hair wellen; *vi* (person) winken; (flag) wehen; (hair) sich wellen; **to —** to *sb* jdm zuwinken; **to —** *sb* goodbye jdm zum Abschied winken; **—length** (lit, fig) Wellenlänge *f*.

waver ['weɪvə*] *vi* (hesitate) schwanken; (flicker) flackern.

wavy ['weɪvɪ] *a* wellig.

wax [wæks] *n* Wachs *nt*; (sealing —) Siegellack *m*; (in ear) Ohrenschmalz *nt*; *vt* floor (ein)wachsen; *vi* (moon) zunehmen; **—works** *pl* Wachsfigurenkabinett *nt*.

way [weɪ] *n* Weg *m*; (road also) Straße *f*; (method) Art und Weise *f*, Methode *f*; (direction) Richtung *f*; (habit) Eigenart *f*, Gewohnheit *f*; (distance) Entfernung *f*; (condition) Zustand *m*; **a long** — away or off weit weg; **to lose one's —** sich verirren; **to make —** for *sb*/*sth* jdm/etw Platz machen; **to be in a bad —** schlecht dransein; **do it this —** machen Sie es so; **give —** (Aut) Vorfahrt achten!; **— of thinking** Meinung *f*; **to get one's own —** seinen Willen bekommen;

one — or another irgendwie; **under —** im Gange; **in a —** in gewisser Weise; **in the —** im Wege; **by the —** übrigens; **by —** of (via) über (+acc); (in order to) um . . . zu; (instead of) als; **'— in'** 'Eingang'; **'— out'** 'Ausgang'; **—lay** *vt irreg* auflauern (+dat); **—ward** *a* eigensinnig.

we [wiː] *pl pron* wir.

weak *a*, **—ly** *ad* [wiːk, -lɪ] schwach; **—en** *vt* schwächen, entkräften; *vi* schwächer werden; nachlassen; **—ling** Schwächling *m*; **—ness** Schwäche *f*.

wealth [welθ] *n* Reichtum *m*; (abundance) Fülle *f*; **—y** *a* reich.

wean [wiːn] *vt* entwöhnen.

weapon ['wepən] *n* Waffe *f*.

wear [wɛə*] *n* (clothing) Kleidung *f*; (use) Verschleiß *m*; *irreg vt* (have on) tragen; smile etc haben; (use) abnutzen; *vi* (last) halten; (become old) (sich) verschleißen; (clothes) sich abtragen; — and tear Abnutzung *f*, Verschleiß *m*; — away *vt* verbrauchen; *vi* schwinden; — down *vt* people zermürben; — off *vi* sich verlieren; — out *vt* verschleißen; person erschöpfen; —er Träger(in *f*) *m*.

wearily ['wɪərɪl] *ad* müde.

weariness ['wɪərɪnəs] *n* Müdigkeit *f*.

weary ['wɪərɪ] *a* (tired) müde; (tiring) ermüdend; *vt* ermüden; *vi* überdrüssig werden (of gen).

weasel ['wiːzl] *n* Wiesel *nt*.

weather ['weðə*] *n* Wetter *nt*; *vt* verwittern lassen; (resist) überstehen; —beaten *a* verwittert; skin wettergegerbt; —cock Wetterhahn *m*; — forecast Wettervorhersage *f*.

weave [wi:v] vt irreg weben; to — one's way through sth sich durch etw durchschlängeln; —r Weber(in f) m.

weaving ['wi:vɪŋ] n Weben nt, Weberei f.

web [web] n Netz nt; (membrane) Schwimmhaut f; —bed a Schwimm-, schwimmhäutig; —bing Gewebe nt.

wed [wed] vt irreg (old) heiraten.

we'd [wi:d] = we had; we would.

wedding ['wedɪŋ] n Hochzeit f; —day Hochzeitstag m; — present Hochzeitsgeschenk nt; — ring Trau- or Ehering m.

wedge [wedʒ] n Keil m; (of cheese etc) Stück nt; vt (fasten) festklemmen; (pack tightly) einkeilen.

Wednesday ['wenzdei] n Mittwoch m.

wee [wi:] a (esp Scot) klein, winzig.

weed [wi:d] n Unkraut nt; vt jäten; —killer Unkrautvertilgungsmittel nt.

week [wi:k] n Woche f; a — today heute in einer Woche; —day Wochentag m; —end Wochenende nt; —ly a ad wöchentlich; wages, magazine Wochen-.

weep [wi:p] vi irreg weinen.

weigh [wei] vt wiegen; — down vt niederdrücken; — up vt prüfen, abschätzen; —bridge Brückenwaage f.

weight [weit] n Gewicht nt; to lose/put on — abnehmen/zunehmen; —lessness Schwerelosigkeit f; —lifter Gewichtheber m; —y a (heavy) gewichtig; (important) schwerwiegend.

weir [wɪə*] n (Stau)wehr nt.

weird [wɪəd] a seltsam.

welcome ['welkəm] n Willkommen nt, Empfang m; vt begrüßen.

welcoming ['welkəmɪŋ] a Begrüßungs-; freundlich.

weld [weld] n Schweißnaht f; vt schweißen; —er Schweißer m; —ing Schweißen nt.

welfare ['welfeə*] n Wohl nt; (social) Fürsorge f; — state Wohlfahrtsstaat m.

well [wel] n Brunnen m; (oil —) Quelle f; a (in good health) gesund; are you —? geht es Ihnen gut?; interj nun, na schön; (starting conversation) nun, tja; —, —! na, na!; ad gut; — over 40 weit über 40; it may — be es kann wohl sein; it would be (as) — to ... es wäre wohl gut, zu ...; you did — (not) to ... Sie haben gut daran getan, (nicht) zu ...; very — (O.K.) nun gut.

we'll [wi:l] = we will, we shall.

well-behaved ['welbɪ'heɪvd] a wohlerzogen.

well-being ['welbi:ɪŋ] n Wohl nt, Wohlergehen nt.

well-built ['wel'bɪlt] a kräftig gebaut.

well-developed ['weldɪ'veləpt] a girl gut entwickelt; economy hochentwickelt.

well-earned ['wel'ɜ:nd] a rest wohlverdient.

well-heeled ['wel'hi:ld] a (col: wealthy) gut gepolstert.

wellingtons ['welɪŋtənz] npl Gummistiefel pl.

well-known ['wel'nəʊn] a person weithin bekannt.

well-meaning ['wel'mi:nɪŋ] a person wohlmeinend; action gutgemeint.

well-off ['wel'ɒf] a gut situiert.
well-read ['wel'red] a (sehr) belesen.
well-to-do ['weltə'du:] a wohlhabend.
well-wisher ['welwɪʃə*] n wohlwollende(r) Freund m, Gönner m.
wench [wentʃ] n (old) Maid f, Dirne f.
went [went] pt of **go**.
were [wɜ:*] pt pl of **be**.
we're [wɪə*] = **we are**.
weren't [wɜ:nt] = **were not**.
west [west] n Westen m; a West-, westlich; ad westwärts, nach Westen; **—erly** a westlich; nach Westen, West-; n (Cine) Western m; **—ward(s)** ad westwärts.
wet [wet] a naß; **—** blanket (fig) Triefel m; **—ness** Nässe f, Feuchtigkeit f; **'— paint'** 'frisch gestrichen'.
we've [wi:v] = **we have**.
whack [wæk] n Schlag m; vt schlagen.
whale [weɪl] n Wal m.
wharf [wɔ:f] n Kai m.
what [wɒt] pron, interj was; a welche(r,s) **—** a hat! was für ein Hut!; **—** money I had das Geld, das ich hatte; **—** about ...? (suggestion) wie wär's mit ...?; **—** about it?, so und? well, **—** about him? was ist mit ihm?; and **—** about me? und ich?; **—** for? wozu?; **—ever** a: **—ever** he says egal, was er sagt; no reason **—ever** überhaupt kein Grund.
wheat [wi:t] n Weizen m.
wheel [wi:l] n Rad nt; (steering **—**) Lenkrad nt; (disc) Scheibe f; vt schieben; vi (revolve) sich drehen; **—barrow** Schubkarren m; **—chair** Rollstuhl m.

wheeze [wi:z] n Keuchen nt; vi keuchen.
when [wen] ad interrog wann; ad,cj (with present ·tense) wenn; (with past tense) als; (with indir question) wann; **—ever** ad wann immer; immer wenn.
where [wɛə*] ad (place) wo; (direction) wohin; **—** from woher; **—abouts** ['wɛərə'bauts] ad wo; n Aufenthalt m, Verbleib m; **—as** [wɛər'æz] cj während, wo ... doch; **—ever** [wɛər'evə*] ad wo (immer).
whet [wet] vt appetite anregen.
whether ['weðə*] cj ob.
which [wɪtʃ] a (from selection) welche(r,s); rel pron der/die/das; (rel: which fact) was; (interrog) welche(r,s); **—ever** (book) he takes welches (Buch) er auch nimmt.
whiff [wɪf] n Hauch m.
while [waɪl] n Weile f; cj während; for a **—** eine Zeitlang.
whim [wɪm] n Laune f.
whimper ['wɪmpə*] n Wimmern nt; vi wimmern.
whimsical ['wɪmzɪkəl] a launisch.
whine . [waɪn] n Gewinsel nt, Gejammer nt; vi heulen, winseln.
whip [wɪp] n Peitsche f; (Parl) Einpeitscher m; vt (beat) peitschen; (snatch) reißen; **—round** (col) Geldsammlung f.
whirl [wɜ:l] n Wirbel m; vti (herum)wirbeln; **—pool** Wirbel m; **—wind** Wirbelwind m.
whirr [wɜ:*] vi schwirren, surren.
whisk [wɪsk] n Schneebesen m; vt cream etc schlagen.
whisker ['wɪskə*] n (of animal) Barthaare pl; **—s** pl (of man) Backenbart m.
whisk(e)y ['wɪskɪ] n Whisky m.

whisper ['wɪspə*] n Flüstern nt; vi flüstern; (leaves) rascheln; vt flüstern, munkeln.

whist [wɪst] n Whist nt.

whistle ['wɪsl] n Pfiff m; (instrument) Pfeife f; vti pfeifen.

white [waɪt] n Weiß nt; (of egg) Eiweiß nt; (of eye) Weiße(s) nt; a weiß; (with fear) blaß; **—collar worker** Angestellte(r) m; **—** lie Notlüge f; **—ness** Weiß nt; **—wash** n (paint) Tünche f; (fig) Ehrenrettung f; vt weißen, tünchen; (fig) reinwaschen.

whiting ['waɪtɪŋ] n Weißfisch m.

Whitsun ['wɪtsn] n Pfingsten nt.

whittle ['wɪtl] vt: **— away or down** stutzen, verringern.

whizz [wɪz] vi sausen, zischen, schwirren; **— kid** (col) Kanone f.

who [huː] pron (interrog) wer; (rel) der/die/das; **—ever** [huːˈevə*] pron wer immer; jeder, der/jede, die/jedes, das.

whole [həʊl] a ganz; (uninjured) heil; n Ganze(s) nt; the **— of the year** das ganze Jahr; on the **—** im großen und ganzen; **—hearted a** rückhaltlos; **—heartedly** ad von ganzem Herzen; **—sale** Großhandel m; a trade Großhandels-; destruction vollkommen, Massen; **—saler** Großhändler m; **—some a** bekömmlich, gesund.

wholly ['həʊlɪ] ad ganz, völlig.

whom [huːm] pron (interrog) wen; (rel) den/die/das/die pl.

whooping cough ['huːpɪŋkɒf] n Keuchhusten m.

whopper ['wɒpə*] n (col) Mordsding nt; faustdicke Lüge f.

whopping ['wɒpɪŋ] a (col) kolossal, Riesen-.

whore [hɔː*] n Hure f.

whose [huːz] pron (interrog) wessen; (rel) dessen/deren/dessen/deren pl.

why [waɪ] ad warum; interj nanu; that's **—** deshalb.

wick [wɪk] n Docht m.

wicked ['wɪkɪd] a böse; **—ness** Bosheit f, Schlechtigkeit f.

wicker ['wɪkə*] n Weidengeflecht nt, Korbgeflecht nt.

wicket ['wɪkɪt] n Tor nt, Dreistab m; (playing pitch) Spielfeld nt.

wide [waɪd] a breit; plain weit; (in firing) daneben; **— of** weitab von; ad weit; daneben; **—angle a lens** Weitwinkel-; **—awake a** hellwach; **—ly** ad weit; known allgemein; **—n** vt erweitern; **—ness** Breite f, Ausdehnung f; **—open a** weit geöffnet; **—spread a** weitverbreitet.

widow ['wɪdəʊ] n Witwe f; **—ed** a verwitwet; **—er** Witwer m.

width [wɪdθ] n Breite f, Weite f.

wield [wiːld] vt schwingen, handhaben.

wife [waɪf] n (Ehe)frau f, Gattin f.

wig [wɪg] n Perücke f.

wiggle ['wɪgl] n Wackeln nt; vt wackeln mit; vi wackeln.

wigwam ['wɪgwæm] n Wigwam m, Indianerzelt nt.

wild [waɪld] a wild; (violent) heftig; plan, idea verrückt; the **—s** pl die Wildnis; **—erness** ['wɪldənəs] Wildnis f, Wüste f; **—goose chase** fruchtlose(s) Unternehmen nt; **—life** Tierwelt f; **—ly** ad wild, ungestüm; exaggerated irrsinnig.

wilful ['wɪlfʊl] a (intended) vorsätzlich; (obstinate) eigensinnig.

will [wɪl] v aux: he **—** come er wird kommen; I **—** do it! ich werde es tun; n (power to choose) Wille m;

(*wish*) Wunsch *m*, Bestreben *nt*; (*Jur*) Testament ·*nt*; *vt* wollen; **—ing** *a* gewillt, bereit; **—ingly** *ad* bereitwillig, gern; **—ingness** (Bereit)willigkeit *f*.

willow ['wıləʊ] *n* Weide *f*.

will power ['wɪl'paʊə*] *n* Willenskraft *f*.

wilt [wɪlt] *vi* (ver)welken.

wily ['waɪlɪ] *a* gerissen.

win [wɪn] *n* Sieg *m*; *irreg vt* gewinnen; *vi* (*be successful*) siegen; **to — sb over** jdn für sich gewinnen, jdn dazu bringen.

wince [wɪns] *n* Zusammenzucken *nt*; *vi* zusammenzucken, zurückfahren.

winch [wɪntʃ] *n* Winde *f*.

wind [waɪnd] *irreg vt rope* winden; *bandage* wickeln; **to — one's way** sich schlängeln; *vi* (*turn*) sich winden; (*change direction*) wenden; **— up** *vt clock* aufziehen; *debate* (ab)schließen.

wind [wɪnd] *n* Wind *m*; (*Med*) Blähungen *pl*; **—fall** Windschutz *m*; **—fall** unverhoffte(r) Glücksfall *m*.

winding ['waɪndɪŋ] *a road* gewunden, sich schlängelnd.

wind instrument ['wɪndɪnstrəmənt] *n* Blasinstrument *nt*.

windmill ['wɪndmɪl] *n* Windmühle *f*.

window ['wɪndəʊ] *n* Fenster *nt*; **— box** Blumenkasten *m*; **— cleaner** Fensterputzer *m*; **— ledge** Fenstersims *m*; **— pane** Fensterscheibe *f*; **—shopping** Schaufensterbummel *m*; **—sill** Fensterbank *f*.

windpipe ['wɪndpaɪp] *n* Luftröhre *f*.

windscreen ['wɪndskriːn], (*US*) **windshield** ['wɪndʃiːld] *n* Windschutzscheibe *f*; **— wiper** Scheibenwischer *m*.

windswept ['wɪndswept] *a* vom Wind gepeitscht; *person* zersaust.

windy ['wɪndɪ] *a* windig.

wine [waɪn] *n* Wein *m*; **—glass** Weinglas *nt*; **— list** Weinkarte *f*; **— merchant** Weinhändler *m*; **— tasting** Weinprobe *f*; **— waiter** Weinkellner *m*.

wing [wɪŋ] *n* Flügel *m*; (*Mil*) Gruppe *f*; **—s** *pl* (*Theat*) Seitenkulisse *f*; **—er** (*Sport*) Flügelstürmer *m*.

wink [wɪŋk] *n* Zwinkern *nt*; *vi* zwinkern, blinzeln; **to — at sb** jdm zublinzeln; **forty —s** Nickerchen *nt*.

winner ['wɪnə*] *n* Gewinner *m*; (*Sport*) Sieger *m*.

winning ['wɪnɪŋ] *a team* siegreich, Sieger-; *goal* entscheidend; *n*: **—s** *pl* Gewinn *m*; **— post** Ziel *nt*.

winter ['wɪntə*] *n* Winter *m*; *a clothes* Winter-; *vi* überwintern; **— sports** *pl* Wintersport *m*.

wintry ['wɪntrɪ] *a* Winter-, winterlich.

wipe [waɪp] *n* Wischen *nt*; *vt* wischen, abwischen; **— out** *vt debt* löschen; (*destroy*) auslöschen.

wire ['waɪə*] *n* Draht *m*; (*telegram*) Telegramm *nt*; *vt* telegrafieren (*sb* jdm, *sth* etw); **—less** Radio(apparat *m*) *nt*.

wiry ['waɪərɪ] *a* drahtig.

wisdom ['wɪzdəm] *n* Weisheit *f*; (*of decision*) Klugheit *f*; **— tooth** Weisheitszahn *m*.

wise [waɪz] *a* klug, weise; **—crack** Witzelei *f*; **—ly** *ad* klug, weise.

wish [wɪʃ] *n* Wunsch *m*; *vt* wünschen; **he —es us to do it** er möchte, daß wir es tun; **with best —es** herzliche Grüße; **to — sb goodbye** jdn verabschieden; **to —**

to do sth etw tun wollen; **—ful
thinking** Wunschdenken *nt*.

wisp [wɪsp] *n* (Haar)strähne *f*; (*of
smoke*) Wölkchen *nt*.

wistful ['wɪstfʊl] *a* sehnsüchtig.

wit [wɪt] *n* (*also* **—s**) Verstand *m
no pl*; (*amusing ideas*) Witz *m*;
(*person*) Witzbold *m*; **at one's —'s
end** mit seinem Latein am Ende;
to have one's —s about one auf
dem Posten sein.

witch [wɪtʃ] *n* Hexe *f*; **—craft**
Hexerei *f*.

with [wɪð, wɪθ] *prep* mit; (*in spite
of*) trotz (+*gen* or *dat*); **— him it's
... bei ihm ist es ...; — to stay —
sb** bei jdm wohnen; **I have no
money — me** ich habe kein Geld
bei mir; **shaking — fright** vor
Angst zitternd.

withdraw [wɪð'drɔ:] *irreg vt*
zurückziehen; *money* abheben;
remark zurücknehmen; *vi* sich
zurückziehen; **—al** Zurückziehung
f; Abheben *nt*; Zurücknahme *f*;
—al symptoms *pl* Entzugser-
scheinungen *pl*.

wither ['wɪðə*] *vi* (ver)welken;
—ed a verwelkt, welk.

withhold [wɪθ'həʊld] *vt irreg*
vorenthalten (*from sb* jdm).

within [wɪð'ɪn] *prep* innerhalb
(+*gen*).

without [wɪð'aʊt] *prep* ohne; **it
goes — saying** es ist selbstverständlich.

withstand [wɪθ'stænd] *vt irreg*
widerstehen (+*dat*).

witness ['wɪtnəs] *n* Zeuge *m*;
Zeugin *f*; *vt* (*see*) sehen, miter-
leben; (*sign document*)
beglaubigen; *vi* aussagen; **— box**,
(*US*) **— stand** Zeugenstand *m*.

witticism ['wɪtɪsɪzəm] *n* witzige
Bemerkung *f*.

witty a, **wittily** *ad* ['wɪtɪ, -lɪ]
witzig, geistreich.

wizard ['wɪzəd] *n* Zauberer *m*.

wobble ['wɒbl] *vi* wackeln.

woe [wəʊ] *n* Weh *nt*, Leid *nt*,
Kummer *m*.

wolf [wʊlf] *n* Wolf *m*.

woman ['wʊmən] *n*, *pl* **women
Frau** *f*; *a* **—** in *f*.

womb [wu:m] *n* Gebärmutter *f*.

women ['wɪmɪn] *npl of* **woman**.

wonder ['wʌndə*] *n* (*marvel*)
Wunder *nt*; (*surprise*) Staunen *nt*,
Verwunderung *f*; *vi* sich wundern;
I — whether ... ich frage mich, ob
...; —ful a wunderbar, herrlich;
—fully *ad* wunderbar.

won't [wəʊnt] = **will not**.

wood [wʊd] *n* Holz *nt*; (*forest*)
Wald *m*; **— carving**
Holzschnitzerei *f*; **—ed** a bewaldet,
waldig, Wald-; **—en** a (*lit, fig*)
hölzern; **—pecker** Specht *m*;
—wind Blasinstrumente *pl*;
—work Holzwerk *nt*; (*craft*)
Holzarbeiten *pl*; **—worm**
Holzwurm *m*.

wool [wʊl] *n* Wolle *f*; **—len**, (*US*)
—en a Woll-; **—ly**, (*US*) **—y** a
wollig; (*fig*) schwammig.

word [wɜ:d] *n* Wort *nt*; (*news*)
Bescheid *m*; **to have a — with sb**
mit jdm reden; **to have —s with
sb** Worte wechseln mit jdm; **by —
of mouth** mündlich; *vt*
formulieren; **—ing** Wortlaut *m*,
Formulierung *f*.

work [wɜ:k] *n* Arbeit *f*; (*Art, Liter*)
Werk *nt*; *vi* arbeiten; *machine*
funktionieren; (*medicine*) wirken;
(*succeed*) klappen; **—s** (*factory*)
Fabrik *f*, Werk *nt*; (*of watch*) Werk
nt; **— off** *vt debt* abarbeiten; *anger*
abreagieren; **— on** *vi*
weiterarbeiten; *vt* (*be engaged in*)

arbeiten an (+ dat); (influence) bearbeiten; — out vi (sum) aufgehen; (plan) klappen; vt problem lösen; plan ausarbeiten; — up to vt hinarbeiten auf (+ acc); to get —ed up sich aufregen; —able a soil bearbeitbar; plan ausführbar; —er Arbeiter(in f) m; —ing class Arbeiterklasse f; —ing-class a Arbeiter-; —ing man Werktätige(r) m; —man Arbeiter m; —manship Arbeit f, Ausführung ·f; —shop Werkstatt f.

world [wɜːld] n Welt f; (animal — etc) Reich nt; out of this — himmlisch; to come into the — auf die Welt kommen; to do sb/sth the — of good jdm/etw sehr gut tun; to be the — to sb jds ein und alles sein; to think the — of sb große Stücke auf jdn halten; —famous a weltberühmt; —ly a weltlich, irdisch; —wide a weltweit.

worm [wɜːm] n Wurm m.

worn [wɔːn] a clothes abgetragen; —out a object abgenutzt; person völlig erschöpft.

worried ['wʌrɪd] a besorgt, beunruhigt.

worrier ['wʌrɪə*] n: he is a — er macht sich (dat) ewig Sorgen.

worry ['wʌrɪ] n Sorge f, Kummer m; vt quälen, beunruhigen; vi (feel uneasy) sich sorgen, sich (dat) Gedanken machen; —ing a beunruhigend.

worse [wɜːs] a comp of bad schlechter, schlimmer; ad comp of badly schlimmer, ärger; n Schlimmere(s) nt, Schlechtere(s) nt; —n vt verschlimmern; vi sich verschlechtern.

worship ['wɜːʃɪp] n Anbetung f, Verehrung f; (religious service) Gottesdienst m; (title) Hoch-

würden m; vt anbeten; —per Gottesdienstbesucher(in f)·m.

worst [wɜːst] a superl of bad schlimmste(r,s), schlechteste(r,s); ad. superl of badly am schlimmsten, am ärgsten; n Schlimmste(s) nt, Ärgste(s) nt.

worsted ['wustɪd] n Kammgarn nt.

worth [wɜːθ] n Wert m; £10 — of food Essen für 10 £; a wert; — seeing sehenswert; it's — £10 es ist 10 £ wert; —less a wertlos; person nichtsnutzig; —while a lohnend, der Mühe wert; ad: it's not —while going es lohnt sich nicht, dahin zu gehen; —y [wɜːðɪ] a (having worth) wertvoll; wert (of gen), würdig (of gen).

would [wud] v aux: she — come sie würde kommen; if you asked he — come wenn Sie ihn fragten, würde er kommen; — you like a drink? möchten Sie etwas trinken? —be a angeblich; —n't = — not.

wound [wuːnd] n (lit, fig) Wunde f; vt verwunden, verletzen (also fig).

wrangle ['ræŋgl] n Streit m; vi sich zanken.

wrap [ræp] n (stole) Umhang m, Schal m; vt (also — up) einwickeln; deal abschließen; —per Umschlag m, Schutzhülle f; —ping paper Einwickelpapier nt.

wreath [riːθ] n Kranz m.

wreck [rek] n Schiffbruch m; (ship) Wrack nt; (sth ruined) Ruine f, Trümmerhaufen m; a nervous — ein Nervenbündel nt; vt zerstören; —age Wrack nt, Trümmer pl.

wren [ren] n Zaunkönig m.

wrench [rentʃ] n (spanner) Schraubenschlüssel m; (twist)

Ruck *m*, heftige Drehung *f*; *vt* reißen, zerren.

wrestle ['resl] *vi* ringen.

wrestling ['reslɪŋ] *n* Ringen *nt*; — match Ringkampf *m*.

wretched [retʃɪd] *a* (*hovel*) elend; (*col*) verflixt; I feel — mir ist elend.

wriggle ['rɪgl] *n* Schlängeln *nt*; *vi* sich winden.

wring [rɪŋ] *vt irreg* wringen.

wrinkle ['rɪŋkl] *n* Falte *f*, Runzel *f*; *vt* runzeln; *vi* sich runzeln; (*material*) knittern.

wrist [rɪst] *n* Handgelenk *nt*; —watch Armbanduhr *f*.

writ [rɪt] *n* gerichtliche(r) Befehl *m*.

write [raɪt] *vti irreg* schreiben; —down *vt* niederschreiben, aufschreiben; — off . *vt* (*dismiss*) abschreiben; — out *vt essay* abschreiben; *cheque* ausstellen; —up *vt* schreiben; —off: it is a off das kann man abschreiben; —r

Verfasser *m*; (*author*) Schriftsteller *m*; —up Besprechung *f*.

writing [raɪtɪŋ] *n* (*act*) Schreiben *nt*; (*hand—*) (Hand)schrift *f*; —s *pl* Schriften *pl*, Werke *pl*; — paper Schreibpapier.

wrong [rɒŋ] *a* (*incorrect*) falsch; (*morally*) unrecht; (*out of order*) nicht in Ordnung; he was — in doing that es war nicht recht von ihm, das zu tun; what's — with your leg? was ist mit deinem Bein los?; to go — (*plan*) schiefgehen; (*person*) einen Fehler machen; *n* Unrecht *nt*; *vt* Unrecht tun (+*dat*); —ful a unrechtmäßig; —ly *ad* falsch; *accuse* zu Unrecht.

wrought [rɔːt] *a*: — iron Schmiedeeisen *nt*.

wry [raɪ] *a* schief, krumm; (*ironical*) trocken; to make a — face das Gesicht verziehen.

X

X, x [eks] *n* X *nt*, x *nt*.

Xmas ['eksməs] *n* (*col*) Weihnachten *nt*.

X-ray ['eks'reɪ] *n* Röntgenaufnahme *f*; *vt* röntgen.

xylophone ['zaɪləfəun] *n* Xylophon *nt*.

Y

Y, y [waɪ] *n* Y *nt*, y *nt*.

yacht [jɒt] *n* Jacht *f*; —ing (Sport-) segeln *nt*; —sman Sportsegler *m*.

Yank [jæŋk] *n* (*col*) Ami *m*.

yap [jæp] *vi* (*dog*) kläffen; (*people*) quasseln.

yard [jɑːd] *n* Hof *m*; (*measure*) (englische) Elle *f*, Yard *n*, 0,91 m;

—stick (*fig*) Maßstab *m*.

yarn [jɑːn] *n* (*thread*) Garn *nt*; (*story*) (Seemanns)garn *nt*.

yawn [jɔːn] *n* Gähnen *nt*; *vi* gähnen.

year [jɪə*] *n* Jahr *nt*; —ly a, ad jährlich.

yearn [jɜːn] *vi* sich sehnen (*for*

nach); **—ing** Verlangen *nt,* Sehnsucht *f.*

yeast [ji:st] *n* Hefe *f.*

yell [jel] *n* gellende(r) Schrei *m; vi* laut schreien.

yellow ['jeləʊ] *a* gelb; *n* Gelb *nt;* **— fever** Gelbfieber *nt.*

yelp [jelp] *n* Gekläff *nt; vi* kläffen.

yeoman ['jəʊmən] *n:* Y— of the Guard Leibgardist *m.*

yes [jes] *ad* ja; *n* Ja *nt,* Jawort *nt;* **—man** Jasager *m.*

yesterday ['jestədeɪ] *ad* gestern; *n* Gestern *nt;* **the day before —** vorgestern.

yet [jet] *ad* noch; *(in question)* schon; *(up to now)* bis jetzt; *and* **—** again und wieder *or* noch einmal; **as —** bis jetzt; *(in past)* bis dahin; *cj* doch, dennoch.

yew [ju:] *n* Eibe *f.*

Yiddish ['jɪdɪʃ] *n* Jiddisch *nt.*

yield [ji:ld] *n* Ertrag *m; vt result, crop* hervorbringen; *interest, profit* abwerfen; *(concede)* abtreten; *vi* nachgeben; *(Mil)* sich ergeben.

yodel ['jəʊdl] *vi* jodeln.

yoga ['jəʊgə] *n* Joga *m.*

yoghurt ['jɒgət] *n* Joghurt *m.*

yoke [jəʊk] *n (lit, fig)* Joch *nt.*

yolk [jəʊk] *n* Eidotter *m,* Eigelb *nt.*

yonder ['jɒndə*] *ad* dort drüben, da drüben; *a* jene(r, s) dort.

you [ju:] *pron (familiar) (sing)* *(nom)* du; *(acc)* dich; *(dat)* dir; *(pl) (nom)* ihr; *(acc, dat)* euch; *(polite) (nom, acc)* Sie; *(dat)* Ihnen; *(indef) (nom)* man; *(acc)* einen; *(dat)* einem.

you'd [ju:d] **= you had; you would.**

you'll [ju:l] **= you will, you shall.**

young [jʌŋ] *a* jung; *npl* die Jungen; **—ish** a ziemlich jung; **—ster** Junge *m,* junge(r) Bursche *m/*junge(s) Mädchen *nt.*

your [jɔ:*] poss a *(familiar) (sing)* dein; *(pl)* euer, eure *pl; (polite)* Ihr.

you're ['jʊə*] **= you are.**

yours ['jɔːz] *poss pron (familiar) (sing)* deine(r, s); *(pl)* eure(r, s); *(polite)* Ihre(r, s).

yourself [jɔː'self] *pron (emphatic)* selbst; *(familiar) (sing) (acc)* dich; *(dat)* dir *(selbst)*; *(pl)* euch *(selbst)*; *(polite)* sich *(selbst)*; **you're not —** mit dir/Ihnen ist etwas nicht in Ordnung.

youth [ju:θ] *n* Jugend *f; (young man)* junge(r) Mann *m; (young people)* Jugend *f;* **—ful** a jugendlich; **— hostel** Jugendherberge *f.*

you've [ju:v] **= you have.**

Z

Z, z [zed] *n* Z *nt,* z *nt.*

zany ['zeɪnɪ] *a* komisch.

zeal [zi:l] *n* Eifer *m;* **—ous** ['zeləs] *a* eifrig.

zebra ['zi:brə] *n* Zebra *nt;* **— crossing** ['zi:brə'krɒsɪŋ] Zebrastreifen *m.*

zenith ['zenɪθ] *n* Zenit *m.*

zero ['zɪərəʊ] *n* Null *f; (on scale)* Nullpunkt *m;* **— hour** die Stunde X.

zest [zest] *n* Begeisterung *f.*

zigzag ['zɪgzæg] *n* Zickzack *m; vi* im Zickzack laufen/fahren.

zinc [zɪŋk] n Zink nt.

Zionism ['zaɪənɪzəm] n Zionismus m.

zip [zɪp] n (also — fastener, —per) Reißverschluß m; vt (also — up) den Reißverschluß zumachen (+ gen)

zither ['zɪðə*] n Zither f.

zodiac ['zəʊdɪæk] n Tierkreis m.

zombie ['zɒmbɪ] n Trantüte f.

zone [zəʊn] n Zone f; (area) Gebiet nt.

zoo [zu:] n Zoo m; —logical [zəʊə'lɒdʒɪkəl] a zoologisch; —logist [zu:'ɒlədʒɪst] Zoologe m; —logy [zu:'ɒlədʒɪ] Zoologie f.

zoom [zu:m] vi (engine) surren; (plane) aufsteigen; (move fast) brausen; (prices) hochschnellen; — lens Zoomobjektiv nt.

Countries, nationalities and languages

I am German/English/Albanian ich bin Deutscher/Engländer/Albanier

a German/an Englishman/an Albanian ein Deutscher/Engländer/Albanier;

a German (woman/girl)/an English woman/girl/an Albanian (woman/girl) eine Deutsche/Engländerin/Albanierin

do you speak German/English/Albanian? sprechen Sie Deutsch/ Englisch/Albanisch?

the Adriatic die Adria.
the Aegean die Ägäis.
Afghanistan Afghanistan nt; Afghan n Afghane m, Afghanin f; a afghanisch.
Africa Afrika nt; African n Afrikaner(in f) m; a afrikanisch.
Albania Albanien nt; Albanian n Albanier(in f) m; a albanisch.
Algeria Algerien nt; Algerian n Algerier(in f) m; a algerisch.
the Alps pl die Alpen pl.
America Amerika nt; American n Amerikaner(in f) m; a amerikanisch.
the Andes pl die Anden pl.
Angola Angola nt; Angolan n Angolaner(in f) m; a angolanisch.
the Antarctic die Antarktis; Antarctic a antarktisch.
Arabia Arabien nt; Arab, Arabian n Araber(in f) m; a arabisch.
the Arctic die Arktis; Arctic a arktisch.
Argentina, the Argentine Argentinien nt; Argentinian n Argentinier(in f) m; a argentinisch.
Asia Asien nt; Asian n Asiat(in f) m; a asiatisch.
Asia Minor Kleinasien nt.
Athens Athen nt.
the Atlantic (Ocean) der Atlantik, der Atlantische Ozean.
Australia Australien nt; Australian n Australier(in f) m; a australisch.
Austria Österreich nt; Austrian n Österreicher(in f) m; a österreichisch.
the Baltic die Ostsee.
Bavaria Bayern nt; Bavarian n Bayer(in f) m; a bay(e)risch.

the **Bay of Biscay** (der Golf von) Biskaya *f.*
Belgium Belgien *nt;* **Belgian** *n* Belgier(in *f*) *m;* a belgisch.
the **Black Forest** der Schwarzwald.
Bolivia Bolivien *nt;* **Bolivian** *n* Bolivianer(in *f*) *m*, Bolivier(in *f*) *m; a* boliv(ian)isch.
Brazil Brasilien *nt;* **Brazilian** *n* Brasilianer(in *f*) *m; a* brasilianisch.
Britain Großbritannien *nt;* **Briton** *n* Brite *m*, Britin *f;* **British** *a* britisch.
Brittany die Bretagne; **Breton** *n* Bretone *m*, Bretonin *f; a* bretonisch.
Brussels Brüssel *nt.*
Bulgaria Bulgarien *nt;* **Bulgarian, Bulgar** *n* Bulgare *m*, Bulgarin *f;* **Bulgarian a** bulgarisch.
Burma Birma *nt;* **Burmese** *n* Birmane *m*, Birmanin *f;* a birmanisch.
California Kalifornien *nt;* **Californian** *n* Kalifornier(in *f*) *m; a* kalifornisch.
Cambodia Kambodscha *nt;* **Cambodian** *n* Kambodschaner(in *f*) *m; a* kambodschanisch.
Canada Kanada *nt;* **Canadian** *n* Kanadier(in *f*) *m; a* kanadisch.
the **Canary Islands** *pl* die Kanarischen Inseln *pl.*
the **Caribbean** die Karibik; **Caribbean** *a* karibisch.
Central America Zentralamerika *nt.*
the **Channel Islands** *pl* die Kanalinseln *pl*, die Normannischen Inseln *pl.*
Chile Chile *nt;* **Chilean** *n* Chilene *m*, Chilenin *f; a* chilenisch.
China China *nt;* **Chinese** *n* Chinese *m*, Chinesin *f; a* chinesisch.
Cologne Köln *nt.*
Colombia Kolumbien *nt;* **Colombian** *n* Kolumbianer(in *f*) *m*, Kolumbier(in *f*) *m; a* kolumb(ian)isch.
Lake Constance der Bodensee.
Cornish a von/aus Cornwall.
Corsica Korsika *nt;* **Corsican** *n* Korse *m*, Korsin *f; a* korsisch.
Crete Kreta *nt;* **Cretan** *n* Kreter(in *f*) *m; a* kretisch.
Cuba Kuba *nt;* **Cuban** *n* Kubaner(in *f*) *m; a* kubanisch.
Cyprus Zypern *nt;* **Cypriot** *n* Zypriot(in *f*) *m; a* zypriotisch.
Czechoslovakia die Tschechoslowakei; **Czech, Czechoslovak(ian)** *n* Tscheche *m*, Tschechin *f;* a tschechisch.
Denmark Dänemark *nt;* **Dane** *n* Däne *m*, Dänin *f;* **Danish** a dänisch.
Dutch *a see* Holland.
East Germany Deutsche Demokratische Republik *f;* **East German** *n* Staatsbürger(in *f*) *m* der Deutschen Demokratischen Republik; **he is an East German** er ist aus der DDR; *a* der DDR; **East German towns** Städte (in) der DDR.
Ecuador Ecuador *nt;* **Ecuadorian** *n* Ecuadorianer(in *f*) *m; a* ecuadorianisch.
Egypt Ägypten *nt;* **Egyptian** *n* Ägypter(in *f*) *m; a* ägyptisch.
Eire ['eərə] (Republik *f*) Irland *nt.*
England England *nt;* **Englishman/-woman** *n* Engländer(in *f*) *m;* **English** a englisch.
the **English Channel** der Ärmelkanal.
Ethiopia Äthiopien *nt;* **Ethiopian** *n* Äthiopier(in *f*) *m; a* äthiopisch.
Europe Europa *nt;* **European** *n* Europäer(in *f*) *m; a* europäisch.
Fiji (Islands) *pl* die Fidschiinseln *pl;* **Fijian** *n* Fidschianer(in *f*) *m; a* fidschianisch.
Filipino *n see* the Philippines.
Finland Finnland *nt;* **Finn** *n* Finne *m*, Finnin *f;* **Finnish** a finnisch.
Flanders Flandern *nt;* **Fleming** *n* Flame *m*, Flämin *f;* **Flemish** a flämisch.

Florence Florenz *nt;* **Florentine** *n* Florentiner(in *f*) *m;* **a** florentinisch.

France Frankreich *nt;* **Frenchman/-woman** *n* Franzose *m,* Französin *f;* **French a** französisch.

Geneva Genf *nt;* **Lake Geneva** der Genfer See.

Germany Deutschland *nt;* **German** *n* Deutsche(r) *m,* Deutsche *f;* **a** deutsch.

Ghana Ghana *nt;* **Ghanaian** *n* Ghanaer(in *f*) *m;* **a** ghanaisch.

Great Britain Großbritannien *nt.*

Greece Griechenland *nt;* **Greek** *n* Grieche *m,* Griechin *f;* **a** griechisch.

the Hague Den Haag.

Haiti Haiti *nt;* **Haitian** *n* Haitianer(in *f*) *m,* Haïtier(in *f*) *m;* **a** haitianisch, haitisch.

Hawaii Hawaii *nt;* **Hawaiian** *n* Hawaiier(in *f*) *m;* **a** hawaiisch.

the Hebrides *pl* die Hebriden *pl.*

the Himalayas *pl* der Himalaja.

Holland Holland *nt;* **Dutchman/-woman** *n* Holländer(in *f*) *m;* **Dutch** **a** holländisch, niederländisch.

Hungary Ungarn *nt;* **Hungarian** *n* Ungar(in *f*) *m;* **a** ungarisch.

Iceland Island *nt;* **Icelander** *n* Isländer(in *f*) *m;* **Icelandic** **a** isländisch.

India Indien *nt;* **Indian** *n* Inder(in *f*) *m;* **a** indisch.

Indonesia Indonesien *nt;* **Indonesian** *n* Indonesier(in *f*) *m;* **a** indonesisch.

Iran (der) Iran; **Iranian** *n* Iraner(in *f*) *m;* **a** iranisch.

Iraq (der) Irak; **Iraqi** *n* Iraker(in *f*) *m;* **a** irakisch.

Ireland Irland *nt;* **Irishman/-woman** *n* Ire *m,* Irin *f;* **Irish** **a** irisch.

Israel Israel *nt;* **Israeli** *n* Israeli *m;* **a** israelisch.

Italy Italien *nt;* **Italian** *n* Italiener(in *f*) *m;* **a** italienisch.

Jamaica Jamaika *nt;* **Jamaican** *n* Jamaikaner(in *f*) *m,* Jamaiker(in *f*) *m;* **a** jamaikanisch, jamaikisch.

Japan Japan *nt;* **Japanese** *n* Japaner(in *f*) *m;* **a** japanisch.

Jordan Jordanien *nt;* **Jordanian** *n* Jordanier(in *f*) *m;* **a** jordanisch.

Kenya Kenia *nt;* **Kenyan** *n* Kenianer(in *f*) *m;* **a** kenianisch.

the Kiel Canal der Nord-Ostsee-Kanal.

Korea Korea *nt;* **Korean** *n* Koreaner(in *f*) *m;* **a** koreanisch.

Laos Laos *nt;* **Laotian** *n* Laote *m,* Laotin *f;* **a** laotisch.

Lapland Lappland *nt;* **Lapp** *n* Lappe *m,* Lappin *f;* **a** lappisch.

Latin America Lateinamerika *nt.*

Lebanon (der) Libanon; **Lebanese** *n* Libanese *m,* Libanesin *f;* **a** libanesisch.

Liberia Liberia *nt;* **Liberian** *n* Liberianer(in *f*) *m;* **a** liberianisch.

Libya Libyen *nt;* **Libyan** *n* Libyer(in *f*) *m;* **a** libysch.

Lisbon Lissabon *nt.*

London London *nt;* **Londoner** *n* Londoner(in *f*) *m;* **London** **a** Londoner *inv.*

Luxembourg Luxemburg *nt;* **Luxembourger** *n* Luxemburger(in *f*) *m.*

Majorca Mallorca *nt;* **Majorcan** *n* Bewohner(in *f*) *m* Mallorcas; **a** mallorkinisch.

Malaysia Malaysia *nt;* **Malaysian** *n* Malaysier(in *f*) *m;* **a** malaysisch.

Malta Malta *nt;* **Maltese** *n* Malteser(in *f*) *m;* **a** maltesisch.

the Mediterranean (Sea) das Mittelmeer.

Mexico Mexiko *nt;* **Mexican** *n* Mexikaner(in *f*) *m;* **a** mexikanisch.

Milan Mailand *nt;* **Milanese** *n* Mailänder(in *f*) *m;* **a** mailändisch.

Mongolia die Mongolei; **Mongolian** *n* Mongole *m,* Mongolin *f;* **a** mongolisch.

Morocco Marokko *nt;* **Moroccan** *n* Marokkaner(in *f*) *m;* **a** marrokkanisch.

Moscow Moskau *nt*; **Muscovite** *n* Moskauer(in *f*) *m*; a moskauisch.

Munich München *nt*.

Naples Neapel *nt*; **Neapolitan** *n* Neapolitaner(in *f*) *m*; a neapolitanisch.

the Netherlands *pl* die Niederlande *pl*.

New Zealand Neuseeland *nt*; **New Zealander** *n* Neuseeländer(in *f*) *m*; New Zealand a neuseeländisch.

Nigeria Nigeria *nt*; **Nigerian** *n* Nigerianer(in *f*) *m*; a nigerianisch.

Normandy die Normandie; **Norman** *n* Normanne *m*, Normannin *f*; a normannisch.

Northern Ireland Nordirland *nt*.

the North Sea die Nordsee.

Norway Norwegen *nt*; **Norwegian** *n* Norweger(in *f*) *m*; a norwegisch.

the Pacific (Ocean) der Pazifik, der Pazifische *or* Stille Ozean.

Pakistan Pakistan *nt*; **Pakistani** *n* Pakistaner(in *f*) *m*; a pakistanisch.

Palestine Palästina *nt*; **Palestinian** *n* Palästinenser(in *f*) *m*; a palästinensisch.

Paraguay Paraguay *nt*; **Paraguayan** *n* Paraguayer(in *f*) *m*; a paraguayisch.

Paris Paris *nt*; **Parisian** *n* Pariser(in *f*) *m*; a Pariser *inv*.

the People's Republic of China die Volksrepublik China.

Persia Persien *nt*; **Persian** *n* Perser(in *f*) *m*; a persisch.

Peru Peru *nt*; **Peruvian** *n* Peruaner(in *f*) *m*; a peruanisch.

the Philippines *pl* die Philippinen *pl*; **Filipino** *n* Philippiner(in *f*) *m*; a, Philippine a philippinisch.

Poland Polen *nt*; **Pole** *n* Pole *m*, Polin *f*; **Polish** a polnisch.

Portugal Portugal *nt*; **Portuguese** *n* Portugiese *m*, Portugiesin *f*; a portugiesisch.

Puerto Rico Puerto Rico *nt*; **Puerto-Rican** *n* Puertoricaner(in *f*) *m*; a puertoricanisch.

the Pyrenees *pl* die Pyrenäen *pl*; **Pyrenean** a pyrenäisch.

the Red Sea das Rote Meer.

Rhodes Rhodos *nt*.

Rhodesia Rhodesien *nt*; **Rhodesian** *n* Rhodesier(in *f*) *m*; a rhodesisch.

Rome Rom *nt*; **Roman** *n* Römer(in *f*) *m*; a römisch.

Ro(u)mania Rumänien *nt*; **Ro(u)manian** *n* Rumäne *m*, Rumänin *f*; a rumänisch.

Russia Rußland *nt*; **Russian** *n* Russe *m*, Russin *f*; a russisch.

the Sahara die Sahara.

Sardinia Sardinien *nt*; **Sardinian** *n* Sarde *m*, Sardin *f*; a sardisch.

Saudi Arabia Saudi-Arabien *nt*; **Saudi (Arabian)** *n* Saudiaraber(in *f*) *m*; a saudiarabisch.

Scandinavia Skandinavien *nt*; **Scandinavian** *n* Skandinave *m*, Skandinavin *f*; a skandinavisch.

Scotland Schottland *nt*; **Scot, Scotsman/-woman** *n* Schotte *m*, Schottin *f*; **Scottish, Scots, Scotch** a schottisch.

Siberia Sibirien *nt*; **Siberian** *n* Sibirier(in *f*) *m*; a sibirisch.

Sicily Sizilien *nt*; **Sicilian** *n* Sizilianer(in *f*) *m*, Sizilier(in *f*) *m*; a sizilianisch, sizilisch.

South Africa Südafrika *nt*; **South African** *n* Südafrikaner(in *f*) *m*; a südafrikanisch.

the Soviet Union die Sowjetunion.

Spain Spanien *nt*; **Spaniard** *n* Spanier(in *f*) *m*; **Spanish** a spanisch.

Sri Lanka Sri Lanka *nt*; **Sri Lankan** *n* Ceylonese *m*, Ceylonesin *f*; a ceylonesisch.

the Sudan der Sudan; **Sudanese** *n* Sudanese *m*, Sudanesin *f*, Sudaner(in *f*) *m*; a sudanesisch.

the Suez Canal der Suez-Kanal.

Sweden Schweden *nt;* **Swede** *n* Schwede *m,* Schwedin *f;* **Swedish** *a* schwedisch.
Switzerland die Schweiz; **Swiss** *n* Schweizer(in *f*) *m;* *a* Schweizer *inv,* schweizerisch.
Syria Syrien *nt;* **Syrian** *n* Syrer(in *f*) *m,* Syrier(in *f*) *m;* *a* syrisch.
Tahiti Tahiti *nt;* **Tahitian** *n* Tahitianer(in *f*) *m;* *a* tahitianisch.
Taiwan Taiwan *nt;* **Taiwanese** *n* Taiwanese(r) *m,* Taiwanesin *f;* *a* taiwanesisch.
Tanzania Tansania *nt;* **Tanzanian** *n* Tansanier(in *f*) *m;* *a* tansanisch.
Tenerife Teneriffa *nt.*
Thailand Thailand *nt;* **Thai** *n* Thailänder(in *f*) *m;* *a* thailändisch.
the Thames die Themse.
the Tyrol Tirol *nt;* **Tyrolean** *n* Tiroler(in *f*) *m;* *a* Tiroler *inv.*
Tunisia Tunesien *nt;* **Tunisian** *n* Tunesier(in *f*) *m;* *a* tunesisch.
Turkey die Türkei; **Turk** *n* Türke *m,* Türkin *f;* **Turkish** *a* türkisch.
Uganda Uganda *nt;* **Ugandan** *n* Ugander(in *f*) *m;* *a* ugandisch.
the United Kingdom das Vereinigte Königreich.
the United States *pl* (of America) die Vereinigten Staaten *pl* (von Amerika).
Uruguay Uruguay *nt;* **Uruguayan** *n* Uruguayer(in *f*) *m;* *a* uruguayisch.
Venezuela Venezuela *nt;* **Venezuelan** *n* Venezolaner(in *f*) *m;* *a* venezolanisch.
Venice Venedig *nt;* **Venetian** *n* Venezianer(in *f*) *m;* *a* venezianisch.
Vienna Wien *nt;* **Viennese** *n* Wiener(in *f*) *m;* *a* wienerisch, Wiener *inv.*
Vietnam Vietnam *nt;* **Vietnamese** *n* Vietnamese *m,* Vietnamesin *f;* *a* vietnamesisch.
Wales Wales *nt;* **Welshman/-woman** *n* Waliser(in *f*) *m;* **Welsh** *a* walisisch.
Warsaw Warschau *nt.*
West Germany die Bundesrepublik (Deutschland); **West German** *n* Bundesdeutsche(r) *m,* Bundesdeutsche *f;* *a* Bundes-, der Bundesrepublik.
the West Indies *pl* Westindien *nt;* **West Indian** *n* Westinder(in *f*) *m;* *a* westindisch.
the Yemen (der) Jemen; **Yemeni, Yemenite** *n* Jemenit(in *f*) *m;* *a* jemenitisch.
Yugoslavia Jugoslawien *nt;* **Yugoslav(ian)** *n* Jugoslawe *m,* Jugoslawin *f;* *a* jugoslawisch.
Zaire Zaire *nt.*
Zambia Sambia *nt;* **Zambian** *n* Sambier(in *f*) *m;* *a* sambisch.

English abbreviations

AD	after (the birth of) Christ *Anno Domini, nach Christi, A.D., n. Chr.*
AGM	annual general meeting *Jahresvollversammlung*
am	before midday (ante meridiem) *vormittags, vorm.;* 1.00am. *1.00 Uhr*
arr	arrival, arrives *Ankunft, Ank.*
asst	assistant *Assistent, Mitarbeiter*
Ave	avenue *Straße, Str.*
BA	Bachelor of Arts *Bakkalaureus der Philosophischen Fakultät*
B and B	bed and breakfast *Zimmer mit Frühstück,* in catalogue: *Zi. m Fr.,* as sign: *Fremdenzimmer*
BAOR	British Army of the Rhine *(britische) Rheinarmee*
BC	before (the birth of) Christ *vor Christi Geburt, v. Chr.*
BO	body odour *Körpergeruch*

Bros	[brɔs] brothers *Gebrüder, Gebr.*
BSc	Bachelor of Science *Bakkalaureus der Naturwissenschaftlichen Fakultät*
Cantab	['kæntæb] Cambridge University (Cantabrigiensis) *Cambridge*
CBI	Confederation of British Industry *Bundesverband der britischen Industrie*
cc	cubic centimetres *Kubikzentimeter, ccm.*
CD	Diplomatic Corps (French: Corps Diplomatique) *Diplomatisches Corps, CD*
CIA	Central Intelligence Agency *CIA*
CID	Criminal Investigation Department *Kriminalpolizei*
cif	cost insurance and freight *Kosten, Versicherung und Fracht einbegriffen*
C-in-C	Commander-in-Chief *Oberkommandierender*
cm	centimetre(s) *Zentimeter, cm*
c/o	care of *bei, c/o*
COD	cash on delivery *gegen Nachnahme*
C of E	Church of England *anglikanische Kirche*
cwt	hundredweight ≈ *Zentner, ztr.*
DA	(*US*) District Attorney *Bezirksstaatsanwalt*
dep	depart(s) *Abfahrt, Abf.*
dept	department *Abteilung, Abt.*
DJ	dinner jacket *Smoking*; disc jockey *Diskjockey*
ed	edited by *herausgegeben, hrsg.*; editor *Herausgeber, Hrsg.*
EEC	European Economic Community *Europäische Wirtschaftsgemeinschaft, EWG*
eg	for example (exempli gratia) *zum Beispiel, z.B.*
ESP	extrasensory perception *übersinnliche Wahrnehmung*
ETA	estimated time of arrival *voraussichtliche Ankunft*
etc	etcetera, and so on *und so weiter, usw., etc.*
FBI	Federal Bureau of Investigation *FBI*
fig	figure, illustration *Abbildung, Abb.*
fob	free on board *frei Schiff*
gbh	grievous bodily harm *schwere Körperverletzung*
GI	(government issue) private in the American Army *amerikanischer Soldat, GI*
govt	government *Regierung*
GP	General Practitioner *praktischer Arzt*
GPO	General Post Office *Britische Post; Hauptpostamt*
HM	His/Her Majesty *Seine/Ihre Majestät*
HMS	His/Her Majesty's Ship *Schiff der Königlichen Marine*
hp	(*Brit*) hire purchase *Abzahlungskauf*; horsepower *Pferdestärke, PS*
HQ	headquarters *Hauptquartier*
hr(s)	hour(s) *Stunde(n), Std.*
HRH	His/Her Royal Highness *Seine/Ihre Hoheit*
ID	identification *Ausweis*

i.e.	that is (id est) *das heißt, d.h.*
IOU	I owe you *Schuldschein*
JP	Justice of the Peace *Friedensrichter*
km	kilometre(s) *Kilometer, km*
kph	kilometres per hour *Stundenkilometer, km/h*
LA	Los Angeles
lb	pound (weight) *Pfund, Pfd.*
LP	long-playing (record), long-player *Langspielplatte, LP*
Ltd	limited (in names of businesses) *Gesellschaft mit beschränkter Haftung, GmbH*
MA	Master of Arts *Magister Artium, M.A.*
max.	maximum *maximal, max*
MI5	department of British Intelligence Service (originally Military Intelligence) *Britischer Geheimdienst*
min	minimum *minimal*
MIT	Massachusetts Institute of Technology
mm	millimetre(s) *Millimeter, mm*
mod cons	[mɔdˈkɔnz] modern conveniences (cooker, lights, *etc*) *mit allem Komfort*
MOT	Ministry of Transport (used for the roadworthiness test of motor vehicles) *Technischer Überwachungsverein, TÜV*
MP	Member of Parliament *Abgeordneter;* military policeman *Militärpolizist, MP*
mpg	miles per gallon *Meilen pro Gallone, Benzinverbrauch*
mph	miles per hour *Meilen pro Stunde*
Mr	[ˈmɪstə] Mister *Herr*
Mrs	[ˈmɪsɪz] Mistress *Frau*
Ms	[məz] *Frau*
NAAFI	[ˈnæfɪ] (*Brit*) Navy, Army and Air Force Institutes (canteen services) *Kantine*
NATO	[ˈneɪtəʊ] North Atlantic Treaty Organization *Nordatlantikpakt, NATO*
NB	note well (nota bene) *notabene, NB*
NCO	non-commissioned officer *Unteroffizier, Uffz.*
no(s)	number(s) *Nummer(n), Nr.*
o.n.o.	or nearest offer *oder höchstes Angebot*
Oxon	[ˈɔksɔn] Oxford University (Oxonia) *Oxford*
oz	ounce(s) (onza) *Unze*
p	page *Seite, S.;* (new) pence *Pence, p*
PA	public address (system) *Lautsprecheranlage*
pa	per year (per annum) *pro Jahr, jährlich, jhrl.*
PC	police constable *Polizeibeamter;* Privy Councillor *Mitglied des Geheimen Staatsrats*
PhD	Doctor of Philosophy *Doktor der Philosophie, Dr. phil.*
PM	Prime Minister *Premierminister*
pm	afternoon (post meridiem) *nachmittags, nachm.;* 10.00pm *22.00 Uhr*

pop	population *Einwohner, Einw.*
POW	prisoner of war *Kriegsgefangener*
pp	pages *Seiten, ff.*, pro persona, for *im Auftrag, I.A.*
PRO	public relations officer *PR-Chef*
PS	postscript *Nachschrift, PS*
pto	please turn over *bitte wenden, b.w.*
QC	Queen's Counsel *Anwalt der königlichen Anwaltskammer*
RADA	Royal Academy of Dramatic Art
RAF	Royal Air Force *britische Luftwaffe*
Rd	road *Straße, Str.*
Rev	Reverend *Herr Pfarrer*
RIP	rest in peace (requiescat in pace) *ruhe in Frieden, R.I.P.*
RSVP	please reply (written on invitations; French: répondez s'il vous plaît) *um Antwort wird gebeten, u.A.w.g.*
Rt Hon	Right Honourable *Anrede für Grafen etc, Abgeordnete und Minister*
s.a.e.	stamped addressed envelope *vorfrankierter Umschlag*
SOS	(save our souls) *SOS*
Sq	square (in town) *Platz, Pl.*
ss	steamship *Dampfer*
St	saint *Sankt, St.*; street *Straße, Str.*
st	stone (weight) *6,35 kg*
STD	subscriber trunk dialling *Selbstwählfernverkehr*
TB	tuberculosis *Tuberkulose, TB*
Tel	telephone *Telefon, Tel.*
TUC	Trades Union Congress *Gewerkschaftsbund*
UFO	['juːfəʊ] unidentified flying object *unbekanntes Flugobjekt, Ufo*
UK	United Kingdom *Vereinigtes Königreich*
UN	United Nations *Vereinte Nationen*
USA	United States of America *Vereinigte Staaten von Amerika, USA;* United States Army *Amerikanische Armee*
USAF	United States Air Force *Amerikanische Luftwaffe*
USN	United States Navy *Amerikanische Marine*
USSR	Union of Soviet Socialist Republics *Sowjetunion, UdSSR*
VAT	[also væt] value added tax *Mehrwertsteuer, Mehrw.St.*
VD	venereal disease *Geschlechtskrankheit*
VHF	very high frequency *Ultrakurzwelle, UKW*
VIP	very important person *wichtige Persönlichkeit, VIP*
viz	[vɪz] namely (videlicet) *nämlich*
VSO	voluntary service overseas *Entwicklungshilfe*
WASP	(US) White Anglo-Saxon Protestant
WC	water closet *Toilette, WC*
ZIP	[zɪp] (US) Zone Improvement Plan (postal code) *Postleitzahl, PLZ*

English irregular verbs

present	pt	ptp	present	pt	ptp
arise (arising)	arose	arisen	cut (cutting)	cut	cut
awake (awaking)	awoke	awaked	deal	dealt	dealt
be (am, is, are; being)	was, were	been	dig (digging)	dug	dug
			do (3rd person: he/she/it/does)	did	done
bear	bore	born(e)	draw	drew	drawn
beat	beat	beaten	dream	dreamed (also dreamt)	dreamed (also dreamt)
become (becoming)	became	become	drink	drank	drunk
befall	befell	befallen	drive (driving)	drove	driven
begin (beginning)	began	begun	dwell	dwelt	dwelt
behold	beheld	beheld	eat	ate	eaten
bend	bent	bent	fall	fell	fallen
beseech	besought	besought	feed	fed	fed
beset (besetting)	beset	beset	feel	felt	felt
bet (betting)	bet (also betted)	bet (also betted)	fight	fought	fought
			find	found	found
bid (bidding)	bid	bid	flee	fled	fled
bind	bound	bound	fling	flung	flung
bite (biting)	bit	bitten	fly (flies)	flew	flown
bleed	bled	bled	forbid (forbidding)	forbade	forbidden
blow	blew	blown	forecast	forecast	forecast
break	broke	broken	forego	forewent	foregone
breed	bred	bred	foresee	foresaw	foreseen
bring	brought	brought	foretell	foretold	foretold
build	built	built	forget (forgetting)	forgot	forgotten
burn	burnt or burned	burnt (also burned)	forgive (forgiving)	forgave	forgiven
burst	burst	burst	forsake (forsaking)	forsook	forsaken
buy	bought	bought	freeze (freezing)	froze	frozen
can	could	(been able)	get (getting)	got	got, (US) gotten
cast	cast	cast	give (giving)	gave	given
catch	caught	caught	go (goes)	went	gone
choose (choosing)	chose	chosen	grind	ground	ground
cling	clung	clung	grow	grew	grown
come (coming)	came	come	hang	hung (also hanged)	hung (also hanged)
cost	cost	cost			
creep	crept	crept			